AMERICA

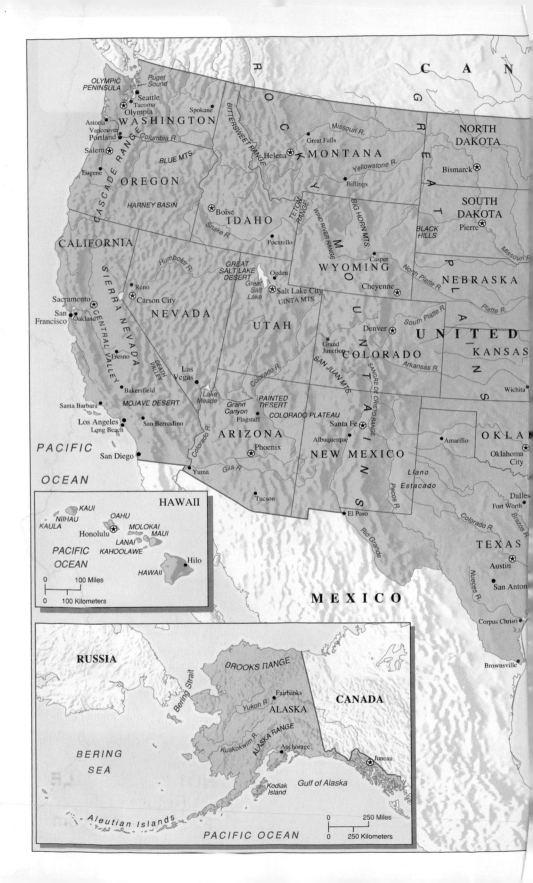

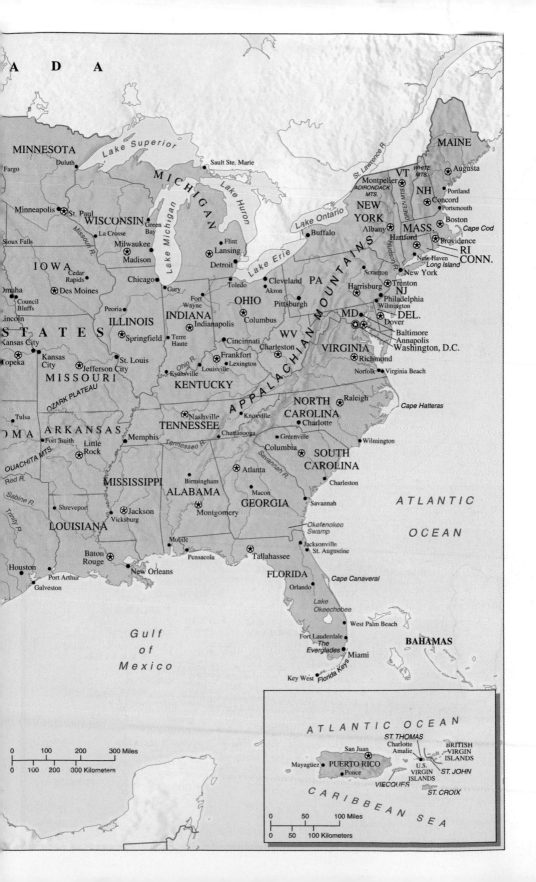

C A N A D A

MINNESOTA

Lake Superior

Fargo

Duluth

Sault Ste. Marie

MICHIGAN

Lake Huron

MAINE

WHITE MTS.

Augusta

VT

Montpelier

St. Lawrence R.

ADIRONDACK MTS.

NH

Portland

Concord

Portsmouth

Minneapolis

St. Paul

WISCONSIN

Green Bay

La Crosse

Lake Michigan

Flint

Lake Ontario

NEW YORK

Albany

Buffalo

Hartford

MASS.

Boston

Cape Cod

Providence

RI

CONN.

GREEN MTS.

Sioux Falls

Milwaukee

Madison

Lansing

Detroit

Lake Erie

Cleveland

PA

Scranton

New Haven

Long Island

Omaha

IOWA

Cedar Rapids

Des Moines

Chicago

Gary

Toledo

Akron

Harrisburg

Trenton

NJ

New York

Hudson R.

Council Bluffs

Peoria

Fort Wayne

OHIO

Pittsburgh

Philadelphia

Wilmington

DEL.

Lincoln

ILLINOIS

INDIANA

Columbus

MD

Dover

STATES

Springfield

Indianapolis

Cincinnati

WV

Baltimore

Annapolis

Kansas City

Terre Haute

Frankfort

Charleston

VIRGINIA

Washington, D.C.

Topeka

Kansas City

St. Louis

Ohio R.

Lexington

Richmond

Jefferson City

Evansville

Louisville

APPALACHIAN MOUNTAINS

Norfolk

Virginia Beach

MISSOURI

KENTUCKY

OZARK PLATEAU

NORTH CAROLINA

Raleigh

Cape Hatteras

Tulsa

ARKANSAS

Nashville

Knoxville

TENNESSEE

Chattanooga

Charlotte

OMA

OUACHITA MTS.

Fort Smith

Little Rock

Memphis

Tennessee R.

Greenville

Columbia

SOUTH CAROLINA

Wilmington

Red R.

Birmingham

Atlanta

Charleston

Sabine R.

MISSISSIPPI

ALABAMA

Macon

GEORGIA

ATLANTIC

Trinity R.

Shreveport

Jackson

Vicksburg

Montgomery

Savannah

OCEAN

LOUISIANA

Mobile

Okefenokee Swamp

Houston

Baton Rouge

Pensacola

Tallahassee

Jacksonville

St. Augustine

Port Arthur

New Orleans

FLORIDA

Cape Canaveral

Galveston

Orlando

Gulf

of

Mexico

Lake Okeechobee

West Palm Beach

Fort Lauderdale

The Everglades

Miami

BAHAMAS

Key West

Florida Keys

0   100   200   300 Miles

0 100 200 300 Kilometers

ATLANTIC OCEAN

ST. THOMAS

Charlotte Amalie

BRITISH VIRGIN ISLANDS

San Juan

Mayagüez   PUERTO RICO

Ponce

U.S. VIRGIN ISLANDS

ST. JOHN

VIEQUES

ST. CROIX

CARIBBEAN SEA

0   50   100 Miles

0   50   100 Kilometers

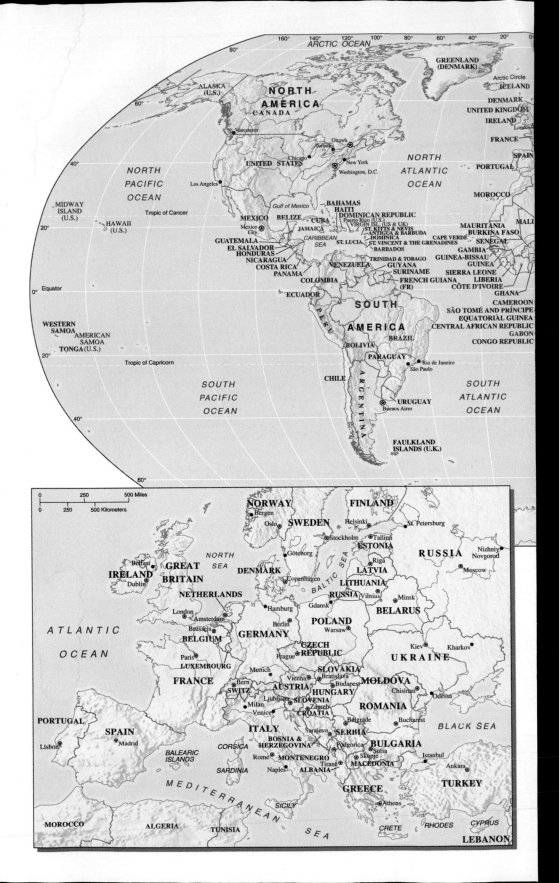

AMERICA

A NARRATIVE HISTORY

Eighth Edition

GEORGE BROWN TINDALL

DAVID EMORY SHI

W · W · NORTON & COMPANY · NEW YORK · LONDON

W. W. Norton & Company has been independent since its founding in 1923, when William Warder Norton and Mary D. Herter Norton first published lectures delivered at the People's Institute, the adult education division of New York City's Cooper Union. The firm soon expanded its program beyond the Institute, publishing books by celebrated academics from America and abroad. By mid-century, the two major pillars of Norton's publishing program—trade books and college texts—were firmly established. In the 1950s, the Norton family transferred control of the company to its employees, and today—with a staff of four hundred and a comparable number of trade, college, and professional titles published each year—W. W. Norton & Company stands as the largest and oldest publishing house owned wholly by its employees.

Editor: Jon Durbin
Manuscript editor: Abby Winograd
Project editor: Melissa Atkin
Emedia editor: Steve Hoge
Print ancillary editor: Rachel Comerford
Production manager: Christine D'Antonio
Editorial assistant: Jason Spears
Book design by Antonina Krass
Composition by TexTech, Inc.
Manufacturing by World Color Press, Inc., Taunton
Cartographer: CARTO-GRAPHICS/Alice Thiede and William Thiede

Library of Congress Cataloging-in-Publication Data

Tindall, George Brown.
    America : a narrative history / George Brown Tindall,
David Emory Shi.—8th ed.
        p.   cm.
    Includes bibliographical references and index.
    ISBN 978-0-393-93405-2
    1. United States—History.   I. Shi, David E.   II. Title.
    E178.1 .T55 2009   2009024625
    973—dc22
        ISBN 978-0-393-93406-9 (pbk.)

W. W. Norton & Company, Inc., 500 Fifth Avenue, New York, NY 10110
www.wwnorton.com

W. W. Norton & Company Ltd., Castle House, 75/76 Wells Street, London W1T 3QT

1 2 3 4 5 6 7 8 9 0

FOR BRUCE AND SUSAN
AND FOR BLAIR

FOR
JASON AND JESSICA

GEORGE B. TINDALL recently of the University of North
Carolina, Chapel Hill, was an award-winning historian
of the South with a number of major books to his credit,
including *The Emergence of the New South, 1913–1945* and
The Disruption of the Solid South.

DAVID E. SHI is a professor of history and the president of
Furman University. He is the author of several books on
American cultural history, including the award-winning
*The Simple Life: Plain Living and High Thinking in American
Culture* and *Facing Facts: Realism in American Thought and
Culture, 1850–1920.*

CONTENTS

List of Maps • *xvii*
Preface • *xxi*

Part One / A NEW WORLD

1 | THE COLLISION OF CULTURES   5

PRE-COLUMBIAN INDIAN CIVILIZATIONS   7   • EUROPEAN VISIONS OF
AMERICA   14   • THE EXPANSION OF EUROPE   16   • THE VOYAGES OF
COLUMBUS   18   • THE GREAT BIOLOGICAL EXCHANGE   21
• PROFESSIONAL EXPLORERS   25   • THE SPANISH EMPIRE   26   •
THE PROTESTANT REFORMATION   40   • CHALLENGES TO THE SPANISH EMPIRE   44

2 | BRITAIN AND ITS COLONIES   52

THE ENGLISH BACKGROUND   52   • SETTLING THE CHESAPEAKE   57
• SETTLING NEW ENGLAND   68   • INDIANS IN NEW ENGLAND   79
• THE ENGLISH CIVIL WAR IN AMERICA   84   • SETTLING THE
CAROLINAS   85   • SETTLING THE MIDDLE COLONIES AND GEORGIA   91
• THRIVING COLONIES   104

3 | Colonial Ways of Life 108

THE SHAPE OF EARLY AMERICA   109   •   SOCIETY AND ECONOMY IN THE
SOUTHERN COLONIES   117   •   SOCIETY AND ECONOMY IN NEW
ENGLAND   129   •   SOCIETY AND ECONOMY IN THE MIDDLE COLONIES   142
•   COLONIAL CITIES   145   •   THE ENLIGHTENMENT   149   •   THE GREAT
AWAKENING   153

4 | The Imperial Perspective 162

ENGLISH ADMINISTRATION OF THE COLONIES   163   •   THE HABIT OF SELF-
GOVERNMENT   168   •   TROUBLED NEIGHBORS   170   •   THE COLONIAL
WARS   176

5 | From Empire to Independence 190

THE HERITAGE OF WAR   191   •   BRITISH POLITICS   192   •   WESTERN LANDS   193
•   GRENVILLE AND THE STAMP ACT   193   •   FANNING THE FLAMES   199
•   DISCONTENT ON THE FRONTIER   204   •   A WORSENING CRISIS   205
•   SHIFTING AUTHORITY   211   •   INDEPENDENCE   218

Part Two / BUILDING A NATION

6 | The American Revolution 231

1776: WASHINGTON'S NARROW ESCAPE   232   •   AMERICAN SOCIETY AT
WAR   236   •   1777: SETBACKS FOR THE BRITISH   239   •   1778: BOTH SIDES
REGROUP   243   •   THE WAR IN THE SOUTH   248   •   NEGOTIATIONS   253
•   THE POLITICAL REVOLUTION   254   •   THE SOCIAL REVOLUTION   258
•   THE EMERGENCE OF AN AMERICAN CULTURE   266

7 | Shaping a Federal Union 270

THE CONFEDERATION   270   •   ADOPTING THE CONSTITUTION   283

8 | THE FEDERALIST ERA   300

A NEW NATION   301   • HAMILTON'S VISION   307   • THE REPUBLICAN
ALTERNATIVE   315   • CRISES FOREIGN AND DOMESTIC   317   • SETTLEMENT OF
NEW LAND   326   • TRANSFER OF POWER   329   • THE ADAMS YEARS   331

9 | THE EARLY REPUBLIC   344

JEFFERSONIAN SIMPLICITY   346   • JEFFERSON IN OFFICE   348
• DIVISIONS IN THE REPUBLICAN PARTY   358   • WAR IN EUROPE   359
• THE WAR OF 1812   364

Part Three / AN EXPANSIVE NATION

10 | NATIONALISM AND SECTIONALISM   383

ECONOMIC NATIONALISM   384   • "GOOD FEELINGS"   389   • CRISES
AND COMPROMISES   394   • JUDICIAL NATIONALISM   398   • NATIONALIST
DIPLOMACY   401   • ONE-PARTY POLITICS   403

11 | THE JACKSONIAN IMPULSE   414

SETTING THE STAGE   417   • NULLIFICATION   421   • JACKSON'S INDIAN
POLICY   428   • THE BANK CONTROVERSY   432   • CONTENTIOUS
POLITICS   435   • VAN BUREN AND THE NEW PARTY SYSTEM   439
• ASSESSING THE JACKSON YEARS   445

12 | THE DYNAMICS OF GROWTH   450

AGRICULTURE AND THE NATIONAL ECONOMY   451   • TRANSPORTATION
AND THE MARKET REVOLUTION   455   • A COMMUNICATIONS REVOLUTION   463
• THE INDUSTRIAL REVOLUTION   465   • THE POPULAR CULTURE   472
• IMMIGRATION   475   • ORGANIZED LABOR   482   • THE RISE OF THE
PROFESSIONS   485   • JACKSONIAN INEQUALITY   488

13 | AN AMERICAN RENAISSANCE: RELIGION, ROMANTICISM, AND REFORM   492

RATIONAL RELIGION   492   •   THE SECOND GREAT AWAKENING   494
•   ROMANTICISM IN AMERICA   503   •   THE FLOWERING OF AMERICAN
LITERATURE   508   •   EDUCATION   512   •   ANTEBELLUM REFORM 516

14 | MANIFEST DESTINY   526

THE TYLER YEARS   527   •   THE WESTERN FRONTIER   530   •   MOVING
WEST   538   •   ANNEXING TEXAS   545   •   POLK'S PRESIDENCY   548
•   THE MEXICAN WAR   553

Part Four / A HOUSE DIVIDED AND REBUILT

15 | THE OLD SOUTH   569

THE DISTINCTIVENESS OF THE OLD SOUTH   570   •   WHITE SOCIETY IN THE SOUTH
576   •   BLACK SOCIETY IN THE SOUTH   581   •   THE CULTURE OF THE
SOUTHERN FRONTIER   591   •   ANTI-SLAVERY MOVEMENTS   592

16 | THE CRISIS OF UNION   602

SLAVERY IN THE TERRITORIES   603   •   THE COMPROMISE OF 1850   610
•   FOREIGN ADVENTURES   618   •   THE KANSAS-NEBRASKA CRISIS   619
•   THE DEEPENING SECTIONAL CRISIS   630   •   THE CENTER COMES APART   639

17 | THE WAR OF THE UNION   648

THE END OF THE WAITING GAME   649   •   THE BALANCE OF FORCE   653
•   THE WAR'S EARLY COURSE   655   •   EMANCIPATION   669
•   THE WAR BEHIND THE LINES   674   •   GOVERNMENT DURING THE WAR   678
•   THE FALTERING CONFEDERACY   684   •   THE CONFEDERACY'S DEFEAT   689
•   A MODERN WAR   698

18 | RECONSTRUCTION: NORTH AND SOUTH   702

THE WAR'S AFTERMATH   702   •   THE BATTLE OVER RECONSTRUCTION   707
•   RECONSTRUCTING THE SOUTH   715   •   THE RECONSTRUCTED SOUTH   720
•   THE GRANT YEARS   727

GLOSSARY   A1

APPENDIX   A77

THE DECLARATION OF INDEPENDENCE   A79   •   ARTICLES OF
CONFEDERATION   A84   •   THE CONSTITUTION OF THE UNITED STATES   A92
•   AMENDMENTS TO THE CONSTITUTION   A104   •   PRESIDENTIAL ELECTIONS   A114
•   ADMISSION OF STATES   A122   •   POPULATION OF THE UNITED STATES   A123
•   IMMIGRATION TO THE UNITED STATES, FISCAL YEARS 1820–2008   A124
•   IMMIGRATION BY REGION AND SELECTED COUNTRY OF LAST RESIDENCE, FISCAL
YEARS 1820–2008   A126   •   PRESIDENTS, VICE PRESIDENTS, AND SECRETARIES
OF STATE   A135

FURTHER READINGS   A141

CREDITS   A160

INDEX   A165

MAPS

The First Migration   6
Pre-Columbian Civilizations in Middle
  and South America   8
Pre-Columbian Civilizations in North America   10
Norse Discoveries   15
Columbus's Voyages   20
Spanish and Portuguese Explorations   25
Spanish Explorations of the Mainland   35
English, French, and Dutch Explorations   45
Land Grants to the Virginia Company   60
Early Virginia and Maryland   67
Early New England Settlements   71
The West Indies, 1600–1800   74
Early Settlements in the South   87
The Middle Colonies   97
European Settlements and Indian Tribes in Early America   102–103
The African Slave Trade, 1500–1800   123
Atlantic Trade Routes   135
Major Immigrant Groups in Colonial America   144
The French in North America   175
Major Campaigns of the French and Indian War   179
North America, 1713   184
North America, 1763   185
Lexington and Concord, April 19, 1775   212
Major Campaigns in New York and New Jersey, 1776–1777   233

Major Campaigns in New York and Pennsylvania, 1777   240
Western Campaigns, 1776–1779   246
Major Campaigns in the South, 1778–1781   249
Yorktown, 1781   249
North America, 1783   255
Western Land Cessions, 1781–1802   273
The Old Northwest, 1785   275
The Vote on the Constitution, 1787–1790   296
Treaty of Greenville, 1795   322
Pinckney's Treaty, 1795   325
The Election of 1800   340
Explorations of the Louisiana Purchase, 1804–1807   356
Major Northern Campaigns of the War of 1812   368
Major Southern Campaigns of the War of 1812   370
The National Road, 1811–1838   387
Boundary Treaties, 1818–1819   391
The Missouri Compromise, 1820   396
The Election of 1828   410
Indian Removal, 1820–1840   430
The Election of 1840   444
Population Density, 1820   454
Population Density, 1860   455
Transportation West, about 1840   456–457
The Growth of Railroads, 1850   460
The Growth of Railroads, 1860   461
The Growth of Industry in the 1840s   470
The Growth of Cities, 1820   474
The Growth of Cities, 1860   475
The Mormon Trek, 1830–1851   503
The Webster-Ashburton Treaty, 1842   529
Wagon Trails West   539
The Election of 1844   549
The Oregon Dispute, 1818–1846   553
Major Campaigns of the Mexican War   559
Cotton Production, 1821   572
Population Growth and Cotton Production, 1821–1859   573
The Slave Population, 1820   584
The Slave Population, 1860   585

The Compromise of 1850   614
The Gadsden Purchase, 1853   621
The Kansas-Nebraska Act, 1854   622
The Election of 1856   628
The Election of 1860   643
Secession, 1860–1861   651
The First Battle of Bull Run, July 21, 1861   656
Campaigns in the West, February–April 1862   662
The Peninsular Campaign, 1862   666
Campaigns in Virginia and Maryland, 1862   667
The Vicksburg Campaign, 1863   685
Campaigns in the East, 1863   686
Grant in Virginia, 1864–1865   692
Sherman's Campaigns, 1864–1865   695
Reconstruction, 1865–1877   725
The Election of 1876   738

PREFACE

This edition of *America: A Narrative History* marks the twenty-fifth anniversary of the book. I very much regret that George Tindall is not alive to celebrate with me. He died on December 2, 2006, in Chapel Hill, North Carolina. He was eighty-five. George was a meticulous, pathbreaking, award winning scholar. He was also an eloquent writer, an engaging teacher, and a caring mentor. And, of course, he wrote a wonderful history of America!

George Tindall developed the idea for a distinctive American history textbook nearly four decades ago. He set out to write a compelling narrative history of the American experience, a succinct narrative that would be animated by colorful characters, informed by balanced analysis and social texture, and guided by the unfolding of events. Those classic principles, combined with the book's handy format and low price, have helped make *America: A Narrative History* one of the most popular and well-respected American history textbooks. It was my good fortune to join George in this worthy endeavor beginning with the Second Edition.

Beginning in 1984, George and I sought to improve *America* with each edition. Each subsequent edition has introduced a new theme designed to show how politics, economics, culture, and society interact to shape the American experience. New themes in previous editions have included the role of immigration, the western experience, work, and the environment. This Eighth Edition of *America* features the theme of religion and its myriad effects on history and society. Religion, of course, is one of the most powerful forces in human life, and it has played a crucial role in the development of the United States. Americans have always been a peculiarly religious people. Native American cultures centered their societies on spiritual life. And most of the first European colonists saw themselves as "a chosen people," agents of divine providence with a mission to spread the gospel to the so-called New World. In 1831 and 1832, the astute Frenchman Alexis de Tocqueville toured the United States and reported that there "is no country in the world where the Christian religion retains a greater influence over the souls of men than in America."

Yet Christianity in America has always assumed many forms. Religious freedom has been as valued a principle as religious belief. And in recent years the United States has witnessed a surge in non-Christian religions. "We are a religious people," said Supreme Court Justice William O. Douglas in 1952. Yet thirteen years later he added that America had become "a nation of Buddhists, Confucianists, and Taoists." Islam, in fact, is the nation's fastest-growing faith; there are more Muslims in America than Episcopalians. The United States is fast becoming a pluralistic, multireligious nation in which toleration is an ever-important outlook. More than the members of any other industrialized society, the vast majority of Americans (90 percent) believe in God, pray, and attend religious services at churches, synagogues, temples, and mosques. To a remarkable degree, many Americans fashion their personal conduct upon their religious principles and their social relationships upon their religious beliefs. Thus diversity characterizes American religious life. There are many different faiths and also quite different expressions of the same faith. Although the U.S. Constitution creates a "wall of separation" between religion and government, Americans are also more apt to mix faith and politics than citizens of other countries. In other words, religion continues to be one of the most dynamic—and most contested—elements of American life.

Some of the additions to the Eighth Edition relating to religious history are outlined here:

- Chapter 1 includes discussions of Aztec religious beliefs and rituals, sixteenth-century European religious life, and Spanish efforts to convert Native Americans to Catholicism.
- Chapter 2 examines the English Reformation and the distinctive characteristics of Anglicanism (the faith of the Church of England), the Native Americans' reverence for nature, and Judaism in British North America.
- Chapter 3 describes the important role of women in colonial religious life, the popularity of Deism among many key Revolutionary leaders, and the social aspects of the Great Awakening.
- Chapter 4 details the impact of the Jesuit missionaries in New France.
- Chapter 8 analyzes the logic of the First Amendment's emphasis on the separation of church and state.

- Chapter 13 explores the changes in religious life during the early nineteenth century.
- Chapter 15 includes new material on religious life in the Old South.
- Chapter 16 features the religious revival of 1857–1859.
- Chapter 17 shows that the armies fighting the Civil War engaged in frequent religious services and revivals.
- Chapter 18 details the role played by religious life in the Reconstruction of the South after the Civil War.
- Chapter 22 summarizes the role that religious fervor played in the populist movement of the 1890s.
- Chapter 23 discusses the role of religion in justifying American imperialism at the end of the nineteenth century.
- Chapter 24 highlights the role of religion in the motives of "progressive" social reformers.
- Chapter 32 describes the efforts of Congress and President Dwight Eisenhower to reaffirm America's belief in God.
- Chapter 33 stresses the crucial role played by religion in the development of the civil rights movement of the 1950s and 1960s.
- Chapter 36 explains the rise of the Republican conservatives and the role that the major revival of evangelical religion played in the conservative ascendancy in American politics.

Beyond those explorations of religious history, I have introduced other new material throughout the Eighth Edition, including new segments on Native Americans, African Americans, and women. In addition, I have incorporated fresh insights from important new scholarly works.

America is a book that students like to read and teachers like to teach. *America*'s consistent narrative voice provides a clear path through the complexities of American history. New, carefully crafted pedagogical features have been added to the Eighth Edition to further help guide students through the narrative. New focus questions and chapter summaries work together seamlessly to highlight core content. Other text features include easy-to-read full-color maps, new chapter chronologies, and new lists of key terms.

Also revised is the outstanding support package that supplements the text. *For the Record: A Documentary History of America*, Fourth Edition, by David E. Shi and Holly A. Mayer (Duquesne University), is the perfect companion reader for *America: A Narrative History*. The new edition has been brought into closer alignment with the main text, and the price has been reduced by nearly 50 percent. *For the Record* now has 225 primary-source readings from diaries, journals, newspaper articles, speeches, government documents, and novels, including a number of readings that highlight the new theme of religion in *America*. If you haven't looked at *For the Record* in a while, now would be a good time to take a look.

America: A Narrative History StudySpace (http://wwnorton.com/study space) provides a proven assignment-driven plan for each chapter. Highlights include chapter outlines, quizzes in the the new Quiz Plus format, iMaps and new iMap quizzes, map worksheets, flashcards, interactive timelines, new U.S. History Tours powered by Google Earth map technology, research topics, and several hundred multimedia primary-source documents. The *Norton Instructor's Resource Disk* provides enhanced PowerPoint lecture outlines with images from the text, four-color maps, the U.S. History Tours in a slideshow format, additional images from the Library of Congress archives, and audio files of historic speeches.

W. W. Norton is pleased to offer adopters the *Norton American History Digital Archive,* a set of seven DVDs, including a new DVD on religion that will help instructors visually tell the story of religion in the American experience.

The *Instructor's Manual and Test Bank,* by Stephen Davis (Kingwood College), Edward Richey (University of North Texas), Michael Krysko (Kansas State University), Brian McKnight (Angelo State University), and David Dewar (Angelo State University), includes a test bank of short-answer and essay questions, as well as detailed chapter outlines, lecture suggestions, and bibliographies. Finally, Norton coursepacks deliver all the instructional materials in a ready-to-use format for your course management system (Blackboard, WebCT, Angel, Moodle, and so on).

It's clear why *America* continues to set the standard when it comes to providing a low-cost book with high-value content. Your students will read it, and they will save money.

In preparing the Eighth Edition, I have benefited from the insights and suggestions of many people. Some of those insights have come from student readers of the text, and I encourage such feedback. I'd particularly like to thank Eirlys Barker (Thomas Nelson Community College), who was a reviewer for us and worked on the wonderful new student pedagogy in the text. Likewise, I'd like to thank Stephen Davis for his work on the *Instructor's*

Manual and Test Bank. I'd like to give special thanks to Brandon Franke (Blinn College, Bryan) for his work on the new PowerPoint lectures. Numerous scholars and survey instructors advised me on the new edition:

Heather Abdelnur (Augusta State University), Alan Autrey (Lamar University), Frank Baglione (Tallahassee Community College), Mario Bennekin (Georgia Perimeter College), William Bush (University of Nevada, Las Vegas), David Castle (Ohio University, Eastern), Craig Coenen (Mercer County Community College), Alice Connally (Purdue University, North Central), Scott Cook (Motlow State Community College), Amy Darty (University of Central Florida), Wade Derden (Pulaski Technical College), Brandon Franke (Blinn College, Bryan), Mark Goldman (Tallahassee Community College), James Good (North Harris College), Shane Hamilton (University of Georgia), Gene Hatfield (Clayton State University), Marc Horger (Ohio State University), Charles Killinger (Valencia Community College), Margaret (Peggy) Lambert (Lone Star College, Kingwood), Pat Ledbetter (North Central Texas College), Robby Luckett (University of Georgia), Lisa Morales (North Central Texas College, Corinth), Bret Nelson (San Jacinto College, North), Michael Nichols (Tarrant County College, Northwest), Yolanda Orizondo-Harding (University of Central Florida), George Pabis (Georgia Perimeter College), Thomas Price (State University of New York, Ulster County Community College), Brooks Simpson (Arizona State University), Alice Taylor-Colbert (University of Arkansas, Fort Smith), John Wegner (Eastern Michigan University), Joseph Whitehorne (Lord Fairfax Community College)

Once again, I thank my friends at W. W. Norton, especially Steve Forman, Jon Durbin, Steve Hoge, Karl Bakeman, Nicole Netherton, Melissa Atkin, Christine D'Antonio, Abigail Winograd, Rachel Comerford, Stephanie Romeo, and Jason Spears for their care and attention along the way.

Part One

A
NEW
WORLD

History is filled with ironies. Luck and accident often shape human affairs. Long before Christopher Columbus accidentally discovered the New World in his effort to find a passage to Asia, the tribal peoples he mislabeled Indians had occupied and shaped the lands of the Western Hemisphere. The first people to settle the New World were nomadic hunters and gatherers who had migrated from northeastern Asia during the last glacial advance of the Ice Age, nearly 20,000 years ago. By the end of the fifteenth century, when Columbus began his voyage west, there were millions of Native Americans living in the Western Hemisphere. Over the centuries they had developed diverse and often highly sophisticated societies, some rooted in agriculture, others in trade or imperial conquest.

The Native American cultures were, of course, profoundly affected by the arrival of peoples from Europe and Africa. Indians were exploited, infected, enslaved, displaced, and exterminated. Yet this conventional tale of tragic conquest oversimplifies the complex process by which Indians, Europeans, and Africans interacted. The Indians were more than passive victims; they were also trading partners and rivals of the transatlantic newcomers. They became enemies and allies, neighbors and advisers, converts and spouses. As such they fully participated in the creation of the new society known as America.

The Europeans who risked their lives to settle in the New World were themselves quite varied. Young and old, men and women, they came from Spain, Portugal, France, the British Isles, the Netherlands, Scandinavia, Italy, and the various German states. A variety of motives inspired them to undertake the often harrowing transatlantic voyage. Some were adventurers and fortune seekers eager to find gold, silver, and spices. Others were fervent Christians determined to create kingdoms of God in the New World. Still others were convicts, debtors, indentured servants, or political or religious exiles. Many were simply seeking a piece of land, higher wages, and greater economic opportunity. A settler in Pennsylvania noted that "poor people (both men and women) of all kinds can here get three times the wages for their labour than they can in England or Wales."

Yet such enticements were not sufficient to attract enough workers to keep up with the rapidly expanding colonial economies. So the Europeans began to force Indians to work for them. But there were never enough laborers to meet the unceasing demand. Moreover, captive Indians often escaped or were so rebellious that their use as slaves was banned in several colonies. The Massachusetts legislature outlawed forced labor because Indians were of such "a malicious, surly and revengeful spirit; rude and insolent in their behavior, and very ungovernable."

Beginning early in the seventeenth century, colonists turned to the African slave trade for their labor needs. In 1619 white traders began transporting captured Africans to the English colonies. This development would transform American society in ways that no one at the time envisioned. Few Europeans during the colonial era saw the contradiction between the New World's promise of individual freedom and the expanding institution of race-based slavery. Nor did they reckon with the problems associated with introducing into the new society people they considered alien and unassimilable.

The intermingling of peoples, cultures, and ecosystems from the continents of Africa, Europe, and North America gave colonial American society its distinctive vitality and variety. In turn, the diversity of the environment and the climate spawned quite different economies and patterns of living in the various regions of North America. As the original settlements grew into prosperous and populous colonies, the transplanted Europeans had to fashion social institutions and political systems to manage growth and control tensions.

At the same time, imperial rivalries among the Spanish, French, English, and Dutch triggered costly wars. The monarchs of Europe struggled to manage often unruly colonies, which, they discovered, played crucial roles in their European wars. Many of the colonists had brought with them to the New World a feisty independence, which led them to resent government interference in their affairs. A British official in North Carolina reported that the residents of the Piedmont region were "without any Law or Order. Impudence is so very high, as to be past bearing." As long as the reins of imperial control were loosely held, the two parties maintained an uneasy partnership. But as the British authorities tightened their control during the mid–eighteenth century, they met resistance, which became revolt and culminated in revolution.

1

THE COLLISION
OF CULTURES

FOCUS QUESTIONS   Ⓢ   wwnorton.com/studyspace

- What civilizations existed in pre-Columbian America?
- Why were European countries, such as Spain and Portugal, prepared to embark on voyages of discovery by the sixteenth century?
- How did contact between the Western Hemisphere and the "Old World" change through the exchange of plants, animals, and pathogens?
- What were the Europeans' reasons for establishing colonies in America?
- What is the legacy of the Spanish presence in North America?
- What effect did the Protestant Reformation have on the colonization of the New World?

The "New World" discovered by Christopher Columbus was in fact home to civilizations thousands of years old. Until recently, archaeologists had long assumed that the first humans in the Western Hemisphere were Siberians who some 12,000 to 15,000 years ago had crossed the Bering Strait on a land bridge to Alaska made accessible by receding waters during the last Ice Age. These nomadic hunters and their descendants, dubbed Paleo-Indians by archaeologists, drifted south in pursuit of vast herds of large mammals: mammoths, musk oxen, bison, and woolly rhinoceroses. Over the next 500 years small bands fanned out across the entire hemisphere, from the Arctic Circle to the tip of South America. Recent archaeological discoveries in Pennsylvania, Virginia, and Chile suggest a much more complicated story of human settlement. The new evidence reveals that prehistoric humans may have arrived by sea much earlier (perhaps 18,000 to 40,000 years ago), however, from various parts of Asia—and some may even have crossed the Atlantic Ocean from southwestern Europe.

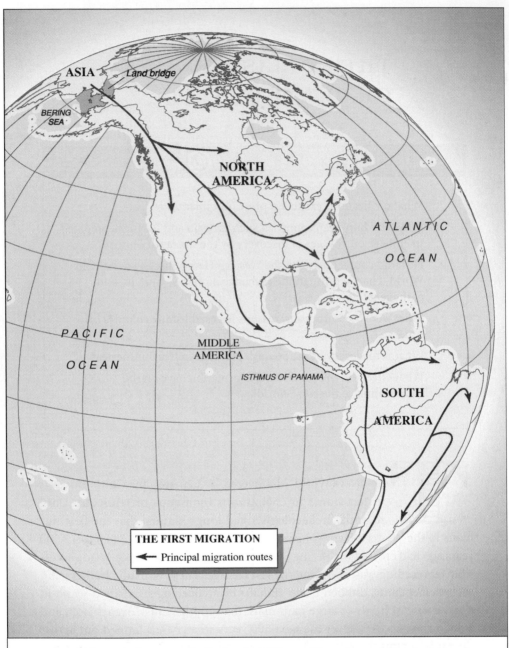

When did people first cross the Bering Sea? What evidence have archaeologists and anthropologists found from the lives of the first people in America? Why did those people travel to North America?

PRE-COLUMBIAN INDIAN CIVILIZATIONS

The first humans in North America discovered an immense continent with extraordinary climatic and environmental diversity. Coastal plains, broad grasslands, harsh deserts, and soaring mountain ranges generated distinct environments, social structures, and cultural patterns. By the time Columbus happened upon the New World, the people living in North America may have numbered over 10 million. They had developed a diverse array of communities in which more than 400 languages were spoken. Yet despite the distances and dialects separating them, the Indian societies created extensive trading networks, which helped spread ideas and innovations. Contrary to the romantic myth of early Indian civilizations' living in perfect harmony with nature and one another, the indigenous societies often exploited the environment and engaged in frequent warfare.

EARLY CULTURES   After centuries of nomadic life, the ancient Indians settled in more permanent villages. Thousands of years after people first appeared in North America, climatic changes and extensive hunting had killed off the largest mammals. Global warming diminished grasslands and stimulated forest growth, which provided plants and small animals for human consumption. The ancient Indians adapted to the new environments by inventing fiber snares, basketry, and mills for grinding nuts, and they domesticated the dog and the turkey. A new cultural stage arrived with the introduction of farming, fishing, and pottery making. Hunting now focused on faster, more elusive mammals: deer, antelope, elk, moose, and caribou. Already by about 5000 B.C., Indians of the Mexican highlands were consuming the plant foods that would become the staples of the New World: chiefly maize (corn), beans, and squash but also chili peppers, avocados, and pumpkins.

THE MAYAS, AZTECS, CHIBCHAS, AND INCAS   Between about 2000 and 1500 B.C., permanent farming towns appeared in Mexico. The more settled life in turn provided time for the cultivation of religion, crafts, art, science, administration—and frequent warfare. From about A.D. 300 to 900, Middle America (Mesoamerica, what is now Mexico and Central America) developed densely populated city centers complete with gigantic pyramids, temples, and palaces, all supported by surrounding peasant villages. Moreover, the Mayas used mathematics and astronomy to devise a calendar more accurate than the one the Europeans were using at the time of Columbus.

In about A.D. 900 the complex Mayan culture collapsed. The Mayas had overexploited the rain forest, upon whose fragile ecosystem they depended.

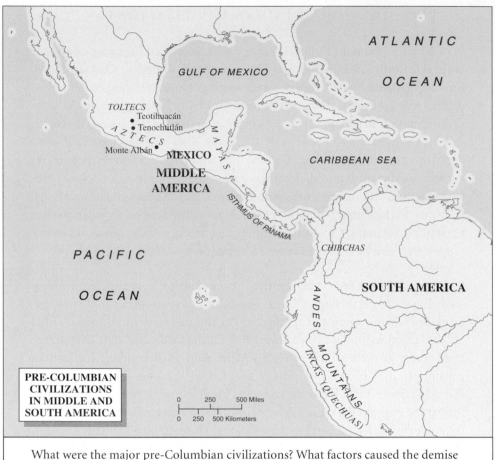

TOLTECS
• Teotihuacán
• Tenochtitlán
AZTECS
Monte Albán • MEXICO
MIDDLE
AMERICA
MAYAS
ISTHMUS OF PANAMA

GULF OF MEXICO

ATLANTIC
OCEAN

CARIBBEAN SEA

CHIBCHAS

SOUTH AMERICA

PACIFIC

OCEAN

ANDES MOUNTAINS INCAS (QUECHUAS)

**PRE-COLUMBIAN
CIVILIZATIONS
IN MIDDLE AND
SOUTH AMERICA**

0   250   500 Miles
0   250   500 Kilometers

What were the major pre-Columbian civilizations? What factors caused the demise of the Mayan civilization? When did the Aztecs build Tenochtitlán?

As an archaeologist has explained, "Too many farmers grew too many crops on too much of the landscape." Deforestation led to hillside erosion and a catastrophic loss of farmland. Overpopulation added to the strain on Mayan society, prompting civil wars. Mayan war parties destroyed one another's cities and took prisoners, who were then sacrificed to the gods in theatrical rituals. Whatever the reasons for the weakening of Mayan society, it succumbed to the Toltecs, a warlike people who conquered most of the region in the tenth century. But around A.D. 1200 the Toltecs mysteriously withdrew.

During the late thirteenth century the Aztecs arrived from the northwest to fill the vacuum in the Basin of Mexico. They founded the city of

Mayan society

A fresco depicting the social divisions of Mayan society. A Mayan lord, at the center, receives offerings.

Tenochtitlán in 1325 and gradually expanded their control over central Mexico. When the Spanish invaded in 1519, the sprawling Aztec Empire ruled over perhaps 5 million people—though estimates range as high as 20 million.

Farther south, in what is now Colombia, the Chibchas built a similar empire on a smaller scale. Still farther south the Quechuas (better known as the Incas, from the name for their ruler) controlled a sprawling empire that by the fifteenth century stretched 1,000 miles along the Andes Mountains from Ecuador to Chile. It was crisscrossed by an elaborate system of roads and organized under an autocratic government.

INDIAN CULTURES OF NORTH AMERICA The pre-Columbian Indians of the present-day United States created three distinct civilizations: the Adena-Hopewell culture of the Ohio River valley (800 B.C.–A.D. 600), the Mississippian culture of the Southeast (A.D. 600–1500), and the Hohokam-Anasazi culture of the Southwest (400 B.C.–present). None of these developed as fully as the civilizations of the Mayas, Aztecs, and Incas to the south. Like the tribes of Mexico and South America, the North American Indians

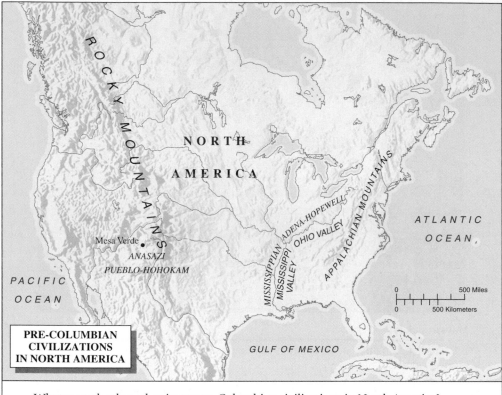

PACIFIC OCEAN

ATLANTIC OCEAN

Mesa Verde•
ANASAZI
PUEBLO-HOHOKAM

**PRE-COLUMBIAN
CIVILIZATIONS
IN NORTH AMERICA**

GULF OF MEXICO

What were the three dominant pre-Columbian civilizations in North America? Where was the Adena-Hopewell culture centered? How was the Mississippian civilization similar to that of the Mayans or Aztecs? What made the Anasazi culture different from the other North American cultures?

often warred with one another. They also enslaved other Indians, tortured captives, and scalped victims. Some tribes practiced ritual cannibalism. Yet they also created sustainable cultures that were as diverse, dynamic, and mobile as those of the peoples of Europe. The Native American tribes of North America shared some fundamental myths and beliefs, especially concerning the sacredness of nature, the necessity of communal living, and respect for elders, but they developed in different ways at different times and in different places. In North America alone, there were probably 240 different tribes when the Europeans arrived.

The Adena-Hopewell culture in what is today the American Midwest left behind enormous earthworks and hundreds of elaborate burial mounds, some of them elaborately shaped like great snakes, birds, and other animals.

The Adena and, later, the Hopewell Indians were gatherers and hunters. Evidence from the burial mounds suggests that they had a complex social structure featuring a specialized division of labor. Moreover, the Hopewells developed an elaborate trade network that spanned the continent.

The Mississippian culture, centered in the southern Mississippi River valley, flourished between 900 and 1350. It resembled the Mayan and Aztec societies in its intensive agricultural economy, which was based on growing corn, beans, and squashes. The Missis-

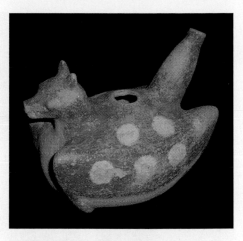

Mississippian artifacts

Mississippians produced finely made pottery, such as this deer-effigy jar.

sippians built substantial towns around central plazas and temples. Like the Aztecs, they developed a highly stratified social structure and spiritual death cults, which involved ceremonial human torture and sacrifice. Like the Hopewells to the north, the Mississippians developed a specialized labor system, an effective governmental structure, and an expansive trading network. The Mississippian culture peaked in the fourteenth century and succumbed first to climate change and finally to pandemic diseases brought by Europeans.

The arid Southwest spawned irrigation-based cultures, elements of which exist today and heirs to which (the Hopis, Zunis, and others) still live in the adobe cliff dwellings (called *pueblos* by the Spanish) erected by their ancestors. About A.D. 500, Hohokam Indians migrated from present-day Mexico into today's southern Arizona. They developed sophisticated irrigation systems in order to grow corn and other crops, and they constructed temple mounds similar to those in Mexico. For unknown reasons, the Hohokam society disappeared during the fifteenth century.

The most widespread and best known of the Southwest cultures were the Anasazi ("Enemy's Ancestors" in the Navajo language). In ancient times they developed extensive settlements in the "four corners," where the states of Arizona, New Mexico, Colorado, and Utah meet. In contrast to the Mesoamerican and Mississippian cultures, Anasazi society lacked a rigid class structure. The religious leaders and warriors labored much as the rest of the people did. In fact, the Anasazi engaged in warfare only as a means of

Cliff dwellings

Ruins of Anasazi cliff dwellings in Mesa Verde National Park, Colorado.

self-defense (*Hopi* means "Peaceful People"). Environmental factors shaped Anasazi culture and eventually caused its decline. Toward the end of the thirteenth century, a lengthy drought and the pressure of migrating Indians from the north threatened the survival of Anasazi society.

NATIVE AMERICANS IN 1500 When Europeans began to arrive in North America in the sixteenth and seventeenth centuries, as many as 4 million Indians lived on a continent crisscrossed by trails and rivers that formed an extensive trading network. The scores of tribes can be clustered according to three major regional groups: the Eastern Woodlands tribes, the Great Plains tribes, and the Western tribes. Although the tribes differed by geography, language, and customs, they shared many attributes and assumptions. They believed that sacred spirits live within plants and animals, and the daily challenge was to keep the spirits satisfied so as to ensure good weather, bountiful harvests, abundant game animals, and victory in battle. Not the least of their shared assumptions was that the European explorers and settlers were trespassing on their lands.

The Eastern Woodlands peoples tended to live along the rivers coursing through primeval forests. They included three distinct regional groups: the Algonquian, the Iroquoian, and the Muskogean. The dozens of Algonquian-speaking tribes stretched far beyond the Eastern Woodlands; those living in the East included the Lenni–Lenape (the Delaware), the Lumbee, the Mahican, the Mohegan, the Pequot, the Narragansett, the Wampanoag, and the Powhatan tribes making up the Confederacy. Their settlements reached from the New England seaboard to lands along the Great Lakes and into the upper Midwest and south to New Jersey, Virginia, and the Carolinas. The Algonquian tribes along the coast were skilled at fishing; the inland tribes excelled at hunting. All of them practiced agriculture to some extent, and they frequently used canoes hollowed out of trees ("dugouts") to navigate rivers and lakes. Most Algonquians lived in small round shelters called wigwams. Their villages typically ranged from 500 to 2,000 inhabitants.

West and south of the Algonquians were the Iroquoian tribes (including the Seneca, Onondaga, Mohawk, Oneida, and Cayuga, and the Cherokee and Tuscarora in the South), whose lands spread from upstate New York south through Pennsylvania and into the upland regions of the Carolinas and Georgia. The Iroquois's skill at growing corn led them to create permanent agricultural villages. Around their villages they constructed log walls and within them they built enormous bark-covered longhouses, which housed several related family clans. Unlike the patriarchal Algonquian culture, Iroquoian society was matriarchal. In part, the matriarchy reflected the frequent absence of Iroquois men. As adept hunters and traders, the men traveled extensively for long periods. Women headed the clans, selected the chiefs, controlled the distribution of property, and planted and harvested the crops.

The third major Indian group in the Eastern Woodlands were the Muskogean-speaking chiefdoms of the South. They included the Creek, Chickasaw, and Choctaw tribes. West of the Mississippi River were the Indian peoples living on the Great Plains and in the Great Basin (present-day Utah and Nevada), many of whom had migrated from the East.

The Native Americans of the Great Plains, the Plains Indians, were a diverse lot. The Blackfeet, Cheyenne, and Arapaho were Algonquian-speaking tribes. The Comanche were Shoshonean, the Apache were Athabaskan, and the Teton Sioux and Crow were Siouan. All were nomadic tribes whose culture focused on hunting the vast herds of bison and growing corn.

The Western tribes, living along the Pacific coast, depended upon fishing, sealing, and whaling. Among them were Salish tribes, including the Tillamook; the Chinook; and the Pomo and Chumash, both speakers of a Hokan language.

Over the centuries the Native Americans of North America had adapted to changing climates and changing environments. Their resilience was remarkable. But they were unprepared for the arrival of Europeans, who were intent upon conquering, converting, exploiting, enslaving, and destroying them. The results were devastating and tragic. Epidemics wiped out millions. Thousands more were killed by European guns and swords. Many Indians were forced to become Christians and to abandon their traditional lands, folkways, and customs. Yet amid the chaos and the carnage, Native Americans proved to be resourceful and resilient. Survivors banded together to reunite families, form new communities, preserve their traditions, and absorb the massive changes transforming their world. What for years was viewed as a simple process of conquest and displacement was in fact much more complex and nuanced. In the process of changing and adapting to new realities in accordance with their own traditions, Native Americans played a crucial role in shaping America and the origins of the United States.

EUROPEAN VISIONS OF AMERICA

The European discovery of America was fueled by curiosity and enabled by advances in nautical technology. Europeans had long imagined what

Vikings in the New World

A Viking settlement at L'Anse aux Meadows, Newfoundland. Reconstructed longhouses in Icelandic Viking style are in the background.

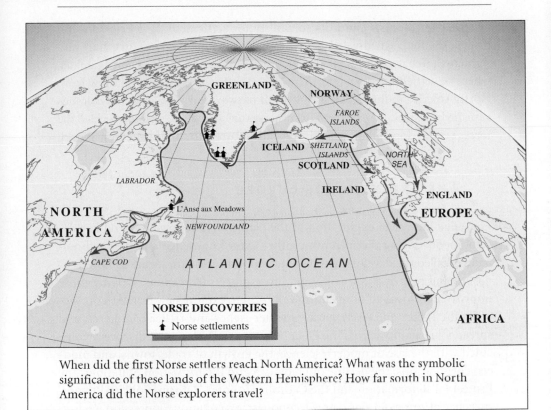

NORSE DISCOVERIES

♦ Norse settlements

When did the first Norse settlers reach North America? What was the symbolic significance of these lands of the Western Hemisphere? How far south in North America did the Norse explorers travel?

lay beyond the western horizon. During the tenth and eleventh centuries the Vikings (Norse peoples who lived in Scandinavia) crisscrossed much of the globe. They were the world's most intrepid explorers and the most feared warriors. They boasted the strongest iron, sharpest swords, and sturdiest and fastest warships. From villages in Norway, Sweden, and Denmark, Viking warriors and traders ventured thousands of miles to the east and the south: down to North Africa, across the Baltic Sea, up Russian rivers, and across the Black Sea to the fabled Turkish capital, Constantinople (present-day Istanbul). The Vikings also headed west, crossing the North Sea and the Atlantic Ocean, raiding towns in Ireland, settling in Iceland, and then exploring the coast of the uppermost reaches of North America.

Around A.D. 985 a Norse Icelander named Erik the Red colonized the west coast of a rocky, fogbound island he called Greenland. The world's largest island, Greenland was almost totally covered by ice and devoid of human inhabitants. The Vikings established a settlement on the southwest coast. Erik the Red ironically named the island Greenland in hopes of misleading prospective colonists about its suitability for settlement. Leif Eriksson, son of Erik the Red, sailed west and south from Greenland about A.D. 1001 and sighted the coast of present-day New Foundland in northeastern Canada, where he settled for the winter. The Norse settlers eventually withdrew from North America in the face of hostile Inuit natives, and the Greenland colonies vanished mysteriously in the fifteenth century. Nowhere in Europe had the forces yet developed that would inspire adventurers to subdue the New World.

THE EXPANSION OF EUROPE

The European exploration of the New World followed several key developments during the fifteenth century. New knowledge and new technologies enabled the development of better ships, more accurate navigation techniques and map-making skills, and more powerful weapons. Driving those improvements was an unrelenting ambition to explore new territories (especially the Indies and Asia), garner greater riches and richer commerce, and spread Christianity across the globe. This remarkable age of discovery coincided with the rise of modern science; the growth of trade, towns, and modern corporations; the decline of feudalism and the formation of nations; the Protestant Reformation and the Catholic Counter-Reformation; and the resurgence of some old sins—greed, conquest, exploitation, oppression, racism, and slavery—that quickly defiled the mythical innocence of the New World.

RENAISSANCE GEOGRAPHY   For more than two centuries before Columbus, the mind of Europe quickened with the so-called Renaissance—the rediscovery of ancient texts, the rebirth of secular learning, the spirit of inquiry, all of which spread more rapidly after Johannes Gutenberg's invention of a printing press with movable type around 1440. Learned Europeans of the fifteenth century held in almost reverential awe the authority of ancient learning. The age of discovery was especially influenced by ancient concepts of geography. As early as the sixth century B.C., Greek mathematicians had taught the sphericity of the earth, and in the third century B.C. the earth's size was accurately computed. Such knowledge was widely accepted in Renaissance universities. So the myth that Columbus was trying to prove that the world is round is one of those falsehoods that will not disappear even in the face of evidence. No informed person at that time thought the earth was flat.

Progress in the art of navigation accompanied the revival of learning. In the fifteenth century, mariners used new instruments to sight stars and find the latitude. Steering across the open sea, however, remained a matter of dead reckoning. A ship's captain set his course along a given latitude and calculated it from the angle of the North Star or, with less certainty, the sun, estimating speed by the eye. Longitude remained a matter of guesswork since accurate timepieces were needed to determine it; ship's clocks remained too inaccurate until the development of more precise chronometers in the eighteenth century.

THE GROWTH OF TRADE, TOWNS, AND NATION-STATES

Europe's interest in exploration derived primarily from the dramatic growth of urban commerce and global trade. In its farthest reaches this commerce moved either overland or through the eastern Mediterranean all the way to east Asia, where Europeans acquired medicine, silks, precious stones, dyewoods, perfumes, and rugs. There they also purchased the much-coveted spices—pepper, nutmeg, clove—so essential for preserving food and enhancing its flavor. The growing trade between Europe and Asia gave rise to a merchant class and to the idea of corporations, through which stockholders would share risks and profits.

The foreign trade was chancy and costly. Goods commonly passed from hand to hand, from ships to pack trains and back to ships, along the way subject to taxes demanded by various rulers. The Muslim world, from Spain across North Africa and into central Asia, straddled the important trade routes, adding to the hazards. Muslims tenaciously opposed efforts to "Christianize" their lands. Little wonder, then, that Europeans should dream of an all-water route to the coveted spices of east Asia and the Indies.

Another spur to global exploration was the rise of centralized nations, ruled by powerful kings and queens who had the power and the money to sponsor the search for foreign riches. The growth of the merchant class went hand in hand with the growth of centralized political power. Merchants wanted uniform currencies, trade laws, and the elimination of trade barriers. They thus became natural allies of the trade-loving monarchs, who could meet their needs. In turn, merchants and university-trained professionals supplied the monarchs with money, lawyers, and government officials. The Crusades—European armies sent between 1095 and 1270 to capture the Holy Land—had also advanced the process of international trade and exploration. The Crusades had brought Europe into contact with the Middle East and had decimated the ranks of the feudal lords, who were killed while fighting Muslims. And new means of warfare—the use of gunpowder and standing armies—further weakened the independence of the nobility relative to royal power.

By 1492 the map of western Europe showed several united kingdoms: France, where in 1453 Charles VII had emerged from the Hundred Years'

War as head of a unified nation; England, where in 1485 Henry VII had emerged victorious after thirty years of civil strife known as the Wars of the Roses; Portugal, where John I had fought off the Castilians to ensure national independence; and Spain, where in 1469 Ferdinand of Aragon and Isabella of Castile had ended an era of chronic civil war when they united two great kingdoms in marriage. The Spanish king and queen were crusading expansionists. On January 1, 1492, after nearly eight centuries of religious warfare between Spanish Christians and Moorish Muslims on the Iberian Peninsula, Ferdinand and Isabella declared victory for Catholicism at Granada, the last Muslim stronghold. They gave the defeated Muslims a desperate choice: convert to Christianity or leave Spain. Soon thereafter Ferdinand and Isabella gave the Sephardi, those Jews living in Spain and Portugal, the same awful ultimatum: convert to Catholicism or leave the kingdom.

These factors—urbanization, world trade, the rise of centralized national states, and advances in knowledge, technology, and firepower—combined with natural human curiosity, greed, and religious zeal to create the outburst of energy that spurred the discovery and conquest of the New World. Beginning in the late fifteenth century, Europeans set in motion the events that, as one historian has observed, bound together "four continents, three races, and a great diversity of regional parts." During the two and a half centuries after 1492, the Spanish developed the most extensive empire the world had ever known. It would span southern Europe and the Netherlands, much of the Western Hemisphere, and parts of Asia. Yet the Spanish Empire grew so vast that its very size and complexity eventually led to its disintegration. In the meantime, the expansion of Spanish influence around the world helped shape much of the development of American society and history.

THE VOYAGES OF COLUMBUS

It was in seafaring Portugal, the westernmost country in Europe, that exploration and discovery began in earnest. In 1422 the Portuguese dispatched a naval expedition to map the West African coast. Driven partly by the hope of outflanking the Islamic world and partly by the hope of lucrative trade, the Portuguese by 1446 had reached the Cape Verde Islands and then the equator and, by 1482, the Congo River. In 1488, Bartholomeu Dias rounded the Cape of Good Hope, at Africa's southern tip. Ten years later Dias's countryman Vasco da Gama went even farther, rounding the Cape of Good Hope and venturing, with four ships, all the way to India.

Christopher Columbus, meanwhile, was learning his trade in the school of Portuguese seamanship. Born in Genoa, Italy, in 1451, the son of a weaver, Columbus took to the sea at an early age, making up for his lack of formal education by teaching himself geography, navigation, and Latin. By the 1480s, Columbus, a tall, white-haired, blue-eyed mariner, was eager to spread Christianity across the globe. Dazzled by the prospect of Asian riches, he developed a bold plan to reach the Indies (India, China, the East Indies, or Japan) by sailing west across the Atlantic. Columbus eventually persuaded Ferdinand and Isabella, the Spanish monarchs, to award him a tenth share of any pearls; gold, silver, or other precious metals; and valuable spices he found in any new territories. The legend that the queen had to hock the crown jewels to finance the voyage is as spurious as the fable that Columbus set out to prove the earth was round.

The Italian Columbus chartered one seventy-five-foot ship, the *Santa María*, and the Spanish city of Palos supplied two smaller caravels, the *Pinta* and the *Niña*. From Palos on August 3, 1492, this little squadron, with about ninety officers and men, most of them Spaniards, set sail westward for what Columbus thought was Asia. As the weeks passed, the crew grew restless and worried. But early on October 12 a lookout yelled, "*Tierra! Tierra!*" (Land! Land!) He had sighted an island in the Bahamas east of Florida that Columbus named San Salvador (Blessed Savior). Once ashore, Columbus and his men raised the Castilian flag, which featured a green cross. Catholicism, not Puritanism, was the first European religion to reach the Americas. Columbus decided, incorrectly, they were near the Indies, so he called the island people *los Indios*. He described the "Indians" as naked people, "very well made, of very handsome bodies and very good faces." He added that "with fifty men they could all be subjugated and compelled to do anything one wishes." It would be easy, he said, "to convert these people [to Catholicism] and make them work for us."

Christopher Columbus

A portrait by Sebastiano del Piombo, ca. 1519 said to be Christopher Columbus.

Columbus continued to search for a passage to the fabled Indies through the Bahamian Cays, down to Cuba, and then eastward to the island he named Española (or Hispaniola, now the site of Haiti and the Dominican Republic), where he first found significant amounts of gold jewelry and was introduced to tobacco. Columbus learned of, but did not encounter until his second voyage, the fierce Caribs of the Lesser Antilles. The Caribbean Sea was named after them, and because of their alleged bad habits the word *cannibal* was derived from a Spanish version of their name (Caníbal).

On the night before Christmas 1492, the *Santa María* ran aground off Hispaniola. Columbus, still believing he had reached Asia, decided to return home. He left about forty men behind and seized a dozen natives to present as gifts to Spain's royal couple. When Columbus reached Spain, he received a hero's welcome. Thanks to the newly invented printing press, news of his discovery spread rapidly across Europe. In Italy, Pope Alexander VI, himself a Spaniard, was so convinced that God favored the conquest of the New World that he awarded Spain the right to control the entire hemisphere so that its pagan natives could be converted to Christianity. Buoyed by such support and by the same burning religious zeal to battle heathens that had

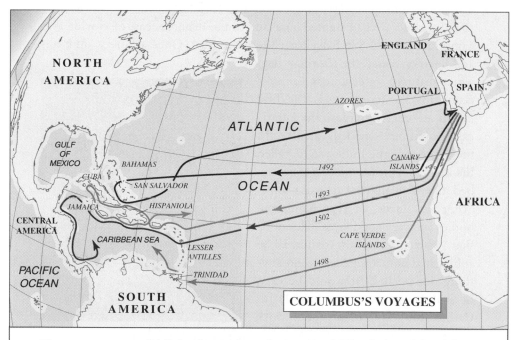

COLUMBUS'S VOYAGES

How many voyages did Columbus make to the Americas? What is the origin of the name for the Caribbean Sea? What happened to the colony that Columbus left on Hispaniola in 1493?

forced the Moors and the Jews into exile or conversion, Ferdinand and Isabella instructed Columbus to prepare for a second voyage. The Spanish monarchs also set about shoring up their legal claim against Portugal's possible pretensions to the newly discovered lands. Spain and Portugal reached a compromise, called the Treaty of Tordesillas (1494), which drew an imaginary line west of the Cape Verde Islands and stipulated that the area to its west would be a Spanish sphere of exploration and settlement.

Columbus returned across the Atlantic in 1493 with seventeen ships, livestock, and over 1,000 men, as well as royal instructions to "treat the Indians very well." Also on board were Catholic priests charged with converting the Indians. Back in the New World, Admiral Columbus discovered that the camp he had left behind was in chaos. The unsupervised soldiers had run amok, raping women, robbing villages, and as Columbus's son later added, "committing a thousand excesses for which they were mortally hated by the Indians." The Indians struck back and killed ten Spaniards. A furious Columbus attacked the villages. The Spaniards, armed with crossbows, guns, and ferocious dogs, decimated the natives and loaded 550 of them onto ships bound for the slave market in Spain.

Columbus then ventured out across the Caribbean Sea before returning to Spain in 1496. On a third voyage, in 1498, Columbus found Trinidad and explored the northern coast of South America. He led a fourth and final voyage in 1502, during which he sailed along the coast of Central America, still looking in vain for Asia. Having been marooned on Jamaica for more than a year, he finally returned to Spain in 1504. He died two years later.

To the end, Columbus insisted that he had discovered the outlying parts of Asia. Full awareness that a great landmass lay between Europe and Asia dawned on the Europeans very slowly. By one of history's greatest ironies, this lag led the New World to be named not for Columbus but for another Italian explorer, Amerigo Vespucci, who sailed to the New World in 1499. Vespucci landed on the coast of South America and reported that it was so large it must be a "new" continent. European mapmakers thereafter began to label the New World using a variant of Vespucci's first name: America.

THE GREAT BIOLOGICAL EXCHANGE

The first European contacts with the place Europeans were soon calling the New World began an unprecedented worldwide biological and social exchange, a diffusion of distinctive elements that ultimately worked in favor of the Europeans at the expense of the natives. Indians, Europeans, and

A land Sort th to the Sausges extreme above all other Torts

Unfamiliar wildlife

A box tortoise drawn by John White, one of the earliest English settlers in America.

eventually Africans intersected to create new religious beliefs and languages, adopt new tastes in food, and develop new modes of dress.

If anything, the plants and animals of the two worlds were more different from each other than were the peoples and their ways of life. Europeans had never seen such creatures as the fearsome (if harmless) iguana, the flying squirrel, fish with whiskers like those of a cat, or the rattlesnake, nor had they seen anything quite like several other species: bison, cougars, armadillos, opossums, sloths, tapirs, anacondas, American eels, toucans, condors, and hummingbirds. Turkeys, guinea pigs, llamas, and alpacas were all new to Europeans. Nor did the Native Americans know of horses, cattle, pigs, sheep, goats, and (maybe) chickens, which soon arrived from Europe in abundance. Yet within a half century whole islands of the Caribbean would be overrun by pigs.

The exchange of plant life between Old and New Worlds worked a revolution in the diets of both hemispheres. Before Columbus's voyage three staples of the modern diet were unknown in Europe: maize (corn), potatoes (sweet and white), and many kinds of beans (snap, kidney, lima, and others). The white potato, although commonly called Irish, actually migrated from South America to Europe and reached North America only with the Scotch-Irish immigrants of the early eighteenth century. Other New World food plants include peanuts, squash, peppers, tomatoes, pumpkins, pineapples, sassafras, papayas, guavas, avocados, cacao (the source of chocolate), and chicle (for chewing gum). Europeans in turn introduced rice, wheat, barley, oats, wine grapes, melons, coffee, olives, bananas, "Kentucky" bluegrass, daisies, and dandelions to the New World.

The beauty of the biological exchange was that the food plants were more complementary than competitive. Corn, it turned out, could flourish almost anywhere—in highland or low, in hot climates or cold, in wetland or dry. It spread quickly throughout the world. Before the end of the 1500s, American maize and sweet potatoes were staple crops in China. The nutritious food crops exported from the Americas thus helped nourish a worldwide population explosion probably greater than any since the invention of agriculture. The dramatic increase in the European populations fueled by the new foods in turn helped provide the surplus of people who colonized the New World.

Europeans, moreover, adopted many Native American devices: canoes, snowshoes, moccasins, hammocks, kayaks, ponchos, dogsleds, and toboggans. The rubber ball and the game of lacrosse have Indian origins. New words entered European languages: *wigwam, tepee, papoose, tomahawk, succotash, hominy, moose, skunk, raccoon, opossum, woodchuck, chipmunk, hickory, pecan,* and hundreds of others. The natives also left the map dotted with place-names of Indian origin long after they were gone, from Miami to Yakima, from Penobscot to Yuma. There were still other New World contributions: tobacco and several other drugs, including curare (a muscle relaxant), coca (for making cocaine), and cinchona bark (for making quinine).

By far the most significant aspect of the biological exchange, however, was the transmission of infectious diseases from Europe and Africa to the Americas. European colonists and enslaved Africans brought with them

Smallpox

Aztec victims of the 1538 smallpox epidemic are covered in shrouds (center) as two others lie dying (at right).

deadly pathogens that Native Americans had never experienced: smallpox, typhus, diphtheria, bubonic plague, malaria, yellow fever, and cholera. The results were catastrophic. Far more Indians—tens of millions—died from contagions than from combat. Major diseases such as typhus and smallpox produced pandemics in the New World on a scale never witnessed in history. Unable to explain or cure the contagions, Indian chiefs and religious leaders often lost their stature. As a consequence, tribal cohesion and cultural life disintegrated, and efforts to resist European assaults collapsed.

Smallpox was an especially ghastly and highly contagious disease in the New World. In central Mexico alone, some 8 million people, perhaps a third of the entire Indian population, died of smallpox within a decade of the arrival of the Spanish. In colonial North America, as Indians died by the tens of thousands, disease became the most powerful weapon of the European invaders. A Spanish explorer noted that "half the natives" died from

Impact of European diseases

This 1592 engraving shows a shaman (top left) in a Brazilian village using his rattle to attract benevolent spirits to heal the diseases brought by Europeans.

smallpox and "blamed us." Many Europeans, however, interpreted such epidemics as diseases sent by God to punish Indians who resisted conversion to Christianity.

PROFESSIONAL EXPLORERS

The news of Columbus's remarkable voyages raced across Europe. Professional explorers, mostly Italians, hired themselves out to look for the elusive western passage to Asia. They probed the shorelines of America during the early sixteenth century in the vain search for an opening and thus increased by leaps and bounds European knowledge of the New World.

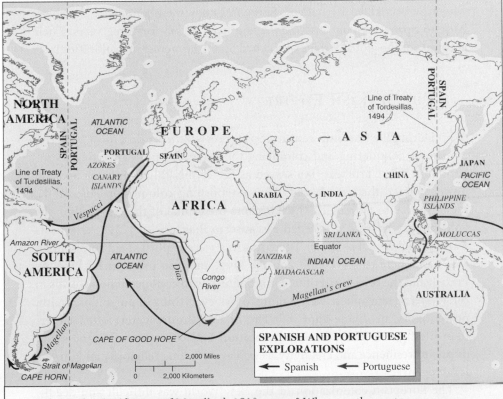

What is the significance of Magellan's 1519 voyage? What was the controversy over the Treaty of Tordesillas? What biological exchanges resulted from these early explorations?

The first to sight the North American continent was John Cabot, a Venetian sponsored by Henry VII of England. Authorized to "conquer and possess" any territory he found, Cabot crossed the North Atlantic in 1497. His landfall at what the king called "the new founde lande," in present-day Canada, gave England the basis for a later claim to all of North America. During the early sixteenth century, however, the English grew so preoccupied with internal divisions and conflicts with France that they failed to capitalize on Cabot's discoveries. In 1513 the Spaniard Vasco Núñez de Balboa became the first European to sight the Pacific Ocean, having crossed the Isthmus of Panama on foot.

The Spanish were eager to find a passage from the Atlantic to the Pacific. To that end, in 1519 Ferdinand Magellan, a haughty Portuguese sea captain hired by the Spanish, discovered the strait at the southern tip of South America that now bears his name. Magellan kept sailing north and west across the Pacific Ocean, discovering Guam and, eventually, the Philippines, where he was killed by natives. Surviving crew members made their way back to Spain, arriving in 1522, having been at sea for three years. Their accounts of the global voyage quickened Spanish interest in exploration.

THE SPANISH EMPIRE

During the sixteenth century, Spain created the world's most powerful empire by conquering and colonizing the Americas and converting its inhabitants. The Caribbean Sea served as the funnel through which Spanish power entered the New World. After establishing colonies on Hispaniola, including Santo Domingo, which became the capital of the West Indies, the gold-hungry Spanish proceeded eastward to Puerto Rico (1508) and westward to Cuba (1511–1514). Their motives were explicit. Said one soldier, "We came here to serve God and the king, and also to get rich." Like the French and the British after them, the Spanish who conquered new worlds in the Western Hemisphere were willing to risk everything in pursuit of wealth, power, glory, or divine approval. The first adventurers were often larger-than-life figures. They displayed ambition and courage, ruthlessness and duplicity, resilience and creativity, as well as crusading religiosity and imperial arrogance.

The European colonization of the New World was difficult and deadly. Most of those in the first wave of settlement died of malnutrition or disease. But the Native Americans suffered even more casualties. Even the most developed Indian societies of the sixteenth century were ill equipped to resist the European cultures invading their world. Disunity everywhere—civil disorder and rebellion plagued the Aztecs and Incas—left the indigenous peoples vulnerable to division and foreign conquest. The onslaught of soldiers and microbes from Europe perplexed and overwhelmed the Indians. Europeans presumed that their civilization was superior to those they discovered in the New World. And such presumed superiority justified in their minds the conquest and enslavement of Indians, the destruction of their way of life, and the seizure of their land and treasures.

A CLASH OF CULTURES The often-violent encounter between Spaniards and Indians involved more than a clash between different peoples. It also involved contrasting forms of technological development. The Indians of Mexico had copper and bronze but no iron. Whereas Indians used dugout canoes for transportation, Europeans sailed heavily armed oceangoing vessels. The Spanish ships not only carried human cargo; they also brought steel swords, firearms, explosives, and armor. These advanced military tools terrified many Indians. A Spanish priest in Florida observed that gunpowder "frightens the most valiant and courageous Indian and renders him slave to the white man's command." Such weaponry helps explain why the Europeans were able to defeat far superior numbers of Indians. Arrows and tomahawks were seldom a match for guns, cannons, and smallpox.

The Europeans enjoyed other cultural advantages. For example, the only domestic four-legged animals in North America were dogs and llamas. The Spaniards, on the other hand, brought with them horses, pigs, and cattle, all of which served as sources of food and leather. Horses provided greater speed in battle and introduced a decided psychological advantage. "The most essential thing in new lands is horses," reported one Spanish soldier. "They instill the greatest fear in the enemy and make the Indians respect the leaders of the army." Even more feared among the Indians were the greyhound dogs that the Spaniards used to guard their camps.

CORTES'S CONQUEST The most dramatic European conquest of a major Indian civilization on the North American mainland occurred in Mexico. The Spanish invasion began on February 18, 1519, when Hernán Cortés, driven by dreams of gold and glory in Mexico, set sail from Cuba with nearly 600 soldiers and sailors. Also on board were 200 Cubans, sixteen horses, and several cannons. After the invaders landed at what is now Veracruz, on the coast of the Gulf of Mexico, they began to move inland, where they assaulted thousands of Indian warriors of Tlaxcala, a confederation of four small kingdoms indendent of, and opposed to, the Aztecs. After

Cortés in Mexico

Page from the Lienzo de Tlaxcala, a historical narrative from the sixteenth century. The scene, in which Cortés is shown seated on a throne, depicts the arrival of the Spaniards in Tlaxcala.

defeating the Tlaxcalans, Cortés shrewdly persuaded the vanquished warriors to join his advance on the hated Aztecs.

Cortés's soldiers, called conquistadores, received no pay; they were military entrepreneurs willing to risk their lives for a share in the expected plunder and slaves. The ruthless Cortés had participated in the Spanish occupation of Cuba and had acquired his own plantations and gold mines. But he yearned for even more wealth and glory. Against the wishes of the Spanish governor in Cuba, who wanted the dazzling riches of the Aztec Empire for himself, Cortés launched the daring invasion of Mexico. The 200-mile march from Veracruz through difficult mountain passes to the magnificent Aztec capital of Tenochtitlán and the subjugation of the Aztecs, who thought themselves "masters of the world," constituted one of the most remarkable feats in history.

THE AZTECS Cortés was one of the most audacious figures in world history. With his small army, the thirty-four-year-old adventurer brashly set out to conquer the opulent Aztec Empire, which extended from central Mexico to what is today Guatemala. The Aztecs—their most accurate name

Aztec sacrifices to the gods

Renowned for military prowess, Aztecs would capture then sacrifice their enemies.

is Mexica—were a once-nomadic people who had wandered south from northern Mexico and settled in the central highlands in the fourteenth century. On marshy islands on the west side of Lake Tetzcoco, the site of present-day Mexico City, they built Tenochtitlán, a dazzling capital city dominated by towering stone temples, broad paved avenues, thriving markets, and some 70,000 adobe huts.

The Aztec Empire was a confederation of city-states remarkable for their military prowess. Aztec culture glorified warfare. Every young Aztec man received military training, and military prowess was the primary source of social stature. Throughout the fourteenth century, the Aztecs systematically conquered neighboring towns and tribes and forced the vanquished to pay tribute in the form of food, clothing, and jewelry. Aztec military strategy focused on capturing rather than killing enemies, for captives were prized as slaves and as sacrifices to the gods.

By 1519, when the Spanish landed on the Mexican coast, the Aztecs were one of the most powerful civilizations in the world. As their empire had expanded across central and southern Mexico, they had developed sophisticated laws and scientific farming techniques and engineering marvels, and a complicated political structure. By 1519, their arts were flourishing; their architecture was magnificent. Aztec rulers were invested with godlike qualities, and nobles, priests, and warrior-heroes dominated the social hierarchy.

AZTEC RELIGION   Like most agricultural peoples, the Aztecs centered their spiritual beliefs on the cosmic forces of nature. Virtually every aspect of life had a deity associated with it. Many of the Aztec gods were aligned with natural forces—the sun, the sky, water, wind, fire—and the gods perpetually struggled with one another for supremacy. The Aztecs divided the cosmos into three multilayered regions: the earth and its human inhabitants, an underworld harboring the dead, and a heavenly arena inaccessible to people. Humans—and gods—circulated between the earth and the underworld through the cycle of birth, life, death, and rebirth. Aztecs believed that the souls of warriors who were killed in battle and women who died in childbirth were transformed into hummingbirds that would follow the sun on its daily journey across the sky. The souls of people who died from less noble causes would go to the underworld.

The greatest of the many Aztec deities, Huitzilopochtli, the god of war and the sun, was engaged in a constant struggle to save the world from the forces of destruction. To bolster Huitzilopochtli's strength, the Aztecs dutifully provided *chalchihuatl*—the vital energy of life—whose only source was human blood. Like most other Mesoamericans, the Aztecs regularly offered human sacrifices—captives, slaves, women, and children—to mollify and support the gods and to promote rain, enable good harvests, and ensure victory in battle. The Aztecs also used the religious obligation to offer sacrifices as a means of justifying their relentless imperial assaults against other tribes. Prisoners of war in vast numbers were needed as sacrificial offerings. In elaborate weekly rituals at temples and in the streets, Aztec priests used stone knives to cut out the beating hearts of live victims. By the early sixteenth century as many as 10,000 people a year were sacrificed at numerous locations across Mesoamerica.

The Spanish were aghast at this "most horrid and abominable custom," but it is important to remember that sixteenth-century Europe also conducted public torture and executions of the most ghastly sort—beheadings, burnings, hangings. In some cases, those convicted of high treason in England and Europe were hanged by the neck until almost dead and then "drawn and quartered." The still-live victim was disemboweled and then the limbs and head were hacked off and put on display. Between 1530 and 1630, England alone executed 75,000 people.

INVADING SPANIARDS   As Cortés and his army marched across Mexico, they heard fabulous accounts of Tenochtitlán. With some 200,000 inhabitants, it was the largest city in the Americas and much larger than Paris or Seville. Graced by wide canals, stunning gardens, and formidable stone pyramids, the fabled lake-encircled capital seemed impregnable. But Cortés made the most of his assets. He forced alliances with Tlaxcalans and other Indians who were resisting the spread of Aztec power. The Spanish also had horses, fighting dogs, guns, and steel swords. By a combination of threats and deceptions, Cortés and his Indian allies entered Tenochtitlán peacefully and made the emperor, Montezuma II, his puppet. Cortés explained to Montezuma why the invasion was necessary: "We Spaniards have a disease of the heart that only gold can cure." Montezuma acquiesced in part because he mistook Cortés for a god.

After taking the Aztecs' gold and silver, the Spanish forced Montezuma to provide laborers to mine more of the precious metals. This state of affairs lasted until the spring of 1520, when disgruntled Aztecs, regarding Montezuma as a traitor, rebelled, stoned him to death, and attacked Cortés's forces. The Spaniards lost about a third of their men as they retreated. Their 20,000 Indian allies remained loyal, however, and Cortés gradually regrouped his men. In 1521, having been reinforced with troops from Cuba and thousands of Indians eager to defeat the Aztecs, he besieged the imperial city for eighty-five days, cutting off its access to water and food and allowing a smallpox epidemic to decimate the inhabitants. As a Spaniard observed, the smallpox "spread over the people as great destruction. Some it covered on all parts—their faces, their heads, their breasts, and so on. There was great havoc. Very many died of it. . . . They could not move; they could not stir." The ravages of smallpox help explain how such a small force of determined Spaniards lusting for gold and silver was able to vanquish a proud nation of nearly 1 million people. Montezuma's nephew led the final assault by the desperate Aztecs. Some 15,000 died in the battle. After the Aztecs surrendered, a merciless Cortés ordered the leaders hanged and the priests devoured by dogs. He and his officers replaced them as rulers over the Aztec Empire. In two years the brilliant Cortés and his disciplined army had conquered a fabled empire that had taken centuries to develop.

Cortés and his army set the style for plundering conquistadores to follow. Within twenty years Spain had established a sprawling empire in the New World. Between 1522 and 1528 various lieutenants of Cortés's conquered the remnants of Indian culture in the Yucatán Peninsula and Guatemala. In 1531, Francisco Pizarro led a band of soldiers down the Pacific coast from Panama toward Peru, where they brutally subdued the Inca Empire. From

Peru, conquistadores had extended Spanish authority south through Chile by about 1553 and north, to present-day Colombia, by 1538.

SPANISH AMERICA As the sixteenth century unfolded, Spain expanded its settlements in the New World and established far-flung governmental and economic centers in Mexico, the Caribbean, Central America, and South America. The Spaniards carried with them a fervent sense of holy mission that bred both intolerance and zeal. They sought to displace the "pagan" civilizations of the Americas with their Catholic-based culture. The crusading conquistadores transferred to America a socioeconomic system known as the *encomienda*, whereby favored officers became privileged landowners who controlled Indian villages or groups of villages. As *encomenderos*, they were called upon to protect and care for the villages and support missionary priests. In turn, they could require Indians to provide them with goods and labor. Spanish America therefore developed from the start a society of extremes: wealthy conquistadores and *encomenderos* at one end of the spectrum and native peoples held in poverty at the other end.

What was left of them, that is. By the mid-1500s native Indians were nearly extinct in the West Indies, reduced more by European diseases than

Missionaries in the New World

A Spanish mission in New Mexico, established to spread the Catholic faith among the native peoples.

by Spanish brutality. To take their place, as early as 1503 the Spanish colonizers began to transport Africans to work as slaves, the first in a wretched traffic that eventually would carry over 9 million people across the Atlantic. In all of Spain's New World empire, by one informed estimate, the Indian population plummeted from about 50 million at the outset to 4 million in the seventeenth century, slowly rising again, to 7.5 million, by the end of the eighteenth century. Whites, who totaled no more than 100,000 in the mid–sixteenth century, numbered over 3 million by the end of the colonial period.

Spain sought to establish a Christian empire in the "New World." Through the various Catholic evangelical orders—Augustinians, Benedictines, Dominicans, Franciscans, and Jesuits—the Spanish (and later the French) launched a massive effort to convert the Indians ("heathens"). During the sixteenth century, thousands of priests fanned out across New Spain (and, later, New France). The missionaries ventured into the remotest areas to spread the gospel, and they often suffered terrible torture and martyrdom for their efforts. Many of them decided that the Indians of Mexico could be converted only by force. "Though they seem to be a simple people," a Spanish friar declared in 1562, "they are up to all sorts of mischief, and are obstinately attached to the rituals and ceremonies of their forefathers. The whole land is certainly damned, and without compulsion, they will never speak the [religious] truth." By the end of the sixteenth century, there were over 300 monasteries or missions in the New World, and Catholicism had become a major instrument of Spanish imperialism.

Not all Spanish officials promoted conversion of the Indians by force. In 1514, Bartolomé de Las Casas, a priest in Cuba, renounced the practice of coercive conversions and spent the next twenty years advocating better treatment for the Indians. But his courageous efforts made little headway against the process of forced evangelization. Most Spanish colonizers believed, as a Spanish bishop in Mexico declared in 1585, that the Indians must be "ruled, governed, and guided" to Christianity "by fear more than by love."

SPANISH EXPLORATION IN NORTH AMERICA During the sixteenth century, Spanish America, also called New Spain, gradually developed into a settled society. The independent conquistadores were succeeded by a second generation of bureaucrats, and the *encomienda* gave way to the hacienda (a great farm or ranch) as the claim to land became a more important source of wealth than the Spanish claim to labor. From the outset, in sharp contrast to the later English experience, the Spanish government regulated every detail of colonial administration. After 1524 the Council of the Indies, issued laws for New Spain, served as the appellate court for civil cases arising in the colonies, and administered the bureaucracy.

Throughout the sixteenth century no European power other than Spain held more than a brief foothold in the New World. Spain had the advantage not only of having arrived first but also of having stumbled onto those regions that would produce the quickest profits. While France and England were struggling with domestic quarrels and religious conflict, Spain had forged an intense national unity. Under Charles V, heir to the throne of Austria and the Netherlands and Holy Roman emperor to boot, Spain dominated Europe as well as the New World during the first half of the sixteenth century. The treasures of the Aztecs and the Incas added to its power, but the single-minded focus on gold and silver also undermined the basic economy of Spain and tempted the government to live beyond its means. The influx of gold and silver also caused inflation throughout Europe.

For most of the colonial period, much of what is now the United States belonged to Spain, and Spanish culture etched a lasting imprint upon American ways of life. Spain's colonial presence lasted more than three centuries, much longer than either England's or France's. New Spain was centered in Mexico, but its frontiers extended from the Florida Keys to Alaska and included areas not currently thought of as formerly Spanish, such as the Deep South and the lower Midwest. Hispanic place-names—San Francisco, Santa Barbara, Los Angeles, San Diego, Tucson, Santa Fe, San Antonio, Pensacola, and St. Augustine—survive to this day, as do Hispanic influences in art, architecture, literature, music, law, and cuisine.

The Spanish encounter with Native American populations and their diverse cultures produced a two-way exchange by which the contrasting societies blended, coexisted, and interacted. Even when locked in mortal conflict and riven by hostility and mutual suspicion, the two cultures necessarily affected each other; both Native Americans and conquerors devised creative adaptations. In other words, New Spain, while permeated with violence, coercion, and intolerance, also produced a mutual accommodation that enabled two living traditions to persist side by side. For example, the Pueblo Indians of the Southwest practiced two religious traditions simultaneously, adopting Spanish Catholicism under duress while retaining the essence of their inherited animistic faith.

The "Spanish borderlands" of the southern United States preserve many reminders of the Spanish presence. The earliest known exploration of Florida was made in 1513 by Juan Ponce de León, then governor of Puerto Rico. Meanwhile, Spanish explorers skirted the Gulf coast from Florida to

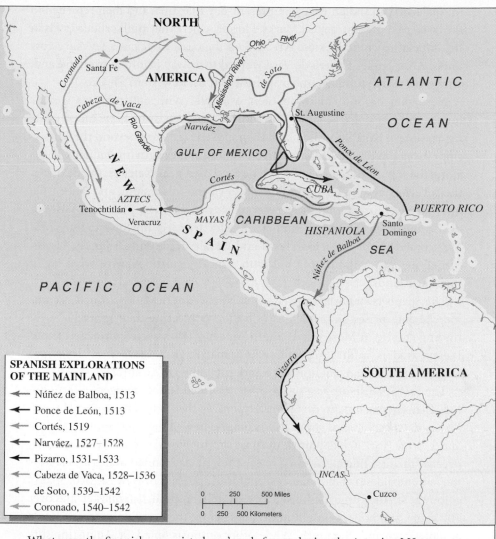

SPANISH EXPLORATIONS
OF THE MAINLAND

←— Núñez de Balboa, 1513

←— Ponce de León, 1513

←— Cortés, 1519

←— Narváez, 1527–1528

←— Pizarro, 1531–1533

←— Cabeza de Vaca, 1528–1536

←— de Soto, 1539–1542

←— Coronado, 1540–1542

What were the Spanish conquistadores' goals for exploring the Americas? How did Cortés conquer the Aztecs? Why did the Spanish first explore North America, and why did they establish St. Augustine, the first European settlement in what would become the United States?

Veracruz, scouted the Atlantic coast from Key West to Newfoundland, and established a short-lived colony on the Carolina coast.

Sixteenth-century knowledge of the North American interior came mostly from would-be conquistadores who sought to plunder the hinterlands. The first, Pánfilo de Narváez, landed in 1528 at Tampa Bay, marched northward to Apalachee, an Indian village in present-day Alabama, and then returned to the coast near present-day St. Marks, Florida, where they built crude vessels in the hope of reaching Mexico. Wrecked on the coast of Texas, a few survivors under Álvar Núñez Cabeza de Vaca worked their way painfully overland and, after eight years, stumbled into a Spanish outpost in western Mexico.

Hernando de Soto followed their example. With 600 men, as well as horses and war dogs, he landed on Florida's west coast in 1539, hiked up as far as western North Carolina, and then moved westward beyond the Mississippi River and up the Arkansas River, looting and destroying Indian villages along the way. In the spring of 1542, de Soto died near Natchez; the next year the survivors among his party floated down the Mississippi, and 311 of the original adventurers found their way to Mexico. In 1540, Francisco Vásquez de Coronado, inspired by rumors of gold, traveled northward into New Mexico and northeast across Texas and Oklahoma as far as Kansas. He returned in 1542 without gold but with a more realistic view of what lay in those arid lands.

The Spanish established provinces in North America not so much as commercial enterprises but as defensive buffers protecting their more lucrative trading empire in Mexico and South America. They were concerned about French traders infiltrating from Louisiana, English settlers crossing into Florida, and Russian seal hunters wandering down the California coast.

The first Spanish outpost in the present United States emerged in response to French encroachments on Spanish claims. In the 1560s, Huguenots (French Protestants) established short-lived colonies in what became South Carolina and Florida. In 1565 a Spanish outpost on the Florida coast, St. Augustine, became the first European town in the present-day United States and is now the nation's oldest urban center, except for the pueblos of New Mexico. Spain's colony at St. Augustine included a fort, church, hospital, fish market, and over 100 shops and houses—all built decades before the first English settlements at Jamestown and Plymouth. While other outposts failed, St. Augustine survived as a defensive base perched on the edge of a continent.

THE SPANISH SOUTHWEST The Spanish eventually established other permanent settlements in what is now New Mexico, Texas, and California. Eager to pacify rather than fight the far more numerous Indians of the region, the Spanish used religion as an effective instrument of colonial control. Missionaries, particularly Franciscans and Jesuits, established isolated Catholic missions, where they imposed Christianity on the Indians. After about ten years a mission would be secularized: its lands would be divided among the converted Indians, the mission chapel would become a parish church, and the inhabitants would be given full Spanish citizenship—including the privilege of paying taxes. The soldiers who were sent to protect the missions were housed in presidios, or forts; their families and the merchants accompanying them lived in adjacent villages.

The land that would later be called New Mexico was the first center of mission activity in the American Southwest. In 1598, Juan de Oñate, the wealthy, imperious son of a Spanish mining family in Mexico, received a land grant for the territory north of Mexico above the Rio Grande. With an expeditionary military force made up mostly of Mexican Indians and mestizos (the offspring of Spanish fathers and Indian mothers), he took possession of New Mexico, established a capital north of present-day Santa Fe, and sent out expeditions to search for gold and silver deposits. He promised the Pueblo leaders that Spanish dominion would bring them peace, justice, prosperity, and protection. Conversion to Catholicism offered even greater benefits: "an eternal life of great bliss" instead of "cruel and everlasting torment."

Some Indians welcomed the missionaries as "powerful witches" capable of easing their burdens. Others tried to use the Spanish invaders as allies against rival tribes. Still others saw no alternative but to submit. The Indians living in Spanish New Mexico were required to pay tribute to their *encomenderos* and perform personal tasks for them, including sexual favors. Disobedient Indians were flogged by soldiers and priests.

Before the end of the province's first year, in December 1598, the Pueblos revolted, killing several soldiers and incurring Oñate's wrath. During three days of relentless fighting, Spanish soldiers killed 500 Pueblo men and 300 women and children. Survivors were enslaved. Pueblo males over

Cultural conflict

This Peruvian illustration, from a 1612–1615 manuscript by Felipe Guamán Poma de Ayala, shows a Dominican friar forcing a native woman to weave.

the age of twenty-five had one foot severed in a public ritual intended to frighten the Indians and keep them from escaping or resisting. Children were taken from their parents and placed under the care of a Franciscan mission, where, Oñate remarked, "they may attain the knowledge of God and the salvation of their souls."

During the first three quarters of the seventeenth century, Spanish New Mexico expanded very slowly. The hoped-for deposits of gold and silver were never found, and a sparse food supply blunted the interest of potential colonists. The Spanish government prepared to abandon the colony, only to realize that Franciscan missionaries had baptized so many Pueblo Indians that they ought not be deserted. In 1608 the government decided to turn New Mexico into a royal province. The following year it dispatched a royal governor, and in 1610, as English settlers were struggling to survive at Jamestown, in Virginia, the Spanish moved the province's capital to Santa Fe, the first permanent seat of government in the present-day United States. By 1630 there were fifty Catholic churches and friaries in New Mexico and some 3,000 Spaniards.

Franciscan missionaries claimed that 86,000 Pueblo Indians had been converted to Christianity. In fact, however, resentment among the Indians increased with time. In 1680 a charismatic Indian leader named Popé organized a massive rebellion, which drove the Spaniards from New Mexico. The Indians burned churches; tortured, mutilated, and executed priests; and destroyed all relics of Christianity. The Pueblo Revolt of 1680 constituted the greatest defeat that natives ever inflicted on European efforts to conquer and colonize the New World. It took fourteen years and four military assaults for the Spaniards to reestablish control over New Mexico. Thereafter, except for sporadic raids by Apaches and Navajos, the Spanish pacified the region. Spanish outposts on the Florida and Texas Gulf coasts and in California did not appear until the eighteenth century.

HORSES AND THE GREAT PLAINS   Another major consequence of the Pueblo Revolt was the opportunity it afforded Indian rebels to acquire hundreds of coveted Spanish horses (Spanish authorities had made it illegal for Indians to own horses). The Pueblos in turn established a thriving horse trade with Navajos, Apaches, and other tribes. By 1690, horses were evident in Texas, and they soon spread across the Great Plains, the vast rolling grasslands extending from the Missouri River valley in the east to the base of the Rocky Mountains in the west.

Horses were a disruptive ecological force in North America. Prior to the arrival of horses, Indians hunted on foot and used dogs as their beasts of burden, hauling supplies on travois, devices made from two long poles connected by leather straps. But dogs are carnivores, and it was difficult to find enough meat to feed them. Horses thus changed everything, providing the Plains Indians with a transforming source of mobility and power. Horses are grazing animals, and the vast grasslands of the Great Plains offered plenty of forage. Horses could also haul up to seven times as much weight as dogs, and their speed and endurance made the Indians much more effective hunters and warriors. In addition, horses enabled Indians to travel farther to trade and fight.

Horses worked a revolution in the economy as well as the ecology of the Great Plains. Tribes such as the Arapaho, Cheyenne, Comanche, Kiowa, and Sioux reinvented themselves as equestrian societies. They left their traditional woodland villages on the fringes of the plains and became nomadic bison (buffalo) hunters. Indians used virtually every part of the bison they killed: meat for food; hides for clothing, shoes, bedding, and shelter; muscles and tendons for thread and bowstrings; intestines for containers; bones for

Plains Indians

The horse-stealing raid depicted in this hide painting demonstrates the essential role horses played in Plains life.

tools; horns for eating utensils; hair for headdresses; and dung for fuel. One scholar has referred to the bison as the "tribal department store."

In the short run the horse brought prosperity and mobility to the Plains Indians. Horses became the center and symbol of Indian life on the plains. Yet the Indians began to kill more bison than the herds could replace. In addition, horses competed with the bison for food, often depleting the prairie grass and compacting the soil in the river valleys during the winter. And as tribes traveled greater distances and encountered more people, infectious diseases spread more widely.

Nonetheless, horses became so valuable that they intensified intertribal warfare. A family's status reflected the number of horses it possessed. Horses eased some of the physical burdens on women but imposed new demands. Women and girls tended to the horses, butchered and dried the buffalo meat and tanned the hides. As the value of the hides grew, male hunters began practicing polygamy: more wives could process more buffalo. The rising economic value of wives eventually led Plains Indians to raid other tribes in search of captive brides as well as horses. The introduction of horses into the Great Plains, then, was a decidedly mixed blessing. By 1800 a white trader could observe that "this is a delightful country, and were it not for perpetual wars, the natives might be the happiest people on earth."

THE PROTESTANT REFORMATION

Sixteenth-century European life was centered on religion. It was an age of faith, with spiritual concerns all-encompassing and deeply felt. Religion inspired, consoled, and united people. In matters of faith, the Roman Catholic Church and the Bible were the pervasive sources of authority. Social life centered on worship services, prayer rituals, and religious festivals and ceremonies. People believed fervently in heaven and hell, devils and witches, demons and angels, magic and miracles, astrology and the occult. Europeans also took for granted the collaboration of church and state; political leaders required religious uniformity. Heresy and blasphemy were not tolerated. Christians were deadly serious about their faith; they were often willing to kill and die for their beliefs. During the Reformation, Catholics and Protestants persecuted, imprisoned, tortured, and killed each other—in large numbers. In France between 1562 and 1629, for example, nine civil wars were fought over religion, with 2 million to 4 million people dying in the widespread conflicts—out of a total population of 19 million. Religion was serious business.

The Protestant Reformation would intensify national rivalries and, by challenging Catholic Spain's power, profoundly affect the course of early American history. When Columbus sailed in 1492, all of western Europe acknowledged the supremacy of the Catholic Church and its pope in Rome. The unity of Christendom began to crack in 1517, however, when Martin Luther (1483–1546), a German monk, priest, and professor, posted on the door of his church in Wittenberg his Ninety-five Theses in protest against Catholic abuses. He especially criticized the sale of indulgences, whereby priests would forgive sins in exchange for money or goods. Sinners, Luther argued, could win salvation neither by doing good works nor by purchasing indulgences but only by receiving the gift of God's grace through the redemptive power of Christ and through a direct personal relationship with God—the "priesthood of all believers."

Lutheranism spread rapidly among the people and their rulers—some of them with an eye to seizing property owned by the Catholic Church. When the pope expelled Luther from the church in 1521, reconciliation became impossible. The German states erupted in religious conflicts; a settlement did not come until 1555, when each prince was allowed to determine the religion of his subjects. Most of northern Germany, along with Scandinavia, became Lutheran. The principle of close association between church and state thus carried over into Protestant lands, but Luther had unleashed volatile ideas that ran beyond his control.

The Protestant Reformation spread rapidly across Europe during the sixteenth century. It was in part a theological dispute, in part a political movement, and in part a catalyst for social change, civil strife, colonial expansion, and imperial warfare. Martin Luther's bold ideas shattered the unity of Catholic Europe and ignited civil wars and societal upheavals. Once unleashed, the flood of Protestant rebellion flowed in directions unexpected and unwanted by Luther and his allies. Other Protestants pursued Luther's rebellious doctrine to its logical end by preaching religious liberty for all. Further divisions on doctrinal matters (baptism, communion, church organization, and so on) spawned various sects, such as the Anabaptists, who rejected infant baptism and favored the separation of church and state. Other offshoots—including the Mennonites, Amish, and Schwenckfeldians—appeared first in Europe and later in America, but the more numerous like-minded groups would be the Baptists and the Quakers, whose origins were English.

CALVINISM Soon after Martin Luther began his revolt against the shortcomings of Catholicism, Swiss Protestants also challenged papal authority. In Geneva the reform movement looked to John Calvin (1509–1564), a

French scholar who had fled to that city and brought it under the sway of his powerful beliefs. In his great theological work, *The Institutes of the Christian Religion* (1536), Calvin set forth a stern doctrine. All people, he taught, were damned by Adam's original sin, but the sacrifice of Christ made possible their redemption. The experience of grace, however, was open only to those whom God had "elected" and thus had predestined to salvation from the beginning of time. Predestination was an uncompromising doctrine, but the infinite wisdom of God was beyond human understanding.

Intoxicated by godliness, Calvin insisted upon strict morality and hard work, values that especially suited the rising middle class. Moreover, he taught that God valued every form of work, however menial it might be. Calvin also permitted lay members a share in the governance of the church through a body of elders and ministers called the presbytery. Calvin's doctrines formed the basis for the German Reformed Church, the Dutch Reformed Church, the Presbyterians in Scotland, some of the Puritans in England (and, eventually, in America), and the Huguenots in France. Through these and other groups, John Calvin exerted a greater effect upon religious belief and practice in the English colonies than did any other leader of the Reformation.

THE REFORMATION IN ENGLAND In England the Reformation followed a unique course. The Church of England, or the Anglican Church, took form through a gradual process of integrating Calvinism with English Catholicism. In early modern England, church and state were united and mutually supportive. The government required citizens to attend religious services and to pay taxes to support the church. The English monarchs also supervised the hierarchy of church officials: two archbishops, twenty-six bishops, and thousands of parish clergy. The royal rulers often instructed the religious leaders to preach sermons in support of particular government policies. As one English king explained, "People are governed by the pulpit more than the sword in time of peace."

Purely political reasons initially led to the rejection of papal authority in England. Brilliant and energetic Henry VIII (r. 1509–1547), the second monarch of the Tudor dynasty, had in fact won from the pope the title Defender of the Faith for refuting Martin Luther's ideas. But Henry's marriage to Catherine of Aragon, his brother's widow, had produced no male heir, and to marry again he required an annulment from the pope. In the past, popes had found ways to accommodate such requests, but Catherine was the aunt of Charles V, king of Spain and ruler of the Holy Roman Empire, whose support was vital to the church. So the pope refused to grant an annulment. Unwilling to accept the rebuff, Henry severed England's nearly nine-hundred-year-old connection with the Catholic Church, named a new archbishop of Canterbury, who granted the annulment, and married his mistress, the lively Anne Boleyn.

In one of history's greatest ironies, Anne Boleyn gave birth not to the male heir that Henry demanded but to a daughter, named Elizabeth. The disappointed king later accused his wife of adultery, ordered her beheaded, and declared the infant Elizabeth a bastard. Yet Elizabeth received a first-rate education and grew up to be quick-witted and nimble, cunning and courageous. After the bloody reigns of her Protestant half brother, Edward VI, and her Catholic half sister, Mary I, she ascended the throne in 1558, at the age of twenty-five. Over the next forty-five years, Elizabeth proved to be the most remarkable female ruler in history. Her long reign over the troubled island kingdom was punctuated by political turmoil, religious tension, economic crises, and foreign wars. Yet Queen Elizabeth came to rule over England's golden age.

Born into a man's world and given a man's role, Elizabeth could not be a Catholic, for in the Catholic view her birth was illegitimate. During her long reign, from 1558 to 1603, therefore, the Church of England became Protestant, but in its own way. The Anglican organizational structure, centered on bishops and archbishops, remained much the same, but the doctrine and practice changed: the Latin liturgy became, with some changes, the English *Book of Common Prayer*, the cult of saints was dropped, and the clergy were permitted to marry. For the sake of unity, the "Elizabethan settlement" allowed some latitude in theology and other matters, but this did not satisfy all. Some Britons tried to enforce the letter of the law, stressing traditional Catholic practices. Many others, however, especially those under Calvinist influence, wished to "purify" the church of all its Catholic remnants and promote widespread spiritual revival. Some of these Puritans would leave England to build their own churches in America. Those who broke altogether with the Church of England were called Separatists. Thus, the religious controversies associated with the English Reformation so dominated the nation's political life that interest in colonizing the New World waned.

Queen Elizabeth I

Shown here in her coronation robes, ca. 1559.

Challenges to the Spanish Empire

The Spanish monopoly on New World colonies remained intact throughout the sixteenth century, but not without challenge from European rivals. The success of Catholic Spain in conquering and exploiting the New World spurred Portugal, France, England, and the Netherlands to develop their own imperial claims in the Western Hemisphere. The French were the first to pose a serious threat. Spanish treasure ships offered tempting targets for French privateers. In 1524 the French king sent the Italian Giovanni da Verrazano in search of a passage to Asia. Sighting land (probably at Cape Fear, North Carolina), Verrazano ranged along the coast as far north as Maine. On a second voyage, in 1528, his life met an abrupt end in the West Indies at the hands of the Caribs.

Unlike the Verrazano voyages, those of Jacques Cartier, beginning in the next decade, led to the first French effort at colonization. During three voyages, Cartier explored the Gulf of St. Lawrence and ventured up the St. Lawrence River, between what would become Canada and New York. Twice he got as far as present-day Montreal, and twice he wintered at or near the site of Quebec, near which a short-lived French colony appeared in 1541–1542. From that time forward, however, French kings lost interest in Canada. France after midcentury plunged into religious civil wars, and the colonization of Canada had to await the coming of Samuel de Champlain, "the Father of New France," after 1600.

From the mid-1500s, greater threats to Spanish power arose from the growing strength of the Dutch and the English. The provinces of the Netherlands, which had passed by inheritance to the Spanish king and become largely Protestant, rebelled against Spanish rule in 1567. A long, bloody struggle for independence ensued. Spain did not accept the independence of the Dutch republic until 1648.

Almost from the beginning of the Protestant Dutch revolt against Catholic Spain, the Dutch "Sea Beggars," privateers working out of English and Dutch ports, plundered Spanish ships in the Atlantic and carried on illegal trade with Spain's colonies. The Sea Beggars soon had their counterpart in the English "sea dogges": John Hawkins, Francis Drake, and others. While Queen Elizabeth steered a tortuous course to avoid open war with Spain, she encouraged both Dutch and English sea captains to engage in smuggling and piracy. In 1577, Drake embarked on his famous adventure around South America, raiding Spanish towns along the Pacific Ocean and surprising a treasure ship from Peru. Eventually he found his way westward around the world and arrived home in 1580. Elizabeth knighted him upon his return.

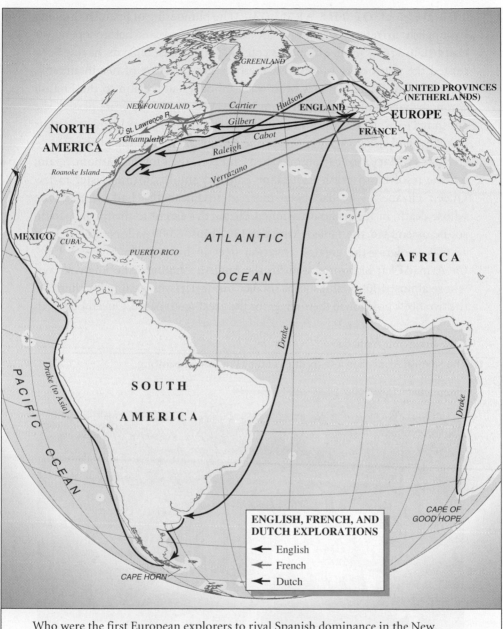

ENGLISH, FRENCH, AND
DUTCH EXPLORATIONS

← English
← French
← Dutch

Who were the first European explorers to rival Spanish dominance in the New World, and why did they cross the Atlantic? Why was the defeat of the Spanish Armada important to the history of English exploration? What was the significance of the voyages of Gilbert and Raleigh?

THE DEFEAT OF THE ARMADA   The plundering of Spanish shipping by English privateers continued for some twenty years before open war erupted. In 1568, Queen Elizabeth's cousin Mary, Queen of Scots, having been ousted the year before by Scottish Presbyterians in favor of her infant son, James, fled to England. Mary, who was Catholic, had a claim to the English throne by virtue of her descent from Henry VII, and as the years passed, she conspired to overthrow the Protestant Elizabeth. In 1587, after learning of plots to kill her and elevate Mary to the throne, Elizabeth ordered Mary beheaded.

News of Mary's execution outraged Philip II, the king of Catholic Spain, and he resolved to crush Protestant England and his former sister-in-law Queen Elizabeth—he had been married to Elizabeth's half sister, Mary, whose death, in 1558, had occasioned Elizabeth's ascent to the throne. To do so, he assembled the fabled Armada: 130 ships, 8,000 sailors, and at least 18,000 soldiers—the greatest invasion fleet in history. On May 28, 1588, the Armada left Lisbon headed for the English Channel. The English navy, whose almost 100 warships were smaller but faster, was waiting for them. As the two fleets positioned themselves for the great naval battle, Queen Elizabeth

"The Invincible Armada"

The Spanish Armada in a sixteenth-century English oil painting.

donned a silver breastplate and told the English forces, "I know I have the body of a weak and feeble woman, but I have the heart and stomach of a king, and a King of England too." As the battle unfolded, the heavy Spanish galleons could not compete with the English vessels. The English fleet harried the Spanish ships through the English Channel on their way to the Netherlands, where the Armada was to pick up more soldiers for an assault on England. But caught up in a powerful "Protestant wind" from the south, the storm-tossed Spanish fleet was swept into the North Sea instead. What was left of it finally found its way home around the British Isles, scattering wreckage on the shores of Scotland and Ireland. The stunning defeat of Catholic Spain's Armada bolstered the Protestant cause across Europe. The ferocious storm that smashed the retreating Spanish ships seemed to be a sign of God's will. Queen Elizabeth commissioned a special medallion to commemorate the successful defense of England. The citation read, "God blew and they were dispersed." Spain's King Philip seemed to agree. Upon learning of the catastrophic defeat, he sighed, "I sent the Armada against men, not God's winds and waves."

Defeat of the Spanish Armada marked the beginning of English naval supremacy and cleared the way for English colonization of America. English colonists could now make their way to North America without fear of Spanish interference. The naval victory was the climactic event of Queen Elizabeth's reign. England at the end of the sixteenth century was in the springtime of its power, filled with a youthful zest for new worlds and new wonders.

ENGLISH EXPLORATION   The history of the English efforts to colonize America begins with Sir Humphrey Gilbert and his half brother, Sir Walter Raleigh. In 1578, Gilbert, who had long been a favorite of the queen's, secured a royal patent to possess "heathen and barbarous landes countries and territories not actually possessed of any Christian prince or people." Significantly, the patent guaranteed to settlers and their descendants in such a colony the rights and privileges of Englishmen "in suche like ample manner and fourme as if they were borne and personally residaunte within our sed Realme of England." Their laws had to be "agreable to the forme of the lawes and pollicies of England."

Gilbert, after two false starts, set out with a colonial expedition in 1583, intending to settle near Narragansett Bay (in present-day Rhode Island). He instead landed in Newfoundland (Canada) and took possession of the land for Elizabeth. With winter approaching and his largest vessels lost, Gilbert resolved to return home. While in transit, however, his ship vanished, and he was never seen again.

RALEIGH'S LOST COLONY The next year, Sir Walter Raleigh persuaded the queen to renew Gilbert's colonizing mission in his own name. The flotilla discovered the Outer Banks of North Carolina and landed at Roanoke Island, where the soil seemed fruitful and the Indians friendly. After several false starts, Raleigh in 1587 sponsored an expedition of about 100 colonists, including women and children, under Governor John White. White spent a month on Roanoke Island and then returned to England for supplies, leaving behind his daughter Elinor and his granddaughter Virginia Dare, the first English child born in the New World. White's return was delayed because of the war with Spain. When he finally landed, in 1590, he discovered that Roanoke had been abandoned and pillaged.

No trace of the "lost colonists" was ever found. Indians may have destroyed the colony, or hostile Spaniards—who had certainly planned to attack—may have done the job. The most recent evidence indicates that the "Lost Colony"

The Arrival of the English in Virginia

The arrival of English explorers on the Outer Banks, with Roanoke Island at left.

fell prey to a horrible drought. Tree-ring samples reveal that the colonists arrived during the driest seven-year period in 770 years. While some may have gone south, the main body of colonists appears to have gone north, to the southern shores of Chesapeake Bay, as they had talked of doing, and lived there for some years until they were killed by local Indians. There was not a single English colonist in North America when Queen Elizabeth died, in 1603.

End of Chapter Review

CHAPTER SUMMARY

- **Pre-Columbian America** At the time of contact, Native American tribes, such as the Aztecs and Mayas of Central America, had developed empires sustained by large-scale agriculture and long-distance trade. North American Indians, however, were less well organized. The Anasazi and the Indians in the Ohio and Mississippi Valleys did establish important trading centers sustained by intensive agriculture.

- **Age of Exploration** By the 1490s, Europe was experiencing a renewed curiosity about the world. New technologies led to the creation of better maps and navigation techniques. Nation-states searching for gold and glory emerged; and Europeans desired silks and spices from Asia.

- **Great Biological Exchange** Contact resulted in a great biological exchange. Crops such as maize, beans, and potatoes became staples in the Old World. Indians incorporated into their culture such Eurasian animals as the horse and pig. The invaders carried pathogens that set off pandemics of smallpox, plague, and other illnesses to which Native Americans had no immunity.

- **Colonizing the Americas** When the Spanish began to colonize the New World, the conversion of Native Americans to Catholicism was important, but the search for gold and silver was primary. In that search, the Spanish demanded goods and labor from their new subjects. As the Indian population declined, the Spanish began to "import" enslaved Africans.

- **Spanish Legacy** Spain left a lasting legacy in the borderlands from California to Florida. Catholic missionaries contributed to the destruction of the old ways of life by actively exterminating "heathen" beliefs in the Southwest, a practice that led to open rebellion in 1598 and 1680.

- **Protestant Reformation** The Protestant Reformation shattered the unity of Catholic Europe. By the time of Elizabeth I of England, religious differences had led to state-supported plunder of Spanish treasure ships, then to open hostility with Spain. England's defeat of the Spanish Armada cleared the path for English dominance in North America.

CHRONOLOGY

by 12,000 B.C.	Humans have migrated to the Americas, most of them from Siberia
A.D. 1492	Columbus, sailing for Spain, makes first voyage of discovery
1497	John Cabot explores Newfoundland
1503	First Africans are brought to the Americas
1513	Juan Ponce de León explores Florida
1517–1648	The Protestant Reformation spurred religious conflict between Catholics and Protestants.
1519	Hernán Cortés begins the Spanish conquest of the Aztec Empire
1531	Francisco Pizarro subdues the Incas of Peru
1541	Jacques Cartier, sailing for France, explores the St. Lawrence River
1561	St. Augustine, the first European colony in present day America, is founded
1584–1587	Raleigh's Roanoke Island venture
1588	The Spanish Armada is defeated by the English
1680	Popé leads rebellion in New Mexico

KEY TERMS & NAMES

Aztec Empire p. 9

Pueblos p. 11

Vikings p. 15

Reformation p. 16

Christopher Columbus p. 19

Amerigo Vespucci p. 21

Hernán Cortés p. 27

conquistadores p. 28

Tenochtitlán p. 28

Francisco Pizarro p. 31

encomienda p. 32

Bartolomé de Las Casas p. 33

Hernando de Soto p. 36

Martin Luther p. 41

Queen Elizabeth I of England p. 43

Jacques Cartier p. 44

Raleigh's Roanoke Island Colony p. 48

2

BRITAIN AND
ITS COLONIES

FOCUS QUESTIONS   Ⓢ   wwnorton.com/studyspace

- What were Britain's reasons for establishing colonies in North America?
- Why did the first English colony, at Jamestown, experience hardships in its first decades?
- How important was religion as a motivation for colonization?
- How did British colonists and Native Americans adapt to each other's presence?
- Why was it possible for England to establish successful colonies by 1700?

The England that Queen Elizabeth bequeathed to the Scottish king James I in 1603, like the colonies it would plant in America, was a unique blend of elements. The language and the people themselves mixed Germanic and Latin backgrounds. The Anglican Church mixed Protestant theology and Catholic rituals. And the growth of royal power paradoxically had been linked to the rise of English liberties, in which even Tudor monarchs took pride. In the course of their history, the English people have displayed a genius for "muddling through," a gift for the pragmatic compromise that at times defies logic but in the light of experience somehow works.

THE ENGLISH BACKGROUND

Dominated by England, the British Isles also included the distinct kingdoms of Wales, Ireland, and Scotland. England, set off from continental Europe by the English Channel, had safe frontiers after the union of the

English and Scottish crowns in 1603. Such comparative isolation enabled the nation to develop institutions quite different from those on the Continent. Unlike the absolute monarchs of France and Spain, the British rulers shared power with the aristocracy and a lesser aristocracy, known as the gentry, whose representatives formed the bicameral legislature known as Parliament, made up of the House of Lords and the House of Commons.

By 1600 the decline of feudal structures and practices was far advanced. The great nobles had been subdued by Tudor monarchs and their ranks filled with men loyal to the Crown. In fact, the only nobles left, strictly speaking, were those who sat in the House of Lords. All others were commoners, and among their ranks the aristocratic pecking order ran through a great class of landholding squires, distinguished mainly by their wealth and bearing the simple titles of "esquire" and "gentleman"—titles held as well by many well-to-do townsmen. They in turn mingled freely, and often intermarried, with the classes of yeomen (small freehold farmers) and merchants.

ENGLISH LIBERTIES It was to these middle classes that the Tudors looked for support and, for want of bureaucrats or a standing army, local government. Self-rule in the counties and towns became a habit—one that, along with the offices of justice of the peace and sheriff, English colonists took with them to America as part of their cultural baggage.

In the making of laws, the monarch's subjects consented through representatives in the House of Commons. Taxes could be enacted only with the consent of Parliament. By its control of the purse strings, Parliament wove together other strands of power. This structure of powers served as an unwritten constitution. The Magna Carta (Great Charter) of 1215 was a statement of privileges wrested by nobles from the king, but it became part of a broader assumption that the people as a whole had rights that even the monarch could not violate. A further safeguard of English liberty was the tradition of common law, which had developed since the twelfth century in royal courts established to check the arbitrary power of local nobles. The courts evolved the principle that people could be arrested or their goods seized only upon a warrant issued by a court and that individuals were entitled to a trial by a jury of their peers (their equals) in accordance with established rules of evidence.

ENGLISH ENTERPRISE This cherished tradition of English liberties inspired a sense of personal initiative and enterprise that spawned prosperity and empire. The ranks of entrepreneurs and adventurers were constantly replenished by the younger sons of the squirearchy, cut off from the estate that the oldest son inherited according to the law of primogeniture (or first-born). At the same time the formation of for-profit joint-stock companies spurred commercial expansion. These entrepreneurial ventures were the ancestors of the modern corporation, in which stockholders, not the government, shared the risks and profits. In the late sixteenth century some of the larger companies managed to get royal charters that entitled them to monopolies in certain territories and even government powers in their outposts. Such companies would become the first instruments of colonization.

For all the vaunted glories of English liberty and enterprise, it was not the best of times for the common people. During the late sixteenth century the "lower sort" in Britain experienced a population explosion that outstripped the economy's ability to support the resulting surplus of workers. An additional strain on the population was the "enclosure" of farmlands on which peasants had lived and worked. As the trade in woolen products grew, landlords decided to "enclose" those farmlands and evict the tenants in favor of sheep. The enclosure movement of the sixteenth century, coupled with the rising population, generated the great number of beggars and vagrants who peopled the literature of Elizabethan times and gained immortality in Mother Goose: "Hark, hark, the dogs do bark. The beggars have come to town." The needs of this displaced peasant population, on the move throughout the British Isles, became a compelling argument for colonial expansion. London served as a powerful magnet for vagabonds. By the seventeenth century the English capital was notorious for its filth, poverty, crime, and class tensions—all of which helped persuade the ruling elite to send idle and larcenous commoners abroad to settle new colonies.

PARLIAMENT AND THE STUARTS Queen Elizabeth, who never married and did not give birth to an heir, died in 1603. With her demise, the Tudor family line ran out, and the throne fell to the first of the Stuarts, whose dynasty would span most of the seventeenth century, a turbulent time during which the English planted their overseas empire. In 1603, James VI of Scotland, son of the ill-fated Mary, Queen of Scots, and great-great-grandson of Henry VII, became King James I of England—as Elizabeth had planned. The new monarch coined the term Great Britain to describe his realm's joining Scotland with England and Ireland. A man of ponderous learning, James fully earned his reputation as the "wisest fool in Christendom." Tall and broad-shouldered, he was bisexual, conceited, profligate,

Stuart kings

(Left) James I, the successor to Queen Elizabeth and the first of England's Stuart kings. (Right) Charles I in a portrait by Gerrit van Honthorst.

and lazy. He lectured the people on every topic but remained blind to English traditions and sensibilities. Whereas the Tudors had wielded power through constitutional forms, James promoted the theory of divine right, by which monarchs answered only to God. And whereas the Puritans hoped to find a Presbyterian ally in their opposition to Anglican trappings, they found instead a testy autocrat who promised to banish them. He even offended Anglicans, by deciding to end his cousin Elizabeth's war with Catholic Spain.

Charles I, who succeeded his father, James, in 1625, proved to be an even more stubborn defender of royal power. He disbanded Parliament from 1629 to 1640 and levied taxes by decree. In the religious arena the archbishop of Canterbury, William Laud, directed a systematic persecution of Puritans but finally overreached himself when he tried to impose Anglican forms of worship on Presbyterian Scots. In 1638, Scotland rose in revolt, and in 1640 King Charles called Parliament to raise money for the defense of his kingdom. The "Long Parliament" impeached Archbishop Laud instead and condemned to death the king's chief minister. In 1642, when the king tried to arrest five members of Parliament, civil war erupted between the "Roundheads," who backed Parliament, and the "Cavaliers," or royalists, who supported the king.

In 1646 parliamentary forces captured the king. Parliament, however, could not agree on a new form of government. A dispute arose between Presbyterians and Independents (who preferred a congregational church government), and in 1648 the Independents purged the Presbyterians, leaving a "Rump Parliament," which then instigated the trial and execution of King Charles I on charges of treason.

Oliver Cromwell, the tenacious commander of the parliamentary army, operated like a military dictator, ruling first through a council chosen by Parliament (the Commonwealth) and, after forcible dissolution of Parliament, as lord protector (the Protectorate). Cromwell extended religious toleration to all Britons except Catholics and Anglicans, but his arbitrary governance and his stern moralistic codes provoked growing public resentment. When, after his death, in 1658, his son proved too weak to carry on, the army once again took control, permitted new elections for Parliament, and in 1660 supported the Restoration of the monarchy under Charles II, son of the martyred king.

Charles II accepted as terms of the Restoration settlement the principle that he must rule jointly with Parliament. By tact or shrewd maneuvering, he managed to hold his throne. His younger brother, the Duke of York (who became James II upon succeeding to the throne in 1685), was less flexible. He openly avowed Catholicism and assumed the same unyielding stance as the first two Stuart kings. The people could bear it so long as they expected one of his Protestant daughters, Mary or Anne, to succeed him. In 1688, however, the birth of a son who would be reared a Catholic brought matters to a crisis. Leaders of Parliament invited Mary Stuart and her husband, William III of Orange, a Dutch prince, to assume the throne jointly, and King James II fled the country.

By this "Glorious Revolution," Parliament finally established its freedom from monarchical control. Under the Bill of Rights, in 1689, William and Mary gave up the royal prerogatives of suspending laws, appointing special courts, keeping a standing army, or levying taxes except by Parliament's consent. They further agreed to hold frequent legislative sessions and allow freedom of speech in Parliament and restrictions against excessive bail and cruel and unusual punishments. The Act of Toleration of 1689 extended a degree of freedom of worship to all Christians except Catholics and Unitarians, although dissenters from the established church still had few political rights.

In 1701 the Act of Settlement ensured Protestant succession through Queen Anne (r. 1702–1714). And by the Act of Union in 1707, England and Scotland became the United Kingdom of Great Britain.

SETTLING THE CHESAPEAKE

During these eventful years all but one of Britain's North American colonies were founded. They began as money-making corporations rather than new countries. In 1606, King James I, having made peace with Spain, chartered a joint-stock enterprise called the Virginia Company, with two divisions, the First Colony of London and the Second Colony of Plymouth. King James assigned to the Virginia Company an explicit religious mission. He decreed that the settlers would bring the "Christian religion" to the natives who "live in darkness and miserable ignorance of the true knowledge and worship of God." But as was true of most colonial ventures, such pious intentions were mixed with the lure of profits. The stockholders viewed the colony as a source of gold and other minerals; products—such as wine, citrus fruits, and olive oil—that would free England from dependence upon Spain; trade with the Indians; pitch, tar, potash, and other forest products needed by the navy. Some investors saw colonization as an opportunity to transplant the growing number of jobless vagrants from Britain to the New World. Few if any foresaw what the first English colony would actually become: a place to grow tobacco.

From the outset the pattern of English colonization diverged significantly from the Spanish pattern, which involved regulating all aspects of colonial life. While interest in America was growing, the English were already involved in planting settlements, or "plantations," in Ireland, which they had conquered by military force under Queen Elizabeth. Within their own pale (or limit) of settlement in Ireland, the English set about transplanting their familiar way of life insofar as possible.

The English would apply the same pattern as they settled North America, subjugating (and converting) the Indians there as they had the Irish in Ireland. Yet in America the English, unlike the Spanish, settled along the Atlantic seaboard, where the native populations were relatively sparse. There was no Aztec or Inca Empire to conquer. The colonists thus had to establish their own communities in the midst of Native American villages. Yet the British colonists who arrived in the seventeenth century rarely *settled* in one place for long. They were migrants more than settlers, people who had been on the move in Britain and continued to pursue new opportunities in different places once they arrived in America.

VIRGINIA   The Virginia Company planted the first permanent colony in Virginia, named after Elizabeth I, "the Virgin Queen." On May 6, 1607, three tiny ships carrying 105 men reached Chesapeake Bay after four storm-tossed months at sea. They chose a river with a northwest bend—in the hope of finding a passage to Asia—and settled about forty miles inland, to hide from marauding Spaniards.

The river they called the James and the colony, Jamestown. The sea-weary colonists built a fort, thatched huts, a storehouse, and a church. They then set to planting, but most were either townsmen unfamiliar with farming or

"Ould Virginia"

A 1624 map of Virginia by John Smith, showing Chief Powhatan in the upper left.

"gentleman" adventurers who scorned manual labor. They had come expecting to find gold, friendly Indians, and easy living. Instead they found disease, drought, starvation, dissension, and death. Ignorant of woodlore, they did not know how to exploit the area's abundant game and fish. Supplies from England were undependable, and only some effective leadership and trade with the Indians, who taught the ill-prepared colonists to grow maize, enabled them to survive.

The Indians of the region were loosely organized. Powhatan was the powerful, charismatic chief of numerous Algonquian-speaking villages in eastern Virginia, representing over 10,000 Indians. The tribes making up the so-called Powhatan Confederacy were largely an agricultural people focused on raising corn. They lived along rivers in fortified settlements and resided in wood houses sheathed with bark. Chief Powhatan collected tribute from the tribes he had conquered—fully 80 percent of the corn that they grew was handed over. Powhatan developed a lucrative trade with the English colonists, exchanging corn and hides for hatchets, swords, and muskets; he realized too late that the newcomers intended to seize his lands and subjugate his people.

The colonists, as it happened, had more than a match for Powhatan in Captain John Smith, a stocky twenty-seven-year-old soldier of fortune with rare powers of leadership and self-promotion. The Virginia Company, impressed by Smith's exploits in foreign wars, had appointed him a member of the council to manage the new colony in America. It was a wise decision. Of the original 105 settlers, only 38 survived the first nine months. With the colonists on the verge of starvation, Smith imposed strict discipline and forced all to labor, declaring that "he that will not work shall not eat." In dealing with the bickering settlers, he imprisoned, whipped, and forced them to labor. Smith also bargained with the Indians and explored and mapped the Chesapeake region. Through his efforts, Jamestown survived, but his dictatorial behavior did not endear him to the colonists.

In 1609 the Virginia Company reinforced Jamestown. More colonists were dispatched, including several women. A new charter replaced the largely ineffective council with an all-powerful governor. The company then lured new investors and attracted new settlers with the promise of free land after seven years of labor. With no gold or silver in Virginia, the company in effect had given up hope of prospering except through the sale of land, which would rise in value as the colony grew. The governor, the noble Lord De La Warr (Delaware), sent as interim governor Sir Thomas Gates. In 1609, Gates set out with a fleet of nine vessels and about 500 passengers and crew.

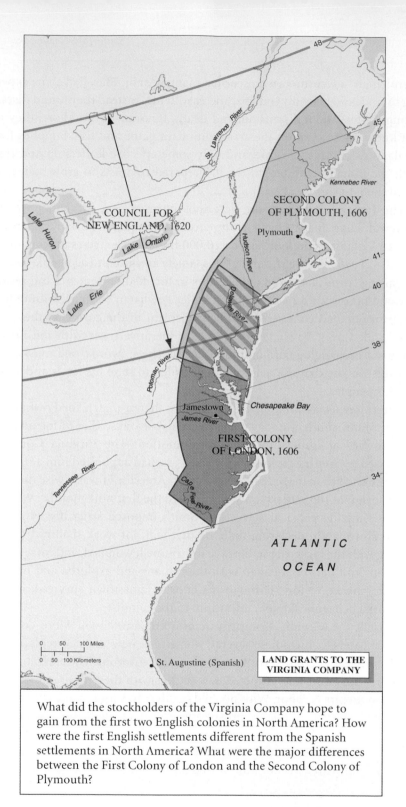

LABELS ON MAP:

48

45

St. Lawrence River

Kennebec River

COUNCIL FOR
NEW ENGLAND, 1620

SECOND COLONY
OF PLYMOUTH, 1606

Plymouth

Lake Huron

Lake Ontario

Hudson River

Delaware River

41

40

Lake Erie

38

Potomac River

Jamestown   Chesapeake Bay

James River

FIRST COLONY
OF LONDON, 1606

Tennessee River

Cape Fear River

34

ATLANTIC

OCEAN

0   50   100 Miles

0   50   100 Kilometers

St. Augustine (Spanish)

**LAND GRANTS TO THE
VIRGINIA COMPANY**

What did the stockholders of the Virginia Company hope to
gain from the first two English colonies in North America? How
were the first English settlements different from the Spanish
settlements in North America? What were the major differences
between the First Colony of London and the Second Colony of
Plymouth?

On the way he was shipwrecked on Bermuda, where he and the other survivors wintered in comparative ease, subsisting on fish, fowl, and wild pigs. (Their story was transformed by William Shakespeare into his play *The Tempest*.)

Most of the fleet did reach Jamestown, however. Some 400 settlers overwhelmed the remnant of about 80. All chance that John Smith might maintain control was lost when he suffered a severe gunpowder burn and sailed back to England. The consequence was anarchy and the "starving time" of the winter of 1609–1610, during which most of the colonists, weakened by hunger, died of disease or starvation. A prolonged drought had hindered efforts to grow food. By May 1610, when Gates and his companions made their way to Jamestown on two small ships built in Bermuda, only about 60 settlers remained. During the winter of 1610, starving colonists consumed their horses, cats, and dogs, then survived on rats and mice. A few even ate the leather from their shoes and boots. Some fled to nearby Indian villages, only to be welcomed with arrows. One man was tortured and executed by his fellow colonists for killing his pregnant wife and feasting on her remains.

Colonial necessities

A list of provisions recommended to new settlers by the Virginia Company in 1622.

THE INCONVENIENCIES
THAT HAVE HAPPENED TO SOME PER-
SONS WHICH HAVE TRANSPORTED THEMSELVES
from *England* to *Virginia*, vvithout prouifions neceffary to fuftaine themfelues, hath *greatly hindred the* Progreffe *of that noble* Plantation: *For preuention of the like diforders* heereafter, that no man fuffer, either through ignorance or mifinformation; it is thought requifite to publifh this fhort declaration: wherein is contained a particular of fuch necef-faries, as either private families or fingle perfons fhall haue caufe to furnifh themfelues with, for their better fupport at their firft landing in Virginia; whereby alfo greater numbers may receiue in part, directions how to prouide themfelues.

Apparrell.	li.	s.	d.		Tooles.	li.	s.	d.
One Monmouth Cap	00	01	10		Fiue broad howes at 2.s. a piece	—	10	—
Three falling bands	—	01	03		Fiue narrow howes at 16.d. a piece	—	06	c8
Three fhirts	—	07	c6		Two broad Axes at 3.s. 8.d.a piece	—	07	c4
One wafte-coate	—	02	02		Fiue felling Axes at 18.d. a piece	—	c7	06
One fuite of Canuafe	—	07	06		Two fteele hand fawes at 16.d. a piece	—	02	08
One fuite of Frize	—	10	00		Two two-hand fawes at 5. s. a piece	—	10	—
One fuite of Cloth	—	15	00		One whip-faw, fet and filed with box, file,			
Three paire of Irifh ftockins	—	c4	—		and wreft	—	10	—
Foure paire of fhooes	—	c8	c8		Two hammers 12.d. a piece	—	02	00
One paire of garters	—	00	10	For a family of 6. perfons and fo after the rate for more.	Three fhouels 18.d. a piece	—	c4	06
One doozen of points	—	00	03		Two fpades at 18.d.a piece	—	03	—
One paire of Canuafe fheets.	—	c8	00		Two augers 6.d. a piece	—	c1	00
Seuen ells of Canuafe, to make a bed and bouliſter, to be filled in *Virginia* 8.s.	c8	00			Sixe chiffels 6.d. a piece	—	03	00
					Two percers ftocked 4.d. a piece	—	00	c8
One Rug for a bed 8. s. which with the bed ſeruing for two men, halfe is					Three gimlets 2.d. a piece	—	00	06
Fiue ells coorfe Canuafe, to make a bed at Sea for two men, to be filled with ftraw, iiij.s.	05	00			Two hatchets 21.d. a piece	—	03	06
					Two froues to cleaue pale 18.d.	—	03	00
					Two hand-bills 20. a piece	—	03	04
One coorfe Rug at Sea for two men, will coft vj.s. is for one	—	—	—		One grindleftone 4.s.	—	c4	00
					Nailes of all forts to the value of	02	00	—
					Two Pickaxes	—	c3	—

Apparrell for one man, and fo after the rate for more.

In June 1610, as the colonists prepared to abandon Jamestown and return to England, the new governor, Lord Delaware, arrived in Virginia with three ships and 150 men. The colonists created new settlements upstream at Henrico (Richmond) and two more downstream, near the mouth of the river. It was a critical turning point for the colony, whose survival required a combination of stern measures and not a little luck. After Lord Delaware returned to England in 1611, Thomas Gates took charge of the colony and established a strict system of laws. When a man was caught stealing oatmeal, the authorities had a long needle thrust through his tongue, chained him to a tree, and let him starve to death as a grisly example to the community. Gates also ordered that the dilapidated Anglican church be repaired and that colonists attend services on Thursdays and Sundays. The church bell rang each morning and afternoon to remind colonists to pray. As Lord Delaware declared, Virginia would be a colony where "God [would be] duly and daily served." Religious uniformity thus became an essential instrument of public policy and civil duty in colonial Virginia.

Desperate men who fled Jamestown to join the Indians were caught and hanged or burned at the stake. The new colonial regime also attacked Indian villages and destroyed their crops. One commander reported that the colonists had marched a captured Indian queen and her children to the river, where they "put the Children to death . . . by throwing them overboard and shooting out their brains in the water."

Over the next seven years the Jamestown colony limped along until it gradually found a lucrative source of revenue: tobacco. The plant had been grown in the West Indies for years, and smoking had become a popular—and addictive—habit in Europe. In 1612, having been introduced to growing tobacco by the Indians, colonist John Rolfe got hold of some seed from the more savory Spanish varieties, and by 1616 the weed had become a profitable export. Even though King James dismissed smoking as "loathsome to the eye, hateful to the nose, harmful to the brain, and dangerous to the lungs," he swallowed his objections to the "noxious weed" when he realized how much revenue it provided the monarchy. Virginia's tobacco production soared during the seventeenth century. Tobacco was such a profitable crop for Virginia planters that they could afford to purchase more indentured servants (colonists who exchanged their labor for the cost of passage to America), thus increasing the flow of immigrants to the colony.

Meanwhile, John Rolfe had made another contribution to stability by marrying Pocahontas, the daughter of Chief Powhatan. Pocahontas (a nickname usually translated as "Frisky"; her given name was Matoaka) had been a familiar figure in Jamestown. In 1607, then only eleven, she figured in perhaps the best-known story of the settlement, her plea for the life of John Smith. Smith had gotten into trouble when he led a small group up the James River. When the Englishmen trespassed on Powhatan's territory, the Indians attacked. Smith was wounded and captured. Others in his scouting party were tortured and disemboweled. Smith was marched to Powhatan's village, interrogated, and readied for execution. At that point, according to Smith, Pocahontas made a dramatic appeal for his life, and Powhatan eventually agreed to release the foreigner in exchange for muskets, hatchets, beads, and trinkets.

Pocahontas

Shown here in European dress, by 1616 Pocahontas was known as "Lady Rebecca."

Schoolchildren still learn the dramatic story of Pocahontas intervening to save Smith. Such dramatic events are magical; they inspire movies, excite our imagination, animate history—and confuse it. Pocahontas and John Smith were never in love. Moreover, the young Indian princess saved the swashbuckling Smith on more than one occasion. Then she herself was captured. In 1614 the Jamestown settlers kidnapped her in an effort to blackmail Powhatan. As the weeks passed, however, she surprised her captors by choosing to join them. She embraced Christianity, was renamed Rebecca, and fell in love with widower John Rolfe. They married and in 1616 moved with their infant son, Thomas, to London. There the young princess drew excited attention from the royal family and curious Londoners. But only a few months after arriving, Rebecca, aged twenty, contracted a lung disease and died.

In 1618, Sir Edwin Sandys, a prominent member of Parliament, became head of the Virginia Company and instituted a series of reforms. First of all he inaugurated a new "headright" policy: anyone who bought a share in the company and could get to Virginia could have fifty acres, and fifty more for any servants they brought along. The following year the company relaxed the colony's military regime and promised that the settlers would have the "rights of Englishmen," including a representative assembly.

A new governor arrived with instructions to put the new order into effect, and on July 30, 1619, the first General Assembly of Virginia, including the governor, six councillors, and twenty-two burgesses, met in the church at Jamestown and deliberated for five days, "sweating & stewing, and battling flies and mosquitoes." It was an eventful year in two other respects. During 1619 a ship arrived with ninety young women, who were to be sold to likely husbands of their own choice for the cost of transportation (about 125 pounds of tobacco). And a Dutch ship stopped by and dropped off "20 Negars," the first Africans known to have reached English America. By this time, Europeans had been selling enslaved Africans for over a century.

The increasingly profitable tobacco trade intensified the settlers' lust for land. They especially coveted Indian fields because they had already been cleared and were ready to be planted. In 1622 the Indians, led by Opechancanough, Powhatan's brother and successor, tried to repel the land-grabbing English. They killed a fourth of the settlers, some 350 colonists, including John Rolfe (who had returned from England). The vengeful English thereafter sought to wipe out the Indian presence along their frontier. The combination of warfare and disease decimated the Indians in Virginia. The 24,000 Algonquians who inhabited the colony in 1607 were reduced to 2,000 by 1669.

Some 14,000 English men, women, and children had migrated to Jamestown since 1607, but most of them had died; the population in 1624 stood at a precarious 1,132. Despite the initial achievements of the company, after about 1617 a handful of insiders appropriated large estates and began to monopolize the indentured workers. Some made fortunes from the tobacco boom, but thousands of Virginia settlers died before the colony become viable. In 1624 an English court dissolved the struggling Virginia Company, and Virginia became a royal colony.

Sir William Berkeley, who arrived as Virginia's royal governor in 1642, presided over the colony's growth for most of the next thirty-five years. The turmoil of Virginia's early days gave way to a more stable period. Tobacco prices peaked, and the large planters began to consolidate their economic gains through political action. They assumed key civic roles as justices of the peace and sheriffs, helped initiate improvements such as roads and bridges, supervised elections, and collected taxes. They also formed the able-bodied men into local militias. Despite the presence of a royal governor, the elected Virginia assembly continued to assert its sovereignty, making laws for the colony and resisting the governor's encroachments.

Virginia at midcentury continued to serve as a magnet for new settlers. By 1650 there were 15,000 white residents. The relentless stream of new settlers and indentured servants into Virginia exerted constant pressure on Indian lands and produced unwanted economic effects. The increase in the number of planters spurred a dramatic rise in agricultural production. That in turn caused the cost of land to soar and the price of tobacco to plummet. To sustain their competitive advantage, the largest planters bought up the most fertile land along the coast, thereby forcing freed servants to become tenants or claim less fertile land inland. In either case the tenants found themselves at a disadvantage. They grew dependent upon planters for land and credit, and small farmers along the western frontier became more vulnerable to Indian attacks.

The plight of the common folk worsened after 1660, when the restored monarchy under Charles II instituted new trade regulations for the colonies. By 1676 a fourth of the free white men in Virginia were landless. Vagabonds roamed the countryside, squatting on private property, working at odd jobs, or poaching game or engaging in other petty crimes in order to survive. Alarmed by the growing social unrest, the large planters who controlled the assembly lengthened terms of indenture, passed more stringent vagrancy laws, stiffened punishments, and stripped the landless of their political rights. Such efforts only increased social friction.

BACON'S REBELLION A variety of simmering tensions—caused by depressed tobacco prices, rising taxes, roaming livestock, and crowds of freed servants greedily eyeing Indian lands—contributed to the tangled events that have come to be labeled Bacon's Rebellion. The roots of the revolt grew out of a festering hatred for the domineering colonial governor, William Berkeley. He catered to the wealthiest planters, granting them most of the frontier land and public offices. He despised commoners. The large planters who dominated the assembly levied high taxes to finance Berkeley's regime, which in turn supported their interests at the expense of the small farmers and servants. With little nearby land available, newly freed indentured servants were forced to migrate westward in their quest for farms. Their lust for land led them to displace the Indians. When Governor Berkeley failed to support the aspiring farmers, they rebelled. The tyrannical governor expected as much. Just before the outbreak of rebellion, Berkeley had remarked that most Virginians were "Poore, Endebted, Discontented and Armed."

STRANGE NEWS

FROM

VIRGINIA;

Being a full and true

ACCOUNT

OF THE

LIFE and DEATH

OF

Nathanael Bacon Esquire,

Who was the only Cause and Original of all the late Troubles in that COUNTRY.

With a full Relation of all the Accidents which have happened in the late War there between the Christians and Indians.

LONDON,
Printed for *William Harris,* next door to the Turn-Stile without *Moor-gate.* 1677.

News of the Rebellion

A broadsheet printed in London provided details about Bacon's Rebellion.

The discontent turned to violence in 1675 when a petty squabble between a frontier planter and Indians on the Potomac River led to the murder of the planter's herdsman and, in turn, to retaliation by frontier militiamen, who killed two dozen Indians. The violence spread. A force of Virginia and Maryland militiamen murdered five Indian chieftains who had sought to negotiate. Enraged Indians took their revenge on frontier settlements. Scattered attacks continued down to the James River, where Nathaniel Bacon's overseer was killed.

By then, their revenge accomplished, the Indians had pulled back. What followed had less to do with a state of war than with a state of hysteria. Governor Berkeley proposed that the assembly erect a series of forts along the frontier. But that would not slake the English thirst for revenge—nor would it open new lands to settlement. Besides, it would be expensive. Some thought Berkeley was out to preserve a profitable fur trade for himself.

In 1676, Nathaniel Bacon defied Governor Berkeley's authority by assuming command of a group of frontier vigilantes. The tall, slender twenty-nine-year-old Bacon, a graduate of Cambridge University, had been in Virginia only two years, but he had been well set up by an English father relieved to get his vain, ambitious, hot-tempered son out of the country. Later historians would praise Bacon as "the Torchbearer of the Revolution" and leader of the first struggle of common folk versus aristocrats. In part that was true. The rebellion he led was largely a battle of servants, small farmers, and even slaves against Virginia's wealthiest planters and political leaders. But Bacon was also a rich squire's spoiled son with a talent for trouble. It was his ruthless assaults against peaceful Indians and his greed for power and land rather than any commitment to democratic principles that sparked his conflict with the governing authorities.

Bacon despised the Indians and resolved to kill them all. Berkeley opposed Bacon's genocidal plan not because he liked Indians but because he wanted to protect his lucrative monopoly over the deerskin trade with them. Bacon ordered the governor arrested. Berkeley's forces resisted—but only feebly—and Bacon's men burned Jamestown. Bacon, however, could not savor the victory long; he fell ill and died a month later.

Governor Berkeley quickly regained control, hanged twenty-three rebels, and confiscated several estates. When his men captured one of Bacon's lieutenants, Berkeley gleefully exclaimed: "I am more glad to see you than any man in Virginia. Mr. Drummond, you shall be hanged in half an hour." For such severity the king denounced Berkeley as a "fool" and recalled him to England, where he died within a year. A royal commission made peace treaties with the remaining Indians, about 1,500 of whose descendants still live in Virginia on tiny reservations guaranteed them by the king in 1677. The result of Bacon's Rebellion was that new lands were opened to the colonists, and the wealthy planters became more cooperative with the small farmers.

MARYLAND In 1634, ten years after Virginia became a royal colony, a neighboring settlement appeared on the northern shores of Chesapeake Bay. Named Maryland in honor of Queen Henrietta Maria, it was granted to Lord Baltimore by King Charles I and became the first *proprietary* colony— that is, it was owned by an individual, not a joint-stock company. Sir George Calvert, the first Lord Baltimore, converted to Catholicism in 1625 and sought the colony as a refuge for English Catholics, who were subjected to discrimination at home. His son, Cecilius Calvert, the second Lord Baltimore, actually founded the colony.

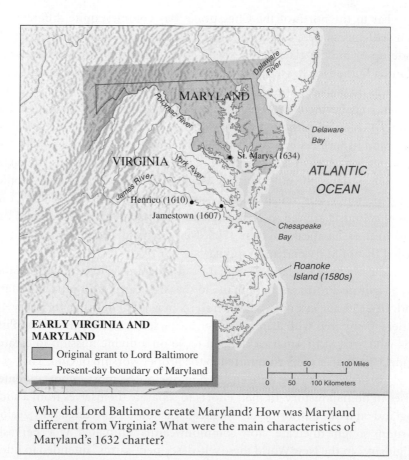

EARLY VIRGINIA AND MARYLAND

☐ Original grant to Lord Baltimore

—— Present-day boundary of Maryland

Why did Lord Baltimore create Maryland? How was Maryland different from Virginia? What were the main characteristics of Maryland's 1632 charter?

In 1634, Calvert planted the first settlement in Maryland at St. Marys, on a small stream near the mouth of the Potomac River. Calvert brought Catholic gentlemen as landholders, but a majority of the servants were Protestants. The charter gave Calvert power to make laws with the consent of the freemen (all property holders). The first legislative assembly met in 1635 and divided into two houses in 1650, with governor and council sitting separately. This action was instigated by the predominantly Protestant freemen—largely immigrants from Virginia and servants who had become landholders. The charter also empowered the proprietor to grant huge manorial estates, and Maryland had some sixty before 1676, but the Lords Baltimore soon found that to recruit settlers they had to offer them small farms, most of which grew tobacco.

SETTLING NEW ENGLAND

Far to the north of the Chesapeake Bay colonies, quite different English settlements were emerging. The New England colonists were generally made up of middle-class families who could pay their own way across the Atlantic. In the Northeast there were relatively few indentured servants, and there was no planter elite. Most male settlers were small farmers, merchants, seamen, or fishermen. New England also attracted more women than did the southern colonies. Although its soil was not as fertile as that of the Chesapeake and its farmers not as wealthy as the southern planters, New England was a much healthier place to settle. Because of its colder climate, the region did not experience the infectious diseases that ravaged the southern colonies. Life expectancy was much longer. During the seventeenth century only 21,000 colonists arrived in New England, compared with the 120,000 who went to the Chesapeake. But by 1700, New England's white population exceeded that of Maryland and Virginia.

Most early New Englanders were devout Puritans, who embraced a much more rigorous Protestant faith than did the Anglicans of Virginia and Maryland. In 1650, for example, Massachusetts boasted 1 minister for every 415 settlers, compared with 1 minister per 3,239 settlers in Virginia. The Puritans who arrived in America claimed to be on a divine mission to create a model Christian society committed to the proper worship of God. They genuinely believed that they were engaged in one of the most important enterprises in human history. In their efforts to separate themselves from a sinful England and its authoritarian Anglican bishops, New England's zealous Puritans sought to create "holy commonwealths" animated by a "pervasive religiosity." In the New World these self-described "saints" intended to purify their churches of all Catholic and Anglican rituals, supervise one another in practicing a communal faith, and enact a code of laws and a government structure based upon biblical principles. Such a holy settlement, they hoped, would provide a beacon of righteousness for a wicked England to emulate.

PLYMOUTH In 1620 a band of Puritan refugees heading for Virginia strayed off course and made landfall at Cape Cod, off the southern coast of what became Massachusetts. These "Pilgrims" belonged to the most radical sect of Puritans, the Separatists (Nonconformists). The Church of England, according to the Puritans, had retained too many vestiges of Catholicism. Viewing themselves as the "godly," they demanded that the Anglican Church rid itself of "papist" rituals. No use of holy water. No elegant robes (vestments). No bejeweled gold crosses. No worship of saints and relics. No kneeling for Communion. No "viperous" bishops and archbishops. No organ music. The Separatists went further. Having decided that the Church of England could not be fixed, they resolved to create their own godly congregations. Such rebelliousness infuriated the Church of England. During the late sixteenth century, Separatists were "hunted & persecuted on every side." English authorities imprisoned Separatist leaders, three of whom were hanged, drawn, and quartered. King James I, who lacked Elizabeth's grace and moderation, resolved to eliminate the Nonconformists. "I shall make them conform," he vowed in 1604, "or I will hurry them out of the land or do worse." Many Separatists had fled to Holland in 1607 to escape persecution. After ten years in the Dutch city of Leiden, they decided to move to the New World.

In 1620, about 100 men, women, and children, led by William Bradford, crammed aboard the tiny *Mayflower*. Their ranks included both "saints" (people recognized as having been selected by God for salvation) and "strangers" (those yet to receive the gift of grace). The latter group included John Alden, a cooper (barrel maker), and Myles Standish, a soldier hired to organize their defenses. The stormy voyage had led them to Cape Cod. "Being thus arrived at safe harbor, and brought safe to land," William Bradford wrote, "they fell upon their knees and blessed the God of Heaven who had brought them over the vast and furious ocean." Since they were outside the jurisdiction of any organized government, forty-one of the Pilgrim leaders entered into a formal agreement to abide by the laws made by leaders of their own choosing—the Mayflower Compact.

On December 26 the *Mayflower* reached harbor at the place the Pilgrims named Plymouth, after the English port from which they had embarked, and they built dwellings on the site of an abandoned Indian village. Nearly half of them died of disease, but in the spring of 1621 the colonists met

New World navigation

Sailors on a sixteenth-century oceangoing vessel navigating by the stars.

Squanto, an Indian who showed them how to grow maize and catch fish. By autumn the Pilgrims had a bumper crop of corn, a flourishing fur trade, and asupply of lumber for shipment. To celebrate, they held a harvest feast with the Indians. That event provided the inspiration for what has become Thanksgiving.

In 1623, the Plymouth Plantation gave up its original communal economy and stipulated that each male settler was to provide for his family from his own land. Throughout its separate existence, until absorbed into Massachusetts in 1691, the Plymouth colony remained in the anomalous position of holding a land grant but no charter of government from any English authority. The government grew instead out of the Mayflower Compact, which was neither exactly a constitution nor a precedent for later constitutions. Rather, it was the obvious recourse of a group that had made a covenant (or agreement)to form a church and believed God had made a covenant with them to provide a way to salvation. Thus the civil government grew naturally out of the church government, and the members of each were identical at

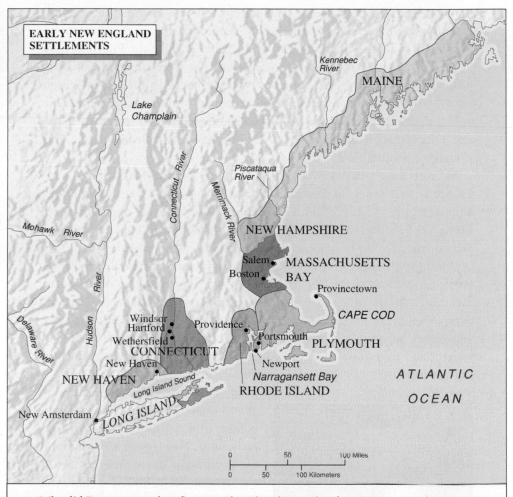

EARLY NEW ENGLAND SETTLEMENTS

Kennebec River

MAINE

Lake Champlain

Piscataqua River

Connecticut River

Merrimack River

Mohawk River

NEW HAMPSHIRE

Salem
Boston

MASSACHUSETTS BAY

Provincetown

CAPE COD

Windsor
Hartford
Wethersfield

Providence

Portsmouth

PLYMOUTH

CONNECTICUT

Hudson River

New Haven

Newport

Narragansett Bay

ATLANTIC

NEW HAVEN

Long Island Sound

RHODE ISLAND

OCEAN

Delaware River

New Amsterdam

LONG ISLAND

0   50   100 Miles

0   50   100 Kilometers

Why did European settlers first populate the Plymouth colony? How were the settlers of the Massachusetts Bay Colony different from those of Plymouth? What was the origin of the Rhode Island colony?

the start. The signers of the compact at first met as the General Court, which chose the governor and his assistants (or council). Later others were admitted as members, or "freemen," but only church members were eligible. Eventually, as the colony grew, the General Court became a body of representatives from the various towns.

MASSACHUSETTS BAY The Plymouth colony's population never rose above 7,000, and after ten years it was overshadowed by its larger neighbor, the Massachusetts Bay Colony. That colony, too, was intended to be a holy commonwealth made up of religious folk bound together in the harmonious worship of God and the pursuit of their "callings." Like the Pilgrims, most of the Puritans who colonized Massachusetts Bay were Congregationalists, who formed self-governing churches with membership limited to "visible saints"—those who could demonstrate receipt of the gift of God's grace. But unlike the Plymouth Separatists, the Puritans still hoped to reform ("purify") the Church of England, and therefore they were called Nonseparating Congregationalists.

In 1629, King Charles I had issued a charter for the Massachusetts Bay Company to a group of English Puritans led by John Winthrop, a lawyer animated by profound religious convictions. Winthrop, tall and strong with a long face, resolved to use the colony as a refuge for persecuted Puritans and as an instrument for building a "wilderness Zion" in America.

Winthrop shrewdly took advantage of a fateful omission in the royal charter for the Massachusetts Bay Company: the usual proviso that the company maintain its home office in England. Winthrop's group took its charter with them, thereby transferring government authority to Massachusetts Bay, where they hoped to ensure local control. So unlike the Virginia Company, which ruled Jamestown from London, the Massachusetts Bay Company was self-governing.

John Winthrop

The first governor of Massachusetts Bay Colony, in whose vision the colony would be as "a city upon a hill."

In 1630 the *Arbella*, with John Winthrop and the charter aboard, embarked with ten other ships for Massachusetts. There were 700 Puritans on board. Some 200 of the exiles died in the crossing. In "A Modell of Christian Charity," a lay sermon delivered on board, Winthrop told his fellow Puritans that they were a chosen people on a divine mission: "We must consider that we shall be a city upon a hill"—a shining example to England of what a godly community could be. They landed in Massachusetts, and by the end of the year seventeen ships bearing 1,000 more colonists had arrived. As settlers—both Puritan and non-Puritan—poured into the region, Boston became the new colony's chief city and capital.

The *Arbella* migrants were the vanguard of a massive movement, the Great Migration, that carried some 80,000 Britons to new settlements around the world over the next decade. Fleeing religious persecution and economic depression at home, they gravitated to Ireland, the Netherlands, and the Rhineland. But the majority traveled to America. They went not only to New England and the Chesapeake but also to new English settlements in the Lesser Antilles: St. Christopher (first settled in 1624), Barbados (1625), Nevis (1632), Montserrat (1632), and Antigua (1632). The West Indian islands started out to grow tobacco but ended up in the more profitable business of producing cane sugar.

The transfer of the Massachusetts charter, whereby an English trading company evolved into a provincial government, was a unique venture in colonization. Under the royal charter, power rested with the Massachusetts General Court, which elected the governor and the assistants. The General Court consisted of shareholders, called freemen (those who had the "freedom of the company"), but only a few besides Winthrop and his assistants had that status. Such a small inner circle suited Winthrop and his friends, but then more than 100 settlers asked to be admitted. Rather than risk trouble, the ruling group finally admitted 118 more freemen in 1631, stipulating that only church members could become freemen.

At first the freemen had no power except to choose "assistants," who in turn chose the governor and deputy governor. In 1634, however, the freemen turned themselves into a representative body called the General Court, with two or three deputies to represent each town. A final stage in the evolution of the government came in 1644, when the General Court, being the supreme judicial as well as legislative body, divided itself into a bicameral assembly, with all decisions requiring a majority in each house.

Thus over a period of fourteen years, the Massachusetts Bay Company, a trading corporation, evolved into the governing body of a holy commonwealth. Membership in a Puritan church replaced the purchase of stock as the means of becoming a freeman, which was to say a voter. The General Court, like Parliament, became a representative body of two houses: the House of Assistants, corresponding roughly to the House of Lords, and the House of Deputies, corresponding to the House of Commons. Although the charter remained unchanged, government was quite different from the original expectation.

It is hard to exaggerate the crucial role played by John Winthrop in establishing the Massachusetts Bay Colony. In England he had been a man of limited means and little stature; in America, however, as the new colony's godly governor, he displayed extraordinary leadership abilities. A devout

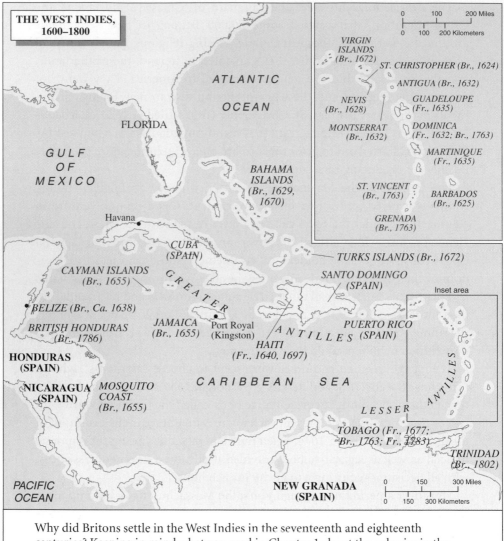

THE WEST INDIES, 1600–1800

ATLANTIC OCEAN

VIRGIN ISLANDS (Br., 1672)
ST. CHRISTOPHER (Br., 1624)
ANTIGUA (Br., 1632)
NEVIS (Br., 1628)
GUADELOUPE (Fr., 1635)
MONTSERRAT (Br., 1632)
DOMINICA (Fr., 1632; Br., 1763)
MARTINIQUE (Fr., 1635)
ST. VINCENT (Br., 1763)
BARBADOS (Br., 1625)
GRENADA (Br., 1763)

FLORIDA

GULF OF MEXICO

BAHAMA ISLANDS (Br., 1629, 1670)

Havana

CUBA (SPAIN)

CAYMAN ISLANDS (Br., 1655)

GREATER

TURKS ISLANDS (Br., 1672)

SANTO DOMINGO (SPAIN)

Inset area

BELIZE (Br., Ca. 1638)

JAMAICA (Br., 1655)
Port Royal (Kingston)

ANTILLES

PUERTO RICO (SPAIN)

BRITISH HONDURAS (Br., 1786)

HAITI (Fr., 1640, 1697)

HONDURAS (SPAIN)

ANTILLES

NICARAGUA (SPAIN)
MOSQUITO COAST (Br., 1655)

CARIBBEAN SEA

LESSER

TOBAGO (Fr., 1677; Br., 1763; Fr., 1783)

TRINIDAD (Br., 1802)

PACIFIC OCEAN

NEW GRANADA (SPAIN)

0   100   200 Miles
0   100   200 Kilometers

0   150   300 Miles
0   150   300 Kilometers

Why did Britons settle in the West Indies in the seventeenth and eighteenth centuries? Keeping in mind what you read in Chapter 1 about the colonies in the West Indies, what products would you expect those colonies to produce? Why would those colonies have had strategic importance to the British?

pragmatist who often governed as an enlightened despot, he steadfastly sought to steer a middle course between clerical absolutists and Separatist zealots. Winthrop prized stability and order and hated democracy, which he called the "worst of all forms of government." His goal was to create a holy commonwealth in Massachusetts, to constrain both religious freedom and

social unrest. His purpose was to enforce Puritan orthodoxy, to compel conformity to the one "true religion." Dissenters, whether they were Catholics,
Anglicans, Quakers, or Baptists, would be punished, banished, or executed. As
an iron-souled man governing a God-saturated community, John Winthrop
provided the foundation not only for a colony but also for major elements in
America's cultural and political development.

RHODE ISLAND   More by accident than design, Massachusetts became
the staging area for the rest of New England as new colonies grew out of
religious quarrels. Puritanism created a volatile mixture: on the one hand,
the search for God's will could lead to a rigid orthodoxy; on the other hand,
it could lead troubled consciences to embrace radical ideas. Young Roger
Williams, who had arrived from England in 1631, was among the first to
cause problems, precisely because he was the purest of Puritans, troubled
by the failure of Massachusetts Nonconformists to repudiate the "whorish"
Church of England entirely. Whereas John Winthrop cherished authority,
Roger Williams championed liberty. Unlike the Puritans and the Pilgrims,
who asserted that God created a covenant with each congregation, Williams
decided that the true covenant was between God and the individual. He
was one of a small but growing number of Puritans who posed a provocative question: If one's salvation depends solely upon God's grace and one
can do nothing to affect it, why bother to have churches at all? Why not
endow individuals with the authority to exercise their free will in worshipping God?

Williams held a brief pastorate in Salem, then moved to Separatist Plymouth. Governor Bradford liked Williams but charged that he "began to fall
into strange opinions," specifically, questioning the king's right to confiscate
Indian lands. Williams then returned to Salem, where he came to love the
Indians. His belief that a true church must include only those who had received God's gift of grace eventually convinced him that no true church was
possible, unless perhaps consisting of his wife and himself.

In Williams's view the purity of the church required complete separation of
church and state and freedom from all coercion in matters of faith. "Forced
worship," he declared, "stinks in God's nostrils." Williams therefore questioned
the authority of government to impose religious conformity. Such radical
views prompted the church of Salem to expel him, whereupon Williams re-
torted so hotly against "ulcered and gangrened" churches that the General
Court in 1635 banished him to England. Governor Winthrop, however, permitted Williams to slip away with his family and a few followers and seek
shelter among the Narragansett Indians. In 1636, Williams established the

The Anabaptift

The Brownift

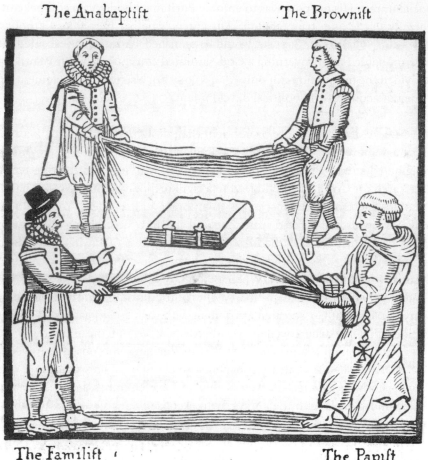

The Familift

The Papift

The diversity of English Protestantism

Religious quarrels within the Puritan fold led to the founding of new colonies. In this seventeenth-century cartoon, four Englishmen, each representing a party in opposition to the established Church of England, are shown fighting over the Bible.

town of Providence at the head of Narragansett Bay, the first permanent settlement in Rhode Island and the first in America to allow freedom of religion. There he welcomed all who fled religious persecution in Massachusetts Bay, including Jews. For their part, Boston officials came to view Rhode Island as a refuge for rogues.

Thus the colony of Rhode Island and Providence Plantations, the smallest in America, grew up in Narragansett Bay as a refuge for dissenters who agreed that the state had no right to coerce religious belief. In 1640 the colony's settlers formed a confederation and in 1643 secured their first charter of incorporation as Providence Plantations. Roger Williams lived until 1683, an active, beloved citizen of the commonwealth he founded, in a society that, during his lifetime at least, lived up to his principles of religious freedom and a government based upon the consent of the people.

Roger Williams was only one of several prominent Puritan dissenters. Another, Anne Hutchinson, quarreled with the Puritan leaders for different reasons. The articulate, strong-willed, intelligent wife of a prominent merchant, she raised thirteen children, served as a healer and midwife, and hosted meetings in her Boston home to discuss sermons. Soon, however, the discussions turned into well-attended forums for Hutchinson's own commentaries on religious matters. Blessed with vast biblical knowledge and a quick wit, she claimed to have experienced direct revelations from the Holy Spirit that convinced her that only two or three Puritan ministers actually preached the appropriate "covenant of grace." The others, she charged, were godless hypocrites, deluded and incompetent; the "covenant of works" they promoted led people to believe that good conduct would ensure salvation. Eventually Hutchinson claimed to know which of her neighbors had been saved and which were damned.

Hutchinson's beliefs were provocative for several reasons. Puritan theology was grounded in the Calvinist doctrine that people could be saved only by God's grace rather than through their own willful actions. But Puritanism in practice also insisted that ministers were necessary to interpret God's will for the people so as to "prepare" them for the possibility of their being selected for salvation. In challenging the very legitimacy of the ministerial community as well as the hard-earned assurances of salvation enjoyed by current church members, Hutchinson was undermining the stability of an already fragile social system. Moreover, her critics likened her claim of direct revelations from the Holy Spirit to the antinomian heresy, a subversive belief that one is freed from obeying the moral law by one's own faith and by God's grace. Unlike Roger Williams, Hutchinson did not advocate religious individualism. Instead, she sought to eradicate the concept of "grace by good works" infecting Puritan orthodoxy. She did not represent a forerunner of modern feminism or freedom of conscience. Instead, she was a proponent of a theocratic extremism that threatened the solidarity of the commonwealth. What made the situation worse in the male-dominated society of seventeenth-century New England was that a *woman* was making such charges. Mrs. Hutchinson had both offended authority and sanctioned a disruptive self-righteousness.

A pregnant Hutchinson was hauled before the General Court in 1637, and for two days she sparred on equal terms with the presiding magistrates and testifying ministers. Her skillful deflections of the charges and her ability to cite chapter-and-verse biblical defenses of her actions led an exasperated Governor Winthrop at one point to explode, "We do not mean to discourse with those of your sex." He found Hutchinson to be "a woman of haughty and fierce carriage, of a nimble wit and active spirit, and a very voluble tongue." As the trial continued, an overwrought Hutchinson was eventually lured into convicting herself by claiming direct revelations from God—blasphemy in the eyes of orthodox Puritans.

Banished in 1638 as a leper not fit for "our society," Hutchinson settled with her family and about sixty followers on an island south of Providence, near what is now Portsmouth, Rhode Island. But the arduous journey had taken its toll. Hutchinson grew sick, and her baby was stillborn, leading her critics in Massachusetts to assert that the "monstrous birth" was God's way of punishing her sins. Hutchinson's spirits never recovered. After her husband's death, in 1642, she moved near New York City, then under Dutch jurisdiction, and the following year she and six of her children were massacred during an Indian attack. Her fate, wrote a vindictive Winthrop, was "a special manifestation of divine justice."

CONNECTICUT Connecticut had a more orthodox beginning than Rhode Island. In 1633 a group from Plymouth settled in the Connecticut River valley. Three years later Thomas Hooker led three entire church congregations from Massachusetts Bay to the Connecticut River towns of Wethersfield, Windsor, and Hartford. In 1637 the inhabitants organized the self-governing colony of Connecticut. Two years later the Connecticut General Court adopted the Fundamental Orders, a series of laws that provided for a "Christian Commonwealth" like that of Massachusetts, except that voting was not limited to church members. The Connecticut constitution specified that the Congregational churches would be the colony's official religion, supported by governmental tax revenues and protected by the civil authorities. The governor was commanded to rule according to "the word of God."

New Haven emerged as a major settlement within Connecticut. A group of English Puritans had migrated first to Massachusetts and then, seeking a place to establish themselves in commerce, to New Haven, on Long Island Sound, in 1638. The New Haven colony became the most rigorously Puritan of all. Like the other offshoots of Massachusetts, it lacked a charter and for a time maintained a self-governing independence. In 1662 it was absorbed into Connecticut under the terms of that colony's first royal charter.

NEW HAMPSHIRE AND MAINE   To the north of Massachusetts, most of what are now the states of New Hampshire and Maine was granted in 1622 by the Council for New England to Sir Ferdinando Gorges and Captain John Mason and their associates. In 1629, Mason and Gorges divided their territory at the Piscataqua River, Mason taking the southern part, which he named New Hampshire, and Gorges taking the northern part, which became the province of Maine. In the 1630s, Puritan immigrants began filtering in, and in 1638 the Reverend John Wheelwright, one of Anne Hutchinson's group, founded Exeter, New Hampshire. Maine at that time consisted of a few scattered settlements, mostly fishing stations.

An ambiguity in the Massachusetts charter brought the proprietorships into doubt, however. The charter set the boundary three miles north of the Merrimack River, and the Bay Colony took that to mean north of the river's northernmost reach, which gave it a claim to nearly the entire Gorges-Mason grant. During the English civil strife in the early 1640s, Massachusetts took over New Hampshire and in the 1650s extended its authority to the scattered settlements in Maine. This led to lawsuits with the heirs of the proprietors, and in 1678 English judges decided against Massachusetts in both cases. In 1679, New Hampshire became a royal colony, but Massachusetts bought out the Gorges heirs and continued to control Maine as its proprietor. A new Massachusetts charter in 1691 finally incorporated Maine into Massachusetts.

INDIANS IN NEW ENGLAND

The English settlers who poured into New England found not a "virgin land" of uninhabited wilderness but a developed region populated by over 100,000 Indians. The white colonists considered the Native Americans wild pagans incapable of fully exploiting nature's bounty. In their view, God meant for the Puritans to take over Indian lands as a reward for their piety and hard work. The town meeting of Milford, Connecticut, for example, voted in 1640 that the land was God's "and that the earth is given to the Saints; voted, we are the Saints."

Indians coped with the newcomers in different ways. Many resisted, others sought accommodation, and still others grew dependent upon European culture. In some areas, Indians survived and even flourished in concert with European settlers. In other areas, land-hungry whites quickly displaced or decimated the native populations. The interactions of the two cultures involved misunderstandings, the mutual need for trade and adaptation, and sporadic outbreaks of epidemics and warfare.

In general, the English colonists adopted a strategy for dealing with the Native Americans quite different from that of the French and the Dutch. Merchants from France and the Netherlands were preoccupied with exploiting the fur trade. To do so, they built permanent trading outposts and established amicable relations with the Indians in the region, who greatly outnumbered them. In contrast, the English colonists were more interested in pursuing their "God-given" right to fish and farm. They sought to exploit Indians rather than deal with them on an equal footing. Their goal was subordination rather than reciprocity.

THE NEW ENGLAND INDIANS   In Maine the Abenakis were primarily hunters and gatherers dependent upon the natural offerings of the land and waters. The men did the hunting and fishing; the women retrieved the

Algonquian ceremony

As with most Indians, the Algonquians' dependence on nature for survival shaped their religious beliefs.

dead game and prepared it for eating. Women were also responsible for setting up and breaking camp, gathering fruits and berries, and raising the children. The Algonquian tribes of southern New England—the Massachusetts, Nausets, Narragansetts, Pequots, and Wampanoags—were more horticultural. Their highly developed agricultural system centered on three primary crops: corn, beans, and pumpkins.

The Indians' dependence upon nature for their survival shaped their religious beliefs. They believed in a Creator who provided them with the land and its bountiful resources. Nature was suffused with spirits. Animals, plants, trees, rivers, and stones harbored spiritual power, and human beings were very much dependent upon such supernatural forces. Indian rituals, ceremonies, and taboos acknowledged their dependence upon the workings of nature. Rain dances, harvest festivals, and pre-battle ceremonies were all intended to honor the spirits at work in nature. The Puritans viewed such animistic beliefs as superstitions fostered by Satan. The Bible, after all, said that Christians were separate from and superior to the natural world, and this reading gave English settlers a biblical rationalization for taking lands from the Indians. God had, after all, granted his followers dominion over "every living thing that moveth upon the earth."

Initially the coastal Indians helped the white settlers develop a subsistence economy. They taught the English settlers how to plant corn and use fish for fertilizer. They also developed a flourishing trade with the newcomers, exchanging furs for manufactured goods and "trinkets." The various Indian tribes of New England often fought among themselves, usually over disputed land. Had they been able to forge a solid alliance, they would have been better able to resist the encroachments of white settlers. As it was, they were not only fragmented but also vulnerable to the infectious diseases carried on board the ships transporting British settlers to the New World. Epidemics of smallpox devastated the Indian population, leaving the coastal areas "a widowed land." Between 1610 and 1675 the Abenakis declined from 12,000 to 3,000 and the southern New England tribes from 65,000 to 10,000. Governor William Bradford of Plymouth reported that the Indians "fell sick of the smallpox, and died most miserably." By the hundreds they died "like rotten sheep."

THE PEQUOT WAR   Indians who survived the epidemics and refused to yield their lands were forced out. In 1636, settlers in Massachusetts accused a Pequot of murdering a colonist. Joined by Connecticut colonists, they exacted their revenge by setting fire to a Pequot village on the Mystic River. As the Indians fled their burning huts, the Puritans shot and killed them—men, women, and children. The militia commander who ordered the massacre declared that God had guided his actions: "Thus the Lord was pleased to smite our Enemies . . . and give us their land for an Inheritance."

Sassacus, the Pequot chief, organized the survivors among his followers and attacked the English. During the Pequot War of 1637, the colonists and their Narragansett allies killed hundreds of Pequots in their village near West Mystic, in the Connecticut River valley. The Puritan minister Cotton Mather later described the slaughter as a "sweet sacrifice" and "gave the praise thereof to God."

Only a few colonists regretted the massacre. Roger Williams warned that the lust for land would become "as great a God with us English as God Gold was with the Spanish." With poignant clarity, Pequot survivors recognized the motives of the English settlers: "We see plainly that their chiefest desire

Pequot fort

The Puritans and their Indian allies, the Narragansetts, mount a ferocious attack on the Pequots at West Mystic, Connecticut (1637).

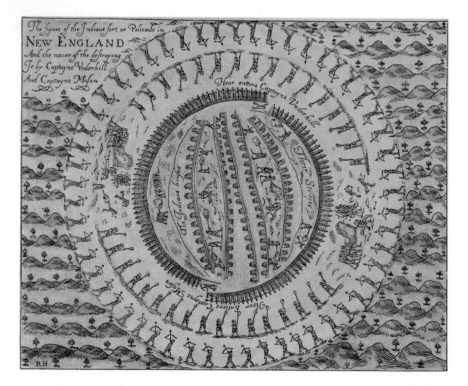

is to deprive us of the privilege of our land, and drive us to our utter ruin." The English colonists captured most of the surviving Pequots and sold them into slavery in Bermuda. Under the terms of the Treaty of Hartford (1638), the Pequot Nation was dissolved.

KING PHILIP'S WAR After the Pequot War the prosperous fur trade contributed to peaceful relations between Europeans and the remaining Indians, but the relentless growth of the New England colonies and the decline of the beaver population began to reduce the eastern tribes to relative poverty. The colonial government repeatedly encroached upon Indian settlements, forcing them to embrace English laws and customs. By 1675 the Native Americans and English settlers had come to know each other well— and fear each other deeply.

The era of peaceful coexistence that had begun with the Treaty of Hartford in 1638 came to a bloody end during the last quarter of the seventeenth century. Tribal leaders, especially the chief of the Wampanoags, Metacomet (known to the colonists as King Philip), resented English efforts to convert Indians to Christianity. During the mid–seventeenth century, the Puritans, led by John Eliot, "Apostle to the Indians," began an aggressive campaign to win Indians over to Christianity. The missionaries insisted, however, that the Indians must abandon their native cultural practices as well as their spiritual beliefs. This meant resettling the Indian converts in what were called praying towns, not unlike the Catholic missions constructed in New Spain. The so-called praying Indians had to adopt English names, cut their hair short, and take up farm work and domestic chores. By 1674, some 1,100 Indian converts were living in fourteen praying towns. But most of the New England Indians resisted such efforts. As one of them asked a Puritan missionary, why should Indians convert to English ways when "our corn is as good as yours, and we take more pleasure than you?"

In the fall of 1674, John Sassamon, a "praying Indian" who had graduated from Harvard College, warned the English that Metacomet and the Wampanoags were preparing for war. A few months later Sassamon was found dead under the ice of a frozen pond. Colonial authorities convicted three Wampanoags of murder and hanged them. Enraged Wampanoag warriors then attacked and burned Puritan farms on June 20, 1675. Three days later an Englishman shot an Indian, and the Wampanoags retaliated by ambushing and beheading a group of Puritans.

Both sides suffered incredible losses in what came to be called King Philip's War, or Metacomet's War. The fighting killed more people and caused more destruction in New England in proportion to the population than any American conflict since. Bands of warriors assaulted fifty towns. Within a year the Indians were threatening Boston itself. The situation was so desperate that the colonies instituted America's first conscription laws, drafting into the militia all males between the ages of sixteen and sixty. Finally, however, shortages of food and ammunition and staggering casualties wore down Indian resistance. Metacomet's wife and son were captured and sold into slavery in Bermuda. Some of the tribes surrendered, a few succumbed to disease, while others fled to the west. Those who remained were forced to resettle in villages supervised by white settlers. Metacomet initially escaped, only to be hunted down and killed in 1676. The victorious colonists marched his severed head to Plymouth, where it sat atop a pole for twenty years, a gruesome reminder of the British determination to control the Indians. King Philip's War devastated the Native American culture in New England. Combat deaths, deportations, and flight cut the region's Indian population in half. Military victory also enabled the Puritan authorities to increase their political, economic, legal, and religious control over the 9,000 Indians who remained.

THE ENGLISH CIVIL WAR IN AMERICA

By 1640, English settlers in New England and around Chesapeake Bay had established two great beachheads on the Atlantic coast, with the Dutch colony of New Netherland in between. After 1640, however, the struggle between king and Parliament in England distracted attention from colonization, and migration to America dwindled to a trickle for more than twenty years. During the English Civil War (1642–1646) and Oliver Cromwell's Puritan dictatorship (1653–1658) the struggling colonies were left pretty much to their own devices.

In 1643, four of the New England colonies—Massachusetts Bay, Plymouth, Connecticut, and New Haven—formed the New England Confederation to provide joint defense against the Dutch, French, and Indians. Two commissioners from each colony met annually to transact business. In some ways the confederation behaved like a sovereign power. It made treaties, and in 1653 it declared war against the Dutch, who were accused of inciting the Indians to attack Connecticut. Massachusetts, far from the scene of trouble, failed to cooperate, greatly weakening the confederation. But the commissioners continued to meet annually until 1684, when Massachusetts lost its charter.

Virginia and Maryland remained almost as independent of English control as New England. At the behest of Governor William Berkeley, the Virginia burgesses in 1649 denounced the Puritans' execution of King Charles and recognized his son, Charles II, as the lawful king. In 1652, however, the assembly yielded to parliamentary commissioners and overruled the governor. In return for the surrender, the commissioners let the assembly choose its own council and governor. The colony grew rapidly in population during its years of independent government, some of the growth coming from the arrival of Royalists, who found a friendly haven in Anglican Virginia.

The parliamentary commissioners who won the submission of Virginia proceeded to Catholic Maryland, where the proprietary governor faced particular difficulties with his Protestant majority. At the governor's suggestion the assembly had passed the Maryland Toleration Act of 1649, an assurance that Puritans would not be molested in the practice of their religion. In 1654 the commissioners revoked the Toleration Act and deprived Lord Baltimore of his governmental rights, though not of his lands and revenues. Still, the more extreme Puritan elements were dissatisfied, and a brief clash in 1654 brought religious civil war to Maryland and led to the deposing of the governor. But Oliver Cromwell took the side of Lord Baltimore and restored his full rights in 1657, whereupon the Toleration Act was reinstated. The act deservedly stands as a landmark to human liberty, albeit enacted more out of expediency than conviction.

Cromwell let the colonies go their own way, but he was not indifferent to Britain's North American empire. He fought trade wars with the Dutch, and his navy harassed England's traditional enemy, Catholic Spain, in the Caribbean. In 1655 a British force wrested Jamaica from Spanish control.

The Restoration of King Charles II in 1660 led to an equally painless restoration of previous governments in the colonies. Agents hastily dispatched by the colonies won reconfirmation of the Massachusetts charter in 1662 and the very first royal charters for Connecticut and Rhode Island in 1662 and 1663. All three retained their status as self-governing corporations. Plymouth still had no charter, but it went unmolested. New Haven, however, disappeared as a separate entity, absorbed into the colony of Connecticut.

SETTLING THE CAROLINAS

The Restoration of Charles II to the British throne in 1660 revived interest in colonial expansion. Within twelve years the English would conquer New Netherland, settle Carolina, and nearly fill out the shape of the colonies. In the middle region, formerly claimed by the Dutch, four new colonies emerged: New York, New Jersey, Pennsylvania, and Delaware. Without exception the new colonies were proprietary, awarded by the king to men who had remained loyal to the monarchy during the civil war, who had brought about his restoration, or in one case, to whom he was indebted. In 1663, for example, King Charles II granted Carolina to eight prominent allies, who became lords proprietors (owners) of the region.

NORTH CAROLINA   Carolina was from the start made up of two widely separated areas of settlement, which eventually became two distinct colonies. The northernmost part, long called Albemarle, had been settled in the 1650s by colonists who had drifted southward from Virginia. For half a century, Albemarle remained a remote scattering of farmers along the shores of Albemarle Sound. Albemarle had no governor until 1664, no assembly until 1665, and not even a town until a group of French Huguenots founded the village of Bath on the Outer Banks in 1704.

SOUTH CAROLINA   The eight lords proprietors to whom the king had given Carolina neglected Albemarle from the outset and focused on more promising sites to the south. They recruited seasoned British planters from the Caribbean island of Barbados to replicate in South Carolina the profitable West Indian sugar-plantation system based on the labor of enslaved Africans. The first British colonists arrived in South Carolina in 1669 at Charles Town (later named Charleston). Over the next twenty years, half the South Carolina colonists came from Barbados.

The government of South Carolina rested upon one of the most curious documents of colonial history, the Fundamental Constitutions of Carolina, drawn up by one of the eight proprietors, Lord Anthony Ashley Cooper, with the help of his secretary, the philosopher John Locke. Its cumbersome frame of government and its provisions for an elaborate nobility had little effect in the colony except to encourage a practice of large land grants. From the beginning, however, smaller headrights (land grants) were given to every immigrant who could afford the cost of transit. The most enticing provision was a grant of religious toleration, designed to encourage immigration, which gave South Carolina a greater degree of religious freedom (extending even to Jews and "heathens") than England or any other colony except Rhode Island and, once it was established, Pennsylvania. South Carolina became a separate royal colony in 1719. North Carolina remained under the proprietors' rule for

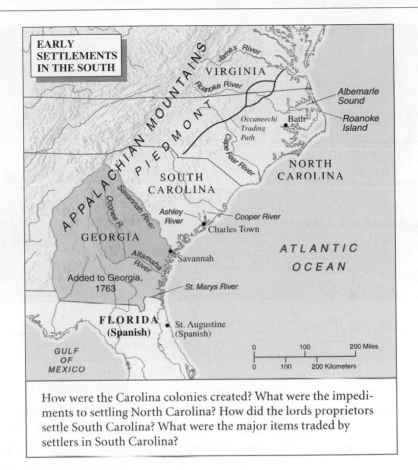

EARLY
SETTLEMENTS
IN THE SOUTH

VIRGINIA
James River
Roanoke River
APPALACHIAN MOUNTAINS
PIEDMONT
Occaneechi
Trading
Path
Bath
Albemarle
Sound
Roanoke
Island
Cape Fear River
NORTH
CAROLINA
SOUTH
CAROLINA
Ashley
River
Cooper River
Charles Town
GEORGIA
Oconee R.
Savannah River
Altamaha
River
Savannah
Added to Georgia,
1763
St. Marys River
ATLANTIC
OCEAN
FLORIDA
(Spanish)
St. Augustine
(Spanish)
GULF
OF
MEXICO

0   100   200 Miles
0   100   200 Kilometers

How were the Carolina colonies created? What were the impediments to settling North Carolina? How did the lords proprietors settle South Carolina? What were the major items traded by settlers in South Carolina?

ten more years, until they transferred their governing rights to the British Crown.

THE SOUTHERN INDIAN TRADE The eight English proprietors (owners) of South Carolina wanted the colony to focus on producing commercial crops (staples). Such production took time to develop, however. Land had to be cleared, crops planted and harvested. These activities required laborers. Some Carolina planters brought enslaved Africans and indentured servants with them. Many more workers were needed, however, yet slaves and servants were expensive. The quickest way to raise capital in the early years of South Carolina's development was through trade with the Indians.

The Broiling of Their Fish over the Flame

In this drawing by John White, Algonquian men in North Carolina broil fish, a dietary staple of coastal societies.

In the late seventeenth century, English merchants—mostly illiterate adventurers—began traveling southward from Virginia into the Piedmont region of Carolina, where they developed a prosperous trade with the Catawba Indians. By 1690, traders from Charles Town, South Carolina, had made their way up the Savannah River to arrange deals with the Cherokees, Creeks, and Chickasaws. Between 1699 and 1715, Carolina exported to England an average of 54,000 deerskins per year. Europeans, in turn, transformed the valuable hides into bookbindings, gloves, belts, hats, and work aprons. The voracious demand for the soft skins almost exterminated the deer population.

The growing trade with the English exposed the Indians to contagious diseases that decimated the population. Commercial activity also entwined the Indians in a dependent relationship that would prove disastrous to their traditional way of life. The English traders began providing the Indians with firearms and rum as incentives to persuade them to capture members of rival tribes to be sold as slaves. While colonists themselves captured and enslaved Indians, most tribes captured other Indians and exchanged the captives for British trade goods, guns, and rum. Colonists, in turn, put some of the Indian captives to work on their plantations. But because Indian captives

Cherokee chiefs

A print depicting seven Cherokee chiefs who had been taken from Carolina to England in 1730.

often ran away, the traders preferred to ship them to New York, Boston, and the West Indies and import enslaved Africans to work in the Carolinas.

The profitability of Indian captives prompted a frenzy of slaving activity among white settlers. Slave traders turned Indian tribes against one another in order to ensure a continuous supply of captives. As many as 50,000 Indians, most of them women and children, were sold as slaves in Charles Town between 1670 and 1715. More enslaved Indians were exported during that period than Africans were imported. Thousands more captured Indians circulated through New England ports. The burgeoning trade in enslaved Indians triggered bitter struggles between tribes, gave rise to unprecedented colonial warfare, and spawned massive internal migrations across the southern colonies.

During the last quarter of the seventeenth century, the trade in enslaved Indians spread across the entire Southeast. Slave raiding became the region's single most important economic activity and a powerful weapon in Britain's global conflict with France and Spain. During the early eighteenth century, Indians armed with British weapons and led by English soldiers crossed into Spanish territory in south Georgia and north Florida. They destroyed thirteen Catholic missions, killed several hundred Indians and Spaniards, and enslaved over 300 Indian men, women, and children. By 1710 the Florida tribes were on the verge of extinction. In 1708, when the total population of

A war dance

The Westo Indians of Georgia, pictured here doing a war dance, were among the first Native Americans to obtain firearms and used this advantage to enslave other Indians throughout Georgia, Florida, and the Carolinas.

South Carolina was 9,580, including 2,900 Africans, there were 1,400 enslaved Indians.

The trade in enslaved Indians led to escalating troubles. Fears of slave raids disrupted the planting cycle in Indian villages. Some tribes fled the South altogether. In 1712 the Tuscaroras of North Carolina attacked German and English colonists who had encroached upon their land. North Carolina authorities appealed to South Carolina for aid, and the colony, eager for more slaves, dispatched two expeditions made up mostly of Indian allies—Yamasees, Cherokees, Creeks, and Catawbas—led by whites. In 1713 they destroyed a Tuscarora town, executed 162 male warriors, and took 392 women and children captive for sale in Charles Town. The surviving Tuscaroras fled north, where they joined the Iroquois Confederacy.

The Tuscarora War in North Carolina sparked more conflict in South Carolina. The Yamasees felt betrayed when white traders paid them less for their Tuscarora captives than they wanted. What made this shortfall so acute was that the Yamasees owed debts to traders totaling 100,000 deerskins—almost five years worth of hunting. To recover their debts, white traders cheated Yamasees, confiscated their lands, and began enslaving their women and children. In April 1715 the enraged Yamasees attacked coastal plantations and killed over 100 whites. Their vengeful assaults continued for months, aided by Creeks. Most of the white traders were killed. Whites throughout the low country of South Carolina panicked; hundreds fled to Charles Town. The governor mobilized all white and black males to defend the colony; other colonies supplied weapons. Not until the governor persuaded the Cherokees (with the inducement of many gifts) to join them against the Yamasees and Creeks did the Yamasee War end—in the spring of 1716. The defeated Yamasees fled to Spanish-controlled Florida. By then hundreds of whites had been killed and dozens of plantations destroyed and abandoned. To prevent another conflict, the colonial government outlawed all private trading with Indians. Commerce between whites and Indians could now occur only through a colonial agency created to end abuses and shift activity from trading enslaved Indians to deerskins.

The end of the Yamasee War did not stop infighting among the Indians, however. For the next ten years or so the Creeks and Cherokees engaged in a costly blood feud, much to the delight of the English. One Carolinian explained that their challenge was to figure out "how to hold both [tribes] as our friends, for some time, and assist them in cutting one another's throats without offending either. This is the game we intend to play if possible." The French played the same brutal game, doing their best to excite hatred between the Choctaws and the Chickasaws. Between 1700 and 1730 the Indian population in the Carolinas dwindled from 15,000 to just 4,000.

SETTLING THE MIDDLE COLONIES AND GEORGIA

NEW NETHERLAND BECOMES NEW YORK During the early seventeenth century, having gained its independence from Spain, the tiny nation of the Netherlands (Holland) emerged as a maritime giant. By 1670 the mostly Protestant Dutch had the largest merchant fleet in the world and the highest standard of living. They controlled northern European commerce and became one of the most diverse societies in Europe. The Dutch welcomed exiles from the constant religious strife in Europe: Iberian and German Jews, French Protestants (Huguenots), and English Puritans. The extraordinary success of the Netherlands also proved to be its downfall, however. Like imperial Spain, the Dutch Empire expanded too rapidly. Netherlanders dominated European trade with China, India, Africa, Brazil, and the Caribbean, but they could not efficiently manage their far-flung possessions. It did not take long for European rivals to exploit the weak points in the lucrative empire. By the mid–seventeenth century, England and the Netherlands were locked in ferocious commercial warfare.

In London, King Charles II resolved to pluck out that old thorn in the side of the English colonies in America: New Netherland. The Dutch colony was older than New England, having been planted when the two Protestant powers allied in opposition to Catholic Spain. The Dutch East India Company (organized in 1602) had hired an English captain, Henry Hudson, to explore America. Sailing along the upper coast of North America in 1609, Hudson had discovered Delaware Bay. He also explored the river named for him, venturing 160 miles, to a point probably beyond what is now Albany, where he and a group of Mohawks began a lasting trade relationship between the Dutch and the Iroquois Nations. In 1610 the Dutch established fur-trading posts on Manhattan Island and upriver at Fort Orange (later Albany). In 1626, Governor Peter Minuit purchased Manhattan from the resident Indians, and a Dutch fort appeared at the lower end of the island. The village of New Amsterdam, which grew up around the fort, became the capital of New Netherland and developed into a rollicking commercial powerhouse, in large part because of its sheltered harbors and deepwater ports. Unlike their Puritan counterparts in Massachusetts Bay, the Dutch in New Amsterdam were preoccupied more with profits and freedoms than with piety and restrictions. They embraced free enterprise and ethnic and religious diversity.

Dutch settlements gradually dispersed in every direction in which furs might be found. In 1638 a Swedish trading company established Fort Christina at the site of present-day Wilmington, Delaware, and scattered a few hundred settlers up and down the Delaware River. The Dutch, at the time allied with the Swedes in the Thirty Years' War, made no move to challenge the claim until 1655, when a force outnumbering the entire Swedish colony subjected them, without bloodshed, to the rule of New Netherland. The chief contribution of the short-lived New Sweden to American culture was the idea of the log cabin, which the Swedes and a few Finnish settlers had brought from the woods of Scandinavia.

Like the French, the Dutch were interested mainly in the fur trade rather than agricultural settlements. The European demand for beaver hats created huge profits. In 1629, however, the Dutch West India Company (organized in 1623) decided that it needed a mass of settlers to help protect the colony's "front door" at the mouth of the Hudson River. It provided that any stockholder might obtain a large estate (a patroonship) in exchange for peopling it with fifty adults within four years. The "patroon" was obligated to supply cattle, tools, and buildings. His tenants, in turn, paid him rent, used his gristmill, gave him first option to purchase surplus crops, and submitted to a court he established. It amounted to transplanting the feudal manor to the New World, and it met with as little luck as similar efforts in Maryland and South Carolina. Volunteers for serfdom were hard to find when there was land to be had elsewhere; most settlers took advantage of the company's provision that one could have as farms (*bouweries*) all the lands one could improve.

The New Netherland government was under the almost absolute control of a governor sent out by the Dutch West India Company. The governors were mostly stubborn autocrats, either corrupt or inept, and especially clumsy at Indian relations. They depended upon a small army garrison for defense, and the inhabitants (including a number of English on Long Island)

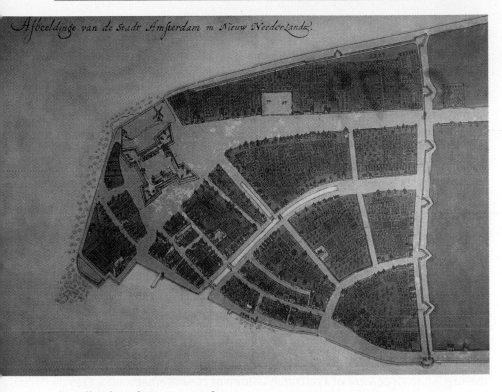

Afbeeldinge van de Stadt Amsterdam m Nieuw Neederlandt.

Castello Plan of New Amsterdam

A map of New Amsterdam in 1660, shortly before the English took the colony from the Dutch and christened it New York.

were hardly devoted to the Dutch government. New Amsterdam was by far the most diverse of the American colonies. Its residents included Swedes, Norwegians, Spaniards, Sephardic Jews, free blacks, English, Germans, and Finns—as well as Dutch. The polyglot colonists prized their liberties and lived in a smoldering state of near mutiny against the colony's governors. In fact, in 1664 they showed almost total indifference when Governor Peter Stuyvesant called them to arms against a threatening British fleet. Almost defenseless, the old soldier Stuyvesant blustered and stomped about on his wooden leg but finally surrendered without firing a shot and stayed on quietly at his farm in what became the English colony of New York.

The plan of conquest had been hatched by the Duke of York, later King James II. As lord high admiral and an investor in the African trade, he had already harassed Dutch shipping and forts in Africa. When he and his advisers counseled that New Netherland could easily be conquered, his brother King Charles II simply granted the region to the Duke of York as proprietor and permitted the hasty gathering of an invasion force. The English thus transformed New Amsterdam into New York and Fort Orange into Albany. The Dutch, however, left a permanent imprint on the land and the language: the Dutch vernacular faded, but place-names such as Block Island, Wall Street (the original wall being for protection against Indians), and Broadway (Breede Wegh) remained, along with family names like Rensselaer, Roosevelt, and Van Buren. The Dutch presence lingered, too, in the Dutch Reformed (Calvinist) Church; in words like *boss, cookie, crib, snoop, stoop, spook*, and *kill* (for "creek"); and in the legendary Santa Claus and in Washington Irving's Rip van Winkle.

Important to the development of the American colonies was New Netherland's political principles, as embodied in the formal document transferring governance of the colony from the Dutch to the British. Called the Articles of Capitulation, the document provided a guarantee of individual rights unparalleled in the English colonies. The articles, which endorsed free trade, religious liberty, and local political representation, were incorporated into the New York City Charter of 1686 and thereafter served as a benchmark for disputes with Britain over colonial rights.

JUDAISM IN NORTH AMERICA   In September 1654, ten years before the English took control of the Dutch colony of New Netherland, a French ship arrived in New Amsterdam (New York) Harbor. On board were twenty-three Sephardi, Jews of Spanish-Portuguese descent. Penniless and weary, they had come seeking refuge from Brazil, where they had earlier fled from Spain and Portugal after being exiled by the Catholic Inquisition. When Portugal took Brazil from the Dutch, the Sephardi again had to flee the Catholic Inquisition. They were the first Jewish settlers to arrive in North America, and they were not readily embraced. Leading merchants as well as members of the Dutch Reformed Church asked Peter Stuyvesant, the dictatorial Dutch director general of New Netherland, to expel them. Stuyvesant despised Jews, Lutherans, Catholics, and Quakers. He characterized Jews as "deceitful," "very repugnant," and "blasphemous." If the Jews were allowed in, then "we cannot refuse the Lutherans and Papists." Stuyvesant's employers at the Dutch West India Company disagreed, however. Early in 1655 they ordered him to accommodate the homeless Jews, explaining that he should "allow every one to have his own belief, as long as he behaves quietly and legally, gives no offense to his neighbor and does not oppose the government."

The autocratic Stuyvesant grudgingly complied, but the Jews in New Amsterdam thereafter had to fight for civil and economic rights, as well as

Jewish heritage

A seventeenth-century Jewish cemetary in New York City.

the right to worship in public. It would not be until the late seventeenth century, years after the English took over New Netherland and renamed it New York, that Jews could worship in public. Such restrictions help explain why the American Jewish community grew so slowly. In 1773, over 100 years after the first Jewish refugees arrived in New Amsterdam, only 242 Jews resided in New York, and Jews represented only one tenth of 1 percent of the entire colonial population. On the eve of the American Revolution, there was not a single rabbi in British America. Not until the nineteenth century would the American Jewish community experience dramatic growth.

THE IROQUOIS LEAGUE One of the most significant effects of European settlement in North America during the seventeenth century was the intensification of warfare among Indian peoples. The same combination of forces that decimated the Indian populations of New England and the Carolinas affected the tribes around New York City and the lower Hudson River valley. Dissension among the Indians and susceptibility to infectious disease left them vulnerable to exploitation by whites and other Indians.

In the interior of New York, however, a different situation arose. There the tribes of the Iroquois (an Algonquian term signifying "Snake" or "Terrifying Man") forged an alliance so strong that the outnumbered Dutch and, later,

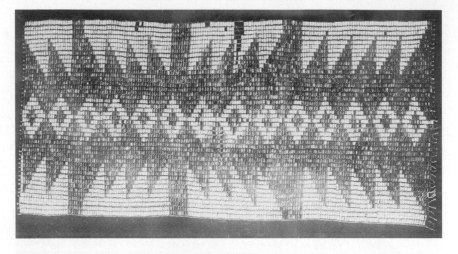

Wampum belt

The diamond shapes at the center of this "covenant chain" belt indicate community alliances. Wampum belts such as this one were often used to certify treaties or record transactions.

English traders were forced to work with the Indians in exploiting the lucrative beaver trade. By the early 1600s some fifty sachems (chiefs) governed the 12,000 members of the Iroquois League, or Iroquois Confederacy. The sachems made decisions for all the villages and mediated tribal rivalries and dissension within the confederacy.

When the Iroquois began to deplete the local game during the 1640s, they used firearms supplied by their Dutch trading partners to seize the Canadian hunting grounds of the neighboring Hurons and Eries. During the so-called Beaver Wars, the Iroquois defeated the western tribes and thereafter hunted the beaver in the region to extinction. During the second half of the seventeenth century, the relentless search for furs and captives led Iroquois war parties to range far across what is today eastern North America. They gained control over a huge area from the St. Lawrence River to Tennessee and from Maine to Michigan. The Iroquois's wars helped reorient the political relationships in the whole eastern half of the continent, especially in the area from the Ohio River valley northward across the Great Lakes Basin. Besieged by the Iroquois League, the western tribes forged defensive alliances with the French.

For over twenty years, warfare raged across the Great Lakes region. In the 1690s the French and their Indian allies gained the advantage over the Iroquois. They destroyed Iroquois crops and villages, infected them with smallpox, and reduced the male population by more than a third. Facing extermination, the Iroquois made peace with the French in 1701. During the first half of the eighteenth century, they maintained a shrewd neutrality in the struggle between the two rival European powers, which enabled them to play the British off against the French while creating a thriving fur trade for themselves.

NEW JERSEY   Shortly after the conquest of New Netherland, the Duke of York granted his lands between the Hudson and Delaware Rivers to Sir George Carteret and Lord John Berkeley (brother of Virginia's governor)

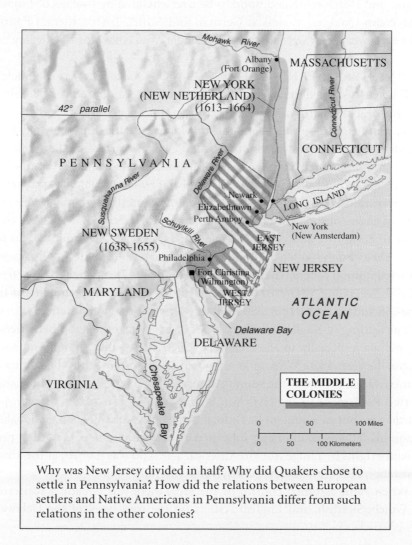

Why was New Jersey divided in half? Why did Quakers chose to settle in Pennsylvania? How did the relations between European settlers and Native Americans in Pennsylvania differ from such relations in the other colonies?

and named the territory for Carteret's native Jersey, an island in the English Channel. In 1676, by mutual agreement, the colony was divided by a diagonal line into East and West Jersey, with Carteret taking the east. Finally, in 1682, Carteret sold out to a group of twelve, including William Penn, who in turn brought into the partnership twelve more proprietors, for a total of twenty-four. In East Jersey, peopled at first by perhaps 200 Dutch who had crossed the Hudson River, new settlements gradually arose: some disaffected Puritans from New Haven founded Newark, Carteret's brother brought a group to found Elizabethtown (Elizabeth), and a group of Scots founded Perth Amboy. In the west, facing the Delaware River, a scattering of Swedes, Finns, and Dutch remained, soon to be overwhelmed by swarms of English and Welsh Quakers, as well as German and Scotch-Irish settlers. In 1702, East and West Jersey were united as the single royal colony of New Jersey.

PENNSYLVANIA AND DELAWARE   The Quaker sect, as the Society of Friends was called in ridicule (because they were supposed to "tremble at the word of the Lord"), became the most influential of many radical religious groups that sprang from the turbulence of the English Civil War. Founded by George Fox in about 1647, the Quakers carried further than any other group the doctrine of individual inspiration and interpretation—the "inner light," they called it. They discarded all formal sacraments and formal ministry, refused deference to persons of rank, used the familiar *thee* and *thou* in addressing everyone, refused to take oaths, claiming they were contrary to Scripture, and embraced pacifism. Quakers were subjected to intense persecution—often in their zeal they seemed to invite it—but never inflicted it upon others. Their tolerance extended to complete religious freedom for everyone, whatever one's belief or disbelief, and to equality of the sexes, including the full participation of women in religious affairs.

The settling of English Quakers in West Jersey encouraged other Friends to migrate, especially to the Delaware River side of the colony. And soon across the river arose William Penn's Quaker commonwealth, the colony of Pennsylvania. Penn was the son of Admiral Sir William Penn, who had supported Parliament in the civil war. Young William was reared as a proper gentleman, but as a student at Oxford University he had become a Quaker. Upon his father's death, Penn inherited a substantial estate, including proprietary rights to a huge tract in America. The land was named, at the king's insistence, for Penn's father: Pennsylvania (literally, "Penn's Woods").

When Penn assumed control of the area, there was already a scattering of Dutch, Swedish, and English settlers on the west bank of the Delaware

Quaker meeting

The presence of women at this meeting is evidence of Quaker views on gender equality.

River. But Penn soon made vigorous efforts to bring more settlers. Unlike John Winthrop in Massachusetts, Penn encouraged people of different religious affiliations (as long as they believed in God) to settle in his new colony. He assumed that believers, regardless of their particular denomination or theology, would set aside their religious differences for the good of the commonwealth ("the holy experiment"). He published glowing descriptions of the colony, which were translated into German, Dutch, and French. By the end of 1681, about 1,000 settlers were living in his province. By that time a town was growing up at the junction of the Schuylkill and Delaware Rivers. Penn called it Philadelphia (City of Brotherly Love). Because of the generous terms on which Penn offered land, the colony grew rapidly.

The relations between the Indians and the Quakers were cordial from the beginning, because of the Quakers' friendliness and Penn's careful policy of purchasing land titles from the Indians. Penn even took the trouble to learn an Indian language, something few colonists ever tried. For some fifty years the settlers and the natives lived side by side in peace.

The colony's government, which rested on three Frames of Government promulgated by Penn, resembled that of other proprietary colonies except that the freemen (taxpayers and property owners) elected the councillors as well as the assembly. The governor had no veto—although Penn, as proprietor, did. Penn hoped to show that a government could operate in accordance with Quaker principles, that it could maintain peace and order without oaths or wars, and that religion could flourish without government support and with absolute freedom of conscience. Because of its tolerance, Pennsylvania became a refuge not only for Quakers but also for a variety of dissenters—as well as Anglicans—and early reflected the ethnic mixture of Scotch-Irish and Germans that became common to the middle colonies and the southern backcountry. Penn himself stayed only four years in the colony.

In 1682 the Duke of York also granted Penn the area of Delaware, another part of the former Dutch territory. At first, Delaware became part of Pennsylvania, but after 1704 it was granted the right to choose its own assembly. From then until the American Revolution, it had a separate assembly but shared Pennsylvania's governor.

GEORGIA   Georgia was the last of the British continental colonies to be established—half a century after Pennsylvania. During the seventeenth century, settlers pushed southward into the borderlands between the Carolinas and Florida. They brought with them their African slaves and a desire to win the Indian trade from the Spanish. Each side used guns, goods, and rum to influence the Indians, and the Indians in turn played off the English against the Spanish in order to gain the most favorable terms.

In 1732, King George II gave the land between the Savannah and Altamaha Rivers to the twenty-one trustees of Georgia. In two respects, Georgia was unique among the colonies: it was set up as a philanthropic experiment and as a military buffer against Spanish Florida. General James E. Oglethorpe, who accompanied the first colonists as resident trustee, represented both concerns: he served as a soldier who organized the defenses and as a philanthropist who championed prison reform and sought a colonial refuge for the poor and the religiously persecuted.

In 1733 a band of about 120 colonists founded Savannah on the coast near the mouth of the Savannah River. Carefully laid out by Oglethorpe, the

Savannah, Georgia

The earliest known view of Savannah, Georgia (1734). The town's layout was carefully planned.

old town, with its geometric pattern and numerous little parks, remains a monument to the city planning of a bygone day. Protestant refugees from Austria began to arrive in 1734, followed by Germans and German-speaking Moravians and Swiss, who made the colony for a time more German than English. The addition of Welsh, Highland Scots, Sephardic Jews, and others gave the early colony a cosmopolitan character much like that of Charleston.

As a buffer against Florida, the colony succeeded, but as a philanthropic experiment it failed. Efforts to develop silk and wine production foundered. Landholdings were limited to 500 acres, rum was prohibited, and the importation of slaves was forbidden, partly to leave room for servants brought on charity, partly to ensure security. But the utopian rules soon collapsed. The regulations against rum and slavery were widely disregarded and finally abandoned. By 1759 all restrictions on landholding had been removed.

In 1754 the trustees' charter expired, and the province reverted to the Crown. As a royal colony, Georgia acquired an effective government for the first time. The province developed slowly over the next decade but grew rapidly in population and wealth after 1763. Instead of wine and silk, as was

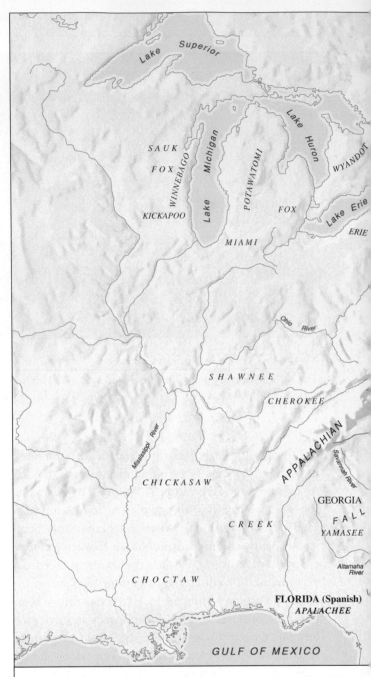

Why did European settlement lead to the expansion of hostilities among the Indians? What were the consequences of the trade and commerce between the English settlers and the southern Indian tribes? How were the relationships between the settlers and the members of the Iroquois League different from those between settlers and tribes in other regions?

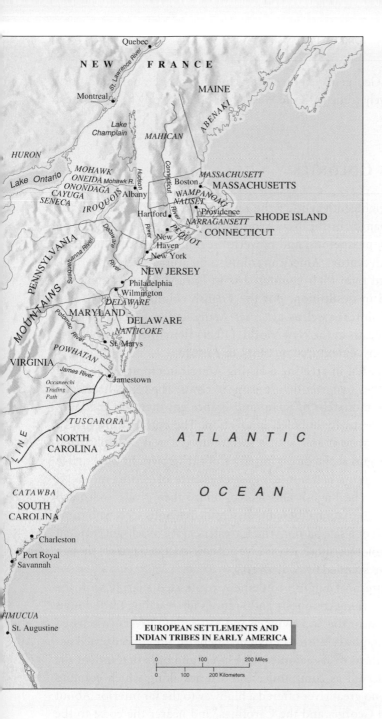

Quebec

NEW FRANCE

MAINE

Montreal

Lake
Champlain

MAHICAN

ABENAKI

HURON

Lake Ontario

MOHAWK
ONEIDA Mohawk R.
ONONDAGA
CAYUGA
SENECA

IROQUOIS

Albany

Hudson

Connecticut

Boston

MASSACHUSETT
MASSACHUSETTS

WAMPANOAG

NAUSET

Providence

RHODE ISLAND

Hartford

NARRAGANSETT

PEQUOT

CONNECTICUT

PENNSYLVANIA

Delaware River

Susquehanna River

MOUNTAINS

New
Haven
New York

NEW JERSEY

Philadelphia
Wilmington

DELAWARE

Potomac River

MARYLAND

DELAWARE

NANTICOKE

St. Marys

POWHATAN

VIRGINIA

James River

Jamestown

Occaneechi
Trading
Path

LINE

TUSCARORA

NORTH
CAROLINA

ATLANTIC

CATAWBA

SOUTH
CAROLINA

OCEAN

Charleston

Port Royal
Savannah

TIMUCUA

St. Augustine

EUROPEAN SETTLEMENTS AND
INDIAN TRIBES IN EARLY AMERICA

0   100   200 Miles

0   100   200 Kilometers

Oglethorpe's plan, Georgians exported rice, indigo, lumber, beef, and pork and carried on a lively trade with the West Indies. The colony had become a commercial success.

Thriving Colonies

By the early eighteenth century the English had outstripped both the French and the Spanish in the New World. British America had become the most populous, prosperous, and powerful region on the continent. By the mid–seventeenth century, American colonists on average were better fed, clothed, and housed than their counterparts in Europe, where a majority of the people lived in destitution. But the English colonization of North America included failures as well as successes. Many settlers found only hard labor and an early death in the New World. Others flourished only because they exploited Indians, indentured servants, or Africans.

The British succeeded in creating a lasting American empire because of crucial advantages they had over their European rivals. The centralized control imposed by the monarchs of Spain and France got them off the mark more quickly but eventually hobbled innovation. The enterprising British acted by private investment and with a minimum of royal control. Not a single colony was begun at the direct initiative of the Crown. In the English colonies poor immigrants had a much greater chance of getting at least a small parcel of land. The English and Dutch, unlike their rivals, welcomed people from a variety of nationalities and dissenting religious sects who came in search of a new life or a safe harbor. And a greater degree of self-government made the English colonies more responsive to new circumstances—though they were sometimes stymied by controversy.

The compact pattern of English settlement contrasted sharply with the pattern of Spain's far-flung conquests and France's far-reaching trade routes to the interior by way of the St. Lawrence and Mississippi Rivers (discussed in Chapter 4). Geography reinforced England's bent for the concentrated occupation and settlement of its colonies. The rivers and bays that indent the Atlantic seaboard served as communication arteries along which colonies first sprang up, but no great river offered a highway to the far interior. About 100 miles inland in Georgia and the Carolinas, and nearer the coast to the north, the fall line of the rivers presented rocky rapids that marked the limit of navigation and the end of the coastal plain. About 100 miles beyond that, and farther back in Pennsylvania, stretched the rolling expanse of the Piedmont, literally, "Foothills." And the final backdrop of English America was the Appalachian Mountain range, some 200 miles from the coast in the South and reaching the coast at points in New England, with only one significant break—up the Hudson and Mohawk River valleys of New York. For 150 years the farthest outreach of British settlement stopped at the slopes of those mountains. To the east lay the wide expanse of ocean, which served not only as a highway for the transport of ideas and ways of life from Europe to America but also as a barrier that separated old ideas from new, allowing the new to evolve in the new environment.

CHAPTER SUMMARY

- **British Colonization** Profit from minerals and exotic products was the overriding objective of the joint-stock Virginia Company, organized to finance the 1607 Jamestown venture. Proprietary colonies, such as Maryland and the Carolinas, were given to individuals who desired wealth but did not usually become colonists themselves. The colonies were also an outlet for Britain's poor.

- **Jamestown Hardships** The early years of Jamestown were grim because food was in short supply except when the Powhatans provided corn. However, relations with the Indians deteriorated, culminating in an Indian uprising in 1622. English investors searched for profits from minerals and trade with Indians, not from agriculture. A high mortality rate caused a scarcity of labor.

- **Religion and Colonization** Religion was the primary motivation for the founding of several colonies. The Plymouth colony was founded by separatists on a mission to build a Christian commonwealth outside the structure of the Anglican Church. The Massachusetts Bay Colony was created by Puritans who wished to purify the established church. Rhode Island was established by Roger Williams, a religious dissenter from Massachusetts. Maryland was founded as a refuge for English Catholics. William Penn, a Quaker, founded Pennsylvania and invited Europe's persecuted religious sects to his colony. The Dutch, with their policy of toleration, allowed members of all faiths to settle in New Netherland.

- **Native American Relations** Settler-Indian relations were complex. Trade with the Powhatans in Virginia enabled Jamestown to survive its early years, but brutal armed conflicts occurred as settlers invaded Indian lands. Puritans retaliated harshly against Indian resistance in the Pequot War of 1637 and in King Philip's War from 1675–1676. Only Roger Williams and William Penn treated natives as equals. Conflicts in the Carolinas—the Tuscarora and Yamasee Wars—occurred because of Indian slave trade and other abuses by traders. France and Spain used natives to further their imperial ambitions, which allowed the Native Americans to play the European powers against each another.

- **British America** By 1700, England was a great trading empire. British America was the most populous and prosperous area of North America. Commercial rivalry between the Dutch and the English led to war, during which the Dutch colony of New Netherland surrendered to the English in 1664. Native allies, such as the Iroquois, traded pelts for English goods. By relying increasingly on slave labor, the Southern colonies provided England with tobacco and other plantation crops.

CHRONOLOGY

1607	Jamestown, Virginia, the first permanent English colony, is established
1616	Pocahontas marries John Rolfe
1620	Plymouth colony is founded; Pilgrims agree to the Mayflower Compact
1622	Indian uprising in Virginia
1630	Massachusetts Bay Colony is founded
1634	Settlement of Maryland begins
1637	Pequot War
1642–1651	English Civil War
1666	Restoration of the English monarchy
1675–1676	King Philip's War
1676	Bacon's Rebellion in Virginia
1681	Pennsylvania is established
1733	Georgia is founded

KEY TERMS & NAMES

Virginia Company p. 57

Chief Powhatan p. 59

Captain John Smith p. 59

Opechancanough p. 64

Bacon's Rebellion p. 65

proprietary colonies
p. 67

Puritans p. 68

John Winthrop p. 72

Roger Williams p. 77

Anne Hutchinson p. 77

Pequot War p. 81

King Philip, or Metacomet
p. 83

New Netherland p. 84

Iroquois League p. 95

Quakers p. 98

3

COLONIAL WAYS OF LIFE

wwnorton.com/studyspace

FOCUS QUESTIONS

- What were the social, ethnic, and economic differences among the southern, middle, and New England colonies?
- What was the attitude of English colonists toward women?
- How important was indentured servitude to the development of the colonies, and why had the system been replaced by slavery in the South by 1700?
- How did the colonies participate in international and imperial trade?
- What were the effects of the Enlightenment in America?
- How did the Great Awakening affect the colonies?

The process of carving a new civilization out of an abundant yet violent frontier involved a clash of European, African, and Indian cultures. War, duplicity, displacement, and enslavement were the tragic results. Yet on another level the process of transforming the "New World" was largely the story not simply of conflict but also of accommodation, a story of thousands of diverse folk engaged in the everyday tasks of building homes, planting crops, trading goods, raising families, enforcing laws, and worshipping their deities. Those who colonized America during the seventeenth and eighteenth centuries were part of a massive social migration occurring throughout Europe and Africa. Everywhere, it seemed, people were moving from farms to villages, from villages to cities, and from homelands to colonies. They moved for different reasons. Most Britons and Europeans were responding to powerful social and economic forces as rapid population growth and the rise of commercial agriculture squeezed people off the land. Many migrants traveled in search of political security or religious freedom. A tragic exception was the Africans, who were captured and transported to new lands against their will.

Those who settled in colonial America were mostly young (over half were under twenty-five), male, and poor. Almost half were indentured servants or slaves, and during the eighteenth century England would transport some 50,000 convicts to the North American colonies. Only about a third of the settlers came with their families. Once in America, many kept moving, trying to take advantage of inexpensive western land or new business opportunities. Whatever their status or ambition, this extraordinary mosaic of ordinary yet adventurous people created America's enduring institutions and values, as well as its distinctive spirit and energy.

THE SHAPE OF EARLY AMERICA

BRITISH FOLKWAYS The vast majority of early European settlers came from the British Isles in four mass migrations over the seventeenth and eighteenth centuries. The first wave involved some 20,000 Puritans who settled Massachusetts between 1630 and 1641. A generation later a smaller group of wealthy Royalist Cavaliers (aristocrats) and their indentured servants migrated from southern England to Virginia. The third wave brought some 23,000 Quakers from the north Midlands of England to the colonies of West Jersey, Pennsylvania, and Delaware. They professed a sense of spiritual equality, a suspicion of class distinctions and powerful elites, and a commitment to plain living and high thinking. The fourth and largest surge of colonization occurred between 1717 and 1775 and included hundreds of thousands of Celtic Britons and Scotch-Irish from northern Ireland; these were mostly poor, feisty, clannish folk who settled in the rugged backcountry along the Appalachian Mountains.

It was long assumed that the strenuous demands of the American frontier served as a great "melting pot" that stripped immigrants of their native identities and melded them into homogeneous Americans. Yet for all of the transforming effects of the New World, British ways of life have persisted to this day. Although most British migrants spoke a common language and shared the Protestant faith, they carried with them—and retained—sharply different cultural attitudes and customs. They spoke distinct dialects, cooked different foods, preferred different architectural styles, and organized their societies differently.

SEABOARD ECOLOGY One of the cherished legends of American history has it that those settling the New World arrived to find an unspoiled

Colonial farm

This plan of a newly cleared American farm shows how trees were cut down and the stumps left to rot.

wilderness little touched by human activity. But that was not the case. For thousands of years, Indian hunting practices had produced what one scholar has called the "greatest known loss of wild species" in the continent's history. Over centuries the Native Americans had regularly burned forests and dense undergrowth in order to provide cropland, ease travel through hardwood forests, and make way for grasses, berries, and other forage for the animals they hunted. This migratory "slash-and-burn" agriculture increased the rate at which plant nutrients were recycled and allowed more sunlight to reach the forest floor. These conditions in turn created rich soil and ideal grazing grounds for elk, deer, turkeys, bears, moose, and beavers.

Equally important in shaping the ecosystem of America was the European attitude toward the environment. Whereas the Native Americans tended to be migratory, considering land and animals communal resources to be shared and consumed only as necessary, most European colonizers viewed natural resources as privately owned commodities to be sold for profit. White settlers thus quickly set about evicting Indians; clearing, fencing, improving, and selling land; cutting timber for masts; and growing surplus crops, trapping game and catching fish for commercial use. These practices transformed the seaboard environment. In many places—Plymouth, Massachusetts, for instance, and St. Marys, Maryland—settlers occupied the sites of former Indian towns, and corn, beans, and squash quickly became colonial staples, along with new crops brought from Europe.

British ships brought to America domesticated animals—cattle, oxen, sheep, goats, horses, and pigs—that were unknown in the New World. By 1650, English farm animals outnumbered the colonists. Rapidly multiplying livestock reshaped the environment and affected Indian life in unexpected ways. Farmers allowed their cows, horses, and pigs to roam freely through the woods, since the labor shortage made it too expensive to pen the animals in barnyards or fence them in pastures. Over time, the failure to constrain farm animals denied the planted fields dung for use as fertilizer. The fertility of the soil declined with each passing year.

Many of the farm animals turned wild (feral), ran amok in Indian cornfields, and devastated native flora and fauna. In New England, rooting pigs devoured the shellfish that local Indians depended upon for subsistence. As livestock herds grew, settlers acquired more land, which often meant seizing Indian land. Trespassing livestock and expanding colonial settlements caused friction with the Indians, which in turn helped ignite such violent confrontations as King Philip's War and Bacon's Rebellion. One historian, in fact, has referred to roaming English livestock as four-legged "agents of empire" invading Indian land. As a frustrated Maryland Indian charged in 1666, "Your hogs & cattle injure us. You come too near us to live & drive us from place to place. We can fly no farther. Let us know where to live & how to be secured for the future from the hogs & cattle."

POPULATION GROWTH   England's first footholds in America were bought at a fearsome price: many settlers died in the first years. But once the brutal seasoning phase was past and the colonies were on their feet, Virginia and its successors grew rapidly. By 1750 the number of colonists had passed 1 million; by 1775 it stood at about 2.5 million. The prodigious increase of the colonial population did not go unnoticed. Benjamin Franklin, a keen observer of many things, published in 1751 his *Observations Concerning the Increase of Mankind*, in which he pointed out two facts of life that distinguished the colonies from Europe: land was plentiful and cheap, and labor was scarce and expensive. The opposite conditions prevailed in the Old World. From this reversal of conditions flowed many of the changes that European culture underwent in America—not the least being that more land and good fortune beckoned the enterprising immigrant and induced settlers to replenish the earth with large families. Where labor was scarce, children could lend a hand and, once grown, find new land for themselves if need be. Colonists tended, as a result, to marry and start families at an earlier age than did their Old World counterparts.

BIRTHRATES AND DEATH RATES   Given the better economic prospects in the colonies, a greater proportion of American white women married, and the birthrate remained much higher than it did in Europe. Whereas in England the average age at marriage for women was twenty-five or twenty-six, in America it dropped to twenty or twenty-one. Men also married younger in the colonies than in the Old World. The birthrate rose accordingly, since women who married earlier had time for about two additional pregnancies during their childbearing years.

Equally responsible for the burgeoning Colonial population was a much lower death rate than that in Europe. After the difficult first years of settlement, infants generally had a better chance of reaching maturity, and adults had a better chance of reaching old age. In seventeenth-century New England, apart from childhood mortality, men could expect to reach seventy and women nearly that age.

This longevity resulted from several factors. Since the land was bountiful, famine seldom occurred after the first year, and although the winters were more severe than those in England, firewood was plentiful. Being younger on the whole—the average age in the new nation in 1790 was sixteen!—Americans were less susceptible to disease than were Europeans. That they were more scattered than in the Old World meant they were also less exposed to infectious diseases. That began to change, of course, as cities grew and trade and travel increased. By the mid–eighteenth century the colonies were beginning to have levels of contagion much like those in Europe.

The greatest variations in these patterns occurred in the earliest years of the southern colonies. From the first century after the Jamestown settlement

John Freake; Mrs. Elizabeth Freake and Baby Mary

Elizabeth married John at age nineteen; Mary, born when Elizabeth was thirty-two, was the Freakes' eighth and last child.

until about 1700, a high rate of mortality and a chronic shortage of women meant that the population increase there could be sustained only by immigration. In the humid southern climate, English settlers contracted malaria, dysentery, and a host of other diseases. The mosquito-infested rice paddies of the Carolina Tidewater were notoriously unhealthy. And ships that docked at the Virginia tobacco plantations brought with their payloads unseen cargoes of smallpox, diphtheria, and other infections.

SEX RATIOS AND THE FAMILY   Whole communities of religious or ethnic groups migrated more often to the northern colonies than to the southern, bringing more women with them. Males, however, were most needed in the early years of new colonies. In fact, as a pamphlet promoting opportunities in America stressed, the infant colonies needed "lusty labouring men . . . capable of hard labour, and that can bear and undergo heat and cold," men adept with the "axe and the hoe." Virginia's seventeenth-century sex ratio of two or three white males to each female meant that many men never married, although nearly every adult woman did. Counting only the unmarried, the ratio was about eight men for every woman.

A population made up largely of bachelors made for instability of a high order in the first years. And the high mortality rates of the early years at Jamestown further loosened family ties. A majority of the women who arrived in the Chesapeake colonies during the seventeenth century were unmarried indentured servants, most of whom died before the age of fifty. Whereas the first generations in New England proved to be long-lived, young people in the seventeenth-century South were apt never to see their grandparents and in fact lose one or both parents before reaching maturity. Eventually, however, the southern colonies reverted to a more even gender ratio, and family sizes approached those of New England. Thus, in contrast to New Spain and New France, British America had far more women, and this different sex ratio largely explains the difference in population growth rates among the European empires competing in the New World.

WOMEN IN THE COLONIES   Most colonists brought to America deeply rooted convictions about the inferiority of women. As one minister stressed, "the woman is a weak creature not endowed with like strength and constancy of mind." The prescribed role of women was clear: to obey and serve their husbands, nurture their children, and endure the taxing labor required to maintain their households. Governor John Winthrop insisted that a "true wife" would find contentment only "in subjection to her husband's authority." Even high-spirited women such as Virginia's Lucy Parke Byrd submitted to their husbands' absolute authority. The imperious patrician William Byrd II of Westover managed his wife's estate without consulting her, kept a tenacious grip on his property—even to the point of forbidding his wife to borrow a book from his library without explicit permission—and saw fit to interfere in her own field of domestic management. In his secret diary he recorded their stormy relationship:

> [April 7] I reproached my wife with ordering the old beef to be kept and the fresh beef to be used first, contrary to good management, on which she was pleased to be very angry . . . then my wife came and begged my pardon and we were friends again. . . .
> [April 8] My wife and I had another foolish quarrel about my saying she listened at the top of the stairs . . . she came soon after and begged my pardon.
> [April 9] My wife and I had another scold about mending my shoes, but it was soon over by her submission.

Both social custom and legal codes ensured that most women in most colonies could not vote, preach, hold office, attend public schools or colleges, bring lawsuits, make contracts, or own property.

Yet there were exceptions to these prevailing gender roles. Circumstances often required or enabled women to exercise leadership outside the domestic sphere. Elizabeth Lucas Pinckney (1722?–1793), for example, emerged as one of America's most enterprising horticulturalists. Born in the West Indies, raised on the island of Antigua, and educated in England, she moved with her family to Charleston, South Carolina, at age fifteen. The following year her father, a British army officer and colonial administrator, was called back to Antigua. He left young Eliza to care for her ailing mother and younger sister—and to manage three plantations worked by slaves. Intelligent and plucky, Eliza decided to try growing indigo, a West Indian plant that produced a much-coveted blue dye for fabric. Within six years she had reaped a bonanza. Exporting indigo became fabulously profitable for her and for other planters on the Carolina coast. She later experimented with other crops, such as flax, hemp, and silk.

In 1744 vivacious Eliza Lucas married widower Charles Pinckney, a prominent attorney and civic leader who was twice her age. Because her husband traveled frequently, she continued to manage the household and the plantations. Within five years she gave birth to four children. She was a devoted wife and loving mother. Her two surviving sons, Charles Cotesworth and Thomas, would play major roles as generals in the American Revolution, in the drafting of the Constitution, and in the political leadership of the new United States of America (both Federalists, they remain the only two brothers to have campaigned for the presidency). When Eliza Pinckney died, she was so revered that President George Washington served as a pallbearer at her funeral.

WOMEN AND RELIGION   During the colonial era, women played a crucial, if restricted, role in religious life. No denomination allowed women to be ordained as ministers. Only the Quakers let women hold church offices and preach ("exhort") in public. Unlike Puritans, who characterized women as "weak vessels" who had succumbed to the original sin in the garden of Eden, Quakers viewed women as equal to men and allowed them authority in their meetings and communities. But the Quakers were unusual in this regard. Most churches (except those of the Baptists and Quakers) did not allow women to vote on congregational issues, such as the appointment of a minister. Puritans cited biblical passages claiming that God required "virtuous" women to submit to male authority and remain "silent" in congregational matters. Governor John Winthrop demanded that women "not meddle in such things as are proper for men" to manage.

Women who challenged ministerial authority were usually prosecuted and punished. Yet by the eighteenth century, as is true today, women made up the overwhelming majority of church members. Their disproportionate attendance at church services and revivals worried many ministers. A feminized church was presumed to be a church in decline. In 1692 the magisterial Boston minister Cotton Mather observed that there "are far more *Godly Women* in the world than there are *Godly Men*." In explaining this phenomenon, Mather put a new twist on the old notion of women being the weaker sex. He argued that the pain associated with childbirth, which had long been interpreted as the penalty women paid for Eve's sinfulness, was in part what drove women "more frequently, & the more fervently" to commit their lives to Christ.

In colonial America the religious roles of black women were quite different from those of their white counterparts. In most West African tribes, women were not subordinate to men, and women frequently served as priests and cult leaders. Furthermore, some enslaved Africans had been exposed to Christianity or Islam in Africa, through slave traders and missionaries. Most of them, however, tried to sustain their traditional African religion once they arrived in the colonies. In America, black women (and men) were often excluded from church membership for fear that Christianized slaves might seek to gain their freedom. To clarify the situation, Virginia in 1667 passed a law specifying that children of slaves would be slaves even if they had been baptised.

WOMEN'S WORK   In the eighteenth century, "women's work" typically involved activities in the house, garden, and yard. Farm women usually rose at four in the morning and prepared breakfast by five-thirty. They then fed and watered the livestock, woke the children, churned butter, tended the garden, prepared lunch, played with the children, worked the garden again, cooked dinner, milked the cows, got the children ready for bed, and cleaned the kitchen before retiring, at about nine. Women also combed, spun, spooled, wove, and bleached wool for clothing, knit linen and cotton, hemmed sheets, pieced quilts, made candles and soap, chopped wood, hauled water, mopped floors, and washed clothes. Female indentured servants in the southern colonies commonly worked as field hands, weeding, hoeing, and harvesting.

Despite the laws and traditions that limited the sphere of women, the scarcity of labor in the colonies created opportunities. In the towns, women

The First, Second, and Last Scene of Mortality

Prudence Punderson's needlework (ca. 1776) shows the domestic path, from cradle to coffin, followed by most colonial women.

commonly served as tavern hostesses and shopkeepers and occasionally also worked as doctors, printers, upholsterers, painters, silversmiths, tanners, and shipwrights—often, but not always, they were widows carrying on their husband's trade.

One of the most lucrative trades among colonial women was the oldest: prostitution. Many servants took up prostitution after their indenture was fulfilled. All of the colonial port cities hosted thriving brothels. They catered especially to sailors and soldiers, but men from all walks of life, married and unmarried, frequented what were called "bawdy houses" or, in Puritan Boston, "disorderly houses." Local authorities frowned on such activities. In Massachusetts convicted prostitutes were stripped to the waist, tied to the back of a cart, and whipped as it moved through the town. In South Carolina, several elected public officials in the seventeenth century were dismissed because they were caught "lying with wenches." New York City officials ordered raids on brothels in 1753. Some two dozen "ladies of pleasure" were arrested, and five of them were subjected to a public whipping. Some slave women whose owners expected sexual favors turned the tables by demanding compensation.

The colonial environment did generate slight improvements in the status of women. The acute shortage of women in the early years made them more highly valued than they were in Europe, and the Puritan emphasis on a well-ordered family life led to laws protecting wives from physical abuse and allowing for divorce. In addition, colonial laws allowed wives greater control over property that they had contributed to a marriage or that was left after a husband's death. But the traditional notion of female subordination and domesticity remained firmly entrenched in colonial America. As a Massachusetts boy self-servingly maintained in 1662, the superior aspect of life was "masculine and eternal; the feminine inferior and mortal."

SOCIETY AND ECONOMY IN THE SOUTHERN COLONIES

CROPS The southern colonies had one unique economic advantage: the climate. The warm weather and plentiful rainfall enabled the colonies to grow exotic staples (profitable market crops) prized by the mother country. Virginia, as Charles I put it, was "founded upon smoke." Tobacco production soared during the seventeenth century. "In Virginia and Maryland," wrote Governor Leonard Calvert in 1629, "Tobacco as our Staple is our All, and indeed leaves no room for anything else." After 1690, rice was as much the profitable staple crop in South Carolina as tobacco was in Virginia. The daily rise and fall of tidewater rivers ideally suited a crop that required the alternate flooding and draining of fields. In addition, southern pine trees provided lumber and key items for the maritime industry. The resin from pine trees could be boiled to make tar, which was in great demand for waterproofing ropes and caulking the seams of wooden ships. From their early leadership in the production of pine tar, North Carolinians would earn the nickname of Tar Heels. In the Carolinas a cattle industry presaged life on the Great Plains—with cowboys, roundups, brandings, and long drives to the market.

English customs records showed that for the years 1698 to 1717, South Carolina and the Chesapeake colonies enjoyed a favorable balance of trade with England. But the surplus revenues earned on goods sold to England were more than offset by "invisible" charges by English "middlemen": freight payments to shippers; commissions, storage charges, and interest payments to English merchants; insurance premiums; inspection and customs duties; and outlays to purchase indentured servants and slaves. Thus began a pattern that would plague southern agriculture for centuries. Planters' investments went into land and slaves while the more profitable enterprises of shipping, trade, investment, and manufacture were conducted by outsiders.

LAND   The economy of the southern colonies centered on the fundamental fact of colonial life that Benjamin Franklin highlighted: land was plentiful, and laborers were scarce. The low cost of land lured most colonists. Under colonial law, land titles rested ultimately upon grants from the Crown, and in colonial practice the evolution of land policy in the first colony set patterns that were followed everywhere save in New England. In 1618 the Virginia Company, lacking any assets other than land, sold each investor a fifty-acre "share-right" and gave each settler a "headright" (acreage) for paying his own way or bringing in others.

If one distinctive feature of the South's agrarian economy was a ready market in England, another was a trend toward large-scale production. Those who planted tobacco discovered that it quickly exhausted the soil, thereby giving an advantage to the planter who had extra fields in which to plant beans and corn or to leave fallow. With the increase of the tobacco crop, moreover, a fall in prices meant that economies of scale might come into play—the large planter with the lower cost per unit might still make a profit. Gradually he would extend his holdings along the riverfronts and thereby secure the advantage of direct access to the oceangoing vessels that plied the waterways of the Chesapeake Bay, discharging goods from London and taking

Virginia plantation

Southern colonial plantations were constructed with easy access to oceangoing vessels, as shown on this 1730 tobacco label.

on tobacco. So easy was the access, in fact, that the Chesapeake colonies never required a city of any size as a center of commerce, and the larger planters functioned as merchants and harbormasters for their neighbors.

LABOR   Voluntary indentured servitude accounted for probably half the white settlers (mostly from England, Ireland, or Germany) in all the colonies outside New England. The name derived from the indenture, or contract, by which a person promised to work for a fixed number of years in return for transportation to America. Not all the servants went voluntarily. The London underworld developed a flourishing trade in "kids" and "spirits," who were "kidnapped" or "spirited" into servitude. After 1717, by act of Parliament, convicts guilty of certain major crimes could escape the hangman by relocating to the colonies.

Once in the colonies, servants contracted with masters. Their rights were limited. They could own property but not engage in trade. Marriage required the master's permission. Runaway servants were hunted down and punished

Indentured servants

An advertisement from the *Virginia Gazette*, October 4, 1779, for indentured servants. The people whose services are being offered secured a life in America, but at a steep price. Servants endured years of labor before their contracts expired and they were granted their freedom.

just as runaway slaves were. Masters could whip servants and extend their indentures for bad behavior. Many servants died from disease or the exhaustion of cultivating tobacco in the broiling sun and intense humidity. In due course, however, usually after four to seven years, the indenture ended, and the servant claimed the "freedom dues" set by custom and law: money, tools, clothing, food, and occasionally small tracts of land. Some former servants did very well for themselves. In 1629 seven members of the Virginia legislature were former indentured servants. Others, including Benjamin Franklin's grandmother, married the men who had originally bought their services. Many servants died before completing their indenture, however, and most of those who served their term remained relatively poor thereafter.

SLAVERY Colonial America was increasingly a land of white opportunity and black slavery. During the eighteenth century there were more than three times as many African or Indian slaves as free immigrants in the British colonies. Black slavery evolved in the Chesapeake Bay region after 1619, when a Dutch vessel dropped off twenty Africans in Jamestown. Some of the first Africans were treated as indentured servants, with a limited term. Those few African servants who worked out their term of indenture gained freedom and some of them acquired slaves and white indentured servants. Gradually, however, with rationalizations based on color difference or "heathenism," lifelong servitude for black slaves became the custom—and law—of the land. By the 1660s colonial legislative assemblies codified lifelong slavery through laws that were later expanded into elaborate and restrictive slave codes.

During the seventeenth and eighteenth centuries, the incredibly profitable sugar islands of the French and British West Indies and the cane fields of Portuguese Brazil had the most voracious appetite for enslaved Africans. By 1675 the British West Indies had over 100,000 slaves while the colonies in North America had only about 5,000. But as staple crops became established on the American continent and as economic growth in England slowed the number of white laborers traveling to the Americas, the demand for mostly male Indian or African slaves grew. Though British North America took less than 5 percent of the total slaves imported to the Western Hemisphere during more than three centuries of that squalid traffic, it offered better chances for survival, if few for human fulfillment. The natural increase of blacks in America approximated that of whites by the end of the colonial period. During the colonial era, slavery was recognized in all the colonies but flourished in the Tidewater South; one colony, South Carolina, had a black majority through the eighteenth century.

AFRICAN ROOTS Enslaved Africans are so often lumped together as a social group that their great ethnic diversity is overlooked. They came from lands as remote from each other as Angola is from Senegal, and they spoke many different languages. Still, the varied peoples of sub-Sahara Africa did share similar kinship and political systems. Like the Native American cultures, the African societies were often matrilineal: property and political status descended through the mother rather than the father. When a couple married, the wife did not leave her family; the husband left his family to join that of his bride.

West African tribes were organized hierarchically. Priests and the nobility lorded over the masses of farmers and craftspeople. Below the masses were the slaves, typically war captives, criminals, or debtors. Slaves in Africa, however, did have certain rights. They could marry and have children. Their servitude was not always permanent, nor were children automatically slaves by virtue of their parentage, as would be the case in the Americas.

TEN DOLLARS
REWARD.

RAN away, on the 23d inft. a handfome active *Mulatto* flave, named A R C H, about 21 years of age, is flender built and of middle ftature, talks fenfible and artful, but if clofly examined is apt to tremble, has a ridge or fcar on

Slavery

A newspaper advertisement placed by Ignatius Davis of Fredericktown, Maryland, in 1741, offering a reward for the capture of a runaway slave.

The West African economy centered on hunting, fishing, planting, and animal husbandry. Men and women typically worked alongside each other in the fields. Religious belief served as the spine of West African life. All tribal groups believed in a supreme Creator and an array of lesser gods tied to specific natural forces, such as rain, fertility, and animal life. West Africans were pantheistic in that they believed that spirits resided in trees, rocks, and streams. People who died were also subjects of reverence, because they served as mediators between the living and the gods.

Africans preyed upon Africans. For centuries rival tribes had conquered and enslaved one another, and during the seventeenth and eighteenth centuries, African middlemen brought captives to the coast to sell to European slave traders. The Europeans preferred male slaves but were forced to take women and children as well. In fact, the proportion of women and children among the Africans taken to America was greater than that among the Europeans who made the transatlantic journey. Once purchased, the people destined for slavery were branded with a company mark, shackled, and packed tightly in horrific slave ships, where they endured a four- to six-week Atlantic voyage, known as the Middle Passage. It was so brutal that one in seven captives died en route. Almost one in every ten slave ships experienced a revolt during the crossing. On average, twenty-five Africans were killed in such uprisings. Far more died of disease.

Once in America, Africans were thrown together indiscriminately and treated like animals before being herded in chains to auctions where they were

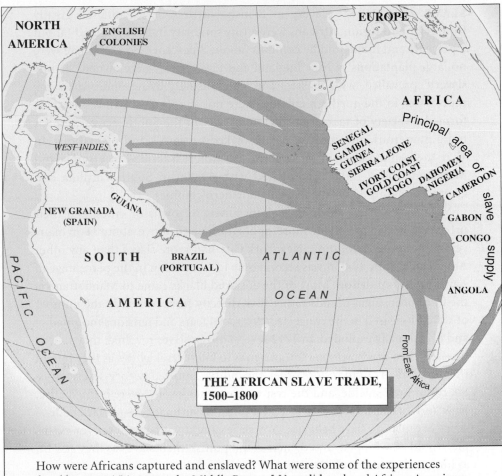

NORTH AMERICA

ENGLISH COLONIES

EUROPE

AFRICA

Principal area of slave supply

WEST INDIES

SENEGAL
GAMBIA
GUINEA
SIERRA LEONE
IVORY COAST
GOLD COAST
TOGO DAHOMEY NIGERIA
CAMEROON

GUIANA

NEW GRANADA (SPAIN)

GABON

CONGO

SOUTH

BRAZIL (PORTUGAL)

ATLANTIC

ANGOLA

AMERICA

OCEAN

PACIFIC OCEAN

From East Africa

THE AFRICAN SLAVE TRADE, 1500–1800

How were Africans captured and enslaved? What were some of the experiences faced by most Africans on the Middle Passage? How did enslaved African Americans create a new culture?

sold. They were often barefoot, ill clothed, and poorly housed and fed. Their role was to dig ditches, drain swamps, build dams, clear and tend fields, and cultivate tobacco and rice. Some rebelled against their new masters, resisting work orders, sabotaging crops and stealing tools, or running away. In a few cases they organized rebellions, which were ruthlessly suppressed. "You would be surprised at their perseverance," noted one white planter. "They often die before they can be conquered." Captured runaway slaves faced ghastly retribution; many were burned at the stake. After rounding up slaves who participated in the Stono Uprising in South Carolina in 1739, enraged planters "cutt off their heads and set them up at every Mile Post."

SLAVE CULTURE   Slavery in British North America differed greatly from region to region. Africans were a tiny minority in New England (about 2 percent) and in the middle colonies (about 8 percent). Because there were no large plantations in New England and fewer slaves were owned, "family slavery" prevailed, with masters and slaves usually living under the same roof. Slaves in the northern colonies were not simply field hands; they performed a variety of tasks, outside and inside. In the South, slaves were far more numerous, and most of them worked on farms and plantations. In 1750 the vast majority of slaves in British America resided in Virginia and Maryland, about 150,000 compared with 60,000 in South Carolina and Georgia and only 33,000 in all of the northern colonies.

Most slaves in the northern colonies lived in towns or cities, and their urban environs gave them more opportunities to move about. For many years before the Revolution, New York City had more slaves than any other American city. By 1740 it was second only to Charleston in the percentage of slaves in its population. Most of the enslaved blacks came to Manhattan via the Caribbean sugar islands rather than directly from Africa. As the number of slaves increased in the congested city, racial fears and tensions mounted—and occasionally exploded. In 1712 several dozen slaves revolted; they started fires and then used swords, axes, and guns to kill several whites as they fought the fires. Called out to restore order, the militia captured twenty-seven slaves. Six committed suicide, and the rest were executed; some were burned alive. New York officials thereafter passed a series of ordinances—a black code—strictly regulating slave behavior. Any slave caught with a weapon, for example, would be whipped, and owners could punish their slaves as they saw fit, as long as they did not kill them.

Yet the punitive regulations did not prevent another major racial incident, which would become Manhattan's version of the Salem witch hunt. In the bitterly cold March of 1741, city dwellers were aghast at a rash of suspicious fires across the city, including one at the governor's house. Their worst fear was that the fires were the result of a slave conspiracy. "The Negroes are rising!" shouted terrified whites. The frantic city council launched a frenzied investigation to find and punish the "villains." A self-promoting prosecutor proved adept at eliciting formulaic confessions. Mary Burton, a sixteen-year-old indentured servant, told authorities that there was indeed a conspiracy among slaves and poor whites to "burn the whole town" and kill the white men among its 11,000 residents, some 2,000 of whom were slaves. The plotters ("seducers of the slaves") were supposedly led by John Hughson, a white trafficker in stolen goods who owned the tavern where Mary Burton worked. His wife, two slaves, and a prostitute were changed as co-conspirators.

Despite their denials, all were convicted and hanged. As in Salem, however, the accusations continued amid an atmosphere of public hysteria. A slave revolt turned into a papal plot. Attracting particular suspicion were people with ties to the Spanish colonies or Catholicism, since England was then at war with Spain and the Spanish had offered freedom to any slave who defected. Within weeks over half of the adult male slaves in the city were in jail. Five Spanish blacks were hanged. Mary Burton then implicated John Ury, a recently arrived teacher whom she claimed was in fact a Jesuit priest and Spanish spy who instigated the conspiracy to burn Manhattan. He, too, was hanged. Mary Burton, meanwhile, kept naming more conspirators. And, as in Salem, the Conspiracy of 1741 ended when some of the most prominent New Yorkers were named as plotters. In the end, twenty-one people—seventeen slaves and four whites—were hanged; thirteen blacks were burned at the stake. Seventy-two other blacks were deported.

Such organized resistance to the abuses and indignities of slavery was rare—in large part because the likelihood of success was so small and the punishments so severe. Much more common were varied forms of creative accommodation and more subtle forms of resistance.

In the process of being forced into lives of bondage in a new world, diverse blacks from diverse homelands forged a new identity as African Americans while leaving entwined in the fabric of American culture more strands of African heritage than historians and anthropologists can ever disentangle. Among them are new words that entered the language, such as *tabby, tote, cooter, goober, yam*, and *banana* and the names of the Coosaw, Pee Dee, and Wando Rivers.

More important are African influences in American music, folklore, and religious practices. On one level, slaves used such cultural activities to distract themselves from their servitude; on another level they used songs, stories, and sermons as coded messages expressing their distaste for masters or overseers. Slave religion, a unique blend of African and Christian beliefs, was frequently practiced in secret. Its fundamental theme was deliverance: God would eventually free African Americans from slavery and open the gates to heaven's promised land. The planters, however, sought to strip slave religion of its liberationist hopes. They insisted that being "born again" as Christians had no effect upon their workers' status as slaves.

Africans brought to America powerful kinship ties. Even though most colonies outlawed slave marriages, many masters believed that slaves would work harder and be more stable if allowed to form families. Though many families were broken up when members were sold, slave culture retained its powerful domestic ties. It also developed gender roles distinct from those of

African heritage

The survival of African culture among enslaved Americans is evident in this late-eighteenth-century painting of a South Carolina plantation. The musical instruments and pottery are of African (probably Yoruban) origin.

white society. Most enslaved women were by necessity field workers as well as wives and mothers responsible for childrearing and household affairs. Since they worked in proximity to enslaved men, they were treated more equally (for good and bad) than were most of their white counterparts.

Slavery gradually expanded to include virtually every activity within the expanding colonial economy. To be sure, the vast majority of slaves worked as field hands. But as the number of slaves grew, so, too, did the variety of their labors and the need for different skills. Virginia and Maryland planters favored slaves from the Bight of Biafra, on the Gulf of Guinea, and the Congo, where the cultivation of yams was similar to the cultivation of tobacco. Fulani from West Africa were prized as cattle herdsmen. Sugar growers preferred Hausa tribesmen from northern Nigeria because of their expertise in producing sugar from cane. South Carolina rice planters purchased slaves from Africa's "Rice Coast," especially Gambia, where rice cultivation was commonplace. Many from the lowlands of Africa used their talent as boatmen in the coastal waterways. Some had linguistic skills that made them useful interpreters. In a new colonial society forced to construct itself, slaves became skilled artisans: blacksmiths, carpenters, coopers, bricklayers, and the like. Some worked as cooks or maids.

Slavery and the growth of a biracial South had economic, political, and cultural effects that would be felt far into the future and would set America on a course that would lead to tragic conflicts. Questions about the beginnings of slavery still have a bearing on the present. Did a deep-rooted color prejudice lead to slavery, for instance, or did the existence of slavery produce the racial prejudice? Clearly slavery evolved because of a demand for labor, and the English joined an African slave trade that had been established by the Portuguese and Spanish more than a century before—the very word *negro* is Spanish for "black." English settlers often enslaved Indian captives, but they did not enslave captured Europeans. Color was the crucial difference, or at least the crucial rationalization.

The English associated the color black with darkness and evil; they stamped the different appearance, behavior, and customs of Africans as "savagery." Most of the self-serving qualities that colonial Virginians imputed to blacks to justify slavery were the same qualities that the English assigned to their own poor to explain *their* status: their alleged bent for laziness, improvidence, treachery, and stupidity, among other shortcomings. Similar traits, moreover, were imputed by ancient Jews to the Canaanites and by the Mediterranean peoples of a later date to the Slavic captives sold among them. The names Canaanite and Slav both became synonymous with slavery—the latter lingers in the very word for the practice. Such expressions would seem to be the product of power relationships and not the other way around. Dominant peoples repeatedly assign ugly traits to those they bring into subjugation.

THE GENTRY   By the early eighteenth century, Virginia and South Carolina were moving into the golden age of the Tidewater gentry, leaving the more isolated and underdeveloped colony of North Carolina as "a valley of humiliation between two mountains of conceit." The first rude huts of Jamestown had given way to frame and brick houses, but it was only as the seventeenth century yielded to the eighteenth that the stately countryseats in the Georgian, or "colonial," style began to emerge along the banks of the great rivers. In South Carolina the eighteenth-century mansions along the Ashley, Cooper, and Wando Rivers boasted spacious gardens and avenues of moss-draped live oaks.

Colonial aristocracy

This painting from about 1710 portrays Henry Darnall III, a youth from one of Maryland's richest families, flanked by a slave. In the background are buildings and gardens that attest to the southern preoccupation with the trappings of English nobility.

The great houses of the new colonial aristocracy became centers of sumptuous living and legendary hospitality. In their zest for the good life, the planters purchased English consumer goods that reflected the latest refinements of London style and fashion, living precariously on credit extended for future crops. Dependence upon outside capital remained a chronic southern problem far beyond the colonial period.

In the social season the carriages of the Chesapeake Bay planter elite rolled to the villages of Annapolis and Williamsburg, and the city of Charleston in South Carolina became the center of political life and high fashion. Throughout much of the year, the outdoors beckoned planters to the pleasures of hunting, fishing, and riding. Gambling on horse races, cards, and dice became consuming passions for men and women alike. But a few colonists, such as Virginia's William Byrd of Westover, pursued learning with a passion. He built a library of some 3,600 volumes and often rose early to read books in Latin, Greek, and Hebrew. The wealthy families commonly sent their sons—and often their daughters—abroad for an education, usually to England, sometimes to France.

RELIGION   After 1642, Virginia governor William Berkeley decided that his colony was to be officially Anglican, and he sponsored laws requiring "all nonconformists . . . to depart the colony with all conveniency." Puritans and Quakers were hounded out. By the end of the seventeenth century, Anglicanism predominated in the Chesapeake region, and it proved especially popular among the large landholders. In the early eighteenth century it became the established (official) church in all the South—and some counties of New York and New Jersey, despite the presence of many dissenters. In the new American environment, however, the Anglican Church evolved into something quite unlike its parent, the state church of England. The scattered population in the colonies, the absence of bishops, and the uneven quality of ministers made centralized control difficult.

It has often been said that Americans during the seventeenth century took religion more seriously than they have at any time since. That may have been true, but many early Americans were not active communicants. One estimate holds that fewer than one in fifteen residents of the southern colonies was a church member. The tone of religious belief and practice in the eighteenth-century South was different from—and less demanding than—that in Puritan New England or Quaker Pennsylvania. As in England, colonial Anglicans tended to be more conservative, rational, and formal in their forms of worship than their Puritan, Quaker, or Baptist counterparts. Anglicans stressed collective rituals over personal religious experience. They did not require members to give a personal, public, and often emotional account of their conversion. Nor did they expect members to practice self-denial. Anglicans disliked "fire-and-brimstone" sermons. They preferred ministers who stressed the reasonableness of Christianity, the goodness of God, and the capacity of humankind to practice benevolence.

SOCIETY AND ECONOMY IN NEW ENGLAND

TOWNSHIPS   In contrast to the seaboard planters, who transformed the English manor into the southern plantation, the Puritans transformed the English village into the New England town, although there were several varieties. Land policy in New England had a stronger social and religious purpose than elsewhere. Towns shaped by English precedent and Puritan policy also were adapted to the environment of a rock-strewn land, confined by sea and mountains and unfit for large-scale agriculture.

Unlike the settlers in the southern colonies or in Dutch New York, few New England colonists received huge tracts of land. Township grants were usually awarded to organized groups. A group of settlers, often already gathered into a church, would petition the general court for a town (what elsewhere was commonly called a township) and then divide its acres according to a rough principle of equity—those who invested more or had larger families or greater status might receive more land—retaining some pasture and woodland in common and holding some for later arrivals. In some early cases the towns arranged each settler's land in separate strips after the medieval practice, but over time the land was commonly divided into separate farms distant from the close-knit village. By the early eighteenth century the colonies were using their remaining land as a source of revenue, selling townships, more often than not to land speculators.

DWELLINGS AND DAILY LIFE   The first colonists in New England initially lived in caves, tents, or "English wigwams," but they soon built simple frame houses clad with hand-split clapboards. The roofs were steeply pitched to reduce the buildup of snow and were covered with thatched grasses or reeds. By the end of the seventeenth century, most New England homes were plain but sturdy dwellings centered on a fireplace. Some had glass windows brought from England. The interior walls were often plastered and whitewashed, but the exterior boards were rarely painted. It was not until the eighteenth century that most houses were painted, usually a dark "Indian" red. New England homes were not commonly painted white until the nineteenth century. The interiors were dark, illuminated only by candles or oil lamps, both of which were expensive; most people usually went to sleep soon after sunset.

Housing in New England

This frame house, built in the 1670s, belonged to Rebecca Nurse, one of the women hanged as a witch in Salem Village in 1692.

Family life revolved around the main room on the ground floor, called the hall, where meals would be cooked in a large fireplace. Food would be served at a table of rough-hewn planks, called the board. The father was sometimes referred to as the chair man because he sat in the only chair (hence the origin of the term *chairman of the board*). The rest of the family usually stood to eat or sat on stools or benches. People in colonial times ate with their hands and wooden spoons. Forks were not introduced until the eighteenth century. The fare was usually corn, boiled meat, and vegetables washed down with beer, cider, rum, or milk. Corn bread was a daily staple, as was cornmeal mush, known as hasty pudding. Colonists also relished succotash, an Indian meal of corn and kidney beans cooked in bear grease.

ENTERPRISE   New England farmers and their families led hard lives. Simply clearing rocks from the glacier-scoured soil might require sixty days of hard labor per acre. The growing season was short, and no profitable crops grew in that harsh climate. The crops and livestock were those familiar to the English countryside: wheat, barley, oats, some cattle, swine, and sheep.

Profitable fisheries

Fishing for, curing, and drying codfish in Newfoundland in the early 1700s. For centuries the rich fishing grounds of the North Atlantic provided New Englanders with a prosperous industry.

With rich fishing grounds that stretched northward to Newfoundland, it is little wonder that New Englanders turned to the sea for their livelihood. The Chesapeake Bay region afforded a rich harvest of oysters, but New England, by its proximity to waters frequented by cod, mackerel, halibut, and other varieties of fish, became the more important maritime center. Whales, too, abounded in New England waters and supplied oil for lighting and lubrication, as well as ambergris, a waxy substance used in the manufacture of perfumes.

The fisheries, unlike the farms, supplied a product that could be profitably exported to Europe, with lesser grades of fish going to the West Indies as food for slaves. Fisheries encouraged the development of shipbuilding, and experience at seafaring spurred commerce. This in turn encouraged wider contacts in the Atlantic world and prompted a self-indulgent materialism and cosmopolitanism that clashed with the Puritan ideal of plain living and high thinking. In 1714 a worried Puritan deplored the "great extravagance that people are fallen into, far beyond their circumstances, in their purchases, buildings, families, expenses, apparel, generally in the whole way of living."

SHIPBUILDING   The abundant forests of New England represented a source of enormous wealth. Old-growth trees were especially prized for use as ships' masts and spars. Early on, the British government claimed the tallest and straightest American trees, mostly white pines and oaks, for use by the Royal Navy. At the same time, British officials encouraged the colonists to develop their own shipbuilding industry. American-built ships quickly became prized for their quality and price. It was much less expensive to purchase ships built in America than to transport American timber to Britain for ship construction, especially since a large ship might require the timber from as many as 2,000 trees.

Nearly a third of all British ships were made in the colonies. Shipbuilding was one of colonial America's first big industries, and it in turn nurtured many related businesses: timbering, sawmills, iron foundries, sail lofts, fisheries, and taverns. Constructing a large ship required as many as thirty skilled trades and 200 workers. The vessel's hull was laid out by master shipwrights, talented maritime carpenters who used axes and adzes to cut and fit together the pieces to form the keel, or spine of the hull. Caulkers made the ship watertight by stuffing the seams with oakum, a loose hemp fiber that was sealed with hot tar.

As the new ship took shape, rope makers created the ship's extensive rigging. After the coils of rope were spun, they were dipped in heated tar to

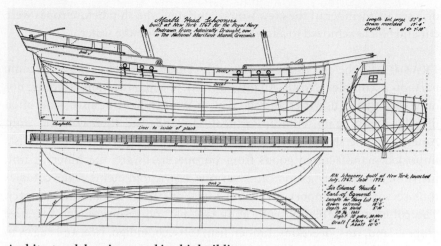

Architectural drawings used in shipbuilding

An architectual drawing of a ship from eighteenth-century New England.

preserve them from saltwater rot. Sailmakers, meanwhile, fashioned sails out of canvas, laying them out in large lofts. Other craftsmen produced the dozens of other items needed for a sailing vessel: Blacksmiths forged iron anchors, chains, hinges, bolts, rudder braces, and circular straps that secured sections of a mast to each other. Block makers created the dozens of metal-strapped wooden pulleys needed to hoist sails. Joiners built hatches, ladders, lockers, and furnishings. Painters finished the trim and interiors. Ship chandlers provided lamps, oil, and candles. Instrument makers fashioned compasses, chronometers, and sextants for navigation.

Such skilled workers were trained in the apprentice-journeyman system then common in England. A master craftsman taught an apprentice the skills of his trade in exchange for wages. After the apprenticeship period, lasting from four to seven years, a young worker would receive a new suit of clothes from the master craftsman and then become a journeyman, literally moving from shop to shop, working for wages as he honed his skills. Over time, journeymen joined local guilds and became master craftsmen, who themselves took on apprentices.

It took four to six months to build a major sailing ship. The ship christenings and launchings were festive occasions that attracted large crowds and dignitaries. Shops and schools would often close to enable workers and students to attend. All of the workers joined the celebration. The ceremony would begin with a clergyman blessing the new vessel. Then the ship's owner or a senior member of the crew would "christen" the ship before ropes were cut and blocks removed to allow the hull to slide into the water.

TRADE   By the end of the seventeenth century, the colonies had become part of a complex North Atlantic commercial connection, trading not only with the British Isles and the British West Indies but also—and often illegally—with Spain, France, Portugal, Holland, and their colonies from America to the shores of Africa. Out of necessity the American colonists imported manufactured goods from Europe: hardware, machinery, paint, instruments for navigation, and various household items. The colonies thus served as an important market for goods from the mother country. The colonies were blessed with abundant natural resources and lucrative crops—land, furs, deerskins, timber, fish, tobacco, indigo, rice, and sugar, to mention a few—but they lacked capital (money to invest in new enterprises) and labor (people to meet the needs of the rapidly expanding economy). The central problem for the colonies was to find the means to pay for the imports—the eternal problem of the balance of trade and the shortage of currency.

The mechanism of trade in New England and the middle colonies differed from that in the South in two respects: the lack of staple crops to exchange for English goods was a relative disadvantage, but the success of their own shipping and mercantile enterprises worked in their favor. After 1660, in order to protect England's agriculture and fisheries, the British government placed prohibitive duties (taxes) on certain major colonial exports—fish, flour, wheat, and meat—while leaving the door open to timber, furs, and whale oil, products in great demand in the home country. New York and New England between 1698 and 1717 bought more from England than they sold there, incurring an unfavorable trade balance.

The northern colonies addressed the trade imbalance partly by using their own ships and merchants, thus avoiding the "invisible" charges by middlemen, and by finding other markets for the staples excluded from England, thus acquiring goods or coins to pay for imports from the mother country. American lumber and fish therefore went to southern Europe, Madeira, and the Azores for money or in exchange for wine; lumber, rum, and provisions went to Newfoundland; and all of these and more went to the West Indies, which became the most important trading outlet of all. American merchants could sell fish, bread, flour, corn, pork, bacon, beef, and horses to West Indian planters, who specialized in sugarcane. In return they got money, sugar, molasses, rum, indigo, dyewoods, and other products, many of which went eventually to England.

These circumstances gave rise to the famous "triangular trade" (more a descriptive convenience than a rigid pattern), in which New Englanders shipped rum to the west coast of Africa, where they bartered for slaves; took the slaves to the West Indies; and returned home with various commodities, including molasses, from which they manufactured rum. In another version they shipped provisions to the West Indies, carried sugar and molasses to England, and returned with goods manufactured in Europe.

The colonies suffered from a chronic shortage of hard currency (coins), which drifted away to pay for imports and shipping charges. Various expedients met the shortage of gold or silver coins: the use of wampum or commodities such as tobacco or rice, the monetary value of which colonial governments tried in vain to set by law. Promissory notes of individuals or colonial treasurers

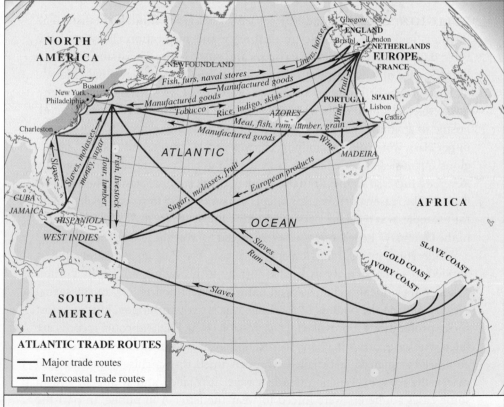

How was overseas trade in the South different from that in New England and the middle colonies? What was the "triangular trade"? What were North America's most important exports?

often passed as a crude sort of paper money. Most of the colonies at one time or another issued bills of credit, on promise of payment later (hence the dollar "bill"), and most set up land banks that issued paper money for loans to farmers on the security of their land, which was mortgaged to the banks. Colonial farmers began to recognize that printing paper money (inflation) led to an inflation of crop prices, and they therefore asked for more and more paper money. Thus began in colonial politics what was to become a recurrent issue in later times, the complex question of currency inflation. Whenever the issue arose, debtors commonly favored growth in the money supply, which would make it easier for them to pay debts, whereas creditors favored a limited money supply, which would increase the value of their capital. Parliament responded to British merchants, who wanted to be paid in hard coins, by outlawing paper money in New England in 1751 and throughout the colonies in 1764.

RELIGION New England was settled by religious fundamentalists. The Puritans looked to the Bible for authority and inspiration. They read the Bible daily and memorized its passages and stories. The Christian faith was a living source of daily inspiration and obligation for most New Englanders.

The Puritans had come to America to create pious, prosperous communities, not to tolerate sinfulness in their new Zion. Yet the picture of the dour Puritan, hostile to anything that gave pleasure, is false. Puritans, especially those of the upper class, wore colorful clothing, enjoyed secular music, and imbibed prodigious quantities of rum. "Drink is in itself a good creature of God," said the Reverend Increase Mather, "but the abuse of drink is from Satan." If found incapacitated by reason of strong drink, a person was subject to arrest. A Salem man, for example, was tried for staggering into a house where he "eased his stomak in the Chimney." Repeat offenders were forced to wear the letter *D* in public.

Moderation in all things except piety was the Puritan guideline, and it applied to sexual activity as well. Contrary to prevailing images of Puritan prudery, they openly acknowledged natural human desires. Of course, sexual activity outside the bounds of marriage was strictly forbidden, but like most social prohibitions it provoked transgression. New England court records are filled with cases of adultery and fornication. A man found guilty of coitus with an unwed woman could be jailed, whipped, fined, disfranchised, and forced to marry the woman. Female offenders were also jailed and whipped, and in some cases adulterers were forced to wear the letter *A* in public. In part the abundance of sex offenses is explained by the disproportionate number of men in the colonies. Many were unable to find a wife and were therefore tempted to satisfy their sexual desires outside marriage.

The Puritans who settled Massachusetts, unlike the Separatists of Plymouth, proposed only to form a purified version of the Anglican Church. They were called non-separating Congregationalists. That is, they remained loyal to the Church of England, the unity of church and state, and the principle of compulsory religious uniformity. But their remoteness from England led them to adopt a congregational form of church government identical with that of the Pilgrim Separatists and for that matter little different from the practice of Anglicans in the southern colonies.

In the Puritan version of John Calvin's theology, God had voluntarily entered into a covenant, or contract, with worshippers through which they could secure salvation. By analogy, therefore, an assembly of true Christians could enter into a church covenant, a voluntary union for the common worship of God. From this idea it was a fairly short step to the idea of a voluntary union for the purpose of government. The history of New England affords examples of several such limited steps toward constitutional government: the Mayflower Compact, the charter of the Massachusetts Bay Colony, the Fundamental Orders of Connecticut, and the informal arrangements whereby the Rhode Island settlers governed themselves until they secured a charter in 1663.

The covenant theory contained certain kernels of democracy in both church and state, but democracy was no part of Puritan political thought, which like so much else in Puritan belief began with an emphasis on original sin. Humanity's innate depravity made government necessary. The Puritan was dedicated to seeking not the will of the people but the will of God, and the ultimate source of authority was the Bible. But biblical passages often had to be interpreted. Hence, most Puritans deferred to a ministerial elite for a true knowledge of God's will. By law every town had to support a church through taxes levied on every household. And every community member was required to attend midweek and Sunday religious services. The average New Englander heard 7,000 sermons in a lifetime.

Religion exercised a pervasive influence over the life of New England towns, but unlike the Church of England and the British government in New England, church and government were technically separate. Thus although Puritan New England has often been called a theocracy, individual congregations were entirely separate from the state—except that the residents were taxed to support the churches. And if not all inhabitants were church members, all were nonetheless required to attend church services.

Yet, for all of their religious convictions, New England Puritans were assailed by doubts, by a fear of falling away from godly living, by the haunting anxiety that despite their best outward efforts they might not be among God's elect. Add such concerns to the long winters that kept families cooped up during

the dark, cold months, and one has a formula for seething resentments and recriminations that, for the sake of peace in the family, were often projected outward, toward neighbors. The New Englanders inhabiting towns they called
peaceable kingdoms therefore built a reputation as the most litigious people on
earth, continually quarreling over property disputes, business dealings, religious concerns, and other issues and building in the process a flourishing legal
profession.

DIVERSITY AND SOCIAL STRAINS   Despite long-enduring myths,
New England towns were not always pious, harmonious, and self-sufficient
utopias populated by praying Puritans. Many communities were founded
not as religious refuges but as secular centers of fishing, trade, or commercial agriculture, and the animating concerns of residents in such commercial
towns tended to be more entrepreneurial than spiritual. After a Puritan minister delivered his first sermon to a congregation in the port of Marblehead,
a crusty fisherman admonished him: "You think you are preaching to the
people of the Bay. Our main end was to catch fish."

In many of the godly inland communities, social strains increased as time
passed, a consequence primarily of population pressure on the land and

School Street, Salem, about 1765

The mansion of a wealthy merchant dominates this street scene, typical of a
prosperous New England port town.

increasing disparities of wealth. "Love your neighbor," said Benjamin Franklin's Poor Richard, "but don't pull down your fence." Initially fathers exercised strong authority over sons through their control of the land. They kept their sons and their families in the town, not letting them set up their own households or get title to their farmland until they reached middle age. In New England, as elsewhere, fathers tended to subdivide their land among all the male children. But by the eighteenth century, with land scarcer, the younger sons were either getting control of the property early or moving on. Often they were forced out, with family help and blessings, to seek land elsewhere or new kinds of work in the commercial cities along the coast or inland rivers. With the growing pressure on land in the settled regions, poverty and social tension increased in what had once seemed a country of unlimited opportunity.

The emphasis on a direct accountability to God, which lies at the base of all Protestant theology, itself caused a persistent tension and led believers to challenge authority in the name of private conscience. Massachusetts repressed such heresy in the 1630s, but it resurfaced during the 1650s among Quakers and Baptists, and in 1659–1660 the Puritan colony hanged four Quakers who persisted in returning after they had been expelled. These acts caused such revulsion—and an investigation by the British government—that they were not repeated, although heretics continued to face harassment and persecution.

More damaging to the Puritan utopia was the growing materialism of New England, which placed strains on church discipline. More and more children of the "visible saints" found themselves unable to give the required testimony of spiritual regeneration. In 1662 an assembly of Boston ministers accepted the Half-Way Covenant, whereby baptized children of church members could be admitted to a "halfway" membership and secure baptism for their own children in turn. Such members, however, could neither vote in church nor take Communion. A further blow to Puritan control came with the Massachusetts royal charter of 1691, which required toleration of dissenters and based the right to vote in public elections on property rather than church membership.

THE DEVIL IN NEW ENGLAND The strains accompanying Massachusetts's transition from Puritan utopia to royal colony reached a tragic climax in the witchcraft hysteria at Salem Village (now the town of Danvers) in 1692. Belief in witchcraft was widespread throughout Europe and New England in the seventeenth century. Prior to the dramatic episode in Salem, almost 300 New Englanders (mostly middle-aged women) had been accused of practicing witchcraft, and more than 30 had been hanged. New England was, in the words of Cotton Mather, "a country . . . extraordinarily alarum'd by the wrath of the Devil."

Still, the Salem episode was distinctive in its scope and intensity. Salem Village was about eight miles from the larger Salem Town, a thriving port. It was a contentious community of independent farm families and people who depended upon the commercial activity of the port. The village struggled to free itself from the influence and taxes of Salem proper. The resulting tensions apparently made the residents especially susceptible to the idea that the devil was at work in their village.

During the winter of 1691–1692, several adolescent girls began meeting in the kitchen of the village minister, the Reverend Samuel Parris. There they gave rapt attention to the African tales told by Tituba, Parris's West Indian slave. As the days passed, the entranced girls began to behave oddly—shouting, barking, groveling, and twitching for no apparent reason. When asked who was tormenting them, the girls replied that three women—Tituba, Sarah Good, and Sarah Osborne—were Satan's servants.

Authorities thereupon arrested the three accused women. At a special hearing before the magistrates, the "afflicted" girls rolled on the floor in convulsive fits as the women were questioned. Tituba shocked everyone by not only confessing to the charge but also divulging the names of many others in the community who she claimed were also performing the devil's work. Within a few months the Salem Village jail was filled with townspeople—men, women, and children—all accused of practicing witchcraft.

As the net of accusation spread wider, extending far beyond the confines of Salem, leaders of the Massachusetts Bay Colony began to worry that the witch hunts were out of control. The governor

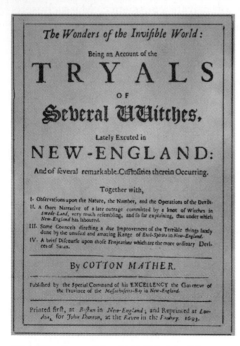

The Wonders of the Invisible World

Title page of the 1693 London edition of Cotton Mather's account of the Salem witchcraft cases. Mather, a prominent Boston minister, advocated the admission of "spectral" evidence in witchcraft trials and warned his congregation that the devil's legions had been set upon New England.

intervened when his own wife was accused of serving the devil. He disbanded the special court in Salem and ordered the remaining suspects released. A year after it had begun, the fratricidal event was finally over. Nineteen people (including some men married to women who had been convicted) had been hanged, one man—the stubborn Giles Corey—was pressed to death by heavy stones, and more than 100 others were jailed. Nearly everybody responsible for the Salem executions later recanted, and nothing quite like it happened in the colonies again.

What explains the witchcraft hysteria at Salem? Some have argued that it may have represented nothing more than a contagious exercise in adolescent imagination intended to enliven the dreary routine of everyday life. Yet adults pressed the formal charges against the accused and provided most of the testimony. This fact has led some scholars to speculate that long-festering local feuds and property disputes may have triggered the prosecutions.

More recently historians have focused on the most salient feature of the accused witches: almost all of them were women. Many of the supposed witches, it turns out, had in some way defied the traditional roles assigned to females. Some had engaged in business transactions outside the home; others did not attend church; some were curmudgeons. Most of them were middle-aged or older and without sons or brothers. They thus stood to inherit property and live independently. The notion of autonomous spinsters flew in the face of prevailing social conventions.

Still another interpretation stresses the hysteria caused in the late seventeenth century by frequent Indian attacks occurring just north of Salem, along New England's northern frontier. Some of the participants in the witch trials were orphan girls from Maine who had witnessed the violence firsthand. Their proximity to such horrific events and the terrifying specter of new Indian attacks exacerbated anxieties and may help explain why witchcraft hysteria developed so rapidly and extensively. "Are you guilty or not?" the Salem magistrate John Hathorne demanded of fourteen-year-old Abigail Hobbs in 1692. "I have seen sights and been scared," she answered.

Whatever the precise cause, there is little doubt that the witchcraft controversy reflected the peculiar social dynamics of the Salem community. Late in 1692, as the hysteria in Salem subsided, several of the afflicted girls were traveling through nearby Ipswich when they encountered an old woman resting on a bridge. "A witch!" they shouted and began writhing as if possessed. But the people of Ipswich were unimpressed. Passersby showed no interest in the theatrics. Unable to generate either sympathy or curiosity, the girls picked themselves up and continued on their way.

SOCIETY AND ECONOMY
IN THE MIDDLE COLONIES

AN ECONOMIC MIX   Both geographically and culturally the middle colonies stood between New England and the South, blending their own influences with elements derived from the older regions on either side. In so doing, they more completely reflected the diversity of colonial life and more fully foreshadowed the pluralism of the American nation than the other regions did. Their crops were those of New England but more bountiful, owing to better land and a longer growing season, and they developed surpluses of foodstuffs for export to the plantations of the South and the West Indies: wheat, barley, oats, and other cereals, flour, and livestock. Three great rivers—the Hudson, the Delaware, and the Susquehanna—and their tributaries gave the middle colonies ready access to the backcountry and to the Indian fur trade, where New York and Pennsylvania long enjoyed friendly relations with the Iroquois, the Delaware, and other tribes. As a consequence, the region's commerce rivaled that of New England, and indeed Philadelphia in time supplanted Boston as the largest city in the colonies.

Land policies in the middle colonies followed the headright system of the South. In New York the early royal governors carried forward, in practice if not in name, the Dutch device of the patroonship, granting influential men vast estates on Long Island and up the Hudson and Mohawk River valleys. These realms most nearly approached the medieval manor. They were self-contained domains farmed by tenants who paid fees to use the landlords' mills, warehouses, smokehouses, and wharves. But with free land available elsewhere, New York's population languished, and the new waves of immigrants sought the promised land of Pennsylvania.

AN ETHNIC MIX   In the makeup of their population, the middle colonies stood apart from both the mostly English Puritan settlements and the biracial plantation colonies to the south. In New York and New Jersey, for instance, Dutch culture and language lingered, along with the Dutch Reformed Church. Along the Delaware River the few Swedes and Finns, the first settlers, were overwhelmed by the influx of English and Welsh Quakers, followed in turn by Germans and Scotch-Irish.

The Germans came mainly from the Rhineland, a region devastated by incessant war. (Until German unification, in 1871, ethnic Germans—those Europeans speaking German as their native language—lived in a variety of areas and principalities in central Europe.) William Penn's brochures encouraging settlement in Pennsylvania circulated throughout central Europe in German translation, and his promise of religious freedom appealed to persecuted sects, especially the Mennonites, German Baptists whose beliefs resembled those of the Quakers.

In 1683 a group of Mennonites founded Germantown, near Philadelphia. They were the vanguard of a swelling migration in the eighteenth century that included Lutherans, Reformed Calvinists, Moravians, and others, a large proportion of whom paid their way as indentured servants, or "redemptioners," as they were commonly called. West of Philadelphia they created a belt of settlement in which the "Pennsylvania Dutch" (a corruption of Deutsch, meaning "German") predominated, as well as a channel for the dispersion of German populations throughout the colonies.

The feisty Scotch-Irish began to arrive later and moved still farther out into the backcountry throughout the eighteenth century. (Scotch-Irish is an enduring misnomer for Ulster Scots, Presbyterians transplanted from Scotland to confiscated lands in northern Ireland to give that country a more Protestant tone.) The Scotch-Irish fled both Anglican persecution and economic disaster caused by English taxation. Between 1717 and 1775 over 250,000 Scots and Scotch-Irish left northern England, southern Scotland, and northern Ireland for America. They settled in Pennsylvania and the fertile valleys stretching southwestward into Virginia and Carolina.

The Germans and Scotch-Irish became the largest non-English elements in the colonies. Other minority ethnic groups enriched the population in New York and the Quaker colonies: Huguenots (whose religious freedom had been revoked in France in 1685), Irish, Welsh, Swiss, and Jews. New York had inherited from the Dutch a tradition of tolerance, which had given the colony a diverse population before the English conquest: French-speaking Walloons (a Celtic people of southern Belgium), French, Germans, Danes, Portuguese, Spaniards, Italians, Bohemians, Poles, and others, including some New England Puritans. The Sephardic Jews who landed in New Netherland in 1654 quickly founded a synagogue there.

What could be said of Pennsylvania as a refuge for the persecuted might be said as well of Rhode Island and South Carolina, which practiced a similar religious toleration. Rhode Island's Newport and South Carolina's Charleston, like New York and Philadelphia, became centers of minuscule Jewish populations. Huguenots (French Protestants) made their greatest mark on South Carolina, more by their enterprise than by their numbers. A number of Highland Scots arrived, especially after the suppression of a rebellion in 1745 on behalf of the Stuart pretender to the throne, Bonnie Prince Charlie.

The eighteenth century was a period of great expansion and population growth in British North America, during which a large increase in the

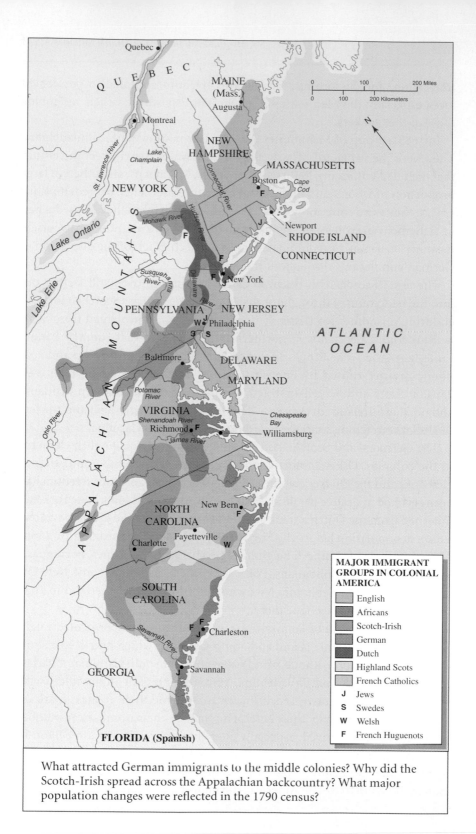

MAJOR IMMIGRANT GROUPS IN COLONIAL AMERICA

- English
- Africans
- Scotch-Irish
- German
- Dutch
- Highland Scots
- French Catholics
- **J** Jews
- **S** Swedes
- **W** Welsh
- **F** French Huguenots

What attracted German immigrants to the middle colonies? Why did the Scotch-Irish spread across the Appalachian backcountry? What major population changes were reflected in the 1790 census?

non-English stock took place. A rough estimate of the national origins of the white population as of 1790 found it to be 61 percent English, 14 percent Scottish and Scotch-Irish, 9 percent German, 5 percent Dutch, French, and Swedish, 4 percent Irish, and 7 percent miscellaneous or unassigned. If one adds to the 3,172,444 whites in the 1790 census the 756,770 nonwhites, without even considering uncounted Indians, it seems likely that only about half the nation's inhabitants, and perhaps fewer, could trace their origins to England. Of the enslaved blacks, about 75 percent had been transported from the bend of the African coastline between the Senegal and Niger Rivers; most of the rest came from the Congo-Angola region.

THE BACKCOUNTRY Pennsylvania in the eighteenth century became the great distribution point for the different ethnic groups of European origin, just as the Chesapeake Bay region and Charleston became the distribution points for African peoples. Before the mid–eighteenth century, settlers in the Pennsylvania backcountry had reached the Appalachian Mountain range. Rather than crossing the steep ridges, the Scotch-Irish and Germans filtered southward along what came to be called the Great Philadelphia Road, the primary internal migration route during the colonial period. It headed west from the port city, traversing Chester and Lancaster Counties, and turned southwest at Harris' Ferry (now Harrisburg), where it crossed the Susquehanna River. Continuing south across western Maryland, the road headed down the Shenandoah River valley of Virginia and on into the Carolina and Georgia backcountry. Germans were the first white settlers in the upper Shenandoah River valley, and Scotch-Irish filled the lower valley.

COLONIAL CITIES

During the seventeenth century the American colonies remained in comparative isolation from one another, evolving distinctive folkways and unfolding separate histories. Boston and New York and Philadelphia and Charleston were more likely to keep in close touch with London than with one another. The Carolina up-country had more in common with the Pennsylvania backcountry than either had with the urban cultures of Charleston or Philadelphia. Since commerce was their chief reason for being, colonial cities hugged the coastline or, like Philadelphia, sprang up on rivers that could be navigated by oceangoing vessels. Never holding more than 10 percent of the colonial population, the large cities exerted a disproportionate influence on commerce, politics, and culture. By the end of the colonial period, Philadelphia, with some 30,000 people, was the largest city in the colonies and second only to London in the British Empire. New York, with about 25,000, ranked second; Boston numbered 16,000; Charleston, 12,000; and Newport, 11,000.

THE SOCIAL AND POLITICAL ORDER   The urban social elite was dominated by the merchants who bartered the products of American farms and forests for the molasses and rum of the West Indies, the manufactured goods of Europe, and the slaves of Africa. After the merchants, who constituted the chief urban aristocracy, came a middle class of retailers, innkeepers, and artisans. Almost two thirds of the urban adult male workers were artisans, people who made their living at handicrafts. They included carpenters and coopers (barrel makers), shoemakers and tailors, silversmiths and blacksmiths, sailmakers, stonemasons, weavers, and potters. At the bottom of the pecking order were sailors and unskilled workers.

Class stratification in the cities became more pronounced as time passed. One study of Boston found that in 1687 the richest 15 percent of the population held 52 percent of the taxable wealth; by 1771 the top 15 percent held about 67 percent and the top 5 percent held some 44 percent. In Philadelphia the concentration of wealth was even more pronounced.

Colonial cities were busy, crowded, and dangerous. They required not only paved roads and streetlights but regulations to protect children and animals from reckless riders. Regulations restrained citizens from tossing their garbage into the street. Fires that on occasion swept through closely packed buildings led to building codes, restrictions on burning rubbish, and the organization of fire companies. Rising crime and violence required more police pro-

The Rapalje Children

John Durand (ca. 1768). These children of a wealthy Brooklyn merchant wear clothing typical of upper-crust urban society.

tection. And in cities the poor became more visible than they were in the countryside. Colonists brought with them to America the English principle of public responsibility for the indigent. The number of Boston's poor receiving public assistance rose from 500 in 1700 to 4,000 in 1736; in New York the number rose from 250 in 1698 to 5,000 in the 1770s. Most of the public assistance went to "outdoor" relief in the form of money, food, clothing, and fuel. Almshouses appeared to house the destitute.

THE URBAN WEB Transit within and between cities was initially difficult. The first roads were Indian trails, which themselves often followed the tracks of bison through the forests. Those trails widened with travel, then were made into roads. Land travel was initially by horse or by foot. The first public stagecoach line opened in 1732. From the main ports good roads might reach thirty or forty miles inland, but all were dirt roads subject to washouts and mud holes.

Taverns were an important aspect of colonial travel, since movement at night was too risky. (During the colonial era it was said that when the Spanish settled an area, they would first build a church; the Dutch, in their settlements, would first construct a fort; and the English, in theirs, would first erect a tavern.) By the end of the seventeenth century, there were more taverns in America than any other business. Indeed, taverns became the most important social institution in the colonies—and the most democratic. By 1690 there were fifty-four taverns in Boston alone, half of them operated by women. Colonial taverns and inns were places to drink, relax, read a newspaper, play cards or billiards, gossip about people or politics, learn news from travelers, or conduct business. Local ordinances regulated them, setting prices and usually prohibiting them from serving liquor to African Americans, Indians, servants, or apprentices.

In 1726 a concerned Bostonian wrote a letter to the community, declaring that "the abuse of strong Drink is becoming Epidemical among us, and it is very justly Supposed . . . that the Multiplication of Taverns has contributed not a little to this Excess of Riot and Debauchery." Despite the objections by some that crowded taverns engendered disease and unruly behavior, colonial taverns and inns continued to proliferate, and by the mid–eighteenth century they would become the gathering place for protests against British rule.

Taverns served as a collective form of communication; long-distance communication, however, was more complicated. Postal service in the seventeenth century was almost nonexistent—people entrusted letters to travelers

Taverns

A tobacconist's business card from 1770 captures the atmosphere of late-eighteenth-century taverns. Here men in a Philadelphia tavern converse while they drink ale and smoke pipes.

or sea captains. Under a parliamentary law of 1710, the postmaster of London named a deputy in charge of the colonies, and a postal system eventually extended the length of the Atlantic seaboard. Benjamin Franklin, who served as deputy postmaster for the colonies from 1753 to 1774, sped up the service with shorter routes and night-traveling post riders, and he increased the volume by lowering rates.

More reliable mail delivery gave rise to newspapers in the eighteenth century. Before 1745 twenty-two newspapers had been started: seven in New England, ten in the middle colonies, and five in the South. An important landmark in the progress of freedom of the press was John Peter Zenger's trial for seditious libel, for publishing criticisms of New York's governor in his newspaper, the *New York Weekly Journal*. Zenger was imprisoned for ten months and brought to trial in 1735. English common law held that one might be punished for criticism that fostered "an ill opinion of the government." The jury's function was only to determine whether the defendant had published the opinion. Zenger's lawyer startled the court with his claim that the editor had published the truth—which the judge ruled an unacceptable defense. The jury, however, agreed with the assertion and held the editor not guilty. The libel law remained standing as before, but editors thereafter were emboldened to criticize officials more freely.

THE ENLIGHTENMENT

By the middle of the eighteenth century, the thirteen colonies were maturing. People increasingly referred to themselves simply as Americans. The population was exploding, fed both by natural increase and by a constant stream of immigrants from diverse lands. Schools and colleges were springing up, and the standard of living was rising as well. More and more colonists had easier access to the latest consumer goods—and the latest ideas percolating in Europe. Through their commercial contacts, newspapers, and other channels, colonial cities became centers for the dissemination of new ideas. Most significant was a burst of intellectual activity known as the Enlightenment. Like the Renaissance, the Enlightenment prized rational inquiry, scientific discoveries, and individual freedom. Curious people wanted to dissect the workings of nature by observation, experimentation, and calculation. Unlike their Renaissance predecessors, however, many enlightened thinkers were willing to discard orthodox religious beliefs in favor of more "rational" ideas and ideals.

DISCOVERING THE LAWS OF NATURE One manifestation of the Enlightenment was a scientific revolution in which the ancient view of an earth-centered universe was overthrown by the heliocentric (sun-centered) system of the sixteenth-century Polish astronomer Nicolaus Copernicus. A climax to the scientific revolution came with Sir Isaac Newton's *Principia* (*Mathematical Principles of Natural Philosophy*, 1687), which set forth his theory of gravitation. Newton challenged biblical notions of the natural order by depicting a mechanistic universe moving in accordance with natural laws that could be grasped by human reason and explained by mathematics. He implied that natural laws govern all things—the orbits of the planets and the orbits of human relations: politics, economics, and society. Reason could make people aware, for instance, that the natural law of supply and demand governs economics or that the natural rights to life, liberty, and property determine the limits and functions of government.

Much of this new enlightened thought could be reconciled with established beliefs: the idea of natural law existed in Christian theology, and religious people could reason that the rational universe of Copernicus and Newton simply demonstrated the glory of God. Yet when people carried Newton's outlook to its ultimate logic, as the Deists did, the idea of natural law reduced God from a daily presence to a remote Creator—as the French philosopher Voltaire put it, the master clockmaker who planned the universe and set it in motion. Evil in the world, in this view, results not from original sin and innate depravity so much as from ignorance, an imperfect understanding of the laws of nature. Humanity, the English philosopher John Locke argued in his *Essay Concerning Human Understanding* (1690), is largely the product of the environment, the mind being a blank tablet on which experience is written. The best way, therefore, to improve both society and human nature was by the application and improvement of Reason, which was the highest Virtue (Enlightenment thinkers often capitalized both words).

THE ENLIGHTENMENT IN AMERICA   However interpreted, such ideas profoundly affected the climate of thought in the eighteenth century. The premises of Newtonian science and the Enlightenment, moreover, fitted the American experience, which placed a premium on observation, experiment, reason, and the need to think anew. America was therefore especially receptive to the new science.

John Winthrop Jr. (1606–1676), three times governor of Connecticut, was one of America's first scientists. His work in chemistry led to his membership in the Royal Society of London. He owned probably the first telescope brought to the colonies. A relative, John Winthrop (1714–1779), was a professional scientist and Harvard professor who introduced to the colonies the study of calculus and ranged over the fields of astronomy, geology, chemistry, and electricity. David Rittenhouse of Philadelphia, a clock maker, became a self-taught scientist who was probably the first to build a telescope in America. John Bartram, also of Philadelphia, spent a lifetime traveling and studying American plant life and developed an extensive botanical garden.

FRANKLIN'S INFLUENCE   Benjamin Franklin epitomized the Enlightenment in the eyes of both Americans and Europeans. Born in Boston in 1706, he was the son of a maker of candles and soap and a descendant of Puritans. Apprenticed to his older brother, a printer, Franklin left home at the age of seventeen, bound for Philadelphia. There, before he was twenty-four, he owned a print shop, where he edited and published the *Pennsylvania Gazette*. When he was twenty-six, he published *Poor Richard's Almanack*, a collection of homely maxims on success and happiness. Before he retired from business, at the age of forty-two, Franklin, among other achievements, had founded a library, organized a fire company, helped start the academy that became the University of Pennsylvania, and organized a debating club that grew into the American Philosophical Society.

Franklin was devoted to science. Skeptical and curious, pragmatic and irreverent, he was a voracious reader and an inventive genius. His wide-ranging experiments traversed the fields of medicine, meteorology, geology, astronomy, and physics, among others. He developed the Franklin stove, the lightning rod, and a glass harmonica.

Franklin's love of commonsensical reason and his pragmatic skepticism clashed with prevailing religious beliefs. Although raised as a Presbyterian, he became a freethinker who had no patience with religious orthodoxy and sectarian squabbles. Franklin prized reason over revelation. He was not burdened with anxieties regarding the state of his soul. Early on, he abandoned the Calvinist assumption that God had predestined salvation for a select few. He found the doctrine of original sin "unintelligible," was skeptical of the divinity of Jesus, and did not accept at face value the Bible as God's word. Franklin quit attending church as a young man, yet he retained a belief in God. Like the European Deists, he came to believe in a God that had created a universe animated by natural laws, laws that inquisitive people could discern through reason. The Deistic God was a distant Creator, not a providential force in human life. Franklin decided that Christian morality, not theology, was the basis of a good life—and a meaningful religious outlook.

Benjamin Franklin

Shown here as a young man in a portrait by Robert Feke.

Benjamin Franklin and other like-minded thinkers, such as Thomas Jefferson, James Madison, and Thomas Paine, derived an outlook of hope and optimism from modern science and Enlightenment rationalism. Unlike Calvinists, they believed people have the capacity, through rational analysis, to unlock the mysteries of the universe and thereby shape their own destinies. "The rapid Progress *true* Science now makes," as Franklin wrote, led him to regret being "born too soon." Jefferson concurred. He, too, envisioned a bright future for humankind: "As long as we may think as we will and speak as we think, the condition of man will proceed in improvement." The evangelical religiosity of traveling revivalists disgusted Jefferson. His "fundamental principle" was that reason, not emotion and "blindfolded fear," should inform decision making: "We are saved by our good works, which are within our power, and not by our faith, which is not in our power."

Jefferson warned against those "despots" in religion and politics who resisted change and still wanted to dictate belief.

Such enlightened thinking, founded on freedom of thought and expression, could not have been more different from the religious assumptions shaping Puritan New England in the seventeenth century. The eighteenth-century Enlightenment thus set in motion intellectual forces that challenged the "truthfulness" of revealed religion and the logic of Christian faith. Those modern forces, however, would inspire stern resistance in the defenders of religious orthodoxy.

EDUCATION IN THE COLONIES   White colonial Americans were among the most literate people in the world. Almost ninety percent of men (more than in England) could read. For the colonists at large, education in the traditional ideas and manners of society—even literacy itself—remained primarily the responsibility of family and church. The modern conception of free public education was slow in coming and failed to win universal acceptance until the twentieth century. Yet colonists were concerned from the beginning that steps needed to be taken to educate their young.

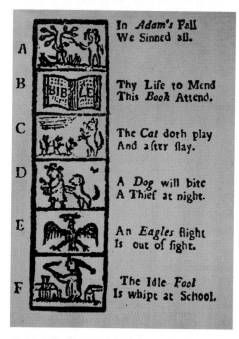

Colonial education

A page from the rhymed alphabet of *The New England Primer*, a popular American textbook first published in the 1680s.

Conditions in New England proved most favorable for the establishment of schools. The Puritan emphasis on reading Scripture, which all Protestants shared to some degree, implied an obligation to ensure literacy. And the compact towns of New England made schools more feasible than they were among the scattered settlers of the southern colonies. In 1647 the Massachusetts Bay Colony enacted the famous "ye olde deluder Satan" act (designed to thwart the evil one), which required every town of fifty or more families to set up a grammar school (a "Latin school" that could prepare a student for college). Although the act was widely evaded, it did signify a serious attempt to promote education.

The Dutch in New Netherland were as interested in education as the New England Puritans. In Pennsylvania the Quakers never heeded William Penn's instructions to establish public schools, but they did finance a number of private schools, where practical as well as academic subjects were taught. In the southern colonies, efforts to establish schools were hampered by the more scattered population and, in parts of the backcountry, by indifference and neglect. Some of the wealthiest southern planters and merchants sent their children to England or hired tutors. In some places wealthy patrons or the people collectively managed to raise some kind of support for "old field" schools (primitive one-room buildings usually made of logs) and academies at the secondary level.

THE GREAT AWAKENING

During the early eighteenth century, the American colonies were "awash in a sea of faith," as one historian has written. Hundreds of new congregations were founded between 1700 and 1750. Most Americans (85 percent) lived in colonies with an "established" church, meaning that the colonial government officially sanctioned—and collected taxes to support—a single official denomination. Anglicanism was the established church in Virginia, Maryland, Delaware, and the Carolinas. Congregationalism was the official faith in New England. In New York, Anglicanism vied with the Dutch Reformed Church for control. Pennsylvania had no single state-supported church, but Quakers dominated the legislative assembly. Like Pennsylvania, New Jersey and Rhode Island had no official denomination and hosted numerous sects.

Most colonies with an established church organized religious life on the basis of well-regulated local parishes, which defined their borders and defended them against dissenters and heretics. No outside preacher could enter the parish and speak in public without permission. Then, in the 1740s, the parish system was thrown into turmoil by the arrival of outspoken traveling (itinerant) evangelists, who claimed that the official parish ministers were incompetent and unregenerate. Many of the evangelists also insisted that Christians must be "reborn" in their convictions and behavior; traditional creeds or articles of faith were unnecessary for rebirth. By emphasizing the individualistic strand embedded in Protestantism, the so-called

Great Awakening ended up invigorating—and fragmenting—American religious life. Unlike the Enlightenment, which affected primarily the intellectual elite, the Great Awakening appealed to the masses. It was the first popular movement before the Revolution that spanned all thirteen colonies. As Benjamin Franklin observed of the Awakening, "Never did the people show so great a willingness to attend sermons. Religion is become the subject of most conversation."

STIRRINGS   During the early eighteenth century the currents of rationalism stimulated by the Enlightenment aroused concerns among orthodox believers in Calvinism. Many people seemed to be drifting away from the moorings of piety. Despite the belief that the Lord had allowed great Puritan and Quaker merchants of Boston and Philadelphia to prosper, there remained a haunting fear that the devil had lured them into the vain pursuit of worldly gain, Deism, and skepticism. And out along the fringes of settlement, many of the colonists were unchurched. On the frontier, people had no minister to preach to them or administer sacraments or perform marriages. According to some ministers, these pioneers had lapsed into a primitive and sinful life, little different from that of the "heathen" Indians. By the 1730s the sense of religious decline had provoked the Great Awakening.

In 1734–1735 a remarkable spiritual revival occurred in the congregation of Jonathan Edwards, a Congregationalist minister in Northampton, in western Massachusetts. One of America's most brilliant philosophers and theologians, Edwards had entered Yale College in 1716, at age thirteen, and graduated as valedictorian four years later. In 1727, Edwards was called to serve the Congregational church in Northampton. There he found the town's spirituality at a low ebb. Edwards claimed that the young people of Northampton were addicted to sinful pleasures, such as "night walking and frequenting the tavern," and indulged in "lewd practices" that "exceedingly corrupted others." Christians, he believed, had become preoccupied with making and spending money. Religion had also become too intellectual, thereby losing its emotional force. Edwards singled out Deists as particularly despicable, for having "cast off the Christian Religion" and for believing that "God has given mankind no other light to walk by but their own reason." Edwards resolved to restore deeply felt spirituality. "Our people," he said, "do not so much need to have their heads stored [with new knowledge] as to have their hearts touched." His own vivid descriptions of the torments of hell and the delights of heaven helped rekindle spiritual fervor among his congregants. By 1735, Edwards could report that "the town seemed to be full of the presence of God; it never was so full of love, nor of joy." To judge the power of the Awakening, he thought, one need only observe that "it was no longer the Tavern" that drew local crowds, "but the Minister's House."

About the same time, William Tennent, an Irish-born Presbyterian revivalist, set up a "Log College" in Neshaminy, Pennsylvania, for the education of ministers to serve the Scotch-Irish Presbyterians living around Philadelphia. Tennent and his sons shocked Presbyterian officials by claiming that many of the local ministers were "cold and sapless"; they showed no evidence of themselves having experienced a convincing conversion experience, nor were they willing to "thrust the nail of terror into sleeping souls." Tennent's oldest son, Gilbert, defended their aggressive (and often illegal) tactics by explaining that he and other traveling evangelists invaded parishes only when the "settled ministry" showed no interest in the "Getting of Grace and Growing in it." The Tennents caused great consternation because they and other unauthorized ministers offered a compelling fire-and-brimstone alternative to the settled parish preachers. They promoted a passionate piety, and they refused to accept the prevailing structure of denominations and clerical authority. Competition was emerging in colonial religious life.

The true catalyst of the Great Awakening was a young English minister, George Whitefield, whose reputation as a spellbinding evangelist preceded him to the colonies. Congregations were lifeless, he claimed, "because dead men preach to them." Too many ministers were "slothful shepherds and dumb dogs." His objective was to restore the fires of religious fervor to American congregations. In the autumn of 1739, Whitefield, then twenty-five, arrived in Philadelphia and began preaching to huge crowds. After visiting Georgia, he made a triumphal procession northward to New England, drawing thousands and releasing "Gales of Heavenly Wind" that blew gusts throughout the colonies.

The cross-eyed Whitefield enthralled audiences with his golden voice, flamboyant style, and unparalleled eloquence. Even the skeptical Benjamin Franklin, who went to see Whitefield preach in Philadelphia, was so carried away that he emptied his pockets into the collection plate. Whitefield urged

George Whitefield

The English minister's dramatic eloquence roused American congregants, inspiring many to experience a religious rebirth.

his listeners to experience a "new birth"—a sudden, emotional moment of conversion and salvation. By the end of his sermon, one listener reported, the entire congregation was "in utmost Confusion, some crying out, some laughing, and Bliss still roaring to them to come to Christ, as they answered, *I will, I will, I'm coming, I'm coming.*"

Jonathan Edwards took advantage of the commotion stirred up by Whitefield to spread his own revival gospel throughout New England. The Awakening reached its peak in 1741 when Edwards delivered his most famous sermon at Enfield, Massachusetts (in present-day Connecticut). Titled "Sinners in the Hands of an Angry God," it represented a devout appeal to repentance. Edwards reminded his congregation that hell is real and that God's vision is omnipotent, his judgment certain. He noted that God "holds you over the pit of hell, much as one holds a spider, or some loathsome insect, over the fire, abhors you, and is dreadfully provoked . . . he looks upon you as worthy of nothing else, but to be cast into the fire." When Edwards finished, he had to wait several minutes for the congregants to quiet down before leading them in a closing hymn.

Women, both white and black, were believed to be more susceptible to fits of spiritual emotion than men. The Tennents, Whitefield, and other traveling evangelists thus targeted women because of their spiritual virtuosity. Whitefield and the other ecstatic evangelists believed that conversion required a visceral, emotional experience. Convulsions, shrieks, and spasms were the physical manifestation of the Holy Spirit at work, and women seemed more willing to let the Spirit move them. Some of the revivalists, especially Baptists, initially loosened traditional restrictions on female participation in worship. Scores of women served as lay exhorters, including Bathsheba Kingsley, who stole her husband's horse in 1741 to spread the gospel among her rural neighbors after receiving "immediate revelations from heaven." Sarah Osborn, a Rhode Island Congregationalist widow, was so inspired by the preachings of Whitefield and Gilbert Tennent that she organized a women's prayer group that same year. By the 1760s her home in Newport had become the locus of a sustained revival. Hundreds of people, white men and women, free and enslaved blacks, converged in her home to pray and embrace Christ. Despite a male friend's advice to "shut up . . . [her] Mouth and doors and creep into obscurity," Osborn persisted. Similarly, Mary Reed of Durham, New Hampshire, so enthralled her minister with her effusions of the Holy Spirit that he allowed her to deliver spellbinding testimonials to the congregation every Wednesday evening for two months. Such ecstatic piety was symptomatic of the Awakening's rekindling of religious enthusiasm. Yet

Sarah Osborn's house

Osborn's house in Newport, Rhode Island, was visited by hundreds of people who came to pray and embrace Christ.

most ministers who encouraged public expressions of female piety refused to link such enhanced participation to the more controversial idea of allowing women to participate in congregational governance. Churches remained male bastions of political authority.

Edwards and Whitefield inspired many imitators, some of whom carried evangelism to extremes. Once unleashed, spiritual enthusiasm is hard to control. In many ways the Awakening backfired on those who had intended it to bolster church discipline and social order. Some of the revivalists began to court those at the bottom of society—laborers, seamen, servants, slaves, and farm folk. The Reverend James Davenport, for instance, a fiery New England Congregationalist, set about shouting, raging, and stomping on the devil, beseeching his listeners to renounce the established clergy and become the agents of their own salvation. The churched and unchurched flocked to his theatrical sermons. Seized by terror and ecstasy, they groveled on the floor or lay unconscious on the benches, to the chagrin of more traditional churchgoers. One never knew, the more conventional clergymen warned, whence came these enthusiasms—perhaps they were devilish delusions intended to discredit the true faith. Critics of the Awakening decried the emotionalism generated by the revivalists. They were especially concerned that evangelicals were encouraging "women, yea, girls to speak" at revivals. One critic of "female exhorters" reminded congregations of the scriptural commandment "let your women keep silence in the churches."

PIETY AND REASON   The Great Awakening undermined many of the established churches by emphasizing that individuals could receive God's grace without the traditional intermediary roles played by the clergy. It also gave people more religious choices. Everywhere the fragmenting force of the Awakening induced splits, especially in the more Calvinistic churches. Presbyterians divided into the "Old Side" and the "New Side," Congregationalists into "Old Light" and "New Light." New England religious life would never be the same. Jonathan Edwards lamented the warring factions. We are "like two armies," he said, "separated and drawn up in battle array, ready to fight one another." Church members chose sides and either dismissed their ministers or deserted them. Many of the New Lights went over to the Baptists, and others flocked to Presbyterian or, later, Methodist groups, which in turn divided and subdivided into new sects.

New England Puritanism disintegrated amid the ecstatic revivals of the Great Awakening. The precarious balance in which the founders had held the elements of emotionalism and reason collapsed. In addition, the Puritan ideal of religious uniformity was shattered. The crusty Connecticut Old Light Isaac Stiles denounced the "intrusion of choice into spiritual matters." In Anglican Virginia some fifty Baptist evangelists were jailed for disturbing the peace during the Great Awakening. New England subsequently attracted more and more Baptists, Presbyterians, Anglicans, and other denominations while the revival frenzy scored its most lasting victories along the frontiers of the middle and southern colonies. In the more sedate churches of Boston, moreover, the principle of rational religion gained the upper hand in a reaction against the excesses of revival emotion. Boston ministers such as Charles Chauncey and Jonathan Mayhew found Puritan theology too forbidding. To them the concept that people could be forever damned by predestination was irrational.

In reaction to taunts that the "born-again" revivalist ministers lacked learning, the Awakening gave rise to the denominational colleges that became characteristic of American higher education. The three colleges already in existence had their origins in religious motives: Harvard College, founded in 1636 because the Puritans dreaded "to leave an illiterate ministry to the church when our present ministers shall lie in the dust"; the College of William and Mary, created in 1693 to strengthen the Anglican ministry; and Yale College, set up in 1701 to educate the Puritans of Connecticut, who believed that Harvard was drifting from the strictest orthodoxy. The College of New Jersey, later Princeton University, was founded by Presbyterians in 1746. In close succession came King's College (1754) in New York, later renamed Columbia University, an Anglican institution; the College of Rhode Island (1764), later called Brown University, which was Baptist; Queens College (1766), later known as Rutgers, which was Dutch Reformed; and Dartmouth College (1769), which was Congregationalist and the outgrowth of a school for Indians. Among the colonial colleges, only the University of Pennsylvania, founded as the Academy of Philadelphia in 1751, arose from a secular impulse.

The Great Awakening subsided by 1750, although revivalism in Virginia continued unabated for another twenty years. The Awakening, like its counterpart, the Enlightenment, influenced the American Revolution and set in motion powerful currents that still flow in American life. It implanted in American culture the evangelical crusade and the emotional appeal of revivalism. The movement weakened the status of the old-fashioned clergy and state-supported churches, encouraged believers to exercise their own judgment, and thereby weakened habits of deference generally. By encouraging the proliferation of denominations, it heightened the need for toleration of dissent. But in some respects the counterpoint between the Awakening and the Enlightenment, between the urgings of the spirit and the logic of reason, led by different roads to similar ends. Both movements emphasized the power and right of individual decision making, and both aroused millennial hopes that America would become the promised land in which people might attain the perfection of piety or reason, if not both.

End of Chapter Review

- **Colonial Differences** Agriculture diversified: tobacco was the staple crop in Virginia, and rice and naval stores were the staples in the Carolinas. Family farms and a mixed economy characterized the middle and New England colonies, while plantation agriculture based on slavery became entrenched in the South. By 1790, German, Scotch-Irish, Welsh, and Irish immigrants had settled in the middle colonies, along with members of religious groups such as Quakers, Jews, Huguenots, and Mennonites.

- **Women in the Colonies** English colonists brought their belief systems with them, including convictions about the inferiority of women. The initial shortage of women gave way to a more equal gender ratio as women immigrated—alone and in family groups—thereby enabling a dramatic population growth in the colonies.

- **Indentured Servants** In response to the labor shortage in the early years, Virginia relied on indentured servants. By the end of the seventeenth century, enslaved Africans had replaced indentured servants in the South. With the supply of slaves seeming inexhaustible, the Carolinas adopted slavery as its primary labor source.

- **Triangular Trade** British America sent raw materials, such as fish and furs, to England in return for manufactured goods. The colonies participated in the triangular trade with Africa and the Caribbean, building ships and exporting manufactured goods, especially rum, while "importing" slaves from Africa.

- **The Enlightenment** The attitudes of the Enlightenment were transported along the trade routes. Isaac Newton's scientific discoveries and John Locke's idea of natural law culminated in the belief that Reason could improve society. Benjamin Franklin, who believed that people could shape their own destinies, became the face of the Enlightenment in America.

- **The Great Awakening** Religious diversity in the colonies increased. By the 1730s a revival of faith, the Great Awakening, swept through the colonies. New congregations formed as older sects were challenged by evangelists, who insisted that Christians be "reborn." Individualism, not orthodoxy, was stressed in this first popular movement in America's history.

CHRONOLOGY

1619	First Africans arrive at Jamestown
1636	Harvard College is established
1662	Puritans initiate the Half-Way Covenant
1662	Virginia enacts law declaring that children of slave women are slaves
1691	Royal charter for Massachusetts is established
1692	Salem witchcraft trials
1730s–1740s	Great Awakening
1735	John Peter Zenger is tried for seditious libel
1739	Stono Uprising
1739	George Whitefield preaches his first sermon in America, in Philadelphia
1741	Jonathan Edward preaches "Sinners in the Hands of an Angry God"

KEY TERMS & NAMES

indentured servants p. 109

Elizabeth Lucas Pinckney p. 114

staple crop, or cash crop p. 117

triangular trade p. 135

Half-Way Covenant p. 139

Enlightenment p. 149

John Locke p. 150

Benjamin Franklin p. 150

Great Awakening p. 153

Jonathan Edwards p. 154

George Whitefield p. 155

4

THE IMPERIAL PERSPECTIVE

FOCUS QUESTIONS   Ⓢ   wwnorton.com/studyspace

- How did the British Empire administer the economy of its colonies?
- How were colonial governments structured, and how independent were they of the mother country?
- How did the presence of the French in North America affect Britain and its colonies?
- What were the causes of the French and Indian War?
- How did victory in the Seven Years' War affect the British colonies in North America?

The English differed from the Spanish and the French in the degree of freedom they initially allowed their American colonies. Unlike New France and New Spain, New England was in effect a self-governing community. There was much less control by the mother country, in part because English leaders were unwilling to incur the expenses of a vast colonial bureaucracy. The constant political struggle between Parliament and the Stuart kings prevented England from perfecting either a systematic colonial policy or effective agencies of imperial control. After the Restoration of Charles II and the Stuart monarchy in 1660, a more comprehensive plan of colonial administration slowly emerged, but even so it lacked coherence and efficiency.

As a result of the often lax colonial administration by the mother country, Americans grew accustomed to loose and often paradoxical imperial policies. For instance, the English government granted local governmental authority to the settlements along the Atlantic coast and then sought to keep them from exercising it. It regarded the English colonists as citizens but refused to grant them the privileges of citizenship. It insisted that the Americans contribute to the expense of maintaining the colonies but refused to allow them a voice in shaping administrative policies. Such inconsistencies spawned grievances and tensions. By the mid–eighteenth century, when Britain tried to tighten control of the colonies, it was too late. Americans had developed a far more powerful sense of their rights than any other colonial people, and in the 1770s they resolved to assert and defend those rights.

ENGLISH ADMINISTRATION OF THE COLONIES

Throughout the colonial period the British monarchy was the source of legal authority in America, and land titles derived ultimately from royal grants to individuals and groups. All the colonies except Georgia received charters from the king before the Glorious Revolution of 1688, when the Crown lost supremacy to Parliament. The colonies therefore continued to stand as "dependencies of the Crown," and the important colonial officials held office at the pleasure of the monarchy. The English Civil War, which lasted from 1642 to 1646, led to Oliver Cromwell's Puritan Commonwealth and Protectorate, and both developments gave the colonies a respite from efforts at royal control.

THE MERCANTILE SYSTEM   As Britain's ruler in the 1650s, Oliver Cromwell showed little passion for regulating daily life in the American colonies, but he had a lively concern for colonial trade, which had fallen largely to Dutch shipping during the civil war. In 1651, therefore, Parliament adopted the Navigation Act, requiring that all goods imported to England or the colonies be carried only on English ships and that the majority of each crew be English.

On economic policy if nothing else, Restoration England under Charles II followed the lead of Cromwell and all the other major European powers of the seventeenth and eighteenth centuries. The new Parliament adopted the mercantile system, or mercantilism, a nationalistic program that assumed that the total of the world's gold and silver remained essentially fixed, with only a nation's share in that wealth subject to change. Thus one nation could gain wealth only at the expense of another—by seizing its gold and silver and dominating its trade. To acquire gold and silver, a government had to control all economic activities, limiting foreign imports and preserving a favorable balance of trade. This required a mercantilist government to encourage manufacturers, through subsidies and monopolies if need be. Mercantilism also required a nation to develop and protect its own shipping and to exploit colonies as sources of raw materials and markets for its manufactured goods.

The Navigation Act of 1660 gave Cromwell's act of 1651 a new twist: ships' crews had to be three-quarters, not just a majority, English, and certain specified goods were to be shipped only to England or other English colonies. The list of "enumerated" products initially included tobacco, cotton, indigo, ginger, and sugar. Rice, hemp, masts, copper ore, and furs, among other items, were added later. Not only did England (and its colonies) become the sole outlet for those "enumerated" colonial exports, but the Navigation Act of 1663 required that *all* colonial imports from Europe to America stop first in England, be offloaded, and have duty paid on them before their reshipment to the colonies. The Navigation Acts, also called the British Acts of Trade, gave England a monopoly over the tobacco and sugar produced in the Chesapeake and the West Indies. The acts also increased customs revenues collected in England, channeled all colonial commerce through English merchants (rather than Europeans), and enriched English shipbuilders. Over time these regulations meant that the commercial activities of the American colonies became ever more important to the strength of the British Empire—and its economy. The Navigation Acts also aroused resentment and resistance in the colonies.

ENFORCING THE NAVIGATION ACTS The Navigation Acts supplied a convenient rationale for a colonial trading system: to serve the economic needs of the mother country. Yet actual enforcement was spotty, and Americans found ingenious ways to avoid the regulations. In 1675, Charles II designated the Lords of Trade, a new government agency, to force the colonies to abide by the mercantile system and to seek out ways to make them more profitable to England and the Crown. The Lords of Trade named colonial governors, wrote or reviewed the governors' instructions, and handled all reports and correspondence dealing with colonial affairs.

During the 1670s, English collectors of customs duties appointed by the Crown appeared in all the colonies, and a surveyor general of customs in the American colonies was named. The most notorious of these, insofar as resentful colonists were concerned, was Edward Randolph, the first man to make a career in the colonial service and the nemesis of insubordinate colonials for a quarter century. Randolph arrived at Boston in 1676 and soon demanded that Massachusetts abide by the Navigation Acts. He set up shop

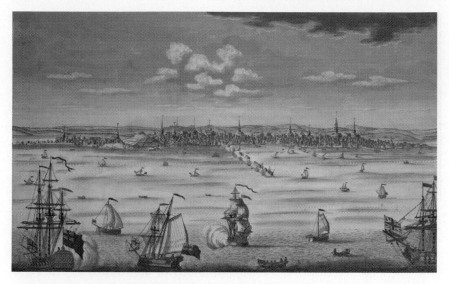

Boston from the southeast

This view of eighteenth-century Boston shows the importance of shipping and its regulation in the colonies, especially in Massachusetts Bay.

as the king's collector of customs in Boston, and within months his efforts to tighten control over commercial activity excited massive resentment. In 1678 a defiant Massachusetts legislature declared that the Navigation Acts had no legal standing in the colony. Eventually, in 1684, the Lords of Trade annulled the charter of Massachusetts. The Puritan utopia was fast becoming a lost cause.

THE DOMINION OF NEW ENGLAND In 1684, the government of Massachusetts Bay was placed in the hands of a special royal commission. Then, in 1685, Charles II died, to be succeeded by his brother the Duke of York, as James II, the first Catholic sovereign since the death of Queen Mary in 1558. James II asserted power more forcefully than his brother had. The new king readily approved a proposal to create a Dominion of New England that included all the colonies south through New Jersey.

The dominion was to have a government named by royal authority; a governor and council would rule without any assembly. The royal governor, Sir Edmund Andros, appeared in Boston in 1686 to establish his rule, which he soon extended over Connecticut and Rhode Island and, in 1688, over New York and East and West Jersey. Andros was a soldier, accustomed

King James II

English monarch from 1685 to 1688.

to taking—and giving—orders. While honest, efficient, and loyal to the Crown, he was often tactless in circumstances that called for the utmost diplomacy—the uprooting of long-established institutions in the face of popular hostility.

A rising resentment greeted Andros's measures, especially in Massachusetts. Taxation was now levied by the governor, without the consent of the General Court. Andros suppressed town governments, enforced the trade laws, and punished smugglers. Most ominous of all, Andros and his lieutenants took over a Puritan church in Boston for Anglican worship. Puritan leaders believed, with good reason, that he was conspiring to break their religious power and spiritual authority.

But the Dominion of New England was scarcely established before the Glorious Revolution of 1688 erupted in England. King James II, like Andros in New England, had aroused resentment by instituting arbitrary measures—and by openly parading his Catholic faith. Parliamentary leaders, their patience exhausted, invited Protestant Mary Stuart and her husband, the Dutch leader William III of Orange, to assume the throne as joint monarchs. James, seeing his support dwindling, fled to France.

THE GLORIOUS REVOLUTION IN AMERICA When news reached Boston that William, the new king, had landed in England, the city staged its own Glorious Revolution. Governor Andros and his councillors were arrested, and Massachusetts reverted to its former government. In rapid sequence the other colonies that had been absorbed into the dominion followed suit. All were permitted to revert to their former status except Massachusetts Bay and Plymouth, which after some delay were united under a new charter in 1691 as the royal colony of Massachusetts Bay.

The new British monarchs, William and Mary, made no effort to restore the Dominion of New England, but they brought more colonies under royal control through the appointment of governors in Massachusetts, New York, and Maryland. Maryland, however, reverted to proprietary status in 1715, after the fourth Lord Baltimore became Anglican. Pennsylvania had an even briefer career as a royal colony, from 1692 to 1694, before reverting to

William Penn's proprietorship. New Jersey became a royal province in 1702, South Carolina in 1719, North Carolina in 1729, and Georgia in 1752.

The Glorious Revolution had significant long-term effects on American history in that the Bill of Rights and the Act of Toleration, passed in England in 1689, influenced attitudes and the course of events in the colonies. Even more significant, the overthrow of James II set a precedent for revolution against the monarch. In defense of that action, the English philosopher John Locke published his *Two Treatises on Government* (1690), which had an enormous impact on political thought in the colonies. Locke's first treatise refuted theories of the "divine" right of kings to govern with absolute power. The more important second treatise set forth Locke's contract theory of government, which claimed that people are endowed with certain natural rights to life, liberty, and property. The need to protect those rights led people to establish governments. Rulers were obligated to protect the property and lives of their subjects. When they failed to do so, the people had the right—in extreme cases—to overthrow the monarch and change their government.

AN EMERGING COLONIAL SYSTEM The accession of William and Mary to the English throne led to a refinement of the existing Navigation Acts. In 1696 two developments created at last the semblance and, to some degree, the reality of a coherent administrative system for governing colonial trade. First, the Act to Prevent Frauds and Abuses of 1696 required colonial governors to enforce the trade laws, allowed customs officials to use "writs of assistance" (general search warrants that did not have to specify the place to be searched), and ordered that accused violators be tried in admiralty courts (because colonial juries habitually refused to convict their peers). Admiralty cases were decided by judges whom the royal governors appointed.

Second, also in 1696, William III created the Lords Commissioners of Trade and Plantations (the Board of Trade) to investigate the enforcement of the Navigation Acts and recommend ways to limit colonial manufactures and encourage the production of raw materials needed by the mother country. At the board's behest, Parliament began paying bounties to encourage the production of ship timber, masts, hemp, rice, indigo, and other strategic commodities.

SALUTARY NEGLECT From 1696 to 1725, the Board of Trade worked vigorously to subject the colonies to a more efficient royal control. After the death of Queen Anne, in 1714, however, its energies waned. The throne went in turn to the Hanoverian monarchs, George I (r. 1714–1727) and George II (r. 1727–1760), German princes who were next in the Protestant line of succession by virtue of descent from James I. Under these monarchs the cabinet emerged as the central agency of administration. Robert Walpole, as first minister (1721–1742), deliberately followed a policy regarding the colonies that the philosopher Edmund Burke later called "a wise and salutary neglect." Walpole's relaxed policy toward the colonies not only gave them greater freedom to pursue their economic interests; it unwittingly also enabled the Americans to pursue greater political independence.

The Habit of Self-Government

Government within the American colonies, like colonial policy, evolved without plan. In broad outline the governor, council, and assembly in each colony corresponded to the king, lords, and commons in England. At the outset all the colonies except Georgia had been founded by trading companies or feudal proprietors holding charters from the Crown, but eight colonies eventually relinquished or forfeited their charters and became royal provinces. In these the Crown named the governor. In Maryland, Pennsylvania, and Delaware the governor remained the choice of a proprietor, although each had an interim period of royal government. Connecticut and Rhode Island were the last of the corporate colonies; they elected their own governors to the end of the colonial period. In the corporate and proprietary colonies and in Massachusetts, the charter served as a rough equivalent to a written constitution. Over the years certain anomalies appeared as colonial governments diverged from that of England. On the one hand, the governors retained powers and prerogatives that the king had lost in the course of the seventeenth century. On the other hand, the assemblies acquired powers, particularly with respect to government appointments, that Parliament had yet to gain for itself.

POWERS OF THE GOVERNORS   The Crown never vetoed acts of Parliament after 1707, but the colonial royal governors, most of whom were mediocre or incompetent, still held an absolute veto over the assemblies, and the Crown could disallow (in effect, veto) colonial legislation. As chief executive the royal governor in each colony could appoint and remove officials, command the militia and naval forces, and grant pardons. In these respects his authority resembled the Crown's, for the king still exercised executive authority and had the power to name administrative officials. For the king those powers often strengthened an effective royal influence in Parliament, since the king could appoint members or their friends to lucrative offices.

The Boston State House

Built in 1713.

While the arrangement might seem a breeding ground for corruption or tyranny, it was often viewed in the eighteenth century as a stabilizing influence, especially by the king's friends. But it was an influence less and less available to the governors. On the one hand, colonial assemblies nibbled away at their power of appointment; on the other hand, the authorities in England more and more drew the control of colonial patronage into their own hands.

POWERS OF THE ASSEMBLIES   Unlike the governor and members of the council, who were appointed by an outside authority, either king or proprietor, the colonial assembly was elected. Whether called the House of Burgesses (Virginia), Delegates (Maryland), or Representatives (Massachusetts) or simply the assembly, the lower houses were chosen by popular vote in counties, towns, or, in South Carolina, parishes. The chief restriction on voting rights was a property qualification, based upon the notion that only men who held a "stake in society" could vote responsibly. Yet the property qualifications generally set low hurdles in the way of potential voters. Property holding was widespread, and a greater proportion of the population could vote in the colonies than anywhere else in the world of the eighteenth century.

Women, Indians, and African Americans were excluded from the political process—as a matter of course—and continued to be excluded for the most part into the twentieth century, but the qualifications excluded few free white adult males. Qualifications for membership in the assembly ran somewhat higher, and officeholders tended to come from the more well-to-do—a phenomenon not unknown today—but there were exceptions. One unsympathetic colonist observed in 1744 that the New Jersey Assembly "was chiefly composed of mechanicks and ignorant wretches; obstinate to the last degree."

By the early eighteenth century the colonial assemblies, like Parliament, held two important strands of power—and they were perfectly aware of the parallel. First, they controlled the budget by their right to vote on taxes and expenditures. Second, they held the power to initiate legislation. Assemblies, because they controlled finance, often won the right to name tax collectors and treasurers. Then they stretched the claim to cover public printers, Indian agents, supervisors of public works and services, and other officers of the government. Throughout the eighteenth century the assemblies expanded their power and influence, sometimes in conflict with the governors, sometimes in harmony with them, and often in the course of routine business passing laws and setting precedents, the collective significance of which neither they nor the imperial authorities fully recognized. Once established, however, these laws and practices became fixed principles, part of the "constitution" of the colonies. Self-government became first a habit, then a "right."

TROUBLED NEIGHBORS

SPANISH AMERICA IN DECLINE   By the start of the eighteenth century, the Spanish were ruling over a huge colonial empire spanning much of North America. Yet their settlements in the borderlands north of Mexico were a colossal failure when compared with the colonies of the other European powers. In 1821, when Mexico declared its independence from Spain and the Spanish withdrew from North America, the most populated Hispanic settlement, Santa Fe, had only 6,000 residents. The next largest, San Antonio and St. Augustine, had only 1,500 each.

The Spanish failed to create thriving colonies in the American Southwest for several reasons. Perhaps the most obvious was that the region lacked the gold and silver, as well as the large native populations, that attracted the

Spanish to Mexico and Peru. In addition, the Spanish were distracted by their need to control the perennial unrest in Mexico among the natives and the mestizos (people of mixed Indian and European ancestry). Moreover, those Spaniards who led the colonization effort in the borderlands were so preoccupied with military and religious exploitation that they failed to produce viable settlements with self-sustaining economies. They never understood that the main factor in creating a successful community was a thriving market economy. Instead, they concentrated on building Catholic missions and forts and looking—in vain—for gold. Whereas the French and the English based their Indian policies on trade (that included supplying Indians with firearms), Spain emphasized conversion to Catholicism, forbade manufacturing within its colonies, and strictly limited trade with the natives.

NEW FRANCE   Permanent French settlements in the New World differed considerably from both the Spanish and the English models. The French settlers were predominantly male but much smaller in number than the English and Spanish settlers. About 40,000 French colonists came to the New World during the seventeenth and eighteenth centuries. The relatively small French population proved to be an advantage in forcing the French to develop cooperative relationships with the Indians. Unlike the English settlers, the French established trading outposts rather than farms, mostly along the St. Lawrence River, on land not claimed by Indians. They thus did not have to confront initial hostility. In addition, the French served as effective mediators among rival Great Lakes tribes. This diplomatic role gave them much more local authority and influence than their English counterparts, who disdained such mediation.

The heavily outnumbered and disproportionately male French settlers sought to integrate themselves with Indian culture rather than eliminate it. Many French traders married Indians, exchanging languages and customs in the process of raising families. This more fraternal bond between the French and the Indians proved to be a source of strength in the wars with the English, enabling New France to survive until 1760 despite the lopsided disparity in numbers between the two colonial powers.

French exploration began when the enterprising Samuel de Champlain landed on the shores of the St. Lawrence River in 1603 and, two years later, at Port Royal, Acadia (later Nova Scotia). In 1608, a year after the English landed at Jamestown, Champlain led another expedition, during which he founded Quebec. While Acadia remained a remote outpost, New France expanded well beyond Quebec, from which Champlain pushed his explorations

Champlain in New France

Samuel de Champlain firing at a group of Iroquois, killing two chiefs (1609).

up the great river and into the Great Lakes as far as Lake Huron, and southward to the lake that still bears his name. There, in 1609, he joined a band of Huron and Algonquian allies in a fateful encounter. When an Iroquois war party attacked Champlain's group, the French explorer shot and killed two chiefs, and the Indians fled. The episode ignited in the Iroquois a hatred for the French that the English would capitalize on. The vengeful Iroquois stood as a buffer against French designs to move toward the English of the middle colonies and as a constant menace on the flank of the French waterways to the interior. For over a century, in fact, Native Americans determined the military balance of power within North America. In 1711 the governor general of New France declared that "the Iroquois are more to be feared than the English colonies."

Until his death, in 1635, Champlain governed New France under a trading company whose charter imposed a fatal weakness. The company won a profitable monopoly of the huge fur trade but had to limit the population to French Catholics. Neither the enterprising, seafaring Huguenots (Protestants) of coastal France nor foreigners of any faith were allowed to populate the country. The colony therefore remained a scattered patchwork of dependent peasants, Jesuit missionaries, priests, soldiers, officials, and *coureurs de bois* (literally, "runners of the woods"), who roamed the interior in quest of furs.

In 1663, King Louis XIV and his chief minister, Jean-Baptiste Colbert, changed New France into a royal colony and pursued a plan of consolidation and stabilization. Colbert dispatched new settlers, including shiploads of young women to lure disbanded soldiers and traders into settled matrimony. He sent out tools and animals for farmers and nets for fishermen and tried to make New France self-sufficient in foodstuffs. The population grew from about 4,000 in 1665 to about 15,000 in 1690.

THE JESUITS IN NEW FRANCE   The lucrative fur trade enticed the French to settle in Canada, but it was the activities of Catholic missionaries that gave New France its dynamism. Like Spain, France aggressively sought to convert the Indians to Catholicism, in part because Christian Indians would become more reliable trading partners and military allies. Jesuit missionaries led the way in New France. The Society of Jesus (the Jesuits) had been founded in 1539, when Ignatius of Loyola, a Spanish soldier and nobleman, and six companions, pledged to lead lives of poverty and chastity—and to defend the Roman Catholic Church. A year later the pope officially recognized the Jesuits as a new religious order and urged them to undertake

Jesuits in New France

Founded in 1539, the Jesuits sought to covert Indians to Catholicism, in part to make them more reliable trading and military partners.

missionary work among the "pagan people." The Jesuits became famous for their religious fervor, intellectual force, and personal courage. They served as the "shock troops" of the Catholic Counter-Reformation, fighting the spread of Protestantism and traversing the globe as earnest missionaries. Some 3,500 Jesuits served in New Spain and New France.

With remarkable tenacity and resilience, French Jesuits in distinctive black robes fanned out from Quebec, walking and canoeing hundreds of miles across the Great Lakes region and down the Mississippi River. Unlike their Spanish counterparts, they were rarely accompanied by soldiers. And unlike the Spanish Franciscans, who required Indian converts to move to missions, many Jesuits lived among the Indians. Jesuits and Indians borrowed from each other's practices and belief systems while never fully abandoning their own folkways. Many of the Indian converts, for example, tolerated the Jesuits but never fully embraced them and their teachings.

FRENCH LOUISIANA   From the Great Lakes, French explorers moved southward. In 1673, Louis Jolliet and Père Jacques Marquette, a Jesuit priest, ventured onto Lake Michigan, up the Fox River from Green Bay, then down the Wisconsin River to the Mississippi and on as far as the Arkansas River. Satisfied that the great Mississippi River flowed to the Gulf of Mexico, they turned back for fear of meeting with Spaniards. Nine years later René-Robert Cavelier, sieur de La Salle, went all the way to the Gulf of Mexico and named the country he explored Louisiana, after King Louis XIV of France.

Settlement of the Louisiana country finally began in 1699, when Pierre Le Moyne, sieur d'Iberville, established a colony near Biloxi, Mississippi. The main settlement then moved to Mobile Bay and, in 1710, to the present site of Mobile, Alabama. For nearly half a century the driving force in Louisiana was Jean-Baptiste Le Moyne, sieur de Bienville, a younger brother of Iberville. Bienville arrived with settlers in 1699, when he was only nineteen, and left the colony for the last time in 1743, when he was sixty-three. Sometimes called the Father of Louisiana, he served periodically as governor, and in 1718 he founded New Orleans, which shortly thereafter became the capital. Louisiana, first a royal colony, then a proprietary colony, and then a corporate colony, again became a royal province in 1731.

In contrast to the English colonies, French Louisiana grew haltingly in the first half of the eighteenth century. Its population in 1732 was only 2,000 whites and about 3,800 slaves. The sweltering climate and mosquito-infested environment enticed few settlers. Poorly administered, dependent upon imports for its sustenance, and expensive to defend, it continued throughout the century to be a financial liability to the French government.

HUDSON BAY

James Bay

HUDSON BAY COMPANY

Newfoundland

French/English

St. Lawrence River

Cape Breton Island

Louisbourg

NEW

Quebec

ACADIA

French/English

FRANCE

Port Royal

Lake Superior

Fort Michilimackinac

Lake Huron

Montreal

Lake Champlain

Wisconsin R.

Green Bay

Lake Michigan

Lake Ontario

Connecticut River

Albany

Lake Erie

Boston

Plymouth

Fox River

Illinois River

Hudson River

New York

Philadelphia

ATLANTIC OCEAN

Missouri River

Vincennes

Ohio River

Cahokia

St. Louis

Kaskaskia

Jamestown

L O U I S I A N A

French/English

A P P A L A C H I A N

Arkansas River

Tennessee River

Charleston

Savannah

Spanish/English

Mobile

Biloxi

St. Augustine

New Orleans

FLORIDA (Spanish)

GULF OF MEXICO

0   500 Miles

0   500 Kilometers

THE FRENCH IN NORTH AMERICA

English possessions

French possessions

Spanish possessions

Disputed territory

Marquette and Jolliet's route, 1673

La Salle's route, 1682

Where were the largest French settlements in North America? How were they different from the Spanish and English colonies? Describe the French colonization of Louisiana.

"France in America had two heads," the historian Francis Parkman wrote, "one amid the snows of Canada, the other amid the canebrakes of Louisiana." The French thus had one enormous advantage: access to the great inland water routes that led to the heartland of the continent. In the Illinois region scattered settlers began farming the fertile soil, and courageous Catholic priests established missions at places such as Terre Haute (High Land) and Des Moines (Some Monks). Because of geography as well as deliberate policy, however, French America remained largely a vast wilderness traversed by a mobile population of traders, trappers, missionaries—and, mainly, Native Americans. In 1750, when the English colonials numbered about 1.5 million, the total French population was no more than 80,000.

Yet in some ways the French had the edge on the British. They offered European goods to Indians in return for furs and encroached far less upon Indian lands. They thereby won Indian allies against the English who came to possess the land. French governors could mobilize for action without any worry about quarreling colonial assemblies or ethnic and religious diversity. The British may have had the greater population, but their separate colonies often worked at cross purposes.

THE COLONIAL WARS

For most of the seventeenth century, the French and British Empires in America developed in relative isolation from each other, and for most of that century the homelands remained at peace with each other. After the Restoration of 1660, Charles II and then James II pursued a policy of friendship with the French king, Louis XIV. The Glorious Revolution of 1688, however, worked an abrupt reversal in English diplomacy. William III, the new king, as leader of the Calvinist Dutch republic, had engaged in a running conflict with the ambitions of Catholic Louis XIV. William's ascent to the throne brought England almost immediately into a Grand Alliance against Louis in the War of the League of Augsburg, known in the American colonies simply as King William's War (1689–1697).

This was the first of four great European and intercolonial wars that would be fought over the next seventy-four years, the others being the War of the Spanish Succession (called Queen Anne's War in the colonies, 1702–1713), the War of the Austrian Succession (called King George's War in the colonies, 1744–1748), and the Seven Years' War (the French and Indian War, which lasted nine years in America, from 1754 to 1763). In all except the last, the battles in America were but a sideshow accompanying greater battles in Europe, where British policy pivoted on keeping a balance of power with the French. The alliances shifted from one fight to the next, but Britain and France were pitted against each other every time.

Thus for much of the eighteenth century, the colonies were embroiled in global wars and rumors of war. The effect on much of the population was devastating. New England, especially Massachusetts, suffered more than the rest, for it was closest to the battlefields of French Canada. It is estimated that 900 Boston men (about 2.5 percent of the men eligible for service) died in the fighting. This meant that the city was faced with assisting a large population of widows and orphans. Even more important, these pro-

From La Roque's *Encyclopédie des Voyages*

An Iroquois warrior in an eighteenth-century French engraving.

longed conflicts had profound consequences for Britain that later would reshape the contours of its relationship with America. The wars with France led the English government to incur an enormous debt, establish a huge navy and a standing army, and excite a militant sense of nationalism. During the early eighteenth century the changes in British financial policy and political culture led critics in Parliament to charge that traditional liberties were being usurped by a tyrannical central government. After the French and Indian War, American colonists began making the same point.

THE FRENCH AND INDIAN WAR   Of the four major wars involving the European powers and their New World colonies, the climactic conflict between Britain and France in North America was the French and Indian War. It began after enterprising Virginians during the early 1750s had crossed the Allegheny Mountains into the Ohio River valley in order to trade with Indians and survey some 200,000 acres granted them by the king. The incursion by the Virginians infuriated the French, and they established forts in what is now western Pennsylvania to defend their interests. When news of these developments reached Williamsburg, the Virginia governor sent out an emissary to warn off the French. An ambitious twenty-one-year-old Virginia militia officer, Major George Washington, whose older brothers owned part of the Ohio Company, a business venture to develop settlements and trade in fertile western Pennsylvania, volunteered for the mission. With a few companions, Washington made his way by horseback and canoe to Fort Le Boeuf in late 1753 and returned with a polite but firm French refusal to budge. The Virginia governor then sent a small force to erect a fort at the strategic fork where the Allegheny and Monongahela Rivers meet to form the great Ohio. No sooner had the English started building than a larger French force appeared and ousted them.

Meanwhile, the earnest young Washington, hungry for combat and yearning for military glory, had been organizing a regiment of Virginians. In the spring of 1754, the tall, muscular surveyor-turned-soldier led his 150 volunteers and Iroquois allies west across the Alleghenies. Their mission was to build a fort at the convergence of the Allegheny, Monongahela, and Ohio Rivers (where the city of Pittsburgh later developed). Along the way, Washington learned that French soldiers had beaten them to the strategic site and erected Fort Duquesne, named for the French governor of Canada. Washington decided to make camp about forty miles from the fort and await reinforcements. The next day the Virginians ambushed a French detachment. Ten French soldiers were killed, including the commander, one escaped, and twenty-one were captured. The Indians then tomahawked and scalped several of the wounded soldiers as a stunned Major Washington looked on. The brave but inexperienced Washington was unaware that the French had been on a peaceful mission to discuss the disputed fort. The mutilated soldiers were the first fatalities in what would become the French and Indian War.

Washington and his troops retreated and hastily constructed a crude stockade at Great Meadows, dubbed Fort Necessity, which a large force of vengeful French soldiers attacked a month later, on July 3, 1754. After a day-long battle, George Washington surrendered, having seen all his horses and cattle killed and a third of his 300 men killed or wounded. The French permitted his surviving troops to withdraw after taking their weapons. Washington's blundering expedition triggered a series of events that would ignite a protracted world war. As a prominent British politician exclaimed, "the volley fired by a young Virginian in the backwoods of America set the world on fire."

Back in London, government officials already had taken notice of the growing conflict in the backwoods of North America and had called com-

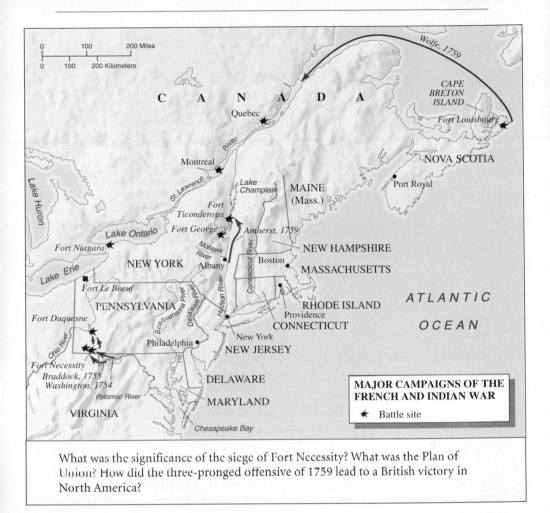

What was the significance of the siege of Fort Necessity? What was the Plan of Union? How did the three-pronged offensive of 1759 lead to a British victory in North America?

missioners from all the colonies as far south as Maryland to a meeting in Albany, New York, to confer on precautions. The Albany Congress (June 19–July 10, 1754), which was meeting when the first shots sounded at Great Meadows, ended with little accomplished. The delegates conferred with Iroquois chieftains and sent them away loaded with gifts in return for some halfhearted promises of support. The congress is remembered mainly for the Plan of Union, worked out by a committee led by Benjamin Franklin and adopted by a unanimous vote of the commissioners. The plan called for a chief executive, a kind of supreme governor, to be called the president general of the United Colonies, appointed and supported by the Crown, and a supreme assembly, called the Grand Council, with forty-eight members

The first American political cartoon

Benjamin Franklin's exhortation to the colonies to unite against the French in 1754 would become popular again twenty years later, when the colonies faced a different threat.

chosen by the colonial assemblies. This federal body would oversee matters of defense, Indian relations, and trade and settlement in the West and would levy taxes to support its programs.

It must have been a good plan, Franklin reasoned, since the assemblies thought it gave too much power to the Crown and the Crown thought it gave too much to the colonies. At any rate the assemblies either rejected or ignored it. Only two substantive results came out of the congress at Albany. Its idea of a supreme commander of British forces in America was adopted, as was its advice that a New Yorker who was a friend of the Iroquois be made British superintendent of the northern Indians.

In London the government decided to force a showdown in America. In 1755 a British fleet captured Nova Scotia and expelled most of its French population. Some 5,000 to 7,000 Acadians who refused to take an oath of allegiance to the British Crown were scattered through the colonies, from Maine to Georgia. Impoverished and homeless, many of them found their way to French Louisiana, where they became the Cajuns (a corruption of *Acadians*), whose descendants still preserve elements of the French language along the remote bayous and in many urban centers.

The colonial backwoods, however, became the scene of one British disaster after another over the next three years. In 1755 a new British commander in chief, General Edward Braddock, arrived in Virginia with two regiments of army regulars. Braddock was a seasoned, confident officer, but neither he nor his red-clad British troops had any experience fighting in the wilderness. Braddock viewed Indians with contempt, and his cocksure ignorance would prove fatal.

With the addition of some colonial troops, including a still-headstrong George Washington as a volunteer staff officer, Braddock hacked a 125-mile road through the mountain wilderness from the upper Potomac River in Maryland to the vicinity of Fort Duquesne. Hauling heavy artillery to surround the French fort, along with a lumbering wagon train of supplies, Braddock's force achieved a great feat of military logistics and was on the verge of success when, six miles from Fort Duquesne, the surrounding woods suddenly came alive with Ojibwa and French soldiers in Indian costume. Beset on three sides by concealed enemies, the British troops panicked and retreated in disarray, abandoning most of their artillery and supplies. Brave but naive General Braddock had several horses shot out from under him before he was mortally wounded. George Washington, his own coat riddled by bullets, helped other officers contain the rout and lead a hasty retreat. More than 900 British and Virginia soldiers were killed or wounded in one of the worst British defeats of the eighteenth century. Braddock died four days later. The overconfident general's last words were prophetic: "We shall know better how to deal with them another time." Twelve of the surviving British soldiers left behind on the battlefield were stripped, bound, and burned at the stake by Indians. A devastated George Washington wrote his brother that the British army had "been scandalously beaten by a trifling body of men." The vaunted redcoats "broke & run as sheep before Hounds," but the Virginians "behaved like Men and died like Soldiers." The French victory demonstrated that backwoods warfare depended upon Indian allies and frontier tactics for success.

A WORLD WAR   For two years, war raged along the American frontier without becoming a cause of war in Europe. In 1756, however, the colonial war became the Seven Years' War in Europe. In the final alignment of European powers, France, Austria, Russia, Saxony, Sweden, and Spain fought against Britain, Prussia, and Hanover. The onset of world war brought into office a new British government, with the eloquent William Pitt as head of the ministry. Pitt's ability and assurance ("I know that I can save England and no one else can") instilled confidence at home and abroad.

A brilliant visionary and a superb administrator, charismatic and supremely self-confident, Pitt decided that America should be the primary theater of conflict with France, and he sought to bludgeon the French with overwhelming force on land and at sea. He eventually mobilized some 45,000 troops in North America, half of whom were British regulars and the other half American colonists. Pitt was able to garner such substantial colonial participation by reversing Britain's administrative policies. His predecessors had demanded that the colonial legislatures help fund the defense effort. Pitt decided to treat the colonies as allies rather than subordinate possessions, offering them subsidies for their participation in the war effort. The colonists readily embraced this invitation to become partners in an imperial crusade, and they contributed key resources and large numbers of men to the war effort.

Pitt's America-first policy had long-term consequences. The massive frontier war with the French and their Indian allies fostered a sense of nationalism among the colonists that would culminate in a war for independence from Britain. Pitt used the powerful British navy to cut off French reinforcements and supplies to the New World—and the goods with which they bought Indian allies. Pitt improved the British forces, gave command to younger men of ability, and carried the battle to the enemy. In 1758 the tides began to turn when the English captured Fort Louisbourg in Canada. The Iroquois, sensing the turn of fortunes, pressed their dependents, the Delawares, to call off the frontier attacks on English settlements.

In 1759 the French and Indian War reached its climax with a series of resounding British victories on land and at sea. Pitt ordered a three-pronged offensive against the French in Canada, along what had become the classic invasion routes: the Niagara River, Lake Champlain, and the St. Lawrence River. On the Niagara expedition the British were joined by a group of Iroquois, and they captured Fort Niagara, virtually cutting the French lifeline to the interior. On Lake Champlain, General Jeffrey Amherst took Forts George and Ticonderoga, then paused to await reinforcements for an advance northward.

Meanwhile, the most decisive battle was shaping up at Quebec, the gateway to Canada. There, British forces led by General James Wolfe waited out the advance of General Louis-Joseph de Montcalm and his French infantry until they were within close range, then loosed volleys that devastated the French ranks—and ended French power in North America for all time. News of the British victory reached London along with similar reports from India, where English forces had reduced French outposts one by one and established the base for expanded British control of India.

The war in North America dragged on until 1763, but the rest was a process of mopping up. In the South, where little significant action had occurred, belated fighting flared up between the settlers and the Cherokee Nation. A force of British regulars and colonial militia broke Cherokee resistance in 1761.

In 1760, King George II died, and the twenty-two-year-old grandson he despised ascended the throne as George III. The new king resolved to seek peace and forced William Pitt out of office. Pitt had wanted to declare war on Spain before the French could bring that other Bourbon monarchy into the conflict. He was forestalled, but Spain belatedly entered the war, in 1761, and during the next year met the same fate as the French: in 1762 British forces took Manila in the Philippines and Havana in Cuba. By 1763 the French and the Spanish were ready to negotiate a surrender. Britain ruled the world.

THE PEACE OF PARIS   The Treaty of Paris of 1763 brought an end to the world war and to French power in North America. Victorious Britain took all French North American possessions east of the Mississippi River (except New Orleans) and all of Spanish Florida. The English invited the Spanish settlers to remain and practice their Catholic religion, but few accepted the offer. The Spanish king ordered them to evacuate the colony and provided free transportation to Spanish possessions in the Caribbean. Within a year most of the Spaniards had sold their property at bargain prices to English speculators and begun an exodus to Cuba and Mexico.

End of the War

With Quebec in the background, France kneels before a victorious Britain (1763).

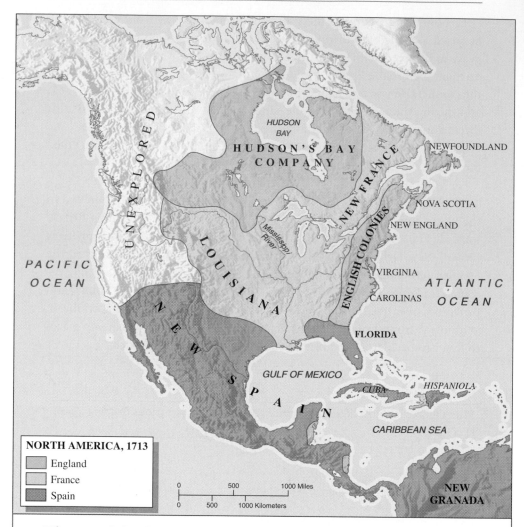

NORTH AMERICA, 1713

- England
- France
- Spain

0   500   1000 Miles
0   500   1000 Kilometers

What events led to the first clashes between the French and the British in the late seventeenth century? Why did New England suffer more than other regions of North America during the wars of the eighteenth century? What were the long-term financial, military, and political consequences of the wars between France and Britain?

When the Indian tribes that had been allied with the French learned of the 1763 peace settlement, they were despondent. Their lands were being given over to the British without consultation. The Shawnees, for instance, demanded to know "by what right the French could pretend" to transfer Indian territory to the British. The Indians also worried that the victorious British

NORTH AMERICA, 1763
England
Spain
— Proclamation line of 1763

0   500   1000 Miles
0   500   1000 Kilometers

How did the map of North America change between 1713 and 1763? How did Spain win Louisiana? What were the consequences of the British winning all the land east of the Mississippi?

had "grown too powerful & seemed as if they would be too strong for God it-self." The Indians had hoped that the departure of the French from the Ohio River valley would mean that the area would revert to their control. Instead, the British cut off the trade and gift-giving practices that had bound the Indi-ans to the French. British forces also moved into the French frontier forts. In a desperate effort to recover their autonomy, tribes struck back in the spring of 1763, capturing most of the British forts around the Great Lakes and in the

Ohio River valley. They also raided colonial settlements in Pennsylvania, Maryland, and Virginia, destroying hundreds of homesteads and killing several thousand people. In the midst of the Indian attack on Fort Pitt (formerly Fort Duquesne), English troops distributed smallpox-infested blankets and handkerchiefs from the fort's hospital to the Indians besieging the garrison. Such efforts at germ warfare were intended to "extirpate this Execrable race" of Indians.

Called Pontiac's Rebellion because of the prominent role played by the Ottawa chief, the far-flung Indian attacks on the frontier forts convinced most American colonists that all Indians must be removed. The British government, meanwhile, negotiated an agreement with the Indians that allowed redcoats to reoccupy the frontier forts in exchange for a renewal of trade and gift giving. Still, as Pontiac stressed, the Indians asserted their independence and denied the legitimacy of the British claim to their territory under the terms of the Treaty of Paris. He told a British official that the "French never conquered us, neither did they purchase a foot of our Country, nor have they a right to give it to you." The British may have won a global empire as a result of the Seven Years' War, but their grip on the American colonies grew ever weaker.

In compensation for the loss of Florida, Spain received Louisiana (New Orleans and all French land west of the Mississippi River) from France. Unlike the Spanish in Florida, however, few of the French settlers left Louisiana after 1763. The French government encouraged them to work with their new Spanish governors to create a bulwark against further English expansion. Spain would hold title to Louisiana for nearly four decades but would never succeed in erasing the territory's French roots. The French-born settlers always outnumbered the Spanish. The loss of Louisiana left France with no territory on the continent of North America. France also gave up several islands in the West Indies. British power reigned supreme over North America east of the Mississippi River.

But a fatal irony would pursue the British victory. In gaining Canada, the British government put in motion a train of events that would end twenty years later with the loss of the rest of British North America. Britain's success against France threatened the Indian tribes of the interior because they had long depended upon playing off one European power against the other. Now, with the British dominant on the continent, American settlers were emboldened to encroach even more upon Indian land. In addition, victory on the battlefields encouraged the British to tighten their imperial control over the American colonists and demand more financial contributions to pay for military defense. Meanwhile, a humiliated France thirsted for revenge. In London, Benjamin Franklin, agent for the colony of Pennsylvania (1764–1775), found the French minister inordinately curious about America and suspected him of wanting to ignite the coals of controversy. Less than three years after Franklin left London and only fifteen years after the conquest of New France, he would be in Paris arranging an alliance on behalf of Britain's rebellious colonists.

CHAPTER SUMMARY

- **Mercantilism** Lords Commissioners of Trade and Plantations administered the economy of the British Empire. The Navigation Acts decreed that enumerated goods had to go directly to England and discouraged manufacturing in the colonies. Raw materials were shipped to the mother country to be processed into manufactured goods. These mercantilist laws were designed to curb direct trade with other countries, such as the Netherlands, and keep the wealth of the empire in British hands.

- **"Salutary Neglect"** Lax administration by the mother country allowed the colonies a measure of self-government. The dynastic problems of the Stuart kings aided the New England colonists in their efforts to undermine the Dominion of New England. The Glorious Revolution of 1688 resulted in a period of "salutary neglect." The American colonies pursued their interests with minimal intervention from the British government, which was preoccupied with European wars.

- **The French in North America** The British and the French peacefully co-existed in North America until the formation of the Louisiana Territory in 1682. Even though the French were more interested in trade than settlement, and in converting natives to Christianity, the British feared their further expansion. During the European wars of the period, New France and the British colonies engaged in armed conflict, with allied Indians fighting on both sides.

- **The French and Indian War** Four wars took place in America between 1689 and 1763 as the British and French confronted each other throughout the world. The Seven Years' War (1754–1763), known as the French and Indian War in the American colonies, was the first world war and was eventually won by the British. A plan to unify all of Britain's American colonies, including those in Canada, proposed by Benjamin Franklin at the Albany Congress, failed to gain colonial support.

- **The Effects of the Seven Years' War** At the Peace of Paris in 1763, France lost all its North American possessions. Britain gained Canada and Florida, while Spain acquired Louisiana. With the war's end, Native Americans were no longer regarded as essential allies and so had no recourse when settlers squatted on their lands. The Treaty of Paris set the stage for conflict between the mother country and the American colonies as Britain tightened control to pay for the colonies' defense.

CHRONOLOGY

1608	Samuel de Champlain founds Quebec
1673	Jolliet and Marquette explore the Mississippi from Canada to the Gulf of Mexico
1684	Dominion of New England is established
1688	Glorious Revolution
1718	New Orleans is founded
1754	Washington is defeated at Fort Necessity
1754	Albany Congress adopts Plan of Union
1754–1763	French and Indian War
1759	Quebec falls to the British
1763	Peace of Paris
1763	Pontiac's Rebellion

KEY TERMS & NAMES

mercantile system p. 163

"enumerated" goods
p. 164

Navigation Acts p. 164

Glorious Revolution
p. 166

Lords Commissioners of
Trade and Plantations (the
Board of Trade) p. 167

salutary neglect p. 167

New France p. 171

Jesuits p. 173

French and Indian War
p. 177

Fort Necessity p. 178

Pontiac's Rebellion p. 186

5

FROM EMPIRE
TO INDEPENDENCE

FOCUS QUESTIONS ⓢ wwnorton.com/studyspace

- How and why did British colonial policy change after 1763?
- How did Whig ideology shape the colonial response to the new British policy?
- What were the main events that led to a break with the mother country?
- Who were the main proponents of revolution; and how did they justify their position?
- How did the individual colonies finally unite to embrace the idea of independence; and how was the goal of independence achieved?

Seldom if ever had England thrilled with such pride as it did during the 1760s. In 1760 young King George III, headstrong and obstinate, had ascended the throne. Three years later the Treaty of Paris declared England the victor in the Seven Years' War, ending fifty years of European fighting, and confirmed a vast new British Empire spanning the globe. Most important, the Treaty of Paris effectively ended the French imperial domain in North America. This in turn influenced the development of the vast region between the Appalachian Mountains and the Mississippi River, from the Gulf of Mexico to Hudson Bay in Canada. After 1763 the maturing American colonies experienced dynamic agricultural and commercial growth, enormously increasing their importance to the British economy. Yet the colonies remained both extraordinarily diverse in composition and peculiarly averse to cooperative efforts. That they would manage to unify themselves and declare independence in 1775 was indeed surprising—even to them.

THE HERITAGE OF WAR

The triumph in what England called the Great War saw Americans celebrating as joyously as Londoners in 1763. Colonists relished their partnership in fostering British liberty, a supportive Parliament, an ancient and revered constitution, and a prosperity fueled by wartime spending. Most Americans, as Benjamin Franklin explained, "submitted willingly to the government of the Crown." He himself proudly proclaimed, "I am a BRITON." But victory celebrations masked festering resentments and new problems spawned by the war. Underneath the pride in the British Empire, an American nationalism was maturing. Colonials were beginning to think and speak of themselves more as Americans than as English or British. With the French out of the way and vast new western lands to exploit, they looked to the future with confidence.

Many Americans had a new sense of importance after fighting a major war with such success. At least a third of military-age New England men had fought in the Seven Years' War. For them army life was both a revelation and an opportunity. Although they admired the courage and discipline of British redcoats under fire, many New Englanders abhorred the carefree cursing, whoring, and Sabbath breaking they observed among the British troops. But most upsetting were the daily "shrieks and cries" resulting from the brutal punishments imposed by British officers on their wayward men. One American soldier recorded in his diary in 1759 that "there was a man whipped to death belonging to the Light Infantry. They say he had twenty-five lashes after he was dead." The brutalities of British army life thus heightened the New Englanders' sense of their separate identity and of their greater worthiness to be God's chosen people. It also emboldened Americans to defy British rule, because the colonists no longer needed military protection from the French.

British forces nevertheless had borne the brunt of the war and had won it for the American colonists, some of whom persisted in trading with the enemy. Molasses in the French West Indies, for instance, continued to draw New England ships like flies. The profitable trade was too important for the colonists to give up but was more than British authorities could tolerate. Along with naval patrols, one important means of disrupting this illegal trade with the French was the use of search warrants that allowed British officers to enter any place during daylight hours to seek evidence of illegal trade.

The peace that secured a global empire in 1763 also laid upon the British government new burdens. How should the British manage the defense and governance of their new global possessions? What should they do about the North American lands inhabited by Indians but coveted by colonists? As an

Ojibwa chief told a British trader, "Although you have conquered the French, you have not yet conquered us." How was the British government to pay both for an unprecedented debt built up during the war and the new expenses of expanded colonial administration and defense? And—the thorniest problem of all, as it turned out—what role should the colonies play in all this? The problems were of a magnitude and a complexity to challenge men of the greatest statesmanship and vision, but those qualities were rare among George III and his advisers.

BRITISH POLITICS

In the English government during the late eighteenth century, nearly every politician called himself a Whig, as did the king. *Whig* was the name given to those who had opposed King James II, led the Glorious Revolution of 1688, and secured the Protestant Hanoverian succession in 1714. The Whigs were the champions of individual liberty and parliamentary supremacy, but with the passage of time Whiggism had drifted into complacency. King George III, a tall, thin, young man with bulging eyes and an obstinate disposition, sought at first to eliminate the Whig influence on the monarchy and establish his own inner circle of obedient advisers, known as the king's friends. They exercised influence by controlling appointments to government offices; they retained their influential positions only by ensuring that they did not contradict the cocksure king.

George III

At age thirty-three, the young king of a victorious empire.

Throughout the 1760s, King George III turned first to one and then to another mediocre prime minister, and the government grew more unstable just as the new problems of world empire required creative solutions. Ministries rose and fell usually because somebody offended the king or somebody's friend failed to get a government post. Colonial policy remained marginal to the chief concerns of British politics. The result was inconsistency and vacillation followed by stubborn inflexibility—and revolution.

WESTERN LANDS

No sooner was peace formally arranged in 1763 than the problem of America's western boundaries overlapping with Indian lands erupted in the form of Pontiac's Rebellion. To keep the peace on the frontier and to keep earlier promises to the Delawares and Shawnees, officials in London postponed further colonial settlement along the frontier. The king also issued the Royal Proclamation of 1763, which drew an imaginary line along the crest of the Appalachians, beyond which white settlers were forbidden to go. It also established the new British colonies of Quebec and East and West Florida. Yet the proclamation line was utterly ineffective. Hardy settlers defied the prohibitions and pushed across the Appalachian ridges onto Indian lands.

GRENVILLE AND THE STAMP ACT

GRENVILLE'S COLONIAL POLICY   Just as the Royal Proclamation of 1763 was being drafted, a new British ministry had begun to grapple with the complex problems of imperial finances. The new chief minister, George Grenville, was much like the king: industrious, honest, and hardheaded. He was a strong-willed accountant whose humorless self-assurance verged on pomposity. George III came to despise him, but the inexperienced king needed the dogged Grenville because they agreed on basic policies: cutting government expenses, reducing the national debt, and generating more revenue from the colonies to pay for their defense. As a colleague said of Grenville, he had "a rage for regulation and restriction."

In developing new policies regulating the American colonies, Grenville took for granted the need to defend the Western frontier. But the sharply rising costs for stationing British troops in America came on top of an already staggering government debt. During the mid-1760s the interest payments on the government's debts consumed 60 percent of Britain's annual budget. Because there was a large tax burden at home and a much lighter one in the colonies, Grenville reasoned that the prosperous Americans should share the cost of their own defense. He also resented the large number of American smugglers who defied British trade regulations. So Grenville issued stern orders to colonial officials to tighten customs enforcement and ordered the British navy to capture smugglers. He also set up a new maritime, or vice-admiralty, court in the Canadian port of Halifax (replacing the ineffectual admiralty courts established in 1696), granting it jurisdiction over all the colonies and ensuring that there would be no juries of colonists sympathetic

The Great Financier, or British Economy for the Years 1763, 1764, 1765

This cartoon, critical of Grenville's tax policies, shows America as an Indian (fourth from the left) groaning under the burden of new taxes.

to smugglers. Under Grenville the period of "salutary neglect" in the enforcement of the Navigation Acts was coming to an end, causing American shippers (and smugglers) great annoyance.

Strict enforcement of the Molasses Act of 1733 posed a serious threat to New England's prosperity. Making rum from molasses was quite profitable. Grenville recognized that the long-neglected molasses tax, if enforced, would devastate a major colonial enterprise. So he put through the Revenue Act of 1764, commonly known as the Sugar Act, which cut the duty on molasses in half. This, he believed, would reduce the temptation to smuggle or to bribe customs officers. In addition, the Sugar Act levied new duties on imports of foreign textiles, wine, coffee, indigo, and sugar. The revenues generated by the Sugar Act, Grenville estimated, would help defray "the necessary expenses of defending, protecting, and securing, the said colonies and plantations." For the first time, Parliament had adopted duties (taxes on imports or exports) designed to raise revenues in the colonies and not merely intended to regulate trade.

Another of Grenville's regulatory measures had an important impact on the colonies: the Currency Act of 1764. The colonies faced a chronic shortage of "hard" money, which kept flowing overseas to pay debts in England. To meet the shortage, they issued their own paper money. British creditors feared payment in such a depreciated currency, however. To alleviate their fears, Grenville prohibited the colonies from printing money. This caused the value of existing paper money to plummet, since nobody was obligated to accept it in payment of debts, even in the colonies. The deflationary impact of the Currency Act, combined with new duties on commodities and stricter enforcement, jolted a colonial economy already suffering a postwar decline.

THE STAMP ACT   George Grenville excelled at doing the wrong thing— repeatedly. The Sugar Act, for example, did not produce additional revenue. Its administrative costs were four times greater than the revenue it generated. Yet he compounded the problem by pushing through still another provocative measure to raise money in America: a stamp tax. On February 13, 1765, Parliament passed the Stamp Act, which created revenue stamps and required that they be purchased and affixed to printed matter and legal documents of all kinds: newspapers, pamphlets, broadsides, almanacs, bonds, leases, deeds, licenses, insurance policies, ship clearances, college diplomas, even playing cards. The requirement was to go into effect on November 1.

That same year, Grenville completed his new system of colonial regulations when he persuaded Parliament to pass the Quartering Act. In effect it was yet another tax. The Quartering Act required the colonies to supply British troops with provisions and provide them with barracks or house them in inns and vacant buildings. It applied to all colonies but affected mainly New York, headquarters of the British forces.

THE IDEOLOGICAL RESPONSE   The cumulative effect of Grenville's measures outraged Americans. Unwittingly this plodding minister of a plodding king stirred up a storm of protest and set in motion a profound exploration of colonial rights and imperial relations. The radical ideas of the minority "Real Whigs" in the English Parliament slowly began to take hold in the colonies. These ideas derived from various sources but above all from John Locke's justification of the Glorious Revolution in his *Two Treatises on Government*. Locke and other Real Whigs viewed English history as a struggle by Parliament to preserve life, liberty, and property against royal tyranny. The Real Whigs harbored an almost paranoid fear of monarchical power. They were convinced that the "King's men" were conspiring against traditional English rights and liberties.

In 1764 and 1765, American colonists adopted the rhetoric of the Real Whigs to express their outrage over new imperial policies. They decided that Grenville and Parliament had loosed upon them the very engines of tyranny from which Parliament had rescued England in the seventeenth century. A standing army was the historic ally of despots, yet now with the French defeated and Canada under English control, thousands of British soldiers remained in the colonies. For what purpose—to protect the colonists or to subdue them? It was beginning to seem clear that it was the latter. Other factors heightened colonial anxiety. Among the fundamental rights of English people were trial by jury and the presumption of innocence, but the new vice-admiralty court in Halifax excluded juries and put the burden of proof on the defendant. Most important, English citizens had the right to be taxed only by their elected representatives. Now, however, Parliament was usurping the colonial assemblies' power of the purse strings. This could lead only to tyranny and enslavement, critics argued. Sir Francis Bernard, the royal governor of Massachusetts, correctly predicted that the new stamp tax "would cause a great Alarm & meet much Opposition" in the colonies. Indeed, the seed of American independence was planted by the heated debates over the stamp tax.

PROTEST IN THE COLONIES   In a flood of colonial pamphlets, speeches, and resolutions, critics of the Stamp Act repeated a slogan familiar to all Americans: "no taxation without representation." The Stamp Act became the chief target of colonial outrage at British arrogance. Unlike the Sugar Act, which affected mainly New England, the Stamp Act burdened all colonists who did any kind of business. And it affected most of all the articulate elements in the community: merchants, planters, lawyers, printer-editors—all strategically placed to influence public opinion. Through the spring and summer of 1765, colonial resentment boiled over at meetings, parades, bonfires, and other demonstrations. The militants, calling themselves Sons of Liberty, met underneath "liberty trees"—in Boston a great elm, in Charleston a live oak.

One day in mid-August 1765, nearly three months before the Stamp Act was to take effect, an effigy of Boston's stamp agent swung from the city's liberty tree. In the evening a mob carried it through the streets, destroyed the stamp office, and used the wood to burn the effigy. Somewhat later another mob sacked the homes of Lieutenant Governor Thomas Hutchinson and the local customs officer. Thoroughly shaken, the Boston stamp agent resigned, and stamp agents throughout the colonies were hounded out of office. Loyalists, those colonists supportive of British policies, deplored the riotous violence, arguing that the American rebels were behaving more tyrannically than the British.

By November 1, its effective date, the Stamp Act was a dead letter. Business went on without the stamps. Newspapers appeared with a skull and

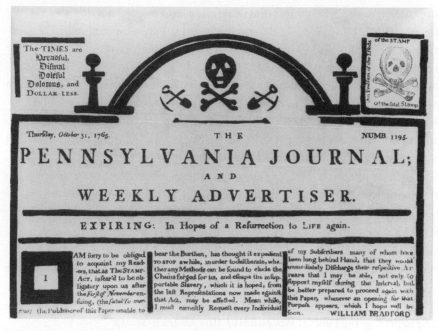

Opposition to the Stamp Act

In protest of the Stamp Act, which was to take effect the next day, *The Pennsylvania Journal* printed a skull and crossbones on its masthead.

crossbones where the stamp belonged. After passage of the Sugar Act, a movement had begun to boycott British goods rather than pay the import duties. Now colonists signed nonimportation agreements, promising not to buy British goods. The purpose was to exert pressure on British merchants. By refusing to buy British goods, Americans exercised real leverage.

The widespread protests involved courageous women as well as men, and the boycotts of British goods encouraged colonial unity as Americans discovered that they had more in common with each other than with London. The Virginia House of Burgesses struck the first blow against the Stamp Act with the Virginia Resolves, a series of resolutions inspired by the fiery young Patrick Henry. Virginians, the burgesses declared, were entitled to the rights of Englishmen, and Englishmen could be taxed only by their own elected representatives. Virginians, moreover, had always been governed by laws passed with their own consent. Newspapers spread the Virginia Resolves throughout the colonies, and other assemblies hastened to copy Virginia's example.

In 1765 the Massachusetts House of Representatives invited the other colonial assemblies to send delegates to confer in New York about their opposition to the Stamp Act. Nine responded, and from October 7 to 25, 1765, the Stamp Act Congress, with twenty-seven delegates, formulated a Declaration of the Rights and Grievances of the Colonies, a petition to the king for relief, and a petition to Parliament for repeal of the Stamp Act. The delegates acknowledged that the colonies owed a "due subordination" to Parliament and recognized its right to regulate colonial trade, but they questioned Parliament's right to levy taxes, which were a free gift granted by the people through their representatives. "The boldness of the minister [Grenville] amazes our people," wrote a New Yorker. "This single stroke has lost Great Britain the affection of all of her Colonies." Grenville responded by denouncing the colonists as "ungrateful."

REPEAL OF THE STAMP ACT   The storm had scarcely broken before Grenville's ministry was out of office, dismissed not because of the colonial turmoil but because Grenville had fallen out with the king over the

The Repeal, or the Funeral Procession of Miss America-Stamp

This 1766 cartoon shows Grenville carrying the dead Stamp Act in its coffin. In the background, trade with America starts up again.

appointment of government officials. The king installed a new first minister, the Marquis of Rockingham, Charles Watson-Wentworth, leader of the "Rockingham Whigs," the "Old Whig" faction, which included Britons who sympathized with the colonies. Pressure from British merchants who feared the economic consequences of the colonial nonimportation movement bolstered Rockingham's resolve to repeal the act. When Parliament assembled early in 1766, Parliamentary leader William Pitt demanded that the Stamp Act be repealed "absolutely, totally, and immediately" but urged that Britain's authority over the colonies "be asserted in as strong terms as possible," except on the point of taxation.

In 1766, Parliament repealed the Stamp Tax but at the same time passed the Declaratory Act, which asserted the full power of Parliament to make laws binding the colonies "in all cases whatsoever." It was a cunning evasion that made no concession with regard to taxes but made no mention of them either. For the moment, however, the Declaratory Act was a face-saving gesture. News of the repeal of the Stamp Act set off excited demonstrations throughout the colonies. In mid-May 1766, Boston church bells signaled the news of Parliament's favorable vote. Grateful New Yorkers commissioned statues to honor George III and William Pitt. Amid the rejoicing and relief on both sides of the Atlantic, few expected that the quarrel between Britain and its American colonies would be reopened within a year. To be sure, the Sugar Act remained on the books, but Lord Rockingham reduced the molasses tax from threepence a gallon to a penny.

FANNING THE FLAMES

Meanwhile, the king continued to play musical chairs with his prime ministers. Rockingham soon lost the confidence of the king and resigned. William Pitt then formed a ministry that included the major factions of Parliament. The ill-matched combination would have been hard to manage even if Pitt had remained in charge, but the old warlord began to slip over the fine line between genius and madness. For a time in 1767, the guiding force in the ministry was the witty and reckless Charles Townshend, chancellor of the exchequer (treasury), whose "abilities were superior to those of all men," according to Horace Walpole, "and his judgement below that of any man." Like George Grenville before him, Townshend held the "factious and turbulent" Americans in contempt and resolved to force their obedience. The erratic Townshend took advantage of Pitt's mental confusion to reopen the question of colonial taxation.

THE TOWNSHEND ACTS In 1767, Townshend put his ill-fated revenue plan through the House of Commons, and a few months later he died, at age forty-two, leaving behind a bitter legacy: the Townshend Acts. With this legislation, Townshend had sought first to bring New York's colonial assembly to its senses. That body had defied the Quartering Act and refused to provide beds or supplies for British troops. Parliament, at Townshend's behest, had suspended all acts of New York's assembly until it would yield. New York protested but finally caved in, inadvertently confirming the British suspicion that too much indulgence had encouraged colonial bad manners. Townshend had followed up with the Revenue Act of 1767, which levied duties on colonial imports of glass, lead, paint, paper, and tea. Third, he had set up a Board of Customs Commissioners at Boston, the colonial hotbed of smuggling. Finally, he had reorganized the vice-admiralty courts, providing four in the continental colonies: at Halifax, Boston, Philadelphia, and Charleston.

The Townshend duties increased government revenues, but the intangible costs were greater. The duties taxed goods exported from England, indirectly hurting British manufacturers, and had to be collected in colonial ports, increasing collection costs. But the highest cost was added conflict with the colonists. The Revenue Act of 1767 posed a more severe threat to colonial assemblies than Grenville's taxes had, for Townshend proposed to use these revenues to pay colonial governors and other officers and thereby release them from financial dependence upon the colonial assemblies.

DICKINSON'S "LETTERS" The Townshend Acts surprised the colonists, but this time the storm gathered more slowly than it had two years before. Once again citizens, including a growing number of women, who called themselves Daughters of Liberty, resolved to resist. They boycotted British goods, made their own clothes, and developed their own manufactures. Once again the colonial press spewed out expressions of protest, most notably the essays of John Dickinson. The son of a Maryland planter, Dickinson was a prosperous Philadelphia lawyer who hoped to resolve the latest dispute by persuasion. Late in 1767 his twelve "Letters from a Farmer in Pennsylvania" (as he chose to style himself) began to appear in the *Pennsylvania Chronicle*, from which they were copied by other newspapers and publishers of pamphlets. His argument repeated in greater detail and more elegance what the Stamp Act Congress had already said. The colonists held that Parliament might regulate commerce and collect duties incidental to that purpose, but it had no right to levy taxes for *revenue*. Dickinson used moderate language. "The cause of Liberty is a cause of too much dignity to be sullied by turbulence and tumult," he argued. "Anger produces anger," he warned. The colonial complaints should "speak at the same time the language of affliction and veneration" so as to avoid "an incurable rage."

SAMUEL ADAMS AND THE SONS OF LIBERTY   But the outraged affliction grew, and veneration of the mother country waned. British officials could neither conciliate moderates like Dickinson nor cope with firebrands like Samuel Adams of Boston, who was emerging as the supreme genius of revolutionary agitation. Born in 1722, Adams graduated from Harvard and soon thereafter inherited the family brewery, which he quickly ran into bankruptcy. Politics, not profit, was his abiding passion, and he spent most of his time debating political issues with sailors, roustabouts, and stevedores at local taverns. Adams insisted that Parliament had no right to legislate at all for the colonies. Massachusetts, he declared, must return to the spirit of its Puritan founders and defend itself from a new conspiracy against its liberties.

Adams became a tireless agitator, whipping up the Sons of Liberty and organizing protests at the Boston town meeting and in the provincial assembly. Early in 1768 he and the Boston attorney James Otis formulated a letter, which the Massachusetts assembly dispatched to the other colonies. The letter's tone was polite and logical: it restated the illegality of taxation without colonial representation in Parliament and invited the support of other colonies. In London the Earl of Hillsborough, just appointed to the new office of secretary of state for the colonies, only made matters worse. He ordered the Massachusetts assembly to withdraw the Adams-Otis letter. The assembly refused and was dissolved by royal decree.

In 1769 the Virginia assembly reasserted its exclusive right to tax Virginians, rather than Parliament, and called upon the colonies to unite in the cause. Virginia's royal governor promptly dissolved the assembly, but the

Samuel Adams

Adams was the fiery organizer of the Sons of Liberty.

members met independently, dubbed themselves a convention after Boston's example, and adopted a new set of nonimportation agreements.

In London the turbulent events across the Atlantic still aroused only marginal interest. The king's long effort to reorder British politics to his liking was coming to fulfillment, and that was the big news. In 1769 new elections for Parliament finally produced a majority of the "king's friends." And George III found a new chief minister to his taste in Frederick, Lord North. In 1770 the king installed a cabinet of the "king's friends," with Lord North as first minister. Lord North, who venerated the traditions of Parliament, was no stooge for the king, but the two worked in harmony.

THE BOSTON MASSACRE By 1770 the nonimportation agreements in the American colonies were strangling British trade and causing unemployment in England. The impact of colonial boycotts had persuaded Lord North to modify the Townshend Acts—just in time to halt a perilous escalation of tensions. The presence of British soldiers in Boston had been a constant provocation. Crowds heckled and ridiculed the red-coated soldiers, many of whom earned the abuse by harassing and intimidating colonists.

On March 5, 1770, in the square outside the Boston customhouse, a group of rowdies began taunting and hurling icicles at the British sentry. His call for help brought reinforcements. Then somebody rang the town fire bell, drawing a larger crowd to the scene. At their head, or so the story goes, was Crispus Attucks, a runaway mulatto slave. Attucks and others continued to bait the British troops. Finally a soldier was knocked down, rose to his feet, and fired into the crowd. When the smoke cleared, five people lay dead or dying, and eight more were wounded. The cause of colonial resistance now had its first martyrs, and the first to die was Attucks. Those involved in the "massacre" were indicted for murder, but they were defended by John Adams, Sam's cousin, who thought they were the victims of circumstance, provoked, he said, by a "motley rabble of saucy boys, negroes and mulattoes, Irish teagues and outlandish Jack tars." All of the British soldiers were acquitted except two, who were convicted of manslaughter and branded on their thumbs.

The so-called Boston Massacre sent shock waves through the colonies—and to London. Late in April 1770, Parliament repealed all the Townshend duties save one. The cabinet, by a fateful vote of 5–4, had advised keeping the tea tax as a token of parliamentary authority. Rebellious colonists insisted that pressure should be kept on British merchants until Parliament gave in

The Bloody Massacre

Paul Revere's partisan engraving of the Boston Massacre.

altogether, but the nonimportation movement soon faded. Parliament, after all, had given up the substance of the taxes, with one exception, and much of the colonists' tea was smuggled in from Holland anyway.

For two years thereafter, colonial discontent remained at a simmer. The Stamp Act was gone, as were all the Townshend duties except that on tea. But most of the Grenville-Townshend innovations remained in effect: the Sugar Act, the Currency Act, the Quartering Act, the vice-admiralty courts. The redcoats had left Boston, but they remained nearby, and the British navy still patrolled the coast. Each remained a source of irritation and the cause of occasional incidents. There was still tinder awaiting a spark, and the most incendiary colonists were eager to provide it. As Sam Adams stressed, "Where there is a spark of patriotick fire, we will enkindle it."

DISCONTENT ON THE FRONTIER

Many colonists had no interest in the disputes over British regulatory policy raging along the seaboard. Parts of the backcountry stirred with quarrels that had nothing to do with the Stamp and Townshend Acts. Rival claims to lands east of Lake Champlain pitted New York against New Hampshire. Eventually the residents of the disputed area would form their own state of Vermont, created in 1777 although not recognized as a member of the Union until 1791. In Pennsylvania sporadic quarrels broke out among land claimants who held grants from Virginia and Connecticut, whose boundaries under their charters overlapped those granted to William Penn, or so they believed.

A more dangerous division in Pennsylvania had arisen in 1763 when a group of frontier ruffians took the law into their own hands. Outraged at the unwillingness of Quakers in the Pennsylvania assembly to suppress marauding Indians, a group called the Paxton Boys, from Paxton, near Harrisburg, took revenge by massacring peaceful Susquehannock Indians in Lancaster County; then they threatened the so-called Moravian Indians, a group of Christian

Paxton Boys

A depiction of the Paxton Boys preparing to attack the Susquehannock Indians.

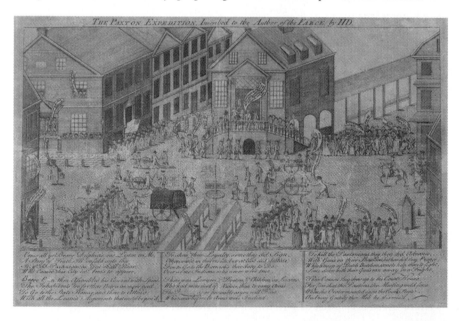

converts near Bethlehem. When the Indians took refuge in Philadelphia, some 1,500 angry Paxton Boys marched on the capital, where Benjamin Franklin persuaded the vengeful frontiersmen to return home by arranging for them to first present their demands to the governor and the assembly.

Farther south, frontier folk of South Carolina also had complaints about the lack of colonial protection—from horse thieves, cattle rustlers, and Indians. Backcountry residents organized societies, called Regulators, to administer vigilante justice in the region and refused to pay taxes until they gained effective government. In 1769 the assembly finally set up six circuit courts in the region but without responding to the backcountry's demand for representation in the legislative assemblies.

In North Carolina the protest was less over the lack of government than over the abuses and extortion by appointees from the eastern part of the colony. Farmers felt especially oppressed by the government's refusal either to issue paper money or to accept produce in payment of taxes, and in 1766 they organized to resist. Efforts of these Regulators to stop seizures of property and other court proceedings led to more disorders and the enactment of a bill that made the rioters guilty of treason. In the spring of 1771, Governor William Tryon led 1,200 militiamen into the Piedmont center of Regulator activity. There his forces defeated some 2,000 ill-organized Regulators in the Battle of Alamance, in which eight were killed on each side. Tryon's men then ranged through the backcountry, forcing some 6,500 Piedmont settlers to sign an oath of allegiance to the king.

These disputes and revolts within the colonies illustrate the fractious diversity of opinion and outlook evident among Americans on the eve of the Revolution. Colonists were of many minds about many things, including British rule. The disputatious frontier in colonial America also helped convince British authorities that the colonies were inherently unstable and required firmer oversight, including the use of military force to ensure civil stability.

A WORSENING CRISIS

Two events in 1772 further eroded the colonies' fragile relationship with the mother country. Near Providence, Rhode Island, the *Gaspee*, a British schooner patrolling for smugglers, accidentally ran aground, and its hungry crew proceeded to comandeer local sheep, hogs, and poultry. An angry crowd from the town boarded the ship, removed the crew, and set fire to the vessel. A commission of inquiry was formed with authority to hold suspects, but no witnesses could be found. Three days after the burning, on June 13, 1772, Governor Thomas Hutchinson told the Massachusetts assembly that his salary thenceforth would come out of customs revenues. Then word came that judges of the Massachusetts Superior Court would be paid from the same source and would no longer be dependent upon the assembly for their income. The assembly feared that this portended "a despotic administration of government."

The existence of the *Gaspee* investigative commission, which bypassed the courts of Rhode Island, and the independent salaries for royal officials in Massachusetts suggested to the residents of other colonies that similar events might be in store for them. The discussion of colonial rights and parliamentary encroachments regained momentum. Ever the agitator, Sam Adams convinced the Boston town meeting to form the Committee of Correspondence, which issued a statement of rights and grievances and invited other towns to do the same. Similar Committees of Correspondence sprang up across Massachusetts and in other colonies. In 1773 the Virginia assembly proposed the formation of such committees on an intercolonial basis, and a network of them spread across the colonies, mobilizing public opinion and keeping colonial resentments at a simmer. In unwitting tribute to their effectiveness, a Massachusetts Loyalist called the committees "the foulest, subtlest, and most venomous serpent ever issued from the egg of sedition."

THE BOSTON TEA PARTY   Lord North soon provided the colonists with the occasion to bring resentment from a simmer to a boil. In 1773 he undertook to help some friends bail out the English East India Company, which had in its warehouses in Britain some 17 million pounds of tea. Under the Tea Act of 1773, the government would allow the grossly mismanaged company to send its south Asian tea directly to America without paying any duties. British tea merchants could thereby undercut their colonial competitors, most of whom were smugglers who bought tea from the Dutch. At the same time, Lord North ordered British authorities in New England to clamp down on American smuggling.

The Committees of Correspondence, backed by colonial merchants, alerted colonists to the new danger. The British government, they said, was trying to purchase colonial acquiescence with cheap tea. Before the end of the year, large shipments of tea had gone out to major colonial ports. In Boston several thousand irate colonists decided that their passion for liberty outweighed their love for tea. On December 16, 1773, a group of sixteen men, disguised as Mohawk Indians, boarded three ships and threw the 342 chests of East India Company tea overboard—cheered on by a crowd

The Able Doctor, or America Swallowing the Bitter Draught

This 1774 engraving shows Lord North, the Boston Port Act in his pocket, pouring tea down America's throat and America spitting it back.

along the shore. Like those who had burned the *Gaspee*, they remained parties unknown—except to hundreds of Bostonians. John Adams relished the vigilante action. The destruction of the disputed tea, he said, was "so bold, so daring, so firm, intrepid and inflexible" that it would have "important consequences."

Yet given a more tactful response from London, the Boston Tea Party might easily have undermined the radicals' credibility. Many Americans, especially merchants, recoiled at the wanton destruction of property. Benjamin Franklin, then serving as an American agent in London trying to improve relations with Britain, declared that the destruction of the tea was a violent injustice. He urged his native city of Boston to reimburse the shipowners for their ruined cargo. Sam Adams dismissed Franklin's reservations. "Franklin may be a good philosopher," Adams said, "but he is a bungling politician."

The Boston Tea Party had pushed British officials to the breaking point. They were now convinced that the very existence of the empire was at stake. The rebels in Boston had instigated what could become a widespread effort to evade royal authority and imperial regulations. A firm response was required. "The colonists must either submit or triumph," a furious George III wrote to Lord North, and North strove to make an example of Boston. In the end, however, he helped make a revolution.

THE COERCIVE ACTS   In 1774, Parliament enacted four harsh measures designed by Lord North to discipline Boston. The Boston Port Act closed the harbor from June 1, 1774, until the city had paid for the lost tea. An Act for the Impartial Administration of Justice let the governor transfer to England the trial of any official accused of committing an offense in the line of duty—no more redcoats would be tried on technicalities. A new Quartering Act directed local authorities to provide lodging for British soldiers, in private homes if necessary. Finally, the Massachusetts Government Act made all of the colony's council and law-enforcement officers appointive rather than elective, declared that sheriffs would select jurors, and stipulated that no town meeting could be held without the governor's consent. In May, General Thomas Gage replaced Hutchinson as governor and assumed command of the 4,000 British soldiers in Boston. Massachusetts now had a military governor.

These Coercive Acts were designed to isolate Boston and make an example of the colony. Instead, they galvanized resistance across the colonies. At last, it seemed to many Americans, their worst fears were being confirmed. If these "Intolerable Acts," as the colonists labeled the Coercive Acts, were not resisted, they would eventually be applied to the other colonies.

Further confirmation of British "tyranny" came with news of the Quebec Act, passed in June of 1774. That act provided that the government in Canada would not have a representative assembly and would instead be led by an appointed royal governor and council. It also gave a privileged position to the Catholic Church. The measure seemed merely another indicator of British authoritarianism. In addition, colonists pointed out that they had lost many lives in an effort to liberate the trans-Appalachian West from the control of French Catholics. Now the British seemed to be

The State Blacksmiths Forging Fetters for the Americans

A British cartoon attacking Parliament's anti-colonial measures of 1775 and 1776.

protecting papists at the expense of their own colonists. What was more, the act placed within the boundaries of Quebec the western lands north of the Ohio River, lands that Virginia and Connecticut claimed.

Meanwhile, colonists rallied to the cause of besieged Boston, raising money, sending provisions, and boycotting, as well as burning, tea. In Williamsburg, when the Virginia assembly met in May, a young member of the Committee of Correspondence, Thomas Jefferson, proposed to set aside June 1, the effective date of the Boston Port Act, as a day of fasting and prayer in Virginia. The royal governor immediately dissolved the assembly, whose members then retired to the Raleigh Tavern and resolved to form a Continental Congress to represent all the colonies. Similar calls were coming from Providence, New York, Philadelphia, and elsewhere, and in June the Massachusetts assembly suggested a meeting in Philadelphia in September. Shortly before George Washington left to represent Virginia at the gathering, he wrote to a friend, "The crisis is arrived when we must assert our rights." Otherwise, he warned, British tyranny "shall make us as tame and abject slaves, as the blacks we rule over with such arbitrary sway."

George Washington's reference to slavery revealed the ugly contradiction in the inflamed rhetoric about American liberties. The colonial leaders who demanded their freedom from British tyranny were quite unwilling to give freedom to slaves. In 1774 in Boston, Phillis Wheatley, an enslaved African-born woman of about twenty-one years of age who had become an accomplished poet, highlighted the hypocrisy of slave-owning patriots when she wrote in a newspaper essay that "the Cry for Liberty" did not extend to her and other slaves. The Revolution would be fought for whites only.

THE CONTINENTAL CONGRESS On September 5, 1774, the First Continental Congress assembled in Philadelphia. It endorsed the Suffolk Resolves, which declared the Coercive, or Intolerable, Acts null and void, urged Massachusetts to arm for defense, and called for economic sanctions against British commerce. The Congress then adopted a Declaration of American Rights, which proclaimed once again the rights of Americans as English citizens, denied Parliament's authority with respect to internal colonial affairs, and proclaimed the right of each colonial assembly to determine the need for British troops within its own province.

Finally, the Continental Congress adopted the Continental Association of 1774, which recommended that every county, town, and city form committees to enforce a boycott of all British goods. These elected committees became the organizational and communications network for the Revolutionary movement, connecting every locality to the leadership and enforcing public behavior. The Continental Association also advocated the nonimportation of British goods (implemented in 1774) and the nonexportation of American goods to Britain (to be implemented in 1775 if colonial grievances were not addressed).

Seven thousand men across the colonies served on the committees of the Continental Association. The committees often required colonists to sign an oath to join the boycotts against British goods. Those who refused to sign were ostracized and intimidated; some were tarred and feathered. The nonimportation movement of the 1760s and 1770s provided women with a significant public role. The Daughters of Liberty resolved to quit buying imported British apparel and make their own clothing ("homespun").

Such efforts to gain economic self-sufficiency helped bind the diverse colonies by ropes of resistance. In this sense the emerging colonial desire for greater political independence involved concrete economic objectives. Gaining economic independence from Britain required not only decreasing imports but also increasing American production of goods heretofore imported from England.

Thousands of ordinary men and women participated in the boycott of British goods, and their sacrifices on behalf of colonial liberties provided the momentum leading to revolution. It was common folk who enforced the boycott, volunteered in local militia units, attended town meetings, and increasingly exerted pressure on royal officials in the colonies. In 1774 more than 4,600 militiamen from Massachusetts lined the streets of Worcester and forced royal officials, hats in hands, to walk a gauntlet while recanting their support for imperial policies. The "Founding Fathers" could not have led the Revolutionary movement without such widespread popular support. As the people of Pittsfield, Massachusetts, declared in a petition, "We have always believed that the people are the fountain of power."

In London the king fumed. He wrote his prime minister that the "New England colonies are in a state of rebellion," and "blows must decide whether they are to be subject to this country or independent." British critics of the American actions reminded the colonists that Parliament had absolute sovereignty. Power could not be shared with the colonies. King George III and Parliament insisted that there would be no negotiation with the rebellious colonies; force was the only option. Yet amid all the furious rhetoric, many colonial rebels still balked at the idea of armed conflict with Britain. In a December 1774 letter, Mercy Otis Warren, sister of James Otis and the colonies' first female playwright, observed that "America stands armed with resolution and virtue; but she still recoils at the idea of drawing the sword against the nation from whence she derived her origin. Yet Britain, like an unnatural parent, is ready to plunge her dagger into the bosom of her affectionate offspring."

In early 1775, Parliament declared Massachusetts in rebellion and prohibited the New England colonies from trading with any nation outside the empire. Lord North's Conciliatory Resolution, adopted on February 27, 1775, was as far as the British would go. Under its terms, Parliament would refrain from using any measures but taxes to regulate trade and would grant to each colony the duties collected within its boundaries, provided the colonies would contribute voluntarily to a quota for defense of the empire. It was a formula, said one English skeptic, not for peace but for new quarrels. In Virginia in March 1775, the colony's leaders met to discuss what had occurred at the Continental Congress in Philadelphia. While most of the participants believed that Britain would relent in the face of united colonial resistance, Patrick Henry was convinced that war was imminent. He urged that the militia begin preparing for combat. Henry claimed that the colonies "have done everything that could be done to avert the storm which is now coming on. We have petitioned; we have remonstrated; we have supplicated; we have prostrated ourselves before the throne," yet such efforts had been met only by "violence and insult." By this point, Henry had whipped himself into a fury. Freedom, he shouted, could be bought only with blood. While staring at his reluctant comrades, he refused to predict what they might do for the cause of liberty. "But as for me," he declared through clenched teeth, "give me liberty"— he paused dramatically, clenched his fist as if it held a dagger, then plunged it as if into his heart— "or give me death."

Shifting Authority

As Patrick Henry had predicted, events during 1775 moved beyond conciliation toward conflict. The king and Parliament had lost control of their colonies; they could neither persuade nor

Patrick Henry

Henry famously declared "Give me Liberty, or give me Death!"

coerce them to accept new regulations and revenue measures. Colonial resistance had become open rebellion. All through late 1774 and early 1775 the defenders of American rights were seizing the initiative. The Continental Congress urged each colony to mobilize its militia units. Royal and proprietary officials were losing control as provincial congresses assumed authority and colonial militias organized, raided military stores, and gathered arms and gunpowder. But British military officials remained smugly confident that the colonists would be inept revolutionaries. Major John Pitcairn wrote home from Boston in 1775, "I am satisfied that one active campaign, a smart action, and burning two or three of their towns, will set everything to rights."

LEXINGTON AND CONCORD   Major Pitcairn soon had his chance to suppress the rebellion. On April 14, 1775, the British military commander and new royal governor of Massachusetts, General Thomas Gage, received secret orders to stop the "open rebellion" in Massachusetts. He decided to arrest rebel leaders and seize the militia's supply depot at Concord, about twenty miles northwest of Boston. On the night of April 18, 700 redcoats gathered on Boston Common and set out by way of Lexington. When local Patriots got wind of the plan, Boston's Committee of Safety sent Paul Revere and William Dawes by separate routes on their famous ride to spread the alarm. Revere reached Lexington about midnight and alerted Hancock and Adams,

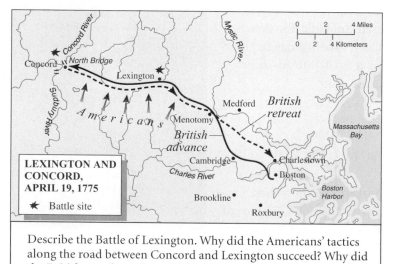

LEXINGTON AND CONCORD, APRIL 19, 1775

✳ Battle site

Describe the Battle of Lexington. Why did the Americans' tactics along the road between Concord and Lexington succeed? Why did the British march on Concord in the first place?

The Battle of Lexington

Amos Doolittle's impression of the Battle of Lexington as combat begins.

who were hiding there. Joined by Dawes and Samuel Prescott, Revere rode on toward Concord. A British patrol intercepted the trio, but Prescott slipped through and delivered the warning.

At dawn on April 19, the British advance guard of 238 redcoats found Captain John Parker and about seventy "Minutemen"—mostly dairy farmers and artisans—lined up on the Lexington green. Parker apparently intended only a silent protest, but Major Pitcairn rode onto the green, swung his sword, and yelled, "Disperse, you damned rebels! You dogs, run!" The Americans had already begun quietly backing away when someone fired a shot, whereupon the British soldiers loosed a volley into the Minutemen, then charged them with bayonets, leaving eight dead and ten wounded.

The British officers hastily brought their men under control and led them to Concord. There the Americans had already carried off most of their munitions, but the British destroyed what they could. At Concord's North Bridge the growing American militia inflicted fourteen casualties on a British platoon, and by about noon the British had begun marching back to Boston. By then, however, the narrow road back to Boston had turned into a gauntlet of death as rebels from "every Middlesex village and farm" sniped from behind stone walls, trees, barns, houses—all the way to the Charlestown Peninsula. Among the Americans were Captain Parker and the reassembled Lexington militia. By nightfall the redcoat survivors were safe under the protection of the fleet and army at Boston, having suffered three times as many casualties as the Americans. A British general reported to London that the Americans had earned his respect: "Whoever looks upon them as an irregular mob will find himself much mistaken." During the fighting along the road leading to Lexington from Concord, a British soldier was searching a house for rebel snipers when he ran into James Hayward of the Acton militia. The redcoat pointed his musket at the American and said, "You're a dead man." Hayward raised his weapon and answered, "So are you." They fired simultaneously.

THE SPREADING CONFLICT   The Revolutionary War had begun. When the Second Continental Congress convened at Philadelphia on May 10, 1775, British-held Boston was under siege by Massachusetts militia units. On the very day that Congress met, Fort Ticonderoga, in northern New York near the Canadian border, fell to a force of "Green Mountain Boys" under the hotheaded Ethan Allen of Vermont and Massachusetts volunteers under Benedict Arnold of Connecticut. Two days later the colonial force took Crown Point, north of Ticonderoga.

The Continental Congress, with no legal authority and no resources, met amid reports of spreading warfare. On June 15 it named George Washington commander in chief of a Continental army. Washington accepted on the condition that he receive no pay. The Congress fastened on Washington because his service in the French and Indian War had made him one of the most experienced officers in America. That he was from influential Virginia, the wealthiest and most populous province, added to his attractiveness. And as many people commented then and later, Washington looked like a leader. He was tall and strong, a superb horseman, and a fearless fighter. As a Philadelphian explained, Washington "had so much martial dignity in his deportment that you would distinguish him as a general and a soldier from among ten thousand people."

On June 17, the very day that Washington was commissioned, the colonials and the British forces engaged in their first major fight, the Battle of Bunker Hill. While the Continental Congress deliberated, American and British forces in and around Boston had increased. Militiamen from Rhode Island, Connecticut, and New Hampshire joined in the siege, as did several freed slaves. British reinforcements included three major generals: William Howe, Sir Henry Clinton, and John Burgoyne. On the day before the battle, American forces fortified the high ground overlooking Boston. Breed's Hill was the battle location, nearer to Boston than Bunker Hill, the site first chosen (and the source of the battle's erroneous name).

View of the Attack on Bunker Hill

The Battle of Bunker Hill and the burning of Charlestown Peninsula.

The rebels were spoiling for a fight. As Joseph Warren, a dapper Boston physician, put it, "The British say we won't fight; by heavens, I hope I shall die up to my knees in blood!" He soon got his wish. With civilians looking on from rooftops and church steeples, the British attacked in the blistering heat, with 2,400 troops moving in tight formation through tall grass. The Americans, pounded by naval guns, watched from behind their earthworks as the waves of British troops in their beautiful but impractical uniforms advanced up the hill. The militiamen waited until the attackers had come within fifteen to twenty paces, then loosed a shattering volley. The Americans cheered as they watched the greatest soldiers in the world retreating in panic.

The British re-formed their lines and attacked again. Another sheet of flames and lead greeted them, and the vaunted redcoats retreated a second time. Still, the proud British generals, led by William Howe, were determined not to let the ragtag rustics humiliate them. On the third attempt, when the colonials began to run out of gunpowder and were forced to throw stones, a bayonet charge ousted them. The British took the high ground, but at the cost of 1,054 casualties. American losses were about 400. Every one of General Howe's aides had been killed or wounded. "A dear bought victory," recorded General Clinton, "another such would have ruined us."

The Battle of Bunker Hill had two profound effects. First, the high number of British casualties made the English generals more cautious in subsequent encounters with the Continental army. Second, the Continental Congress recommended that all able-bodied men enlist in a militia. This tended to divide the male population into Patriot and Loyalist camps. A middle ground was no longer tenable.

In early March 1776, American forces occupied Dorchester Heights, to the south of Boston, and the city threatened with cannons and mortars. General Howe retreated by water to Halifax, Canada. The last British forces, along with fearful American Loyalists, embarked on March 17, 1776. By that time the British forces were facing not the suppression of a rebellion but the re-conquest of a continent.

While American forces held Boston under siege, the Continental Congress pursued the dimming hope of a compromise settlement. On July 6 and 8, 1775, the delegates issued two major documents: an appeal to the king known as the Olive Branch Petition and a Declaration of the Causes and Necessity of Taking Up Arms. The Olive Branch Petition, written by Pennsylvanian John Dickinson, professed continued loyalty to George III and begged the king to refrain further hostilities pending a reconciliation. The declaration, also largely Dickinson's work, traced the history of the controversy, denounced the British for the unprovoked assault at Lexington, and rejected independence but affirmed the colonists' purpose to fight for their rights rather than submit to slavery. When the Olive Branch Petition reached London, George III refused even to look at it. On August 22 he declared the American colonists "open and avowed enemies." The next day he issued a proclamation of rebellion.

Before the end of July 1775, the Congress had authorized an ill-fated attack on British troops in the walled city of Quebec, in the vain hope of rallying support from the French inhabitants of Canada. One force, under Richard Montgomery, advanced toward Quebec by way of Lake Champlain; another, under Benedict Arnold, struggled through the Maine woods. The American units arrived outside Quebec in September, exhausted and hungry. Then they were ambushed by a silent killer: smallpox. "The small pox [is] very much among us," wrote one soldier. As the deadly virus raced through the American camp, General Montgomery faced a brutal dilemma. Most of his soldiers had signed up for short tours of duty, many of which were scheduled to expire at the end of the year. He could not afford to wait until spring for the epidemic to subside. Seeing little choice but to fight, Montgomery ordered a desperate attack on the British forces at Quebec during a blizzard, on December 31, 1775. The assault was a disaster. Montgomery was killed early in the battle. Over 400 Americans were taken prisoner. The rest of the Patriot force retreated to its camp outside the walled city and appealed to the Continental Congress for reinforcements.

By May 1776 there were only 1,900 American soldiers left outside Quebec, and 900 of them were infected with smallpox. Sensing the weakness of the American force, the British attacked and sent the ragtag Patriots on a frantic retreat up the St. Lawrence River to the American-held city of Montreal and eventually back to New York and New England. The sick were left behind, but the smallpox virus traveled with the fleeing soldiers.

Quebec was the first military setback for the Revolutionaries. It would not be the last. And smallpox would continue to bedevil the American war effort. The veterans of the failed Canadian campaign brought home both smallpox and demoralizing stories about the disease, spreading the epidemic to civilians and making the recruitment of new soldiers more difficult. Men who might risk British gunfire balked at the more terrifying thought of contracting smallpox in a military camp.

In the South, Virginia's royal governor raised a Loyalist force, including slaves recruited with the promise of freedom, but met defeat in December 1775. In North Carolina, Loyalist Highland Scots, joined by some former Regulators, lost a battle with a Patriot force at Moores Creek Bridge. The Loyalists had set out for Wilmington to join a British expeditionary force under Lord Charles Cornwallis and Sir Henry Clinton. That plan frustrated, the British commanders decided to attack Charleston instead. The Patriot militia there had partially finished a palmetto-log fort on Sullivans Island (later named in honor of its commander, Colonel William Moultrie), and when the British fleet attacked, on June 28, 1776, the spongy palmetto logs absorbed the naval fire, and Fort Moultrie's cannon returned it with devastating effect. The fleet, with over 200 casualties and every ship damaged, was forced to retire. South Carolina would honor the palmetto tree by putting it on its state flag.

As the fighting spread north into Canada and south into Virginia and the Carolinas, the Continental Congress appointed commissioners to negotiate treaties of peace with Indian tribes, organized a Post Office Department with Benjamin Franklin as postmaster general, and authorized the formation of a navy and a marine corps.

The delegates continued to hold back from declaring independence. Yet through late 1775 and early 1776, word came of one British action after another that proclaimed rebellion and war. In December 1775 a Prohibitory Act declared the colonies closed to all British commerce. The king and cabinet also recruited mercenaries (hired foreign soldiers) in Europe. Eventually almost 30,000 Germans served, about 17,000 of them from the principality of Hesse-Cassel—thus *Hessian* became the name applied to all of them. Parliament remained deaf to members who warned that the reconquest of America would not only be costly in itself but also might lead to another great war with France and Spain.

COMMON SENSE   In 1776, Thomas Paine's stirring pamphlet *Common Sense* was published anonymously in Philadelphia. Paine had arrived there from England thirteen months before. Coming from a humble Quaker background, Paine had distinguished himself chiefly as a drifter, a failure in marriage and business. At age thirty-seven he had set sail for America with a letter of introduction from Benjamin Franklin and the purpose of setting up a school for young ladies. When the school did not work out, he moved into the political controversy as a freelance writer, and, with *Common Sense*, he proved himself the consummate Revolutionary rhetorician. Until his pamphlet appeared, the squabble had been mainly with Parliament; few colonists considered independence an option. Paine, however, directly attacked allegiance to the monarchy, which had remained the last frayed connection to Britain, and he refocused the hostility previously vented on Parliament. The "common sense" of the matter, it seemed, was that King George III bore the responsibility for the malevolence toward the colonies. Americans should consult their own interests, abandon George III, and declare their independence: "The blood of the slain, the weeping voice of nature cries, 'TIS TIME TO PART."

INDEPENDENCE

Within three months more than 150,000 copies of Paine's pamphlet were in circulation, an enormous number for the time. "*Common Sense* is working a powerful change in the minds of men," Washington said. A visitor to North Carolina's Provincial Congress could "hear nothing praised but *Common Sense* and independence." One by one the provincial governments

The coming revolution

The Continental Congress votes for independence, July 2, 1776.

authorized their delegates in the Continental Congress to take the final step. On June 7, Richard Henry Lee of Virginia moved "that these United Colonies are, and of right ought to be, free and independent states." Lee's resolution passed on July 2, a date that "will be the most memorable epoch in the history of America," John Adams wrote to his wife, Abigail. The memorable date, however, became July 4, 1776, when the Congress adopted the Declaration of Independence, a statement of political philosophy that still retains its dynamic force.

JEFFERSON'S DECLARATION   Although Thomas Jefferson is often called the author of the Declaration of Independence, he is more accurately termed its draftsman. In June 1776 the Continental Congress appointed a committee of five men—Jefferson, Benjamin Franklin, John Adams, Robert Livingston of New York, and Roger Sherman of Connecticut—to write a public explanation of the reasons for colonial discontent and to provide a rationale for independence. The group asked Adams and Jefferson to produce a first draft, whereupon Adams deferred to Jefferson because of the thirty-three-year-old Virginian's reputation as an eloquent writer.

During two days in mid-June 1776, in his rented lodgings in Philadelphia, Jefferson wrote the first statement of American grievances and principles. He later explained that his purpose was "not to find out new principles, or new arguments, never before thought of, not merely to say things which had never been said before; but to place before mankind the common

sense of the subject, in terms so plain and firm as to command their assent."
He intended his words to serve as "an expression of the American mind,
and to give to that expression the proper tone and spirit called for by the
occasion."

Jefferson drew primarily upon two sources: his own draft preamble to the
Virginia Constitution, written a few weeks earlier, and George Mason's draft
of Virginia's Declaration of Rights, which had appeared in Philadelphia
newspapers in mid-June. It was Mason's text that inspired many of Jefferson's most famous phrases. Mason, for example, had written that "all men
are born equally free and independent, and have certain inherent natural
Rights, . . . among which are the Enjoyment of Life and Liberty, with the
Means of acquiring and possessing Property, and pursuing and obtaining
Happiness and Safety."

The Declaration of Independence

Members of the Continental Congress made eighty-six
changes to Jefferson's draft.

Jefferson shared his draft with the committee members, and they made several minor revisions before submitting the document to the Congress. The legislators made eighty-six changes in Jefferson's declaration, including the insertion of two references to God and the deletion of a section blaming the English monarch for imposing African slavery on the colonies (delegates from Georgia and South Carolina had protested that it smacked of abolitionism).

The resulting Declaration of Independence constitutes a compelling restatement of John Locke's contract theory of government—the theory, in Jefferson's words, that governments derive "their just Powers from the consent of the people," who are entitled to "alter or abolish" those that deny their "unalienable rights" to "life, Liberty, and the pursuit of Happiness." The appeal was no longer simply to "the rights of Englishmen" but to the broader "laws of Nature and Nature's God." Parliament, which had no proper authority over the colonies, was never mentioned by name. The enemy was a king who had tried to establish "an absolute Tyranny over these States." The "Representatives of the United States of America," therefore, declared the thirteen "United Colonies" to be "Free and Independent States." General George Washington ordered the Declaration read to every unit in the Continental army in New York. He prayed that the muscular statement of colonial principles would "serve as a fresh incentive to every officer, and soldier, to act with Fidelity and Courage." An equally excited but more realistic John Adams recognized that "the Toil and Blood and Treasure, that it will cost Us to maintain this Declaration" would be immense. Benjamin Franklin acknowledged how high the stakes were: "Well, Gentlemen," he told the Congress, "we must now hang together, or we shall most assuredly hang separately."

"WE ALWAYS HAD GOVERNED OURSELVES" So it had come to this, thirteen years after Britain acquired domination of North America with the Treaty of Paris in 1763. American Patriots were willing to fight for their freedom against the most formidable military power in the modern world. In explaining the causes of the Revolution, historians have advanced many theories and explanations: the excessive British regulation of colonial trade, the restrictions on settling western lands, the tax burden, the mounting debts to British merchants, the growth of a national consciousness, the lack of representation in Parliament, the ideologies of Whiggery and the Enlightenment, the abrupt shift from a mercantile to an "imperial" policy after 1763, class conflict, and revolutionary agitators.

Each factor contributed something to the collective grievances that rose to a climax in a gigantic failure of British statesmanship. A conflict between British sovereignty and American rights had come to a point of confrontation that adroit statesmanship might have avoided, sidestepped, or outflanked. Irresolution and vacillation in the British ministry finally gave way to the stubborn determination to force an issue long permitted to drift. The colonists, conditioned by the Whig interpretation of history, saw the tightening of British regulations as the conspiracy of a corrupted oligarchy—and finally, they decided, of a despotic king—to impose an "absolute Tyranny."

The individual motives of the Revolutionaries varied considerably. The most frequent explanation for rebelling against British authority was the necessity of preserving traditional English rights and freedoms. George Washington, for example, saw in British policies a conspiracy to "fix the Shackles of Slavery upon us." Yet colonists sought liberty from British tyranny for many reasons, not all of which were selfless or noble. The Boston merchant John Hancock, for example, embraced the Patriot cause in part because he was the region's foremost smuggler. Paying British taxes would have cost him a fortune. Likewise, South Carolina's Henry Laurens and Virginia's Landon Carter, wealthy planters, were concerned about the future of slavery under British control. The seeming contradiction between American slaveholders demanding liberty from British oppression was not lost on observers at the time. John Fletcher, a leading Methodist in Britain, wrote in 1776 that the Americans were "hypocritical friends of liberty who buy and sell and whip their fellow men as if they were brutes, and absurdly complain that they are enslaved." Likewise, the talented writer Phillis Wheatley, the first African American to see her poetry published in America, highlighted the hypocritical "absurdity" of white colonists' demanding their freedom from British tyranny while continuing to exercise "oppressive power" over enslaved Africans. Slave owner George Washington was not devoid of self-interest in his opposition to British policies. He owned 60,000 acres of land west of the Appalachians and very much resented British efforts to restrict white settlement on the frontier.

Perhaps the last word on the complex causes of the Revolution should belong to an obscure participant, Levi Preston, a Minuteman from Danvers, Massachusetts. Asked sixty-seven years after Lexington and Concord about British oppressions, the ninety-one-year-old veteran responded, as his young interviewer reported later:

"What were they? Oppressions? I didn't feel them." "What, were you not oppressed by the Stamp Act?" "I never saw one of those stamps . . . I am certain I never paid a penny for one of them." "Well, what then about the tea-tax?" "Tea-tax! I never drank a drop of the stuff; the boys threw it all overboard." "Well, then, what was the matter? and what did you mean in going to the fight?" "Young man, what we meant in going for those redcoats was this: we always had governed ourselves, and we always meant to. They didn't mean we should."

End of Chapter Review

- **British Colonial Policy** After the French and Indian War, the British government was saddled with an enormous national debt. To reduce that imperial burden, the British government concluded that the colonies ought to help pay for their own defense. Thus, the ministers of King George III began to implement various acts and impose new taxes.

- **Colonial Justification to Resistance** Whig ideology was based on the writings of John Locke and others who justified the Glorious Revolution of 1688. American colonists adopted that ideology to justify their resistance to increasing royal control over the colonies. They viewed their opposition to King George as an outgrowth of Parliament's long constitutional struggle to preserve life, liberty, and property against royal tyranny.

- **Road to the American Revolution** Colonial reaction to the Stamp Act of 1765 was the first intimation of real trouble for imperial authorities: colonists argued that citizens should be taxed only by their elected representatives. Conflict intensified when the British government imposed additional taxes. Spontaneous resistance led to the Boston Massacre; organized protesters staged the Boston Tea Party. The British response, the Coercive Acts, sparked further violence. Compromise became less likely, if not impossible.

- **Taxation without Representation** Colonists based their resistance to the Crown on the idea that taxation without direct colonial representation in Parliament violated their rights. They viewed George III as a tyrant who had ignored the contractual nature of government. Patrick Henry protested the Stamp Act in Virginia on those grounds; Samuel Adams and the Sons of Liberty used the same arguments to incite mobs. It was Thomas Paine, in *Common Sense*, who first argued clearly that independence was not only necessary in response to royal actions but also economically viable.

- **Declaration of Independence** The colonists were united through what was increasingly regarded as the unreasonable and unconstitutional demands that the mother country had made on them since 1763. George III's refusal to compromise after violence erupted at Concord alienated many among the colonial elite who might have argued for restraint. In June 1776, Richard Henry Lee introduced a motion for independence at the Continental Congress. Its passage, on July 2, 1776, created a new country, the United States of America. Lee's motion has been overshadowed throughout history by the document issued two days later, the Declaration of Independence.

CHRONOLOGY

1760	King George III accedes to the throne
1763	French and Indian War ends
1764	Parliament passes the Revenue (Sugar) Act
1765	Parliament passes the Stamp Act; colonists hold Stamp Act Congress
1766	Parliament repeals the Stamp Act and passes the Declaratory Act
1767	Parliament levies the Townshend duties
1770	Boston Massacre
1772	*Gaspee* incident
1773	Colonists stage the Boston Tea Party
1774	Parliament passes the Coercive Acts; colonists hold First Continental Congress
1775	Battles of Lexington and Concord
1775	Colonists hold Second Continental Congress
1776	Thomas Paine's *Common Sense* is published; Declaration of Independence is signed

KEY TERMS & NAMES

Whigs p. 192

Sons of Liberty p. 196

Stamp Act Congress p. 198

Declaratory Act p. 199

John Dickinson's "Letters from a Farmer in Pennsylvania" p. 200

Samuel Adams p. 201

Lord North p. 202

Crispus Attucks p. 202

Patrick Henry p. 211

Paul Revere p. 212

Minutemen p. 213

Thomas Paine's *Common Sense* p. 218

Thomas Jefferson p. 219

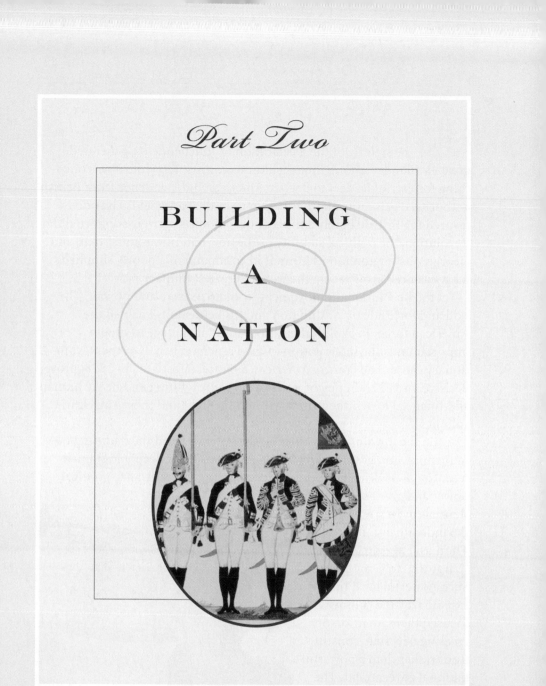

Part Two

BUILDING

A

NATION

The signing of the Declaration of Independence generated great excitement among the rebellious colonists. Yet while it was one thing for Patriot leaders to declare American independence from British authority, it was quite another to win it on the battlefield. The odds favored the British: barely a third of the colonists actively supported the Revolution, the political stability of the new nation was uncertain, and George Washington found himself in command of a poorly supplied, inexperienced army facing the world's greatest military power.

Yet the Revolutionary movement would persevere and prevail. The skill and fortitude of Washington and his lieutenants enabled the American forces to exploit their geographic advantages. Equally important was the intervention of the French on behalf of the Revolutionary cause. The Franco-American alliance, negotiated in 1778, proved decisive. In 1783, after eight years of sporadic fighting and heavy human and financial losses, the British gave up the fight and their American colonies.

Amid the Revolutionary turmoil the Patriots faced the daunting task of forming new governments for themselves. Their deeply ingrained resentment of British imperial rule led them to decentralize political power and grant substantial sovereignty to the individual states. As Thomas Jefferson declared, "Virginia, Sir, is my country." Such powerful local ties help explain why the colonists focused their attention on creating new state constitutions rather than a powerful national government. The Articles of Confederation, ratified in 1781, provided only the semblance of national authority. Final power to make and execute laws remained with the states.

After the end of the Revolutionary War, the flimsy political bonds authorized by the Articles of Confederation proved inadequate to the needs of the new—and rapidly expanding—nation. This realization led to the Constitutional Convention in 1787. The process of drafting and ratifying the new constitution prompted a heated debate on the relative significance of national power, local control, and individual freedom that has provided the central theme of American political thought ever since.

The Revolution involved much more than the apportionment of political power, however. It also unleashed social forces that would help reshape the very fabric of American culture. What would be the role of women, African Americans, and Native Americans in the new republic? How would the quite different economies of the various regions of the new United States be developed? Who would control access to the vast territories to the west of the original thirteen states? How would the new republic relate to the other nations of the world?

These controversial questions helped foster the first national political parties in the United States. During the 1790s, Federalists, led by Alexander Hamilton, and Republicans, led by Thomas Jefferson and James Madison, furiously debated the political and economic future of the new nation. With Jefferson's election as president in 1800, the Republicans gained the upper hand in national politics for the next quarter century. In the process they presided over a maturing republic that aggressively expanded westward at the expense of the Native Americans, ambivalently embraced industrial development, fitfully engaged in a second war with Great Britain, and ominously witnessed a growing sectional controversy over slavery.

6

THE AMERICAN REVOLUTION

FOCUS QUESTIONS $Ⓢ$ wwnorton.com/studyspace

- What were the military strategies and problems for both the Americans and the British?

- What were the war's major turning points?

- Who were the Loyalists; and what became of them?

- Why was it possible to gain European allies; and how important were European allies to the war's successful conclusion?

- To what extent was the American Revolution a social revolution in matters of gender equality, race relations, and religious freedom?

Few foreign observers thought that the upstart American revolutionaries could win a war against the world's greatest empire and most powerful military force—and the Americans did lose most of the battles in the Revolutionary War. But they eventually forced the British to sue for peace and grant their independence, a stunning result that reflects the tenacity of the Patriots as well as the peculiar difficulties facing the British as they tried to conduct a far-flung campaign thousands of miles from home. The British Empire dispatched two thirds of its entire army and one half of its formidable navy to suppress the American revolt. The costly military commitments that the British maintained elsewhere around the globe further complicated their war effort, and the intervention of the French on behalf of the Americans in 1778 proved to be the war's key turning point.

Fighting in the New World was not an easy task for either side, however. The Americans had to create and sustain a military force from scratch. Recruiting, supplying, equipping, training, and paying soldiers were monumental challenges, especially for a fledgling nation in the midst of forming its first governments. The Patriot army encircling British-controlled Boston in 1775 was little more than a rustic militia made up of volunteers who had enlisted for six months. The citizen-soldiers lacked training and discipline. They came and went as they pleased, often chose not to salute officers, gambled frequently, and drank liquor freely. General George Washington recognized immediately that the foremost needs of the new Continental army were capable officers, intensive training, strict discipline, and longer enlistment contracts. He soon began whipping his army into shape. Recruits who violated army rules were placed in the stockade, flogged, or sent packing. Yet the tenacity of Washington and the Revolutionaries bore fruit as war-weariness and political dissension in London hampered British efforts to suppress the rebel forces.

Like all major military events, the Revolution had unexpected consequences affecting political, economic, and social life. It not only secured American independence, generated a sense of nationalism, and created a unique system of self-governance; it also began a process of societal definition and change that has yet to run its course. The turmoil of revolution upset traditional class and social relationships and helped transform the lives of people who had long been relegated to the periphery of social status— African Americans, women, and Indians. In important ways, then, the Revolution was much more than simply a war for independence. It was an engine for political experimentation and social change.

1776: WASHINGTON'S NARROW ESCAPE

On July 2, 1776, the day that Congress voted for independence, British redcoats landed on undefended Staten Island, across New York Harbor from Manhattan. They were the vanguard of a gigantic effort to reconquer America and the first elements of an enormous force that gathered around the harbor over the next month. By mid-August, British Major General William Howe, with the support of a fleet under his older brother, Admiral Richard, Lord Howe, had some 32,000 men at his disposal, the largest single force mustered by the British in the eighteenth century. George Washington transferred most of his troops to New York from Boston, but he could gather only about 19,000 poorly trained militiamen and members of the new Continental army—much too small a force to defend New York, but Congress wanted it held. This meant that Washington had to expose his men to entrapments

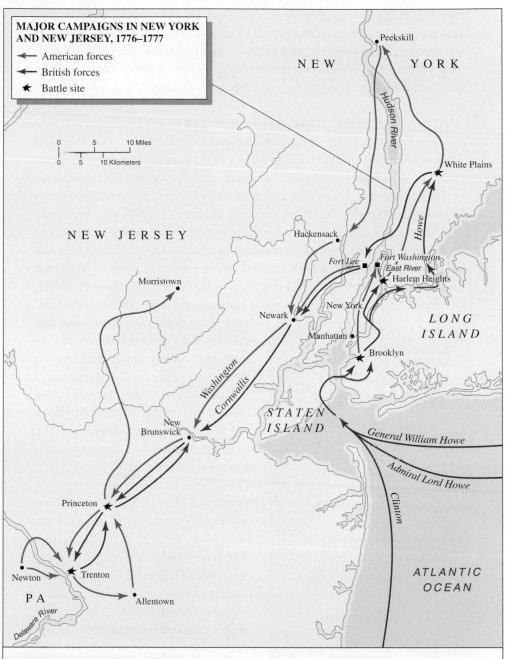

MAJOR CAMPAIGNS IN NEW YORK AND NEW JERSEY, 1776–1777

← American forces

← British forces

★ Battle site

0   5   10 Miles
0   5   10 Kilometers

NEW YORK

Peekskill

Hudson River

White Plains

NEW JERSEY

Hackensack

Howe

Fort Lee

Fort Washington

East River

Harlem Heights

Morristown

Newark

New York

LONG ISLAND

Manhattan

Washington

Cornwallis

Brooklyn

New Brunswick

STATEN ISLAND

General William Howe

Admiral Lord Howe

Princeton

Clinton

Newton

Trenton

ATLANTIC OCEAN

PA

Allentown

Delaware River

Why did Washington lead his army from Brooklyn to Manhattan and from there to New Jersey? How could General Howe have ended the rebellion in New York? What is the significance of the Battle of Trenton?

from which they escaped more by luck and Howe's caution than by any strategic genius on the part of the American commander. Although a veteran of frontier fighting, Washington had never commanded a large unit or supervised artillery. In 1776 he was still learning the art of generalship, and the New York campaign taught him some expensive lessons.

FIGHTING IN NEW YORK AND NEW JERSEY   By occupying New York, the British hoped to sever New England from the rest of the rebellious colonies. The British enjoyed complete naval superiority as well as overwhelming advantages in men and weaponry. In late August 1776 the massive British armada of 427 warships and transports began landing 30,000 troops on Long Island. It was the largest seaborne military expedition in world history. Although short of munitions, greatly outnumbered, and leading a force in which a quarter of the men were suffering from smallpox, Washington was determined to defend New York. It was a colossal mistake. The new American army suffered a humiliating defeat at the Battle of Long Island. British invaders caught Washington's forces by surprise, and only a timely rainstorm, with strong winds, high tides, and fog, enabled the retreating Americans to cross the harbor from Brooklyn to Manhattan under cover of darkness.

Had General Howe moved more quickly, he could have trapped Washington's army in lower Manhattan. The main American force, however, withdrew northward, crossed the Hudson River, and retreated slowly across New Jersey and over the Delaware River into Pennsylvania. As the ragged remnants of the American army fled across New Jersey, the British buglers giving chase mocked them by trumpeting fox-hunting calls.

At the end of August 1776, General Washington had had more than 28,000 men under his command. By December he had only 3,000. The supreme commander was disconsolate; the American war effort was in desperate straits. Thousands of militiamen had simply gone home. Unless a

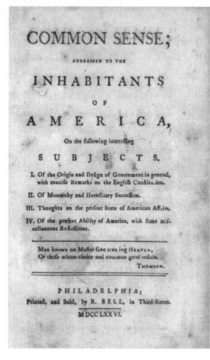

Common Sense

Thomas Paine's inspiring pamphlet was originally published anonymously because of its treasonous content.

new army could be raised quickly, Washington warned, "I think the game is pretty near up." But it wasn't. In the retreating American army marched a British volunteer, Thomas Paine. Having opened the eventful year of 1776 with his inspiring pamphlet *Common Sense*, which in plain terms encouraged American independence, Paine now composed *The American Crisis*, in which he penned these immortal lines:

> These are the times that try men's souls: The summer soldier and the sunshine patriot will, in this crisis, shrink from the service of his country; but he that stands it NOW deserves the love and thanks of man and woman. Tyranny, like Hell, is not easily conquered. Yet we have this consolation with us, that the harder the conflict, the more glorious the triumph.

The stirring pamphlet, ordered read in the American army camps, bolstered the shaken morale of the Patriots—as events would soon do more decisively.

General Howe, firmly—and luxuriously—based in New York (which the British held throughout the war), settled down with his mistress to wait out the winter. Washington, however, was not ready to hibernate. He knew that the morale of his men and the hopes of a new nation required "some stroke" of good news in the face of their devastating losses in New York. So he seized the initiative with a desperate gamble to achieve a much-needed first victory before more of his soldiers returned home once their initial enlistment contracts expired. On Christmas night 1776 he led some 2,400 men across the icy Delaware River. Near dawn at Trenton, New Jersey, the Americans surprised a garrison of 1,500 sleeping Hessians (German mercenaries). It was a total rout, from which only 500 Hessians escaped death or capture. Yet only 6 of Washington's men were wounded, one of whom was Lieutenant James Monroe, the future president. A week later, at nearby Princeton, the Americans repelled three regiments of British redcoats before taking refuge in winter quarters at Morristown, in the hills of northern New Jersey.

The campaigns of 1776 had ended, after repeated defeats, with two minor victories that bolstered the Patriot cause. The unexpected victories at Princeton and Trenton may well have saved the cause of independence. Having learned of the American triumphs in New Jersey, a Virginian loyal to Britain glumly reported that a few days before, the Revolutionaries "had given up the cause for lost. Their late successes have turned the scale and now they are all liberty mad again." General Howe had missed his great chance—indeed, several chances—to bring the rebellion to a speedy end. Grumbled one British officer, the Americans had "become a formidable enemy" even though they had yet to win a full-scale conventional battle.

In fact, George Washington had painfully come to realize that the only way to defeat the British was to wear them down in a long war of attrition

George Washington at Princeton

By Charles Willson Peale.

and exhaustion. As the combat in New York had shown, he could not beat the British army in a conventional battle. The only hope of winning the war was not to lose it. Time became his greatest weapon. Over the next eight years he and his troops would outlast the invaders through a strategy of evasion and maneuver punctuated by selective confrontations.

AMERICAN SOCIETY AT WAR

CHOOSING SIDES The American Revolution was as much a civil war as it was a struggle against a foreign nation. The act of choosing sides divided families and friends, towns and cities. Benjamin Franklin's illegitimate son, William, for example, was the royal governor of New Jersey. He sided with Great Britain during the Revolution, and his Patriot father later removed him from his will. The passions unleashed by the Revolution erupted in brutalities on both sides. Mobs of Patriots executed Tories (or Loyalists, as the British sympathizers were sometimes known), and state governments confiscated their homes and property. One Loyalist, John Stevens, testified that he "was dragged by a rope fixed about his neck" across the Susquehanna River because he refused to sign an oath supporting the rebellion. In Virginia, the planter Charles Lynch set up vigilante courts to punish Tories by "lynching" them—which in this case meant having them whipped.

Opinion among the colonists concerning the war divided in three ways: Patriots, or Whigs (as the Revolutionaries called themselves); Tories; and an indifferent middle group swayed mostly by the better organized and more energetic radicals. That the Loyalists were numerous is evident from the departure, during and after the war, of roughly 100,000 of them, more than 3 percent of the total population. But the Patriots were probably the largest of the three groups. There was a like division in British opinion. The aversion of so many English to the war was one reason for the government's hiring German mercenaries to fight with the British army.

Estimating how many Americans remained loyal to Britain was a central concern of English military planners, for they based many of their decisions on such figures. Throughout most of the war, the British sought to align themselves with an elusive Tory majority that the Loyalists kept telling them was waiting only for British regulars to show the flag. Often they miscalculated. Generally Tories were concentrated in the seaport cities, but they came from all walks of life. Governors, judges, and other royal officials were almost all Loyalists; most Anglican ministers also preferred the mother country; colonial merchants might be tugged one way or the other, depending upon how much they had benefited or suffered from mercantilist regulation; the wealthy southern planters were swayed one way by dependence upon British crop bounties, another by their debts to British merchants. In the backcountry of New York and the Carolinas, many humble folk rallied to the Crown. Where planter aristocrats tended to be Whig, as in North Carolina, backcountry farmers (many of them recently Regulators) leaned toward the Tories.

In few places, however, there were enough Tories to assume control without the presence of British troops, but nowhere for very long. Repeatedly the British forces were frustrated by both the failure of Loyalists to materialize in strength and the collapse of Loyalist militia units once regular detachments pulled out. Even more disheartening was what one British officer called "the licentiousness of the [Loyalist] troops, who committed every species of rapine and plunder" and thereby converted potential friends to enemies. British and Hessian regulars, brought up in a hard school of warfare, tended to treat all civilians as hostile.

The inability of the British to use Loyalists effectively led them to abandon areas once they had conquered them. Because Patriot militias quickly returned whenever the British left an area, any Loyalists in the region faced a difficult choice: either accompany the British and leave behind their property or stay and face the wrath of the Patriots. In addition, the British policy of offering slaves their freedom in exchange for their loyalty and service alienated large numbers of neutral or even Tory planters dependent upon slave labor.

The Patriot militia sprang to life whenever redcoats appeared nearby, and all adult white males, with few exceptions, were obligated under state law to serve when called. And sooner or later nearly every colonial county experienced military action that called for armed resistance. The war itself, then, whether through British and Loyalist behavior or the call of the militia, mobilized the apathetic to make at least an appearance of support for the American cause. Once made, this commitment was seldom reversed.

MILITIA AND ARMY   American militiamen served two purposes: they constituted a home guard, defending their communities, and they helped augment the Continental army. Dressed in hunting shirts and armed with

American militia

This sketch of militiamen by a French soldier at Yorktown, Virginia, shows one of those ubiquitous American frontiersmen turned soldier (second from right), and it is also one of the earliest depictions of an African American soldier.

muskets, they preferred to ambush their opponents or engage them in hand-to-hand combat rather than fight in traditional European formations. They also tended to kill unnecessarily and to torture prisoners. To repel an attack, the militia somehow materialized; the danger past, it evaporated, for there were chores to do at home. They "come in, you cannot tell how," Washington said in exasperation, "go, you cannot tell when, and act you cannot tell where, consume your provisions, exhaust your stores, and leave you at last at a critical moment."

The Continental army, by contrast, was on the whole better trained and more reliable. Unlike the professional soldiers in the British army, Washington's troops were citizen soldiers, mostly poor native-born Americans or immigrants who had been indentured servants or convicts. Many found camp life debilitating and combat horrifying. As General Nathanael Greene, Washington's ablest commander, pointed out, few of the Patriots had ever engaged in mortal combat, and they were hard-pressed to "stand the shocking scenes of war, to march over dead men, to hear without concern the groans of the wounded." Desertions grew as the war dragged on. At times, General Washington could put only 2,000 to 3,000 men in the field. Regiments were organized by state, and the states were supposed to keep them filled with volunteers or with conscripts if need be, but Washington could never be sure that his troop requisitions would be met.

PROBLEMS OF FINANCE AND SUPPLY Congress found it difficult to supply the army. None of the states provided more than a part of its designated share of the war's expenses, and Congress reluctantly let army agents take supplies directly from farmers in return for promises of future payment. Many of the states found a ready source of revenue in the sale of abandoned Loyalist estates. Nevertheless, Congress and the states fell short of funding the war's cost and resorted to printing paper money.

Congress did better at providing munitions than at providing other supplies. In 1777 it established a government arsenal at Springfield, Massachusetts, and during the war, states offered bounties for the manufacture of guns and powder. Still, most munitions were supplied either by wartime captures or by importation from France, whose government was all too glad to help the rebels fight its archenemy.

During the harsh New Jersey winter at Morristown (1776–1777), George Washington's army nearly disintegrated as enlistments expired and deserters fled the hardships of brutally cold weather, inadequate food, and widespread disease. Smallpox continued to wreak havoc among the American armies. By 1777, Washington had come to view the virus with greater dread than "the Sword of the Enemy." On any given day, a fourth of the American troops were deemed unfit for duty, usually because of smallpox. The threat of smallpox to the war effort was so great that in early 1777 Washington ordered a mass inoculation, which he managed to keep secret from the British. Inoculating an entire army was an enormous, risky undertaking. Washington's daring gamble paid off. The successful inoculation of the American army marks one of his greatest strategic accomplishments of the war.

Only about 1,000 Continentals and a few militiamen stuck out the Morristown winter. With the spring thaw, however, recruits began arriving to claim the bounty of $20 and 100 acres of land offered by Congress to those who would enlist for three years or for the duration of the conflict, if less. With some 9,000 regulars, Washington began sparring and feinting with Howe's British Forces in northern New Jersey. Howe had been making plans, however, and so had other British officers.

1777: SETBACKS FOR THE BRITISH

Overconfidence, poor communications, and indecision plagued British military planning in the campaigns of 1777. After the removal of General Gage during the siege of Boston, Gentleman Johnny Burgoyne took command of the northern British armies. He proposed to bisect the colonies. His

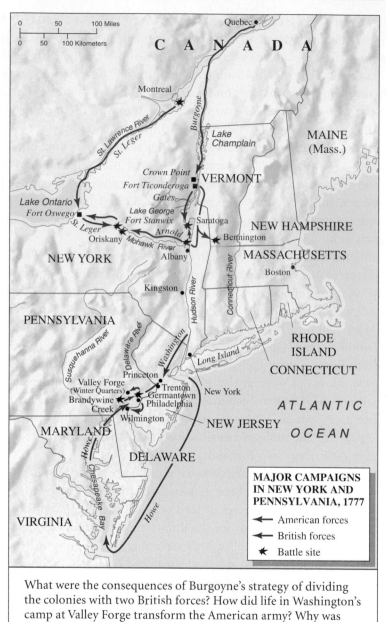

What were the consequences of Burgoyne's strategy of dividing the colonies with two British forces? How did life in Washington's camp at Valley Forge transform the American army? Why was Saratoga a turning point in the American Revolution?

men would advance southward from Canada to the Hudson River while another force moved eastward from Oswego, in western New York, down the Mohawk River valley toward Albany. General Howe, meanwhile, would lead a third force up the Hudson from New York City. Howe had in fact proposed a similar plan, combined with an attack on New England. Had the British followed that plan, Howe might have cut the colonies in two and delivered them a disheartening blow. But he changed his mind and decided to move against the Patriot capital, Philadelphia, expecting that the Pennsylvania Tories would rally to the Crown and secure the colony.

Washington, sensing Howe's purpose, withdrew most of his men from New Jersey to meet the new threat. At Brandywine Creek, southwest of Philadelphia, Howe outmaneuvered and routed Washington's forces on September 11, and fifteen days later the British occupied Philadelphia. Washington counterattacked in a dense fog at Germantown on October 4, but British reinforcements from Philadelphia under General Charles Cornwallis arrived in time to repulse the Americans. Washington retired with his army to winter quarters at Valley Forge, Pennsylvania, while Howe and his men remained for the winter in the relative comfort of Philadelphia, twenty miles away (eighteenth-century armies rarely fought during the winter months). Howe's plan had succeeded, up to a point. He had taken Philadelphia—or as Benjamin Franklin put it, Philadelphia had taken him. But the Tories there proved fewer than Howe had expected, and his decision to move on Philadelphia from the south, by way of Chesapeake Bay, put his forces even farther from Burgoyne's army. Meanwhile, Burgoyne was stumbling into disaster in the north.

General John Burgoyne

Commander of Britain's northern forces. Burgoyne and most of his troops surrendered to the Americans at Saratoga on October 17, 1777.

SARATOGA General Burgoyne moved south from Canada toward Lake Champlain in 1777 with about 7,000 men, his mistress, and a baggage train that included some thirty carts carrying his personal belongings and a large supply of champagne. Such heavily laden forces struggled to cross the wooded, marshy terrain. Burgoyne sent part of his forces down the St. Lawrence River with Lieutenant Colonel Barry St. Leger, and at

Oswego they were joined by a force of Iroquois allies. The combined force then headed east toward Albany.

The American army in New York had dwindled since 1776. When Burgoyne brought his cannon to bear on Fort Ticonderoga, the Continentals abandoned the fort, with a substantial loss of gunpowder and supplies. An angry Congress thereupon fired the American commander and replaced him with Horatio Gates, a favorite of the New Englanders. Fortunately for the American forces, Burgoyne delayed at Ticonderoga, enabling American reinforcements to arrive from the south and New England.

The more mobile Patriots inflicted two serious "defeats" on the British forces. At Oriskany, New York, on August 6, 1777, a band of militiamen repulsed an ambush by Tories and Indians under St. Leger and gained time for General Benedict Arnold to bring 1,000 Continentals to the relief of Fort Stanwix. Convinced that they faced an even greater force than they actually did, the Indians deserted, and the Mohawk River valley was secured for the Patriot forces. To the east, at Bennington, Vermont, on August 16, New England militiamen, led by Colonel John Stark, decimated a British foraging party. Stark had pledged that morning, "We'll beat them before night, or Molly Stark will be a widow." As American reinforcements continued to gather and after two other defeats by the Americans, Burgoyne pulled back to Saratoga, New York, where General Horatio Gates's forces surrounded him.

On October 17, 1777, Burgoyne, resplendent in his scarlet, gold, and white uniform, surrendered to the plain, blue-coated Gates, and most of his 5,700 soldiers were imprisoned in Virginia. Gates allowed Burgoyne himself to return to England, where he received an icy reception. Gates was ecstatic. He wrote his wife, "If old England is not by this lesson taught humility, then she is an obstinate old slut, bent upon her ruin."

ALLIANCE WITH FRANCE   In early December 1777, news of the surprising American triumph at Saratoga reached Paris, where it was celebrated almost as if it were a French victory. In 1776 the French had taken their first step toward aiding the colonists, sending fourteen ships with crucial military supplies to America; most of the Continental army's gunpowder in the first years of the war came from France. The Spanish government added a donation and soon established its own supply company.

Word of the American victory at Saratoga led in early 1778 to the signing of two crucial treaties. Under the Treaty of Amity and Commerce, France recognized the new United States and offered trade concessions, including important privileges to American shipping. Under the Treaty of Alliance, both parties agreed, first, that if France entered the war, both countries would fight until

American independence was won; second, that neither would conclude a "truce or peace" without "the formal consent of the other first obtained"; and third, that each guaranteed the other's possessions in America "from the present time and forever against all other powers." France further bound itself to seek neither Canada nor other British possessions on the mainland of North America.

By June 1778, British vessels had fired on French ships, and the two nations were at war. The French decision to join the infant United States in its war for independence was by far the most important factor in America's winning the Revolutionary War. In 1779, Spain entered the war as an ally of France but not of the United States. In 1780, Britain declared war on the Dutch, who persisted in a profitable trade with the French and the Americans. The rebellious farmers at Lexington and Concord had indeed fired a shot "heard round the world." Like Washington's encounter with the French in 1754, it was the start of world war, and the fighting now spread to the Mediterranean, Africa, India, the West Indies, and the high seas.

1778: BOTH SIDES REGROUP

After the British defeat at Saratoga, Lord North knew that the war was unwinnable, but the king refused to let him either resign or make peace. On March 16, 1778, the House of Commons in effect granted all the demands that the Americans had made prior to independence. Parliament repealed the Townshend tea duty, the Massachusetts Government Act, and the Prohibitory Act, which had closed the colonies to commerce, and sent peace commissioners to Philadelphia to negotiate an end to hostilities. But Congress refused to begin any negotiations until Britain recognized American independence or withdrew its forces.

Unbeknownst to the British peace commissioners, the Crown had already authorized the evacuation of British troops from Philadelphia, a withdrawal that further weakened what little bargaining power they had. After Saratoga, General Howe had resigned his command, and Sir Henry Clinton had replaced him, with orders to pull out of Philadelphia and, if necessary, New York but to keep Newport, Rhode Island. He was to supply troops for an expedition in the South, where the government believed a latent Tory sentiment in the backcountry needed only a British presence for its release. The ministry was right, up to a point, but the Loyalist sentiment turned out once again, as in other theaters of war, to be weaker than it had seemed.

For Washington's army at Valley Forge, the winter of 1777–1778 had been a season of intense suffering. The American force, encamped near Philadelphia,

Valley Forge

During the winter of 1777–1778, Washington's army battled starvation, disease, and freezing temperatures.

endured unrelenting cold, hunger, and disease. Some troops lacked shoes and blankets. Their makeshift log-and-mud huts offered little protection from the howling winds and bitter cold. Most of the army's horses died of exposure or starvation. By February, 7,000 troops were too ill for duty. More than 2,500 soldiers died at Valley Forge; another 1,000 deserted. Fifty officers resigned on one December day. Several hundred more left before winter's end.

Desperate for relief, Washington sent troops on foraging expeditions into New Jersey, Delaware, and the Eastern Shore of Maryland, confiscating horses, cattle, and hogs in exchange for "receipts" to be honored by the Continental Congress. By March 1778 the once-gaunt troops at Valley Forge saw their strength restored. Their improved health enabled Washington to begin a rigorous training program, designed to bring unity to his motley array of forces. Because few of the regimental commanders had any formal military training, their troops lacked leadership, discipline, and skill. To remedy this defect, Washington turned to an energetic Prussian soldier of fortune, Friedrich Wilhelm, baron von Steuben. Steuben used an interpreter and frequent profanity to instruct the troops, teaching them the fundamentals of close-order drill: how to march in formation and how to handle their weapons.

Steuben was one of several foreign volunteers who joined the American army at Valley Forge. Among the Europeans was also a twenty-year-old red-haired Frenchman named, in short, Gilbert du Motier, the Marquis de Lafayette. A wealthy idealist excited by the American cause, Lafayette offered to serve for no pay in exchange for being named a major general. General Washington was initially skeptical of the young French patriot, but Lafayette soon became the commander in chief's most trusted aide. The French general proved to be a courageous soldier and able diplomat.

By the end of the winter, the ragtag American soldiers at Valley Forge were beginning to resemble a professional army. The army's morale stiffened when Congress promised extra pay and bonuses after the war. The good news from France about the formal military alliance also helped raise their spirits. As General Clinton's British forces withdrew eastward toward New York, Washington pursued them across New Jersey. On June 28 he engaged the British in an indecisive battle at Monmouth Court House. But the battle was significant for revealing Washington's temper and leadership qualities. In the midst of the fighting, he discovered that his potbellied subordinate, General Charles Lee, was retreating rather than attacking. Infuriated, Washington swore at Lee "till the leaves shook the trees." Then Washington rallied the troops just in time to stave off defeat. Clinton's redcoats slipped away to New York City while Washington's men took up a position at White Plains, north of the city. From that time on, the northern theater, scene of the major campaigns and battles in the first years of the war, settled into a long stalemate, interrupted by minor and mostly inconclusive engagements.

ACTIONS ON THE FRONTIER The one major American success of 1778 occurred far from the New Jersey battlefields. Out to the west the British, under Colonel William Hamilton at Forts Niagara and Detroit, had incited frontier Tories and Indians to raid western settlements and offered to pay bounties for American scalps. To end the English-led attacks, young George Rogers Clark took 175 frontiersmen on flatboats down the Ohio River early in 1778, marched through the woods, and on the evening of July 4 took English-controlled Kaskaskia (in present-day Illinois) by surprise. The French inhabitants, terrified at first, "fell into transports of joy" at news of the French alliance with the Americans. Then, without bloodshed, Clark took Cahokia (opposite St. Louis) and Vincennes (in present-day Indiana). After the British retook Vincennes, Clark marched his men (almost half of them French volunteers) through icy rivers and flooded prairies, sometimes in water neck deep, and laid siege to the astonished British garrison. Clark,

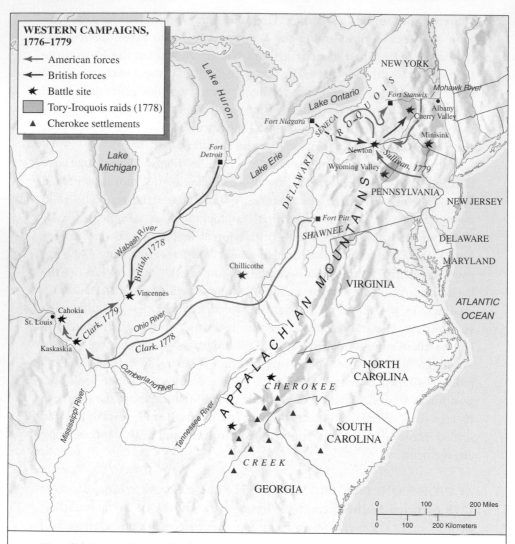

How did George Rogers Clark secure Cahokia and Vincennes? Why did the American army destroy Iroquois villages in 1779? Why were the skirmishes between settlers and Indian tribes significant for the future of the trans-Appalachian frontier?

the hardened woodsman, tomahawked Indian captives in sight of the fort to show that the British afforded them no protection. He spared the British captives when they surrendered, however.

While Clark's captives traveled eastward, a much larger American expedition moved through western Pennsylvania to attack Iroquois strongholds in western New York. There the Tories and Indians had terrorized frontier settlements throughout the summer of 1778. Led by the charismatic Mohawk Joseph Brant, the Iroquois had killed hundreds of militiamen along the Pennsylvania frontier. In response, Washington dispatched an expedition of 4,000 men under General John Sullivan. At Newton, New York, (near Elmira), on August 29, 1779, Sullivan defeated the only serious opposition and proceeded to carry out Washington's instruction that the Iroquois country be not "merely overrun but destroyed." The American force burned about forty Seneca and Cayuga villages, together with their orchards and food supplies, leaving many of the Indians homeless and without enough provisions to survive. The action broke the

Joseph Brant

This 1786 portrait of Thayendanegea (Joseph Brant) by Gilbert Stuart features the Mohawk leader who fought against the Americans in the Revolution.

power of the Iroquois Confederacy for all time, but it did not completely pacify the frontier. Sporadic encounters with various tribes continued to the end of the war.

In the Kentucky territory, Daniel Boone and his small band of settlers risked constant attack by the Shawnees and their British and Tory allies. During the Revolution they survived frequent ambushes, at least seven skirmishes, and three pitched battles. In 1778, Boone and some thirty men, aided by their wives and children, held off an assault by more than 400 Indians at Boonesborough (now Boonesboro). Thereafter, Boone himself was twice shot and twice captured. Indians killed two of his sons, a brother, and two brothers-in-law. His daughter was captured, and another brother was wounded four times. Despite such ferocious fighting and dangerous circumstances, the white settlers refused to leave Kentucky.

In early 1776 a delegation of northern Indians—Shawnees, Delawares, and Mohawks—had talked the Cherokees into striking at frontier settlements in Virginia and the Carolinas. Swift retaliation had followed as Carolina militia men burned Cherokee towns and destroyed corn. By weakening the major Indian tribes along the frontier, the American Revolution cleared the way for rapid settlement of the trans-Appalachian West after the war.

The War in the South

At the end of 1778, the focus of the British military efforts shifted suddenly to the South. The whole region from Virginia southward had been free of major action since 1776. Now the British would test King George's belief that a sleeping Tory power in the South needed only the presence of a few redcoats to be awakened. The British commander, General Henry Clinton, decided to take Savannah, on the southeast Georgia coast, and roll northeast, gathering momentum from the Loyalist countryside. For a while the idea seemed to work, but it ran afoul of two developments: first, the Loyalist strength was less than estimated, and second, the British forces behaved so harshly that they drove even Loyalists into rebellion.

SAVANNAH AND CHARLESTON   In November 1778 a British force attacked Savannah. The invaders quickly overwhelmed the Patriots, took the town, and hurried northeast toward Charleston, plundering plantation houses along the way. The Carolina campaign took a major turn when British general Clinton, accompanied by General Charles Cornwallis, bottled up an American force led by General Benjamin Lincoln on the Charleston Peninsula. On May 12, 1780, Lincoln surrendered the port city and its 5,500 defenders, the greatest single American loss of the war. At that point, Congress, against Washington's advice, turned to the victor of Saratoga, Horatio Gates, to take command and sent him south. General Cornwallis, in charge of the British troops in the South, surprised Gates's force at Camden, South Carolina, routing his new army, which retreated all the way to Hillsborough, North Carolina, 160 miles away.

THE CAROLINAS   From the point of view of British imperial goals, the southern colonies were ultimately more important than the northern ones because they produced valuable staple crops, such as tobacco, indigo, and naval supplies (tar, pitch, and turpentine). Eventually the war in the Carolinas not only involved opposing British and American armies but also degenerated into brutal guerrilla-style civil conflicts between local Loyalists and local Patriots.

General Cornwallis had South Carolina just about under British control, but two subordinates, Sir Banastre Tarleton and Patrick Ferguson, who mobilized Tory militiamen, overreached themselves in their effort to subdue the Whigs. The British officers often let their men execute Patriots who surrendered. Ferguson sealed his doom when he threatened to march over the mountains and hang the backcountry Patriot leaders. Instead, the feisty

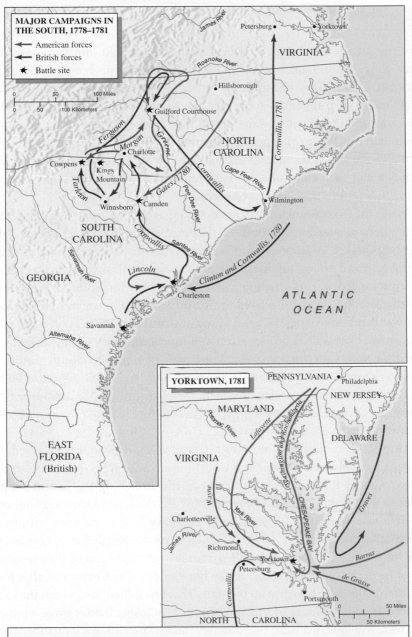

MAJOR CAMPAIGNS IN THE SOUTH, 1778–1781

← American forces
← British forces
★ Battle site

0   50   100 Miles
0   50   100 Kilometers

James River · Petersburg · Yorktown

VIRGINIA

Roanoke River

· Hillsborough

★ Guilford Courthouse

Ferguson

Morgan · Charlotte

NORTH CAROLINA

Greene

Cornwallis, 1781

Cape Fear River

Cowpens ★ ★ Kings Mountain

Tarleton

Gates, 1780

Pee Dee River

Cornwallis

· Wilmington

Winnsboro · Camden

SOUTH CAROLINA

Cornwallis

Santee River

Clinton and Cornwallis, 1780

GEORGIA

Savannah River

Lincoln

· Charleston

ATLANTIC OCEAN

Savannah

Altamaha River

EAST FLORIDA (British)

YORKTOWN, 1781

PENNSYLVANIA · Philadelphia

NEW JERSEY

MARYLAND

Potomac River

Lafayette

Washington and Rochambeau

DELAWARE

VIRGINIA

Wayne

York River

CHESAPEAKE BAY

Graves

Charlottesville

James River

Richmond ·

Yorktown ★

Petersburg ·

Barras

de Grasse

Cornwallis

Portsmouth

0   50 Miles
0   50 Kilometers

NORTH   CAROLINA

Why did the British suddenly shift their campaign to the South? Why were the battles at Savannah and Charleston major victories for the British? How did Nathanael Greene undermine British control of the Deep South? Why did Cornwallis march to Virginia and camp at Yorktown? How was the French navy crucial to the American victory? Why was Cornwallis forced to surrender?

"overmountain men" went after Ferguson. They caught him and his Tories near Kings Mountain, just across the North Carolina border. There, on October 7, 1780, they decimated his force. By then, feelings were so strong that American militiamen continued firing on Tories trying to surrender and later indiscriminately slaughtered Tory prisoners. The Battle of Kings Mountain was the turning point of the war in the South. By proving that the British were not invincible, it emboldened small farmers to join guerrilla bands under such colorful leaders as Francis Marion, "the Swamp Fox," and Thomas Sumter, "the Carolina Gamecock."

While the overmountain men were closing in on Ferguson, Congress chose a new commander for the southern theater, General Nathanael Greene, "the fighting Quaker" of Rhode Island. A man of infinite patience, skilled at managing men and saving supplies, careful to avoid needless risks, he was suited to a prolonged war of attrition against the British forces. From Charlotte, North Carolina, where he arrived in December 1780, Greene moved his army eastward and sent General Daniel Morgan with about 700 men on a sweep to the west of Cornwallis's headquarters at Winnsboro, South Carolina. Taking a position near Cowpens, a cow-grazing area in northern South Carolina, Morgan's force engaged Tarleton's army on January 17, 1781. Once the battle was joined, Tarleton rushed his men forward, only to be ambushed by Morgan's cavalry. Tarleton escaped, but over 100 of his men were killed, and more than 700 were taken prisoner.

Morgan then fell back into North Carolina and linked up with General Greene's main force at Guilford Courthouse (near what became Greensboro). Greene lured Cornwallis's army north, stretching the British supply lines to the breaking point. The Americans attacked the redcoats at Guilford Courthouse on March 15, 1781, inflicted heavy losses, and then withdrew. Cornwallis marched off toward Wilmington, on the North Carolina coast, to lick his wounds and take on supplies from British ships. Greene then resolved to go back into South Carolina in the hope of drawing Cornwallis after him or forcing the British to give up the state. There he joined forces with the local guerrillas and in a series of brilliant actions kept losing battles while winning the war. "We fight, get beat, rise, and fight again," he said. By September 1781 he had narrowed British control in the Deep South to Charleston and Savannah, although for more than a year longer Whigs and Tories slashed at each other "with savage fury" in the backcountry, where there was "nothing but murder and devastation in every quarter," Greene said.

Meanwhile, Cornwallis had headed north, away from Greene, reasoning that Virginia must be eliminated as a source of reinforcement before the Carolinas could be subdued. In May 1781 the British force marched into

Virginia. There, since December 1780, Benedict Arnold, now a *British* general, had been engaged in a war of maneuver against the American forces. Arnold, until September 1780, had been the American commander at West Point, New York. Overweening in ambition, lacking in moral scruples, and a reckless spender on his fashionable wife, Arnold had nursed a grudge against Washington over an official reprimand for his extravagances as commander of reoccupied Philadelphia. Traitors have a price, and Arnold had found his: he had crassly plotted to sell out the American garrison at West Point to the British, and he even suggested how they might seize George Washington himself. Only the fortuitous capture of the British go-between, Major John André, had ended Arnold's plot. Warned that his plan had been discovered, Arnold had joined the British in New York while André was hanged by the Americans as a spy.

YORKTOWN   When Cornwallis linked up with Arnold at Petersburg, Virginia, their combined British forces totaled 7,200 men, far more than the small American army in the South. The arrival of American reinforcements led Cornwallis to pick Yorktown, Virginia, on Chesapeake Bay, as a defensible site. There appeared to be little reason to worry about a siege, since Washington's main land force seemed preoccupied with attacking New York, and the British navy controlled American waters.

To be sure, there was a small American navy, but it was no match for the British fleet. Yet American privateers distracted and wounded the British massive ships. Most celebrated were the exploits of Captain John Paul Jones. Off England's coast on September 23, 1779, Jones and his crew won a desperate battle with a British frigate, which the Americans captured and occupied before their own ship sank. This was the occasion for Jones's stirring and oft-repeated response to a British demand for surrender: "I have not yet begun to fight."

Still, such heroics were little more than nuisances to the British. But at a critical point, thanks to the French navy, the British lost naval control of Chesapeake Bay. Indeed, it is impossible to imagine an American victory in the Revolution without the assistance of the French. As long as the British navy maintained supremacy at sea, the Americans could not hope to force a settlement to their advantage. For three years, George Washington had waited to get some strategic military benefit from the French alliance. In July 1780 the French had finally landed 6,000 soldiers at Newport, Rhode Island, which the British had given up to concentrate on the South, but the French force had sat there for a year, blockaded by the British fleet.

Then, in 1781, the elements for a combined action suddenly fell into place. In May, as Cornwallis moved into Virginia, George Washington persuaded the commander of the French army to join forces for an attack on New York. The two armies linked up in July, but before they could strike at New York, word came from the West Indies that Admiral François-Joseph-Paul de Grasse was bound for the Chesapeake Bay with his entire French fleet and some 3,000 soldiers. Washington immediately began moving his army south toward Yorktown. Meanwhile, French ships slipped out of the British blockade at Newport and also headed toward Chesapeake Bay.

On August 30, Admiral de Grasse's fleet reached Yorktown, and French troops landed to join the American force confronting Cornwallis's army. On September 6, the day after a British fleet appeared, de Grasse gave battle and forced the British to give up the effort to relieve Cornwallis, whose fate was quickly sealed. De Grasse then sent ships up the Chesapeake to ferry down the allied armies, bringing the total American and French armies to more than 16,000, or better than double the size of Cornwallis's besieged British army.

The siege of Yorktown began on September 28. On October 14 two major outposts guarding the left of the British line fell to French and American attackers, the latter led by Washington's aide, Alexander Hamilton. A British counterattack failed to retake them. Later that day a squall forced Cornwallis to abandon a desperate plan to escape across the York River. On October 17, 1781, Cornwallis sued for peace, and on October 19, as colors cased (that is, their flag lowered as a sign of surrender), the British force of more than

Surrender of Lord Cornwallis

By John Trumbull. The artist completed his painting of the pivotal British surrender at Yorktown in 1781.

7,000 marched out as its band played somber tunes along with the English nursery rhyme "The World Turned Upside Down." Cornwallis himself claimed to be too ill to appear. His dispatch to his superior was telling: "I have the mortification to inform your Excellency that I have been forced to . . . surrender the troops under my command."

NEGOTIATIONS

Whatever lingering hopes of victory the British may have harbored vanished at Yorktown. "Oh God, it's all over," Lord North groaned at news of the surrender. On February 27, 1782, the House of Commons voted against continuing the war, and on March 20 Lord North resigned. The Continental Congress named commissioners to negotiate a peace treaty, including John Adams, who was on state business in the Netherlands; John Jay, minister to Spain; and Benjamin Franklin, already in Paris. Franklin and Jay did most of the work.

The French commitment to Spain complicated the treaty negotiations. Spain and the United States were allied with France but not with each other. America was bound by its alliance to fight on until the French made peace, and the French were bound to help the Spanish recover Gibraltar from England. Unable to deliver Gibraltar, or so the tough-minded Jay reasoned, the French might try to bargain off American land west of the Appalachians in its place. Fearful that the French were angling for a separate peace with the British, Jay persuaded Franklin to meet with British diplomats separately. On November 30, 1782, the talks produced a preliminary treaty with Great Britain. If it violated the spirit of the alliance with France, it did not violate the strict letter of the treaty, for the French

American Commissioners of the Preliminary Peace Negotiations with Great Britain

An unfinished painting from 1782 by Benjamin West. From left, John Jay, John Adams, Benjamin Franklin, Henry Laurens, and Franklin's grandson William Temple Franklin.

minister was notified the day before it was signed, and final agreement still depended upon a Franco-British settlement.

THE TREATY OF PARIS   Early in 1783, France and Spain gave up on Gibraltar and reached an armistice with Britain. The final signing of the Treaty of Paris came on September 3, 1783. In accord with the bargain already struck, Great Britain recognized the independence of the United States and agreed to a Mississippi River boundary to the west. Both the northern and the southern borders left ambiguities that would be disputed for years. Florida, as it turned out, passed back to Spain. The British further granted the Americans the "liberty" of fishing off Newfoundland and in the Gulf of St. Lawrence and the right to dry their catch on the unsettled Atlantic coast of Canada. On the matter of prewar debts, the best the British could get was a promise that their merchants should "meet with no legal impediment" in seeking to collect money owed them by Americans. And on the tender point of Loyalists whose estates had been confiscated, the negotiators agreed that Congress would "earnestly recommend" to the states the restoration of confiscated property. Each of the last two points was little more than a face-saving gesture to the British.

THE POLITICAL REVOLUTION

REPUBLICAN IDEOLOGY   The Americans had won their War of Independence. Had they undergone a political revolution as well? Years later John Adams offered an answer: "The Revolution was effected before the war commenced. The Revolution was in the minds and hearts of the people. . . . This radical change in the principles, opinions, sentiments, and affections of the people, was the real American Revolution." Yet Adams's observation ignores the fact that the Revolutionary War itself served as the catalyst for a prolonged debate about what new forms of government would best serve an independent republic. Americans promoted a "republican" system as opposed to the aristocratic or monarchical governments that had long dominated Europe. In its simplest sense the new American republic was a nation whose citizens (property-holding white men) were deemed equal before the law and governed themselves through elected and appointed representatives. Classical republican theory cherished individual liberty and feared centralized power. To preserve the delicate balance between liberty and power, republicans believed that their new governments must be designed to protect individual liberty and states' rights. Governments must be structured

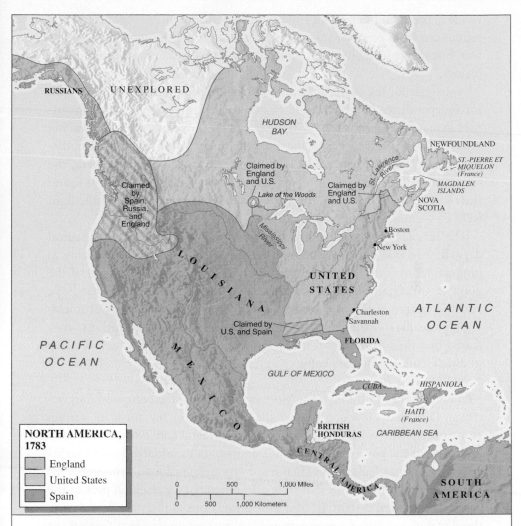

NORTH AMERICA, 1783

- England
- United States
- Spain

RUSSIANS

UNEXPLORED

HUDSON BAY

NEWFOUNDLAND

ST.-PIERRE ET MIQUELON (France)

Claimed by England and U.S.

MAGDALEN ISLANDS

Claimed by Spain, Russia, and England

Lake of the Woods

Claimed by England and U.S.

St. Lawrence River

NOVA SCOTIA

Mississippi River

Boston

New York

UNITED STATES

ATLANTIC OCEAN

LOUISIANA

Claimed by U.S. and Spain

Charleston

Savannah

FLORIDA

PACIFIC OCEAN

MEXICO

GULF OF MEXICO

CUBA

HISPANIOLA

HAITI (France)

BRITISH HONDURAS

CARIBBEAN SEA

CENTRAL AMERICA

SOUTH AMERICA

0 500 1,000 Miles

0 500 1,000 Kilometers

How did France's treaties with Spain complicate the peace-treaty negotiations with the British? What were the terms of the Treaty of Paris? Why might the ambiguities in the treaty have led to conflicts among the Americans, the Spanish, and the British?

to create counterbalancing forces to prevent tyranny from emerging. The conventional British model of mixed government sought to balance monarchy, aristocracy, and the common people and thereby protect individual liberty. Because of the more democratic nature of their society, however, Americans knew that they must devise new political assumptions and institutions. They had no monarchy or aristocracy. Yet how could sovereignty reside in the common people? How could Americans ensure the survival of a republican form of government, long assumed to be the most fragile? The war thus sparked a spate of state constitution making that remains unique in history.

A struggle for the rights of English citizens in the colonies became a fight for independence in which those rights found expression in governments that were new yet deeply rooted in the colonial experience and the prevailing viewpoints of Whiggery and the Enlightenment. With the Loyalists displaced or dispersed, such ideas as the contract theory of government, the sovereignty of the people, the separation of powers, and natural rights found their way into the new state constitutions that were devised while the fight went on—amid other urgent business.

The very idea of representative ("republican") government was a radical departure in that day. A republic, it was presumed, would endure only as long as the majority of the people were virtuous and willingly placed the good of society above the self-interest of individuals. Herein lay the hope and the danger of the new American experiment in popular government: even as leaders enthusiastically fashioned new state constitutions, they feared that their experiments in republicanism would fail because of a lack of civic virtue among the people.

STATE CONSTITUTIONS   Most of the political experimentation between 1776 and 1787 occurred at the state level in the form of written constitutions in which the people were sovereign and delegated limited authority to the government. In addition, the states initiated bills of rights guaranteeing particular individual freedoms and fashioned procedures for constitutional conventions that have also remained an essential part of the American political system. In sum, the innovations at the state level during the Revolution created a reservoir of ideas and experience that formed the basis for the creation of the federal constitution in 1787.

The first state constitutions varied mainly in detail. They formed governments much like the colonial governments, but with elected governors and senates instead of appointed governors and councils. Generally they embodied a separation of powers (legislative, executive, and judicial) as a safeguard against abuses. Most of them also included a bill of rights that protected the time-honored rights of petition, freedom of speech, trial by jury, freedom from self-incrimination, and the like. Most tended to limit the powers of governors and increase the powers of the legislatures, which had led the people in their quarrels with the colonial governors.

THE ARTICLES OF CONFEDERATION The national American government, the Continental Congress, had exercised powers without any constitutional sanction before March 1781. Plans for a permanent frame of government emerged very early, however. Richard Henry Lee's motion for independence included a call for a plan of confederation. As early as July 1776, a committee headed by John Dickinson had produced a draft constitution, the Articles of Confederation and Perpetual Union. For more than a year, Congress had debated the articles in between more urgent matters and had finally adopted them in November 1777. All states ratified them promptly except Maryland, which insisted that the seven states claiming western lands should cede them to the authority of Congress. Maryland did not relent until early 1781, when Virginia gave up its claims, under the old colonial charter, to the vast region north of the Ohio River. New York had already relinquished a dubious claim based upon its "jurisdiction" over the Iroquois, and the other states eventually abandoned their claims to western lands as well.

When the Articles of Confederation became effective, in March 1781, they did little more than legalize the status quo. "The United States of America in Congress Assembled" had a multitude of responsibilities but little authority to carry them out. Congress was intended not as a legislature, nor as a sovereign entity unto itself, but as a collective substitute for the monarch. In essence it was to be a legislative body serving as the nation's executive rather than a parliament. It had full power over foreign affairs and questions of war and peace; it could decide disputes between the states; it had authority over coinage, the postal service, and Indian affairs and responsibility for the government of the western territories. But it had no courts and no power to enforce its resolutions and ordinances at either the state or an individual level. It also had no power to levy taxes and had to rely on requisitions, which state legislatures could ignore.

The states, after their battles with Parliament, were in no mood for a strong central government. Congress in fact had less power than the colonists had once accepted in Parliament, since it could not regulate interstate and foreign commerce. For certain important acts, moreover, a "special majority" was required. Nine states had to approve measures dealing with war, treaties, coinage, finances, and the army and navy. Unanimous approval of the states was needed to levy tariffs (often called duties) on imports. Amendments to the Articles also required unanimous ratification by all the states. The Confederation had neither an executive nor a judicial branch; there was no administrative head of government (only the president of Congress, chosen annually), and there were no federal courts.

For all its weaknesses, however, the Confederation government represented the most pragmatic structure for the new nation fighting for its very survival. After all, the Revolution on the battlefields had yet to be won, and America's statesmen could not risk the prolonged and divisive debates over the distribution of power that other forms of government would have entailed.

THE SOCIAL REVOLUTION

Political revolutions and the chaos of war often spawn social revolutions. What did the Revolution mean to those workers, servants, farmers, and freed slaves who participated in the Stamp Act demonstrations, supported the boycotts, idolized Tom Paine, and fought with Generals Washington, Gates, and Greene? Many laboring folk hoped that the Revolution would remove, not reinforce, the elite's traditional political and social advantages. The more conservative Patriots would have been content to replace royal officials with the rich, the wellborn, and the able and let it go at that. But more radical revolutionaries raised the question not only of home rule but also of who should rule at home.

EQUALITY AND ITS LIMITS   This spirit of equality found outlet in several directions, one of which was simply a weakening of old habits of deference. A Virginia gentleman remembered being in a tavern when a group of farmers came in, spitting and pulling off their muddy boots without regard for the sensibilities of the gentlemen present: "The spirit of independence was converted into equality," he wrote, "and every one who bore arms, esteems himself upon a footing with his neighbors. . . . No doubt each of these men considers himself, in every respect, my equal."

Participation in the army or militia excited men who had taken little interest in politics before. The new political opportunities afforded by the creation of state governments led more ordinary citizens to participate than ever before. The social base of the new legislatures was thus much broader than that of the old assemblies. Men fighting for their liberty found it difficult to justify denying other white men the rights of suffrage and representation. The property qualifications for voting, which already admitted an overwhelming majority of white men, were lowered still further. In Pennsylvania, Delaware, North Carolina, and Georgia, any male taxpayer could vote, although candidates for elector offices usually had to meet more stringent property requirements. Men who had argued against taxation without representation now questioned the denial of proportional representation for

Social democracy

In this watercolor by Benjamin Latrobe, a gentleman plays billiards with artisans, suggesting that "the spirit of independence was converted into equality."

the backcountry, which generally enlarged its presence in the legislatures. More often than not, the political newcomers were men with less property and little formal education. All states concentrated power in a legislature chosen by a wide suffrage, but not even Pennsylvania, which adopted the most radical of the state constitutions, went quite so far as to grant universal male suffrage.

New developments in land tenure that grew out of the Revolution extended the democratic trends of suffrage requirements. All state legislatures seized Tory estates. These properties were of small consequence, however, in contrast to the unsettled areas formerly at the disposal of the Crown and proprietors but now in the hands of popular assemblies. Much of that land was now used for bonuses to reward veterans of the war. Moreover, western lands, formerly closed by the Royal Proclamation of 1763 and the Quebec Act of 1774, were soon thrown open to settlers.

THE PARADOX OF SLAVERY Members of the Revolutionary generation of leaders were the first to consider abolishing slavery. The principles of liberty and equality invoked in debates over British policies had clear implications for enslaved Americans. Before the Revolution only Rhode Island, Connecticut, and Pennsylvania had halted the importation of slaves. After independence all the states except Georgia stopped the traffic, although South Carolina later reopened it.

African American soldiers or sailors were present at most major battles from Lexington to Yorktown, most on the Loyalist side. When the Revolution began, the British had promised freedom to slaves, as well as to indentured servants, who would bear arms for the Loyalist cause. In December 1775, Lord Dunmore, the royal governor of Virginia, issued such an offer and within a month had attracted 300 former servants and slaves to the British army. Within a year the number had grown to almost 1,000, although Dunmore himself refused to release his own slaves. The overseer of Mount Vernon reported to General George Washington that his slaves and servants would leave if they got the chance. "Liberty is sweet," he bitterly added. Dunmore's effort to recruit slaves into the "Ethiopian Regiment" infuriated Washington and other Virginia planters. Washington predicted that if Dunmore were "not crushed" soon, the number of slaves joining him would "increase as a Snow ball by Rolling." For all of the revolutionary rhetoric about liberty, the war for independence was intended to liberate whites only. As a New England soldier named Josiah Atkins noticed when he was sent to the southern theater, the ideals of the war were "strikingly inconsistent" with the widespread practice of slavery in Virginia and the Carolinas. Independence was for whites only.

In December 1775 a Patriot militia defeated Lord Dunmore and his army of blacks and forced the British units to flee Norfolk, Virginia, and board ships in the Chesapeake Bay. No sooner had the former slaves crowded onto the British ships than they contracted smallpox. The epidemic raced through the fleet, eventually forcing the Loyalist forces to disembark on an offshore island. During the winter and spring of 1776, disease devastated the primitive camp. "Dozens died daily from Small Pox and rotten Fevers by which diseases they are infected," wrote a visitor. Before the Loyalists fled the island in the summer of 1776, over half of the troops, most of them former slaves, had died.

In response to the British recruitment of American slaves, General Washington, at the end of 1775, reversed the policy of excluding blacks from the American forces—except the few already in militia companies—and Congress quickly approved the new policy. Only two states, South Carolina and Georgia, refused to allow blacks to serve in the Patriot forces. No more than about 5,000 African Americans were admitted to the total American forces of about 300,000, and most of them were free blacks from northern states. They served mainly in white units, although Massachusetts did organize two all-black companies, and Rhode Island organized one.

Slaves who supported the cause of independence won their freedom and, in some cases, received land bounties as well. But the British army, which liberated tens of thousands of slaves during the war, was a greater instrument of emancipation than the American forces. Most of the newly freed blacks found their way to Canada or to British colonies in the Caribbean. American Whigs had shown no mercy to blacks caught aiding or abetting the British cause. A Charleston mob hanged and then burned Thomas Jeremiah, a free African American who was convicted of telling slaves that the British "were come to help the poor Negroes." White Loyalists who were caught encouraging slave militancy were tarred and feathered.

Elizabeth Freeman ("Mum Bett")

Also known as Mum Bett, Freeman was born around 1742 and sold as a slave to a Massachusetts family. She won her freedom by claiming in court that the Bill of Rights and the new state constitution gave liberty to all, and her case contributed to the eventual abolition of slavery in Massachusetts. One of Freeman's great grandchildren was the scholar and civil rights leader W. E. B. Du Bois.

In the northern states, which had fewer slaves than the southern states, the doctrines of liberty led swiftly to emancipation for all, either during the fighting or shortly afterward. The Vermont Constitution of 1777 specifically forbade slavery. The Massachusetts Constitution of 1780 proclaimed the "inherent liberty" of all. In 1780, Pennsylvania declared that all children born thereafter to slave mothers would become free at age twenty-eight, after enabling their owners to recover their initial cost. In 1784, Rhode Island provided freedom to all children of slaves born thereafter, at age twenty-one for males, eighteen for females. New York lagged until 1799 in granting freedom to mature slaves born after enactment of its constitution, but an act of 1817 set July 4, 1827, as the date for emancipation of all remaining "people in slavery."

In the states south of Pennsylvania, emancipation was less popular. Yet even there, slaveholders expressed moral qualms. Thomas Jefferson wrote in his *Notes on the State of Virginia* (1785): "Indeed I tremble for my country when I reflect that God is just; that his justice cannot sleep forever." But he, like many other white southerners, could not bring himself to free his slaves. In the southern states anti-slavery sentiment went no further than a relaxation of the manumission laws, under which owners might free their slaves through individual acts. Some 10,000 enslaved Virginians were manumitted during the 1780s. A much smaller number would be shipped back to Africa during the early nineteenth century. By the outbreak of the Civil War, in 1861, approximately half the African Americans living in Maryland were free.

Manumission freed slaves by the action of a white owner. But slaves, especially in the upper South, also earned freedom through their own actions during the Revolutionary era, frequently by running away. They often gravitated to the growing number of African American communities in the North. Because of emancipation laws in the northern states, and with the formation of free black neighborhoods in the North and in several southern cities, runaways found refuge and the opportunities for new lives. It is estimated that 80,000 to 100,000 slaves, nearly one out of five, fled to freedom during the Revolution. Angry slave owners often hunted down the runaways, executing some of them and whipping the rest. At the end of the war, the British took more than 3,000 former slaves to Canada.

THE STATUS OF WOMEN   The logic of liberty spawned by the Revolution applied to the status of women as much as to that of African Americans. Women in the colonies had remained essentially confined to the domestic sphere during the eighteenth century. They could not vote or preach or hold office. Few had access to formal education. Only rarely could women own property or execute contracts. Divorces were extremely difficult to obtain.

Yet the Revolution offered women new opportunities. Women were drawn at least temporarily into new pursuits. Women supported the armies in various roles: by handling supplies, serving as couriers, and working as camp followers—cooking, cleaning, and nursing the soldiers. Wives often followed their husbands to camp and on occasion took their place in the line, as Margaret Corbin did at Fort Washington when her husband fell at his artillery post and as Mary Ludwig Hays (better known as Molly Pitcher) did when her husband collapsed of heat exhaustion. An exceptional case was Deborah Sampson, who joined a Massachusetts regiment as Robert Shurtleff and served from 1781 to 1783 by the "artful concealment" of her sex.

To be sure, most women retained the constricted domestic outlook that had long been imposed upon them by society. But a few free-spirited reformers demanded equal treatment. In an essay titled "On the Equality of the Sexes," written in 1779 and published in 1790, Judith Sargent Murray of Gloucester, Massachusetts, stressed that women were perfectly capable of excelling outside the domestic sphere.

Molly Pitcher

At Fort Washington, Molly Pitcher took her husband's place at the cannon during the American Revolution.

Early in the Revolutionary struggle, Abigail Adams, one of the most learned, spirited, and independent women of the time, wrote to her husband, John: "In the new Code of Laws which I suppose it will be necessary for you to make I desire you would remember the Ladies. . . . Do not put such unlimited power into the hands of the Husbands." Since men were "Naturally Tyrannical," she wrote, "why then, not put it out of the power of the vicious and the Lawless to use us with cruelty and indignity with impunity." Otherwise, "if particular care and attention is not paid to the Ladies we are determined to foment a Rebellion, and will not hold ourselves bound by any Laws in which we have no voice, or Representation." Husband John expressed surprise that women might be discontented, but he clearly knew the privileges enjoyed by males and was determined to retain them: "Depend upon it, we know better than to repeal our Masculine systems." Thomas Jefferson was of one mind with Adams on the matter. When asked about women's voting rights, he replied that "the tender breasts of ladies were not formed for political convulsion."

The legal status of women did not improve dramatically as a result of the Revolutionary ferment. Married women in most states still forfeited

A symbolic frontispiece from *Lady's Magazine*

Lady's Magazine printed extensive extracts from Mary Wollstonecraft's *A Vindication of the Rights of Woman* (1792).

control of their own property to their husbands, and women gained no permanent political rights. Under the 1776 New Jersey Constitution, which neglected to specify an exclusively male franchise because the delegates apparently took the distinction for granted, women who met the property qualifications for voting exercised the right until they were denied access early in the nineteenth century.

INDIANS AND THE REVOLU-TION The war for American independence had profound effects on the Indians in the southern backcountry and in the Old Northwest region west of New York and Pennsylvania. Most tribes sought to remain neutral in the conflict, but both British and American agents lobbied the chiefs to fight on their side. The result was the disintegration of the alliance among the six tribes making up the Iroquois League. The Mohawks, for example, succumbed to British promises to protect them from encroachments by American settlers on their lands. The Oneidas, on the other hand, fought on the side of the American Patriots. The result of such alliances was chaos on the frontier. Indians on both sides attacked villages, burned crops, and killed civilians. The new American government assured its Indian allies that it would respect their lands and their rights. In December 1777 the Continental Congress promised Oneida leaders that "we shall [always] love and respect you. As our trusty friends, we shall protect you; and shall at all times consider your welfare as our own." But in various places local Revolutionaries adopted a very different goal: they sought to use the turmoil of war to displace and destroy Native Americans. In 1777 South Carolina militiamen were ordered to "cut up every Indian cornfield, and burn every Indian town and every Indian taken shall be slave and property of the taker and . . . the [Indian] nation be extirpated and the lands become the property of the public." Once the war ended and independence was secured, the U.S. government turned its back on most of the pledges made to Native Americans. By the end of the eighteenth century, land-hungry American whites were again pushing into Indian territories on the western frontier.

FREEDOM OF RELIGION   The Revolution also tested traditional religious loyalties and set in motion a transition from the toleration of religious dissent to a complete freedom of religion as embodied in the principle of separation of church and state. The Anglican Church, established as the official religion in five colonies and parts of two others, was especially vulnerable. Anglicans tended to be pro-British. And non-Anglican dissenters, most notably Baptists and Methodists, outnumbered Anglicans in all states except Virginia. All but Virginia eliminated tax support for the church before the fighting was over, and Virginia did so soon afterward. Although Anglicanism survived in the form of the new Episcopal Church, it never regained its pre-Revolutionary size or stature. Newer denominations, such as Methodists and Baptists, as well as Presbyterians, filled the vacuum created by the shrinking Anglican Church.

In 1776 the Virginia Declaration of Rights guaranteed the free exercise of religion, and in 1786 the Virginia Statute of Religious Freedom (written by

Religious development

The Congregational Church developed a national presence in the early nineteenth century, and Lemuel Haynes, depicted here, was its first African American preacher.

Thomas Jefferson) declared that "no man shall be compelled to frequent or support any religious worship, place or ministry whatsoever" and "that all men shall be free to profess, and by argument to maintain, their opinions in matters of religion." These statutes and the Revolutionary ideology that justified them helped shape the course that religion would take in the new United States: pluralistic and voluntary rather than state supported and monolithic.

In churches as in government, the Revolution set off a period of constitution making as some of the first national church bodies emerged. In 1784 the Methodists, who at first were an offshoot of the Anglicans, gathered for a general conference at Baltimore under Bishop Francis Asbury. The Anglican Church, rechristened the Episcopal Church, gathered in a series of meetings that by 1789 had united the various dioceses in a federal union; in 1789 the Presbyterians also held their first general assembly in Philadelphia. That same year the Catholic Church got its first higher official in the United States when John Carroll was named bishop of Baltimore.

THE EMERGENCE OF AN AMERICAN CULTURE

The Revolution helped excite a sense of common nationality. One of the first ways in which a national consciousness was forged was through the annual celebration of the new nation's independence from Great Britain. On July 2, 1776, when the Second Continental Congress had resolved "that these United Colonies are, and of right ought to be, free and independent states," John Adams had written his wife, Abigail, that future generations would remember that date as their "day of deliverance." People, he predicted, would celebrate the occasion with "solemn acts of devotion to God Almighty" and with "pomp and parade, with shows, games, sports, guns, bells, bonfires and illuminations [fireworks] from one end of this continent to the other, from this time forward, forever more."

Adams got everything right but the date. Americans fastened not upon July 2 but upon July 4 as their Independence Day. To be sure, it was on the Fourth that Congress formally adopted the Declaration of Independence and ordered it to be printed and distributed throughout the states, but America by then had been officially independent for two days. As luck would have it, July 4 became Independence Day by accident. In 1777, Congress forgot to make any acknowledgment of the first anniversary of independence until July 3, when it was too late to honor July 2. As a consequence, the Fourth won by default.

The celebration of Independence Day quickly became the most important public ritual in the United States. Huge numbers of people from all walks of life suspended their normal routine in order to devote a day to parades, formal orations, and fireworks displays. In the process the infant republic began to create its own myth of national identity that transcended local or regional concerns. "What a day!" exclaimed the editor of the *Southern Patriot* in 1815. "What happiness, what emotion, what virtuous triumph must fill the bosoms of Americans!"

AMERICA'S "DESTINY" American nationalism embodied a stirring idea. This first new nation, unlike the Old World nations of Europe, was not rooted in antiquity. Its people, except for the Native Americans, had not inhabited it over the centuries, nor was there any notion of a common ethnic descent. "The American national consciousness," one observer wrote, "is not a voice crying out of the depth of the dark past, but is proudly a product of the enlightened present, setting its face resolutely toward the future."

Many people, at least since the time of the Pilgrims, had thought of America as singled out for a special identity, a special mission. Jonathan Edwards said God had chosen America as "the glorious renovator of the world," and later John Adams proclaimed the opening of America "a grand scheme and design in Providence for the illumination and the emancipation of the slavish part of mankind all over the earth." This sense of mission was neither limited to New England nor rooted solely in Calvinism. From the democratic rhetoric of Thomas Jefferson to the pragmatism of George Washington to heady toasts bellowed in South Carolina taverns, patriots everywhere articulated a special role for American leadership in history. The mission was now a call to lead the world toward greater liberty and equality. Meanwhile, however, Americans had to address more immediate problems created by their new nationhood. The Philadelphia doctor and scientist Benjamin Rush issued a prophetic statement in 1787: "The American war is over: but this is far from being the case with the American Revolution. On the contrary, but the first act of the great drama is closed."

CHAPTER SUMMARY

- **Military Strategies** The Americans had to create an army—the Continental army—from scratch and sustain it. To defeat the British, Washington realized that the Americans had to wage a war of attrition, given that the British army was fighting a war thousands of miles from its home base. To defeat the Americans, Britain's initial strategy was to take New York and sever the troublesome New England colonies from the rest.

- **Turning Points** The American victory at Saratoga in 1777 was the first major turning point of the war. Washington's ability to hold his forces together despite daily desertions and two especially difficult winters was a second major turning point. The British lost support from the southern colonies when they executed the rebels they captured in backcountry skirmishing.

- **Loyalists, "Tories"** The American Revolution was a civil war, dividing families and communities. There were at least 100,000 Tories, or Loyalists, in the colonies. They included royal officials, Anglican ministers, wealthy southern planters, and the elite in large seaport cities; they also included many humble people, especially recent immigrants. After the hostilities ended, most Loyalists, including slaves who had fled their plantations to support the British cause, left for Canada, the West Indies, or England.

- **Worldwide Conflict** The French were prospective allies from the beginning of the conflict, because they resented their losses to Britain in the Seven Years' War. After the British defeat at Saratoga, France and the colonies agreed to fight together until independence was won. Further agreements with Spain and the Netherlands helped to make the Revolution a worldwide conflict. French supplies and the presence of the French fleet ensured the Americans' victory at Yorktown.

- **A Social Revolution** The American Revolution disrupted and transformed traditional class and social relationships. More white men gained the vote as property requirements were removed. Northern states began to free slaves, but southerner states were reluctant. Although many women had undertaken nontraditional roles during the war, they remained largely confined to the domestic sphere afterward, with no changes to their legal or political status. The Revolution had catastrophic effects on the Native Americans, regardless of which side they had embraced. American settlers seized Native American land, often in violation of existing treaties.

CHRONOLOGY

1776	General Washington's troops cross the Delaware River; Battle of Trenton
1776–1777	Washington's troops winter at Morristown, New Jersey
1777	Battle of Saratoga; General Burgoyne surrenders
1777–1778	Washington's troops winter at Valley Forge, Pennsylvania
1778	Americans and French form an alliance
1781	Battles of Cowpens and Guildford Courthouse
1781	General Cornwallis surrenders at Yorktown, Virginia
1781	Articles of Confederation are ratified
1783	Treaty of Paris is signed
1786	Virginia adopts the Statute of Religious Freedom

KEY TERMS & NAMES

General George Washington p. 232

General William Howe p. 232

Tories p. 236

Continental army p. 237

Saratoga p. 241

General John Burgoyne p. 241

General Charles Cornwallis p. 241

Benedict Arnold p. 242

Marquis de Lafayette p. 245

Joseph Brant p. 247

Nathanael Greene p. 250

surrender at Yorktown p. 252

John Adams p. 253

Abigail Adams p. 263

7

SHAPING
A FEDERAL UNION

FOCUS QUESTIONS   Ⓢ   wwnorton.com/studyspace

- What were the achievements of the Confederation government?
- What were the shortcomings of the Articles of Confederation?
- Why did the delegates to the Constitutional Convention draft a completely new constitution?
- How important was the issue of slavery in the Constitution?
- What were the main issues in the debate over ratification of the Constitution?

In an address to fellow graduates at the Harvard commencement ceremony in 1787, young John Quincy Adams lamented "this critical period" when the country was "groaning under the intolerable burden of . . . accumulated evils." The same phrase, "critical period," has often been used to label the history of the United States under the Articles of Confederation, between 1781 and 1787. Fear of a British-like central government dominated the period, and the result was fragmentation and stagnation. Yet while the Confederation had its weaknesses, it also generated major achievements. Moreover, lessons learned under the Confederation would prompt the formulation of a new national constitution that better balanced central and local authority.

THE CONFEDERATION

The Congress of the Confederation had little authority. "It could ask for money but not compel payment," as one historian wrote; "it could enter into treaties but not enforce their stipulations; it could provide for raising of armies but not fill the ranks; it could borrow money but take no proper measures for repayment; it could advise and recommend but not command." Congress was virtually helpless to cope with foreign relations and a postwar economic depression that would have challenged the resources of a much stronger government. It was not easy to find men of stature to serve in such a weak congress, and it was often hard to gather a quorum of those who did. Yet in spite of its handicaps, the Confederation Congress somehow managed to survive and to lay important foundations. It concluded the Treaty of Paris in 1783, ending the Revolutionary War. It created the first executive departments. And it formulated principles of land distribution and territorial government that would guide westward expansion all the way to the Pacific coast.

Throughout most of the War of Independence, the members of Congress distrusted and limited executive power. They assigned administrative duties to numerous committees and thereby imposed a painful burden on conscientious members. John Adams, for instance, served on some eighty committees at one time or another. In 1781, however, Congress addressed the problem by establishing three executive departments: Foreign Affairs, Finance, and War, each with a single head responsible to Congress.

FINANCE   The closest thing to an executive leader of the Confederation was Robert Morris, who as superintendent of finance in the final years of the war became the most influential figure in the government. Morris wanted to make both himself and the Confederation government more powerful. He envisioned a coherent program of taxation and debt management to make the national government financially stable; "a public debt supported by public revenue will prove the strongest cement to keep our confederacy together," he confided to a friend. The powerful financiers who had lent the new government funds to buy supplies and pay its bills would, Morris believed, give stronger support to a government committed to paying its debts. Morris therefore welcomed the chance to enlarge the national debt by issuing new government bonds that would help pay off wartime debts. With a sounder federal Treasury—certainly one with the power to raise taxes—the bonds could be expected to rise in value, creating new capital with which to finance banks and economic development.

To anchor his plan, Morris in 1781 secured a congressional charter for the Bank of North America, which would hold government cash, lend money to the government, and issue currency. Though a national bank, it was in part privately owned and was expected to turn a profit for Morris and other shareholders, in addition to performing a crucial public service. But Morris's program depended ultimately upon the government's having a secure income, and it foundered on the requirement of unanimous state approval for amendments to the Articles of Confederation. Local interests and the fear of a central authority—a fear strengthened by the recent quarrels with king and Parliament—hobbled action.

To carry their point, Morris and his nationalist friends in 1783 risked a dangerous gamble. George Washington's army, encamped at Newburgh, New York, on the Hudson River, had grown restless in the final winter of the war. The soldiers' pay was late as usual, and the officers feared that the land grants promised them by the government might never be honored once their service was no longer needed. A delegation of concerned officers traveled to Philadelphia, where they soon found themselves drawn into a scheme to line up army officers and public creditors with nationalists in Congress and confront the states with the threat of a coup d'état unless they yielded more power to Congress. Alexander Hamilton, congressman from New York and former aide-de-camp to General Washington, sought to bring his old commander into the plan.

General Washington sympathized with the basic purpose of Hamilton's scheme. If congressional powers were not enlarged, he had told a friend, "anarchy and confusion must ensue." But Washington was just as deeply convinced that a military coup would be both dishonorable and dangerous. In March 1783, when he learned that some of the plotting officers had planned an unauthorized meeting, he confronted the conspirators. He told them that any effort to intimidate the government by threatening a mutinous coup violated the very purposes for which the war was being fought and directly challenged his own integrity. While agreeing that the officers had been poorly treated by the government and deserved their long-overdue back pay and future pensions, Washington expressed his "horror and detestation" of any effort by the officers to assume dictatorial powers. A military revolt would open "the flood-gates of civil discord" and "deluge our rising empire in blood." It was a virtuoso performance. When Washington finished, his officers, many of them fighting back tears, unanimously adopted resolutions denouncing the recent "infamous propositions," and the so-called Newburgh Conspiracy came to a sudden end.

In the end the Confederation never did put its finances in order. The currency issued by the Continental Congress had become worthless. It was never redeemed. The national debt, domestic and foreign, grew from $11 million to $28 million as Congress paid off citizens' and soldiers' claims. Each year, Congress ran a deficit in its operating expenses.

LAND POLICY The Confederation Congress might ultimately have drawn an independent income from the sale of western lands. Thinly populated by

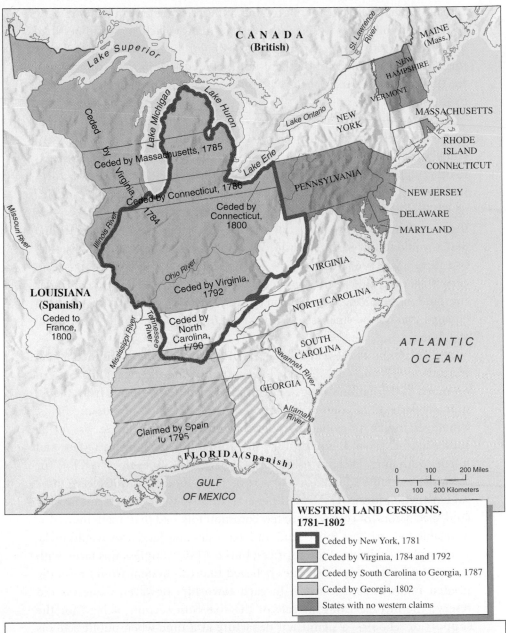

WESTERN LAND CESSIONS, 1781–1802

- Ceded by New York, 1781
- Ceded by Virginia, 1784 and 1792
- Ceded by South Carolina to Georgia, 1787
- Ceded by Georgia, 1802
- States with no western claims

Why were there so many overlapping claims to the western lands? What were the terms of the Land Ordinance of 1785? How did it arrange for future states to enter the Union?

Indians, French settlers, and a growing number of American squatters, the region north of the Ohio River and west of the Appalachian Mountains had long been the site of overlapping claims by colonies and speculators. Under the Articles of Confederation, land not included within the boundaries of the thirteen original states became public domain, owned and administered by the national government.

As early as 1779, Congress had declared that it would not treat the western lands as dependent colonies. The delegates resolved instead that western lands "shall be . . . formed into distinct Republican states," equal in all respects to other states. Between 1784 and 1787 the Confederation Congress set forth three major ordinances for the development of the West. These documents, which rank among the Confederation's greatest achievements—and among the most important in American history—set precedents that the United States would follow in its expansion all the way to the Pacific. Thomas Jefferson in fact was prepared to grant self-government to western states at an early stage, allowing settlers to meet and choose their own officials. Under the land ordinance that Jefferson wrote in 1784, when the population equaled that of the smallest existing state, the territory would achieve full statehood.

A year later, in the Land Ordinance of 1785, the delegates outlined a plan of land surveys and sales that would eventually stamp a rectangular pattern on much of the nation's surface, a rectilinear grid that is visible from the air in many parts of the country today because of the layout of roads and fields. Wherever Indian titles had been extinguished, the Northwest was to be surveyed and six-mile-square townships established along east-west and north-south lines. Each township was in turn divided into thirty-six lots (or sections) one mile square (or 640 acres). The 640-acre sections were to be sold at auction for no less than $1 per acre, or $640 total. Such terms favored land speculators, of course, since few common folk had that much money or were able to work that much land. In later years new land laws would make smaller plots available at lower prices; but in 1785, Congress was faced with an empty Treasury, and delegates believed that this system would raise the needed funds most effectively. In each township, however, Congress did reserve the income from the sale of the sixteenth section of land for the support of schools—a significant departure at a time when public schools were rare.

THE NORTHWEST ORDINANCE   Spurred by the plans for land sales and settlement, Congress drafted a more specific frame of territorial government to replace Jefferson's ordinance of 1784. The new plan backed off from

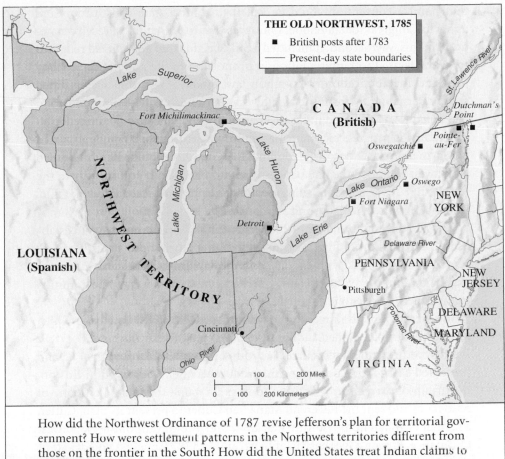

THE OLD NORTHWEST, 1785

■ British posts after 1783
— Present-day state boundaries

CANADA
(British)

Lake Superior

Fort Michilimackinac

Lake Huron

Lake Michigan

NORTHWEST

LOUISIANA
(Spanish)

TERRITORY

Detroit

Lake Erie

Lake Ontario

Oswego

Fort Niagara

St. Lawrence River

Dutchman's Point

Pointe-au-Fer

Oswegatchie

NEW YORK

Delaware River

PENNSYLVANIA

NEW JERSEY

Pittsburgh

Cincinnati

Ohio River

DELAWARE

Potomac River

MARYLAND

VIRGINIA

0   100   200 Miles
0   100   200 Kilometers

How did the Northwest Ordinance of 1787 revise Jefferson's plan for territorial government? How were settlement patterns in the Northwest territories different from those on the frontier in the South? How did the United States treat Indian claims to territory in the West?

Jefferson's recommendation of early self-government. Because of the trouble that might be expected from squatters who were clamoring for free land, the Northwest Ordinance of 1787 required a period of preparation for statehood. At first the territory fell subject to a governor, a secretary, and three judges, all chosen by Congress. Eventually there would be three to five territories in the region, and when any one of them had a population of 5,000 free male adults, it could choose an assembly. Congress then would name a council of five from ten names proposed by the assembly. The governor would have a veto over actions by the territorial assembly, and so would Congress.

The resemblance to the old royal colonies is clear, but there were three significant differences. First, the ordinance anticipated statehood when any territory's population reached a population of 60,000 "free inhabitants." At that point a convention could be called to draft a state constitution and apply to Congress for statehood. Ohio was the first territory to receive statehood in this way. Second, it included a bill of rights that guaranteed religious freedom, legislative representation in proportion to the population, trial by jury, and the application of common law. Finally, the ordinance excluded slavery permanently from the Northwest—a proviso that Thomas Jefferson had failed to get accepted in his ordinance of 1784. This proved a fateful decision. As the progress of emancipation in the existing states gradually freed all slaves above the Mason-Dixon line, the Ohio River boundary of the Old Northwest extended the line between freedom and slavery all the way to the Mississippi River, encompassing what would become the states of Ohio, Indiana, Illinois, Michigan, and Wisconsin.

The Northwest Ordinance of 1787 had a larger importance, beyond establishing a formal procedure for transforming territories into states. It represented a sharp break with the imperialistic assumption behind European expansion into the Western Hemisphere: the new states were to be admitted to the American republic as equals.

In seven mountain ranges to the west of the Ohio River, an area in which recent treaties had voided Indian titles, surveying began in the mid-1780s. But before any land sales occurred, a group of speculators from New England presented cash-poor Congress with a seductive offer. Organized in Boston, the group of former army officers took as its name the Ohio Company of Associates and sent the Reverend Manasseh Cutler to present its plan. Cutler, a former chaplain in the Continental army and a co-author of the Northwest Ordinance, proved a persuasive lobbyist, and in 1787 Congress voted a grant of 1.5 million acres for about $1 million in certificates of indebtedness to Revolutionary War veterans. The arrangement had the dual merit, Cutler argued, of reducing the national debt and encouraging new settlement and sales of federal land.

The lands south of the Ohio River followed a different line of development. Title to the western lands remained with Georgia, North Carolina, and Virginia for the time being, but settlement proceeded at a far more rapid pace during and after the Revolution, despite the Indians' fierce resentment of encroachments upon their hunting grounds. The Iroquois and Cherokees, badly battered during the Revolution, were in no position to resist encroachments by American settlers. By the Treaty of Fort Stanwix (1784), the Iroquois were forced to cede land in western New York and Pennsylvania. With the Treaty of Hopewell (1785), the Cherokees gave up all claims in South Carolina, much of western North Carolina, and large portions of present-day Kentucky and Tennessee. Also in 1785 the major Ohio tribes dropped their claim to most of Ohio, except for a chunk bordering the western part of Lake Erie. The Creeks, pressed by the state of Georgia to cede portions of their lands in 1784–1785, went to war in the summer of 1786 with covert aid from Spanish-controlled Florida. When Spanish aid diminished, however, the Creek chief traveled to New York and in 1791 finally struck a bargain that gave the Creeks favorable trade arrangements with the United States but did not restore the lost land.

TRADE AND THE ECONOMY In its economic life, as in planning westward expansion, the young nation dealt vigorously with difficult problems. Congress had little to do with achievements in the economy, but neither could it bear the blame for an acute economic contraction that occurred between 1770 and 1790, the result primarily of the war and separation from the British Empire. Although farmers enmeshed in local markets maintained their livelihood during the Revolutionary era, commercial agriculture dependent upon trade with foreign markets collapsed during the war. Virginia planters saw many of their enslaved workers liberated by the British. Chesapeake planters also lost their lucrative foreign markets. The tobacco trade was especially hard hit. The British decision to close its West Indian colonies to American commerce devastated what had been a thriving market for timber, wheat, and other foodstuffs.

After the war, British trade with America did resume, and American ships were allowed to deliver American products to Britain and return to the United States with British goods. American ships could not carry British goods anywhere else, however. The pent-up demand for goods imported from London created a vigorous market in postwar exports to America. The result was a quick cycle of postwar boom and bust, a buying spree followed by a money shortage and economic troubles that lasted several years.

In colonial days the chronic trade deficit with Britain had been offset by the influx of coins from trade with the West Indies. Now American ships found themselves excluded altogether from the British West Indies. The islands, however, still needed wheat, fish, and lumber, and American shippers had not lost their talent for smuggling. By 1787 American seaports were flourishing as never before. Trade treaties opened new markets with the Dutch (1782), the Swedes (1783), the Prussians (1785), and the Moroccans (1787), and American shippers found new outlets on their own in Europe, Africa, and Asia. The most spectacular new development, if not the largest, was trade with China. It began in 1784–1785, when the *Empress of China*

Merchants' counting house

Americans involved in overseas trade, such as the merchants depicted here, had been sharply affected by the dislocations of war.

sailed from New York to Canton (Kuang-Chou)* and back, around the tip of South America. Profits from its cargo of silks and tea encouraged the outfitting of other ships, which carried American goods to exchange for the luxury goods of east Asia.

By 1790 the dollar value of American commerce and exports had far exceeded the trade of the colonies. Merchants had more ships than they had had before the war. Farm exports were twice what they had been. Although most of the exports were the products of forests, fields, and fisheries, during and after the war more Americans had turned to small-scale manufacturing, mainly for domestic markets.

DIPLOMACY   Yet while postwar trade flourished, the shortcomings and failures of the Articles of Confederation prompted a growing chorus of com-

---

*The traditional (Wade-Giles) spelling is used here. Nearly two centuries after these events, the Chinese government adopted pinyin transliterations, which became more widely used after 1976, so that, for example, Peking became Beijing and, in this case, Kuang-Chou became Guanzhou.

plaints. In the diplomatic arena, there remained the nagging problems of relations with Great Britain and Spain, both of which still kept military posts on American soil and conspired with Indians to foment unrest. The British, despite pledges made in the peace treaty of 1783, held on to a string of forts along the Canadian border. They argued that their continued occupation was justified by the failure of Americans to pay their prewar debts to British creditors. According to one Virginian, a common question in his state was, "If we are now to pay the debts due to British merchants, what have we been fighting for all this while?"

Another major irritant in U.S.-British relations was the American confiscation of Loyalist property. The Treaty of Paris had encouraged Congress to end confiscations of Tory property, to guarantee immunity to Loyalists for twelve months, during which they could return from Canada or Great Britain and wind up their affairs, and to recommend that the states give back confiscated property. Persecutions, even lynchings, of Loyalists occurred even after the end of the war. Some Loyalists who had fled returned unmolested, however, and resumed their lives in their former homes. By the end of 1787, moreover, at the request of Congress, all the states had rescinded any laws that were in conflict with the peace treaty.

With Spain the chief issues were the disputed southern boundary of the United States and the right for Americans to navigate the Mississippi River. According to the preliminary treaty with Britain, the United States claimed a southern boundary line as far south as the 31st parallel; Spain held out for the line running eastward from the mouth of the Yazoo River (at 32°28′N), which it claimed as the traditional boundary. The Treaty of Paris had also given the Americans the right to ship goods by barge and boat down the Mississippi River to its mouth. Still, the international boundary ran down the middle of the river for most of its length, and the Mississippi was entirely within Spanish Louisiana in its lower reaches. The right to send boats or barges down the Mississippi was crucial to the growing American settlements in Kentucky and Tennessee, but in 1784 Louisiana's Spanish governor closed the river to American commerce and began to intrigue with Indians against the American settlers and with settlers against the United States.

THE CONFEDERATION'S PROBLEMS The problems of land-hungry trans-Appalachian settlers with the British and the Spanish seemed remote from the everyday concerns of most Americans, however. Most people were more affected by economic troubles and the acute currency shortage after the war. Merchants who found themselves prevented from reviving old trade relationships with colonies in the British Empire agitated for reprisals against the British. State governments, in response, imposed special taxes on British vessels and special tariffs on the goods they brought to the United States. State action alone, however, failed to work because of a lack of uniformity among the states. British ships could be diverted to states whose import duties were less restrictive. The other states tried to meet this problem by taxing British goods that flowed across state lines, creating the impression that states were involved in commercial war with each other. Chaos ensued. By 1787 there was a clear need—it seemed to commercial interests—for the national government to regulate interstate trade.

After the Revolution, mechanics (skilled workers who made, used, or repaired tools and machines) and artisans (skilled workers who made products) developed new industries. Their products ranged from crude iron nails to the fine silver bowls of such smiths as Paul Revere. These skilled workers wanted reprisals against British goods as well as British ships. They sought, and to various degrees obtained from the states, tariffs (taxes) on foreign goods that competed with theirs. Nearly all the states gave some preference to American goods, but again the lack of uniformity in their laws put them at cross-purposes, and so urban artisans along with merchants were drawn into the movement calling for a stronger central government in the interest of uniform regulation.

Domestic industry

American craftsmen, such as this cabinet-maker, favored tariffs on foreign goods that competed with their own products.

The shortage of cash and other economic difficulties gave rise to more immediate demands for paper currency, for postponement of tax and debt payments, and for laws to "stay" (delay) the foreclosure of mortgages. Farmers who had profited during the war found themselves squeezed afterward by depressed crop prices and mounting debts while merchants opened up new trade routes. Creditors demanded to be paid in gold or silver coins, but such "hard money" was in short supply—and paper money was almost nonexistent after the depreciation of the Continental currency. By 1785 the demand for new paper money became the most divisive issue in state politics. Debtors promoted the use of paper money as a means of easing repayment, and farmers saw paper money as an inflationary means of raising commodity prices.

In 1785–1786 seven states (Pennsylvania, New York, New Jersey, South Carolina, Rhode Island, Georgia, and North Carolina) began issuing paper money. It served in five of those states—Pennsylvania, New York, New Jersey, South Carolina, and Rhode Island—as a means of extending credit to hard-pressed farmers through state loans on farm mortgages. It was variously used to fund state debts and to pay off the claims of veterans. In spite of the cries of calamity at the time, the money never seriously depreciated in Pennsylvania, New York, and South Carolina. In Rhode Island, however, the debtor party ran wild. In 1786 the Rhode Island legislature issued more paper money than any other state in proportion to its population and declared it legal tender in payment of all debts. Creditors fled the state to avoid being paid in worthless paper.

SHAYS'S REBELLION Newspapers throughout the country followed the chaotic developments in Rhode Island. The little commonwealth, stubbornly independent since its founding, became the prime example of democracy run riot—until its riotous neighbor, Massachusetts, provided the final proof (some said) that the new nation was poised on the brink of anarchy: Shays's Rebellion. There the trouble was not too much paper money but too little, as well as too much taxation.

After 1780, Massachusetts had remained in the grip of a rigidly conservative state government, which levied ever-higher poll and land taxes to pay off a massive war debt, held mainly by wealthy creditors in Boston. The taxes fell most heavily upon beleaguered farmers and the poor in general. When the Massachusetts legislature adjourned in 1786 without providing paper money or any other relief from taxes and debts, three western agricultural counties erupted in revolt.

Armed bands of angry farmers closed the courts and prevented farm foreclosures. A ragtag "army" of some 1,200 unruly farmers led by Daniel Shays, a destitute war veteran, advanced upon the federal arsenal at Springfield in 1787. Shays and his followers sought a more flexible monetary policy, laws allowing them to use corn and wheat as money, and the right to postpone paying taxes until the postwar agricultural depression lifted.

The state responded to the uprising by sending 4,400 militiamen armed with cannons. The soldiers scattered the debtor army with a single volley that left four farmers dead. The rebels nevertheless had a victory of sorts. The new state legislature decided to relieve the agricultural crisis by eliminating some

Shays's Rebellion

Shays and his followers demanded a more flexible monetary policy and the right to postpone paying taxes until the postwar agricultural depression lifted.

of the taxes on farmers. But a more important consequence was the impetus that Shays's Rebellion gave to conservatism and nationalism.

Rumors greatly exaggerated, at times deliberately, the extent of this pathetic rebellion of desperate men. The Shaysites were rumored to be linked to the conniving British and were accused of seeking to pillage the wealthy. Panic set in among the Republic's elite. "Good God!" George Washington exclaimed when he heard of the incident. He worried that the rebellion might tempt other disgruntled groups around the country to adopt similar measures. In a letter to Thomas Jefferson, Abigail Adams tarred the Shaysites as "ignorant, restless desperadoes, without conscience or principles, . . . mobbish insurgents [who] are for sapping the foundation" of the struggling young government. Thomas Jefferson disagreed. If Abigail Adams and others were overly critical of Shays's Rebellion, Jefferson was, if anything, too complacent. From his post as the American minister in Paris (the term *ambassador* was not used until the 1890s), he wrote to a friend back home, "The tree of liberty must be refreshed from time to time with the blood of patriots and tyrants." Abigail Adams was so infuriated by Jefferson's position that she refused to correspond with him for months.

CALLS FOR A STRONGER GOVERNMENT   Well before the turmoil in New England, the advocates of a stronger central authority had been calling for a convention to revise the Articles of Confederation to strengthen the national government. Many bankers, merchants, and mechanics promoted a stronger central government as the only alternative to anarchy. Americans were gradually losing the fear of a strong central government as they saw evidence that tyranny might come from other quarters, including the common people themselves.

Such developments led many of the Founding Fathers to revise their assessment of the American character. "We have, probably," concluded George Washington in 1786, "had too good an opinion of human nature in forming our confederation." Washington and other so-called Federalists concluded that the new republic must now depend for its success upon the constant virtue of the few rather than the public-spiritedness of the many.

In 1785, delegates from Virginia and Maryland had met at Mount Vernon, at George Washington's invitation, to promote commerce and economic development and to settle outstanding questions about the navigation of the Potomac River and the Chesapeake Bay. Washington had a personal interest in the river flowing by his door: it was a potential route to the West, where he owned substantial property. The delegates agreed on interstate cooperation, and Maryland suggested a further pact with Pennsylvania and Delaware to encourage water transportation between the Chesapeake Bay and the Ohio River; the Virginia legislature agreed and, at James Madison's suggestion, invited all thirteen states to a general discussion of commercial problems. Nine states named representatives, but those from only five appeared at the Annapolis Convention in 1786—not represented were the New England states, the Carolinas, and Georgia. Apparent failure soon turned into success, however, when the alert Alexander Hamilton, representing New York, presented a resolution for still another national convention, in Philadelphia, to consider all measures necessary "to render the constitution of the Federal Government adequate to the exigencies of the Union."

ADOPTING THE CONSTITUTION

THE CONSTITUTIONAL CONVENTION   After stalling for several months, Congress fell in line in 1787 with a resolution endorsing a convention in Philadelphia "for the sole and express purpose of revising the Articles of Confederation." By then five states had already named delegates; before the meeting, called to begin on May 14, 1787, six more states had acted. New Hampshire delayed until June, its delegates arriving in July. Fearful of

Drafting the Constitution

George Washington presides over a session of the Constitutional Convention in Philadelphia.

consolidated power, tiny Rhode Island kept aloof throughout. (Critics labeled the fractious little state Rogue Island.) Virginia's Patrick Henry, an implacable foe of centralized government, claimed to "smell a rat" and refused to represent his state. Twenty-nine delegates from nine states began work on May 25. Altogether, the state legislatures had elected seventy-three men. Fifty-five attended at one time or another, and after four months of deliberations in stifling summer heat, thirty-nine signed the constitution they drafted. Only three of the delegates refused to sign it.

The durability and flexibility of that document testify to the remarkable men who made it. The delegates were surprisingly young: forty-two was the average age. They were farmers, merchants, lawyers, and bankers, many of them widely read in history, law, and political philosophy. Yet they were also practical men of experience, tested in the fires of the Revolution. Twenty-one had served in the conflict, seven had been state governors, most had been members of the Continental Congress, and eight had signed the Declaration of Independence.

The magisterial George Washington served as presiding officer but participated little in the debates. Eighty-one year-old Benjamin Franklin, the oldest delegate, also said little from the floor but provided a wealth of experience, wit, and common sense behind the scenes. More active in the debates were James Madison, the ablest political philosopher in the group; Massachusetts's dapper Elbridge Gerry, a Harvard graduate who earned the nickname Old Grumbletonian because, as John Adams once said, he "opposed everything he did not propose"; George Mason, the author of the Virginia Declaration of Rights and a slaveholding planter with a deep-rooted suspicion of all government; the witty, eloquent, arrogant New York aristocrat Gouverneur Morris, who harbored a venomous contempt for the masses; Scottish-born James Wilson of Pennsylvania, one of the ablest lawyers in the new nation and next in importance at the convention only to Washington and Madison; and Roger Sherman of Connecticut, a self-trained lawyer adept at negotiating compromises. John Adams, like Jefferson, was serving abroad on a diplomatic mission. Also conspicuously absent during most of the convention was Alexander Hamilton, the staunch nationalist who regretfully went home when the other two New York delegates walked out to protest what they saw as the loss of states' rights.

James Madison emerged as the central figure at the convention. Small of stature—barely over five feet tall—and frail in health, the thirty-six-year-old bookish bachelor was descended from wealthy slaveholding Virginia planters. He suffered from chronic headaches and was painfully shy. Crowds made him nervous, and he hated to use his high-pitched voice in public, much less in open debate. But the Princeton graduate possessed an agile mind and had a voracious appetite for learning. The convincing eloquence of his arguments proved decisive. "Every person seems to acknowledge his greatness," wrote one delegate. Madison had arrived in Philadelphia with trunks full of books and a head full of ideas. He had been preparing for the convention for months and probably knew more about historic forms of government than any other delegate.

For the most part the delegates' differences on political philosophy fell

James Madison

Madison was only thirty-six when he assumed a major role in the drafting of the Constitution. This miniature (1783) is by Charles Willson Peale.

within a narrow range. On certain fundamentals they generally agreed: that government derives its just powers from the consent of the people but that society must be protected from the tyranny of the majority; that the people at large must have a voice in their government but that any one group must be kept from abusing power; that a stronger central authority was essential but that all power is subject to abuse. Most of the delegates assumed, with Madison, that even the best people are naturally selfish and government, therefore, could not be founded altogether upon a trust in goodwill and virtue. By a careful arrangement of checks and balances, by checking power with countervailing power, the Founding Fathers hoped to devise institutions that could constrain individual sinfulness and channel self-interest to benefit the public good.

THE VIRGINIA AND NEW JERSEY PLANS   At the outset of the Constitutional Convention, the delegates unanimously elected George Washington president of the assembly. James Madison drafted the framework of the discussions. His proposals, which came to be called the Virginia Plan, embodied a revolutionary idea: that the delegates scrap their instructions to revise the Articles of Confederation and submit an entirely new document to the states. Madison's plan proposed separate legislative, executive, and judicial branches and a truly national government to make laws binding upon individual citizens as well as states. The new Congress would be divided into two houses: a lower house chosen by popular vote and an upper house of senators elected by the state legislatures. Congress could disallow state laws under the plan and would itself define the extent of its and the states' authority.

On June 15, delegates critical of some aspects of Madison's proposals submitted the New Jersey Plan, which sought to keep the existing structure of equal representation of the states in a unicameral Congress but give Congress the power to levy taxes and regulate commerce and the authority to name a plural executive (with no veto) and a supreme court.

The plans presented the convention with two major issues: (1) whether simply to amend the Articles of Confederation or to draft a new document and (2) whether to determine congressional representation by state or by population. On the first point the convention voted to work toward establishing a national government as envisioned by Madison and the other Virginians. Regarding the powers of this government, there was little disagreement except in the details. Experience with the Articles of Confederation had persuaded the delegates that an effective central government, as distinguished from a confederation, needed the power to levy taxes, regulate commerce, fund an army and navy, and make laws binding upon individual citizens. The painful lessons of the 1780s suggested to them, moreover, that in the interest of order and uniformity the states must be denied certain powers: to issue money, abrogate contracts, make treaties, wage war, and levy tariffs.

But these issues sparked furious disagreements. The first clash in the convention involved congressional representation, and it was resolved by the Great Compromise (sometimes called the Connecticut Compromise, as it was proposed by Roger Sherman), which gave both groups their way. The more populous states won apportionment by population in the House of Representatives; the states that sought to protect states' power won equality in the Senate, with the vote by individuals, not by states.

An equally contentious struggle ensued between northern and southern delegates over slavery and the regulation of trade, an omen of sectional controversies to come. Of all the issues that emerged during the Constitutional Convention of 1787, none was more volatile than the question of slavery. During the eighteenth century the economies of Virginia and the Carolinas had become dependent upon enslaved workers, and delegates from those states were determined to protect the future of slavery. A South Carolinian stressed that his delegation and the Georgians would oppose any constitution that failed to protect slavery. Few if any of the framers of the Constitution even considered the notion of abolition, and they carefully avoided using the term *slavery* in the final document. In this they reflected the prevailing attitudes among white Americans. Most agreed with South Carolina's John Rutledge when he asserted, "Religion and humanity [have] nothing to do with this [slavery] question. Interest alone is the governing principle of nations."

The "interest" of southern delegates, with enslaved African Americans so numerous in their states, dictated that slaves be counted as part of the population in determining the number of a state's congressional representatives. Northerners were willing to count slaves when deciding each state's share of taxes but not for purposes of representation. The delegates finally compromised on this issue by counting a slave as three fifths of a citizen as a basis for apportioning both representatives and direct taxes to those states with slaves.

A more sensitive issue for the delegates involved an effort to prevent the government from stopping the slave trade with Africa. Virginia's George Mason, himself a slaveholder, condemned the "infernal traffic," which his state had already outlawed. He argued that the issue concerned "not the importing states alone but the whole union." People in the western territories were "already calling out for slaves for their new lands." He feared that they would

Slave trade

This cross-sectional view of the British slave ship *Brookes* shows the crowded conditions that enslaved Africans endured in the international slave trade.

"fill the country" with enslaved people. Such a development would bring forth "the judgment of Heaven" on the country. Southern delegates rejected Mason's reasoning. They argued that the continued importation of African slaves was vital to their states' economies.

To resolve the question, the delegates established a time limit: Congress could not forbid the transatlantic slave trade before 1808, but it could levy a tax of $10 a head on all imported Africans. In both provisions a sense of delicacy—and hypocrisy—dictated the use of euphemisms. The Constitution spoke of "free Persons" and "all other persons," of "such persons as any of the States Now existing shall think proper to admit," and of persons "held to Service of Labor." The odious word *slavery* did not appear in the Constitution until the Thirteenth Amendment (1865) abolished the "peculiar institution." The success of southern delegates in getting slaves counted for purposes of calculating a state's representation in the House of Representatives and the Electoral College, coupled with the decision not to prohibit American involvement with the African slave trade, would lead abolitionist William Lloyd Garrison to declare in the 1830s that the drafters of the Constitution had forged a "covenant with death and an agreement with hell."

If the delegates found the slavery issue fraught with peril, they considered irrelevant any discussion of the legal or political role of women under the new constitution. The Revolutionary rhetoric of liberty prompted some women to demand political equality. "The men say we have no business [with politics]," Eliza Wilkinson of South Carolina observed as the Constitution was being framed, "but I won't have it thought that because we are the weaker sex as to bodily strength we are capable of nothing more than domestic concerns." Her complaint, however, fell on deaf ears. There was never any formal discussion of women's rights at the convention. The new nationalism still defined politics and government as outside the realm of female endeavor.

The Constitution also said little about the processes of immigration and naturalization, and most of what it said was negative. In Article II, Section 1, the Constitution prohibits any future immigrant from becoming president, limiting that office to a "natural born Citizen." In Article I, Sections 2 and 3, respectively, it stipulates that no person can serve in the House of Representatives who has not "been seven Years a Citizen of the United States" or in the Senate who has not "been nine Years a Citizen." On the matter of defining citizenship, the Constitution gives Congress the authority "to establish an uniform Rule of Naturalization" but offers no further guidance on the matter. As a result, naturalization policy (citizenship for immigrants) has changed significantly over the years in response to fluctuating social attitudes and political moods. In 1790 the first Congress passed a naturalization law that allowed "free white persons" who had been in the country for as few as two years to be made naturalized citizens in any court. This meant that persons of African descent were denied citizenship by the federal government; it was left to individual states to determine whether free blacks were citizens. And because Indians were not "free white persons," they were also treated as aliens rather than citizens. Not until 1924 would Native Americans be granted citizenship—by an act of Congress rather than a constitutional amendment.

THE SEPARATION OF POWERS   The details of the government structure embedded in the Constitution aroused less debate than the basic issues pitting the large states against the small and the northern states against the southern. Existing state constitutions, several of which already separated powers among legislative, executive, and judicial branches, set an example that reinforced the convention's resolve to disperse centralized power with checks and balances. Although the Founding Fathers hated royal tyranny, most of them also feared rule by the people and favored various mechanisms to check public passions. Some delegates displayed a thumping disdain for any democratizing of the political system. Elbridge Gerry asserted that most of the nation's problems "flow from an excess of democracy." Alexander Hamilton once called the people "a great beast."

Those elitist views were accommodated by the Constitution's mixed legislative system. The lower house of Congress was designed to be closer to the voters, who elected its delegates every two years. It would be, according to Virginia's George Mason, "the grand repository of the democratic principle of the Government." House members should "sympathize with their constituents, should think as they think, & feel as they feel; and for these purposes should even be residents among them." The upper house, or Senate, its members elected by the state legislatures, was intended to be more detached from the voters. Staggered six-year terms for senators prevent the choice of a majority in any given year and thereby further isolate senators from the passions of moment.

The delegates to the Constitutional Convention struggled over issues related to the new executive branch. The decision that a single person be made the chief executive caused the delegates "considerable pause," according to James Madison. George Mason protested that this would create a "fetus of monarchy." Indeed, several of the chief executive's powers actually exceeded those of the British monarch. This was the sharpest departure from the recent experience in state government, where the office of governor had commonly been diluted because of the recent memory of struggles with royal governors. The new president would have a veto over acts of Congress, subject to being overridden by a two-thirds vote in each house, whereas the royal veto had long since fallen into complete disuse. The president was named commander in chief of the armed forces and responsible for the execution of the laws. The chief executive could make treaties with the advice and consent of two thirds of the Senate and had the power to appoint diplomats, judges, and other officers with the consent of a majority of the Senate. The president was instructed to report annually on the state of the nation and was authorized to recommend legislation, a provision that presidents eventually would take as a mandate to promote extensive legislative programs.

But the president's powers were limited in certain key areas. The chief executive could neither declare war nor make peace; those powers were reserved for Congress. Unlike the British monarch, moreover, the president could be removed from office. The House could impeach (indict) the chief executive—and other civil officers—on charges of treason, bribery, or "other high crimes and misdemeanors," and upon conviction the Senate could remove an impeached president by a two-thirds vote. The presiding officer at the trial of a president would be the chief justice, since the usual presiding officer of the Senate (the vice president) would have a personal stake in the outcome.

The leading nationalists—men like James Madison, James Wilson, and Alexander Hamilton—wanted to strengthen the independence of the executive by entrusting the choice to popular election. But an elected executive was still too far beyond the American experience. Besides, a national election would have created enormous problems of organization and voter qualification. Wilson suggested instead that the people of each state choose presidential electors equal to the number of their senators and representatives. Others proposed that the legislators make the choice. Finally, the convention voted to let the legislature decide the method in each state. Before long nearly all the states were choosing the presidential electors by popular vote, and the electors were acting as agents of the party will, casting their votes as they had pledged them before the election. This method diverged from the original expectation that the electors would deliberate and make their own choices.

On the third branch of government, the judiciary, there was surprisingly little debate. Both the Virginia and the New Jersey Plans had called for a supreme court, which the Constitution established, providing specifically for a chief justice of the United States and leaving up to Congress the number of other justices. Although the Constitution nowhere authorizes the courts to declare laws void when they conflict with the Constitution, the power of the Supreme Court to review congressional actions is implied. Such "judicial review" was soon exercised in cases involving both state and federal laws. Article VI declares the federal Constitution, federal laws, and treaties to be "the supreme Law of the Land," state laws or constitutions "to the Contrary notwithstanding." The advocates of states' rights thought this a victory, since it eliminated the proviso in the Virginia Plan for Congress to settle all conflicts between the federal government and individual states. As it turned out, however, the clause became the basis for an important expansion of judicial review of legislative actions.

Signing the Constitution, September 17, 1787

Thomas Pritchard Rossiter's painting shows George Washington presiding over what Thomas Jefferson called "an assembly of demi gods" in Philadelphia.

Although the Constitution extended vast new powers to the national government, the delegates' mistrust of unchecked power is apparent in repeated examples of countervailing forces: the separation of the three branches of government, the president's veto, the congressional power of impeachment and removal, the Senate's power to approve or reject treaties and appointments, the courts' implied right of judicial review. In addition, the new form of government specifically forbade Congress to pass bills of attainder (criminal condemnation by a legislative act) or ex post facto laws (laws adopted after an event to criminalize deeds that have already been committed). It also reserved to the states large areas of sovereignty—a reservation soon made explicit by the Tenth Amendment. By dividing sovereignty between the people and the government, the framers of the Constitution provided a distinctive contribution to political theory. That is, by vesting ultimate authority in the people, they divided sovereignty *within* the government. This constituted a dramatic break with the colonial tradition. The British had always insisted that the sovereignty of the king in Parliament was indivisible.

The most glaring defect of the Articles of Confederation, the rule of state unanimity that defeated every effort to amend them, led the delegates to provide a less forbidding, though still difficult, method of amending the Constitution. Amendments can be proposed either by a two-thirds vote of each house in the national Congress or by a convention specially called, upon application of two thirds of the state legislatures. Amendments can be ratified by approval of three fourths of the states acting through their legislatures or in special conventions. The national convention has never been used, however, and state conventions have been called only once—in 1933 to ratify the repeal of the Eighteenth Amendment, which had prohibited "the manufacture, sale, or transportation of" alcoholic beverages.

THE FIGHT FOR RATIFICATION   The final article of the Constitution provided that it would become effective upon ratification by nine states (not quite the three-fourths majority required for amendment). The Confederation Congress submitted the draft of the Constitution to the states on September 28, 1787.

In the ensuing political debate, advocates of the Constitution assumed the name Federalists. Opponents, who favored a more decentralized federal system, became anti-Federalists. The Federalists had several advantages. Their leaders had been members of the convention and were already familiar with the document and the arguments on each point. They were not only better prepared but also better organized and, on the whole, made up of the more able leaders in the political community.

Historians have hotly debated the motivation of the advocates of the Constitution. For more than a century the tendency to idolize the Founding Fathers prevailed. In 1913, however, historian Charles A. Beard's book *An Economic Interpretation of the Constitution* argued that the Philadelphia convention was made up of men who had a selfish economic interest in the outcome. Beard claimed that the delegates represented an economic elite of speculators in western lands, holders of depreciated government securities, and creditors whose wealth was mostly in "paper": mortgages, stocks, bonds, and the like. The owners of western lands and government bonds would benefit financially from a stronger federal government. Creditors generally stood to gain from the prohibitions against state currency issues and the impairment of contract, provisions clearly aimed at the paper-money issues and at the stay laws that were then effective in many states. Stay laws prevented people to whom money was owed from enforcing their contractual rights to foreclose on debtors.

Beard's thesis provided a useful antidote to unquestioning hero worship and still contains a germ of truth, but the historian exaggerated. Most of the delegates, according to evidence unavailable to Beard, had no compelling stake in government bonds, and most were far more involved in landholding. Many prominent nationalists, including "the Father of the Constitution," James Madison, had no western lands or bonds or much other personal property. Some opponents of the Constitution, on the other hand, held large blocks of land and securities. Economic interests certainly figured in the ratification process, but they functioned in a complex interplay of state, sectional, group, and individual interests that turned largely on how well people had fared under the Confederation.

The most notable aspect of the new American republic was not selfishness but cooperation. The American Revolution had led not to general chaos and terror, as would occur during the French Revolution, but to "an outbreak of constitution-making." From the 1760s through the 1780s, Americans engaged in a prolonged debate over the fundamental issues of government, which in its scope and depth—and in the durability of its outcome—is without parallel in world history.

THE FEDERALIST Among the supreme legacies of the debate over the Constitution is *The Federalist,* a collection of essays originally published in New York newspapers between 1787 and 1788. Instigated by Alexander Hamilton, the eighty-five articles published under the name Publius include about fifty by Hamilton, thirty by James Madison, and five by New Yorker John Jay. Written in support of ratification, the essays defended the principle of a supreme national authority, but sought to reassure doubters that the people and the states had little reason to fear tyranny in the new government.

In perhaps the most famous *Federalist* essay, Number 10, Madison argued that the very size and diversity of the expanding nation would make it impossible for any single faction to form a majority that could dominate the government. This contradicted the conventional wisdom of the time, which insisted that republics could survive only in small, homogeneous countries like Switzerland and the Netherlands. Large republics, on the other hand, would fragment, dissolving into anarchy and tyranny through the influence of factions. Quite the contrary, Madison insisted. Given a balanced federal government, a republic could work in large, diverse nations probably better than in smaller nations. "Extend the sphere," he wrote, "and you take in a greater variety of parties and interests; you make it less probable that a majority of the whole will have a common motive to invade the rights of other citizens."

Madison and the other Federalists also insisted that the new union would promote prosperity by reducing taxes, paying off the war bonds, and expanding the money supply. The anti-Federalists, however, highlighted the dangers of power in terms that had become familiar during the centuries-long struggles with Parliament and the crown. They especially noted the absence of a bill of rights to protect the rights of individuals and states. They found the process of ratification highly irregular, as it was—indeed, it was illegal under the Articles of Confederation. Not only did Patrick Henry refuse to attend the Constitutional Convention, but he later demanded (unsuccessfully) that it be investigated as a conspiracy. The anti-Federalist leaders— George Mason, Patrick Henry, and Richard Henry Lee of Virginia, George Clinton of New York, Samuel Adams and Elbridge Gerry of Massachusetts, Luther Martin of Maryland—were often men whose careers and reputations had been established well before the Revolution. The Federalist leaders were more likely to be younger men whose careers had begun in the Revolution— men such as Hamilton, Madison, and Jay.

The two groups disagreed more over means than ends, however. Both sides, for the most part, acknowledged that a stronger national authority was needed and that it required an independent source of revenue to function properly. Both were convinced that the people must erect safeguards against tyranny, even the tyranny of the majority. Few of the Constitution's supporters liked it in its entirety, but most believed that it was the best document obtainable; few of its opponents found it unacceptable in its entirety. Once the new government had become an accomplished fact, few wanted to undo the work of the Philadelphia convention.

THE DECISION OF THE STATES   Ratification of the new constitution gained momentum before the end of 1787, and several of the smaller states were among the first to act, apparently satisfied that they had gained all the safeguards they could hope for in equality of representation in the Senate. Delaware, New Jersey, and Georgia voted unanimously in favor. Massachusetts, still sharply divided in the aftermath of Shays's Rebellion, was the first state in which the outcome was close. There the Federalists finally carried the day. Massachusetts approved the Constitution by 187 to 168 on February 6, 1788.

New Hampshire was the ninth state to ratify the Constitution, allowing it to be put into effect, but the Union could hardly succeed without the approval of Virginia, the most populous state, or New York, which had the third highest population and occupied a key position geographically. Both states harbored strong opposition groups. In Virginia, Patrick Henry became the chief spokesman for backcountry farmers who feared the powers of the new government, but wavering delegates were won over by the same strategem as in Massachusetts. When it was proposed that the convention should recommend a bill of rights, Edmund Randolph, who had refused to sign the finished document, announced his conversion to the cause.

Upon notification that New Hampshire had become the ninth state to ratify the Constitution, the Confederation Congress began to draft plans for the

RATIFICATION OF THE CONSTITUTION

Order of Ratification	State	Date of Ratification
1	Delaware	December 7, 1787
2	Pennsylvania	December 12, 1787
3	New Jersey	December 18, 1787
4	Georgia	January 2, 1788
5	Connecticut	January 9, 1788
6	Massachusetts	February 6, 1788
7	Maryland	April 28, 1788
8	South Carolina	May 23, 1788
9	New Hampshire	June 21, 1788
10	Virginia	June 25, 1788
11	New York	July 26, 1788
12	North Carolina	November 21, 1789
13	Rhode Island	May 29, 1790

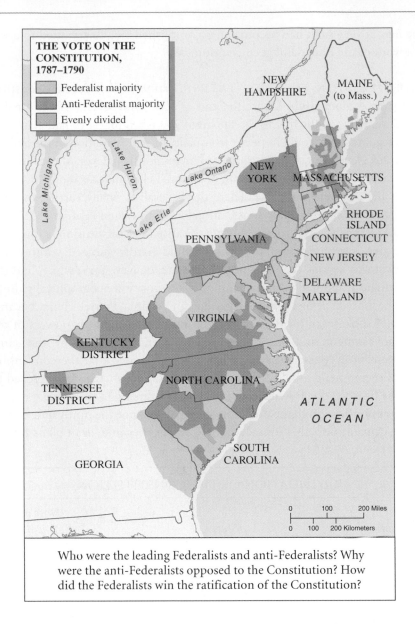

THE VOTE ON THE CONSTITUTION, 1787–1790

- Federalist majority
- Anti-Federalist majority
- Evenly divided

Who were the leading Federalists and anti-Federalists? Why were the anti-Federalists opposed to the Constitution? How did the Federalists win the ratification of the Constitution?

transfer of power to the new federal government created by the Constitution. On September 13, 1788, it selected New York City as the initial capital of the new government and fixed the date for elections. On October 10, 1788, the Confederation Congress transacted its last business and passed into history.

"Our constitution is in actual operation," the elderly Benjamin Franklin wrote to a friend; "everything appears to promise that it will last; but in this

Sixth pillar

An engraving published in 1788 in *The Massachusetts Centinel* after Massachusetts became the sixth state to ratify the Constitution. By the end of 1788, five more states would approve and the Constitution would go into effect. The last two states to ratify were North Carolina in 1789 and Rhode Island in 1790.

world nothing is certain but death and taxes." George Washington was even more uncertain about the future under the new plan of government. He had told a fellow delegate as the convention adjourned, "I do not expect the Constitution to last for more than twenty years."

The Constitution has lasted much longer, of course, and in the process it has provided a model of resilient republican government whose features have been repeatedly borrowed by other nations through the years. Yet what makes the U.S. Constitution so distinctive is not its specific provisions or many compromises but its remarkable harmony with the particular "genius of the people" it governs. The Constitution has provided a flexible system of government that presidents, legislators, judges, and the people have adjusted to changing social, economic, and political circumstances. In this sense the Founding Fathers not only created "a more perfect Union" in 1787; they also engineered a frame of government whose resilience has enabled later generations to continue to perfect their republican experiment. But the framers of the Constitution failed in one significant respect: in skirting the issue of slavery so as to cement the Union, they unknowingly allowed tensions over the "peculiar institution" to reach the point where there would be no political solution—only civil war.

CHAPTER SUMMARY

- **Confederation Government** Despite the weak form of government deliberately crafted under the Articles of Confederation, the Confederation government managed to construct alliances, wage the Revolutionary War to a successful conclusion, and negotiate the Treaty of Paris. It created executive departments and established the way in which western lands would be organized and governments would be formed in the territories.

- **Articles of Confederation** Postwar economic conditions were difficult because British markets were closed to the new nation and the Articles had not provided for a means to raise taxes or stimulate economic recovery. Shays's Rebellion made many Americans fear that anarchy would destroy the new republic and led them to clamor for a stronger national government.

- **Constitutional Convention** Delegates gathered at the convention in Philadelphia to revise the existing government, but almost immediately they proposed scrapping the Articles of Confederation. An entirely new document emerged, delineating separate executive, legislative, and judicial branches. Argument about representation was resolved by establishing a two-house legislature, with equal representation by state in the Senate and by population in the House of Representatives.

- **Slavery and the Constitution** Southern delegates would not support a constitution that failed to protect the institution of slavery and provide for the international slave trade. In determining how enslaved people would be counted for the sake of apportioning direct taxes and representation in the lower house, it was agreed that three-fifths of the enslaved population would be counted. It was also agreed that Congress would not forbid participation in the transatlantic slave trade before 1808. Nevertheless, the framers of the Constitution avoided using the word *slavery* in the Constitution.

- **Ratification of the Constitution** Ratification of the Constitution was difficult, especially in the key states of Virginia and New York. Anti-Federalists such as Virginia's Patrick Henry favored a decentralized federal system and feared that the absence of a bill of rights would lead to a loss of individual and states' rights. To sway New York State toward ratification, Alexander Hamilton, James Madison, and John Jay wrote *The Federalist*, a series of articles defending a strong national authority. Ratification became possible only with the promise of a bill of rights.

CHRONOLOGY

1781	Articles of Confederation take effect
1783	General Washington puts an end to the Newburgh Conspiracy
1784	Treaty of Fort Stanwix forces the Iroquois to give up land in New York and Pennsylvania
1785	Land Ordinance outlines a plan for surveying and selling government lands
1786	Delegates to the Annapolis Convention decide to call for a constitutional convention
1786–1787	Shays's Rebellion
1787	Northwest Ordinance outlines a detailed plan for organizing western territories
1787	The Constitutional Convention is held in Philadelphia
1787–1788	*The Federalist Papers* are published
1788	Confederation government is phased out
1790	Rhode Island becomes the last state to ratify the Constitution

KEY TERMS & NAMES

Robert Morris p. 271

Alexander Hamilton p. 272

Northwest Ordinance
p. 274

bill of rights p. 276

Shays's Rebellion p. 281

Annapolis Convention
p. 283

James Madison p. 285

Virginia Plan p. 286

New Jersey Plan p. 286

separation of powers
p. 289

anti-Federalists p. 292

The Federalist p. 293

8

THE FEDERALIST ERA

FOCUS QUESTIONS wwnorton.com/studyspace

- What were the main challenges facing Washington's administration?
- What was Hamilton's vision of the new republic?
- How did religious freedom become a reality for the new country?
- How did European affairs complicate the internal political and diplomatic problems of the new country?
- Why did Madison and Jefferson lead the opposition to Hamilton's policies?

The Constitution, ratified in 1788, was a bundle of deft compromises intended to create a more powerful central government better capable of managing a sprawling—and rapidly growing—new republic. Although the U.S. Constitution has become the world's most enduring national charter, skeptics in the late eighteenth century doubted that it would survive more than a few years. A Massachusetts anti-Federalist said that governing such an "extensive empire . . . upon republican principles" was impossible. It was one thing to draft a dramatic new constitution but quite another to exercise such expanded powers. The Constitution's ideals were profound, but its premises and theories were untested. Creating a "more perfect union" would prove to be a long, complicated, and painful process. During the 1790s the new federal government would confront civil rebellions, threats of secession, international intrigues, and foreign wars. In 1789, Americans wildly celebrated the inauguration of George Washington as the nation's first president. But amid the excitement was a powerful undercurrent of uncertainty, suspicion, and anxiety. The

Constitution provided a framework but not a blueprint; it left unanswered many questions about the actual structure and conduct of the new government. As James Madison had acknowledged, "We are in a wilderness without a single footstep to guide us."

A NEW NATION

In 1789 the United States and the western territories reached from the Atlantic Ocean to the Mississippi River and hosted almost 4 million people. This vast new republic, much larger than any in Europe, harbored distinct regional differences. A southerner highlighted such distinctions when he said that "men who come from New England are different from us." Although still characterized by small farms and bustling seaports, New England was on the verge of developing a manufacturing sector. The middle Atlantic states boasted the most well-balanced economy, the largest cities, and the most diverse collection of ethnic and religious groups. The South was an

New beginnings

An engraving from the title page of *The Universal Asylum and Columbian Magazine* (published in Philadelphia in 1790). America is represented as a woman laying down her shield to engage in education, art, commerce, and agriculture.

agricultural region whose British and European settlers were more ethnically homogeneous and increasingly dependent upon enslaved laborers. By 1790 the southern states were exporting as much tobacco as they had been before the Revolution. Most important, however, was the surge in southern cotton. Between 1790 and 1815 the annual production of cotton soared from less than 3 million pounds to 93 million pounds. The invention of the cotton gin, to separate the seeds from the cotton fibers, played a key role in the soaring production.

Overall, the United States in 1790 was predominantly a rural society. Eighty percent of households were involved in agricultural production. Only a few cities had more than 5,000 residents. The first national census, taken in 1790, counted 750,000 African Americans, almost a fifth of the population. Most of them lived in the five southernmost states; less than ten percent lived outside the South. Most African Americans, of course, were enslaved, but there were many free blacks as a result of the Revolution. In fact, the proportion of free to enslaved blacks was never higher than in 1790.

The 1790 census did not even count the many Indians still living east of the Mississippi River. Most Americans viewed the Native Americans as those people whom the Declaration of Independence had dismissed as "merciless Indian Savages." There were over eighty tribes totaling perhaps as many as 150,000 people in 1790. In the Old Northwest along the Great Lakes, the British continued to arm the Indians and encouraged them to resist American encroachments. Between 1784 and 1790, Indians killed or captured some 1,500 settlers in Kentucky alone. Such bloodshed generated a ferocious reaction. "The people of Kentucky," observed an official frustrated by his inability to negotiate a treaty between whites and Indians, "will carry on private expeditions against the Indians and kill them whenever they meet them, and I do not believe there is a jury in all Kentucky that will punish a man for it." In the South the five most powerful tribes—the Cherokees, Chickasaws, Choctaws, Creeks, and Seminoles—numbered between 50,000 and 100,000. They steadfastly refused to recognize U.S. authority and used Spanish-supplied weapons to thwart white settlement on their lands.

Only about 125,000 whites and blacks lived west of the Appalachian Mountains in 1790. But that was soon to change. The great theme of nineteenth-century American history would be the ceaseless stream of migrants flowing westward from the Atlantic seaboard. By foot, horse, boat, and wagon, pioneers and adventurers headed west. Kentucky, still part of Virginia but destined for statehood in 1792, harbored 75,000 settlers in 1790. In 1776 there had been only 150 pioneers there. Rapid population growth, cheap land, and new economic opportunities fueled the western migration. The average white woman gave birth to eight children, and the white population doubled approximately every twenty-two years. This made for a very young population on average. In 1790 almost half of all white Americans were under the age of sixteen.

A NEW GOVERNMENT   The men who drafted the Constitution knew that many questions were left unanswered, and they feared that putting the new frame of government into practice would pose unexpected challenges. On the appointed date, March 4, 1789, the new Congress of the United States, meeting in New York City, could muster only eight senators and thirteen representatives. A month passed before both chambers gathered a quorum. Only then could the presiding officer of the Senate certify the foregone conclusion that George Washington, with 69 votes, was the unanimous choice of the Electoral College for president. John Adams, with 34 votes, the second-highest number, became vice president.

Washington was a reluctant first president. He greeted the news of his election with "a heart filled with distress" because he imagined "the ten thousand embarrassments, perplexities and troubles to which I must again be exposed." He told a friend as he prepared to assume office in New York City that he felt like a "culprit who is going to the place of his execution." Yet Washington agreed to serve because he had been "summoned by my country." A self-made man with little formal education, he brought to his new office a remarkable capacity for moderation and mediation that helped keep the infant republic from disintegrating. In his inaugural address, Washington appealed for national unity, pleading with the new Congress to abandon "local prejudices" and "party animosities" in order to create the "national" outlook necessary for the fledgling republic to thrive. Within a few months the new president would see his hopes dashed. Personal rivalries, sectional tensions, and partisan conflict characterized political life in the 1790s.

THE GOVERNMENT'S STRUCTURE   President Washington had a larger staff at his Mount Vernon estate in northern Virginia than he did as president. During the summer of 1789, Congress created executive departments corresponding to those formed under the Confederation. To head the Department of State, Washington named Thomas Jefferson, recently back from his diplomatic duties in France. To head the Department of the Treasury, Washington picked his devoted wartime aide, Alexander Hamilton, now a prominent lawyer in New York. The new position of attorney general was occupied by Edmund Randolph, former governor of Virginia.

John Jay

Chief Justice of the Supreme Court. Jay favored a strong union and emphatically supported the Constitution.

Washington routinely called these men to sit as a group to discuss matters of policy. This was the origin of the president's cabinet, an advisory body for which the Constitution made no formal provision. The office of vice president also took on what would become its typical character. "The Vice-Presidency," John Adams wrote his wife, Abigail, is the most "insignificant office . . . ever . . . contrived."

The structure of the federal court system, like that of the executive departments, was left to Congress, except for a chief justice and the Supreme Court. Congress set the membership of the highest court at six (now nine)—the chief justice and five associates—and created thirteen federal district courts. From these, appeals might go to one of three circuit courts, composed of two Supreme Court justices and the district judge, who met twice a year in each district. Members of the Supreme Court, therefore, were initially itinerant judges riding the circuit during a good part of the year. All federal cases originated in a district court and, if appealed on issues of procedure or legal interpretation, went to the circuit courts and from there to the Supreme Court.

Washington named John Jay as the first chief justice of the Supreme Court, a post Jay held until 1795. Born in New York City in 1745, Jay graduated from King's College (now Columbia University). His reputation as the state's finest lawyer had led New York to send him as its representative to the First and Second Continental Congresses. After serving as president of the Continental Congress in 1778–1779, Jay became the American minister in Spain. While in Europe he helped John Adams and Benjamin Franklin negotiate the Treaty of Paris in 1783. After the Revolution, Jay served as secretary of foreign affairs. He joined James Madison and Alexander Hamilton as co-author of the *The Federalist* and became one of the most effective champions of the Constitution.

THE BILL OF RIGHTS The ratification of the Constitution did not end the debate about the centralization of power in the federal government.

Debates over ratification

This satirical, eighteenth-century engraving illustrates some of the major issues in Connecticut politics on the eve of ratification.

Amid the debates over ratification of the Constitution, four states—Massachusetts, New York, Virginia, and North Carolina—requested that a "bill of rights" be added to protect individual freedoms, state's rights, and civil liberties. To address such concerns, Congressman James Madison presented to Congress in May 1789 a cluster of constitutional amendments that have since become known as the Bill of Rights. After considerable discussion and debate, Congress approved the amendments in September 1789, and a few days later President George Washington officially transmitted the amendments to the states for ratification. By the end of 1791, the necessary three fourths of the states had approved ten of the twelve proposed amendments.

The first eight Amendments to the Constitution were modeled after the Virginia Declaration of Rights that George Mason had written in 1776. They provide safeguards for specified rights of individuals: freedom of religion, press, speech, and assembly; the right to own firearms; the right to refuse to house soldiers in a private home; protection against unreasonable searches and seizures; the right to refuse to testify against oneself; the right to a speedy public trial, with legal counsel present, before an impartial jury; and protection against "cruel and unusual" punishment.

The Ninth and Tenth Amendments address the demand for specific statements that the enumeration of rights in the Constitution "shall not be construed to deny or disparage others retained by the people" and that "powers not delegated to the United States by the Constitution, nor prohibited by it to the States, are reserved to the States respectively, or to the people." The ten amendments constituting the Bill of Rights became effective on December 15, 1791. The Bill of Rights, it should be noted, provided no rights or legal protection to African Americans or Indians.

RELIGIOUS FREEDOM   The debates over the Constitution and the Bill of Rights generated a religious revolution as well as a political revolution. Unlike the New England Puritans, who sought to ensure that governments explicitly supported their particular religious beliefs, the men who drafted and amended the Constitution made no direct mention of God. They were determined to protect freedom of religion from government interference. The First Amendment declares that "Congress shall make no law respecting an establishment of religion or prohibiting the free exercise thereof." This statement has since become one of the most important—and most disputed—principles of American government. In the late eighteenth century the United States was virtually alone among nations in refusing to establish a single government-mandated and tax-supported religion. In addition, at the time the Bill of Rights was ratified, all but two states—New York and Virginia—still sponsored some form of official religion or maintained a religious requirement for holding political office. In 1789 many people feared that the new national government might impose a particular religious faith on the people. The First Amendment was intended to create a pluralistic framework within which people of all religious persuasions could flourish. It prohibits the federal government from endorsing or supporting any particular religion or interfering with the religious choices that people make. As Thomas Jefferson later explained, the First Amendment was intended to erect a "wall of separation between church and State."

RAISING REVENUE   Raising money to operate its affairs was the new federal government's most critical task. When George Washington took office, the nation's finances were in shambles. The federal treasury was virtually empty. To raise funds, James Madison proposed a modest federal tariff (a tax on imports) for revenue only, but the demands of manufacturers in the northern states for tariffs high enough to protect them from foreign competition forced a compromise that imposed higher tariffs on specified items. Madison linked the tariff to a proposal for a mercantile system that would levy extra tonnage duties (fees) on foreign ships and an especially heavy duty on countries that had no commercial treaty with the United States.

Madison's goal was to wage economic war against Great Britain, which had no such treaty but more foreign trade with the new nation than any other country. Northern businessmen, however, fearing any disruption in the economy, were in no mood for a renewal of economic pressures. In the end the only discrimination built into the Tonnage Act of 1789 was between U.S. and all foreign ships: U.S. ships paid an import duty of 6¢ per ton; American-built foreign-owned ships paid 30¢; and ships that were foreign built and owned paid 50¢ per ton.

The disagreements created by the trade measures were portents of quarrels yet to come. One unanswered question was whether U.S. economic policy should favor Britain or France. The more persistent question was whether tariff and tonnage duties should penalize farmers in the interest of northern manufacturers and shipowners. Tariffs and tonnage duties resulted in higher prices on goods bought by Americans, most of whom were tied to the farm economy. This raised a basic and perennial question: should rural consumers be forced to subsidize the nation's infant manufacturing sector? This issue became a volatile political question pitting South against North.

HAMILTON'S VISION

The tariff and tonnage duties, linked as they were to other issues, marked but the beginning of the effort to get the new country on sound fiscal footing. In 1789 thirty-four-year-old Alexander Hamilton seized the initiative. The first secretary of the Treasury was an unlikely protégé of President Washington. Born out of wedlock on a Caribbean island and deserted by his ne'er-do-well Scottish father, Hamilton was left an orphan at thirteen by the death of his mother. With the help of friends and relatives, he found his way, at seventeen, to New York, attended King's College, and entered the Continental army, where he became Washington's favorite aide. After the war he studied law, passed the bar examination, established a thriving legal practice in New York City, and became a self-made aristocrat, serving as a collector of revenues and as a member of the Confederation Congress. An early convert to nationalism, Hamilton played a major role in promoting the new federal constitution. Shrewd, energetic, determined, and combative, the

Alexander Hamilton

Secretary of the Treasury from 1789 to 1795.

red-haired, blue-eyed attorney was consumed with social and political ambition. As he recognized at age fourteen, "To confess my weakness, my ambition is prevalent." The same could be said of most of the Founding Fathers.

During the Revolutionary War, Hamilton had witnessed the near-fatal weaknesses of the Confederation Congress. Its lack of authority and money almost lost the war. Now, as the nation's first secretary of the Treasury, he was determined to transform an economically weak and fractious cluster of states into a powerful nation and global force. To flourish in a warring world, Hamilton believed, the United States needed to unleash the energy and ambition of its citizens so as to create a vibrant economy driven by the engines of capitalism. He wanted to nurture the hustling, bustling, aspiring spirit that he believed distinguished Americans from others. Just as he had risen from poverty and shame to success, he wanted to ensure that Americans would always have such opportunities. To that end he envisioned a limited but assertive government that encouraged new fields of enterprise and fostered investment and entrepreneurship. Thriving markets and new industries would best ensure the fate of the Republic, and a secure federal debt would give investors a stake in the success of the new national government. The young but confident Hamilton sought to use economic growth as the new nation's source of energy and cohesion. His success in creating a budget, a funded debt, a federal tax system, a national bank, a customs service, and a coast guard provided the foundations for American capitalism.

ESTABLISHING THE PUBLIC CREDIT In a series of brilliant reports submitted to Congress between January 1790 and December 1791, Hamilton outlined his visionary program for government finances and the economic development of the United States. The first of two "Reports on Public Credit" dealt with the vexing issue of war-generated debt. Both the federal government and the individual states had emerged from the

Revolution owing substantial sums. France, Spain, and Holland had lent the United States money and supplies to fight the war, and Congress had incurred more debt by printing paper money and selling government bonds to investors. State governments had also accumulated huge debts. After the war some states had started paying off their debts, but the efforts were uneven. Only the federal government could wipe the entire slate clean. Hamilton insisted that the state debts from the Revolution were a *national* responsibility because all Americans had benefited from independence. He also knew that the federal government's willingness to assume responsibility for paying off the state debts would heighten a sense of nationalism by helping the people see the benefits of a strong central government.

Hamilton's controversial report on public credit made two key recommendations: first, it called for funding the federal debt at face value, which meant that citizens holding deflated war bonds could exchange them for new interest-bearing bonds, and second, it declared that the federal government should assume state debts from the Revolution. Holders of state bonds would exchange them for new national bonds.

The funding scheme was controversial because many farmers and former soldiers in immediate need of money had sold their securities for a fraction of their value to speculators who were eager to buy them up after reading Hamilton's first report. The original bondholders argued that they should be reimbursed for their losses; otherwise, the speculators would gain a windfall from the new government's funding of bonds at face value. Hamilton sternly resisted their pleas. The speculators, he argued, had "paid what the commodity was worth in the market, and took the risks." Therefore, they should reap the profits. In fact, Hamilton insisted, the government should favor the speculative investors because they represented the bedrock of a successful capitalist economy.

The report sparked lengthy debates before its substance was adopted. Then, in short order, Hamilton authored three more reports: the second of the "Reports on Public Credit," which included a proposal for a liquor tax to raise revenue to cover the nation's debts; a report recommending the establishment of a national bank and a national mint (to provide coins and currency), which were set up in 1791–1792; and the "Report on Manufactures," which proposed an extensive program of government aid and other encouragement to stimulate the development of manufacturing enterprises so as to reduce America's dependence on imported goods.

Hamilton's economic program was substantially the one that Robert Morris had urged upon the Confederation a decade before and Hamilton had strongly endorsed at the time. "A national debt," he had written Morris in

1781, "if it is not excessive, will be to us a national blessing; it will be a powerful cement of our union. It will also create a necessity for keeping up taxation to a degree which without being oppressive, will be a spur to industry." Payment of the national debt, in short, would be not only a point of national honor and sound finance, ensuring the country's credit for the future; it would also be an occasion to assert the federal power of taxation and thus instill respect for the authority of the new national government. Not least, the plan would win the new government the support of wealthy, influential creditors who would now have a direct financial stake in the survival of the government.

THE EMERGENCE OF SECTIONAL DIFFERENCES   Hamilton's brilliant financial proposals created a political firestorm. The Virginian James Madison, who had been Hamilton's close ally in promoting ratification of the Constitution, broke with him over the matter of a national debt. Madison did not question whether the debt should be paid; he was troubled, however, that speculators would become the chief beneficiaries. That the far greater portion of the national debt was owed to northerners than to southerners further troubled him. Madison, whom Hamilton had expected to champion his program in the House, proposed an alternative plan, one that gave a larger share to the first owners of the government bonds than to the speculators who purchased them. Madison's opposition to Hamilton's plan ignited a vigorous debate, but Hamilton carried his point by a margin of 3 to 1 when the House brought it to a vote.

Madison's opposition to Hamilton's plan to have the federal government assume responsibility for state debts got more support, however, and clearly signaled a political division along geographic lines. The southern states, with the exception of South Carolina, had whittled down their war debts. New England, with the largest unpaid debts, stood to be the greatest beneficiary of Hamilton's plan for the federal government to pay off the state debts. Rather than see Virginia victimized, Madison held out yet another alternative. Why not, he suggested, have the government assume state debts as they stood in 1783, at the conclusion of the peace treaty? Debates on this point deadlocked the whole question of debt funding and assumption, and Hamilton grew so frustrated with the legislative stalemate that he considered resigning.

The gridlock ended in the summer of 1790, when Jefferson, Hamilton, and Madison agreed to a compromise. In return for northern votes in favor of locating the permanent national capital on the Potomac River, Madison pledged to seek enough southern votes to pass the debt assumption plan, with the further arrangement that those states with smaller debts would get in effect outright grants from the federal government to equalize the difference. These arrangements secured enough votes to carry Hamilton's funding and assumption proposals. The national capital would be moved from New York City to Philadelphia for ten years, after which it would be settled at a new federal city on the Potomac River, the site to be chosen by the president. Jefferson later claimed to have been "duped" by Hamilton into agreeing to the "Compromise of 1790" because he did not fully understand the implications of the debt-assumption plan. It is more likely that Jefferson had been outsmarted. He only later realized how relatively insignificant the location of the national capital was when compared with the far-reaching effects of Hamilton's economic program.

A NATIONAL BANK   Hamilton's initiatives generated from nowhere, as if by magic, a great sum of capital for the federal government. Having solidified the national government's ability to pay its debts, the relentless Hamilton moved on to a related measure essential to his vision of national greatness: a national bank modeled on the Bank of England, which by issuance of bank notes (paper money) might provide a uniform national paper currency that

The Bank of the United States

Proposed by Alexander Hamilton, the bank opened in Philadelphia in 1791.

would address the chronic American shortage of gold and silver. Government bonds held by the bank would back up the value of its new bank notes. The national bank, chartered by Congress, would remain under government control, but private investors would supply four fifths of the $10 million capital and name twenty of the twenty-five directors; the government would provide the other fifth of the capital and name five directors.

The bank, Hamilton explained, would serve many purposes. Like the national banks of Europe, it would provide a stable, flexible national currency and a source of capital for loans to fund business and commercial development. What is more, the bank would be a safe place to keep government funds; it could provide "pecuniary aids" in the event of sudden emergencies, and through the use of bookkeeping entries it could readily transfer funds between branch offices, eliminating the need for the more costly and cumbersome shipment of metals.

Once again James Madison rose to lead the opposition to Hamilton, arguing that he could find no basis in the Constitution for a national bank. That was enough to raise in President Washington's mind serious doubts as to the constitutionality of the measure, which Congress passed fairly quickly over Madison's objections. The vote in Congress revealed the growing sectional division in the young United States. Representatives from the northern states voted 33 to 1 in favor of the national bank; southern congressmen opposed the bank 19 to 6.

Before signing the bill into law, President Washington sought the advice of his cabinet, where he found an equal division of opinion. The result was the first great debate on constitutional interpretation. Should there be a strict or a broad construction of the document? Were the powers of Congress only those explicitly stated, or were others implied? The argument turned chiefly on Article I, Section 8, which authorizes Congress to "make all Laws which shall be necessary and proper for carrying into Execution the foregoing Powers."

Such language left room for disagreement and led to a confrontation between Jefferson and Hamilton. Secretary of State Jefferson pointed to the Tenth Amendment, which reserves to the states and the people powers not delegated to Congress. "To take a single step beyond the boundaries thus specially drawn around the powers of Congress," he wrote, "is to take possession of a boundless field of power, no longer susceptible of any definition." A bank might be a convenient aid to Congress in collecting taxes and regulating the currency, but it was not, as Article I, Section 8, specified, *necessary.*

In a lengthy report to the president, Hamilton countered that the power to charter corporations was included in the sovereignty of any government, whether or not expressly stated. And in a classic summary he expressed his opinion on constitutionality:

> This criterion is the *end,* to which the measure relates as a *mean.* If the *end* be clearly comprehended within any of the specified powers, collecting taxes and regulating the currency, and if the measure have an obvious relation to that *end,* and is not forbidden by any particular provision of the Constitution, it may safely be deemed to come within the compass of the national authority.

Hamilton's sophisticated analysis convinced Washington to sign the controversial bank bill. In doing so, the president had indeed, in Jefferson's words, opened up "a boundless field of power," which in the coming years would lead to a further broadening of implied powers with the approval of the Supreme Court. Under the leadership of Chief Justice John Marshall, the Court would eventually adopt Hamilton's words almost verbatim. On July 4, 1791, stock in the new Bank of the United States was put up for sale, and it sold out within an hour.

ENCOURAGING MANUFACTURES   Hamilton's audacious ambitions for the new country were not yet exhausted. In the last of his great reports, the "Report on Manufactures," he set in place the capstone of his design for a modern national economy: the active governmental encouragement of manufacturing to provide productive uses for the new capital created by his funding, assumption (of state debts), and banking schemes. Hamilton believed that several advantages would flow from the aggressive development of manufactures: the diversification of labor in a country given over too much to farming; improved productivity through greater use of machinery; paid work for those not ordinarily employed outside the home, such as women and children; the promotion of immigration to provide industrial workers; a greater scope for the diversity of talents in business; more ample and various opportunities for entrepreneurial activity; and a better domestic market for agricultural products.

To secure his ends, Hamilton proposed to use the means to which other countries had resorted: tariffs (taxes) on imported foreign goods, or in Hamilton's words, "protecting duties," which in some cases might be raised so high as to deter imports altogether; restraints on the export of raw materials; government-paid bounties and premiums to encourage certain industries; tariff exemptions for imported raw materials needed for American manufacturing; government encouragement of inventions and discoveries; regulations for

Certificate of the New York Mechanick Society

An illustration of the growing diversification of labor, by Abraham Godwin (ca. 1785).

the inspection of commodities; and finally, the financing of improvements in transportation, including the development of roads, canals, and rivers.

Some of Hamilton's tariff proposals were enacted in 1792. Otherwise the program was filed away—but not forgotten. It provided an arsenal of arguments for the advocates of manufactures in years to come. Hamilton denied that there was any necessary economic conflict between the northern and southern regions of the Union. If, as seemed likely, the northern and middle Atlantic states should become the chief scenes of manufacturing, they would create robust markets for agricultural products, some of which the southern states were peculiarly qualified to produce. Both North and South would benefit, he argued, as more commerce moved between those regions than across the Atlantic, thus strengthening the Union.

HAMILTON'S ACHIEVEMENT Largely owing to the skillful Hamilton, the Treasury Department during the early 1790s began to retire the Revolutionary War debt, and foreign capital began to flow in once again.

Economic growth, so elusive in the 1780s, flourished by the end of the century. A Bostonian reported in late 1790 that the United States had never "had a brighter sunshine of prosperity. . . . Our agricultural interest smiles, our commerce is blessed, our manufactures flourish." But Hamilton's policies had done much more than revive the economy. Against fierce opposition, Hamilton had established the foundations for a powerful capitalist republic. In the process he helped Americans see beyond their local interests. Hamilton was a consummate nationalist. As an immigrant he never developed the intense loyalty to a state felt by most Americans. And during the Revolutionary War he had seen how shortsighted and selfish the states could be in refusing to provide adequate support for the Continental army. He dreamed of the United States' becoming a commercial and industrial empire, a world power remarkable for its ability to balance individual freedom with government power. As he recognized, "Liberty may be endangered by the abuses of liberty as well as by the abuses of power."

Yet however profound Hamilton's economic insights were and however beneficial his policies were to the nation's long-term economic development, they provoked fierce opposition. By championing industry and commerce as well as the expansion of federal authority at the expense of the states, Hamilton infuriated a growing number of people, especially in the agricultural South. Competition between Jefferson and Hamilton boiled over into a nasty feud between the government's two most talented men. The concerted opposition to Hamilton's politics and policies soon fractured Washington's cabinet and spawned the nation's first political parties.

THE REPUBLICAN ALTERNATIVE

Hamilton's controversial financial ideas became the foundation of the party known as the Federalists; in opposition, Madison and Jefferson led those who took the name Republicans (also called the Democratic Republicans), thereby implying that the Federalists aimed at a monarchy. Neither side in the disagreement over national policy deliberately set out to create organized political parties. But there were growing differences of both philosophy and self-interest that would not subside. At the outset, Madison assumed leadership of Hamilton's opponents in Congress. Madison, like Thomas Jefferson, was rooted in Virginia, where opposition to Hamilton's economic policies predominated. Patrick Henry, for example, proclaimed that Hamilton's policies were "dangerous to the rights and subversive of the interests of the people."

Thomas Jefferson

A portrait by Charles Willson Peale
(1791).

After the Compromise of 1790, which assured the federal assumption of state debts, Madison and Jefferson ever more resolutely opposed Hamilton's policies: his effort to place a tax on whiskey, which laid a burden especially on the trans-Appalachian farmers, whose livelihood depended upon the production and sale of the beverage; his proposal for the national bank; and his "Report on Manufactures." As the differences built, hostility between Jefferson and Hamilton festered within the cabinet, much to the distress of President Washington.

Thomas Jefferson, twelve years Hamilton's senior, was in most respects his opposite. Jefferson was an agrarian aristocrat, his father a successful surveyor and land speculator, his mother a Randolph, from one of the first families of Virginia. Like Hamilton, Jefferson was brilliant. He developed a breadth of cultivated interests that ranged widely in science, the arts, and the humanities. He read or spoke seven languages. He was an architect of distinction (Monticello, the Virginia state capitol, and the University of Virginia are monuments to his talent), a courtly gentleman who understood mathematics and engineering, an inventor, and an agronomist. He knew music and practiced the violin, although one wit remarked that only Patrick Henry played it worse.

Hamilton and Jefferson represented opposite visions of the character of the Union and defined certain contrasting philosophical and political issues that still echo more than two centuries later. Hamilton was a hardheaded realist who foresaw a diversified capitalist economy, with agriculture balanced by commerce and industry, and was thus the better prophet. Jefferson was an agrarian idealist who feared that the growth of crowded cities would divide society into a capitalist aristocracy on the one hand and a deprived proletariat on the other. Hamilton feared anarchy and loved order; Jefferson feared tyranny and loved liberty.

Hamilton championed a strong central government actively engaged in encouraging capitalist enterprise. Jefferson wanted to preserve a decentralized agrarian republic made up primarily of small farmers. "Those who labor in the earth," he wrote, "are the chosen people of God, if ever he had a chosen people, whose breasts He has made His peculiar deposit for genuine and substantial virtue." Jefferson did not oppose all forms of manufacturing; he simply feared that the unlimited expansion of commerce and industry would produce a growing class of wage laborers who were dependent upon others for their livelihood and therefore subject to political manipulation and economic exploitation.

In their quarrel, Hamilton isolated Jefferson as the leader of the opposition to his policies. In the summer of 1791, Jefferson and Madison set out on a "botanizing" excursion up the Hudson River in New York and into New England. The supposed vacation trip was actually a cover for consultations with New York political figures who personally and politically opposed Hamilton. Although the significance of that single trip was exaggerated, there did ultimately arise an informal alliance of Jeffersonian Republicans in the South and New York that would become a constant if sometimes divisive feature of the new party and its successor, the Democratic party. By mid-1792, Hamilton and Jefferson could no longer disguise their disdain for each other. Jefferson told a friend that the two rivals "daily pitted in the cabinet like two cocks."

Still, amid the rising political tensions, there was little opposition in either party to Washington, who longed to end his exile from his beloved Mount Vernon and had even begun drafting a farewell address but was urged by both Hamilton and Jefferson to continue in public life. In the fragile infancy of the new nation, Washington was the only man who could transcend party differences and hold things together with his unmatched prestige. In 1792, Washington was unanimously reelected, the only president ever to garner such uniform support.

CRISES FOREIGN AND DOMESTIC

During George Washington's second term, the problems of foreign relations surged to center stage, delivered by the consequences of the French Revolution, which had begun in 1789, during the first months of his presidency. Americans followed the tumultuous events in France with almost universal sympathy, up to a point. By the spring of 1792, however, the French experiment in liberty, equality, and fraternity had transformed itself into a monster. France plunged into war with Austria and Prussia. The French Revolution began devouring its own children, along with its enemies, during the Terror of 1793–1794. The revolutionary rulers executed thousands of political prisoners, and barbarism ruled the streets of Paris. Secretary of State Thomas Jefferson wholeheartedly endorsed the efforts of French revolutionaries to replace the monarchy with a republican form of government. By contrast, Vice President John Adams decided that the French Revolution had run amok; it had become barbarous and godless. Such conflicting attitudes toward the French Revolution transformed the first decade of American politics into one of the most fractious periods in the nation's history.

The French Revolution also transformed international relations and set in motion a series of complex European alliances and prolonged wars that would frustrate the desire of the young United States to remain neutral in world affairs. After the execution of King Louis XVI, early in 1793, Great Britain and Spain entered into the coalition of monarchies at war with the chaotic French republic. For the next twenty-two years, Britain and France were at war, with only a brief respite, until the final defeat of the French forces under Napoléon in 1815. The European war presented George Washington, just beginning his second term in 1793, with an awkward decision. By the 1778 Treaty of Alliance, the United States was a perpetual ally of France, obligated to defend that nation's possessions in the West Indies.

But Americans wanted no part of the European war. They were determined to maintain their lucrative trade with both sides. And besides, the Americans had no navy with which to wage a war. Neutrality was the only sensible policy. For their part, Hamilton and Jefferson found in the neutrality policy one issue on which they could agree. Where they differed was in how best to implement it. Hamilton had a simple answer: declare the French alliance invalid because it had been made with a French government that no longer existed. Jefferson preferred to delay and use the alliance as a bargaining point with the British. In the end, however, Washington followed the advice of neither. Taking a middle course, the president issued a neutrality proclamation on April 22, 1793, that declared the United States "friendly and impartial toward the belligerent powers" and warned U.S. citizens that they might be prosecuted for "aiding or abetting hostilities" or taking part in other nonneutral acts. Instead of settling matters in his cabinet, however, Washington's proclamation brought to a boil the personal and partisan feud between Hamilton and Jefferson. Jefferson dashed off an angry letter to James Madison, urging his ally to "take up your pen" and cut Hamilton "to pieces" in the newspapers.

CITIZEN GENET   At the same time, Washington accepted Jefferson's argument that the United States should recognize the new French republican government (becoming the first country to do so) and welcome its new ambassador to the United States, the headstrong, indiscreet Edmond-Charles-Édouard Genet. Early in 1793, Citizen Genet landed at Charleston, South

Carolina to a hero's welcome. Along the route to Philadelphia, the enthusiasm of his American sympathizers gave the swaggering Genet an inflated notion of his influence. In Charleston he had engaged privateers to capture British ships, and in Philadelphia he continued the process. He also conspired with frontiersmen and land speculators to organize an attack on Spanish Florida and Louisiana.

Genet quickly became an embarrassment even to his Republican friends. The cabinet unanimously agreed that the French troublemaker had to go; in August 1793, President Washington demanded his recall. Meanwhile, a new party of radicals had gained power in France and sent its own minister with a warrant for Genet's arrest. Instead of returning to Paris and risk the guillotine, Genet sought asylum in the United States.

Genet's foolishness and the growing excesses of the French radicals were fast cooling U.S. support for France's wayward revolution. To Hamilton's followers, what was occurring in France began to resemble their worst nightmares of democratic anarchy. The French radicals made it hard even for American Republicans to retain sympathy, but they swallowed hard and made excuses. "The liberty of the whole earth was depending on the issue of the contest," the genteel Jefferson wrote, "and . . . rather than it should have failed, I would have seen half the earth devastated." Nor did the British make it easy for Federalists to rally to their side. Near the end of 1793, they informed the U.S. government that they intended to occupy their Great Lakes forts indefinitely.

The French and British causes deeply divided American opinion. In the contest, it seemed, one had to either be a Republican and support liberty, reason, and the "atheistic" revolutionaries ruling France or become a Federalist and support order, religious faith, and Britain. The division gave rise to curious loyalties: slaveholding planters like Thomas Jefferson joined the cheers for radical revolutionaries who dispossessed aristocrats in France, and they supported the protest against British seizures of New England ships; Massachusetts shippers still profited from the British trade and kept quiet. Boston, once a hotbed of revolution, became a bastion of Federalism. Jefferson was so disgusted by Washington's refusal to support the French Revolution and by his own ideological warfare with Hamilton that he resigned as secretary of state at the end of 1793.

JAY'S TREATY   By 1794 a prolonged foreign-policy crisis between the United States and Great Britain threatened to renew warfare between the old enemies. In late 1793 the British government violated international law by ordering naval commanders to begin seizing any American ship that carried

Trade limitations

A 1794 watercolor of Fort Detroit, a major center of Indian trade that the British agreed to evacuate under the terms of Jay's Treaty.

French goods or was sailing for a French port. By early 1794 several hundred American ships in the West Indies had been confiscated. Their crews were given the terrible choice of joining the British navy or being imprisoned. At the same time, British troops in the Ohio River valley armed Indians who attacked American settlers. Early in 1794 the Republican leaders in Congress were gaining support for commercial retaliation to end British trade abuses when the British gave President Washington a timely opening for a settlement. They stopped seizing American ships, and on April 16, 1794, Washington named Chief Justice John Jay as a special envoy to Great Britain. Jay left with instructions to settle all major issues: to get the British out of their forts along the Great Lakes and to secure reparations for the losses of American shippers, compensation for southern slaves carried away by British ships in 1783, and a new commercial treaty that would legalize American trade with the British West Indies.

To win his objectives, Jay accepted the British definition of neutral rights—that exports of tar, pitch, and other products needed for warships were contraband and that such military products could not go in neutral ships to enemy ports—and the "rule of 1756" prevailed, meaning that trade that was prohibited in peacetime because of mercantilist restrictions could not be opened in wartime. Through Jay's negotiations, Britain also gained most-favored-nation treatment in American commerce and a promise that French privateers would not be outfitted in American ports. Finally, Jay conceded that the British need not compensate U.S. citizens for the enslaved people who had escaped during the war and that the pre-Revolutionary American debts to British merchants would be paid by the U.S. government. In return for these concessions, the chief justice won three important points: British evacuation of their six northwestern forts by 1796, reparations for the seizures of American ships and cargo in 1793–1794, and the right of American merchants to trade with the British West Indies. But the last of these (Article XII) was hedged with restrictions.

Public outrage greeted the terms of Jay's Treaty (also known as the Treaty of London of 1794). The debate was so intense that some Americans feared civil war might erupt. Jefferson and the Democratic Republicans who favored France in its war with Britain were furious; they wanted no concessions to the hated British. They took to the streets, hanged Jay in effigy, and claimed that the treaty was unconstitutional. The heated dispute helped to crystallize the differences between the nation's first competing political parties, the Republicans and the Federalists. Even Federalist shippers, ready for a settlement with the British on almost any terms, were disappointed by the limitations on their trading privileges in the British West Indies. But much of the outcry was simply an expression of disappointment by Republican partisans who had sought an escalation of the conflict with the hated Great Britain. Some of it, too, was the outrage of Virginia planters at the concession on old debts to British merchants and the failure to get reparations for slaves liberated by British forces during the Revolution. George Washington himself wrestled with doubts over the treaty. He worried that his opponents were prepared to separate "the Union into Northern & Southern." Once he endorsed Jay's Treaty, there were even calls for his impeachment. Yet the president, while acknowledging that the proposed agreement was imperfect, concluded that adopting it was the only way to avoid a war with Britain that America was bound to lose. Still, the Senate debated the treaty in secret, and without a single vote to spare Jay's Treaty got the necessary two-thirds majority on June 24, 1795, with Article XII (the provision regarding the West Indies) expunged. The major votes in Congress were again aligned by region: 80 percent of the votes for the treaty came from New England or the middle Atlantic states; 74 percent of those voting against the treaty were southerners.

President Washington reluctantly signed the flawed treaty, concluding that it was the best he was likely to get. In the House, opponents, spurred on by James Madison, went so far as to demand that the president produce all papers relevant to the treaty, but the president refused on the grounds that approval of treaties was solely the business of the Senate. He thereby set an important precedent of executive privilege (a term not used at the time), and the House finally relented, supplying by a close vote the money required to carry out the terms of the treaty. The desperate effort to thwart Jay's Treaty cost James Madison his friendship with George Washington.

FRONTIER TENSIONS Other events also had an important bearing on Jay's Treaty, adding force to the importance of its settlement of the Canadian frontier and strengthening Spain's conviction that it needed to settle long-festering problems along America's southwestern frontier. While Jay was haggling in London, frontier conflict with Indians escalated, with U.S. troops twice crushed by northwestern tribes. At last, President Washington named General Anthony Wayne to head a military expedition into the Northwest Territory. In the fall of 1793, Wayne marched into Indian country with some 2,600 men, built Fort Greenville, and with reinforcements from Kentucky went on the offensive in 1794.

In August some 2,000 Shawnee, Ottawa, Chippewa, and Potawatomi warriors, reinforced by Canadian militias, attacked Wayne's troops in the Battle of Fallen Timbers, south of Detroit. The Americans repulsed them and then destroyed their fields and villages. The Indians, frustrated by their inability

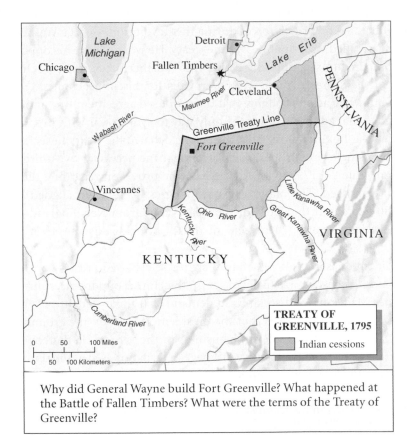

Why did General Wayne build Fort Greenville? What happened at the Battle of Fallen Timbers? What were the terms of the Treaty of Greenville?

to stop the relentless waves of white settlers encroaching upon their tribal lands, finally agreed to the Treaty of Greenville, signed in August 1795. According to the terms of the treaty, the United States bought from twelve tribes the rights to the southeastern quarter of the Northwest Territory (now Ohio and Indiana) and enclaves at the sites of Detroit, Chicago, and Vincennes, Indiana.

THE WHISKEY REBELLION   Soon after the Battle of Fallen Timbers, the Washington administration resolved on another show of strength in the backcountry, against the so-called Whiskey Rebellion. Alexander Hamilton's federal tax on liquor, levied in 1791, had outraged frontier farmers because it taxed their most profitable commodity. During the eighteenth and early nineteenth centuries nearly all Americans regularly drank alcoholic beverages: beer, hard cider, ale, wine, rum, brandy, or whiskey. In the areas west of the Appalachian Mountains, the primary cash commodity was liquor distilled from grain or fruit. Such emphasis on distilling reflected a practical problem. Many farmers could not afford to transport bulky crops of corn and rye across the mountains or down the Mississippi River to the seaboard markets. Instead, it was much more profitable to distill liquor from corn and rye or apples and peaches. Unlike grain crops, distilled spirits could be easily stored, shipped, or sold—and at higher profits. A bushel of corn worth 25¢ could yield two and a half gallons of liquor, worth ten times as much.

Western farmers were also suspicious of the new federal government in Philadelphia. The frontiersmen considered the whiskey tax another part of Hamilton's scheme to pick the pockets of the poor to enrich urban speculators. All through the backcountry, from Georgia to Pennsylvania and beyond, the whiskey tax provoked resistance and evasion.

In the summer of 1794, discontent over the federal tax on whiskey exploded into open rebellion in western Pennsylvania. Vigilantes began terrorizing federal revenue officers. They blew up the stills of those who paid the tax, robbed the mails, stopped court proceedings, and threatened an assault on Pittsburgh. On August 7, 1794, President Washington issued a proclamation ordering the insurgents home and calling out 12,900 militiamen from Virginia, Maryland, Pennsylvania, and New Jersey. Getting no response from the "Whiskey boys," he ordered the army to suppress the rebellion.

Under the command of General Henry Lee, 13,000 soldiers marched out from Harrisburg across the Alleghenies with Alexander Hamilton in their midst, itching to smite the insurgents. But the rebels vanished into the hills, and the troops met with little opposition. They finally rounded up twenty

Whiskey Rebellion

George Washington as commander in chief reviews the troops mobilized to quell the Whiskey Rebellion in 1794.

barefoot, ragged prisoners, whom they paraded down Market Street in Philadelphia and clapped into prison. Two of them were found guilty of treason, but they were pardoned by Washington on the grounds that one was a "simpleton" and the other "insane." Although Washington had overreacted, the government had made its point and gained "reputation and strength," claimed Hamilton, by suppressing the elusive rebellion—one that, according to Jefferson, "could never be found." The use of such excessive force, however, led many who sympathized with the frontiersmen to become Republicans, and Jefferson's party scored heavily in the next Pennsylvania elections. Nor was it the end of whiskey rebellions, which continued in an unending war of wits between moonshiners and federal tax officers, known as revenuers.

PINCKNEY'S TREATY   While these stirring events were transpiring in Pennsylvania, the Spanish were encouraging the Creeks, Choctaws, Chickasaws, and Cherokees in the Old Southwest to create the same turmoil that the British had fomented along the Ohio River. In Tennessee white settlers reacted by burning and leveling Indian villages. The defeat of their Indian allies, combined with Britain's concessions in the North and worries about possible American intervention in Louisiana, led the Spanish to enter into treaty negotiations with the Americans. U.S. negotiator Thomas Pinckney pulled off a diplomatic triumph in 1795 when he won acceptance of a boundary at the 31st parallel, open access to the Mississippi River, the right to transport goods to Spanish-controlled New Orleans, a commission to settle American claims against Spain, and a promise by each side to refrain

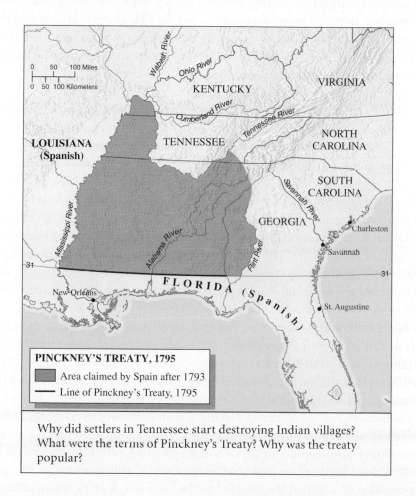

PINCKNEY'S TREATY, 1795

▪ Area claimed by Spain after 1793
━ Line of Pinckney's Treaty, 1795

Why did settlers in Tennessee start destroying Indian villages? What were the terms of Pinckney's Treaty? Why was the treaty popular?

from inciting Indian attacks on the other side. Ratification of Pinckney's Treaty came quickly. In fact, it was immensely popular, especially among westerners eager to use the Mississippi River to transport their crops to market.

Settlement of New Land

Now that Jay and Pinckney had settled matters with Britain and Spain and the army in the Northwest and white settlers in the South had suppressed the Indians, the West was prepared for a renewed surge of settlers. New lands, ceded by the Indians in the Treaty of Greenville, revealed a Congress once again divided on the issue of federal land policy. There were two basic viewpoints on the matter: federal land should serve mainly as a source of revenue, or it was more important to get the new country settled quickly, an endeavor that required low land prices. In the long run the evolution of policy would be from the first to the second viewpoint, but for the time being the federal government's need for revenue took priority.

LAND POLICY   Opinions on land policy, like opinions on other issues, separated Federalists from Republicans. Influential Federalists, like Hamilton and Jay, preferred to build the population of the eastern states first, lest the East lose both political influence and a labor force important to the growth of manufactures. Men of their persuasion favored high prices for federal land to enrich the Treasury, the sale of relatively large parcels to speculators rather than small parcels to settlers, and the development of compact settlements. Jefferson and Madison were reluctantly prepared to go along for the sake of reducing the national debt, but Jefferson expressed the hope for a plan by which the lands could be more readily settled by the masses. In any case, he suggested, frontiersmen would do as they had done before: "They will settle the lands in spite of everybody."

For the time being, however, Federalist policy prevailed. With the Land Act of 1796, Congress extended the rectangular surveys ordained in 1785 but doubled the price to $2 per acre, with only one year in which to complete payment. Half the townships would be sold in 640-acre sections, making the minimum cost $1,280, and alternate townships would be sold in blocks of eight sections, or 5,120 acres, making the minimum cost $10,240. Either price was well beyond the means of ordinary settlers and a bit much even for speculators, who could still pick up state-owned lands at lower prices. By 1800 federal land offices had sold fewer than 50,000 acres under the act. Continuing criticism in the West led to the Land Act of 1800, which reduced the minimum unit to 320 acres and spread payments over four years. Thus, with a down payment of $160, one could buy a farm. Under the Land Act of 1804, the minimum unit was reduced to 160 acres, which became the traditional homestead, and the price per acre went down to $1.64.

THE WILDERNESS ROAD   The lure of western lands led thousands of settlers to follow pathfinder Daniel Boone into the territory known as Kentucky, or Kaintuck, from the Cherokee name Ken-Ta-Ke (Great Meadow). In the late eighteenth century, the Indian land in Kentucky was a farmer's fantasy and a hunter's paradise, with its fertile soil and abundant forests teeming with buffalo, deer, and wild turkeys.

Boone himself was the product of a pioneer background. Born on a small farm in 1734 in central Pennsylvania, he was a deadeye marksman by the age

The emergence of agriculture

This American Folk painting by Edward Hicks shows the residence of David Twining, a Pennsylvania farmer, as it appeared in 1787.

of twelve and would soon become an experienced farmer and an accomplished woodsman. In 1750 the Boone family moved to western North Carolina. There Boone emerged as the region's greatest hunter, trading animal skins for salt and other household needs. After hearing numerous reports about the territory over the mountains, Boone set out alone in 1769 to find a trail into Kentucky. Armed with a long rifle, tomahawk, and hunting knife, he found what was called the Warriors' Path, a narrow foot trail that buffalo, deer, and Indians had worn along the steep ridges. It took him through the Cumberland Gap in southwestern Virginia.

In 1773, Boone led the first group of settlers through the Appalachian Mountains at the Cumberland Gap. Two years later he and thirty woodsmen used axes to widen the Warriors' Path into what became known as the Wilderness Road, a passage that more than 300,000 settlers would use over the next twenty-five years. At a point where a branch of the Wilderness Road intersected with the Kentucky River, near what is now Lexington, Boone built the settlement of Boonesborough in an area called Transylvania.

A steady stream of settlers, mostly Scotch-Irish from Pennsylvania, Virginia, and North Carolina, poured into Kentucky during the last quarter of the eighteenth century. That they were trespassing on Indian lands did not faze them. The backcountry pioneers came on foot or horseback, often leading a mule or a cow that carried their few tools and other possessions. On a good day they might cover fifteen miles. Near a creek or spring they would buy a parcel or stake out a claim and mark its boundaries by chopping notches into "witness trees." They would then build a lean-to for temporary shelter and clear the land for planting. The larger trees, those that could not be felled with an ax, were girdled: a cut would be made around the trunk, and the tree would be left to die. Because the process often took years, a farmer had to hoe and plant a field filled with stumps. The pioneers grew melons, beans, turnips, and other

The Wilderness Road

Daniel Boone Escorting Settlers through the Cumberland Gap by George Caleb Bingham.

vegetables, but corn was the preferred crop because it kept well and had so many uses. Ears were roasted and eaten on the cob, and kernels were ground into meal for making mush, hominy grits, and hoecakes, or johnnycakes (dry flour cakes, suitable for travelers, that were originally called journey-cakes). Pigs provided pork, and cows supplied milk, butter, and cheese. Many frontier families also built crude stills to manufacture a potent whiskey they called corn likker.

TRANSFER OF POWER

By 1796, President Washington had decided that two terms in office were enough. Weary of the increasingly bitter political quarrels and the venom of the partisan newspapers, he was ready to retire at last to his beloved home in northern Virginia, Mount Vernon. He would leave behind a formidable record of achievement: the organization of a new national government with demonstrated power, a secure national credit, the recovery of territory from Britain and Spain, a stable northwestern frontier, and the admission of three new states: Vermont (1791), Kentucky (1792), and Tennessee (1796).

WASHINGTON'S FAREWELL With the considerable help of Alexander Hamilton, Washington drafted a valedictory speech to the nation. His farewell address, dated September 17, 1796, called for unity among the people in backing their new government. Washington decried the rising spirit of partisanship and sectionalism; he feared the emergence of regional political parties promoting local interests. In foreign relations, Washington said, the United States should avoid both "an habitual hatred" and "an habitual fondness" for other countries. Europe, he noted, "has a set of primary interests which to us have none or a very remote relation. Hence she must be engaged in frequent controversies, the causes of which are essentially foreign to our concerns." The United States should keep clear of those quarrels. It was, moreover, "our true policy to steer clear of permanent alliances with any portion of the foreign world." A key word here is *permanent*. Washington opposed permanent alliances like the one with France, still technically in effect, but he endorsed "temporary alliances for extraordinary emergencies." Washington's warning against permanent foreign entanglements served as a fundamental principle in U.S. foreign policy until the early twentieth century.

Mount Vernon

George Washington and the Marquis de Lafayette at Mount Vernon in 1784. Washington enlarged the estate, which overlooks the Potomac River, to nearly 8,000 acres, dividing it among five farms.

THE ELECTION OF 1796 With George Washington out of the race, the United States had its first partisan election for president. The logical choice of the Federalists would have been Washington's protégé, Alexander Hamilton, the chief architect of their programs. But Hamilton's policies had left scars and made enemies. Nor did he suffer fools gladly, a common affliction of Federalist leaders, including the man on whom the choice fell. In Philadelphia a caucus of Federalist congressmen chose John Adams of Massachusetts as their heir apparent, with Thomas Pinckney of South Carolina, fresh from his diplomatic triumph in Spain, as the nominee for vice president. As expected, the Republicans drafted Thomas Jefferson and added geographic balance to the ticket with Senator Aaron Burr of New York.

The campaign of 1796 was intensely partisan. Republicans caricatured John Adams as "His Rotundity" because of his short, paunchy body. They also labeled him a pro-British monarchist. The Federalists countered that Jefferson was a French-loving atheist eager to incite another war with Great Britain. They also charged that the philosophical Jefferson was unsuited to executive leadership; he was not decisive enough. The increasing strength of the Republicans, fueled by the smoldering resentment of Jay's Treaty, very nearly swept Jefferson into office and perhaps would have but for the French ambassador's public appeals for his election—an action that backfired. Then, despite a Federalist majority among the electors, Hamilton hatched an impulsive scheme that very nearly threw the election away after all. Hamilton decided that Pinckney would be more subject to his influence than would the strong-minded Adams. He therefore sought to have the South Carolina Federalists withhold a few votes for Adams and bring Pinckney in first. The Carolinians more than cooperated—they divided their vote between Pinckney and Jefferson—but the New Englanders got wind of the scheme and dropped Pinckney. The upshot of Hamilton's scheme was to cut Pinckney out of both the presidency and the vice presidency and elect Jefferson as vice president with 68 electoral votes to Adams's 71.

THE ADAMS YEARS

Vain and cantankerous, John Adams had crafted a distinguished career as a Massachusetts lawyer, as a leader in the Revolutionary movement, as the hardest working member of the Continental Congress, as a diplomat in France, Holland, and Britain, and as George Washington's vice president. His political philosophy fell somewhere between Jefferson's and Hamilton's. He shared neither the one's faith in the common people nor the other's fondness for a financial aristocracy of "paper wealth." Adams feared the concept of democracy and considered equality a fanciful notion. He favored the classic mixture of aristocratic, democratic, and monarchical elements, though his use of *monarchical* interchangeably with *executive* exposed him to the attacks of Republicans who saw a monarchist in every Federalist. Adams was always haunted by a feeling that he was never properly appreciated—and he may have been right. Yet on the overriding issue of his administration, war and peace, he kept his head when others about him were losing theirs— probably at the cost of his reelection.

John Adams

Political philosopher and politician, Adams was the first president to take up residence in the White House, in early 1801.

THE WAR WITH FRANCE As America's second president, Adams faced the daunting task of succeeding the most popular man in the nation. He also inherited an undeclared naval war with France, a by-product of Jay's Treaty. When Jay accepted the British demand that food supplies and naval products, as well as war matériel, be treated as contraband subject to seizure, the French reasoned that American cargo headed for British ports was subject to the same interpretation. The French loosed their corsairs in the British West Indies, with an even more devastating effect on American shipping than the British had had in 1793–1794. By the time of Adams's inauguration, in 1797, the French had plundered some 300 American ships and broken diplomatic relations with the United States. As ambassador to Paris, Monroe had become so pro-French and so hostile to Jay's Treaty that George Washington had removed him for his indiscretions. France, grown haughty and contemptuous with Napoléon's military conquests, had then refused to accept Monroe's replacement, Charles Cotesworth Pinckney (brother of Thomas), and ordered him out of the country.

Conflict with France

A cartoon indicating the anti-French sentiment generated by the XYZ affair. The three American negotiators (at left) reject the Paris Monster's demand for money.

John Adams immediately acted to restore relations with France in the face of an outcry for war from the "high Federalists," including Secretary of State Timothy Pickering. Alexander Hamilton agreed with Adams on this point and approved his last-ditch effort for a diplomatic settlement. In 1797, Pinckney returned to Paris with John Marshall, a Virginia Federalist, and Elbridge Gerry, a Massachusetts Republican, for further negotiations. After nagging delays the three commissioners were accosted by three French officials (whom Adams labeled X, Y, and Z in his report to Congress). The French diplomats confided that negotiations could begin only if the Americans paid a bribe of $250,000.

Such bribes were common eighteenth-century diplomatic practice, but the answer from the American side, according to the commissioners' report, was "no, no, not a sixpence." When the so-called XYZ affair was reported in Congress and the public press, the response was translated into the more stirring slogan "Millions for defense but not one cent for tribute." Thereafter, the expressions of hostility toward France rose in a crescendo and even the most partisan Republicans—with the exception of Thomas Jefferson—quit making excuses for the French, and many of them joined the cry for war. Yet President Adams resisted a formal declaration of war; the French would have to bear the onus for that. Congress, however, authorized the capture of armed French ships, suspended commerce with France, and renounced the 1778 Treaty of Alliance, which was already a dead letter.

In 1798, George Logan, a Pennsylvania Quaker and Republican sympathizer, visited Paris at his own expense, hoping to head off war. He secured the release of some American seamen and won assurances that a new U.S. minister to France would be welcomed. The fruit of his mission, otherwise, was passage of the Logan Act (1799), still in effect, which forbids private citizens to negotiate with foreign governments without official authorization.

Amid a nation churning with patriotism and war fever, Adams strengthened American defenses. Militias marched and mobilized, and a navy began to emerge. An American navy had ceased to exist at the end of the Revolution. No armed ships were available when Algerian brigands began to prey on American commerce in the Mediterranean in 1794. As a result, Congress had authorized the arming of six ships. The job was still incomplete in 1796, however, when President Washington bought peace with the Algerians, but Congress allowed work on three of the ships to continue: the *Constitution,* the *United States,* and the *Constellation,* all completed in 1797. In 1798, Congress authorized a Department of the Navy, and by the end of the year, an undeclared naval war had begun in the West Indies with the French capture of an American schooner.

While the naval war was being fought, Congress, in 1798, authorized an army of 10,000 men to serve three years. Adams called George Washington from retirement to be its commander, and Washington agreed only on condition that Alexander Hamilton be his second in command. Adams relented but resented the slight to his authority as commander in chief. The rift among the Federalists thus widened further.

Peace overtures began to come from the French by the autumn of 1798, before the naval war was fully under way. In 1799, Adams dispatched a team of three Americans to negotiate with a new French government under First Consul Napoléon Bonaparte. By the Convention of 1800, they won the best terms they could from the triumphant Napoléon. In return for giving up all claims of indemnity for American losses, they got official suspension of the 1778 perpetual alliance with France and an end to the quasi naval war. The Senate ratified the agreement, contingent upon outright abrogation of the alliance, and it became effective on December 21, 1801.

THE WAR AT HOME   The simmering naval conflict with France mirrored a ferocious ideological war at home between Federalists and Republicans. Already-heated partisan politics had begun boiling over during the latter years of Washington's administration. The rhetoric grew so personal and tempers grew so short that opponents commonly resorted to duels. Federalists and Republicans saw each other as traitors to the principles of the American Revolution. Jefferson, for example, decided that Hamilton, Washington, Adams, and other Federalists were suppressing individual liberty in order to promote selfish interests. He adamantly opposed Jay's Treaty because it was pro-British and anti-French, and he was disgusted by the army's forceful suppression of the Whiskey Rebellion.

Such volatile issues forced Americans to take sides, and the Revolutionary generation of leaders, a group that John Adams had called the band of brothers, began to fragment into die-hard factions. Long-standing political friendships disintegrated amid the partisan attacks, and sectional divisions between North and South grew more fractious. Jefferson observed that a "wall of separation" had come to divide the nation's political leaders. "Politics and party hatreds," he told his daughter, "destroy the happiness of every being here."

Ironically, Jefferson's combative tactics contributed directly to the partisan tensions. He frequently planted rumors about his opponents in the press, wrote anonymous newspaper attacks, and asked others to disparage his opponents. As vice president under Adams, he displayed a gracious deviousness.

He led the Republican faction opposed to Adams and actively schemed to embarrass him. In 1797, Jefferson secretly hired a rogue journalist, James Callender, to produce a scurrilous pamphlet that described President Adams as a deranged monarchist intent upon naming himself king. By the end of the century, Jefferson had become an ardent advocate of polarized party politics: "I hold it as immoral to pursue a middle line, as between parties of Honest men and Rogues, into which every country has divided."

THE PROVIDENTIAL DETECTION

The partisan divide

The war with France deepened the division between the Federalists and Republicans.

For his part, John Adams refused to align himself completely with the Federalists, preferring instead to mimic George Washington and retain his independence as chief executive. He was too principled and too prickly to toe a party line. Soon after his election he invited Jefferson to join him in creating a bipartisan administration. After all, they had worked well together in the Continental Congress and in France, and they harbored great respect for each other. After consulting with James Madison, however, Jefferson refused to accept the new president's offer. Within a year he and Adams were at each other's throats. Adams expressed regret at losing Jefferson as a friend but "felt obliged to look upon him as a man whose mind is warped by prejudice." Jefferson had become "a child and the dupe" of the Republican faction in Congress, which was led by Madison.

The conflict with France only deepened the partisan divide emerging in the young United States. The real purpose of the French crisis all along, the more ardent Republicans suspected, was to provide Federalists with an excuse to suppress their American critics. The infamous Alien and Sedition Acts of 1798 lent credence to their suspicions. These and two other acts, passed in the wave of patriotic war fever, limited freedom of speech and the press and the liberty of aliens. Proposed by extreme Federalists in Congress, the acts did not originate with Adams but had his blessing. Goaded by his wife, Abigail, his primary counselor, Adams signed the controversial statutes and in doing so made the greatest mistake of his presidency. Timothy Pickering, his secretary of state, claimed that Adams had acted without consulting "any member of the government and for a reason truly remarkable—because he knew we should all be opposed to the measure." By succumbing to the partisan hysteria and enacting the vindictive acts, Adams seemed to bear out what Benjamin Franklin had said about him years before: he "means well for his country, is always an honest man, often a wise one, but sometimes and in some things, absolutely out of his senses."

Three of the four repressive acts engineered by the Federalists reflected hostility to foreigners, especially the French and the Irish, a large number of whom had become active Republicans and were suspected of revolutionary intent. The Naturalization Act lengthened from five to fourteen years the residency requirement for citizenship. The Alien Act empowered the president to deport "dangerous" aliens. The Alien Enemies Act authorized the president in time of declared war to expel or imprison enemy aliens at will. Finally, the Sedition Act defined as a high misdemeanor any conspiracy against legal measures of the government, including interference with federal officers and insurrection or rioting. What is more, the law forbade writing, publishing, or speaking anything of "a false, scandalous and malicious" nature against the government or any of its officers.

The Sedition Act was designed to punish Republicans, whom Federalists lumped together with French revolutionary radicals and American traitors. To be sure, partisan Republican journalists published scandalous lies and misrepresentations, but so did Federalists; it was a time when both sides seemed afflicted with paranoia. But the fifteen indictments brought under the Sedition Act, with ten convictions, were all directed at Republicans.

The most conspicuous targets of prosecution were Republican editors and a Republican congressman, Matthew Lyon of Vermont, a rough-and-tumble Irishman who castigated Adams's "continual grasp for power" and "unbounded thirst for ridiculous pomp, foolish adulation, and selfish avarice." Lyon was imprisoned for four months and fined $1,000, but from his cell he continued to write articles and letters for the Republican papers. The few convictions under the act only created martyrs to the cause of freedom of speech and the press and exposed the vindictiveness of Federalist judges.

Lyon and the others based their defense on the unconstitutionality of the Sedition Act, but Federalist judges dismissed the notion. It ran against the Republican grain, anyway, to have federal courts assume the authority to declare laws unconstitutional. To offset the "reign of witches" unleashed by the Alien and Sedition Acts, therefore, Jefferson and Madison drafted what

Dispute in the House

Republican representative Matthew Lyon and Connecticut Federalist Roger
Griswold attack each other on the floor of the House (1798). Lyon soon became
a target of the Sedition Act.

came to be known as the Kentucky and Virginia Resolutions. These passed
the legislatures of their respective states in 1798, and more Kentucky Resolutions, adopted in 1799, responded to counterresolutions from northern
states. The Kentucky and Virginia Resolutions, much alike in their arguments, denounced the Alien and Sedition Acts as "alarming infractions" of
constitutional rights. Since the Constitution arose as a compact among the
states, the resolutions argued, the states should decide when Congress had
exceeded its powers. The Virginia Resolutions, drafted by James Madison,
declared that states "have the right and are in duty bound to interpose for arresting the progress of the evil." The second set of Kentucky Resolutions, in
restating the states' right to judge violations of the Constitution, added,
"That a nullification of those sovereignties, of all unauthorized acts done
under color of that instrument, is the rightful remedy."

These doctrines of interposition and nullification, reworked and edited
by later theorists, were destined to be used for causes unforeseen by their
authors. (Years later, Madison would disclaim the doctrine of nullification as
developed by John C. Calhoun, but his own doctrine of interposition would

resurface as late as the 1950s as a device to oppose racial integration.) At the time, it seems, both men intended the resolutions to serve chiefly as propaganda, the opening guns in the political campaign of 1800. Neither Kentucky nor Virginia took steps to nullify or interpose its authority in the enforcement of the Alien and Sedition Acts. Instead, both called upon the other states to help them win a repeal. In Virginia, citizens talked of armed resistance to the federal government. Jefferson counseled against any thought of violence: it was "not the kind of opposition the American people will permit." He assured a fellow Virginian that the Federalist "reign of witches" would soon end, that it would be discredited by the arrival of the tax collector more than anything else.

REPUBLICAN VICTORY As the presidential election of 1800 approached, civil unrest boiled over. Grievances mounted against Federalist policies: taxation to support an unneeded army; the Alien and Sedition Acts, which cast the Federalists as anti-liberty; the lingering fears of "monarchism"; the hostilities aroused by Alexander Hamilton's economic programs; the suppression of the Whiskey Rebellion; and Jay's Treaty. When Adams opted for peace with France in 1800, he probably doomed his one chance for reelection—a wave of patriotic war fever with a united party behind him. His decision gained him much goodwill among Americans at large but left the Hamiltonians angry and his party divided. In 1800 the Federalists summoned enough unity to name as their candidates Adams and Charles Cotesworth Pinckney; they agreed to cast all their electoral votes for both. But the Hamiltonian Federalists continued to snipe at Adams and his policies, and soon after his renomination Adams removed two of them from his cabinet. A furious Hamilton struck back with a pamphlet questioning Adams's fitness to be president, citing his "disgusting egotism." Intended for private distribution among Federalist leaders, the pamphlet reached the hands of New York Republican Aaron Burr, who put it in general circulation.

Jefferson and Burr, as the Republican presidential candidates, once again represented the alliance of Virginia and New York. Jefferson, perhaps even more than Adams, was attacked by Federalists as a supporter of the radical French revolutionaries and an atheist. His election would supposedly bring civil war—"dwellings in flames, hoary hairs bathed in blood, female chastity violated . . . children writhing on the pike and halberd." Jefferson kept quiet, refused to answer the attacks, and directed the campaign by mail from his home at Monticello. His supporters portrayed him as the farmers' friend, the champion of states' rights, frugal government, liberty, and peace.

Adams proved more popular than his party, whose candidates generally fared worse than the president, but the Republicans edged him out by 73 electoral votes to 65. The decisive states were New York and South Carolina, either of which might have given the victory to Adams. But in New York former senator Aaron Burr's organization won control of the legislature, which cast the electoral votes. In South Carolina, Charles Pinckney (cousin of the Federalist Pinckneys) won over the legislature by well-placed promises of Republican patronage. Still, the result was not final, for Jefferson and Burr had tied with 73 votes each, and the choice of the president was thrown into the House of Representatives, where Federalist diehards tried vainly to give the election to Burr. This was too much for Hamilton, who opposed Jefferson but held a much lower opinion of Burr. The stalemate in the House continued for thirty-five ballots. The deadlock was broken only when a confidant of Jefferson's assured a Delaware congressman that Jefferson, if elected, would refrain from the wholesale removal of Federalists appointed to federal offices and would uphold Hamilton's financial policies. The representative resolved to vote for Jefferson, and several other Federalists agreed simply to cast blank ballots, permitting Jefferson to win without any of them having to vote for him.

Before the Federalists relinquished power to the Jeffersonian Republicans on March 4, 1801, their lame-duck Congress passed the Judiciary Act of 1801. Intended to ensure Federalist control of the judicial system, this act provided that the next vacancy on the Supreme Court would not be filled, created sixteen federal circuit courts with a new judge for each, and increased the number of federal attorneys, clerks, and marshals. Before he left office, Adams named John Marshall to the vacant office of chief justice and appointed Federalists to all the new positions, including forty-two justices of the peace for the new District of Columbia. The Federalists, defeated and destined never to regain national power, had in the words of Jefferson "retired into the judiciary as a stronghold."

The election of 1800 marked a major turning point in American political history. It was the first time that one political party, however ungracefully, relinquished power to the opposition party. Jefferson's victory signaled the emergence of a new, more democratic political system, dominated by parties, partisanship, and wider public participation—at least by white men. Before and immediately after independence, politics was popular but not democratic: people took a keen interest in public affairs, but socially prominent families, the "rich, the able, and the wellborn," dominated political life. However, the fierce political battles of the late 1790s, culminating in 1800 with Jefferson's election as the nation's third president, wrested control of

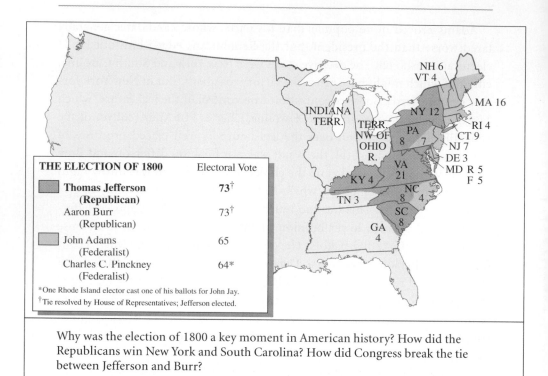

THE ELECTION OF 1800	Electoral Vote
Thomas Jefferson (Republican)	**73**[†]
Aaron Burr (Republican)	73[†]
John Adams (Federalist)	65
Charles C. Pinckney (Federalist)	64[*]

[*] One Rhode Island elector cast one of his ballots for John Jay.
[†] Tie resolved by House of Representatives; Jefferson elected.

Why was the election of 1800 a key moment in American history? How did the Republicans win New York and South Carolina? How did Congress break the tie between Jefferson and Burr?

politics from the governing elite and established the right of more people to play an active role in governing the young republic. With the gradual elimination of property qualifications for voting and the proliferation of newspapers, pamphlets, and other publications, the "public sphere" in which political issues were debated and decided expanded enormously in the early nineteenth century.

The Republican victory in 1800 also marked the political triumph of the slaveholding South. Three Virginia slaveholders—Thomas Jefferson, James Madison, and James Monroe—would control the White House for the next twenty-four years. While Republicans celebrated democracy, many of them also prospered because of slavery. The tensions between republican ideals and plantation slavery would eventually lead to civil war.

John Adams regretted the democratization of politics and the rise of fractious partisanship. "Jefferson had a party, Hamilton had a party, but the commonwealth had none," he sighed. The defeated president was so distraught at the turn of events that he decided not to participate in Jefferson's inauguration in the new capital, Washington, D.C. Instead, he boarded a stagecoach for the 500-mile trip to his home in Quincy, Massachusetts. He and Jefferson would not communicate for the next twelve years. As Adams returned to work on his Massachusetts farm, he reported that he had exchanged "honors and virtue for manure." He told his son John Quincy, who would become president himself, that the American president "has a hard, laborious, and unhappy life."

CHAPTER SUMMARY

- **Formation of the Government** The Constitution left many questions unanswered about the structure and conduct of the government. Congress had to create executive departments and organize the federal judiciary. The ratification of the first ten amendments, the Bill of Rights, was a leading issue; however, strengthening the economy was the highest priority.

- **Hamiltonian Vision** Hamilton wanted to create a vibrant economy. He succeeded in establishing a sound foundation for American capitalism by crafting a budget with a funded national debt, a federal tax system, a national bank, and a customs service.

- **Religious Freedom** In terms of religion, the Constitution does not mention a deity and the First Amendment guarantees people the right to worship freely, regardless of their religious persuasion.

- **Neutrality** With the outbreak of European-wide war during the French Revolution, Washington's policy of neutrality violated the terms of the 1778 treaty with France, which had established a perpetual alliance. The French began seizing British and American ships and an undeclared war was under way. The resulting unrest contributed to the creation of the first two political parties: Hamiltonian Federalists and Jeffersonian Republicans.

- **Jeffersonian Vision** James Madison and Thomas Jefferson became increasingly critical of Hamilton's policies, which favored a strong federal government and weaker state governments. Jefferson, on the other hand, championed an agrarian vision, in which independent small farmers were the backbone of American society. He feared that the growth of cities would enrich the aristocracy and widen divisions between the rich and the poor.

CHRONOLOGY

1789	President George Washington is inaugurated
1789	French Revolution begins
1791	Bill of Rights is ratified
1791	Bank of the United States is created
1793	Washington issues a proclamation of neutrality
1794	Jay's Treaty is negotiated with England
1794	Whiskey Rebellion
1795	By the Treaty of Greenville, the United States purchases western lands from Native Americans
1795	Pinckney's Treaty is negotiated with Spain
1796	Washington delivers his farewell address
1797	XYZ affair
1798	Alien and Sedition Acts are passed

KEY TERMS & NAMES

Alexander Hamilton's "Report on Manufactures" p. 309

Bank of the United States p. 311

Republicans p. 315

Citizen Genet p. 318

Jay's Treaty p. 319

Whiskey Rebellion p. 323

Daniel Boone p. 327

XYZ affair p. 333

Alien and Sedition Acts p. 335

Kentucky and Virginia Resolutions p. 337

9

THE EARLY REPUBLIC

FOCUS QUESTIONS ⓢ wwnorton.com/studyspace

- What were the main achievements of Jefferson's administration?
- What was the impact of the Marshall court on the U.S. government?
- How did the Louisiana Purchase change the United States?
- What were the causes of the War of 1812?
- What were the effects of the War of 1812?

The early years of the new American republic laid the foundation for the nation's development as the first society in the world organized by the principle of democratic capitalism and its promise of equal opportunity for all—except African Americans, Native Americans, and women. Americans in the fifty years after independence were on the move and on the make. Their prospects seemed unlimited, their optimism unrestrained. As John Adams observed, "There is no people on earth so ambitious as the people of America . . . because the lowest can aspire as freely as the highest."

Land sales west of the Appalachian Mountains soared in the early nineteenth century as aspiring farmers shoved Indians aside in order to establish homesteads of their own. Enterprising, mobile, and increasingly diverse in religion and national origin, tens of thousands of ordinary folk uprooted themselves from settled communities and went west in search of personal advancement, occupying more territory in a single generation than had been settled in the 150 years of colonial history. "Never again," as the historian Joyce Appleby wrote, "would so large a portion of the nation live in new settlements." Between 1800 and 1820 the trans-Appalachian population soared from 300,000 to 2 million. By 1840, over 40 percent of Americans lived west of the Appalachians in eight new states.

The migrants flowed westward in three streams between 1780 and 1830. One ran from the Old South—Maryland, Virginia, and the Carolinas—through Georgia into the newer states of Alabama and Mississippi. Another wave traversed the Blue Ridge Mountains from Maryland and Virginia, crossing into Kentucky and Tennessee. The third route was in the North, taking New Englanders westward into upstate New York, Pennsylvania, Ohio, and Michigan. Many of the pioneers stayed only a few years before continuing westward in search of cheaper and more fertile land.

The spirit of opportunistic independence affected free African Americans as well as whites, Indians as well as immigrants. Free blacks were the fastest-growing segment of the population during the early nineteenth century. Many enslaved Americans had gained their freedom during the Revolutionary War by escaping, joining the British forces, or serving in American military units. Every state except South Carolina and Georgia promised freedom to slaves who fought the British. Afterward, state after state in the North outlawed slavery, and anti-slavery societies blossomed, exerting increasing pressure on the South to end the degrading practice. Pressure of another sort affected the besieged Indian tribes. The westward migration of whites brought incessant conflict with Native Americans. Indians fiercely resisted the invasion of their ancestral lands but ultimately succumbed to a federal government and a federal army determined to displace them.

Most whites, however, were less concerned about Indians and slavery than they were about seizing their own opportunities. Politicians suppressed the volatile issue of slavery; their priorities were elsewhere. Westward expansion, economic growth, urban development, and the democratization of politics preoccupied a generation of Americans born after 1776—especially outside the South. In 1790 nine out of ten Americans lived on the land and engaged in what is called household production; their sphere of activity was local. But with each passing year, farmers increasingly focused on producing surplus crops and livestock to sell in regional markets. Such commercial agriculture was especially evident in the South. As cotton prices soared, the Deep South grew ever more committed to a plantation economy dependent upon slave labor, New England merchants and shippers, and world markets. The burgeoning market economy produced boom-and-bust cycles, but overall the years from 1790 to 1830 were quite prosperous, with young Americans experiencing unprecedented opportunities for economic gain and geographic mobility.

The colonial economy had been organized according to what Great Britain demanded from its New World possessions. This dependency brought the hated imperial restrictions on manufacturing, commerce, and shipping. With independence, however, Americans could create new industries, pursue new careers, and exploit new markets. It was not simply Alexander Hamilton's financial initiatives and the capitalistic energies of wealthy investors and speculators that sparked America's dramatic commercial growth in these years. It was also the strenuous efforts of ordinary men and women who were willing to take risks, uproot families, use unstable paper money issued by unregulated local banks, purchase factory-made goods, and tinker with new machines and tools. Free enterprise was the keynote of the era.

While most Americans continued to work as farmers, a growing number found employment in new or greatly expanded enterprises: textiles, banking, transportation, publishing, retailing, teaching, preaching, medicine, law, construction, and engineering. Technological innovations (steam power, power tools, and new modes of transportation) and their social applications (mass communication, turnpikes, the postal service, banks, and corporations) fostered an array of new industries and businesses. The emergence of a factory system transformed the nature of work for many Americans. Proud apprentices, journeymen, and master craftsmen, who controlled their labor and invested their work with an individualistic emphasis on quality rather than quantity, resented the proliferation of mills and factories populated by masses of "half-trained" workers dependent upon an hourly wage and subject to the sharp fluctuations of the larger economy.

In short, the decentralized agrarian republic of 1776, nestled along the Atlantic seaboard, had by 1830 become a sprawling commercial nation connected by networks of roads and canals and cemented by economic relationships—all animated by a restless spirit of enterprise, experimentation, and expansion.

JEFFERSONIAN SIMPLICITY

On March 4, 1801, the fifty-seven-year-old Thomas Jefferson, tall and thin, with red hair and a ruddy complexion, became the first president to be inaugurated in the new federal city, Washington, District of Columbia. The new capital city was still a motley array of buildings around two centers, Capitol Hill and the executive mansion. Congress, having met in eight towns and cities since 1774, had at last found a permanent home but enjoyed few amenities. There were only two places of amusement, one a racetrack, the other a theater thick with "tobacco smoke, whiskey breaths, and other stenches."

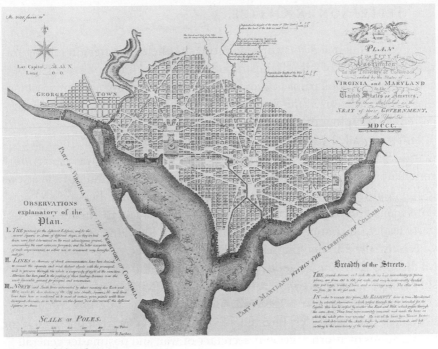

The new federal city

Plan of Washington, D.C., from 1792.

Jefferson's informal inauguration befitted the primitive surroundings. The new president left his lodgings and walked down a stump-strewn Pennsylvania Avenue to the unfinished Capitol. He entered the Senate chamber, took the oath administered by Chief Justice John Marshall, read his inaugural address in a barely audible voice, and returned to his boardinghouse for dinner. A tone of simplicity and conciliation ran through his inaugural speech. The campaign between Federalists and Republicans had been so fierce that some had predicted civil war. Jefferson now appealed for unity. "We are all Republicans—we are all Federalists. If there be any among us who would wish to dissolve this Union or to change its republican form, let them stand undisturbed as monuments of the safety with which error of opinion may be tolerated where reason is left free to combat it." Jefferson concluded with a summary of the "essential principles" that would guide his administration: "Equal and exact justice to all men . . . ; peace, commerce, and honest friendship with all nations, entangling alliances with none . . . ; freedom of religion; freedom of the press; and freedom of person, under the protection of the habeas corpus; and trial by juries impartially selected. . . . The wisdom of our sages and the blood of our heroes have been devoted to their attainment."

JEFFERSON IN OFFICE

The deliberate display of republican simplicity at Jefferson's inauguration set the style of his administration. Although a man of expensive personal tastes, he took pains to avoid the occasions of pomp and circumstance that had characterized the Federalist administrations and to his mind suggested the trappings of monarchy.

Jefferson called his election the "revolution of 1800," but the electoral margin had been razor thin, and the policies that he followed were more conciliatory than revolutionary. His overwhelming reelection in 1804 attests to the popularity of his philosophy. Jefferson placed in policy-making positions men of his own party, and he was the first president to pursue the role of party leader, cultivating congressional support at his dinner parties and elsewhere. In the cabinet the leading figures were Secretary of State James Madison, a longtime neighbor and political ally, and Secretary of the Treasury Albert Gallatin, a Swiss-born Pennsylvania Republican whose financial skills had won him the respect of the Federalists. In an effort to cultivate Federalist-controlled New England, Jefferson chose men from that region for the positions of attorney general, secretary of war, and postmaster general.

In lesser offices, however, Jefferson often succumbed to pressure from the Republicans to remove Federalists. In one area he removed the offices rather than the appointees. In 1802, Congress repealed the Judiciary Act of 1801

The executive mansion

A watercolor of the president's house during Jefferson's term in office. Jefferson described it as "big enough for two emperors, one pope, and the grand lama in the bargain."

and so abolished the circuit judgeships and other offices to which John Adams had made his "midnight appointments."

MARBURY V. MADISON The midnight appointments that John Adams made just before leaving office sparked the pathbreaking case of *Marbury v. Madison* (1803), the first in which the Supreme Court declared a federal law unconstitutional. The case involved the appointment of the Maryland Federalist William Marbury, a prominent land speculator, as justice of the peace in the District of Columbia. Marbury's letter of appointment, or commission, signed by President Adams two days before he left office, was still undelivered when Madison took office as secretary of state, and Jefferson directed him to withhold it. Marbury then sued for a court order (a writ of mandamus) directing Madison to deliver his commission.

The Court's unanimous opinion, written by Chief Justice John Marshall, a brilliant Virginia Federalist and ardent critic of Jefferson, his distant relative, held that Marbury deserved his commission but denied that the Court had jurisdiction in the case. Section 13 of the Federal Judiciary Act of 1789, which gave the Court original jurisdiction in mandamus proceedings, was unconstitutional, the Court ruled, because the Constitution specified that the Court should have original jurisdiction only in cases involving foreign ambassadors or states. The Court, therefore, could issue no order in the case. With one bold stroke the Federalist Marshall had chastised the Jeffersonians while avoiding an awkward confrontation with an administration that might have defied his order. At the same time he established the stunning precedent of the Court's declaring a federal law invalid on the grounds that it violated provisions of the Constitution. Marshall stressed that it "is emphatically the province and duty of the judicial department to say what the law is." In other words, the Supreme Court was assuming the right of judicial review, meaning that it would decide whether acts of Congress were constitutional. So even though Marbury never gained his judgeship, Marshall established the Supreme Court as the final judge of constitutional interpretation. Since the Marbury decision, the Court has struck down over 150 acts of Congress and over 1,100 acts of state legislatures.

The *Marbury* decision, about which President Jefferson could do nothing, confirmed his fear of judicial partisanship, and he resolved to counter the Federalist influence in the federal court system. In 1804, Republicans used the impeachment power against two of the most partisan Federalist judges and succeeded in ousting one of them, District Judge John Pickering of New Hampshire. Pickering was clearly insane, which was not a "high crime or misdemeanor," but he also delivered profane, drunken harangues from the bench, which the Senate quickly decided was an impeachable offense.

The bitter feud between Thomas Jefferson and John Marshall over the *Marbury* case revealed fundamental divisions over the nature of the new nation. Jefferson and other Republicans remained committed to the idea that the individual states should remain the primary agents of political power. In contrast, Marshall and the Federalists insisted that modern nationhood required a powerful central government capable of creating and enforcing laws for all the American people. Marshall got the better of the argument. During his long tenure as chief justice (1801–1835), which spanned the administrations of five presidents, he established the foundations for American jurisprudence, the authority of the Supreme Court, and the constitutional supremacy of the national government over the states.

DOMESTIC REFORMS   Jefferson's first term produced a succession of triumphs in both domestic and foreign affairs. The president did not set out to dismantle Alexander Hamilton's economic program, despite his criticism of it. Under the tutelage of Treasury Secretary Gallatin, he learned to accept the national bank as an essential convenience. Jefferson detested Hamilton's belief that a federal debt was a national "blessing" because it gave the bankers and investors who lent money to the U.S. government a direct stake in the success of the new republic. Jefferson believed that a large federal debt would bring only high taxes and government corruption, so he set about reducing government expenses and paying down the debt. At the same time, he won the repeal of the whiskey tax, much to the relief of backwoods distillers, drinkers, and grain farmers.

Without income from such taxes, frugality was all the more necessary to a federal government dependent chiefly upon tariffs and the sale of western lands for its revenue. Happily for the Treasury, both sources of income flourished. The continuing Napoleonic Wars in Europe increased American shipping traffic and thus padded the federal Treasury. At the same time, settlers flocked to western land they purchased from the government. Ohio's admission to the Union in 1803 increased to seventeen the number of states.

Jefferson's commitment to "wise and frugal government" enabled the United States to live within its income, like a prudent farmer. The basic formula was simple: cut back on military expenses. A large peacetime army menaced a free society anyway, Jefferson believed. It therefore should be kept to a minimum and the national defense left, in Jefferson's words, to state militias. The navy, which the Federalists had already reduced, ought to be reduced further. Coastal defense, Jefferson argued, should rely upon land-based fortifications and a "mosquito fleet" of small gunboats.

In 1807, Jeffersonian reforms culminated in an act that outlawed the foreign slave trade as of January 1, 1808, the earliest date possible under the

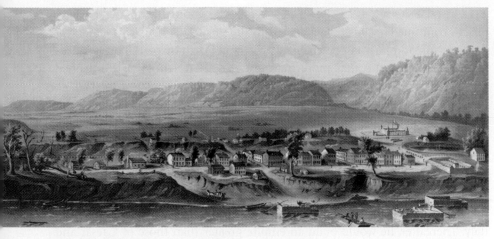

Cincinnati in 1800

Though its population was only about 750, boosters were already promoting Cincinnati as "the metropolis of the North Western Territory."

Constitution. At the time, South Carolina was the only state that still permitted the trade, having reopened it in 1803. But for years to come, an illegal traffic would continue. By one informal estimate perhaps 300,000 enslaved blacks were smuggled into the United States between 1808 and 1861.

THE BARBARY PIRATES   Issues of foreign relations emerged early in Jefferson's first term, when events in the Mediterranean gave him second thoughts about the need for a navy. On the Barbary Coast of North Africa, the rulers of Morocco, Algiers, Tunis, and Tripoli had for years practiced piracy and extortion. After the Revolution, Mediterranean pirates captured American vessels and enslaved the crews. The new U.S. government made blackmail payments, first to Morocco in 1786, then to the others in the 1790s. In 1801, however, the pasha of Tripoli upped his demands and declared war on the United States by the symbolic gesture of chopping down the flagpole at the U.S. consulate. Jefferson sent warships to blockade Tripoli.

A wearisome war dragged on until 1805, punctuated in 1804 by the notable exploit of Lieutenant Stephen Decatur, who slipped into Tripoli Harbor by night and set fire to the frigate *Philadelphia,* which had been captured (along with its crew) after it ran aground. The pasha finally settled for a $60,000 ransom and released the *Philadelphia*'s crew, whom he had held hostage for more than a year. It was still tribute, but less than the $300,000 the pasha had demanded at first and much less than the cost of war.

THE LOUISIANA PURCHASE   While the conflict with the Barbary pirates continued, events elsewhere led to the greatest single achievement of the Jefferson administration. The vast Louisiana Purchase of 1803 was a brilliant diplomatic coup that more than doubled the territory of the United States. Its estimated 875,000 square miles, from which would be formed six states in their entirety and most or part of nine more, comprised the entire Mississippi River valley west of the river itself. Louisiana, settled by the French, had been ceded to Spain in 1763, following the Seven Years' War, with Great Britain receiving Florida from Spain in an exchange of sorts. Since that time the dream of retaking Louisiana had stirred the French, and the audacious general Napoléon Bonaparte had retrieved it for France in 1800. In 1797, Napoléon had made his first conquest when his army defeated the Austrians in northern Italy. Thereafter, he would build an empire greater than those of Caesar and Charlemagne. He became the most feared man in Europe—and in America.

When word of the deal between Spain and France reached Washington in 1801, Jefferson sent Robert R. Livingston to Paris as the new U.S. minister to France. Spain in control of the Mississippi River outlet was bad enough, but the power-hungry Napoléon in control could only mean serious trouble. "The day that France takes possession of New Orleans," Jefferson wrote Livingston, "we must marry ourselves to the British fleet and nation," an unhappy prospect for the French-loving Jefferson.

Negotiations with the French dragged into 1803 while Spanish forces remained in control in Louisiana, awaiting the arrival of the French. Early that year, Jefferson sent his trusted Virginia friend James Monroe to assist Livingston in Paris. But no sooner had Monroe arrived than the French surprised Livingston by asking if the United States would like to buy the whole of the Louisiana Territory. Livingston snapped up the offer. Napoléon was willing to sell the Louisiana Territory because his French army in Haiti had been decimated not only by a slave revolt but also by yellow fever. Some 24,000 soldiers died in Haiti. Concerned about financing another round of warfare in Europe, Napoléon decided to cut French losses in the New World by selling the Louisiana Territory.

By the Treaty of Cession, dated April 30, 1803, the United States obtained the Louisiana Territory for about $15 million. The surprising turn of events presented President Jefferson with a "noble bargain," but also with a constitutional dilemma. Nowhere did the Constitution mention the purchase of territory. Jefferson at first suggested a constitutional amendment, but his advisers argued against delay lest Napoléon change his mind. The power to purchase territory, they reasoned, resided in the power to make treaties. Jefferson relented, trusting, he said, "that the good sense of our country will correct the evil of loose construction [of the Constitution] when it shall produce ill effects."

Jefferson and other Republicans supported the Louisiana Purchase for several reasons. Acquiring the immense territory, the president explained, would be "favorable to the immediate interests of our Western citizens" and would promote "the peace and security of the nation in general" by removing French power from the region and by creating a protective buffer separating the United States from the rest of the world. Jefferson also hoped that the new territory might become a haven for free blacks and thereby diminish racial tensions along the Atlantic seaboard. New Englanders, however, were not convinced by such arguments. Many of them worried that the growing westward exodus was driving up wages and lowering the value of real estate in their region. New England Federalists boggled at the prospect of new western states that would probably strengthen the Jeffersonian party. They lambasted a proviso in the treaty that the inhabitants be "incorporated in the Union" as citizens. In a reversal that anticipated many more reversals on constitutional issues, Federalists found themselves arguing for strict construction of the Constitution while Jefferson and the Republicans brushed aside their scruples in favor of implied presidential power. Gaining over 800,000 square miles of new territory trumped any legal reservations.

The Senate ratified the treaty by an overwhelming vote of 26 to 6, and on December 20, 1803, U.S. officials took formal possession of the sprawling Louisiana Territory. For the time being the Spanish kept West Florida, but within a decade that area would be ripe for the plucking. In 1808, Napoléon put his brother on the throne of Spain. With the Spanish colonial administration in disarray, American settlers in 1810 staged a rebellion in Baton Rouge and proclaimed the republic of West Florida, which was quickly annexed and occupied by the United States as far east as the Pearl River. In 1812, upon becoming the Union's eighteenth state, Louisiana absorbed the region, still known as the Florida parishes. In 1813, with Spain itself a battlefield for French and British forces, Americans took over the rest of West Florida, the Gulf coast of the future states of Mississippi and Alabama. Legally, the U.S. government has claimed ever since, all these areas were included in the Louisiana Purchase. Jefferson's decision to swallow his constitutional scruples and acquire the vast territory proved to be one of the most important factors shaping America's development.

LEWIS AND CLARK   A longtime amateur scientist, Thomas Jefferson was eager to learn about the mysterious region west of the Mississippi River, its geography, its flora and fauna, and its prospects for trade and agriculture. He envisioned the United States as an "empire of liberty" spanning the continent. Thus in 1803 he asked Congress to finance a mapping and scientific expedition to the far Northwest, beyond the Mississippi River, in what was still foreign territory. Congress approved, and Jefferson assigned as commanders the twenty-nine-year-old Meriwether Lewis, his former private secretary, and another Virginian, a former army officer, William Clark.

In 1804 the "Corps of Discovery," numbering nearly fifty, set out from a small village near St. Louis to ascend the muddy Missouri River. Forced to live off the land, they quickly adapted to the new environment. Local Indians introduced them to clothes made from deer hides, taught them hunting techniques, and traded horses. Lewis and Clark kept detailed journals of their travels and drew maps of the unexplored regions. As they moved up the Missouri, the landscape changed from forest to prairie grass. They saw immense herds of bison and other animals. They passed trappers and traders headed south with rafts and boats laden with furs. Six months after leaving St. Louis, near the Mandan Sioux villages in what would become North Dakota, they built Fort Mandan and wintered in relative comfort, sending downriver a barge loaded with maps, soil samples, and live specimens, such as the prairie dog and the magpie, previously unknown in America.

One of Lewis and Clark's journals

Lewis and Clark kept detailed journals during their entire journey.

In the spring, Lewis and Clark added to their main party a remarkable young Shoshone woman named Sacagawea, who proved an enormous help as a guide, translator, and negotiator as the group headed westward into uncharted territory. At the head of the Missouri River, they took the north fork, which they named the Jefferson River, crossed the Rocky Mountains at Lemhi Pass, and in canoes descended the Snake and Columbia Rivers to the Pacific. Near the future site of Astoria, Oregon, at the mouth of the Columbia River, they built Fort Clatsop, where they spent the winter, struggling to find enough to eat. The following spring they split into two parties, with Lewis heading back by almost the same route and Clark going by way of the Yellowstone River. They rejoined at the juncture of the Missouri and Yellowstone Rivers, returning together to St. Louis in 1806, having been gone nearly two and a half years. Along the way they had been chased by grizzly bears, attacked and aided by Indians, buffeted by blizzards and illness, and forced by starvation to eat their own horses. "I have been wet and as cold in every part as I ever was in my life," William Clark wrote in his journal. "Indeed I was at one time fearful my feet would freeze in the thin moccasins which I wore." But the intrepid discoverers had, in their own words, "proceeded on" day after day against the odds.

No longer was the Far West unknown country. It would be nearly a century before a good edition of the *Journals of the Lewis and Clark Expedition* appeared in print; many of the explorers' findings came out piecemeal, however, including an influential map in 1814. Their reports of friendly Indians and abundant beaver pelts quickly attracted traders and trappers to the region and gave the United States a claim to the Oregon Country by right of discovery and exploration.

POLITICAL SCHEMES Thomas Jefferson's policies, including the Louisiana Purchase, brought him solid support in the South and the West.

One of Lewis and Clark's maps

In their journals, Lewis and Clark sketched detailed maps of unexplored regions.

Even New Englanders were moving to his side. By 1809, John Quincy Adams, the son of the second president, would become a Republican. Other Federalists

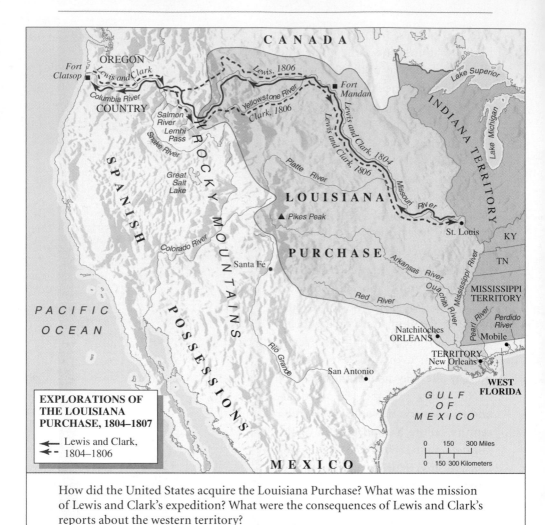

EXPLORATIONS OF THE LOUISIANA PURCHASE, 1804–1807

← Lewis and Clark, 1804–1806

How did the United States acquire the Louisiana Purchase? What was the mission of Lewis and Clark's expedition? What were the consequences of Lewis and Clark's reports about the western territory?

panicked. The acquisition of a vast new empire in the West would reduce New England and the Federalist party to insignificance in political affairs. Under the leadership of Thomas Pickering, secretary of state under Washington and Adams and now a U.S. senator, a group of ardent Massachusetts Federalists, called the Essex Junto, considered seceding from the Union, an idea that would simmer in New England circles for another decade.

Federalists also hatched a scheme to link New York to New England. To that end, they contacted Vice President Aaron Burr, a prominent New Yorker who had been on the outs with the Jeffersonians. Their plan, which depended

Exploring the far Northwest

Captain Clark and His Men Shooting Bears, from a book of engravings of the Lewis and Clark expedition (ca. 1810).

upon Burr's election as governor of New York, could not win the support of even the extreme Federalists: Alexander Hamilton bitterly opposed it on the grounds that Burr was "a dangerous man, and one who ought not to be trusted with the reins of government."

Those remarks led to Hamilton's famous duel with Burr, in July 1804 at Weehawken, New Jersey, across the Hudson River from New York City. Hamilton's sense of honor compelled him to meet the vice president's challenge and demonstrate his courage—yet he was determined not to fire at his opponent. Burr had no such scruples; he shot Hamilton through the heart. Hamilton's death ended both Pickering's scheme and Burr's political career—but not Burr's intrigues. Burr would lose the gubernatorial election.

In the meantime the presidential campaign of 1804 began when a congressional caucus of Republicans renominated Jefferson and chose the New Yorker George Clinton for vice president. (By then, to avoid the problems associated with parties running multiple candidates for the presidency, Congress had passed, and the states would soon ratify, the Twelfth Amendment, providing that electors use separate ballots to vote for the president and vice president.) Opposed by the Federalists Charles C. Pinckney and Rufus King, Jefferson and Clinton won 162 of the 176 electoral votes. It was the first landslide election in American history.

DIVISIONS IN THE REPUBLICAN PARTY

JOHN RANDOLPH AND THE OLD REPUBLICANS   Freed from a strong opposition—Federalists made up only a quarter of the new Congress— the Republican majority began to fragment. The Virginian John Randolph— known as John Randolph of Roanoke—initially a loyal Jeffersonian, became the most conspicuous of the dissidents. He was a powerful combination of principle, eccentricity, and rancor. Famous for his venomous assaults delivered in a shrill soprano, the colorful congressman strutted about the House floor with a whip in his hand, a symbol of his relish for contrarian positions. Few colleagues had the stomach for his tongue lashings.

Randolph became the crusty spokesman for a shifting group of "Old Republicans," whose adherence to party principles had rendered them more Jeffersonian than Jefferson himself. The Old Republicans were mostly southerners who defended states' rights and strict construction of the Constitution. They opposed any compromise with the Federalists and promoted an agrarian way of life. The Jeffersonian, or moderate, Republicans tended to be more pragmatic and nationalist in their orientation. As Thomas Jefferson himself demonstrated, they were willing to go along with tariffs on imports and a national bank.

THE BURR CONSPIRACY   For all of his popularity, Jefferson in some quarters aroused intense opposition. Aaron Burr, for example, despised the president. Sheer brilliance and opportunism had carried Burr to the vice presidency in 1800. He might easily have become Jefferson's heir apparent, but a taste for backroom deal making was the tragic flaw in his character. Caught up in the dubious schemes of Federalist diehards in 1800 and again in 1804, he ended his political career for good when he killed Alexander Hamilton. Indicted for murder and heavily in debt, the vice president fled to Spanish-held Florida. Once the furor subsided, he boldly returned to Washington to preside over the Senate. As long as he stayed out of New York and New Jersey, he was safe from arrest.

But Burr focused his attention less on the Senate than on a cockeyed scheme to carve out a personal empire for himself in the West. What came to be known as the Burr conspiracy was hatched when Burr met with General James Wilkinson. Just what Wilkinson and Burr were up to may never be known. The most likely explanation is that they conspired to get the Louisiana Territory to secede and set up an independent republic. Earlier Burr had solicited British support for his scheme to separate "the western part of the United States in its whole extent."

Whatever the goal, Burr learned in early 1807 that Jefferson had ordered his arrest. He tried to flee to Florida but was caught and taken to Richmond, Virginia. Charged with treason, Burr was brought for trial before Chief Justice John Marshall. The case established two major constitutional precedents. First, Jefferson ignored a subpoena requiring him to appear in court with certain papers in his possession. He refused, as had George Washington, to submit the papers to Congress on the grounds that the independence of the executive branch would be compromised if the president were subject to a court writ. The second major precedent was Marshall's rigid definition of treason. Treason under the Constitution, Marshall wrote, consists of "levying war against the United States or adhering to their enemies" and requires "two witnesses to the same overt act" for

Aaron Burr

Burr graduated from what is now Princeton University, where he changed his course of study from theology to law.

conviction. Since the prosecution failed to produce two witnesses to an overt act of treason by Burr, the jury found him not guilty.

Whether or not Burr escaped his just deserts, Marshall's strict construction of the Constitution protected the United States, as its framers clearly intended, from the capricious judgments of "treason" that governments through the centuries have used to terrorize dissenters. As for Burr, with further charges pending, he skipped bail and took refuge in France, but he returned unmolested in 1812 to practice law in New York. He survived to a virile old age. At seventy-eight, shortly before his death in 1836, he was divorced on the grounds of adultery.

WAR IN EUROPE

Oppositionists of whatever stripe were more an annoyance than a threat to Jefferson. The more intractable problems of his disastrous second term involved the renewal of the European war pitting Napoleonic France against Great Britain—and most of Europe—in 1803, which helped resolve the problem of Louisiana but put more strains on Jefferson's desire to avoid "entangling alliances" with European nations. In 1805, Napoléon's crushing defeat of Russian and Austrian forces left him in control of western Europe. The same year, Britain's defeat of the French and Spanish fleets in the Battle of Trafalgar secured control of the seas. The war then turned into a battle of elephant and whale, Napoléon's French armies dominant on land, the British navies dominant on the water, neither able to strike a decisive blow at the other and neither restrained by concerns over neutral shipping rights or international law.

HARASSMENT BY BRITAIN AND FRANCE   For two years after the renewal of European warfare, American shippers reaped the benefits, taking over trade with the French and Spanish West Indies. But in the case of the *Essex* (1805), a British court ruled that the practice of shipping French and Spanish goods through U.S. ports on their way elsewhere did not neutralize enemy goods. The practice violated the British rule of 1756, under which trade closed in time of peace remained closed in time of war. Goods shipped in violation of the rule would be seized. In 1807 the commercial provisions of Jay's Treaty expired, and the British interference with American shipping increased, not just in a desperate effort to keep supplies from Napoléon's continent but also to hobble U.S. competition with British merchant ships.

In a series of decrees in 1806 and 1807, the British government set up a "paper blockade" of Europe. Vessels headed for European ports were required to get British licenses and were subject to British inspection. It was a paper blockade because even the powerful British navy was not large enough to monitor every European port. Napoléon retaliated with his "Continental System," proclaimed in the Berlin Decree of 1806 and the Milan Decree of 1807. In the Berlin Decree he declared his own blockade of the British Isles and barred British ships from ports under French control. In the Milan Decree he ruled that neutral ships that complied with British regulations were subject to seizure when they reached Continental ports. The situation presented American shippers with a dilemma: if they complied with the demands of one side, they were subject to seizure by the other.

The prospects for profits were so great, however, that American shippers ran the risk. For seamen the danger was heightened by a renewal of the practice of impressment. The use of press-gangs to kidnap men in British (and colonial) ports was a long-standing method of recruitment used by the British navy. The seizure of British subjects from American vessels became a new source of recruits, justified on the principle that British citizens remained British subjects for life: "Once an Englishman, always an Englishman." Mistakes might be made, of course, since it was sometimes hard to distinguish British subjects from Americans; indeed, a flourishing trade in fake citizenship papers arose in American ports. Impressment was mostly confined to merchant vessels, but on at least two occasions before 1807 vessels of the U.S. Navy had been stopped on the high seas and seamen removed.

Preparation for war to defend commerce

In 1806 and 1807, American shipping was caught in the crossfire of the war between Britain and France.

In the summer of 1807, the British frigate *Leopard* accosted a U.S. naval vessel, the *Chesapeake*, just outside territorial waters off Norfolk, Virginia. After the *Chesapeake*'s captain refused to be searched, the *Leopard* opened fire, killing three Americans and wounding eighteen. The *Chesapeake*, unready for battle, was forced to strike its colors. A British search party seized four men, one of whom was later hanged for desertion from the British navy. Soon after the *Chesapeake* limped back into Norfolk, the *Washington Federalist* editorialized: "We have never, on any occasion, witnessed . . . such a thirst for revenge." Public wrath was so aroused that Jefferson could have had a war on the spot. Had Congress been in session, he might have been forced into one. But Jefferson, like John Adams before him, resisted war fever—and suffered politically as a result. One Federalist called him a "dish of skim milk curdling at the head of our nation."

THE EMBARGO   Instead of rushing to war, Jefferson resolved to use public indignation at the British to promote "peaceable coercion." In 1807 he persuaded Congress to pass the sweeping Embargo Act, which stopped all exports of American goods and prohibited American ships from leaving for foreign ports. The constitutional basis of the embargo was the power granted Congress to regulate commerce, which in this case Republicans interpreted broadly as the power to prohibit commerce.

Jefferson's ill-considered embargo failed from the beginning, however, because few Americans were willing to make the necessary sacrifices. The idealistic spirit that had made economic pressures effective in the pre-Revolutionary crises was lacking. Illegal trade with Britain and France flourished despite the risks, and violation of Jefferson's embargo was almost laughably easy. While American ships sat idle in ports, their crews laid off and unpaid, smugglers abounded and the British enjoyed a near monopoly on legitimate trade. As it turned out, France was little hurt by the embargo. The lack of American cotton pinched some British manufacturers and workers, but British shippers benefited. With American ports closed, they found a new trade in Latin American ports thrown open by the colonial authorities when Napoléon's armies occupied the mother countries of Spain and Portugal.

American resistance to the embargo revived the Federalist party in New England, which charged that Jefferson was in league with the French. At the same time, large farmers in the South and West suffered for want of foreign outlets for their grain, cotton, and tobacco. After fifteen months of

The election of 1808

This 1807 Federalist cartoon compares Washington and Jefferson. Washington (left) is flanked by the British lion and the American eagle, while Jefferson (right) is flanked by a snake and a lizard. Below Jefferson are volumes by French philosophers.

ineffectiveness, Jefferson accepted failure and repealed the embargo in 1809, shortly before he relinquished the "splendid misery" of the presidency.

In the election of 1808 the presidential succession passed to another Virginian, Secretary of State James Madison. George Clinton was again the candidate for vice president. The Federalists, backing Charles C. Pinckney of South Carolina and Rufus King of New York, revived enough as a result of the embargo to win 47 electoral votes to Madison's 122.

THE DRIFT TO WAR   The brilliant Madison proved to be a mediocre chief executive. From the beginning his presidency was entangled in foreign affairs and crippled by naïveté. Madison and his advisers repeatedly overestimated the young republic's diplomatic leverage and military strength. The result was humiliation. Still insisting on freedom of the seas, Madison continued Jefferson's policy of "peaceable coercion" by different but no more effective means. In place of the embargo, Congress reopened trade with all countries except France and Great Britain and authorized the president to reopen trade with whichever of these gave up its restrictions on American trade. The British minister in Washington, David Erskine, assured Madison's secretary of state that Britain would revoke its restrictions in 1809. With that assurance, Madison reopened trade with Britain, but Erskine had acted on his own, and his superiors repudiated his action and recalled him. Madison's trade restrictions proved as ineffective as the embargo. The president's policies created an economic recession and brought no change in British behavior. In the vain search for an alternative, Congress in 1810 reversed itself and adopted a measure introduced by Nathaniel Macon of North Carolina, Macon's bill number 2, which reopened trade with the warring powers but provided that if either dropped its restrictions, the United States would embargo trade with the other.

This time, Napoléon took a turn at trying to bamboozle Madison. The French foreign minister, the Duke de Cadore, informed the U.S. minister in Paris that he had withdrawn the Berlin and Milan Decrees, but the carefully worded Cadore letter had strings attached: revocation of the decrees depended upon the British doing likewise. The strings were plain to see, but Madison either misunderstood or, more likely, foolishly went along in the hope of putting pressure on the British. The British initially refused to give in, and on June 1, 1812, Madison reluctantly asked Congress to declare war. On June 16, however, the British foreign minister, facing an economic crisis, ended restraints on U.S. trade. Britain preferred not to risk war with the United States on top of its war with Napoléon. But on June 18, not having heard of the British action, Congress concurred with Madison's request.

With more time or more patience, Madison's policy would have been vindicated without resort to war.

THE WAR OF 1812

CAUSES   The main cause of the war—the violation of American shipping rights—dominated Madison's war message and provided the most evident reason for a mounting hostility toward the British. Yet the geographic distribution of the congressional vote for war raises a troubling question. The preponderance of the vote came from members of Congress representing the farm regions from Pennsylvania southward and westward. The maritime states of New York and New England, the region that bore the brunt of British attacks on U.S. shipping, voted against the declaration of war. One explanation for this seeming anomaly is simple enough: the farming regions suffered damage to their markets for grain, cotton, and tobacco while New England shippers made profits from smuggling in spite of the British restrictions.

Other plausible explanations for the sectional vote, however, include frontier Indian attacks that were blamed on British agents, western land hunger, and the desire for new land in Canada and the Floridas. Conflicts with Indians were endemic to a rapidly expanding West. Land-hungry settlers and speculators kept moving out ahead of government surveys and sales in search of fertile acres. The constant pressure to sell tribal lands repeatedly forced or persuaded Indians to sign treaties they did not always understand. It was an old story, dating from the Jamestown settlement, but one that took a new turn with the rise of two Shawnee leaders, Tecumseh and his twin brother, Tenskwatawa, "the Prophet."

Tecumseh saw with blazing clarity the consequences of Indian disunity. From his base on the Tippecanoe River in northern Indiana, he traveled from Canada to the Gulf of Mexico in an effort to form a confederation of tribes to defend Indian hunting grounds, insisting that no land cession was valid without the consent of all tribes, since they held the land in common. His brother supplied the inspiration of a religious revival, calling upon Indians to worship "the Master of Life," resist the white man's liquor, and lead a simple life within their means. By 1811, Tecumseh had matured his plans and headed south to win the Creeks, Cherokees, Choctaws, and Chickasaws to his cause.

William Henry Harrison, the governor of the Indiana Territory, learned of Tecumseh's plans, met with him twice, and pronounced him "one of those uncommon geniuses who spring up occasionally to produce revolutions and overturn the established order of things." In the fall of 1811, Harrison decided that Tecumseh must be stopped. He gathered 1,000 troops and advanced on Tecumseh's capital, Prophetstown, on the Tippecanoe River, while the leader was away. Tecumseh's followers attacked Harrison's encampment on the river, although Tecumseh had warned against any fighting in his absence. The Shawnees lost a bloody engagement that left about a quarter of Harrison's men dead or wounded. Only later did Harrison realize that he had inflicted a defeat on the Indians, who had become so demoralized that many fled to Canada. Harrison burned the town and destroyed its supplies. Tecumseh's dreams of an Indian confederacy went up in smoke, and Tecumseh himself fled to British protection in Canada.

The Battle of Tippecanoe reinforced suspicions that British agents in the

Tecumseh

The Shawnee leader who tried to unite Indian tribes in defense of their lands. Tecumseh was killed in 1813 at the Battle of the Thames.

Great Lakes region were inciting the Indians. Actually the incident was mainly Harrison's doing. With little hope of help from war-torn Europe, British officials in Canada had steered a careful course, discouraging warfare but seeking to keep the Indians' friendship and fur trade. To eliminate the Indian menace, Americans reasoned, they needed to remove its foreign support, and they saw the Canadian province of Ontario as a pistol pointing at the United States. Conquest of Canada would accomplish a twofold purpose: it would eliminate British influence among the Indians and open a new empire for land-hungry Americans. It was also one place where the British, in case of war, were vulnerable to an American attack. Madison and others acted on the mistaken assumption that the Canadians were eager to be liberated from British control. Thomas Jefferson had told Madison that the American "acquisition of Canada" was simply a "matter of marchin" north with a military force. To the far south the British were also vulnerable. East Florida, still under Spanish control, posed a similar threat to the Americans. Spain was too weak or simply unwilling to prevent sporadic Indian attacks across the border with Georgia. In addition, the British were suspected of smuggling goods through Florida and intriguing with the Indians on the southwestern border.

Such concerns helped generate war fever. In the Congress that assembled in late 1811, new members from southern and western districts clamored for war in defense of "national honor." Among them were Henry Clay and Richard Mentor Johnson of Kentucky, Felix Grundy of Tennessee, and John C. Calhoun of South Carolina. John Randolph of Roanoke christened these "new boys" the war hawks. After they entered the House, Randolph said, "We have heard but one word—like the whip-poor-will, but one eternal monotonous tone—Canada! Canada! Canada!" The young senator Henry Clay, a tall, rawboned westerner known for his combative temperament and propensity for dueling, yearned for war. "I am for resistance by the *sword*," he vowed. He promised that the Kentucky militia stood ready to march on Canada and acquire its lucrative fur trade.

PREPARATIONS   As it turned out, the war hawks would get neither Canada nor Florida, for James Madison had carried into war a nation that was ill prepared both financially and militarily. The Republican emphasis on small federal budgets and military cutbacks was not an effective way to win a war. And Madison, a studious, soft-spoken man, lacked anything resembling the martial qualities needed to inspire national confidence and resolve. He was no George Washington.

Moreover, the national economy was not prepared for war. In 1811, despite earnest pleas from Treasury Secretary Gallatin, Congress had let the twenty-year charter of the Bank of the United States expire. Furthermore, many state banks were being mismanaged. Trade had dried up, and tariff revenues had declined. Loans were now needed to cover about two thirds of the war costs, and northeastern opponents of the war were reluctant to lend money.

The military situation was almost as bad. War had become more and more likely for nearly a decade, but Republican defense cutbacks had prevented preparations. When the War of 1812 began, the army numbered only 6,700 men, ill trained, poorly equipped, and led by aging officers past their prime. A young Virginia officer named Winfield Scott, destined for military distinction, commented that most of the veteran commanders "had very generally slunk into either sloth, ignorance, or habits of intemperate drinking."

The navy, on the other hand, was in comparatively good shape, with able officers and trained men whose seamanship had been tested in the fighting against France and Tripoli. Its ships were well outfitted and seaworthy—all sixteen of them. In the first year of the war, it was the navy that produced the only U.S. victories, in isolated duels with British vessels, but their effect was

The American navy

John Bull (the personification of England) "stung to agony" by *Wasp* and *Hornet*, two American ships that won early victories in the War of 1812.

mainly an occasional boost to morale. Within a year the British had blockaded the U.S. coast, except for New England, where they hoped to cultivate anti-war feeling, and most of the little American fleet was bottled up in port.

THE WAR IN THE NORTH   The only place where the United States could effectively strike at the British was Canada. The Madison administration opted for a three-pronged assault: along the Lake Champlain route toward Montreal, with General Henry Dearborn in command; along the Niagara River, with forces under General Stephen Van Rensselaer; and into Upper Canada (north of Lake Erie) from Detroit, with General William Hull and some 2,000 men.

In 1812, Hull marched his men across the Detroit River but was pushed back by the British. Sickly and senile, Hull procrastinated in Detroit while his position worsened. The British commander cleverly played upon Hull's worst fears. Gathering what redcoats he could to parade in view of Detroit's defenders, he announced that thousands of Indian allies were at the rear and

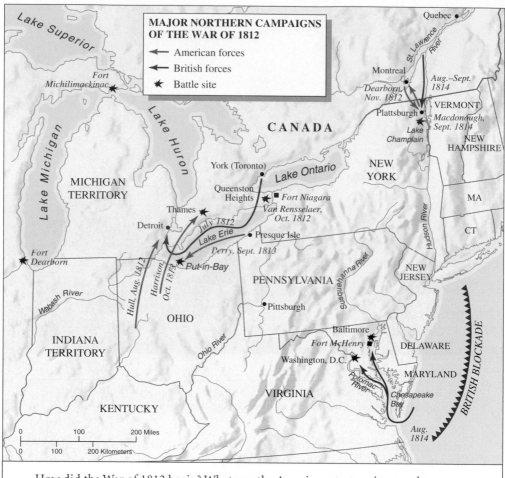

MAJOR NORTHERN CAMPAIGNS OF THE WAR OF 1812

← American forces
← British forces
✴ Battle site

Lake Superior

Quebec •

Fort Michilimackinac ✴

Montreal •

CANADA

St. Lawrence River

Dearborn, Nov. 1812

Aug.–Sept. 1814

Plattsburgh •

VERMONT

Macdonough, Sept. 1814

Lake Champlain

NEW HAMPSHIRE

Lake Huron

Lake Michigan

MICHIGAN TERRITORY

York (Toronto) •

Lake Ontario

NEW YORK

MA

Queenston Heights ✴

Thames ✴

■ Fort Niagara

Van Rensselaer, Oct. 1812

Hudson River

CT

Detroit •

Lake Erie

July 1812

Presque Isle •

Fort Dearborn ✴

Perry, Sept. 1813

Put-in-Bay ✴

Hull, Aug. 1812

Harrison, Oct. 1813

PENNSYLVANIA

NEW JERSEY

Wabash River

Pittsburgh •

Susquehanna River

INDIANA TERRITORY

OHIO

Ohio River

Baltimore •

Fort McHenry ■

DELAWARE

Washington, D.C. ✴

MARYLAND

BRITISH BLOCKADE

VIRGINIA

Potomac River

Chesapeake Bay

KENTUCKY

Aug. 1814

0   100   200 Miles
0   100   200 Kilometers

How did the War of 1812 begin? What was the American strategy in regard to Canada? Describe the battle that is the subject of "The Star-Spangled Banner."

that once fighting began, he would be unable to control them. Fearing a massacre, Hull surrendered his entire force.

Along the Niagara River front, General Van Rensselaer was more aggressive. An advance party of 600 Americans crossed the river and worked their way up the bluffs on the Canadian side. The stage was set for a major victory, but the New York militia refused to reinforce Van Rensselaer's men, claiming that their military service did not obligate them to leave the country. They complacently remained on the New York side and watched their outnumbered countrymen fall to a superior force across the river.

On the third front, the old invasion route via Lake Champlain, General Dearborn led his army north from Plattsburgh, New York, toward Montreal.

He marched them up to the border, where the state militia once again stood on its alleged constitutional rights and refused to cross, so Dearborn marched them back to Plattsburgh.

Madison's navy secretary now pushed vigorously for American control of inland waters. At Presque Isle (near Erie), Pennsylvania, in 1813, twenty-eight-year-old Oliver Hazard Perry, already a fourteen-year veteran, was building ships from the wilderness lumber. By the end of the summer, Commodore Perry set out in search of the British, whom he found at Lake Erie's Put-in-Bay on September 10. After completing the preparations for battle, Perry told an aide, "This is the most important day of my life."

Two British warships used their superior weapons to pummel the *Lawrence,* Perry's flagship. After four hours of intense shelling, none of the *Lawrence*'s guns was working, and most of the crew was dead or wounded. The British expected the Americans to flee, but Perry refused to quit. He had himself rowed to another vessel, carried the battle to the enemy, and finally accepted the surrender of the entire British squadron. Hatless and bloodied, Perry sent to General William Henry Harrison the long-awaited message: "We have met the enemy and they are ours."

American naval control of Lake Erie forced the British to evacuate Upper Canada. They gave up Detroit, and an American army defeated them at the Battle of the Thames on October 5. British power in Upper Canada was eliminated. In the course of the battle, Tecumseh fell, his dream of Indian unity dying with him.

THE WAR IN THE SOUTH In the South, too, the war flared up in 1813. On August 30, Creeks allied with the British attacked Fort Mims, on the Alabama River above Mobile, killing 553 people and scalping half of them. The news found Andrew Jackson at home in Tennessee, recovering from a street brawl with Thomas Hart Benton, later a senator from Missouri. As major general of the Tennessee militia, Jackson summoned about 2,000 volunteers and set out on a vengeful campaign across Alabama that crushed the Creek resistance. The decisive battle occurred on March 27, 1814, at Horseshoe Bend, on the Tallapoosa River, in the heart of Upper Creek country in east-central Alabama. Jackson's Cherokee allies played a crucial role in the battle. Only 200 of the 1,000 Creeks survived the fighting. By contrast, less than fifty of Jackson's men and Indian allies were killed. With the Treaty of Fort Jackson, the Creeks ceded two thirds of their land to the United States, including part of Georgia and most of Alabama. Red Eagle, the chief of the Creeks, told Jackson: "I am in your power. . . . My people are all gone. I can do no more but weep over the misfortunes of my nation."

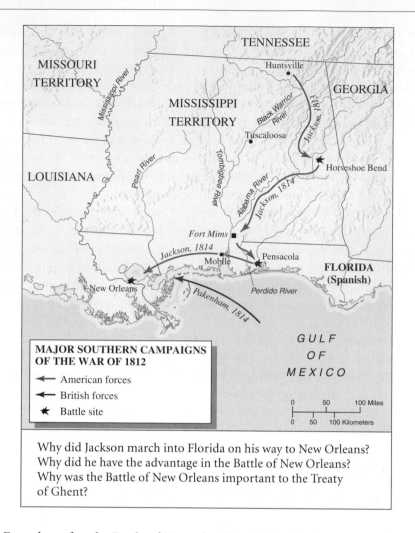

MAJOR SOUTHERN CAMPAIGNS OF THE WAR OF 1812

← American forces
← British forces
✴ Battle site

Why did Jackson march into Florida on his way to New Orleans? Why did he have the advantage in the Battle of New Orleans? Why was the Battle of New Orleans important to the Treaty of Ghent?

Four days after the Battle of Horseshoe Bend, Napoléon's empire collapsed with the defeat of his French army in Europe. Now free to deal solely with the United States, the British in 1814 invaded America from Canada. They also extended the naval blockade to New England, subjecting coastal towns to raids. The final piece of the British war plan was to seize New Orleans in order to cut American access to the Mississippi River, lifeline of the West.

MACDONOUGH'S VICTORY   The main British military effort focused on launching from Canada a massive invasion of the United States. The outnumbered American defenders were saved only by the superb ability of Commodore Thomas Macdonough, commander of the U.S. naval squadron on Lake Champlain. England's army bogged down while its flotilla engaged Macdonough's ships in a battle that ended with the entire British fleet either destroyed or captured.

FIGHTING IN THE CHESAPEAKE   Meanwhile, however, U.S. forces suffered the most humiliating experience of the war as the British captured and burned Washington, D.C. In 1814, a British force landed at Benedict, Maryland, and headed for Washington, thirty miles away. To defend the capital, the Americans had a timid militia force of about 7,000.

The redcoats marched unopposed into the American capital, where British officers ate a meal in the White House that had been prepared for President Madison and his wife, Dolley. The vengeful British then burned the White House, the Capitol, and most other government buildings. A tornado the next day compounded the damage, but a violent thunderstorm dampened both the fires and the enthusiasm of the British forces, who headed north to assault Baltimore.

The British attack on Baltimore was a surprising failure for the British forces. About 1,000 Americans held Fort McHenry on an island in the harbor. The British fleet bombarded the fort to no avail, and the invaders abandoned the attack. Francis Scott Key, a Washington lawyer and occasional poet, watched the siege from the harbor. The sight of the American flag still in place at dawn inspired him to draft the verses of what came to be called "The Star-Spangled Banner." Later revised and set to the tune of an English drinking song, it eventually became America's national anthem.

THE BATTLE OF NEW ORLEANS   The British failure to capture Baltimore followed by three days their defeat on Lake Champlain; their offensive against New Orleans, however, had yet to run its course. Along the Gulf coast, forty-seven-year-old Major General Andrew Jackson had been busy shoring up the defenses of Mobile and New Orleans. Without authorization he invaded the Panhandle region of Spanish Florida and took Pensacola, putting an end to British efforts to organize Indian attacks on American settlements. Back in Louisiana he began to erect defensive barriers on the approaches to New Orleans as the British fleet, with some 8,000 soldiers under General Sir Edward Pakenham, took up positions just south of New Orleans, the second busiest port in the United States (after New York).

Pakenham's painfully careful approach—he waited weeks until all his artillery was available—gave Jackson time to build defensive earthworks

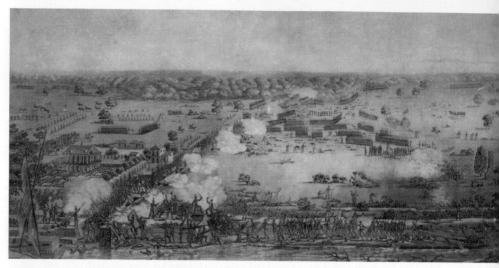

Jackson's army defends New Orleans

Andrew Jackson's defeat of the British at New Orleans, January 1815.

bolstered by barrels and casks of sugar. It was an almost invulnerable position, but Pakenham, contemptuous of Jackson's much smaller multiethnic and multiracial force of 4,000 frontier militiamen, Creole aristocrats, free blacks, a few slaves, and several notorious pirates rashly ordered a frontal assault at dawn on January 8, 1815. His brave but blundering redcoats ran into a murderous hail of artillery shells and rifle fire. Before the British withdrew, about 2,000 had been wounded or killed, including Pakenham himself. A British officer, after watching his battered and retreating troops, wrote that there "never was a more complete failure."

The slow pace of transatlantic communications during the early nineteenth century meant that the Battle of New Orleans occurred after a peace treaty had already been signed in Europe. But this is not to say that the battle had no effect on the outcome of the war, for the treaty was yet to be ratified and the British might have exploited the possession of New Orleans had they won control of the city. The battle did ensure that both governments acted quickly to ratify the treaty. The unexpected American victory at New Orleans would also generate a wave of patriotic nationalism that would help transform a victorious general, Andrew Jackson, into a dynamic president.

THE TREATY OF GHENT Efforts to negotiate an end to the war had begun in 1812, even before hostilities got under way. The British, after all, had repealed their violations of U.S. shipping rights two days before the declaration of war and expected at least an armistice. Secretary of State James Monroe, however, had told the British that they would have to quit boarding U.S. ships and seizing British-born sailors (the practice of impressment). Meanwhile, Czar Alexander of Russia had offered to mediate the dispute, hoping to relieve the pressure on Great Britain, his ally against Napoleonic France. Madison had sent Albert Gallatin and James Bayard to join John Quincy Adams, the U.S. minister to Russia, in St. Petersburg. They arrived in 1813, but the czar was at the war front, and they waited impatiently for six months. At that point the British refused Russia's mediation and instead offered to negotiate directly with the American diplomats. Madison then appointed Henry Clay and Jonathan Russell to join the other three commissioners in peace talks that finally got under way in 1814 in the Flemish city of Ghent in August.

The American delegates demanded that the British abandon impressment and provide compensation for the seizure of American ships. The British opened the discussions with demands for territory in New York and Maine, removal of U.S. warships from the Great Lakes, the creation of an Indian buffer state in the Northwest, trading rights on the Mississippi River, and abandonment of U.S. fishing rights off Labrador and Newfoundland. If the British insisted on such a position, the Americans informed them, the negotiations would be at an end.

But the British were stalling, awaiting news of hoped-for victories to strengthen their hand. The news of the U.S. victory on Lake Champlain arrived in October, 1814, and weakened the British resolve. The British will to fight was further eroded by a continuing power struggle with Napoléon and France, by the eagerness of British merchants to renew trade with America, and by the war-weariness of a tax-burdened public. The British finally decided that the American war was not worth the cost. One by one, demands were dropped on both sides, until the envoys agreed to end the war, return the prisoners, restore the previous boundaries, and settle nothing else. The questions of fisheries and disputed boundaries were referred to commissions for future settlement. The Treaty of Ghent was signed on Christmas Eve of 1814.

THE HARTFORD CONVENTION While the diplomats converged on a peace settlement in Europe, an entirely different kind of meeting was taking place in Hartford, Connecticut. The Hartford Convention represented the climax of New England's disaffection with "Mr. Madison's war." New England had managed to keep aloof from the war and extract a profit from illegal trading and privateering. Both Massachusetts and Connecticut had refused to contribute militias to the war effort; merchants had continued to sell supplies to British troops in Canada. After the fall of Napoléon in 1815, however, the British extended their blockade to New England, occupied Maine, and conducted several raids along the coast. Even Boston seemed threatened. Instead of rallying to the American flag, however, Federalists in the Massachusetts legislature voted in October 1814 to hold a convention of New England states to plan independent action.

On December 15 the Hartford Convention assembled with delegates chosen by the legislatures of Massachusetts, Rhode Island, and Connecticut as well as two delegates from Vermont and one from New Hampshire—twenty-two in all. The convention proposed seven constitutional amendments designed to limit Republican (and southern) influence: abolishing the counting of slaves in apportioning state representation in Congress, requiring a two-thirds vote to declare war or admit new states, prohibiting embargoes lasting more than sixty days, excluding foreign-born individuals from holding federal office, limiting the president to one term, and forbidding successive presidents from the same state.

Their call for a later convention in Boston carried the unmistakable threat of secession if the demands were ignored. Yet the threat quickly evaporated. In February 1815, when messengers from Hartford reached Washington, D.C., they found the battered capital celebrating the good news from Ghent and New Orleans. "Their position," according to a French diplomat, was "awkward, embarrassing, and lent itself to cruel ridicule," and they swiftly withdrew their recommendations. The consequence was a fatal blow to the Federalist party, which never recovered from the stigma of disloyalty stamped on it by the Hartford Convention.

THE AFTERMATH For all the fumbling ineptitude with which the War of 1812 was fought, it generated an intense patriotism. Despite the standoff with which it ended at Ghent, Americans nourished a sense of victory, courtesy of Andrew Jackson and his men at New Orleans as well as the heroic exploits of American frigates in their duels with British ships. Under Republican leadership the nation had survived a "second war of independence" against the greatest power on earth and emerged with new symbols of nationhood and a new gallery of heroes. The war also launched the United States toward economic independence as the interruption of trade with Europe had encouraged the growth of American manufactures. After forty years of independence, it dawned on the world that the new American republic might be emerging as a world power.

As if to underline the point, Congress authorized a quick, decisive blow at the pirates of the Barbary Coast. During the War of 1812, North Africans had again set about plundering American ships in the Mediterranean. On March 3, 1815, little more than two weeks after the Senate ratified the Treaty of Ghent, Congress sent Captain Stephen Decatur with ten vessels to the Mediterranean. Decatur seized two Algerian ships and then sailed boldly into the harbor of Algiers. On June 30, 1815, the Algerian ruler agreed to cease molesting American ships and to give up all U.S. prisoners. Decatur's show of force

We Owe Allegiance to No Crown

The War of 1812 generated a renewed spirit of nationalism.

induced similar treaties from other North African countries. This time the United States would not pay blackmail; this time, for a change, the Barbary pirates paid for the damage they had done. This time, victory put an end to the region's tradition of piracy and extortion.

One of the strangest results of the War of 1812 and its aftermath was a reversal of roles by the Republicans and the Federalists. Out of the wartime experience the Republicans had learned some lessons in nationalism. Certain needs and inadequacies revealed by the war had "Federalized" Madison or "re-Federalized" this Father of the Constitution. Perhaps, he reasoned, a peacetime army and navy were necessary. The lack of a national bank had added to the problems of financing the war. Now Madison wanted it back. The rise of new industries during the war prompted calls for increased tariffs on imports to protect the infant American companies from foreign competition. Madison went along. The problems of overland transportation in the West experienced by American armies had revealed the need for internal improvements. Madison agreed, but on that point kept his constitutional scruples. He wanted a constitutional amendment. So while Madison embraced nationalism and broad construction of the Constitution, the Federalists took up the Jeffersonians' position of states' rights and strict construction in an effort to oppose Madison's policies. It was the first great reversal of roles in constitutional interpretation. It would not be the last.

CHAPTER SUMMARY

- **Jefferson's Administration** Thomas Jefferson did not dismantle much of Hamilton's program, but he did promptly repeal the whiskey tax and cut back on government expenditures. He involved the navy in subduing the Barbary pirates and negotiated with the Spanish and then with the French to ensure that the Mississippi River remained open to American commerce. The purchase of the Louisiana Territory through negotiations with French Emperor Napoleon dramatically expanded the boundaries of the United States.

- **Marshall Court** John Marshall, a Federalist, played influential roles in many crucial decisions during his long tenure as chief justice of the Supreme Court. In *Marbury v. Madison*, the Court declared a federal act unconstitutional for the first time. With that decision, the Court assumed the right of judicial review over acts of Congress. As chief justice, Marshall established the constitutional supremacy of the federal government over state governments.

- **Louisiana Purchase** The Louisiana Purchase led to a debate on the nature of the Constitution, in which Federalists feared the addition of new territories would strengthen the Republicans. Jefferson's "Corps of Discovery," led by Meriwether Lewis and William Clark, explored the new region's resources, captured the public imagination, and gave the United States a claim to the Oregon Country.

- **War of 1812** Renewal of the European war in 1803 created conflicts with Britain and France. Neither country wanted its enemy to purchase U.S. goods, so both declared blockades. In retaliation, Jefferson had Congress pass the Embargo Act, which prohibited all foreign trade. James Madison ultimately declared war over the issue of neutral shipping rights and the fear that the British were inciting Native Americans to attack frontier settlements.

- **Aftermath of the War of 1812** The Treaty of Ghent, signed in 1814, ended the War of 1812 without settling any of the disputes. One effect of the conflict over neutral shipping rights was to launch the economic independence of the United States, as goods previously purchased from Britain were now manufactured at home. Federalists and Republicans seemed to exchange roles: delegates from the waning Federalist party met at the Hartford Convention to consider states' rights and secession, whereas Republicans embraced nationalism and a broad interpretation of the Constitution.

CHRONOLOGY

1803	*Marbury v. Madison*
1803	Louisiana Purchase
1804–1806	Lewis and Clark expedition
1807	*Chesapeake* affair
1807	Embargo Act is passed
1808	International slave trade is outlawed
1811	Battle of Tippecanoe
1814	Battle of Horseshoe Bend
1814	Treaty of Ghent
1814	Hartford Convention
1815	Battle of New Orleans

KEY TERMS & NAMES

Marbury v. Madison p. 349

Chief Justice John Marshall
p. 349

Barbary pirates p. 351

"Corps of Discovery"
p. 354

Aaron Burr p. 356

impressment p. 360

Tecumseh p. 364

war hawks p. 366

Andrew Jackson p. 369

Francis Scott Key p. 371

Treaty of Ghent p. 372

Hartford Convention
p. 373

Part Three

AN
EXPANSIVE
NATION

housands of Americans during the early nineteenth century spilled over the Appalachian Mountains, crossed the Mississippi River, and in the 1840s reached the Pacific Ocean. Wagons, canals, flatboats, steamboats, and eventually railroads helped transport them. The feverish expansion of the United States into new western territories brought Americans into more conflict with Native Americans, Mexicans, the British, and the Spanish. Only a few people, however, expressed moral reservations about displacing others. Most Americans believed it was the "manifest destiny" of the United States to spread throughout the continent—at whatever cost and at whomever's expense. Americans generally believed that they enjoyed the blessing of Providence in their efforts to consolidate the continent and bring it under their control.

During the early nineteenth century most Americans continued to earn their living from the soil, but textile mills and manufacturing plants began to dot the landscape and transform the nature of work and the pace of life. By midcentury the United States was emerging as one of the world's major industrial powers. In addition, the lure of cheap land and plentiful jobs, as well as the promise of political equality and religious freedom, attracted hundreds of thousands of immigrants from Europe. The newcomers, mostly from Germany and Ireland, faced ethnic prejudices, religious persecution, and language barriers that made assimilation into American culture difficult.

These developments gave life in the second quarter of the nineteenth century a dynamic quality. The United States, said the philosopher-poet Ralph Waldo Emerson, was "a country of beginnings, of projects, of designs, of expectations." A restless optimism character-ized the period. People of a lowly social status who heretofore had accepted their lot in life now strove to climb the social ladder and enter the political arena. The patrician republic espoused by Jefferson and Madison gave way to the frontier democracy promoted by the Jacksonians. Americans were no longer content to be governed by a small, benevolent aristocracy of talent and wealth. They began to demand—and obtain—government of, by, and for the people.

The fertile economic environment during the antebellum era helped foster the egalitarian idea that individuals (except African Americans,

Native Americans, and women) should have an equal opportunity to better themselves and should be granted political rights and privileges. In America, observed a journalist in 1844, "one has as good a chance as another according to his talents, prudence, and personal exertions."

The exuberant individualism embodied in such mythic expressions of economic equality and political democracy spilled over into the cultural arena during the first half of the century. The so-called Romantic movement applied democratic ideals to philosophy, religion, literature, and the fine arts. In New England, Ralph Waldo Emerson and Henry David Thoreau joined other "transcendentalists" in espousing a radical individualism. Other reformers were motivated more by a sense of spiritual mission than by democratic individualism. Reformers sought to promote public-supported schools, abolish slavery, promote temperance, and improve the lot of the disabled, the insane, and the imprisoned. Their efforts ameliorated some of the problems created by the frenetic economic growth and territorial expansion. But reformers made little headway against slavery. It would take a brutal civil war to dislodge America's "peculiar institution."

10 NATIONALISM AND SECTIONALISM

FOCUS QUESTIONS

  wwnorton.com/studyspace

- How did economic policies after the War of 1812 reflect the nationalism of the period?
- What characterized the Era of Good Feelings?
- What were the various issues that promoted sectionalism?
- How did the Supreme Court under John Marshall strengthen the federal government and the national economy?
- What were the main diplomatic achievements of these years?

Amid the jubilation that followed the War of 1812, Americans began to transform their young nation. Hundreds of thousands of people streamed westward at the same time that the largely local economy was being transformed into a national market. The spread of plantation slavery and the cotton culture into the Old Southwest—Alabama, Mississippi, Arkansas, Louisiana, and Texas as well as the frontier areas of Tennessee, Kentucky, and Florida—disrupted family ties and transformed social life. In the North and the West, meanwhile, a dynamic urban middle class began to emerge and grow in towns and cities. Such dramatic changes prompted vigorous political debates over economic policies, transportation improvements, and the extension of slavery into the new territories. In the process the nation began to divide into three powerful regional blocs—North, South, and West—whose shifting alliances would shape the political landscape until the Civil War.

ECONOMIC NATIONALISM

Immediately after the War of 1812, Americans experienced a new surge of nationalism. The young United States was growing from a loose confederation of territories into a fully functioning nation-state that spanned almost an entire continent. An abnormal economic prosperity after the war fed a feeling of well-being and enhanced the prestige of the national government. Thomas Jefferson's embargo ironically had spawned the factories that he abhorred. During the war the idea spread that the young nation needed a more balanced economy of farming, commerce, and manufacturing. After a generation of war, shortages of farm products in Europe forced up the prices of American products and stimulated agricultural expansion—indeed, they induced a wild speculation in farmland. Southern cotton, tobacco, and rice would form about two thirds of U.S. exports. At the same time, the postwar market was flooded with cheap English goods that threatened America's new manufacturing sector.

President James Madison, in his first annual message to Congress after the war, recommended several steps to strengthen the government and the national economy: improved fortifications, a permanent army and a strong navy, a new national bank, protection of new industries from foreign competition, a system of canals and roads for commercial and military use, and to top it off, a

The Union Manufactories of Maryland in Patapsco Falls, Baltimore County (ca. 1815)

A textile mill established during the embargo of 1807. The Union Manufactories would eventually employ more than 600 people.

great national university. "The Republicans have out-Federalized Federalism," one New Englander remarked. Congress responded by authorizing a standing army of 10,000 and strengthening the navy as well.

THE BANK OF THE UNITED STATES   The trinity of ideas promoting postwar economic nationalism—proposals for a second national bank; for a protective tariff; and for government-financed roads, canals, and eventually railroads, called internal improvements—inspired the greatest controversies. Issues related to money—the reliability and availability of currency, the relative value of paper money and "specie" (silver and gold coins), and the structure and regulation of the banking system—often dominated political debates. After the first national bank expired, in 1811, the country fell into a financial muddle. State-chartered local banks mushroomed with little or no control, and their bank notes (paper money) flooded the channels of commerce with currency of uncertain value. Because state banks were loosely and poorly regulated, they often issued paper money for loans far in excess of the "hard money" they stored in their vaults. Such loose lending practices led initially to an economic boom but was followed by a dramatic inflation fed by the excess of paper money circulating in the economy. Eventually the inherent value of the excess bank notes would plummet and the bubble would burst, causing recession and depression. Because hard money had been in such short supply during the war (because coins were typically required to pay off foreign debts), many state banks suspended specie payments, meaning that they stopped exchanging coins for paper money submitted by depositors. The result was chronic instability and occasional chaos in the banking sector. The absence of a central national bank had also become a source of financial embarrassment to the government, which had neither a ready means of floating loans nor a way of transferring funds across the country.

In the face of this growing financial turmoil, President Madison and most of the younger generation of Republicans swallowed their constitutional reservations about a powerful national bank. The issue of a central bank, Madison said, had been decided "by repeated recognitions . . . of the validity of such an institution in acts of the legislative, executive, and judicial branches of the Government, accompanied by . . . a concurrence of the general will of the nation." In 1816, Congress adopted, over the protest of Old Republicans, a provision for a new Bank of the United States, which would be located in Philadelphia. Once again the charter would run for twenty years, and the federal government owned a fifth of the stock and named five of the twenty-five directors, with the B.U.S., as it was called, serving as the government depository for federal funds. Its bank notes were accepted in payments to the government. In return for its privileges, the bank had to handle the government's funds without charge, lend the government up to $5 million upon demand, and pay the government a cash bonus of $1.5 million.

The bitter debate over the B.U.S., then and later, helped set the pattern of regional alignment for most other economic issues. Missouri senator Thomas Hart Benton predicted that the currency-short western towns would be at the mercy of a centralized eastern bank. "They may be devoured by it any moment! They are in the jaws of the monster! A lump of butter in the mouth of a dog! One gulp, one swallow, and all is gone!"

The debate over the Bank of the United States was also noteworthy because of the leading roles played by the era's greatest statesmen: John C. Calhoun of South Carolina, Henry Clay of Kentucky, and Daniel Webster of New Hampshire. Calhoun, still in his youthful phase as a war-hawk nationalist, introduced the banking bill and pushed it through, justifying its constitutionality by citing the congressional power to regulate the currency. Clay, who had long opposed a national bank, reversed himself; he now asserted that circumstances had made one indispensable. Webster, on the other hand, led the opposition of the New England Federalists, who did not want the banking center moved from Boston to Philadelphia. Later, after he had moved from New Hampshire to Massachusetts, Webster would return to Congress as the champion of a much stronger national government, whereas events would steer Calhoun toward a defiant embrace of states' rights.

A PROTECTIVE TARIFF   The shift of investment capital from commerce to manufactures, begun during the embargo of 1807, had speeded up during the war. But new American manufacturers needed "protection" from foreign competitors. After the War of 1812 ended, a sudden renewal of cheap British imports generated pleas for tariffs (taxes on imports) to "protect" infant American industries from foreign competition. The self-interest of the manufacturers, who as yet had little political influence, was reinforced by a patriotic desire for economic independence from Britain. New England shippers and southern farmers opposed tariffs, but in both regions sizable minorities believed that the promotion of new industry by means of tariffs enhanced both local economic interests and the national welfare.

The Tariff of 1816, the first intended more to protect industry against foreign competition than to raise revenue, easily passed in Congress. New England supported the tariff and the South opposed it, and the middle Atlantic states and the Old Northwest cast only five negative votes altogether. The minority of southerners who voted for the tariff, led by John Calhoun, did so because they hoped that the South might itself become a manufacturing center. South Carolina was then developing a few textile mills. According to the census of 1810, the southern states had approximately as many manufacturers as New England. Within a few years, however, New England would move well ahead of the South and Calhoun would do an about-face and oppose tariffs. The tariff would then become a sectional issue, with manufacturers, wool processors, and food, sugar, and hemp growers favoring higher tariffs while southern cotton planters and northern shipping interests would favor lower duties.

INTERNAL IMPROVEMENTS The third major issue of the time involved government support for internal improvements: the building of roads and the development of water transportation. The war had highlighted the shortcomings of the nation's transportation network: the movement of troops through the western wilderness had proved very difficult. At the same time, settlers found that unless they located themselves near navigable waters, they were cut off from trade.

The federal government had entered the field of internal improvements under Thomas Jefferson. Jefferson and both of his successors recommended a constitutional amendment to give the federal government undisputed

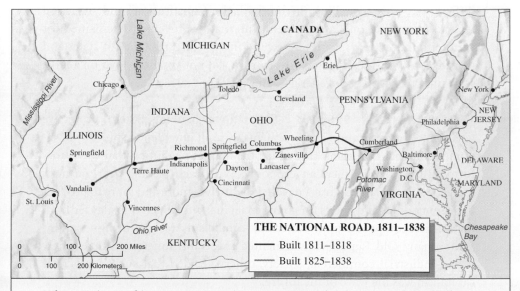

Why were internal improvements so important? How did the National Road affect agriculture and trade? What were the constitutional issues that limited the federal government's ability to enact internal improvements?

authority to improve the national transportation system. Lacking that, the constitutional grounds for federal action rested mainly on the provision of national defense and the expansion of the postal system. In 1803, when Ohio became a state, Congress decreed that 5 percent of the proceeds from land sales in the state would go to building a National Road from the Atlantic coast into Ohio and beyond as the territory developed. Construction of the National Road began in 1815.

Originally called the Cumberland Road, it was the first federally financed interstate roadway. By 1818 it was open from Cumberland, Maryland, to Wheeling, Virginia (now West Virginia), on the Ohio River. By 1838 it extended all the way to Vandalia, Illinois. By reducing transportation costs and opening up new markets, the National Road and other privately financed turnpikes helped accelerate the commercialization of agriculture.

In 1817, John C. Calhoun put through the House a bill to fund internal improvements. He believed that western development would help his native South by opening up trading relationships. Opposition to federal spending on transportation projects centered in New England and the South, which expected to gain the least from federal projects intended to spur western development, and support came largely from the West, which badly needed good roads. On his last day in office, President Madison vetoed the bill. While sympathetic to its purpose, he could not overcome his "insuperable difficulty . . . in reconciling the bill with the Constitution" and suggested instead a constitutional amendment. Internal improvements remained for another hundred years, with few exceptions, the responsibility of states and private enterprise. The federal government did not enter the field on a large scale until passage of the Federal Highways Act of 1916.

THE AMERICAN SYSTEM   The national banking system, protective tariffs, and transportation improvements were all intended to spur the development of what historians have called the market revolution that was transforming the young American economy. With each passing year, farmers, merchants, and manufacturers devoted themselves more and more to producing commodities and goods for commercial markets, which often lay far from the sources of production. American capitalism was maturing—rapidly. While many Old Republicans lamented the transition to an increasingly urban-industrial-commercial society, others decided that such democratic capitalism was the wave of the future.

Henry Clay emerged during the first half of the nineteenth century as the foremost spokesman for what he came to call the American System. Born and raised in Virginia, Clay became a successful attorney in Lexington,

Kentucky, before launching a political career. He was fond of gambling, liquor, and women, and like his foe Andrew Jackson, he had a brawling temper that led to several duels. During the 1820s, as Speaker of the House, Clay became the chief proponent of economic nationalism. Prosperity, he insisted, depended upon the federal government's assuming an active role in shaping the economy. He scoffed at the old Jeffersonian fear that an urban-industrial society would necessarily grow corrupt. Clay instead promoted the "market revolution" and the rapid development of the new western states and territories. The American System he championed included several measures: (1) high tariffs to impede the import of European products and thereby "protect" fledgling American industries, (2) higher prices for federal lands, the proceeds of which would be distributed to the states to finance internal improvements that would facilitate the movement of goods to markets, and (3) a strong national bank to regulate the nation's money supply and thereby ensure sustained economic growth.

Clay's American System aroused intense support—and opposition. Some critics argued that higher prices for federal lands would discourage western migration. Others believed that tariffs benefited industrialists at the expense of farmers and "common" folk, who paid higher prices for the goods produced by tariff-protected manufacturers. And many feared that the B.U.S. was potentially a tyrannical force, dictating the nation's economic future and in the process centralizing power at the expense of states' rights and individual freedoms. The debates grew in scope and intensity during the first half of the nineteenth century. In the process, they would aggravate sectional tensions to the breaking point.

"GOOD FEELINGS"

JAMES MONROE   As James Madison approached the end of a turbulent presidency, he, like Thomas Jefferson, turned to a fellow Virginian, another secretary of state, to be his successor. For Madison that man would be James Monroe. And Monroe won the Republican nomination. In the 1816 election he overwhelmed his Federalist opponent, Rufus King of New York, with 183 to 34 votes in the Electoral College. The "Virginia dynasty" continued. Like three of the four presidents before him, Monroe was a Virginia planter, but with a difference: his plantation holdings were much smaller. At the outbreak of the Revolution, he was just beginning his studies at the College of William and Mary. He joined the army at the age of sixteen, fought with Washington during the Revolution, and later studied law with Jefferson.

James Monroe

Portrayed as he entered the presidency in 1817.

Monroe had served as a representative in the Virginia assembly, as governor of the state, as a representative in the Confederation Congress, as a U.S. senator, and as U.S. minister in Paris, London, and Madrid. Under Madison he was secretary of state and doubled as secretary of war. Monroe, with his powdered wig, cocked hat, and knee breeches, was the last of the Revolutionary generation to serve in the White House and the last president to dress in the old style.

Firmly grounded in traditional Republican principles, Monroe failed to keep up with the onrush of the "new nationalism." He accepted as an accomplished fact the Bank of the United States and the protective tariff, but during his tenure there was no further extension of economic nationalism. Indeed, there was a minor setback: he permitted the National Road to be extended, but in his veto of the 1822 Cumberland Road bill, he denied the authority of Congress to collect tolls to pay for its repair and maintenance. Like Jefferson and Madison, he urged a constitutional amendment to remove all doubt about federal authority in the field of internal improvements.

Monroe surrounded himself with some of the ablest young Republican leaders. John Quincy Adams became secretary of state. William H. Crawford of Georgia continued as secretary of the Treasury. John C. Calhoun headed the War Department after Henry Clay refused the job in order to stay on as Speaker of the House. The new administration found the country in a state of well-being: America was at peace, and the economy was flourishing. Soon after his inauguration, in 1817, Monroe embarked on a goodwill tour of New England. In Boston, lately a hotbed of wartime dissent, a Federalist newspaper commented upon the president's visit under the heading "Era of Good Feelings." The label became a popular catchphrase for Monroe's administration, one that historians would later seize upon.

In 1820 the president was reelected without opposition. The Federalists were too weak to put up a candidate. Monroe won all the electoral votes except three abstentions and one vote from New Hampshire for John Quincy Adams. The Republican party was dominant—for the moment. In fact, it was about to follow the Federalists into oblivion. Amid the general political contentment of the era, the first party system was fading away, but rivals for the succession soon began forming new parties.

RELATIONS WITH BRITAIN   Fueling the contentment after the War of 1812 was a growing trade with Britain (and India). The Treaty of Ghent had ended the war but left unsettled a number of minor disputes. Subsequently two important compacts, the Rush-Bagot Agreement of 1817 and the Convention of 1818, removed several potential causes of irritation. In the first, resulting from an exchange of letters between Acting Secretary of State Richard Rush and the British minister to the United States, Charles Bagot, the threat of naval competition on the Great Lakes vanished with an arrangement to limit forces there to several U.S. ships collecting customs duties. Although the exchange made no reference to the land boundary between the United States and Canada, its cooperative spirit gave rise to the tradition of an unfortified border, the longest in the world.

The Convention of 1818 covered three major points. It settled the northern limit of the Louisiana Purchase by extending the national boundary

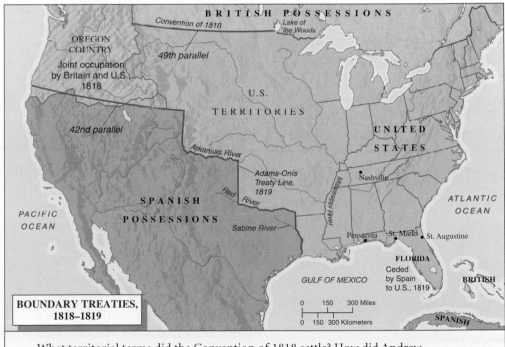

BOUNDARY TREATIES, 1818–1819

What territorial terms did the Convention of 1818 settle? How did Andrew Jackson's actions in Florida help John Quincy Adams claim the territory from Spain? What were the terms of the treaty with Spain?

along the 49th parallel west from Lake of the Woods in what would become Minnesota to the crest of the Rocky Mountains. West of that point the Oregon Country would be open to joint occupation by the British and the Americans, but the boundary remained unsettled. The right of Americans to fish off Newfoundland and Labrador, granted in 1783, was acknowledged once again.

The chief remaining problem was Britain's exclusion of American ships from the British West Indies in order to reserve that lucrative trade for the British. This remained a chronic irritant, and the United States retaliated with several measures. Under the Navigation Act of 1817, importation of West Indian products was restricted to American vessels or vessels belonging to West Indian merchants. In 1818, U.S. ports were closed to all British vessels arriving from a colony that was legally closed to vessels of the United States. In 1820, Monroe approved an act of Congress that specified total "nonintercourse"—with British vessels, with all British colonies in the Americas, and even in goods taken to England and reexported. The rapprochement with Britain therefore fell short of perfection.

THE EXTENSION OF BOUNDARIES The year 1819 was one of the more fateful years in American history. Controversial efforts to expand U.S. territory, an intense financial panic, a tense debate over the extension of slavery, and several landmark Supreme Court cases combined to bring an unsettling end to the Era of Good Feelings. The new nationalism reached a climax with the acquisition of Florida and the extension of America's southwestern boundary to the Pacific, but nationalism quickly began to run afoul of domestic crosscurrents that would submerge the country in sectional squabbles.

Unrest in Florida

Portrait of an escaped slave who lived with the Seminoles in Florida.

In the calculations of global power, it had perhaps long been reckoned that Florida would someday pass to the United States. Spanish sovereignty there was more a technicality than an actuality. Spain, once dominant in the Americas, was now a declining power, unable to enforce its obligations, under Pinckney's Treaty of 1795, to pacify the Florida frontier. In 1816, U.S. forces clashed with a group of escaped slaves who had taken over a British fort on the Apalachicola River in west Florida. Seminoles were soon fighting white settlers in the area, and in 1817, Americans burned a Seminole border settlement, killed five of its inhabitants, and dispersed the rest across the border into Florida.

At that point, Secretary of War Calhoun authorized the use of federal troops against the Seminoles, and he summoned General Andrew Jackson from Nashville to take command. Jackson's orders allowed him to pursue the offenders into Spanish territory but not to attack any Spanish posts. A frustrated Jackson pledged to President Monroe that if the United States wanted Florida, he could wind up the whole controversy in sixty days.

When it came to Spaniards or Indians, few white Tennesseans—and certainly not Andrew Jackson—bothered with technicalities. In early 1818, without presidential approval, Jackson ordered his force of 2,000 federal troops, Tennessee volunteers, and Creek allies to cross the border into Spanish Florida from their encampment in south Georgia. In April the Americans assaulted a Spanish fort at St. Marks and destroyed Seminole villages. They also captured and court-martialed two Indian chiefs and two British traders accused of inciting Indian attacks. Jackson ordered their immediate execution, an act that outraged the British government and caused great consternation among President Monroe's cabinet. But the Tennessee general kept moving. In May he captured Pensacola, the Spanish capital of West Florida, established a provisional American government, and then returned to Tennessee.

Jackson's exploits excited American expansionists and aroused anger in Madrid and concern in Washington. Spain demanded the return of its territory and the punishment of Jackson, but Spain's impotence was plain for all to see. Monroe's cabinet was at first prepared to disavow Jackson's actions, especially his direct attack on Spanish posts. Secretary of War Calhoun was inclined, at least officially, to discipline Jackson for disregard of orders—a stand that would later cause bad blood between the two men—but privately confessed a certain pleasure at Jackson's expedition. In any case a man as popular as Jackson was almost invulnerable. And he had one important friend, Secretary of State John Quincy Adams, who realized that Jackson's conquest of West Florida had strengthened his own hand in negotiations under way with the Spanish minister to purchase the

Andrew Jackson

Victor at the Battle of New Orleans, Indian fighter, and future president.

territory. U.S. forces withdrew from Florida, but negotiations resumed with the knowledge that the United States could retake Florida at any time.

With the fate of Florida a foregone conclusion, John Quincy Adams turned his eye to a larger purpose, a definition of the ambiguous western boundary of the Louisiana Purchase and—his boldest stroke—extension of its boundary to the Pacific coast. In lengthy negotiations with Spain, Adams gradually gave ground on claims to Texas but stuck to his demand for a transcontinental line for the Louisiana Territory, extending its boundary to the Pacific. Agreement on what came to be called the Transcontinental Treaty was reached early in 1819. Spain ceded all of Florida in return for the U.S. government's agreement to pay Americans who had sued Spain for financial losses resulting from Spanish actions. The western boundary of the Louisiana Purchase would run along the Sabine River and then, in stair-step fashion, up to the Red River, along the Red, and up to the Arkansas River. From the source of the Arkansas, it would go north to the 42nd parallel and thence west to the Pacific coast. A dispute over land claims held up ratification for another two years, but those claims were revoked and final ratifications were exchanged in 1821. Florida became a U.S. territory, and its first governor, albeit briefly, was Andrew Jackson. In 1845, Florida would achieve statehood.

CRISES AND COMPROMISES

THE PANIC OF 1819   John Quincy Adams's Transcontinental Treaty of 1819 (also called the Adams-Onís Treaty) was a diplomatic triumph and the climactic event of the postwar nationalism. Even before it was signed, however, two thunderclaps signaled the end of the brief Era of Good Feelings and gave warning of stormy weather ahead: the financial panic of 1819 and the controversy over Missouri statehood. The occasion for the panic was the sudden collapse of cotton prices. At one point in 1818, cotton had soared to 32.5¢ per pound. The high prices prompted British textile mills to turn from American plantations to cheaper East Indian cotton, and by 1819, cotton was averaging only 14.3¢ per pound. The price collapse set off a decline in the demand for other American goods and suddenly revealed the fragility of the prosperity that had begun after the War of 1812.

New American factories struggled to find markets for their goods. Even the Tariff of 1816 had not been a strong enough force to eliminate British competition. Moreover, businessmen, farmers, and land speculators had recklessly borrowed money to fuel their entrepreneurial schemes. The sources of this credit were both government and the banks. Under the Land Act of 1800, the government had extended four years' credit to those who bought western land. After 1804, one could buy as little as 160 acres at a minimum price of $1.64 per acre (although in auctions the best land went for more). In many cases, speculators purchased large tracts, paying only a fourth down, and then sold them to settlers with the understanding that the settlers would pay the remaining installments. With the collapse of crop prices and, subsequently, land values, both speculators and settlers saw their income plummet.

The reckless practices of the state banks compounded the inflation of credit. To enlarge their loans, the state banks issued more bank notes than they could redeem with gold or silver coins. Even the second Bank of the United States, which was supposed to introduce some order to the chaotic financial arena, got caught up in the easy-credit mania. Its first president yielded to the contagion of the get-rich-quick fever that was sweeping the country. The proliferation of branches, combined with little supervision by the central bank, carried the national bank into the same reckless extension of loans that state banks had pursued. In 1819, just as alert businessmen began to take alarm, newspapers revealed a case of extensive fraud and embezzlement in the Baltimore branch of the Bank of the United States. The disclosure prompted the appointment of Langdon Cheves, a former congressman from South Carolina, as the bank's new president.

Cheves reduced salaries and other costs, postponed the payment of dividends, restrained the extension of credit, and presented for redemption the state bank notes that came in, thereby forcing the state-chartered banks to keep specie reserves. Cheves rescued the bank from near ruin, but only by putting pressure on the state banks. State banks in turn put pressure on their debtors, who found it harder to renew old loans or get new ones. In 1822, considering his task completed, Cheves retired and was succeeded in the following year by Nicholas Biddle of Philadelphia. The Cheves policies were the result rather than the cause of the panic, but they pinched debtors. Hard times lasted about three years, and many people blamed the bank. After the panic passed, resentment of the national bank lingered in the South and the West.

THE MISSOURI COMPROMISE Just as the financial panic spread over the country, another cloud appeared on the horizon: the onset of a fierce sectional controversy over slavery. By 1819 the country had an equal number of slave states and free states—eleven of each. The line between them was defined by the southern and western boundaries of Pennsylvania and the Ohio River. Although slavery lingered in some places north of the

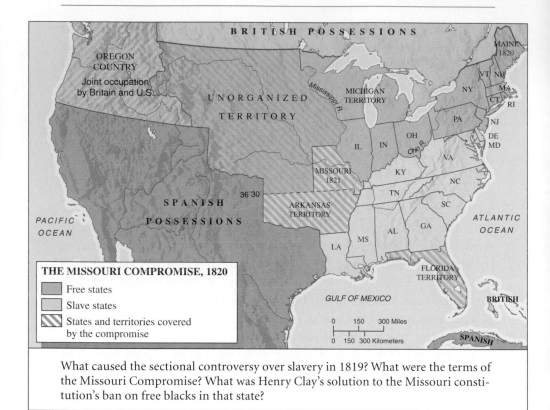

THE MISSOURI COMPROMISE, 1820

Free states

Slave states

States and territories covered by the compromise

What caused the sectional controversy over slavery in 1819? What were the terms of the Missouri Compromise? What was Henry Clay's solution to the Missouri constitution's ban on free blacks in that state?

line, it was on its way to extinction there. Beyond the Mississippi River, however, no move had been made to extend the dividing line across the Louisiana Territory, where slavery had existed since the days when France and Spain had colonized the area. At the time, the Missouri Territory encompassed all of the Louisiana Purchase except the state of Louisiana and the Arkansas Territory. The old French town of St. Louis became the funnel through which settlers, largely southerners who brought their slaves with them, rushed westward beyond the Mississippi.

In 1819 the House of Representatives was asked to approve legislation enabling the Missouri Territory to draft a state constitution, its population having passed the minimum of 60,000. At that point, Representative James Tallmadge Jr., a New York congressman, proposed a resolution prohibiting the transport of more slaves into Missouri, which already had some 10,000, and providing freedom at age twenty-five to those slaves born after the territory's admission as a state. After brief but fiery exchanges, the House passed the Tallmadge amendment on an almost strictly sectional vote. The Senate rejected it by a similar tally, but with several northerners joining in the opposition. With population growing faster in the North, a balance between the two sections could be held only in the Senate. In the House, slave states had 81 votes while free states had 105; a balance was unlikely ever to be restored there.

Maine's coincidental application for statehood made it easier to arrive at an agreement. Since colonial times, Maine had been the northern province of Massachusetts. The Senate linked its request for separate statehood with Missouri's and voted to admit Maine as a free state and Missouri as a slave state, thus maintaining the balance between free and slave states in the Senate. A senator further extended the compromise by an amendment to exclude slavery from the rest of the Louisiana Purchase north of 36°30′, Missouri's southern border. Slavery thus would continue in the Arkansas Territory and in the new state of Missouri but would be excluded from the remainder of the area. People at that time presumed that what remained was the Great American Desert, unlikely ever to be settled. Thus the arrangement seemed to be a victory for the slave states. By a very close vote it passed the House on March 2, 1820.

Then another problem arose. The pro-slavery faction that dominated Missouri's constitutional convention inserted in the proposed state constitution a proviso excluding free blacks and mulattoes from the state. This clearly violated the requirement of Article IV, Section 2, of the federal Constitution: "The Citizens of each State shall be entitled to all Privileges and Immunities of Citizens in the several States." Free blacks were citizens of many states, including the slave states of North Carolina and Tennessee, where until the mid-1830s they also enjoyed voting privileges.

The renewed controversy threatened final approval of Missouri's admission as a state until Henry Clay formulated a "second" Missouri Compromise: admission of Missouri as a state would depend upon assurance from the Missouri legislature that it would never construe the offending clause in such a way as to

Henry Clay

Clay entered the Senate at twenty-eight despite the requirement that senators be at least thirty years old.

sanction the denial of privileges that citizens held under the Constitution. It was one of the more artless dodges in American history, for it required the legislature to affirm that the state constitution did not mean what it clearly said, yet the compromise worked. The Missouri legislature duly adopted the pledge while denying that the legislature had any power to bind the people of the state to it. On August 10, 1821, President Monroe proclaimed the admission of Missouri as the twenty-fourth state. For the moment the controversy subsided. "But this momentous question," Thomas Jefferson wrote to a friend after the first compromise, "like a firebell in the night awakened and filled me with terror. I considered it at once as the knell of the Union."

JUDICIAL NATIONALISM

JOHN MARSHALL, CHIEF JUSTICE Meanwhile, the spirit of nationalism still flourished in the Supreme Court, where Chief Justice John Marshall preserved Hamiltonian Federalism for yet another generation, establishing the power of the Supreme Court by his force of mind and crystalline logic. During Marshall's early years on the Court (he served thirty-four years altogether), he affirmed the principle of judicial review of legislative actions. In *Marbury v. Madison* (1803) and *Fletcher v. Peck* (1810), the Court struck down first a federal law and then a state law as unconstitutional. In the cases of *Martin v. Hunter's Lessee* (1816) and *Cohens v. Virginia* (1821), the Court assumed the right to consider appeals from state courts on the grounds that the Constitution, the laws, and the treaties of the United States could be kept uniformly the supreme law of the land only if the Court could review decisions of state courts. In the first case the Court overruled Virginia's confiscation of Loyalist property after the Revolution because it violated treaties with Great Britain; in the second the Court upheld Virginia's right to forbid the sale of lottery tickets.

PROTECTING CONTRACT RIGHTS In the fateful year of 1819, John Marshall and the Supreme Court made two more decisions of major importance in checking the states and building the power of the central government. One of them, *Dartmouth College v. Woodward*, involved an attempt by the New Hampshire legislature to alter a provision in Dartmouth's charter, under which the college's trustees became a self-perpetuating board. In 1816 the state's Republican legislature, offended by this relic of monarchy and even more by the Federalist majority on the board, placed Dartmouth under a new board named by the governor. The original trustees sued and lost in the state courts but, with Daniel Webster as counsel, won on appeal to the Supreme Court. The college's original charter, Marshall said, was a valid contract that the legislature had impaired, an act forbidden by the Constitution. This decision implied a new and enlarged definition of *contract* that seemed to put private corporations beyond the reach of the states that chartered them. Thereafter states commonly wrote into the charters incorporating businesses and other organizations provisions making them subject to modification. Such provisions were then part of the "contract."

John Marshall

Chief Justice and pillar of judicial nationalism.

STRENGTHENING THE FEDERAL GOVERNMENT   The second major Supreme Court case of 1819 was John Marshall's single most important interpretation of the constitutional system: *McCulloch v. Maryland*. James McCulloch, a clerk in the Baltimore branch of the Bank of the United States, had failed to affix state revenue stamps to bank notes as required by a Maryland law taxing the notes. Indicted by the state, McCulloch, acting for the bank, appealed to the Supreme Court, which handed down a unanimous judgment upholding the power of Congress to charter the bank and denying any right of the state to tax it. In a lengthy opinion, Marshall rejected Maryland's argument that the federal government was the creature of sovereign states. Instead, he argued, it arose directly from the people acting through the state conventions that had ratified the Constitution. Whereas sovereignty was divided between the states and the national government, the latter, "though limited in its powers, is supreme within its sphere of action."

Marshall went on to endorse the doctrine of the federal government's having implied constitutional powers. The "necessary and proper" clause of the Constitution, he argued, did not mean "absolutely indispensable." The test of constitutionality was, in his view, a practical one: "Let the end be legitimate, let it be within the scope of the Constitution, and all means which are appropriate, which are plainly adapted to that end, which are not prohibited, but consistent with the letter and spirit of the Constitution, are constitutional."

Maryland's effort to tax the national bank conflicted with the supreme law of the land. One great principle that "entirely pervades the Constitution,"

Marshall wrote, was "that the Constitution and the laws made in pursuance thereof are supreme: . . . they control the Constitution and laws of the respective states, and cannot be controlled by them." The effort by a state to tax a federal bank therefore was unconstitutional, for the "power to tax involves the power to destroy"—which was precisely what the legislatures of Maryland and several other states had in mind with respect to the national bank.

REGULATING INTERSTATE COMMERCE   John Marshall's last great decision, *Gibbons v. Ogden* (1824), established national supremacy in regulating interstate commerce. In 1808, Robert Fulton and Robert R. Livingston (Jefferson's minister to France in 1801), who pioneered commercial use of the steamboat, won from the New York legislature the exclusive right to operate steamboats on the state's rivers and lakes. Fulton and Livingston then gave Aaron Ogden the exclusive right to navigate the Hudson River between New York and New Jersey. Thomas Gibbons, however, operated ships under a federal license that competed with Ogden. On behalf of a unanimous Court,

Deck life on the *Paragon* (1811–1812)

The *Paragon*, "a whole floating town," was the third steamboat operated on the Hudson River by Robert Fulton and Robert R. Livingston.

Marshall ruled that the monopoly granted by the state to Ogden conflicted with the federal Coasting Act, under which Gibbons operated. Congressional power to regulate commerce, the Court said, "like all others vested in Congress, is complete in itself, may be exercised to its utmost extent, and acknowledges no limitations other than are prescribed in the Constitution."

The opinion stopped just short of designating an exclusive federal power over commerce, and later cases would clarify the point that states had a concurrent jurisdiction so long as it did not come into conflict with federal action. For many years there was in fact little federal regulation of commerce, so that in striking down the monopoly created by the state, Marshall had opened the way to extensive development of steamboat navigation and, soon afterward, railroads. Economic expansion often depended upon judicial nationalism.

NATIONALIST DIPLOMACY

THE NORTHWEST   In foreign affairs, too, nationalism prevailed. Within a few years of final approval of John Quincy Adams's Transcontinental Treaty in 1819, the secretary of state drew another important transcontinental boundary line. Spain had abandoned its claim to the Oregon Country above the 42nd parallel, but in 1821 the Russian czar claimed the Pacific coast as far south as the 51st parallel, which in the American view lay within the Oregon Country. In 1823, Secretary of State Adams contested "the right of Russia to any territorial establishment on this continent." The U.S. government, he informed the Russian minister, assumed "that the American continents are no longer subjects for any new European colonial establishments." His protest resulted in a treaty signed in 1824, whereby Russia, which had more pressing concerns in Europe, accepted the line of 54°40′ as the southern boundary of its claim. In 1825 a similar agreement between Russia and Britain gave the Oregon Country clearly defined boundaries, although it was still subject to joint occupation by the United States and Great Britain under their agreement of 1818. In 1827 both countries agreed to extend indefinitely the provision for joint occupation of the Oregon region, subject to termination by either power.

THE MONROE DOCTRINE   Secretary of State Adams's disapproval of further hemispheric colonization had clear implications for Latin America as well. One consequence of the Napoleonic Wars raging across Europe and the French occupation of Spain and Portugal was a series of wars of liberation in colonial Latin America. Within little more than a decade after the flag of rebellion was first raised in 1811, Spain had lost almost its entire empire in the Americas. All that was left were the islands of Cuba and Puerto Rico and the colony of Santo Domingo on the island of Hispaniola.

In 1823, rumors emerged that France wanted to restore the Spanish king's power over Spain's American empire. President James Monroe and Secretary of War John C. Calhoun were alarmed at the possibility, although Secretary of State John Quincy Adams took the more realistic view that any such action was unlikely. The British foreign minister, George Canning, told the U.S. minister to London that the two countries should jointly oppose any incursions by France or Spain in the Western Hemisphere.

Monroe at first agreed, with the support of his advisers Jefferson and Madison. Secretary of State Adams, however, urged Monroe and the cabinet to proclaim a unilateral policy against the restoration of Spain's control over its colonies. "It would be more candid," Adams said, "as well as more dignified, to avow our principles explicitly to Russia and France, than to come in as a cockboat in the wake of the British man-of-war." Adams knew that the British navy would stop any action by European powers in Latin America. The British, moreover, wanted the United States to agree not to acquire any more Spanish territory, including Cuba, Texas, and California, but Adams preferred to avoid such a commitment.

President Monroe incorporated the substance of Adams's views into his annual message to Congress in 1823. The Monroe Doctrine, as it was later called, comprised four major points: (1) that "the American continents . . . are henceforth not to be considered as subjects for future colonization by any European powers"; (2) that the political system of European powers was different from that of the United States, which would "consider any attempt

Forefather's advice

In this letter, Monroe asked former president Jefferson for advice on foreign policy.

on their part to extend their system to any portion of this hemisphere as dangerous to our peace and safety"; (3) that the United States would not interfere with existing European-controlled colonies; and (4) that the United States would keep out of the internal affairs of European nations and their wars.

At the time the statement drew little attention, either in the United States or abroad. The Monroe Doctrine, not even so called until 1852, became one of the cherished principles of American foreign policy, but for the time being it slipped into obscurity for want of any occasion to invoke it. In spite of Adams's affirmation, the United States came in as a cockboat in the wake of the British man-of-war after all, for the effectiveness of the doctrine depended upon British naval supremacy. The doctrine had no standing in international law. It was merely a statement of intent sent by an American president to Congress and did not even draw enough interest at the time for European powers to acknowledge it.

ONE-PARTY POLITICS

Almost from the start of James Monroe's second term, in 1821, the jockeying for the presidential succession began. Three members of Monroe's cabinet were active candidates: Secretary of War John C. Calhoun, Secretary of the Treasury William H. Crawford, and Secretary of State John Quincy Adams. Speaker of the House Henry Clay also hungered for the office. And on the fringes of the Washington scene, a new force appeared in the person of former general Andrew Jackson, the scourge of the British, Spanish, Creeks, and Seminoles, the epitome of what every frontiersman admired, who became a senator from Tennessee in 1823. All were Republicans, for again no Federalist stood a chance, but they were competing in a new political world, complicated by the crosscurrents of nationalism and sectionalism. With only one party there was in effect no party, for there existed no generally accepted method for choosing a "regular" candidate.

PRESIDENTIAL NOMINATIONS The tradition of selecting presidential candidates by congressional caucus, already under attack in 1816, had disappeared in the wave of unanimity that reelected Monroe in 1820 without the formality of a nomination. The friends of William Crawford sought in vain to breathe life back into "King Caucus," but only a minority of congressmen appeared in answer to the call. In 1824 they duly named Crawford for president, but the endorsement was so weak as to be more a handicap than an advantage. Crawford was in fact the logical successor to the Virginia dynasty, a native of the state though now a resident of Georgia. He had flirted with nationalism but swung back to states' rights and assumed leadership of the Radicals, a faction that included Old Republicans and those who distrusted the nationalism of John Quincy Adams and John Calhoun. Crawford's candidacy foundered from the beginning, for the candidate had been stricken in 1823 by a disease that left him half-paralyzed and half-blind. His friends protested that he would soon be well, but he never did fully recover.

Long before the Crawford caucus met in early 1824, indeed for two years before, the country had broken out in a rash of presidential endorsements by state legislatures and public meetings. In 1822 the Tennessee legislature named Andrew Jackson as their choice to succeed Monroe. In 1824 a mass meeting of Pennsylvanians added their endorsement. Jackson, who had previously kept silent, responded that while the presidency should not be sought, it should not be declined. The same meeting in Pennsylvania named Calhoun for vice president, and Calhoun accepted. The youngest of the candidates, he was content to take second place and bide his time. Meanwhile, the Kentucky legislature had named its favorite son, Henry Clay, in 1822. The Massachusetts legislature nominated John Quincy Adams in 1824.

Of the four candidates, only two had clearly defined programs, and the outcome was an early lesson in the danger of committing oneself on the issues too soon. Crawford's friends emphasized his devotion to states' rights and strict construction of the Constitution. Clay, on the other hand, took his stand for the "American System": the national bank, the protective tariff, and a program of federally funded internal improvements to bind the country together and strengthen its economy. Adams was close to Clay, openly dedicated to internal improvements but less strongly committed to the tariff. Jackson, where issues were concerned, carefully avoided commitment so as to capitalize on his popularity as the hero of the Battle of New Orleans at the end of the War of 1812.

THE "CORRUPT BARGAIN"   The 1824 election featured squabbling personalities and sectional partisanship more than substantive issues. Adams, the only northern candidate, carried New England, the former bastion of Federalism, and won most of New York's electoral votes. Clay took Kentucky, Ohio, and Missouri. Crawford carried Virginia, Georgia, and Delaware. Jackson swept the South, along with Illinois and Indiana, and, with Calhoun's support, the Carolinas, Pennsylvania, Maryland, and New Jersey. All candidates got scattered votes elsewhere. In New York, where Clay was strong, his supporters were outmaneuvered by the Adams forces in the legislature, which still chose the presidential electors.

The result of the 1824 election was inconclusive. In the Electoral College, Jackson had 99 votes, Adams 84, Crawford 41, Clay 37. In the popular vote the trend ran about the same: Jackson, 154,000; Adams, 109,000; Crawford, 47,000; and Clay, 47,000. Whatever else might have been said about the outcome, one thing seemed apparent—it was a defeat for Clay's American System promoting national economic development: New England and New York opposed him on internal improvements; the South and the Southwest rejected his promotion of the protective tariff. Sectionalism had defeated the national economic program.

Yet Clay, the dynamic advocate of economic nationalism, now assumed the role of president maker, as the deadlocked election was thrown into the House of Representatives, where the Speaker's influence was decisive. Clay disdained all three of the candidates, but he had little trouble choosing, since he regarded Jackson as a "military chieftain" unfit for the office. "I cannot believe," he muttered, "that killing 2,500 Englishmen at New Orleans qualifies for the various, difficult and complicated duties of the Chief Magistracy." He eventually threw his support to John Quincy Adams. Clay disliked Adams, and vice versa, but Adams endorsed the high tariffs, internal transportation

The presidential "race" of 1824

John Adams, William Crawford, and Andrew Jackson stride to the finish line (on the left) as Henry Clay lags behind (far right).

improvements, and strong national bank that comprised Clay's American System. Clay also expected Adams to name him secretary of state. Whatever the reasons, Clay's decision to support Adams backfired on the Kentuckian's own aspirations for the White House. The final vote in the House, which was by state, carried Adams to victory with 13 votes to Jackson's 7 and Crawford's 4.

It was a costly victory, for the result united Adams's foes and crippled his administration before it got under way. Andrew Jackson dismissed Clay as "the Judas of the West," who thereafter would be burdened by the charge that he had entered into a selfishly "corrupt bargain" with Adams to gain the presidency. There is no evidence that Adams entered into any "corrupt bargain" with Clay to win his support. Still, the charge was widely believed after Adams named Clay secretary of state and thus put him in the office from which three successive presidents had risen. Adams's Puritan conscience could never quite overcome a sense of guilt at the maneuverings that were necessary to gain his election. Jackson supporters launched a campaign to elect him president in 1828 almost immediately after the 1824 decision. The Crawford people, including Martin Van Buren, "the Little Magician" of New York politics, soon moved into the Jackson camp. So, too, did the new vice president, John Calhoun, of South Carolina, who had run on the ticket with both Adams and Jackson but favored the general from Tennessee.

JOHN QUINCY ADAMS   Short, plump, peppery John Quincy Adams was one of the ablest men, hardest workers, and finest intellects ever to enter the White House. Yet he also was one of the most ineffective presidents. Like

John Quincy Adams

Adams was known as a brilliant man but an ineffective leader.

his father, the aristocratic Adams lacked the common touch and the politician's gift for compromise. A stubborn, snobbish man who saw two brothers and two sons die from alcoholism, he suffered from chronic bouts of depression that aroused in him a grim self-righteousness and self-pity, qualities that did not endear him to fellow politicians. His idealism also irritated the party faithful. He refused to play the game of patronage, arguing that it would be dishonorable to dismiss "able and faithful political opponents to provide [government jobs] for my own partisans." In four years he removed only twelve officeholders. His first message to Congress included a grandiose blueprint for national development, set forth in such a blunt way that it became a disaster of political ineptitude.

In the boldness and magnitude of its conception, Adams's vision of an expanded federal government outdid the plans of both Alexander Hamilton and Henry Clay. The central government, the president proposed, should promote internal improvements (roads, canals, harbors, and bridges), set up a national university, finance scientific explorations, build astronomical observatories, and create a department of the interior. To refrain from using broad federal powers, Adams insisted, "would be treachery to the most sacred of trusts."

The merits of Adams's bold message to Congress were obscured by an unhappy choice of language. For the son of John Adams to praise the example "of the nations of Europe and of their rulers" was downright suicidal. At one fell swoop he had revived all the Republican suspicions of the Adamses as closet monarchists and provoked the emergence of a new party system. The minority who cast their lot with the economic nationalism of Adams and Clay were turning into National Republicans; the opposition, the growing party of Jacksonians, now called themselves the Democratic Republicans; they would eventually drop the name Republican and become Democrats.

Adams's headstrong plunge into nationalism and his refusal to play the game of backroom politics condemned his administration to utter frustration. Congress ignored his domestic proposals, and in foreign affairs the triumphs that he had scored as secretary of state had no sequels. The climactic effort of Adams's opponents to discredit him centered on the tariff issue. The panic of 1819 had elicited calls in 1820 for a higher tariff, but the effort failed by one vote in the Senate. In 1824 the tariff advocates renewed the effort, with greater success. The Tariff of 1824 favored the middle Atlantic and New England manufacturers by raising duties on imported woolens, cotton, iron, and other finished goods. Clay's Kentucky won a tariff on hemp, and a tariff on raw wool brought the wool-growing interests to the support of the measure. Additional revenues were raised with duties on sugar, molasses, coffee, and salt.

At this point, Jackson's supporters saw a chance to advance their candidate through an awkward scheme hatched by John Calhoun. The plan was to present an alternative tariff bill with such outrageously high duties on raw materials that the manufacturers of the East would join the commercial interests there and, with the votes of the agricultural South and Southwest, defeat the measure. In the process, Jackson supporters in the Northeast could take credit for supporting the tariff, and wherever it fit their interests, other Jacksonians elsewhere could take credit for opposing it—while Jackson himself remained in the background. John Randolph of Roanoke saw through the ruse. The bill, he asserted, "referred to manufactures of no sort or kind, but the manufacture of a President of the United States."

The complicated scheme helped elect Jackson, but in the process Calhoun became a victim of his own machinations. Instead of being defeated, the high tariffs ended up becoming law. Calhoun had calculated upon neither the defection of Van Buren, who supported a crucial amendment to satisfy the woolens manufacturers, nor the growing strength of manufacturing interests in New England. Daniel Webster, now a senator from Massachusetts, explained that he was ready to deny all he had said against the tariff because New England had built up its manufactures on the understanding that high tariffs would continue to protect them from foreign competition.

When the tariff bill passed, in May 1828, it was Calhoun's turn to explain his newfound opposition to the gospel of tariff protection, and nothing so well illustrates the flexibility of constitutional principles as the switch in positions by Webster and Calhoun. Back in South Carolina, Calhoun prepared the *South Carolina Exposition and Protest* (1828), which was issued anonymously along with a series of resolutions by the South Carolina legislature. In that document, Calhoun declared that a state could nullify an act of Congress that it found unconstitutional.

THE ELECTION OF ANDREW JACKSON   Thus the stage was set for the contentious election of 1828, which might more truly than that of 1800 be called a revolution. But if the issues of the day had anything to do with the election, they were hardly visible in the campaign, in which politicians on both sides reached depths of scurrilousness that had not been plumbed since 1800. Those campaigning for Adams denounced Jackson as a hot-tempered,

The bloody deeds of General Andrew Jackson

This anti-Jackson handbill, published during the 1828 campaign, depicts Jackson as a merciless frontier ruffian.

ignorant barbarian, a participant in repeated duels and frontier brawls, a man whose fame rested upon his reputation as a killer. In addition, his enemies dredged up the story that Jackson had lived in adultery with his wife, Rachel, before they were legally married; in fact they had lived together for two years in the mistaken belief that her divorce from her former husband was final. As soon as the official divorce had come through, Andrew and Rachel had remarried. A furious Jackson blamed Henry Clay for the campaign slurs against his wife's chastity. He bitterly dismissed his longtime enemy as "the basest, meanest scoundrel that ever disgraced the image of his god."

The Jacksonians, however, got in their licks against Adams, condemning him as a man who had lived his adult life on the public treasury, who had been corrupted by foreigners in the courts of Europe, and who had allegedly delivered up an American girl to serve the lust of Czar Alexander I while serving as minister to Russia. They called Adams a gambler and a spendthrift for having bought a billiard table and a chess set for the White House and a puritanical hypocrite for despising the common people and warning Congress to ignore the will of its constituents. He had gained the presidency in 1824, the Jacksonians claimed, by a "corrupt bargain" with Henry Clay.

In the campaign of 1828, Jackson held most of the advantages. As a military victor, he projected patriotism. As a son of the West and a fabled Indian fighter, he was a hero in the frontier states. As a farmer, lawyer, and slaveholder, he had the trust of southern planters. Debtors and local bankers who hated the national bank also turned to Jackson. In addition, his vagueness on the issues protected him from attack by interest groups. Not least of all, Jackson benefited from a growing spirit of democracy in which the common folk were no longer satisfied to look to their betters for leadership, as they had done in the eighteenth century. It had become politically fatal to be labeled an aristocrat.

Since the Revolution and especially since 1800, the opportunity for white men to vote

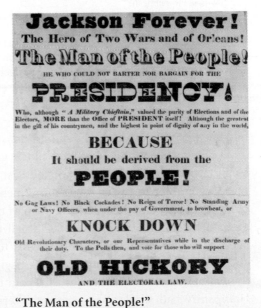

"The Man of the People!"

This 1828 handbill identifies Jackson with the democratic impulse of the time.

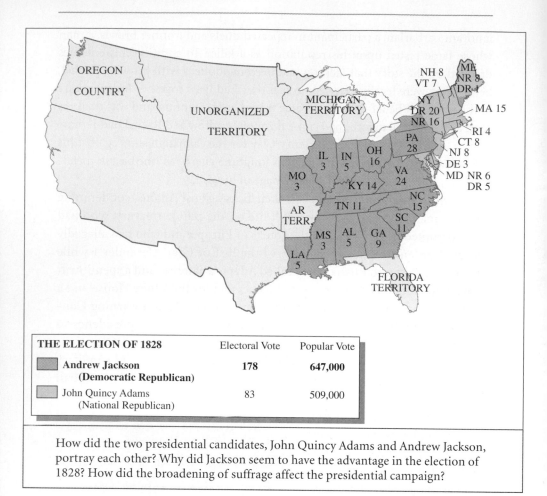

OREGON
COUNTRY

UNORGANIZED
TERRITORY

MICHIGAN
TERRITORY

NH 8
VT 7

ME
NR 8
DR 1

NY
DR 20
NR 16

MA 15

RI 4
CT 8
NJ 8
DE 3
MD NR 6
DR 5

PA
28

IL
3

IN
5

OH
16

VA
24

MO
3

KY 14

AR
TERR.

TN 11

NC
15

SC
11

MS
3

AL
5

GA
9

LA
5

FLORIDA
TERRITORY

THE ELECTION OF 1828	Electoral Vote	Popular Vote
Andrew Jackson (Democratic Republican)	178	647,000
John Quincy Adams (National Republican)	83	509,000

How did the two presidential candidates, John Quincy Adams and Andrew Jackson, portray each other? Why did Jackson seem to have the advantage in the election of 1828? How did the broadening of suffrage affect the presidential campaign?

had been gaining ground. The traditional story is that a surge of Jacksonian democracy came out of the West like a great wave, supported mainly by small farmers, leading the way for the East. But in the older seaboard states there were other forces enabling more men to vote: the Revolutionary doctrine of equality and the feeling on the part of the workers, artisans, and small merchants of the towns, as well as small farmers and landed gentry, that broader voting rights provided a means to combat the rising commercial and manufacturing interests. From the beginning, Pennsylvania had opened the ballot box to all adult males who paid taxes; by 1790, Georgia and New Hampshire had similar arrangements. Vermont, in 1791, became the first state with universal manhood suffrage, having first adopted it in 1777. Kentucky, admitted to the Union in 1792, became the second. Tennessee, admitted in 1796, had only a modest taxpaying qualification. New Jersey in 1807 and Maryland and South Carolina in 1810 abolished property and tax-paying requirements for voting, and after 1815 the new states of the West came in with either white manhood suffrage or a low taxpaying requirement. Connecticut in 1818, Massachusetts in 1821, and New York in 1821 abolished their property requirements for voting.

Along with the broadening of white male suffrage went a liberalization of other features of government. Representation was reapportioned more nearly in line with the population. An increasing number of officials, even judges, were chosen by popular vote rather than appointment. Final disestablishment of the Congregational Church in New England as the official state church came in Vermont in 1807, in New Hampshire in 1817, in Connecticut in 1818, in Maine in 1820, and in Massachusetts in 1834. In 1824 six state legislatures still chose presidential electors. By 1828 the popular vote prevailed in all but South Carolina and Delaware and by 1832 in all but South Carolina.

The extension of voting rights to the poorest people brought a new type of politician to the fore: the man who had special appeal to the masses or knew how to organize the people for political purposes and who became a vocal advocate of the people's right to rule. Jackson fit the ideal of this more democratic political world, a rustic leader sprung from the people rather than a member of the aristocracy, a frontiersman of humble origin who had scrambled up the political ladder by will and tenacity. "Adams can write," went one of the campaign slogans, "Jackson can fight." He could write, too, but he once said that he had no respect for a man who could think of only one way to spell a word.

When the 1828 election returns came in, Jackson had won by a comfortable margin. The electoral vote was 178 to 83, and the popular vote was about 647,000 to 509,000 (the figures vary). Adams had won New Jersey, Delaware, all of New England (except 1 of Maine's 9 electoral votes), 16 of the 36 from New York, and 6 of the 11 from Maryland. All the rest belonged to Jackson. The new president was eager to launch a new era in American political development.

CHAPTER SUMMARY

- **Economic Policies** The Tariff of 1816 protected American manufacturing, and the second Bank of the United States provided a stronger currency, thus strengthening the national economy. Henry Clay's American System anticipated an active economic role for the federal government with its vision of a national bank, a protective tariff, and federally funded internal improvements, such as roads.

- **Era of Good Feelings** James Monroe's term in office was initially dubbed the Era of Good Feelings because it began with peace and prosperity. The demise of the Federalists ended the first party system in America, leaving the Republicans as the only political party in the nation. The seeming unity of the Republicans was shattered by the election of 1824, which Andrew Jackson lost as a result of what he believed was a "corrupt bargain" between John Quincy Adams and Henry Clay.

- **Sectionalism** The growth of the cotton culture transformed life in the South, in part by encouraging the expansion of slavery. As settlers streamed west, the extension of slavery into the new territories became the predominant concern of southern politicians. The Missouri Compromise, a short-term solution, exposed the emotions and turmoil that the problem generated. During this time, the North changed as well—an urban middle class emerged.

- **Strengthening the Federal Government** The Marshall court used the "necessary and proper" clause to endorse the exercise of implied constitutional powers of the federal government. In striking down a federal law and a state law, the Court confirmed the primacy of the national judiciary. Further decisions of the Marshall court protected contract rights against state action and established the federal government's supremacy over interstate commerce.

- **The Monroe Doctrine** The main diplomatic achievements of the period between the end of the War of 1812 and the coming civil war concerned America's boundaries and the resumption of trade with its old enemy, Great Britain. The Monroe Doctrine expressed the idea that America was no longer open to colonization and proclaimed American neutrality in European affairs.

CHRONOLOGY

1810	Supreme Court issues *Fletcher v. Peck* decision
1815	Construction of the National Road begins
1816	Second Bank of the United States is established
	First protective tariff goes into effect
1819	Supreme Court issues *McCulloch v. Maryland* decision
	United States and Spain agree to the Transcontinental (Adams-Onís) Treaty
	Tallmadge amendment
1821	Florida becomes a territory
	Missouri becomes a state
1823	President Monroe enunciates the principles of the Monroe Doctrine
1824	Supreme Court issues *Gibbons v. Ogden* decision
	John Quincy Adams wins the presidential election by what some critics claim is a "corrupt bargain" with Henry Clay
1828	John C. Calhoun publishes the *South Carolina Exposition and Protest*

KEY TERMS & NAMES

Daniel Webster p. 386

Henry Clay p. 386

John C. Calhoun p. 386

Tariff of 1816 p. 386

American System p. 388

James Monroe p. 389

John Quincy Adams p. 390

Oregon Country p. 392

panic of 1819 p. 394

second Bank of the United States p. 395

Missouri Compromise p. 395

36°30′ p. 397

Monroe Doctrine p. 401

"corrupt bargain" p. 404

11

THE JACKSONIAN IMPULSE

FOCUS QUESTIONS   Ⓢ   wwnorton.com/studyspace

- To what extent did Andrew Jackson's election initiate a new era in American politics?

- What was Jackson's attitude toward federal involvement in the economy?

- How did Jackson respond to the nullification controversy?

- What happened to the Indians living east of the Mississippi River by 1840?

- Why did a new party system of Democrats and Whigs emerge?

The election of Andrew Jackson initiated a new era in American politics and social development. Jackson was the first president not to come from a prominent colonial family. As a self-made soldier, politician, and slave-owning land speculator from the backcountry, he symbolized the changing social scene and the emergence of the "common" man in political life. The nation he prepared to govern was vastly different from that led by George Washington and Thomas Jefferson. In 1828 the United States boasted twenty-four states and nearly 13 million people, many of them recent arrivals from Germany and Ireland. The national population was growing at a phenomenal rate, doubling every twenty-three years. An extraordinary surge in foreign demand for cotton and other goods, along with British investment in American enterprises, helped fuel an economic boom and a transportation revolution. Textile mills sprouted like mushrooms across the New England countryside, their ravenous spinning looms fed by cotton grown in the newly cultivated lands

All Creation Going to the White House

The scene following Jackson's inauguration as president, according to the satirist Robert Cruikshank.

of Alabama and Mississippi. This fluid new economic environment fostered a mad scramble for material gain and political advantage. People of all back grounds engaged in a frenzied effort to acquire land and wealth and thereby gain social status and prestige.

Cities increasingly became the dynamic centers of the nation's commerce, industry, finance, and politics. The urban population grew twice as fast as the rural population during the second quarter of the nineteenth century. A more urban society and a more specialized and speculative economy created more instability as people took greater risks to make money. A more stratified social order also emerged, with some people acquiring great wealth while most others worked for wages.

An agrarian economy that earlier had produced crops and goods for household use or local exchange expanded into a market-oriented capitalist economy engaged in national and international commerce. New canals and roads opened up eastern markets to western farmers in the Ohio River valley. The new "market economy" brought with it greater regional specialization. The South grew more dependent upon cotton while the Northeast witnessed the first stages of industrialization. As more land was put into cultivation and commercial farmers came to rely upon banks for credit to buy land, seed, and tools, they were subject to greater risks and the volatility of the commodities markets. In the midst of periodic financial panics and sharp business depressions, farmers unable to pay their debts lost their farms to "corrupt" banks, which they believed had engaged in reckless speculative ventures and benefited from government favoritism.

For many people the transition from household farming to market-based commercial agriculture and capitalist manufacturing was painful and unsettling. A traditional "Jeffersonian" economy of artisans and craftsmen and subsistence farmers was giving way to a modern system of centralized workshops, mills, and factories dependent upon large numbers of wage laborers. Chartered corporations and commercial banks began to dominate local economies. With the onset of the factory system and urban commerce, rural people migrated from farms and shops to towns and factories and in the process became dependent upon others for their food, clothing, and livelihood. This transformation called into question the traditional assumption of Thomas Jefferson and others that a republic could survive only if most of its citizens were independent, self-reliant property owners, neither too rich to dominate other people nor too poor to become dependent and subservient.

Amid these profound economic and social changes was a widespread effort to democratize the political process. The Jacksonians sought to expand economic opportunity and political participation. Yet to call the Jacksonian era the age of the common man, as many historians have, is misleading. While political participation increased during the Jacksonian era, most of the common folk remained *common* folk. The period never produced true economic and social equality. Power and privilege, for the most part, remained in the hands of an "uncommon" elite of powerful men. Jacksonians in power often proved to be as opportunistic and manipulative as the patricians they displaced. And they never embraced the principle of economic equality. "Distinctions in society will always exist under every just government," Andrew Jackson observed. "Equality of talents, or education, or of wealth cannot be produced by human institutions." He and other Jacksonians wanted every American to have an equal chance to compete in the marketplace and in the political arena, but they never sanctioned equality of results. "True republicanism," one commentator declared, "requires that every man shall have an equal chance—that every man shall be free to become as unequal as he can." But in the afterglow of Jackson's electoral victory, few observers troubled with such distinctions. It was time to celebrate the "commoner's" ascension to the presidency.

SETTING THE STAGE

Andrew Jackson's father had died before Andrew was born, and his mother scratched out a meager living as a housekeeper before dying of cholera when her son was fifteen. Jackson grew to be proud, gritty, and short-tempered, and he became a good hater. During the Revolution, when he was a young boy, two of his brothers were killed by redcoats, and the young Jackson was gashed and scarred by a British officer's saber. He also carried with him the conviction that it was not enough for a man to be right; he had to be tough—even ferocious—as well, qualities that inspired his soldiers to nickname him Old Hickory. During a duel with a man reputed to be the best shot in Tennessee, Jackson nevertheless let his opponent fire first. For his gallantry the future president received a bullet that wedged itself next to his heart. He nevertheless straightened himself, patiently took aim, and killed his foe. "I should have hit him," Jackson claimed, "if he had shot me through the brain."

Andrew Jackson was the most popular politician since George Washington. Born in poverty and raised in hardship, he was a commanding figure with a cutthroat ambition who championed the common people; he could not have been more different from the aloof aristocrat John Quincy Adams. "I was born for a storm," he once boasted; "a calm does not suit me." Tall and lean, the rough-hewn Jackson looked gaunt and haggard—as well as intrepid and domineering. His ashen skin, chiseled features, penetrating eyes, jutting chin, and iron-gray hair accentuated his steely personality. A British visitor said he had a "gamecock look." By nature, Jackson was combative—a fearless fighter governed by an explosive temper and strong prejudices. He assaulted one opponent with a cane, another with his fists, and engaged in three duels. Two bullets remained lodged in his body most of his life. "His passions are terrible," said Thomas Jefferson, who deemed the volatile Jackson "dangerous" and "unfit" for the presidency.

As a victorious, wildly popular general, Jackson often behaved as a tyrant. He not only had deserters and captives executed; he once had a teenager shot for refusing to comply with an officer's order. During and then after the Battle of New Orleans, in 1815, he took control of the chaotic city, declared martial law, and ruled with an iron fist for two months, imposing a nightly curfew, censoring the newspaper, jailing city officials (including judges), and threatening to execute dissenters. After retiring from the army, Jackson became an attorney, a planter, a Tennessee legislator, and a U.S. senator. Now, as the nation's seventh president, he was determined to change the structure and tone of the federal government. The charismatic new president appealed to the masses. Senator Daniel Webster scoffed at the huge, unruly crowd attending Jackson's inauguration: "Persons have come 500 miles to see Genl. Jackson; & they really seem to think that the Country is rescued from some dreadful danger."

Jackson did view himself as a savior of sorts, a crusading president with the courage to assault the "rich and the powerful" in an effort to create the egalitarian republic envisioned by Thomas Jefferson. National politics, he had decided, had fallen under the sway of wealthy bankers and corrupt public officials preoccupied with promoting their self-interest at the expense of the public good. Jackson vowed to eliminate such corrupting elitism. Yet ironies abounded as the audacious new president assumed leadership of a self-conscious democratic revival. An ardent Jeffersonian whom Jefferson himself distrusted, the slave-owning Jackson championed equality (for white men). He also wanted to lower taxes, reduce government spending, shrink the federal bureaucracy, pay off the federal debt, destroy the national bank, and cleanse politics of what he viewed as the corrosive effects of naked self-interest. And he was determined to remove the "ill-fated race" of Indians from all of the states so that white Americans could exploit their lands. Yet he wanted to do all of those things while bolstering states' rights and diminishing federal power. In pursuing these occasionally conflicting goals, Jackson acted quickly—and decisively.

APPOINTMENTS AND RIVALRIES   Jackson believed that politicians should serve a term in government, then return to the status of private citizen, for officials who stayed in office too long grew corrupt. So he vowed to replace federal officials. During his first year in office, however, Jackson replaced only about 9 percent of the appointed officials in the federal government and during his entire term replaced fewer than 20 percent.

Jackson's administration was from the outset divided between the partisans of Secretary of State Martin Van Buren and those of Vice President John C. Calhoun. Much of the political history of the next few years would turn upon the rivalry of these two statesmen as each jockeyed for position as Jackson's successor. Van Buren held most of the advantages, foremost among them his skill at timing and tactics. Jackson, new to political administration, leaned heavily upon him for advice. Van Buren had perhaps more skill at maneuvering than Calhoun and certainly more freedom to maneuver because his home base of New York was more secure politically than Calhoun's base in South Carolina. But Calhoun, a humorless man of towering intellect and apostolic zeal, could not be taken lightly. A visitor remarked after a three-hour discussion with the bushy-browed Calhoun, "I hate a man who makes me think so much . . . and I hate a man who makes me feel my own inferiority." As vice president, Calhoun was determined to defend southern interests, especially the preservation of slavery, against the worrisome advance of northern industrialism and abolitionism.

THE EATON AFFAIR   In his battle with Calhoun over political power, Van Buren had luck on his side. Fate handed him a trump card: the succulent scandal known as the Peggy Eaton affair. The daughter of an Irish tavern owner, Margaret (Peggy) O'Neale was a vivacious widow whose husband had supposedly committed suicide upon learning of her affair with the Tennessee senator John Eaton, a close friend of Jackson. Her marriage to Eaton, three months before he became Jackson's secretary of war, had scarcely made a virtuous woman of her in the eyes of the proper ladies of Washington. Floride Calhoun, the vice president's wife, especially objected to Peggy Eaton's lowly origins and unsavory past. She pointedly snubbed her, and the cabinet wives followed suit.

Political scandal

This political cartoon depicts Jackson and his Cabinet welcoming a popular French dancer and actress to the White House. This cartoon has long been associated with the Eaton affair.

Peggy's plight reminded Jackson of the gossip that had pursued his own wife, Rachel, and he pronounced Peggy Eaton "chaste as a virgin." To a friend he wrote, "I did not come here to make a Cabinet for the Ladies of this place, but for the Nation." His cabinet members, however, were unable to cure their wives of what Van Buren dubbed "the Eaton Malaria." Mrs. Eaton finally gave in to the chill and withdrew from the social scene in Washington. The outraged Jackson linked his nemesis, Calhoun, to what he called a conspiracy against her and drew even closer to Van Buren.

INTERNAL IMPROVEMENTS While Washington social life weathered the gossip-filled winter of 1829–1830, Van Buren delivered some additional blows to Calhoun. It was easy to persuade Jackson to oppose federal financing of transportation improvements, programs with which Calhoun had long been identified. Jackson did not oppose road building per se, but he had the same constitutional scruples as Madison and Monroe about using federal funds to pay for local projects in a single state. In 1830 the Maysville Road bill, passed by Congress, offered Jackson a happy chance for a dual thrust at rivals John Calhoun and Henry Clay. The bill authorized the government to buy stock in a road from Maysville, Kentucky, to Clay's hometown of Lexington. The proposed road, to be constructed by the Maysville Turnpike Road Company, lay entirely within the state of Kentucky, and though part of a larger scheme to link up with the National Road via Cincinnati, it could be viewed as a purely local undertaking. On that ground, Jackson vetoed the bill, calling it unconstitutional, and his decisive action garnered widespread popular acclaim.

King Andrew the First

Opponents considered Jackson's veto of the Maysville Road bill an abuse of power. This cartoon shows "King Andrew" trampling on the Constitution, internal improvements, and the Bank of the United States.

Yet while Jackson continued to oppose federal aid to local projects, he supported interstate projects such as the National Road. Even so, Jackson's opposition to the Maysville Road set an important precedent, on the eve of the railroad age, for limiting federal support of transportation improvements. The early railroads would be built altogether by state and private capital until at least 1850.

NULLIFICATION

CALHOUN'S THEORY   There is a fine irony to Vice President John Calhoun's plight in the Jackson administration, for the South Carolinian was now midway between his early phase as a war-hawk nationalist and his later phase as a states' rights sectionalist. Conditions in his home state had brought on the change. Suffering from prolonged agricultural depression, South Carolina lost almost 70,000 residents to emigration during the 1820s and was fated to lose nearly twice that number in the 1830s. Most South Carolinians blamed the protective tariff for raising the price of manufactured goods from Europe. Insofar as tariffs discouraged the sale of foreign goods in the United States, they reduced the ability of British and French traders to buy southern cotton. This situation worsened already existing problems of low cotton prices and farmland exhausted from perennial planting. Compounding the South Carolinians' malaise was growing anger over the North's moral criticism of slavery. Hardly had the country emerged from the Missouri controversy of 1819–1820 when Charleston, South Carolina, was thrown into panic by the Denmark Vesey slave insurrection of 1822, though the uprising was quickly—and brutally—put down.

The unexpected passage of the Tariff of 1828, called the tariff of abominations by its critics, left Calhoun no choice but to join those in opposition or give up his base of political support in his home state. Calhoun's *South Carolina Exposition and Protest*, written in opposition to the new tariff, had actually been an effort to check the most extreme states' rights advocates with

John C. Calhoun

During the Civil War, the Confederate government printed, but never issued, a one-cent postage stamp bearing this likeness of Calhoun.

finespun theory, in which nullification stopped short of secession from the Union. The unsigned statement accompanied resolutions of the South Carolina legislature protesting the tariff and urging its repeal. Calhoun, it was clear, had not entirely abandoned his earlier nationalism. He wanted to preserve the Union by protecting the minority rights that the agricultural and slaveholding South claimed. The fine balance he struck between states' rights and federal authority was actually not as far removed from Jackson's own philosophy as it might have seemed, but growing tensions between the two men would complicate the issue. The flinty Jackson, in addition, was determined to draw the line at any state defiance of federal law.

Nor would Calhoun's theory permit any state to take up such defiance lightly. His concept of nullification, or interposition, whereby a state could in effect repeal a federal law, followed that by which the original thirteen states had ratified the Constitution. He proposed that a special state convention, like the ratifying conventions, which embody the sovereign power of the people, could declare a federal law null and void within the state's borders because it violated the Constitution. One of two outcomes would then be possible: the federal government would have to abandon the law, or it would have to propose a constitutional amendment removing all doubt as to its validity. The immediate issue was the constitutionality of a tariff designed mainly to protect American industries from foreign competition. The South Carolinians argued that the Constitution authorized tariffs for revenue only.

THE WEBSTER-HAYNE DEBATE   South Carolina's leaders hated the tariff because it helped northern manufacturers and forced South Carolina planters to pay higher prices. But they had postponed any action against its enforcement, awaiting with hope the election of 1828, in which anti-tariff Calhoun was the Jacksonian candidate for vice president. Yet after Jackson assumed the presidency in early 1829, neither he nor Congress saw fit to reduce the tariff duties. There the issue stood until 1830, when the great Webster-Hayne debate sharpened the lines between states' rights and the Union and provoked a national crisis.

The immediate occasion for the debate, however, was the question of public land. The federal government owned immense tracts of unsettled land, and what to do with them set off an intense sectional debate. Late in 1829, Senator Samuel A. Foot of Connecticut proposed that the federal government restrict land sales in the West. When the Foot Resolution came before the Senate in January 1830, Thomas Hart Benton of Missouri denounced it as a northern effort to slow the settlement of the West so that the

East might maintain its supply of cheap factory labor and its political leverage. Senator Robert Y. Hayne of South Carolina took Benton's side. Hayne saw in the issue a chance to strengthen the political alliance of South and West reflected in the vote for Jackson. Perhaps by promoting the sale of federal land in the West, southerners could gain western support for lower tariffs. The government, said Hayne, endangered the Union by imposing any policy that would cause a hardship on one section of the nation to the benefit of another.

Senator Daniel Webster of Massachusetts then rose to defend the East. Possessed of a thunderous voice and a theatrical flair, Webster was the nation's foremost orator and lawyer. With the gallery hushed, he denied that the East had ever shown a restrictive policy toward the West. Webster then lured Hayne into defending states' rights and upholding the doctrine of nullification instead of pursuing a coalition with the West.

Hayne took the bait. He defended John Calhoun's *South Carolina Exposition*, appealed to the example of the Virginia and Kentucky Resolutions of 1798, and called attention to the Hartford Convention of 1814, in which New Englanders had taken much the same position against federal measures

Daniel Webster

The eloquent Massachusetts senator stands to rebut the argument for nullification in the Webster-Hayne debate.

as South Carolina now did. The Union constituted a compact of the states, Hayne argued, and the federal government, which was their "agent," could not be the judge of its own powers, else its powers would be unlimited. Rather, the states must judge when their agent—the federal government— had overstepped the bounds of its constitutional authority. The right of state interposition was "as full and complete as it was before the Constitution was formed."

In rebutting the idea that a state could thwart a federal law, "the God-like" Webster defined a nationalistic view of the Constitution. From the beginning, he asserted, the American Revolution had been fought by a united nation rather than by separate colonies. True sovereignty resided in the people as a whole, for whom both federal and state governments acted as agents in their respective spheres. If a single state could nullify a law of the national government, Webster insisted, then the Union would be a "rope of sand," a practical absurdity. A state could neither nullify a federal law nor secede from the Union. The practical outcome of nullification, Webster predicted, would be a confrontation leading to civil war.

The spectators in the Senate galleries and much of the country at large thrilled to Webster's eloquence. Webster's closing statement became an American classic, reprinted in textbooks and committed to memory by young orators: "Liberty and Union, now and forever, one and inseparable." In the practical world of coalition politics, Webster had the better argument, for the Union and majority rule meant more to westerners, including President Jackson, than the abstractions of state sovereignty and nullification. As for the sale of public land, the Foot Resolution was soon defeated anyway. And whatever one might argue about the origins of the Union, its evolution would validate Webster's position: the states could not act separately from the national government.

THE RIFT WITH CALHOUN   As yet, however, Jackson had not spoken out on the issue. Like John C. Calhoun he was a slaveholder, and he might have been expected to sympathize with South Carolina, his native state. Soon all doubt was removed, at least on the point of nullification. On April 13, 1830, the Democratic party hosted the annual Jefferson Day dinner in Washington to honor the birthday of the former president. Jackson and Secretary of State Van Buren agreed that Jackson should present a toast proclaiming his opposition to nullification. When his turn came, after twenty-four other toasts, many of them extolling states' rights, Jackson raised his glass, glared at Calhoun, and announced, "Our Union—It must be preserved!"

Calhoun, who followed, tried to parry Jackson's criticism with a toast to "the Union, next to our liberty most dear! May we all remember that it can only be preserved by respecting the rights of the States and distributing equally the benefit and the burden of the Union!" But Jackson had set off a bombshell that exploded the plans of the states' righters.

Nearly a month afterward a final nail was driven into the coffin of Calhoun's presidential ambitions. On May 12, 1830, Jackson saw for the first time a letter confirming reports of Calhoun's stand in 1818, when as secretary of war in the Monroe administration he had proposed disciplining General Jackson for his unauthorized invasion of Spanish-held Florida. A tense correspondence between Jackson and Calhoun followed, ending with a curt note from Jackson cutting it off. "Understanding you now," Jackson wrote two weeks later, "no further communication with you on this subject is necessary."

The Rats Leaving a Falling House

During his first term, Jackson was beset by dissension within his administration. Here "public confidence in the stability of this administration" is toppling.

The acidic rift between the two proud men prompted Jackson to take a dramatic step: he removed all Calhoun partisans from the cabinet. Before the end of the summer of 1831, the president had a new cabinet, one entirely loyal to him. He named Martin Van Buren, who had resigned from his post as secretary of state, minister (ambassador) to England, and Van Buren departed for London. Van Buren's friends now urged Jackson to repudiate his previous intention of serving only one term. They believed it might be hard to win the 1832 nomination for the New Yorker, who had been charged with intrigues against Calhoun, and the still-popular Carolinian might yet gain the presidency.

Jackson relented and in the fall of 1831 announced his readiness for one more term, with the idea of bringing Van Buren back from London in time to win the presidency in 1836. But in 1832, when the Senate reconvened, Van Buren's enemies opposed his London appointment and gave Calhoun, as vice president, a chance to reject the nomination with a tie-breaking vote. "It will kill him, sir, kill him dead," Calhoun told Senator Thomas Hart Benton. Benton disagreed: "You have broken a minister, and elected a Vice-President." So, it turned out, he had. Calhoun's peevish vote against Van Buren evoked popular sympathy for the New Yorker, who returned from London and would soon be nominated to succeed Calhoun as vice president.

Now that his presidential hopes were blasted, Calhoun openly opposed Jackson by assuming public leadership of the South Carolina nullificationists. They thought that tariff rates remained too high and represented an unconstitutional tax designed to enrich the industrial North at the expense of the agricultural South. Jackson accepted the principle of using tariffs to protect new American industries from foreign competition. Nevertheless, he had called upon Congress in 1829 to reduce tariffs on goods "which cannot come in competition with our own products." Late in the spring of 1830, Congress lowered tariff duties on such consumer products as tea, coffee, salt, and molasses. That and the Maysville veto, coming at about the same time, mollified a few South Carolinians, but nullifiers regarded the two actions as "nothing but sugar plums to pacify children." By the end of 1831, Jackson was calling for further tariff reductions to take the wind out of the nullificationists' sails. The Tariff of 1832, pushed through by John Quincy Adams (back in Washington as a congressman), reduced duties on many items, but tariffs on cloth and iron remained high.

THE SOUTH CAROLINA ORDINANCE White South Carolinians, living in the only state where slaves were a majority of the population, feared that the federal authority to impose tariffs might eventually be used to end slavery. In the state elections of 1832, attention centered on the nullification issue. The nullificationists took the initiative in organization and agitation, and the newly formed Unionist party was left with distinguished leaders but little public support. A state convention overwhelmingly adopted an ordinance of nullification that repudiated the federal tariff acts of 1828 and 1832 and forbade federal agents in Charleston to collect the tariff duties after February 1, 1833. The reassembled state legislature then provided that any citizen whose property was seized by federal authorities for failure to pay the duty could get a state court order to recover twice its value. The legislature chose Robert Hayne as governor and elected John Calhoun to succeed him as senator. Calhoun promptly resigned as vice president in order to defend nullification on the Senate floor.

JACKSON'S FIRM RESPONSE   In the nullification crisis, South Carolina found itself standing alone: other southern states expressed sympathy, but none endorsed nullification. President Jackson's response was measured but not rash—at least not in public. He viewed nullification as an act of treason. In private he threatened to hang Calhoun and all other traitors—and later expressed regret that he had failed to hang at least Calhoun, whom he detested. In his annual message, on December 4, 1832, Jackson announced his firm intention to enforce the tariff but once again urged Congress to lower the rates. On December 10 he followed up with a proclamation that characterized the doctrine of nullification as an "impractical absurdity." He appealed to the people of his native state not to follow false leaders: "The laws of the United States must be executed. . . . Those who told you that you might peaceably prevent their execution, deceived you. . . . Their object is disunion. But be not deceived by names. Disunion by armed force is treason."

CLAY'S COMPROMISE   Jackson then sent federal soldiers to South Carolina. The nullifiers mobilized the state militia. In 1833 the president requested from Congress a "force bill" authorizing him to use the army to compel compliance with federal law in South Carolina. Under existing legislation he already had such authority, but this affirmation would strengthen his hand. At the same time he supported a bill in Congress that would have lowered tariff duties substantially within two years.

The nullifiers postponed enforcement of their ordinances in anticipation of a compromise. Passage of the compromise bill depended upon the support of the shrewd Kentucky senator Henry Clay, who finally yielded to those urging him to save the day. On February 12, 1833, he circulated a plan to reduce the tariff gradually until 1842. It was less than South Carolina preferred, but it got the nullifiers out of the dilemma they had created.

On March 1, 1833, Congress passed the compromise tariff and the force bill, and the next day Jackson signed both. The South Carolina convention then met and rescinded its nullification of the tariff acts. In a face-saving gesture, it nullified the force bill, for which Jackson no longer had any need. Both sides were able to claim victory. Jackson had upheld the supremacy of the Union, and South Carolina had secured a reduction of the federal tariff. A sulking Calhoun, worn out by the controversy, returned to his plantation. "The struggle, so far from being over," he ominously wrote, "is not more than fairly commenced."

JACKSON'S INDIAN POLICY

If Jackson's firm stance against nullification constituted his finest hour, his effort to displace Indians from their ancestral lands was one of his lowest moments. During the 1820s and 1830s the United States was fast becoming a multicultural nation, home to people from many countries. Most whites, however, were openly racist in their treatment of African Americans and Indians. As economic growth reinforced the institution of slavery and accelerated westward expansion, policy makers struggled to pre-serve white racial homogeneity and hegemony. "Next to the case of the black race within our bosom," declared former president James Madison, "that of the red [race] on our borders is the problem most baffling to the policy of our country."

Yet Andrew Jackson saw nothing baffling about Indian policy. He viewed Native Americans as barbarians who were better off out of the way. Jackson believed that a "just, humane, liberal policy toward Indians" dictated moving all of them onto territory west of the Mississippi River, to the Great Ameri-can Desert, which white settlers would never covet since it was believed to be fit mainly for lizards and rattlesnakes.

INDIAN REMOVAL In response to a request by Jackson, Congress in 1830 approved the Indian Removal Act. It authorized the president to give Indians federal land west of the Mississippi River in exchange for the land they occupied in the East and the South. By 1835 some 46,000 people were relocated at government expense. The policy was enacted with remarkable speed, but even that was too slow for state authorities in the South and Southwest. Unlike the Ohio River valley and the Great Lakes region, where the flow of white settlement had constantly pushed Indians westward before it, in the Old Southwest, settlement moved across Kentucky and Tennessee and down the Mississippi, surrounding the Creeks, Choctaws, Chickasaws, Seminoles, and Cherokees. These "civilized tribes" had over the years taken on many of the features of white society. The Cherokees, for example, had developed a constitution and a written language and owned African American slaves.

Most of the northern tribes were too weak to resist the offers of federal commissioners who, if necessary, used bribery and alcohol to woo the chiefs. On the whole, there was remarkably little resistance. In Illinois and the Wisconsin Territory an armed clash erupted in 1832, which came to be known as the Black Hawk War. Under Chief Black Hawk, the Sauk and Fox sought to reoccupy land they had abandoned the previous year. Facing famine and hostile Sioux west of the Mississippi, they were simply seeking a place to raise a crop of corn. The Illinois militia mobilized to expel them, chased them into the Wisconsin Territory, and massacred women and

The Trail of Tears

Elias Boudinot (Gallegina Watie), editor of the *Cherokee Phoenix,* signed the Indian removal treaty in 1835 and was subsequently murdered.

children as they tried to escape across the Mississippi. The Black Hawk War came to be remembered, however, less because of the atrocities inflicted on the Indians than because among the participants were two native Kentuckians later pitted against each other: Lieutenant Jefferson Davis of the regular army and Captain Abraham Lincoln of the Illinois volunteers.

In the South two Indian nations, the Seminoles and the Cherokees, put up a stubborn resistance to the federal removal policy. The Seminoles of Florida fought a protracted guerrilla war in the Everglades from 1835 to 1842. But their resistance waned after 1837, when their leader, Osceola, was seized by treachery under a flag of truce, imprisoned, and left to die at Fort Moultrie near Charleston Harbor. After 1842 only a few hundred Seminoles remained, hiding out in the swamps. Most of the rest had been banished to the West.

THE TRAIL OF TEARS   The Cherokees had, by the end of the eighteenth century, fallen back into the mountains of northern Georgia and western North Carolina, settling on land guaranteed to them in 1791 by a treaty with the U.S. government. But when Georgia ceded its western lands to

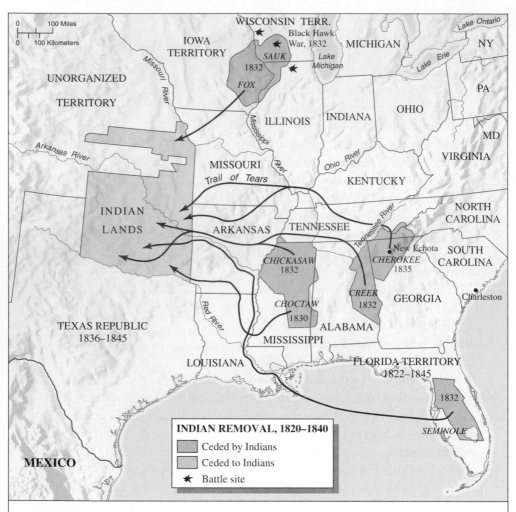

Why did Congress exile the Choctaws, Chickasaws, Creeks, Seminoles, and Cherokees to territory west of Arkansas and Missouri? How far did the tribes have to travel, and what were the conditions on the journey? Why were the Indians not forced to move before the 1830s?

the federal government in 1802, it did so on the ambiguous condition that the United States extinguish all Indian titles within the state "as early as the same can be obtained on reasonable terms." In 1827 the Cherokees, relying upon their established treaty rights, adopted a constitution in which they declared pointedly that they were not subject to the laws or control of any other state or nation. In 1828, shortly after Jackson's election, Georgia declared that after June 1, 1830, the authority of state law would extend to the Cherokees living within the boundaries of the state.

The discovery of gold in north Georgia in 1829 whetted the whites' appetite for Cherokee land and brought bands of prospectors into the country. The Cherokees sought relief in the Supreme Court, but in *Cherokee Nation v. Georgia* (1831) Chief Justice John Marshall ruled that the Court lacked jurisdiction because the Cherokees were a "domestic dependent nation" rather than a foreign state in the meaning of the Constitution. Marshall added, however, that the Cherokees had "an unquestionable right" to their lands "until title should be extinguished by voluntary cession to the United States." In 1830 a Georgia law had required whites in the Cherokee territory to obtain licenses authorizing their residence there and to take an oath of allegiance to the state. Two New England missionaries among the Indians refused to abide by the law and were sentenced to four years at hard labor. On appeal their case reached the Supreme Court as *Worcester v. Georgia*

The Trail of Tears and the rush for gold

Native Americans were exiled to territory west of Arkansas and Missouri, largely as a result of the discovery of gold in the Cherokee Nation. Thousands of miners flooded the area by late 1829.

(1832). The Marshall court held that the Cherokee Nation was "a distinct political community" within which Georgia law had no force. The Georgia law was therefore unconstitutional.

Six years earlier, Georgia had faced down President John Quincy Adams when he tried to protect the rights of the Creeks. Now Georgia faced down the Supreme Court with the tacit consent of another president. Andrew Jackson did nothing to enforce the Court's decision, claiming that he had no authority to intervene in Georgia. In fact, Jackson regarded any treaties with Indians as "an absurdity." Under the circumstances there was nothing for the Cherokees to do but give in and sign a treaty, which they did in 1835. They gave up their land in the Southeast (about 100 million acres) in exchange for tracts in the Indian Territory west of Arkansas, $5 million from the federal government, and expenses for transportation.

By 1838, 17,000 Cherokees had departed westward on the "Trail of Tears," following other tribes on an 800-mile journey marked by the cruelty and neglect of soldiers and private contractors and scorn and pilferage by whites along the way. Four thousand of the refugees died on the Trail of Tears. A few held out in the mountains and acquired title to federal land in North Carolina; thenceforth they were the "Eastern Band" of Cherokees. Some Seminoles were able to hide out in the swamps of the Everglades in south Florida, and a few of the others, especially mixed-blood Creeks who could pass for white, remained scattered in the Southeast. Only 8,000 of the exiles survived the forced march to Oklahoma.

THE BANK CONTROVERSY

THE BANK'S OPPONENTS   The overriding national issue in the presidential campaign of 1832 was neither Jackson's Indian policy nor South Carolina's obsession with the tariff. It was the question of rechartering the Bank of the United States. Andrew Jackson had absorbed the western attitude of hostility toward the bank after the panic of 1819. He believed that "hard" money—gold and silver coins—was the only legitimate medium of exchange. He remained skeptical of all forms of paper currency, and he was convinced that the central bank was unconstitutional—no matter what Chief Justice John Marshall had said in *McCulloch v. Maryland*.

Under the astute management of haughty Nicholas Biddle, the Bank of the United States had prospered and grown. With twenty-nine branches and a third of the nation's bank deposits, it had facilitated business expansion and supplied a stable currency by forcing the 464 state banks to keep a specie (gold or silver) reserve on hand to back their paper currency. The bank also acted as the collecting and disbursing agent for the federal government, which held a fifth of the bank's $35 million capital stock. From the start this combination of private and public functions caused problems for the Bank of the United States. As the government's revenues soared, the bank became the most powerful lending institution in the country, a central bank, in effect, whose huge size enabled it to determine the amount of credit available for the nation.

Arrayed against the bank were powerful enemies: some of the state and local banks that had been forced to reduce their volume of paper money, groups of debtors who suffered from the reduction, and businessmen and speculators on the make, who wanted easier credit. States' rights groups questioned the bank's constitutionality. Financiers on New York's Wall Street resented the supremacy of the bank, which was located on Philadelphia's Chestnut Street.

Like Jackson, many westerners and workingmen believed that the bank was, in Thomas Hart Benton's word, a "Monster," a financial monopoly controlled by a wealthy few. "I think it right to be perfectly frank with you," Jackson told Biddle in 1829. "I do not dislike your Bank any more than [I dislike] all banks." Jackson characterized bankers as "vipers and thieves." He was perhaps right in his instinct that the national bank lodged too much power in private hands, but he was mistaken in his understanding of the bank's policies. By issuing paper money of its own, the bank provided a stable, uniform currency for the expanding economy as well as a mechanism to control the pace of growth.

In 1829, in his first annual message, the president questioned the bank's constitutionality and asserted (whatever the evidence to the contrary) that it had failed to maintain a sound, uniform currency. Jackson talked of a compromise, perhaps a bank completely owned by the government with its operations confined chiefly to government deposits, its profits payable to the government, and its authority to set up branches in any state dependent upon the state's wishes. But Jackson never revealed the precise terms of compromise. The defense of the bank was left up to Biddle.

THE RECHARTER EFFORT   The bank's twenty-year charter would run through 1836, but Biddle could not afford the uncertainty of waiting until then for a renewal. He pondered whether to force the issue of recharter before the election of 1832 or after. On this point, leaders of the National Republicans, especially Henry Clay and Daniel Webster (who was legal counsel to the bank as well as a senator), argued that the time to move was

Rechartering the Bank

President Andrew Jackson battling the "Hydra-headed" Bank of the United States.

before the election. Clay, already the presidential candidate of the National Republicans, proposed making the renewal of the bank charter the central election issue. Friends of the bank held a majority in Congress, and Jackson would risk loss of support in the election if he vetoed its renewal. But Biddle and his allies failed to grasp the depth of public suspicion of the bank and succeeded mainly in handing Jackson a popular issue on the eve of the election. "The Bank," Jackson told Martin Van Buren in May 1832, "is trying to kill me. But I will kill it."

Both houses of Congress passed the recharter by a comfortable margin but without the two-thirds majority needed to override a veto. On July 10, 1832, Jackson vetoed the bill, sending it back to Congress with a ringing denunciation of the bank's monopoly and the financial elite. Jackson argued that the bank was unconstitutional no matter what the Court and Congress said: "The opinion of the judges has no more authority over Congress than the opinion of Congress had over the judges, and on that point the President is independent of both." Besides, there were substantive objections apart from the question of constitutionality. Foreign stockholders in the bank had an undue influence. The bank, Jackson added, had shown favors to members of Congress and exercised an improper power over state banks. He called the B.U.S. a "Monster," a "hydra of corruption" that was "dangerous to our liberties." An effort to overrule Jackson's veto failed in the Senate, thus setting the stage for a nationwide financial crisis and a dramatic presidential campaign.

CONTENTIOUS POLITICS

CAMPAIGN INNOVATIONS   In 1832, for the first time in a presidential election, a third party entered the field. The Anti-Masonic party grew out of popular hostility toward the Masonic fraternal order, members of which were suspected of having kidnapped and murdered a New Yorker for revealing the "secrets" of his lodge. Opposition to a fraternal order was hardly the foundation upon which to build a lasting political party, but the Anti-Masonic party had three important firsts to its credit: in addition to

The Verdict of the People

George Caleb Bingham's painting depicts the increasingly democratic politics of the mid–nineteenth century.

being the first third party, it was the first party to hold a national nominating convention and the first to announce a platform, both of which it accomplished in 1831 when 116 delegates from thirteen states nominated William Wirt of Maryland for president.

The major parties followed its example by holding national conventions of their own. In December 1831 the delegates of the National Republican party assembled in Baltimore to nominate Henry Clay, the charming, charismatic, and witty legislative genius from Kentucky whose arrogance was matched only by his burning ambition to be president. Jackson endorsed the idea of a nominating convention for the Democratic party (the name Republican was now formally dropped) to demonstrate popular support for its candidates. To that purpose the convention, also meeting at Baltimore, first adopted the two-thirds rule for nomination (which prevailed until 1936, when it became a simple majority) and then named Martin Van Buren as Jackson's running mate. The Democrats, unlike the other two parties, adopted no formal platform at their first convention and relied to a substantial degree upon hoopla and the popularity of the president to carry their cause.

The outcome was an overwhelming endorsement of Jackson in the Electoral College, with 219 votes to 49 for Clay, and a less overwhelming but solid victory in the popular vote, 688,000 to 530,000. William Wirt carried only Vermont, winning several electoral votes. South Carolina, preparing for nullification and unable to stomach either Jackson or Clay, delivered its 11 votes to Governor John Floyd of Virginia.

THE REMOVAL OF GOVERNMENT DEPOSITS   Andrew Jackson interpreted his reelection as a mandate to further weaken the Bank of the United States. He asked Congress to investigate the safety of government deposits in the bank. After a committee had checked on the bank's operations, the Calhoun and Clay forces in the House of Representatives passed a resolution affirming that government deposits were safe and could be continued. The resolution passed on March 2, 1833, by chance the same day that Jackson signed the compromise tariff and the force bill. With the nullification issue out of the way, Jackson was free to wage war on the bank. He now resolved to remove all government deposits from the national bank.

When Secretary of the Treasury Louis McLane balked, Jackson fired him. In the reshuffling, Attorney General Roger B. Taney moved to the Treasury Department, where he gladly complied with the presidential wishes, which corresponded to his own views. Taney continued to draw on government accounts with Biddle's bank but deposited all new federal receipts in state banks. By the end of 1833, twenty-three state banks—"pet banks," as they came to be called—had the benefit of federal deposits. Transferring the government's deposits was a highly questionable action under the law, and the Senate voted to censure Jackson for it. Biddle refused to surrender. "This worthy President," he declared, "thinks that because he has scalped Indians and imprisoned Judges he is to have his way with the Bank. He is mistaken." Biddle ordered that the B.U.S. curtail loans throughout the nation and demand the redemption of state bank notes in gold or silver as quickly as possible. He sought to bring the economy to a halt, create a sharp depression, and reveal to the nation the importance of maintaining the bank.

Biddle's contraction policy, however, unwittingly unleashed a speculative binge encouraged by the deposit of government funds in the pet banks. With the restraint of Biddle's bank removed, the state banks unleashed their wild-cat tendencies. New banks mushroomed, printing bank notes with abandon for the purpose of lending money to speculators. Sales of public lands rose from 4 million acres in 1834 to 15 million in 1835 and 20 million in 1836. At the same time, the states plunged heavily into debt to finance the building of roads and canals, inspired by the success of New York's Erie Canal. By 1837 total state indebtedness had soared to $170 million. The supreme irony of Jackson's war on the bank was that it sparked the speculative mania that he most feared.

FISCAL MEASURES   The surge of cheap paper money reached its peak in 1836, when events combined suddenly to deflate it. Most important among these were the Distribution Act and the Specie Circular. Distribution of the government's surplus funds to the states had long been a pet project of Henry Clay's. One of its purposes was to eliminate the federal surplus, thus removing one argument for cutting the tariff. Much of the federal surplus, however, resulted from the "land-office business" in western property sales and was therefore in the form of bank notes that had been issued to speculators. Many westerners thought that the solution to the surplus was simply to lower the price of land; southerners preferred to lower the tariff—but such action would now upset the delicate compromise achieved with the Tariff of 1833. For a time the annual surpluses could be applied to paying off the government debt, but the debt, reduced to $7 million by 1832, was entirely paid off by 1835.

Still, the federal surplus continued to mount. Clay again proposed distributing the funds to the states, but Jackson had constitutional scruples about the process. Finally a compromise was worked out whereby the government would distribute most of the surplus as loans to the states. To satisfy Jackson's concerns, the funds were technically deposits, but in reality the government never asked to be repaid. Distribution of the surplus was to be in proportion to each state's representation in the two houses of Congress and was to be paid out in quarterly installments beginning in 1837.

The Specie Circular, issued by the secretary of the Treasury at Jackson's order, applied the president's hard-money conviction to the sale of public lands. According to his order, the government would accept only gold or silver coins in payment for land. The purposes declared in the circular were to "repress frauds," to withhold support "from the monopoly of the public lands in the hands of speculators and capitalists," and to discourage the "ruinous extension" of bank notes and credit.

Irony dogged Jackson to the end on this matter. Since few settlers had gold or silver coins, they were now left all the more at the mercy of speculators for land purchases. Both the Distribution Act and the Specie Circular put many state banks in a plight. The distribution of the surplus to the state governments resulted in federal funds' being withdrawn from the state banks. In turn the state banks had to require many borrowers to pay back their loans immediately in order to be able to transfer the federal funds to the state governments. This situation caused greater disarray in the already chaotic state banking community. At the same time the new requirement that only hard money be accepted for federal land purchases put an added strain on the supplies of gold and silver.

BOOM AND BUST   But the boom-and-bust cycle of the 1830s had causes larger even than Andrew Jackson, causes that were beyond his control. The soaring inflation of the mid-1830s was rooted not so much in a prodigal expansion of bank notes, as it seemed at the time, but in an increase of gold and silver payments from England, France, and especially Mexico for investment and for the purchase of American cotton and other products. At the same time, British credits enabled Americans to buy British goods without having to export gold or silver. Meanwhile, the flow of hard coins to China, where silver had been much prized, decreased. Now the Chinese took in payment for their goods British credits, which they could in turn use to cover rapidly increasing imports of opium from British India.

Contrary to appearances, therefore, the reserves of gold and silver in U.S. banks kept pace with the increase of bank notes despite reckless behavior on the part of some banks. But by 1836 a tighter British economy had caused a decline in both British investments and British demand for American cotton just when the new western lands were creating a rapid increase in the cotton supply. Fortunately for Jackson, the financial panic of 1837 did not erupt until he was out of the White House. His successor would serve as the scapegoat.

In May 1837, New York banks suspended gold and silver payments on their bank notes, and fears of bankruptcy set off runs on banks around the country, many of which were soon overextended. A brief recovery followed in 1838, stimulated in part by a bad wheat harvest in England, which forced the British to buy American wheat. But by 1839 that stimulus had passed. A bumper cotton crop overloaded the market, and a collapse of cotton prices set off a depression from which the economy did not fully recover until the mid-1840s.

VAN BUREN AND THE NEW PARTY SYSTEM

THE WHIG COALITION   Before the depression set in, however, the Jacksonian Democrats reaped a political bonanza. Jackson had slain the dual monsters of nullification and the bank, and the people loved him for it. The hard times following the contraction of the economy turned Americans against Biddle and the Bank of the United States but not against Jackson, the professed friend of "the people" and foe of the "selfish" interests of financiers and speculators. But in 1834, Jackson's opponents began to pull together a new coalition of diverse elements, united chiefly by their hostility to him. The imperious demeanor of the feisty champion of democracy had given rise to the name King Andrew I. Jackson's followers therefore were Tories, supporters of the "tyrannical" king, and his opponents became Whigs, a name that linked them to the Patriots of the American Revolution.

The diverse coalition making up the Whigs clustered around the National Republican party of John Quincy Adams, Henry Clay, and Daniel Webster. Into the combination came remnants of the Anti-Masonic and Democratic parties, who for one reason or another were alienated by Jackson's stand on the bank or states' rights. Of the forty-one Democrats in Congress who had voted to recharter the bank, twenty-eight had joined the Whigs by 1836. For the next twenty years the Whigs and the Democrats would be the two major political parties.

Whiggery always had about it an atmosphere of social conservatism and superiority. The core Whigs were the supporters of Henry Clay and his economic nationalism. In the South the Whigs enjoyed the support of the urban banking and commercial interests, as well as their planter associates, owners of most of the slaves in the region. In the West, farmers who valued government-funded internal improvements joined the Whig ranks. Most states' rights supporters eventually dropped away, and by the early 1840s the Whigs were becoming more clearly the party of Henry Clay's economic nationalism, even in the South. Unlike the Democrats, who attracted Catholics from Germany and Ireland, Whigs tended to be native-born or British-American evangelical Protestants—Presbyterians, Baptists, and Congregationalists—who were active in promoting social reforms such as abolition and temperance.

THE ELECTION OF 1836 By the presidential election of 1836, a two-party system was emerging from the Jackson and anti-Jackson forces, a system that would remain in even balance for twenty years. In 1835, eighteen months before the election, the Democrats held their second national convention, nominating Jackson's handpicked successor, Vice President Martin Van Buren. The Whig coalition, united chiefly in its opposition to Jackson, held no convention but adopted a strategy of multiple candidacies, hoping to throw the election into the House of Representatives.

The result was a free-for-all reminiscent of 1824, except that this time one candidate stood apart from the rest. It was Van Buren against the field. The Whigs put up three favorite sons: Daniel Webster, named by the Massachusetts legislature; Hugh Lawson White, chosen by anti-Jackson Democrats in the Tennessee legislature; and William Henry Harrison of Indiana, nominated by a predominantly Anti-Masonic convention in Harrisburg, Pennsylvania. In the South the Whigs made heavy inroads on the Democratic vote by arguing that Van Buren would be soft on anti-slavery advocates and that the South could trust only a southerner—that is, Hugh White—as president. In the popular vote, Van Buren outdistanced the entire Whig field, with 765,000 votes to 740,000 for the Whigs, most of which were cast for Harrison. Van Buren won 170 electoral votes; Harrison, 73; White, 26; and Webster, 14.

Martin Van Buren

Van Buren earned the nickname the "Little Magician."

Martin Van Buren, the eighth president, was the first of Dutch ancestry. The son of a tavern keeper in Kinderhook, New York, he had attended a local academy, studied law, and entered politics. Although he kept up a limited legal practice, he had been for most of his adult life a professional politician, so skilled in the arts of organization and manipulation that he came to be known as the Little Magician. In 1824 he supported Crawford, then switched his allegiance to Jackson in 1828 but continued to look to the Old Republicans of Virginia as the southern anchor of his support. Elected governor of New York, he quickly resigned to join Jackson's cabinet and because of the president's favor became vice president.

THE PANIC OF 1837 Van Buren inherited a financial panic. An already precarious economy was tipped over by a depression in England, which resulted in a drop in the price of American cotton and caused English banks and investors to cut back their American commitments and refuse extensions of loans. This was a particularly hard blow because much of America's economic expansion depended upon European—and mainly

Jacksonian Treasury note

A parody of the often-worthless fractional notes issued by banks and businesses in lieu of coins. These notes proliferated during the panic of 1837, with the emergency suspension of gold and silver payments. In the main scene, Martin Van Buren, a monster on a wagon driven by John C. Calhoun, is about to pass through an arch labeled "Wall Street" and "Safety Fund Banks."

English—investment capital. On top of everything else, in 1836 there had been a failure of the wheat crop, the export of which in good years helped offset the drain of payments abroad. As creditors hastened to foreclose, the inflationary spiral went into reverse. States curtailed ambitious plans for roads and canals and in many cases felt impelled to repudiate their debts. In the crunch many of the wildcat state banks succumbed.

The working class, as always, was particularly hard hit during the economic slump and largely had to fend for itself. By the fall of 1837, a third of the workforce was jobless, and those still fortunate enough to have jobs saw their wages cut by 30 to 50 percent within two years. At the same time, prices for food and clothing soared. As the winter of 1837 approached, a journalist reported that in New York City 200,000 people were "in utter and hopeless distress with no means of surviving the winter but those provided by charity." There was no government aid; churches and charitable societies were the major sources of support for the indigent.

Van Buren's advisers and supporters blamed the depression on speculators and bankers, at the same time expecting the evildoers to get what they deserved in a healthy shakeout that would restabilize the economy. Van Buren did not believe that he or the government had any responsibility to rescue hard-pressed farmers or businessmen or to provide relief for the jobless and homeless. He did feel obliged to keep the government itself in a healthy financial situation, however. To that end he called a special session of Congress in 1837, which quickly voted to postpone indefinitely the distribution of the surplus because of a probable upcoming deficit and approved an issue of Treasury notes (currency) to cover immediate expenses.

AN INDEPENDENT TREASURY Van Buren believed that the government should cease risking its deposits in shaky state banks and set up an independent Treasury. Under this plan the government would keep its funds in its own vaults and do business entirely in hard money. The Independent Treasury Act elicited opposition from a combination of Whigs and conservative Democrats who feared deflation. It had taken Van Buren several years of maneuvering to get what he wanted. Calhoun signaled a return to the Democratic fold, after several years of flirting with the Whigs, when he came out for the Treasury act. Van Buren gained western support by backing a more liberal policy regarding federal land sales. Congress finally passed the Independent Treasury Act on July 4, 1840. Although it lasted little more than a year (the Whigs repealed it in 1841), it would be restored in 1846.

The drawn-out struggle over the Treasury was only one of several squabbles that preoccupied politicians during the Van Buren years. A flood of petitions for Congress to abolish slavery and the slave trade in the District of Columbia brought on tumultuous debate, especially in the House of Representatives. Border incidents growing out of a Canadian insurrection in 1837 and a dispute over the Maine boundary kept British-American animosity at a simmer, but General Winfield Scott, the president's ace troubleshooter, managed to keep the hotheads in check along the border. The spreading malaise was rooted in the depressed condition of the economy, which lasted through Van Buren's term. Fairly or not, the administration became the target of growing discontent. The president won renomination easily enough but could not get the Democratic convention to

Uncle Sam's Pet Pups!

A woodcut showing William Henry Harrison luring "Mother Bank," Andrew Jackson, and Martin Van Buren into a barrel of hard cider. While Jackson and Van Buren sought to destroy the Bank of the United States, Harrison promised to reestablish it, hence his providing "Mother Bank" a refuge in this scene.

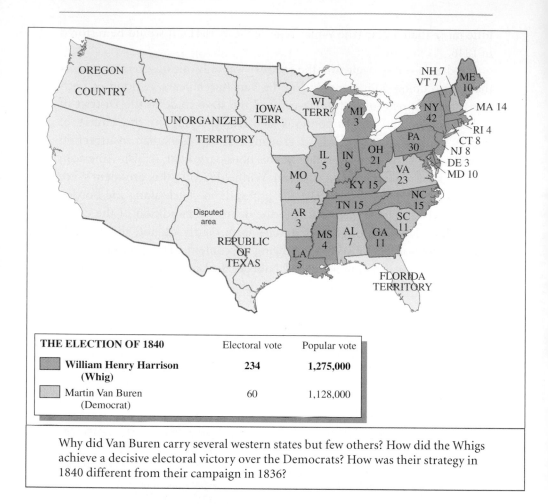

THE ELECTION OF 1840	Electoral vote	Popular vote
■ William Henry Harrison (Whig)	234	1,275,000
□ Martin Van Buren (Democrat)	60	1,128,000

Why did Van Buren carry several western states but few others? How did the Whigs achieve a decisive electoral victory over the Democrats? How was their strategy in 1840 different from their campaign in 1836?

agree on his vice-presidential choice, which was left up to the Democratic electors.

THE "LOG CABIN AND HARD CIDER" CAMPAIGN The Whigs got an early start on their campaign when they met at Harrisburg, Pennsylvania, on December 4, 1839, to choose a candidate. Henry Clay expected 1840 to be his year and had soft-pedaled talk of his economic nationalism in the interest of building broader support. Although Clay led on the first ballot, the convention sought a Whiggish Jackson, as it were, a military hero who could enter the race with few known political convictions or enemies, and the delegates finally turned to the colorless William Henry Harrison.

Harrison's credentials were impressive: victor at the Battle of Tippecanoe against the Shawnees in 1811, former governor of the Indiana Territory, briefly congressman and senator from Ohio, more briefly minister to Colombia. Another advantage of Harrison's was that the Anti-Masons liked him. To rally their states' rights wing, the Whigs chose for vice president John Tyler of Virginia, a close friend of Clay's.

The Whigs had no platform. Taking a stand on issues would have risked dividing a coalition united chiefly by opposition to the Democrats. But they had a catchy slogan, "Tippecanoe and Tyler Too." And they soon had a rousing campaign theme, which a Democratic newspaper unwittingly supplied: the *Baltimore Republican* declared sardonically "that upon condition of his receiving a pension of $2,000 and a barrel of cider, General Harrison would no doubt consent to withdraw his pretensions, and spend his days in a log cabin on the banks of the Ohio." The Whigs seized upon the cider and log cabin symbols to depict Harrison as a simple man sprung from the people. Actually, he sprang from one of the first families of Virginia and lived in a large farmhouse.

The Whig "Log Cabin and Hard Cider" campaign featured portable log cabins rolling through the streets along with barrels of cider. All the devices of hoopla were mobilized: placards, emblems, campaign buttons, floats, effigies, great rallies, and a campaign newspaper, the *Log Cabin*. Building on the example of the Jacksonians' campaign to discredit John Quincy Adams, the Whigs pictured Van Buren, who unlike Harrison really did have humble origins, as an aristocrat living in luxury at "the Palace."

The Whig party had not only learned its lessons well, but it had also improved upon its teachers in the art of campaigning. "Van! Van! Is a Used-Up Man!" went one campaign refrain, and down he went by the thumping margin of 234 votes to 60 in the Electoral College. In the popular vote it was closer: 1,275,000 for Harrison; 1,128,000 for Van Buren.

ASSESSING THE JACKSON YEARS

The Whigs may have won in 1840, but the Jacksonian impulse had permanently altered American politics. People were much more involved in the political process. By 1840 both parties were organized down to the precinct level, and the proportion of white men who voted in the presidential election had tripled, from 27 percent in 1824 to 78 percent in 1840. That much is beyond dispute, but the phenomenon of Jackson, the heroic symbol for an age, continues to spark historical debate.

The earliest historians of the Jackson era belonged largely to an eastern elite nurtured in a "Whiggish" culture, men who could never quite forgive Jackson for instituting the "spoils system," which in their view excluded the fittest from office. A later school of "progressive" historians depicted Jackson as the leader of a vast democratic movement that welled up in the West and mobilized a farmer-labor alliance to sweep the "Monster" national bank into the dustbin of history. Some historians have recently focused on local power struggles, in which the great national debates of the time often seemed empty rhetoric or at most snares to catch the voters. One view of Jackson makes him out to be essentially a frontier opportunist for whom democracy "was good talk with which to win the favor of the people."

Most recently scholars have highlighted the fact that Jacksonian "democracy" was for white males only; it did not apply to African Americans, Indians, or women. These revisionist historians have also stressed that greater participation in politics was much more a northern development than a southern development. As late as 1857, for example, North Carolina's fifty-acre property requirement for voting disenfranchised almost half the state's voters.

Yet there seems little question that whatever else Jackson and his supporters had in mind, they followed an ideal of republican virtue, of returning to the Jeffersonian vision that the federal government would play as limited a role as possible. In the Jacksonian view the alliance of government and business was always an invitation to special favors and an eternal source of corruption. The national bank was the epitome of such evil. The right policy for government, at the national level in particular, was to refrain from granting special privileges and to let free competition in the marketplace regulate the economy.

In the bustling world of the nineteenth century, however, the idea of a return to agrarian simplicity was a futile exercise in nostalgia. Instead, free-enterprise policies opened the way for a host of aspiring entrepreneurs eager to replace the established economic elite with a new order of free-enterprise capitalism. And in fact there was no great conflict in the Jacksonian mentality between the farmer or planter who delved in the soil and the independent speculator and entrepreneur who grew wealthy by other means. Jackson himself was both. What the Jacksonians did not foresee was the degree to which, in a growing country, unrestrained enterprise could lead to new centers of economic power largely independent of government regulation. But history is forever marked by unintended consequences. Here the ultimate irony would be that the laissez-faire rationale for republican simplicity eventually became the justification for the growth of unregulated corporate powers far greater than any ever wielded by Biddle's bank.

CHAPTER SUMMARY

- **Jacksonian Democracy** Jackson's America was very different from the America of 1776. Most white men had gained the vote when states removed property qualifications for voting. The Jacksonians sought to democratize economic opportunity; thus politics changed with the advent of national conventions, at which party leaders chose their party's candidates and platforms. Powerful elites remained in charge of society and politics, however.

- **Jacksonian Policies** Jackson wanted to lower taxes and reduce government spending. He vetoed bills to use federal funds for internal improvements, and his belief that banks were run by corrupt businessmen for their own ends led him to veto a bill for the rechartering of the second Bank of the United States.

- **Nullification Controversy** When a South Carolina convention nullified the Tariffs of 1828 and 1832, Jackson requested that Congress pass a "force bill" authorizing the army to compel compliance with the tariffs. After South Carolina accepted a compromise tariff put forth by Henry Clay, the state convention nullified the force bill. Nullification, an extreme states' rights ideology, had been put into action. The crisis was over, but both sides claimed victory.

- **Indian Removal Act of 1830** The Indian Removal Act of 1830 authorized the relocation of eastern Indians to federal lands west of the Mississippi River. The Cherokees used the federal court system to try to block this relocation, but despite the Marshall court's decision in their favor, federal troops forced them to move; the event and the route they took came to be known as in the Trail of Tears. By 1840 only a few Seminoles and Cherokees remained, hiding in remote areas of the Southeast.

- **Democrats and Whigs** Jackson's arrogant behavior, especially his use of the veto, led many to regard him as "King Andrew." Groups who opposed him coalesced in a new party, known as the Whigs, thus forming the country's second party system. The panic of 1837, during Martin Van Buren's administration, ensured Whig victory in the election of 1840 despite the party's lack of a coherent political program.

CHRONOLOGY

1828	Tariff of abominations goes into effect
1830	Congress passes the Indian Removal Act
	Andrew Jackson vetoes the Maysville Road Bill
1831	Supreme Court issues *Cherokee Nation v. Georgia* decision
1832	Supreme Court issues *Worcester v. Georgia* decision
	South Carolina issues ordinance of nullification
	Andrew Jackson vetoes the Bank Recharter Bill
1833	Congress passes Henry Clay's compromise tariff
1836	Martin Van Buren is elected president
1837	Financial panic follows a drop in the price of cotton
1837–1838	Eastern Indians are forced west on the Trail of Tears
1840	William Henry Harrison, a Whig, is elected president

KEY TERMS & NAMES

Martin Van Buren p. 418

Peggy Eaton p. 419

Webster-Hayne debate p. 422

Tariff of 1832 p. 426

"force bill" p. 427

Osceola p. 429

Trail of Tears p. 429

Nicholas Biddle p. 432

Anti-Masonic party p. 435

"pet banks" p. 436

Whig party p. 445

"spoils system" p. 446

12

THE DYNAMICS
OF GROWTH

FOCUS QUESTIONS   Ⓢ   wwnorton.com/studyspace

- How did the explosive growth of industry, agriculture, and transportation change America?
- What were some inventions that economically and socially improved the country?
- How had immigration changed by the mid nineteenth century?
- Why did early labor unions emerge?

The Jacksonian-era political debate between democratic ideals and elitist traditions was rooted in a profound transformation of American social and economic life. Between 1815 and 1850 the United States became a transcontinental power, expanding all the way to the Pacific coast. An industrial revolution in the Northeast began to reshape the region's economy and propel an unrelenting process of urbanization. In the West, commercial agriculture began to emerge, focused on the surplus production of corn, wheat, and cattle. In the South, cotton became king, and its reign required the expanding institution of slavery. At the same time, innovations in transportation—larger horse-drawn wagons, called Conestogas; canals; steamboats; and railroads—knit together an expanding national market for goods and services. In sum, the eighteenth-century economy based primarily upon small-scale farming and local commerce was maturing rapidly into a far-flung capitalist marketplace entwined with world markets. These economic developments in turn helped expand prosperity and freedom. The dynamic economy generated changes in every other area of life, from politics to the legal system, from the family to social values, from work to recreation.

AGRICULTURE AND THE NATIONAL ECONOMY

The first stage of industrialization brought with it an expansive commercial and urban outlook that supplanted the agrarian philosophy espoused by Thomas Jefferson and many others. "We are greatly, I was about to say fearfully, growing," South Carolina's John C. Calhoun told his congressional colleagues in 1816, and many other statesmen shared his ambivalent outlook. Would the agrarian Republic retain its virtue and cohesion amid the chaotic commercial development? In the brief Era of Good Feelings after the War of 1812, such a troublesome question was easily brushed aside. Economic opportunities seemed abundant, especially in Calhoun's native South Carolina. The reason was cotton, the profitable new cash crop of the South, which spread rapidly from South Carolina and Georgia into the fertile lands of Mississippi, Alabama, Louisiana, and Arkansas.

COTTON Cotton has been used from ancient times, but the Industrial Revolution and its spread of textile mills created a rapidly growing global market for the fluffy fiber. Cotton cloth had remained for many years rare and expensive because of the need for hand labor to separate the lint from tenacious seeds. One person working all day could separate barely one pound by hand. The profitability of cotton depended upon finding a better way to separate the seeds from the fiber.

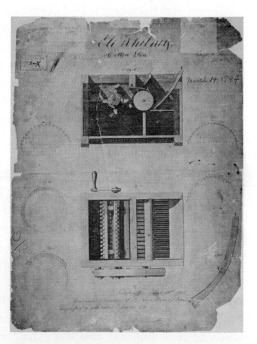

Whitney's cotton gin

Eli Whitney's drawing, which accompanied his 1794 federal patent application, shows the side and top of the machine as well as the sawteeth that separated the seeds from the fiber.

At a plantation called Mulberry Grove in coastal Georgia, the home of Catharine Greene, widow of the Revolutionary War hero Nathanael Greene, discussion often focused on the problem of separating cotton seeds from the cotton fiber. In 1792 young Eli Whitney, recently graduated from Yale, visited Mulberry Grove, where he devised a mechanism for removing the seeds from upland cotton. In the spring of 1793, Whitney's cotton "gin" (short for *engine*) enabled the operator to separate fifty times as much cotton as a worker could separate by hand.

Whitney's invention had unwittingly launched a revolution. Green-seed cotton first engulfed the up-country hills of South Carolina and Georgia and after the War of 1812 migrated into the former Indian lands to the west. Cotton prices and production soared, and in the process planters found a profitable new use for slavery. A lucrative trade in the sale of slaves emerged from the coastal South to the Southwest. The cotton culture became a way of life that tied the Old Southwest to the coastal Southeast in a common interest.

Cotton also became a major export commodity. From the mid-1830s to 1860, cotton accounted for more than half the value of all exports in the nation. The South supplied the North with both raw materials and markets for manufactures. Income from the North's role in handling the cotton trade then provided surpluses for capital investment in new factories and businesses. Cotton thereby became a crucial element of the national economy—and the driving force behind the expansion of slavery.

FARMING THE WEST   The westward flow of planters and their slaves to Alabama and Mississippi during these flush times mirrored another migration through the Ohio River valley and the Great Lakes region, where the Indians had been steadily—and forcibly—pushed westward. By 1860 more than half the nation's population resided in trans-Appalachia, and the restless migrants had long since spilled across the Mississippi River and touched the shores of the Pacific.

North of the expanding cotton belt, the fertile woodland soil, riverside bottomlands, and black loam of the prairies drew farmers from the rocky lands of New England and the exhausted soils of the Southeast. A new national land law of 1820, passed after the panic of 1819, reduced the price of federal land. A settler could get a farm for as little as $100, and over the years the proliferation of state banks made it possible to continue buying land on credit. Even that was not enough for westerners, however, who began a long—and eventually victorious—agitation for further relaxation of the federal land laws. They favored "preemption," the right of squatters to purchase land at the minimum price, and graduation, the progressive reduction of the price of land that did not sell immediately.

Congress eventually responded to the land mania with two bills. Under the Preemption Act of 1830, squatters could stake out claims ahead of the land surveys and later get 160 acres at the minimum price of $1.25 per acre. Under the Graduation Act of 1854, prices of unsold lands were to be lowered in stages over thirty years.

The process of settling new lands followed the old pattern of clearing trees, grubbing out the stumps and underbrush, and settling down at first to a crude subsistence. The development of effective iron plows greatly eased the backbreaking job of tilling the soil. In 1819, Jethro Wood of New York developed an improved iron plow with separate replaceable parts. Further improvements would follow, including John Deere's steel plow (1837) and James Oliver's chilled-iron and steel plow (1855).

Other technological improvements quickened the growth of commercial agriculture. By the 1840s new mechanical seeders had replaced the process of sowing seed by hand. Even more important, twenty-two-year-old Cyrus Hall McCormick of Virginia in 1831 invented a mechanical reaper to harvest

McCormick's Reaping Machine

This illustration appeared in the catalog of the Great Exhibition, held at the Crystal Palace in London in 1851. The plow eased the transformation of rough plains into fertile farmland, and the reaping machine accelerated farm production.

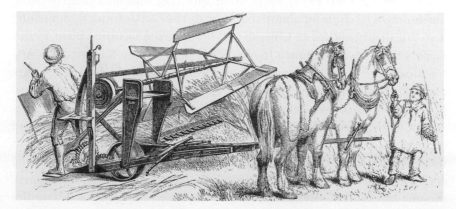

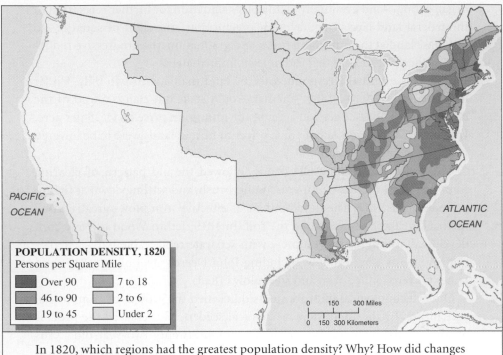

POPULATION DENSITY, 1820
Persons per Square Mile

Over 90
46 to 90
19 to 45
7 to 18
2 to 6
Under 2

In 1820, which regions had the greatest population density? Why? How did changes in the 1820 land law encourage western expansion? What events caused the price of land to decrease between 1800 and 1841?

wheat, a development as significant to the agricultural economy of the West as the cotton gin was to the South. After tinkering with his strange-looking horse-drawn machine for almost a decade, in 1847 McCormick began selling it so fast that he moved to Chicago and built a manufacturing plant for his reapers and mowers. Within a few years he had sold thousands of machines, transforming the scale of agriculture. Using a handheld sickle, a farmer could harvest half an acre of wheat a day; with a McCormick reaper two people could work twelve acres a day.

McCormick's success inspired other manufacturers and inventors, and soon there were mechanical threshers to separate the grains of wheat from the straw. By the 1850s, farming had become a major commercial activity. As the volume of agricultural products soared, prices dropped, income rose, and the standard of living improved for many farm families in the West.

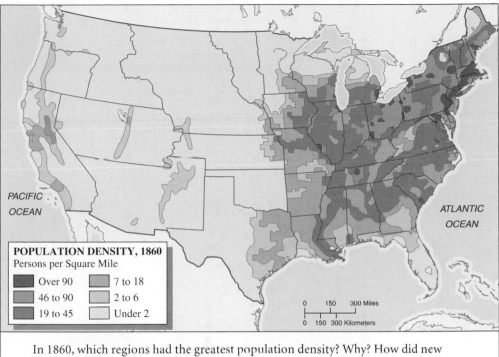

POPULATION DENSITY, 1860
Persons per Square Mile

- Over 90
- 46 to 90
- 19 to 45
- 7 to 18
- 2 to 6
- Under 2

In 1860, which regions had the greatest population density? Why? How did new technologies allow farmers to grow more crops on larger pieces of land?

TRANSPORTATION AND THE MARKET REVOLUTION

NEW ROADS Transportation improvements helped spur the development of a national market. As settlers moved west, people demanded better roads. In 1795 the Wilderness Road, along the trail blazed by Daniel Boone twenty years before, was opened to wagon and stagecoach traffic, thereby easing the route through the Cumberland Gap into Kentucky and along the Walton Road, completed the same year, into Tennessee. Even so, travel remained difficult. Stagecoaches crammed with as many as a dozen people crept along at four miles per hour. South of these roads there were no similar major highways. South Carolinians and Georgians pushed westward on whatever trails or rutted roads had appeared.

To the northeast a movement for graded and paved roads (macadamized with packed-down crushed stones) gathered momentum after completion of the Philadelphia-Lancaster Turnpike in 1794 (the term *turnpike* derives from a pole, or pike, at the tollgate, which was turned to admit the traffic). By 1821 some 4,000 miles of turnpikes had been completed.

TRANSPORTATION WEST, ABOUT 1840

ᴗᴗᴗ Canals ═══ Roads

━━━ Navigable rivers

Why were river towns important commercial centers? What was the impact of the steamboat and the flatboat on travel in the West? How did the Erie Canal transform the economy of New York and the Great Lakes region?

WATER TRANSPORTATION By the early 1820s the turnpike boom was giving way to developments in water transportation: river steamboats, flatboats, and canal barges carried people and commodities far more cheaply than did wagons on the National Road. The first commercially successful steamboat appeared when Robert Fulton and Robert R. Livingston sent the *Clermont* up New York's Hudson River in 1807. Thereafter the use of steamboats spread rapidly to other eastern rivers and to the Ohio and Mississippi,

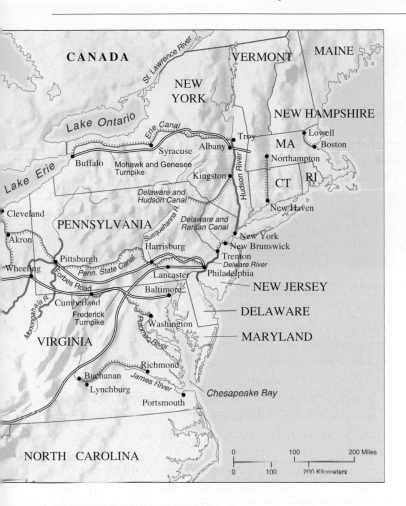

opening nearly half a continent to water traffic. Steamboats transformed inland water transportation. To travel downstream from Pittsburgh to New Orleans on a flatboat took up to six weeks. And because flatboats could not make the return trip upstream, they were chopped up in New Orleans for firewood, and the crews had to make their way back home by other means. In 1815 the first steamboat made the trip upriver from New Orleans to Pittsburgh; it took twenty-five days.

By 1836, 361 steamboats were navigating the western waters, reaching ever farther up the tributaries that fed into the Mississippi River. The durable flatboat, however, still carried to market most of the western wheat, corn, flour, meal, bacon, ham, pork, whiskey, soap and candles (byproducts

Traveling the western waters

Steamboats at the levee at St. Paul, Minnesota, in 1859.

of slaughterhouses), lead from Missouri, copper from Michigan, timber from the Rockies, and ironwork from Pittsburgh. But the steamboat, by bringing two-way traffic to the Mississippi River valley, created a transcontinental market and an agricultural empire that became the nation's new breadbasket. Villages at strategic trading points along the streams evolved into centers of commerce and urban life. The port of New Orleans grew in the 1830s and 1840s to lead all others in exports.

But by then the Erie Canal in New York was drawing eastward much of the midwestern trade that earlier had been forced to make the long journey down the Ohio and Mississippi Rivers to the Gulf of Mexico. This development would have major economic and political consequences, tying together the West and the East while further isolating the Deep South. In 1817 the New York legislature had endorsed Governor DeWitt Clinton's dream (President Jefferson called the idea "madness") of connecting the Hudson River with Lake Erie to the west across New York. Eight years later, in 1825, the Erie Canal, forty feet wide and four feet deep, was open for the entire 363 miles from Albany to Buffalo; branches soon put most of the state within its reach. The Erie Canal brought a "river of gold" to New York City and caused small towns such as Syracuse, Rochester, and Buffalo in New York, as well as Cleveland, Ohio, and Chicago, Illinois, to blossom into major commercial cities.

The Erie Canal was the longest canal in the world. It virtually revolutionized American economic development. It reduced travel time from New York City to Buffalo from twenty days to six, and the cost of moving a ton of

The Erie Canal

Junction of the Northern and Western Canals (1825), an aquatint by John Hill.

freight plummeted from $100 to $5. After 1828 the Delaware and Hudson Canal linked New York to the coalfields of northeastern Pennsylvania. The speedy success of the New York system inspired a mania for canals in other states that lasted more than a decade and spawned about 3,000 miles of waterways by 1837. But no canal ever matched the spectacular success of the Erie, which rendered the entire Great Lakes region an economic tributary to the port of New York City. With the further development of canals spanning Ohio and Indiana from north to south, much of the upper Ohio River valley also came within the economic sphere of New York.

RAILROADS   The financial panic of 1837 and the subsequent depression cooled the canal fever. Meanwhile, a more versatile form of transportation was gaining on the canal: the railroad. In 1825, the year the Erie Canal was completed, the world's first commercial steam railway began operation in England. By the 1820s the American port cities of Baltimore, Charleston, and Boston were alive with schemes to connect the port cities to the hinterlands by rail. Over the next twenty years, railroads grew nearly tenfold, covering 30,626 miles; more than two thirds of that total was built in the 1850s.

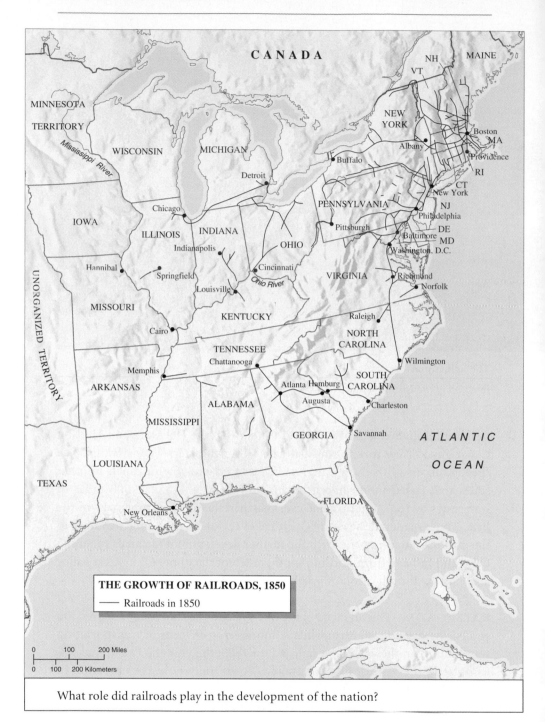

THE GROWTH OF RAILROADS, 1850

—— Railroads in 1850

0   100   200 Miles

0   100   200 Kilometers

What role did railroads play in the development of the nation?

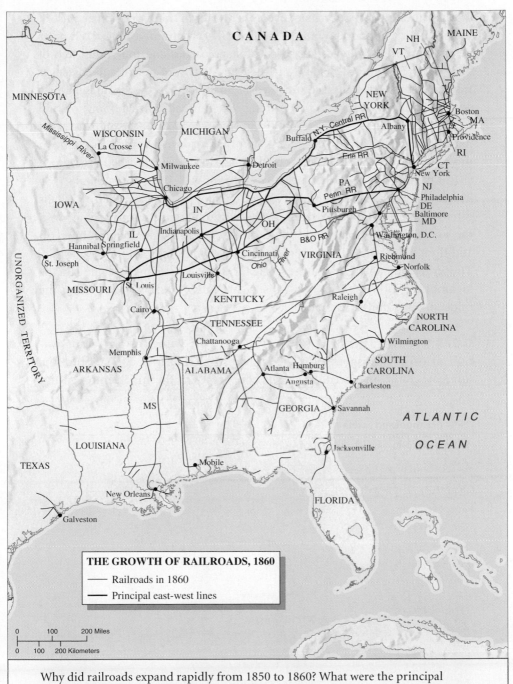

THE GROWTH OF RAILROADS, 1860

— Railroads in 1860
— Principal east-west lines

0   100   200 Miles
0   100   200 Kilometers

Why did railroads expand rapidly from 1850 to 1860? What were the principal east-west lines?

The railroad gained supremacy over other forms of transportation because of its speed, carrying capacity, and reliability. The early trains averaged ten miles per hour, more than twice the speed of stagecoaches and four times that of boats. By 1859, railroads had greatly reduced the cost of freight and passenger transportation. Railroads also provided indirect benefits, by encouraging new settlement and the expansion of farming. The railroads' demand for iron and equipment of various kinds created an enormous market for the industries that made these capital goods. And the ability of railroads to operate year-round in most kinds of weather gave them an advantage in carrying finished goods, too.

But the railroad boom had negative effects as well. By opening up possibilities for quick and shady profits, it helped corrupt political life. Railroad titans often bribed legislators. By opening up access to the trans-Appalachian West, the railroad helped accelerate the decline of Native American culture. In addition, it dramatically quickened the tempo and mobility of everyday life. The writer Nathaniel Hawthorne spoke for many Americans when he said the locomotive, with its unsettling whistle, brought "the noisy world into the midst of our slumberous space."

OCEAN TRANSPORTATION   The year 1845 witnessed a great innovation in ocean transport with the launching of the first clipper ship, the *Rainbow*. Built for speed, the sleek clippers were the nineteenth-century

New oceangoing vessels

Clipper ship in New York Harbor in the 1840s.

equivalent of the supersonic jetliner. They doubled the speed of the older merchant ships. Long and lean, with taller masts and more sails, they cut dashing figures during their brief but colorful career, which lasted less than two decades. What prompted the clipper boom was the lure of Chinese tea, a drink long coveted in America but in scarce supply. Asian tea leaves were a perishable commodity that had to reach the market quickly after harvest, and the new clipper ships made this possible. Even more important, the discovery of California gold in 1848 lured thousands of prospectors and entrepreneurs from the Atlantic seaboard. The massive wave of miners generated an urgent demand for goods, and the clippers met it. In 1854 the *Flying Cloud* took eighty-nine days and eight hours to travel from New York to San Francisco. But clippers, while fast, lacked ample cargo space, and after the Civil War they would give way to the steamship.

THE ROLE OF GOVERNMENT   The dramatic transportation improvements of the antebellum era were financed by both state governments and private investors. After the panic of 1837, however, the states left railroad development mainly to private corporations. Still, several southern and western states built their own lines, and most states granted generous tax concessions to railroad companies.

The federal government helped too, despite ferocious debates over whether direct involvement in internal improvements was constitutional. The national government bought stock in turnpike and canal companies and, after the success of the Erie Canal, extended land grants to several western states for the support of canal projects. Congress provided for railroad surveys by government engineers and reduced the tariff duties on iron used in railroad construction. In 1850, Senator Stephen A. Douglas of Illinois and others prevailed upon Congress to extend a major land grant to support a north-south rail line connecting Chicago and Mobile, Alabama. Regarded at the time as a special case, the 1850 grant set a precedent for other bounties that totaled about 20 million acres by 1860—a small amount compared with the land grants that Congress awarded transcontinental railroads during the 1860s.

A COMMUNICATIONS REVOLUTION

The transportation revolution also helped spark dramatic improvements in communications. At the beginning of the century, it took days— often weeks—for news to travel along the Atlantic seaboard. For example, after George Washington died in 1799 in Virginia, the news of his death did not appear in New York City newspapers until a week later. Naturally, news took even longer to travel to and from Europe. It took forty-nine days for news of the peace treaty ending the War of 1812 to reach New York from Europe.

The speed of communications accelerated greatly as the nineteenth century unfolded. The construction of turnpikes, canals, railroads, and scores of post offices, as well as the development of steamships and the telegraph, generated a communications revolution. By 1830 it was possible to "convey" Andrew Jackson's inaugural address from Washington, D.C., to New York City in sixteen hours. It took six days to reach New Orleans. Mail began to be delivered by "express," a system in which riders could mount fresh horses at a series of relay stations. Still, even with such advances the states and territories west of the Appalachian Mountains struggled to get timely deliveries and news.

AMERICAN TECHNOLOGY   During the nineteenth century, Americans became famous for their "practical" inventiveness. One of the most striking examples of the connection between pure research and innovation was in the work of Joseph Henry, a Princeton physicist. His research in electromagnetism provided the basis for Samuel F. B. Morse's invention of the telegraph and for the invention of electric motors. In 1846, Henry became head of the new Smithsonian Institution, founded in Washington, D.C., with a bequest from the Englishman James Smithson "for the increase and diffusion of knowledge." Two years later, in 1848, the American Association for the Advancement of Science was founded to "advance science and serve society."

Technological advances helped improve living conditions: houses could be larger, better heated, and better illuminated. Although working-class residences had few creature comforts, the affluent were able to afford indoor plumbing, central heating, gas lighting, bathtubs, and iceboxes. Even the lower classes were able to afford new coal-burning cast-iron cooking stoves, which facilitated the preparation of more varied meals, improved heating, and lightened the daily burdens of women. The first sewer systems helped cities begin to rid their streets of human and animal waste, while underground water lines enabled firemen to use hydrants rather than bucket brigades. Machine-made clothes usually fit better and were cheaper than those sewed by hand from homespun cloth; newspapers and magazines were more abundant and affordable, as were clocks and watches.

A spate of inventions in the 1840s generated dramatic changes. In 1844, Charles Goodyear patented a process for "vulcanizing" rubber, which made the product stronger and more elastic. In 1846, Elias Howe patented his design of the sewing machine, soon improved upon by Isaac Merrit Singer. The sewing machine, incidentally, actually slowed the progress of the factory. Since it was adapted to use in the home, enabling women to work for pay from home.

In 1844 the first intercity telegraph message was transmitted, from Baltimore to Washington, D.C., on the device Samuel Morse had invented back in 1832. The telegraph may have triggered more social changes than any other invention. Until it appeared, communications were conveyed by boat, train, or horseback or delivered by hand. With the telegraph, people could learn of events and exchange messages instantaneously.

Taken together, the communications and transportation improvements of the first half of the nineteenth century reshaped the contours of economic, social, and political life. Steamboats, canals, and railroads helped unite the western areas of the country with the East, boost trade, open up the West for settlement, and spark dramatic growth of cities such as Buffalo, Cleveland, and Chicago. Between 1800 and 1860 an undeveloped land dotted with scattered farms, primitive roads, and modest local markets was transformed into an engine of capitalist expansion, audacious investment, urban energy, and global reach.

THE INDUSTRIAL REVOLUTION

While the South and the West developed the agricultural basis for a national economy, the Northeast was initiating an industrial revolution. Technological breakthroughs such as the cotton gin, mechanical harvester, and railroad had quickened agricultural development and to some extent decided its direction. But technology altered the economic landscape even more profoundly, by giving rise to the factory system.

EARLY TEXTILE MANUFACTURES   In the eighteenth century, Great Britain enjoyed a long head start in industrial production. The foundations of Britain's advantage were the invention of the steam engine in 1705, its improvement by James Watt in 1765, and a series of inventions that mechanized the production of textiles. Britain carefully guarded its hard-won secrets, forbidding the export of machines or the publication of descriptions of them, even restricting the emigration of informed mechanics. But the secrets could not be kept. In 1789, Samuel Slater arrived in America from England with the plan of a water-powered spinning machine in his head. He contracted with an enterprising merchant-manufacturer in Rhode Island to build a mill in Pawtucket, and in that little mill, completed in 1790, nine

New England Factory Village (ca. 1830)

Mills and factories gradually transformed the New England landscape in the early nineteenth century.

children turned out a satisfactory cotton yarn, which was then worked up by the putting-out system.

The growth of textile production was slow and faltering until Thomas Jefferson's embargo in 1807 stimulated domestic production. Policies adopted during the War of 1812 further restricted imports and encouraged the merchant capitalists of New England to transfer their resources from shipping to manufacturing. By 1815 textile mills numbered in the hundreds. A flood of British imports after the War of 1812 dealt a temporary setback to the infant American industry. But the foundations of textile manufacture were laid, and they spurred the growth of garment trades and a machine-tool industry that built and serviced the mills.

THE LOWELL SYSTEM   The factory system sprang full-blown upon the American scene at Waltham, Massachusetts, in 1813, in the plant of the Boston Manufacturing Company, formed by the Boston Associates, one of whom was Francis Cabot Lowell. Their plant was the first factory in which the processes of spinning and weaving by power machinery were brought together under one roof, with every process mechanized, from the production of the raw material to that of finished cloth. In 1822 the Boston

Associates developed a new water-powered center at a village along the Merrimack River, which they renamed Lowell.

The founders of the Lowell mills sought to design model factory communities. To avoid the drab, crowded, and wretched life of the English mill villages, they located their mills in the countryside and established an ambitious program of paternal supervision of the workers.

The Lowell factory workers were mostly young women from New England farm families. Employers preferred to hire women because of their dexterity in operating machines and their willingness to work for wages lower than those paid to men. Moreover, by the 1820s there was a surplus of women in the region because so many men had migrated westward in search of cheap land and new economic opportunities. In the early 1820s a steady stream of single women began flocking toward Lowell. To reassure worried parents, the mill owners promised to provide the "Lowell girls" with tolerable work, prepared meals, comfortable boardinghouses, moral discipline, and educational and cultural opportunities.

Merrimack Mills and Boarding-Houses (1848)

One of the textile companies in Lowell, Massachusetts.

Initially the "Lowell idea" worked pretty much according to plan. Visitors commented on the well-designed red-brick mills with their lecture halls and libraries. The "Lowell girls" appeared "healthy and happy." The female workers lived in dormitories staffed by matronly supervisors who enforced mandatory church attendance and curfews. Despite thirteen-hour days and six-day workweeks spent tending the knitting looms, some of the women found the time and energy to form study groups, publish a literary magazine, and attend lectures. But Lowell soon lost its innocence as it experienced mushrooming growth. By 1840 there were thirty-two mills and factories in operation, and the blissful rural town had become an industrial city—bustling, grimy, and bleak.

Other factory centers sprouted up across New England, displacing forests and farms and engulfing villages, filling the air with smoke, noise, and stench. Between 1820 and 1840 the number of Americans engaged in manufacturing increased eightfold, and the number of city dwellers more than doubled. Booming growth transformed the Lowell experiment. By 1846 a concerned worker told young farm women thinking about taking a mill job that "it will be better for you to stay at home on your fathers' farms than to run the risk of being ruined in a manufacturing village."

Mill girls

Massachusetts mill workers of the mid–nineteenth century, photographed holding shuttles. Although mill work initially provided women with an opportunity for independence and education, conditions soon deteriorated as profits took precedence.

During the 1830s, as textile prices and mill wages dropped, relations between workers and managers deteriorated. A new generation of owners and foremen began stressing efficiency and profit margins over community values. They worked employees and machines at a faster pace. In response, the women organized strikes to protest deteriorating conditions. In 1834, for instance, they unsuccessfully "turned out" (went on strike) against the mills after learning of a proposed sharp cut in their wages.

The "Lowell girls" drew attention less because they were typical than because they were special. An increasingly common pattern in industrial New England was the family system, sometimes called the Rhode Island system or the Fall River system, which prevailed in textile companies outside northern New England. The Rhode Island factories, which relied upon waterpower, were often built in unpopulated areas, and the complexes included tenements or mill villages. Whole families might be hired, the men for heavy labor, the women and children for lighter work. Like the Lowell model, the Rhode Island system promoted paternalism. Employers dominated the life of the mill villages. Employees worked from sunup to sunset and longer in winter—a sixty-eight- to seventy-two-hour week. Such hours were common on the farms of the time, but in textile mills the work was more intense and less varied, with no slow season.

INDUSTRIALIZATION AND THE ENVIRONMENT   Between 1820 and 1850 some forty textile and flour mills were built along the Merrimack River, which runs from New Hampshire through northeastern Massachusetts. In pre-industrial England and America the common-law tradition required that water be permitted to flow as it had always flowed; the right to use it was reserved to those who owned land adjoining streams and rivers. In other words, running water, by nature, could not be converted into private property. People living along rivers could divert water for domestic use or to water livestock but could not use naturally flowing water to irrigate land or drive machinery.

The rise of the water-powered textile industry challenged those long-standing assumptions. Entrepreneurs acquired water rights by purchasing land adjoining rivers and buying the acquiescence of nearby landowners; then, in the 1820s, they began renting the water that flowed to the textile mills. Water suddenly became a commodity independent of the land. It was then fully incorporated into the industrial process. Canals, locks, and dams were built to facilitate the needs of the proliferating mills. Flowing water was transformed from a societal resource to a private commodity.

The changing uses of water transformed the region's ecology. Rivers shape regions far beyond their banks, and the changing patterns of streams now affected marshlands, meadows, vegetation, and the game and other wildlife that depended upon those habitats. The dams built to harness water to turn the mill wheels that ground corn and wheat flooded pastures and decimated fish populations, spawned urban growth that in turn polluted the rivers, and aroused intense local resentment, particularly among the New Hampshire residents far upstream of the big Massachusetts textile

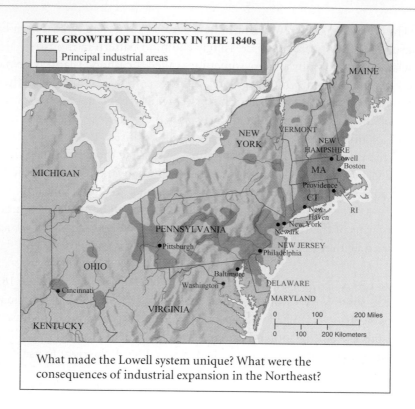

THE GROWTH OF INDUSTRY IN THE 1840s

Principal industrial areas

What made the Lowell system unique? What were the consequences of industrial expansion in the Northeast?

factories. In 1859 angry farmers, loggers, and fishermen tried to destroy a massive dam in Lake Village, New Hampshire. But their axes and crowbars caused little damage. By then the Industrial Revolution could not be stopped. The textile system was not only transforming lives and property; it was re-shaping nature as well.

INDUSTRIALIZATION AND CITIES The rapid growth of commerce and industry spurred the growth of cities. In terms of the census definition of *urban*, as a place with 8,000 inhabitants or more, the proportion of urban to rural populations grew from 3 percent in 1790 to 16 percent in 1860. Because of their strategic locations, the four great Atlantic seaports of New York, Philadelphia, Baltimore, and Boston remained the largest cities. New Orleans became the nation's fifth-largest city from the time of the Louisiana Purchase. Its focus on cotton exports to the neglect of imports eventually caused it to lag behind its northeastern competitors, however. New York outpaced all its competitors and the nation as a whole in its

Milling and the environment

A milldam on the Appomattox River near Petersburg, Virginia, in 1865. Milldams were used to produce a head of water for operating a mill.

population growth. By 1860 it was the first city to reach a population of more than 1 million, largely because of its superior harbor and its unique access to commerce.

Pittsburgh, at the head of the Ohio River, was already a center of iron production by 1800, and Cincinnati, at the mouth of the Little Miami River, soon surpassed all other meatpacking centers. Louisville, because it stood at the falls of the Ohio River, became an important trading center. On the Great Lakes the leading cities—Buffalo, Cleveland, Detroit, Chicago, and Milwaukee—also stood at important breaking points in water transportation. Chicago was well located to become a hub of both water and rail transportation, connecting the Northeast, the South, and the trans-Mississippi West. During the 1830s, St. Louis tripled in size mainly because most of the western fur trade was funneled down the Missouri River. By 1860, St. Louis and Chicago were positioned to challenge Baltimore and Boston for third and fourth places.

Broadway and Canal Street, New York City (1836)

New York's economy and industry, like those of many other cities, grew rapidly in the early nineteenth century.

THE POPULAR CULTURE

During the colonial era, Americans had little time for play or amusement. Most adults worked from dawn to dusk six days a week. In rural areas free time was often spent in communal activities, such as barn raisings and corn-husking parties, shooting matches and footraces, while residents of the seacoast sailed and fished. In colonial cities, people attended balls, went on sleigh rides and picnics, and played "parlor games" at home—billiards, cards, and chess. By the early nineteenth century, however, a more urban society enjoyed more diverse forms of recreation. As more people moved to cities in the first half of the nineteenth century, they created a distinctive urban culture. Laborers and shopkeepers sought new forms of leisure and entertainment as pleasant diversions from their long workdays.

URBAN RECREATION Social drinking was pervasive during the first half of the nineteenth century. In 1829 the secretary of war estimated that three quarters of the nation's laborers drank at least four ounces of "hard liquor" daily. This drinking culture cut across all regions, races, and classes. Taverns and social or sporting clubs in the burgeoning cities served as the nexus of recreation and leisure. So-called blood sports were also a popular form of amusement. Cockfighting and dogfighting at saloons attracted excited crowds and frenzied betting. Prizefighting, also known as boxing, eventually displaced the animal contests. Imported from Britain, boxing proved popular with all social classes. The early contestants tended to be Irish or English immigrants, often sponsored by a neighborhood fire company, fraternal association, or street gang. In the antebellum era, boxers fought with bare knuckles, and the results were brutal. A match ended only when a contestant could not continue. A bout in 1842 lasted 119 rounds and ended when one fighter died in his corner. Such deaths prompted several cities to outlaw the practice, only to see it reappear as an underground activity.

THE PERFORMING ARTS   Theaters were the most popular form of indoor entertainment during the first half of the nineteenth century. People of all classes flocked to opera houses, playhouses, and music halls to watch a wide spectrum of performances: Shakespeare's tragedies, "blood and thunder" melodramas, comedies, minstrel shows, operas, performances by acrobatic troupes, and local pageants. Audiences were predominantly young and middle aged men. "Respectable" women rarely attended; the prevailing "cult of domesticity" kept women in the home. Behavior in antebellum theaters was raucous. Audiences cheered the heroes and heroines and hissed at the

Bare Knuckles

Blood sports emerged as popular urban entertainment for men of all social classes.

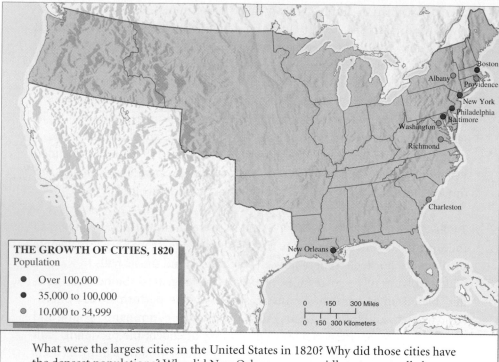

THE GROWTH OF CITIES, 1820
Population

● Over 100,000
● 35,000 to 100,000
● 10,000 to 34,999

What were the largest cities in the United States in 1820? Why did those cities have the densest populations? Why did New Orleans grow rapidly yet eventually lag behind its northeastern counterparts?

villains. If an actor did not meet expectations, spectators hurled curses, nuts, eggs, fruit, shoes, or chairs.

The 1830s witnessed the emergence of the first uniquely American form of mass entertainment: blackface minstrel shows, featuring white performers made up as blacks. "Minstrelsy" drew upon African American subjects and re-inforced prevailing racial stereotypes. It featured banjo and fiddle music, "shuffle" dances, and lowbrow humor. Between the 1830s and the 1870s, minstrel shows were immensely popular, especially among northern working-class ethnic groups and southern whites.

The most popular minstrel songs were written by a young white composer named Stephen Foster. Born near Pittsburgh on July 4, 1826, Foster was a self-taught musician who could pick up any tune by ear. In 1846 he composed "Oh! Susanna," which immediately became a national favorite. Its popularity catapulted Foster into the national limelight, and equally popular tunes followed, such as "Old Folks at Home" (popularly known as "Way Down upon the Swanee River"), "Massa's in de Cold, Cold Ground," "My

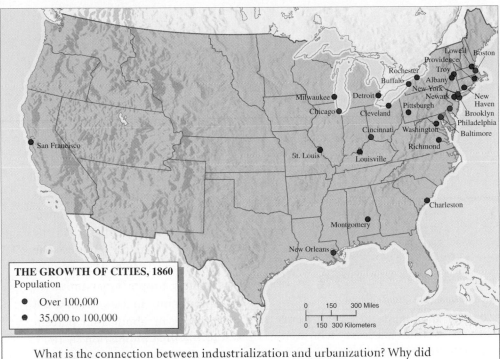

THE GROWTH OF CITIES, 1860
Population

● Over 100,000

● 35,000 to 100,000

0   150   300 Miles

0   150 300 Kilometers

What is the connection between industrialization and urbanization? Why did Chicago, Pittsburgh, Cincinnati, and St. Louis become major urban centers in the mid–nineteenth century?

Old Kentucky Home," and "Old Black Joe," all of which perpetuated the sentimental myth of contented slaves, and none of which used actual African American melodies.

IMMIGRATION

Throughout the nineteenth century, land and jobs in America were plentiful. The United States thus remained a strong magnet for immigrants, offering them chances to take up farming or urban employment. Glowing reports from early arrivals who made good reinforced romantic views of American opportunity and freedom. "Tell Miriam," one immigrant wrote, "there is no sending children to bed without supper, or husbands to work without dinner in their bags." A German immigrant in Missouri applauded America's "absence of overbearing soldiers, haughty clergymen, and inquisitive tax collectors." In 1834 an English immigrant reported that America is

The Crow Quadrilles

This sheet-music cover, printed in 1837, shows eight vignettes caricaturing African Americans. Minstrel shows enjoyed nationwide popularity while reinforcing racial stereotypes.

ideal "for a poor man that is industrious, for he has to want for nothing."

During the forty years from the outbreak of the Revolution to the end of the War of 1812, immigration had slowed to a trickle. The French Revolution and the Napoleonic Wars restricted travel from Europe until 1815. Thereafter, however, the number of immigrants to America rose steadily. After 1845 the tempo picked up rapidly. The years from 1845 to 1854 saw the greatest proportional influx of immigrants in U.S. history, 2.4 million, or about 14.5 percent of the total population in 1845. In 1860, America's population was 31 million, with more than one of every eight residents foreign-born. The three largest groups were the Irish (1.6 million), the Germans (1.2 million), and the British (588,000).

THE IRISH What caused so many Irish to flee their homeland in the nineteenth century was the onset of a prolonged depression that brought immense social hardship. The most densely populated country in Europe, Ireland was so ravaged by its economic collapse that in rural areas the average age at death declined to nineteen. After an epidemic of potato rot in 1845, called the Irish potato famine, killed more than 1 million peasants, the flow of Irish immigrants to Canada and the United States became a flood. Thousands died of dysentery, typhus, and malnutrition during the six-week ocean crossing on what came to be called "coffin ships." In 1847 alone 40,000 Irish perished at sea.

By 1850 the Irish constituted 43 percent of the foreign-born population of the United States. Unlike the German immigrants, who were predominantly male, the Irish newcomers were divided evenly by sex; in fact a slight majority of them were women. Most of the Irish arrivals had been tenant farmers, but their rural sufferings left them with little taste for farmwork and little money with which to buy land in America. Great numbers of the men hired on with the construction crews building canals and railways. Others worked in iron foundries, steel mills, warehouses, mines, and shipyards. Many Irish women found jobs as servants, laundresses, or workers in textile mills in New England. In 1845 the Irish constituted only 8 percent of the workforce in the Lowell mills; by 1860 they made up 50 percent. Relatively few immigrants found their way to the South, where land was expensive and industries scarce. The widespread use of slavery also left few opportunities in the region for immigrant laborers.

Too poor to move inland, most of the destitute Irish immigrants congregated in the eastern cities, in or near their port of entry. By the 1850s the Irish made up over half the population of Boston and New York City and were almost as prominent in Philadelphia. They typically crowded into filthy, poorly ventilated tenements, plagued by high rates of crime, infectious disease, prostitution, alcoholism, and infant mortality. The archbishop of New York at midcentury described the Irish as "the poorest and most wretched population that can be found in the world."

But many enterprising Irish immigrants forged remarkable careers. Twenty years after arriving in New York, Alexander T. Stewart became the owner of the nation's largest department store and thereafter accumulated vast real estate holdings in Manhattan. Michael Cudahy, who began work in a Milwaukee meatpacking business at age fourteen, became head of the Cudahy Packing Company and developed a process for the curing of meats under refrigeration. Dublin-born Victor Herbert emerged as one of

Irish immigration

In 1847 nearly 214,000 Irish immigrated to the United States and Canada aboard the ships of the White Star Line and other companies. Despite promises of spacious, well-lit, well-ventilated, and heated accommodations on ships, 30 percent of these immigrants died on board.

America's most revered composers, and Irish dancers and playwrights came to dominate the stage. Irishmen were equally successful in the boxing arena and on the baseball diamond.

These accomplishments, however, did little to quell the anti-Irish sentiments prevalent in nineteenth-century America. Irish immigrants confronted demeaning stereotypes and intense anti-Catholic prejudices. Protestants remained fearful of a "papist plot" to turn America into a Catholic nation. And ethnic prejudice was widespread. Many employers posted "No Irish Need Apply" signs. But Irish Americans could be equally contemptuous of other groups, such as free African Americans, who competed with them for low-status jobs. In 1850 the *New York Tribune* expressed concern that the Irish, having themselves escaped from "a galling, degrading bondage" in their homeland, voted against proposals for equal rights for blacks and frequently arrived at the polls shouting, "Down with the Nagurs! Let them go back to Africa, where they belong." For their part, many African Americans viewed the Irish with equal disdain. In 1850 a slave expressed a common sentiment: "My Master is a great tyrant, he treats me badly as if I were a common Irishman."

After becoming citizens, the Irish formed powerful voting blocs. Drawn mainly to the party of Andrew Jackson, they set a crucial example of identification with the Democrats, one that other ethnic groups by and large followed. In Jackson the Irish immigrants found a hero. Himself the son of Scots-Irish colonists, he was also popular for having defeated the hated English at New Orleans. In addition, the Irish immigrants' loathing of aristocracy, which they associated with English rule, attracted them to a politician and a party claiming to represent "the common man." Although property requirements initially kept most Irish Americans from voting, a New York State law extended the franchise in 1821, and five years later the state removed the property qualification altogether. In the 1828 election, masses of Irish voters made the difference in the race between Jackson and John Quincy Adams. One newspaper expressed alarm at this new force in politics: "It was emphatically an Irish triumph. The foreigners have carried the day." With African Americans, women, and Native Americans still years from enfranchisement, Irish men became perhaps the first "minority group" to exert a remarkable political influence.

Perhaps the greatest collective achievement of the Irish immigrants was stimulating the growth of the Catholic Church in the United States. Years of persecution had instilled in Irish Catholics a fierce loyalty to the doctrines of the church as "the supreme authority over all the affairs of the world." Such passionate attachment to Catholicism generated both community cohesion among Irish Americans and fears of Roman Catholicism among American Protestants. By 1860, Catholicism had become the largest denomination in the United States.

THE GERMANS   A new wave of German immigration peaked in 1854, just a few years after the crest of Irish arrivals, when 215,000 Germans disembarked in U.S. ports. These immigrants included a large number of learned, cultured professional people—doctors, lawyers, teachers, engineers—some of them refugees from the failed German revolution of 1848. In addition to an array of political opinions, the Germans brought with them a variety of religious preferences. A third of the new arrivals were Catholics, most were Protestants (usually Lutherans), and a significant number were Jews or freethinking atheists or agnostics. By the end of the century, some 250,000 German Jews had emigrated to the United States.

Unlike the Irish, more Germans settled in rural areas than in cities, and the influx included many independent farmers, skilled workers, or shopkeepers who arrived with the means to get themselves established on the land or in skilled jobs. More so than the Irish, they migrated in families and groups rather than individually, and this clannish quality helped them better sustain elements of their language and culture in the New World. More of them also

German Beer Garden, New York (1825)

German immigrants established their own communities, where they maintained the traditions of their homeland.

tended to return to their native country. About 14 percent of the Germans eventually went back to their homeland, compared with 9 percent of the Irish.

Among the German immigrants who prospered in the New World were Ferdinand Schumacher, who began peddling flaked oatmeal in Ohio and whose business eventually became part of the Quaker Oats Company; Heinrich Steinweg, a piano maker who in America changed his name to Steinway and became famous for the quality of his instruments; and Levi Strauss, a Jewish tailor who followed the gold rushers to California and began making durable work pants that were later dubbed blue jeans, or Levi's. Major centers of German settlement developed in southwestern Illinois and Missouri (around St. Louis), Texas (near San Antonio), Ohio, and Wisconsin (especially around Milwaukee). The larger German communities developed traditions of bounteous food, beer, and music, along with German turnvereins (gymnastic societies), sharpshooter clubs, fire-engine companies, and kindergartens.

THE BRITISH, SCANDINAVIANS, AND CHINESE British immigrants continued to arrive in the United States in large numbers during the first half of the nineteenth century. They included professionals, independent farmers, and skilled workers. Two other groups that began to arrive in noticeable numbers during the 1840s and 1850s served as the vanguard for greater numbers of their compatriots. Annual arrivals from Scandinavia did not exceed 1,000 until 1843, but by 1860, 72,600 Scandinavians were living in the United States. The Norwegians and Swedes gravitated to Wisconsin and Minnesota, where the climate and woodlands reminded them of home. By the 1850s the rapid development of California was attracting Chinese, who, like the Irish in the East, did the heavy work of construction. Infinitesimal in number until 1854, the Chinese in America numbered 35,500 by 1860.

NATIVISM Not all Americans welcomed the flood of immigrants. Many "natives" resented the newcomers, with their alien languages and mysterious customs. The flood of Irish and German Catholics aroused Protestant hostility to "popery." A militant Protestantism growing out of the evangelical revivals of the early nineteenth century fueled the anti-Catholic hysteria. There were also fears that German communities were fomenting political radicalism and that the Irish were forming ethnic voting blocs, but above all hovered the "menace" of unfamiliar religious practices. Catholic authoritarianism was widely perceived as a threat to hard-won liberties—religious and political.

A Know-Nothing cartoon

The Catholic Church supposedly attempts to control American religious and political life through Irish immigration.

In 1834 a series of anti-Catholic sermons by Lyman Beecher, a popular Congregationalist minister who served as president of Lane Theological Seminary in Cincinnati, incited a mob to attack and burn the Ursuline Convent in Charlestown, Massachusetts. In 1844 armed clashes between Protestants and Catholics in Philadelphia caused widespread injuries and deaths. Sporadically the nativist spirit took organized form in groups that claimed to prove their patriotism by hating foreigners and Catholics.

As early as 1837, a Native American Association emerged in Washington D.C., but the most significant such group was the Order of the Star-Spangled Banner, founded in New York City in 1849. Within a few years this group had grown into a formidable third party known as the American party, which had the trappings of a secret fraternal order. Members pledged never to vote for any foreign-born or Catholic candidate. When asked about the organization, they were to say, "I know nothing." In popular parlance the American party became the Know-Nothing party. For a season it appeared to be on the brink of achieving major-party status. In state and local campaigns during 1854, the Know-Nothings carried one election after another.

They swept the Massachusetts legislature, winning all but two seats in the lower house. That fall they elected more than forty congressmen. For a while the Know-Nothings threatened to control New England, New York, and Maryland and showed strength elsewhere, but the anti-Catholic movement subsided when slavery became the focal issue of the 1850s.

The Know-Nothings demanded the exclusion of immigrants and Catholics from public office and the extension of the period for naturalization (citizenship) from five to twenty-one years, but the American party never gathered the political strength to enact such legislation. Nor did Congress restrict immigration in any way during that period.

ORGANIZED LABOR

Skilled workers in American cities before and after the Revolution were called artisans, craftsmen, or mechanics. They made or repaired shoes, hats, saddles, ironware, silverware, jewelry, glass, ropes, furniture, tools, weapons, and an array of wooden products, and printers published books, pamphlets, and newspapers. These skilled workers operated within a guild system, a centuries-old economic and social structure developed in medieval Europe to serve the interests of particular crafts.

Like medieval guilds, skilled workers in the United States organized themselves by individual trades. These trade associations pressured politicians for tariffs to protect them from foreign imports, provided insurance benefits, and drafted regulations to improve working conditions, ensure quality control, and provide equitable treatment of apprentices and journeymen. In addition, they sought to control the total number of tradesmen in their profession so as to maintain wage levels. The New York shoemakers, for instance, complained about employers taking on too many apprentices, insisting that "two was as many as one man can do justice by."

The use of slaves as skilled workers also caused controversy among tradesmen. White journeymen in the South objected to competing with enslaved laborers. Other artisans refused to take advantage of slave labor. The Baltimore Carpenters' Society, for example, admitted as members only those employers who refused to use forced labor.

During the 1820s and 1830s, artisans who emphasized quality and craftsmanship for a custom trade found it hard to meet the low prices made possible by the new factories and mass-production workshops. At the time few workers belonged to unions, but a growing fear that they were losing status led artisans in the major cities to become involved in politics and unions.

EARLY UNIONS   Early labor unions faced serious legal obstacles—they were prosecuted as unlawful conspiracies. In 1806, for instance, Philadelphia shoemakers were found guilty of a "combination to raise their wages." The court's decision broke the union. Such precedents were used for many years to hamstring labor organizations, until the Massachusetts Supreme Judicial Court made a landmark ruling in *Commonwealth v. Hunt* (1842). In this case the court declared that forming a trade union was not in itself illegal, nor was a demand that employers hire only members of the union. The court also declared that workers could strike if an employer hired nonunion laborers.

Until the 1820s labor organizations took the form of local trade unions, confined to one city and one craft. From 1827 to 1837, however, organization on a larger scale began to take hold. In 1834 the National Trades' Union was set up to federate the city societies. At the same time, national craft unions were established by the shoemakers, printers, combmakers, carpenters, and handloom weavers, but all the national groups and most of the local ones vanished in the economic collapse of 1837.

LABOR POLITICS   With the widespread removal of property qualifications for voting, working-class politics flourished briefly during the Jacksonian era, especially in Philadelphia. A Workingmen's party, formed there in 1828, gained the balance of power in the city council that fall. This success inspired other Workingmen's parties in about fifteen states. The Workingmen's parties were broad reformist groups devoted to the interests of labor, but they faded quickly. The inexperience of labor politicians left the parties prey to manipulation by political professionals. In addition, some of

The Shoemaker, from *The Book of Trades* (1807)

When Philadelphia boot makers and shoemakers went on strike in 1806, a court found them guilty of a "conspiracy to raise their wages."

their issues were co-opted by the major parties. Labor parties also proved vulnerable to charges of radicalism, and the courts typically sided with management.

Once the labor parties had faded, many of their supporters found their way into a radical wing of the Jacksonian Democrats. This faction acquired the name Locofocos in 1835, when their opponents in New York City's regular Democratic organization, Tammany Hall, turned off the gaslights at one of their meetings and they produced candles, lighting them with the new friction matches known as locofocos. The Locofocos soon faded as a separate group but endured as a radical faction within the Democratic party.

While the working-class parties elected few candidates, they did succeed in drawing notice to their demands, many of which attracted the support of middle-class reformers. Above all they promoted free public education for all children and the abolition of imprisonment for debt, causes that won widespread popular support. The labor parties and unions actively promoted the ten-hour workday to prevent employers from abusing workers. In 1836, President Andrew Jackson established the ten-hour workday at the Naval Shipyard in Philadelphia in response to a strike, and in 1840 President Martin Van Buren extended the limit to all government offices and projects. In private jobs the ten-hour workday became increasingly common, although by no means universal, before 1860. Other reforms put forward by the Workingmen's parties included mechanics' lien laws, to protect workers from nonpayment of wages; limits on the militia system, which allowed the rich to escape military service with fines but forced poor resisters to face jail terms; the abolition of "licensed monopolies," especially banks; measures to ensure payment in hard money and to protect workers from inflated banknote currency; measures to restrict competition from prison labor; and the abolition of child labor.

THE REVIVAL OF UNIONS   After the financial panic of 1837, the infant labor movement declined, and unions did not begin to revive until business conditions improved in the early 1840s. Even then unions remained local and weak. Often they came and went with a single strike. The greatest labor dispute before the Civil War occurred on February 22, 1860, when shoemakers at Lynn and Natick, Massachusetts, walked out after their requests for higher wages were denied. Before the strike ended, it had spread through New England, involving perhaps twenty-five towns and 20,000 workers. The strike stood out not just for its size but also because the workers won. Most of the employers agreed to wage increases, and some also agreed to recognize the union as a bargaining agent.

By the mid–nineteenth century the labor union movement was maturing. Workers began to emphasize the importance of union recognition and regular collective-bargaining agreements. They also shared a growing sense of solidarity. In 1852 the National Typographical Union revived the effort to organize skilled crafts on a national scale. Others followed, and by 1860 about twenty such organizations had appeared, although none was yet strong enough to do much more than hold national conventions and pass resolutions.

Symbols of organized labor

A pocket watch with an International Typographical Union insignia.

THE RISE OF THE PROFESSIONS

The dramatic social changes of the first half of the nineteenth century opened up an array of new professions. Bustling new towns required new services—retail stores, printing shops, post offices, newspapers, schools, banks, law firms, medical practices, and others—that created more high-status jobs than had ever existed before. By definition, professional workers are those who have specialized knowledge and skills that ordinary people lack. To be a professional in Jacksonian America, to be a self-governing individual exercising trained judgment in an open society, was the epitome of the democratic ideal, an ideal that rewarded hard work, ambition, and merit.

The rise of various professions resulted from the rapid expansion of new communities, public schools, and institutions of higher learning; the emergence of a national market economy; and the growing sophistication of American life and society, which was fostered by new technologies. In the process, expertise garnered special prestige. In 1849, Henry Day delivered a lecture titled "The Professions" at the Western Reserve School of Medicine. He declared that the most important social functions in modern life were the professional skills. In fact, Day claimed, American society had become utterly dependent upon "professional services."

TEACHING   Teaching was one of the fastest-growing vocations in the antebellum period. Public schools initially preferred men as teachers, usually hiring them at age seventeen or eighteen. The pay was so low that few stayed in the profession their entire career, but for many educated, restless young adults, teaching was a convenient first job that offered independence and stature, as well as an alternative to the rural isolation of farming. Church groups and civic leaders started private academies, or seminaries, for girls. Initially viewed as finishing schools for young women, these institutions soon added courses in the liberal arts: philosophy, music, literature, Latin, and Greek.

LAW, MEDICINE, AND ENGINEERING   Teaching was a common stepping-stone for men who became lawyers. In the decades after the Revolution, young men, often hastily or superficially trained, swelled the ranks of

Medical training

This nineteenth-century surgical amphitheater allowed students to observe operations from seats surrounding the operating table.

the legal profession. They typically would teach for a year or two before clerking for a veteran attorney, who would train them in the law in exchange for their labors. The absence of formal standards for legal training helps explain why there were so many attorneys in the antebellum period. In 1820 eleven of the twenty-three states required no specific length or type of study for aspiring lawyers.

Like attorneys, physicians in the early nineteenth century often had little formal academic training. Healers of every stripe and motivation assumed the title of *doctor* and established a medical practice without regulation. Most of them were self-taught or had learned their profession by assisting a doctor for several years, occasionally supplementing such internships with a few classes at the handful of new medical schools, which in 1817 graduated only 225 students. That same year there were almost 10,000 physicians in the nation. By 1860 there were 60,000 self-styled physicians, and quackery was abundant. As a result, the medical profession lost its social stature and the public's confidence.

The industrial expansion of the United States during the first half of the nineteenth century spurred the profession of engineering, a field that has since become the single largest professional occupation for men in the United States. Specialized expertise was required for the building of canals and railroads, the development of machine tools and steam engines, and the construction of roads and bridges. Beginning in the 1820s, Americans gained access to technical knowledge in mechanics' institutes, scientific libraries, and special schools that sprouted up across the young nation. By the outbreak of the Civil War, engineering had become one of the largest professions in the nation.

WOMEN'S WORK   Women during the first half of the nineteenth century still worked primarily in the home. The prevailing assumption was that women by nature were most suited to marriage, motherhood, and domesticity. The only professions readily available to women were nursing (often midwifery, the delivery of babies) and teaching, both of which were extensions of the domestic roles of health care and child care. Teaching and nursing commanded relatively lower status and pay than did the male-dominated professions.

Many middle-class and affluent women spent their time outside the home engaged in religious and benevolent work. They were unstinting volunteers in churches and reform societies. A very few women, however, courageously pursued careers in male-dominated professions. Harriet Hunt of Boston was a teacher who, after nursing her sister through a serious illness, set up shop in 1835 as a self-taught physician and persisted in medical practice although she was twice rejected for admission by the Harvard Medical School. Elizabeth Blackwell of Ohio managed to gain admission to the Geneva Medical College of Western New York despite the disapproval of the faculty. When she arrived at her first class, "a hush fell upon the class as if each member had been struck with paralysis." Blackwell had the last laugh when she finished first in her class in 1849, but thereafter the medical school refused to admit any more women. Blackwell went on to found the New York Infirmary for Women and Children and later had a long career as a professor of gynecology at the London School of Medicine for Women.

JACKSONIAN INEQUALITY

During the years before the Civil War, the American legend of young men rising from rags to riches was a durable myth. Speaking to the Senate in 1832, Kentucky's Henry Clay claimed that almost all the successful factory owners he knew were "enterprising self-made men, who have whatever wealth they possess by patient and diligent labor." The legend had just enough basis in fact to gain credence. John Jacob Astor, the wealthiest man in America (worth more than $20 million at his death in 1848), came of humble if not exactly destitute origins. The son of a minor official in Germany, he arrived in the United States in 1784 with little or nothing and made a fortune on the western fur trade, which he then parlayed into a much larger fortune in New York real estate. But his and similar cases were more exceptional than common.

While men of moderate means could sometimes turn an inheritance into a fortune by good management and prudent speculation, those who started out poor and uneducated seldom made it to the top. In 1828 the top 1 percent of New York's families (worth $34,000 or more) held 40 percent of the wealth, and the top 4 percent held 76 percent. Similar circumstances prevailed in Philadelphia, Boston, and other cities.

A supreme irony of the times was that the age of the so-called common man, the age of Jacksonian democracy, seems actually to have been an age of growing economic and social inequality. Why that happened is difficult to say, except that the boundless wealth of the untapped frontier narrowed as the land was taken up and claims on various entrepreneurial opportunities were staked out. Such developments had taken place in New England towns even before the end of the seventeenth century. But despite growing social distinctions, it seems likely that the white population of America, at least, was better off than the general run of Europeans. New frontiers, both geographic and technological, raised the level of material well-being for all. And religious as well as political freedoms continued to attract people eager for, liberty in a new land.

CHAPTER SUMMARY

- **Transportation and Communication Revolutions** While the cotton culture booms in the South, with a resultant increase in slavery, commercial agriculture emerged in the West, aided by a demand for corn, wheat, and cattle and by many inventions. The first stages of the Industrial Revolution in the Northeast reshaped the region's economy and led to the explosive growth of cities and factories. The Erie Canal contributed to New York City's status as the nation's economic center and spurred the growth of Chicago and other midwestern cities. The revolution in transportation and communication linked rural communities to a worldwide marketplace.

- **Inventions and the Economy** Inventions in agriculture included the cotton gin, which increased cotton production in the South. Other inventions, such as John Deere's steel plow and Cyrus McCormick's mechanized reaper, helped Americans, especially westerners, farm their land more efficiently and more profitably. Canals and other improvements in transportation allowed goods to reach markets quicker and more cheaply than ever before. The railroads, which expanded rapidly during the 1850s, and the telegraph diminished the isolation of the West and united the country economically and socially.

- **Immigration** The promise of cheap land and good wages drew millions of immigrants to America. Those who arrived in the 1840s came not just from the Protestant regions of Britain and Europe that had supplied most of America's previous immigrants. The devastating potato famine led to an influx of destitute Irish Catholic families. Also, Chinese laborers were drawn to California's goldfields, where nativists objected to their presence because of their poverty and their religion.

- **Workers Organize** The first unions, formed by artisans who feared a loss of status in the face of mechanization, were local and based on individual crafts. An early attempt at a national union collapsed with the panic of 1837. Unions faced serious legal obstacles even after a Massachusetts court ruled in 1842 that the formation of unions was legal. Weak national unions had reappeared by 1860.

CHRONOLOGY

1793	Eli Whitney invents the cotton gin
1794	Philadelphia-Lancaster Turnpike is completed
1795	Wilderness Road opens
1807	*Clermont*, the first successful steamboat, sails to Albany
1825	Erie Canal opens
1831	Cyrus McCormick invents a mechanical reaper
1834	National Trades' Union is organized
1837	John Deere invents the steel plow
1842	Massachusetts Supreme Judicial Court issues *Commonwealth v. Hunt* decision
1845	*Rainbow*, the first clipper ship, is launched
1846	Elias Howe invents the sewing machine
1848	California gold rush begins

KEY TERMS & NAMES

Conestoga wagons p. 450

Eli Whitney p. 452

Cyrus Hall McCormick
p. 454

Erie Canal p. 458

Samuel F. B. Morse p. 464

Lowell system p. 466

"cult of domesticity" p. 473

"minstrelsy" p. 474

Irish potato famine
p. 476

"coffin ships" p. 476

Levi Strauss p. 480

nativism p. 480

Know-Nothing party
p. 481

13

AN AMERICAN RENAISSANCE: RELIGION, ROMANTICISM, AND REFORM

FOCUS QUESTIONS   Ⓢ wwnorton.com/studyspace

- What were the main changes in the practice of religion in America during the early nineteenth century?
- Which religious sects flourished during this time?
- What were the distinguishing characteristics of American literature during the antebellum period?
- What were the goals of the social-reform movement?
- What was the status of women during this period?

The American novelist Nathaniel Hawthorne once lamented the difficulty of writing "about a country where there is no shadow, no antiquity, no mystery, no picturesque and gloomy wrong." Unlike nations of the Old World, which had long been steeped in history and romance, the United States in the nineteenth century was an infant republic swaddled in the rational ideas of the Enlightenment. Those ideas, most vividly set forth in Thomas Jefferson's Declaration of Independence, would influence religion, literature, and various social-reform movements during the first half of the nineteenth century.

RATIONAL RELIGION

After the Revolution many Americans assumed that the United States had a mission to provide the world with a shining example of republican virtue, much as Puritan New England had once stood before erring humanity as an example of an ideal Christian community. The concept of America's having a special mission still carried strong spiritual overtones, for the religious fervor that quickened in the Great Awakening had reinforced the idea of the nation's fulfilling a providential purpose. This idea infused the national character with an element of perfectionism—and an element of impatience when reality fell short of expectations. The combination of widespread religious energy and fervent social idealism brought major reforms and advances in human rights during the first half of the nineteenth century. It also brought disappointments that at times triggered cynicism and alienation.

DEISM The currents of the rational Enlightenment and the spiritual Great Awakening, now mingling, now parting, flowed on into the nineteenth century and in different ways eroded the remnants of Calvinist orthodoxy. As time passed, the puritanical image of a just but stern God promising predestined hellfire and damnation gave way to a more optimistic religious outlook. Enlightenment rationalism stressed humankind's inherent goodness rather than its depravity and encouraged a belief in social progress and the promise of individual perfectibility.

Many leaders of the Revolutionary War era, such as Thomas Jefferson and Benjamin Franklin, were Deists. After the American Revolution, and especially during the 1790s, when the French Revolution generated excited attention in the United States, interest in Deism increased. In every major city "deistical societies" were formed, and college students especially took delight in criticizing conventional religion. By the use of reason, Deists believed, people might grasp the natural laws governing the universe. Deists rejected the belief that every statement in the Bible is literally true. They were skeptical of miracles and questioned the divinity of Jesus. Deists also defended free speech and opposed religious coercion of all sorts.

UNITARIANISM AND UNIVERSALISM Orthodox Christians could hardly distinguish Deism from atheism, but Enlightenment rationalism soon began to make deep inroads into American Protestantism. The old Puritan churches around Boston proved most vulnerable. Boston's progress—or, some would say, its degeneration—from Puritanism to prosperity had persuaded many affluent families that they were anything but sinners in the hands of an angry God. By the end of the eighteenth century, many well-educated New Englanders were embracing Unitarianism, a belief that emphasizes the oneness and benevolence of a loving God, the inherent goodness of humankind, and the primacy of reason and conscience over established creeds and confessions. Unitarians believe that Jesus was a saintly man but he was not divine. People are not inherently depraved, Unitarians stress; they are capable of doing tremendous good, and *all* are eligible for salvation. Boston was the center of the Unitarian movement, and it flourished chiefly within Congregational churches. During the early nineteenth century more and more "liberal" churches adopted the name *Unitarian.*

William Ellery Channing of Boston's Federal Street Congregational Church emerged as the most inspiring Unitarian leader. "I am surer that my rational nature is from God," he said, "than that any book is an expression of his will." The American Unitarian Association in 1826 had 125 churches (all but a handful of them in Massachusetts). That same year, when the Presbyterian minister Lyman Beecher moved to Boston, he deplored the inroads that had been made by the new rationalist faith: "All the literary men of Massachusetts were Unitarian; all the trustees and professors of Harvard College were Unitarian; all the elite of wealth and fashion crowded Unitarian churches."

A parallel anti-Calvinist movement, Universalism, attracted a different—and much larger—social group: working-class people of a humbler status. In 1779, John Murray, a British ex-Methodist clergyman, founded the first Universalist church, in Gloucester, Massachusetts. Universalism stresses the salvation of all people, not just a predestined few. God, it teaches, is too merciful to condemn anyone to eternal punishment. "Thus, the Unitarians and Universalists were in fundamental agreement," wrote one historian of religion, "the Universalists holding that God was too good to damn man; the Unitarians insisting that man was too good to be damned." Although both sects remained relatively small, they exercised a powerful influence over intellectual life, especially in New England.

THE SECOND GREAT AWAKENING

By the end of the eighteenth century, Enlightenment secularism had made deep inroads into American thought. Yet for all the impact of rationalism among the intellectual elite, most Americans remained a profoundly religious people, as they have been ever since. There was, the perceptive French visitor Alexis de Tocqueville observed, "no country in the world where the Christian religion retains a greater influence over the souls of men than in America."

After the Revolution, American religious life witnessed a profound transformation. The established denominations gave way to newer, more democratic sects. Anglicanism was affected the most. It suffered the stigma of being aligned with the Church of England, and it lost its status as the official religion in most states. To diminish their pro-British image, Virginia Anglicans renamed themselves Episcopalians. But even the new name did not prevent the denomination from losing its traditional leadership position in the South.

John Wesley

Wesley's gravestone reads, "Lord let me not live to be useless."

At the same time that Anglicanism was losing stature and support, a new denomination—Methodism—was experiencing dramatic growth. In 1784, Methodists met in Baltimore and announced that they were abandoning Anglicanism and forming a distinct new denomination committed to the aggressive conversion of all people: men, women, Indians, and African Americans. The restless, energetic reform-minded Methodists, inspired by their founder, the English Anglican priest John Wesley, abandoned the gloomy predestination of Calvinism in favor of a life of unceasing "cheerful activism." Methodists abandoned the Anglican prayer book, loved singing hymns, welcomed the working poor and the oppressed, and emphasized the possibility of Christian perfection in their earthly lives.

Around 1800, fears that secularism was taking root among many well-educated Americans sparked a counterattack in the form of an intense series of revivals that soon grew into the Second Great Awakening. An early revivalist leader, Timothy Dwight, became president of Yale College in 1795 and resolved to purify a campus that had turned into "a hotbed of infidelity." Like his grandfather Jonathan Edwards, Dwight helped launch a series of revivals that captivated Yale students and spread to all of New England. Over the next forty years the flames of revivalism crisscrossed the United States. By the time those flames died down, the landscape of American religious life had been turned topsy-turvy. The once-dominant Congregational and Anglican churches were displaced by newer sects, such as the Baptists and the Methodists. By the mid–nineteenth century, there would be more Methodist churches by far than those of any other denomination. The percentage of Americans who joined Protestant churches increased sixfold between 1800 and 1860.

The Second Great Awakening involved two very different centers of activity. One emerged among the elite New England colleges, especially Yale, and then spread west across New York into Pennsylvania and Ohio, Indiana and Illinois. The other center of revivalism coalesced in the backwoods of Tennessee and Kentucky and spread across rural America. What both forms of Protestant revivalism shared was a simple message: salvation is available not just to a select few but to anyone who repents and embraces Christ.

FRONTIER REVIVALS   In its frontier phase the Second Great Awakening, like the first, generated great excitement and dramatic behavior. It gave birth, moreover, to two religious phenomena—the backwoods circuit-riding preacher and the camp meeting—that helped keep the fires of revivalism burning in the backwoods. Evangelists found ready audiences among lonely frontier folk hungry for spiritual intensity and a sense of community. Revivals were often unifying events; they bridged many social, economic, political, and even racial divisions. Women especially flocked to the rural revivals and sustained religious life on the frontier. In the backwoods and in small rural hamlets, the traveling revival was as welcome an event as the traveling circus—and as entertaining.

Among the established sects, Presbyterianism was entrenched among the Scotch-Irish, from Pennsylvania to Georgia. Presbyterians gained further from the Plan of Union, worked out in 1801 with the Congregationalists of Connecticut and later with Congregationalists of other states. Since the Presbyterians and the Congregationalists agreed on doctrine and differed mainly on the form of church government they adopted, they were able to form unified congregations and call a minister from either church. The result through much of the Old Northwest was that New Englanders became Presbyterians by way of the "Presbygational" churches.

The Baptists, often unschooled, embraced a simplicity of doctrine and organization that appealed especially to rural people. Their theology was grounded in the infallibility of the Bible and the recognition of humankind's innate depravity. But they replaced the Calvinist notion of predestination and selective salvation with the concepts of free will and universal redemption and highlighted the ritual of adult baptism. They also stressed the equality of all before God, regardless of wealth, social standing, or education. Since each congregation was its own highest authority, a frontier church had no denominational hierarchy to report to.

The Methodists, who shared with the Baptists an emphasis on salvation by free will, established a much more centralized church structure. They also developed the most effective evangelical method of all: the minister on horseback, who sought out rural converts in the most remote areas with the message of salvation as a gift free for the taking. The "circuit rider" system began with Francis Asbury, a tireless British-born revivalist who scoured the trans-Appalachian frontier for lost souls, traversing fifteen states and preaching thousands of sermons. Asbury established a mobile evangelism perfectly suited to the frontier environment and the new democratic age. After Asbury, Peter Cartwright emerged as the most successful circuit rider and grew justly famous for his highly charged sermons. Cartwright roamed across Kentucky, Tennessee, Ohio, and Indiana, preaching a sermon a day for over twenty years. His message was simple: salvation is free for all to embrace. By the 1840s the Methodists had grown into the largest Protestant church in the country.

African Americans were especially attracted to the new Methodist and Baptist churches. Richard Allen, who would later help found the African Methodist Episcopal (AME) Church, said in 1787 that "there was no religious sect or denomination that would suit the capacity of the colored people as well as the Methodist." He decided that the "plain and simple gospel suits best for any people; for the unlearned can understand [it]." But even more important, the Methodists actively recruited blacks. They were "the first people," Allen noted, "that brought glad tidings to the colored people." The Baptists did as well. Like the Methodists, they offered a gospel of salvation open to all, regardless of wealth, social standing, gender, or race. As free as well as enslaved African Americans joined white Baptist or Methodist churches, they infused the congregations with exuberant energy and emotional music.

During the early nineteenth century the energies of the Great Revival, as the Second Great Awakening was called, spread through the West and into more settled regions back East. Camp meetings were typically held in late summer or fall, when farmwork slackened. People came from far and wide, camping in wagons, tents, or crude shacks. African Americans, whether enslaved or free, were allowed to set up their own adjacent camp revivals. The largest camp meetings tended to be ecumenical affairs, with Baptist, Methodist, and Presbyterian ministers working as a team. The crowds often numbered in the thousands, and the unrestrained atmosphere made for chaos. If a particular hymn or sermon excited participants, they would shout, dance, or repeat the phrase. Mass excitement swept up even the most skeptical onlookers, and infusions of the spirit moved participants to strange and often hysterical manifestations. Some went into trances; others contracted the "jerks," laughed "the holy laugh," babbled in unknown tongues, or got down on all fours and barked like dogs to "tree the devil," as a hound might tree a raccoon.

But dwelling on the bizarre aspects of the camp meetings distorts an activity that offered a redemptive social outlet to isolated rural folk. This was especially true for women, for whom the camp meetings provided an alternative to the rigors and loneliness of farm life. Women, in fact, played the predominant role, as they had in earlier revivals. Evangelical ministers repeatedly applauded the spiritual energies of women and affirmed their right to give witness to their faith in public. Camp meetings provided opportunities for women to participate as equals in large public rituals. In addition, the various organizational needs of large revivals offered numerous opportunities for women to exercise leadership roles outside the home, including service as traveling evangelists themselves. Phoebe Worrall Palmer, for example, hosted revival meetings in her New York City home, then traveled across the United States as a camp meeting evangelist. Such opportunities to assume traditional male roles bolstered women's self-confidence and expanded their horizons beyond the domestic sphere. Their religious enthusiasm often inspired them to work on behalf of various social-reform efforts, including expanded educational opportunities for women and the right to vote. So in many ways and on many levels, the energies of the revivals helped spread a more democratic faith among people living on the frontier. The evangelical impulse also led

Religious revival

An aquatint of a backwoods Methodist camp meeting in 1819.

to an array of interdenominational initiatives intended to ensure that new converts sustained their faith. Various denominations, for example, joined forces to create the American Bible Society and the American Sunday School Union. The Bible Society gave free Bibles to new converts, and the Sunday School Union provided weekly educational instruction, including basic literacy, even in backwoods communities.

CHARLES FINNEY AND THE BURNED-OVER DISTRICT Regions swept by revival fevers were compared to forests devastated by fire. Western New York, in fact, experienced such intense levels of evangelical activity that it was labeled the burned-over district. The most successful evangelist in the burned-over district was an energetic former lawyer named Charles Grandison Finney (1792–1875). In the winter of 1830–1831, he preached for six months in upstate New York and helped generate 100,000 conversions. Finney wrestled with a question that had plagued Protestantism for centuries: what role can the individual play in earning salvation? Orthodox Calvinists had long argued that people could neither earn nor choose salvation of their own accord. Grace was a gift of God to a select few, a predetermined decision incapable of human understanding or control. In contrast, Finney insisted that the only thing preventing conversion was the individual. And what most often discouraged the individual from choosing to be "saved" was the terrifying loneliness of the decision. So Finney transformed revivals into well-organized popular spectacles: collective conversion experiences in which spectacular public events displaced private communion. At his marathon revivals, often lasting for hours, Finney would call people forward to the "anxious bench," a front pew where they struggled to confess their sins and seek conversion and forgiveness, assisted by friends and neighbors helping to "pray them through" the intense experience.

Finney compared his theatrical methods with those of politicians who used advertising and showmanship to attract attention. He carried the methods of the frontier revival to the cities and factories of the East and as far as Great Britain. His gospel combined faith and good works: revival led to efforts at social reform. By embracing Christ, a convert could thereafter be free of sin, but Christians also had an obligation to improve the larger society. Finney therefore helped found an array of groups designed to reform various social ills: alcoholism, prostitution, war, and slavery. The revivals thus provided one of the most powerful motives for the reform impulse that characterized the age. Lyman Beecher, one of the towering champions of revivalism, stressed that the Second Great Awakening was not focused simply on promoting individual conversions; it was also intended to "reform human society."

In 1835, Finney accepted the professorship of theology at the newly established Oberlin College, founded by pious New Englanders in northern Ohio's Western Reserve. Later he served as its president. From the start, Oberlin College radiated a spirit of reform predicated on faith; it was the first college in America to admit women and blacks, and it was a hotbed of anti-slavery agitation.

THE MORMONS   The burned-over district crackled with spiritual fervor and gave rise to several religious movements, the most important of which was the Church of Jesus Christ of Latter-day Saints, or the Mormons. Its founder, Joseph Smith, was the barely literate child of wandering Vermont farmers who finally settled in the village of Palmyra in western New York. In 1820 young Smith, then fourteen, declared that he had seen God and Christ, both of whom had forgiven his sins and announced that all religious denominations were false. Three and a half years later, in 1823, Smith, who had become a relentless seeker of buried treasure and an ardent believer in folk magic and the occult, reported that an angel named Moroni had visited him. Moroni was supposedly the son of the prophet Mormon and the last survivor of the Nephites, descendants of ancient Hebrews who had traveled to America 2,000 years before Columbus and had been visited by Jesus after his crucifixion and resurrection. According to Smith, Moroni led him to a hillside near his father's farm, where he unearthed golden tablets on which was etched the Book of Mormon, supposedly a lost "gospel" of the Bible buried some 1,400 years earlier.

On the same September day for each of the next three years, Smith went back to the hill and talked with the angel, who let him view the thin golden plates each time, but it was not until 1827 that Moroni allowed Smith to take them home. There, over the course of a year, Smith used supernatural "seer" stones to decipher the strange hieroglyphic language etched into the plates. (Smith said that Moroni thereafter retrieved the plates, and they have never been seen again.) The resulting 588-page Book of Mormon, published in 1830, includes large portions of the King James Bible but claims that a new prophet will visit the Americas to herald the millennium, during which the human race will be redeemed and the Native American "Lamanites," whose dark skin betray their sinfulness, will be rendered "white and delightsome" people again.

With the remarkable Book of Mormon as his gospel, the charismatic Smith set about forming his own church. He dismissed all Christian denominations as frauds, denied that there was a hell, opposed slavery, and promised that the Second Coming was imminent. Within a few years, Smith, whom the Mormons simply called Joseph, had gathered thousands of devout converts, most of them poor New England farmers who, like Smiths' family, had migrated to western New York. These religious seekers, many of them cut off from organized communities and traditional social relationships, found in Mormonism the promise of a pure kingdom of Christ in America. Mormons rejected the notion of original sin staining the human race in favor of an optimistic creed stressing human goodness.

A new Christianity

The Mormon temple in Nauvoo, Illinois, ca. 1840.

From the outset the Mormon "saints" upset their "gentile" neighbors and the political authorities with their close-knit sense of community, their eerily secret rituals, their assurance of righteousness, and their refusal to abide by local laws and conventions. Joseph Smith denied the legitimacy of civil governments and the federal Constitution. As a result, no community wanted to host him and his "peculiar people." In their search for a refuge from persecution and for the "promised land," the ever-growing contingent of Mormons moved from western New York to Ohio, then to Missouri, and finally, in 1839, to the half-built Mississippi River town of Commerce, Illinois, which they renamed Nauvoo. Within a few years, Nauvoo had become a bustling, well-planned community of 12,000 centered on an impressive neoclassical temple overlooking the river. In the process of developing Nauvoo, Joseph Smith, "the Prophet," became the community's leading entrepreneur and political czar: he owned the hotel and general store, served as mayor and as lieutenant general of the city's militia (the Nauvoo Legion), and was the trustee of the church. Smith's lust for power grew as well. He began excommunicating dissidents and announced his intention to become president of the United States.

Smith also excited outrage by practicing "plural marriage," whereby he accumulated two dozen wives and encouraged other Mormon leaders to do the same. In 1844 a crisis arose when Mormon dissidents, including Smith's first wife, Emma, denounced his polygamy. The upshot was not only a schism in the church but also an attack on Nauvoo by non-Mormons from the neighboring counties. When Smith ordered Mormons to destroy an opposition newspaper, he and his brother Hyrum were arrested and charged with treason. On June 27, 1844, an anti-Mormon mob of masked men stormed the feebly defended Nauvoo jail and killed Joseph and Hyrum Smith.

In Brigham Young (1801–1877), the remarkable successor to Joseph Smith, the Mormons found a stern new leader who was strong-minded, intelligent, and authoritarian (and husband to twelve wives). A Vermont carpenter and an early convert to Mormonism, Young succeeded Smith and promised Illinois officials that the Mormons would leave the state. Their new destination was 1,300 miles away, near the Great Salt Lake in Utah, a vast, sparsely populated area owned by Mexico. In early 1846, in wagons and on foot, 12,000 Mormon migrants started their grueling trek to the "promised land" of Utah. The first to arrive at Salt Lake, in July 1847, found only "a broad and barren plain hemmed in by the mountains . . . the paradise of the lizard, the cricket and the rattlesnake." By the end of 1848, however, the Mormons had developed an efficient irrigation system, and over the next decade they brought about a spectacular greening of the desert. At first they organized their own state, named Deseret (meaning "Land of the Honeybee," according to Young), but their independence was short-lived. In 1848, having been defeated by U.S. troops, Mexico signed the Treaty of Guadalupe Hidalgo, ceding to the United States what is now California, Nevada, Utah, Texas, and parts of Arizona, New Mexico, Colorado, and Wyoming. Two years later, Congress incorporated the Utah Territory, including the Mormons' Salt Lake settlement, into the United States. Nevertheless, with Brigham Young named the territorial governor, the new arrangement afforded the Mormons virtual independence. For over twenty

Brigham Young

Young was the president of the Mormons for thirty years.

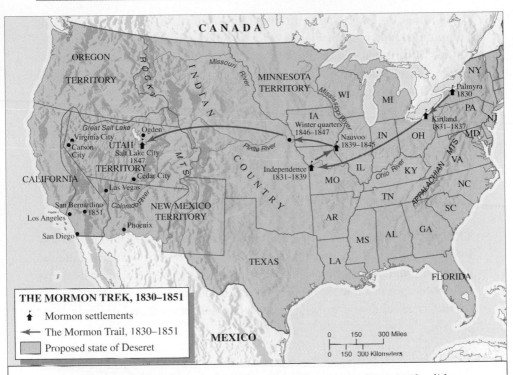

THE MORMON TREK, 1830–1851

🛆 Mormon settlements

◄— The Mormon Trail, 1830–1851

▢ Proposed state of Deseret

Where were Mormon settlements established between 1830 and 1851? Why did Joseph Smith initially lead his congregation west? Why was the Utah Territory an ideal place for the Mormons to settle at least initially?

years, Young successfully defied federal authority. By 1869 some 80,000 Mormons had settled in Utah, and they had developed an aggressive program to convert the 20,000 Indians in the territory.

ROMANTICISM IN AMERICA

The revival of emotional piety and the founding of new religions during the early 1800s represented a widespread tendency throughout the United States and Europe to accentuate the stirrings of the spirit and the heart rather than the dry logic of reason. Another great victory of heart over head was the Romantic movement in thought, literature, and the arts. By the 1780s a revolt was brewing in Europe against the well-ordered world of scientific rationalism. Were there not, after all, more things in this world than reason and logic could box up and explain: moods, impressions, and feelings; mysterious, unknown, and half-seen things? Americans also took readily to the Romantics' emphasis on individualism, idealizing now the virtues of common people, now the idea of original or creative genius in the artist, the author, or the great personality.

The German philosopher Immanuel Kant gave the transatlantic Romantic movement a summary definition in the title of his *Critique of Pure Reason* (1781), an influential book that emphasized the limits of science and reason in explaining the universe. People have innate conceptions of conscience and beauty, the Romantics believed, and religious impulses too strong to be dismissed as illusions. In areas in which science could neither prove nor disprove concepts, people were justified in having faith. The impact of such ideas elevated intuitive knowledge at the expense of rational knowledge.

TRANSCENDENTALISM   The most intense proponents of such Romantic ideals were the transcendentalists of New England, America's first cohesive group of public intellectuals. The transcendental movement drew its name from its emphasis on those things that transcend (or rise above) the limits of reason. Transcendentalism, said one of its apostles, meant an interest in areas

Kaaterskill Falls, 1825

Thomas Cole's painting captures the Romantic ideals that swept America in the wake of the Enlightenment.

"a little beyond" the scope of reason. If transcendentalism drew much of its inspiration from Immanuel Kant, it was also a reaction against Calvinist orthodoxy and the "corpse-cold" rationalism of Unitarianism. It had a close affinity with the Quaker doctrine of the inner light. The inner light, a gift from God's grace, was transformed by transcendentalists into intuition, a faculty of the mind. In both cases, adherents believed that everyone contains a spark of divinity. Transcendentalism during the 1830s became the most influential intellectual and spiritual force in American culture.

An element of mysticism had always lurked in Puritanism, even if viewed as a heresy—Anne Hutchinson, for instance, had been banished from the Massachusetts Bay Colony for claiming direct revelations from God. The reassertion of mysticism had something in common, too, with the meditative religions of Asia, a continent with which New England now had a flourishing trade. Transcendentalists steeped themselves in the teachings of the Buddha, the Sufis of Islam, the Upanishads, and the Bhagavad Gita.

In 1836 an informal discussion group known as the Transcendental Club began to meet in Boston and Concord, Massachusetts, to discuss philosophy, literature, and religion. It was a loosely knit association of diverse individualists who shared a rejection of traditional conventions and a relentless intellectual curiosity. Some were focused on individual freedom while others stressed collective efforts to reform society. They were united by their differences. The transcendentalists called themselves the "club of the like-minded," quipped a Boston preacher, "because no two . . . thought alike." A woman who participated in the discussions more tartly noted that the transcendentalists "dove into the infinite, soared into the illimitable, and never paid cash." They asserted the right of individuals to interpret life in their own way. The club included liberal clergymen and militant reformers such as Theodore Parker, George Ripley, and James Freeman Clarke; writers such as Henry David Thoreau, Bronson Alcott, Nathaniel Hawthorne, and Orestes Brownson; and learned women such as Elizabeth Peabody and her sister Sophia (who married Hawthorne in 1842) and Margaret Fuller. Fuller edited the group's quarterly review, the *Dial* (1840–1844), for two years before the duty fell to Ralph Waldo Emerson, soon to become the acknowledged high priest of transcendentalism.

RALPH WALDO EMERSON More than any other person, Emerson embodied and championed the transcendentalist gospel. Sprung from a line of New England ministers, he set out to be a Unitarian parson but quit the "cold and cheerless" denomination before he was thirty. After traveling in

Ralph Waldo Emerson

Emerson is most remembered for leading the transcendentalist movement.

Europe, where he met England's greatest Romantic writers, Emerson settled in Concord to take up the life of an essayist, poet, and popular speaker on the lecture circuit, preaching the sacredness of Nature, the good news of optimism, self-reliance, and the individual's unlimited potential. Having found pure reason "cold as a cucumber," he was determined to *transcend* the limitations of inherited conventions and rationalism in order to penetrate the inner recesses of the self.

The spirit of freedom in Emerson's lectures and writings, often stated in maddeningly vague language, expressed the core of the transcendentalist worldview. His notable address "The American Scholar," delivered at Harvard in 1837, urged young Americans to put aside their awe of European culture and explore their own new world. It was "our intellectual Declaration of Independence," said one observer.

Emerson's essay on "Self-Reliance" (1841) has a timeless appeal to youth, with its message of individualism and independence. Like most of Emerson's writings, it is crammed with pungent quotations:

> Whoso would be a man, must be a nonconformist. . . . Nothing is at last sacred but the integrity of your own mind. . . . It is easy in the world to live after the world's opinion; it is easy in solitude to live after our own; but the great man is he who in the midst of a crowd keeps with perfect sweetness the independence of solitude. . . . A foolish consistency is the hobgoblin of little minds, adored by little statesmen and philosophers and divines. . . . Speak what you think now in hard words and tomorrow speak what tomorrow thinks in hard words again, though it contradict everything you said today. . . . To be great is to be misunderstood.

HENRY DAVID THOREAU Emerson's young friend and Concord neighbor Henry David Thoreau practiced the reflective self-reliance that Emerson preached. "I like people who can do things," Emerson stressed, and

Thoreau, fourteen years his junior, could do many things well: carpentry, masonry, painting, surveying, sailing, gardening. The philosophical son of a man who was a pencil maker and a woman who was a domineering abolitionist, Thoreau displayed a sense of uncompromising integrity, outdoor vigor, and prickly individuality that Emerson found captivating. "If a man does not keep pace with his companions," Thoreau wrote, "perhaps it is because he hears a different drummer."

Thoreau himself marched to a different drummer all his life. After Harvard, where he exhausted the resources of the library in gargantuan bouts of reading, and after a brief stint as a teacher, during which he got in trouble for refusing to cane his students, Thoreau settled down to eke out a living by making pencils with his father. But he made frequent escapes to drink in the beauties of nature. Thoreau revered Nature as a living Bible. He showed no interest in the contemporary scramble for wealth, for it too often corrupted the pursuit of happiness. "The mass of men," he wrote, "lead lives of quiet desperation."

Determined to practice plain living and high thinking, Thoreau boarded with the Emersons for a time and then embarked upon an experiment in self-reliance. On July 4, 1845, he took to the woods to live in a cabin he had built on Emerson's land beside Walden Pond. Thoreau wanted to free himself from the complexities and hypocrisies of conventional life so as to devote his time to observation, reflection, and writing. His purpose was not to lead a hermit's life. He frequently walked the mile or so to Concord to dine with his friends and often welcomed guests at his cabin. "I went to the woods because I wished to live deliberately," he wrote in *Walden, or Life in the Woods* (1854), ". . . and not, when I came to die, discover that I had not lived."

While Thoreau was at Walden Pond, the Mexican War erupted. Seeing the conflict as an unjust war to advance the cause of slavery, he refused to pay his poll tax as a gesture of opposition, for which he was put in jail (for only one night; an aunt paid the tax). The incident was so trivial as to be almost comic, but out of it grew the classic essay "Civil Disobedience"

Henry David Thoreau
Thoreau was a lifelong abolitionist.

(1849), which would influence the passive-resistance movements of Mahatma Gandhi in India and Martin Luther King Jr. in the American South. "If the law is of such a nature that it requires you to be an agent of injustice to another," Thoreau wrote, "then, I say, break the law."

The broadening ripples of influence more than a century after Thoreau's death show the impact that a contemplative person can have on the world of action. Thoreau and the other transcendentalists taught a powerful lesson: people must follow their conscience. Promoters of transcendentalism portrayed the movement as a profound expression of moral idealism; critics dismissed it as an outrageous expression of egotism. Though the transcendentalists attracted only a small following in their own time, they inspired reform movements and were the quickening force for a generation of writers that produced the first great age of American literature.

The Flowering of American Literature

The half decade of 1850 to 1855 witnessed an outpouring of extraordinary literature. It saw the publication of *Representative Men* by Emerson, *Walden* by Thoreau, *The Scarlet Letter* and *The House of the Seven Gables* by Nathaniel Hawthorne, *Moby-Dick* by Herman Melville, and *Leaves of Grass* by Walt Whitman. As a noted literary critic wrote, "You might search all the rest of American literature without being able to collect a group of books equal to these in imaginative quality." The flowering of New England literature featured, too, a foursome of poets who shaped the American imagination in a day when poetry was popular among the public: Henry Wadsworth Longfellow, John Greenleaf Whittier, Oliver Wendell Holmes Sr., and James Russell Lowell.

LITERARY GIANTS Nathaniel Hawthorne, the supreme writer of the New England group, never shared the sunny optimism of his neighbors or their perfectionist belief in reform. A sometime resident of Concord, Massachusetts, but a native and longtime inhabitant of Salem, he was haunted by the knowledge of evil bequeathed to him by his Puritan forebears, one of whom (John Hathorne) had been a judge at the Salem witchcraft trials. After college he worked in obscurity in Salem, gradually began to sell a few stories, and finally earned a degree of fame with his collection of *Twice-Told Tales* (1837). In these, as in most of his later work, he presented powerful moral allegories. His central themes examined sin and its consequences: pride and selfishness, secret guilt, and the impossibility of rooting sin out of the human soul.

Emily Dickinson, the most strikingly original and elusive of the New England poets, remained a slim, white-gowned recluse in her second-story bedroom in Amherst, Massachusetts. She found solace in writing poetry that few people read during her lifetime. As she once prophetically wrote, "Success is counted sweetest / By those who ne'er succeed." Only a few of her almost 1,800 poems were published (anonymously) before her death, in 1886. Born in Amherst in 1830, she received a first-rate secondary education and attended the new Mount Holyoke Female Seminary. Neither she nor her sister married, and they lived

Emily Dickinson

Dickinson offered the world of New England literature a fresh female voice.

out their lives in their parents' home. Like the transcendentalists, Dickinson cherished and protected her individualism. As she told a friend, "There is always one thing to be grateful for—that one is one's self & not somebody else." Perhaps it was Dickinson's severe eye trouble during the 1860s that induced her solitary withdrawal from the larger society; perhaps it was the aching despair generated by her unrequited love for a married minister. Whatever the reason, her intense isolation and lifelong religious doubts led her to probe her own shifting psychological state. Her often abstract themes were elemental: life, death, fear, loneliness, nature, and above all, God, a "Force illegible," a "distant, stately lover."

Edgar Allan Poe, born in Boston but reared in Virginia, was a master of gothic horror and the inventor of the detective story. He delighted in evoking terror and nursing suspense. He judged prose by its ability to provoke emotional tension, and since he considered fear to be the most powerful emotion, he focused his efforts on making the grotesque and the supernatural seem disturbingly real to his readers. Anyone who has read "The Tell-Tale Heart" or "The Pit and the Pendulum" can testify to his success.

Herman Melville was a New Yorker who went to sea as a youth. After eighteen months aboard a whaler, he arrived in the Marquesas Islands, in the South Seas, and jumped ship with a companion. He spent several weeks with a friendly tribe in "the valley of the Typees" before signing on with an Australian whaler. He joined a mutiny in Tahiti and finally returned home as a seaman aboard a U.S. Navy frigate. An embroidered account of his exotic

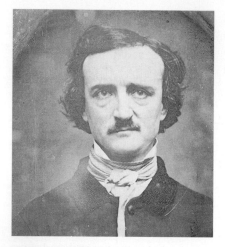

Edgar Allan Poe

Poe has had immense influence on poets and prose writers in America and abroad.

adventures, *Typee* (1846), became an instant popular success, which he repeated in *Omoo* (1847), based on his stay in Tahiti.

In 1851, Melville produced one of the world's greatest novels. In *Moby-Dick*, the story of Captain Ahab's obsessive quest for the white whale that devoured his leg, Melville explored the darker recesses of the soul. The book was aimed at two audiences. On one level it is a ripping good yarn of adventure on the high seas. But on another level it explores profound philosophical and psychological realms: Ahab's single-minded mission to slay the evildoer turns the captain into a monster of destruction who sacrifices his ship, his crew, and himself to his folly, leaving as the one survivor the narrator of the story. Yet neither the public nor the critics at the time accepted the novel on either level. Melville's career wound down into futility. He supported himself for years with a job in the New York Customhouse and turned to poetry, much of which, especially the Civil War *Battle-Pieces* (1866), won acclaim in later years.

The most provocative writer during the antebellum period was Walt Whitman, a vibrant personality who disdained inherited conventions and artistic traditions. There was something elemental in Whitman's overflowing character, something bountiful and generous and compelling—even his faults and inconsistencies were ample. Born on a Long Island farm, he moved with his family to Brooklyn and from the age of twelve worked mainly as a handyman and journalist, frequently taking the ferry across the harbor to bustling Manhattan. The city fascinated him, and he gorged himself on the urban spectacle: shipyards, crowds, factories, shop windows. From such material he drew his editorial opinions and poetic inspiration, but he remained relatively obscure until the first edition of *Leaves of Grass* (1855) caught the eye and aroused the ire of readers. Emerson found it "the most extraordinary piece of wit and wisdom that America has yet contributed," but more conventional critics shuddered at Whitman's explicit sexual references and groused at his indifference to rhyme and meter as well

The Perilous Situation of Whalemen (ca. 1861)

A harpooned whale breaks the surface of the water, as described by Herman Melville in *Moby-Dick*.

as his buoyant egotism. The jaunty Whitman was a startling figure, with his frank sexuality and homoerotic overtones. He also stood out from the pack of his fellow writers in rejecting the idea that a woman's proper sphere is in a supportive and dependent role. Thoreau described Whitman as "the greatest democrat the world has seen."

NEWSPAPERS   The flowering of American literature during the first half of the nineteenth century coincided with a massive expansion in newspaper readership. Technology had sparked a reading revolution. The steam-driven Napier press, introduced from England in 1825, could print 4,000 sheets of newsprint in an hour. Richard Hoe of New York improved upon it, inventing in 1847 the rotary press, which printed 20,000 sheets an hour. The availability of daily newspapers costing only a penny each transformed daily reading into a form of popular entertainment. Newspaper circulation skyrocketed. The "penny dailies," explained one editor, "are to be found in every street, lane, and alley; in every hotel, tavern, countinghouse, [and] shop."

Politics in an Oyster House (1848) by Richard Caton Woodville

Newspapers often fueled public discussions and debates.

The United States had more newspapers than any other nation in the world. It needed them to forge a network of communications across the expanding republic. As readership soared, the content of the papers expanded beyond political news and commentary to include society gossip, sports, and reports of sensational crimes and accidents. The proliferation of newspapers was largely a northern and western phenomenon. Literacy rates in the South lagged behind those of the rest of the country. Before any state had even been formed in the Northwest Territory, for example, the region boasted thirteen newspapers while North Carolina had only four.

EDUCATION

A literate and well-informed citizenry equipped with knowledge not only for obtaining a vocation but also for promoting self-government and self-culture was one of the animating ideals of the Founding Fathers. Literacy in Jacksonian America was surprisingly widespread. In 1840, according to census data, some 78 percent of the total population and 91 percent of the white population could read and write. Ever since the colonial period, in fact, Americans had had the highest literacy rate in the Western world. Most children were taught to read in church or in private "dame" schools, by formal tutors, or by their families. By 1830 no state had a school system in the modern sense, although for nearly two centuries Massachusetts had required towns to maintain schools.

EARLY PUBLIC SCHOOLS   In the 1830s the demand for public schools peaked. Workers wanted free schools to give their children an equal chance to pursue the American dream. In 1830 the Workingmen's party of Philadelphia called for "a system of education that shall embrace equally all the children of the state, of every rank and condition." Education, it was

Greek class at the Western Reserve Eclectic Institute at Hiram, Ohio, 1853

At front right are the young James A. Garfield and his future wife, Lucretia Randolph.

argued, would improve manners and at the same time reduce crime and poverty.

Horace Mann of Massachusetts led the early drive for statewide school systems. Trained as a lawyer, he sponsored the creation of a state board of education, then served as its leader. Mann went on to sponsor many reforms in Massachusetts, including the first state-supported "normal school" for the training of teachers, a state association of teachers, and a minimum school year of six months. He repeatedly promoted the public-school system as the way to achieve social stability and equal opportunity.

In the South, North Carolina led the way in state-supported education. By 1860, North Carolina had enrolled more than two thirds of its white school-age population for an average term of four months, kept so low because of the rural state's need for children to do farmwork. But the educational pattern in the South continued to reflect the aristocratic pretensions of the region: the South had a higher percentage of college students than any other region but a lower percentage of public-school students. And the South had some 500,000 white illiterates, more than half the total number in the young nation.

For all the effort to establish state-supported schools, conditions for public education were seldom ideal. Funds were insufficient for buildings, books, and equipment; teachers were poorly paid and often poorly pre-pared. Most students going beyond the elementary grades attended private academies, often subsidized by church and public funds. Such schools, begun in colonial days, multiplied until in 1850 there were more than 6,000 of them. In 1821 the Boston English High School opened as the first free public secondary school, set up mainly for students not going on to college. By a law of 1827, Massachusetts required a high school in every town of 500; in towns of 4,000 or more, the school had to offer Latin, Greek, rhetoric, and other college-preparatory courses. Public high schools became well estab-lished only after the Civil War. In 1860 there were barely 300 in the whole country.

HIGHER EDUCATION   The post-Revolutionary proliferation of col-leges continued after 1800 with the spread of small church-supported schools and state universities. The nine colleges founded in the colonial period sur-vived, but not many of the fifty that had sprung up between 1776 and 1800 lasted. Of the seventy-eight colleges and universities in 1840, thirty-five had been founded after 1830, almost all affiliated with a religious denomination. A post-Revolutionary movement for state-supported universities flourished in those southern states that had had no colonial university. Federal policy abetted the spread of universities in the West. When Congress granted state-hood to Ohio in 1803, it set aside two townships for the support of a state university and kept up that policy in other new states.

The coexistence of state and religious colleges led to conflicts over fund-ing and curriculum, however. Beset by the need for funds, as colleges usually were, denominational schools often competed with tax-supported schools. Regarding curricula, many of the denominational colleges emphasized the-ology at the expense of science and the humanities. On the other hand, America's development required broader access to education and programs geared to vocations. The University of Virginia, "Mr. Jefferson's University," founded in 1819, introduced a curriculum modeled on Jefferson's view that education ought to combine pure knowledge with "all the branches of sci-ence useful to us, and at this day." The model influenced the other new state universities of the South and those of the West.

Technical education grew slowly. The U.S. Military Academy at West Point, founded in 1802, and the U.S. Naval Academy at Annapolis, opened in 1845, trained a limited number of engineers. More young men learned technical skills through practical experience with railroad and canal companies and by apprenticeship to experienced technologists. The president of Brown Univer-sity remarked that there were no colleges to provide "the agriculturalist, the manufacturer, the mechanic, and the merchant with any kind of professional preparation."

Elementary education for girls met with general acceptance, but training beyond that level did not. Most people viewed higher education as unsuited to a woman's destiny in life. Some did argue that education would produce better wives and mothers, but few were ready to demand equality on principle. Progress began with the academies, some of which taught boys and girls alike. Good "female seminaries," like those founded by Emma Willard at Troy, New York (1821), and by Mary Lyon at South Hadley, Massachusetts (1837), grew into colleges. The curricula in female seminaries usually differed from the courses in men's schools, giving more attention to the social amenities and such "embellishments" as music and art. Vassar, opened at Poughkeepsie, New York, in 1861, is usually credited with being the first women's college to give priority to academic standards. In general, the West gave the greatest impetus to coeducation, with state universities in the lead. But once admitted, female students remained in a subordinate status. At Oberlin College in Ohio, for instance, they were expected to clean male

The George Barrell Emerson School, Boston, ca. 1850

Although higher education for women initially met with some resistance, seminaries like this one, started in the 1820s and 1830s, taught women mathematics, physics, and history, as well as music, art, and the social graces.

students' rooms and were not allowed to speak in class or recite at graduation exercises. Coeducation did not mean equality.

Antebellum Reform

The United States in the antebellum period was awash in reform movements. The urge to eradicate evil had its roots in the widespread sense of spiritual zeal and moral mission, which in turn drew upon the growing faith in human perfectibility promoted by both revivalists and Romantic idealists. Reformers tackled such issues as observance of the Sabbath, dueling, crime and punishment, the hours and conditions of work, poverty, vice, care of the disabled, pacifism, foreign missions, temperance, women's rights, and the abolition of slavery.

While an impulse to "perfect" people and society helped excite the reform movements of the Jacksonian era, social and economic changes helped supply the reformers themselves, most of whom were women. The rise of an urban middle class offered affluent women greater time to devote to societal concerns. Prosperity enabled them to hire cooks and maids, often Irish immigrants, who in turn freed them from the performance of household chores. Many affluent women joined churches and charitable organizations, most of which were led by men. Some reformers proposed legislative remedies for social ills; others stressed personal conversion or private philanthropy. Whatever the method or approach, earnest social reformers mobilized in great numbers during the second quarter of the nineteenth century.

TEMPERANCE   The temperance crusade was perhaps the most widespread of all. The census of 1810 reported some 14,000 distilleries producing 25 million gallons of alcoholic spirits each year. William Cobbett, an English reformer who traveled in the United States, noted in 1819 that one could "go into hardly any man's house without being asked to drink wine or spirits, even *in the morning.*"

The temperance movement rested on a number of arguments. Foremost was the religious concern that "soldiers of the cross" should lead blameless lives. The bad effects of distilled beverages on body and mind were noted by the respected physician Benjamin Rush as early as 1784. The dynamic new economy, with factories and railroads moving on strict schedules, made tippling by the labor force a far more dangerous habit than it had been in a simpler time. Humanitarians also emphasized the relationship between drinking and poverty. Much of the movement's propaganda focused on the sufferings of innocent mothers and children. "Drink," said a pamphlet from the Sons of Temperance, "is the prolific source (directly or indirectly) of nearly all the ills that afflict the human family."

In 1826 a group of ministers in Boston organized the American Society for the Promotion of Temperance, which worked through lectures, press campaigns, an essay contest, and the formation of local and state societies. A favorite device was to ask each person who took the pledge to put by his or her signature a T for "total abstinence." With that a new word entered the language: *teetotaler*.

In 1833 the society called a national convention in Philadelphia, where the American Temperance Union was formed. Like

The temperance crusade

A temperance banner, ca. 1850, depicts a young man being tempted by a woman offering him a glass of wine.

nearly every reform movement of the day, temperance had a wing of absolutists. They would brook no compromise with Demon Rum and carried the day with a resolution that liquor traffic was morally wrong and ought to be prohibited by law. The Temperance Union, at its spring convention in 1836, called for abstinence from all alcoholic beverages, a costly victory in that it caused moderates to abstain from the temperance movement instead.

PRISONS AND ASYLUMS The Romantic era's liberal belief that people are innately good and capable of improvement brought about major changes in the treatment of prisoners, the disabled, and dependent children. Public institutions arose that were dedicated to the treatment and cure of social ills. Earlier these had been "places of last resort," the historian David Rothman has written. Now they "became places of first resort, the preferred solution to the problems of poverty, crime, delinquency, and insanity." If removed from society, the theory went, the needy and the deviant could be made whole again. Unhappily, however, the asylums had a way of turning into breeding grounds for brutality and neglect.

Gradually the idea of the penitentiary developed. It would be a place where the guilty experienced penitence and underwent rehabilitation, not just punishment. An early model of the new system, widely copied, was the Auburn Penitentiary, which opened in New York in 1816. The prisoners at Auburn had separate cells and gathered only for meals and group labor. Discipline was severe. The men were marched out in lockstep and never put face-to-face or allowed to talk. But prisoners were at least reasonably secure from abuse by their fellow prisoners. The system, its advocates argued, had a beneficial effect on the prisoners and saved money since the workshops supplied prison needs and produced goods for sale at a profit. By 1840 there were twelve penitentiaries of the Auburn type scattered across the nation.

The reform impulse also found outlet in the care of the insane. The charter of the Pennsylvania Hospital, founded in 1751 and one of the first such institutions in the country, provided for the care of "lunaticks," but before 1800 few other hospitals provided care for the mentally ill. The insane were usually confined at home with hired keepers or in jails or almshouses. In the years after 1815, however, asylums that separated the disturbed from the criminal began to appear.

The most important figure in heightening the public's awareness of the plight of the mentally ill was Dorothea Lynde Dix. A pious Boston school-teacher, she was called upon to instruct a Sunday-school class at the East Cambridge House of Correction in 1841. There she found a roomful of insane people completely neglected, without even heat on a cold March day. Dix was so disturbed by the scene that she commenced a two-year investigation of jails and almshouses in Massachusetts. In a report to the state legislature in 1843, she revealed that insane people were confined "in *cages, closets, cellars, stalls, pens! Chained, naked, beaten with rods,* and *lashed* into obedience." Keepers of the institutions dismissed her charges as "slanderous lies," but she won the support of leading reformers. From Massachusetts she carried her campaign throughout the country and abroad. By 1860 she had persuaded twenty states to heed her advice, thereby helping to transform social attitudes toward mental illness.

WOMEN'S RIGHTS   Whereas Dorothea Dix stood out as an example of the opportunity that social reform gave middle-class women to enter public life, Catharine Beecher, a leader in the education movement and founder of women's schools in Connecticut and Ohio, published a guide prescribing the domestic sphere for women. *A Treatise on Domestic Economy* (1841) became the leading handbook of what historians have labeled the cult of domesticity. While Beecher upheld high standards in women's education, she also accepted the prevailing view that the "woman's sphere" was the home and argued that young women should be trained in the domestic arts.

The social custom of assigning the sexes different roles was not new, of course. In earlier agrarian societies gender-based functions were closely tied to the household and often overlapped. As the more complex economy of the nineteenth century matured, economic production came to be increasingly separated from the home, and the home in turn became a refuge from the outside world, with separate and distinct functions for men and women. Some have argued that the home be-

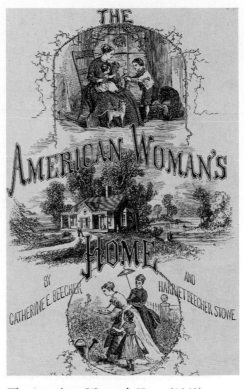

***The American Woman's Home* (1869)**

An illustrated page from a book by Catharine Beecher and her sister, Harriet Beecher Stowe.

came a trap for women, a prison that hindered fulfillment. But others have noted that it often gave women a sphere of independence in which they might exercise a degree of initiative and leadership. The so-called cult of domesticity idealized a woman's moral role in civilizing husband and family.

The official status of women during this period remained much as it had been in the colonial era. Women were barred from the ministry and most other professions. Higher education was hardly an option. Women could not serve on juries, nor could they vote. A wife often had no control over her property or even over her children. A wife could not make a will, sign a contract, or bring suit in court without her husband's permission. Her legal status was like that of a minor, a slave, or a free black.

Gradually, however, women began to protest their status, and men began to listen. The organized movement for women's rights had its origins in 1840, when the anti-slavery movement split over the question of women's

**Elizabeth Cady Stanton and
Susan B. Anthony**

Stanton (left) "forged the thunderbolts and Miss Anthony hurled them."

right to participate. Women decided then that they needed to organize on behalf of their own emancipation, too.

In 1848 two prominent moral reformers and advocates of women's rights, Lucretia Mott, a Philadelphia Quaker, and Elizabeth Cady Stanton, a graduate of Troy Female Seminary who refused to be merely "a household drudge," called a convention to discuss "the social, civil, and religious condition and rights of women." The hastily organized Seneca Falls Convention, the first of its kind, issued on July 19, 1848, a clever paraphrase of Thomas Jefferson's Declaration of Independence. Called the Declaration of Sentiments, it proclaimed the self-evident truth that "all men and women are created equal," and the attendant resolutions held that all laws that placed women "in a position inferior to that of men, are contrary to the great precept of nature, and therefore of no force or authority." Such language was too strong for most of the 1,000 delegates, and only about a third of them signed the document. Yet the Seneca Falls gathering represented an important first step in the evolving campaign for women's rights.

From 1850 until the Civil War, the leaders of the women's rights movement held annual conventions and carried on a program of organizing, lecturing, and petitioning. The movement struggled in the face of meager funds and anti-feminist women and men. Its success resulted from the work of a few undaunted women who refused to be cowed by the odds against them. Susan B. Anthony, already active in temperance and anti-slavery groups, joined the crusade in the 1850s. Unlike Stanton and Mott, she was unmarried and therefore able to devote most of her attention to the women's crusade. As one observer put it, Stanton "forged the thunderbolts and Miss Anthony hurled them." Both were young when the movement started, and both lived into the twentieth century, focusing after the Civil War on demands for women's suffrage. Many of the feminists, like Elizabeth Stanton and

Lucretia Mott, had supportive husbands, and the movement won prominent male champions, such as Ralph Waldo Emerson, Walt Whitman, William Ellery Channing, and William Lloyd Garrison.

The fruits of the women's rights movement ripened slowly. Women did not gain the vote but did make some legal gains. In 1839, Mississippi became the first state to grant married women control over their property; by the 1860s eleven more states had such laws. Still, the only jobs open to educated women in any number were nursing and teaching, both of which extended the domestic roles of health care and nurture to the outside world. Both brought relatively lower status and pay than "man's work" despite the skills, training, and responsibility involved.

UTOPIAN COMMUNITIES Amid the pervasive climate of reform during the Jacksonian era, the quest for utopia flourished. Plans for ideal communities had long been an American passion, at least since the Puritans set out to build a wilderness Zion in New England. More than 100 utopian communities sprang up between 1800 and 1900. Those founded by the

The Shaker Dance

During the Shaker dancing ritual, dancers wore thin, slipper-like shoes. Upon entering the dancing area, they walked on tip-toe.

Shakers, officially the United Society of Believers in Christ's Second Appearing, proved to be long lasting. Ann Lee (Mother Ann Lee) arrived in New York from England with eight followers in 1774. Believing religious fervor to be a sign of inspiration from the Holy Ghost, Mother Ann and her followers had strange fits in which they saw visions and prophesied. These manifestations later evolved into a ritual dance—hence the name Shakers. Shaker doctrine held God to be a dual personality: in Christ the masculine side was manifested; in Mother Ann, the feminine element. Mother Ann preached celibacy to prepare Shakers for the perfection that was promised them in heaven.

Mother Ann died in 1784, but the group found new leaders. From the first community, at New Lebanon, New York, the movement spread into New England, Ohio, and Kentucky. By 1830 about twenty groups were flourishing. In these Shaker communities all property was held in common. The Shakers' farms were among the nation's leading sources of garden seed and medicinal herbs, and many of their manufactures, including clothing, household items, and especially furniture, were prized for their simple beauty.

John Humphrey Noyes, founder of the Oneida Community, had a quite different model of the ideal community. The son of a Vermont congressman, educated at Dartmouth and Yale Divinity School, Noyes was converted at one of Charles Grandison Finney's revivals and entered the ministry. He was forced out, however, when he declared that with true conversion came perfection and a complete release from sin. In 1836 he gathered a group of "Perfectionists" around his home in Putney, Vermont. Ten years later, Noyes announced a new doctrine, "complex marriage," which meant that every man in the community was married to every woman and vice versa. "In a holy community," he claimed, "there is no more reason why sexual intercourse should be restrained by law, than why eating and drinking should be." Authorities thought otherwise, and Noyes was arrested for practicing his "free love" theology. He fled to New York State and in 1848 established the Oneida Community, which numbered more than 200 by 1851.

In contrast to these religious-based communities, Robert Owen's New Harmony was based upon a secular principle. A British capitalist who worried about the degrading social effects of the factory system, Owen set forth a scheme for a model community in his pamphlet *A New View of Society* (1813). Later he bought the town of Harmonie, Indiana, promptly christening it New Harmony. In 1825 a varied group of about 900 colonists gathered there for a period of transition from Owen's ownership to the new system of cooperation. After a trial period of only nine months, Owen turned over management of the colony to a town meeting of all residents and a council of town officers. The high proportion of learned participants generated a certain intellectual electricity about the place. For a time it looked like a brilliant success, but New Harmony soon fell into discord. Every idealist wanted his own plan put into practice. In 1827, Owen returned from a visit to England to find New Harmony insolvent. The following year he dissolved the project.

Brook Farm in Massachusetts was the most celebrated of all the utopian communities because it grew out of the transcendental movement. George Ripley, a Unitarian minister and transcendentalist, conceived of Brook Farm as a kind of early-day think tank, combining high thinking and plain living. In 1841 he and several dozen other like-minded utopians moved to the 175-acre farm eight miles southwest of Boston. Brook Farm became America's first secular utopian community. One of its members, the novelist Nathaniel Hawthorne, called Brook Farm "our beautiful scheme of a noble and unselfish life." The social experiment attracted great attention and hundreds of visitors. Its residents shared the tasks of maintaining the buildings, tending the fields, and preparing the meals. They also organized picnics, dances, lectures, and discussions. The place survived, however, mainly because of an excellent community school that drew tuition-paying students from outside. In 1846, Brook Farm's main building burned down, and the community spirit expired in the embers.

Utopian communities, with few exceptions, quickly ran out of steam. The communal social experiments, performed in relative isolation, had little effect on the outside world, where reformers wrestled with the sins of the multitudes. Among all the targets of the reformers' wrath, one great evil would finally take precedence over the others: human bondage. The transcendentalist reformer Theodore Parker declared that slavery was "the blight of this nation, the curse of the North and the curse of the South." The paradox of American slavery coupled with American freedom, of "the world's fairest hope linked with man's foulest crime," in the novelist Herman Melville's words, would inspire the climactic crusade of the age, abolitionism, one that would ultimately move to the center of the political stage and sweep the nation into an epic civil war.

CHAPTER SUMMARY

- **Second Great Awakening** The Second Great Awakening, an evangelical move-ment, generated revivals, especially in the backwoods. The Calvinist doctrine of predestination was often replaced by the concept of salvation by free will. The more democratic sects, such as Baptists and Methodists, gained members. Evan-gelists preached to enslaved people that everyone is equal in the eyes of God.

- **Religious Movements** The burned-over district was the birthplace of several religious movements, including the Church of Jesus Christ of Latter-day Saints, whose followers call themselves Mormons. Largely because they allowed mul-tiple marriages, Mormons were persecuted and their "prophet," Joseph Smith, lost his life. Smith's successor, Brigham Young, led the Mormons on a trek to then-isolated Utah in the hope that they could worship freely there. Another sect of this period, the Shakers, established celibate communities and believed that the Second Coming of Christ was imminent.

- **Romanticism** The transcendentalists embraced the Romantic movement in reaction to scientific rationalism and Calvinist orthodoxy, producing works that transcended reason and the material world. At the same time, improved technology and communication allowed the works of novelists, essayists, and poets to reach a mass market.

- **Social Reform Movements** America had an astonishingly high literacy rate, and reformers sought to establish statewide school systems. New colleges, most with religious affiliations, also sprang into existence. A few institutions, such as Vassar College, aimed to provide women with an education equal to that available to men at the best colleges. Social reformers sought to eradicate such evils as excessive drinking. They were active in the Sunday-school movement and in reforming prisons and asylums. With the Seneca Falls Convention of 1848, social reformers also launched the women's rights movement.

- **Cult of Domesticity** The cult of domesticity relegated women to the home. Middle-class women were educated to manage the household, inculcate in their children a strong sense of morality, and please their husbands. Married women had few rights under the law; women could not vote.

CHRONOLOGY

1826	Ministers organize the American Society for the Promotion of Temperance
1830–1831	Charles G. Finney begins preaching in upstate New York
1830	Joseph Smith reveals the Book of Mormon
1836	Transcendental Club holds its first meeting
1839	Mormons establish the community of Nauvoo, Illinois
1841	Catharine Beecher's *Treatise on Domestic Economy* is published
1846	Mormons, led by Brigham Young, undertake trek to Utah
1848	At Seneca Falls Convention, women issue the Declaration of Sentiments
	John Humphrey Noyes establishes the Oneida Community
1854	Henry David Thoreau's *Walden, or Life in the Woods* is published
1855	Walt Whitman's *Leaves of Grass* is published

KEY TERMS & NAMES

deism p. 493

Unitarianism p. 493

Second Great Awakening
p. 494

burned-over district p. 499

Church of Jesus Christ of
Latter-day Saints; Mormons
p. 500

Joseph Smith p. 500

Brigham Young p. 502

transcendentalism p. 504

Ralph Waldo Emerson
p. 505

Horace Mann p. 513

Dorothea Dix p. 518

Elizabeth Cady Stanton
p. 520

Shakers p. 522

utopian communities
p. 523

14

MANIFEST DESTINY

FOCUS QUESTIONS
Ⓢ wwnorton.com/studyspace

- What were the dominant issues in national politics in the 1840s?
- Why did settlers migrate west, and what conditions did they face?
- Why did Texas declare independence from Mexico in 1836, and why were many Americans reluctant to accept it as a new state in the Union?
- What were the causes of the Mexican War?
- What territories did the United States gain from the Mexican War, and what controversial issue consequently arose?

In the American experience the West has always had a mythical magic and allure. Moving westward was one of the primary sources of energy and hope in the development of the United States. The West—whether, initially, the enticing lands over the Allegheny Mountains that became Ohio and Kentucky or, later, the fertile prairies watered by the Mississippi River or, at last, the spectacular lands on the Pacific coast that became the states of California, Oregon, and Washington—served as a powerful magnet for adventurous people dreaming of freedom and self-fulfillment. During the 1840s and after, Americans moved west in droves, seeking a better chance and more space. "If hell lay to the west," one pioneer declared, "Americans would cross heaven to get there." Millions of Americans crossed the Mississippi River and endured unrelenting hardships in order to fulfill their "providential destiny" to subdue the entire continent. By 1860 some 4.3 million people had settled in the trans-Mississippi West.

Most of these settlers and adventurers sought to exploit the many economic opportunities afforded by the new land. Trappers and farmers, miners and merchants, hunters, ranchers, teachers, domestics, and prostitutes, among others, headed west seeking their fortune. Others sought religious freedom or new converts to Christianity. Whatever the reason, the pioneers formed an unceasing migratory stream flowing across the Great Plains and the Rocky Mountains. Of course, the West was not empty land waiting to be developed by hardy pioneers, trappers, and miners. Others had been there long before the American migration. The Indian and Mexican inhabitants of the region soon found themselves swept aside by successive waves of American settlement.

THE TYLER YEARS

When President William Henry Harrison took office in 1841, elected, like Andrew Jackson, mainly on the strength of his military record and his lack of a public stand on key issues, the Whig leaders expected him to be a pliant figurehead, a tool in the hands of the era's most prominent—and most cunning—statesmen, Daniel Webster and Henry Clay. Webster became secretary of state. Clay, who preferred to stay in the Senate, tried to fill the cabinet with his friends. Within a few days of the inauguration, signs of strain appeared between Harrison and Clay, whose disappointment at missing the nomination had made him peevish. At one point an exasperated Harrison exploded: "Mr. Clay, you forget that I am the President." But the quarrel never had a chance to fester, for Harrison served the shortest term of any president. At the inauguration, held on a chilly, rainy day, he caught cold after delivering a two-hour speech. On April 4, 1841, exactly one month after the inauguration, the sixty-eight-year-old military hero died of pneumonia. He was the first president to die in office.

Thus mild-mannered John Tyler of Virginia, the first vice president to succeed upon the death of a president, served practically all of Harrison's term. And if there was ambiguity about where Harrison stood, there was none about Tyler's convictions. At age fifty-one, the slave-owning Virginian was the youngest president to date, but he had already had a long career as legislator, governor, congressman, and senator, and his opinions on all the important issues had been forcefully stated and were widely known. Although officially a Whig, at an earlier time he might have been called an Old Republican: he was stubbornly opposed to everything associated with the "American System," Henry Clay's program of economic nationalism—protective tariffs, a national bank, and internal improvements at national expense—and, like Thomas Jefferson, was in favor of states' rights, strict construction of the Constitution, and territorial expansion.

Webster-Ashburton Treaty

A political cartoon of Webster and Ashburton negotiating.

When asked about the concept of nationalism, Tyler replied that he had "no such word in my political vocabulary." Originally a Democrat, he had broken with the party over Andrew Jackson's "condemnation" of South Carolina's attempt to nullify federal laws and Jackson's heavy-handed use of executive authority. In 1840, Tyler had been chosen to "balance" the Whig ticket, with no expectation that he would wield power. Acid-tongued John Quincy Adams said that Tyler was "a political sectarian of the slave-driving, Virginian, Jeffersonian school, principled against all improvement, with all the interests and passions and vices of slavery rooted in his moral and political constitution."

DOMESTIC AFFAIRS Given more finesse on Henry Clay's part, he might have bridged the divisions among the Whigs over financial issues. But for once, driven by an unrelenting quest to be president, the Great Compromiser lost his instinct for compromise. When Congress met in a special session in 1841, Clay introduced a series of resolutions designed to supply the platform that the party had evaded in the previous election. The chief points were repeal of the Independent Treasury Act, establishment of a third Bank of the United States, distribution to the states of money from federal land sales, and higher tariffs. The "haughty and imperious" Clay then set out to push his program through Congress. "Tyler dares not resist. I will drive him before me," he said.

Tyler, it turned out, was not easily driven. Although he agreed to the repeal of the Independent Treasury Act and signed a higher tariff bill in 1842, Tyler vetoed Clay's bill for a new national bank on August 16, 1841. Clay was furious. The domineering leader of the Senate developed a ferocious hatred for Tyler, calling him a traitor who had abandoned his party and accusing him of "pride, vanity, and egotism." Tyler's bank veto also prompted his entire cabinet to resign in September, with the exception of Secretary of State Daniel Webster. Tyler replaced the defectors with anti-Jackson Democrats who, like him, had become Whigs. Irate congressional Whigs expelled Tyler from the party, and Democrats viewed him as an untrustworthy renegade. By 1842, Clay's legislative program was in ruins. Yet by opposing Clay and the Whigs, Tyler had become a president without a party, shunned by both Whigs and Democrats. Such political turmoil was occurring amid the worst economic depression in the history of the young nation. Bank failures mounted. Unemployment soared.

FOREIGN AFFAIRS In foreign relations, tensions with Great Britain captured President Tyler's attention. In 1841, British ships patrolling off the coast of Africa threatened to board and search vessels flying the American flag to see if they carried slaves. Relations were further strained late in 1841 when 135 slaves on the *Creole*, bound from Hampton Roads, Virginia, to be sold in New Orleans, mutinied and sailed into Nassau, in the Bahamas, where the British set them free. Secretary of State Daniel Webster demanded that the slaves be returned as American property, but the British refused (the dispute was not settled until 1853, when England paid $110,000 to the owners of the freed slaves).

At this point a new British government decided to accept Webster's overtures for negotiations and sent Lord Ashburton to Washington, D.C. The

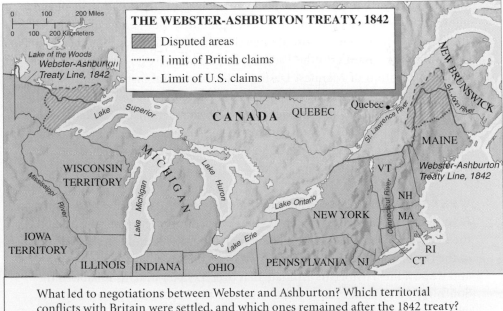

THE WEBSTER-ASHBURTON TREATY, 1842

What led to negotiations between Webster and Ashburton? Which territorial conflicts with Britain were settled, and which ones remained after the 1842 treaty? In addition to settling the dispute over land, what other issues did the Webster-Ashburton Treaty settle?

meetings were fruitful. The disputed Maine boundary was resolved in what Webster later called "the battle of the maps." Webster settled for about seven twelfths of the contested land along the Maine boundary, and except for Oregon, which remained under joint occupation, he settled the other border disputes with Great Britain by accepting the existing line between the Connecticut and St. Lawrence Rivers and compromising on the line between Lake Superior and Lake of the Woods. The Webster-Ashburton Treaty (1842) also provided for joint naval patrols off Africa to suppress the slave trade.

THE WESTERN FRONTIER

In the early 1840s most Americans were no more stirred by the quarrels of John Tyler and Henry Clay over such issues as the banking system and the tariff policy than students of history would be at a later date. What aroused public interest was the ongoing depression and the mounting evidence that the "empire of freedom" was hurdling the barriers of the Great American Desert and the Rocky Mountains, reaching out toward the Pacific coast. In 1845 a New York newspaper editor and Democratic-party propagandist named John L. O'Sullivan gave a name to this aggressive spirit of expansion. "Our manifest destiny," he wrote, "is to overspread the continent allotted by Providence for the free development of our yearly multiplying millions." God, in other words, deemed that the United States should extend itself from the Atlantic to the Pacific—and beyond. At its best this much-trumpeted notion of Manifest Destiny offered a moral justification for expansion, a prescription for what an enlarged United States could and should be. At its worst it was a cluster of flimsy rationalizations for naked greed and imperial ambition. Whatever the case, settlers began streaming into the Far West in the aftermath of the panic of 1837 and the prolonged economic depression.

WESTERN INDIANS   The sprawling territory across the Mississippi River was a new environment as well as a new culture. The Great Plains and the Far West were already occupied by Indians and Mexicans, who had lived in the region for centuries and had established their own distinctive customs and ways of life. Historians estimate that over 325,000 Indians inhabited the Southwest, the Great Plains, California, and the Pacific Northwest in 1840, when the great migration of white settlers began to pour into the region. The Native Americans often competed with and warred against one another. They were divided into more than 200 tribes, each with its own language,

Buffalo Hunt, Chasing Back (1860s)

This painting by George Catlin shows a hunter outrunning a buffalo.

religion, economic base, kinship practices, and system of governance. Some were primarily farmers; others were nomadic hunters who preyed upon game animals, as well as other Indians.

Many tribes resided on the Great Plains, a vast grassland stretching from the Mississippi River west to the Rocky Mountains and from Canada south to Mexico. This region had been virtually devoid of a human presence until the Spaniards introduced the horse and the gun in the late sixteenth century. Horses dramatically increased the mobility of the Plains Indians, enabling them to leave their villages and follow the migrating buffalo herds. The Indians used buffalo meat for food and transformed the skins into clothing, bedding, and tepee coverings. The bones and horns served as tools and utensils. Buffalo manure could be dried and burned for heat.

Plains Indians such as the Arapaho, Blackfoot, Cheyenne, Kiowa, and Sioux were horse-borne nomads; they migrated across the grasslands, carrying their tepees with them. Quite different Indian tribes lived to the south and west of them. In the arid region including what is today Arizona, New Mexico, and southern Utah were the peaceful Pueblo tribes: Acoma, Hopi, Laguna, Taos, Zia, Zuni. They were sophisticated farmers who lived in adobe villages along rivers that irrigated their crops of corn, beans, and squash. Their rivals were the Apache and the Navajo, warlike hunters who roamed the countryside in small bands and preyed upon the Pueblos. They, in turn, were periodically harassed by their powerful enemies, the Comanches.

To the north, in the Great Basin between the Rocky Mountains and the Sierra Nevadas, Paiutes and Gosiutes struggled to survive in the harsh, arid region of what is today Nevada, Utah, and eastern California. They traveled in family groups and subsisted on berries, pine nuts, insects, and rodents. West of the mountains, along the California coast, Indians lived in small villages. They gathered wild plants and acorns and were adept at fishing in the rivers and bays.

The Indian tribes living in the Pacific Northwest—the Nisqually, Spokane, Yakama, Chinook, Klamath, and Nez Perce (Pierced Nose)—enjoyed the most abundant natural resources and the most temperate climate. The ocean and rivers provided bountiful supplies of food: whales, seals, salmon, crabs. The lush inland forests harbored game, berries, and nuts. And the majestic forests of fir, redwood, and cedar offered wood for cooking and shelter.

All these Indian tribes eventually felt the unrelenting pressure of white expansion and conquest. Because Native American life on the plains depended upon the buffalo, the influx of white settlers and hunters posed a direct threat to the Indians' cultural survival. When federal officials could not coerce, cajole, or confuse Indian leaders into selling the title to their tribal lands, fighting ensued. And after the discovery of gold in California in 1848, the tidal wave of white expansion flowed all the way to the west coast.

THE SPANISH WEST AND MEXICAN INDEPENDENCE   As American settlers moved westward, they also encountered Spanish-speaking peoples. Many whites were as contemptuous of Hispanics as they were of Indians. Senator Lewis Cass, the expansionist from Michigan, expressed the sentiment of many Americans during a debate over the annexation of New Mexico. "We do not want the people of Mexico," he declared, "either as citizens or as subjects. All we want is a portion of territory." The vast majority of the Spanish-speaking people in what is today the American Southwest resided in New Mexico. Most of them were of mixed Indian and Spanish blood and were ranch hands or small farmers and herders.

The centuries-old Spanish efforts at colonization had been less successful in Arizona and Texas than in New Mexico and Florida. The Yuma and Apache Indians in Arizona and the Comanches and Apaches in Texas thwarted Spanish efforts to establish Catholic missions. After years of fruitless missionary efforts among the Pueblo Indians, one Spaniard complained that "most [of them] have never forsaken idolatry, and they appear to be Christians more by force than to be Indians who are reduced to the Holy Faith." By 1790 the Latino population in Texas numbered only 2,510, while in New Mexico it exceeded 20,000.

In 1807, French forces had occupied Spain and imprisoned the king, creating consternation and confusion throughout Spain's colonial possessions, including Mexico. Miguel Hidalgo y Costilla, a creole priest (born in the New World of European ancestry), took advantage of the fluid situation to convince Indians and mestizos to revolt against Spanish rule in Mexico. But the poorly organized uprising failed miserably. In 1811, Spanish troops captured Hidalgo and executed him. Other Mexicans, however, continued to yearn for independence. In 1820, Mexican creoles again tried to liberate themselves from Spanish authority. By then the Spanish forces in Mexico had lost much of their cohesion and dedication. Facing a growing revolt, the last Spanish officials withdrew in 1821, and Mexico became an independent nation. The infant Mexican republic struggled to develop a stable government,

"¡Viva El Cura Hidalgo!"

This patriotic broadside celebrating Mexican independence shows Father Miguel Hidalgo in an oval medallion.

however, and an effective economy. Localism and corruption flourished. And Americans were eager to take advantage of Mexico's instability.

Mexican independence from Spain unleashed tremors throughout the Southwest. American fur traders streamed into New Mexico and Arizona and developed a lucrative commerce in beaver pelts. American entrepreneurs also flooded into the western Mexican province of California and soon became a powerful force for change; by 1848, Americans made up half the non-Indian population. In Texas, American adventurers decided to promote their own independence from a newly independent—and chaotic—Mexican government. Suddenly, it seemed, the Southwest was ripe for a new phase of American exploitation and settlement.

THE ROCKY MOUNTAINS AND OREGON COUNTRY During the early nineteenth century the Far Northwest consisted of the Nebraska, Washington, and Oregon Territories. Fur traders especially were drawn to the Missouri River, with its many tributaries. By the mid-1820s the "rendezvous

Fur Traders Descending the Missouri (1845)

One of George Caleb Bingham's paintings from his winter in central Missouri. A bear cub is depicted at the bow.

system" had developed, in which trappers, traders, and Indians from the Rocky Mountain territories gathered annually at some designated place, usually in or near the Grand Tetons, to trade pelts and hides. But by 1840 the great days of the western fur trade were over. The streams no longer teemed with beavers.

During the 1820s and 1830s the fur trade had inspired a reckless breed of "mountain men" who deserted civilization in pursuit of beavers and reverted to a primitive existence in the wilderness. The rugged trappers lived sometimes in splendid isolation, sometimes in the shelter of primitive forts, and sometimes among Indians. They were the first whites to find their way around the Rocky Mountains, and they pioneered the trails that settlers by the 1840s were beginning to travel as they flooded the Oregon Country and trickled across the border into California.

Beyond the mountains the Oregon Country stretched from the 42nd parallel north to 54°40′, a region in which Spain and Russia had given up their rights, leaving Great Britain and the United States as the only claimants. By the Convention of 1818, the two countries had agreed to "joint occupation" of the region. Until the 1830s, however, joint occupation had been a legal technicality, because the only American presence was the occasional mountain man who wandered across the Sierra Nevadas or the infrequent trading vessel from Boston or New York.

Word of Oregon's fertile soil, plentiful rainfall, and magnificent forests gradually spread eastward. By the late 1830s, during the economic hard times after the panic of 1837, a trickle of emigrants was flowing along the Oregon Trail. Soon, however, "Oregon fever" swept the nation. In 1841 and 1842 the first sizable wagon trains made the trip, and in 1843 the movement became a mass migration. "The Oregon fever has broke out," wrote a settler in 1843, "and is now raging like any other contagion." By 1845 there were about 5,000 settlers in Oregon's Willamette River valley.

THE SETTLEMENT OF CALIFORNIA California was also an alluring attraction for new settlers and entrepreneurs. It had first felt the influence of European culture in 1769, when Spain grew concerned about Russian seal traders moving south along the Pacific coast from their base in Alaska. To thwart Russian intentions, Spain sent a naval expedition to settle the region. The Spanish discovered San Francisco Bay and constructed presidios (military garrisons) at San Diego and Monterey. Even more important, Franciscan friars, led by Junípero Serra, established a Catholic mission at San Diego.

CALIFORNIA'S MISSIONS Over the next fifty years, Franciscans built twenty more missions, spaced a day's journey apart along the coast from San Diego northward to San Francisco. The mission-centered culture created by the Hispanic settlers who migrated to California from Mexico was quite different from the patterns of conquest and settlement in Texas and New Mexico. In those more settled regions the original missions were converted into secular parishes, and the property was divided among the Indians. In California the missions were much larger, more influential, and longer lasting.

Franciscan missionaries, aided by Spanish soldiers, gathered most of the coastal Indian population in California under their control. They viewed the Indians as ignorant, indolent heathens living in a "free and undisciplined" society. The friars were determined to convert them to Catholicism and make them useful members of the Spanish Empire. Viewing the missions as crucial outposts of their empire, the Spanish government provided military support, annual cash grants, and supplies from Mexico. The Franciscan friars enticed the local Indians into the adobe-walled, tile-roofed missions by offering gifts or impressing them with their "magical" religious rituals. Once inside the missions, the Indians were baptized as Catholics, taught the Spanish language, and stripped of their native heritage. Soldiers living in the missions enforced the will of the friars.

The California mission served multiple roles. It was church, fortress, home, town, farm, and imperial agent. The missions were economic as well as religious and cultural institutions: they quickly became substantial agricultural enterprises. Missions produced crops, livestock, clothing, and household goods, both for profit and to supply the neighboring presidios (forts). Indians provided the labor. The Franciscans viewed regimented Indian labor as more than a practical necessity: they saw it as a morally enriching responsibility essential to transforming unproductive Indians into industrious Christians.

Sketch of a college of the order of San Francisco in the former mission of Santa Barbara

From Edward Vischer's collection of reminiscences of California under Spain and Mexico.

A mission's daily routine began at dawn with the ringing of a bell, which summoned the community to prayer. Work began an hour later and did not end until an hour before sunset. Indians worked at the missions six days a week; they did not work on Sundays and religious holidays. Children and the elderly were expected to work as well. Most Indian men performed manual labor in the fields. Some were trained in special skills, such as masonry, carpentry, or leatherwork. Women handled domestic chores, such as cooking, sewing, cleaning, and shucking corn. During harvest season everyone was expected to help in the fields. In lieu of wages the Indians received clothing, food, housing, and religious instruction.

The Franciscans used overwhelming force to maintain the captive labor system in the missions. Rebellious Indians were whipped or imprisoned. Mission Indians died at an alarming rate. One Franciscan friar reported that "of every four Indian children born, three die in their first or second year, while those who survive do not reach the age of twenty-five." Infectious disease was the primary threat, but the grueling labor regimen took a high toll as well. The Indian population along the California coast declined from 72,000 in 1769 to 18,000 by 1821. Saving souls cost many lives.

EARLY DEVELOPMENT OF CALIFORNIA   For all of its rich natural resources, California remained thinly populated by Indians and mission friars well into the nineteenth century. In 1821, when Mexico wrested its independence from Spain, Californians took comfort in the fact that Mexico City was so far away it would exercise little effective control over its farthermost state. During the next two decades, Californians, including many recent

American arrivals, staged ten revolts against the Mexican governors dispatched to lord over them.

Yet the shift from Spanish to Mexican rule did produce a dramatic change in California history. In 1824, Mexico passed a colonization act that granted hundreds of huge "rancho" estates to Mexican settlers. With free labor extracted from Indians, who were treated like slaves, the rancheros lived a life of self-indulgent luxury and ease, roaming their lands, gambling, horse racing, bull baiting, and dancing. The freebooting rancheros soon cast covetous eyes on the vast estates controlled by the Franciscan missions. In 1833–1834 they persuaded the Mexican government to confiscate the missions, exile the Franciscan friars, release the Indians from church control, and make the mission lands available to new settlement. Within a few years some 700 new rancho grants of 4,500 to 50,000 acres were issued along the California coast. Organized like feudal estates, these ranches resembled southern plantations—but the death rate among Indian workers was twice as high as that of enslaved blacks in the Deep South.

Few accounts of life in California took note of the brutalities inflicted upon the Indians, however. Instead, they portrayed the region as a proverbial land of milk and honey, ripe for development. Such a natural paradise could not long remain a secret. By the late 1820s, American trappers had wandered in from time to time, and American ships had begun to enter the "hide and tallow" trade: the ranchos of California produced cowhide and beef tallow in large quantities, and both products enjoyed a brisk demand, cowhides mainly for shoes and tallow chiefly for candles. By the mid-1830s shipping companies had stationed representatives in California to buy the hides and store them until a

Sutter's Fort in 1847

Renamed Fort Sacramento during the Mexican War.

company ship arrived. One of these agents, Thomas O. Larkin at Monterey, would play a leading role in the acquisition of California by the United States.

The most noteworthy of the traders, however, was not American but Swiss. John A. Sutter had abandoned his family in Europe in order to avoid arrest for bankruptcy. He found his way to California and persuaded the Mexican governor to give him land on which to plant a colony of Swiss émigrés. At the juncture of the Sacramento and American Rivers (later the site of Sacramento), Sutter built an enormous enclosure that guarded an entire village of settlers and shops. At New Helvetia (Americans called it Sutter's Fort), completed in 1843, no Swiss colony materialized, but the baronial estate, worked by local Indians, became a magnet for Americans bent on settling the Sacramento country. It stood at the end of what became the most traveled route through the Sierra Nevadas, the California Trail, which forked off the Oregon Trail and led through the mountains near Lake Tahoe. By the start of 1846, there were perhaps 800 Americans in California, along with 8,000 to 12,000 Californios (settlers of Hispanic descent).

MOVING WEST

Most of the western pioneers during the second quarter of the nineteenth century were American-born whites from the Upper South and the Midwest. Only a few African Americans joined in the migration. Although some emigrants traveled by sea to California, most went overland. Between 1841 and 1867 some 350,000 men, women, and children made the arduous trek to California or Oregon, while hundreds of thousands of others settled along the way, in Colorado, Texas, Arkansas, and other areas.

THE SANTA FE TRAIL   After gaining its independence in 1821, the new government of Mexico was much more interested in trade with the United States than Spain had been. In Spanish-controlled Santa Fe, in fact, all commerce with the United States had been banned. After 1821, however, trade flourished. Hundreds of entrepreneurs made the 1,000-mile trek from St. Louis to Santa Fe, forging a route that became known as the Santa Fe Trail. Soon Mexican traders began leading caravans east to Missouri. By the 1830s there was so much commercial activity between Mexico and St. Louis that the Mexican silver peso had become the primary medium of exchange in Missouri.

Thousands of Americans risked their lives along the Santa Fe Trail to exploit the commercial opportunities afforded by trade with the Mexicans. On a good day their wagons might travel twelve to fourteen miles through rough terrain. Water was scarce, as was forage for their livestock. Indians occasionally raided the wagon trains. In 1847 almost fifty pioneers were killed, 330 wagons destroyed, and 6,500 animals stolen by hostile Indians. The traders who survived pioneered more than a new trail. They showed that heavy wagons could cross the plains and the mountains, and they developed the technique of organized caravans for common protection.

THE OVERLAND TRAILS   Like those on the Santa Fe Trail, travelers bound for Oregon and California rode in wagon caravans. But on the Overland Trails to the West Coast, most of the pioneers were settlers rather than traders,

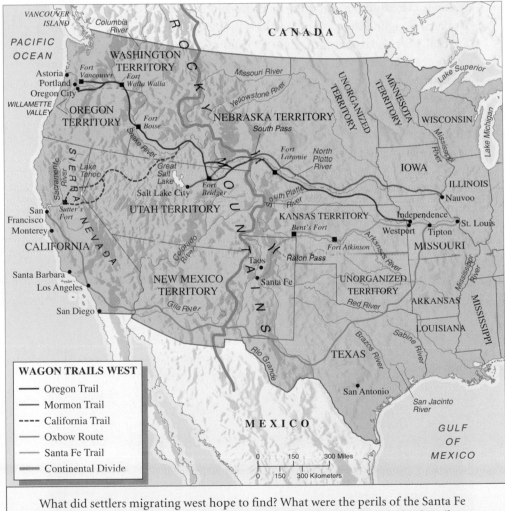

WAGON TRAILS WEST

—— Oregon Trail
—— Mormon Trail
---- California Trail
—— Oxbow Route
······· Santa Fe Trail
══════ Continental Divide

What did settlers migrating west hope to find? What were the perils of the Santa Fe Trail? Describe the experience of a typical settler traveling on the Overland Trails.

and they traveled mostly in family groups and came from all over the United States. The Oregon-bound wagon trains followed the trail west from Independence, Missouri, along the North Platte River into what is now Wyoming, through South Pass down to Fort Bridger (abode of the celebrated mountain man Jim Bridger), then down the Snake River to the Columbia River and along the Columbia to their goal in Oregon's fertile Willamette River valley. They usually left Missouri in late spring, completing the grueling 2,000-mile trek in six months. Traveling in ox-drawn canvas-covered wagons nicknamed prairie schooners, they jostled their way across the dusty or muddy trails and rugged mountains. By 1845 some 5,000 people were making the arduous journey annually. The discovery of gold in California in 1848 brought some 30,000 pioneers along the Oregon Trail in 1849. By 1850, the peak year of travel along the trail, the annual count had risen to 55,000.

Contrary to the mythology, Indians rarely attacked wagon trains. Less than 4 percent of the fatalities associated with the Overland Trails experience were the result of Indian attacks. More often, Native Americans either allowed the settlers to pass through their tribal lands unmolested or demanded payment. Many wagon trains never encountered a single Indian, and others received generous aid from Indians who served as guides, advisers, or traders.

Gathering buffalo chips

Women on the Overland Trails not only cooked and washed and took care of their children but also gathered dried buffalo dung to use as fuel as their wagons crossed the treeless plains.

The Indians, one female pioneer noted, "proved better than represented." To be sure, as the number of pioneers increased dramatically during the 1850s, disputes with Indians over land and water increased, but never to the degree portrayed in novels and films.

Still, the journey west was extraordinarily difficult. The diary of Amelia Knight, who set out for Oregon in 1853 with her husband and seven children, reveals the mortal threats along the trail: "Chatfield quite sick with scarlet fever. A calf took sick and died before breakfast. Lost one of our oxen; he dropped dead in the yoke. I could hardly help shedding tears. Yesterday my eighth child was born." Cholera claimed many lives. On average there was one grave every eighty yards along the trail.

Initially the pioneers along the Overland Trails adopted the same division of labor used back East. Women cooked, washed, sewed, and monitored the children while men drove the wagons, tended the horses and cattle, and did the heavy labor. But the unique demands of the western trails soon dissolved such neat distinctions and posed new tasks. Women found themselves gathering buffalo dung for fuel, pitching in to dislodge a wagon mired in mud, helping to construct a makeshift bridge, or participating in a variety of other "unladylike" tasks.

The hard labor of the trails understandably provoked tensions within families and powerful yearnings for home. Many a tired pioneer could identify with the following comment in a girl's journal: "Poor Ma said only this morning, 'Oh, I wish we had never started.' She looks so sorrowful and dejected." Another woman wondered "what had possessed my husband, anyway, that he should have thought of bringing us away out through this God forsaken country." Some turned back, but most continued on. And once in Oregon or California they set about establishing stable communities. Noted one settler: "Friday, October 27. — Arrived at Oregon City at the falls of the Willamette. Saturday, October 28. —Went to work."

THE INDIANS AND GREAT PLAINS ECOLOGY The massive migrations along the Overland Trails wreaked havoc on the environment of the Great Plains.

Wagon-wheel ruts near Guernsey, Wyoming

The wheels of thousands of wagons traveling to Oregon cut into solid rock as oxen strained up hillsides, leaving indentations that are still visible today.

Hundreds of thousands of settlers and traders brought with them millions of animals—horses, cattle, oxen, and sheep—all of which consumed huge amounts of prairie grass. The wagons and herds trampled vegetation and gouged ruts in the landscape that survive to this day. With the onset of the California gold rush in 1849, Plains Indians, led by Cheyennes, began supplying buffalo meat and skins to the white pioneers. Tracking and killing buffalo required many horses, and the four-legged creatures added to the strain on the prairie grasslands and river bottoms. A major climatic change coincided with the mass migrations sparked by the discovery of gold in California. In 1849 a prolonged drought struck the region west of the Mississippi River and produced widespread suffering. Starving Indians demanded or begged for food from passing wagon trains. Tensions between Native Americans and white travelers brought additional federal cavalry units to the plains, exacerbating the shortage of forage grasses.

In 1851, U.S. officials invited the Native Americans tribes from the northern plains to a conference in the grassy valley along the North Platte River, near Fort Laramie in what is now southeastern Wyoming. Almost 10,000 Indians—men, women, and children—attended the treaty council. What made the huge gathering even more remarkable is that so many of the tribes

Indian rendering of the Fort Laramie Treaty

This buffalo-hide robe commemorates the 150th anniversary of the signing of the Fort Laramie Treaty.

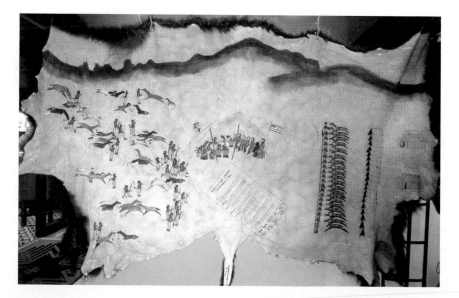

were at war with one another. After nearly three weeks of heated discussions, during which the chiefs were presented with a mountain of gifts, federal negotiators and tribal leaders agreed to what became known as the Fort Laramie Treaty. The government promised to provide an annual cash payment to the Indians as compensation for the damage caused by wagon trains traversing their hunting grounds. In exchange the Indians agreed to stop harassing white caravans, allow federal forts to be built, and confine themselves to a specified area "of limited extent and well-defined boundaries."

Several tribes, however, refused to accept the provisions. The most powerful, the Lakota Sioux, reluctantly signed the agreement but thereafter failed to abide by its restrictions. "You have split my lands and I don't like it," declared Black Hawk, a Sioux chief at Fort Laramie. "These lands once belonged to the Kiowas and the Crows, but we whipped these nations out of them, and in this we did what the white men do when they want the lands of the Indians." Yet despite the dissension, the Fort Laramie Treaty was significant. As the first comprehensive treaty with the Plains Indians, it foreshadowed the "reservation" concept of Indian management.

THE DONNER PARTY   The most tragic story of the Overland Trails involved the party led by George Donner, a prosperous sixty-two-year-old farmer from Illinois, who led his family and a train of other settlers along the Oregon Trail in 1846. They made every mistake possible: starting too late in the year, overloading their wagons, and taking a foolish shortcut to California across the Wasatch Mountains in the Utah Territory. In the Wasatch they were joined by a group of thirteen other pioneers, bringing the total to eighty-seven. Finding themselves lost on their "shortcut," they backtracked before finding their way across the mountains and into the desert leading to the Great Salt Lake. Crossing the desert exacted a terrible toll. They lost over 100 oxen and were forced to abandon several wagons and their precious supplies.

When the Donner party reached Truckee Pass, the last mountain barrier before the Sacramento River valley, a two-week-long snowfall trapped them in two separate camps. By December, eighty-one settlers, half of them children, were marooned with only enough food to last through the end of the month. Seventeen of the strongest members decided to cross the pass on their own, only to be trapped by more snow on the western slope. Two of them died of exposure and starvation. Just before he died, Billy Graves urged his daughters to eat his body. The daughters were appalled by the prospect of cannibalism but a day later saw no other choice. The group struggled on, and when two more died, they, too, were consumed. Only seven lived to reach the Sacramento River valley.

Back at the main camps, at Alder Creek and Truckee Lake, the survivors had slaughtered and eaten the last of the livestock, then proceeded to boil hides and bones. When the rescue party finally reached them, they discovered a grisly scene. Thirteen people had died, and cannibalism had become commonplace; one pioneer had noted casually in his diary, "Mrs. Murphy said here yesterday that she thought she would commence on Milt and eat him." As the rescuers led the forty-seven survivors over the pass, George Donner, so weakened that he was unable to walk, stayed behind to die. His wife chose to remain with him.

THE PATHFINDER: JOHN FRÉMONT Despite the hardships and dangers of the overland crossing, the Far West proved an irresistible attraction. The most enthusiastic champion of American settlement in Mexican California and the Far West was John Charles Frémont, "the Pathfinder" — who mainly "found" paths that mountain men showed him. Born in Savannah, Georgia, and raised in the South, he had a robust love of the outdoors and an exuberant, self-promoting personality. Frémont was commissioned a second lieutenant in the U.S. Topographical Corps in 1838. In the early 1840s his new father-in-law, Missouri senator Thomas Hart Benton, arranged the explorations that made Frémont famous. In 1842, Frémont mapped the eastern half of the Oregon Trail—and met Christopher "Kit" Carson, one of the most knowledgeable of the mountain men, who became his frequent associate. In 1843–1844, Frémont, typically clad in a deerskin shirt, blue army trousers, and moccasins, went on to Oregon, then horrified his

superior officers when he impetuously launched a "military" expedition. Frémont swept down the eastern slopes of the Sierra Nevadas, headed southward through the central valley of Mexican California, bypassed the mountains in the south, and returned via the Great Salt Lake. His excited reports on both expeditions, published together in 1845, gained a wide circulation and played a crucial role in prompting the mass migration to Oregon and California.

"The Pathfinder"

John Charles Frémont became a national hero early in life.

CALIFORNIA IN TURMOIL American presidents beginning with Andrew Jackson had tried to purchase from Mexico at least northern California, down to San Francisco Bay. Jackson reasoned that as a free state, California would balance the future admission of Texas as a slave state. But Jackson's agent had to be recalled after a clumsy effort to bribe Mexican officials. Rumors flourished that the British and the French were scheming to grab California, though neither government actually had such intentions. Political conditions in Mexico left the remote territory in near anarchy much of the time as governors came and went in rapid succession. Amid the chaos many Californios reasoned that they would be better off if they cut ties to Mexico altogether. Some favored California's becoming an independent nation, perhaps under French or British protection. A larger group wanted to join the United States.

ANNEXING TEXAS

AMERICAN SETTLEMENTS   The lust for new land focused on the most accessible of all the Mexican borderlands, Texas. By the 1830s, Texas was rapidly turning into a province of the United States, for Mexico initially welcomed white American settlers, known as Anglos. Foremost among the promoters of American settlement in Texas was Stephen F. Austin, a Missouri resident who gained from Mexico a huge land grant originally given to his father by Spanish authorities. Before Mexican independence from Spain was fully won, the twenty-eight-year-old Austin had started a colony on the lower Brazos River, in central Texas, late in 1821, and by 1824 more than 2,000 hardy souls had settled on his land. Most of the newcomers were southern farmers drawn to rich new cotton land selling for only a few cents an acre. By 1830 the coastal region of Texas had about 20,000 white settlers and 1,000 black slaves brought in to work the cotton.

The Mexican government, opposed to slavery, grew alarmed at the flood of strangers engulfing its Texas province and in 1830 forbade further immigration. But illegal immigrants from the United States moved across the long border as easily as illegal Mexican immigrants would later cross in the opposite direction. By 1835 the Anglo population in Texas had grown to around 30,000, about ten times the Mexican population there. Friction mounted in 1832 and 1833 as Americans organized conventions to demand a state of their own. Ignoring the request, General Antonio López de Santa Anna, who had seized political power in Mexico, dissolved the national congress late in 1834 and became dictator. Anglo Texans feared that the Mexicans intended to free "our slaves and to make slaves of us." In the fall of 1835, Texans rebelled against Santa Anna's "despotism." A furious Santa

Anna ordered all Americans expelled, all Texans disarmed, and all rebels arrested. As fighting erupted, volunteers from southern states rushed to assist the 30,000 Texans in their revolution against a Mexican nation of 7 million people.

TEXAS INDEPENDENCE   At San Antonio the Mexican army assaulted a small garrison of Texans and southern allies holed up behind the adobe walls of an abandoned mission called the Alamo. Led by the twenty-six-year-old colonel William B. Travis, a hot-tempered young lawyer from Alabama, who had been in Texas since 1831, the troops included not only Tejanos (Texas settlers of Mexican or Spanish descent) but also American volunteers, the most celebrated of whom was David Crockett, the Tennessee frontiersman who had fought Indians under Andrew Jackson and served as a Whig congressman. Full of bounce and brag, Crockett was thoroughly expert at killing. As he once told his men, "Pierce the heart of the enemy as you would a feller that spit in your face, knocked down your wife, burnt up your houses, and called your dog a skunk! Cram his pesky carcass full of thunder and lightning like a stuffed sassidge . . . and bite his nose off into the bargain."

On February 23, 1836, Santa Anna demanded that the 189 defenders of the Alamo surrender. They answered with a cannon shot. The Mexicans then launched a series of assaults against the outnumbered defenders. For twelve days the Mexicans were repulsed, suffering huge losses. Then, on March 6, the defenders of the Alamo were awakened by the sound of Mexican bugles playing the dreaded "Degüello" ("No Mercy to the Defenders"). Soon thereafter Santa Anna's men attacked from every side. They were twice repulsed, but on the third try the Mexicans broke through the battered north wall. Colonel Travis was killed by a bullet to the forehead. The frontiersmen used their muskets as clubs, but soon they were all killed or wounded. The notorious slave smuggler, Indian fighter, and inventor of the Bowie knife, James Bowie, his pistols emptied, his famous knife bloodied, and his body riddled with Mexican bullets, lay dead on his cot.

Santa Anna ordered the wounded Americans hacked to death with swords and their bodies burned with the rest. The only survivors were sixteen women, children, and servants. It was a complete victory for the Mexicans, but a costly one. Fewer than 200 defenders of the Alamo had given their lives at the price of twice as many Mexicans, and their heroic stand inspired the rest of the Anglos in Texas to stage a fanatical resistance. While Santa Anna dictated a glorious victory declaration, his aide wrote in his diary, "One more such 'glorious victory' and we are finished."

On March 2, 1836, while the siege of the Alamo continued, delegates from all fifty-nine Texas towns met at the village of Washington-on-the-Brazos and signed a declaration of independence. Over the next seventeen days the delegates drafted a constitution for the Republic of Texas and established an interim government. The delegates then hastily adjourned as Santa Anna's troops, fresh from their victory at the Alamo, bore down upon them.

The commander in chief of the Texas forces was Sam Houston, a Tennessee frontiersman who had learned war under the tutelage of Andrew Jackson, later represented the Nashville district in Congress, and had moved to Texas only three years before. After learning of the Anglo defeat at the Alamo, Houston beat a strategic retreat eastward from Gonzales, gathering reinforcements as he went, including volunteers from the United States. Just west of the San Jacinto River he paused near the site of the city that later bore his name, and on April 21, 1836, his forces surprised a Mexican encampment there. The Texans charged, yelling "Remember the Alamo," and overwhelmed the panic-stricken Mexican force. Santa Anna was captured trying to escape. The Mexican dictator bought his freedom by signing a treaty recognizing the independence of Texas, with the Rio Grande as the boundary. The Mexican congress repudiated the treaty and never officially recognized the loss of its northern province, but the war was at an end.

Sam Houston

Houston was commander in chief of the Texas forces.

NEGOTIATIONS FOR ANNEXATION   In 1836 the Lone Star Republic drafted a constitution that legalized slavery and banned free blacks, made Sam Houston its first president, and voted for annexation to the United States. The American president then was Houston's old friend Andrew Jackson, who desperately wanted Texas to join the Union, but even Old Hickory could be discreet when delicacy demanded it. The addition of Texas as a new slave state in 1836 threatened a serious sectional quarrel that might endanger the election of Martin Van Buren, his handpicked successor. Worse than that, it raised the specter of war with Mexico. Jackson delayed official recognition of the Republic of Texas until his last day in office, and Van Buren shied away from the issue of annexation during his term as president.

Rebuffed in Washington, Texans began to talk of expanding their new nation to the Pacific, thus rivaling the United States. France and Britain extended formal recognition to the republic and began to develop trade relations. Meanwhile, thousands more Americans poured into Texas. The population grew from 40,000 in 1836 to 150,000 in 1845. Many settlers were attracted by the low land prices. And most brought with them a desire to join the United States.

Most Texans never abandoned their hope of annexation, although reports of growing British influence in Texas created anxieties in the U.S. government and among southern slaveholders, who became the chief advocates of annexation. Soon after John Tyler became president, in 1841, he promoted the idea of annexing Texas. Secret negotiations with Texas began in 1843, and that April, John C. Calhoun, then secretary of state, completed an annexation treaty that went to the Senate for ratification.

Calhoun chose this moment to send the British minister to the United States a letter instructing him on the blessings of slavery and stating that the annexation of Texas was needed to foil the British abolitionists. Publication of the note fostered the claim that annexation was planned less in the national interest than to promote the expansion of slavery. It was so worded, one observer wrote to Andrew Jackson, as to "drive off every northern man from the support of the measure." Sectional division, plus fear of a war with Mexico, contributed to the Senate's overwhelming rejection of the Texas annexation treaty in 1843. Solid Whig opposition was the most important factor behind its defeat.

POLK'S PRESIDENCY

THE ELECTION OF 1844   Although adding Texas to the Union was an enormously popular idea among the citizenry, prudent leaders in both political parties had hoped to keep the divisive issue out of the 1844 presidential campaign. Whig Henry Clay and Democrat Martin Van Buren, the leading candidates, had reached the same conclusion about pro-slavery Texas: when the annexation treaty was submitted to the Senate, both wrote letters opposing it for fear the debate might spark civil war. The two letters, dated three days apart, appeared in two Washington newspapers on April 27, 1844. Clay's "Raleigh letter" (written while he was on a southern tour) stated that annexation was "dangerous to the integrity of the Union . . . and not called for by any general expression of public opinion." Clay feared that the furor over Texas would distract the nation from more important issues. He also worried that John Calhoun and other southern Democrats were using the Texas issue in a deliberate attempt to outflank the Whig party and divide the nation along sectional lines. The outcome of the Whig Convention, held in Baltimore, seemed to bear out his view. Party leaders showed no qualms about Clay's stance. The convention nominated Clay unanimously, and the Whig platform omitted any reference to Texas.

The Democratic Convention was a different story. Martin Van Buren's southern supporters, including Andrew Jackson, abandoned him because of his opposition to Texas annexation. Jackson wrote his former vice president a brutally frank letter, conveying his intense disappointment with Van Buren's anti-Texas stance. He told the New Yorker that his chances of being elected were now about as great as those of reversing the flow of the Mississippi River. A future president, James Buchanan, the head of the Pennsylvania Democrats, declared that Van Buren's principled stance against annexing

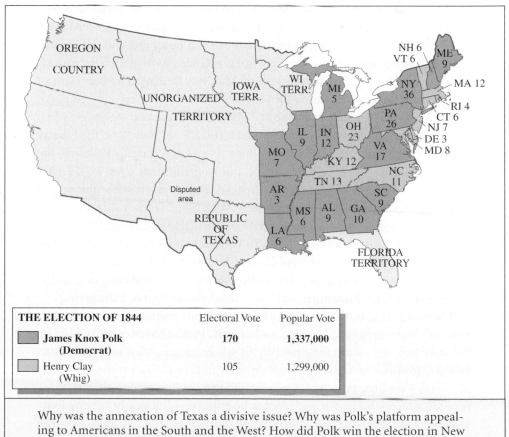

THE ELECTION OF 1844	Electoral Vote	Popular Vote
James Knox Polk (Democrat)	170	1,337,000
Henry Clay (Whig)	105	1,299,000

Why was the annexation of Texas a divisive issue? Why was Polk's platform appealing to Americans in the South and the West? How did Polk win the election in New York, and why was winning that state important?

Texas would cost him the party's nomination. Van Buren was like a "dead cock in the pit." With the Democratic Convention deadlocked, expansionists, including Andrew Jackson, nominated James Knox Polk, former Speaker of the House and governor of Tennessee, an ardent expansionist. On the ninth ballot he became the first "dark horse" candidate to win a major-party nomination. The party platform embraced territorial expansion, and to win support in the North and the West as well as in the South, it called for the annexation of both Oregon and Texas. Missouri senator Thomas Hart Benton, a Van Buren supporter, lamented what had taken place at the convention. The single-minded preoccupation with Texas among the southern delegates foreshadowed national disaster. "Under the pretext of getting Texas into the Union," he observed, "the scheme is to get the South out of it."

The Democratic combination of southern and western expansionism offered a winning strategy, one so popular it forced the Whig Henry Clay to alter his position on Texas; now he claimed that he had "no personal objection to the annexation" if it could be achieved "without dishonor, without war, with the common consent of the Union, and upon just and fair terms." His explanation seemed clear enough, but prudence was no match for spread-eagle oratory and the emotional pull of Manifest Destiny. The net result of Clay's stand was to turn more anti-slavery votes to the new Liberty party, which increased its count from about 7,000 in 1840 (the year it was founded) to more than 62,000 in 1844. In the western counties of New York, the Liberty party drew enough votes from the Whigs to give the state to Polk and the Democrats. Had he carried New York, the overconfident Clay would have won the election by 7 electoral votes. Instead, Polk won a narrow plurality of 38,000 popular votes (the first president since John Quincy Adams to win without a majority) but a clear majority of the Electoral College, 170 to 105. Clay had lost his third and last effort to win the presidency. His rival, Daniel Webster, blamed the savagely ambitious Clay for the Whig defeat, declaring that he had behaved as if he were willing to say or do anything to gain the White House, and "his temper was bad—resentful, violent & unforgiving."

The humiliated but still haughty Clay could not understand how a statesman of his stature could have lost to James K. Polk, a "third-rate" politician. Yet Polk had been surprising people his whole career. Born near Charlotte, North Carolina, and trained in mathematics and the classics at the University of North Carolina, Polk had moved to Tennessee as a young man. Having become a successful lawyer and planter, he entered politics early, serving fourteen years in Congress (four as Speaker of the House) and two as governor of Tennessee. "Young Hickory," as his partisans liked to call him, was a short, slender man with a shock of grizzled hair and a seemingly permanent grimace.

Humorless and dogmatic, he had none of Andrew Jackson's charisma but shared Jackson's opposition to a national bank and other Whig economic policies. Although America's youngest president up to that time, Polk worked so hard during his four years in the White House that his health deteriorated, and he died in 1849, at age fifty-three just three months after leaving office. He died knowing that his strenuous efforts had paid off. Polk was one of the few presidents to accomplish all of his major objectives.

POLK'S PROGRAM   In domestic affairs, "Young Hickory" Polk reflected the growing influence of the slaveholding South on the Democratic party. Abolitionism, Polk warned, could destroy the Union. Anti-slavery northerners had already begun to drift from the Democratic party, which they complained was coming to represent southern slaveholding interests. Polk himself had slaves on his Tennessee and Mississippi plantations. Like Andrew Jackson and most Americans of the time, Polk was a racist who sought to avoid any public discussion of slavery.

Polk's major objectives were tariff reduction, reestablishment of Van Buren's independent Treasury, settlement of the Oregon boundary dispute with Britain, and acquisition of California from Mexico. He gained them all. The Walker Tariff of 1846, in keeping with Democratic tradition, reduced the tariff rates. In the same year, Polk persuaded Congress to restore the independent Treasury, which the Whigs had eliminated. Twice Polk vetoed internal-improvement bills. In each case his blows to the economic nationalism of Henry Clay's Whigs satisfied the urges of the slaveholding South, but at the cost of annoying northerners who wanted higher tariffs and westerners who longed for internal improvements in the form of roads and harbors.

THE STATE OF TEXAS   Polk's chief concern was geographic expansion. He pledged to annex Texas, but he privately vowed to acquire California and New Mexico as well, preferably by purchase. The acquisition of slaveholding Texas was already under way when Polk took office. In his final months in office, President John Tyler, taking Polk's election as a mandate to act, had asked Congress to accomplish annexation by joint resolution, which required only a simple majority in each house and avoided the two-thirds Senate vote needed to ratify a treaty. Congress had read the election returns too, and after a bitter debate over slavery, the resolution passed by votes of 27 to 25 in the Senate and 120 to 98 in the House. The Whig leader Daniel Webster was aghast. He felt "sick at heart" to see Congress take a step toward civil strife because of the "greediness for more slave Territory and for the greater increase of Slavery!" On March 1, 1845, just before leaving office, President

Tyler signed the resolution, offering to admit Texas to the Union. The new state formally entered the Union on December 29, 1845. An outraged Mexico dispatched troops to the Rio Grande border.

OREGON Meanwhile, the Oregon boundary issue heated up as expansionists insisted that President Polk abandon previous offers to settle with Britain on the 49th parallel and stand by the Democrats' platform pledge to take all of Oregon ("54°40′ or Fight"). The expansionists were prepared to risk war with Britain over the Oregon issue. "All of Oregon or none," they cried. In his inaugural address, Polk had claimed that the American title to Oregon was "clear and unquestionable," but privately he favored a prudent compromise.

Fortunately for Polk the British government had no enthusiasm for war over a remote wilderness territory at the cost of profitable trade relations with the United States. So in 1846 the British government submitted a draft treaty that extended the border along the 49th parallel and through the main channel south of Vancouver Island and kept the right to navigate all of the Columbia River. On June 15, James Buchanan, now Polk's secretary of state,

Polk's Dream (1846)

The devil advises Polk to pursue 54° 40′ even if "you deluge your country with seas of blood, produce a servile insurrection and dislocate every joint of this happy and prosperous union!!!"

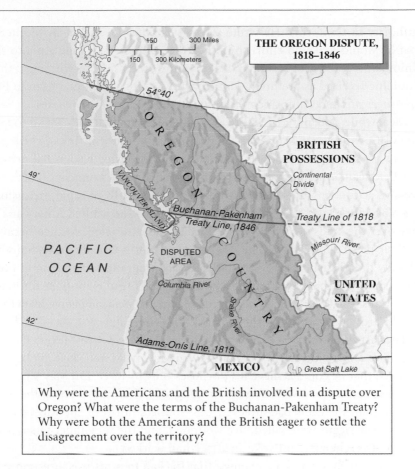

Why were the Americans and the British involved in a dispute over Oregon? What were the terms of the Buchanan-Pakenham Treaty? Why were both the Americans and the British eager to settle the disagreement over the territory?

signed it, and three days later the Buchanan-Pakenham Treaty was ratified in the Senate. The only opposition came from a group of expansionists who wanted more, but most of the country was satisfied. Southerners cared less about Oregon than about Texas, and northern business interests valued British trade more than they valued trying to gain all of the Oregon Territory. Besides, the country by then was at war with Mexico.

THE MEXICAN WAR

THE OUTBREAK OF WAR   On March 6, 1845, two days after James Polk took office, the Mexican government broke off relations with the United States to protest the American annexation of Texas. When an effort at negotiation failed, the hard-driving Polk focused his efforts on subverting Mexican authority in California. He wrote Consul Thomas O. Larkin in Monterey that he would make no effort to induce the admission of California to the Union, but "if the people should desire to unite their destiny with ours, they would be received as brethren." Larkin, who could take a hint, began to line up Americans and Californios who wanted to join the United States.

Meanwhile, Polk ordered U.S. troops under General Zachary Taylor to take up positions around Corpus Christi, near the Rio Grande in Texas. These positions lay in territory that was doubly disputed: Mexico recognized neither the American annexation of Texas nor the Rio Grande boundary. Polk's aggressive actions in Texas gained widespread support from rabid expansionists. The editor John L. O'Sullivan exclaimed that God wanted Americans to take over the lands owned by the "imbecile and distracted" Mexico because of their racial superiority. "The Anglo-Saxon foot is already on its borders. Already the irresistible army of Anglo-Saxon emigration has begun to pour down upon it, armed with the plow and the rifle." O'Sullivan spoke for many Americans who believed it their duty to redeem the Mexican people from their "backward" civilization and their chaotic government.

The last hope for peace died when John Slidell, sent to Mexico City to negotiate a settlement, gave up on his mission in March 1846. Polk then resolved that he could achieve his purposes only by force. On May 9 he won cabinet approval of a war message to Congress. That very evening the news arrived that Mexicans had attacked U.S. soldiers north of the Rio Grande. Eleven Americans were killed, five wounded, and the remainder taken prisoner. Polk's scheme to provoke an attack had worked.

In his war message, Polk claimed that his call to arms was a response to Mexican aggression, a recognition that war had been forced upon the United States. Mexico, he reported, "has invaded our territory, and shed American blood upon the American soil." Congress quickly passed the war resolution, and Polk signed the declaration of war on May 13, 1846. But support for the war was guarded. The House authorized a call for 50,000 volunteers and a war appropriation of $10 million, but sixty-seven Whigs voted against the measure, a sign of rising opposition, especially in the North, where people assumed that the southerner Polk wanted a war with Mexico in order to acquire more territory for the expansion of slavery.

OPPOSITION TO THE WAR   In the Mississippi River valley, where expansion fever ran high, the war with Mexico was immensely popular. Bonfires were lit, parades held, poems and songs composed, and patriotic speeches delivered. Men rushed to volunteer; thousands had to be turned back. In Illinois, efforts to form four regiments produced fourteen. In New England, however, there was much less enthusiasm for "Mr. Polk's war." Whig opinion ranged from lukewarm to hostile. Congressman John Quincy Adams, who voted against participation, called it "a most unrighteous war." An obscure congressman from Illinois named Abraham Lincoln, upon taking his seat in 1847, began introducing "spot resolutions," calling on President Polk to name the spot where American blood had been shed on American soil, implying that U.S. troops may, in fact, have been in Mexico when fired upon. The Whig leader Daniel Webster was convinced that the outbreak of war with Mexico was driven by a Democratic party scheme to add more slave states to the Union. The Massachusetts senator worried that an "expensive and bloody war" would end up fragmenting the Union. He was "quite alarmed for the state of the Country." Many other New Englanders denounced the war as the work of pro-slavery southerners seeking new territories. The fiery abolitionist William Lloyd Garrison charged that the unjust war was one "of aggression, of invasion, of conquest, and rapine—marked by ruffianism, perfidy, and every other feature of national depravity." But before the war ended, some anti-slavery leaders had a change of heart. Mexican territory seemed so unsuited to slave-based agriculture that they endorsed expansion in the hope of enlarging the area of free soil. The lure of more land and the idea of Manifest Destiny exerted a potent influence even upon those who opposed the war because they opposed the expansion of slavery.

PREPARING FOR BATTLE   Both the United States and Mexico approached the war ill prepared. American policy had been incredibly reckless, risking war with both Britain and Mexico while doing nothing to strengthen the armed forces until war came. At the outset of the war, the regular army numbered barely over 7,000, in contrast to the Mexican force of 32,000. Before the war ended, the U.S. military had grown to 78,718 troops, of whom about 31,000 were regular army troops and marines. Most of the new soldiers were six- and twelve-month volunteers. The volunteer militia companies, often filled with frontier toughs, lacked uniforms, standard equipment, and discipline. Repeatedly, despite the best efforts of the commanding generals, these undisciplined forces engaged in plunder, rape, and murder.

Yet the motley American troops outmatched larger Mexican forces, which had their own problems with training, discipline, morale, supplies, and munitions. Many of the Mexicans had been pressed into service or recruited from prisons, and they made less than enthusiastic fighters. Mexican artillery pieces were generally obsolete, and the gunpowder was so faulty that American soldiers could often dodge cannonballs that fell short and bounced ineffectively along the ground.

The Mexican War would be fought on four fronts: southern Texas, central Mexico, New Mexico, and California. And it would last two years, from March 1846 to April 1848. The United States entered the war without even a tentative plan of action, and politics complicated matters. President Polk sought to manage every detail of the conflict. What Polk wanted, Thomas Hart Benton wrote later, was "a small war, just large enough to require a treaty of peace, and not large enough to make military reputations, dangerous for the presidency." Winfield Scott, general-in-chief of the army, was a politically ambitious Whig. Nevertheless, Polk at first named him to take charge of the southern Texas front. When Scott quarreled with Polk's secretary of war, however, the exasperated president withdrew the appointment.

There now seemed a better choice for commander. General Zachary Taylor's men had scored two victories over Mexican forces north of the Rio Grande, at Palo Alto (May 8) and Resaca de la Palma (May 9). On May 18, Taylor crossed the Rio Grande and occupied Matamoros, which a demoralized and bloodied Mexican army had abandoned. These quick victories brought Taylor instant popularity, and the president responded willingly to the demand that he be made commander for the conquest of Mexico. Old "Rough-and-Ready" Taylor impressed Polk as less of a political threat than Scott. Without a major battle he had achieved Polk's main objective, the conquest of Mexico's northern provinces.

THE ANNEXATION OF CALIFORNIA   Along the Pacific coast, conquest was under way before definitive news of the Mexican War erupting arrived. Near the end of 1845, John C. Frémont recruited a band of sixty frontiersmen, ostensibly for another exploration of California and Oregon. When the Mexican commanding officer at Monterey, California, ordered him out of the Salinas River valley, Frémont at first refused to go, but he soon changed his mind and headed for Oregon. In 1846 he and his men again moved south, this time into California's Sacramento River valley. Americans in the area captured Sonoma on June 14, proclaimed the Republic of California, and hoisted the hastily designed flag: a grizzly bear and star painted on white cloth, a version of which would become the state flag.

But the Bear Flag Republic lasted only a month. In July, John D. Sloat, commodore of the U.S. Pacific Fleet, having heard of the outbreak of hostilities with Mexico, sent troops ashore to raise the American flag and proclaim California part of the United States. Most Californians of whatever origin welcomed a change that promised order in preference to the confusion of the Bear Flag Republic.

The Battle of the Plains of Mesa

This sketch was made at the battle, which took place just before U.S. forces entered Los Angeles.

Before the end of July, a new navy commodore, Robert F. Stockton, began preparations to move against Mexican forces in southern California. Stockton's forces occupied Santa Barbara and Los Angeles. By mid-August, Mexican resistance had dissipated. On August 17, Stockton declared himself governor, with Frémont as military commander in the north. At the same time another expedition in New Mexico was closing on Santa Fe. On August 18, Colonel Stephen Kearny and 1,600 U.S. soldiers entered Santa Fe. After naming a civilian governor, Kearny divided his force, leading 300 men west toward California.

In southern California, where most of the poorer Mexicans and Mexicanized Indians resented American rule, a rebellion broke out. By the end of October, the rebels had ousted the token American force. Kearny's troops met up with Stockton's forces at San Diego and joined them in the reconquest of southern California, which they achieved after two brief clashes, entering Los Angeles on January 10, 1847. Rebel forces capitulated three days later.

TAYLOR'S BATTLES   Both California and New Mexico had been taken from Mexican control before General Zachary Taylor fought his first major battle in northern Mexico. Having waited for more men and munitions, he finally moved out of his Matamoros base in September 1846 and assaulted the fortified city of Monterrey, which he took after a five-day siege. President Polk, however, disliked the easy terms of surrender to which Taylor agreed, and worried about Taylor's growing popularity. The whole episode merely confirmed the president's impression that Taylor was too passive to be trusted further with the major campaign. Besides, his victories, if flawed, were leading to talk of General Taylor as the next Whig candidate for president. Polk's greatest flaw as commander in chief was that he sought to manage the war for partisan political purposes. Most of the generals he appointed were selected for their political views rather than their military skill. He wanted to defeat both Mexico and the Whigs—at the same time.

Yet Polk's grand strategy was itself flawed. Having never seen the Mexican desert, the president wrongly assumed that Taylor's men could live off the land and need not depend upon resupply. Polk therefore misunderstood the general's reluctance to strike out across several hundred miles of barren land just north of Mexico City. On another point the president was simply duped. The old dictator General Antonio López de Santa Anna, forced out of power in 1845, got word to Polk from his exile in Cuba that in return for the right considerations he would bring about a settlement of the Mexican War. Polk in turn assured the exiled Mexican leader that the U.S. government would pay well for any territory taken from Mexico. In August 1846, on Polk's orders, Santa Anna was permitted to pass through the American blockade into Veracruz. Soon he was again in command of the Mexican army and was named president once more. Polk's scheme had unintentionally put the ablest Mexican general back in command, where he busily organized his forces to strike at Taylor.

By then another American front had been opened, and Taylor was ordered to wait in place, outside Matamoros. In October 1846, Polk and his cabinet decided to assault Mexico City by way of Veracruz, a port city on the Gulf of Mexico southeast of Mexico City. Polk named General Winfield Scott to the field command. Taylor, miffed at his reduction to a minor role, disobeyed orders and moved west to attack Mexican forces near the hacienda of Buena Vista. Santa Anna met Taylor's untested volunteers with a large but ill-trained and tired army. The Mexican general invited the outnumbered Americans to surrender. "Tell him to go to hell," Taylor replied. In the hard-fought Battle of Buena Vista (February 22–23, 1847), Taylor's son-in-law, Colonel Jefferson Davis, the future president of the Confederacy, led a regiment that broke up a Mexican cavalry charge. Neither side could claim victory. It was the last major action on the central Mexican front, and Taylor was granted leave to return home. The general's growing popularity forced Polk to promote him, despite the president's concerns about his political aspirations. In a self-serving moment, Polk recorded in his diary that Taylor was a "hard fighter" but had "none of the other qualities of a great general." For his part, Taylor came to view Polk with contempt.

Why did John C. Frémont initially settle in the Salinas River valley before marching north, only to march south to San Francisco? How did Polk's fear of Zachary Taylor's popularity undermine the Americans' military strategy?

SCOTT'S TRIUMPH Meanwhile, the long-planned assault on Mexico City had begun on March 9, 1847, when Winfield Scott's army landed on the beaches south of Veracruz. It was the first major amphibious operation by U.S. military forces and was carried out without loss. Veracruz surrendered on March 27 after a weeklong siege. Scott then set out on the route taken by Cortés and his Spanish troops more than 300 years before. Santa Anna tried to set a trap for him at the mountain pass of Cerro Gordo, but Scott's men took more than 3,000 Mexican prisoners.

On May 15, Scott's army entered Puebla, the second-largest Mexican city. There Scott lost about a third of his army because men whose twelve-month enlistments had expired felt free to go home, leaving Scott with about 7,000 troops in all. There was nothing to do but hang on until reinforcements and supplies came up from the coast. Finally, after three months, with his numbers almost doubled, Scott set out on August 7 through the mountain passes into the Valley of Mexico, cutting his supply line to the coast.

Scott directed a brilliant flanking operation around the lakes and marshes that guard the eastern approaches to Mexico City. After a series of battles in which they overwhelmed Mexican defenses, U.S. forces entered Mexico City on September 13, 1847. At the national palace a battalion of marines raised the American flag and occupied "the halls of Montezuma." News of the victory led some expansionists to new heights of land lust. The editor John O'Sullivan, who had coined the term *manifest destiny*, shouted, "More, More, More! Why not take all of Mexico?"

THE TREATY OF GUADALUPE HIDALGO After the fall of the capital, Santa Anna resigned and a month later left the country. Meanwhile, Polk had appointed as peace negotiator Nicholas P. Trist, chief clerk of the State Department and a Virginia Democrat. Formal talks got under way on January 2, 1848, at the village of Guadalupe Hidalgo, just outside the capital, and dragged on through the month. By the Treaty of Guadalupe Hidalgo, signed on February 2, 1848, Mexico gave up all claims to Texas above the Rio Grande and ceded California and New Mexico to the United States. In return the United States agreed to pay Mexico $15 million and assume the claims of U.S. citizens against Mexico up to $3.25 million. Like the Louisiana Purchase, it was a remarkable bargain.

Polk submitted the treaty to the Senate. A growing movement to annex all of Mexico briefly excited the president, but as Polk confided in his diary, rejecting the treaty would be too risky. If he should spurn a treaty made in accord with his own original terms in order to gain more territory, "the probability is that Congress would not grant either men or money to prosecute the war." In that case he might eventually have to withdraw the army and lose everything. So the Treaty of Guadalupe Hidalgo went to the Senate, which ratified it on March 10, 1848. By the end of July, the last remaining U.S. soldiers had left Mexico.

THE WAR'S LEGACIES The Mexican War cost the United States 1,733 killed in battle, 4,152 wounded, and, as usual, far more—11,550—dead of disease, mostly dysentery and chronic diarrhea ("Montezuma's revenge"). It remains the deadliest war in American history in terms of the percentage of combatants killed. Out of every 1,000 soldiers in Mexico, some 110 died. The next highest death rate would be in the Civil War, with 65 dead out of every 1,000 participants.

The Mexican War was a crushing defeat for Mexico and a defining event for the United States. As a result of the conflict, the United States acquired more than 500,000 square miles of territory (almost 1 million, counting Texas), including the splendid Pacific harbors of San Diego, Monterey, and San Francisco. Except for a small addition made by the Gadsden Purchase of 1853, these annexations rounded out the continental United States and doubled its size.

Several important firsts are associated with the Mexican War: the first successful offensive American war, the first occupation of an enemy capital, the first war in which martial law was declared on foreign soil, the first in which West Point graduates played a major role, and the first reported by war correspondents. It was also the first significant combat experience for a group of junior officers who would later serve as leading generals during the Civil War: Robert E. Lee, Ulysses S. Grant, Thomas "Stonewall" Jackson, George B. McClellan, George Meade, and others.

Initially the victory in Mexico unleashed a surge of national pride, but as the years passed, the Mexican War was increasingly seen as a war of conquest directed by a president bent on expansion. Ulysses S. Grant later called it "one of the most unjust ever waged by a stronger against a weaker nation." America's terrible Civil War fifteen years later, he added, was "our punishment" for the unholy Mexican War. For a brief season the glory of conquest added political luster to the names of Generals Zachary Taylor and Winfield Scott. Despite Polk's best efforts, he had manufactured the next, and last, two Whig candidates for president. One of them, Taylor, would replace him in the White House, with the storm of sectional conflict already on the horizon.

The acquisition of Oregon, Texas, California, and the New Southwest made the United States a transcontinental nation. Extending authority over this vast new land greatly expanded the scope of the federal government. In 1849, for example, Congress created the Department of the Interior to supervise the distribution of land, the creation of new territories and states, and the "protection" of the Indians and their land. President Polk naively assumed that the dramatic expansion of American territory to the Pacific would strengthen "the bonds of Union." He was wrong. No sooner was Texas annexed and gold discovered in California than a violent debate erupted over the extension of slavery into the new territories. That debate would culminate in a war that would nearly destroy the Union.

End of Chapter Review

- **Nationalism** Nationalism and westward expansion were the dominant issues in the 1840s, although President John Tyler, a Whig, vetoed traditional Whig policies, such as a new national bank and higher tariffs. Boundaries with Canada were finally settled. The desire for westward expansion culminated in the Mexican War.

- **Westward Migration** Many Americans believed that the West was divinely ordained to be part of the United States. Although populated by Indians and Latinos, the West was portrayed as an empty land. The lure of cheap, fertile land led to Oregon fever, and settlers moved along the Overland Trails, enduring great physical hardships.

- **Texas Republic** Many southerners had moved to the Mexican province of Texas to grow cotton, taking their slaves with them. The Mexican government opposed slavery and in 1830 forbade further immigration. American settlers declared Texas independent in 1836, and the slaughter at the Alamo made the independence of Texas a popular cause in the United States. As soon as Mexico recognized the Texas Republic, many Texans clamored for annexation. The notion was unpopular among the growing anti-slavery faction, however, because it meant adding another slave state to the Union; thus, Texas remained independent for nearly a decade.

- **Mexican War** Annexation of Texas, declared by a joint resolution of Congress in 1845, infuriated Mexico. The newly elected president, James K. Polk, sought to acquire California and New Mexico as well as Texas, but negotiations soon failed. When Mexican troops crossed the Rio Grande, Polk urged Congress to declare war.

- **Results of the Mexican War** In 1848, in the Treaty of Guadalupe Hidalgo, Mexico ceded California and New Mexico to the United States and gave up claims to land north of the Rio Grande. The vast acquisition did not strengthen the Union, however, because a fierce debate immediately erupted allowing slavery in the new territories.

CHRONOLOGY

1821	Mexico gains independence from Spain
1836	Americans are defeated at the Alamo
1841	John Tyler becomes president
1842	Americans and British agree to the Webster-Ashburton Treaty
1845	United States annexes Texas
	Mexican War begins
1846	Most of the Donner party die en route to California
1848	Treaty of Guadalupe Hidalgo ends the Mexican War
1849	California gold rush begins
1851	Plains Indians agree to the Fort Laramie Treaty

KEY TERMS & NAMES

Manifest Destiny p. 530

mountain men p. 534

Oregon fever p. 534

Franciscan missions p. 537

Overland Trails p. 539

John C. Frémont, "the Pathfinder" p. 544

Stephen F. Austin p. 545

Tejanos p. 546

Battle of the Alamo p. 546

Sam Houston p. 547

Lone Star Republic p. 547

James Knox Polk, "Young Hickory" p. 550

Winfield Scott p. 556

Zachary Taylor p. 556

Bear Flag Republic p. 556

General Antonio López de Santa Anna p. 558

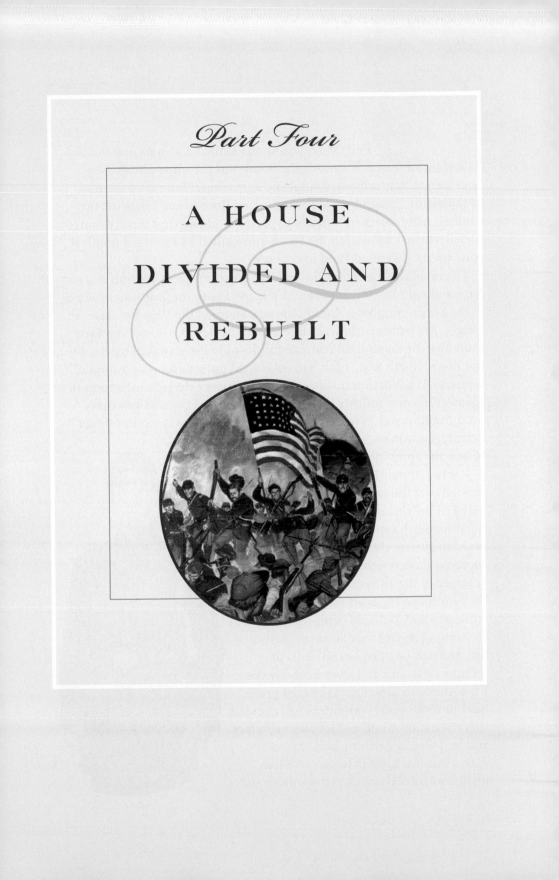

Part Four

A HOUSE
DIVIDED AND
REBUILT

Of all the regions of the United States during the first half of the nineteenth century, the South was the most distinctive. Southern society remained rural and agricultural long after the rest of the nation had embraced the Industrial Revolution. Likewise, the southern elite's tenacious desire to preserve and expand slavery muted social-reform impulses in the South and ignited a prolonged political controversy that would end in civil war.

The rapid settlement of the western territories set in motion a ferocious competition between North and South for political influence in the burgeoning West. Would the new states in the West be "slave" or "free"? The issue of allowing slavery into the new territories involved more than humanitarian concern for the plight of enslaved blacks. By the 1840s, North and South had developed quite different economic interests. The North wanted high tariffs on imported manufactures to "protect" its new industries from foreign competition. Southerners, on the other hand, favored free trade because they wanted to import British goods in exchange for the profitable cotton they provided British textile mills.

A series of political compromises had glossed over the fundamental differences between the regions during the first half of the nineteenth century. But abolitionists refused to give up their crusade against slavery. Moreover, a new generation of politicians emerged in the 1850s, leaders from both the North and the South who were less willing to seek political compromises. The continuing debate over allowing slavery into the new western territories kept sectional tensions at a fever pitch. By the time Abraham Lincoln was elected president in 1860, many Americans had decided that the nation could not survive half-slave and half-free; something had to give.

In a last-ditch effort to preserve the institution of slavery, eleven southern states seceded from the Union and created a separate confederate nation. That, in turn, prompted northerners such as Lincoln to support a civil war to preserve the Union. No one realized in 1861 how prolonged and costly the War between the States would become. Over 630,000 soldiers and sailors would die of wounds or disease. The colossal carnage caused even the most seasoned observers to blanch in disbelief. As President Lincoln confessed in his second inaugural address, in 1865, no one expected the war to become so "fundamental and astonishing."

Nor did anyone envision how sweeping the war's effects would be upon the future of the country. The northern victory in 1865 restored the Union and in the process helped accelerate America's transformation into a modern nation-state. National power and a national consciousness began to displace the sectional emphases of the antebellum era. A Republican-led Congress enacted federal legislation to foster industrial and commercial development and western expansion. In the process the United States began to leave behind the Jeffersonian dream of a decentralized agrarian republic.

The Civil War also ended slavery, yet the status of the freed African Americans remained precarious. Former slaves found themselves legally free, but few of them had property, a home, education, or training. Although the Fourteenth Amendment (1868) set forth guarantees for the civil rights of African Americans and the Fifteenth Amendment (1870) provided that black men could vote, southern officials found ingenious and often violent—ways to avoid the spirit and the letter of the new laws.

The restoration of the former Confederate states to the Union did not come easily. Bitterness and resistance festered among the vanquished. Although Confederate leaders were initially disenfranchised, they continued to exercise considerable authority in political and economic matters. In 1877, when the last federal troops were removed from the occupied South, former Confederates declared themselves "redeemed" from the stain of military occupation. By the end of the nineteenth century, most states of the former Confederacy had devised a system of legal discrimination against blacks that re-created many aspects of slavery.

15

THE OLD SOUTH

FOCUS QUESTIONS ⓢ wwnorton.com/studyspace

- How diverse was the South's economy, and what was its unifying feature?
- How did dependence on agriculture and slavery shape the distinctive culture of the Old South? Why did southern whites who did not hold slaves defend the "peculiar institution"?
- What led to the anti-slavery movement? How did white southerners respond to it?
- How did enslaved people respond to their bondage during the antebellum period? How did free persons of color fit into southern society?

Southerners, a North Carolina editor once wrote, are "a mythological people, created half out of dream and half out of slander, who live in a still legendary land." Most Americans, including southerners themselves, have long harbored a cluster of myths and stereotypes about the South. Perhaps the most enduring myths come from the classic movie *Gone with the Wind* (1939). The South portrayed in such romanticized Hollywood productions is a stable agrarian society led by paternalistic white planters and their families, who live in white-columned mansions and represent a "natural" aristocracy of virtue and talent within their communities. In *Gone with the Wind* and similar accounts, southerners are kind to their slaves and devoted to the rural values of independence and chivalric honor, values celebrated by Thomas Jefferson.

By contrast, a much darker myth about the Old South emerged from abolitionist pamphlets and Harriet Beecher Stowe's best-selling novel, *Uncle*

Tom's Cabin (1852). Those exposés of southern culture portrayed the planters as arrogant aristocrats who raped enslaved women, brutalized enslaved workers, and lorded over their communities with haughty disdain for the rights and needs of others. They bred slaves like cattle, broke up slave families, and sold slaves "down the river" to certain death in the Louisiana sugar mills and rice plantations.

Such contrasting myths die hard, in large part because each one is rooted in reality. Nonetheless, efforts to get at what set the Old South apart from the rest of the nation generally pivot on two lines of thought: the impact of the environment (climate and geography) and the effects of human decisions and actions. The South's warm, humid climate was ideal for the cultivation of commercial crops such as tobacco, cotton, rice, and sugarcane. The growth of those lucrative cash crops helped foster the plantation system and its dependence upon enslaved labor. The lust for profits trumped concerns over the morality of slavery. In the end the profitability of slavery and the racist attitudes it engendered brought about the sectional conflict over the extension of slavery that ignited the Civil War.

The Distinctiveness of the Old South

While geography was and is a key determinant of the South's economy and culture, much of southern distinctiveness resulted from the institution of slavery. The resolve of slaveholders to retain control of their socioeconomic order created a sense of racial unity that bridged class divisions among whites. Yet the biracial character of the population exercised an even greater influence over southern culture. In shaping patterns of speech and folklore, music, religion, literature, and recreation, black southerners immeasurably influenced and enriched the region's development.

The South differed from other sections of the country, too, in the high proportion of native-born Americans in its population, both whites and blacks. Despite a great diversity of origins in the colonial population, the South drew few overseas immigrants after the Revolution. One reason was that the main shipping lines went from Europe to northern ports; another, that the prospect of competing with slave labor deterred immigrants. During the first half of the nineteenth century, the South increasingly became a consciously minority region. The South's population growth lagged behind that of other sections of the country. The South's determination to preserve and expand slavery in the face of growing criticism in the North and around the world further isolated and defined the region. A prickly defensiveness increasingly shaped southern attitudes and actions.

The South also differed from the rest of the nation in its architecture; its penchant for fighting, guns, and the military; and its attachment to an agrarian ideal. The preponderance of farming remained a distinctive regional characteristic, whether pictured as the Jeffersonian small farmer living by the sweat of his brow or the lordly planter dispatching his slave gangs. But in the end what made the South distinctive was its people's belief—and other people's belief—that the region *was* so distinctive.

Slavery in the South

Slave quarters on a South Carolina plantation.

DIVERGENT SOUTHS   For all of the common threads tying the Old South together, it in fact included three distinct regions with quite different economic interests and diverging degrees of commitment to slavery. The seven states making up the Lower South (South Carolina, Georgia, Florida, Alabama, Mississippi, Louisiana, and Texas) grew increasingly dependent upon labor-intensive cotton production and slave labor. By 1860, slaves represented nearly half the population of the Lower South. The states of the Middle South (Virginia, North Carolina, Tennessee, and Arkansas) had more diversified agricultural economies and included large areas without slavery. In the Upper or Border South (Delaware, Maryland, Kentucky, and Missouri), slavery was beginning to decline by 1860. The shifting differences among these three regions help explain the different degrees of concern, and the intensity of feelings, about the fate of slavery. With a disproportionately large investment in slavery, the states of the Lower South took the lead in the sectional debates over restricting slavery in the new western territories.

RELIGION IN THE OLD SOUTH   The growing defensiveness of the South with respect to slavery was especially evident in the region's religious life. The South was overwhelmingly Protestant. Although there were pockets of Catholicism and Judaism in the large coastal cities—Baltimore, Richmond, Charleston, Savannah, and New Orleans—the vast majority of southerners were Baptist or Methodist. In the eighteenth century the first generation of Baptists and Methodists condemned slavery, welcomed blacks to their congregations, and accorded women important roles in their churches. By the early nineteenth century, however, having grown concerned about the diminishing participation of white men in their churches, the two denominations had changed their stance. Ministers began to mute their opposition to slavery. In 1785 the Methodists formally abandoned their policy of denying church membership to slaveholders. By the 1830s most Protestant preachers in the South had switched from attacking slavery to defending it as a divinely ordained social system evident in the Bible. Most of the ministers who refused to promote slavery left the region.

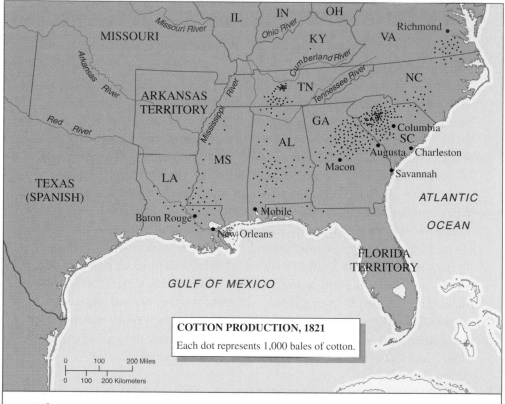

COTTON PRODUCTION, 1821

Each dot represents 1,000 bales of cotton.

Why was cotton an appealing staple crop? What regions produced the most cotton in 1821? Keeping in mind what you read about cotton in Chapter 12, what innovations would you suppose allowed farmers to move inland and produce cotton more efficiently?

STAPLE CROPS   The idea of the Cotton Kingdom is itself something of a mythic stereotype. Although cotton was the most important of the "staple," or most profitable, crops, it was a latecomer. Tobacco, the first staple crop, had been the mainstay of Virginia and Maryland during the colonial era and was common in North Carolina. After the Revolution the tobacco economy spread into Kentucky and as far as Missouri. Indigo, an important crop in colonial South Carolina, vanished with the loss of British bounties for this source of a valuable blue dye. Since rice production required substantial capital for floodgates, irrigation ditches, and machinery, it was limited to the relatively few large plantations that could afford it, and those were in the Tidewater areas of North and South Carolina and Georgia, where fields could easily be flooded and drained.

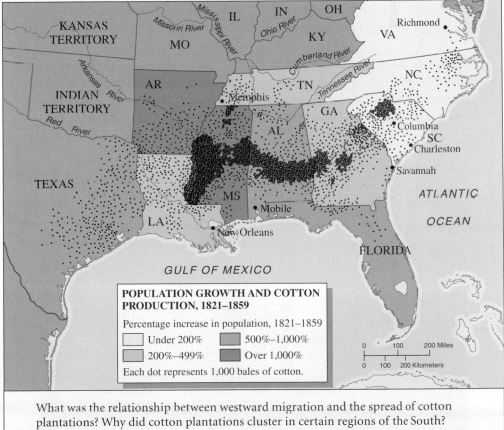

POPULATION GROWTH AND COTTON PRODUCTION, 1821–1859

Percentage increase in population, 1821–1859

Under 200%   500%–1,000%
200%–499%   Over 1,000%

Each dot represents 1,000 bales of cotton.

What was the relationship between westward migration and the spread of cotton plantations? Why did cotton plantations cluster in certain regions of the South? What were the environmental and economic consequences of the South's emphasis on cotton?

Sugar, like rice, required a heavy capital investment—in machinery to grind the cane. Since sugar needed the prop of a protective tariff to enable its farmers to compete with foreign suppliers, it produced the anomaly in southern politics of pro-tariff congressmen from Louisiana, where sugar was king.

Cotton, the last of the major staple crops, eventually outpaced all the others put together. At the end of the War of 1812, annual cotton production was less than 150,000 bales; in 1860 it was 4 million. Two factors accounted for the dramatic growth: British and French textile manufacturers' voracious appetite for American cotton and the cultivation of farmlands in the newer states of Alabama, Mississippi, Arkansas, and Louisiana. Much of the story of the southern people—white and black—from 1820 to 1860 is their mass movement from Virginia and the Carolinas to more fertile cotton lands farther west. By 1860 the center of the cotton belt stretched from eastern North Carolina, South Carolina, and Georgia through the fertile Alabama-Mississippi black belt (so called for the color of the soil), through Louisiana, on to Texas, and up the Mississippi River valley as far as southern Illinois.

AGRICULTURAL DIVERSITY   The focus on cotton and the other cash crops has obscured the degree to which the antebellum South fed itself from its own fields. Southern farms also grew enormous amounts of corn, wheat, and potatoes and raised plenty of cattle and hogs. Yet the story of the southern

Southern agriculture

Planting sweet potatoes on James Hopkinson's plantation, Edisto Island, South Carolina, April 1862.

economy was hardly one of unbroken prosperity. The South's cash crops, planted year after year, quickly exhausted the soil. In low-country South Carolina, Senator Robert Y. Hayne spoke of "fields abandoned; and hospitable mansions of our fathers deserted." The older farmlands had trouble competing with the newer soil farther west. But lands in the states bordering the Gulf of Mexico also began to show wear and tear. By 1855, an Alabama senator had noted, "Our small planters, after taking the cream off their lands . . . are going further west and south in search of other virgin lands which they may and will despoil and impoverish in like manner."

MANUFACTURING AND TRADE   So the South faced a growing sense of economic crisis as the nineteenth century advanced. Some sought to deal with the loss of the soil's fertility by promoting "scientific agriculture." Researchers encouraged farmers to rotate the types of crops they planted each year and use new forms of fertilizer. By 1840 other southerners had concluded that the farm-centered region desperately needed to develop its own manufacturing and trade. The cotton-growing mania had led the South to become increasingly dependent upon northern industry and commerce: cotton and tobacco were exported mainly in northern vessels; southerners also relied upon northern merchants for imported goods—economically the South had become a kind of colonial dependency of the North. The merchants of northern cities, a southerner said, "export our . . . valuable productions, and import our articles of consumption and from this agency they derive a profit which has enriched them . . . at our expense."

Southern concerns about their overdependence upon northern merchants and bankers prompted interest in a more diversified economy. Factories and mills were needed to balance agriculture and trade. Southern publicists called attention to the section's great resources: its raw materials, labor supply, waterpower, wood and coal, and markets. In Richmond the Tredegar Iron Works grew into the single most important manufacturing enterprise in the Old South. It used mostly slave labor to produce cannons, shot, and shells, as well as axes, saws, girders, boilers, and steam engines, including locomotives. Yet despite such efforts the region still lagged well behind the North in its industrial development and commercial network.

ECONOMIC DEVELOPMENT   During the antebellum years two major explanations were put forward for the lag in southern industrial development. First, blacks were presumed unsuited to factory work. Second, the ruling elite of the Old South had developed a lordly disdain for industrial production. A certain aristocratic prestige derived from owning land and

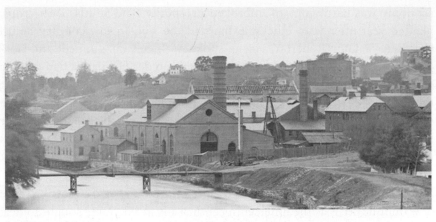

Iron manufacturing

By 1873, the Tredegar Iron Works in Richmond, Virginia, employed 1,200 workers.

holding slaves. But any argument that African American labor was incompatible with industrial work simply flew in the face of the evidence, since southern factory owners bought or hired enslaved blacks to operate just about every kind of manufacture. Given the opportunity, any number of African Americans displayed managerial skills as overseers.

The notion that aristocratic planters were not sufficiently motivated by profits to promote industrial development is also a myth. While the profitability of slavery has been a long-standing subject of controversy, in recent years economic historians have concluded that slaves on average supplied about a 10 percent annual return on their cost. At the time that was an enticing profit margin, just as it is now. By a strictly economic calculation, slaves and land on which cotton could be grown were the most profitable investments available in the antebellum South. Some slaveholders, particularly in the newer cotton lands of the Old Southwest, were incredibly rich.

WHITE SOCIETY IN THE SOUTH

If an understanding of the Old South must begin with a knowledge of social myths, it must end with a sense of tragedy. Since colonial days white southerners had won short-term gains at the cost of both long-term development and moral isolation in the eyes of the world. The concentration on agriculture and slaves at the expense of urban development and immigration

King Cotton Captured

This engraving shows cotton being trafficked in Louisiana.

deprived the South of the most dynamic sources of innovation. The slave-holding South hitched its wagon not to a star but to the (largely British) demand for cotton. During the late 1850s cotton production became so profitable that it blinded many people to reality and fostered some tragic misperceptions. The South, "safely entrenched behind her cotton bags . . . can defy the world—for the civilized world depends on the cotton of the South," said a Mississippi newspaper in 1860. "No power on earth dares to make war upon it," said James H. Hammond of South Carolina. "Cotton is king." What such naive southern boosters could not perceive was what they could least afford: the imminent slackening of the world demand for cotton. The heyday of expansion in British textiles had ended by 1860, but by then the Deep South was locked into large-scale cotton production for generations to come.

PLANTERS   Although there were only a few giant plantations in each southern state, they set the tone for economic and social life. What distinguished the plantation from the farm, in addition to its size, was the use of a large labor force, under separate control and supervision, to grow primarily staple crops (cotton, rice, tobacco, and sugarcane) for profit. A clear-cut distinction between management and labor set the planter apart from the small slaveholder, who often worked side by side with slaves at the same tasks.

If, to be called a planter, one had to hold 20 slaves, only 1 out of every 30 whites in the South in 1860 was a planter. Fewer than 11,000 held 50 or more slaves, and only 2,300 held over 100. The census listed only 11 planters with 500 slaves and just 1 with as many as 1,000. Yet this privileged elite exercised disproportionate influence. The planter group, making up under 4 percent of the white men in the South, held more than half the slaves and produced most of the cotton, tobacco, and hemp and all of the sugar and rice. The number of slaveholders was only 383,637 out of a total white population of 8 million. But assuming that each family numbered five people, then whites with some proprietary interest in slavery constituted 1.9 million, or roughly a fourth of the South's white population. While the preponderance of southern whites belonged to the small-farmer class, they tended to defer to the large planters. After all, many small farmers aspired to become planters themselves.

THE PLANTATION MISTRESS The mistress of the plantation, like the master, seldom led a life of idle leisure. She supervised the domestic household in the same way the planter took care of the business, overseeing the supply and preparation of food and linens, the housecleaning and care of the sick, and a hundred other details. Mary Boykin Chesnut of South Carolina complained that "there is no slave like a wife." The wives of all but the most wealthy planters supervised the domestic activities of the household and managed the slaves. The son of a Tennessee slaveholder remembered that his mother and grandmother were "the busiest women I ever saw."

White women living in a slaveholding culture confronted a double standard in terms of moral and sexual behavior. While they were expected to behave as exemplars of Christian piety and sexual purity, their husbands, brothers, and sons often followed an

MRS. CHESTNUT
of South Carolina

Mary Chestnut

Mary Chestnut's diary describing the Civil War was republished in 1981 and won the Pulitzer Prize.

unwritten rule of self-indulgent hedonism. "God forgive us," Mary Chesnut wrote in her diary,

> but ours is a monstrous system. Like the patriarchs of old, our men live all in one house with their wives and their [enslaved] concubines; and the mulattoes one sees in every family partly resemble the white children. Any lady is ready to tell you who is the father of all the mulatto children in everybody's household but her own. Those, she seems to think, drop from the clouds.

Such a double standard both illustrated and reinforced the arrogant authoritarianism displayed by many male planters. Yet for all their private complaints and daily burdens, few plantation mistresses engaged in public criticism of the prevailing social order and racist climate.

THE MIDDLE CLASS Overseers on the largest plantations generally came from the middle class of small farmers or skilled workers or were younger sons of planters. Most aspired to become slaveholders themselves. Occasionally there were black overseers, but the highest management position to which a slave could aspire was usually that of "driver," placed in charge of a small group of slaves with the duty of getting them to work without creating dissension.

The most numerous white southerners were the small farmers (yeomen), those who lived with their families in simple two-room cabins rather than columned mansions. They raised a few hogs and chickens, grew some corn and cotton, and traded with neighbors more than they bought from stores. Women worked in the fields during harvesttime but spent most of their days attending to domestic chores. Many of these "middling" farmers owned a handful of slaves, but most had none.

Southern farmers were typically mobile folk, ever willing to pull up stakes and move west or southwest in pursuit of better land. They tended to be fiercely independent and suspicious of government authority, and they overwhelmingly identified with the Democratic party of Andrew Jackson and the spiritual fervor of evangelical Protestantism. Even though only a minority of the middle-class farmers held slaves, most of them supported the slave system. They feared that the slaves, if freed, would compete with them for land, and they enjoyed the privileged status that racially based slavery afforded them. As a white farmer told a northern traveler, "Now suppose they was free. You see they'd all think themselves as good as we." Such racist sentiments pervaded the Deep South—and much of the rest of the nation.

"POOR WHITES" Visitors to the Old South often had trouble telling yeomen apart from the true "poor whites," a degraded class relegated to the least desirable land, living on the fringes of polite society. The "poor whites," given over to hunting and fishing, to hound dogs and moonshine whiskey, often displayed a pronounced lankness and sallowness. Speculation had it that they were descended from indentured servants or convicts transported to the colonies from Britain or that they were the weakest of the frontier population, forced to take refuge in the sand land, the pine barrens, and the swamps after having been pushed aside by the more enterprising and the more successful. But the problem was less heredity than environment, the consequence of infections and dietary deficiencies that gave rise to a trilogy of "lazy diseases": hookworm, malaria, and pellagra, all of which produced an enervating lethargy. Around 1900, researchers discovered the causes of and cures for these diseases. By 1930 they had practically disappeared, taking with them many of the stereotypes.

HONOR AND VIOLENCE From colonial times most southern white men prided themselves on adhering to a moral code centered on a prickly sense of honor. Such a preoccupation with masculine honor was common among Germanic and Celtic peoples (the Scottish, Irish, Scotch-Irish, Cornish, and Welsh), from whom most white southerners were descended. It flourished in hierarchical rural societies, where face-to-face relations governed social manners. The dominant ethical code for the southern white elite included a combative sensitivity to slights; loyalty to family, locality, state, and region; deference to elders and social "betters"; and an almost theatrical hospitality. Southern men displayed a fierce defense of female purity and a propensity to magnify personal insults to the point of capital offenses.

The preoccupation of southern white men with a sense of honor steeped in violence found outlets in several popular rituals. Like their Celtic and English ancestors, white southerners hunted, rode, and gambled—over cards, dice, horse racing, and cockfighting. All those activities provided arenas for masculine camaraderie as well as competition.

Southern men of all social classes often promoted a reckless manliness. Duels were the ultimate expression of personal honor and manly courage. Although not confined to the South, dueling was much more common there than in the rest of the young nation, a fact that gave rise to the observation that southerners would be polite until they were angry enough to kill you. Dueling was outlawed in the northern states after Aaron Burr killed Alexander

Hamilton in 1804, and several southern states banned the practice as
well—but the prohibition was rarely
enforced. Amid the fiery antebellum
political debates over nullification,
abolition, and the fate of slavery in the
territories, clashing opinions often
ended in duels. Many of the most
prominent southern leaders—congressmen, senators, governors, editors,
and planters—engaged in duels. The
roster of participants included Andrew
Jackson, Henry Clay, Sam Houston,
and Jefferson Davis.

Scene in Washington

BLACK SOCIETY IN THE SOUTH

This caricature of the prominent Whig
newspaper editor James Watson Webb
appeared after Webb provoked a duel
between two congressmen in 1838. He
is shown armed with a sword cane, a
musket, a knife, and several pistols and
is trailed by a turkey, a symbol of his
arrogance.

For all of its evils, slavery was
one of the fastest growing elements
of American life during the first half
of the nineteenth century. In 1790
there were fewer than 700,000 enslaved blacks in the United States. By
1830 there were more than 2 million, and by 1860 there were almost 4 million. Throughout the seventeenth and well into the eighteenth century, slavery was largely an uncodified system of forced labor practiced in most
New World colonies. Enslaved workers were treated largely like indentured
servants. After the American Revolution, however, slavery became a highly
regulated institution limited to the South. People referred to it as the "peculiar institution" because it so flagrantly violated the principle of individual freedom that served as the basis of the Declaration of Independence.
During the antebellum era, slavery became such a powerful engine of
economic development—for both the southern cotton crop and the New
England textile industry—that its mushrooming significance defied domestic and international criticism. By 1860 the dollar value of southern slavery
outstripped the value of all banks, railroads, and factories combined. Slavery
was the most important force shaping American history in the first half of

the nineteenth century. Yet by no means was it monolithic in character, nor was it necessarily inescapable.

"FREE PERSONS OF COLOR" In the Old South free persons of color occupied an uncertain status, balanced somewhere between slavery and freedom, subject to racist legal restrictions not imposed upon whites. Free blacks attained their status in a number of ways. Over the years some slaves were able to purchase their freedom, and some gained it as a reward for wartime military service. Others were freed by conscientious masters. By 1860 there were some 260,000 free blacks in the slave states.

Among them were a large number of mulattoes, people of mixed racial ancestry. The census of 1860 reported 412,000 people of mixed parentage in the United States, or about 10 percent of the black population, probably a drastic undercount. In cities such as Charleston and especially New Orleans, "colored" society became virtually a third caste, a new people who occupied a status somewhere between that of blacks and that of whites. Some mulattoes built substantial fortunes and even became slaveholders. They often operated inns serving a white clientele. Jehu Jones, for instance, was the "colored" proprietor of one of Charleston's best hotels. In Louisiana a mulatto, Cyprien Ricard, paid $250,000 for an estate that had ninety-one slaves. In Natchez, Mississippi, William Johnson, son of a white father and a mulatto mother, operated three barbershops, owned 1,500 acres of land, and held several slaves.

Yarrow Mamout

Mamout, an African Muslim who had been sold into slavery, purchased his freedom, acquired property, and settled in Georgetown (now part of Washington, D.C.). Charles Willson Peale executed this portrait in 1819, when Mamout was over 100 years old.

Black slaveholders were few in number, however. The 1830 census revealed that 3,775 free blacks, about 2 percent of the total free black population, held 12,760 slaves. Some blacks held slaves for humanitarian purposes. One minister, for instance, bought slaves and then enabled them to purchase their freedom from him on easy terms. Most often, black slaveholders were free blacks who bought their own family members with the express purpose of freeing them.

THE TRADE IN SLAVES

The rise in the slave population mainly occurred naturally, especially after the African slave trade was outlawed in 1808. The rise in the cash value of enslaved workers brought better treatment. "Massa was purty good," one ex-slave recalled. "He treated us jus' 'bout like you would a good mule." Another said his master "fed us reg'lar on good, 'stantial food, jus' like you'd tend to you hoss, if you had a real good one." Some slaveholders hired wage laborers, often Irish immigrants, for ditching and other dangerous work rather than risk the lives of the more valuable slaves.

Free blacks

This badge, issued in Charleston, South Carolina, was worn by a free black so that he would not be mistaken for someone's "property."

The end of the foreign slave trade increased the importance of the domestic trading network, with slaves moving mainly from the used-up lands of the Southeast into the booming new country of the Old Southwest. The slave trade peaked just before 1837, then slacked off, first because of economic depression, then because agricultural reform and recovery renewed the demand for slaves in the Upper South. Many slaves moved south and west with the planters who owned them, but selling slaves became big business, with brokers, pens, and auctioneers. The worst aspect of the domestic slave trade was the separation of children from parents and husbands from wives. Only Louisiana and Alabama (from 1852) forbade separating a child under ten from his or her mother, and no state forbade the separation of husband from wife.

PLANTATION SLAVERY

Most slaves labored on large plantations. The preferred jobs were household servant and skilled worker, including blacksmith and carpenter, or a special assignment, such as boatman or cook. Field hands were usually housed in one- or two-room wooden shacks with dirt floors. A set of clothes was distributed twice a year, but shoes were generally provided only in winter. About half of all slave babies died in the first year of life, a mortality rate more than twice that of whites. Field hands worked long hours, from dawn to dusk. The difference between a good owner and a bad

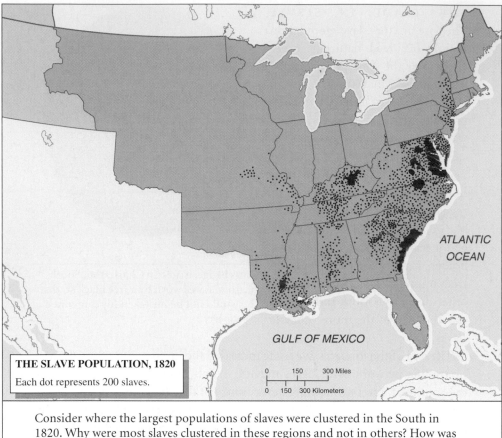

THE SLAVE POPULATION, 1820

Each dot represents 200 slaves.

ATLANTIC OCEAN

GULF OF MEXICO

0   150   300 Miles

0   150   300 Kilometers

Consider where the largest populations of slaves were clustered in the South in 1820. Why were most slaves clustered in these regions and not in others? How was the experience of plantation slavery different for men and women?

one, according to one ex-slave, was the difference between one "who did not whip you too much" and one who "whipped you till he'd bloodied you and blistered you." Over 50,000 slaves a year escaped. Those not caught often headed for Mexico, the northern states, or Canada.

THE EXPERIENCE OF SLAVE WOMEN   Although black men and women often performed similar labors, they did not experience slavery in the same way. Once slaveholders realized how profitable a fertile female slave could be over time, giving birth every two and a half years to a child who eventually could be sold, they began to encourage reproduction through a variety of incentives. Pregnant slaves were given less work to do and more food. Some plantation owners rewarded new mothers with dresses and silver dollars.

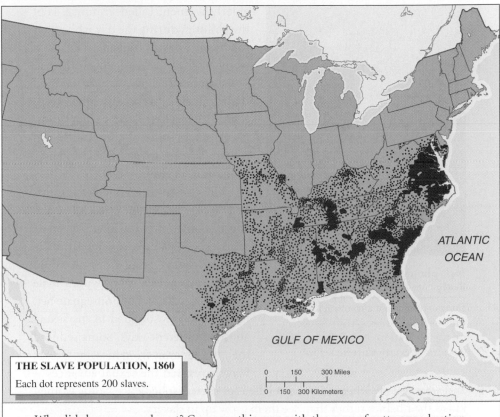

THE SLAVE POPULATION, 1860

Each dot represents 200 slaves.

0   150   300 Miles

0   150   300 Kilometers

Why did slavery spread west? Compare this map with the map of cotton production on page 573. What patterns do you see? Why would slaves have resisted migrating west?

But if motherhood endowed enslaved women with stature and benefits, it also entailed exhausting demands. Within days after childbirth, the mother was put to work spinning, weaving, or sewing. A few weeks thereafter mothers were sent back to the fields; breast-feeding mothers were often forced to take their babies to the fields with them. Enslaved women were expected to do "man's work" outside: cut trees, haul logs, plow fields with mules, dig ditches, spread fertilizer, slaughter animals, hoe corn, and pick cotton. As a slave who escaped reported, "Women who do outdoor work are used as bad as men."

Once women passed their childbearing years, around the age of forty, their workload was increased. Slaveholders put middle-aged women to work full-time in the fields or performing other outdoor labor. On larger plantations

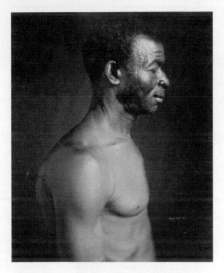

***Jack*, photographed by Joseph T. Zealy**

Daguerreotype of a man identified only as Jack, a driver from Guinea, on the plantation of B. F. Taylor of Columbia, South Carolina, 1850.

elderly women, called grannies, kept the children during the day while their mothers worked outside. Enslaved women of all ages usually worked in sex-segregated gangs, which enabled them to form close bonds with one another. To enslaved African Americans, developing a sense of community and camaraderie meant emotional and psychological survival.

Unlike enslaved men, enslaved girls and women faced the threat of sexual abuse. Sometimes a white master or overseer would rape a woman in the fields or cabins. Sometimes he would lock a woman in a cabin with a male slave whose task was to impregnate her. Female slaves responded to the sexual abuse in different ways. Some seduced their master away from his wife. Others fiercely resisted the sexual advances— and were usually whipped or even killed for their disobedience. Some women killed their babies rather than see them grow up in slavery.

CELIA   Occasionally a single historical incident involving ordinary people can illustrate the web of laws and customs within a society. Such is the case of a teenage slave named Celia. In 1850 fourteen-year-old Celia was purchased by Robert Newsom, a prosperous, respected Missouri farmer who told his daughters that he had bought Celia to work as their domestic servant. In fact, however, the recently widowed Newsom wanted a sexual slave. After purchasing Celia, he raped the girl while taking her back to his farm. For the next five years, Newsom treated Celia as his mistress, even building her a brick cabin fifty yards from his house. During that time she gave birth to two children, presumably his offspring. By 1855, Celia had fallen in love with another slave, George, who demanded that she "quit the old man." Desperate for relief from her tormentor, Celia appealed to Newsom's two grown daughters, but they either could not or would not intervene.

Soon thereafter, on June 23, 1855, the sixty-five-year-old Newsom entered Celia's cabin, ignored her frantic appeals, and kept advancing until she struck and killed him with a large stick. Celia was not allowed to testify at

The business of slavery

The offices of Price, Birch and Company, dealers in slaves, Alexandria, Virginia.

her trial because she was a slave. Her attorneys, all of them slaveholders, argued that the right of white women to defend themselves against sexual assault should be extended to enslaved women. The prevailing public opinion in the slave states, however, stressed that the rape of a slave by an owner was not a crime. The judge and jury, all white men, pronounced Celia guilty. On December 21, 1855, after two months of trials and futile appeals, Celia was hanged.

The grim story of Celia's brief life and abused condition highlights the skewed power structure in southern society before the Civil War. Celia bore a double burden, that of a slave and that of a woman living in a male-dominated society rife with racism and sexism.

SLAVE REBELLIONS Organized slave resistance was difficult in the face of overwhelming white authority and firepower. The nineteenth-century South witnessed only three major slave insurrections, two of which were betrayed before they got under way. In 1800 a slave named Gabriel on a plantation near Richmond hatched a plot involving perhaps 1,000 others to seize key points in the city and start a general slaughter of whites. Twenty-five of his conspirators were executed, and ten others were deported to the West Indies.

The Denmark Vesey plot in Charleston, discovered in 1822, involved an effort to assault the white population, seize ships in the harbor, burn the city, and head for Santo Domingo. It never got off the ground. Instead, thirty-five

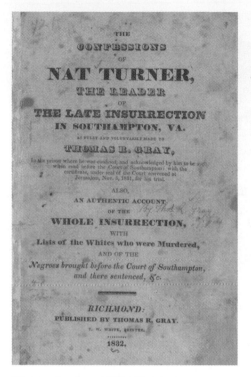

The confessions of Nat Turner

Published account of Turner's rebellion, written by Turner's lawyer, Thomas Gray.

supposed slave rebels were executed, and thirty-four were deported. The city also responded by curtailing the liberties of free blacks. In Charleston, blacks outnumbered whites, and the ruling elite was hysterically determined to quash any slave uprising.

Only the Nat Turner insurrection of August 1831, in rural Southampton County, Virginia, got beyond the planning stage. Turner, a black overseer, was also a religious exhorter who professed a divine mission in leading a slave rebellion. The revolt began when a small group of slaves killed the adults and children in Turner's master's household and set off down the road, repeating the process at other farmhouses, where other slaves joined in. Before it ended, at least fifty-five whites had been killed. The Virginia militia indiscriminately killed many slaves in the process of putting down the rebels. Seventeen slaves were hanged.

Most slaves, however, did not rebel or run away. Instead, they more often retaliated against oppression by malingering or engaging in sabotage. Yet there were constraints on such behavior, for laborers would likely eat better on a prosperous plantation than on a struggling one. And the shrewdest slaveholders knew that they would more likely benefit from offering rewards than from inflicting pain. Plantations based upon the profit motive fostered mutual dependency between slaves and their masters, as well as natural antagonism. And in an agrarian society in which personal relations counted for much, blacks could win concessions that moderated the harshness of slavery, permitting them a certain degree of individual and community development.

FORGING A SLAVE COMMUNITY   To generalize about slavery is to miss its variety from place to place and time to time. The experience was as varied as people are. Enslaved African Americans were certainly victims, but to stop at so obvious a reality would be to miss an important story of endurance, resilience, and achievement. If ever there was an effective melting pot in American history, it may have been that in which Africans with a variety of ethnic, linguistic, and tribal origins fused to form a new community and a new culture as African Americans. Slave culture incorporated many African elements, especially in areas with few whites. Among the Gullahs of the South Carolina and Georgia coast, for example, a researcher found as late as the 1940s more than 4,000 words still in use from the languages of twenty-one African tribes. Elements of African culture have thus survived, adapted, and interacted with those of the other cultures with which they came in contact.

SLAVE RELIGION AND FOLKLORE Among the most important manifestations of slave culture was its dynamic religion, a mixture of African and Christian elements. Slaves found in religion both balm for the soul and release for their emotions. Most Africans brought with them to the Americas a concept of a Creator, or Supreme God, whom they could recognize in the Christian Jehovah, and lesser gods, whom they might identify with Christ, the Holy Ghost, and the saints, thereby reconciling their African beliefs with Christianity. Alongside the church they maintained beliefs in spirits (many of them benign), magic, and conjuring. Belief in magic is in fact a common response to conditions of danger or helplessness.

Slaves found great comfort in religion. Masters sought to instill lessons of Christian humility and obedience, but African Americans identified their plight with that of the Israelites in Egypt or the Christ who suffered as they did. And the ultimate hope of a better world gave solace in this one. Some slaveholders encouraged religious meetings among their slaves, many of them believing that an enslaved Christian would be a better slave. "Church was what they called it," one former slave remembered, "but all that [white] preacher talked about was for us slaves to obey our masters and not to lie and steal."

Such a manipulated Christianity alienated many African Americans, and most sought to create a genuine faith that spoke to their own spiritual and human needs. This often required worship in secret, stealing away from the slave quarters to hold "bush meetings." A slave preacher explained that the "way in which we worshiped is almost indescribable. The singing helped provoke a certain ecstasy of emotion, clapping of hands, tossing of heads, which would continue without cessation about half an hour. The old house partook of the ecstasy; it rang with their jubilant shouts, and shook in all its joints."

Slaves found the Bible edifying in its tributes to the poor and oppressed, and they embraced its promise of salvation through Jesus. Likewise, the lyrics of religious "spirituals" helped slaves endure the strain of field labor and provided them with a musical code with which to express their own desire for freedom on earth. The former slave Frederick Douglass stressed that "slaves sing most when they are most unhappy," and spirituals offered them deliverance from their worldly woes.

THE SLAVE FAMILY Slave marriages had no legal status, but many slaveholders accepted marriage as a stabilizing influence on the plantation. Sometimes they performed the marriages themselves or had a minister celebrate a formal wedding. Whatever the formalities, the norm for the slave community, as for the white, was the nuclear family, with the father regarded as head of the household. Most slave children were socialized by means of the nuclear family, which afforded some degree of independence from white influence. Childhood was short for slaves. At five or six years of age, children

Plantation of J. J. Smith, Beaufort, South Carolina, 1862

Several generations of a family raised in slavery.

were put to work: they collected trash and firewood, picked cotton, scared away crows, weeded, and ran errands. By age ten they were full-time field hands. Children were often sold to new masters. In Missouri an enslaved woman saw six of her seven children, aged one to eleven, sold to six different masters.

THE CULTURE OF THE SOUTHERN FRONTIER

There was substantial social and cultural diversity within the South during the three decades before the Civil War. The region known as the Old Southwest, for example, is perhaps the least well known. It includes the states and territories west of Georgia—Alabama, Mississippi, Arkansas, Louisiana, and Texas—as well as the frontier areas of Tennessee, Kentucky, and Florida.

Largely unsettled until the 1820s, this region bridged the South and the West, exhibiting characteristics of both areas. Raw and dynamic, marked by dangers, uncertainties, and opportunities, it served as a powerful magnet, luring thousands of settlers from Virginia, Georgia, and the Carolinas when the seaboard economy faltered during the 1820s and 1830s. The migrating southerners carved out farms, built churches, established towns, and eventually brought culture and order to a raw frontier. As they took up new lives and occupations, the southern pioneers transplanted many practices and institutions from the coastal states. But they also fashioned a distinct new set of cultural values and social customs.

THE DECISION TO MIGRATE By the late 1820s the agricultural economy of the Upper South was suffering from falling crop prices and soil exhaustion. The dwindling economic opportunities in the Carolinas and Virginia led many residents of those states to migrate to the Old Southwest. Like their northern counterparts, restless southern sons of the planter and professional elite wanted to make it on their own, to be "self-made men," economically self-reliant and socially independent.

Women were underrepresented among migrants to the Old Southwest. Few were interested in relocating to a disease-ridden, violent, and primitive territory. As a Carolina woman prepared to depart for Alabama, she confided to a friend that "you *cannot* imagine the state of despair that I am in." Another said that "my heart bleeds within me" at the thought of the "many tender cords [of kinship] that are now severed forever." Others feared that life on the frontier would produce a "dissipation" of morals. They heard vivid stories of lawlessness, drunkenness, gambling, and miscegenation.

Enslaved blacks had many of the same reservations. Almost 1 million captive blacks were taken to the Old Southwest during the antebellum era, most of them in the 1830s. Like the white women, they feared the harsh working conditions and torpid heat and humidity of the new territory. They were also despondent at the breakup of their family ties.

A MASCULINE CULTURE   The frontier environment in the Old Southwest prompted important changes in gender roles, and relations between men and women became even more inequitable. Young men indulged themselves in activities that would have generated disapproval in the more settled seaboard society. They drank, gambled, fought, and gratified their sexual desires. In 1834 a South Carolina migrant urged his brother to move west and join him because "you can live like a fighting cock with us." Alcohol consumption hit new heights. Most Old Southwest plantations had their own stills to manufacture whiskey, and alcoholism ravaged frontier families. Violence was also commonplace. A Virginian who settled in Mississippi fought in fourteen duels, killing ten men in the process. The frequency of fights, stabbings, shootings, and murders shocked visitors. So, too, did the propensity of white men to take sexual advantage of enslaved women. An Alabama woman married to a lawyer and politician was outraged by the "beastly passions" of the white men who fathered slave children and then sold them like livestock. She also recorded in her diary instances of men regularly beating their wives. Wives, it seems, had little choice but to endure the mistreatment because, as one woman wrote about a friend whose husband abused her, she was "wholly dependent upon his care."

ANTI-SLAVERY MOVEMENTS

EARLY OPPOSITION TO SLAVERY   The first organized emancipation movement appeared with the formation, in 1817, of the American Colonization Society, which proposed to return freed slaves to Africa. Its supporters included such prominent figures as James Madison, James Monroe, Henry Clay, John Marshall, and Daniel Webster. Some backed it because of their opposition to slavery, while others saw it as a way to bolster slavery by getting rid of potentially troublesome free blacks. Leaders of the free black community denounced it from the start. America, they stressed, was their native land. Nevertheless, in 1821, agents of the American Colonization Society acquired from local chieftains in West Africa a parcel of land that became the nucleus of a new country. In 1822 the first freed slaves arrived there, and twenty-five years later the society relinquished control to the Free and Independent Republic of Liberia. But given its uncertain purpose, the African colonization movement received only meager support from either anti-slavery or pro-slavery elements. In all only about 15,000 blacks migrated to Africa up to 1860, approximately 12,000 with the help of the Colonization Society. The number was infinitesimal compared with the number of slave births.

FROM GRADUALISM TO ABOLITIONISM   Meanwhile, in the early 1830s the anti-slavery movement took a new route. Its initial efforts to promote a gradual end to slavery by prohibiting it in the new western territories and encouraging manumission gave way to demands for immediate abolition everywhere. In 1831, William Lloyd Garrison launched in Boston a new anti-slavery newspaper, the *Liberator*. Garrison, who had risen from poverty in Newburyport, Massachusetts, had been apprenticed to a newspaper publisher and had edited a number of anti-slavery papers but had grown impatient with the strategy of moderation. In the first issue of the *Liberator*, he renounced "the popular but pernicious doctrine of gradual emancipation." In calling for abolition, he vowed, "I will be as harsh as truth, and as uncompromising as justice."

Garrison's militancy outraged slaveholders. Their anger soared after the Nat Turner insurrection in August 1831. Garrison, they assumed, bore a large part of the responsibility for the uprising, but there is no evidence that Nat Turner had ever heard of him, and Garrison said that he had not a single subscriber in the South at the time. What is more, however violent his language, Garrison was a pacifist, opposed to the use of force.

During the 1830s, Garrison became the nation's most fervent, principled, and unyielding foe of slavery. In 1831 he and his followers set up the New England Anti-Slavery Society. Two years later Garrison and others helped two wealthy New York merchants, Arthur and Lewis Tappan, found the American Anti-Slavery Society in the hope of exploiting the publicity generated when the British anti-slavery movement, also in 1833, induced Parliament to end slavery, and compensate slaveholders, throughout the British Empire.

William Lloyd Garrison

Garrison was a vocal abolitionist and advocate of immediate emancipation.

The American Anti-Slavery Society stressed that "slaveholding is a heinous crime in the sight of God, and that the duty, safety, and best interests of all concerned, require its *immediate abandonment,* without expatriation." The society went beyond the issue of emancipation to argue that blacks should "share an equality with the whites, of civil and religious privileges." The group issued a barrage of propaganda for its cause, including periodicals, tracts, agents, lecturers, organizers, and fund-raisers.

A SPLIT IN THE MOVEMENT   As the anti-slavery movement spread, debates over tactics intensified. The Garrisonians, mainly New Englanders, felt that American society had been corrupted from top to bottom and needed universal reform. Garrison embraced every important reform movement of the day: abolition, temperance, pacifism, and women's rights. He also championed equal social and legal rights for African Americans. He broke with the organized church, which to his mind was in league with slavery. The federal government was all the more so. The Constitution, he said, was "a covenant with death and an agreement with hell." Garrison therefore refused to vote.

Other reformers were less dogmatic and sweeping. They saw American society as fundamentally sound and concentrated on purging it of slavery. Garrison struck them as an impractical fanatic. A showdown came in 1840 on the issue of women's rights. Women had joined the abolition movement from the start, but largely in groups without men. Then the activities of the Grimké sisters brought the issue of women's rights to center stage.

Sarah and Angelina Grimké, daughters of a prominent South Carolina slaveholding family, had broken with their parents and moved north to embrace Quakerism, abolitionism, feminism, and other reforms. As anti-slavery activists, they set out speaking first to audiences of women and eventually to both men and women. Their behavior inspired the Congregational clergy of Massachusetts to chastise them for engaging in unfeminine activity. The chairman of the Connecticut Anti-Slavery Society declared, "No woman shall speak or vote where I am a moderator." Catharine Beecher reminded the activist sisters that women occupy "a subordinate relation in society to the other sex" and should therefore limit their activities to the "domestic and social circle." Angelina Grimké stoutly rejected such conventional arguments. "It is a woman's right," she insisted, "to have a voice in all laws and regulations by which she is to be governed, whether in church or in state."

The debate over the role of women in the anti-slavery movement crackled and simmered until it finally exploded in 1840. At the Anti-Slavery Society's meeting that year, the Garrisonians convinced a majority of delegates that women should participate equally in the organization. They did not commit

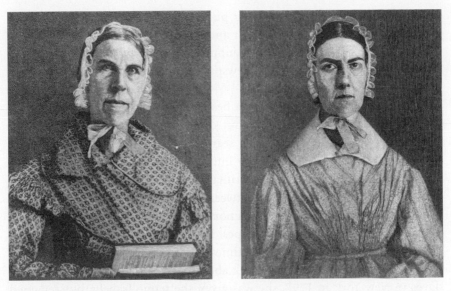

Sarah (left) and Angelina (right) Grimké

After moving away from their slaveholding family, the Grimké sisters devoted themselves to abolitionism and feminism.

the group to women's rights in any other way, however. Contrary opinion, mainly from the Tappans' New York group, ranged from outright anti-feminism to the fear of scattering shots over too many reforms. The New Yorkers thus broke away to form the American and Foreign Anti-Slavery Society.

BLACK ANTI-SLAVERY ACTIVITY White male abolitionists also balked at granting full recognition to black abolitionists of either sex. White abolitionists expected free blacks to take a backseat in the movement. Despite the invitation to form separate groups, African American leaders were active in the white societies from the beginning. Three attended the organizational meeting of the American Anti-Slavery Society in 1833, and some—notably former slaves, who could speak from firsthand experience—became outstanding agents for the movement. Garrison pronounced men such as Henry Bibb and William Wells Brown, both escapees from Kentucky, and Frederick Douglass, who had fled Maryland, "the best qualified to address the public on the subject of slavery."

Douglass, blessed with an imposing frame and a simple eloquence, became the best-known black man in America. "I appear before the immense assembly this evening as a thief and a robber," he told a Massachusetts group in 1842. "I stole this head, these limbs, this body from my master, and ran off with them." Fearful of capture after publishing his *Narrative of the Life of Frederick Douglass* (1845), he left for an extended lecture tour of the British Isles, returning two years later with enough money to purchase his freedom. He then started an abolitionist newspaper for blacks, the *North Star,* in Rochester, New York.

Douglass's *Narrative* was but the best known among hundreds of such accounts. Escapees often made it out of slavery on their own—Douglass borrowed a pass from a free black seaman—but many were aided by the Underground Railroad, which grew into a vast system of secret routes and safe stopping places that concealed runaways and spirited them to freedom, often over the Canadian border. Between 1810 and 1850, tens of thousands of southern slaves ran away and fled north. A few intrepid refugees returned to the slave states to organize escapes. Fearless Harriet Tubman, the most celebrated, ventured back nineteen times and helped 300 slaves escape.

Equally courageous was the black abolitionist Sojourner Truth. Born to slaves in New York in 1797, she was given the name Isabella but renamed herself in 1843 after experiencing a conversation with God, who told her "to travel up and down the land" preaching against the sins of slavery. She did just that, crisscrossing the country during the 1840s and 1850s, exhorting audiences to support abolition and women's rights. Having been a slave

Frederick Douglass (left) and Sojourner Truth (right)

Both Douglass and Truth were leading abolitionists and captivating orators.

until freed by a New York law in 1827, Sojourner Truth was able to speak with conviction and knowledge about the evils of the "peculiar institution" and the inequality of women. As she told a gathering of the Ohio Women's Rights Convention in 1851, "I have plowed, and planted, and gathered into barns, and no man could head me—and ar'n't I a woman? I have borne thirteen children, and seen 'em mos' all sold off into slavery, and when I cried out with a mother's grief, none but Jesus heard—and ar'n't I a woman?"

Through such compelling testimony, Sojourner Truth demonstrated the powerful intersection of abolitionism and feminism, and in the process she tapped the distinctive energies that women brought to reformist causes. "If the first woman God ever made was strong enough to turn the world upside down all alone," she concluded in her address to the Ohio gathering, "these women together ought to be able to turn it back, and get it right side up again!"

REACTIONS TO ABOLITION   Racism was a national problem in the nineteenth century. Even in the North, abolitionists had to face down hostile crowds who disliked blacks or found anti-slavery agitation bad for business. In 1837 a mob in Illinois killed the anti-slavery newspaper editor Elijah P. Lovejoy, giving the movement a martyr to the causes of both abolition and freedom of the press.

Lovejoy had begun his career as a Presbyterian minister in New England. He moved to St. Louis, in slaveholding Missouri, where he published a newspaper that repeatedly denounced alcohol, Catholicism, and slavery. When a pro-slavery mob destroyed his printing office, he moved across the Mississippi River to Alton, Illinois. There mobs twice more destroyed his printing press. When a new press arrived, Lovejoy and several of his supporters armed themselves and took up defensive positions. On November 7, 1837, thugs gathered outside, hurling stones and firing shots into the building. One of Lovejoy's allies fired back, killing one of the rioters. The mob then set fire to the warehouse, shouting, "Kill every damned abolitionist as he leaves." A shotgun blast killed Lovejoy. His murder aroused a frenzy of indignation. John Quincy Adams said that Lovejoy's death sent "a shock as of an earthquake throughout the continent." At one of the hundreds of memorial services across the North a grizzled, lean John Brown rose, raised his right hand, and declared, "Here, before God, in the presence of these witnesses, from this time, I consecrate my life to the destruction of slavery!" Brown and other militants decided that only violence would dislodge the sin of slavery.

In the 1830s, abolition took a political turn, focusing at first on Congress. One shrewd strategy was to deluge Congress with petitions for abolition in the District of Columbia. Most such petitions were presented by former

Abolition under attack

This color engraving depicts the riot at Alton, Illinois, in 1837, in which the abolitionist Elijah Lovejoy was killed.

president John Quincy Adams, elected to the House from Massachusetts in 1830. In 1836, however, the House adopted a rule to lay abolition petitions automatically on the table, in effect ignoring them. Adams, "Old Man Eloquent," stubbornly fought this "gag rule" as a violation of the First Amendment and hounded its supporters until the rule was repealed in 1844.

Meanwhile, in 1840, a small group of abolitionists organized a national political convention in Albany, New York, and launched the Liberty party, with James G. Birney, a onetime slaveholder in Alabama and Kentucky, as its candidate for president. Birney, converted to abolitionism, had moved to Ohio and in 1837 had become executive secretary of the American Anti-Slavery Society. In the 1840 election he polled only 7,000 votes, but in 1844 he won 60,000, and from that time forth an anti-slavery party contested every national election until Abraham Lincoln won the presidency in 1860.

THE DEFENSE OF SLAVERY   James Birney was but one of several southerners propelled north during the 1830s by the South's growing hostility to the abolition of slavery. The anti-slavery movement in the Upper South had its last stand in 1831–1832, when the Virginia legislature debated a plan of gradual emancipation and African colonization, then rejected it by a vote of 73 to 58. Thereafter, leaders of southern thought worked out an elaborate intellectual defense of slavery, presenting it in a positive light. In 1837, South Carolina's John C. Calhoun told the Senate that slavery was not evil. Instead, it was "good—a great good." He brazenly asserted that the Africans brought to America "had never existed in so comfortable, so respectable, or so civilized a condition, as that which is now enjoyed in the Southern states."

The evangelical Christian churches, which had widely condemned slavery at one time, gradually turned pro-slavery, at least in the South. Biblical passages were cited to buttress slaveholding. Had not the patriarchs of the Hebrew Bible held people in bondage? Had not Saint Paul advised servants to obey their masters and told a fugitive servant to return to his master? And had not Jesus remained silent on the subject, at least so far as the Gospels reported his words? In 1844–1845, disputes over slavery split two great denominations along sectional lines and led to the formation of the Southern Baptist Convention and the Methodist Episcopal Church, South. Presbyterians, the only other major denomination to divide by regions, did not do so until the Civil War.

A more fundamental feature of the pro-slavery argument stressed the racial inferiority of blacks. Other arguments took a more "practical" view. Not only was slavery profitable, one argument went, but it was also a matter of social necessity. Thomas Jefferson, for instance, in his *Notes on the State of Virginia* (1785), argued that whites and emancipated slaves could not live together without the risk of a race war triggered by the resentment of past injustices. What is more, it seemed clear to some defenders of slavery that blacks could not be expected to work under conditions of freedom. They were too shiftless and improvident, the argument went, and in freedom would be a danger to themselves as well as to others. White workers, on the other hand, feared the competition for jobs if slaves were freed.

A new argument on behalf of slavery arose in the late 1850s. The Virginian George Fitzhugh and others began to defend slavery as better for workers than freely chosen employment. Why? Fitzhugh claimed that slaves enjoyed security in sickness and old age, unlike the "wage slavery" practiced by northern factory owners, which exploited workers for profit and then cast them away. Within one generation such ideas had triumphed in the white South over the post-Revolutionary apology for slavery as an evil bequeathed by the nation's forefathers. Opponents of the orthodox faith in slavery as a "positive good" were either silenced or exiled. Freedom of thought in the Old South had become a victim of the region's growing obsession with the preservation and expansion of slavery—at all costs.

CHAPTER SUMMARY

- **The Southern Economy** Cotton was not the only profitable crop in the South. The Border South and Middle South became increasingly diversified, producing tobacco and indigo. Sugar and other crops were grown along with cotton in the Lower South. Despite the belief that slaves were unsuited for factory work, some manufacturing ventures in the South employed slaves. Slavery was the unifying element in all southern enterprises.

- **Southern Culture** Throughout the antebellum era the American South became increasingly committed to a cotton economy, which in turn was dependent upon slave labor. Despite efforts to diversify the economy, the wealth and status associated with cotton prompted the westward expansion of the plantation culture. In defense of slavery, evangelical churches declared that it was sanctioned by the Bible; southerners proclaimed it a "positive good" for African Americans. Whereas only a quarter of white southerners held slaves, the planter elite set the standard for southern white culture. Its dominant features were a strict social hierarchy based on race, a preoccupation with masculine honor, and the glorification of white women's chastity.

- **Anti-Slavery Movement** Northern opponents of slavery promoted several solutions, including deportation of African Americans to colonies in Africa, gradual emancipation, and immediate abolition. Radical abolitionist efforts in the North provoked a strong reaction among southern whites, stirring fears for their safety and resentment of interference. Yet many northerners shared the belief in the racial inferiority of Africans.

- **Southern Black Culture** The enslaved responded to their oppression in a variety of ways. Although many slaves attempted to run away, only a few openly rebelled. Some survived by relying on their own communities, family ties, and Christian faith. Although nominally free, blacks who won their freedom were not permitted to vote or testify against whites in court.

CHRONOLOGY

1808	Participation in the international slave trade is outlawed
1816	American Colonization Society is founded
1822	Denmark Vesey conspiracy is discovered in Charleston, South Carolina
1831	Nat Turner leads slave insurrection in Virginia
	William Lloyd Garrison begins publication of the *Liberator*
1833	American Anti-Slavery Society is founded
1837	Abolitionist editor Elijah Lovejoy is murdered
1840	Abolitionists form the Liberty party
1845	*Narrative of the Life of Frederick Douglass* is published
1851	Sojourner Truth delivers her famous speech *Ain't I a Woman?*
1852	Harriet Beecher Stowe's *Uncle Tom's Cabin* is published

KEY TERMS & NAMES

planters p. 570

yeomen p. 579

"peculiar institution" p. 581

Nat Turner p. 588

abolition p. 593

gradualism p. 593

William Lloyd Garrison p. 593

Liberator p. 593

Sarah and Angelina Grimké p. 594

Frederick Douglass p. 595

Sojourner Truth p. 596

Harriet Tubman p. 596

Underground Railroad p. 596

"gag rule" p. 598

16

THE CRISIS OF UNION

FOCUS QUESTIONS

Ⓢ wwnorton.com/studyspace

- Who were the members of the free-soil coalition, and what arguments did they use to demand that slavery not spread to the territories?

- Why did the issue of statehood for California precipitate a crisis for the Union?

- What were the major elements of the Compromise of 1850?

- How did the Kansas-Nebraska Act initiate the collapse of the second party system?

- Why did the southern states secede?

John C. Calhoun of South Carolina and Ralph Waldo Emerson of Massachusetts had little in common, but both men sensed in the Mexican War the omens of a national disaster. Mexico was "the forbidden fruit; the penalty of eating it would be to subject our institutions to political death," Calhoun warned. "The United States will conquer Mexico," Emerson conceded, "but it will be as the man swallows the arsenic. . . . Mexico will poison us." Wars, as both men knew, have a way of corrupting ideals and breeding new wars, often in unforeseen ways. America's victory in the war with Mexico spawned heated quarrels over newly acquired land, quarrels that set in motion a series of fractious disputes, which led to a crisis of union.

SLAVERY IN THE TERRITORIES

THE WILMOT PROVISO   The Mexican War was less than three months old when the seeds of a new political conflict began to sprout. On August 8, 1846, a freshman Democratic congressman from Pennsylvania, David Wilmot, delivered a provocative speech to the House in which he endorsed the annexation of Texas as a slave state. But slavery had come to an end in the rest of Mexico, and if new Mexican territory should be acquired, Wilmot declared, "God forbid that we should be the means of planting this institution [slavery] upon it." If any additional land should be acquired from Mexico, Wilmot proposed, then "neither slavery nor involuntary servitude shall ever exist" there.

The proposed Wilmot Proviso ignited the festering debate over slavery. For a generation, since the Missouri controversy of 1819–1821, the issue had been lurking in the wings. Now, for the next two decades, it would never be far from center stage. The House adopted the Wilmot Proviso, but the Senate balked. When Congress reconvened in December 1846, President James K. Polk, who believed a debate over slavery had no place in the conduct of the war in Mexico and dismissed the proviso as "mischievous and foolish," prevailed upon Wilmot to withhold his amendment from any bill dealing with the annexation of Mexican territory. By then, however, others were ready to take up the cause. In one form or another, Wilmot's idea kept cropping up in Congress. Abraham Lincoln later recalled that during his one term as a congressman, in 1847–1849, he voted for it "as good as forty times."

Senator John Calhoun of South Carolina, meanwhile, devised a thesis to counter the proviso, which he set before the Senate on February 19, 1847. Calhoun began by reasserting his pride in being a slaveholding cotton planter. He made no apologies for holding slaves and insisted that slaveholders had an unassailable right to take their slaves into any territories. Wilmot's effort to exclude slaves from territories acquired from Mexico, Calhoun declared, would violate the Fifth Amendment, which forbids Congress to deprive any person of life, liberty, or property without due process of law, and slaves were property. By this clever stroke of logic, Calhoun took that basic guarantee of liberty, the Bill of Rights, and turned it into a basic guarantee of slavery. The irony was not lost on his critics, but the point became established southern dogma—echoed by his colleagues and formally endorsed by the Virginia legislature.

The burly senator Thomas Hart Benton of Missouri, himself a slaveholder but also a nationalist eager to calm sectional tensions, found in Calhoun's stance a set of abstractions "leading to no result." Wilmot and Calhoun between them, he said, had fashioned a pair of shears. Neither blade alone would cut very well, but joined together they could sever the nation in two.

POPULAR SOVEREIGNTY   Senator Benton and others sought to bypass the brewing conflict over slavery in the new territories. President Polk was among the first to suggest extending the Missouri Compromise, dividing free and slave territory at the latitude of 36°30′, all the way to the Pacific Ocean. Senator Lewis Cass of Michigan suggested that the citizens of a territory "regulate their own internal concerns in their own way," like the citizens of a state. Such an approach would take the contentious issue of allowing slavery in new territories out of the national arena and put it in the hands of those directly affected.

Popular sovereignty, or "squatter sovereignty," as the idea was also called, appealed to many Americans. Without directly challenging the slaveholders' access to the new lands, it promised to open the lands quickly to nonslaveholding farmers, who would almost surely dominate the territories. With this tacit understanding the idea prospered in the Midwest, where Senator Stephen A. Douglas of Illinois and other prominent Democrats soon endorsed it.

In 1848, when the Mexican War ended, the issue of introducing slavery into the new territories was no longer hypothetical. Nobody doubted that Oregon would become a free-soil (nonslave) territory, but it, too, was drawn into the growing controversy. Territorial status for Oregon, pending since 1846, was delayed because its provisional government had excluded slavery. To concede that provision would imply an authority drawn from the powers of Congress, since a territory was created by Congress. After much wrangling, an exhausted Congress let Oregon organize without slavery but postponed a decision on the Southwest territories. President Polk signed the bill on the principle that Oregon was north of 36°30′, the latitude that had formed the basis of the Missouri Compromise in 1820.

Polk had promised to serve only one term; exhausted and having accomplished his major goals, he refused to run again. At the 1848 Democratic Convention, Michigan senator Lewis Cass won the presidential nomination, but the party refused to endorse Cass's "squatter sovereignty" plan. Instead, it simply denied the power of Congress to interfere with slavery in the states and criticized all efforts by anti-slavery activists to bring the question before Congress. The Whigs devised an even more artful shift. Once again, as in 1840, they passed over their party leader, Henry Clay, this time, for a general, Zachary Taylor, whose fame had grown since the Battle of Buena Vista.

Taylor, a Louisiana resident who held more than 100 slaves, was an apolitical figure who had never voted in a national election. Once again, also as in 1840, the Whig party adopted no platform. Stunned that his party had deserted him in favor of a "wholly incompetent" general with no political experience, Henry Clay concluded that the Whigs were on the verge of dissolution.

THE FREE-SOIL COALITION   But the anti-slavery impulse was not easily squelched. Congressman David Wilmot had raised a standard for resisting the expansion of slavery, to which a broad coalition could rally. Americans who shied away from abolition could readily endorse the exclusion of slavery from the western territories. The Northwest Ordinance and the Missouri Compromise supplied honored precedents. Free soil in the new territories, therefore, rather than abolition in the slave states, became the rallying point for those opposed to slavery—and also the name of a new political party.

Three major groups combined to form the free-soil coalition: rebellious northern Democrats, anti-slavery Whigs, and members of the Liberty party, which dated from 1840. Disaffection among the Democrats centered in New York, where the Van Burenite "Barnburners" seized upon the free-soil issue as a moral imperative. Free-soil principles among the Whigs centered in Massachusetts, where a group of "Conscience" Whigs battled the "Cotton" Whigs, a coalition of northern businessmen and southern planters. Conscience Whigs rejected the slaveholding nominee of their party, Zachary Taylor.

In 1848 these groups—Van Burenite Democrats, Conscience Whigs, and followers of the Liberty party—organized the Free-Soil party at a convention at Buffalo, New York, and nominated Martin Van Buren for president. The party's platform endorsed the Wilmot Proviso's declaration that slavery would not be allowed in the new territories acquired from Mexico. The Free-Soil party entered the campaign with the catchy slogan of "free soil, free speech, free labor, and free men." The new party infuriated John Calhoun and other southern Democrats committed to the expansion of slavery. Calhoun called Van Buren a "bold, unscrupulous and vindictive demagogue." Other Democrats, both northern and southern, denounced Van Buren as a traitor and a hypocrite, while the New Yorker's supporters praised his service as a "champion of freedom."

The impact of the new Free-Soil party on the election was mixed. The Free-Soilers split the Democratic vote enough to throw New York to the Whig Zachary Taylor, and they split the Whig vote enough to give Ohio to the Democrat Lewis Cass, but Van Buren's 291,000 votes lagged well behind the totals of 1,361,000 for Taylor and 1,222,000 for Cass. Taylor won with 163 to 127 electoral votes, and both major parties retained a national following. Taylor

THE BUFFALO HUNT.

Martin Van Buren

Martin Van Buren was nominated as the presidential candidate for the Free-Soil party, at the party's convention in Buffalo, New York. In this cartoon, he is shown riding a buffalo past the Democratic and Whig party candidates.

took eight slave states and seven free; Cass, just the opposite: seven slave and eight free.

THE CALIFORNIA GOLD RUSH   Meanwhile, a new dimension had been introduced into the vexing question of the western territories: on January 24, 1848, gold was discovered in the Mexican province of California, which nine days later would be ceded to the United States as a result of the treaty ending the Mexican War. Word spread quickly, and the California gold rush constituted the greatest mass migration in American history—and one of the most significant events in the first half of the nineteenth century. The infusion of California gold into the U.S. economy triggered a surge of prosperity and dramatic growth that eventually helped finance the Union military effort in the Civil War. New business enterprises emerged to serve the burgeoning population of miners, including one dedicated to the production of sturdy denim trousers made of sailcloth, their pockets reinforced by copper rivets. The blue jeans, known to this day as Levi's, were developed by the German Jewish immigrant Levi Strauss. The gold rush also shifted the nation's center of gravity westward, spurred the construction of railroads and telegraph lines, and

California News (1850) by William Sidney Mount

During the California gold rush, San Francisco quickly became a cosmopolitan city as the population increased almost fiftyfold in a few months.

excited dreams of an eventual American empire based in the Pacific. During 1849 some 80,000 gold seekers reached California, half of them Americans, and by 1854 the number would top 300,000. The massive migration to California had profound effects nationwide. So many men left New England, for instance, that it would be years before the region's gender ratio evened out again. The "forty-niners" included people from every social class and every state and territory, as well as slaves brought by their owners. Most forty-niners went overland; the rest, by ship. The influx of gold seekers quickly reduced the 14,000 Mexicans to a minority, and sporadic conflicts with the Indians of the Sierra Nevada foothills decimated California's Native Americans.

Unlike the land-hungry pioneers who traversed the Overland Trails, the miners were mostly unmarried young men with varied ethnic and cultural backgrounds. Few were interested in establishing a permanent settlement. They wanted to strike it rich and return home. The mining camps in California's valleys and canyons and along its creek beds thus sprang up like mushrooms and disappeared almost as rapidly. As soon as rumors of a new strike made the rounds, miners converged on the area, joined soon thereafter by a

Gold miners, ca. 1850

Daguerreotype of miners panning for gold at their claim.

hodgepodge of merchants and camp followers. When no more gold could be found, they picked up and moved on.

The mining camps and shantytowns may have had colorful names—Whiskey Flat, Lousy Ravine, Petticoat Slide, Piety Hill—but the male-dominated communities were in fact dismal, dirty, disorderly, and often lawless places. Vigilante justice prevailed in camps speckled with saloons and gambling halls. One newcomer reported that "in the short space of twenty-four days, we have had murders, fearful accidents, bloody deaths, a mob, whippings, a hanging, an attempt at suicide, and a fatal duel." Within six months of arriving in California in 1849, one gold seeker in every five was dead. The goldfields and mining towns were so dangerous that insurance companies refused to provide coverage. The town of Marysville had seventeen murders in one week. Suicides were common, and disease was rampant. Cholera and scurvy plagued every camp.

Women were as rare in the mining camps as liquor and guns were abundant. In 1850 less than 8 percent of California's population was female, and even fewer women dared to live in the camps. Those who did could demand a premium for their work, as cooks, laundresses, entertainers, and prostitutes. In the polyglot mining camps white Americans often looked with disdain upon the Hispanics and Chinese, who were most often employed as wage laborers to help in the panning process, separating gold from sand and gravel. But the white Americans focused their contempt on the Indians in particular. In the mining culture it was not a crime to kill Indians or work them to death. American miners tried several times to outlaw foreigners in the mining country but had to settle for a tax on foreign miners, which was applied to Mexicans in express violation of the treaty ending the Mexican War.

CALIFORNIA STATEHOOD   In 1849 the new president, Zachary Taylor, decided to use California's request for statehood as a lever to end the stalemate in Congress brought about by the slavery issue. Born in Virginia and raised in Kentucky, Taylor had been a soldier most of his life. Constantly on the move, he had acquired a home in Louisiana and a plantation in Mississippi. Southern Whigs had rallied to his support, expecting him to uphold the cause of slavery. Instead, he turned out to be a southern man who championed Union principles. Inexperienced in politics, Taylor had a soldier's practical mind. Slavery should be upheld where it existed, he believed, but he had little patience with abstract theories about slavery in territories where it probably could not exist. Why not make California and New Mexico free states immediately, he reasoned, and bypass the vexing issue of slavery?

But the Californians, in desperate need of organized government, were ahead of him. By December 1849, without consulting Congress, California had put a free-state (no-slavery) government into operation. New Mexico responded more slowly, but by 1850 Americans there had adopted a free-state constitution. The Mormons around Salt Lake, meanwhile, drafted a basic law for the state of Deseret, which embraced most of the Mexican cession, including a slice of the coast from Los Angeles to San Diego. In his annual message on December 4, 1849, President Taylor endorsed immediate statehood for California and urged Congress to avoid injecting slavery into the issue. The new Congress, however, was in no mood for simple solutions. By 1850, tensions over the morality and the future of slavery were boiling over. At the same time that tempers were flaring over the issue of allowing slavery into the new western territories, anti-slavery members of the House of Representatives were proposing legislation to ban slavery in the District of Columbia. Further complicating the political debate was the claim by Texas, a slave state, to half of the New Mexico Territory. These were only a few of the complex dilemmas confronting the nation's statesmen as they assembled in Washington, D.C., for the 1850 legislative session.

THE COMPROMISE OF 1850

The spotlight fell on the Senate, where a stellar cast—the triumvirate of Henry Clay, John Calhoun, and Daniel Webster, with William H. Seward, Stephen A. Douglas, and Jefferson Davis in supporting roles—enacted one of the great dramas of American politics: the Compromise of 1850. With southerners threatening secession, seventy-three-year-old Henry Clay had become so concerned about the fate of the Union that he had come out of retirement to return to the Senate after a seven-year absence. After arriving in Washington, D.C., he observed that the "feeling for disunion among some intemperate Southern politicians is stronger than I supposed it could be." At the end of 1849, southerners fumed over President Taylor's efforts to bring California and New Mexico into the union as free states. After all, some of them reasoned, southerners had fought disproportionately in the Mexican War; their concerns about the expansion of slavery should be given more weight. Other southerners demanded a federal fugitive slave law that would require northern authorities to arrest and return runaways. Irate southerners threatened to leave the Union. "I avow before this House and country, and in the presence

Drama in American politics

This cartoon attacks Democratic presidential candidate Franklin Pierce for his party's endorsement of the Compromise of 1850.

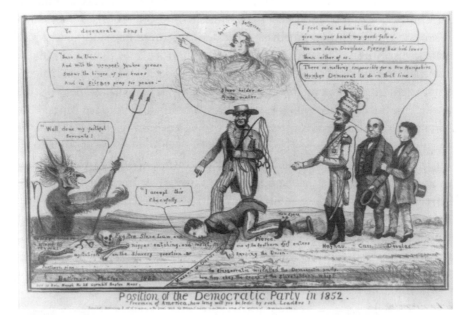

of the living God," shouted Robert Toombs, a Georgia congressman, "that if by your legislation you seek to drive us [slaveholders] from the territories of California and New Mexico . . . and to abolish slavery in this District [of Columbia] . . . *I am for disunion.*"

By 1850 the United States was facing its greatest political crisis. Henry Clay was so devoted to the preservation of the Union that he was willing to alienate southern supporters by once again assuming the role of Great Compromiser, which he had played in the Missouri and nullification controversies earlier in the century.

THE GREAT DEBATE   In January 1850, having gained the support of Daniel Webster, Clay presented to Congress a package of eight resolutions meant to settle the "controversy between the free and slave States." His proposals represented what he called a "great national scheme of compromise and harmony." He proposed to (1) admit California as a free state, (2) organize the territories of New Mexico and Utah without restrictions on slavery, allowing the residents to decide the issue for themselves, (3) deny Texas its extreme claim to much of New Mexico, (4) compensate Texas by having the federal government pay the pre-annexation Texas debts, (5) retain slavery in the District of Columbia, but (6) abolish the slave trade across its boundaries, (7) adopt a more effective federal fugitive slave act, and (8) deny congressional authority to interfere with the interstate slave trade. His complex cluster of proposals became in substance the Compromise of 1850, but only after the most celebrated debate in the annals of Congress.

On February 5–6, Clay summoned all his eloquence in promoting the proposed settlement to the Senate. In the interest of "peace, concord and harmony," he called for an end to "passion, passion—party, party—and intemperance." Otherwise, he warned, continued sectional bickering would lead to a "furious, bloody" civil war. To avoid such a catastrophe, Clay stressed, California should be admitted as a free state on the terms that its own citizens had approved. He begged the opposing sides "by all of their love of liberty—by all their veneration for their ancestors—by all their regard for posterity . . . to pause—solemnly to pause—at the edge of the precipice, before the fearful and disastrous leap is taken into the yawning abyss below." No sooner had Clay finished than a crowd rushed forward to shake his hand and kiss his cheek.

The congressional debate continued sporadically through February, with the Texan Sam Houston rising to the support of Clay's compromise and Mississippi's Jefferson Davis defending the slavery cause on every point. President Taylor believed that slavery in the South could best be protected if southerners avoided injecting the issue into any dispute over new territories.

Unlike John Calhoun, he did not believe the new western territories were suitable for slave-based agriculture. Because in his mind the issue of bringing slaves into the western territories was moot, he continued to urge Congress to admit California and New Mexico without reference to slavery. But few others embraced such a simple solution. In fact, a rising chorus of pugnacious southern leaders, labeled Ultras, threatened to secede from the Union if slavery were not allowed in California.

On March 4, John Calhoun left his sickbed to sit in the Senate chamber, a gaunt, pallid figure draped in a black cloak, as a colleague read his defiant speech. "I have, Senators, believed from the first that the agitation of the subject of slavery would, if not prevented by some timely and effective measure, end in disunion," said James M. Mason on Calhoun's behalf. Neither Clay's compromise nor Taylor's efforts would serve the Union, he added. The South simply needed an acceptance of its rights: equality of treatment in the territories, the return of fugitive slaves, and some guarantee of "an equilibrium between the sections." Otherwise, Calhoun warned, the "cords which bind" the Union would be severed.

Three days later Calhoun, who would die in three weeks, returned to the Senate to hear Daniel Webster speak. The "godlike Daniel" no longer possessed the thunderous voice of his youth, nor did his shrinking frame project its once-magisterial aura, but he remained a formidable presence, especially when fortified by brandy. He chose as the central theme of his three-hour speech the preservation of the Union: "I wish to speak today, not as a Massachusetts man, not as a Northern man, but as an American. . . . I speak today for the preservation of the Union." The geographic extent of slavery had already been determined, Webster insisted, by the Northwest Ordinance, by the Missouri Compromise, and in the new territories by the law of nature. He criticized extremists on both sides. Both northerners and southerners, to be sure, had legitimate grievances: on the one hand the excesses of "infernal fanatics and abolitionists" in the North and on the other hand southern efforts to expand slavery and heap southern slurs on northern workingmen. But "Secession! Peaceable secession! Sir, your eyes and mine are never destined to see that miracle." Instead of looking into such "caverns of darkness," let "men enjoy the fresh air of liberty and union. Let them look to a more hopeful future."

Webster's conciliatory March 7 speech brought down a storm upon his head. New England anti-slavery leaders lambasted this "Benedict Arnold" who had betrayed his region. On March 11, William Seward, the Whig senator from New York, gave the anti-slavery reply to Webster. He declared that any compromise with slavery was "radically wrong and essentially vicious."

There was, he said, "a higher law than the Constitution," and it demanded the abolition of slavery.

In mid-April a select committee of thirteen senators bundled Henry Clay's suggestions (insofar as they concerned the Mexican cession) into one comprehensive bill and presented it to the Senate early in May. President Taylor continued to oppose Clay's compromise, and their feud threatened to split the Whig party wide open. As the weeks and months passed, Clay worked tirelessly to convince opponents that compromise by all parties was essential to preserving the Union. Yet as the stalemate continued and the atmosphere in Congress became more fevered and violent, he grew frustrated and peevish. "Mr. Clay with all his talents," Daniel Webster told a friend, "is not a good leader. . . . He is irritable, impatient, and occasionally overbearing; & he drives people off." Another crisis loomed near the end of June when word came that New Mexico was applying for statehood, with President Taylor's support and on the basis of boundaries that conflicted with the Texas claim to the east bank of the Rio Grande.

TOWARD A COMPROMISE On July 4, 1850, supporters of the Union staged a grand rally at the base of the unfinished Washington Monument. Zachary Taylor went to hear the speeches, lingering in the hot sun and humid heat. Five days later he died of a gastrointestinal affliction possibly caused by tainted food or water.

President Taylor's sudden death strengthened the chances of a congressional compromise. The soldier in the White House was replaced by a politician, Vice President Millard Fillmore. The son of a poor upstate New York farmer, Fillmore had succeeded despite few opportunities or advantages. Largely self-educated, he had made his own way in the profession of law and the rough-and-tumble world of New York politics. Experience had taught him caution, which some interpreted as indecision, but he had made up his mind to support Henry Clay's compromise and had so informed Taylor. It was a strange switch: Taylor, the Louisiana slaveholder, had

Millard Fillmore

Fillmore's support of the Compromise of 1850 helped the Union muddle through the crisis.

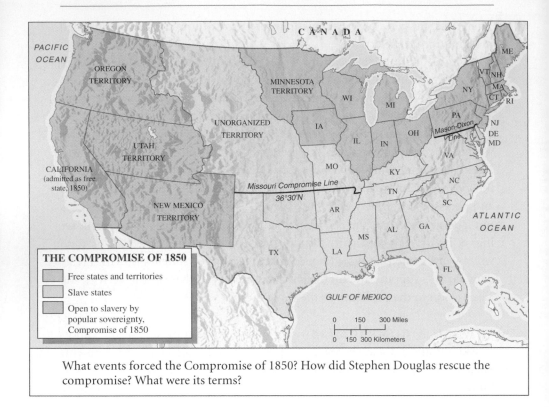

PACIFIC
OCEAN

CANADA

OREGON
TERRITORY

MINNESOTA
TERRITORY

WI

MI

ME

VT NH

NY MA
CT RI

UNORGANIZED
TERRITORY

IA

PA

NJ
DE
MD

OH   Mason-Dixon
Line

IL   IN

UTAH
TERRITORY

VA

CALIFORNIA
(admitted as free
state, 1850)

MO

KY

NC

Missouri Compromise Line

36°30′N

TN

NEW MEXICO
TERRITORY

AR

SC

ATLANTIC
OCEAN

MS   AL   GA

TX   LA

FL

THE COMPROMISE OF 1850

Free states and territories

Slave states

Open to slavery by
popular sovereignty,
Compromise of 1850

GULF OF MEXICO

0   150   300 Miles

0 150 300 Kilometers

What events forced the Compromise of 1850? How did Stephen Douglas rescue the
compromise? What were its terms?

been ready to make war on his native region; Fillmore, who southerners
thought opposed slavery, was ready to make peace.

At this point the young senator Stephen A. Douglas of Illinois, a rising star in
the Democratic party, rescued Clay's faltering compromise. Short and stocky,
brash and brilliant, Douglas was nicknamed the Little Giant. His capacity for
liquor was only exceeded by his appetite for hard work. Douglas's strategy
was in fact the same one Clay had used to pass the Missouri Compromise
thirty years before. Reasoning that nearly everybody objected to one or
another provision of Clay's "comprehensive scheme," Douglas decided to
break it up into six (later five) separate measures. Few members were prepared to vote for all of them, but from different elements Douglas hoped to
mobilize a majority for each.

The plan worked. By September 20, President Fillmore had signed the last
of the measures into law. The Union had muddled through, and the settlement went down in history as the Compromise of 1850. For a time it defused

an explosive situation, settled each of the major points at issue, and post-poned secession and civil war for ten years.

In its final version, the Compromise of 1850 included the following ele-ments: *First*, California entered the Union as a free state, ending forever the old balance of free and slave states. *Second*, the Texas–New Mexico Act made New Mexico a territory and set the Texas boundary at its present location. In return for giving up its claims, Texas was paid $10 million, which secured payment of the state's debt. *Third*, the Utah Act set up the Utah Territory. The territorial act in each case omitted reference to slavery except to give the territorial legislature authority over "all rightful subjects of legislation" with provision for appeal to the federal courts. For the sake of agreement, the de-liberate ambiguity of the statement was its merit. Northern congressmen could assume that the territorial legislatures might act to exclude slavery; southern congressmen assumed that they could not.

Fourth, a new Fugitive Slave Act put the matter of apprehending runaway slaves wholly under federal jurisdiction and stacked the cards in favor of slave catchers. *Fifth*, as a gesture to anti-slavery forces, the slave trade, but not slavery itself, was abolished in the District of Columbia. The awful spec-tacle of chained-together slaves passing through the streets of the capital, to be sold at public auctions, was brought to an end.

President Millard Fillmore pronounced the five measures making up the Compromise of 1850 "a final settlement." Still, doubts lingered that both North and South could be reconciled to the measures permanently. In the South the disputes of 1846–1850 had transformed the abstract doctrine of secession into a growing movement animated by "fire-eaters" such as Robert Barnwell Rhett of South Carolina, William Lowndes Yancey of Alabama, and Edmund Ruffin of Virginia.

But once the furies aroused by the Wilmot Proviso had been spent, the compromise left little on which to focus pro-slavery agitation. The state of California was an accomplished fact and, ironically, tended to elect pro-slavery men to Congress. New Mexico and Utah were far away and in any case at least hypothetically open to slavery. Both in fact adopted slave codes, but the census of 1860 reported no slaves in New Mexico and only twenty-nine in Utah. The Fugitive Slave Act was something else again. It was the one clear-cut victory for the cause of slavery, but would the North enforce it?

THE FUGITIVE SLAVE ACT   Southern insistence on the Fugitive Slave Act as part of the Compromise of 1850 outraged abolitionists. The act did more than strengthen the hand of slave catchers; it offered a strong temptation

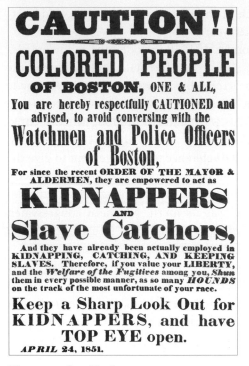

Threats to free blacks

An 1851 notice to the free blacks of Boston to avoid "the watchmen and police officers . . . empowered to act as kidnappers and slave catchers."

to kidnap free blacks. The law denied alleged fugitives a jury trial. In addition, federal marshals could require citizens to help locate and capture runaways; violators could be imprisoned for up to six months and fined $1,000.

"This filthy enactment was made in the nineteenth century, by people who could read and write," Ralph Waldo Emerson marveled in his journal. He advised neighbors to break the new law "on the earliest occasion." The occasion soon arose in Detroit, Michigan, where only military force stopped the rescue of an alleged fugitive by an outraged mob in October 1850.

There were relatively few such incidents, however. In the first six years of the act, only three fugitives were forcibly rescued from slave catchers. On the other hand, probably fewer than 200 were returned to bondage during those years. The Fugitive Slave Act had the tremendous effect of arousing the antislavery impulse in the North.

UNCLE TOM'S CABIN   Anti-slavery forces found their most persuasive appeal not in the Fugitive Slave Act but in the fictional drama of Harriet Beecher Stowe's best-selling novel, *Uncle Tom's Cabin* (1852). The daughter, sister, and wife of Congregationalist ministers, Stowe epitomized the powerful religious underpinnings of the abolitionist movement. She had decided to write the novel because of her disgust with the Fugitive Slave Act of 1850. *Uncle Tom's Cabin* depicts a combination of unlikely saints and sinners, stereotypes, fugitive slaves, and melodramatic escapades—and it was a smashing commercial success. The long-suffering slave Uncle Tom, the villainous planter Simon Legree, the angelic Eva, the desperate Eliza carrying her child to freedom across the icy Ohio River—all became stock characters in American folklore. Slavery, seen through Stowe's eyes, was an abominable sin. Southern slaveholders were incensed by Stowe's best-selling book. One of them mailed Stowe an anonymous parcel containing the severed ear of a disobedient slave. Yet it took time for the novel to work its effect on public opinion. At the time of its publication, the country was enjoying a surge of prosperity fueled by California gold, and the course of the presidential campaign in 1852 reflected a common desire to lay sectional quarrels to rest.

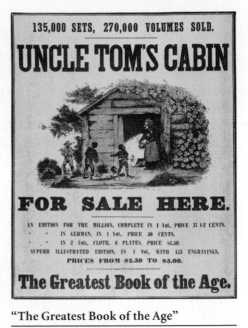

"The Greatest Book of the Age"

Uncle Tom's Cabin, as this advertisement indicates, was a best seller.

THE ELECTION OF 1852

In 1852 the Democrats chose Franklin Pierce of New Hampshire as their presidential candidate; their platform endorsed the Compromise of 1850. The party's candidates and platform generated a surprising reconciliation of its factions. Pierce rallied both the southern rights' advocates and the Van Burenite Democrats. The third-party Free-Soilers, as a consequence, mustered only 156,000 votes, for John P. Hale, in contrast to the 291,000 they had tallied for Van Buren in 1848.

The Whigs repudiated the lackluster Millard Fillmore, who had faithfully supported the Compromise of 1850, and once again tried to exploit martial glory. It took fifty-three ballots, but the convention finally chose General Winfield Scott, the hero of the Mexican War and a Virginia native backed mainly by northern Whigs. The Whig Convention dutifully endorsed the compromise, but with some opposition from the North. Scott, an able army commander but an inept politician, had gained a reputation for anti-slavery and nativist sentiments, alienating German- and Irish-American voters. In the end, Scott carried only Tennessee, Kentucky, Massachusetts, and Vermont. Pierce overwhelmed him in the Electoral College, 254 to 42, although the popular vote was close: 1.6 million to 1.4 million.

Forty-eight-year-old Franklin Pierce, an undistinguished but engaging former congressman, senator, and soldier in Mexico, was, like James Polk, touted as another Andrew Jackson. But the youngest president to date was unable to unite the warring factions of his party. He was neither a statesman nor a leader. After the election, Pierce wrote a poignant letter to his wife in which he expressed his frustration at the prospect of keeping North and South together. "I can do no right," he sighed. "What am I to do, wife? Stand by me." By the end of Pierce's first year in office, the leaders of his own party had decided he was a failure. By trying to be all things to all people, Pierce looked more and more like a "Northern man with Southern principles."

FOREIGN ADVENTURES

CUBA   During the early 1850s foreign diversions sporadically distracted attention from domestic quarrels. Cuba, one of Spain's first possessions in the New World, continued to tempt American expansionists. In the early 1850s Americans tried to incite Cubans to rebel against Spain. Spanish authorities retaliated by harassing American ships. In response the Pierce administration in 1854 offered $130 million for Cuba, which Spain spurned. The U.S. then joined France and Britain in drafting the Ostend Manifesto, which declared that if Spain, "actuated by stubborn pride and a false sense of honor, refused to sell," then the United States must ask itself, "Does Cuba, in the possession of Spain, seriously endanger our internal peace and the existence of our cherished Union?" If so, "then, by every law, human and divine, we shall be justified in wresting it from Spain." Publication of the supposedly confidential dispatch left the administration no choice but to disavow what northern opinion widely regarded as a "slaveholders' plot" to acquire Cuba.

DIPLOMATIC GAINS IN ASIA   In the Pacific, U.S. diplomacy scored some important achievements. American trade with China dated from 1784–1785 but was allowed only through the port of Canton. In 1844 the United States and China signed the Treaty of Wanghsia, which opened four ports, including Shanghai, to U.S. trade. The Treaty of Tientsin (1858) opened eleven more ports and granted Americans the right to travel and trade throughout China. Protestant missionaries had also developed a keen interest in China. About fifty were already there by 1855, and for nearly a century China remained the most active site for American missionaries.

Japan, meanwhile, had for two centuries remained closed to U.S. trade. Moreover, American whalers wrecked on the shores of Japan had been forbidden to leave the country. Mainly in their interest, President Fillmore entrusted a special Japanese expedition to Commodore Matthew Perry, who arrived in Tokyo in 1853. Negotiations led to the Treaty of Kanagawa (1854). Japan agreed to allow a U.S. consulate, promised to treat castaways cordially, and permitted American ships to enter certain ports to take on supplies and make repairs. Broader commercial relations came after the first U.S. envoy, Townsend Harris, negotiated the Harris Convention of 1858, which opened five Japanese ports to American trade.

Expedition to Japan, 1853

A woodcut by the Japanese artist Hiroshige Utagawa depicts Commodore Perry's steamship.

THE KANSAS-NEBRASKA CRISIS

American commercial interests in Asia helped spark a growing desire for a transcontinental railroad line connecting the eastern seaboard with the Pacific coast. During the 1850s the only land added to the United States was a barren stretch of some 30,000 square miles south of the Gila River in present-day New Mexico and Arizona. This Gadsden Purchase of 1853, for which the United States paid Mexico $10 million, provided land offering a likely route for a transcontinental railroad. The idea of building a railroad linking the far-flung regions of the new continental domain of the United States reignited sectional rivalries and reopened the slavery issue. Among the many possible transcontinental routes, the four most important were a northern route from Milwaukee to the Columbia River in northern Oregon, a central route from St. Louis to San Francisco, another from Memphis to Los Angeles, and a more southerly route from Houston to Los Angeles via the Gadsden Purchase.

DOUGLAS'S PROPOSAL   In 1852 and 1853, Congress debated several proposals for a transcontinental rail line. For various reasons, including terrain, climate, and sectional interests, Secretary of War Jefferson Davis favored the southern route and promoted the Gadsden Purchase. Any other route, moreover, would go through the territories granted to Indians, which stretched from Texas to the Canadian border.

Senator Stephen Douglas of Illinois had an even better idea: Chicago should be the transcontinental railroad's eastern terminus. Since 1845, therefore, Douglas and his supporters had offered bills for a new territory west of Missouri and Iowa bearing the Indian name Nebraska. In 1854, as chairman of the Committee on Territories, Senator Douglas proposed yet another Nebraska bill, which became the Kansas-Nebraska Act. Unlike the others, this one included the entire unorganized portion of the Louisiana Purchase, extending to the Canadian border. Political necessity then began to transform Douglas's proposal from a railroad bill into a pro-slavery bill, thus reopening the controversy over the extension of slavery into the territories. To grant territorial status to Nebraska required the support of southerners in Congress, and to win that support Douglas needed to make some concession on slavery in the new territories. This he did by writing the principle of popular sovereignty into the bill, allowing voters in each territory to decide whether to allow slavery.

It was a clever dodge since the 1820 Missouri Compromise would exclude slaves until a territorial government had made a decision. Southerners quickly spotted the barrier, and Douglas just as quickly made two more concessions. He supported an amendment for repeal of the Missouri Compromise insofar as it excluded slavery north of 36°30', and he agreed to the creation of two territories, Kansas, west of Missouri, and Nebraska, west of Iowa and Minnesota.

Douglas's motives remain unclear. Railroads were surely foremost in his mind, but he was also influenced by the desire to win support for his bill in the South, by the hope that his promotion of "popular sovereignty" would quiet the slavery issue and open the Great Plains to development, or by a chance to split the Whigs over the issue. But whatever his

Stephen Douglas, ca. 1852

Author of the Kansas-Nebraska Act.

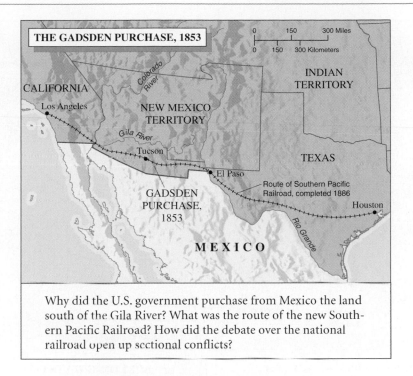

THE GADSDEN PURCHASE, 1853

Why did the U.S. government purchase from Mexico the land south of the Gila River? What was the route of the new Southern Pacific Railroad? How did the debate over the national railroad open up sectional conflicts?

reasoning, he had blundered, damaging his presidential chances and setting the country on the road to civil war. In replacing the long-standing Missouri Compromise boundary line with the concept of popular sovereignty, enabling territorial residents to decide the issue of slavery for themselves, Douglas renewed sectional tensions and forced moderate political leaders to align with the extremes. In the end the Kansas-Nebraska Act would destroy the Whig party, fragment the Democratic party, and spark a territorial civil war between pro- and anti-slavery settlers in Kansas.

The tragic flaw in Douglas's reasoning was his failure to appreciate the growing intensity of anti-slavery sentiment spreading across the country. Douglas himself preferred that the territories vote against slavery. Their climate and geography excluded plantation agriculture, he reasoned, and he could not comprehend how people could get so wrought up over the abstract right of taking their slaves into territories unsuited for slave labor. Yet he had in fact opened the possibility that slavery might gain a foothold in Kansas.

Douglas's proposal to repeal the Missouri Compromise was less than a week old when six anti-slavery congressmen published a protest, the "Appeal of the Independent Democrats." Their moral indignation quickly spread

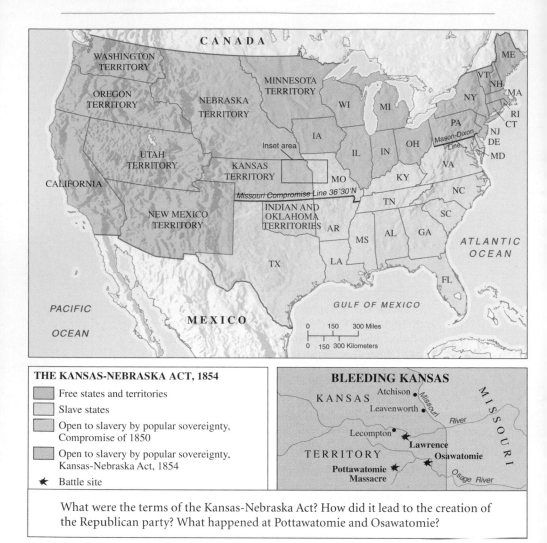

THE KANSAS-NEBRASKA ACT, 1854

- Free states and territories
- Slave states
- Open to slavery by popular sovereignty, Compromise of 1850
- Open to slavery by popular sovereignty, Kansas-Nebraska Act, 1854
- ✱ Battle site

BLEEDING KANSAS

What were the terms of the Kansas-Nebraska Act? How did it lead to the creation of the Republican party? What happened at Pottawatomie and Osawatomie?

among those who opposed Douglas. The document dismissed his bill "as a gross violation of a sacred pledge" and as "part and parcel of an atrocious plot" to create "a dreary region of despotism, inhabited by masters and slaves." The anti-slavery Democrats called upon Americans to protest this "atrocious crime."

Across the North, editorials, sermons, speeches, and petitions echoed this indignation. What had been the opinion of a radical minority was fast becoming the common view of northerners. But in Congress, Douglas had the votes for his Kansas-Nebraska Act, and he forced the issue with tireless energy. The inept President Pierce impulsively added his support. Southerners lined up behind Douglas, with notable exceptions, such as Texas senator Sam Houston, who denounced the act's violation of two solemn compacts: the Missouri Compromise and the confirmation of the territory deeded to the Indians "as long as grass shall grow and water run." He was not the only one concerned about the Indians, however. Federal agents were already busy hoodwinking or bullying Indians into relinquishing their lands. Douglas and Pierce whipped reluctant Democrats into line (though about half the northern Democrats refused to yield), pushing the passage of the Kansas-Nebraska bill by a vote of 37 to 14 in the Senate and 113 to 100 in the House.

Very well, many in the North reasoned, if the Missouri Compromise was not a sacred pledge, then neither was the Fugitive Slave Act that was part of the Compromise of 1850. On June 2, 1854, Boston witnessed the most dramatic demonstration against the act. A runaway Virginia slave named Anthony Burns had been taken in by free blacks in Boston when federal marshals arrived to arrest and return him. Incensed by what had happened, a crowd of 2,000 abolitionists led by a minister stormed the jail in an effort to free Burns. In the melee a federal marshal was killed. At Burns's trial, held to determine whether he indeed was a fugitive, a compromise was proposed that would have allowed Bostonians to buy Burns his freedom, but the plan was scuttled by President Pierce, who was determined to enforce the Fugitive Slave Act. On June 2, the day that state militia and federal troops marched Burns through Boston to a ship waiting to return him to Virginia, some 50,000 people lined the streets. Many of them shouted insults at the federal officials.

Over the next several weeks, demonstrations against the Fugitive Slave Act grew in scope and intensity. At a July 4 rally in Framingham, Massachusetts, the abolitionist editor William Lloyd Garrison burned copies of the Fugitive Slave Act and the Constitution. Later in the day the Transcendentalist Henry David Thoreau delivered a fiery speech in which he charged that the trial of Burns was "really the trial of Massachusetts." Prominent New Englanders despised President Pierce for his handling of the Burns case. In a letter to the White House, one of them wrote: "To the chief slave-catcher of the United States. You damned, infernal scoundrel, if I only had you here in Boston, I would murder you!" As it happened, Anthony Burns was the last fugitive slave to be returned from Boston and was soon freed through purchase by the African American community of Boston.

THE EMERGENCE OF THE REPUBLICAN PARTY By the mid-1850s the sharp tensions over slavery were fracturing the nation. The national organizations of Baptists and Methodists, for instance, had split over slavery by 1845 and formed new northern and southern organizations. The national parties were also beginning to buckle under the strain of slavery. The Democrats managed to postpone disruption for a while, but their congressional delegation lost heavily in the North, enhancing the influence of their southern wing.

The strain of the Kansas-Nebraska Act soon destroyed the Whig party. Southern Whigs now tended to abstain from voting, while northern Whigs gravitated toward two new parties. One was the American (Know-Nothing) party, which had raised the banner of nativism and the hope of serving the patriotic cause of Union. The other, which attracted even more northern Whigs, was formed in 1854 when those Whigs joined with independent Democrats and Free-Soilers to form the Republican party.

"BLEEDING KANSAS"   After passage of the Kansas-Nebraska Act in 1854, attention swung to the plains of Kansas, where opposing elements gathered to stage a rehearsal for civil war. Whereas all had agreed that Nebraska would be a free state, Kansas soon exposed the potential for mischief in the idea of popular sovereignty. The ambiguity of the law, useful to Douglas in getting it passed, only added to the chaos. The people of Kansas were "perfectly free to form and regulate their domestic institutions in their own way, subject only to the Constitution." That in itself invited conflicting interpretations, but the law was completely silent as to the time of any decision, adding to each side's sense of urgency in getting political control of the 50-million-acre territory.

The settlement of Kansas therefore differed from the typical pioneering efforts. Groups sprang up in North and South to hurry right-minded transplants westward. Most of the settlers were from Missouri and its surrounding states. Although few of them held slaves, they were not sympathetic to abolitionism; racism was prevalent even among nonslaveholding whites. Many of the Kansas settlers wanted to keep all blacks, enslaved or free, out of the territory. "I kem to Kansas to live in a free state," declared a minister, "and I don't want niggers a-trampin' over my grave." By 1860 there were only 627 African Americans in the territory.

When Kansas's first federal governor arrived, in 1854, he found several thousand settlers there. He ordered a census and scheduled an election for a territorial legislature in 1855. On election day several thousand "border ruffians" crossed over from Missouri, illegally swept the polls for pro-slavery forces, and vowed to kill every "God-damned abolitionist in the Territory." The governor denounced the vote as a fraud but did nothing to alter the results, for fear of being killed. The territorial legislature expelled its few anti-slavery members, adopted a drastic slave code, and made it a capital offense

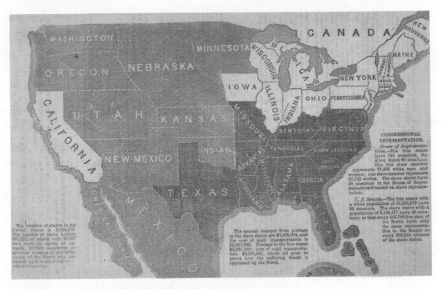

"The Border Ruffian Code in Kansas" (1856)

This map, which appeared in a pamphlet published by Horace Greeley's *New York Tribune*, shows the country divided into slave states (dark), free states (white), and those in the middle (gray). It attempts to "prove how the suffering South is oppressed by the North."

to aid a fugitive slave and a felony even to question the legality of slavery in the territory.

Outraged free-state advocates rejected this "bogus" government and moved directly toward application for statehood. In 1855 a constitutional convention, the product of an extralegal election, met in Topeka, drafted a state constitution excluding both slavery and free blacks from Kansas, and applied for admission to the Union. By 1856 a free-state "governor" and "legislature" were functioning in Topeka; thus there were two illegal governments in the Kansas territory. The prospect of getting any government to command authority seemed dim, and both sides began to arm.

Finally, the tense confrontation began to slip into violent conflict. In May 1856 a pro-slavery mob entered the free-state town of Lawrence, Kansas, destroyed newspaper presses, set fire to the free-state governor's home, stole property, and demolished the Free-State Hotel.

The "sack of Lawrence" resulted in just one casualty, but the excitement aroused a zealous Free-Soiler named John Brown, who had a history of mental instability. Two days after Lawrence was sacked, Brown set out with four of his sons and three other men for Pottawatomie, the site of a pro-slavery

The "sack of Lawrence"

This sheet music cover for an anti-slavery song portrays (in the circle) the burning of the Free-State Hotel in Lawrence, Kansas, by a pro-slavery mob in 1856. Shalor Eldridge, the hotel's owner, rebuilt the hotel in 1857 and again in 1865, after it was destroyed by William Quantrill and his raiders in 1863.

settlement, where they dragged five men from their houses and hacked them to death in front of their screaming families.

The Pottawatomie Massacre (May 24–25, 1856) set off a guerrilla war in the Kansas Territory that lasted through the fall. On August 30, Missouri ruffians raided the free-state settlement at Osawatomie, Kansas. They looted and burned the houses and shot John Brown's son Frederick through the heart. The elder Brown, who barely escaped, looked back at the site being devastated by "Satan's legions" and swore to his surviving sons and followers, "I have only a short time to live—only one death to die, and I will die fighting for this cause." Three years later he would do just that, in a futile uprising at Harpers Ferry, Virginia, that inflamed sentiment in the North and the South. Altogether, by the end of 1856, about 200 settlers had been killed in Kansas and $2 million in property destroyed during the territorial civil war. Approximately 1,500 federal troops were dispatched to restore some semblance of order.

VIOLENCE IN THE SENATE   The violence in Kansas over slavery spilled over into Congress. On May 22, 1856, the day after the burning of Lawrence and two days before the Pottawatomie Massacre, a sudden flash of violence on the Senate floor electrified the whole country. Just two days earlier, Senator Charles Sumner of Massachusetts, an unyielding foe of slavery, had delivered an inflammatory speech on "The Crime against Kansas." Sumner, elected five years earlier by a coalition of Free-Soilers and Democrats, was a brilliant orator with a sharp tongue and a self-righteous manner. His two-day speech, delivered from memory, was an exercise in studied insult. The pro-slavery Missourians who crossed into Kansas, he charged, were

"Bully" Brooks's attack on Charles Sumner

The incident worsened the strains on the Union.

"hirelings picked from the drunken spew and vomit of an uneasy civilization." Their treatment of Kansas was "the rape of a virgin territory," he said, "and it may be clearly traced to a depraved longing for a new slave State, the hideous offspring of such a crime." Sumner singled out the elderly senator Andrew Pickens Butler of South Carolina for censure. Butler, Sumner charged, had "chosen a mistress . . . who . . . though polluted in the sight of the world, is chaste in his sight—I mean the harlot, Slavery."

Sumner's indignant rudeness might well have backfired had it not been for Butler's kinsman Preston S. Brooks, a fiery-tempered South Carolina congressman. For two days, Brooks brooded over the insult to his relative, knowing that Sumner would refuse a challenge to a duel. On May 22 he found Sumner writing at his Senate desk after an adjournment, accused him of slander against South Carolina and Butler, and commenced beating him about the head with a cane while stunned colleagues looked on. Sumner, struggling to rise, wrenched the desk from the floor and collapsed. Brooks kept beating the unconscious Sumner until his cane broke.

Brooks had satisfied his rage but in doing so had created a martyr for the anti-slavery cause. For two and a half years, Sumner's empty Senate seat was a solemn reminder of the violence done to him. When the House censured Brooks, he resigned, only to return after being triumphantly reelected. His southern admirers sent him new canes. The editor of the *Richmond Enquirer* urged Brooks to cane Sumner again: "These vulgar abolitionists in the Senate . . . must be lashed into submission." Northerners hastened to Sumner's defense. The news of the beating drove John Brown "crazy," his eldest son remembered, *"crazy."* People on each side, appalled at the behavior of the other, decided that North and South had developed into different civilizations with incompatible standards of honor. "I do not see," Ralph Waldo Emerson confessed, "how a barbarous community and a civilized community can constitute one state. We must either get rid of slavery, or get rid of freedom."

SECTIONAL POLITICS Within the span of five days in May of 1856, "Bleeding Kansas," "Bleeding Sumner," and "Bully Brooks" had set the tone for another presidential election. The major parties could no longer evade

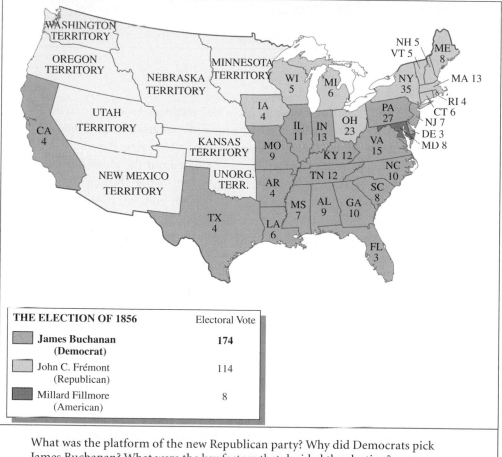

THE ELECTION OF 1856	Electoral Vote
James Buchanan (Democrat)	174
John C. Frémont (Republican)	114
Millard Fillmore (American)	8

What was the platform of the new Republican party? Why did Democrats pick James Buchanan? What were the key factors that decided the election?

the slavery issue. Already in February it had split the infant American party wide open. Southern delegates, with help from New York, killed a resolution to restore the Missouri Compromise and nominated Millard Fillmore for president. Later what was left of the Whig party endorsed him as well. But as a friend wrote Fillmore, the "outrageous proceedings in Kansas & the assault on Mr. Sumner have contributed very much to strengthen the [new] Republican Party."

At its first national convention the Republican party passed over its leading figure, New York senator William H. Seward, who was awaiting a better chance in 1860. Following the Whig tradition, the party sought out a military hero, John C. Frémont, "the Pathfinder," who had led the conquest of Mexican California. The Republican platform also owed much to the Whigs. It favored a transcontinental railroad and, in general, more government-financed internal improvements. It condemned the repeal of the Missouri Compromise, the Democratic policy of territorial expansion, and "those twin relics of barbarism—Polygamy and Slavery." The campaign slogan echoed that of the Free-Soilers: "Free soil, free speech, and Frémont." It was the first time a major-party platform had taken a stand against slavery.

The Democrats, meeting two weeks earlier in June, had rejected Franklin Pierce, the hapless victim of so much turmoil. Pierce, who struggled most of his life with alcoholism and self-doubt, may have been the most hated person in the nation by 1852. A Boston newspaper vilified him for promoting sectionalism. "Who but you, Franklin Pierce, have . . . kindled the flames of civil war on the desolated plains of Kansas?" A Philadelphia newspaper was even blunter. The Pierce presidency, it charged, was one of "weakness, indecision, rashness, ignorance, and an entire and utter absence of dignity." Pierce remains the only elected president to be denied renomination by his party. Stephen Douglas, too, was left out, because of the damage done by his Kansas-Nebraska Act. The party therefore turned to James Buchanan of Pennsylvania, a former Senator and secretary of state who had long sought the nomination. The party and its candidate nevertheless supported Pierce's policies. The Democratic platform endorsed the Kansas-Nebraska Act, called for vigorous enforcement of the fugitive slave law, and stressed that Congress should not interfere with slavery in either states or territories. The party reached out to its newly acquired Irish and German voters by condemning nativism and endorsing religious liberty.

The campaign of 1856 resolved itself as a sectional contest in which parties vied for northern or southern votes. The Republicans had few southern supporters and only a handful in the border states, where fear of disunion held many Whigs in line. Buchanan thus went into the campaign as the candidate of the only remaining national party. Frémont swept the north-ernmost states with 114 electoral votes, but Buchanan added five free states—Pennsylvania, New Jersey, Illinois, Indiana, and California—to his southern majority for a total of 174.

The sixty-five-year-old Buchanan, America's first unmarried president, brought to the White House a portfolio of impressive achievements in politics and diplomacy. His political career went back to 1815, when he served as a Federalist legislator in Pennsylvania before switching to Andrew Jackson's party in the 1820s. He had served in Congress for over twenty years and had been ambassador to Russia and Britain and James K. Polk's secretary of state. His long quest for the presidency had been built on his commitment to states' rights and his aggressive promotion of territorial expansion. His political debts reinforced his belief that saving the Union depended upon concessions to the South. Republicans charged that he lacked the backbone to stand up to the southerners who dominated the Democratic majorities in Congress. His choice of four slave-state men and only three free-state men for his cabinet seemed another bad omen. It was.

THE DEEPENING SECTIONAL CRISIS

During James Buchanan's first six months in office in 1857, three major events caused his undoing: (1) the Supreme Court decision in the *Dred Scott* case, (2) new troubles in Kansas, and (3) a financial panic that sparked a widespread economic depression. For all of Buchanan's experience as a legislator and diplomat, he failed to handle those and other key issues in a statesmanlike manner. The new president proved to be a mediocre chief executive.

THE *DRED SCOTT* CASE   On March 6, 1857, two days after Buchanan's inauguration, the Supreme Court rendered a decision in the long-pending case of *Dred Scott v. Sandford*. Dred Scott, born a slave in Virginia in about 1800, had been taken to St. Louis in 1830 and sold to an army surgeon, who took him to Illinois, then to the Wisconsin Territory (later Minnesota), and finally back to St. Louis in 1842. While in the Wisconsin Territory, Scott had married Harriet Robinson, and they eventually had two daughters.

After his master's death, in 1843, Scott had tried to buy his freedom. In 1846, Harriet Scott persuaded her husband to file suit in the Missouri courts, claiming that residence in Illinois and the Wisconsin Territory had made him free. A jury decided in his favor, but the state supreme court ruled against him. When the case rose on appeal to the Supreme Court, the nation anxiously awaited its opinion on whether freedom once granted could be lost by returning to a slave state.

Eight of the nine justices filed separate opinions; one concurred with Chief Justice Roger B. Taney of Maryland. By different lines of reasoning, seven justices ruled that Scott remained a slave. The aging Taney, who wrote the Court's majority opinion, ruled that Scott lacked legal standing because he lacked citizenship. Taney argued that one became a U.S. citizen either by birth or by naturalization, and both of those methods ruled out any former slave. He then mistakenly argued that no state had ever accorded citizenship to blacks.

Chief Justice Roger B. Taney

Taney played a critical role in the Supreme Court's decision in the *Dred Scott* case, which fanned the flames of sectional discord.

At the time the Constitution was adopted, Taney further said, blacks "had for more than a century been regarded as . . . so far inferior, that they had no rights which the white man was bound to respect."

Taney declared that Scott's residency in a free state had not freed him since, in line with precedent, the decision of the state court governed. This left the question of residency in a free territory. On that point, Taney argued that the Missouri Compromise of 1820 had deprived citizens of property by prohibiting slavery, an action "not warranted by the Constitution." He strongly implied, but never said explicitly, that the Missouri Compromise had violated the due-process clause of the Fifth Amendment, as John C. Calhoun had earlier argued.

The upshot was that Chief Justice Taney and the rest of the Supreme Court had declared an act of Congress unconstitutional for the first time since *Marbury v. Madison* (1803). Congress had repealed the Missouri Compromise in the Kansas-Nebraska Act three years earlier, but the *Dred Scott* decision now challenged the concept of popular sovereignty. If Congress itself could not exclude slavery from a territory, then presumably neither could a territorial government created by an act of Congress.

By this decision the Supreme Court had tried to settle a question that Congress had dodged ever since the Wilmot Proviso had surfaced. But far from settling it, Taney's ruling had fanned the flames of dissension. Little wonder that Republicans protested the *Dred Scott* decision: the Court had declared their anti-slavery program unconstitutional. It had also reinforced the suspicion that the slavocracy was hatching a conspiracy. Were not all but one of the justices who had joined Taney southerners? And President Buchanan had sought to influence the Court's decision both before and during his inaugural ceremony. Besides, if Dred Scott were not a citizen and had no standing in court, there was no case before the Court. The majority ruling was an obiter dictum—a statement not essential to deciding the case and therefore not binding, "entitled to just so much moral weight as would be the judgment of a majority of those congregated in any Washington bar-room."

Pro-slavery elements of course greeted the Court's opinion as binding. Now the most militant among them were emboldened to make yet another demand. It was not enough to deny Congress the right to interfere with slavery in the territories; Congress had an obligation to protect the property of slaveholders, making a federal slave code the next step in the militant effort to defend slavery.

THE LECOMPTON CONSTITUTION   Out in Kansas, meanwhile, the struggle over slavery continued. Just before Buchanan's inauguration, in early 1857, the pro-slavery legislature called for a constitutional convention. Since no provision was made for a referendum on the constitution, however, the governor vetoed the measure, and then the legislature overrode his veto. The Kansas governor resigned on the day Buchanan took office, and the new president replaced him with Robert J. Walker. A native Pennsylvanian who had made a political career in Mississippi and a former member of Polk's cabinet, Walker had greater prestige than his predecessors, and he put the Union above slavery. In Kansas he scented a chance to advance the cause of both the Union and his party. Under popular sovercignty fair elections would produce a state that would be both free and Democratic.

Walker arrived in Kansas in 1857, and with Buchanan's approval the new governor pledged to the free-state Kansans that the new constitution would be submitted to a fair vote. But in spite of his pleas, he arrived too late to persuade free-state men to vote for convention delegates in elections they were sure had been rigged against them. Later, however, Walker did persuade the free-state leaders to vote in the election of a new territorial legislature.

As a result a polarity arose between an anti-slavery legislature and a pro-slavery constitutional convention. The convention, meeting at Lecompton, Kansas, drew up a constitution under which Kansas would become a slave state. Although Kansas had only about 200 slaves at the time, free-state men boycotted the vote on the new constitution on the claim that it, too, was rigged. At that point, President Buchanan took a fateful step. Influenced by southern advisers and politically dependent upon southern congressmen, he decided to renege on his pledge to Governor Walker and support the action of the pro-slavery Lecompton convention. Walker resigned, and the election went according to form: 6,226 for the constitution with slavery, 569 for the constitution without slavery. Meanwhile, the acting governor had convened the anti-slavery legislature, which called for another election to vote the Lecompton Constitution up or down. Most of the pro-slavery settlers boycotted this election, and the result, on January 4, 1858, was overwhelming: 10,226 against the constitution, 138 for the constitution with slavery, 24 for the constitution without slavery.

The combined results suggested a clear majority against slavery, but the pro-southern Buchanan stuck to his support of the Lecompton Constitution, driving another wedge into the Democratic party. Senator Stephen Douglas, up for reelection, broke dramatically with the president in a tense confrontation, but Buchanan persisted in trying to get the Lecompton Constitution approved by Congress. In the Senate, administration forces held firm, and in 1858 the Lecompton Constitution was passed. In the House enough anti-Lecompton Democrats combined to put through an amendment for a new and carefully supervised popular vote in Kansas. Enough senators went along to permit passage of the House bill. Southerners were confident the vote would favor slavery because to reject it the voters would have to reject the constitution, an action that would postpone statehood until the population reached 90,000. On August 2, 1858, Kansas voters nevertheless rejected Lecompton, 11,300 to 1,788. With that vote, Kansas, now firmly in the hands of its anti-slavery legislature, largely ended its provocative role in the sectional controversy.

THE PANIC OF 1857   The third emergency of Buchanan's first half year in office, a financial crisis, occurred in August 1857. It was brought on by a reduction in foreign demand for American grain, overly rapid railroad construction, a surge in manufacturing that outran the growth of markets, and the continued weakness and confusion of the state banknote system. The failure of the Ohio Life Insurance and Trust Company on August 24, 1857, precipitated the panic, which was followed by an economic slump from which the country did not emerge until 1859.

Everything in those years seemed to get drawn into the vortex of sectional conflict, and business troubles were no exception. Northern businessmen tended to blame the depression on the Democratic Tariff of 1857, which had set rates on imports at their lowest level since 1816. The agricultural South weathered the crisis better than the North. Cotton prices fell, but slowly, and world markets for cotton quickly recovered. The result was an exalted notion of King Cotton's importance to the world and apparent confirmation of the growing argument that the southern system of slave-based agriculture was superior to the free-labor system of the North.

THE REVIVAL OF 1857–1859   The business panic and depression coincided with a widespread national revival of religious life. In New York City, where over 30,000 people had lost their jobs, Jeremiah Lanphier, a business executive–turned–lay missionary, grew despondent at the suffering in the city as well as an alarming decline in church membership. God, he later claimed, led him to begin a weekly prayer service in the Wall Street financial district so that executives might commune with God. He began on September 23, 1857, with six people attending. Within a few months, though, the number of participants soared. To accommodate the overflow crowds (largely male), nondenominational prayer meetings were offered daily at locations across the city. Soon the daily prayer ritual spread across the nation, especially in the northern tier of states. Women were eventually encouraged to attend the meetings, but they were rarely allowed to speak.

The "prayer-meeting" revivals generated excited discussion; stories about the latest "awakening" dominated big-city newspapers, some of which created regular sections to report the daily progress of the crusade. Between 1857 and 1859 over half a million people joined churches. The revivals of the late 1850s were distinctive in several respects. Unlike the Second Great Awakening of the 1830s and 1840s, the prayer-meeting revivals were largely uninterested in social reform. In fact, prayers about controversial issues, such as slavery, were expressly prohibited at the meetings. The focus of the meetings was personal spiritual renewal, not social transformation. The transcendentalist minister and militant reformer Theodore Parker denounced the revivalists for ignoring the evils of slavery. The Revival of 1857–1859 also differed from earlier awakenings in that it did not feature charismatic ministers or fire-and-brimstone evangelizing. Instead, it was largely a lay movement focused on discreet prayer.

DOUGLAS VERSUS LINCOLN   Amid the recriminations over the *Dred Scott* decision, Kansas, and the floundering economy, the center could not hold. The controversy over slavery in Kansas put severe strains on the most substantial cord of union that was left, the Democratic party. To many, Senator Stephen Douglas seemed the best hope for unity and union, one of the few remaining Democratic leaders with support in both the North and the South. But now Douglas was being whipsawed by the extremes. The passage of the Kansas-Nebraska Act had cast him in the role of a doughface, a southern sympathizer. Yet his opposition to the Lecompton Constitution, the fraudulent fruit of popular sovereignty, had alienated him from Buchanan's southern junta. But for all his flexibility and opportunism, Douglas had convinced himself that popular sovereignty was a point of principle, a bulwark of democracy and local self-government. In 1858 he faced reelection to the Senate against the opposition of both Buchanan Democrats and Republicans. The year 1860 would give him a chance for the presidency, but first he had to secure his home base in Illinois.

To oppose him, Illinois Republicans named Abraham Lincoln of Springfield, the lanky, rawboned former Whig state legislator and one-term congressman, a small-town lawyer. Lincoln's early life had been the hardscrabble existence of the frontier farmer. Born in a Kentucky log cabin in 1809 and raised on farms in Indiana and Illinois, the young Lincoln had worked at various farm tasks, operated a ferry, and made two trips down to New Orleans as a flatboatman. Striking out on his own, he managed a general store in New Salem, Illinois, learned surveying, served in the Black Hawk War in 1832, won election to the legislature in 1834 (at the age of twenty-five), read law, and was admitted to the bar in 1836. Lincoln stayed in the Illinois legislature until 1842 and in 1846 won a seat in Congress. After a single term he retired from active politics to cultivate his law practice in Springfield.

In 1854 the Kansas-Nebraska Act drew Lincoln back into the political arena. When Douglas appeared in Springfield to defend his idea of popular sovereignty, Lincoln countered from the same platform. Lincoln abhorred slavery but was no abolitionist. He did not believe the two races could coexist as equals, but he did oppose any further extension of slavery into new territories, assuming that over time the institution would die a "natural death." Slavery, he said in the 1840s, was a vexing but "minor question on its way to extinction." Now, in 1854 in Peoria, he preached an old but oft-neglected doctrine: hate the sin but not the sinner:

> When Southern people tell us they are no more responsible for the origin of slavery, than we, I acknowledge the fact. When it is said that the institution exists; and that it is very difficult to get rid of it, in any satisfactory way, I can understand and appreciate the saying. . . .
>
> But all this, to my judgment, furnishes no more excuses for permitting slavery to go into our own free territory, than it would for reviving the African slave trade by law.

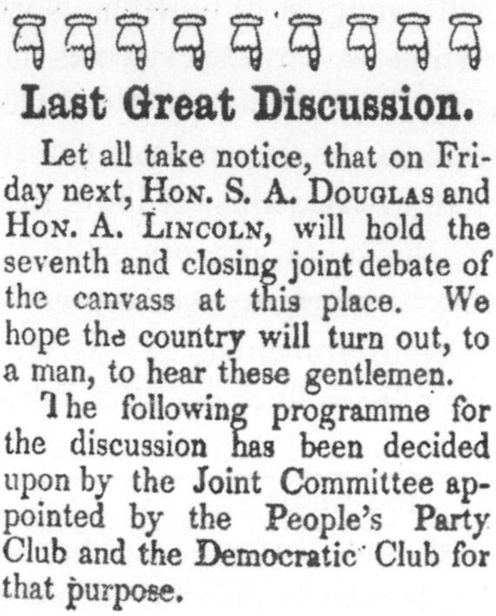

Last Great Discussion.

Let all take notice, that on Friday next, HON. S. A. DOUGLAS and HON. A. LINCOLN, will hold the seventh and closing joint debate of the canvass at this place. We hope the country will turn out, to a man, to hear these gentlemen.

The following programme for the discussion has been decided upon by the Joint Committee appointed by the People's Party Club and the Democratic Club for that purpose.

Debate announcement

An announcement for the seventh and final Lincoln-Douglas debate.

At first Lincoln had held back from the rapidly growing Republican party, but in 1856 he had joined it and had given some fifty speeches for the Frémont ticket in Illinois and nearby states. By 1858, as the obvious choice to oppose Douglas for the Senate seat, he was resorting to the classic ploy of the underdog: he challenged the favorite to debate him. Douglas agreed to meet him in seven places around the state.

Thus the legendary Lincoln-Douglas debates took place, from August 21 to October 15, 1858. They attracted thousands of spectators and transformed a contest for a Senate seat into a battle for the very future of the Republic. The two men could not have presented a more striking contrast. Lincoln was well over six feet tall, sinewy and craggy featured with a singularly long neck and deep-set, brooding eyes. Unassuming in manner, dressed in homely, well-worn clothes, and walking with a shambling gait, he lightened his essentially serious demeanor with a refreshing sense of humor. To sympathetic observers he conveyed an air of simplicity, sincerity, and common sense. Douglas, on the other hand, was short, rotund, stern, and cocky, attired in the finest custom-tailored suits. A man of considerable abilities and even greater ambition, he strutted to the platform with the pugnacious air of a predestined champion. Douglas traveled to the debate sites in a private railroad car; Lincoln rode alone on his horse.

At the time and since, much attention focused on the second debate, at Freeport, where Lincoln asked Douglas how he could reconcile popular sovereignty with the *Dred Scott* ruling that citizens had the right to carry slaves into any territory. Douglas's answer, thenceforth known as the Freeport Doctrine, was to state the obvious: whatever the Supreme Court might say about slavery, it could not exist anywhere unless supported by local police regulations.

Douglas tried to set some traps of his own. He intimated that Lincoln belonged to the fanatic sect of abolitionists who advocated racial equality. Lincoln responded with caution. There was, he said, "a physical difference between the white and black races" that would "forever forbid the two races living together on terms of social and political equality." But Lincoln insisted that blacks had an "equal" right to freedom and the fruits of their labor. The basic difference between the two men, Lincoln insisted, lay in Douglas's professed indifference to the moral question of slavery.

If Lincoln had the better of the argument, at least in the long view Douglas had the better of a close election in traditionally Democratic Illinois. Douglas retained his Senate seat, but Lincoln's energetic campaign had made him a national figure well positioned to become the Republican presidential candidate in 1860. Across the country, however, Democrats did not fare as well as Douglas in 1858. Most congressional candidates aligned with President Buchanan lost their elections, thus signaling in the North and the West the political shift toward the new Republican party and the politics of anti-slavery.

At the same time that the political balance in the North was beginning to shift from the Democrats to the Republicans, political tensions over slavery were becoming more intractable—and violent. In 1858, members of Congress engaged in the largest brawl ever on the floor of the House of Representatives. Harsh words about slavery incited the melee, which involved more than fifty legislators shoving, punching, and wrestling one another. The fracas culminated when John "Bowie Knife" Potter of Wisconsin yanked off the wig of a Mississippi congressman and claimed, "I've scalped him." Like the scuffling congressmen, more and more Americans began to feel that slavery could be ended or defended only with violence. The editor of a Kansas newspaper exclaimed that he yearned to kill an abolitionist: "If I can't kill a man, I'll kill a woman; and if I can't kill a woman, I'll kill a child."

John Brown

Although his anti-slavery efforts were based in Kansas, Brown was a native of Connecticut.

JOHN BROWN'S RAID The gradual return of prosperity in 1859 offered hope that the sectional storms of the 1850s might yet pass. But the slavery issue remained tornadic. In October 1859, John Brown once again surfaced, this time in the East. Since the Pottawatomie Massacre in 1856, he had led a furtive existence, engaging in fund-raising and occasional bushwhacking. His heartfelt commitment to abolish the "wicked curse of slavery" and promote complete racial equality, meanwhile, had intensified to a fever pitch. Self-righteous and de-manding, he was driven by a sense of crusading zeal and puritanical righteous-ness. His penetrating gray eyes and flowing beard and the religious certainty that he was an instrument of God struck fear into supporters and opponents alike.

On October 16, 1859, Brown launched his supreme gesture. From a Mary-land farm he crossed the Potomac River with about twenty men, including five blacks. Under cover of darkness, they occupied the federal arsenal in Harpers Ferry, Virginia (now West Virginia). Brown planned to arm the slaves in the area, who he assumed would flock to his cause; then he would set up a black stronghold in the mountains of western Virginia, thus provid-ing a nucleus of support for slave insurrections across the South.

What Brown actually did was to take the arsenal by surprise, seize eleven hostages, and hole up in the fire-engine house, where he was surrounded by militiamen and townspeople. The next morning, Brown sent his son Watson and another supporter out under a white flag, hoping to trade his hostages for his freedom, but the enraged crowd shot them both. Intermittent shoot-ing continued, and another Brown son was wounded. He begged his father to kill him to end his suffering, but the righteous Brown lashed out, "If you must die, die like a man." A few minutes later the son was dead.

That night Lieutenant Colonel Robert E. Lee arrived with his aide, Lieu-tenant J. E. B. Stuart, and a force of U.S. marines, having been dispatched from Washington by President Buchanan. The following morning, Octo-ber 18, Stuart and his troops, with thousands of spectators cheering, broke down the barricaded doors and rushed into the fire-engine house. A young lieutenant found Brown kneeling with his rifle cocked. Before Brown could fire, however, the marine used the hilt of his sword to beat Brown uncon-scious. The siege was over. Altogether, Brown's men had killed four people and wounded nine. Of their own force, ten died (including two of Brown's sons), seven were captured, and five escaped.

Brown was quickly tried for treason and conspiracy to incite insurrection. He was convicted on October 31 and hanged on December 2. Six others died on the gallows later. If Brown had failed in his purpose, he had achieved two things: he had become a martyr for the anti-slavery cause, and he had set off a panic throughout the slaveholding South. At his sentencing he delivered one of America's classic speeches: "Now, if it is deemed necessary that I should forfeit my life for the furtherance of the ends of justice, and mingle my blood further with the blood of my children and with the blood of mil-lions in this slave country whose rights are disregarded by wicked, cruel, and unjust enactments, I say, let it be done."

When John Brown, still unflinching, met his end, there were solemn observances in the North. "That new saint," Ralph Waldo Emerson said, ". . . will make the gallows glorious like the cross." By far the gravest effect of Brown's raid was to encourage pro-slavery southerners to equate the militant abolitionism of John Brown with the Republican party. All through the fall and winter of 1859–1860, rumors of abolitionist conspiracies and slave insurrections swept through the slave states. Every northern visitor, commercial traveler, or schoolteacher came under suspicion, and many were driven out. "We regard every man in our midst an enemy to the institutions of the South," said the *Atlanta Confederacy*, "who does not boldly declare that he believes African slavery to be a social, moral, and political blessing."

THE CENTER COMES APART

THE DEMOCRATS DIVIDE   Amid such emotional hysteria the nation ushered in another presidential election, destined to be the most fateful in its history. In April 1860 the Democrats gathered in Charleston, a pro-slavery hotbed, for their presidential convention. Illinois senator Stephen Douglas's supporters at the convention reaffirmed the platform of 1856, which simply promised congressional noninterference with slavery. Southern firebrands,

"Prospect of a Smash Up" (1860)

This cartoon shows the Democratic party—the last remaining national party—about to be split by sectional differences and the onrush of Republicans, led by Abraham Lincoln.

PROGRESSIVE DEMOCRACY—PROSPECT OF A SMASH UP.

however, demanded federal protection for slavery in the territories. Buchanan supporters, hoping to stop Douglas, encouraged the strategy. The platform debate reached a heady climax when the Alabama hotspur William Yancey informed the northern Democrats that their error had been the failure to defend slavery as a positive good. An Ohio senator offered a blunt reply. "Gentlemen of the South," he said, "you mistake us—you mistake us. We will not do it."

When the pro-slavery planks lost, Alabama's delegates walked out of the convention, followed by those representing most of the other southern states. "We say, go your way," exclaimed a Mississippi delegate to Douglas's supporters, "and we will go ours." The convention then decided to leave the overwrought atmosphere of Charleston and reassemble in Baltimore on June 18. The Baltimore convention finally nominated Stephen Douglas and reaffirmed the 1856 platform. The Charleston seceders met first in Richmond and then in Baltimore, where they adopted the slave-code platform defeated in Charleston and named Vice President John C. Breckinridge of Kentucky as their candidate for president. Thus another cord of union had snapped: the last remaining national party had fragmented.

LINCOLN'S ELECTION   The Republicans, meanwhile, gathered in Chicago. There everything suddenly came together for Abraham Lincoln, the uncommon common man. He had emerged on the national scene during his unsuccessful Illinois senatorial campaign two years before and had since taken a stance designed to make him available for the nomination. He was strong enough on the containment of slavery to satisfy the abolitionists yet moderate enough to seem less threatening than they were. In 1860 he had gone east to address an audience of influential Republicans at Cooper Union, a newly established art and engineering college in New York City, where he emphasized his view of slavery "as an evil, not to be extended, but to be tolerated and protected only because of and so far as its actual presence among us makes that toleration and protection a necessity."

At the Chicago Republican Convention, New York senator William H. Seward was the early leader among the presidential nominees, but he had been tagged, perhaps wrongly, as an extremist for his earlier statements about a looming "irrepressible conflict" over slavery. On the first ballot, Lincoln finished in second place. On the next ballot he drew almost even with Seward, and when he came within one and a half votes of a majority on the third count, Ohio quickly switched four votes to put him over the top.

The Republican party platform denounced both the Supreme Court's *Dred Scott* decision allowing slavery in all federal territories and John

Brown's raid as "among the gravest of crimes." It also promised "the right of each state to order and control its own domestic institutions." The party reaffirmed its resistance to the extension of slavery and, in an effort to gain broader support, endorsed a higher protective tariff for manufacturers, free homesteads on federal lands, a more liberal naturalization law for immigrants, and internal improvements, including a transcontinental railroad. With this platform, Republicans made a strong appeal to eastern businessmen, western farmers, and the large immigrant population.

Abraham Lincoln

Republican candidate for president, June 1860.

Both major conventions revealed that opinions tended to become more radical in the Upper North and the Deep South. Attitude followed latitude. In the border states a sense of moderation aroused the die-hard Whigs to make one more try at reconciliation. Meeting in Baltimore a week before the Republicans met in Chicago, they reorganized as the Constitutional Union party and nominated John Bell of Tennessee for president. Their only platform was a vague statement promoting "the Constitution of the Country, the Union of the States, and the Enforcement of the Laws."

None of the four candidates generated a national following, and the campaign devolved into a choice between Lincoln and Douglas in the North (Lincoln was not even on the ballot in the South), Breckinridge and Bell in the South. One consequence of the separate campaigns was that each section gained a false impression of the other. The South never learned to distinguish Lincoln from the militant abolitionists; the North, and especially Lincoln, failed to gauge the force of southern intransigence. Lincoln stubbornly refused to offer the South assurances or to clarify his position, which he said was a matter of public record.

The one man who attempted to penetrate the veil that was falling between the North and the South was Douglas, who tried to mount the first nationwide campaign tour. Only forty-seven but weakened by excessive drink, ill health, and disappointments, he wore himself out in one final, glorious campaign. Early in October 1860, at Cedar Rapids, Iowa, he learned of

Republican victories in the Pennsylvania and Indiana state legislatures. "Mr. Lincoln is the next President," he said. "We must try to save the Union. I will go South." Down through the hostile states of Tennessee, Georgia, and Alabama, Douglas carried appeals on behalf of the Union. "I do not believe that every Breckinridge man is a disunionist," he said, "but I do believe that every disunionist is a Breckinridge man." He was in Mobile, Alabama, when the presidential election was held.

By midnight on November 6, Lincoln's victory was clear. In the final count he had 39 percent of the total popular vote but a clear majority, with 180 votes, in the Electoral College. He carried every one of the eighteen free states, and by a margin wide enough to elect him even if the votes for the other candidates had been combined. But hidden in the balloting was an ominous development: for the first time a president had been elected by a clear sectional vote. Among all the candidates, only Douglas had won electoral votes from both slave and free states, but his total of 12 was but a pitiful remnant of Democratic unionism. Bell took Virginia, Kentucky, and Tennessee for 39 votes, and Breckinridge swept the other slave states to come in second with 72.

SECESSION OF THE DEEP SOUTH   Soon after Lincoln's election, South Carolina held a special election to choose delegates to a state convention. In Charleston on December 20, 1860, the convention unanimously endorsed an Ordinance of Secession, declaring the state's ratification of the Constitution repealed and its union with the other states dissolved. A Declaration of the Causes of Secession reviewed the threats to slavery and asserted that a purely sectional (Republican) party had elected to the presidency a man "whose opinions and purposes are hostile to slavery," who had declared "government cannot endure permanently half slave, half free" and that slavery "is in the course of ultimate extinction."

By February 1, 1861, Mississippi, Florida, Alabama, Georgia, Louisiana, and Texas had also seceded. Three days later a convention of the seven states met in Montgomery, Alabama, where they adopted a provisional constitution for the Confederate States of America, and two days later they elected Mississippi's Jefferson Davis as president. He was inaugurated on February 18, with Alexander Stephens of Georgia as vice president.

In all seven Deep South states a solid majority had voted for secessionist delegates, but their combined vote would not have been a majority of the presidential vote in November. What happened, it seemed, was what often happens in revolutionary situations: a determined minority acted quickly in

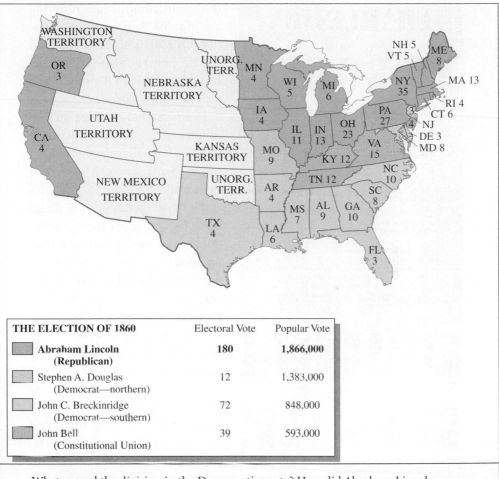

THE ELECTION OF 1860	Electoral Vote	Popular Vote
Abraham Lincoln **(Republican)**	**180**	**1,866,000**
Stephen A. Douglas (Democrat—northern)	12	1,383,000
John C. Breckinridge (Democrat—southern)	72	848,000
John Bell (Constitutional Union)	39	593,000

What caused the division in the Democratic party? How did Abraham Lincoln position himself to win the Republican nomination? What were the major factors that led to Lincoln's electoral victory?

an emotionally charged climate and carried out its program over the weak objections of a confused and indecisive opposition.

BUCHANAN'S WAITING GAME   History is full of might-have-beens. A bold stroke, even a bold statement, by the lame-duck president at this point might have changed the course of events. But James Buchanan lacked boldness. Besides, a bold stroke might simply have hastened the conflict. No bold stroke came from Lincoln either, nor would he consult with the

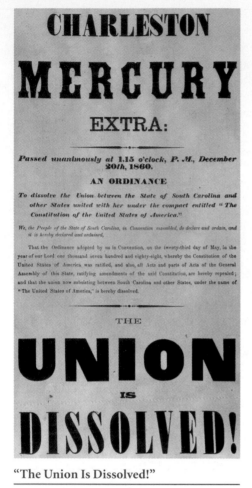

"The Union Is Dissolved!"

A handbill announcing South Carolina's
secession from the Union.

Buchanan administration during the months before his inauguration on March 4. He inclined all too strongly to the belief that secession was just another bluff and kept his public silence.

In his annual message on December 3, President Buchanan criticized northern agitators for trying to interfere with "slavery in the southern states." He then declared that secession was illegal but that he lacked the constitutional authority to coerce a state to rejoin the Union. The president did reaffirm his duty to "take care that the laws be faithfully executed" insofar as he was able. If the president could enforce the law upon all citizens, he would have no need to "coerce" a state. Indeed, his position became the policy of the Lincoln administration, which ended up fighting a civil war on the theory that individuals, but not states, were in rebellion.

The feckless Buchanan held firm to his resolve, with some slight stiffening by the end of December 1860, when secession became a fact, but he refrained from taking provocative actions. As the secessionists seized federal property, arsenals, and forts, this policy soon meant holding federal facilities at Fort Pickens in Pensacola Harbor, some remote islands off southern Florida, and Fort Sumter in Charleston Harbor.

Fort Sumter was commanded by Major Robert Anderson, a Kentucky Unionist, when South Carolina secessionists demanded withdrawal of all federal forces. Buchanan sharply rejected the South Carolina ultimatum. He dispatched a steamer, *Star of the West*, to Fort Sumter with reinforcements and provisions. As the ship approached Charleston Harbor, Confederate batteries opened fire on January 9, 1861, and drove it away. It was in fact an act of war, but Buchanan chose to ignore the challenge. He decided instead to hunker down and ride out the remaining weeks of his term, hoping against hope that one of several compromise efforts would prevail.

FINAL EFFORTS AT COMPROMISE Desperate efforts at a compromise that would avoid a civil war continued in Congress. On December 18, 1860, Senator John J. Crittenden of Kentucky had proposed a series of amendments and resolutions that allowed for slavery in the territories south of 36°30' and guaranteed the maintenance of slavery where it already existed. Meanwhile, a peace conference met at Willard's Hotel in Washington, D.C., in February 1861. Twenty-one states sent delegates, and former president John Tyler presided, but the convention's proposal, substantially the same as the Crittenden Compromise, failed to win the support of either house of Congress. The only proposal that met with any success was a constitutional amendment guaranteeing slavery where it existed. Many Republicans, including Lincoln, were prepared to go that far to save the Union, but they were unwilling to repudiate their stand against slavery in the territories. As it happened, after passing the House, the amendment passed the Senate without a vote to spare, by 24 to 12, on the dawn of inauguration day. It would have become the Thirteenth Amendment, with the first use of the word *slavery* in the Constitution, but the states never ratified it. When a Thirteenth Amendment was ratified, in 1865, it did not guarantee slavery— it abolished it.

CHAPTER SUMMARY

- **Free-Soil Coalition** David Wilmot's declaration that the Mexican territories had been free and therefore should remain so attracted a broad coalition of Americans, including many northern Democrats and anti-slavery Whigs, as well as members of the new Liberty party. Like the Wilmot Proviso, the Free-Soil party demanded that slavery not be expanded to the territories.

- **California Statehood** Californians wanted their territory to enter the Union as a free state. Southerners feared that they would loose federal protection of their "peculiar institution" if more free states than slave states emerged. Whereas Senator John C. Calhoun maintained that slavery could not constitutionally be banned in any of the territories, anti-slavery forces demanded that all the territories remain free.

- **Compromise of 1850** It had been agreed that popular sovereignty would settle the status of the territories, but when the territories applied for statehood, the debate over slavery was renewed. The Compromise of 1850 was the result of the impassioned debate over whether to allow slavery in the territories gained from Mexico, which had banned slavery. By the Compromise of 1850, California entered the Union as a free state, the territories of Texas, New Mexico, and Utah were established without direct reference to slavery, the slave trade (but not slavery itself) was banned in Washington, D.C., and a new, stronger fugitive slave act was passed.

- **Kansas-Nebraska Act** The proposal to overturn the Missouri Compromise by opening to slavery the territories north of 36°30′ outraged the nation's growing anti-slavery faction. The Kansas-Nebraska Act destroyed the Whig party, limited the influence of the Democrats, and led to the creation of the Republican party, which absorbed many Free-Soilers and Know-Nothings.

- **Southern Secession** The Democrats' split into northern and southern factions contributed to the success of Abraham Lincoln and the new Republican party in the election of 1860. The Republicans' victory was the immediate cause of secession. Southerners, reeling from John Brown's raid at Harpers Ferry, equated anti-slavery violence with the Republican party. More important, the Republican victory showed that the South no longer had enough votes in Congress to protect its "peculiar institution."

CHRONOLOGY

1848	Free-Soil party is organized
	California gold rush begins
1853	With the Gadsden Purchase, the United States acquires 30,000 square miles from Mexico
1854	President Pierce's administration disavows the Ostend Manifesto, in which the United States declared its intention to seize Cuba from Spain
	Congress passes the Kansas-Nebraska Act
	The Republican party emerges
1856	A pro-slavery mob sacks Lawrence, Kansas; John Brown stages the Pottawatomie Massacre in retaliation
	Charles Sumner of Massachusetts is caned and seriously injured by a pro-slavery congressman in the U.S. Senate
1857	U.S. Supreme Court issues the *Dred Scott* decision
	Lecompton Constitution declares that slavery will be allowed in Kansas
1858	Abraham Lincoln debates Stephen A. Douglas during the 1858 Illinois Senate race
October 1859	John Brown and his followers stage raid at Harpers Ferry, Virginia, in an attempt to incite a massive slave insurrection
December 1860	South Carolina secedes from the Union
	Crittenden Compromise is proposed

KEY TERMS & NAMES

Wilmot Proviso p. 603

popular sovereignty p. 604

Stephen A. Douglas p. 604

Free-Soil party p. 605

Compromise of 1850 p. 610

secession p. 610

Fugitive Slave Act p. 615

Commodore Matthew Perry p. 619

Kansas-Nebraska Act p. 620

John Brown p. 625

"Bleeding Kansas" p. 628

Dred Scott v. Sandford p. 630

Abraham Lincoln p. 635

Lincoln-Douglas debates p. 636

Freeport Doctrine p. 636

17

THE WAR OF THE UNION

FOCUS QUESTIONS

Ⓢ wwnorton.com/studyspace

- What events led to the firing of the first shots of the Civil War?
- What were the major strategies of the Civil War?
- How did the war affect the home front in both the North and the South?
- What were the reasons for the Emancipation Proclamation?
- How did most enslaved people become free in the United States?

During the four long months between his election in November 1860 and his inauguration in March 1861, Abraham Lincoln said little about future policies and less about past positions. "If I thought a repetition would do any good I would make it," he wrote to an editor in St. Louis. "But my judgment is it would do positive harm. The secessionists per se, believing they had alarmed me, would clamor all the louder." So he stayed in Illinois until mid-February 1861, biding his time. He then boarded a train for a long, roundabout trip to Washington D.C., and began to discuss his shifting outlook along the way. He told the New Jersey legislature that he was "devoted to peace" but warned that "it may be necessary to put the foot down." At the end of the journey, reluctantly yielding to rumors of plots against his life, he passed unnoticed on a night train through Baltimore and slipped into Washington before daybreak on February 23, 1861.

THE END OF THE WAITING GAME

In early 1861, as the possibility of civil war captured the attention of a divided nation, no one imagined that a conflict of horrendous scope and intensity lay ahead. On both sides, people believed that any fighting would be over quickly and that their daily lives would go on as usual.

LINCOLN'S INAUGURATION　In his March 4 inaugural address, Lincoln repeated his pledge not "to interfere with the institution of slavery in the States where it exists." But the immediate question had shifted from slavery to secession, and most of the speech emphasized Lincoln's view that "the Union of these States is perpetual." No state, he insisted, "can lawfully get out of the Union." Lincoln promised to hold federal forts in the South, collect taxes, and deliver the mail unless repelled, but beyond that "there will be no invasion, no using of force against or among the people anywhere." In the final paragraph of the speech, Lincoln offered an eloquent appeal for regional harmony:

> I am loath to close. We are not enemies, but friends. We must not be enemies. Though passion may have strained, it must not break our bonds of affection. The mystic chords of memory, stretching from every battlefield and patriot grave to every living heart and hearthstone all over this broad land, will yet swell the chorus of the Union, when again touched, as surely they will be, by the better angels of our nature.

Lincoln not only entered the White House amid the gravest crisis yet faced by a president, but he also confronted unusual problems of transition. Republicans, in power for the first time, crowded Washington, hungry for government appointments. Four of the seven new cabinet members had been rivals for the presidency: William H. Seward at the State Department, Salmon P. Chase at the Treasury Department, Simon Cameron at the War Department, and Edward Bates as attorney general. Four were former Democrats, and three were former Whigs. They formed a group of better-than-average ability, though most were so strong-minded they thought themselves better qualified to lead than Lincoln. Only later did they acknowledge with Seward that Lincoln "is the best man among us."

THE FALL OF FORT SUMTER　On March 5, 1861, the day after Lincoln took office, word arrived from South Carolina that time was running out at the federal garrison at Fort Sumter in Charleston harbor. Major Robert Anderson, in charge of the federal forces at Fort Sumter, had enough supplies for only a

War begins

An interior view of the ruins of Fort Sumter.

month to six weeks, and Confederates were encircling the fort with a "ring of fire." On April 4, 1861, Lincoln decided to resupply the sixty-nine men at Fort Sumter. On April 9, President Jefferson Davis and his Confederate cabinet in Montgomery, Alabama, decided to oppose any effort to resupply the fort. On April 11 the Confederate general Pierre G. T. Beauregard, a dapper Louisiana creole who had studied the use of artillery under Robert Anderson at West Point, demanded a speedy surrender of Fort Sumter. Anderson refused, and at four-thirty on the morning of April 12 the shelling of Fort Sumter began. After more than thirty hours, his ammunition exhausted, Anderson lowered the flag on April 13 and the following day the Union troops left the fort.

The guns of Charleston signaled the end of the waiting game. On April 15, Lincoln called upon the loyal states to supply 75,000 militiamen to subdue the rebel states. Volunteers rallied around the flag at the recruiting stations. On April 19, Lincoln proclaimed a naval blockade of southern ports, which, as the Supreme Court later ruled, confirmed the existence of war.

TAKING SIDES Lincoln's war proclamation prompted four more southern states to join the Confederacy. Virginia acted first. Its convention passed an Ordinance of Secession on April 17. The Confederate Congress then chose Richmond, Virginia, as its new capital, and the government moved there in June. Three other states followed Virginia in little over a month: Arkansas on May 6, Tennessee on May 7, and North Carolina on May 20. All four of the holdout states, especially Tennessee and Virginia, had areas (mainly in the mountains) where slaves were scarce and Union support ran strong. In east

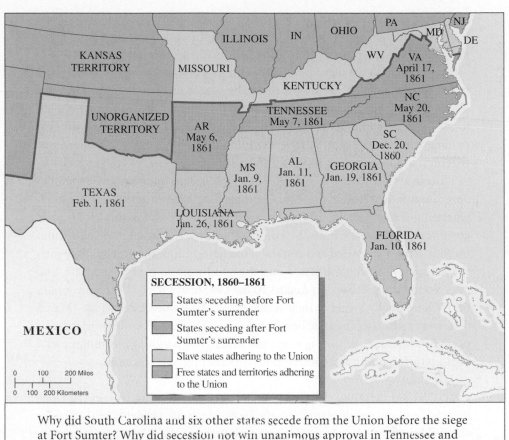

KANSAS TERRITORY

ILLINOIS   IN   OHIO   PA   NJ

MISSOURI   WV   VA April 17, 1861   MD   DE

KENTUCKY

UNORGANIZED TERRITORY

NC May 20, 1861

AR May 6, 1861

TENNESSEE May 7, 1861

SC Dec. 20, 1860

MS Jan. 9, 1861

AL Jan. 11, 1861

GEORGIA Jan. 19, 1861

TEXAS Feb. 1, 1861

LOUISIANA Jan. 26, 1861

FLORIDA Jan. 10, 1861

MEXICO

SECESSION, 1860–1861

States seceding before Fort Sumter's surrender

States seceding after Fort Sumter's surrender

Slave states adhering to the Union

Free states and territories adhering to the Union

0   100   200 Miles
0   100   200 Kilometers

Why did South Carolina and six other states secede from the Union before the siege at Fort Sumter? Why did secession not win unanimous approval in Tennessee and Virginia? How did Lincoln keep Missouri and Kentucky in the Union?

Tennessee the mountain counties would supply more volunteers to the Union than to the Confederate cause. Unionists in western Virginia, bolstered by a Union army from Ohio under General George B. McClellan, contrived a loyal government of Virginia that formed a new state. In 1863, Congress admitted West Virginia to the Union with a constitution that provided for gradual emancipation of the few slaves there.

Of the other slave states, Delaware remained firmly in the Union, but Maryland, Kentucky, and Missouri went through bitter struggles to decide which side to support. The secession of Maryland would have isolated Washington, D.C., within the Confederacy. To hold on to that crucial state, Lincoln took drastic measures of dubious legality: he suspended the writ of habeas corpus (under which judges can require arresting officers to produce their prisoners and justify their arrest) and rounded up pro-Confederate leaders and threw them in jail. The fall elections ended the threat of Maryland's secession by returning a solidly Unionist majority in the state.

Kentucky, native state of both Abraham Lincoln and Jefferson Davis, harbored divided loyalties. Its fragile neutrality lasted until September 3, when a Confederate force occupied several towns. General Ulysses S. Grant then moved Union soldiers into Paducah. Thereafter, Kentucky, though divided in allegiance, for the most part remained with the Union. It joined the Confederacy, some have said, only after the war.

Lincoln's effort to hold a middle course in Missouri ran afoul of the maneuvers of less patient men in the state. Elections for a convention brought an overwhelming Union victory, whereas a pro-Confederate militia under the state governor began to gather near St. Louis. In that city, Unionist forces rallied, and on May 10 they surprised and disarmed the rebel militia at its camp. They pursued the pro-Confederate forces into the southwestern part of the state, and after a temporary setback on August 10 the Unionists pushed the Confederates back again, finally breaking their resistance at the Battle of Pea Ridge (March 6–8, 1862), just over the state line in Arkansas. Thereafter border warfare continued in Missouri, pitting against each other rival bands of gunslingers who kept up their feuding and banditry for years after the war was over.

CHOOSING SIDES   Virginian Robert E. Lee's decision to join the Confederacy epitomized the agonizing choice facing many residents of the border states. The son of Light-Horse Harry Lee, a Revolutionary War hero, and married to a descendant of Martha Washington's, Lee had served in the U.S. Army for thirty years. When Fort Sumter was attacked, he was summoned by General Winfield Scott, another Virginian, and offered command of the Federal forces. After a sleepless night spent pacing the floor, Lee told Scott that he could not go against his "country," meaning Virginia. Although Lee failed to "see the good of secession," he could not "raise my hand against my birthplace, my home, my children." So Lee resigned his U.S. Army commission, retired to his Arlington estate across the Potomoc River from Washington, D.C., and soon answered a call to the Virginia—later the Confederate—service.

On the other hand, many southerners made great sacrifices to remain loyal to the Union. Some left their native region once the fighting began. Others remained in the South but found ways to support the Union. In every Confederate state except South Carolina, whole regiments were organized to fight for the Union. Some 100,000 men from the southern states fought against the Confederacy. One out of every five soldiers from Arkansas killed in the war fought on the Union side.

THE BALANCE OF FORCE

Shrouded in an ever-thickening mist of larger-than-life mythology, the Union triumph in the Civil War has acquired an aura of inevitability. The Confederacy's fight for independence, on the other hand, has taken on the aura of a romantic lost cause, doomed from the start by the region's sparse industrial development, smaller pool of able-bodied men, paucity of gold and warships, and spotty transportation network.

But in 1861 the military situation seemed by no means so clear-cut. For all of the South's obvious disadvantages, it initially enjoyed a captive labor force (slaves) and the benefits of fighting a defensive campaign on familiar territory. Jefferson Davis and other Confederate leaders were confident that their cause would prevail. The outcome of the Civil War was not inevitable: it was determined as much by human decisions and human willpower as by physical resources.

ECONOMIC ADVANTAGES   The South seceded in part out of a growing awareness of its minority status in the nation; a balance sheet of the regions in 1861 shows the accuracy of that perception. The Union held

Union soldiers at Harpers Ferry, Virginia, in 1862

Neither side in the Civil War was prepared for the magnitude of this first "modern" war.

twenty-three states, including four border slave states, while the Confederacy had eleven. The population count was about 22 million in the Union to 9 million in the Confederacy, and about 4 million of the latter were enslaved African Americans. The Union therefore had an edge of about four to one in human resources. To help redress the imbalance, the Confederacy mobilized 80 percent of its military-age white men, a third of whom would die during the prolonged war.

An even greater advantage for the North was its industrial development. The states that joined the Confederacy produced just 7 percent of the nation's manufactures on the eve of the war. The Union states produced 97 percent of the firearms and 96 percent of the railroad equipment. The North's advantage in transportation weighed heavily as the war went on. The Union had more wagons, horses, and ships than the Confederacy and an impressive edge in railroads.

As the Civil War began, the Confederacy enjoyed a major geographic advantage: it could fight a defensive war on its own territory. In addition, the South had more experienced military leaders. Some of those advantages were soon countered, however, by the Union navy's blockade of the major

The U.S. Watervliet Arsenal in Watervliet, New York

The North had an advantage in industrial development, and its foundries turned out most of the nation's firearms.

southern ports. On the inland waters Federal gunboats and transports played an even more direct role in securing the Union's control of the Mississippi River and its larger tributaries, which provided easy invasion routes into the center of the Confederacy.

THE WAR'S EARLY COURSE

After the fall of Fort Sumter, partisans on both sides hoped that the war might end with one sudden bold stroke, the capture of Washington or the fall of Richmond. Nowhere was this naive optimism more clearly displayed than at the First Battle of Bull Run (or Manassas).* An eager public pressured both sides to strike quickly. Jefferson Davis allowed the battle-hungry General Beauregard to hurry the main Confederate army to the railroad center at Manassas Junction, Virginia, about twenty-five miles west of Washington. Lincoln decided that General Irvin McDowell's hastily assembled Union army of some 37,000 might overrun the outnumbered Confederates and quickly march on to Richmond, the Confederate capital.

It was a hot, dry day on July 21, 1861, when McDowell's raw recruits encountered Beauregard's army dug in behind a meandering stream called Bull Run. The two generals, former classmates at West Point, adopted markedly similar plans: each would try to turn the other's left flank. The Federals almost achieved their purpose early in the afternoon, but Confederate reinforcements, led by General Joseph E. Johnston, poured in to check the Union offensive. Amid the fury a South Carolina officer rallied his men by pointing to Thomas Jackson's brigade: "Look! there is Jackson with his Virginians, standing like a stone wall!" The reference thereafter served as Jackson's nickname.

After McDowell's last assault faltered, his army's frantic retreat turned into a panic as fleeing soldiers and terrified civilians clogged the Washington road. An Ohio congressman and several colleagues tried to rally the frenzied soldiers. "We called them cowards, denounced them in the most offensive terms, pulled out our heavy revolvers and threatened to shoot them, but in vain; a cruel, crazy, mad, hopeless panic possessed them." But the Confederates were

---

*The Federals most often named battles for natural features; the Confederates, for nearby towns—thus Bull Run (Manassas), Antietam (Sharpsburg), Stones River (Murfreesboro), and the like.

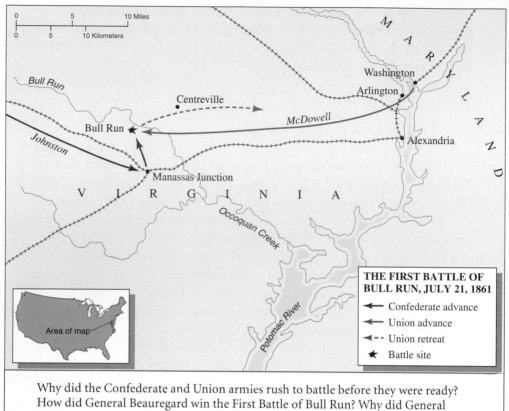

THE FIRST BATTLE OF
BULL RUN, JULY 21, 1861

← Confederate advance
← Union advance
◄-- Union retreat
★ Battle site

Why did the Confederate and Union armies rush to battle before they were ready?
How did General Beauregard win the First Battle of Bull Run? Why did General
Jackson not pursue the Union army?

about as disorganized and exhausted by the battle as the Yankees were, and
they failed to give chase.

The Battle of Bull Run was a sobering experience for both sides. Much of
the romance—the splendid uniforms, bright flags, rousing songs—gave way
to the agonizing realization that this would be a long, costly struggle.
Harper's Weekly bluntly warned: "From the fearful day at Bull Run dates war.
Not polite war, not incredulous war, but war that breaks hearts and blights
homes."

THE WAR'S EARLY PHASE   The Battle of Bull Run demonstrated
that the war would not be decided with one sudden stroke. General Winfield
Scott, the seventy-five-year-old commander of the Union armies, had predicted
as much, and now Lincoln fell back upon Scott's three-pronged "anaconda"

strategy. It called first for the Union Army of the Potomac to defend Washington, D.C., and exert constant pressure on the Confederate capital at Richmond. At the same time the navy would blockade the southern ports and dry up the Confederacy's access to foreign goods and weapons. The final component of the plan would divide the Confederacy by invading the South along the main water routes: the Mississippi, Tennessee, and Cumberland Rivers. This strategy would slowly entwine and crush the southern resistance, like an anaconda strangling its prey.

The Confederate strategy was simpler. If the Union forces could be stalemated, Jefferson Davis and others hoped, then the cotton-hungry British or French might be persuaded to join their cause, or perhaps public sentiment in the North would force Lincoln to seek a negotiated settlement. So at the same time that armies were forming in the South, Confederate diplomats were seeking assistance in London and Paris, and Confederate sympathizers in the North were urging an end to the North's war effort.

NAVAL ACTIONS   The one great threat to the Union navy's blockade of southern ports proved to be short-lived. The Confederates in Norfolk, Virginia, fashioned an ironclad ship from an abandoned Union steam frigate, the *Merrimack*. Rechristened the *Virginia*, it ventured out on March 8, 1862, and began attacking Union ships. But as luck would have it, a new Union ironclad, the *Monitor*, arrived from New York in time to engage the *Virginia* on the next day. They fought to a draw, and the *Virginia* returned to port, where the Confederates destroyed it when they had to give up Norfolk soon afterward.

Thereafter the Union navy tightened its grip on southern ports. In late 1861 a Federal flotilla appeared at Port Royal, south of Charleston, pounded the fortifications into submission, and seized the port and nearby sea islands. The navy extended its bases farther down the Carolina coast in the late summer and fall of 1862. From there its progress extended southward along the Georgia-Florida coast. In the spring of 1862, Admiral David Farragut forced open the lower Mississippi near its mouth and surprised the Confederate defenders of New Orleans.

FORMING ARMIES   Once the fighting began, the Federal Congress recruited 500,000 more men and after the Battle of Bull Run added another 500,000. By the end of 1861, the first half million had enlisted. This rapid mobilization left the army with a large number of "political" officers, commissioned by state governors or elected by the recruits.

The U.S. Army recruiting office in City Hall Park, New York City

The sign advertises the money offered to those willing to serve: $677 to new recruits, $777 to veteran soldiers, and $15 to anyone who brought in a recruit.

The nineteenth-century army often organized its units along community and ethnic lines. The Union army, for example, included a Scandinavian regiment (the 15th Wisconsin Infantry), a Highland Scots unit (the 79th New York Infantry), a French regiment (the 55th New York Infantry), and a mixed unit of Poles, Hungarians, Germans, Spaniards, and Italians (the 39th New York Infantry).

In the Confederacy, Jefferson Davis initially called up 100,000 twelve-month volunteers. Once the fighting started, he was authorized to raise up to 400,000 three-year volunteers "without the delay of a formal call upon the respective states." Thus by early 1862 most of the veteran Confederate soldiers were nearing the end of their enlistment without having encountered much significant action. They were also resisting bonuses and furloughs offered as incentives for reenlistment. The Confederate government thus turned to conscription. By an act passed on April 16, 1862, all white male citizens aged eighteen to thirty-five were declared members of the army for three years, and those already in service were required to serve out three years. In 1862 the upper age was raised to forty-five, and in 1864 the age limit was further extended from seventeen to fifty, with those under eighteen and over forty-five reserved for state defense.

The conscription law included two loopholes, however. First, a draftee might escape service either by providing an able-bodied substitute who was not of draft age or by paying $500 in cash. Second, exemptions, designed to protect key civilian work, were subject to abuse by men seeking "bombproof" jobs. The exemption of one white man for each plantation with twenty or more slaves led to bitter complaints about "a rich man's war and a poor man's fight."

The Union took nearly another year to force men into service. In 1863 the government began to draft men aged twenty to forty-five. Exemptions were granted to specified federal and state officeholders and to others on medical or compassionate grounds. For $300 one could avoid service. Widespread public opposition to the draft impeded its enforcement in both the North and the South. In New York City the an-

New York Sprouts Violence

picked out, shot, and fell dead in the midst of his imprecations and threats. Some four or five hundred rioters were killed by the military. Victims of the mob numbered eight-

ATTENTION!

By Resolution of a large Meeting of the Merchants and Bankers of New York, held at two o'clock, at the Merchants' Exchange. Merchants are requested to close their Stores, and meet with their Employees on South side of Wall St., for immediate organization.
July 14, 2 P. M.

Call for merchants and clerks to defend their shops during the Draft Riots, 1863.

een, eleven of whom were colored men who were strung up to lamp posts and either shot or strangled to death. About fifty buildings were burned and destroyed, and the property

Draft riots

This broadside called upon storeowners to defend their shops during the New York draft riots of 1863.

nouncement of a draft lottery on July 11, 1863, incited a week of rioting. Roving bands of working-class toughs, many of them Irish Catholic immigrants, took control of the streets. Although provoked by feelings that the draft loopholes catered to the wealthy, the riots also exposed racial and ethnic tensions. The mobs directed their wrath most furiously at African Americans. They blamed blacks for causing the war and for threatening to take their own unskilled jobs. The violence ran completely out of control; over 100 people were killed before five regiments of battle-weary soldiers brought from Gettysburg, Pennsylvania, restored order.

CONFEDERATE DIPLOMACY While the Union and the Confederate armies mobilized, Confederate diplomacy focused on gaining foreign supplies, diplomatic recognition, and perhaps even military intervention. The first Confederate emissaries to England and France took hope when the British foreign minister received them after their arrival in London in 1861; they even won a promise from France's Napoléon III to recognize the Confederacy if Britain would lead the way. But the British foreign minister refused to receive the Confederates again, partly in response to Union pressure and partly out of British self-interest.

One incident early in the war threatened to upset British neutrality. In November 1861 a Union warship stopped a British ship, the *Trent*, and took into custody two Confederate agents, James M. Mason and John Slidell. Celebrated as a heroic deed by a northern public still starved for victories, the *Trent* affair roused a storm of protest in Britain. The British government sent Lincoln an ultimatum for the captives' release. To interfere with a neutral ship on the high seas violated a long-settled American principle, and federal officials reluctantly decided to release the two agents. Mason and Slidell were more useful as martyrs to their own cause than they could ever be in London and Paris.

Confederate agents in Europe were far more successful in getting supplies than in gaining official recognition of the Confederacy as a sovereign nation. The most spectacular feat was the purchase of raiding ships designed to attack Union vessels around the world. Although British law forbade the sale of warships to belligerents, a Confederate commissioner contrived to have ships built and then, on trial runs, escape to the Azores or elsewhere to be outfitted with guns. In all, eighteen such ships were activated and saw action in the Atlantic, Pacific, and Indian Oceans, where they sank hundreds of Yankee ships and terrified the rest.

THE WEST AND THE CIVIL WAR   During the Civil War western settlement continued unabated. New discoveries of gold and silver in eastern California and in Montana and Colorado lured thousands of prospectors and their suppliers. New transportation and communication networks emerged to serve the growing population in the West. Telegraph lines sprouted above the plains, and stagecoach lines fanned out to serve the new communities. Dakota, Colorado, and Nevada gained territorial status in 1861, Idaho and Arizona in 1863, and Montana in 1864. Silver-rich Nevada gained statehood in 1864.

With the firing on Fort Sumter, many of the regular army units assigned to frontier outposts in the West began to head east to meet the Confederate threat. Texas was the only western state to join the Confederacy. For the most part, the federal government maintained its control of the western territories during the war. But it was not easy. Fighting in Kansas and the Indian Territory was widespread. By 1862, Lincoln had been forced to dispatch new units to the West. He had two primary concerns: to protect the shipments of gold and silver and to win over western political support for the war and his presidency.

The most intense fighting in the West occurred along the Kansas-Missouri border. There the disputes between the pro-slavery and anti-slavery settlers of the 1850s turned into brutal guerrilla warfare. The most prominent pro-Confederate leader in the area was William Quantrill. He and his pro-slavery followers, mostly teenagers, fought under a black flag, meaning that they gave no quarter. In destroying Lawrence, Kansas, in 1863, Quantrill ordered his forces to "kill every male and burn every house." By the end of the day, 182 boys and men had been killed. Their opponents, the Jayhawkers, responded in kind. They tortured and hanged pro-Confederate prisoners, burned houses, and destroyed livestock.

Many Indian tribes found themselves caught up in the war. Indian regiments fought on both sides, and in Oklahoma they fought against each other. Indians among the "Five Civilized Tribes" held African American slaves and felt a natural bond with southern whites. Oklahoma's proximity to Texas influenced the Choctaws and Chickasaws to support the Confederacy. The Cherokees, Creeks, and Seminoles were more divided in their loyalties. For those tribes the Civil War served as a wedge that fractured their unity. The Cherokees, for example, split in two, some supporting the Union and others supporting the South.

ACTIONS IN THE WESTERN THEATER   Little happened of military significance in the eastern theater (east of the Appalachians) before May 1862. On the other hand, the western theater (from the Appalachians to the Mississippi River) flared up with several encounters and an important penetration of the Confederate states. In western Kentucky, the Confederate general Albert Sidney Johnston had perhaps 40,000 men stretched over some 150 miles. Early in 1862, General Ulysses S. Grant made the first Union thrust against the weak center of Johnston's overextended lines. Moving out of Cairo, Illinois, and Paducah, Kentucky, with a gunboat flotilla, he swung southward up the Tennessee River and captured Fort Henry in northern Tennessee on February 6. Grant then moved quickly overland to attack nearby Fort Donelson. On February 16 a force of 12,000 Confederates surrendered.

SHILOH   After suffering defeats in Kentucky and Tennessee, the Confederate forces regrouped at Corinth, in northern Mississippi, near the Tennessee border. Ulysses Grant, meanwhile, moved his Union army southward along the Tennessee River during the early spring of 1862. Grant then made a costly

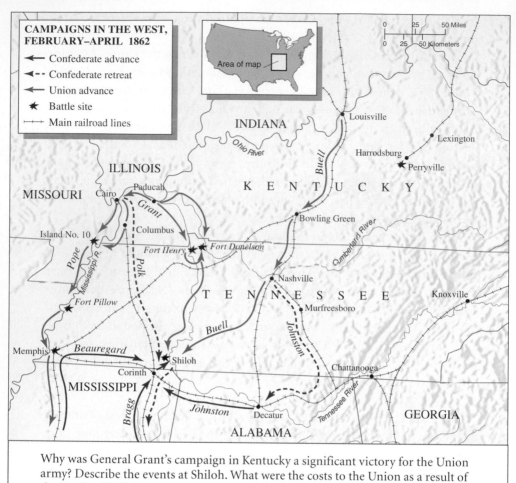

CAMPAIGNS IN THE WEST,
FEBRUARY–APRIL 1862

← Confederate advance
◄-- Confederate retreat
← Union advance
★ Battle site
+--+ Main railroad lines

Why was General Grant's campaign in Kentucky a significant victory for the Union army? Describe the events at Shiloh. What were the costs to the Union as a result of the Battle of Shiloh?

mistake. While planning his attack on Corinth, he exposed his 42,000 troops on a rolling plateau between two creeks flowing into the Tennessee River and failed to dig defensive trenches. General Albert Johnston shrewdly recognized Grant's oversight, and on the morning of April 6 the Kentuckian ordered an attack on the vulnerable Federals, urging his men to be "worthy of your race and lineage; worthy of the women of the South."

The 44,000 Confederates struck suddenly at Shiloh, the site of a log church in the center of the Union camp in southwestern Tennessee. They found most of Grant's troops still sleeping or eating breakfast; many died in their bedrolls. After a day of carnage and confusion, the Union soldiers were pinned against the river. The Union army might well have been defeated had General Johnston not been mortally wounded at the peak of the battle; his second in command called off the attack. Bolstered by reinforcements, Grant took the offensive the next day, and the Confederates glumly withdrew to Corinth, leaving the Union army too battered to pursue. Casualties on both sides totaled over 20,000.

Shiloh, a Hebrew word meaning "Place of Peace," was the costliest battle in which Americans had ever engaged, although worse was yet to come. Grant observed that the ground was "so covered with dead one could walk across the field without touching the ground." Like so many battles thereafter, Shiloh was a story of missed opportunities and debated turning points punctuated by lucky incidents and accidents. Throughout the Civil War, winning armies would fail to pursue their retreating foes, thus allowing the wounded opponent to slip away and fight again.

After the battle at Shiloh, General Henry Halleck, already jealous of Grant's success, spread the false rumor that Grant had been drinking during the battle. Some called upon Lincoln to fire Grant, but the president refused: "I can't spare this man; he fights." Halleck, however, took Grant's place as field commander, and as a result the Union thrust southward ground to a halt. For the remainder of 1862, the chief action in the western theater was a series of inconclusive maneuvers punctuated by sharp engagements.

MCCLELLAN'S PENINSULAR CAMPAIGN   The eastern theater remained fairly quiet for nine months after Bull Run. In the wake of the Union defeat, Lincoln had replaced McDowell with General George B. McClellan, Stonewall Jackson's classmate at West Point. As head of the Army of the Potomac, McClellan set about building a powerful, well-trained army that would be ready for its next battle. When General Winfield Scott retired in November, Lincoln appointed McClellan general in chief. McClellan exuded confidence and poise. Yet for all his organizational ability and dramatic flair, his innate caution would prove crippling. Time passed, and McClellan kept building and training his army to meet the superior numbers he claimed the Confederates were deploying. Lincoln wanted the army to move directly toward Richmond, but McClellan, who dismissed the president as a "well-meaning baboon," sought to enter Richmond by the side door, so to speak, up the neck of land between the York and James Rivers, site of Jamestown, Williamsburg, and Yorktown.

In mid-March 1862, McClellan's army finally moved down the Potomac River and the Chesapeake Bay to the Virginia peninsula southeast of

Camp Winfield Scott

General George McClellan's headquarters during the siege of Yorktown, 1862.

Richmond. This bold move put the Union forces within sixty miles of the Confederate capital. Thousands of Richmond residents fled the city in panic, but McClellan waited to strike, failing to capitalize on his advantages.

President Jefferson Davis, at the urging of his adviser Robert E. Lee, sent Stonewall Jackson's army into the Shenandoah Valley in western Virginia on what proved to be a brilliant diversionary action. From March 23 to June 9, Jackson's 18,000 men pinned down two separate Union armies with more than twice their numbers in the western Virginia mountains. While the Union army under General McDowell braced to defend Washington, D.C., Jackson hastened back to defend Richmond against McClellan.

On May 31 the Confederate general Joseph E. Johnston struck at McClellan's forces along the Chickahominy River. In the Battle of Seven Pines (Fair Oaks), only the arrival of federal reinforcements, who somehow crossed the swollen river, prevented a disastrous Union defeat. Both sides took heavy casualties, and General Johnston was severely wounded.

At this point, Robert E. Lee assumed command of the Army of Northern Virginia, a development that changed the course of the war. Tall, erect, and broad shouldered, Lee projected a commanding presence. At the start of the

Civil War, the West Point graduate was considered the most promising army officer in the United States. Dignified yet fiery, Lee was an audacious commander. He led by example, and his men loved him. Unlike Joseph Johnston, Lee enjoyed Jefferson Davis's trust. More important, he knew how to use the talents of his superb field commanders: Stonewall Jackson, the pious, fearless mathematics professor from the Virginia Military Institute; James Longstreet, Lee's deliberate but tireless "warhorse"; sharp-tongued D. H. Hill, the former engineering professor at Davidson College; Ambrose P. Hill, the consummate fighter who challenged one commander to a duel and feuded with Stonewall Jackson; and J. E. B. Stuart, the colorful young cavalryman who once said, "All I ask of fate is that I may be killed leading a cavalry charge." He would get his wish.

Once in command, Lee attacked the Union lines east of Richmond but failed to dislodge the Union forces. McClellan's army was still near Richmond. On July 9, when Lincoln visited McClellan's headquarters, the general complained that the administration had failed to support him adequately and instructed the president at length on military strategy. Such insubordination was ample reason to remove McClellan. Lincoln returned to Washington and on July 11 called Henry Halleck from the West to take charge as general in chief. Miffed at his demotion, McClellan angrily dismissed Halleck as an officer "whom I know to be my inferior."

SECOND BULL RUN   Lincoln and Halleck ordered McClellan to leave the Virginia peninsula and join the Washington defense force, now under the command of the bombastic John Pope, who had been called back from the West for a new overland assault on Richmond. In a letter to his wife, McClellan predicted that "Pope will be thrashed and disposed of" by Lee. As McClellan's Army of the Potomac began to pull out of the Tidewater, Lee moved northward to strike Pope before McClellan's troops arrived. Dividing his forces, Lee sent Jackson's "foot cavalry" around Pope's right flank to attack his supply lines. At the Second Battle of Bull Run (or Manassas), fought on almost the same site as the earlier battle, Pope assumed that he faced only Jackson, but Lee's main army by that time had joined in. On August 30 a crushing attack on Pope's flank drove the Federals from the field. In the next few days the Union forces pulled back to Washington, where McClellan once again took command and reorganized. He displayed his unflagging egotism in a letter to his wife: "Again I have been called upon to save the country." The disgraced Pope was dispatched to Minnesota to fight Indians.

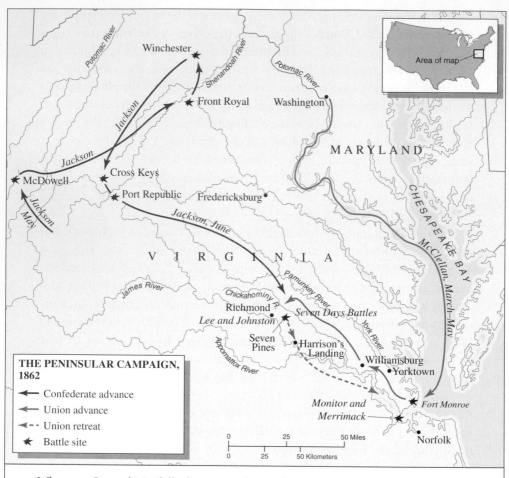

THE PENINSULAR CAMPAIGN, 1862

◄— Confederate advance
◄— Union advance
◄- - Union retreat
✴ Battle site

What was General McClellan's strategy for attacking Richmond? How did General Jackson divert the attention of the Union army? Why did President Lincoln demote McClellan after the Peninsular campaign?

ANTIETAM A victorious Lee then made a momentous decision: he would invade the North and perhaps thereby gain foreign recognition and military supplies for the Confederacy. He and his battle-tested troops pushed into western Maryland in September 1862, headed for Pennsylvania. But Lee's bold strategy was uncovered when a Union soldier picked up a bundle of cigars and discovered a secret order from Lee wrapped around them. The paper revealed that Lee had again divided his army, sending Stonewall Jackson off to take Harpers Ferry, Virginia. McClellan boasted upon seeing the captured document, "Here is a paper with which, if I cannot whip Bobby

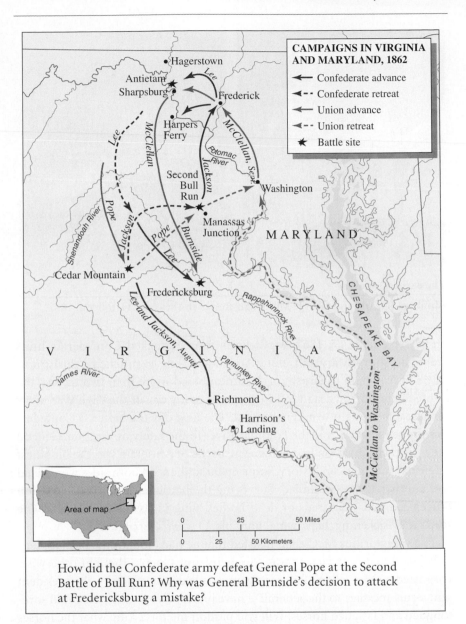

CAMPAIGNS IN VIRGINIA AND MARYLAND, 1862

◄── Confederate advance
◄-- Confederate retreat
◄── Union advance
◄-- Union retreat
★ Battle site

How did the Confederate army defeat General Pope at the Second Battle of Bull Run? Why was General Burnside's decision to attack at Fredericksburg a mistake?

Lee, I will be willing to go home." Instead of seizing his unexpected opportunity, however, he delayed for sixteen crucial hours, still worried—as always—about enemy strength. Lee was thereby able to reassemble most of his tired army behind Antietam Creek. Still, McClellan was optimistic, and Lincoln, too, relished the chance for a truly decisive blow. "God bless you and all with you," he wired McClellan. "Destroy the rebel army if possible."

The early campaigns

Abraham Lincoln and George McClellan confer at Antietam, October 4, 1862.

On September 17, 1862, McClellan's forces attacked Confederate units near Sharpsburg, Maryland, along Antietam Creek, commencing the furious Battle of Antietam (Sharpsburg). Outnumbered more than two to one, the Confederates forced a standoff in the most costly day of the Civil War, a day participants thought would never end. The next day the battered Confederates slipped south across the Potomac River to the safety of Virginia. General Lee's northern invasion had failed. The Battle of Antietam was the bloodiest single day in American history. Some 6,400 soldiers on both sides were killed and another 15,000 wounded. Surveying the battlefield afterward, a Union officer counted "hundreds of dead bodies lying in rows and in piles." The scene was "sickening, harrowing, horrible. O what a terrible sight!"

The vainglorious McClellan insisted that he had "fought the battle splendidly" and that "our victory was complete," but Lincoln thought otherwise. Disgusted by McClellan's failure to gain a truly decisive victory, the president sent a curt message to the general: "I have just read your dispatch about sore-tongued and fatigued horses. Will you pardon me for asking what the horses of your army have done . . . that fatigues anything?" Failing to receive a satisfactory answer, Lincoln assigned McClellan to recruiting duty in New Jersey. Never again would he command troops.

FREDERICKSBURG   The Battle of Antietam was the turning point in the war. It revived sagging Northern morale, emboldened Abraham Lincoln to issue the Emancipation Proclamation, freeing all slaves in the Confederate states, and dashed the Confederacy's hopes of foreign recognition. Yet the war was far from over. In his search for a fighting general, Lincoln now made the worst choice of all. He turned to Ambrose E. Burnside, who had twice before turned down the job on the grounds that he felt unfit for so large a command. But if the White House wanted him to fight, he would attack, even in the face of the oncoming winter.

On December 13, 1862, Burnside sent the Army of the Potomac across the icy Rappahannock River to assault Lee's forces, who were well entrenched on ridges and behind stone walls west of Fredericksburg, Virginia, between Richmond and Washington. Confederate artillery and muskets chewed up the blue columns as they crossed a mile of open land outside the town. It was, a Federal general sighed, "a great slaughter-pen." The scene was both awful and awesome, prompting Lee to remark, "It is well that war is so terrible—we should grow too fond of it." After taking more than 12,000 casualties, compared with fewer than 6,000 for the Confederates, Burnside wept as he gave the order to withdraw.

The year 1862 ended with forces in the East deadlocked and the Union advance in the West stalled since midyear. Union morale plummeted: northern Democrats were calling for a negotiated peace. At the same time, Lincoln was under pressure from the so-called Radical Republicans, who were pushing for more stringent war measures and questioning the president's competence. General Burnside, too, was under fire, with some of his own officers ready to testify publicly to his shortcomings.

But amid the dissension the deeper currents of the war were turning in favor of the Union: in the lengthening war its superior resources began to tell. In both the eastern and the western theaters the Confederate counterattack had been repulsed. And while the armies clashed, Lincoln, by the stroke of a pen, changed the conflict from a war to restore the Union to a revolutionary struggle for the abolition of slavery. On January 1, 1863, he signed the Emancipation Proclamation.

EMANCIPATION

At the war's outset, Lincoln had promised to restore the Union but maintain slavery where it existed. Congress, too, endorsed that position. Once fighting began, the need to hold the border states in the Union dictated caution on the volatile issue of emancipation. Beyond that, several other considerations deterred action. For one, Lincoln had to cope with a deep-seated racial prejudice in the North. Whereas most abolitionists promoted both complete emancipation and the social integration of the races, many anti-slavery activists wanted slavery prohibited only in the new western territories and states. They were willing to allow slavery to continue in the South and were uneasy about racial integration. Lincoln himself harbored doubts about his authority to emancipate slaves so long as he clung to the view that the rebellious states remained legally in the Union. The only way around the problem would be to justify emancipation as a military necessity.

A MEASURE OF WAR   The expanding war forced the issue. As Federal forces pushed into the Confederacy, fugitive slaves began to turn up in Union army camps, and generals did not know whether to declare them free. Some put the "contrabands" to work building fortifications; others set them free. Lincoln, meanwhile, began to edge toward emancipation. In March 1862 he proposed that federal compensation be offered any state that began gradual emancipation. The plan failed in Congress because of border-state opposition, but on April 16, 1862, Lincoln signed an act that abolished slavery in the District of Columbia; on June 19 another act excluded slavery from the territories, without offering owners compensation. A Second Confiscation Act, passed on July 17, liberated the slaves held by anyone aiding the rebellion. Still another act forbade the army to help return runaways to their border-state owners.

To save the Union, Lincoln finally decided, emancipation of Confederate slaves would be required for several reasons: slave labor bolstered the Rebel war effort, sagging morale in the North needed the boost of a moral cause,

Contrabands

Former slaves on a farm in Cumberland Landing, Virginia, 1862.

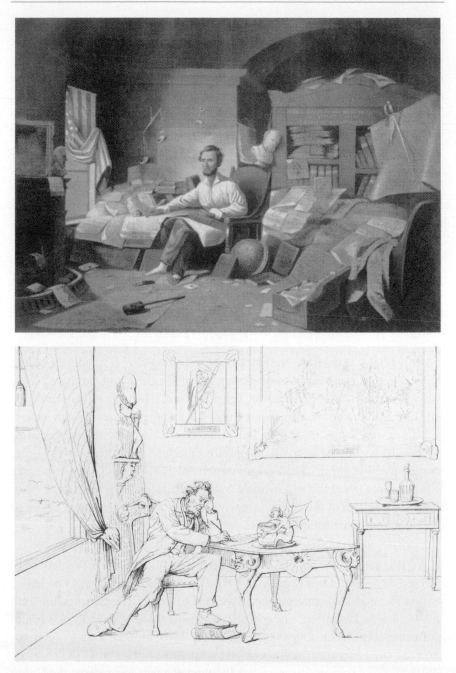

Two views of the Emancipation Proclamation

The Union view (top) shows a thoughtful Lincoln composing the proclamation, the Constitution and the Holy Bible in his lap. The Confederate view (bottom) shows a demented Lincoln, his foot on the Constitution and his inkwell held by the devil.

and public opinion was swinging toward emancipation as the war dragged on. Proclaiming a war on slavery, moreover, would end forever any chance that France or Britain would support the Confederacy. In July 1862, Lincoln first confided to his cabinet that he was considering issuing a proclamation that under his war powers would free the slaves of the enemy. At the time, Secretary of State William Seward advised him to wait for a Union victory in order to avoid any semblance of desperation.

The time to act came at last after the Battle of Antietam. On September 22, 1862, five days after Lee's Confederates had been forced to retreat from Maryland, Lincoln issued a proclamation in which he repeated that his object was mainly to restore the Union and that he favored proposals for paying slaveholders for their losses. But the main burden of the document was his warning that on January 1, 1863, all slaves in the Rebel states would be "forever free." On January 1, 1863, Lincoln urged blacks to abstain from violence except in self-defense, and he added that free blacks would now be received into the armed services of the United States. As he wrote his name on the Emancipation Proclamation, Lincoln said, "I never, in my life, felt more certain that I was doing the right thing than I do in signing this paper."

REACTIONS TO EMANCIPATION   Among the Confederate states, Tennessee and the Union-controlled parts of Virginia and Louisiana were exempted from the Emancipation Proclamation. Thus no slaves who were within Union lines at the time were freed. But many enslaved African Americans in those areas claimed their freedom anyway. "In a document proclaiming liberty," wrote the historian Benjamin Quarles, "the unfree never bother to read the fine print." The African American abolitionist leader Frederick Douglass was overjoyed at Lincoln's "righteous decree." By contrast, Democratic newspapers in the North savagely attacked the proclamation, calling it dictatorial, unconstitutional, and catastrophic.

BLACKS IN THE MILITARY   Lincoln's Emancipation Proclamation sparked new efforts to organize all-black Union military units, to be led by white officers. Massachusetts organized one of the first such units, the 54th Massachusetts Regiment, under Colonel Robert Gould Shaw. Rhode Island and other states soon followed suit. In May 1863 the War Department authorized the general recruitment of African Americans across the country. This was a momentous decision, for it changed a war to preserve the Union into a revolution to transform the social, economic, and racial status quo in the South.

By mid-1863, African American units were involved in significant action. On July 18, 1863, Colonel Shaw, a Harvard graduate and the son of a prominent abolitionist, led his troops in a courageous assault against Fort Wagner, a massive earthwork barrier guarding Charleston, South Carolina. During the battle almost half the members of the 54th Regiment were killed, including Colonel Shaw. The courageous performance of the 54th Regiment did much to win acceptance for both black soldiers and emancipation. Commenting on Union victories at Port Hudson and Milliken's Bend, Louisiana, Lincoln reported that "some of our commanders . . . believe that . . . the use of colored troops constitutes the heaviest blow yet dealt to the rebels."

By the end of the war, almost 180,000 African Americans had served in the U.S. Colored Troops, providing around 10 percent of the Union army total. Some 80 percent of the "colored troops" were former slaves or free blacks from the South. Some 38,000 gave their lives. In the navy, African Americans accounted for about a fourth of all enlistments; of these more than 2,800 died.

As the war entered its final months, freedom emerged more fully as a legal reality. Three major steps occurred in January 1865, when both Missouri

The 107th U.S. Colored Infantry

From early in the war, Union commanders found "contrabands" useful as informants and guides to unfamiliar terrain.

"Drummer" Jackson

This photograph of a former slave who served in the 79th U.S. Colored Troops was used to encourage African Americans to enlist.

and Tennessee abolished slavery by state action and the U.S. House of Representatives passed an abolition amendment. Upon ratification by three fourths of the reunited states, the Thirteenth Amendment became part of the Constitution on December 18, 1865, and removed any lingering doubts about the legality of emancipation. By then, in fact, slavery remained only in the border states of Kentucky and Delaware.

THE WAR BEHIND THE LINES

The scale and scope of the Civil War affected everyone—not simply the combatants. Feeding, clothing, and supplying the vast armies required tremendous sacrifices on the home fronts. The fighting knew no boundaries, as farms and villages were transformed into battlefields and churches became makeshift hospitals. Gender roles were transformed, as women assumed new duties managing households and farms, raising funds, and volunteering as nurses by the thousands. At the same time, federal and state governments assumed expansive new powers in an effort to support a war effort that turned out to be much longer and more expensive than anyone anticipated.

WOMEN AND THE WAR   While breaking the bonds of slavery, the Civil War also loosened traditional restraints on female activity. "No conflict in history," a journalist wrote at the time, "was such a woman's war as the Civil War." Women on both sides played prominent roles in the conflict. They sewed uniforms, composed patriotic poems and songs, and raised money and supplies. Thousands of northern women worked with the U.S. Sanitary Commission, which organized medical relief and other services for soldiers. Others, black and white, supported the freedmen's aid movement to help impoverished freed slaves.

In the North alone, some 20,000 women served as nurses or other health-related volunteers. The most famous nurses were Dorothea Dix and Clara Barton, both untiring volunteers in service to the wounded and the dying. Dix, the earnest reformer of the nation's insane asylums, became the Union army's first superintendent of women nurses. She soon found herself flooded with applications from around the country. Dix explained that nurses should be "sober, earnest, self-sacrificing, and self-sustained" women between the ages of thirty-five and fifty who could "bear the presence of suffering and exercise entire self control" and who could be "calm, gentle, quiet, active, and steadfast in duty."

The departure of hundreds of thousands of men for the battlefield forced women to assume the public and private roles the men left behind. In many southern towns and counties the home front became a world of white women and children and African American slaves. A resident of Lexington, Virginia, reported in 1862 that there were "no men left" in town by mid-1862. Women suddenly found themselves farmers or plantation managers, clerks, munitions-plant workers, and schoolteachers. Some 400 women disguised themselves as men and fought in the war; dozens served as spies; others traveled with the armies, cooking meals, writing letters, and assisting with amputations.

The war's unrelenting carnage took a terrible toll on the nation's women. A North Carolina mother lost seven sons in the fighting; another lost four. Women who bore such losses or who witnessed daily suffering while serving as nurses were transformed by the experience. The number of widows,

Nursing and the war

Clara Barton oversaw the distribution of medicines to Union troops. She later helped found the American Red Cross of which she remained president until the age of 83.

spinsters, and orphans mushroomed. Many bereaved women on both sides came to look upon the war with what the poet Emily Dickinson called a "chastened stare."

RELIGION AND THE CIVIL WAR Wars intensify religious convictions (and vice versa), and this was certainly true of the Civil War. Religious concerns pervaded the conflict. Both sides believed they were fighting a holy war with God's divine favor. The Confederate constitution, unlike the U.S. Constitution, explicitly invoked the guidance of Almighty God. Southern leaders thus asserted that the Confederacy was the only truly Christian nation. Clergymen in the North and the South—Protestant, Catholic, and Jewish—saw the war as a righteous crusade. They were among the most partisan advocates of the war, in part because they were so certain that God was on their side and would ensure victory.

During the war both President Lincoln and President Davis proclaimed numerous official days of fasting and prayer in the aftermath of important battles. Such national rituals were a means of mourning the "martyrs" who had given their lives for the righteous cause. Salmon P. Chase, the U.S. secretary of the Treasury, added the motto "In God We Trust" to American coins as a means of expressing the nation's religious zeal. Many soldiers were armed with piety as well as muskets. William Pendleton, the chief artillery officer under Robert E. Lee, named his favorite four cannons after the four Gospels of the Christian scriptures: Matthew, Mark, Luke, and John. His orders revealed his faith: "While we will kill their bodies, may the Lord have mercy on their sinful souls—FIRE!"

Every regiment on both sides had an ordained chaplain, and devotional services in military camps were regularly held and widely attended. More than 1,300 clergymen served in the military camps, with the Methodists providing the largest number. By late 1862, Christian religious revivals were sweeping through both northern and southern armies. To facilitate such battlefield conversions, religious organizations distributed millions of Bibles and religious tracts to soldiers and sailors. During the winter of 1863–1864, the widespread conversions among the Union army camped in northern Virginia led one reporter to claim that the soldiers' martial piety might "win the whole nation to Christ." The revivals in the Confederate camps were even larger. Mary Jones, the wife of a Confederate minister in Georgia whose son was a soldier, reported the good news that "revivals in our army are certainly the highest proofs we can possible desire or receive of the divine favor" shrouding the Confederacy. Abraham Lincoln took keen interest in the religious fervor among Confederate soldiers. He expressed concern that

Religion in the army

The 69th New York State Militia having a religious service in 1861.

"rebel soldiers are praying with a great deal more earnestness" than Union soldiers.

With so many ministers away at the front, lay people, especially women, assumed even greater responsibility for religious activities in churches and synagogues. The war also transformed the religious life of African Americans, who saw the war as a recapitulation of the biblical Exodus: God's miraculous intervention in history on behalf of a chosen people. In those areas of the South taken over by Union armies, freed slaves were able to create their own churches for the first time.

Of course, as the war continued, it became evident that God would not bring victory to both sides. In the South, many Christians were deeply perplexed by the shifting tide of battle. What had happened to God's righteous providence? Seventeen-year-old Emma LeConte of South Carolina anguished in her diary over God's seeming desertion of the Confederacy: "They say *right* always triumphs, but what cause could have been more just than ours?" Religious leaders explained military defeats as God's way of chastening and purifying southerners. The editors of a southern Presbyterian newspaper insisted that God "chastens" only "those he loves."

In the end the war revealed how much religion mattered in American life. It also showed how problematic it is to claim that God is on any particular side. Abraham Lincoln was never sure whose side God was on when he reflected on the transcendent meaning of the horrible war. Yes, he observed, both sides claimed providential sanction. In this regard, he said, "Both *may* be, and one *must* be wrong. God can not be *for* and *against* the same thing at the same time." After all, Lincoln noted, God could give victory to either side at any moment. "Yet the contest proceeds." Thus Lincoln was one of the few Americans to suggest that God's divine purpose might be something different from simple victory or defeat.

GOVERNMENT DURING THE WAR

Freeing 4 million slaves and loosening the restraints on female activity constituted a momentous social and economic revolution. But an even broader revolution began as power in Congress shifted from South to North during the Civil War. Before the war, southern congressmen exercised disproportionate influence, but once the secessionists had abandoned Congress to the Republicans, a dramatic change occurred. Several projects that had been stalled by sectional controversy were adopted before the end of 1862. Congress passed a higher tariff bill to deter imports and thereby "protect" American manufacturers. A transcontinental railroad was approved, to run through Omaha, Nebraska, to Sacramento, California. A Homestead Act granted 160 acres to settlers who agreed to work the land for five years. The National Banking Act followed in 1863. Two other key pieces of legislation were the Morrill Land Grant Act (1862), which provided federal aid to state colleges teaching "agriculture and mechanic arts," and the Contract Labor Act (1864), which encouraged the importation of immigrant labor. All of these had long-term significance for the expansion of the national economy—and the federal government.

UNION FINANCES   Congress focused on three options to finance the war: raising taxes, printing paper money, and borrowing. The taxes came chiefly in the form of the Morrill Tariff on imports and taxes on manufactures and nearly every profession. A butcher, for example, had to pay 30¢ for every head of beef he slaughtered, 10¢ for every hog, 5¢ for every sheep.

In 1862, Congress passed the Internal Revenue Act, which created an Internal Revenue Service to implement a new income tax.

But federal tax revenues trickled in so slowly—in the end they would meet only 21 percent of wartime expenditures—that Congress in 1862 resorted to printing paper money. Beginning with the Legal Tender Act of 1862, Congress ultimately authorized $450 million in paper currency, which soon became known as greenbacks because of the bills' color. The congressional decision to allow the Treasury to print paper money was a profoundly important development for the U.S. economy, then and since. Unlike previous paper currencies issued by local banks, the federal greenbacks could not be exchanged for gold or silver. Instead, their value relied upon public trust in the government. Many bankers were outraged by the advent of the greenbacks. "Gold and silver are the only true measure of value," one financier declared. "These metals were prepared by the Almighty." But the crisis of the Union and the desperate need to finance the expanding war demanded such a solution. As the months passed, the greenbacks helped ease the Union's financial crisis without causing the ruinous inflation that the unlimited issue of paper money caused in the Confederacy.

The federal government also relied upon the sale of bonds to help finance the war effort. A Philadelphia banker named Jay Cooke (sometimes tagged the Financier of the Civil War) mobilized a nationwide campaign to sell government bonds to private investors. Eventually bonds generated $2 billion in federal revenue.

Union bank note

Bank notes were promissory notes. Generally, the better the art on the note, the more it was trusted.

For many businessmen, war-related ventures brought quick riches. Some suppliers and financiers bilked the government or provided shoddy goods. Not all the wartime fortunes were made dishonestly, however. And the war-related expenditures by the Union helped promote the capital accumulation with which businesses fueled later expansion. Wartime business thus laid the groundwork for the postwar economic boom and for the fortunes of tycoons such as J. Pierpont Morgan, John D. Rockefeller, Andrew W. Mellon, and Andrew Carnegie.

CONFEDERATE FINANCES   Confederate finances were a disaster from the start. In the first year of its existence, the Confederacy enacted a tax of one half of 1 percent on most forms of property, which should have yielded a hefty income, but the Confederacy farmed out its collection of the taxes to the states. The result was chaos. In 1863 the desperate Confederate Congress began taxing nearly everything, but enforcement of the taxes was poor and evasion easy. Altogether, taxes covered no more than 5 percent of Confederate costs; bond issues accounted for less than 33 percent; and treasury notes (paper money), for more than 66 percent. Altogether the Confederacy turned out more than $1 billion in paper money and sparked a steep inflation. By 1864 a turkey sold in the Richmond market for $100, flour brought $425 a barrel, and bacon was $10 a pound.

UNION POLITICS AND CIVIL LIBERTIES   On the home front, the crisis of war brought no moratorium on partisan politics, northern or southern. Within his own party, Lincoln faced a Radical wing in Congress composed mainly of prewar abolitionists. Led by House members such as Thaddeus Stevens and George Washington Julian and senators such as Charles Sumner, Benjamin Franklin Wade, and Zachariah Chandler, the Radical Republicans pushed for confiscation of plantations, immediate emancipation of slaves, and a more vigorous prosecution of the war. The majority of Republicans, however, continued to back Lincoln's more cautious approach. The party was generally united on economic policy.

The Democratic party suffered the loss of its southern wing and the death of its leader, Stephen A. Douglas, in June 1861. By and large, northern Democrats supported a war for the Union "as it was" before 1860, giving reluctant support to Lincoln's policies but opposing restraints on civil liberties and the new economic legislation. "War Democrats," such as Tennessee senator Andrew Johnson and Secretary of War Edwin M. Stanton fully supported Lincoln's policies, while a peace wing of the party preferred an end to the fighting, even if that meant risking the Union. An extreme fringe of the peace wing even flirted with outright disloyalty. The Copperheads, as they were called, were strongest in states such as Ohio, Indiana, and Illinois, all leavened with native southerners, some of whom were pro-Confederate.

Such open sympathy for the enemy led Lincoln to crack down hard. Early in the war he assumed emergency powers, including the power to suspend the writ of habeas corpus, which guarantees arrested citizens a speedy hearing. The Constitution states that habeas corpus may be suspended only in cases of rebellion or invasion, but congressional leaders argued that Congress alone had the authority to take such action. By the Habeas Corpus Act of 1863, Congress authorized the president to suspend the writ.

There were probably more than 14,000 arrests made without recourse to a writ of habeas corpus. Most of those arrested were Confederate citizens accused of slipping vessels through the Union blockade, or they were foreign nationals. But Union citizens were also detained. One celebrated case arose in 1863 when Federal soldiers hustled the Democrat Clement L. Vallandigham

"Abraham's Dream!"

This cartoon depicts President Lincoln having a nightmare about the election of 1864. Lady Liberty brandishes the severed head of a black man at the door of the White House as General McClellan mounts the steps and Lincoln runs away.

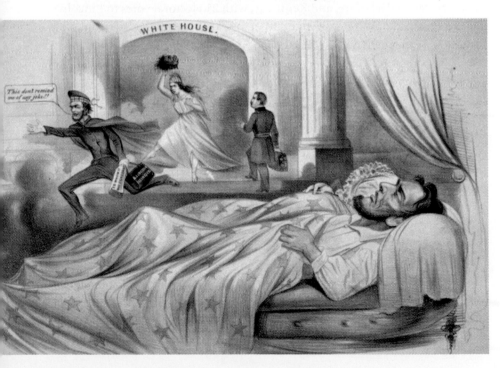

out of his home in Dayton, Ohio, and a military court condemned Ohio's most prominent Confederate sympathizer to confinement for the duration of the war. The muzzling of a political opponent proved such an embarrassment to Lincoln that he commuted the sentence, but only by another irregular device: banishment behind Confederate lines. Vallandigham eventually found his way to Canada.

At their 1864 national convention in Chicago, the Democrats called for an immediate end to the war, to be followed by a national convention that would restore the Union. They named General George B. McClellan as their candidate, but McClellan distanced himself from the peace platform by declaring that agreement on Union would have to precede peace.

Radical Republicans, who still regarded Lincoln as soft on treason, tried to thwart his nomination for a second term, but he outmaneuvered them at every turn. Lincoln promoted the vice-presidential nomination of Andrew Johnson, a "war Democrat" from Tennessee, on the "National Union" ticket, so named to promote bipartisanship. As the war dragged on through 1864, however, with Grant's army taking heavy losses in Virginia, Lincoln fully expected to lose the 1864 election. Then Admiral David Farragut's capture of Mobile, Alabama, in August and General William Tecumseh Sherman's capture of Atlanta on September 2, 1864, turned the tide. McClellan carried only New Jersey, Delaware, and Kentucky, with 21 electoral votes to Lincoln's 212, and he won only 1.8 million popular votes (45 percent) to Lincoln's 2.2 million (55 percent).

CONFEDERATE POLITICS   Unlike Lincoln, Jefferson Davis never had to face a presidential contest. He and his vice president, Alexander Stephens, were elected without opposition in 1861 for a six-year term. But discontent flourished as the war dragged on. Food grew scarce, and prices skyrocketed. A bread riot in Richmond on April 2, 1863, ended only when Davis himself threatened to shoot the protesters (mostly women). After the Confederate congressional elections of 1863, about a third of the legislators were ardent critics of Davis. Although parties as such did not figure in the elections, it was noteworthy that many ex-Whigs and other opponents of secession were chosen.

Davis's greatest challenge came from the politicians who had embraced secession and then guarded states' rights against the authority of the central government of the Confederacy as zealously as they had against that of the Union. Georgia and, to a lesser degree, North Carolina were strongholds of such sentiments. The states' rights advocates challenged, among other things, the legality of the military draft, taxes on farm produce, and above all the suspension of habeas corpus. Vice President Alexander Stephens carried on a running battle against Davis's effort to establish "military despotism," and he eventually left Richmond to sulk at his Georgia home for eighteen months.

Among other fatal flaws, the Confederacy suffered from an excess of dogma. Where Lincoln was the consummate pragmatist, Davis was a brittle ideologue with a waspish temper. Once he made a decision, nothing could change his mind. One southern politician said that Davis was "as stubborn as a mule." Davis could never admit a mistake. Such a personality was ill suited to the chief executive of an infant—and fractious—nation.

Jefferson Davis

President of the Confederacy.

THE ENVIRONMENT AND THE CIVIL WAR Wars not only kill and maim people; they also transform the environment. The Civil War devastated the ecology of the South. While well over half a million soldiers died of wounds, disease, or accidents, equally appalling numbers of animals, especially horses and mules but also cattle and pigs, were killed in battle or for food. During the final year of the war, nearly 500 horses a day died of shell fire, starvation, overwork, or disease.

Fighting during the Civil War also destroyed much of the landscape. In 1864 a Confederate major wrote that near Chickamauga, Georgia, just south of Chattanooga, Tennessee, the road was "covered with the skeletons of horses, and every tree bears the mark of battle. Many strong trunks were broken down by artillery fire." Hundreds of bridges and levees were also destroyed during the war, as were endless miles of fences, which foraging soldiers used for firewood. The loss of levees caused massive flooding; the loss of fencing meant that much of the postwar South would revert to open-range grazing. Craters gouged out by cannonballs pockmarked the landscape and provided breeding grounds for mosquitoes. The loss of so many animals meant that the mosquitoes focused on humans for their blood meal, thus increasing the spread of malaria. Hundreds of miles of trenches dug for military defense scarred the land and accelerated erosion. All told, the environment was as much a victim of the warfare as were the soldiers, and it would take years to heal nature's wounds across the South.

The Faltering Confederacy

CHANCELLORSVILLE   After the Union disaster at Fredericksburg at the end of 1862, Lincoln's search for a capable general had turned to one of Burnside's disgruntled lieutenants, Joseph Hooker, whose pugnacity had earned him the nickname Fighting Joe. With a force of 130,000 men, the largest Union army yet gathered, and a brilliant plan, Hooker failed his leadership test at Chancellorsville, Virginia, on May 1–5, 1863. Robert E. Lee, with perhaps half that number of troops, staged what became a textbook example of daring and maneuver. On May 2, the Confederates surprised the Federals at the edge of a densely wooded area called the Wilderness, but the fighting died out in confusion as darkness fell. General Stonewall Jackson rode out beyond the skirmish line to locate the Union forces. Shooting erupted in the darkness, and nervous Confederates mistakenly opened fire on Jackson, who was struck by three bullets that shattered his left arm and right hand. The next day a surgeon amputated his arm. The indispensable Jackson seemed to be recovering well but then contracted pneumonia and died. Jackson had been a fearless general famous for leading rapid marches, bold flanking movements, and furious assaults. "I have lost my right arm," Lee lamented, and "I do not know how to replace him." The next day, Lee forced Hooker's Union army to retreat. It was the peak of Lee's career, but Chancellorsville was his last significant victory.

Stonewall Jackson

Jackson was mortally wounded by his own men.

VICKSBURG   While Lee's army held the Federals at bay in the East, Ulysses Grant, his appointment as field commander reinstated, had been inching his army down the Mississippi River toward the Confederate stronghold of Vicksburg, in western Mississippi. If Union forces could gain control of the Mississippi River, they could split the Confederacy in two. Grant marched his army into

Louisiana, and while the navy ran gunboats and transports past the Confederate batteries along the river at Vicksburg, he moved south to meet them at the end of April 1863. From there Grant swept eastward on a campaign that Lincoln later called "one of the most brilliant in the world," taking Jackson, Mississippi, where he seized or destroyed supplies, and then turning westward and on May 18 pinning the 30,000 Confederates inside Vicksburg. He resolved to wear them down by bombardment and starvation.

GETTYSBURG   The plight of besieged Vicksburg put the Confederate high command in a quandary. General Joseph E. Johnston, now in charge of

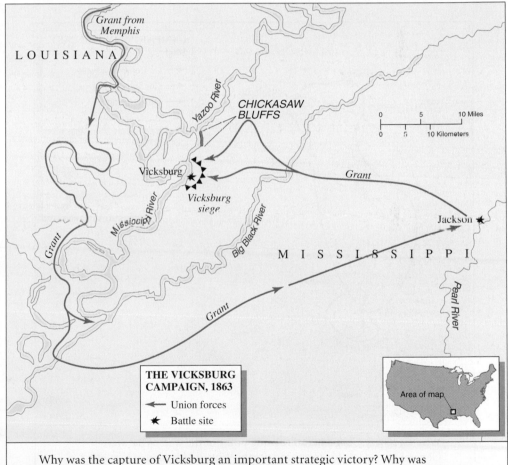

Why was the capture of Vicksburg an important strategic victory? Why was Vicksburg difficult to seize from the Confederacy? How did General Lee hope to save Vicksburg from the Union siege?

the western Confederate forces, wanted to lure Grant's army into Tennessee and thereby relieve the siege of Vicksburg. Lee had another idea for a diversion. Once more he sought to win a major battle on northern soil, this time in the hope of not just saving Vicksburg but also persuading northern public opinion to end the war. In June he again moved his army northward across Maryland.

Neither side chose Gettysburg, Pennsylvania, as the site for the war's climactic battle, but a Confederate scavenging party entered the town in search of shoes and encountered units of Union cavalry on June 30, 1863. The main forces quickly converged on that point. On July 1 the Confederates pushed the Federals out of the town, but into stronger positions on high ground

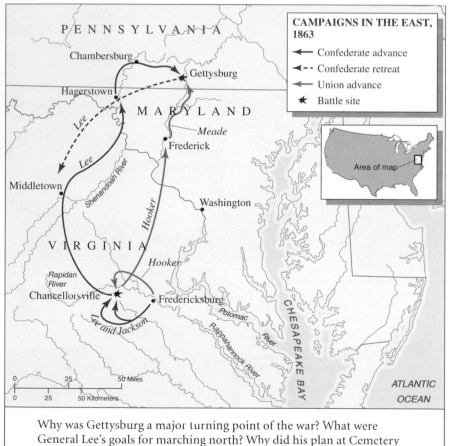

CAMPAIGNS IN THE EAST, 1863

← Confederate advance
◄- - Confederate retreat
← Union advance
★ Battle site

Why was Gettysburg a major turning point of the war? What were General Lee's goals for marching north? Why did his plan at Cemetery Ridge fail?

to the south. The new Union commander, General George Meade, hastened reinforcements to his new lines along the heights. On July 2, Confederate units assaulted Meade's army, but in vain.

The next day, July 3, Lee staked everything on one final assault on the Union center at Cemetery Ridge. At about two in the afternoon, General George Pickett's 15,000 Confederate troops emerged from the woods into the brilliant sunlight, formed neat ranks, and began their suicidal advance uphill across open ground commanded by Union artillery. The few Confederates who got within range of hand-to-hand combat were quickly overwhelmed. At the head of Pickett's division were the University Greys, thirty-one college students from Mississippi. Within an hour of their assault, every one of them had been killed or wounded. As he watched the few survivors returning from the bloody field, General Lee muttered, "All this has been my fault." He then ordered Pickett to regroup his division to repulse a possible counterattack, only to have Pickett tartly reply, "General Lee, I have no division now." Pickett never forgave Lee. Years later he charged, "That old man had my division slaughtered."

With nothing left to do but retreat, on July 4 Lee's mangled army, with about a third of its number gone, began to slog south through a driving rain.

"A Harvest of Death"

Timothy H. O'Sullivan's grim photograph of the dead at Gettysburg.

They had failed in all their purposes, not the least being to relieve the pressure on Vicksburg. On that same July 4, the Confederate commander at Vicksburg surrendered his entire garrison after a forty-seven-day siege. The Confederacy was now split in two. Had Meade pursued Lee, he might have ended the war, but yet again the winning army failed to capitalize on its victory.

After the fighting at Gettysburg had ended, a group of northern states funded a military cemetery for the 6,000 soldiers killed in the battle. On November 19, 1863, the new cemetery was officially dedicated. In his brief remarks, since known as the Gettysburg Address, President Lincoln eloquently expressed the pain and sorrow of the brutal civil war. The prolonged conflict was testing whether a nation "dedicated to the proposition that all men are created equal . . . can long endure." Lincoln declared that all living Americans must ensure that the "honored dead" had not "died in vain." In stirring words that continue to inspire, Lincoln predicted that "this nation, under God, shall have a new birth of freedom—and that government of the people, by the people, and for the people, shall not perish from the earth."

CHATTANOOGA   The third great Union victory of 1863 occurred in fighting around Chattanooga, the railhead of eastern Tennessee and gateway to northern Georgia. In the late summer a Union army led by General William Rosecrans took Chattanooga and then rashly pursued General Braxton Bragg's Rebel forces into Georgia, where they met at Chickamauga. The battle (September 19–20) had the makings of a Union disaster, since it was one of the few times the Confederates had a numerical advantage (about 70,000 to 56,000). Only the stubborn stand of Union troops under George H. Thomas (thenceforth dubbed the Rock of Chickamauga) prevented a rout. The battered Union forces fell back into Chattanooga while Bragg held the city virtually under siege from the heights to the south and the east.

Rosecrans seemed stunned and apathetic, but Lincoln urged him to hang on: "If we can hold Chattanooga, and East Tennessee, I think rebellion must dwindle and die." The Union command sent reinforcements. General Grant, given overall command of the western theater of operations, replaced Rosecrans with Thomas. On November 24 the Federal troops took Lookout Mountain in what was mainly a feat of mountaineering. The next day Union forces dislodged the Rebels atop Missionary Ridge.

The Union victory at Missionary Ridge confirmed the impression of Grant's genius. Lincoln had at last found his fighting general. In 1864, Grant arrived in Washington to assume the rank of lieutenant general and a new position as general in chief.

THE CONFEDERACY'S DEFEAT

During the winter of 1863–1864, Confederates began to despair of victory. A War Department official in Richmond noted in his diary a spreading "sense of hopelessness." Union leaders, sensing the momentum swinging their way, stepped up their pressure on Confederate forces. The Union command's main targets now were Lee's army in Virginia and General Joseph Johnston's forces in Georgia. Grant personally would accompany George Meade, who retained direct command over the Army of the Potomac; operations in the West were entrusted to Grant's longtime lieutenant, William T. Sherman. As Sherman put it later, Grant "was to go for Lee, and I was to go for Joe Johnston."

Grant brought with him a new strategy against Lee. Where all his predecessors had hoped for the climactic single battle, he adopted a policy of aggressive attrition. Grant's unyielding faith that the Union armies were destined for victory enabled him to impose his tenacious will upon his troops; his unflappable calmness in the face of adversity and danger inspired his troops, enabling them to survive defeats and endure savage losses. With the benefit of far more soldiers and better supplies than Lee, Grant planned to attack, attack, attack, keeping the pressure on the Confederates, grinding down their numbers and their will to fight. As he ordered Meade, "Wherever Lee goes, there you will go also." Grant would now wage total war, confiscating or destroying civilian property of use to the military. It was a brutal and costly—but effective—plan.

Ulysses S. Grant

At his headquarters in City Point (now Hopewell), Virginia.

GRANT'S PURSUIT OF LEE

In May 1864, the Union's Army of the Potomac, numbering about 115,000 to Lee's 65,000, moved south across the Rappahannock and Rapidan Rivers into the Wilderness of eastern Virginia, where Hooker had come to grief in the Battle of Chancellorsville. In the nightmarish Battle of the Wilderness (May 5–6), the armies

"Sheridan's Ride"

This sketch, attributed to Alfred Waud, depicts General Philip Sheridan's ride at the Battle of Cedar Creek, Virginia, October 19, 1864. Artists traveling with the soldiers rendered quick, accurate sketches of battle scenes.

fought blindly through the woods, the horror and suffering of the scene heightened by crackling brushfires. Grant's men suffered heavier casualties than the Confederates, but the Rebels were running out of replacements. Always before when bloodied by Lee's troops, Union forces had pulled back to nurse their wounds, but Grant slid off to his left and continued to push southward, engaging Lee's men near Spotsylvania Court House. "Whatever happens," he assured Lincoln, "we will not retreat."

Again Grant's forces slid off to the left of Lee's army and kept moving. Along the banks of the Chickahominy River, the two sides clashed again at Cold Harbor (June 1–3), ten miles east of Richmond. Grant ordered his troops to assault the heavily entrenched Confederate lines. As the Confederates had discovered at Gettysburg, such a frontal assault was murder. The Union army was massacred at Cold Harbor: in twenty minutes almost 7,000 attacking Federals were killed or wounded. Grant later admitted that the attack was his greatest mistake. Critics called him the Butcher after Cold Harbor. Yet the relentless Grant brilliantly maneuvered his battered forces around Lee and headed for Petersburg, south of Richmond, where the major railroads converged.

The two armies then dug in for a siege along lines that extended for twenty-five miles above and below Petersburg. Grant telegraphed Lincoln

The tattered colors of the 56th and 36th Massachusetts Regiments

Union soldiers march through Virginia in 1864.

that he intended "to fight it out on this line if it takes all summer." Lincoln replied, "Hold on with a bulldog grip, and chew and choke as much as possible." For nine months the two armies faced each other down while Grant's troops tried to cut the railroad arteries that were Lee's lifeline. During that time, Grant's troops, twice as numerous as the Confederate army, were generously supplied by Union vessels moving up the James River, while Lee's forces, beset by hunger, cold, and desertion, wasted away. Petersburg had become Lee's prison while disasters piled up for the Confederacy elsewhere.

SHERMAN'S MARCH   When Grant's army headed south from northern Virginia, General William T. Sherman moved south from Tennessee toward the railroad hub of Atlanta, with 90,000 men against Joseph Johnston's 60,000. Johnston's skillful defensive tactics caused an impatient President Jefferson Davis to replace him with the reckless John B. Hood, a natural fighter but an inept strategist who did not know the meaning of retreat. Having had an arm crippled by a bullet at Gettysburg and most of one leg shot off at Chickamauga, he had to be strapped to his horse. Three times in eight days, Hood's Confederate army lashed out at the Union lines, each time meeting a bloody rebuff. Sherman at first resorted to a siege of Atlanta, then slid off to

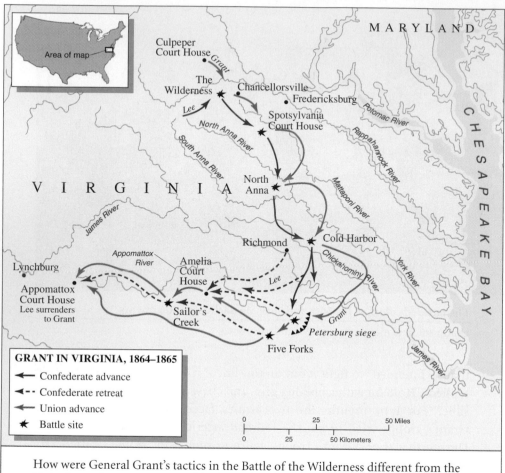

Area of map

MARYLAND

Culpeper
Court House
Grant

The
Wilderness
Chancellorsville
Fredericksburg
Potomac River

Lee
North Anna River
Spotsylvania
Court House

South Anna River

VIRGINIA

North
Anna

Mattaponi River

Rappahannock River

James River

Appomattox
River

Richmond
Cold Harbor
Chickahominy River

Lynchburg
Amelia
Court
House
Lee

York River

Appomattox
Court House
Lee surrenders
to Grant
Sailor's
Creek
Grant
Petersburg siege

James River

Five Forks

C H E S A P E A K E   B A Y

GRANT IN VIRGINIA, 1864–1865

◄— Confederate advance

◄-- Confederate retreat

◄— Union advance

✱ Battle site

0   25   50 Miles

0   25   50 Kilometers

How were General Grant's tactics in the Battle of the Wilderness different from the Union's previous encounters with General Lee's army? Why did Grant have the advantage at Petersburg?

the right again, cutting the rail lines below the city. Hood evacuated Atlanta on September 1 but kept his army intact.

Sherman now laid plans for a march south through central Georgia, where no organized Confederate armies remained. His intention was to "whip the rebels, to humble their pride, to follow them into their inmost recesses, and make them fear and dread us." Hood, meanwhile, had hatched an equally audacious plan: he would slip out of Georgia into northern Alabama and push northward into Tennessee, forcing Sherman into pursuit. Sherman refused to take the bait, although he did send a Union force, led by General George

Thomas, back to Tennessee to keep watch. So unfolded the curious spectacle of the main armies' moving off in opposite directions. But it was a measure of the Confederates' plight that Sherman could cut a swath of destruction across Georgia with impunity while Hood's army was soon outnumbered again, this time in Tennessee.

In the Battle of Franklin (November 30), near Nashville, Hood sent his army across two miles of open ground defended by entrenched Union troops backed by massed artillery. It was suicide. Six waves broke against the Union lines, leaving the ground strewn with Confederate dead. A Confederate captain from Texas, scarred by the battle's senseless butchery, wrote that the "wails

William Tecumseh Sherman

Sherman's campaign developed into a war of maneuver, but without the pitched battles of Grant's campaign.

and cries of the widows and orphans made at Franklin, Tennessee will heat up the fires of the bottomless pit to burn the soul of General J. B. Hood for murdering their husbands and fathers." With what he had left, Hood dared not attack Nashville, nor did he dare withdraw for fear of final disintegration. Finally, in the Battle of Nashville (December 15–16), the Federals scattered what was left of the Confederate Army of Tennessee. The Confederate front west of the Appalachians had collapsed.

Meanwhile, William T. Sherman's Union army was marching through Georgia, waging war against the people's resources and their will to resist. In his effort to demoralize the civilian populace, Sherman was determined to "make Georgia howl." The Union army moved southeast from Atlanta, living off the land and destroying any provisions that might serve Confederate forces. Bands of stragglers and deserters from both armies joined in looting along the flanks while Union cavalry destroyed Rebel supplies to keep them out of enemy hands.

More than any other Civil War general, Sherman recognized the connections among the South's economy, its morale, and its ability to wage war. He explained that "we are not only fighting hostile armies, but a hostile people" who must be made to "feel the hard hand of war." He wanted the Rebels to "fear and dread us." When, after a month of ravaging the Georgia countryside, Sherman's army arrived in Savannah, on the coast, his forces had freed

"Ruins of Depot, Blown Up on Sherman's Departure" (1864)

In the wake of Sherman's march, burned depots, abandoned locomotives, and twisted rails marked Atlanta's destruction.

over 40,000 slaves and burned plantations. A Macon, Georgia, newspaper wrote that Sherman was a "demon" willing to plumb the "depths of depravity" in wreaking his campaign of vengeance. Yet Sherman scoffed at such criticism. "Those people made war on us, defied and dared us to come south to their country, where they boasted they would kill us and do all manner of terrible things. We accepted their challenge, and now for them to whine and complain of the natural and necessary results is beneath contempt." Sherman's troops, in fact, rarely committed the atrocities later attributed to them. To be sure, they confiscated food and livestock, destroyed railroads and mills, and burned plantations, but most houses were left untouched, and Union soldiers committed few serious crimes against individuals. Sherman's goal was to defeat Confederate morale and reunite the nation, not destroy Georgia or the South physically. After the war a Confederate officer acknowledged that Sherman's march through Georgia was in fact well conceived and well managed. "I don't think there was ever an army in the world that would have behaved better, in a similar expedition, in an enemy country. Our army certainly wouldn't."

Pushing across the Savannah River into South Carolina, that "hell-hole of secession," Sherman's men wrought even greater destruction. More than a

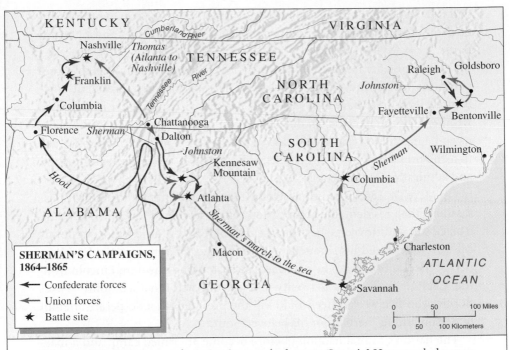

SHERMAN'S CAMPAIGNS, 1864–1865
← Confederate forces
← Union forces
★ Battle site

What was General Sherman's goal as he marched across Georgia? How much damage did Sherman do in Georgia and South Carolina? How did Sherman's march affect the Confederate war effort?

dozen towns were burned in whole or part, including the state capital of Columbia, which was captured on February 17, 1865. Meanwhile, Charleston's defenders abandoned the city and headed north to join a ragtag Rebel army that Joseph E. Johnston was desperately pulling together in North Carolina. Johnston mounted an attack on Sherman's army at Bentonville (March 19–20), but that would be his last major battle.

During the late winter and early spring of 1865, the Confederacy found itself besieged on all sides. Defeat was in the air. Some Rebel leaders wanted to negotiate a peace settlement. Confederate secretary of war John C. Breckinridge, the Kentuckian who had served as vice president under James Buchanan and had run for president in 1860, urged Robert E. Lee to negotiate an honorable end to the war. "This has been a magnificent epic," he said. "In God's name, let it not terminate in a farce." But Jefferson Davis dismissed any talk of surrender. If the Confederate armies should be defeated, he wanted the soldiers to disperse and fight a guerrilla war. "The war came and now it must go on," he stubbornly insisted, "till the last man of this generation falls in his tracks, and his children seize his musket and fight our battle."

While Confederate forces made their last stands, Abraham Lincoln prepared for his second term as president. He was the first president since Andrew Jackson to have been reelected. The weary commander in chief had weathered constant criticism during his first term, but with the war nearing its end, Lincoln now garnered deserved praise. The *Chicago Tribune* observed that the president "has slowly and steadily risen in the respect, confidence, and admiration of the people."

On March 4, 1865, amid rumors of a Confederate attempt to abduct or assassinate the president, the six-foot-four-inch rawboned Lincoln, dressed in a black suit and stovepipe hat, his face weathered by prairie wind and political worry, delivered his eloquent second inaugural address on the East Portico of the Capitol. Not a hundred feet away, looking down on Lincoln from the Capitol porch, was a twenty-six-year-old actor named John Wilkes Booth, who five weeks later would kill the president in a desperate attempt to do something "heroic" for his beloved South.

The nation's capital had long before become an armed camp and a massive military hospital. Sick and wounded soldiers were scattered everywhere: in hotels, warehouses, schools, businesses, and private homes. Thousands of Confederate deserters roamed the streets. After a morning of torrential rains, the sun broke through the clouds just as Lincoln began to speak to the mud-spattered audience of some 35,000, half of whom were African Americans. While managing a terrible civil war, the president had experienced personal tragedy (the loss of a second child and a wife plagued by mental instability) and chronic depression. What had kept him from unraveling were a principled pragmatism and a godly foundation that endowed his life with purpose.

Lincoln's second inaugural address was more a sermon than a speech, the reflections of a somber statesman still struggling to understand the relation between divine will and human endeavor. Rather than detailing the progress of the war effort or indulging in self-congratulatory celebration, Lincoln focused on the origins and paradoxes of the war. Slavery, he said, had "somehow" caused the war, and everyone bore some guilt for the national shame of racial injustice and its bloody expiation. Both sides had known before the fighting began that war was to be avoided at all costs, but "one of them would *make* war rather than let the nation survive; and the other would *accept* war rather than let it perish."

The weary but resolute commander in chief longed for peace. "Fondly do we hope—fervently do we pray—that this mighty scourge of war may speedily pass away." He wondered aloud why the war had lasted so long and had been so brutal. "The Almighty," he acknowledged, "has His own purposes." Lincoln noted the paradoxical irony of both sides in this civil war reading the same Bible, praying to the same God, and appealing for divine support in its fight against the other. The God of Judgment, however, would not be misled or denied. If God willed that the war continue until "every drop of blood drawn with the lash, shall be paid with another drawn by the sword, as was said three thousand years ago, so still it must be said 'the judgments of the Lord are true and righteous altogether.'" After four years of escalating combat, the war had grown "incomprehensible" in its scope and horrors. Now the president, looking gaunt and tired, urged the Union forces "to finish the work we are in," bolstered with "firmness in the right insofar as God gives us to see the right."

As Lincoln looked ahead to the end of the fighting and a "just and lasting peace," he stressed the need to "bind up the nation's wounds" by exercising the Christian virtues of forgiveness and mercy. Vengeance must be avoided at all costs. Reconciliation must be pursued "with malice toward none; with charity for all." Those eight words marvelously captured Lincoln's hopes for a restored Union. Redemption was his goal; victory was less important than peace. The sublime majesty of Lincoln's brief speech revealed how the rigors of war had transformed and elevated him from the obscure congressman who had entered the White House in 1861. The abolitionist leader Frederick Douglass proclaimed Lincoln's second inaugural address "a sacred effort."

APPOMATTOX During the spring of 1865, General Grant's army kept pushing, probing, and battering the entrenched Rebels around Petersburg, Virginia, twenty miles south of Richmond. The badly outnumbered Confederates were slowly starving. Their trenches were filled with rats and lice; scurvy and dysentery were rampant. News of Sherman's progress through Georgia and South Carolina added to the gloom and heightened the impulse of weary Rebels to desert. Lee began to lay plans for his forces to escape and join Johnston's army in North Carolina. On April 2, 1865, Lee's army abandoned Richmond and Petersburg in a desperate flight southwest toward Lynchburg and railroads leading south. President Davis, exhausted but still defiant, too stubborn and vain to concede, gathered what archives and treasure he could and fled by train ahead of the advancing Federals, only to be captured in Georgia by Union cavalry on May 10.

Robert E. Lee

Mathew Brady took this photograph in Richmond eleven days after Lee's surrender at Appomattox.

By then the Confederacy was dead. Lee had moved out of Petersburg with Grant in hot pursuit and soon found his escape route cut off. Lee recognized that there was no need to prolong the inevitable. As he told the Union officer who delivered the terms of a proposed surrender, "There is nothing left for me to do but go and see General Grant, and I would rather die a thousand deaths." On April 9 (Palm Sunday) the tall, stately Lee donned a crisp dress uniform and met the mud-spattered Grant in the parlor of Wilmer McLean's home at Appomattox Court House to tender his surrender. Grant, at Lee's request, let the Rebel officers keep their sidearms and permitted soldiers to keep their personal horses and mules. As the gaunt, hungry Confederate troops formed ranks for the last time, Joshua Chamberlain, the Union general in charge of the surrender ceremony, ordered his Federal soldiers to salute their foes as they paraded past. His Confederate counterpart signaled his men to do likewise. General Chamberlain remembered that there was not a sound—no trumpets or drums, no cheers or jeers, simply an "awed stillness . . . as if it were the passing of the dead." On April 18, General Joseph Johnston surrendered his Confederate army to General Sherman near Durham, North Carolina. The remaining Confederate forces surrendered during May. The brutal war was at last over.

A MODERN WAR

The Civil War was in many respects the first modern war. Its scope was unprecedented. One out of every twelve adult American men served in the war, and few families were unaffected by the event. Over 630,000 Americans died in the conflict from wounds or disease, 50 percent more than in World War II. Of the survivors, 50,000 returned home with one or more limbs amputated. Disease, however, was the greatest threat to soldiers, killing twice as many as were lost in battle.

The Civil War was also modern in that much of the killing was distant, impersonal, and mechanical. Men were killed without knowing who had fired the shot that felled them. The opposing forces used an array of new weapons and instruments of war: artillery with "rifled," or grooved, barrels for greater accuracy, repeating rifles, ironclad ships, observation balloons, and wire entanglements.

Historians have provided conflicting assessments of the reasons for the Union victory. Some have focused on the inherent weaknesses of the Confederacy: its lack of industry, the fractious relations between the states and the central government in Richmond, poor political and military leadership, faulty coordination and communication, the burden of slavery, and the disparities in population and resources compared with those of the North. Still others have highlighted the erosion of Confederate morale in the face of chronic food shortages and horrific human losses. The debate over why the North won and the South lost the Civil War will probably never end, but as in other modern wars, firepower and manpower were essential factors. Robert E. Lee's own explanation of the Confederate defeat retains an enduring legitimacy: "After four years of arduous service marked by unsurpassed courage and fortitude, the Army of Northern Virginia has been compelled to yield to overwhelming numbers and resources."

CHAPTER SUMMARY

- **Civil War Begins** In his inaugural address, Abraham Lincoln made it clear that secession was unconstitutional but that the North would not invade the South. War came when the federal government attempted to resupply forts in the South. When South Carolinians shelled Fort Sumter, in Charleston Harbor, Lincoln issued his call to arms. Other southern states seceded at that point, and the American Civil War was under way.

- **Civil War Strategies** The Confederates had a geographic advantage in that they were fighting to defend their own soil. They expected support from Britain and France because of those nations' dependence on southern cotton for their textile industries. The Union quickly launched a campaign to seize the Confederate capital, Richmond, Virginia. Initial hopes for a rapid victory died at the First Battle of Bull Run. The Union then adopted the "anaconda plan," which involved imposing a naval blockade on southern ports and slowly crushing resistance on all fronts. The Union's industrial might was a deciding feature in a long war of attrition.

- **Wartime Home Fronts** Both sides passed conscription laws. Most of the fighting took place in the South; thus, although the North had more casualties, the impact on the South was greater. Its population was smaller, and its civilians experienced local violence and food shortages. The landscape, food supply, and wildlife were destroyed in many areas. In both the North and the South, women played nontraditional roles on farms and even at the battlefront.

- **Emancipation Proclamation** Initially, President Lincoln declared that the war's aim was to restore the Union and that slavery would be maintained where it existed. Gradually, he came to see that the Emancipation Proclamation was justified as a military necessity because it would deprive the South of its labor force. He hoped that southern states would return to the Union before his January 1863 deadline, when all slaves under Confederate control were declared free.

- **Freedom from Slavery** Many slaves freed themselves by escaping to Union camps. Although the Emancipation Proclamation announced the war aim of abolishing slavery, it freed only those people enslaved in areas still under Confederate control. The Thirteenth Amendment freed all enslaved people throughout the United States.

CHRONOLOGY

March 4, 1861	Abraham Lincoln is inaugurated president
April 1861	Fort Sumter falls to Confederate forces; Lincoln issues call to arms
July 1861	First Battle of Bull Run (Manassas)
November 1861	The *Trent* affair commences when a Union warship stops a British ship on the high seas and takes two Confederate agents into custody
March 1862	Battle of the *Merrimack* (the *Virginia*) and the *Monitor*
March–July 1862	Peninsular campaign
April, August, September 1862	Battles of Shiloh, Second Bull Run, and Antietam
January 1, 1863	Lincoln signs the Emancipation Proclamation
May–July, November 1863	Siege of Vicksburg, Battles of Gettysburg and Chattanooga
April 9, 1865	Robert E. Lee surrenders at Appomattox Court House
1865	Thirteenth Amendment is ratified

KEY TERMS & NAMES

Fort Sumter p. 649

Jefferson Davis p. 650

George B. McClellan p. 651

Robert E. Lee p. 652

Ulysses S. Grant p. 652

Battles of Bull Run (First and Second Manassas) p. 655

Thomas "Stonewall" Jackson p. 655

anaconda strategy p. 656

Battle of the *Merrimack* (the *Virginia*) and the *Monitor* p. 657

Emancipation Proclamation p. 668

Radical Republicans p. 669

Thirteenth Amendment p. 674

Battle of Gettysburg p. 685

William T. Sherman's March through Georgia p. 691

18

RECONSTRUCTION: NORTH AND SOUTH

FOCUS QUESTIONS   wwnorton.com/studyspace

- What were the different approaches to Reconstruction?
- How did white southerners respond to the end of the old order in the South?
- To what extent did blacks function as citizens in the reconstructed South?
- What were the main issues in national politics in the 1870s?
- Why did Reconstruction end in 1877?

In the spring of 1865, the Civil War was finally over. At a frightful cost of 630,000 lives and the destruction of the southern economy and much of its landscape, the Union had emerged triumphant, and some 4 million enslaved Americans had seized their freedom. Ratification of the Thirteenth Amendment in December 1865 abolished slavery throughout the Union. Now the nation faced the task of reuniting, coming to terms with the abolition of slavery, and "reconstructing" a ravaged and resentful South.

THE WAR'S AFTERMATH

In the war's aftermath difficult questions faced the victors: Should the Confederate leaders be tried for treason? How should new governments be formed? How and at whose expense was the South's economy to be rebuilt?

Should debts incurred by the Confederate state governments be honored? Who should pay to rebuild the South's railroads and public buildings, dredge the clogged southern harbors, and restore damaged levees? What was to be done for the freed slaves? Were they to be given land? social equality? education? voting rights? Such complex questions required sober reflection and careful planning, but policy makers did not have the luxury of time or the benefit of consensus. Some northerners wanted the former Confederate states returned to the Union with little or no changes in the region's social, political, and economic life. Others wanted southern society punished and transformed. The editors of the nation's foremost magazine, *Harper's Weekly*, expressed this vengeful attitude when they declared at the end of 1865 that "the forgive-and-forget policy . . . is mere political insanity and suicide."

DEVELOPMENT IN THE NORTH   To some Americans the Civil War had been more truly a social revolution than the War of Independence, for it reduced the once-dominant influence of the South's planter elite in national politics and elevated the power of the northern "captains of industry." Government, both federal and state, became more friendly to business leaders and more unfriendly to those who would probe into their activities. The wartime Republican Congress had delivered on the party's major platform promises of 1860.

In the absence of southern members, the wartime Congress had centralized national power and enacted the Republican economic agenda. It passed the Morrill Tariff, which doubled the average level of import duties. The National Banking Act created a uniform system of banking and bank-note currency and helped finance the war. Congress also decided that the first transcontinental railroad would run along a north-central route, from Omaha, Nebraska, to Sacramento, California, and it donated public land and sold bonds to ensure its financing. In the Homestead Act of 1862, moreover, Congress provided free federal homesteads of 160 acres to settlers, who had only to occupy the land for five years to gain title. No cash was needed. The Morrill Land Grant Act of the same year conveyed to each state 30,000 acres of federal land per member of Congress from the state. The sale of some of the land provided funds to create colleges of "agriculture and mechanic arts." Such measures helped stimulate the North's economy in the years after the Civil War.

DEVASTATION IN THE SOUTH   The postwar South offered a sharp contrast to the victorious North. Along the path of General William T. Sherman's Union army, one observer reported in 1866, the countryside

A street in the "burned district"

Ruins of Richmond, Virginia, in the spring of 1865.

"looked for many miles like a broad black streak of ruin and desolation."
Columbia, South Carolina, said another witness, was "a wilderness of ruins";
Charleston, a place of "vacant houses, of widowed women, of rotting
wharves, of deserted warehouses, of weed-wild gardens, of miles of grass-
grown streets, of acres of pitiful and voiceless barrenness."

Throughout the South, property values had collapsed. Confederate bonds
and paper money were worthless; most railroads were damaged or destroyed.
Cotton that had escaped destruction was seized by federal troops. Emancipation wiped out $4 billion invested in human flesh and left the labor system
in disarray. The great age of expansion in the cotton market was over. Not
until 1879 would the cotton crop again equal the record harvest of 1860;
tobacco production did not regain its prewar level until 1880; the sugar crop
of Louisiana did not recover until 1893; and the old rice industry of the
Tidewater and the hemp industry of the Kentucky Bluegrass never regained
their prewar status.

A TRANSFORMED SOUTH   The defeat of the Confederacy transformed much of southern society. The freeing of slaves, the destruction of
property, and the collapse of land values left many planters destitute and
homeless. Amanda Worthington, a planter's wife from Mississippi, saw her

whole world destroyed. In the fall of 1865, she assessed the damage: "None of us can realize that we are no longer wealthy—yet thanks to the yankees, the cause of all unhappiness, such is the case."

Union soldiers who fanned out across the defeated South to impose order were cursed and spat upon. A Virginia woman expressed a spirited defiance common among her circle of friends: "Every day, every hour, that I live increases my hatred and detestation, and loathing of that race. They [Yankees] disgrace our common humanity. As a people I consider them vastly inferior to the better classes of our slaves." Fervent southern nationalists, both men and women, implanted in their children a similar hatred of Yankees and a defiance of northern rule. One mother said that she trained her children to "fear God, love the South, and live to avenge her."

LEGALLY FREE, SOCIALLY BOUND In the former Confederate states the newly freed slaves often suffered most of all. A few northerners argued that what the ex-slaves needed most was their own land. But even abolitionists shrank from proposals to confiscate white-owned land and distribute it to the freed slaves. Citizenship and legal rights were one thing, wholesale confiscation of property and land redistribution quite another. Nonetheless, discussions of land distribution fueled false rumors that freed slaves would get "forty acres and a mule," a slogan that swept the

Freed slaves in Richmond, Virginia

According to a former Confederate general, freed slaves had "nothing but freedom."

South at the end of the war. Instead of land or material help, the freed slaves more often got advice about proper behavior.

THE FREEDMEN'S BUREAU   On March 3, 1865, while the war was still raging, Congress set up within the War Department the Bureau of Refugees, Freedmen, and Abandoned Lands to provide "such issues of provisions, clothing, and fuel" as might be needed to relieve "destitute and suffering refugees and freedmen and their wives and children." It was the first federal experiment in social welfare, albeit temporary. Agents of what came to be called the Freedmen's Bureau negotiated labor contracts (something new for both blacks and white planters), provided medical care, and set up schools. The bureau had its own courts to deal with labor disputes and land titles, and its agents were authorized to supervise trials involving blacks in other courts. The intensity of racial prejudice in the South thwarted the efforts of Freedmen's Bureau agents to protect and assist the former slaves.

Freedmen's school in Virginia

Throughout the former Confederate states the Freedmen's Bureau set up schools such as this one.

THE BATTLE OVER RECONSTRUCTION

The question of how to reconstruct the South's political structure centered on deciding which governments would constitute authority in the defeated states. As Union forces advanced into the South, President Lincoln in 1862 named military governors for conquered Tennessee, Arkansas, and Louisiana. By the end of the following year, he had formulated a plan for regular governments in those states and any others that might be liberated from Confederate rule.

LINCOLN'S PLAN AND CONGRESS'S RESPONSE In late 1863, President Lincoln had issued a Proclamation of Amnesty and Reconstruction, under which any former Rebel state could form a Union government whenever a number equal to 10 percent of those who had voted in 1860 took an oath of allegiance to the Constitution and the Union and had received a presidential pardon. Participants also had to swear support for laws and proclamations dealing with emancipation. Certain groups, however, were excluded from the pardon: Confederate officials; senior officers of the Confederate army and navy; judges, congressmen, and military officers of the United States who had left their federal posts to aid the rebellion; and those accused of failure to treat captured African American soldiers and their officers as prisoners of war.

Under this plan, governments loyal to the Union appeared in Tennessee, Arkansas, and Louisiana, but Congress recognized neither their representatives nor their 1864 electoral votes. In the absence of specific provisions for Reconstruction in the Constitution, politicians disagreed as to where authority to restore Rebel states properly rested. Lincoln claimed the right to direct Reconstruction under the clause that set forth the presidential power to grant pardons and under the constitutional obligation of the United States to guarantee each state a republican form of government. Republican congressmen, however, argued that this obligation implied that Congress, not the president, should supervise Reconstruction.

A few conservative and most moderate Republicans supported Lincoln's program of immediate restoration. The small but influential group of Radical Republicans, however, favored a sweeping transformation of southern society based upon granting freed slaves full-fledged citizenship. The Radicals hoped to reconstruct southern society so as to dismantle the old planter class and the Democratic party.

The Radical Republicans were talented, earnest legislators who insisted that Congress control the Reconstruction program. To this end in 1864 they helped pass the Wade-Davis Bill, sponsored by Senator Benjamin Wade of Ohio and Representative Henry Winter Davis of Maryland. In contrast to Lincoln's 10 percent plan, the Wade-Davis Bill required that a majority of white male citizens declare their allegiance and that only those who could take an "ironclad" oath (required of federal officials since 1862) attesting to their *past* loyalty could vote or serve in the state constitutional conventions. The conventions, moreover, would have to abolish slavery, exclude from political rights high-ranking civil and military officers of the Confederacy, and repudiate debts incurred during the conflict.

Passed during the closing day of the session, the Wade-Davis Bill never became law: Lincoln vetoed it. In retaliation furious Republicans penned the Wade-Davis Manifesto, which accused the president of usurping power and attempting to use readmitted states to ensure his reelection, among other sins. Lincoln offered his last view of Reconstruction in his final public address, on April 11, 1865. Speaking from the White House balcony, he pronounced that the Confederate states had never left the Union. Those states were simply "out of their proper practical relation with the Union," and the object was to get them back "into their proper practical relation." At a cabinet meeting, Lincoln proposed the creation of new southern state governments before Congress met in December. He shunned the vindictiveness of the Radicals. He wanted "no persecution, no bloody work," no radical restructuring of southern social and economic life.

THE ASSASSINATION OF LINCOLN   On the evening of April 14, 1865, Lincoln went to Ford's Theatre and his rendezvous with death. With his trusted bodyguard called away to Richmond and the policeman assigned to his box away from his post, Lincoln was helpless as John Wilkes Booth slipped into the unguarded presidential box. Booth, a crazed actor and Confederate zealot, fired his derringer point-blank at the president's head. He then stabbed Lincoln's aide and jumped from the box to the stage, crying "*Sic semper tyrannis*" (Thus always to tyrants), the motto of Virginia. The president died nine hours later. Accomplices of Booth had also targeted Vice President Andrew Johnson and Secretary of State William Seward. Seward and four others, including his son, were victims of severe but not fatal stab wounds. Johnson escaped injury, however, because his would-be assassin got cold feet and wound up tipsy in the barroom of the vice president's hotel.

The nation extracted a full measure of vengeance from the conspirators. Booth was pursued into Virginia and killed in a burning barn. Three of his

Mourning a fallen president

President Lincoln's funeral procession on Pennsylvania Avenue.

collaborators were convicted by a military court and hanged, along with the woman at whose boardinghouse they had plotted. Three others got life sentences, including a Maryland doctor who set the leg Booth had broken when he jumped to the stage. President Johnson eventually pardoned them all, except one who died in prison.

JOHNSON'S PLAN Lincoln's death elevated to the White House Andrew Johnson of Tennessee, a combative man who lacked most presidential virtues. Essentially illiterate, Johnson was provincial and bigoted—he harbored fierce prejudices. He was also short-tempered and impetuous. At the inaugural ceremonies in early 1865, he had delivered his vice-presidential address in a state of slurring drunkenness that embarrassed Lincoln and the nation. Johnson was a war (pro-Union) Democrat who had been put on the National Union ticket in 1864 as a gesture of unity. Of origins as humble as Lincoln's, Johnson was an orphan who had moved as a youth from his birthplace in Raleigh, North Carolina, to Greeneville, Tennessee, where he became the proprietor of a tailor shop. Self-educated with the help of his wife, he

Andrew Johnson

A pro-Union Democrat from Tennessee.

had served as mayor, congressman, governor, and senator, then as the Unionist military governor of Tennessee before he became vice president. In the process he had become an advocate of the small farmers in opposition to the privileges of the large planters—"a bloated, corrupted aristocracy." He also shared the racist attitudes of most white yeomen. "Damn the negroes," he exclaimed to a friend during the war, "I am fighting those traitorous aristocrats, their masters."

Some Radicals at first thought Johnson, unlike Lincoln, to be one of them. Johnson had, for example, once asserted that treason "must be made infamous and traitors must be impoverished." Senator Benjamin Wade loved such vengeful language. "Johnson, we have faith in you," he promised. "By the gods, there will be no trouble now in running this government." But Wade would soon find Johnson as unsympathetic as Lincoln, if for different reasons.

Johnson's loyalty to the Union sprang from a strict adherence to the Constitution and a fervent belief in limited government. When discussing what to do with the former Confederate states, Johnson preferred the term *restoration* to *reconstruction*. In 1865, Johnson declared that "there is no such thing as reconstruction. Those States have not gone out of the Union. Therefore reconstruction is unnecessary." Like many other whites he also opposed the growing Radical sentiment to grant the vote to African Americans.

Johnson's plan to restore the Union thus closely resembled Lincoln's. A new Proclamation of Amnesty, issued in May 1865, excluded not only those Lincoln had excluded from pardon but also everybody with taxable property worth more than $20,000. Those wealthy planters, bankers, and merchants were the people Johnson believed had led the South to secede. Those in the excluded groups might make special applications for pardon directly to the president, and before the year was out Johnson had issued some 13,000 pardons.

Johnson followed up his amnesty proclamation with his own plan for readmitting the former Confederate states. In each state a native Unionist became provisional governor, with authority to call a convention of men elected by loyal voters. Lincoln's 10 percent requirement was omitted. Johnson called upon the state conventions to invalidate the secession ordinances, abolish slavery, and repudiate all debts incurred to aid the Confederacy. Each state, moreover, must ratify the Thirteenth Amendment. In his final public address, Lincoln had endorsed a limited black suffrage. Johnson repeated Lincoln's advice. He reminded the provisional governor of Mississippi, for example, that the state conventions might "with perfect safety" extend suffrage to African Americans with education or with military service so as to "disarm the adversary," the adversary being "radicals who are wild upon" giving all African Americans the right to vote.

The state conventions for the most part met Johnson's requirements. But Carl Schurz, a German immigrant and war hero who became a prominent Missouri politician, found during a visit to the South "an *utter absence of national feeling* . . . and a desire to preserve slavery . . . as much and as long as possible." Southern whites had accepted the situation because they thought so little had changed after all. Emboldened by Johnson's indulgence, they ignored his pleas for moderation and conciliation. Suggestions of black suffrage were scarcely raised in the state conventions and promptly squelched when they were.

SOUTHERN INTRANSIGENCE When Congress met in December 1865, for the first time since the end of the war it faced the fact that the new state governments in the postwar South were remarkably like the old ones. Southern voters had acted with extreme disregard for northern feelings. Among the new members presenting themselves to Congress were Georgia's Alexander Stephens, former vice president of the Confederacy, now claiming a seat in the Senate, four Confederate generals, eight colonels, and six cabinet members. The Congress forthwith denied seats to all such officials. It was too much to expect, after four bloody years, that the Unionists in Congress would welcome back ex-Confederate leaders.

Furthermore, the new southern state legislatures, in passing repressive "black codes" restricting the freedom of African Americans, demonstrated that they intended to preserve slavery as nearly as possible. As one white southerner stressed, "The ex-slave was not a free man; he was a free Negro," and the black codes were intended to highlight the distinction.

The black codes varied from state to state, but some provisions were common. Existing marriages, including common-law marriages, were recognized (although interracial marriages were prohibited), and testimony of blacks was accepted in legal cases involving blacks—and in six states in all cases.

"(?) Slavery Is Dead (?)"

Thomas Nast's cartoon suggests that in 1866 slavery was not dead.

Blacks could own property. They could sue and be sued in the courts. On the other hand, they could not own farmland in Mississippi or city lots in South Carolina; they were required to buy special licenses to practice certain trades in Mississippi. Blacks who worked for whites were required to enter into labor contracts with their employers, to be renewed annually. Unemployed ("vagrant") blacks were often arrested and punished with severe fines, and if unable to pay they were forced to labor in the fields of those who paid the courts for this source of cheap labor. In other words, aspects of slavery were simply being restored in another guise.

Faced with such blatant evidence of southern intransigence, moderate Republicans in Congress drifted toward the Radicals' views. The new Congress set up a Joint Committee on Reconstruction, with nine members from the House and six from the Senate, to gather evidence of southern efforts to thwart Reconstruction. Initiative fell to determined Radical Republicans who knew what they wanted: Benjamin Wade of Ohio, George Julian of Indiana, and—most conspicuously of all—Thaddeus Stevens of Pennsylvania and Charles Sumner of Massachusetts.

THE RADICAL REPUBLICANS Most Radical Republicans had been connected with the anti-slavery cause for decades. In addition, few could escape the bitterness bred by the long war or remain unaware of the partisan advantage that would come to the Republican party from black suffrage. The Republicans needed African American votes to maintain their control of Congress and the White House. They also needed to disenfranchise former Confederates to keep them from helping to elect Democrats who would restore the old southern ruling class to power. In public, however, the Radical Republicans rarely disclosed such partisan self-interest. Instead, they asserted that the Republicans, the party of Union and freedom, could best guarantee the fruits of victory and that extending voting rights to African Americans would be the best way to promote their welfare.

Senator Charles Sumner

A leading Radical Republican.

The growing conflict of opinion over Reconstruction policy brought about an inversion in constitutional reasoning. Secessionists—and Andrew Johnson—were now arguing that the Rebel states had in fact remained in the Union, and some Radical Republicans were contriving arguments that they had left the Union after all. Thaddeus Stevens argued that the Confederate states should be viewed as conquered provinces, subject to the absolute will of the victors, and that the "whole fabric of southern society must be changed." Most Republicans, however, held that the Confederate states continued to exist as entities, but by the acts of secession and war they had forfeited "all civil and political rights under the Constitution." And Congress, not the president, was the proper authority to determine how and when such rights might be restored.

JOHNSON'S BATTLE WITH CONGRESS A long year of political battling remained, however, before this idea triumphed. By the end of 1865, the Radical Republicans' views had gained a majority in Congress, if one not yet large enough to override presidential vetoes. But the critical year of 1866 saw the gradual waning of Andrew Johnson's power and influence, much of which was self-induced. Johnson first challenged Congress in 1866, when he vetoed a bill to extend the life of the Freedmen's Bureau. The measure, he said, violated the Constitution in several ways: it made the federal government responsible for the care of indigents, it was passed by a Congress in which

"The Cruel Uncle and the Vetoed Babes in the Wood"

A cartoon depicting Andrew Johnson leading two children, "Civil Rights" and "Bureau," into the "Veto Wood."

eleven ex-Confederate states had been denied seats, and it used vague language in defining the "civil rights and immunities" of African Americans. For the time being, Johnson's prestige remained sufficiently intact that the Senate upheld his veto.

Three days after the veto, however, during an impromptu speech, Johnson undermined his already weakening authority with a fiery assault upon the Radical Republican leaders. From that point forward, moderate Republicans deserted a president who had opened himself to counterattack. The Radical Republicans took the offensive. Johnson was "an alien enemy of a foreign state," Stevens declared. Sumner called him "an insolent drunken brute," a charge Johnson was open to because of his behavior at the 1865 inauguration.

In mid-March 1866 the Radical-led Congress passed the Civil Rights Act. A response to the black codes and the neo-slavery system created by unrepentant southern state legislatures, it declared that "all persons born in the United States and not subject to any foreign power, excluding Indians not taxed," were citizens entitled to "full and equal benefit of all laws." The granting of citizenship to native-born blacks, Johnson fumed, exceeded the scope of federal power. It would, moreover, "foment discord among the races." Johnson vetoed the bill, but this time, on April 9, Congress overrode the presidential veto. On July 16 it enacted a revised Freedmen's Bureau Bill, again overriding a veto. From that point on, Johnson steadily lost both public and political support.

THE FOURTEENTH AMENDMENT   To remove all doubt about the constitutionality of the new Civil Rights Act, the joint committee recommended a new constitutional amendment, which passed Congress on June 16, 1866, and was ratified by the states on July 28, 1868. The Fourteenth Amendment went far beyond the Civil Rights Act, however. It reaffirms the state and federal citizenship of persons born or naturalized in the United States,

and it forbids any state (the word *state* would be important in later litiga-
tion) to "abridge the privileges or immunities of citizens," to deprive any
person (again an important term) "of life, liberty, or property, without due
process of law," or to "deny any person . . . the equal protection of the
laws." These three clauses have been the subject of many lawsuits, resulting
in applications not widely, if at all, foreseen at the time. The "due-process
clause" has come to mean that state as well as federal power is subject to the
Bill of Rights, and it has been used to protect corporations, as legal "persons," from "unreasonable" regulation by the states. Other provisions of the
amendment have had less far-reaching effects. One section specified that
the debt of the United States "shall not be questioned" by the former Confederate states and declared "illegal and void" all debts contracted in aid of
the rebellion.

Johnson's home state was among the first to ratify the Fourteenth Amendment. In Tennessee, which had more Unionists than any other Confederate
state, the government had fallen under Radical Republican control. The
state's governor, in reporting the results to the secretary of the Senate, added,
"Give my respects to the dead dog of the White House." His words illustrate
the growing acrimony on both sides of the Reconstruction debates. In May
and July, race riots in Memphis and New Orleans added fuel to the flames.
Both incidents involved indiscriminate massacres of blacks by local police
and white mobs. The carnage, Radical Republicans argued, was the natural
fruit of Andrew Johnson's lenient policy. "Witness Memphis, witness New
Orleans," Senator Sumner cried. "Who can doubt that the President is the
author of these tragedies?"

RECONSTRUCTING THE SOUTH

THE TRIUMPH OF CONGRESSIONAL RECONSTRUCTION   As
1866 drew to an end, the congressional elections promised to be a referendum on the growing split between Andrew Johnson and the Radical Republicans. To win votes, Johnson went on a speaking tour of the Midwest, which
turned into an undignified shouting contest between the president and his
critics. In Cleveland he described the Radical Republicans as "factious, domineering, tyrannical" men, and he foolishly exchanged hot-tempered insults
with a heckler. At another stop, while Johnson was speaking from the back
of a railway car, the engineer mistakenly pulled the train out of the station,
making the president appear quite the fool. Such incidents tended to confirm
his image as a "ludicrous boor" and a "drunken imbecile," which Radical

Republicans promoted. The 1866 congressional elections were a devastating defeat for Johnson; Republicans won more than a two-thirds majority in each house, a comfortable margin with which to override presidential vetoes.

Congress in fact enacted a new program even before the new members took office. Two acts passed in 1867 extended voting rights to African Americans in the District of Columbia and the territories. Another law provided that the new Congress would convene on March 4 instead of the following December, depriving Johnson of a breathing spell. On March 2, 1867, two days before the old Congress expired, it passed, over Johnson's vetoes, three laws promoting congressional Reconstruction: the Military Reconstruction Act, the Command of the Army Act (an amendment to an army appropriation), and the Tenure of Office Act.

The first of the three acts prescribed conditions under which the formation of southern state governments should begin all over again. The other two sought to block any effort by the president to obstruct the process. The Command of the Army Act required that all orders from the commander in chief go through the headquarters of the general of the army, then Ulysses Grant. The Radical Republicans trusted Grant, who was already leaning their way. The Tenure of Office Act required Senate permission for the president to remove any federal officeholder whose appointment the Senate had confirmed. The purpose of at least some congressmen was to retain Secretary of War Edwin Stanton, the one Radical Republican sympathizer in Johnson's cabinet. But an ambiguity had crept into the wording of the act. Cabinet officers, it said, should serve during the term of the president who appointed them—and Lincoln had appointed Stanton, although, to be sure, Johnson was serving out Lincoln's term.

The Military Reconstruction Act was hailed—or denounced—as the triumphant victory of Radical Reconstruction. The act declared that "no legal state governments or adequate protection for life and property now exists in the rebel States." One state, Tennessee, which had ratified the Fourteenth Amendment, was exempted from the application of the new act. The other ten southern states were divided into five military districts, and the commanding officer of each was authorized to keep order and protect the "rights of persons and property." The Johnson governments remained intact for the time being, but new constitutions were to be framed "in conformity with the Constitution of the United States," in state conventions elected by male citizens aged twenty-one and older "of whatever race, color, or previous condition." Each state constitution had to provide the same universal male suffrage. Then, once the constitution was ratified by a majority of voters and accepted by Congress, other criteria had to be met. The new state legislature had to ratify the Fourteenth Amendment, and once the amendment became part of the Constitution, any given state would be entitled to representation in Congress. Persons excluded from officeholding by the proposed amendment were also excluded from participation in the process.

Johnson reluctantly appointed military commanders under the new act, but the situation remained uncertain for a time. Some people expected the Supreme Court to strike down the act, and no process existed for the new elections. Congress quickly remedied that on March 23, 1867, with the Second Reconstruction Act, which directed the army commanders to register all adult men who swore they were qualified. A Third Reconstruction Act, passed on July 19, directed registrars to go beyond the loyalty oath and determine each person's eligibility to take it and authorized district army commanders to remove and replace officeholders of any existing "so-called state" or division thereof. Before the end of 1867, new elections had been held in all the states but Texas.

Having clipped the president's wings, the Republican Congress moved a year later to safeguard its Reconstruction program from possible interference by the Supreme Court. On March 27, 1868, Congress simply removed the power of the Supreme Court to review cases arising under the Military Reconstruction Act, which Congress clearly had the right to do under its power to define the Court's appellate jurisdiction. The Court accepted this curtailment of its authority on the same day it affirmed the principle of an "indestructible Union" in *Texas v. White* (1869). In that case the Court also asserted the right of Congress to reframe state governments, thus endorsing the Radical Republican point of view.

THE IMPEACHMENT AND TRIAL OF JOHNSON By 1868, Radical Republicans were convinced not only that the power of the Supreme Court and the president needed to be curtailed but also that Andrew Johnson himself had to be removed from office. Johnson, though hostile to the congressional Reconstruction program, had gone through the motions required of him. He continued to pardon former Confederates, however, and transferred several of the district military commanders who had displayed Radical sympathies. Johnson lacked Lincoln's resilience and pragmatism and allowed his temper to get the better of his judgment. He castigated the Radical Republicans as "a gang of cormorants and bloodsuckers who have been fattening upon the country."

The Republicans unsuccessfully tried to impeach Johnson early in 1867, alleging a variety of flimsy charges, none of which represented an indictable crime. Then Johnson himself provided the occasion for impeachment when he deliberately violated the Tenure of Office Act in order to test its constitutionality. Secretary of War Edwin Stanton had become a thorn in Johnson's side, refusing to resign despite his disagreements with the president's Reconstruction policy. On August 12, 1867, during a congressional recess, Johnson suspended Stanton and named General Ulysses S. Grant in his place. When the Senate refused to confirm Johnson's action, however, Grant returned the office to Stanton.

The Radical Republicans now saw their chance to remove the president. On February 24, 1868, the Republican-dominated House passed eleven articles of impeachment by a party-line vote of 126 to 47. Of the eleven articles, eight focused on the charge that Johnson had unlawfully removed Secretary of War Stanton. Article 9 accused the president of issuing orders in violation of the Command of the Army Act. The last two articles of impeachment in effect claimed that the president had undermined Congress by "inflammatory and scandalous harangues." Article 11 also accused him of "unlawfully devising and contriving" to violate the Reconstruction Acts, contrary to his obligation to execute the laws. At the very least, it stated, Johnson had tried to obstruct Congress's will while observing the letter of the law.

The trial of Andrew Johnson

House of Representatives managers of the impeachment proceedings. Among them were Benjamin Franklin Butler (Republican of Massachusetts, seated left) and Thaddeus Stevens (Republican of Pennsylvania, seated with cane).

The Senate trial began on March 5, 1868, and continued until May 26, with Chief Justice Salmon P. Chase presiding. It was a great spectacle before a packed gallery. As the five-week trial ended and the voting began in May 1868, seven moderate Republicans and all twelve Democrats voted to acquit. The final tally was 35 to 19 for conviction, only one vote short of the two thirds needed for removal from office. Although the Senate failed to remove Johnson, the trial crippled his already weakened presidency. During the remaining ten months of his term, he initiated no other clashes with Congress. In 1868, Johnson sought the Democratic presidential nomination but lost to New York governor Horatio Seymour, who then lost to the Republican, Ulysses Grant, in the general election. The impeachment of Johnson was in the end a great political mistake, for the failure to remove the president damaged Radical Republican morale and support. Nevertheless, the Radical cause did gain something: to stave off impeachment, Johnson agreed not to obstruct the process of Reconstruction. Thereafter Radical Reconstruction began in earnest.

REPUBLICAN RULE IN THE SOUTH   In June 1868, Congress agreed that seven southern states, all but Virginia, Mississippi, and Texas, had met the more stringent conditions for readmission to the Union. Congress rescinded Georgia's admission, however, when the state legislature expelled twenty-eight African American members and seated former Confederate leaders. The federal military commander in Georgia then forced the legislature to reseat the black members and remove the Confederates, and the state was compelled to ratify the Fifteenth Amendment before being admitted in July 1870. Mississippi, Texas, and Virginia had returned earlier in 1870, under the added requirement that they, too, ratify the Fifteenth Amendment. That amendment, submitted to the states in 1869 and ratified in 1870, forbids the states to deny any person the vote on grounds of "race, color, or previous condition of servitude."

Long before the new governments were established, Republican groups had begun to spring up in the South, chiefly sponsored by the Union League, founded in Philadelphia in 1862 to promote support for the Union. League recruiters in the South enrolled African Americans and loyal whites, initiated them into the secrets and rituals of the order, and instructed them "in their rights and duties." Their recruiting efforts were so successful that in 1867, on the eve of South Carolina's choice of convention delegates, the league reported eighty-eight chapters, which claimed to have enrolled almost every adult black male in the state.

The Reconstructed South

THE FREED SLAVES African Americans in the postwar South were active agents in affecting the course of Reconstruction. It was not an easy road, though. Many former Confederates displayed deeply ingrained racial prejudices. During the era of Reconstruction, whites used terror, intimidation, and violence to suppress black efforts to gain social and economic equality. In July 1866, for instance, a black woman in Clinch County, Georgia, was arrested and given sixty-five lashes for "using abusive language" during an encounter with a white woman. The Civil War had brought freedom to enslaved African Americans, but it did not bring them protection against exploitation or abuse.

Participation in the Union army or navy had provided many freedmen with training in leadership. Black military veterans would form the core of the first generation of African American political leaders in the postwar South. Military service provided many former slaves with the first opportunities to learn to read and write. Army life also alerted them to new opportunities for economic advancement, social respectability, and civic leadership. Fighting for the Union cause also instilled a fervent sense of nationalism. A Virginia freedman explained that the United States was "now *our* country—made emphatically so by the blood of our brethren."

Former slaves established churches after the war, which quickly formed the foundation of African American community life. Blacks preferred the Baptist denomination, in part because its decentralized structure allowed each congregation to worship in its own way. By 1890 over 1.3 million African Americans in the South had become Baptists, nearly three times as many as had joined any other black denomination. In addition to forming viable new congregations, freed African Americans organized thousands of fraternal, benevolent, and mutual-aid societies, as well as clubs, lodges, and associations. Memphis, for example, had over 200 such organizations; Richmond boasted twice that number.

Freed slaves also hastened to reestablish their families. Marriages that had been prohibited during slavery were now legitimized through the assistance of the Freedmen's Bureau. By 1870 a preponderant majority of former slaves were living in two-parent households. With little money or technical training, freed slaves faced the prospect of becoming wage laborers. Yet many husbands and wives instead chose sharecropping, in which the crop produced was divided between the tenant and the landowner. This choice enabled mothers and wives to devote more of their time to domestic duties while contributing to the family's income.

The First African Church

On the eve of its move to a new building, the First African Church of Richmond, Virginia, was featured in a short article, including illustrations such as the one above, in *Harper's Weekly*, in June 1874.

African American communities in the postwar South also sought to establish schools. The antebellum planter elite had denied education to blacks because they feared that literate slaves would read abolitionist literature and organize uprisings. After the war the white elite worried that formal education would encourage poor whites and poor blacks to leave the South in search of better social and economic opportunities. Economic leaders wanted to protect the competitive advantage afforded by the region's low-wage labor market. "They didn't want us to learn nothin'," one former slave recalled. "The only thing we had to learn was how to work." White opposition to education for blacks made education all the more important to African Americans. South Carolina's Mary McLeod Bethune, the fifteenth child of former slaves, reveled in the opportunity to gain an education: "The whole world opened to me when I learned to read." She walked five miles to school as a child, earned a scholarship to college, and went on to become the first black woman to found a school that became a four-year college, Bethune-Cookman, in Daytona Beach, Florida. African American churches and individuals helped raise the money and often built the schools and paid the teachers. Soldiers who had acquired some literacy skills often served as the teachers, and the students included adults as well as children.

AFRICAN AMERICANS IN SOUTHERN POLITICS In the postwar South the new role of African Americans in politics caused the most controversy. If largely illiterate and inexperienced in the rudiments of politics, southern blacks were little different from the millions of newly enfranchized propertyless whites in the age of Andrew Jackson's political reforms or immigrants in postwar cities. Some freedmen frankly confessed their disadvantages. Beverly Nash, an African American delegate to the South Carolina convention of 1868, told his colleagues: "I believe, my friends and fellow-citizens, we are not prepared for this suffrage. But we can learn. Give a man tools and let him commence to use them, and in time he will learn a trade. So it is with voting."

Several hundred African American delegates participated in the statewide political conventions. Most had been selected by local political meetings or churches, fraternal societies, Union Leagues, or black army units from the North, although a few simply appointed themselves. The African American delegates "ranged all colors and apparently all conditions," but free mulattoes from the cities played the most prominent roles. At Louisiana's Republican

Freedmen voting in New Orleans

The Fifteenth Amendment, ratified in 1870, guaranteed at the federal level the right of citizens to vote regardless of "race, color, or previous condition of servitude." But former slaves had been registering to vote—and voting in large numbers—in state elections since 1867, as in this scene.

state convention, for instance, nineteen of the twenty black delegates had been born free.

By 1867, however, former slaves had begun to gain political influence and vote in large numbers, and this development revealed emerging tensions within the African American community. Some southern blacks resented the presence of northern brethren who moved south after the war, while others complained that few ex-slaves were represented in leadership positions. Northern blacks and the southern free black elite, most of whom were urban dwellers, often opposed efforts to redistribute land to the rural freedmen, and many insisted that political equality did not mean social equality. As a black Alabama leader stressed, "We do not ask that the ignorant and degraded shall be put on a social equality with the refined and intelligent." In general, however, unity rather than dissension prevailed, and African Americans focused on common concerns such as full equality under the law.

Brought suddenly into politics in times that tried the most skilled of statesmen, many African Americans served with distinction. Nonetheless, the derisive label "black Reconstruction," used by later critics, exaggerates

African American political figures of Reconstruction

Blanche K. Bruce (left) and Hiram Revels (right) served in the U.S. Senate. Frederick Douglass (center) was a major figure in the abolitionist movement.

African American political influence, which was limited mainly to voting. Such criticism also overlooks the political clout of the large number of white Republicans, especially in the mountain areas of the Upper South, who also favored the Radical plan for Reconstruction. Only one of the new state conventions, South Carolina's, had a black majority, seventy-six to forty-one. Louisiana's was evenly divided racially, and in only two other conventions were more than 20 percent of the members black: Florida's, with 40 percent, and Virginia's, with 24 percent. The Texas convention was only 10 percent black, and North Carolina's was 11 percent—but that did not stop a white newspaper from calling it a body consisting of "baboons, monkeys, mules . . . and other jackasses."

In the new state governments any African American participation was a novelty. Although some 600 blacks—most of them former slaves—served as state legislators, no black man was ever elected governor, and only a few served as judges. In Louisiana, however, Pinckney Pinchback, a northern black and former Union soldier, won the office of lieutenant governor and served as acting governor when the white governor was indicted for corruption. Several African Americans were elected lieutenant governor, state treasurer, or secretary of state. There were two black senators in Congress, Hiram Revels and Blanche K. Bruce, both Mississippi natives who had been educated in the North, and fourteen black members of the House of Representatives during Reconstruction.

CARPETBAGGERS AND SCALAWAGS   The top positions in postwar southern state governments went for the most part to white Republicans, whom the opposition whites labeled carpetbaggers and scalawags, depending upon their place of birth. Northerners who allegedly rushed South with all their belongings in carpetbags to grab the political spoils were more often than not Union veterans who had arrived as early as 1865 or 1866, drawn South by the hope of economic opportunity and other attractions that many of them had seen in their Union service. Many other so-called carpetbaggers were teachers, social workers, or preachers animated by a sincere missionary impulse.

The scalawags, or native white Republicans, were even more reviled and misrepresented. A Nashville newspaper editor called them the "merest trash." Most scalawags had opposed secession, forming a Unionist majority in many mountain counties as far south as Georgia and Alabama and especially in the hills of eastern Tennessee. Among the scalawags were several distinguished figures, including the former Confederate general James Longstreet, who decided after Appomattox that the Old South must change its ways. He became a successful cotton broker in New Orleans, joined the Republican party, and supported the Radical Reconstruction program. Other scalawags were former Whigs attracted by the Republican party's economic program of industrial and commercial expansion.

THE RADICAL REPUBLICAN RECORD Former Confederates resented the new state constitutions because of their provisions allowing for black voting and civil rights. Yet most of those constitutions remained in effect for some years after the end of Radical Republican control, and later constitutions incorporated many of their features. Conspicuous among the Radical innovations were such steps toward greater democracy as requiring

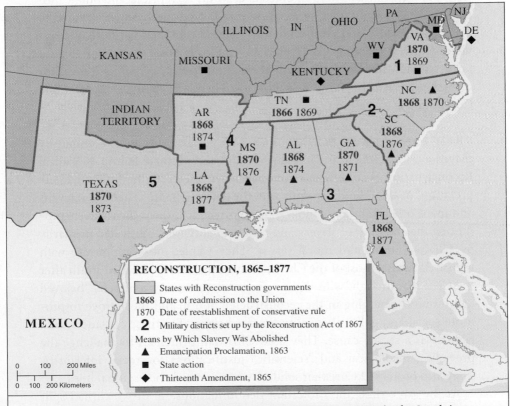

RECONSTRUCTION, 1865–1877

States with Reconstruction governments
1868 Date of readmission to the Union
1870 Date of reestablishment of conservative rule
2 Military districts set up by the Reconstruction Act of 1867
Means by Which Slavery Was Abolished
▲ Emancipation Proclamation, 1863
■ State action
◆ Thirteenth Amendment, 1865

How did the Military Reconstruction Act reorganize governments in the South in the late 1860s and 1870s? What did the former Confederate states have to do to be readmitted to the Union? Why did "Conservative" parties gradually regain control of the South from the Republicans in the 1870s?

universal manhood suffrage, reapportioning legislatures more nearly according to population, and making more state offices elective.

Given the hostile circumstances under which the Radical governments operated, their achievements were remarkable. They constructed an extensive
railroad network and established state-supported public school systems. Some
600,000 black pupils were enrolled in southern schools by 1877. State governments under the Radicals also gave more attention to the poor and to orphan-
ages, asylums, and institutions for the deaf and the blind of both races. Public
roads, bridges, and buildings were repaired or rebuilt. African Americans
achieved rights and opportunities that would never again be taken away, at
least in principle: equality before the law and the rights to own property, carry
on business, enter professions, attend schools, and learn to read and write.

Yet several of these Republican state regimes also engaged in corrupt practices. Bids for contracts were accepted at absurdly high prices, and public officials took their cut. Public money and public credit were often awarded to
privately owned corporations, notably railroads, under conditions that invited influence peddling. Corruption was not invented by the Radical Republican regimes, nor did it die with them. Louisiana's "carpetbag" governor
recognized as much. "Why," he said, "down here everybody is demoralized.
Corruption is the fashion."

RELIGION AND RECONSTRUCTION The religious community
played a critical role in the implementation and ultimate failure of Radical
Reconstruction. And religious commentators offered quite different interpretations of what should be done with the defeated South. Thaddeus Stevens
and many other Radical Republican leaders who had spent their careers promoting the abolition of slavery and racial equality were motivated primarily
by religious ideals and moral fervor. They wanted no compromise with
racism. Likewise, most of the Christian missionaries who headed south after
the Civil War brought with them a progressive vision of a biracial "beloved
community" emerging in the reconstructed South, and they strove to promote social and political equality for freed slaves. For these crusaders, civil
rights was a sacred cause. They used Christian principles to challenge the
prevailing theological and "scientific" justifications for racial inferiority.
They also promoted Christian solidarity across racial and regional lines.

At the same time, the Protestant denominations, all of which had split
into northern and southern branches over the issues of slavery and secession, struggled to reunite after the war. A growing number of northern ministers promoted reconciliation between the warring regions after the Civil
War. These "apostles of forgiveness" prized white unity over racial equality.

For example, the Reverend Henry Ward Beecher, the powerful New York minister whose sister Harriet Beecher Stowe wrote *Uncle Tom's Cabin*, wanted white southern planters—rather than federal officials or African Americans themselves—to oversee Reconstruction. Not surprisingly, Beecher's views gained widespread support among evangelical ministers in the South.

The collapse of the Confederacy did not prompt southern whites to abandon their belief that God was on their side. In the wake of defeat and emancipation, white southern ministers reassured their congregations that they had no reason to question the moral foundations of their region or their defense of white racial superiority. For African Americans, the Civil War and emancipation demonstrated

The "white republic"

This cartoon illustrates white unity over racial equality.

that God was on their side. Emancipation was in their view a redemptive act through which God wrought national regeneration. African American ministers were convinced that the United States was indeed a divinely inspired nation and that blacks had a providential role to play in its future. Yet neither black nor idealistic white northern ministers could stem the growing chorus of whites who were willing to abandon goals of racial equality in exchange for national religious reconciliation. By the end of the nineteenth century, mainstream American Protestantism promoted the image of a "white republic" that conflated whiteness, godliness, and nationalism.

THE GRANT YEARS

THE ELECTION OF 1868   Ulysses S. Grant, who presided during the collapse of Republican rule in the South, brought to the White House little political experience. But in 1868 northern voters supported the Lion of Vicksburg because of his record as the Union army commander. He was the most popular man in the nation. Both parties wooed him, but his falling-out with President Johnson had pushed him toward the Republicans. They were,

"The Working-Man's Banner"

This campaign banner makes reference to the working-class origins of Ulysses S. Grant and his vice-presidential candidate, Henry Wilson, by depicting Grant as a tanner and Wilson as a shoemaker.

as Thaddeus Stevens said, ready to "let him into the church."

The Republican party platform of 1868 endorsed congressional Reconstruction. One plank cautiously defended black suffrage as a necessity in the South but a matter each northern state should settle for itself. Another urged payment of the national debt "in the utmost good faith to all creditors," which meant in gold. More important than the platform were the great expectations of a soldier-president and his slogan, "Let us have peace."

The Democrats took opposite positions on both Reconstruction and the debt. The Republican Congress, the Democratic party platform charged, instead of restoring the Union had "so far as in its power, dissolved it, and subjected ten states, in the time of profound peace, to military despotism and Negro supremacy." As for the federal debt, the party endorsed Representative George H. Pendleton's "Ohio idea" that, since most war bonds had been bought with depreciated greenbacks, they should be paid off in greenbacks rather than in gold. With no conspicuously available candidate in sight, the Democratic Convention turned to Horatio Seymour, wartime governor of New York. Seymour neither sought nor embraced the nomination, leading opponents to call him the Great Decliner. Yet the Democrats made a closer race of it than the electoral vote revealed. While Grant swept the Electoral College by 214 to 80, his popular majority was only 307,000 out of a total of over 5.7 million votes. More than 500,000 African American voters accounted for Grant's margin of victory.

Grant had proved himself a great military leader, but as the youngest president ever (forty-six years old at the time of his inauguration), he was often blind to the political forces and influence peddlers around him. He was awestruck by men of wealth and unaccountably loyal to some who betrayed his trust, and he passively followed the lead of Congress. This approach at first endeared him to Republican party leaders, but at last it left him ineffective and others disillusioned with his leadership.

At the outset, Grant consulted nobody on his seven cabinet appointments. Some of his choices indulged personal whims; others simply displayed bad judgment. In some cases, appointees learned of their nomination from the newspapers. As time went by, Grant betrayed a fatal gift for losing men of talent and integrity from his cabinet. Secretary of State Hamilton Fish of New York turned out to be a happy exception; he guided foreign policy throughout the Grant presidency. Other than Fish, however, the Grant cabinet overflowed with incompetents.

THE GOVERNMENT DEBT Financial issues dominated Grant's presidency. After the war the Treasury had assumed that the $432 million worth of greenbacks issued during the conflict would be retired from circulation and that the nation would revert to a "hard-money" currency—gold coins. Many agrarian and debtor groups resisted any contraction of the money supply resulting from the elimination of greenbacks, believing that it would mean lower prices for their crops and more difficulty repaying long-term debts. They were joined by a large number of Radical Republicans who thought that a combination of high tariffs and inflation would generate more rapid economic growth. As Senator John Sherman explained, "I prefer gold to paper money. But there is no other resort. We must have money or a fractured government." In 1868 congressional supporters of such a "soft-money" policy halted the retirement of greenbacks. There matters stood when Grant took office.

The "sound-money" (or hard-money) advocates, mostly bankers and merchants, claimed that Grant's election was a mandate to save the country from the Democrats' "Ohio idea" of using greenbacks to repay government bonds. Quite influential in Republican circles, the hard-money advocates also reflected the deeply ingrained popular assumption that gold coins were morally preferable to paper currency. Grant agreed as well, and in his inaugural address he endorsed payment of the national debt in gold as a point of national honor. On March 18, 1869, the Public Credit Act, which endorsed that principle, became the first act of Congress that Grant signed. The following year, under the Refunding Act of 1870, the Treasury was able to replace 6 percent Civil War bonds with a new bond issue promising purchasers a return of 4 to 5 percent in gold.

SCANDALS   The complexities of the "money question" exasperated Grant, but that was the least of his worries, for his administration soon fell into a cesspool of scandal. In the summer of 1869, two unscrupulous financial buccaneers, Jay Gould and James Fisk, connived with the president's brother-in-law to corner the nation's gold market. That is, they would create a public craze for gold by purchasing massive quantities of the precious yellow metal and convincing traders and the general public that the price would keep climbing. As more buyers joined the frenzy, the value of gold would soar. The only danger to the scheme lay in the federal Treasury's selling large amounts of gold, which would deflate its value.

Grant apparently smelled a rat from the start, but he was seen in public with the speculators. As the rumor spread on Wall Street that the president had bought the argument, gold rose from $132 to $163 an ounce. Finally, on Black Friday, September 24, 1869, Grant ordered the Treasury to sell a large quantity of gold, and the bubble burst. Fisk got out by repudiating his agreements and hiring thugs to intimidate his creditors. "Nothing is lost save honor," he said.

The plot to corner the gold market was only the first of several scandals that rocked the Grant administration. During the campaign of 1872, the public learned about the financial crookery of the Crédit Mobilier, a sham construction company composed of directors of the Union Pacific Railroad who had milked the Union Pacific for exorbitant fees in order to line the pockets of the insiders who controlled both firms. Union Pacific shareholders were left holding the bag. The schemers bought political support by giving congressmen stock in the enterprise. This chicanery had transpired before Grant's election in 1868, but it now touched a number of prominent Republicans. The beneficiaries included Speaker of the House Schuyler Colfax, later vice president, and Representative James A. Garfield, later president. Of the thirteen members of Congress involved, only two were censured.

Even more odious disclosures soon followed, some involving the president's cabinet. The secretary of war, it turned out, had accepted bribes from merchants who traded with Indians at army posts in the West. He was impeached, but he resigned in time to elude a Senate trial. Post-office contracts, it was revealed, went to carriers who offered the highest kickbacks. The secretary of the Treasury had awarded a political friend a commission of 50 percent for the collection of overdue taxes. In St. Louis a "whiskey ring" bribed tax collectors to bilk the government out of millions of dollars in revenue. Grant's private secretary was enmeshed in that scheme, taking large sums of money and other valuables in return for inside information. There is no evidence that Grant himself was ever involved in, or personally profited from, any of the fraud, but his poor choice of associates and his gullibility earned him widespread criticism.

WHITE TERROR President Grant initially fought hard to enforce the federal efforts to reconstruct the postwar South. By the time he became president, southern resistance to "Radical rule" had turned violent. In Grayson County, Texas, three whites murdered three former slaves because they felt the need to "thin the niggers out and drive them to their holes."

"Worse Than Slavery"

This Thomas Nast cartoon chides the Ku Klux Klan and the White League for promoting conditions "worse than slavery" for southern blacks after the Civil War.

The prototype of all the terrorist groups was the Ku Klux Klan (KKK), organized in 1866 by some young men of Pulaski, Tennessee, as a social club, with the costumes and secret rituals common to fraternal groups. At first a group of pranksters, its members soon turned to intimidation of blacks and white Republicans. The KKK and its imitators, like Louisiana's Knights of the White Camelia, spread rapidly across the South in answer to the Republican party's Union League. Klansmen rode about the countryside, hiding behind masks and under robes, spreading horrendous rumors, issuing threats, harassing African Americans, and occasionally wreaking violence and destruction. "We are going to kill all the Negros," a white supremacist declared during one massacre.

Klansmen focused their terror on prominent Republicans, black and white. Racial violence was widespread and horrific. In Mississippi they killed a black Republican leader in front of his family. Three white "scalawag" Republicans were murdered in Georgia in 1870. That same year an armed mob of whites assaulted a Republican political rally in Alabama, killing four blacks and wounding fifty-four. In South Carolina white supremacists were especially active—and violent. Virtually the entire white male population of York County joined the Klan, and they were responsible for eleven murders and hundreds of whippings. In 1871 some 500 masked men laid siege to the Union County jail and eventually lynched eight black prisoners.

At the urging of President Grant, who showed true moral courage in try-ing to protect the former slaves, Congress struck back with three Enforce-ment Acts (1870–1871) to protect black voters. The first of these measures levied penalties on anyone who interfered with any citizen's right to vote. A second placed the election of congressmen under surveillance by federal election supervisors and marshals. The third (the Ku Klux Klan Act) out-lawed the characteristic activities of the Klan—forming conspiracies, wear-ing disguises, resisting officers, and intimidating officials—and authorized the president to suspend habeas corpus where necessary to suppress "armed combinations." In 1871 the federal government singled out nine counties in up-country South Carolina as an example, suspended habeas corpus, and pursued mass prosecutions. In general, however, the Enforcement Acts suf-fered from weak and inconsistent execution. As time passed, President Grant vacillated between clamping down on the Klan and capitulating to racial intimidation. The strong tradition of states' rights and local autonomy in the South, as well as racial prejudice, resisted federal force. The unrelenting efforts of white racists to use violence to thwart Reconstruction continued into the 1870s. On Easter Sunday in 1873 in Colfax, Louisiana, a mob of white vigilantes attacked a group of black Republicans, slaughtering eighty-one. White southerners had lost the war, but during the 1870s they were winning the peace with their reactionary behavior. In the process, the goals of racial justice and civil rights were blunted.

REFORM AND THE ELECTION OF 1872   Long before President Grant's first term ended, a reaction to Radical Reconstruction and incompe-tence and corruption in the administration had incited mutiny within the Republican ranks. A new faction, called Liberal Republicans, favored free trade, the redemption of greenbacks with gold, a stable currency, an end to federal Re-construction efforts in the South, the restoration of the rights of former Con-federates, and civil service reform. In 1872 the Liberal Republicans held their own national convention, in which they produced a compromise platform condemning the Republicans' Reconstruction policy and favoring civil service reform, but they remained silent on the protective tariff. The delegates em-braced a quixotic presidential candidate: Horace Greeley, the prominent editor of the *New York Tribune*, a longtime champion of just about every reform available. Greeley had promoted vegetarianism, socialism, and spiritualism. His image as an eccentric was complemented by his record of hostility to the Democrats, whose support the Liberals needed. The Democrats nevertheless swallowed the pill and gave their nomination to Greeley as the only hope of beating Grant.

"What I Know about Raising the Devil"

With the tail and cloven hoof of the devil, Horace Greeley (center) leads a small band of Liberal Republicans in pursuit of incumbent president Ulysses S. Grant and his supporters in this 1872 cartoon.

The result was a foregone conclusion. Republican regulars duly endorsed Grant, Radical Reconstruction, and the protective tariff. Greeley, despite an exhausting tour of the country—still unusual for a presidential candidate—carried only six southern and border states and none in the North. Grant won by 3,598,235 votes to Greeley's 2,834,761.

CONSERVATIVE RESURGENCE   The Klan's impact on southern politics varied from state to state. In the Upper South it played only a modest role in facilitating a Democratic resurgence. But in the Deep South, Klan violence and intimidation had more substantial effects. In overwhelmingly black Yazoo County, Mississippi, vengeful whites used violence to reverse the political balance of power. In the 1873 elections the Republicans cast 2,449 votes and the Democrats 638; two years later the Democrats polled 4,049 votes, the Republicans 7. Throughout the South the activities of the Klan and other white supremacists weakened black and Republican morale, and in the North they encouraged a growing weariness with the whole "southern question." "The plain truth is," noted *The New York Herald*, "the North has got tired of the Negro."

The erosion of northern interest in civil rights resulted from more than weariness, however. Western expansion, Indian wars, new economic opportunities, and political controversy over the tariff and the currency distracted attention from southern outrages against Republican rule and black rights. In addition, after a business panic that occurred in 1873 and an ensuing depression, desperate economic circumstances in the North and the South created new racial tensions that helped undermine federal efforts to promote racial justice in the former Confederacy. Republican control in the South gradually loosened as "Conservative" parties—a name used by Democrats to mollify former Whigs— mobilized the white vote. Prewar political leaders reemerged to promote the antebellum Democratic goals of limited government, states' rights, and free trade. They politicized the race issue to excite the white electorate and intimidate black voters. The Republicans in the South became increasingly an organization limited to African Americans and federal officials. Many scalawags and carpetbaggers drifted away from the Radical Republican ranks under pressure from their white neighbors. Few of them had joined the Republicans out of concern for black rights in the first place. And where persuasion failed to work, Democrats were willing to use chicanery. As one enthusiastic Democrat boasted, "The white and black Republicans may outvote us, but we can outcount them."

Republican political control collapsed in Virginia and Tennessee as early as 1869; in Georgia and North Carolina it collapsed in 1870, although North Carolina had a Republican governor until 1876. Reconstruction lasted longest in the Deep South states with the largest black population, where whites abandoned Klan masks for barefaced intimidation in paramilitary groups such as the Mississippi Rifle Club and the South Carolina Red Shirts. By 1876, Radical Republican regimes survived only in Louisiana, South Carolina, and Florida, and those collapsed after the elections of that year.

PANIC AND REDEMPTION   Economic distress followed close upon the public scandals besetting the Grant administration. Such developments help explain why northerners lost interest in Reconstruction. A contraction of the nation's money supply resulting from the withdrawal of greenbacks and investments in new railroads helped precipitate a financial crisis. During 1873 the market for railroad bonds turned sour as some twenty-five railroads defaulted on their interest payments. The prestigious investment bank of Jay Cooke and Company went bankrupt on September 18, 1873. The ensuing stampede of investors eager to exchange securities for cash forced the stock market to close for ten days. The panic of 1873 set off a depression that lasted six years, the longest and most severe that Americans had yet suffered.

Thousands of businesses went bankrupt, millions of people lost their jobs, and as usually occurs, voters blamed the party in power for their economic woes.

Hard times and political scandals hurt Republicans in the midterm elections of 1874. The Democrats won control of the House of Representatives and gained seats in the Senate. The new Democratic House launched inquiries into the scandals and unearthed further evidence of corruption in high places. The financial panic, meanwhile, focused attention once more on greenback currency.

Since the value of greenbacks was lower than that of gold, greenbacks had become the chief circulating medium. Most people spent greenbacks first and held their gold or used it to settle foreign accounts, thereby draining much gold out of the country. The postwar reduction of greenbacks in circulation, from $432 million to $356 million, had made for tight money. To relieve the currency shortage and stimulate business expansion, the Treasury issued more greenbacks. As usually happened during economic hard times in the nineteenth century, debtors, the people hurt most by depression, called upon the federal government to inflate the money supply so as to make it easier for them to pay their obligations.

For a time the advocates of paper money were riding high. But in 1874, Grant vetoed a bill to issue more greenbacks. Then, in his annual message, he called for the redemption of greenbacks in gold, making greenbacks "good as gold" and raising their value to a par with that of the gold dollar. Congress obliged by passing the Specie Resumption Act of 1875. The payment in gold to people who turned in their paper money began on January 1, 1879, after the Treasury had built a gold reserve for that purpose and reduced the value of the greenbacks in circulation. This act infuriated those promoting an inflationary monetary policy and prompted the formation of the Greenback party, which elected fourteen congressmen in 1878. The much-debated and very complex "money question" was destined to remain one of the most divisive issues in American politics.

THE COMPROMISE OF 1877   President Grant, despite the controversies swirling around him, wanted to run again in 1876, but many Republicans balked at the prospect of the nation's first three-term president. After all, the Democrats had devastated the Republicans in the 1874 congressional elections: the decisive Republican majority in the House had evaporated, and the Democrats had taken control. In the summer of 1875, Grant acknowledged the growing opposition to his renomination and announced his retirement. James Gillespie Blaine of Maine, former Speaker of the House and one of the

The Compromise of 1877

This illustration represents the compromise between Republicans and southern Democrats that ended Radical Reconstruction.

nation's favorite orators, emerged as the Republican front-runner, but he, too, bore the taint of scandal. Letters in the possession of James Mulligan of Boston linked Blaine to dubious railroad dealings, and the "Mulligan letters" found their way into print.

The Republican Convention therefore eliminated Blaine and several other hopefuls in favor of Ohio's favorite son, Rutherford B. Hayes. Elected governor of Ohio three times, most recently as an advocate of gold rather than greenbacks, Hayes had also made a name for himself as a civil service reformer. But his chief virtue was that he offended neither Radicals nor reformers. As a journalist put it, he was "a third rate nonentity, whose only recommendation is that he is obnoxious to no one."

The Democratic Convention was abnormally harmonious from the start. The nomination went on the second ballot to Samuel J. Tilden, a millionaire corporation lawyer and reform governor of New York who had directed a campaign to overthrow the notorious Tweed ring controlling New York City politics.

The 1876 campaign generated no burning issues. Both candidates favored the trend toward relaxing federal authority and restoring white conservative rule in the South. In the absence of strong differences, Democrats aired the Republicans' dirty linen. In response, Republicans waved "the bloody shirt," which is to say that they linked the Democratic party to secession and the outrages committed against Republicans in the South. As one Republican speaker insisted, "The man that assassinated Abraham Lincoln was a Democrat. . . . Soldiers, every scar you have on your heroic bodies was given you by a Democrat!"

Early election returns pointed to a Tilden victory. Tilden enjoyed a 254,000-vote edge in the balloting and had won 184 electoral votes, just one short of a majority. Hayes had only 165 electoral votes, but the Republicans also claimed 19 doubtful votes from Florida, Louisiana, and South Carolina. The Democrats laid a counterclaim to 1 of Oregon's 3 electoral votes, but the Republicans had clearly carried that state. In the South the outcome was less certain, and given the fraud and intimidation perpetrated on both sides, nobody will ever know what might have happened if, to use a slogan of the day, "a free ballot and a fair count" had prevailed.

In all three of the disputed southern states, rival canvasing boards sent in different returns. The Constitution offered no guidance in this unprecedented situation. Finally, on January 29, 1877, the Congress decided to set up a special Electoral Commission with fifteen members, five each from the House, the Senate, and the Supreme Court. The commission's decision went by a vote of 8 to 7 along party lines, in favor of Hayes. After much bluster and the threat of a filibuster by the Democrats, the House voted on March 2 to accept the report and declared Hayes elected by an electoral vote of 185 to 184.

Critical to this outcome was the defection of southern Democrats, who had made several informal agreements with the Republicans. On February 26, 1877, prominent Ohio Republicans (including future president James A. Garfield) and powerful southern Democrats struck a secret bargain at Wormley's Hotel in Washington. The Republicans promised that if Hayes were elected, he would withdraw the last federal troops from Louisiana and South Carolina, letting the Republican governments there collapse. In return, the Democrats promised to withdraw their opposition to Hayes, accept in good faith the Reconstruction amendments (including civil rights for blacks), and refrain from partisan reprisals against Republicans in the South.

Southern Democrats could now justify deserting Tilden because this so-called Compromise of 1877 ended Radical Reconstruction and brought a return to "home rule," which actually meant rule by white Democrats. As a former slave observed in 1877, "The whole South—every state in the South—has got [back] into the hands of the very men that held us as slaves." Other, more informal promises, less noticed by the public, were made at the "Wormley Conference." Hayes's friends pledged more support for rebuilding Mississippi River

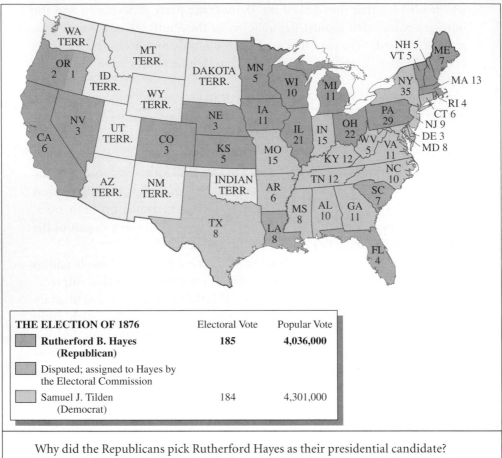

THE ELECTION OF 1876	Electoral Vote	Popular Vote
Rutherford B. Hayes (Republican)	**185**	**4,036,000**
Disputed; assigned to Hayes by the Electoral Commission		
Samuel J. Tilden (Democrat)	184	4,301,000

Why did the Republicans pick Rutherford Hayes as their presidential candidate? Why were the electoral votes of several states disputed? What was the Compromise of 1877?

levees and other internal improvements, including a federal subsidy for a transcontinental railroad along a southern route. Southerners extracted a further promise that Hayes would name a white southerner as postmaster general, the cabinet position with the most patronage jobs at hand. In return, southerners would let the Republicans make James Garfield the Speaker of the new House. Such a deal illustrates the relative weakness of the presidency compared with Congress during the postwar era.

THE END OF RECONSTRUCTION In 1877 the new president withdrew federal troops from Louisiana and South Carolina, and those states'

Republican governments collapsed soon thereafter—along with much of Hayes's claim to legitimacy. The president chose a Tennessean and former Confederate as postmaster general. But most of the other Wormley Conference promises were either renounced or forgotten. As for southern promises to protect the civil rights of African Americans, only a few Democratic leaders, such as the new governors of South Carolina and Louisiana, remembered them for long. Over the next three decades the protection of black civil rights crumbled under the pressure of restored white rule in the South and the force of Supreme Court decisions narrowing the application of the Reconstruction amendments.

Radical Reconstruction never offered more than an uncertain commitment to black civil rights and social equality. Yet it left an enduring legacy—the Thirteenth, Fourteenth, and Fifteenth Amendments—not dead but dormant, waiting to be awakened. If Reconstruction did not provide social equality or substantial economic opportunities for African Americans, it did create the foundation for future advances. It was a revolution, sighed former governor of North Carolina Jonathan Worth, and "nobody can anticipate the action of revolutions."

End of Chapter Review

CHAPTER SUMMARY

- **Reconstruction** Abraham Lincoln and his successor, the southerner Andrew Johnson, wanted a lenient and quick plan for Reconstruction. Lincoln's assassination made many northerners favor the Radical Republicans, who wanted to end the grasp of the old planter class on the South's society and economy. Congressional Reconstruction included the stipulation that to reenter the Union, former Confederate states had to ratify the Fourteenth and Fifteenth Amendments. Congress also passed the Military Reconstruction Act, which attempted to protect the voting rights and civil rights of African Americans.

- **Southern Violence** Many white southerners blamed their poverty on freed slaves and Yankees. White mobs attacked blacks in 1866 in Memphis and New Orleans. That year the Ku Klux Klan was formed as a social club; its members soon began to intimidate freedmen and white Republicans. Despite government action, violence continued and even escalated in the South.

- **Freed Slaves** Newly freed slaves suffered economically. Most did not have the resources to succeed in the aftermath of the war's devastation. There was no redistribution of land; former slaves were given their freedom but nothing else. The Freedmen's Bureau attempted to educate and aid freed slaves and reunite families. Many former slaves found comfort in their families and the independent churches they established. Some took part in state and local government under the last, radical phase of Reconstruction.

- **Grant Administration** During Ulysses Grant's administration fiscal issues dominated politics. Paper money (greenbacks) was regarded as inflationary; and agrarian and debtor groups opposed its withdrawal from circulation. Many members of Grant's administration were corrupt; scandals involved an attempt to corner the gold market, construction of the intercontinental railroad, and the whiskey ring's plan to steal millions of dollars in tax revenue.

- **End of Reconstruction** Most southern states had completed the requirements of Reconstruction by 1876. The presidential election returns of that year were so close that a special commission was established to count contested electoral votes. A decision hammered out at a secret meeting gave the presidency to the Republican, Rutherford B. Hayes; in return, the Democrats were promised that the last federal troops would be withdrawn from Louisiana and South Carolina, putting an end to the Radical Republican administrations in the southern states.

CHRONOLOGY

1862	Congress passes the Morrill Land Grant Act
	Congress guarantees the construction of a transcontinental railroad
	Congress passes the Homestead Act
1864	Lincoln refuses to sign the Wade-Davis Bill
1865	Congress sets up the Freedmen's Bureau
April 14, 1865	Lincoln is assassinated
1866	Ku Klux Klan is organized
	Congress passes the Civil Rights Act
1867	Congress passes the Military Reconstruction Act
	Congress passes the Tenure of Office Act
1868	Fourteenth Amendment is ratified
	Congress impeaches President Andrew Johnson; the Senate fails to convict him
1877	Compromise of 1877 ends Reconstruction

KEY TERMS & NAMES

Freedmen's Bureau p. 706

John Wilkes Booth p. 708

Andrew Johnson p. 708

black codes p. 711

Thaddeus Stevens p. 712

Fourteenth Amendment p. 714

Fifteenth Amendment p. 719

carpetbaggers p. 724

scalawags p. 724

greenbacks p. 728

Crédit Mobilier scandal p. 730

Horace Greeley p. 732

Compromise of 1877 p. 735

GLOSSARY

36°30′ According to the Missouri Compromise, any part of the Louisiana Purchase north of this line (Missouri's southern border) was to be excluded from slavery.

54th Massachusetts Regiment After President Abraham Lincoln's Emancipation Proclamation, the Union army organized all black military units, which white officers led. The 54th Massachusetts Regiment was one of the first of such units to be organized.

Abigail Adams (1744–1818) As the wife of John Adams, she endured long periods of separation from him while he served in many political roles. During these times apart, she wrote often to her husband; and their correspondence has provided a detailed portrait of life during the Revolutionary War.

abolition In the early 1830s, the anti-slavery movement shifted its goal from the gradual end of slavery to the immediate end or abolition of slavery.

John Adams (1735–1826) He was a signer of the Declaration of Independence and a delegate to the First and Second Continental Congress. During the Revolutionary War, he worked as a diplomat in France and Holland and negotiated the peace treaty with Britain. After the Revolutionary War, he served as the minister to Britain as well as the vice president and the second president of the United States. As president, he passed the Alien and Sedition Acts and endured a stormy relationship with France, which included the XYZ affair.

John Quincy Adams (1767–1848) As secretary of state under President Monroe, he negotiated agreements to define the boundaries of the Oregon country and the Transcontinental Treaty. He urged President Monroe to issue the Monroe Doctrine, which incorporated Adams's views. As president, Adams envisioned an expanded federal government and a broader use of federal powers. Adams's nationalism and praise of European leaders caused a split in his party. Some Republicans suspected him of being a closet monarchist and left to form the Democrat party. In the presidential election 1828, Andrew Jackson claimed that Adams had gained the presidency through a "corrupt bargain" with Henry Clay, which helped Jackson win the election.

Samuel Adams (1722–1803) A genius of revolutionary agitation, he believed that English Parliament had no right to legislate for the colonies. He organized the Sons of Liberty as well as protests in Boston against the British.

Jane Addams (1860–1935) As the leader of one of the best known settlement houses, she rejected the "do-goodism" spirit of religious reformers. Instead, she focused on solving the practical problems of the poor and tried to avoid the assumption that she and other social workers knew what was best for poor immigrants. She established child care for working mothers, health clinics, job training, and other social programs. She was also active in the peace movement and was awarded the Noble Peace Prize in 1931 for her work on its behalf.

Agricultural Adjustment Act (1933) New Deal legislation that established the Agricultural Adjustment Administration (AAA) to improve agricultural prices by limiting market supplies; declared unconstitutional in *United States v. Butler* (1936).

Emilio Aguinaldo (1869?–1964) He was a leader in Filipino struggle for independence. During the war of 1898, Commodore George Dewey brought Aguinaldo back to the Philippines from exile to help fight the Spanish. However, after the Spanish surrendered to Americans, America annexed the Philippines and Aguinaldo fought against the American military until he was captured in 1901.

Alamo, Battle of the Siege in the Texas War for Independence of 1836, in which the San Antonio mission fell to the Mexicans. Davy Crockett and Jim Bowie were among the courageous defenders.

Alien and Sedition Acts (1798) Four measures passed during the undeclared war with France that limited the freedoms of speech and press and restricted the liberty of noncitizens.

American Federation of Labor Founded in 1881 as a federation of trade unions made up of skilled workers, the AFL under president Samuel Gompers successfully pushed for the eight-hour workday.

American Indian Movement Fed up with the poor conditions on Indian reservations and the federal government's unwillingness to help, Native Americans founded the American Indian Movement (AIM) in 1963. In 1973, AIM led 200 Sioux in the occupation of Wounded Knee. After a ten-week standoff with the federal authorities, the government agreed to reexamine Indian treaty rights and the occupation ended.

American Protective Association Nativist, anti-Catholic secret society founded in Iowa in 1887 and active until the end of the century.

American Recovery and Reinvestment Act Hoping to restart the weak economy, President Obama signed this $787 billion economic stimulus bill in February of 2009. The bill included cash distributions to states, funds for food stamps, unemployment benefits, construction projects to renew the nation's infrastructure, funds for renewable-energy systems, and tax reductions.

American System Program of internal improvements and protective tariffs promoted by Speaker of the House Henry Clay in his presidential campaign of 1824; his proposals formed the core of Whig ideology in the 1830s and 1840s.

anaconda strategy Union General Winfield Scott developed this three-pronged strategy to defeat the Confederacy. Like a snake strangling its prey, the Union army would crush its enemy through exerting pressure on Richmond, blockading Confederate ports, and dividing the South by invading its major waterways.

Annapolis Convention In 1786, all thirteen colonies were invited to a convention in Annapolis to discuss commercial problems, but only representatives from five states attended. However, the convention was not a complete failure because the delegates decided to have another convention in order to write the constitution.

anti-Federalists Forerunners of Thomas Jefferson's Democratic-Republican party; opposed the Constitution as a limitation on individual and states' rights, which led to the addition of a Bill of Rights to the document.

Anti-Masonic party This party grew out of popular hostility toward the Masonic fraternal order and entered the presidential election of 1832 as a third party. It was the first party to run as a third party in a presidential election as well as the first to hold a nomination convention and announce a party platform.

Benedict Arnold (1741–1801) A traitorous American commander who planned to sell out the American garrison at West Point to the British, but his plot was discovered before it could be executed and he joined the British army.

Atlanta Compromise Speech to the Cotton States and International Exposition in 1895 by educator Booker T. Washington, the leading black spokesman of the day; black scholar W. E. B. Du Bois gave the speech its derisive name and criticized Washington for encouraging blacks to accommodate segregation and disenfranchisement.

Atlantic Charter Issued August 12, 1941, following meetings in Newfoundland between President Franklin D. Roosevelt and British Prime Minister Winston Churchill, the charter signaled the allies' cooperation and stated their war aims.

Crispus Attucks (1723–1770) During the Boston Massacre, he was supposedly at the head of the crowd of hecklers who baited the British troops. He was killed when the British troops fired on the crowd.

Stephen F. Austin (1793–1836) He established the first colony of Americans in Texas, which eventually attracted 2,000 people.

Axis powers In World War II, the nations of Germany, Italy, and Japan.

Aztec Empire Mesoamerican people who were conquered by the Spanish under Hernando Cortés, 1519–1528.

baby boom Markedly higher birth rate in the years following World War II; led to the biggest demographic "bubble" in American history.

Bacon's Rebellion Unsuccessful 1676 revolt led by planter Nathaniel Bacon against Virginia governor William Berkeley's administration, because it had failed to protect settlers from Indian raids.

Bank of the United States Proposed by the first Secretary of the Treasury Alexander Hamilton, the bank opened in 1791 and operated until 1811 to issue a uniform currency, make business loans, and collect tax monies. The second Bank of the United States was chartered in 1816 but was not renewed by President Andrew Jackson twenty years later.

barbary pirates Plundering pirates off the Mediterranean coast of Africa; President Thomas Jefferson's refusal to pay them tribute to protect

American ships sparked an undeclared naval war with North African nations, 1801–1805.

Battle of the Bulge On December 16, 1944, the German army launched a counter attack against the Allied forces, which pushed them back. However, the Allies were eventually able to recover and breakthrough the German lines. This defeat was a great blow to the Nazi's morale and their army's strength. The battle used up the last of Hitler's reserve units and opened a route into Germany's heartland.

Bear Flag Republic On June 14, 1846, a group of Americans in California captured Sonoma from the Mexican army and declared it the Republic of California whose flag featured a grizzly bear. In July, the commodore of the U.S. Pacific Fleet landed troops on California's shores and declared it part of the United States.

Beats A group of writers, artists, and musicians whose central concern was the discarding of organizational constraints and traditional conventions in favor of liberated forms of self expression. They came out of the bohemian underground in New York's Greenwich Village in the 1950s and included the writers Jack Kerouac, Allen Ginsberg, and William Burroughs. Their attitudes and lifestyles had a major influence on the youth of the 1960s.

beatnik A name referring to almost any young rebel who openly dissented from the middle-class life. The name itself stems from the Beats.

Nicholas Biddle (1786–1844) He was the president of the second Bank of the United States. In response to President Andrew Jackson's attacks on the bank, Biddle curtailed the bank's loans and exchanged its paper currency for gold and silver. He was hoping to provoke an economic crisis to prove the bank's importance. In response, state banks began printing paper without restraint and lent it to speculators, causing a binge in speculating and an enormous increase in debt.

Bill of Rights First ten amendments to the U.S. Constitution, adopted in 1791 to guarantee individual rights and to help secure ratification of the Constitution by the states.

Osama bin Laden (1957–) He is the leader of al Qaeda whose members attacked America on September 11, 2001. Years before the attack, he had declared *jihad* (holy war) on the United States, Israel, and the Saudi monarchy. In Afghanistan, the Taliban leaders gave Osama bin Laden a safe haven in exchange for aid in fighting the Northern Alliance, who were rebels opposed to the Taliban. After the 9/11 terrorist attacks, the United States asked the Taliban to turn over bin Laden. Following their refusal, America and multinational coalition invaded Afghanistan and overthrew the Taliban, but they did not capture bin Laden.

black codes Laws passed in southern states to restrict the rights of former slaves; to combat the codes, Congress passed the Civil Rights Act of 1866 and the Fourteenth Amendment and set up military governments in southern states that refused to ratify the amendment.

black power A more militant form of protest for civil rights that originated in urban communities, where nonviolent tactics were less effective than in the South. Black power encouraged African Americans to take pride in their racial heritage and forced black leaders and organizations to focus attention on the plight of poor inner-city blacks.

James Gillepsie Blaine (1830–1893) As a Republican congressman from Maine, he developed close ties with business leaders, which contributed to him losing the presidential election of 1884. He later opposed President Cleveland's efforts to reduce tariffs, which became a significant issue in the 1888 presidential election. Blaine served as secretary of state under President Benjamin Harrison and his flamboyant style often overshadowed the president.

"bleeding" Kansas Violence between pro- and antislavery settlers in the Kansas Territory, 1856.

blitzkrieg The German "lightening war" strategy used during World War II; the Germans invaded Poland, France, Russia, and other countries with fast-moving, well-coordinated attacks using aircraft, tanks, and other armored vehicles, followed by infantry.

Bolsheviks Under the leadership of Vladimir Lenin, this Marxist party led the November 1917 revolution against the newly formed provisional government in Russia. After seizing control, the Bolsheviks negotiated a peace treaty with Germany, the Treaty of Brest-Litovsk, and ended their participation in World War I.

Bonus Expeditionary Force Thousands of World War I veterans, who insisted on immediate payment of their bonus certificates, marched on Washington in 1932; violence ensued when President Herbert Hoover ordered their tent villages cleared.

Daniel Boone (1734–1820) He found and expanded a trail into Kentucky, which pioneers used to reach and settle the area.

John Wilkes Booth (1838?–1865) He assassinated President Abraham Lincoln at the Ford's Theater on April 14, 1865. He was pursued to Virginia and killed.

Bourbons In post–Civil War southern politics, the opponents of the Redeemers were called Bourbons. They were known for having forgotten nothing and learned nothing from the ordeal of the Civil War.

Joseph Brant (1742?–1807) He was the Mohawk leader who led the Iroquois against the Americans in the Revolutionary War.

brinkmanship Secretary of State John Foster Dulles believed that communism could be contained by bringing America to the brink of war with an aggressive communist nation. He believed that the aggressor would back down when confronted with the prospect of receiving a mass retaliation from a country with nuclear weapons.

John Brown (1800–1859) He was willing to use violence to further his antislavery beliefs. In 1856, a pro-slavery mob sacked the free-state town of Lawrence, Kansas. In response, John Brown went to the pro-slavery settlement of Pottawatomie, Kansas and hacked to death several people, which led to a guerrilla war in the Kansas territory. In 1859, he attempted to raid the federal arsenal at Harpers Ferry. He had hoped to use the stolen weapons to arm slaves, but he was captured and executed. His failed raid instilled panic throughout the South, and his execution turned him into a martyr for his cause.

***Brown v. Board of Education of Topeka* (1954)** U.S. Supreme Court decision that struck down racial segregation in public education and declared "separate but equal" unconstitutional.

William Jennings Bryan (1860–1925) He delivered the pro-silver "cross of gold" speech at the 1896 Democratic Convention and won his party's nomination for president. Disappointed pro-gold Democrats chose to walk out of the convention and nominate their own candidate, which split the Democratic party and cost them the White House. Bryan's loss also crippled the Populist movement that had endorsed him.

"Bull Moose" Progressive party In the 1912 election, Theodore Roosevelt was unable to secure the Republican nomination for president. He left the Republican party and formed his own party of progressive Republicans, called the "Bull Moose" party. Roosevelt and Taft split the Republican vote, which allowed Democrat Woodrow Wilson to win.

Bull Run, Battles of (First and Second Manassas) First land engagement of the Civil War took place on July 21, 1861, at Manassas Junction, Virginia, at which surprised Union troops quickly retreated; one year later, on August 29–30, Confederates captured the federal supply depot and forced Union troops back to Washington.

Martin Van Buren (1782–1862) During President Jackson's first term, he served as secretary of state and minister to London. He often politically fought Vice President John C. Calhoun for the position of Jackson's successor. A rift between Jackson and Calhoun led to Van Buren becoming vice president during Jackson's second term. In 1836, Van Buren was elected president, and he inherited a financial crisis. He believed that the government should not continue to keep its deposits in state banks and set up an independent Treasury, which was approved by Congress after several years of political maneuvering.

General John Burgoyne (1722–1792) He was the commander of Britain's northern forces during the Revolutionary War. He and most of his troops surrendered to the Americans at the Battle of Saratoga.

burned-over district Area of western New York strongly influenced by the revivalist fervor of the Second Great Awakening; Disciples of Christ and Mormons are among the many sects that trace their roots to the phenomenon.

Aaron Burr (1756–1836) Even though he was Thomas Jefferson's vice president, he lost favor with Jefferson's supporters who were Republicans. He sought to work with the Federalists and run as their candidate for the governor of New York. Alexander Hamilton opposed Burr's candidacy and his stinging remarks on the subject led to Burr challenging him to duel in which Hamilton was killed.

George H. W. Bush (1924–) He had served as vice president during the Reagan administration and then won the presidential election of 1988. During his presidential campaign, Bush promised not to raise taxes. However, the federal deficit had become so big that he had to raise taxes. Bush chose to make fighting illegal drugs a priority. He created the Office of National Drug Control Policy, but it was only moderately successful in stopping drug use. In 1989, Bush ordered the invasion of Panama and the capture of Panamanian leader Manuel Noriega, who was wanted in America on drug charges. He was captured, tried, and convicted. In 1990, Saddam Hussein invaded Kuwait; and Bush sent the American military to Saudi Arabia on a defensive mission. He assembled a multinational force and launched Operation Desert Storm, which took Kuwait back from Saddam in 1991. The euphoria over the victory in Kuwait was short lived as the country slid into a recession. He lost the 1992 presidential election to Bill Clinton.

George W. Bush (1946-) In the 2000 presidential election, Texas governor George W. Bush ran as the Republican nominee against Democratic nominee Vice President Al Gore. The election ended in controversy over the final vote tally in Florida. Bush had slightly more votes, but a recount was required by state law. However, it was stopped by Supreme Court and Bush was declared president. After the September 11 terrorist attacks, he launched his "war on terrorism." President George W. Bush adapted the Bush Doctrine, which claimed the right to launch preemptive military attacks against enemies. The United States invaded Afghanistan and Iraq with unclear outcomes leaving the countries divided. In the summer of 2006, Hurricane Katrina struck the Gulf Coast and left destruction across several states and three-quarters of New Orleans flooded. Bush was attacked for the unpreparedness of the federal government to handle the disaster as well as his own slowness to react. In September 2008, the nation's economy nosedived as a credit crunch spiraled into a global economic meltdown. Bush signed into law the bank bailout fund called Troubled Asset Relief Program (TARP), but the economy did not improve.

***Bush v. Gore* (2000)** The close 2000 presidential election came down to Florida's decisive twenty-five electoral votes. The final tally in Florida gave Bush a slight lead, but it was so small that a recount was required by state law. While the votes were being recounted, a legal battle was being waged to stop the recount. Finally, the case, *Bush v. Gore*, was present to the Supreme Court who ruled 5–4 to stop the recount and Bush was declared the winner.

Bush Doctrine Believing that America's enemies were now terrorist groups and unstable rogue nations, President George W. Bush adapted a foreign policy that claimed the right to launch preemptive military attacks against enemies.

buying (stock) on margin The investment practice of making a small down payment (the "margin") on a stock and borrowing the rest of money need for the purchase from a broker who held the stock as security against a down market. If the stock's value declined and the buyer failed to meet a margin call for more funds, the broker could sell the stock to cover his loan.

John C. Calhoun (1782–1850) He served in both the House of Representatives and the Senate for South Carolina before becoming secretary of war under President Monroe and then John Quincy Adams's vice president. He introduced the bill for the second national bank to Congress and led the minority of southerners who voted for the Tariff of 1816. However, he later chose to oppose tariffs. During his time as secretary of war under President Monroe, he authorized the use of federal troops against the Seminoles who were attacking settlers. As John Quincy Adams's vice president, he supported a new tariffs bill to win presidential candidate Andrew Jackson additional support. Jackson won the election, but the new tariffs bill passed and Calhoun had to explain why he had changed his opinion on tariffs.

Camp David Accords Peace agreement between Israeli Prime Minister Menachem Begin and Egyptian President Anwar Sadat, brokered by President Jimmy Carter in 1978.

"Scarface" Al Capone (1899–1947) He was the most successful gangster of the Prohibition era whose Chicago-based criminal empire included bootlegging, prostitution, and gambling.

Andrew Carnegie (1835–1919) He was a steel magnate who believed that the general public benefited from big business even if these companies employed harsh business practices. This philosophy became deeply ingrained in the conventional wisdom of some Americans. After retiring, he devoted himself to philanthropy in hopes of promoting social welfare and world peace.

carpetbaggers Northern emigrants who participated in the Republican governments of the reconstructed South.

Jimmy Carter (1924–) Jimmy Carter, an outsider to Washington, capitalized on the post-Watergate cynicism and won the 1976 presidential election. He created departments of Energy and Education and signed into law several environmental initiatives. However, his efforts to support the Panama Canal Treaties and his unwillingness to make deals with legislators caused other bills to be either gutted or stalled in Congress. Despite his efforts to improve the economy, the recession continued and inflation increased. In 1978, he successfully brokered a peace agreement between Israel and Egypt called the Camp David Accords. Then his administration was plagued with a series of crises. Fighting in the Middle East produced a fuel shortage in the United States. The Soviets invaded Afghanistan and Carter responded with the suspension of an arms-control treaty with the Soviets, the halting of grain shipments to the Soviet Union, and a call for a boycott of the Olympic Games in Moscow. In Iran, revolutionaries toppled the shah's government and seized the American embassy, taking hostage those inside. Carter struggled to get the hostages released and was unable to do so until after he lost the 1980 election to Ronald Reagan. He was awarded the Nobel Peace Prize in 2002 for his efforts to further peace and democratic elections around the world.

Jacques Cartier (1491–1557) He led the first French effort to colonize North America and explored the Gulf of St. Lawrence and reached as far as present day Montreal on the St. Lawrence River.

Bartolomé de Las Casas (1484–1566) A Catholic missionary who renounced the Spanish practice of coercively converting Indians and advocated the better treatment for them. In 1552, he wrote *A Brief Relation of the Destruction of the Indies*, which described the Spanish's cruel treatment of the Indians.

Fidel Castro (1926–) In 1959, his Communist regime came to power in Cuba after two years of guerrilla warfare against the dictator Fulgenico Batista. He enacted land redistribution programs and nationalized all foreign-owned property. The latter action as well as his political trials and summary executions damaged relations between Cuba and America. Castro was turned down when he asked for loans from the United States. However, he did receive aid from the Soviet Union.

Carrie Chapman Catt (1859–1947) She was a leader of a new generation of activists in the women's suffrage movement who carried on the work started by Elizabeth Cady Stanton and Susan B. Anthony.

Cesar Chavez (1927–1993) He founded the United Farm Workers (UFW) in 1962 and worked to organize migrant farm workers. In 1965, the UFW joined Filipino farm workers striking against corporate grape farmers in California's San Joaquin Valley. In 1970, the strike and a consumer boycott on grapes compelled the farmers to formally recognize the UFW. As the result of Chavez's efforts, wages and working conditions improved for migrant workers. In 1975, the California state legislature passed a bill that required growers to bargain collectively with representatives of the farm workers.

Chinese Exclusion Act (1882) The first federal law to restrict immigration on the basis of race and class. Passed in 1882, the act halted Chinese immigration for ten years, but it was periodically renewed and then indefinitely extended in 1902. Not until 1943 were the barriers to Chinese immigration finally removed.

Church of Jesus Christ of Latter-day Saints / Mormons Founded in 1830 by Joseph Smith, the sect was a product of the intense revivalism of the burned-over district of New York; Smith's successor Brigham Young led 15,000 followers to Utah in 1847 to escape persecution.

Winston Churchill (1874–1965) The British prime minister who led the country during World War II. Along with Roosevelt and Stalin, he helped shape the post-war world at the Yalta Conference. He also coined the term "iron curtain," which he used in his famous "The Sinews of Peace" speech.

"city machines" Local political party officials used these organizations to dispense patronage and favoritism amongst voters and businesses to ensure their loyal support to the political party.

Civil Rights Act of 1957 First federal civil rights law since Reconstruction; established the Civil Rights Commission and the Civil Rights Division of the Department of Justice.

Civil Rights Act of 1964 Outlawed discrimination in public accommodations and employment.

Henry Clay (1777–1852) In the first half of the nineteenth century, he was the foremost spokesman for the American system. As speaker of the House in the 1820s, he promoted economic nationalism, "market revolution," and the rapid development of western states and territories. He formulated the "second" Missouri Compromise, which denied the Missouri state legislature the power to exclude the rights of free blacks and mulattos. In the deadlocked presidential election of 1824, the House of Representatives decided the election. Clay supported John Quincy Adams, who won the presidency and appointed Clay to secretary of state. Andrew Jackson claimed that Clay had entered into a "corrupt bargain" with Adams for his own selfish gains.

Hillary Rodham Clinton (1947–) In the 2008 presidential election, Senator Hillary Clinton, the spouse of former President Bill Clinton, initially was the front-runner for the Democratic nomination, which made her the first woman with a serious chance to win the presidency. However,

Senator Barack Obama's Internet-based and grassroots-orientated campaign garnered him enough delegates to win the nomination. After Obama became president, she was appointed secretary of state.

William Jefferson Clinton (1946–) The governor of Arkansas won the 1992 presidential election against President George H. W. Bush. In his first term, he pushed through Congress a tax increase, an economic stimulus package, the adoption of the North America Free Trade Agreement, welfare reform, a raise in the minimum wage, and improved public access to health insurance. However, he failed to institute major health-care reform, which had been one of his major goals. In 1996, Clinton defeated Republican presidential candidate Bob Dole. Clinton was scrutinized for his investment in the fraudulent Whitewater Development Corporation, but no evidence was found of him being involved in any wrongdoing. In 1998, he was revealed to have had a sexual affair with a White House intern. Clinton had initially lied about the affair and tried to cover up it, which led to a vote in Congress on whether or not to begin an impeachment inquiry. The House of Representatives voted to impeach Clinton, but the Senate found him not guilty. Clinton's presidency faced several foreign policy challenges. In 1994, he used U.S. forces to restore Haiti's democratically elected president to power after he had been ousted during a coup. In 1995, the Clinton Administration negotiated the Dayton Accords, which stopped the ethnic strife in the former Yugoslavia and the Balkan region. Clinton sponsored peace talks between Arabs and Israelis, which culminated in Israeli Prime Minister Yitzhak Rabin and the Palestine Liberation Organization leader Yasir Arafat signing the Oslo Accords in 1993. This agreement provided for the restoration of Palestinian self-rule in specific areas in exchange for peace as provided in UN Security Council resolutions.

Coercive Acts / Intolerable Acts (1774) Four parliamentary measures in reaction to the Boston Tea Party that forced payment for the tea, disallowed colonial trials of British soldiers, forced their quartering in private homes, and set up a military government.

coffin ships Irish immigrants fleeing the potato famine had to endure a six-week journey across the Atlantic to reach America. During these voyages, thousands of passengers died of disease and starvation, which led to the ships being called "coffin ships."

Christopher Columbus (1451–1506) The Italian sailor who persuaded King Ferdinand and Queen Isabella of Spain to fund his expedition across the Atlantic to discover a new trade route to Asia. Instead of arriving at China or Japan, he reached the Bahamas in 1492.

Committee on Public Information During World War I, this committee produced war propaganda that conveyed the Allies' war aims to Americans as well as attempted to weaken the enemy's morale.

Committee to Re-elect the President (CREEP) During Nixon's presidency, his administration engaged in a number of immoral acts, such as attempting to steal information and falsely accusing political appointments of sexual improprieties. These acts were funded by money illegally collected through CREEP.

Thomas Paine's *Common Sense* This pamphlet refocused the blame for the colonies' problems on King George III rather than on Parliament and advocated a declaration of independence, which few colonialists had considered prior to its appearance.

Compromise of 1850 Complex compromise mediated by Senator Henry Clay that headed off southern secession over California statehood; to appease the South it included a stronger fugitive slave law and delayed determination of the slave status of the New Mexico and Utah territories.

Compromise of 1877 Deal made by a special congressional commission on March 2, 1877, to resolve the disputed presidential election of 1876; Republican Rutherford B. Hayes, who had lost the popular vote, was declared the winner in exchange for the withdrawal of federal troops from the South, marking the end of Reconstruction.

Conestoga wagons These large horse-drawn wagons were used to carry people or heavy freight long distances, including from the East to the western frontier settlements.

conquistadores Spanish term for "conqueror," applied to European leaders of campaigns against indigenous peoples in central and southern America.

consumer culture In the post–World War II era, affluence seemed to be forever increasing in America. At the same time, there was a boom in construction as well as products and appliances for Americans to buy. As a result, shopping became a major recreational activity. Americans started spending more, saving less, and building more shopping centers.

containment U.S. strategy in the cold war that called for containing Soviet expansion; originally devised in 1947 by U.S. diplomat George F. Kennan.

Continental army Army authorized by the Continental Congress, 1775–1784, to fight the British; commanded by General George Washington.

Contras The Reagan administration ordered the CIA to train and supply guerrilla bands of anti-Communist Nicaraguans called Contras. They were fighting the Sandinista government that had recently come to power in Nicaragua. The State Department believed that the Sandinista government was supplying the leftist Salvadoran rebels with Soviet and Cuban arms. A cease-fire agreement between the Contras and Sandinistas was signed in 1988.

Calvin Coolidge "Silent Cal" (1872–1933) After President Harding's death, his vice president, Calvin Coolidge, assumed the presidency. Coolidge believed that the nation's welfare was tied to the success of big business, and he worked to end government regulation of business and industry as well as reduce taxes. In particular, he focused on the nation's industrial development.

Hernán Cortés (1485–1547) The Spanish conquistador who conquered the Aztec Empire and set the precedent for other plundering conquistadores.

General Charles Cornwallis (1738–1805) He was in charge of British troops in the South during the Revolutionary War. His surrendering to George Washington at the Battle of Yorktown ended the Revolutionary War.

Corps of Discovery Meriwether Lewis and William Clark led this group of men on an expedition of the newly purchased Louisiana territory, which took them from Missouri to Oregon. As they traveled, they kept detailed journals and drew maps of the previously unexplored territory. Their reports attracted traders and trappers to the region and gave the United States a claim to the Oregon country by right of discovery and exploration.

"corrupt bargain" A vote in the House of Representatives decided the deadlocked presidential election of 1824 in favor of John Quincy Adams, who Speaker of the House Henry Clay had supported. Afterward, Adams appointed Clay secretary of state. Andrew Jackson charged Clay with having made a "corrupt bargain" with Adams that gave Adams the presidency and Clay a place in his administration. There was no evidence of such a deal, but it was widely believed.

the counterculture "Hippie" youth culture of the 1960s, which rejected the values of the dominant culture in favor of illicit drugs, communes, free sex, and rock music.

court-packing plan President Franklin D. Roosevelt's failed 1937 attempt to increase the number of U.S. Supreme Court justices from nine to fifteen in order to save his Second New Deal programs from constitutional challenges.

covenant theory A Puritan concept that believed true Christians could enter a voluntary union for the common worship of God. Taking the idea one step further, the union could also be used for the purposes of establishing governments.

Coxey's Army Jacob S. Coxey, a Populist, led this protest group that demanded the federal government provide the unemployed with meaningful employment. In 1894, Coxey's Army joined other protests groups in a march on Washington D.C. The combination of the march and the growing support of Populism scared many Americans.

Credit Mobilier scandal Construction company guilt of massive overcharges for building the Union Pacific Railroad were exposed; high officials of the Ulysses S. Grant administration were implicated but never charged.

George Creel (1876–1953) He convinced President Woodrow Wilson that the best approach to influencing public opinion was through propaganda rather than censorship. As the executive head of the Committee on Public Information, he produced propaganda that conveyed the Allies' war aims.

"Cross of Gold" Speech In the 1896 election, the Democratic party split over the issue of whether to use gold or silver to back American currency. Significant to this division was the "Cross of Gold" speech that William Jennings Bryan delivered at the Democratic convention. This pro-silver speech was so well received that Bryan won the nomination to be their presidential candidate. Disappointed pro-gold Democrats chose to walk out of the convention and nominate their own candidate.

Cuban missile crisis Caused when the United States discovered Soviet offensive missile sites in Cuba in October 1962; the U.S.–Soviet confrontation was the cold war's closest brush with nuclear war.

cult of domesticity The belief that women should stay at home to manage the household, educate their children with strong moral values, and please their husbands.

George A. Custer (1839–1876) He was a reckless and glory-seeking Lieutenant Colonel of the U.S. Army who fought the Sioux Indians in the Great Sioux War. In 1876, he and his detachment of soldiers were entirely wiped out in the Battle of Little Bighorn.

D-day June 6, 1944, when an Allied amphibious assault landed on the Normandy coast and established a foothold in Europe from which Hitler's defenses could not recover.

Jefferson Davis (1808–1889) He was the president of the Confederacy during the Civil War. When the Confederacy's defeat seemed invitable in early 1865, he refused to surrender. Union forces captured him in May of that year.

Eugene V. Debs (1855–1926) He founded the American Railway Union, which he organized against the Pullman Palace Car Company during the Pullman strike. Later he organized the Social Democratic party, which eventually became the Socialist Party of America. In the 1912 presidential election, he ran as the Socialist party's candidate and received more than 900,000 votes.

Declaratory Act Following the repeal of the Stamp Act in 1766, Parliament passed this act which asserted Parliament's full power to make laws binding the colonies "in all cases whatsoever."

deism Enlightenment thought applied to religion; emphasized reason, morality, and natural law.

détente In the 1970s, the United States and Soviet Union began working together to achieve a more orderly and restrained competition between each other. Both countries signed an agreement to limit the number of Intercontinental Long Range Ballistic Missiles (ICBMs) that each country could possess and to not construct antiballistic missiles systems. They also signed new trade agreements.

George Dewey (1837–1917) On April 30, 1898, Commodore George Dewey's small U.S. naval squadron defeated the Spanish warships in Manila Bay in the Philippines. This quick victory aroused expansionist fever in the United States.

John Dewey (1859–1952) He is an important philosopher of pragmatism. However, he preferred to use the term *instrumentalism*, because he saw ideas as instruments of action.

Ngo Dinh Diem (1901–1963) Following the Geneva Accords, the French, with the support of America, forced the Vietnamese emperor to accept Dinh Diem as the new premier of South Vietnam. President Eisenhower sent advisors to train Diem's police and army. In return, the United States expected Diem to enact democratic reforms and distribute land to the peasants. Instead, he suppressed his political opponents, did little or no land distribution, and let corruption grow. In 1956, he refused to participate in elections to reunify Vietnam. Eventually, he ousted the emperor and declared himself president.

Dorothea Dix (1802–1887) She was an important figure in increasing the public's awareness of the plight of the mentally ill. After a two-year investigation of the treatment of the mentally ill in Massachusetts, she presented her findings and won the support of leading reformers. She eventually convinced twenty states to reform their treatment of the mentally ill.

Dixiecrats Deep South delegates who walked out of the 1948 Democratic National Convention in protest of the party's support for civil rights legislation and later formed the States' Rights (Dixiecrat) party, which nominated Strom Thurmond of South Carolina for president.

dollar diplomacy The Taft administration's policy of encouraging American bankers to aid debt-plagued governments in Haiti, Guatemala, Honduras, and Nicaragua.

Donner party Forty-seven surviving members of a group of migrants to California were forced to resort to cannibalism to survive a brutal winter trapped in the Sierra Nevadas, 1846–1847; highest death toll of any group traveling the Overland Trail.

Stephen A. Douglas (1812–1861) As a senator from Illinois, he authored the Kansas-Nebraska Act. Once passed, the act led to violence in Kansas between pro- and antislavery factions and damaged the Whig party. These damages prevented Senator Douglas from being chosen as the presidential candidate of his party. Running for senatorial reelection in 1858, he engaged Abraham Lincoln in a series of public debates about slavery in the territories. Even though Douglas won the election, the debates gave Lincoln a national reputation.

Frederick Douglass (1818–1895) He escaped from slavery and become an eloquent speaker and writer against slavery. In 1845, he published his autobiography entitled *Narrative of the Life of Frederick Douglass* and two years later he founded an abolitionist newspaper for blacks called the *North Star*.

dot-coms In the late 1990s, the stock market soared to new heights and defied the predictions of experts that the economy could not sustain such a performance. Much of the economic success was based on dot-com enterprises, which were firms specializing in computers, software, telecommunications, and the internet. However, many of the companies' stock market values were driven higher and higher by speculation instead of financial success. Eventually the stock market bubble burst.

Dred Scott v. Sandford (1857) U.S. Supreme Court decision in which Chief Justice Roger B. Taney ruled that slaves could not sue for freedom and that Congress could not prohibit slavery in the territories, on the grounds that such a prohibition would violate the Fifth Amendment rights of slaveholders.

W. E. B. Du Bois (1868–1963) He criticized Booker T. Washington's views on civil rights as being accommodationist. He advocated "ceaseless agitation" for civil rights and the immediate end to segregation and an enforcement of laws to protect civil rights and equality. He promoted an education for African Americans that would nurture bold leaders who were willing to challenge discrimination in politics.

John Foster Dulles (1888–1959) As President Eisenhower's secretary of state, he institutionalized the policy of containment and introduced the strategy of deterrence. He believed in using brinkmanship to halt the spread of communism. He attempted to employ it in Indochina, which led to the United States' involvement in Vietnam.

"Dust Bowl" Great Plains counties where millions of tons of topsoil were blown away from parched farmland in the 1930s; massive migration of farm families followed.

Peggy Eaton (1796–1879) The wife of John Eaton, President Jackson's secretary of war, was the daughter of a tavern owner with an unsavory past. Supposedly her first husband had committed suicide after learning that she was having an affair with John Eaton. The wives of members of Jackson's cabinet snubbed her because of her lowly origins and past. The scandal that resulted was called the Eaton Affair.

Jonathan Edwards (1703–1758) New England Congregationalist minister, who began a religious revival in his Northampton church and was an important figure in the Great Awakening.

Election of 1912 The presidential election of 1912 featured four candidates: Wilson, Taft, Roosevelt, and Debs. Each candidate believed in the basic assumptions of progressive politics, but each had a different view on how progressive ideals should be implemented through policy. In the end, Taft and Roosevelt split the Republican party votes and Wilson emerged as the winner.

Queen Elizabeth I of England (1533–1603) The protestant daughter of Henry VIII, she was Queen of England from 1558-1603 and played a major role in the Protestant Reformation. During her long reign, the doctrines and services of the Church of England were defined and the Spanish Armada was defeated.

General Dwight D. Eisenhower (1890–1969) During World War II, he commanded the Allied Forces landing in Africa and was the supreme Allied commander as well as planner for Operation Overlord. In 1952, he was elected president on his popularity as a war hero and his promises to clean up Washington and find an honorable peace in the Korean War. His administration sought to cut the nation's domestic programs and budget, but he left the basic structure of the New Deal intact. In July of 1953, he announced the end of fighting in Korea. He appointed Earl Warren to the Supreme Court whose influence helped the court become an important force for social and political change. His secretary of state, John Foster Dulles, institutionalized the policies of containment and deterrence. Eisenhower supported the withdrawal of British forces from the Suez Canal and established the Eisenhower doctrine, which promised to aid any nation against aggression by a communist nation. Eisenhower preferred that state and local institutions to handle civil rights issues, and he refused to force states to comply with the Supreme Court's civil rights decisions. However, he did propose the legislation that became the Civil Rights Act of 1957.

Ellis Island Reception center in New York Harbor through which most European immigrants to America were processed from 1892 to 1954.

Emancipation Proclamation (1863) President Abraham Lincoln issued a preliminary proclamation on September 22, 1862, freeing the slaves in the Confederate states as of January 1, 1863, the date of the final proclamation.

Ralph Waldo Emerson (1803–1882) As a leader of the transcendentalist movement, he wrote poems, essays, and speeches that discussed the sacredness of nature, optimism, self-reliance, and the unlimited potential of the individual. He wanted to transcend the limitations of inherited conventions and rationalism to reach the inner recesses of the self.

encomienda System under which officers of the Spanish conquistadores gained ownership of Indian land.

Enlightenment Revolution in thought begun in the seventeenth century that emphasized reason and science over the authority of traditional religion.

enumerated goods According to the Navigation Act, these particular goods, like tobacco or cotton, could only be shipped to England or other English colonies.

Erie Canal Most important and profitable of the barge canals of the 1820s and 1830s; stretched from Buffalo to Albany, New York, connecting the Great Lakes to the East Coast and making New York City the nation's largest port.

ethnic cleansing The act of killing an entire group of people in a region or country because of its ethnic background. After the collapse of the former Yugoslavia in 1991, Serbs in Bosnia attacked communities of Muslims, which led to intervention by the United Nations. In 1998, fighting broke out again in the Balkans between Serbia and Kosovo. Serbian police and military attacked, killed, raped, or forced Muslim Albanian Kosovars to leave their homes.

Fair Employment Practices Commission Created in 1941 by executive order, the FEPC sought to eliminate racial discrimination in jobs; it possessed little power but represented a step toward civil rights for African Americans.

Farmers' Alliance Two separate organizations (Northwestern and Southern) of the 1880s and 1890s that took the place of the Grange, worked for similar causes, and attracted landless, as well as landed, farmers to their membership.

Federal Writers' Project During the Great Depression, this project provided writers, such as Ralph Ellison, Richard Wright, and Saul Bellow, with work, which gave them a chance to develop as artists and be employed.

The Federalist Collection of eighty-five essays that appeared in the New York press in 1787–1788 in support of the Constitution; written by Alexander Hamilton, James Madison, and John Jay but published under the pseudonym "Publius."

Geraldine Ferraro (1935–) In the 1984 presidential election, Democratic nominee, Walter Mondale, chose her as his running mate. As a member of the U.S. House of Representatives from New York, she was the first woman to be a vice-presidential nominee for a major political party. However, she was placed on the defensive because of her husband's complicated business dealings.

Fifteenth Amendment This amendment forbids states to deny any person the right to vote on grounds of "race, color or pervious condition of servitude." Former Confederate states were required to ratify this amendment before they could be readmitted to the Union.

the "final solution" The Nazi party's systematic murder of some 6 million Jews along with more than a million other people including, but not limited to, gypsies, homosexuals, and handicap individuals.

Food Administration After America's entry into World War I, the economy of the home front needed to be reorganized to provide the most efficient means of conducting the war. The Food Administration was a part of this effort. Under the leadership of Herbert Hoover, the organization sought to increase agricultural production while reducing civilian consumption of foodstuffs.

force bill During the nullification crisis between President Andrew Jackson and South Carolina, Jackson asked Congress to pass this bill, which authorized him to use the army to force South Carolina to comply with federal law.

Gerald Ford (1913–2006) He was President Nixon's vice president and assumed the presidency after Nixon resigned. President Ford issued Nixon a pardon for any crimes related to the Watergate scandal. The American public's reaction was largely negative; and Ford never regained the public's confidence. He resisted congressional pressure to both reduce taxes and increase federal spending, which sent the American economy into the deepest recession since the Great Depression. Ford retained Kissinger as his secretary of state and continued Nixon's foreign policy goals, which included the signing of another arms-control agreement with the Soviet Union. He was heavily criticized following the collapse of South Vietnam.

Fort Laramie Treaty (1851) Restricted the Plains Indians from using the Overland Trail and permitted the building of government forts.

Fort Necessity After attacking a group of French soldiers, George Washington constructed and took shelter in this fort from vengeful French troops. Washington eventually surrendered to them after a day-long battle. This conflict was a significant event in igniting the French and Indian War.

Fort Sumter First battle of the Civil War, in which the federal fort in Charleston (South Carolina) Harbor was captured by the Confederates on April 14, 1861, after two days of shelling.

"forty-niners" Speculators who went to northern California following the discovery of gold in 1848; the first of several years of large-scale migration was 1849.

Fourteen Points President Woodrow Wilson's 1918 plan for peace after World War I; at the Versailles peace conference, however, he failed to incorporate all of the points into the treaty.

Fourteenth Amendment (1868) Guaranteed rights of citizenship to former slaves, in words similar to those of the Civil Rights Act of 1866.

Franciscan Missions In 1769, Franciscan missioners accompanied Spanish soldiers to California and over the next fifty years established a chain of missions from San Diego to San Francisco. At these missions, friars sought to convert Indians to Catholicism and make them members of the Spanish empire. The friars stripped the Indians of their native heritage and used soldiers to enforce their will.

Benjamin Franklin (1706–1790) A Boston-born American, who epitomized the Enlightenment for many Americans and Europeans, Franklin's wide range of interests led him to become a publisher, inventor, and statesman. As the latter, he contributed to the writing of the Declaration of Independence, served as the minister to France during the Revolutionary War, and was a delegate to the Constitutional Convention.

Free-Soil party Formed in 1848 to oppose slavery in the territory acquired in the Mexican War; nominated Martin Van Buren for president in 1848, but by 1854, most of the party's members had joined the Republican party.

Freedmen's Bureau Reconstruction agency established in 1865 to protect the legal rights of former slaves and to assist with their education, jobs, health care, and landowning.

freedom riders In 1961, the Congress of Racial Equality had this group of black and white demonstrators ride buses to test the federal court ruling that had banned segregation on buses and trains and in terminals. Despite being attacked, they never gave up. Their actions drew national attention and generated respect and support for their cause.

John C. Frémont "the Pathfinder" (1813–1890) He was an explorer and surveyor who helped inspire Americans living in California to rebel against the Mexican government and declare independence.

French and Indian War Known in Europe as the Seven Years' War, the last (1755–1763) of four colonial wars fought between England and France for control of North America east of the Mississippi River.

Sigmund Freud (1865–1939) He was the founder of psychoanalysis, which suggested that human behavior was motivated by unconscious and irrational forces. By the 1920s, his ideas were being discussed more openly in America.

Fugitive Slave Act of 1850 Gave federal government authority in cases involving runaway slaves; so much more punitive and prejudiced in favor of slaveholders than the 1793 Fugitive Slave Act had been that Harriet Beecher Stowe was inspired to write *Uncle Tom's Cabin* in protest; the new law was part of the Compromise of 1850, included to appease the South over the admission of California as a free state.

fundamentalism Anti-modernist Protestant movement started in the early twentieth century that proclaimed the literal truth of the Bible; the name came from *The Fundamentals*, published by conservative leaders.

"gag rule" In 1831, the House of Representatives adopted this rule, which prevented the discussion and presentation of any petitions for the abolition of slavery to the House. John Quincy Adams, who was elected to the House after his presidency ended, fought the rule on the grounds that it violated the First Amendment. In 1844, he succeeded in having it repealed.

William Lloyd Garrison (1805–1879) In 1831, he started the anti-slavery newspaper *Liberator* and helped start the New England Anti-Slavery Society. Two years later, he assisted Arthur and Lewis Tappan in the founding of the American Anti-Slavery Society. He and his followers believed that America had been thoroughly corrupted and needed a wide range of reforms. He embraced every major reform movement of the day: abolition, temperance, pacifism, and women's rights. He wanted to go beyond just freeing slaves and grant them equal social and legal rights.

Marcus Garvey (1887–1940) He was the leading spokesman for Negro Nationalism, which exalted blackness, black cultural expression, and black exclusiveness. He called upon African Americans to liberate themselves from the surrounding white culture and create their own businesses, cultural centers, and newspapers. He was also the founder of the Universal Negro Improvement Association.

Citizen Genêt (1763–1834) As the ambassador to the United States from the new French Republic, he engaged American privateers to attack British ships and conspired with frontiersmen and land speculators to organize an attack on Spanish Florida and Louisiana. His actions and the French radicals excessive actions against their enemies in the new French Republic caused the French Revolution to lose support among Americans.

Geneva Accords In 1954, the Geneva Accords were signed, which ended French colonial rule in Indochina. The agreement created the independent nations of Laos and Cambodia and divided Vietnam along the 17th parallel until an election in 1956 would reunify the country.

German U-boat German submarines, or U-boats, were used to attack enemy merchant ships in the waters around the British Isles during World War I. The sinking of the ocean liner *Lusitania* by a German submarine caused a public outcry in America, which contributed to the demands to expand the United States' military.

Gettysburg, Battle of Fought in southern Pennsylvania, July 1–3, 1863; the Confederate defeat and the simultaneous loss at Vicksburg spelled the end of the South's chances in the Civil War.

Ghost Dance movement This spiritual and political movement came from a Paiute Indian named Wovoka (or Jack Wilson). He believed that a messiah would come and rescue the Indians and restore their lands. To hasten the arrival of the messiah, the Indians needed to take up a ceremonial dance at each new moon.

Newt Gingrich (1943–) He led the Republican insurgency in Congress in the mid 1990s through mobilizing religious and social conservatives. Along with other Republican congressmen, he created the Contract with America, which was a ten-point anti-big government program. However, the program fizzled out after many of its bills were not passed by Congress.

The Gilded Age Mark Twain and Charles Dudley Warner's 1873 novel, the title of which became the popular name for the period from the end of the Civil War to the turn of the century.

glasnost Soviet leader Mikhail Gorbachev instituted this reform, which brought about a loosening of censorship.

Glorious Revolution In 1688, the Protestant Queen Mary and her husband, William of Orange, took the British throne from King James II in a bloodless coup. Afterward, Parliament greatly expanded its power and passed the Bill of Rights and the Act of Toleration, both of which would influence attitudes and events in the colonies.

Barry Goldwater (1909–1998) He was a leader of the Republican right whose book, *The Conscience of a Conservative*, was highly influential to that segment of the party. He proposed eliminating the income tax and overhauling Social Security. In 1964, he ran as the Republican presidential candidate and lost to President Johnson. He campaigned against Johnson's war on poverty, the tradition of New Deal, the nuclear test ban and the Civil Rights Act of 1964. He advocated the wholesale bombing of North Vietnam.

Samuel Gompers (1850–1924) He served as the president of the American Federation of Labor from its inception until his death. He focused on achieving concrete economic gains such as higher wages, shorter hours, and better working conditions.

"good neighbor" policy Proclaimed by President Franklin D. Roosevelt in his first inaugural address in 1933, it sought improved diplomatic relations between the United States and its Latin American neighbors.

Mikhail Gorbachev (1931–) In the late 1980s, Soviet leader Mikhail Gorbachev attempted to reform the Soviet Union through his programs of *perestroika* and *glasnost*. He pursued a renewal of détente with America and signed new arms-control agreements with President Reagan. Gorbachev chose not to involve the Soviet Union in the internal affairs of other Communist countries, which removed the threat of armed Soviet crackdowns on reformers and protesters in Eastern Europe. Gorbachev's decision allowed the velvet revolutions of Eastern Europe to occur without outside interference. Eventually the political, social, and economic upheaval he had unleashed would lead to the break-up of the Soviet Union.

Al Gore (1948–) He served as a senator of Tennessee and then as President Clinton's vice president. In the 2000 presidential election, he was the Democratic candidate and campaigned on preserving Social Security, subsidizing prescription-medicine expenses for the elderly, and protecting the environment. His opponent was Governor George W. Bush, who promoted compassionate conservatism and the transferring of power from the federal government to the states. The election ended in controversy. The close election came down to Florida's electoral votes. The final tally in Florida gave Bush a slight lead, but it was so small that a recount was required by state law. While the votes were being recounted, a legal battle was being waged to stop the recount. Finally, the case, *Bush v. Gore*, was presented to the Supreme Court who ruled 5–4 to stop the recount and Bush was declared the winner.

Jay Gould (1836–1892) As one of the biggest railroad robber barons, he was infamous for buying rundown railroads, making cosmetic improvements and then reselling them for a profit. He used corporate funds for personal investments and to bribe politicians and judges.

gradualism This strategy for ending slavery involved promoting the banning of slavery in the new western territories and encouraging the release of slaves from slavery. Supporters of this method believed that it would bring about the gradual end of slavery.

Granger movement Political movement that grew out of the Patrons of Husbandry, an educational and social organization for farmers founded in 1867; the Grange had its greatest success in the Midwest of the 1870s, lobbying for government control of railroad and grain elevator rates and establishing farmers' cooperatives.

Ulysses S. Grant (1822–1885) After distinguishing himself in the western theater of the Civil War, he was appointed general in chief of the Union army in 1864. Afterward, he defeated General Robert E. Lee through a policy of aggressive attrition. He constantly attacked Lee's army until it was grind down. Lee surrendered to Grant on April 9th, 1865 at the Appomattox Court House. In 1868, he was elected President and his tenure suffered from scandals and fiscal problems including the debate on whether or not greenbacks, paper money, should be removed from circulation.

Great Awakening Fervent religious revival movement in the 1720s through the 1740s that was spread throughout the colonies by ministers like

New England Congregationalist Jonathan Edwards and English revivalist George Whitefield.

great black migration After World War II, rural southern blacks began moving to the urban North and Midwest in large numbers in search of better jobs, housing, and greater social equality. The massive influx of African American migrants overwhelmed the resources of urban governments and sparked racial conflicts. In order to cope with the new migrants and alleviate racial tension, cities constructed massive public-housing projects that segregated African Americans into over-crowded and poor neighborhoods.

Great Compromise (Connecticut Compromise) Mediated the differences between the New Jersey and Virginia delegations to the Constitutional Convention by providing for a bicameral legislature, the upper house of which would have equal representation and the lower house of which would be apportioned by population.

Great Depression Worst economic depression in American history; it was spurred by the stock market crash of 1929 and lasted until World War II.

Great Sioux War In 1874, Lieutenant Colonel Custard led an exploratory expedition into the Black Hills, which the United States government had promised to the Sioux Indians. Miners soon followed and the army did nothing to keep them out. Eventually, the army attacked the Sioux Indians and the fight against them lasted for fifteen months before the Sioux Indians were forced to give up their land and move onto a reservation.

Great Society Term coined by President Lyndon B. Johnson in his 1965 State of the Union address, in which he proposed legislation to address problems of voting rights, poverty, diseases, education, immigration, and the environment.

Horace Greeley (1811–1872) In reaction to Radical Reconstruction and corruption in President Ulysses S. Grant's administration, a group of Republicans broke from the party to form the Liberal Republicans. In 1872, the Liberal Republicans chose Horace Greeley as their presidential candidate who ran on a platform of favoring civil service reform and condemning the Republican's Reconstruction policy.

greenbacks Paper money issued during the Civil War. After the war ended, a debate emerged on whether or not to remove the paper currency from circulation and revert back to hard-money currency (gold coins).

Opponents of hard-money feared that eliminating the greenbacks would shrink the money supply, which would lower crop prices and make it more difficult to repay long-term debts. President Ulysses S. Grant, as well as hard-currency advocates, believed that gold coins were morally preferable to paper currency.

Greenback party Formed in 1876 in reaction to economic depression, the party favored issuance of unsecured paper money to help farmers repay debts; the movement for free coinage of silver took the place of the greenback movement by the 1880s.

Nathanael Greene (1742–1786) He was appointed by Congress to command the American army fighting in the South during the Revolutionary War. Using his patience and his skills of managing men, saving supplies, and avoiding needless risks, he waged a successful war of attrition against the British.

Sarah Grimké (1792–1873) and **Angelina Grimké (1805–1879)** These two sisters gave anti-slavery speeches to crowds of mixed gender that caused some people to condemn them for engaging in unfeminine activities. The sisters rejected this opinion and made the role of women in the anti-slavery movement a prominent issue. In 1840, William Lloyd Garrison convinced the Anti-Slavery Society to allow women equal participation in the organization. A group of members that did not agree with this decision left the Anti-Slavery Society to form the American and Foreign Anti-Slavery Society.

Half-Way Covenant Allowed baptized children of church members to be admitted to a "halfway" membership in the church and secure baptism for their own children in turn, but allowed them neither a vote in the church, nor communion.

Alexander Hamilton (1755–1804) His belief in a strong federal government led him to become a contributor to *The Federalist* and leader of the Federalists. As the first secretary of the Treasury, he laid the foundation for American capitalism through his creation of a federal budget, funded debt, a federal tax system, a national bank, a customs service, and a coast guard. His "Reports on Public Credit" and "Reports on Manufactures" outlined his vision for economic development and government finances in America. He died in a duel against Aaron Burr.

Warren Harding (1865–1923) In the 1920 presidential election, he was the Republican nominee who promised Americans a "return to normalcy," which would mean a return to conservative values and a turning away from President Wilson's internationalism. His message resonated with voters' conservative postwar mood; and he won the election. Once in office, Harding's administration dismantled many of the social and economic components of progressivism and pursued a pro-business agenda. Harding appointed four pro-business Supreme Court Justices and his administration cut taxes, increased tariffs and promoted a lenient attitude towards government regulation of corporations. However, he did speak out against racism and ended the exclusion of African Americans from federal positions. His administration did suffer from a series of scandals as the result of him appointing members of the Ohio gang to government positions.

Harlem Renaissance African American literary and artistic movement of the 1920s and 1930s centered in New York City's Harlem district; writers Langston Hughes, Jean Toomer, Zora Neale Hurston, and Countee Cullen were among those active in the movement.

Hartford Convention Meeting of New England Federalists on December 15, 1814, to protest the War of 1812; proposed seven constitutional amendments (limiting embargoes and changing requirements for officeholding, declaration of war, and admission of new states), but the war ended before Congress could respond.

Patrick Henry (1736–1799) He inspired the Virginia Resolves, which declared that Englishmen could only be taxed by their elected representatives. In March of 1775, he met with other colonial leaders to discuss the goals of the upcoming Continental Congress and famously declared "Give me liberty or give me death." During the ratification process of the U.S. Constitution, he became one of the leaders of the anti-federalists.

Hideki Tōjō (1884–1948) He was Japan's war minister and later prime minister during World War II.

Alger Hiss (1904–1996) During the second Red Scare, Alger Hiss, who had served in several government departments, was accused of being a spy for the Soviet Union and was convicted of lying about espionage. The case was politically damaging to the Truman administration because the president called the charges against Hiss a "red herring." Richard

Nixon, then a California congressman, used his persistent pursuit of the case and his anti-Communist rhetoric to raise his national profile and to win election to the Senate.

Adolph Hitler "*Führer*" (1889–1945) The leader of the Nazis who advocated a violent anti-Semitic, anti-Marxist, pan-German ideology. He started World War II in Europe and orchestrated the systematic murder of some 6 million Jews along with more than a million others.

HIV/AIDS Human Immunodeficiency Virus (HIV) is a virus that attacks the body's T-cells, which are necessary to help the immune system fight off infection and disease. Acquired Immunodeficiency Syndrome (AIDS) occurs after the HIV virus has destroyed the body's immune system. HIV is transferred when body fluids, such as blood or semen, which carry the virus, enter the body of an uninfected person. The virus appeared in America in the early 1980s. The Reagan administration was slow to respond to the "AIDS Epidemic," because effects of the virus were not fully understood and they deemed the spread of the disease as the result of immoral behavior.

Homestead Act (1862) Authorized Congress to grant 160 acres of public land to a western settler, who had only to live on the land for five years to establish title.

Herbert Hoover (1874–1964) Prior to becoming president, Hoover served as the secretary of commerce in both the Harding and Coolidge administrations. During his tenure at the Commerce Department, he pursued new markets for business and encouraged business leaders to share information as part of the trade-association movement. The Great Depression hit while he was president. Hoover believed that the nation's business structure was sound and sought to revive the economy through boosting the nation's confidence. He also tried to restart the economy with government constructions projects, lower taxes and new federal loan programs, but nothing worked.

House Un-American Activities Committee (HUAC) Formed in 1938 to investigate subversives in the government; best-known investigations were of Hollywood notables and of former State Department official Alger Hiss, who was accused in 1948 of espionage and Communist party membership.

Sam Houston (1793–1863) During Texas's fight for independence from Mexico, Sam Houston was the commander in chief of the Texas forces, and he led the attack that captured General Antonio López de Santa Anna. After Texas gained its independence, he was name its first president.

Jacob Riis' *How the Other Half Lives* Jacob Riis was an early muckraking journalist who exposed the slum conditions in New York City in his book *How the Other Half Lives.*

General William Howe (1729–1814) As the commander of the British army in the Revolutionary War, he seized New York City from Washington's army, but failed to capture it. He missed several more opportunities to quickly end the rebellion, and he resigned his command after the British defeat at Saratoga.

Saddam Hussein (1937–2006) The former dictator of Iraq who became the head of state in 1979. In 1980, he invaded Iran and started the eight-year-long Iran-Iraq War. In 1990, he invaded Kuwait, which caused the Gulf War of 1991. In 2003, he was overthrown and captured when the United States invaded. He was sentenced to death by hanging in 2006.

Anne Hutchinson (1591–1643) The articulate, strong-willed, and intelligent wife of a prominent Boston merchant, who espoused her belief in direct divine revelation. She quarreled with Puritan leaders over her beliefs; and they banished her from the colony.

impressment The British navy used press-gangs to kidnap men in British and colonial ports who were then forced to serve in the British navy.

"Indian New Deal" This phrase refers to the reforms implemented for Native Americans during the New Deal era. John Collier, the commissioner of the Bureau of Indian Affairs (BIA), increased the access Native Americans had to relief programs and employed more Native Americans at the BIA. He worked to pass the Indian Reorganization Act. However, the version of the act passed by Congress was a much-diluted version of Collier's original proposal and did not greatly improve the lives of Native Americans.

indentured servant Settler who signed on for a temporary period of servitude to a master in exchange for passage to the New World; Virginia and Pennsylvania were largely peopled in the seventeenth and eighteenth centuries by English indentured servants.

Indian Removal Act (1830) Signed by President Andrew Jackson, the law permitted the negotiation of treaties to obtain the Indians' lands in exchange for their relocation to what became Oklahoma.

Indochina This area of Southeast Asian consists of Laos, Cambodia, became and Vietnam and was once controlled by France as a colony. After the Viet Minh defeated the French, the Geneva Accords were signed, which ended French colonial rule. The agreement created the independent nations of Laos and Cambodia and divided Vietnam along the 17th parallel until an election would reunify the country. Fearing a communist take over, the United States government began intervening in the region during the Truman administration, which led to President Johnson's full-scale military involvement in Vietnam.

Industrial Workers of the World A radical union organized in Chicago in 1905, nicknamed the Wobblies; its opposition to World War I led to its destruction by the federal government under the Espionage Act.

internationalists Prior to the United States' entry in World War II, internationalists believed that America's national security depended on aiding Britain in its struggle against Germany.

internment of Japanese Americans In 1942, President Roosevelt issued an executive order to have all Japanese Americans forcibly relocated to relocation camps. More than 60 percent of the more than 100,000 internees were American citizens.

interstate highway system In the late 1950s, construction began on a national network of interstate superhighways for the purpose of commerce and defense. The interstate highways would enable the rapid movement of military convoys and the evacuation of cities after a nuclear attack.

Iranian Hostage Crisis In 1979, a revolution in Iran placed the Ayatollah Ruhollah Khomeini, a fundamental religious leader, in power. In November 1979, revolutionaries seized the American embassy in Tehran and held those inside hostage. President Carter struggled to get the hostages. He tried pressuring Iran through appeals to the United Nations, freezing Iranian assets in the United States and imposing a trade embargo. During an aborted rescue operation, a helicopter collided with a transport plane and killed eight U.S. soldiers. Finally, Carter un-froze several billion dollars in Iranian assets, and the hostages were re-leased after being held for 444 days; but not until Ronald Reagan had become president of the United States.

Iran-Contra affair Scandal of the second Reagan administration involving sale of arms to Iran in partial exchange for release of hostages in Lebanon and use of the arms money to aid the Contras in Nicaragua, which had been expressly forbidden by Congress.

Irish Potato Famine In 1845, an epidemic of potato rot brought a famine to rural Ireland that killed over 1 million peasants and instigated a huge increase in the number or Irish immigrating to America. By 1850, the Irish made up 43 percent of the foreign-born population in the United States; and in the 1850s, they made up over half the population of New York City and Boston.

iron curtain Term coined by Winston Churchill to describe the cold war divide between western Europe and the Soviet Union's Eastern European satellites.

Iroquois League An alliance of the Iroquois tribes that used their strength to force Europeans to work with them in the fur trade and to wage war across what is today eastern North America.

Andrew Jackson (1767–1837) As a major general in the Tennessee militia, he defeated the Creek Indians, invaded the panhandle of Spanish Florida and won the Battle of New Orleans. In 1818, his successful campaign against Spanish forces in Florida gave the United States the upper hand in negotiating for Florida with Spain. As president, he ve-toed bills for the federal funding of internal improvements and the re-chartering of the Second National Bank. When South Carolina nul-lified the Tariffs of 1828 and 1832, Jackson requested that Congress pass a "force bill" that would authorize him to use the army to compel the state to comply with the tariffs. He forced eastern Indians to move west of the Mississippi River so their lands could be used by white set-tlers. Groups of those who opposed Jackson come together to form a new political part called the Whigs.

Jesse Jackson (1941–) An African American civil rights activist who had been one of Martin Luther King Jr.'s chief lieutenants. He is most famous for founding the social justice organization the Rainbow

Coalition. In 1988, he ran for the Democratic presidential nomination, which became a race primarily between him and Michael Dukakis. Dukakis won the nomination, but lost the election to Republican nominee Vice President George H. W. Bush.

Thomas "Stonewall" Jackson (1824–1863) He was a Confederate general who was known for his fearlessness in leading rapid marches, bold flanking movements, and furious assaults. He earned his nickname at the Battle of the First Bull Run for standing courageously against Union fire. During the battle of Chancellorsville, his own men accidently mortally wounded him.

William James (1842–1910) He was the founder of Pragmatism and one of the fathers of modern psychology. He believed that ideas gained their validity not from their inherent truth, but from their social consequences and practical application.

Jay's Treaty Treaty with Britain negotiated in 1794 by Chief Justice John Jay; Britain agreed to vacate forts in the Northwest Territories, and festering disagreements (border with Canada, prewar debts, shipping claims) would be settled by commission.

Thomas Jefferson (1743–1826) He was a plantation owner, author, the drafter of the Declaration Independence, ambassador to France, leader of the Republican party, secretary of state, and the third president of the United States. As president, he purchased the Louisiana territory from France, withheld appointments made by President Adams leading to *Marybury v. Madison*, outlawed foreign slave trade, and was committed to a "wise and frugal" government.

Jesuits A religious order founded in 1540 by Ignatius Loyola. They sought to counter the spread of Protestantism during the Protestant Reformation and spread the Catholic faith through work as missionaries. Roughly 3,500 served in New Spain and New France.

"Jim Crow" laws In the New South, these laws mandated the separation of races in various public places that served as a way for the ruling whites to impose their will on all areas of black life.

Andrew Johnson (1808–1875) As President Abraham Lincoln's vice president, he was elevated to the presidency after Lincoln's assassination. In order to restore the Union after the Civil War, he issued an amnesty proclamation and required former Confederate states to ratify the Thirteenth Amendment. He fought Radical Republicans in Congress over whether he or Congress had the authority to restore states rights to the former Confederate states. This fight weakened both his political and public support. In 1868, the Radical Republicans attempted to impeach Johnson but fell short on the required number of votes needed to remove him from office.

Lyndon B. Johnson (1908–1973) Former member of the United States House of Representatives and the former Majority Leader of the United States Senate, Vice President Lyndon Johnson, assumed the presidency after President Kennedy's assassination. He was able to push through Congress several pieces of Kennedy's legislation that had been stalled including the Civil Rights Act of 1964. He declared "war on poverty" and promoted his own social program called the Great Society, which sought to end poverty and racial injustice. In 1965, he signed the Immigration and Nationality Service Act, which abolished the discriminatory quotas system that had been the immigration policy since the 1920s. Johnson greatly increased America's role in Vietnam. By 1969, there were 542,000 U.S. troops fighting in Vietnam and a massive anti-war movement had developed in America. In 1968, Johnson announced that he would not run for re-election.

Kansas-Nebraska Act (1854) Law sponsored by Illinois senator Stephen A. Douglas to allow settlers in newly organized territories north of the Missouri border to decide the slavery issue for themselves; fury over the resulting nullification of the Missouri Compromise of 1820 led to violence in Kansas and to the formation of the Republican party.

Florence Kelley (1859–1932) As the head of the National Consumer's League, she led the crusade to promote state laws to regulate the number of working hours imposed on women who were wives and mothers.

George F. Kennan (1904–2005) While working as an American diplomat, he devised the strategy of containment, which called for the halting of Soviet expansion. It became America's choice strategy throughout the cold war.

John F. Kennedy (1917–1963) Elected president in 1960, he was interested in bringing new ideas to the White House. Despite the difficulties he had in getting his legislation through Congress, he did establish the Alliance for Progress programs to help Latin America, the Peace Corps, the Trade

Expansion Act of 1962, and funding for urban renewal projects and the space program. He mistakenly proceeded with the Bay of Pigs invasion, but he successfully handled the Cuban missile crisis. In Indochina, his administration became increasingly involved in supporting local governments through aid, advisors, and covert operations. In 1963, he was assassinated by Lee Harvey Oswald in Dallas, Texas.

Kent State During the spring of 1970, students on college campuses across the country protested the expansion of the Vietnam War into Cambodia. At Kent State University, the National Guard attempted to quell the rioting students. The guardsmen panicked and shot at rock-throwing demonstrators. Four student bystanders were killed.

Kentucky and Virginia Resolutions (1798–1799) Passed in response to the Alien and Sedition Acts, the resolutions advanced the state-compact theory that held states could nullify an act of Congress if they deemed it unconstitutional.

Francis Scott Key (1779–1843) During the War of 1812, he watched British forces bombard Fort McHenry, but fail to take it. Seeing the American flag still flying over the fort at dawn inspired him to write "The Star-Spangled Banner," which became the American national anthem.

Keynesian economics A theory of economics developed by John Maynard Keynes. He argued that increased government spending, even if it increased the nation's deficit, during an economic downturn was necessary to reinvigorate a nation's economy. This view was held by Harry Hopkins and Harold Ickes who advised President Franklin Roosevelt during the Great Depression.

Martin Luther King Jr. (1929–1968) As an important leader of the civil rights movement, he urged people to use nonviolent civil disobedience to demand their rights and bring about change. He successfully led the Montgomery bus boycott. While in jail for his role in demonstrations, he wrote his famous "Letter from Birmingham City Jail," in which he defended his strategy of nonviolent protest. In 1963, he delivered his famous "I Have a Dream Speech" from the steps of the Lincoln Memorial as a part of the March on Washington. A year later, he was awarded the Nobel Peace Prize. In 1968, he was assassinated.

King William's War (War of the League of Augsburg) First (1689–1697) of four colonial wars between England and France.

King Philip (?–1676) or Metacomet The chief of the Wampanoages, who the colonists called King Philip. He resented English efforts to convert Indians to Christianity and waged a war against the English colonists in which he was killed.

Henry Kissinger (1923–) He served as the secretary of state and national security advisor in the Nixon administration. He negotiated with North Vietnam for an end to the Vietnam War. In 1973, an agreement was signed between America, North and South Vietnam, and the Viet Cong to end the war. The cease-fire did not last; and South Vietnam fell to North Vietnam. He helped organize Nixon's historic trips to China and the Soviet Union. In the Middle East, he negotiated a cease-fire between Israel and its neighbors following the Yom Kippur War and solidified Israel's promise to return to Egypt most of the land it had taken during the 1967 war.

Knights of Labor Founded in 1869, the first national union picked up many members after the disastrous 1877 railroad strike, but lasted under the leadership of Terence V. Powderly, only into the 1890s; supplanted by the American Federation of Labor.

Know-Nothing party Nativist, anti-Catholic third party organized in 1854 in reaction to large-scale German and Irish immigration; the party's only presidential candidate was Millard Fillmore in 1856.

Ku Klux Klan Organized in Pulaski, Tennessee, in 1866 to terrorize former slaves who voted and held political offices during Reconstruction; a revived organization in the 1910s and 1920s stressed white, Anglo-Saxon, fundamentalist Protestant supremacy; the Klan revived a third time to fight the civil rights movement of the 1950s and 1960s in the South.

Marquis de Lafayette (1757–1834) A wealthy French idealist excited by the American cause, he offered to serve in Washington's army for free in exchange for being named a major general. He overcame Washington's initial skepticism to become one of his most trusted aides.

Land Ordinance of 1785 Directed surveying of the Northwest Territory into townships of thirty-six sections (square miles) each, the sale of the sixteenth section of which was to be used to finance public education.

Bartolomé de Las Casas (1484–1566) A Catholic missionary who renounced the Spanish practice of coercively converting Indians and advocated the better treatment for them. In 1552, he wrote *A Brief Relation of the Destruction of the Indies*, which described the Spanish's cruel treatment of the Indians.

League of Nations Organization of nations to mediate disputes and avoid war established after World War I as part of the Treaty of Versailles; President Woodrow Wilson's "Fourteen Points" speech to Congress in 1918 proposed the formation of the league.

Mary Elizabeth Lease (1850–1933) She was a leader of the farm protest movement who advocated violence if change could not be obtained at the ballot box. She believed that the urban-industrial East was the enemy of the working class.

Robert E. Lee (1807–1870) Even though he had served in the United States Army for thirty years, he chose to fight on the side of the Confederacy and took command of the Army of North Virginia. Lee was excellent at using his field commanders; and his soldiers respected him. However, General Ulysses S. Grant eventually wore down his army, and Lee surrendered to Grant at the Appomattox Court House on April 9, 1865.

Lend-Lease Act (1941) Permitted the United States to lend or lease arms and other supplies to the Allies, signifying increasing likelihood of American involvement in World War II.

John Dickinson's "Letters from a Farmer in Pennsylvania" These twelve letters appeared in the *Pennsylvania Chronicle* and argued that Parliament could regulate colonial commerce and collect duties that related to that purpose, but it did not have the right to levy taxes for revenue.

Levittown First low-cost, mass-produced development of suburban tract housing built by William Levitt on Long Island, New York, in 1947.

Lexington and Concord, Battle of The first shots fired in the Revolutionary War, on April 19, 1775, near Boston; approximately 100 Minutemen and 250 British soldiers were killed.

Liberator William Lloyd Garrison started this anti-slavery newspaper in 1831 in which he renounced gradualism and called for abolition.

Queen Liliuokalani (1838–1917) In 1891, she ascended to the throne of the Hawaiian royal family and tried to eliminate white control of the Hawaiian government. Two years later, Hawaii's white population revolted and seized power with the support of American marines.

Abraham Lincoln (1809–1865) His participation in the Lincoln-Douglas debates gave him a national reputation and he was nominated as the Republican party candidate for president in 1860. Shortly after he was elected president, southern states began succeeding from the Union and in April of 1861 he declared war on the succeeding states. On January 1, 1863, Lincoln signed the Emancipation Proclamation, which freed all slaves. At the end of the war, he favored a reconstruction strategy for the former Confederate states that did not radically alter southern social and economic life. However, before his plans could be finalized, John Wilkes Booth assassinated Lincoln at Ford's Theater on April 14, 1865.

Lincoln-Douglas debates Series of senatorial campaign debates in 1858 focusing on the issue of slavery in the territories; held in Illinois between Republican Abraham Lincoln, who made a national reputation for himself, and incumbent Democratic senator Stephen A. Douglas, who managed to hold onto his seat.

John Locke (1632–1704) An English philosopher whose ideas were influential during the Enlightenment. He argued in his *Essay on Human Understanding* (1690) that humanity is largely the product of the environment, the mind being a blank tablet, *tabula rasa*, on which experience is written.

Henry Cabot Lodge (1850–1924) He was the chairman of the Senate Foreign Relations Committee who favored limiting America's involvement in the League of Nations' covenant and sought to amend the Treaty of Versailles.

de Lôme letter Spanish ambassador Depuy de Lôme wrote a letter to a friend in Havana in which he described President McKinley as "weak" and a seeker of public admiration. This letter was stolen and published in the *New York Journal*, which increased the American public's dislike of Spain and moved the two countries closer to war.

Lone Star Republic After winning independence from Mexico, Texas became its own nation that was called the Lone Star Republic. In 1836, Texans drafted themselves a constitution, legalized slavery, banned free blacks, named Sam Houston president, and voted for the annexation to the United States. However, quarrels over adding a slave state and fears of instigating a war with Mexico delayed Texas's entrance into the Union until December 29, 1845.

Huey Long (1893–1935) He began his political career in Louisiana where he developed a reputation for being an unscrupulous reformer. As a U.S. senator, he became a critic of President Roosevelt's New Deal Plan and offered his alternative called the Share-the-Wealth program. He was assassinated in 1935.

Lords Commissioners of Trade and Plantations (the Board of Trade) William III created this organization in 1696 to investigate the enforcement of the Navigations Act, recommend ways to limit colonial manufactures, and encourage the production of raw materials in the colonies that were needed in Britain.

Louisiana Purchase President Thomas Jefferson's 1803 purchase from France of the important port of New Orleans and 828,000 square miles west of the Mississippi River to the Rocky Mountains; it more than doubled the territory of the United States at a cost of only $15 million.

Lowell System Lowell mills were the first to bring all the processes of spinning and weaving cloth together under one roof and have every aspect of the production mechanized. In addition, the Lowell mills were designed to be model factory communities that provided the young women employees with meals, a boardinghouse, moral discipline, and educational and cultural opportunities.

Martin Luther (1483–1546) A German monk who founded the Lutheran church. He protested abuses in the Catholic Church by posting his Ninety-five Theses, which began the Protestant Reformation.

General Douglas MacArthur (1880–1964) During World War II, he and Admiral Chester Nimitz dislodged the Japanese military from the Pacific Islands they had occupied. Following the war, he was in charge of the occupation of Japan. After North Korea invaded South Korea, Truman sent the U.S. military to defend South Korea under the command of MacArthur. Later in the war, Truman expressed his willingness to negotiate the restoration of prewar boundaries which MacArthur attempted to undermine. Truman fired MacArthur for his open insubordination.

James Madison (1751–1836) He participated in the Constitutional Convention during which he proposed the Virginia Plan. He believed in a strong federal government and was a leader of the Federalists and a contributor to *The Federalist*. However, he also presented to Congress the Bill of Rights and drafted the Virginia Resolutions. As the secretary of state, he withheld a commission for William Marbury, which led to the landmark *Marbury v. Madison* decision. During his presidency, he declared war on Britain in response to violations of American shipping rights, which started the War of 1812.

Alfred Thayer Mahan's *The Influence of Sea Power Upon History, 1660–1783* Alfred Thayer Mahan was an advocate for sea power and Western imperialism. In 1890, he published *The Influence of Sea Power Upon History*, 1660–1783 in which he argued that a nation's greatness and prosperity comes from maritime power. He believed that America's "destiny" was to control the Caribbean, build the Panama Canal, and spread Western civilization across the Pacific.

Malcolm X (1925–1964) The most articulate spokesman for black power. Originally, the chief disciple of Elijah Muhammad, the black Muslim leader in the United States, Malcolm X broke away from him and founded his own organization committed to establishing relations between African Americans and the nonwhite peoples of the world. Near the end of his life, he began to preach a biracial message of social change. In 1964, he was assassinated by members of a rival group of black Muslims.

Manchuria incident The northeast region of Manchuria was an area contested between China and Russia. In 1931, the Japanese claimed that they needed to protect their extensive investments in the area and moved their army into Manchuria. They quickly conquered the region and set up their own puppet empire. China asked both the United States and the League of Nations for help and neither responded.

Manifest Destiny Imperialist phrase first used in 1845 to urge annexation of Texas; used thereafter to encourage American settlement of European colonial and Indian lands in the Great Plains and Far West.

Horace Mann (1796–1859) He believed the public school system was the best way to achieve social stability and equal opportunity. As a reformer of education, he sponsored a state board of education, the first state-supported "normal" school for training teachers, a state association for teachers, the minimum school year of six months, and led the drive for a statewide school system.

***Marbury v. Madison* (1803)** First U.S. Supreme Court decision to declare a federal law—the Judiciary Act of 1801—unconstitutional; President John Adams's "midnight appointment" of Federalist judges prompted the suit.

March on Washington Civil rights demonstration on August 28, 1963, where the Reverend Martin Luther King Jr. gave his "I Have a Dream" speech on the steps of the Lincoln Memorial.

George C. Marshall (1880–1959) As the chairman of the Joint Chiefs of Staff, he orchestrated the Allied victories over Germany and Japan in World War II. In 1947, he became President Truman's secretary of state and proposed the massive reconstruction program for western Europe called the Marshall Plan.

Chief Justice John Marshall (1755–1835) During his long tenure as chief justice of the supreme court (1801–1835), he established the foundations for American jurisprudence, the authority of the Supreme Court, and the constitutional supremacy of the national government over states.

Marshall Plan U.S. program for the reconstruction of post–World War II Europe through massive aid to former enemy nations as well as allies; proposed by General George C. Marshall in 1947.

massive resistance In reaction to the *Brown v. Board of Education* decision of 1954, U.S. Senator Harry Byrd encouraged southern states to defy federally mandated school integration.

Senator Joseph R. McCarthy (1908–1957) In 1950, this senator became the shrewdest and most ruthless exploiter of America's anxiety of communism. He claimed that the United States government was full of Communists and led a witch hunt to find them, but he was never able to uncover a single communist agent.

George B. McClellan (1826–1885) In 1861, President Abraham Lincoln appointed him head of the Army of the Potomac and, later, general in chief of the U.S. Army. He built his army into well trained and powerful force. However, he often delayed taking action against the enemy even though Lincoln wanted him to attack. After failing to achieve a decisive victory against the Confederacy, Lincoln removed McClellan from command in 1862.

Cyrus Hall McCormick (1809–1884) In 1831, he invented a mechanical reaper to harvest wheat, which transformed the scale of agriculture. By hand a farmer could only harvest a half an acre a day, while the McCormick reaper allowed two people to harvest twelve acres of wheat a day.

William McKinley (1843–1901) As a congressman, he was responsible for the McKinley Tariff of 1890, which raised the duties on manufactured products to their highest level ever. Voters disliked the tariff and McKinley, as well as other Republicans, lost their seats in Congress the next election. However, he won the presidential election of 1896 and raised the tariffs again. In 1898, he annexed Hawaii and declared war on Spain. The war concluded with the Treaty of Paris, which gave America control over Puerto Rico, Guam, and the Philippines. Soon America was fighting Filipinos, who were seeking independence for their country. In 1901, McKinley was assassinated.

Robert McNamara (1916–) He was the secretary of defense for both President Kennedy and President Johnson and a supporter of America's involvement in Vietnam.

McNary-Haugen Bill Vetoed by President Calvin Coolidge in 1927 and 1928, the bill to aid farmers would have artificially raised agricultural prices by selling surpluses overseas for low prices and selling the reduced supply in the United States for higher prices.

Andrew Mellon (1855–1937) As President Harding's secretary of the Treasury, he sought to generate economic growth through reducing government spending and lowering taxes. However, he insisted that the tax reductions mainly go to the rich because he believed the wealthy would reinvest their money and spur economic growth. In order to bring greater efficiency and nonpartisanship to the government's budget process, he persuaded Congress to pass the Budget and Accounting Act of 1921, which created a new Bureau of the Budget and a General Accounting Office.

mercantile system A nationalistic program that assumed that the total amount of the world's gold and silver remained essentially fixed with only a nation's share of that wealth subject to change.

James Meredith (1933–) In 1962, the governor of Mississippi defied a Supreme Court ruling and refused to allow James Meredith, an African American, to enroll at the University of Mississippi. Federal marshals were sent to enforce the law which led to clashes between a white mob and the marshals. Federal troops intervened and two people were killed and many others were injured. A few days later, Meredith was able to register at the university.

Merrimack* (ship renamed the *Virginia*) and the *Monitor First engagement between ironclad ships; fought at Hampton Roads, Virginia, on March 9, 1862.

Metacomet (?–1676) or King Philip The chief of the Wampanoages, who the colonists called King Philip. He resented English efforts to convert Indians to Christianity and waged a war against the English colonists in which he was killed.

militant nonviolence After the success of the Montgomery bus boycott, people were inspired by Martin Luther King Jr.'s use of this nonviolent form of protest. Throughout the civil rights movement, demonstrators used this method of protest to challenge racial segregation in the South.

Ho Chi Minh (1890–1969) He was the Vietnamese communist resistance leader who drove the French and the United States out of Vietnam. After the Geneva Accords divided the region into four countries, he controlled North Vietnam, and ultimately became the leader of all of Vietnam at the conclusion of the Vietnam War.

minstrelsy A form of entertainment that was popular from the 1830s to the 1870s. The performances featured white performers who were made up as African Americans or blackface. They performed banjo and fiddle music, "shuffle" dances and lowbrow humor that reinforced racial stereotypes.

Minutemen Special units organized by the militia to be ready for quick mobilization.

***Miranda v. Arizona* (1966)** U.S. Supreme Court decision required police to advise persons in custody of their rights to legal counsel and against self-incrimination.

Mississippi Plan In 1890, Mississippi instituted policies that led to a near-total loss of voting rights for blacks and many poor whites. In order to vote, the state required that citizens pay all their taxes first, be literate, and have been residents of the state for two years and one year in an electoral district. Convicts were banned from voting. Seven other states followed this strategy of disenfranchisement.

Missouri Compromise Deal proposed by Kentucky senator Henry Clay to resolve the slave/free imbalance in Congress that would result from Missouri's admission as a slave state; in the compromise of March 20, 1820, Maine's admission as a free state offset Missouri, and slavery was prohibited in the remainder of the Louisiana Territory north of the southern border of Missouri.

Model T Ford Henry Ford developed this model of car so that it was affordable for everyone. Its success led to an increase in the production of automobiles which stimulated other related industries such steel, oil, and rubber. The mass use of automobiles increased the speed goods could be transported, encouraged urban sprawl, and sparked real estate booms in California and Florida.

modernism As both a mood and movement, modernism recognized that Western civilization had entered an era of change. Traditional ways of thinking and creating art were being rejected and replaced with new understandings and forms of expression.

Molly Maguires Secret organization of Irish coal miners that used violence to intimidate mine officials in the 1870s.

Monroe Doctrine President James Monroe's declaration to Congress on December 2, 1823, that the American continents would be thenceforth closed to colonization but that the United States would honor existing colonies of European nations.

Montgomery bus boycott Sparked by Rosa Parks's arrest on December 1, 1955, a successful year-long boycott protesting segregation on city buses; led by the Reverend Martin Luther King Jr.

moral majority Televangelist Jerry Falwell's political lobbying organization, the name of which became synonymous with the religious right— conservative evangelical Protestants who helped ensure President Ronald Reagan's 1980 victory.

J. Pierpont Morgan (1837–1913) As a powerful investment banker, he would acquire, reorganize, and consolidate companies into giant trusts. His biggest achievement was the consolidation of the steel industry into the United States Steel Corporation, which was the first billion-dollar corporation.

James Monroe (1758–1831) He served as secretary of state and war under President Madison and was elected president. As the latter, he signed the Transcontinental Treaty with Spain which gave the United States Florida and expanded the Louisiana territory's western border to the Pacific coast. In 1823, he established the Monroe Doctrine. This foreign policy proclaimed the American continents were no longer open to colonization and America would be neutral in European affairs.

Robert Morris (1734–1806) He was the superintendent of finance for the Congress of the Confederation during the final years of the Revolutionary War. He envisioned a national finance plan of taxation and debt management, but the states did not approve the necessary amendments to the Articles of Confederation need to implement the plan.

Samuel B. Morse (1791–1872) In 1832, he invented the telegraph and revolutionized the speed of communication.

mountain men Inspired by the fur trade, these men left civilization to work as trappers and reverted to a primitive existence in the wilderness. They were the first whites to find routes through the Rocky Mountains, and they pioneered trails that settlers later used to reach the Oregon country and California in the 1840s.

muckrakers Writers who exposed corruption and abuses in politics, business, meat-packing, child labor, and more, primarily in the first decade of the twentieth century; their popular books and magazine articles spurred public interest in progressive reform.

Mugwumps Reform wing of the Republican party that supported Democrat Grover Cleveland for president in 1884 over Republican James G. Blaine, whose influence peddling had been revealed in the Mulligan letters of 1876.

Benito Mussolini "*Il Duce*" (1883–1945) The Italian founder of the Fascist party who came to power in Italy in 1922 and allied himself with Adolf Hitler and the Axis powers during World War II.

My Lai Massacre In 1968, Lieutenant William Calley and his soldiers massacred 347 Vietnamese civilians in the village of My Lai. Twenty-five army officers were charged with complicity in the massacre and its cover-up but only Calley was convicted. Later, President Nixon granted him parole.

NAFTA Approved in 1993, the North American Free Trade Agreement with Canada and Mexico allowed goods to travel across their borders free of tariffs; critics argued that American workers would lose their jobs to cheaper Mexican labor.

National Industrial Recovery Act (1933) Passed on the last of the Hundred Days; it created public-works jobs through the Federal Emergency Relief Administration and established a system of self-regulation for industry through the National Recovery Administration, which was ruled unconstitutional in 1935.

National Recovery Administration This organization's two goals were to stabilize business and generate purchasing power for consumers. The first goal was to be achieved through the implementation industry-wide codes that set wages and prices, which would reduce the chaotic competition. To provide consumers with purchasing power, the administration would provide jobs, define workplace standards, and raise wages.

National Socialist German Workers' Party (Nazi) Founded in the 1920s, this party gained control over Germany under the leadership of Adolf Hitler in 1933 and continued in power until Germany's defeat at the end of World War II. It advocated a violent anti-Semitic, anti-Marxist, pan-German ideology. The Nazi party systematically murdered some 6 million Jews along with more than a million others.

nativism Anti-immigrant and anti-Catholic feeling in the 1830s through the 1850s; the largest group was New York's Order of the Star-Spangled Banner, which expanded into the American, or Know-Nothing party in 1854. In the 1920, there was a surge in nativism as Americans grew to fear immigrants who might be political radicals. In response, new strict immigration regulations were established.

nativist A native-born American who saw immigrants as a threat to his way of life and employment. During the 1880s, nativist groups worked to stop the flow of immigrates into the United States. Of these groups, the most successful was the American Protective Association who promoted government restrictions on immigration, tougher naturalization requirements, the teaching of English in schools and workplaces that refused to employ foreigners or Catholics.

Navigation Acts Passed by the English Parliament to control colonial trade and bolster the mercantile system, 1650–1775; enforcement of the acts led to growing resentment by colonists.

new conservatism The political philosophy of those who led the conservative insurgency of the early 1980s. This brand of conservatism was personified in Ronald Reagan who believed in less government, supply-side economics, and "family values."

New Deal Franklin D. Roosevelt's campaign promise, in his speech to the Democratic National Convention of 1932, to combat the Great Depression with a "new deal for the American people;" the phrase became a catchword for his ambitious plan of economic programs.

New France The name used for the area of North America that was colonized by the French. Unlike Spanish or English colonies, New France had a small number of colonists, which forced them to initially seek good relations with the indigenous people they encountered.

New Freedom Democrat Woodrow Wilson's political slogan in the presidential campaign of 1912; Wilson wanted to improve the banking system, lower tariffs, and, by breaking up monopolies, give small businesses freedom to compete.

New Frontier John F. Kennedy's program, stymied by a Republican Congress and his abbreviated term; his successor Lyndon B. Johnson had greater success with many of the same concepts.

New Jersey Plan The delegations to the Constitutional Convention were divided between two plans on how to structure the government: New Jersey wanted one legislative body with equal representation for each state.

New Nationalism Platform of the Progressive party and slogan of former President Theodore Roosevelt in the presidential campaign of 1912; stressed government activism, including regulation of trusts, conservation, and recall of state court decisions that had nullified progressive programs.

"new Negro" In the 1920s, a slow and steady growth of black political influence occurred in northern cities where African Americans were freer to speak and act. This political activity created a spirit of protest that expressed itself culturally in the Harlem Renaissance and politically in "new Negro" nationalism.

New Netherlands Dutch colony conquered by the English to become four new colonies New York, New Jersey, Pennsylvania, and Delaware.

New South *Atlanta Constitution* editor Henry W. Grady's 1886 term for the prosperous post–Civil War South: democratic, industrial, urban, and free of nostalgia for the defeated plantation South.

William Randolph Hearst's *New York Journal* In the late 1890s, the *New York Journal* and its rival, the *New York World*, printed sensationalism on the Cuban revolution as part of their heated competition for readership. The *New York Journal* printed a negative letter from the Spanish ambassador about President McKinley and inflammatory coverage of the sinking of the *Maine* in Havana Harbor. These two events roused the American public's outcry against Spain.

Joseph Pulitzer's *New York World* In the late 1890s, the *New York World* and its rival, *New York Journal*, printed sensationalism on the Cuban revolution as part of their heated competition for readership.

Admiral Chester Nimitz (1885–1966) During World War II, he was the commander of central Pacific. Along with General Douglas MacArthur, he dislodged the Japanese military from the Pacific Islands they had occupied.

Nineteenth Amendment (1920) Granted women the right to vote.

Richard Nixon (1913–1994) He first came to national prominence as a congressman involved in the investigation of Alger Hiss. Later he served as vice president during the Eisenhower administration. In 1960, he ran as the Republican nominee for president and lost to John Kennedy. In 1968, he ran and won the presidency against Democratic nominee Hubert Humphrey. During his campaign, he promised to bring about "peace with honor" in Vietnam. He told southern conservatives that he would slow the federal enforcement of civil rights laws and appoint pro-southern justices to the Supreme Court. After being elected, he fulfilled the latter promise attempted to keep the former. He opened talks with the North Vietnamese and began a program of Vietnamization of the war. He also bombed Cambodia. In 1973, America, North and South Vietnam, and the Viet Cong agreed to end the war and the United States withdrew. However, the cease-fire was broken, and the South Vietnam fell to North Vietnam. In 1970, Nixon changed U.S. foreign policy. He declared that the America was no longer the world's policemen and he would seek some partnerships with Communist countries. With his historic visit to China, he ended twenty years of diplomatically isolating China and he began taking steps towards cultural exchanges and trade. In 1972, Nixon travelled to Moscow and signed agreements with the Soviet Union on arms control and trade. That same year, Nixon was reelected, but the Watergate scandal erupted shortly after his victory. When his knowledge of the break-in and subsequent cover-up was revealed, Nixon resigned the presidency under threat of impeachment.

No Child Left Behind President George W. Bush's education reform plan that required states to set and meet learning standards for students and make sure that all students were "proficient" in reading and writing by 2014. States had to submit annual reports of students' standardized test scores. Teachers were required to be "proficient" in their subject area.

Schools who failed to show progress would face sanctions. States criticized the lack of funding for remedial programs and noted that poor school districts would find it very difficult to meet the new guidelines.

Lord North (1732–1792) The first minister of King George III's cabinet whose efforts to subdue the colonies only brought them closer to revolution. He helped bring about the Tea Act of 1773, which led to the Boston Tea Party. In an effort to discipline Boston, he wrote, and Parliament passed, four acts that galvanized colonial resistance.

North Atlantic Treaty Organization (NATO) Defensive alliance founded in 1949 by ten western European nations, the United States, and Canada to deter Soviet expansion in Europe.

Northwest Ordinance Created the Northwest Territory (area north of the Ohio River and west of Pennsylvania), established conditions for self-government and statehood, included a Bill of Rights, and permanently prohibited slavery.

nullification Concept of invalidation of a federal law within the borders of a state; first expounded in the Kentucky and Virginia Resolutions (1798), cited by South Carolina in its Ordinance of Nullification (1832) of the Tariff of Abominations, used by southern states to explain their secession from the Union (1861), and cited again by southern states to oppose the *Brown v. Board of Education* decision (1954).

Nuremberg trials At the site of the annual Nazi party rallies, twenty-one major German offenders faced an international military tribunal for Nazi atrocities. After a ten-month trial, the court acquitted three and sentenced eleven to death, three to life imprisonment, and four to shorter terms.

Barack Obama (1961–) In the 2008 presidential election, Senator Barack Obama mounted an innovative Internet based and grassroots orientated campaign that garnered him enough delegates to win the Democratic nomination. As the nation's economy nosedived in the fall of 2008, Obama linked the Republican economic philosophy with the country's dismal financial state and promoted a message of "change" and "politics of hope," which resonated with voters. He decisively won the presidency and became America's first person of colored to be elected president.

Sandra Day O'Connor (1930–) She was the first woman to serve on the Supreme Court of the United States and was appointed by President Reagan. Reagan's critics charged that her appointment was a token gesture and not a sign of any real commitment to gender equality.

Ohio gang In order to escape the pressures of the White House, President Harding met with a group of people, called the "Ohio gang," in a house on K Street in Washington D.C. Members of this gang were given low-level positions in the American government and they used their White House connection to "line their pockets" by granting government contracts without bidding, which led to a series of scandals, most notably the Teapot Dome Scandal.

Frederick Law Olmsted (1822–1903) In 1858, he constructed New York's Central Park, which led to a growth in the movement to create urban parks. He went on to design parks for Boston, Brooklyn, Chicago, Philadelphia, San Francisco, and many other cities.

Opechancanough (?–1644) The brother and successor of Powhatan who led his tribe in an attempt to repel the English settlers in Virginia in 1622.

Open Door Policy In hopes of protecting the Chinese market for U.S. exports, Secretary of State John Hay unilaterally announced in 1899 that Chinese trade would be open to all nations.

Operation Desert Shield After Saddam Hussein invaded Kuwait in 1990, President George H. W. Bush sent American military forces to Saudi Arabia on a strictly defensive mission. They were soon joined by a multinational coalition. When the coalition's mission changed to the retaking of Kuwait, the operation was renamed Desert Storm.

Operation Desert Storm Multinational allied force that defeated Iraq in the Gulf War of January 1991.

Operation Overlord The Allies' assault on Hitler's "Atlantic Wall," a seemingly impregnable series of fortifications and minefields along the French coastline that German forces had created using captive Europeans for laborers.

J. Robert Oppenheimer (1904–1967) He led the group of physicists at the laboratory in Los Alamos, New Mexico, who constructed the first atomic bomb.

Oregon Country The Convention of 1818 between Britain and the United States established the Oregon Country as being west of the crest of the

Rocky Mountains and the two countries were to jointly occupy it. In 1824, the United States and Russia signed a treaty that established the line of 54°40′ as the southern boundary of Russia's territorial claim in North America. A similar agreement between Britain and Russia finally gave the Oregon Country clearly defined boarders, but it remained under joint British and American control.

Oregon fever Enthusiasm for emigration to the Oregon Country in the late 1830s and early 1840s.

Osceola (1804?–1838) He was the leader of the Seminole nation who resisted the federal Indian removal policy through a protracted guerilla war. In 1837, he was treacherously seized under a flag of truce and imprisoned at Fort Moultrie, where he was left to die.

Overland (Oregon) Trail Route of wagon trains bearing settlers from Independence, Missouri, to the Oregon Country in the 1840s to 1860s.

A. Mitchell Palmer (1872–1936) As the attorney general, he played an active role in government's response to the Red Scare. After several bombings across America, including one at Palmer's home, he and other Americans became convinced that there was a well-organized Communist terror campaign at work. The federal government launched a campaign of raids, deportations, and collecting files on radical individuals.

Panic of 1819 Financial collapse brought on by sharply falling cotton prices, declining demand for American exports, and reckless western land speculation.

panning A method of mining that used a large metal pan to sift gold dust and nuggets from riverbeds during the California gold rush of 1849.

Rosa Parks (1913–2005) In 1955, she refused to give up her seat to a white man on a city bus in Montgomery, Alabama, which a local ordinance required of blacks. She was arrested for disobeying the ordinance. In response, black community leaders organized the Montgomery bus boycott.

Alice Paul (1885–1977) She was a leader of the women's suffrage movement and head of the Congressional Committee of National Women Suffrage Association. She instructed female suffrage activists to use more militant tactics, such as picketing state legislatures, chaining themselves to public buildings, inciting police to arrest them, and undertaking hunger strikes.

Norman Vincent Peale (1898–1993) He was a champion of the upbeat and feel-good theology that was popular in the 1950s religious revival. He advocated getting rid of any depressing or negative thoughts and replacing them with "faith, enthusiasm and joy," which would make an individual popular and well liked.

"peculiar institution" This term was used to describe slavery in America because slavery so fragrantly violated the principle of individual freedom that served as the basis for the Declaration of Independence.

Pentagon papers Informal name for the Defense Department's secret history of the Vietnam conflict; leaked to the press by former official Daniel Ellsberg and published in the *New York Times* in 1971.

Pequot War Massacre in 1637 and subsequent dissolution of the Pequot Nation by Puritan settlers, who seized the Indians' lands.

perestroika Soviet leader Mikhail Gorbachev introduced these political and economic reforms, which included reconstructing the state bureaucracy, reducing the privileges of the political elite, and shifting from a centrally planned economy to a mixed economy.

Commodore Matthew Perry (1794–1858) In 1854, he negotiated the Treaty of Kanagawa, which was the first step in starting a political and commercial relationship between the United States and Japan.

John J. Pershing (1860–1948) After Pancho Villa had conducted several raids into Texas and New Mexico, President Woodrow Wilson sent troops under the command of General John J. Pershing into Mexico to stop Villa. However, after a year of chasing Villa and not being able to catch him, they returned to the United States. During World War I, Pershing commanded the first contingent of U.S. soldiers sent to Europe and advised the War Department to send additional American forces.

"pet banks" During President Andrew Jackson's fight with the national bank, Jackson resolved to remove all federal deposits from it. To comply with Jackson's demands, Secretary of Treasury Taney continued to draw on government's accounts in the national bank, but deposit all new federal receipts in state banks. The state banks that received these deposits were called "pet banks."

Pilgrims Puritan Separatists who broke completely with the Church of England and sailed to the New World aboard the *Mayflower*, founding Plymouth Colony on Cape Cod in 1620.

Dien Bien Phu The defining battle in the war between French colonialists and the Viet Minh. The Viet Minh's victory secured North Vietnam for Ho Chi Minh and was crucial in compelling the French to give up Indochina as a colony.

Gifford Pinchot (1865–1946) As the head of the Division of Forestry, he implemented a conservation policy that entailed the scientific management of natural resources to serve the public interest. His work helped start the conservation movement. In 1910, he exposed to the public the decision of Richard A. Ballinger's, President Taft's secretary of the interior, to open up previously protected land for commercial use. Pinchot was fired, but the damage to Taft's public image resulted in the loss of many pro-Taft candidates in 1910 congressional election.

Elizabeth Lucas Pinckney (1722? –1793) One of the most enterprising horticulturists in colonial America, she began managing her family's three plantations in South Carolina at the age of sixteen. She had tremendous success growing indigo, which led to many other plantations growing the crop as well.

Pinckney's Treaty Treaty with Spain negotiated by Thomas Pinckney in 1795; established United States boundaries at the Mississippi River and the 31st parallel and allowed open transportation on the Mississippi.

Francisco Pizarro (1478?–1541) In 1531, he lead his Spanish soldiers to Peru and conquered the Inca Empire.

planters In the antebellum South, the owner of a large farm worked by twenty or more slaves.

James Knox Polk "Young Hickory" (1795–1849) As President, his chief concern was the expansion of the United States. In 1846, his administration resolved the dispute with Britain over the Oregon Country border. Shortly, after taking office, Mexico broke off relations with the United States over the annexation of Texas. Polk declared war on Mexico and sought to subvert Mexican authority in California. The United States defeated Mexico; and the two nations signed the Treaty of Guadalupe Hidalgo in which Mexico gave up any claims on Texas north of the Rio Grande River and ceded New Mexico and California to the United States.

Pontiac's Rebellion The Peace Treaty of 1763 gave the British all French land east of the Mississippi River. This area included the territory of

France's Indian allies who were not consulted about the transfer of their lands to British control. In an effort to recover their autonomy, Indians captured British forts around the Great Lakes and in the Ohio Valley as well as attacked settlements in Pennsylvania, Maryland, and Virginia.

popular sovereignty Allowed settlers in a disputed territory to decide the slavery issue for themselves.

Populist / the People's party Political success of Farmers' Alliance candidates encouraged the formation in 1892 of the People's party (later renamed the Populist party); active until 1912, it advocated a variety of reform issues, including free coinage of silver, income tax, postal savings, regulation of railroads, and direct election of U.S. senators.

Chief Powhatan Wahunsonacock He was called Powhatan by the English after the name of his tribe, and was the powerful, charismatic chief of numerous Algonquian-speaking towns in eastern Virginia representing over 10,000 Indians.

pragmatism William James founded this philosophy in the early 1900s. Pragmatists believed that ideas gained their validity not from their inherent truth, but from their social consequences and practical application.

Proclamation of 1763 Royal directive issued after the French and Indian War prohibiting settlement, surveys, and land grants west of the Appalachian Mountains; although it was soon over-ridden by treaties, colonists continued to harbor resentment.

proprietary colonies A colony owned by an individual, rather than a joint-stock company.

pueblos The Spanish term for the adobe cliff dwellings of the indigenous people of the southwestern United States.

Pullman Strike Strike against the Pullman Palace Car Company in the company town of Pullman, Illinois, on May 11, 1894, by the American Railway Union under Eugene V. Debs; the strike was crushed by court injunctions and federal troops two months later.

Puritans English religious group that sought to purify the Church of England; founded the Massachusetts Bay Colony under John Winthrop in 1630.

Quakers George Fox founded the Quaker religion in 1647. They rejected the use of formal sacraments and ministry, refused to take oaths and embraced pacifism. Fleeing persecution, they settled and established the colony of Pennsylvania.

Radical Republicans Senators and congressmen who, strictly identifying the Civil War with the abolitionist cause, sought swift emancipation of the slaves, punishment of the rebels, and tight controls over the former Confederate states after the war.

Raleigh's Roanoke Island Colony English expedition of 117 settlers, including Virginia Dare, the first English child born in the New World; colony disappeared from Roanoke Island in the Outer Banks sometime between 1587 and 1590.

A. Philip Randolph (1889–1979) He was the head of the Brotherhood of Sleeping Car Porters who planned a march on Washington D.C. to demand an end to racial discrimination in the defense industries. To stop the march, Roosevelt administration negotiated an agreement with the Randolph group. The demonstration would be called off and an executive order would be issued that forbid discrimination in defense work and training programs and set up the Fair Employment Practices Committee.

range wars In the late 1800s, conflicting claims over land and water rights triggered violent disputes between farmers and ranchers in parts of the western United States.

Ronald Reagan (1911–2004) In 1980, the former actor and governor of California was elected president. In office, he reduced social spending, cut taxes, and increased defense spending. He was criticized for cutting important programs, such as housing and school lunches and increasing the federal deficit. By 1983, prosperity had returned to America and Reagan's economic reforms appeared to be working, but in October of 1987 the stock market crashed. Some blamed the federal debt, which had tripled in size since Reagan had taken office. In the early 1980s, HIV/AIDS cases were beginning to be reported in America, but the Reagan administration chose to do little about the growing epidemic. Reagan believed that most of the world's problems came from the Soviet Union, which he called the "evil empire." In response, he conducted a major arms build up. Then in 1987, he signed an arms-control treaty with the Soviet Union. He authorized covert CIA operations in Central America. In 1986, the Iran-Contra scandal came to light which revealed arms sales were being conducted with Iran in a partial exchange for the release of hostages in Lebanon. The arms money was being used to aid the Contras.

Reaganomics Popular name for President Ronald Reagan's philosophy of "supply side" economics, which combined tax cuts, less government spending, and a balanced budget with an unregulated marketplace.

Reconstruction Finance Corporation Federal program established in 1932 under President Herbert Hoover to loan money to banks and other institutions to help them avert bankruptcy.

Red Scare Fear among many Americans after World War I of Communists in particular and noncitizens in general, a reaction to the Russian Revolution, mail bombs, strikes, and riots.

Redeemers In post–Civil War southern politics, redeemers were supporters of postwar Democratic leaders who supposedly saved the South from Yankee domination and the constraints of a purely rural economy.

Dr. Walter Reed (1851–1902) His work on yellow fever in Cuba led to the discovery that the fever was carried by mosquitoes. This understanding helped develop more effective controls of the worldwide disease.

Reformation European religious movement that challenged the Catholic Church and resulted in the beginnings of Protestant Christianity. During this period, Catholics and Protestants persecuted, imprisoned, tortured, and killed each other in large numbers.

reparations As a part of the Treaty of Versailles, Germany was required to confess its responsibility for World War I and make payments to the victors for the entire expense of the war. These two requirements created a deep bitterness among Germans.

Alexander Hamilton's Report on Manufactures First Secretary of the Treasury Alexander Hamilton's 1791 analysis that accurately foretold the future of American industry and proposed tariffs and subsidies to promote it.

"return to normalcy" In the 1920 presidential election, Republican nominee Warren G. Harding campaigned on the promise of a "return to normalcy," which would mean a return to conservative values and a turning away from President Wilson's internationalism.

Paul Revere (1735–1818) On the night of April 18, 1775, British soldiers marched towards Concord to arrest American Revolutionary leaders and seize their depot of supplies. Paul Revere famously rode through the night and raised the alarm about the approaching British troops.

Roaring Twenties In 1920s, urban America experienced an era of social and intellectual revolution. Young people experimented with new forms of recreation and sexuality as well as embraced jazz music. Leading young urban intellectuals expressed a disdain for old-fashioned rural and small-town values. The Eastern, urban cultural shift clashed with conservative and insular midwestern America, which increased the tensions between the two regions.

Jackie Robinson (1919–1972) In 1947, he became the first African American to play major league baseball. He won over fans and players and stimulated the integration of other professional sports.

rock-and-roll music Alan Freed, a disc jockey, noticed white teenagers were buying rhythm and blues records that had been only purchased by African Americans and Hispanic Americans. Freed began playing these records, but called them rock-and-roll records as a way to overcome the racial barrier. As the popularity of the music genre increased, it helped bridge the gap between "white" and "black" music.

John D. Rockefeller (1839–1937) In 1870, he founded the Standard Oil Company of Ohio, which was his first step in creating his vast oil empire. Eventually, he perfected the idea of a holding company: a company that controlled other companies by holding all or at least a majority of their stock. During his lifetime, he donated over $500 million in charitable contributions.

Romanticism Philosophical, literary, and artistic movement of the nineteenth century that was largely a reaction to the rationalism of the previous century; Romantics valued emotion, mysticism, and individualism.

Eleanor Roosevelt (1884–1962) She redefined the role of the presidential spouse and was the first woman to address a national political convention, write a nationally syndicated column and hold regular press conferences. She travelled throughout the nation to promote the New Deal, women's causes, organized labor, and meet with African American leaders. She was her husband's liaison to liberal groups and brought women activists and African American and labor leaders to the White House.

Franklin D. Roosevelt (1882–1945) Elected during the Great Depression, Roosevelt sought to help struggling Americans through his New Deal programs that created employment and social programs, such as Social Security. Prior to American's entry into World War II, he supported Britain's fight against Germany through the lend-lease program. After the bombing of Pearl Harbor, he declared war on Japan and Germany and led the country through most of World War II before dying of cerebral hemorrhage. In 1945, he met with Winston Churchill and Joseph Stalin at the Yalta Conference to determine the shape of the post-War world.

Theodore Roosevelt (1858–1919) As the assistant secretary of the navy, he supported expansionism, American imperialism and war with Spain. He led the First Volunteer Cavalry, or Rough Riders, in Cuba during the war of 1898 and used the notoriety of this military campaign for political gain. As President McKinley's vice president, he succeeded McKinley after his assassination. His forceful foreign policy became known as "big stick diplomacy." Domestically, his policies on natural resources helped start the conversation movement. Unable to win the Republican nomination for president in 1912, he formed his own party of progressive Republicans called the "Bull Moose" party.

Roosevelt Corollary to the Monroe Doctrine (1904) President Theodore Roosevelt announced in what was essentially a corollary to the Monroe Doctrine that the United States could intervene militarily to prevent interference from European powers in the Western Hemisphere.

Rough Riders The First U.S. Volunteer Cavalry, led in battle in the Spanish-American War by Theodore Roosevelt; they were victorious in their only battle near Santiago, Cuba; and Roosevelt used the notoriety to aid his political career.

Nicola Sacco (1891–1927) In 1920, he and Bartolomeo Vanzetti were Italian immigrants who were arrested for stealing $16,000 and killing a paymaster and his guard. Their trial took place during a time of numerous bombings by anarchists and their judge was openly prejudicial. Many liberals and radicals believe that the conviction of Sacco and Vanzetti was based on their political ideas and ethnic origin rather than the evidence against them.

"salutary neglect" Edward Burke's description of Robert Walpole's relaxed policy towards the American colonies, which gave them greater independence in pursuing both their economic and political interests.

Sandinista Cuban-sponsored government that came to power in Nicaragua after toppling a corrupt dictator. The State Department believed that the Sandinistas were supplying the leftist Salvadoran rebels with Cuban and Soviet arms. In response, the Reagan administration ordered the CIA to train and supply guerrilla bands of anti-Communist Nicaraguans called Contras. A cease-fire agreement between the Contras and Sandinistas was signed in 1988.

Margaret Sanger (1883–1966) As a birth-control activist, she worked to distribute birth control information to working-class women and opened the nation's first family-planning clinic in 1916. She organized the American Birth Control League, which eventually changed its name to Planned Parenthood.

General Antonio López de Santa Anna (1794–1876) In 1834, he seized political power in Mexico and became a dictator. In 1835, Texans rebelled against him and he led his army to Texas to crush their rebellion. He captured the missionary called the Alamo and killed all of its defenders, which inspired Texans to continue to resistance and Americans to volunteer to fight for Texas. The Texans captured Santa Anna during a surprise attack and he bought his freedom by signing a treaty recognizing Texas's independence.

Saratoga, Battle of Major defeat of British general John Burgoyne and more than 5,000 British troops at Saratoga, New York, on October 17, 1777.

scalawags White southern Republicans—some former Unionists—who served in Reconstruction governments.

Phyllis Schlafly (1924–) She was a right-wing Republican activist who spearheaded the anti-feminism movement. She believed feminist were "anti-family, anti-children, and pro-abortion." She worked against the equal-rights amendment for women and civil rights protection for gays.

Winfield Scott (1786–1866) During the Mexican War, he was the American general who captured Mexico City, which ended the war. Using his popularity from his military success, he ran as a Whig party candidate for President.

Sears Roebuck and Company By the end of the nineteenth century, this company dominated the mail-order industry and helped create a truly national market. Its mail-order catalog and low prices allowed people living in rural areas and small towns to buy products that were previously too expensive or available only to city dwellers.

secession Shortly after President Abraham Lincoln was elected, southern states began dissolving their ties with the United States because they believed Lincoln and the Republican party were a threat to slavery.

second Bank of the United States In 1816, the second Bank of the United States was established in order to bring stability to the national economy, serve as the depository for national funds, and provide the government with the means of floating loans and transferring money across the country.

Second Great Awakening Religious revival movement of the early decades of the nineteenth century, in reaction to the growth of secularism and rationalist religion; began the predominance of the Baptist and Methodist churches.

Second New Deal To rescue his New Deal program form judicial and political challenges, President Roosevelt launched a second phase of the New Deal in 1935. He was able to convince Congress to pass key pieces of legislation including the National Labor Relations act and Social Security Act. Roosevelt called the latter the New Deal's "supreme achievement" and pensioners started receiving monthly checks in 1940.

Seneca Falls Convention First women's rights meeting and the genesis of the women's suffrage movement; held in July 1848 in a church in Seneca Falls, New York, by Elizabeth Cady Stanton and Lucretia Coffin Mott.

"separate but equal" Principle underlying legal racial segregation, which was upheld in *Plessy v. Ferguson* (1896) and struck down in *Brown v. Board of Education* (1954).

separation of powers The powers of government are split between three separate branches (executive, legislative, and judicial) who check and balance each other.

September 11 On September 11, 2001, Islamic terrorists, who were members of al Qaeda terrorist organization, hijacked four commercial airliners. Two were flown into the World Trade Center and a third into the Pentagon. A fourth plane was brought down in Shanksville, Pennsylvania, when its passengers attacked the cockpit. In response, President George W. Bush launched his "war on terrorism." His administration assembled an international coalition to fight terrorism, and they invaded Afghanistan after the country's government would not turn over al Qaeda's leader, Osama bin Laden. However, bin Laden evaded capture. Fearful of new attacks, Bush created the Office of Homeland Security and the Transportation Security Administration.

Bush and Congress passed the U.S.A. Patriot Act, which allowed government agencies to try suspected terrorists in secret military courts and eavesdrop on confidential conversations.

settlement houses Product of the late nineteenth-century movement to offer a broad array of social services in urban immigrant neighborhoods; Chicago's Hull House was one of hundreds of settlement houses that operated by the early twentieth century.

Shakers Founded by Mother Ann Lee Stanley in England, the United Society of Believers in Christ's Second Appearing settled in Watervliet, New York, in 1774 and subsequently established eighteen additional communes in the Northeast, Indiana, and Kentucky.

sharecropping Type of farm tenancy that developed after the Civil War in which landless workers—often former slaves—farmed land in exchange for farm supplies and a share of the crop; differed from tenancy in that the terms were generally less favorable.

Share-the-Wealth program Huey Long, a critic of President Roosevelt, offered this program as an alternative to the New Deal. The program proposed to confiscate large personal fortunes, which would be used to guarantee every poor family a cash grant of $5,000 and every worker an annual income of $2,500. Under this program, Long promised to provide pensions, reduce working hours, pay veterans' bonuses, and ensures a college education to every qualified student.

Shays's Rebellion Massachusetts farmer Daniel Shays and 1,200 compatriots, seeking debt relief through issuance of paper currency and lower taxes, stormed the federal arsenal at Springfield in the winter of 1787 but were quickly repulsed.

William T. Sherman's March through Georgia Union General William T. Sherman believed that there was a connection between the South's economy, morale, and ability to wage war. During his March through Georgia, he wanted to demoralize the civilian populace and destroy the resources they needed to fight. His army seized food and livestock that the Confederate Army might have used as well as wrecked railroads and mills and burned plantations.

Sixteenth Amendment (1913) Legalized the federal income tax.

Alfred E. Smith (1873–1944) In the 1928 presidential election, he won the Democratic nomination, but failed to win the presidency. Rural voters distrusted him for being Catholic and the son of Irish immigrants as well as his anti-Prohibition stance.

Captain John Smith (1580–1631) A swashbuckling soldier of fortune with rare powers of leadership and self-promotion, he was appointed to the resident council to manage Jamestown.

Joseph Smith (1805–1844) In 1823, he claimed that the Angel Moroni showed him the location of several gold tablets on which the Book of Mormon was written. Using the Book of Mormon as his gospel, he founded the Church of Jesus Christ of Latter-day Saints, or Mormons. Joseph and his followers upset non-Mormons living near them so they began looking for a refuge from persecution. In 1839, they settled in Commerce, Illinois, which they renamed Nauvoo. In 1844, Joseph and his brother were arrested and jailed for ordering the destruction of a newspaper that opposed them. While in jail, an anti-Mormon mob stormed the jail and killed both of them.

social Darwinism Application of Charles Darwin's theory of natural selection to society; used the concept of the "survival of the fittest" to justify class distinctions and to explain poverty.

social gospel Preached by liberal Protestant clergymen in the late nineteenth and early twentieth centuries; advocated the application of Christian principles to social problems generated by industrialization.

social justice An important part of the Progressive's agenda, social justice sought to solve social problems through reform and regulation. Methods used to bring about social justice ranged from the founding of charities to the legislation of a ban on child labor.

Sons of Liberty Organized by Samuel Adams, they were colonialists with a militant view against the British government's control of the colonies.

Hernando de Soto (1500?–1542) A conquistador who explored the west coast of Florida, western North Carolina and along the Arkansas river from 1539 till his death in 1542.

Southern Christian Leadership Conference (SCLC) Civil rights organization founded in 1957 by the Reverend Martin Luther King Jr., and other civil rights leaders.

"southern strategy" This strategy was a major reason for Richard Nixon's victory in the 1968 presidential election. To gain support in the South, Nixon assured southern conservatives that he would slow the federal enforcement of civil rights laws and appoint pro-southern justices to the Supreme Court. As president, Nixon fulfilled these promises.

Spanish flu Unprecedentedly lethal influenza epidemic of 1918 that killed more than 22 million people worldwide.

Herbert Spencer (1820–1903) As the first major proponent of social Darwinism, he argued that human society and institutions are subject to the process of natural selection and that society naturally evolves for the better. Therefore, he was against any form of government interference with the evolution of society, like business regulations, because it would help the "unfit" to survive.

spoils system The term—meaning the filling of federal government jobs with persons loyal to the party of the president—originated in Andrew Jackson's first term; the system was replaced in the Progressive Era by civil service.

stagflation During the Nixon administration, the economy experienced inflation and a recession at the same time, which is syndrome that defies the orthodox laws of economics. Economists named this phenomenon "stagflation."

Joseph Stalin (1879–1953) The Bolshevik leader who succeeded Lenin as the leader of the Soviet Union in 1924 and ruled the country until his death. During his totalitarian rule of the Soviet Union, he used purges and a system of forced labor camps to maintain control over the country. During the Yalta Conference, he claimed vast areas of Eastern Europe for Soviet domination. After the end of World War II, the alliance between the Soviet Union and the Western powers altered into the tension of the cold war and Stalin erected the "iron curtain" between Eastern and Western Europe.

Stalwarts Conservative Republican party faction during the presidency of Rutherford B. Hayes, 1877–1881; led by Senator Roscoe B. Conkling of New York, Stalwarts opposed civil service reform and favored a third term for President Ulysses S. Grant.

Stamp Act Congress Twenty-seven delegates from nine of the colonies met from October 7 to 25, 1765 and wrote a Declaration of the Rights and Grievances of the Colonies, a petition to the King and a petition to Parliament for the repeal of the Stamp Act.

Standard Oil Company of Ohio John D. Rockefeller found this company in 1870, which grew to monopolize 90 to 95 percent of all the oil refineries in the country. It was also a "vertical monopoly" in that the company controlled all aspects of production and the services it needed to conduct business. For example, Standard Oil produced their own oil barrels and cans as well as owned their own pipelines, railroad tank cars, and oil-storage facilities.

Elizabeth Cady Stanton (1815–1902) She was a prominent reformer and advocate for the rights of women, and she helped organize the Seneca Falls Convention to discuss women's rights. The convention was the first of its kind and produced the Declaration of Sentiments, which proclaimed the equality of men and women.

staple crop, or cash crop A profitable market crop, such as cotton or tobacco.

Thaddeus Stevens (1792–1868) As one of the leaders of the Radical Republicans, he argued that the former Confederate states should be viewed as conquered provinces, which were subject to the demands of the conquerors. He believed that all of southern society needed to be changed, and he supported the abolition of slavery and racial equality.

Adlai E. Stevenson (1900–1965) In the 1952 and 1956 presidential elections, he was the Democratic nominee who lost to Dwight Eisenhower. He was also the U.S. Ambassador to the United Nations and is remembered for his famous speech in 1962 before the UN Security Council that unequivocally demonstrated that the Soviet Union had built nuclear missile bases in Cuba.

Strategic Defense Initiative ("Star Wars") Defense Department's plan during the Reagan administration to build a system to destroy incoming missiles in space.

Levi Strauss (1829–1902) A Jewish tailor who followed miners to California during the gold rush and began making durable work pants that were later dubbed blue jeans or Levi's.

Students for a Democratic Society (SDS) Major organization of the New Left, founded at the University of Michigan in 1960 by Tom Hayden and Al Haber.

suburbia The postwar era witnessed a mass migration to the suburbs. As the population in cities areas grew, people began to spread further out within the urban areas, which created new suburban communities. By 1970 more people lived in the suburbs (76 million) than in central cities (64 million).

Sunbelt The label for an arc that stretched from the Carolinas to California. During the postwar era, much of the urban population growth occurred in this area.

the "surge" In early 2007, President Bush decided he would send a "surge" of new troops to Iraq and implement a new strategy. U.S. forces would shift their focus from offensive operations to the protection of Iraqi civilians from attacks by terrorist insurgents and sectarian militias. While the "surge" reduced the violence in Iraq, Iraqi leaders were still unable to develop a self-sustaining democracy.

Taliban A coalition of ultraconservative Islamists who rose to power in Afghanistan after the Soviets withdrew. The Taliban leaders gave Osama bin Laden a safe haven in their country in exchange for aid in fighting the Northern Alliance, who were rebels opposed to the Taliban. After September 11 terrorist attacks, the United States asked the Taliban to turn over bin Laden. After they refused, America invaded Afghanistan, but bin Laden evaded capture.

Tammany Hall The "city machine" used by "Boss" Tweed to dominate politics in New York City until his arrest in 1871.

Tariff of 1816 First true protective tariff, intended strictly to protect American goods against foreign competition.

Tariff of 1832 This tariff act reduced the duties on many items, but the tariffs on cloth and iron remained high. South Carolina nullified it along with the tariff of 1828. President Andrew Jackson sent federal troops to the state and asked Congress to grant him the authority to enforce the tariffs. Henry Clay presented a plan of gradually reducing the tariffs until 1842, which Congress passed and ended the crisis.

TARP In 2008 President George W. Bush signed into law the bank bailout fund called Troubled Asset Relief Program (TARP), which required the Treasury Department to spend $700 billion to keep banks and other financial institutions from collapsing.

Zachary Taylor (1784–1850) During the Mexican War, he scored two quick victories against Mexico, which made him very popular in America. President Polk chose him as the commander in charge of the war. However, after he was not put in charge of the campaign to capture Mexico City, he chose to return home. Later he used his popularity from his military victories to be elected the president as a member of the Whig party.

Taylorism In his book *The Principles of Scientific Management*, Frederick W. Taylor explained a management system that claimed to be able to reduce waste through the scientific analysis of the labor process. This system called Taylorism, promised to find the optimum technique for the average worker and establish detailed performance standards for each job classification.

Teapot Dome Harding administration scandal in which Secretary of the Interior Albert B. Fall profited from secret leasing to private oil companies of government oil reserves at Teapot Dome, Wyoming, and Elk Hills, California.

Tecumseh (1768–1813) He was a leader of the Shawnee tribe who tried to unite all Indians into a confederation that could defend their hunting grounds. He believed that no land cessions could be made without the consent of all the tribes since they held the land in common. His beliefs and leadership made him seem dangerous to the American government and they waged war on him and his tribe. He was killed at the Battle of the Thames.

Tejanos Texas settlers of Spanish or Mexican descent.

Teller Amendment On April 20, 1898, a joint resolution of Congress declared Cuba independent and demanded the withdrawal of Spanish forces. The Teller amendment was added to this resolution, and it declaimed any designs the United States had on Cuban territory.

Tenochtitlán The capital city of the Aztec Empire. The city was built on marshy islands on the western side of Lake Tetzcoco, which is the site of present-day Mexico City.

Tet offensive Surprise attack by the Viet Cong and North Vietnamese during the Vietnamese New Year of 1968; turned American public opinion strongly against the war in Vietnam.

Thirteenth Amendment This amendment to the U.S. Constitution freed all slaves in the United States. After the Civil War ended, the former confederate states were required to ratify this amendment before they could be readmitted to the Union.

Gulf of Tonkin incident On August 2 and 4 of 1964, North Vietnamese vessels attacked two American destroyers in Gulf of Tonkin off the coast of North Vietnam. President Johnson described the attacks as unprovoked. In reality, the U.S. ships were monitoring South Vietnamese attacks on North Vietnamese islands that America advisors had planned. The incident spurred the Tonkin Gulf resolution.

Tonkin Gulf resolution (1964) Passed by Congress in reaction to supposedly unprovoked attacks on American warships off the coast of North Vietnam; it gave the president unlimited authority to defend U.S. forces and members of SEATO.

Tories Term used by Patriots to refer to Loyalists, or colonists who supported the Crown after the Declaration of Independence.

Trail of Tears Cherokees' own term for their forced march, 1838–1839, from the southern Appalachians to Indian lands (later Oklahoma); of 15,000 forced to march, 4,000 died on the way.

Transcendentalism Philosophy of a small group of mid-nineteenth-century New England writers and thinkers, including Ralph Waldo Emerson, Henry David Thoreau, and Margaret Fuller; they stressed "plain living and high thinking."

Transcontinental railroad First line across the continent from Omaha, Nebraska, to Sacramento, California, established in 1869 with the linkage of the Union Pacific and Central Pacific railroads at Promontory, Utah.

triangular trade Means by which exports to one country or colony provided the means for imports from another country or colony. For example, merchants from colonial New England shipped rum to West Africa and used it to barter for slaves who were then taken to the West Indies. The slaves were sold or traded for materials that the ships brought back to New England including molasses which is need to make rum.

Treaty of Ghent The signing of this treaty in 1814 ended the War of 1812 without solving any of the disputes between Britain and the United States.

Harry S. Truman (1884–1972) As President Roosevelt's vice president, he succeeded him after his death near the end of World War II. After the war, Truman wrestled with the inflation of both prices and wages, and his attempts to bring them both under control led to clashes with organized labor and Republicans. He did work with Congress to pass the National Security Act, which made the Joint Chiefs of Staff a permanent position and created the National Military Establishment and the Central Intelligence Agency. He banned racial discrimination in the hiring of federal employees and ended racial segregation in the armed forces. In foreign affairs, he established the Truman Doctrine to contain communism and the Marshall Plan to rebuild Europe. After North Korea invaded South Korea, Truman sent the U.S. military to defend

South Korea under the command of General Douglas MacArthur. Later in the war, Truman expressed his willingness to negotiate the restoration of prewar boundaries which MacArthur attempted to undermine. Truman fired MacArthur for his open insubordination.

Truman Doctrine President Harry S. Truman's program of post–World War II aid to European countries—particularly Greece and Turkey—in danger of being undermined by communism.

Sojourner Truth (1797? –1883) She was born into slavery, but New York State freed her in 1827. She spent the 1840s and 1850s travelling across the country and speaking to audiences about her experiences as slave and asking them to support abolition and women's rights.

Harriet Tubman (1820–1913) She was born a slave, but escaped to the North. Then she returned to the South nineteen times and guided 300 slaves to freedom.

Nat Turner (1800–1831) He was the leader of the only slave revolt to get past the planning stages. In August of 1831, the revolt began with the slaves killing the members of Turner's master's household. Then they attacked other neighboring farmhouses and recruited more slaves until the militia crushed the revolt. At least fifty-five whites were killed during the uprising and seventeen slaves were hanged afterwards.

Tuskegee Airmen During World War II, African Americans in the armed forces usually served in segregated units. African American pilots were trained at a separate flight school in Tuskegee, Alabama, and were known as Tuskegee Airmen.

Mark Twain (1835–1910) Born Samuel Langhorne Clemens in Missouri, he became a popular humorous writer and lecturer and established himself as one of the great American authors. Like other authors of the local-color movement, his stories expressed the nostalgia people had for rural culture and old folkways as America became increasingly urban. His two greatest books, *The Adventures of Tom Sawyer* and *The Adventures of Huckleberry Finn*, drew heavily on his childhood in Missouri.

"Boss" Tweed (1823–1878) An infamous political boss in New York City, Tweed used his "city machine," the Tammany Hall ring, to rule, plunder and sometimes improve the city's government. His political domination of New York City ended with his arrest in 1871 and conviction in 1873.

Twenty-first Amendment (1933) Repealed prohibition on the manufacture, sale, and transportation of alcoholic beverages, effectively nullifying the Eighteenth Amendment.

Underground Railroad Operating in the decades before the Civil War, the "railroad" was a clandestine system of routes and safehouses through which slaves were led to freedom in the North.

Unitarianism Late eighteenth-century liberal offshoot of the New England Congregationalist church; Unitarianism professed the oneness of God and the goodness of rational man.

United Nations Security Council A major agency within the United Nations which remains in permanent session and has the responsibility of maintaining international peace and security. Originally, it consisted of five permanent members, (United States, Soviet Union, Britain, France, and the Republic of China), and six members elected to two-year terms. After 1965, the number of rotating members was increased to ten. In 1971, the Republic of China was replaced with the People's Republic of China and the Soviet Union was replaced by the Russian Federation in 1991.

Utopian communities These communities flourished during the Jacksonian era and were attempts to create the ideal community. They were social experiments conducted in relative isolation, so they had little impact on the world outside of their communities. In most cases, the communities quickly ran out of steam and ended.

Cornelius Vanderbilt (1794–1877) In the 1860s, he consolidated several separate railroad companies into one vast entity, New York Central Railroad.

Bartolomeo Vanzetti (1888–1927) In 1920, he and Nicola Sacco were Italian immigrants who were arrested for stealing $16,000 and killing a paymaster and his guard. Their trial took place during a time of numerous bombings by anarchists and their judge was openly prejudicial. Many liberals and radicals believe that the conviction of Sacco and Vanzetti was based on their political ideas and ethnic origin rather than the evidence against them.

Amerigo Vespucci (1455–1512) Italian explorer who reached the New World in 1499 and was the first to suggest that South America was a new continent. Afterward, European mapmakers used a variant of his first name, America, to label the New World.

Viet Cong In 1956, these guerrilla forces began attacking South Vietnam's government and in 1960 the resistance groups coalesced as the National Liberation Front.

Vietnamization President Nixon's policy of equipping and training the South Vietnamese so that they could assume ground combat operations in the place of American soldiers. Nixon hoped that a reduction in U.S. forces in Vietnam would defuse the anti-war movement.

Vikings Norse people from Scandinavia who sailed to Newfoundland about A.D. 1001.

Pancho Villa (1877–1923) While the leader of one of the competing factions in the Mexican civil war, he provoked the United States into intervening. He hoped attacking the United States would help him build a reputation as an opponent of the United States, which would increase his popularity and discredit Mexican President Carranza.

Virginia Company A joint stock enterprise that King James I chartered in 1606. The company was to spread Christianity in the New World as well as find ways to make a profit in it.

Virginia Plan The delegations to the Constitutional Convention were divided between two plans on how to structure the government: Virginia called for a strong central government and a two-house legislature apportioned by population.

George Wallace (1919–1998) An outspoken defender of segregation. As the governor of Alabama, he once attempted to block African American students from enrolling at the University of Alabama. He ran as the presidential candidate for the American Independent party in 1968. He appealed to voters who were concerned about rioting anti-war protestors, the welfare system, and the growth of the federal government.

War Hawks In 1811, congressional members from the southern and western districts who clamored for a war to seize Canada and Florida were dubbed "war hawks."

Warren Court The U.S. Supreme Court under Chief Justice Earl Warren, 1953–1969, decided such landmark cases as *Brown v. Board of Education* (school desegregation), *Baker v. Carr* (legislative redistricting), and *Gideon v. Wainwright* and *Miranda v. Arizona* (rights of criminal defendants).

Booker T. Washington (1856–1915) He founded a leading college for African Americans in Tuskegee, Alabama, and become the foremost black educator in America by the 1890s. He believed that the African American community should establish an economic base for its advancement before striving for social equality. His critics charged that his philosophy sacrificed educational and civil rights for dubious social acceptance and economic opportunities.

George Washington (1732–1799) In 1775, the Continental Congress named him the commander in chief of the Continental Army. He had previously served as an officer in the French and Indian War, but had never commanded a large unit. Initially, his army was poorly supplied and inexperienced, which led to repeated defeats. Washington realized that he could only defeat the British through wearing them down, and he implemented a strategy of evasion and selective confrontations. Gradually, the army developed into an effective force and, with the aid of the French, defeated the British. In 1787, he was the presiding officer over the Constitutional Convention, but participated little in the debates. In 1789, the Electoral College chose Washington to be the nation's first president. He assembled a cabinet of brilliant minds, which included Thomas Jefferson, James Madison, and Alexander Hamilton. Together, they would lay the foundations of American government and capitalism. Washington faced the nation's first foreign and domestic crises. In 1793, the British and French were at war. Washington chose to keep America neutral in the conflict even though France and the United States had signed a treaty of alliance. A year later, the Whiskey Rebellion erupted in Pennsylvania, and Washington sent militiamen to suppress the rebels. After two terms in office, Washington chose to step down; and the power of the presidency was peacefully passed to John Adams.

Watergate Washington office and apartment complex that lent its name to the 1972–1974 scandal of the Nixon administration; when his knowledge of the break-in at the Watergate and subsequent cover-up was revealed, Nixon resigned the presidency under threat of impeachment.

Daniel Webster (1782–1852) As a representative from New Hampshire, he led the New Federalists in opposition to the moving of the second national bank from Boston to Philadelphia. Later, he served as representative and a senator for Massachusetts and emerged as a champion of a stronger national government. He also switched from opposing to supporting tariffs because New England had built up its manufactures with the understanding tariffs would protect them from foreign competitors.

Webster-Ashburton Treaty Settlement in 1842 of U.S.–Canadian border disputes in Maine, New York, Vermont, and in the Wisconsin Territory (now northern Minnesota).

Webster-Hayne debate U.S. Senate debate of January 1830 between Daniel Webster of Massachusetts and Robert Hayne of South Carolina over nullification and states' rights.

Ida B. Wells (1862–1931) After being denied a seat on a railroad car because she was black, she became the first African American to file a suit against such discrimination. As a journalist, she criticized Jim Crow laws, demanded that blacks have their voting rights restored and crusaded against lynching. In 1909, she helped found the National Association for the Advancement of Colored People (NAACP).

western front The military front that stretched from the English Channel through Belgium and France to the Alps during World War I.

Whig party Founded in 1834 to unite factions opposed to President Andrew Jackson, the party favored federal responsibility for internal improvements; the party ceased to exist by the late 1850s, when party members divided over the slavery issue.

Whigs Another name for revolutionary Patriots.

Whiskey Rebellion Violent protest by western Pennsylvania farmers against the federal excise tax on corn whiskey, 1794.

Eli Whitney (1765–1825) He invented the cotton gin which could separate cotton from its seeds. One machine operator could separate fifty times more cotton than worker could by hand, which led to an increase in cotton production and prices. These increases gave planters a new profitable use for slavery and a lucrative slave trade emerged from the coastal South to the Southwest.

George Whitefield (1714–1770) A true catalyst of the Great Awakening, he sought to reignite religious fervor in the American congregations. During his tour of the American Colonies in 1739, he gave spellbinding sermons and preached the notion of "new birth"—a sudden, emotional moment of conversion and salvation.

Wilderness Road Originally an Indian path through the Cumberland Gap, it was used by over 300,000 settlers who migrated westward to Kentucky in the last quarter of the eighteenth century.

Roger Williams (1603–1683) Puritan who believed that the purity of the church required a complete separation between church and state and freedom from coercion in matters of faith. In 1636, he established the town of Providence, the first permanent settlement in Rhode Island and the first to allow religious freedom in America.

Wendell L. Willkie (1892–1944) In the 1940 presidential election, he was the Republican nominee who ran against President Roosevelt. He supported aid to the Allies and criticized the New Deal programs. Voters looked at the increasingly dangerous world situation and chose to keep President Roosevelt in office for a third term.

Wilmot Proviso Proposal to prohibit slavery in any land acquired in the Mexican War, but southern senators, led by John C. Calhoun of South Carolina, defeated the measure in 1846 and 1847.

Woodrow Wilson (1856–1924) In the 1912 presidential election, Woodrow Wilson ran under the slogan of New Freedom, which promised to improve of the banking system, lower tariffs, and break up monopolies. He sought to deliver on these promises through passage of the Underwood-Simmons Tariff, the Federal Reserve Act of 1913, and new antitrust laws. Though he was weak on implementing social change and showed a little interest in the plight of African Americans, he did eventually support some labor reform. At the beginning of World War I, Wilson kept America neutral, but provided the Allies with credit for purchases of supplies. However, the sinking of U.S. merchant ships and the news of Germany encouraging Mexico to attack America caused Wilson to ask Congress to declare war on Germany. Following the war, Wilson supported the entry of America into the League of Nations and the ratification of the Treaty of Versailles; but Congress would not approve the entry or ratification.

John Winthrop Puritan leader and Governor of the Massachusetts Bay Colony who resolved to use the colony as a refuge for persecuted Puritans and as an instrument of building a "wilderness Zion" in America.

Women Accepted for Voluntary Emergency Services (WAVES) During World War II, the increased demand for labor shook up old prejudices about gender roles in workplace and in the military. Nearly 200,000 women served in the Women's Army Corps or its naval equivalent, Women Accepted for Volunteer Emergency Service (WAVES).

Women's Army Corps (WAC) During World War II, the increased demand for labor shook up old prejudices about gender roles in workplace and in the military. Nearly 200,000 women served in the Women's Army

Corps or its naval equivalent, Women Accepted for Volunteer Emergency Service (WAVES).

Woodstock In 1969, roughly a half a million young people converged on a farm near Bethel, New York, for a three-day music festival that was an expression of the flower children's free spirit.

Wounded Knee, Battle of Last incident of the Indians Wars took place in 1890 in the Dakota Territory, where the U.S. Cavalry killed over 200 Sioux men, women, and children who were in the process of surrender.

XYZ affair French foreign minister Tallyrand's three anonymous agents demanded payments to stop French plundering of American ships in 1797; refusal to pay the bribe led to two years of sea war with France (1798–1800).

Yalta Conference Meeting of Franklin D. Roosevelt, Winston Churchill, and Joseph Stalin at a Crimean resort to discuss the postwar world on February 4–11, 1945; Soviet leader Joseph Stalin claimed large areas in eastern Europe for Soviet domination.

yeomen Small landowners (the majority of white families in the South) who farmed their own land and usually did not own slaves.

surrender at Yorktown Last battle of the Revolutionary War; General Lord Charles Cornwallis along with over 7,000 British troops surrendered at Yorktown, Virginia, on October 17, 1781.

Brigham Young (1801–1877) Following Joseph Smith's death, he became the leader of the Mormons and promised Illinois officials that the Mormons would leave the state. In 1846, he led the Mormons to Utah and settled near the Salt Lake. After the United States gained Utah as part of the Treaty of Guadalupe Hidalgo, he became the governor of the territory and kept the Mormons virtually independent of federal authority.

youth culture The youth of the 1950s had more money and free time than any previous generation which allowed a distinct youth culture to emerge. A market emerged for products and activities that were specifically for young people such as transistor radios, rock records, *Seventeen* magazine, and Pat Boone movies.

APPENDIX

THE DECLARATION OF INDEPENDENCE (1776)

WHEN IN THE COURSE OF HUMAN EVENTS, it becomes necessary for one people to dissolve the political bands which have connected them with another, and to assume the Powers of the earth, the separate and equal station to which the Laws of Nature and of Nature's God entitle them, a decent respect to the opinions of mankind requires that they should declare the causes which impel them to the separation.

We hold these truths to be self-evident, that all men are created equal, that they are endowed by their Creator with certain unalienable rights, that among these are Life, Liberty, and the pursuit of Happiness. That to secure these rights, Governments are instituted among Men, deriving their just powers from the consent of the governed. That whenever any Form of Government becomes destructive of these ends, it is the Right of the People to alter or to abolish it, and to institute new Government, laying its foundation on such principles and organizing its powers in such form, as to them shall seem most likely to effect their Safety and Happiness. Prudence, indeed, will dictate that Governments long established should not be changed for light and transient causes; and accordingly all experience hath shown, that mankind are more disposed to suffer, while evils are sufferable, than to right themselves by abolishing the forms to which they are accustomed. But when a long train of abuses and usurpations, pursuing invariably the same Object evinces a design to reduce them under absolute Despotism, it is their right, it is their duty, to throw off such Government, and to provide new Guards for their future security.—Such has been the patient sufferance of these Colonies; and such is now the necessity which constrains them to alter their former Systems of Government. The history of the present King of Great Britain is a history of repeated injuries and usurpations, all having in direct object the establishment of an absolute Tyranny over these States. To prove this, let Facts be submitted to a candid world.

He has refused his Assent to Laws, the most wholesome and necessary for the public good.

He has forbidden his Governors to pass Laws of immediate and pressing importance, unless suspended in their operation till his Assent should be obtained; and when so suspended, he has utterly neglected to attend to them.

He has refused to pass other Laws for the accommodation of large districts of people, unless those people would relinquish the right of Representation in the Legislature, a right inestimable to them and formidable to tyrants only.

He has called together legislative bodies at places unusual, uncomfortable, and distant from the depository of their public Records, for the sole purpose of fatiguing them into compliance with his measures.

He has dissolved Representative Houses repeatedly, for opposing with manly firmness his invasions on the rights of the people.

He has refused for a long time, after such dissolutions, to cause others to be elected; whereby the Legislative powers, incapable of Annihilation, have returned to the People at large for their exercise; the State remaining in the mean time exposed to all dangers of invasion from without, and convulsions within.

He has endeavoured to prevent the population of these States; for that purpose obstructing the Laws of Naturalization of Foreigners; refusing to pass others to encourage their migrations hither, and raising the conditions of new Appropriations of Lands.

He has obstructed the Administration of Justice, by refusing his Assent to Laws for establishing Judiciary powers.

He has made Judges dependent on his Will alone, for the tenure of their offices, and the amount and payment of their salaries.

He has erected a multitude of New Offices, and sent hither swarms of Officers to harass our People, and eat out their substance.

He has kept among us, in times of peace, Standing Armies without the Consent of our legislatures.

He has affected to render the Military independent of and superior to the Civil Power.

He has combined with others to subject us to a jurisdiction foreign to our constitution, and unacknowledged by our laws; giving his Assent to their Acts of pretended Legislation:

For quartering large bodies of armed troops among us:

For protecting them, by a mock Trial, from Punishment for any Murders which they should commit on the Inhabitants of these States:

For cutting off our Trade with all parts of the world:

For imposing taxes on us without our Consent:

For depriving us of many cases, of the benefits of Trial by jury:

For transporting us beyond Seas to be tried for pretended offences:

For abolishing the free System of English Laws in a neighbouring Province, establishing therein an Arbitrary government, and enlarging its

Boundaries so as to render it at once an example and fit instrument for introducing the same absolute rule into these Colonies:

For taking away our Charters, abolishing our most valuable Laws, and altering fundamentally the Forms of our Governments:

For suspending our own Legislatures, and declaring themselves in vested with Power to legislate for us in all cases whatsoever.

He has abdicated Government here, by declaring us out of his Protection and waging War against us.

He has plundered our seas, ravaged our Coasts, burnt our towns, and destroyed the lives of our people.

He is at this time transporting large armies of foreign mercenaries to compleat the works of death, desolation, and tyranny, already begun with circumstances of Cruelty & perfidy scarcely paralleled in the most barbarous ages, and totally unworthy the Head of a civilized nation.

He has constrained our fellow Citizens taken Captive on the high Seas to bear Arms against their Country, to become the executioners of their friends and Brethren, or to fall themselves by their Hands.

He has excited domestic insurrections amongst us, and has endeavoured to bring on the inhabitants of our frontiers, the merciless Indian Savages, whose known rule of warfare, is an undistinguished destruction of all ages, sexes, and conditions.

In every stage of these Oppressions We have Petitioned for Redress in the most humble terms: Our repeated Petitions have been answered only by repeated injury. A Prince, whose character is thus marked by every act which may define a Tyrant, is unfit to be the ruler of a free people.

Nor have We been wanting in attention to our British brethren. We have warned them from time to time of attempts by their legislature to extend an unwarrantable jurisdiction over us. We have reminded them of the circumstances of our emigration and settlement here. We have appealed to their native justice and magnanimity, and we have conjured them by the ties of our common kindred to disavow these usurpations, which, would inevitably interrupt our connections and correspondence. They too must have been deaf to the voice of justice and of consanguinity. We must, therefore, acquiesce in the necessity, which denounces our Separation, and hold them, as we hold the rest of mankind, Enemies in War, in Peace Friends.

WE, THEREFORE, the Representatives of the UNITED STATES OF AMERICA, in General Congress, Assembled, appealing to the Supreme Judge of the world for the rectitude of our intentions, do, in the Name, and by Authority of the good People of these Colonies, solemnly publish and declare, That these United Colonies are, and of Right ought to be FREE AND INDEPENDENT STATES; that they are Absolved from all Allegiance to the

British Crown, and that all political connection between them and the State of Great Britain, is and ought to be totally dissolved; and that as Free and Independent States, they have full Power to levy War, conclude Peace, contract Alliances, establish Commerce, and to do all other Acts and Things which Independent States may of right do. And for the support of this Declaration, with a firm reliance on the Protection of Divine Providence, we mutually pledge to each other our Lives, our Fortunes, and our sacred Honor.

The foregoing Declaration was, by order of Congress, engrossed, and signed by the following members:

John Hancock

NEW HAMPSHIRE
Josiah Bartlett
William Whipple
Matthew Thornton

MASSACHUSETTS BAY
Samuel Adams
John Adams
Robert Treat Paine
Elbridge Gerry

RHODE ISLAND
Stephen Hopkins
William Ellery

CONNECTICUT
Roger Sherman
Samuel Huntington
William Williams
Oliver Wolcott

NEW YORK
William Floyd
Philip Livingston
Francis Lewis
Lewis Morris

NEW JERSEY
Richard Stockton
John Witherspoon
Francis Hopkinson
John Hart
Abraham Clark

PENNSYLVANIA
Robert Morris
Benjamin Rush
Benjamin Franklin
John Morton
George Clymer
James Smith
George Taylor
James Wilson
George Ross

DELAWARE
Caesar Rodney
George Read
Thomas M'Kean

MARYLAND
Samuel Chase
William Paca
Thomas Stone
Charles Carroll, of Carrollton

VIRGINIA
George Wythe
Richard Henry Lee
Thomas Jefferson
Benjamin Harrison
Thomas Nelson, Jr.
Francis Lightfoot Lee
Carter Braxton

NORTH CAROLINA
William Hooper
Joseph Hewes
John Penn

SOUTH CAROLINA
Edward Rutledge
Thomas Heyward, Jr.
Thomas Lynch, Jr.
Arthur Middleton

GEORGIA
Button Gwinnett
Lyman Hall
George Walton

Resolved, that copies of the declaration be sent to the several assemblies, conventions, and committees, or councils of safety, and to the several commanding officers of the continental troops; that it be proclaimed in each of the united states, at the head of the army.

ARTICLES OF
CONFEDERATION (1778)

To ALL TO WHOM these Presents shall come, we the undersigned Delegates of the States affixed to our Names send greeting.

Whereas the Delegates of the United States of America in Congress assembled did on the fifteenth day of November in the Year of our Lord One Thousand Seven Hundred and Seventy-seven, and in the Second Year of the Independence of America agree to certain articles of Confederation and perpetual Union between the States of Newhampshire, Massachusetts-bay, Rhodeisland and Providence Plantations, Connecticut, New York, New Jersey, Pennsylvania, Delaware, Maryland, Virginia, North-Carolina, South-Carolina and Georgia in the Words following, viz.

Articles of Confederation and perpetual Union between the States of Newhampshire, Massachusetts-bay, Rhodeisland and Providence Plantations, Connecticut, New-York, New-Jersey, Pennsylvania, Delaware, Maryland, Virginia, North-Carolina, South-Carolina and Georgia.

ARTICLE I. The stile of this confederacy shall be "The United States of America."

ARTICLE II. Each State retains its sovereignty, freedom and independence, and every power, jurisdiction and right, which is not by this confederation expressly delegated to the United States, in Congress assembled.

ARTICLE III. The said States hereby severally enter into a firm league of friendship with each other, for their common defence, the security of their liberties, and their mutual and general welfare, binding themselves to assist each other, against all force offered to, or attacks made upon them, or any of them, on account of religion, sovereignty, trade or any other pretence whatever.

ARTICLE IV. The better to secure and perpetuate mutual friendship and intercourse among the people of the different States in this Union, the free inhabitants of each of these States, paupers, vagabonds and fugitives from justice excepted, shall be entitled to all privileges and immunities of free citizens in the several States; and the people of each State shall have free ingress and regress to and from any other State, and shall enjoy therein all the privileges of trade and commerce, subject to the same duties, impositions and restrictions as the inhabitants thereof respectively, provided that such restrictions shall not extend so far as to prevent the removal of property imported into any State, to any other State of which the owner is an inhabitant; provided also that no imposition, duties or restriction shall be laid by any State, on the property of the United States, or either of them.

If any person guilty of, or charged with treason, felony, or other high misdemeanor in any State, shall flee from justice, and be found in any of the United States, he shall upon demand of the Governor or Executive power, of the State from which he fled, be delivered up and removed to the State having jurisdiction of his offence.

Full faith and credit shall be given in each of these States to the records, acts and judicial proceedings of the courts and magistrates of every other State.

ARTICLE V. For the more convenient management of the general interests of the United States, delegates shall be annually appointed in such manner as the legislature of each State shall direct, to meet in Congress on the first Monday in November, in every year, with a power reserved to each State, to recall its delegates, or any of them, at any time within the year, and to send others in their stead, for the remainder of the year.

No State shall be represented in Congress by less than two, nor by more than seven members; and no person shall be capable of being a delegate for more than three years in any term of six years; nor shall any person, being a delegate, be capable of holding any office under the United States, for which he, or another for his benefit receives any salary, fees or emolument of any kind.

Each State shall maintain its own delegates in a meeting of the States, and while they act as members of the committee of the States.

In determining questions in the United States, in Congress assembled, each State shall have one vote.

Freedom of speech and debate in Congress shall not be impeached or questioned in any court, or place out of Congress, and the members of Congress shall be protected in their persons from arrests and imprisonments, during the time of their going to and from, and attendance on Congress, except for treason, felony, or breach of the peace.

ARTICLE VI. No State without the consent of the United States in Congress assembled, shall send any embassy to, or receive any embassy from, or enter into any conference, agreement, alliance or treaty with any king, prince or state; nor shall any person holding any office of profit or trust under the United States, or any of them, accept of any present, emolument, office or title of any kind whatever from any king, prince or foreign state; nor shall the United States in Congress assembled, or any of them, grant any title of nobility.

No two or more States shall enter into any treaty, confederation or alliance whatever between them, without the consent of the United States in Congress assembled, specifying accurately the purposes for which the same is to be entered into, and how long it shall continue.

No State shall lay any imposts or duties, which may interfere with any stipulations in treaties, entered into by the United States in Congress assembled, with any king, prince or state, in pursuance of any treaties already proposed by Congress, to the courts of France and Spain.

No vessels of war shall be kept up in time of peace by any State, except such number only, as shall be deemed necessary by the United States in Congress assembled, for the defence of such State, or its trade; nor shall any body of forces be kept up by any State, in time of peace, except such number only, as in the judgment of the United States, in Congress assembled, shall be deemed requisite to garrison the forts necessary for the defence of such State; but every State shall always keep up a well regulated and disciplined militia, sufficiently armed and accoutred, and shall provide and constantly have ready for use, in public stores, a due number of field pieces and tents, and a proper quantity of arms, ammunition and camp equipage.

No State shall engage in any war without the consent of the United States in Congress assembled, unless such State be actually invaded by enemies, or shall have received certain advice of a resolution being formed by some nation of Indians to invade such State, and the danger is so imminent as not to admit of a delay, till the United States in Congress assembled can be consulted: nor shall any State grant commissions to any ships or vessels of war, nor letters of marque or reprisal, except it be after a declaration of war by the United States in Congress assembled, and then only against the kingdom or state and the subjects thereof, against which war has been so declared, and under such regulations as shall be established by the United States in Congress assembled, unless such State be infested by pirates, in which case vessels of war may be fitted out for that occasion, and kept so long as the danger shall continue, or until the United States in Congress assembled shall determine otherwise.

ARTICLE VII. When land-forces are raised by any State of the common defence, all officers of or under the rank of colonel, shall be appointed by the Legislature of each State respectively by whom such forces shall be raised, or in such manner as such State shall direct, and all vacancies shall be filled up by the State which first made the appointment.

ARTICLE VIII. All charges of war, and all other expenses that shall be incurred for the common defence or general welfare, and allowed by the United States in Congress assembled, shall be defrayed out of a common treasury, which shall be supplied by the several States, in proportion to the value of all land within each State, granted to or surveyed for any person, as such land and the buildings and improvements thereon shall be estimated according to such mode as the United States in Congress assembled, shall from time to time direct and appoint.

The taxes for paying that proportion shall be laid and levied by the authority and direction of the Legislatures of the several States within the time agreed upon by the United States in Congress assembled.

ARTICLE IX. The United States in Congress assembled, shall have the sole and exclusive right and power of determining on peace and war, except in the cases mentioned in the sixth article—of sending and receiving ambassadors—entering into treaties and alliances, provided that no treaty of commerce shall be made whereby the legislative power of the respective States shall be restrained from imposing such imposts and duties on foreigners, as their own people are subjected to, or from prohibiting the exportation or importation of and species of goods or commodities whatsoever—of establishing rules for deciding in all cases, what captures on land or water shall be legal, and in what manner prizes taken by land or naval forces in the service of the United States shall be divided or appropriated—of granting letters of marque and reprisal in times of peace—appointing courts for the trial of piracies and felonies committed on the high seas and establishing courts for receiving and determining finally appeals in all cases of captures, provided that no member of Congress shall be appointed a judge of any of the said courts.

The United States in Congress assembled shall also be the last resort on appeal in all disputes and differences now subsisting or that hereafter may arise between two or more States concerning boundary, jurisdiction or any other cause whatever; which authority shall always be exercised in the manner following. Whenever the legislative or executive authority or lawful agent of any State in controversy with another shall present a petition to Congress, stating the matter in question and praying for a hearing, notice thereof shall be given by order of Congress to the legislative or executive authority of the other State in controversy, and a day assigned for the appearance of the parties by their lawful agents, who shall then be directed to appoint by joint consent, commissioners or judges to constitute a court for hearing and determining the matter in question: but if they cannot agree, Congress shall name three persons out of each of the United States, and from the list of such persons each party shall alternately strike out one, the petitioners beginning, until the number shall be reduced to thirteen; and from that number not less than seven, nor more than nine names as Congress shall direct, shall in the presence of Congress be drawn out by lot, and the persons whose names shall be so drawn or any five of them, shall be commissioners or judges, to hear and finally determine the controversy, so always as a major part of the judges who shall hear the cause shall agree in the determination: and if either party shall neglect to attend at the day appointed, without reasons, which Congress shall judge sufficient, or being present shall refuse to strike, the Congress shall proceed to nominate three persons out of each State, and the Secretary of Congress shall strike in behalf of such party absent or refusing; and the judgment and sentence of the court to be appointed, in the manner before prescribed, shall be final and conclusive; and if any of the parties shall refuse to submit to the authority of such court, or to appear or defend their claim or cause, the court shall nevertheless proceed to pronounce sentence, or judgment, which shall in like manner be final and decisive, the judgment or sentence and other proceedings being in either case transmitted to Congress, and lodged among the acts of Congress for the security of the parties concerned: provided that every commissioner, before he sits in judgment, shall take an oath to be administered by one of the judges of the supreme or superior court of the State where the case shall be tried, "well and truly to hear and determine the matter in question, according to the best of his judgment, without favour, affection or hope of reward:" provided also that no State shall be deprived of territory for the benefit of the United States.

All controversies concerning the private right of soil claimed under different grants of two or more States, whose jurisdiction as they may respect such lands, and the states which passed such grants are adjusted, the said grants or either of them being at the same time claimed to have originated antecedent to such settlement of jurisdiction, shall on the petition of either party to the Congress of the United States, be finally determined as near as may be in the same manner as is before prescribed for deciding disputes respecting territorial jurisdiction between different States.

The United States in Congress assembled shall also have the sole and exclusive right and power of regulating the alloy and value of coin struck by their own authority, or by that of the respective States—fixing the standard of weights and measures throughout the United States—regulating the trade and managing all affairs with the Indians, not members of any of the States, provided that the legislative right of any State within its own limits be not infringed or violated—establishing and regulating post-offices from one State to another, throughout all of the United States, and exacting such postage on the papers passing thro' the same as may be requisite to defray the expenses of the said office—appointing all officers of the land forces, in the service of the United States, excepting regimental officers—appointing all the officers of the naval forces, and commissioning all officers whatever in the service of the United States—making rules for the government and regulation of the said land and naval forces, and directing their operations.

The United States in Congress assembled shall have authority to appoint a committee, to sit in the recess of Congress, to be denominated "a Committee of the States," and to consist of one delegate from each State; and to appoint such other committees and civil officers as may be necessary for managing the general affairs of the United States under their direction—to appoint one of their number to preside, provided that no person be allowed to serve in the office of president more than one year in any term of three years; to ascertain the necessary sums of money to be raised for the service of the United States, and to appropriate and apply the same for defraying the public expenses—to borrow money, or emit bills on the credit of the United States, transmitting every half year to the respective States an account of the sums of money so borrowed or emitted,—to build and equip a navy—to agree upon the number of land forces, and to make requisitions from each State for its quota, in proportion to the number of white inhabitants in such State; which requisition shall be binding, and thereupon the Legislature of each State shall appoint the regimental officers, raise the men and cloath, arm and equip them in a soldier like manner, at the expense of the United States; and the officers and men so cloathed, armed and equipped shall march to the place appointed, and within the time agreed on by the United States in Congress assembled: but if the United States in Congress assembled shall, on consideration of circumstances judge proper that any State should not raise men, or should raise a smaller number of men than the quota thereof, such extra number shall be raised, officered, cloathed, armed and equipped in the same manner as the quota of such State, unless the legislature of such State shall judge that such extra number cannot be safely spared out of the same, in which case they shall raise officer, cloath, arm and equip as many of such extra number as they judge can be safely spared. And the officers and men so cloathed, armed and equipped, shall march to the place appointed, and within the time agreed on by the United States in Congress assembled.

The United States in Congress assembled shall never engage in a war, nor grant letters of marque and reprisal in time of peace, nor enter into any treaties or alliances, nor coin money, nor regulate the value thereof, nor ascertain the sums and expenses necessary for the defence and welfare of the United States, or any of them, nor emit bills, nor borrow money on the credit of the United States, nor appropriate money, nor agree upon the number of vessels to be built or purchased, or the number of land or sea forces to be raised, nor appoint a commander in chief of the army or navy, unless nine States assent to the same: nor shall a question on any other point, except for adjourning from day to day be determined, unless by the votes of a majority of the United States in Congress assembled.

The Congress of the United States shall have power to adjourn to any time within the year, and to any place within the United States, so that no period of adjournment be for a longer duration than the space of six months, and shall publish the journal of their proceedings monthly, except such parts thereof relating to treaties, alliances or military operations, as in their judgment require secresy; and the yeas and nays of the delegates of each State on any question shall be entered on the Journal, when it is desired by any delegate; and the delegates of a State, or any of them, at his or their request shall be furnished with a transcript of the said journal, except such parts as are above excepted, to lay before the Legislatures of the several States.

ARTICLE X. The committee of the States, or any nine of them, shall be authorized to execute, in the recess of Congress, such of the powers of Congress as the United States in Congress assembled, by the consent of nine States, shall from time to time think expedient to vest them with; provided that no power be delegated to the said committee, for the exercise of which, by the articles of confedcration, the voice of nine States in the Congress of the United States assembled is requisite.

ARTICLE XI. Canada acceding to this confederation, and joining in the measures of the United States, shall be admitted into, and entitled to all the advantages of this Union: but no other colony shall be admitted into the same, unless such admission be agreed to by nine States.

ARTICLE XII. All bills of credit emitted, monies borrowed and debts contracted by, or under the authority of Congress, before the assembling of the United States, in pursuance of the present confederation, shall be deemed and considered as a charge against the United States, for payment and satisfaction whereof the said United States, and the public faith are hereby solemnly pledged.

ARTICLE XIII. Every State shall abide by the determinations of the United States in Congress assembled, on all questions which by this confederation are submitted to them. And the articles of this confederation shall be inviolably observed by every State, and the Union shall be perpetual; nor shall any alteration at any time hereafter be made in any of them; unless such alteration be agreed to in a Congress of the United States, and be afterwards confirmed by the Legislatures of every State.

And whereas it has pleased the Great Governor of the world to incline the hearts of the Legislatures we respectively represent in Congress, to approve of, and to authorize us to ratify the said articles of confederation and perpetual union. Know ye that we the undersigned delegates, by virtue of the power and authority to us given for that purpose, do by these presents, in the name and in behalf of our respective constituents, fully and entirely ratify and confirm each and every of the said articles of confederation and perpetual union, and all and singular the matters and things therein contained: and we do further solemnly plight and engage the faith of our respective constituents, that they shall abide by the determinations of the United States in Congress assembled, on all questions, which by the said confederation are submitted to them. And that the articles thereof shall be inviolably observed by the States we respectively represent, and that the Union shall be perpetual.

In witness thereof we have hereunto set our hands in Congress. Done at Philadelphia in the State of Pennsylvania the ninth day of July in the year of our Lord one thousand seven hundred and seventy-eight, and in the third year of the independence of America.

THE CONSTITUTION OF THE
UNITED STATES (1787)

WE THE PEOPLE OF THE UNITED STATES, in order to form a more perfect Union, establish Justice, insure domestic Tranquility, provide for the common defence, promote the general Welfare, and secure the Blessings of Liberty to ourselves and our Posterity, do ordain and establish this Constitution for the United States of America.

ARTICLE. I.

Section. 1. All legislative Powers herein granted shall be vested in a Congress of the United States, which shall consist of a Senate and House of Representatives.

Section. 2. The House of Representatives shall be composed of Members chosen every second Year by the People of the several States, and the Electors in each State shall have the Qualifications requisite for Electors of the most numerous Branch of the State Legislature.

No Person shall be a Representative who shall not have attained to the Age of twenty five Years, and been seven Years a Citizen of the United States, and who shall not, when elected, be an Inhabitant of that State in which he shall be chosen.

Representatives and direct Taxes shall be apportioned among the several States which may be included within this Union, according to their respective Numbers, which shall be determined by adding to the whole Number of free Persons, including those bound to Service for a Term of Years, and excluding Indians not taxed, three fifths of all other Persons. The actual Enumeration shall be made within three Years after the first Meeting of the Congress of the United States, and within every subsequent Term of ten Years, in such

Manner as they shall by Law direct. The Number of Representatives shall not exceed one for every thirty Thousand, but each State shall have at Least one Representative; and until such enumeration shall be made, the State of New Hampshire shall be entitled to chuse three, Massachusetts eight, Rhode-Island and Providence Plantations one, Connecticut five, New-York six, New Jersey four, Pennsylvania eight, Delaware one, Maryland six, Virginia ten, North Carolina five, South Carolina five, and Georgia three.

When vacancies happen in the Representation from any state, the Executive Authority thereof shall issue Writs of Election to fill such Vacancies.

The House of Representatives shall chuse their Speaker and other Officers; and shall have the sole Power of Impeachment.

Section. 3. The Senate of the United States shall be composed of two Senators from each State, chosen by the legislature thereof, for six Years; and each Senator shall have one Vote.

Immediatcly after they shall be assembled in Consequence of the first Election, they shall be divided as equally as may be into three Classes. The Seats of the Senators of the first Class shall be vacated at the Expiration of the second Year, of the second Class at the Expiration of the fourth Year, and of the third Class at the Expiration of the sixth Year, so that one third maybe chosen every second Year; and if Vacancies happen by Resignation, or otherwise, during the Recess of the Legislature of any State, the Executive thereof may make temporary Appointments until the next Meeting of the Legislature, which shall then fill such Vacancies.

No Person shall be a Senator who shall not have attained to the Age of thirty Years, and been nine Years a Citizen of the United States, and who shall not, when elected, be an Inhabitant of that State for which he shall be chosen.

The Vice President of the United States shall be President of the Senate, but shall have no Vote, unless they be equally divided.

The Senate shall chuse their other Officers, and also a President pro tempore, in the Absence of the Vice President, or when he shall exercise the Office of President of the United States.

The Senate shall have the sole Power to try all Impeachments. When sitting for that Purpose, they shall be on Oath or Affirmation. When the President of the United States is tried, the Chief Justice shall preside: And no Person shall be convicted without the Concurrence of two thirds of the Members present.

Judgment in Cases of Impeachment shall not extend further than to removal from Office, and disqualification to hold and enjoy any Office of honor, Trust or Profit under the United States: but the Party convicted shall nevertheless be liable and subject to Indictment, Trial, Judgment and Punishment, according to Law.

Section. 4. The Times, Places and Manner of holding Elections for Senators and Representatives, shall be prescribed in each State by the Legislature thereof; but the Congress may at any time by Law make or alter such Regulations, except as to the Places of chusing Senators.

The Congress shall assemble at least once in every Year, and such Meeting shall be on the first Monday in December, unless they shall by Law appoint a different Day.

Section. 5. Each House shall be the Judge of the Elections, Returns and Qualifications of its own Members, and a Majority of each shall constitute a Quorum to do Business; but a smaller Number may adjourn from day to day, and may be authorized to compel the Attendance of absent Members, in such Manner, and under such Penalties as each House may provide.

Each House may determine the Rules of its Proceedings, punish its Members for disorderly Behaviour, and, with the Concurrence of two thirds, expel a Member.

Each House shall keep a Journal of its Proceedings, and from time to time publish the same, excepting such Parts as may in their Judgment require Secrecy; and the Yeas and Nays of the Members of either House on any question shall, at the Desire of one fifth of those Present, be entered on the Journal.

Neither House, during the Session of Congress, shall, without the Consent of the other, adjourn for more than three days, not to any other Place than that in which the two Houses shall be sitting.

Section. 6. The Senators and Representatives shall receive a Compensation for their Services, to be ascertained by Law, and paid out of the Treasury of the United States. They shall in all Cases, except Treason, Felony and Breach of the Peace, be privileged from Arrest during their Attendance at the Session of their respective Houses, and in going to and returning from the same; and for any Speech or Debate in either House, they shall not be questioned in any other Place.

No Senator or Representative shall, during the Time for which he was elected, be appointed to any civil Office under the Authority of the United States, which shall have been created, or the Emoluments whereof shall have been encreased during such time; and no Person holding any Office under the United States, shall be a Member of either House during his Continuance in Office.

Section. 7. All Bills for raising Revenue shall originate in the House of Representatives; but the Senate may propose or concur with Amendments as on other Bills.

Every Bill which shall have passed the House of Representatives and the Senate shall, before it become a Law, be presented to the President of the United States; If he approve he shall sign it, but if not he shall return it, with his Objections to that House in which it shall have originated, who shall enter the Objections at large on their Journal, and proceed to reconsider it. If after such Reconsideration two thirds of that House shall agree to pass the Bill, it shall be sent, together with the Objections, to the other House, by which it shall likewise be reconsidered, and if approved by two thirds of that House, it shall become a Law. But in all such Cases the Votes of both Houses shall be determined by yeas and Nays, and the Names of the Persons voting for and against the Bill shall be entered on the Journal of each House respectively. If any Bill shall not be returned by the President within ten Days (Sundays excepted) after it shall have been presented to him, the Same shall be a Law, in like Manner as if he had signed it, unless the Congress by their Adjournment prevent its Return, in which Case it shall not be a Law.

Every Order, Resolution, or Vote to which the Concurrence of the Senate and House of Representatives may be necessary (except on a question of Adjournment) shall be presented to the President of the United States; and before the Same shall take Effect, shall be approved by him, or being disapproved by him, shall be repassed by two thirds of the Senate and House of Representatives, according to the Rules and Limitations prescribed in the Case of a Bill.

Section. 8. The Congress shall have Power To lay and collect Taxes, Duties, Imposts and Excises, to pay the Debts and provide for the common Defence and general Welfare of the United States; but all Duties, Imposts and Excises shall be uniform throughout the United States;

To borrow Money on the credit of the United States;

To regulate Commerce with foreign Nations, and among the several States, and with the Indian Tribes;

To establish an uniform Rule of Naturalization, and uniform Laws on the subject of Bankruptcies throughout the United States;

To coin Money, regulate the Value thereof, and of foreign Coin, and fix the Standard of Weights and Measures;

To provide for the Punishment of counterfeiting the Securities and current Coin of the United States;

To establish Post Offices and Post Roads;

To promote the Progress of Science and useful Arts, by securing for limited Times to Authors and Inventors the exclusive Right to their respective Writings and Discoveries;

To constitute Tribunals inferior to the supreme Court;

To define and punish Piracies and Felonies committed on the high Seas, and Offences against the Law of Nations;

To declare War, grant Letters of Marque and Reprisal, and make Rules concerning Captures on land and Water;

To raise and support Armies, but no Appropriation of Money to that Use shall be for a longer Term than two Years;

To provide and maintain a Navy;

To make Rules for the Government and Regulation of the land and naval Forces;

To provide for calling forth the Militia to execute the Laws of the Union, suppress Insurrections and repel Invasions;

To provide for organizing, arming, and disciplining, the Militia, and for governing such Part of them as may be employed in the Service of the United States, reserving to the States respectively, the Appointment of the Officers, and the Authority of training the Militia according to the discipline prescribed by Congress.

To exercise exclusive Legislation in all Cases whatsoever, over such District (not exceeding ten Miles square) as may, by Cession of Particular States, and the Acceptance of Congress, become the Seat of the Government of the United States, and to exercise like Authority over all Places purchased by the Consent of the Legislature of the State in which the Same shall be, for the Erection of Forts, Magazines, Arsenals, dock-Yards, and other needful Buildings;—And

To make all Laws which shall be necessary and proper for carrying into Execution the foregoing Powers, and all other Powers vested by this Constitution in the Government of the United States, or in any Department or Officer thereof.

Section. 9. The Migration or Importation of such Persons as any of the States now existing shall think proper to admit, shall not be prohibited by the Congress prior to the Year one thousand eight hundred and eight, but a Tax or duty may be imposed on such Importation, not exceeding ten dollars for each Person.

The Privilege of the Writ of Habeas Corpus shall not be suspended, unless when in Cases of Rebellion or Invasion the public Safety may require it.

No Bill of Attainder or ex post facto Law shall be passed.

No Capitation, or other direct, Tax shall be laid, unless in Proportion to the Census or Enumeration herein before directed to be taken.

No Tax or Duty shall be laid on Articles exported from any State.

No Preference shall be given by any Regulation of Commerce or Revenue to the Ports of one State over those of another: nor shall Vessels bound to, or from, one State, be obliged to enter, clear, or pay Duties in another.

No Money shall be drawn from the Treasury, but in Consequence of Appropriations made by Law; and a regular Statement and Account of the Receipts and Expenditures of all public Money shall be published from time to time.

No Title of Nobility shall be granted by the United States: And no Person holding any Office of Profit or trust under them, shall, without the Consent of the Congress, accept of any present, Emolument, Office, or Title, of any kind whatever, from any King, Prince, or foreign State.

Section 10. No State shall enter into any Treaty, Alliance, or Confederation; grant Letters of Marque and Reprisal; coin Money; emit Bills of Credit; make any Thing but gold and silver Coin a Tender in Payment of Debts; pass any Bill of Attainder, ex post facto Law, or Law impairing the Obligation of Contracts, or grant any Title of Nobility.

No State shall, without the Consent of the Congress, lay any Imposts or Duties on Imports or Exports, except what may be absolutely necessary for executing its inspection Laws: and the net Produce of all Duties and Imposts, laid by any State on Imports or Exports, shall be for the Use of the Treasury of the United States; and all such Laws shall be subject to the Revision and Controul of the Congress.

No State shall, without the Consent of Congress, lay any Duty of Tonnage, keep Troops, or Ships of War in time of Peace, enter into any Agreement or Compact with another State, or with a foreign Power, or engage in War, unless actually invaded, or in such imminent Danger as will not admit of delay.

ARTICLE. II.

Section. 1. The executive Power shall be vested in a President of the United States of America. He shall hold his Office during the term of four Years, and, together with the Vice President, chosen for the same Term, be elected, as follows:

Each State shall appoint, in such Manner as the Legislature thereof may direct, a Number of Electors, equal to the whole Number of Senators and Representatives to which the State may be entitled in the Congress: but no Senator or Representative, or Person holding an Office of Trust or Profit under the United States, shall be appointed an Elector.

The Electors shall meet in their respective States, and vote by Ballot for two Persons, of whom one at least shall not be an Inhabitant of the same State with themselves. And they shall make a List of all the Persons voted for, and of the Number of Votes for each; which List they shall sign and certify, and transmit sealed to the Seat of the Government of the United States, directed to the President of the Senate. The President of the Senate shall, in the Presence of the Senate and House of Representatives, open all the Certificates, and the Votes shall then be counted. The Person having the greatest Number of Votes shall be the President, if such Number be a Majority of the whole Number of Electors appointed; and if there be more than one who have such Majority, and have an equal Number of Votes, then the House of Representatives shall immediately chuse by Ballot one of them for President; and if no Person have a Majority, then from the five highest on the List the said House shall in like Manner chuse the President. But in chusing the President, the Votes shall be taken by States, the Representation from each State having one Vote; A quorum for this Purpose shall consist of a Member or Members from two thirds of the States, and a Majority of all the States shall be necessary to a Choice. In every Case, after the Choice of the President, the Person having the greatest Number of Votes of the Electors shall be the Vice President. But if there should remain two or more who have equal Votes, the Senate shall chuse from them by Ballot the Vice President.

The Congress may determine the Time of chusing the Electors, and the Day on which they shall give their Votes; which Day shall be the same throughout the United States.

No Person except a natural born Citizen, or a Citizen of the United States, at the time of the Adoption of this Constitution, shall be eligible to the Office of President; neither shall any Person be eligible to that Office who shall not have attained to the Age of thirty five Years, and been fourteen Years a Resident within the United States.

In Case of the Removal of the President from Office, or of his Death, Resignation, or Inability to discharge the Powers and Duties of the said Office, the Same shall devolve on the Vice President, and the Congress may by Law provide for the Case of Removal, Death, Resignation or Inability, both of the President and Vice President, declaring what Officer shall then act as President, and such Officer shall act accordingly, until the Disability be removed, or a President shall be elected.

The President shall, at stated Times, receive for his Services, a Compensation, which shall neither be encreased or diminished during the Period for which he shall have been elected, and he shall not receive within that Period any other Emolument from the United States, or any of them.

Before he enters on the Execution of his Office, he shall take the following Oath or Affirmation:—"I do solemnly swear (or affirm) that I will faithfully execute the Office of President of the United States, and will to the best of my Ability, preserve, protect and defend the Constitution of the United States."

Section. 2. The President shall be Commander in Chief of the Army and Navy of the United States, and of the Militia of the several States, when called into the actual Service of the United States; he may require the Opinion, in writing, of the principal Officer in each of the executive Departments, upon any Subject relating to the Duties of their respective Offices, and he shall have Power to grant Reprieves and Pardons for Offences against the United States, except in Cases of Impeachment.

He shall have Power, by and with the Advice and Consent of the Senate, to make Treaties, provided two thirds of the Senators present concur; and he shall nominate, and by and with the Advice and Consent of the Senate, shall appoint Ambassadors, other public Ministers and Consuls, Judges of the supreme Court, and all other Officers of the United States, whose Appointments are not herein otherwise provided for, and which shall be established by Law; but the Congress may by Law vest the Appointment of such inferior Officers, as they think proper, in the President alone, in the Courts of Law, or in the Heads of Departments.

The President shall have Power to fill up all Vacancies that may happen during the Recess of the Senate, by granting Commissions which shall expire at the End of their next Session.

Section. 3. He shall from time to time give to the Congress Information of the State of the Union, and recommend to their Consideration such Measures as he shall judge necessary and expedient; he may, on extraordinary Occasions, convene both Houses, or either of them, and in Case of Disagreement between them, with Respect to the Time of Adjournment, he may adjourn them to such Time as he shall think proper; he shall receive Ambassadors and other public Ministers; he shall take Care that the Laws be faithfully executed, and shall Commission all the Officers of the United States.

Section. 4. The President, Vice President and all civil Officers of the United States, shall be removed from Office on Impeachment for, and Conviction of, Treason, Bribery, or other high Crimes and Misdemeanors.

Article. III.

Section. 1. The judicial Power of the United States, shall be vested in one supreme Court, and in such inferior Courts as the Congress may from time to time ordain and establish. The Judges, both of the supreme and inferior Courts, shall hold their Offices during good Behavior, and shall, at stated Times, receive for their Services, a Compensation, which shall not be diminished during their Continuance in Office.

Section. 2. The judicial Power shall extend to all Cases, in Law and Equity, arising under this Constitution, the Laws of the United States, and Treaties made, or which shall be made, under their Authority;—to all Cases affecting Ambassadors, other public Ministers and Consuls;—to all Cases of admiralty and maritime Jurisdiction;—the Controversies to which the United States shall be a Party;—to Controversies between two or more States;—between a State and Citizens of another State;—between Citizens of different States;—between Citizens of the same State claiming Lands under Grants of different States, and between a State, or the Citizens thereof, and foreign States, Citizens or Subjects.

In all cases affecting Ambassadors, other public Ministers and Consuls, and those in which a State shall be Party, the supreme Court shall have original Jurisdiction. In all the other Cases before mentioned, the supreme Court shall have appellate Jurisdiction, both as to Law and Fact, with such Exceptions, and under such Regulations as the Congress shall make.

The Trial of all Crimes, except in Cases of Impeachment, shall be by Jury; and such Trial shall be held in the State where the said Crimes shall have been committed; but when not committed within any State, the Trial shall be at such Place or Places as the Congress may by Law have directed.

Section. 3. Treason against the United States, shall consist only in levying War against them, or in adhering to their Enemies, giving them Aid and Comfort. No Person shall be convicted of Treason unless on the Testimony of two Witnesses to the same overt Act, or on Confession in open Court.

The Congress shall have Power to declare the Punishment of Treason, but no Attainder of Treason shall work Corruption of Blood, or Forfeiture except during the Life of the Person attainted.

ARTICLE. IV.

Section. 1. Full Faith and Credit shall be given in each State to the public Acts, Records, and judicial Proceedings of every other State. And the Congress may by general Laws prescribe the Manner in which such Acts, Records and Proceedings shall be proved, and the Effect thereof.

Section. 2. The Citizens of each State shall be entitled to all Privileges and Immunities of Citizens in the several States.

A Person charged in any State with Treason, Felony, or other Crime, who shall flee from Justice, and be found in another State, shall on Demand of the executive Authority of the State from which he fled, be delivered up, to be removed to the State having Jurisdiction of the Crime.

No Person held to Service or Labour in one State, under the Laws thereof, escaping into another, shall, in Consequence of any Law or Regulation therein, be discharged from such Service or Labour, but shall be delivered up on Claim of the Party to whom such Service or Labour may be due.

Section. 3. New States may be admitted by the Congress into this Union; but no new State shall be formed or erected within the Jurisdiction of any other State; nor any State be formed by the Junction of two or more States, or Parts of States, without the consent of the Legislatures of the States concerned as well as of the Congress.

The Congress shall have Power to dispose of and make all needful Rules and Regulations respecting the Territory or other Property belonging to the United States; and nothing in this Constitution shall be so construed as to Prejudice any Claims of the United States, or of any particular States.

Section. 4. The United States shall guarantee to every State in this Union a Republican Form of Government, and shall protect each of them against Invasion; and on Application of the Legislature, or of the Executive (when the Legislature cannot be convened) against domestic Violence.

ARTICLE. V.

The Congress, whenever two thirds of both Houses shall deem it necessary, shall propose Amendments to this Constitution, or, on the Application of the

Legislatures of two thirds of the several States, shall call a Convention for proposing Amendments, which, in either Case, shall be valid to all Intents and Purposes, as Part of this Constitution, when ratified by the Legislatures of three fourths of the several States, or by Conventions in three fourths thereof, as the one or the other Mode of Ratification may be proposed by the Congress; Provided that no Amendment which may be made prior to the Year One thousand eight hundred and eight shall in any Manner affect the first and fourth Clauses in the Ninth Section of the first Article; and that no State, without its Consent, shall be deprived of its equal Suffrage in the Senate.

ARTICLE. VI.

All Debts contracted and Engagements entered into, before the Adoption of this Constitution, shall be as valid against the United States under this Constitution, as under the Confederation.

This Constitution, and the Laws of the United States which shall be made in Pursuance thereof; and all Treaties made, or which shall be made, under the Authority of the United States, shall be the supreme Law of the Land; and the Judges in every State shall be bound thereby, any Thing in the Constitution or Laws of any State to the Contrary notwithstanding.

The Senators and Representatives before mentioned, and the Members of the several State Legislatures, and all executive and judicial Officers, both of the United States and of the several States, shall be bound by Oath or Affirmation, to support this Constitution; but no religious Test shall ever be required as a Qualification to any Office or public Trust under the United States.

ARTICLE. VII.

The Ratification of the Conventions of nine States, shall be sufficient for the Establishment of this Constitution between the States so ratifying the Same.

Done in Convention by the Unanimous Consent of the States present the Seventeenth Day of September in the Year of our Lord one thousand seven hundred and Eighty seven and of the Independence of the United States of America the Twelfth. In witness thereof We have hereunto subscribed our Names,

Go. WASHINGTON—Presdt.
and deputy from Virginia.

New Hampshire	John Langdon Nicholas Gilman	Delaware	Geo: Read Gunning Bedford jun John Dickinson Richard Bassett Jaco: Broom
Massachusetts	Nathaniel Gorham Rufus King		
Connecticut	Wm Saml Johnson Roger Sherman	Maryland	James McHenry Dan of St Thos Jenifer Danl Carroll
New York: . . .	Alexander Hamilton		
New Jersey	Wil: Livingston David A. Brearley. Wm Paterson. Jona: Dayton	Virginia	John Blair— James Madison Jr.
Pennsylvania	B Franklin Thomas Mifflin Robt Morris Geo. Clymer Thos FitzSimons Jared Ingersoll James Wilson Gouv Morris	North Carolina	Wm Blount Richd Dobbs Spaight. Hu Williamson
		South Carolina	J. Rutledge Charles Cotesworth Pinckney Charles Pinckney Pierce Butler.
		Georgia	William Few Abr Baldwin

AMENDMENTS TO THE CONSTITUTION

ARTICLES IN ADDITION TO, and Amendment of the Constitution of the United States of America, proposed by Congress, and ratified by the Legislatures of the several States, pursuant to the fifth Article of the original Constitution.

AMENDMENT I.

Congress shall make no law respecting an establishment of religion, or prohibiting the free exercise thereof; or abridging the freedom of speech, or of the press; or the right of the people peaceably to assemble, and to petition the Government for a redress of grievances.

AMENDMENT II.

A well regulated Militia, being necessary to the security of a free State, the right of the people to keep and bear Arms, shall not be infringed.

AMENDMENT III.

No Soldier shall, in time of peace be quartered in any house, without the consent of the Owner, nor in time of war, but in a manner to be prescribed by law.

AMENDMENT IV.

The right of the people to be secure in their persons, houses, papers, and effects, against unreasonable searches and seizures, shall not be violated, and no Warrants shall issue, but upon probable cause, supported by Oath or affirmation, and particularly describing the place to be searched, and the persons or things to be seized.

AMENDMENT V.

No person shall be held to answer for a capital, or otherwise infamous crime, unless on a presentment or indictment of a Grand Jury, except in cases arising in the land or naval forces, or in the Militia, when in actual service in time of War or public danger; nor shall any person be subject for the same offence to be twice put in jeopardy of life or limb; nor shall be compelled in any criminal case to be a witness against himself, nor be deprived of life, liberty, or property, without due process of law; nor shall private property be taken for public use, without just compensation.

AMENDMENT VI.

In all criminal prosecutions, the accused shall enjoy the right to a speedy and public trial, by an impartial jury of the State and district wherein the crime shall have been committed, which district shall have been previously ascertained by law, and to be informed of the nature and cause of the accusation; to be confronted with the witnesses against him; to have compulsory process for obtaining witnesses in his favor, and to have the Assistance of Counsel for his defence.

AMENDMENT VII.

In Suits at common law, where the value in controversy shall exceed twenty dollars, the right of trial by jury shall be preserved, and no fact tried by a jury, shall be otherwise re-examined in any Court of the United States, than according to the rules of the common law.

AMENDMENT VIII.

Excessive bail shall not be required, nor excessive fines imposed, nor cruel and unusual punishments inflicted.

Amendment IX.

The enumeration in the Constitution, of certain rights, shall not be construed to deny or disparage others retained by the people.

Amendment X.

The powers not delegated to the United States by the Constitution, nor prohibited by it to the States, are reserved to the States respectively, or to the people. [The first ten amendments went into effect December 15, 1791.]

Amendment XI.

The Judicial power of the United States shall not be construed to extend to any suit in law or equity, commenced or prosecuted against one of the United States by Citizens of another State, or by Citizens or Subjects of any Foreign State. [January 8, 1798.]

Amendment XII.

The Electors shall meet in their respective states, and vote by ballot for President and Vice-President, one of whom, at least, shall not be an inhabitant of the same state with themselves; they shall name in their ballots the person voted for as President, and in distinct ballots the person voted for as Vice-President, and they shall make distinct lists of all persons voted for as President, and of all persons voted for as Vice President, and of the number of votes for each, which lists they shall sign and certify, and transmit sealed to the seat of the government of the United States, directed to the President of the Senate;—The President of the Senate shall, in the presence of the Senate and House of Representatives, open all the certificates and the votes shall then be counted;—The person having the greatest number of votes for President, shall be the President, if such number be a majority of the whole number of Electors appointed; and if no person have such majority, then from the persons having the highest numbers not exceeding three on the list of those voted for as President, the House of Representatives shall choose immediately, by ballot, the President. But in choosing the President, the votes shall be taken by states, the representation from each state having one vote; a quorum for this purpose shall consist of a member or members from two-thirds of the states, and a majority of all the states shall be necessary to a choice. And if the House of Representatives shall not choose a President whenever the right of choice shall devolve upon them, before the fourth day of March next following, then the Vice-President shall act as President, as in the case of the death or other constitutional disability of the President.— The person having the greatest number of votes as Vice-President, shall be the Vice-President, if such number be a majority of the whole number of Electors appointed, and if no person have a majority, then from the two highest numbers on the list, the Senate shall choose the Vice-President; a quorum for the purpose shall consist of two-thirds of the whole number of Senators, and a majority of the whole number shall be necessary to a choice. But no person constitutionally ineligible to the office of President shall be eligible to that of Vice-President of the United States. [September 25, 1804.]

AMENDMENT XIII.

Section 1. Neither slavery nor involuntary servitude, except as a punishment for crime whereof the party shall have been duly convicted, shall exist within the United States, or any place subject to their jurisdiction.

Section 2. Congress shall have power to enforce this article by appropriate legislation. [December 18, 1865.]

AMENDMENT XIV.

Section 1. All persons born or naturalized in the United States, and subject to the jurisdiction thereof, are citizens of the United States and of the State wherein they reside. No State shall make or enforce any law which shall abridge the privileges or immunities of citizens of the United States; nor shall any State deprive any person of life, liberty, or property, without due process of law; nor deny to any person within its jurisdiction the equal protection of the laws.

Section 2. Representatives shall be apportioned among the several States according to their respective numbers, counting the whole number of persons in each State, excluding Indians not taxed. But when the right to vote at any election for the choice of electors for President and Vice President of the United States, Representatives in Congress, the Executive and Judicial officers of a State, or the members of the Legislature thereof, is denied to any of the male inhabitants of such State, being twenty-one years of age, and citizens of the United States, or in any way abridged, except for participation in rebellion, or other crime, the basis of representation therein shall be reduced in the proportion which the number of such male citizens shall bear to the whole number of male citizens twenty-one years of age in such State.

Section 3. No person shall be a Senator or Representative in Congress, or elector of President and Vice President, or hold any office, civil or military, under the United States, or under any State, who, having previously taken an oath, as a member of Congress, or as an officer of the United States, or as a member of any State legislature, or as an executive or judicial officer of any State, to support the Constitution of the United States, shall have engaged in insurrection or rebellion against the same, or given aid or comfort to the enemies thereof. But Congress may by a vote of two-thirds of each House, remove such disability.

Section 4. The validity of the public debt of the United States, authorized by law, including debts incurred for payment of pensions and bounties for services in suppressing insurrection or rebellion, shall not be questioned. But neither the United States nor any State shall assume or pay any debt or obligation incurred in aid of insurrection or rebellion against the United States, or any claim for the loss or emancipation of any slave; but all such debts, obligations and claims shall be held illegal and void.

Section 5. The Congress shall have power to enforce, by appropriate legislation, the provisions of this article. [July 28, 1868.]

AMENDMENT XV.

Section 1. The right of citizens of the United States to vote shall not be denied or abridged by the United States or by any State on account of race, color, or previous condition of servitude—

Section 2. The Congress shall have power to enforce this article by appropriate legislation.—[March 30, 1870.]

AMENDMENT XVI.

The Congress shall have power to lay and collect taxes on incomes, from whatever source derived, without apportionment among the several

States, and without regard to any census or enumeration. [February 25, 1913.]

AMENDMENT XVII.

The Senate of the United States shall be composed of two senators from each State, elected by the people thereof, for six years; and each Senator shall have one vote. The electors in each State shall have the qualifications requisite for electors of the most numerous branch of the State legislature.

When vacancies happen in the representation of any State in the Senate, the executive authority of such State shall issue writs of election to fill such vacancies: *Provided,* That the legislature of any State may empower the executive thereof to make temporary appointments until the people fill the vacancies by election as the legislature may direct.

This amendment shall not be so construed as to affect the election or term of any senator chosen before it becomes valid as part of the Constitution. [May 31, 1913.]

AMENDMENT XVIII.

After one year from the ratification of this article, the manufacture, sale, or transportation of intoxicating liquors within, the importation thereof into, or the exportation thereof from the United States and all territory subject to the jurisdiction thereof for beverage purposes is hereby prohibited.

The Congress and the several States shall have concurrent power to enforce this article by appropriate legislation.

This article shall be inoperative unless it shall have been ratified as an amendment to the Constitution by the legislatures of the several States, as provided in the Constitution, within seven years from the date of the submission thereof to the States by Congress. [January 29, 1919.]

AMENDMENT XIX.

The right of citizens of the United States to vote shall not be denied or abridged by the United States or by any State on account of sex.

The Congress shall have power by appropriate legislation to enforce the provisions of this article. [August 26, 1920.]

AMENDMENT XX.

Section 1. The terms of the President and Vice-President shall end at noon on the twentieth day of January, and the terms of Senators and Representatives at noon on the third day of January, of the years in which such terms would have ended if this article had not been ratified; and the terms of their successors shall then begin.

Section 2. The Congress shall assemble at least once in every year, and such meeting shall begin at noon on the third day of January, unless they shall by law appoint a different day.

Section 3. If, at the time fixed for the beginning of the term of the President, the President-elect shall have died, the Vice-President-elect shall become President. If a President shall not have been chosen before the time fixed for the beginning of his term, or if the President-elect shall have failed to qualify, then the Vice-President-elect shall act as President until a President shall have qualified; and the Congress may by law provide for the case wherein neither a President-elect nor a Vice-President-elect shall have qualified, declaring who shall then act as President, or the manner in which one who is to act shall be selected, and such person shall act accordingly until a President or Vice-President shall have qualified.

Section 4. The Congress may by law provide for the case of the death of any of the persons from whom the House of Representatives may choose a President whenever the right of choice shall have devolved upon them, and for the case of the death of any of the persons from whom the Senate may choose a Vice-President whenever the right of choice shall have devolved upon them.

Section 5. Sections 1 and 2 shall take effect on the 15th day of October following the ratification of this article.

Section 6. This article shall be inoperative unless it shall have been ratified as an amendment to the Constitution by the legislatures of three-fourths of the several States within seven years from the date of its submission. [February 6, 1933.]

AMENDMENT XXI.

Section 1. The eighteenth article of amendment to the Constitution of the United States is hereby repealed.

Section 2. The transportation or importation into any State, Territory or possession of the United States for delivery or use therein of intoxicating liquors, in violation of the laws thereof, is hereby prohibited.

Section 3. This article shall be inoperative unless it shall have been ratified as an amendment to the Constitution by convention in the several States, as provided in the Constitution, within seven years from the date of the submission thereof to the States by the Congress. [December 5, 1933.]

AMENDMENT XXII.

Section 1. No person shall be elected to the office of the President more than twice, and no person who has held the office of President, or acted as President, for more than two years of a term to which some other person was elected President shall be elected to the office of the President more than once. But this Article shall not apply to any person holding the office of President when this Article was proposed by the Congress, and shall not prevent any person who may be holding the office of President, or acting as President, during the term within which this Article becomes operative from holding the office of President or acting as President during the remainder of such term.

Section 2. This article shall be inoperative unless it shall have been ratified as an amendment to the Constitution by the legislatures of three-fourths of the several states within seven years from the date of its submission to the States by the Congress. [February 27, 1951.]

AMENDMENT XXIII.

Section 1. The District constituting the seat of government of the United States shall appoint in such manner as the Congress may direct:
A number of electors of President and Vice-President equal to the whole number of Senators and Representatives in Congress to which the District would be entitled if it were a State, but in no event more than the least

populous State; they shall be in addition to those appointed by the States, but they shall be considered, for the purposes of the election of President and Vice-President, to be electors appointed by a State; and they shall meet in the District and perform such duties as provided by the twelfth article of amendment.

Section 2. The Congress shall have the power to enforce this article by appropriate legislation. [March 29, 1961.]

AMENDMENT XXIV.

Section 1. The right of citizens of the United States to vote in any primary or other election for President or Vice President, for electors for President or Vice President, or for Senator or Representative in Congress, shall not be denied or abridged by the United States or any State by reason of failure to pay any poll tax or other tax.

Section 2. The Congress shall have power to enforce this article by appropriate legislation. [January 23, 1964.]

AMENDMENT XXV.

Section 1. In case of the removal of the President from office or of his death or resignation, the Vice President shall become President.

Section 2. Whenever there is a vacancy in the office of Vice President, the President shall nominate a Vice President who shall take office upon confirmation by a majority vote of both Houses of Congress.

Section 3. Whenever the President transmits to the President pro tempore of the Senate and the Speaker of the House of Representatives his written declaration that he is unable to discharge the powers and duties of his office, and until he transmits to them a written declaration to the contrary, such powers and duties shall be discharged by the Vice President as Acting President.

Section 4. Whenever the Vice President and a majority of either the principal officers of the executive departments or of such other body as Congress may by law provide, transmit to the President pro tempore of the Senate and the Speaker of the House of Representatives their written declaration that the President is unable to discharge the powers and duties of his office, the Vice President shall immediately assume the powers and duties of the office as Acting President.

Thereafter, when the President transmits to the President pro tempore of the Senate and the Speaker of the House of Representatives his written declaration that no inability exists, he shall resume the powers and duties of his office unless the Vice President and a majority of either the principal officers of the executive departments or of such other body as Congress may by law provide, transmit within four days to the President pro tempore of the Senate and the Speaker of the House of Representatives their written declaration that the President is unable to discharge the powers and duties of his office. Thereupon Congress shall decide the issue, assembling within forty-eight hours for that purpose if not in session. If the Congress, within twenty-one days after receipt of the latter written declaration, or, if Congress is not in session, within twenty-one days after Congress is required to assemble, determines by two-thirds vote of both Houses that the President is unable to discharge the powers and duties of his office, the Vice President shall continue to discharge the same as Acting President; otherwise, the President shall resume the powers and duties of his office. [February 10, 1967.]

AMENDMENT XXVI.

Section 1. The right of citizens of the United States, who are eighteen years of age or older, to vote shall not be denied or abridged by the United States or by any State on account of age.

Section 2. The Congress shall have power to enforce this article by appropriate legislation [June 30, 1971.]

AMENDMENT XXVII.

No law, varying the compensation for the services of the Senators and Representatives shall take effect, until an election of Representatives shall have intervened. [May 8, 1992.]

PRESIDENTIAL ELECTIONS

Year	Number of States	Candidates	Parties	Popular Vote	% of Popular Vote	Electoral Vote	% Voter Participation
1789	11	**GEORGE WASHINGTON**	No party designations			69	
		John Adams				34	
		Other candidates				35	
1792	15	**GEORGE WASHINGTON**	No party designations			132	
		John Adams				77	
		George Clinton				50	
		Other candidates				5	
1796	16	**JOHN ADAMS**	Federalist			71	
		Thomas Jefferson	Democratic-Republican			68	
		Thomas Pinckney	Federalist			59	
		Aaron Burr	Democratic-Republican			30	
		Other candidates				48	
1800	16	**THOMAS JEFFERSON**	Democratic-Republican			73	
		Aaron Burr	Democratic-Republican			73	
		John Adams	Federalist			65	
		Charles C. Pinckney	Federalist			64	
		John Jay	Federalist			1	
1804	17	**THOMAS JEFFERSON**	Democratic-Republican			162	
		Charles C. Pinckney	Federalist			14	

Year	Number of States	Candidates	Parties	Popular Vote	% of Popular Vote	Electoral Vote	% Voter Participation
1808	17	**JAMES MADISON**	Democratic-Republican			122	
		Charles C. Pinckney	Federalist			47	
		George Clinton	Democratic-Republican			6	
1812	18	**JAMES MADISON**	Democratic-Republican			128	
		DeWitt Clinton	Federalist			89	
1816	19	**JAMES MONROE**	Democratic-Republican			183	
		Rufus King	Federalist			34	
1820	24	**JAMES MONROE**	Democratic-Republican			231	
		John Quincy Adams	Independent			1	
1824	24	**JOHN QUINCY ADAMS**	Democratic-Republican	108,740	30.5	84	26.9
		Andrew Jackson	Democratic-Republican	153,544	43.1	99	
		Henry Clay	Democratic-Republican	47,136	13.2	37	
		William H. Crawford	Democratic-Republican	46,618	13.1	41	
1828	24	**ANDREW JACKSON**	Democratic	647,286	56.0	178	57.6
		John Quincy Adams	National-Republican	508,064	44.0	83	

Year	Number of States	Candidates	Parties	Popular Vote	% of Popular Vote	Electoral Vote	% Voter Participation
1832	24	**ANDREW JACKSON**	Democratic	688,242	54.5	219	55.4
		Henry Clay	National-Republican	473,462	37.5	49	
		William Wirt	Anti-Masonic	101,051	8.0	7	
		John Floyd	Democratic			11	
1836	26	**MARTIN VAN BUREN**	Democratic	765,483	50.9	170	57.8
		William H. Harrison	Whig			73	
		Hugh L. White	Whig	739,795	49.1	26	
		Daniel Webster	Whig			14	
		W. P. Mangum	Whig			11	
1840	26	**WILLIAM H. HARRISON**	Whig	1,274,624	53.1	234	80.2
		Martin Van Buren	Democratic	1,127,781	46.9	60	
1844	26	**JAMES K. POLK**	Democratic	1,338,464	49.6	170	78.9
		Henry Clay	Whig	1,300,097	48.1	105	
		James G. Birney	Liberty	62,300	2.3		
1848	30	**ZACHARY TAYLOR**	Whig	1,360,967	47.4	163	72.7
		Lewis Cass	Democratic	1,222,342	42.5	127	
		Martin Van Buren	Free Soil	291,263	10.1		
1852	31	**FRANKLIN PIERCE**	Democratic	1,601,117	50.9	254	69.6
		Winfield Scott	Whig	1,385,453	44.1	42	
		John P. Hale	Free Soil	155,825	5.0		
1856	31	**JAMES BUCHANAN**	Democratic	1,832,955	45.3	174	78.9
		John C. Frémont	Republican	1,339,932	33.1	114	
		Millard Fillmore	American	871,731	21.6	8	

Year	Number of States	Candidates	Parties	Popular Vote	% of Popular Vote	Electoral Vote	% Voter Participation
1860	33	**ABRAHAM LINCOLN**	Republican	1,865,593	39.8	180	81.2
		Stephen A. Douglas	Democratic	1,382,713	29.5	12	
		John C. Breckinridge	Democratic	848,356	18.1	72	
		John Bell	Constitutional Union	592,906	12.6	39	
1864	36	**ABRAHAM LINCOLN**	Republican	2,206,938	55.0	212	73.8
		George B. McClellan	Democratic	1,803,787	45.0	21	
1868	37	**ULYSSES S. GRANT**	Republican	3,013,421	52.7	214	78.1
		Horatio Seymour	Democratic	2,706,829	47.3	80	
1872	37	**ULYSSES S. GRANT**	Republican	3,596,745	55.6	286	71.3
		Horace Greeley	Democratic	2,843,446	43.9	66	
1876	38	Rutherford B. Hayes	Republican	4,036,572	48.0	185	81.8
		Samuel J. Tilden	Democratic	4,284,020	51.0	184	
1880	38	**JAMES A. GARFIELD**	Republican	4,453,295	48.5	214	79.4
		Winfield S. Hancock	Democratic	4,414,082	48.1	155	
		James B. Weaver	Greenback-Labor	308,578	3.4		
1884	38	**GROVER CLEVELAND**	Democratic	4,879,507	48.5	219	77.5
		James G. Blaine	Republican	4,850,293	48.2	182	
		Benjamin F. Butler	Greenback-Labor	175,370	1.8		
		John P. St. John	Prohibition	150,369	1.5		
1888	38	**BENJAMIN HARRISON**	Republican	5,477,129	47.9	233	79.3
		Grover Cleveland	Democratic	5,537,857	48.6	168	
		Clinton B. Fisk	Prohibition	249,506	2.2		
		Anson J. Streeter	Union Labor	146,935	1.3		

Year	Number of States	Candidates	Parties	Popular Vote	% of Popular Vote	Electoral Vote	% Voter Participation
1892	44	**GROVER CLEVELAND**	Democratic	5,555,426	46.1	277	74.7
		Benjamin Harrison	Republican	5,182,690	43.0	145	
		James B. Weaver	People's	1,029,846	8.5	22	
		John Bidwell	Prohibition	264,133	2.2		
1896	45	**WILLIAM MCKINLEY**	Republican	7,102,246	51.1	271	79.3
		William J. Bryan	Democratic	6,492,559	47.7	176	
1900	45	**WILLIAM MCKINLEY**	Republican	7,218,491	51.7	292	73.2
		William J. Bryan	Democratic; Populist	6,356,734	45.5	155	
		John C. Wooley	Prohibition	208,914	1.5		
1904	45	**THEODORE ROOSEVELT**	Republican	7,628,461	57.4	336	65.2
		Alton B. Parker	Democratic	5,084,223	37.6	140	
		Eugene V. Debs	Socialist	402,283	3.0		
		Silas C. Swallow	Prohibition	258,536	1.9		
1908	46	**WILLIAM H. TAFT**	Republican	7,675,320	51.6	321	65.4
		William J. Bryan	Democratic	6,412,294	43.1	162	
		Eugene V. Debs	Socialist	420,793	2.8		
		Eugene W. Chafin	Prohibition	253,840	1.7		
1912	48	**WOODROW WILSON**	Democratic	6,296,547	41.9	435	58.8
		Theodore Roosevelt	Progressive	4,118,571	27.4	88	
		William H. Taft	Republican	3,486,720	23.2	8	
		Eugene V. Debs	Socialist	900,672	6.0		
		Eugene W. Chafin	Prohibition	206,275	1.4		

Year	Number of States	Candidates	Parties	Popular Vote	% of Popular Vote	Electoral Vote	% Voter Participation
1916	48	**WOODROW WILSON**	Democratic	9,127,695	49.4	277	61.6
		Charles E. Hughes	Republican	8,533,507	46.2	254	
		A. L. Benson	Socialist	585,113	3.2		
		J. Frank Hanly	Prohibition	220,506	1.2		
1920	48	**WARREN G. HARDING**	Republican	16,143,407	60.4	404	49.2
		James M. Cox	Democratic	9,130,328	34.2	127	
		Eugene V. Debs	Socialist	919,799	3.4		
		P. P. Christensen	Farmer-Labor	265,411	1.0		
1924	48	**CALVIN COOLIDGE**	Republican	15,718,211	54.0	382	48.9
		John W. Davis	Democratic	8,385,283	28.8	136	
		Robert M. La Follette	Progressive	4,831,289	16.6	13	
1928	48	**HERBERT C. HOOVER**	Republican	21,391,993	58.2	444	56.9
		Alfred E. Smith	Democratic	15,016,169	40.9	87	
1932	48	**FRANKLIN D. ROOSEVELT**	Democratic	22,809,638	57.4	472	56.9
		Herbert C. Hoover	Republican	15,758,901	39.7	59	
		Norman Thomas	Socialist	881,951	2.2		
1936	48	**FRANKLIN D. ROOSEVELT**	Democratic	27,752,869	60.8	523	61.0
		Alfred M. Landon	Republican	16,674,665	36.5	8	
		William Lemke	Union	882,479	1.9		
1940	48	**FRANKLIN D. ROOSEVELT**	Democratic	27,307,819	54.8	449	62.5
		Wendell L. Willkie	Republican	22,321,018	44.8	82	
1944	48	**FRANKLIN D. ROOSEVELT**	Democratic	25,606,585	53.5	432	55.9
		Thomas E. Dewey	Republican	22,014,745	46.0	99	

Year	Number of States	Candidates	Parties	Popular Vote	% of Popular Vote	Electoral Vote	% Voter Participation
1948	48	**HARRY S. TRUMAN**	Democratic	24,179,345	49.6	303	53.0
		Thomas E. Dewey	Republican	21,991,291	45.1	189	
		J. Strom Thurmond	States' Rights	1,176,125	2.4	39	
		Henry A. Wallace	Progressive	1,157,326	2.4		
1952	48	**DWIGHT D. EISENHOWER**	Republican	33,936,234	55.1	442	63.3
		Adlai E. Stevenson	Democratic	27,314,992	44.4	89	
1956	48	**DWIGHT D. EISENHOWER**	Republican	35,590,472	57.6	457	60.6
		Adlai E. Stevenson	Democratic	26,022,752	42.1	73	
1960	50	**JOHN F. KENNEDY**	Democratic	34,226,731	49.7	303	62.8
		Richard M. Nixon	Republican	34,108,157	49.5	219	
1964	50	**LYNDON B. JOHNSON**	Democratic	43,129,566	61.1	486	61.9
		Barry M. Goldwater	Republican	27,178,188	38.5	52	
1968	50	**RICHARD M. NIXON**	Republican	31,785,480	43.4	301	60.9
		Hubert H. Humphrey	Democratic	31,275,166	42.7	191	
		George C. Wallace	American Independent	9,906,473	13.5	46	
1972	50	**RICHARD M. NIXON**	Republican	47,169,911	60.7	520	55.2
		George S. McGovern	Democratic	29,170,383	37.5	17	
		John G. Schmitz	American	1,099,482	1.4		

Year	Number of States	Candidates	Party	Popular Vote	Percentage of Popular Vote	Electoral Vote	Percentage of Voter Participation
1976	50	**JIMMY CARTER** Gerald R. Ford	Democratic Republican	40,830,763 39,147,793	50.1 48.0	297 240	53.5
1980	50	**RONALD REAGAN** Jimmy Carter John B. Anderson Ed Clark	Republican Democratic Independent Libertarian	43,901,812 35,483,820 5,719,437 921,188	50.7 41.0 6.6 1.1	489 49	52.6
1984	50	**RONALD REAGAN** Walter F. Mondale	Republican Democratic	54,451,521 37,565,334	58.8 40.6	525 13	53.1
1988	50	**GEORGE H. W. BUSH** Michael Dukakis	Republican Democratic	47,917,341 41,013,030	53.4 45.6	426 111	50.1
1992	50	**BILL CLINTON** George H. W. Bush H. Ross Perot	Democratic Republican Independent	44,908,254 39,102,343 19,741,065	43.0 37.4 18.9	370 168	55.0
1996	50	**BILL CLINTON** Bob Dole H. Ross Perot	Democratic Republican Independent	47,401,185 39,197,469 8,085,295	49.0 41.0 8.0	379 159	49.0
2000	50	**GEORGE W. BUSH** Al Gore Ralph Nader	Republican Democrat Green	50,455,156 50,997,335 2,882,897	47.9 48.4 2.7	271 266	50.4
2004	50	**GEORGE W. BUSH** John F. Kerry	Republican Democrat	62,040,610 59,028,444	50.7 48.3	286 251	60.7
2008	50	**BARACK OBAMA** John McCain	Democrat Republican	69,456,897 59,934,814	52.92% 45.66%	365 173	63.0

Candidates receiving less than 1 percent of the popular vote have been omitted. Thus the percentage of popular vote given for any election year may not total 100 percent.

Before the passage of the Twelfth Amendment in 1804, the electoral college voted for two presidential candidates; the runner-up became vice president.

ADMISSION OF STATES

Order of Admission	State	Date of Admission	Order of Admission	State	Date of Admission
1	Delaware	December 7, 1787	26	Michigan	January 26, 1837
2	Pennsylvania	December 12, 1787	27	Florida	March 3, 1845
3	New Jersey	December 18, 1787	28	Texas	December 29, 1845
4	Georgia	January 2, 1788	29	Iowa	December 28, 1846
5	Connecticut	January 9, 1788	30	Wisconsin	May 29, 1848
6	Massachusetts	February 7, 1788	31	California	September 9, 1850
7	Maryland	April 28, 1788	32	Minnesota	May 11, 1858
8	South Carolina	May 23, 1788	33	Oregon	February 14, 1859
9	New Hampshire	June 21, 1788	34	Kansas	January 29, 1861
10	Virginia	June 25, 1788	35	West Virginia	June 30, 1863
11	New York	July 26, 1788	36	Nevada	October 31, 1864
12	North Carolina	November 21, 1789	37	Nebraska	March 1, 1867
13	Rhode Island	May 29, 1790	38	Colorado	August 1, 1876
14	Vermont	March 4, 1791	39	North Dakota	November 2, 1889
15	Kentucky	June 1, 1792	40	South Dakota	November 2, 1889
16	Tennessee	June 1, 1796	41	Montana	November 8, 1889
17	Ohio	March 1, 1803	42	Washington	November 11, 1889
18	Louisiana	April 30, 1812	43	Idaho	July 3, 1890
19	Indiana	December 11, 1816	44	Wyoming	July 10, 1890
20	Mississippi	December 10, 1817	45	Utah	January 4, 1896
21	Illinois	December 3, 1818	46	Oklahoma	November 16, 1907
22	Alabama	December 14, 1819	47	New Mexico	January 6, 1912
23	Maine	March 15, 1820	48	Arizona	February 14, 1912
24	Missouri	August 10, 1821	49	Alaska	January 3, 1959
25	Arkansas	June 15, 1836	50	Hawaii	August 21, 1959

POPULATION OF THE UNITED STATES

Year	Number of States	Population	% Increase	Population per Square Mile
1790	13	3,929,214		4.5
1800	16	5,308,483	35.1	6.1
1810	17	7,239,881	36.4	4.3
1820	23	9,638,453	33.1	5.5
1830	24	12,866,020	33.5	7.4
1840	26	17,069,453	32.7	9.8
1850	31	23,191,876	35.9	7.9
1860	33	31,443,321	35.6	10.6
1870	37	39,818,449	26.6	13.4
1880	38	50,155,783	26.0	16.9
1890	44	62,947,714	25.5	21.1
1900	45	75,994,575	20.7	25.6
1910	46	91,972,266	21.0	31.0
1920	48	105,710,620	14.9	35.6
1930	48	122,775,046	16.1	41.2
1940	48	131,669,275	7.2	44.2
1950	48	150,697,361	14.5	50.7
1960	50	179,323,175	19.0	50.6
1970	50	203,235,298	13.3	57.5
1980	50	226,504,825	11.4	64.0
1985	50	237,839,000	5.0	67.2
1990	50	250,122,000	5.2	70.6
1995	50	263,411,707	5.3	74.4
2000	50	281,421,906	6.8	77.0
2008	50	304,059,724	8.0	79.6

IMMIGRATION TO THE UNITED STATES, FISCAL YEARS 1820–2008

Year	Number	Year	Number	Year	Number	Year	Number
1820–1989	**55,457,531**	**1871–80**	**2,812,191**	**1921–30**	**4,107,209**	**1971–80**	**4,493,314**
1820	8,385	1871	321,350	1921	805,228	1971	370,478
1821–30	**143,439**	1872	404,806	1922	309,556	1972	384,685
1821	9,127	1873	459,803	1923	522,919	1973	400,063
1822	6,911	1874	313,339	1924	706,896	1974	394,861
1823	6,354	1875	227,498	1925	294,314	1975	386,914
1824	7,912	1876	169,986	1926	304,488	1976	398,613
1825	10,199	1877	141,857	1927	335,175	1976	103,676
1826	10,837	1878	138,469	1928	307,255	1977	462,315
1827	18,875	1879	177,826	1929	279,678	1978	601,442
1828	27,382	1880	457,257	1930	241,700	1979	460,348
1829	22,520	**1881–90**	**5,246,613**	**1931–40**	**528,431**	1980	530,639
1830	23,322	1881	669,431	1931	97,139	**1981–90**	**7,338,062**
1831–40	**599,125**	1882	788,992	1932	35,576	1981	596,600
1831	22,633	1883	603,322	1933	23,068	1982	594,131
1832	60,482	1884	518,592	1934	29,470	1983	559,763
1833	58,640	1885	395,346	1935	34,956	1984	543,903
1834	65,365	1886	334,203	1936	36,329	1985	570,009
1835	45,374	1887	490,109	1937	50,244	1986	601,708
1836	76,242	1888	546,889	1938	67,895	1987	601,516
1837	79,340	1889	444,427	1939	82,998	1988	643,025
1838	38,914	1890	455,302	1940	70,756	1989	1,090,924
1839	68,069	**1891–1900**	**3,687,564**	**1941–50**	**1,035,039**	1990	1,536,483
1840	84,066	1891	560,319	1941	51,776	**1991–2000**	**9,090,857**
1841–50	**1,713,251**	1892	579,653	1942	28,781	1991	1,827,167
1841	80,289	1893	439,730	1943	23,725	1992	973,977
1842	104,565	1894	285,631	1944	28,551	1993	904,292
		1895	258,536	1945	38,119	1994	804,416
		1896	343,267	1946	108,721		

Year	Number	Year	Number	Year	Number	Year	Number
1843	52,496	1897	230,832	1947	147,292	1995	720,461
1844	78,615	1898	229,299	1948	170,570	1996	915,900
1845	114,371	1899	311,715	1949	188,317	1997	798,378
1846	154,416	1900	443,572	1950	249,187	1998	660,477
1847	234,968					1999	644,787
1848	226,527	**1901–10**	**8,795,386**	**1951–60**	**2,515,479**	2000	841,002
1849	297,024	1901	487,918	1951	205,717	**2001–8**	**8,330,011**
1850	369,980	1902	648,743	1952	265,520	2001	1,058,902
		1903	857,046	1953	170,434	2002	1,059,356
1851–60	**2,598,214**	1904	812,870	1954	208,177	2003	705,827
1851	379,466	1905	1,026,499	1955	237,790	2004	957,883
1852	371,603	1906	1,100,735	1956	321,625	2005	1,122,373
1853	368,645	1907	1,285,349	1957	326,867	2006	1,266,129
1854	427,833	1908	782,870	1958	253,265	2007	1,052,415
1855	200,877	1909	751,786	1959	260,686	2008	1,107,126
1856	200,436	1910	1,041,570	1960	265,398		
1857	251,306						
1858	123,126	**1911–20**	**5,735,811**	**1961–70**	**3,321,677**		
1859	121,282	1911	878,587	1961	271,344		
1860	153,640	1912	838,172	1962	283,763		
		1913	1,197,892	1963	306,260		
1861–70	**2,314,824**	1914	1,218,480	1964	292,248		
1861	91,918	1915	326,700	1965	296,697		
1862	91,985	1916	298,826	1966	323,040		
1863	176,282	1917	295,403	1967	361,972		
1864	193,418	1918	110,618	1968	454,448		
1865	248,120	1919	141,132	1969	358,579		
1866	318,568	1920	430,001	1970	373,326		
1867	315,722						
1868	138,840						
1869	352,768						
1870	387,203						

Source: U.S. Department of Homeland Security.

IMMIGRATION BY REGION AND SELECTED COUNTRY OF LAST RESIDENCE, FISCAL YEARS 1820–2008

Region and country of last residence	1820 to 1829	1830 to 1839	1840 to 1849	1850 to 1859	1860 to 1869	1870 to 1879	1880 to 1889	1890 to 1899
Total	128,502	538,381	1,427,337	2,814,554	2,081,261	2,742,137	5,248,568	3,694,294
Europe	99,272	422,771	1,369,259	2,619,680	1,877,726	2,251,878	4,638,677	3,576,411
Austria-Hungary	—	—	—	—	3,375	60,127	314,787	534,059
Austria	—	—	—	—	2,700	54,529	204,805	268,218
Hungary	—	—	—	—	483	5,598	109,982	203,350
Belgium	28	20	3,996	5,765	5,785	6,991	18,738	19,642
Bulgaria	—	—	—	—	—	—	—	52
Czechoslovakia	—	—	—	—	—	—	—	—
Denmark	173	927	671	3,227	13,553	29,278	85,342	56,671
Finland	—	—	—	—	—	—	—	—
France	7,694	39,330	75,300	81,778	35,938	71,901	48,193	35,616
Germany	5,753	124,726	385,434	976,072	723,734	751,769	1,445,181	579,072
Greece	17	49	17	32	51	209	1,807	12,732
Ireland	51,617	170,672	656,145	1,029,486	427,419	422,264	674,061	405,710
Italy	430	2,225	1,476	8,643	9,853	46,296	267,660	603,761
Netherlands	1,105	1,377	7,624	11,122	8,387	14,267	52,715	29,349
Norway-Sweden	91	1,149	12,389	22,202	82,937	178,823	586,441	334,058
Norway	—	—	—	—	16,068	88,644	185,111	96,810
Sweden	—	—	—	—	24,224	90,179	401,330	237,248
Poland	19	366	105	1,087	1,886	11,016	42,910	107,793
Portugal	177	820	196	1,299	2,083	13,971	15,186	25,874
Romania	—	—	—	—	—	—	5,842	6,808
Russia	86	280	520	423	1,670	35,177	182,698	450,101
Spain	2,595	2,010	1,916	8,795	6,966	5,540	3,995	9,189
Switzerland	3,148	4,430	4,819	24,423	21,124	25,212	81,151	37,020
United Kingdom	26,336	74,350	218,572	445,322	532,956	578,447	810,900	328,759
Yugoslavia	—	—	—	—	—	—	—	—
Other Europe	3	40	79	4	9	590	1,070	145

Asia	34	55	121	36,080	54,408	134,128	71,151	61,285
China	3	8	32	35,933	54,028	133,139	65,797	15,268
Hong Kong	9	38	33	42	50	166	—	102
India	—	—	—	—	—	—	247	102
Iran	—	—	—	—	—	—	—	—
Israel	—	—	—	—	—	—	—	—
Japan	—	—	—	—	138	193	1,583	13,998
Jordan	—	—	—	—	—	—	—	—
Korea	—	—	—	—	—	—	—	—
Philippines	—	—	—	—	—	—	—	—
Syria	—	—	—	—	—	—	—	—
Taiwan	—	—	—	—	—	—	—	—
Turkey	19	8	45	94	129	382	2,478	27,510
Vietnam	—	—	—	—	—	—	—	—
Other Asia	3	1	11	11	63	248	1,046	4,407
America	9,655	31,905	50,516	84,145	130,292	345,010	524,826	37,350
Canada and Newfoundland	2,297	11,875	34,285	64,171	117,978	324,310	492,865	3,098
Mexico	3,835	7,187	3,069	3,446	1,957	5,133	2,405	734
Caribbean	3,061	11,792	11,803	12,447	8,751	14,285	27,323	31,480
Cuba	—	—	—	—	—	—	—	—
Dominican Republic	—	—	—	—	—	—	—	—
Haiti	—	—	—	—	—	—	—	—
Jamaica	—	—	—	—	—	—	—	—
Other Caribbean	3,061	11,792	11,803	12,447	8,751	14,285	27,323	31,480
Central America	57	94	297	512	70	173	279	649
Belize	—	—	—	—	—	—	—	—
Costa Rica	—	—	—	—	—	—	—	—
El Salvador	—	—	—	—	—	—	—	—
Guatemala	—	—	—	—	—	—	—	—
Honduras	—	—	—	—	—	—	—	—
Nicaragua	—	—	—	—	—	—	—	—
Panama	—	—	—	—	—	—	—	—
Other Central America	57	94	297	512	70	173	279	649
South America	405	957	1,062	3,569	1,536	1,109	1,954	1,389
Argentina	—	—	—	—	—	—	—	—
Bolivia	—	—	—	—	—	—	—	—

Region and country of last residence	1820 to 1829	1830 to 1839	1840 to 1849	1850 to 1859	1860 to 1869	1870 to 1879	1880 to 1889	1890 to 1899
Brazil	—	—	—	—	—	—	—	—
Chile	—	—	—	—	—	—	—	—
Colombia	—	—	—	—	—	—	—	—
Ecuador	—	—	—	—	—	—	—	—
Guyana	—	—	—	—	—	—	—	—
Paraguay	—	—	—	—	—	—	—	—
Peru	—	—	—	—	—	—	—	—
Suriname	—	—	—	—	—	—	—	—
Uruguay	—	—	—	—	—	—	—	—
Venezuela	—	—	—	—	—	—	—	—
Other South America	405	957	1,062	3,569	1,536	1,109	1,954	1,389
Other America	—	—	—	—	—	—	—	—
Africa	15	50	61	84	407	371	763	432
Egypt	—	—	—	—	4	29	145	51
Ethiopia	1	8	5	7	43	52	21	9
Liberia	—	—	—	—	—	—	—	—
Morocco	—	—	—	—	35	48	23	9
South Africa	14	42	56	77	325	242	574	363
Other Africa	3	7	14	166	187	9,996	12,361	4,704
Oceania	—	—	—	—	—	—	—	—
Australia	2	1	2	15	187	8,930	7,250	3,098
New Zealand	—	—	—	—	—	39	21	12
Other Oceania	1	6	12	151	187	1,027	5,090	1,594
Not Specified	19,523	83,593	7,366	74,399	18,241	754	790	14,112

Total	8,202,388	6,347,380	4,295,510	699,375	856,608	2,499,268	3,213,749	6,244,379
Europe	7,572,569	4,985,411	2,560,340	444,399	472,524	1,404,573	1,133,443	668,866
Austria-Hungary	2,001,376	1,154,727	60,891	12,531	13,574	113,015	17,571	20,437
Austria	532,416	589,174	31,392	5,307	8,393	81,354	27,590	15,374
Hungary	685,567	565,553	29,499	7,224	5,181	31,661	10,019	5,063
Belgium	37,429	32,574	21,511	4,013	12,473	18,885	9,647	7,028
Bulgaria	34,651	27,180	2,824	1,062	449	97	598	1,124
Czechoslovakia	—	—	101,182	17,757	8,475	1,624	2,758	5,678
Denmark	61,227	45,830	34,406	3,470	4,549	10,518	9,797	4,847
Finland			16,922	2,438	2,230	4,923	4,310	2,569
France	67,735	60,335	54,842	13,761	36,954	50,113	46,975	32,066
Germany	328,722	174,227	386,634	119,107	119,506	576,505	209,616	85,752
Greece	145,402	198,108	60,774	10,599	8,605	45,153	74,173	37,729
Ireland	344,940	166,445	202,854	28,195	15,701	47,189	37,788	22,210
Italy	1,930,475	1,229,916	528,133	85,053	50,509	184,576	200,111	55,562
Netherlands	42,463	46,065	29,397	7,791	13,877	46,703	37,918	11,234
Norway-Sweden	426,981	192,445	170,329	13,452	17,326	44,224	36,150	13,941
Norway	182,542	79,488	70,327	6,901	8,326	22,806	17,371	3,835
Sweden	244,439	112,957	100,002	6,551	9,000	21,418	18,779	10,106
Poland			223,316	25,555	7,577	6,465	55,742	63,483
Portugal	65,154	82,489	44,829	3,518	6,765	13,928	70,568	42,685
Romania	57,322	13,566	67,810	5,264	1,254	914	2,339	24,753
Russia	1,501,301	1,106,998	61,604	2,463	605	453	2,329	33,311
Spain	24,818	53,262	47,109	3,669	2,774	6,880	40,793	22,783
Switzerland	32,541	22,839	31,772	5,990	9,904	17,577	19,193	8,316
United Kingdom	469,518	371,878	341,552	61,813	131,794	195,709	220,213	153,644
Yugoslavia	—	—	49,215	6,920	2,039	6,966	17,990	16,267
Other Europe	514	6,527	22,434	9,978	5,584	11,756	6,845	3,447
Asia	299,836	269,736	126,740	19,231	34,532	135,844	358,605	2,391,356
China	19,884	20,916	30,648	5,874	16,072	8,836	14,060	170,897
Hong Kong	—	—	—	—	—	13,781	67,047	112,132
India	3,026	3,478	2,076	554	1,692	1,850	18,638	231,649
Iran	—	—	208	198	1,144	3,195	9,059	98,141
Israel	—	—	—	—	98	21,376	30,911	43,669

Region and country of last residence	1900 to 1909	1910 to 1919	1920 to 1929	1930 to 1939	1940 to 1949	1950 to 1959	1960 to 1969	1980 to 1989
Japan	139,712	77,125	42,057	2,683	1,557	40,651	40,956	44,150
Jordan	—	—	—	—	—	4,899	9,230	28,928
Korea	—	—	—	—	83	4,845	27,048	322,708
Philippines	—	—	—	391	4,099	17,245	70,660	502,056
Syria	—	—	5,307	2,188	1,179	1,091	2,432	14,534
Taiwan	—	—	—	—	—	721	15,657	119,051
Turkey	127,999	160,717	40,450	1,327	754	2,980	9,464	19,208
Vietnam	—	—	—	—	—	290	2,949	200,632
Other Asia	9,215	7,500	5,994	6,016	7,854	14,084	40,494	483,601
America	277,809	1,070,539	1,591,278	230,319	328,435	921,610	1,674,172	2,695,329
Canada and Newfoundland	123,067	708,715	949,286	162,703	160,911	353,169	433,128	156,313
Mexico	31,188	185,334	498,945	32,709	56,158	273,847	441,824	1,009,586
Caribbean	100,960	120,860	83,482	18,052	46,194	115,661	427,235	790,109
Cuba	—	—	12,769	10,641	25,976	73,221	202,030	132,552
Dominican Republic	—	—	—	1,026	4,802	10,219	83,552	221,552
Haiti	—	—	—	156	823	3,787	28,992	121,406
Jamaica	—	—	—	—	—	7,397	62,218	193,874
Other Caribbean	100,960	120,860	70,713	6,229	14,593	21,037	50,443	120,725
Central America	7,341	15,692	16,511	6,840	20,135	40,201	98,560	339,376
Belize	77	40	285	193	433	1,133	4,185	14,964
Costa Rica	—	—	—	431	1,965	4,044	17,975	25,017
El Salvador	—	—	—	597	4,885	5,094	14,405	137,418
Guatemala	—	—	—	423	1,303	4,197	14,357	58,847
Honduras	—	—	—	679	1,874	5,320	15,078	39,071
Nicaragua	—	—	—	405	4,393	7,812	10,383	31,102
Panama	—	—	—	1,452	5,282	12,601	22,177	32,957
Other Central America	7,264	15,652	16,226	2,660	—	—	—	—

South America	399,862	250,754	78,418	19,662	9,990	43,025	39,938	15,253
Argentina	23,442	49,384	16,346	3,108	1,067	—	—	—
Bolivia	9,798	6,205	2,759	893	50	—	—	—
Brazil	22,944	29,238	11,547	3,653	1,468	4,627	—	—
Chile	19,749	12,384	4,669	1,320	347	—	—	—
Colombia	105,494	68,371	15,567	3,454	1,027	—	—	—
Ecuador	48,015	34,107	8,574	2,207	244	—	—	—
Guyana	85,886	4,546	1,131	596	131	—	—	—
Paraguay	3,518	1,249	576	85	33	—	—	—
Peru	49,958	19,783	5,980	1,273	321	—	—	—
Suriname	1,357	612	299	130	25	—	—	—
Uruguay	7,235	4,089	1,026	754	112	—	—	—
Venezuela	22,405	20,758	9,927	2,182	1,155	—	—	—
Other South America	61	28	17	7	4,010	38,398	39,938	15,253
Other America	83	22,671	60,314	25,375	25	29	—	—
Africa	141,990	23,780	13,016	6,720	2,120	6,362	8,867	6,326
Egypt	26,744	5,581	1,996	1,613	781	1,063	—	—
Ethiopia	12,927	804	302	28	10	—	—	—
Liberia	6,420	841	239	37	35	—	—	—
Morocco	3,471	2,880	2,733	879	73	—	—	—
South Africa	15,505	4,360	2,278	1,022	312	5,299	8,867	6,326
Other Africa	76,923	9,314	5,448	3,141	909	—	—	—
Oceania	41,432	23,630	11,353	14,262	3,306	9,860	12,339	12,355
Australia	16,901	14,986	8,275	11,201	2,260	8,404	11,280	11,191
New Zealand	6,129	3,775	1,799	2,351	790	935	—	—
Other Oceania	18,402	4,869	1,279	710	256	521	1,059	1,164
Not Specified	305,406	119	12,472	135	—	930	488	33,493

Region and country of last residence	1990 to 1999	2000	2001	2002	2003	2004	2005	2006	2007	2008
Total	9,775,398	841,002	1,058,902	1,059,356	703,542	957,883	1,122,257	1,266,129	1,052,415	1,107,126
Europe	1,348,612	131,920	176,892	177,059	102,546	135,663	180,396	169,156	120,759	121,146
Austria-Hungary	27,529	2,009	2,303	4,004	2,176	3,689	4,569	2,991	2,057	2,576
Austria	18,234	986	996	2,650	1,160	2,442	3,002	1,301	849	1,505
Hungary	9,295	1,023	1,307	1,354	1,016	1,247	1,567	1,690	1,208	1,071
Belgium	7,077	817	997	834	515	746	1,031	891	733	829
Bulgaria	16,948	4,779	4,273	3,476	3,706	4,042	5,451	4,690	3,766	2,805
Czechoslovakia	8,970	1,407	1,911	1,854	1,472	1,871	2,182	2,844	1,851	1,650
Denmark	6,189	549	732	651	435	568	714	738	505	551
Finland	3,970	377	497	365	230	346	549	513	385	287
France	35,945	4,063	5,379	4,567	2,926	4,209	5,035	4,945	3,680	5,246
Germany	92,207	12,230	21,992	20,977	8,061	10,270	12,864	10,271	8,640	8,456
Greece	25,403	5,113	1,941	1,486	900	1,213	1,473	1,544	1,152	943
Ireland	65,384	1,264	1,531	1,400	1,002	1,518	2,083	2,038	1,599	1,499
Italy	75,992	2,652	3,332	2,812	1,890	2,495	3,179	3,406	2,682	2,738
Netherlands	13,345	1,455	1,888	2,296	1,321	1,713	2,150	1,928	1,482	1,423
Norway-Sweden	17,825	1,967	2,544	2,082	1,516	2,011	2,264	2,111	1,604	1,557
Norway	5,211	508	582	460	385	457	472	532	388	386
Sweden	12,614	1,459	1,962	1,622	1,131	1,554	1,792	1,579	1,216	1,171
Poland	172,249	9,750	12,308	13,274	11,004	14,048	14,836	16,704	9,717	7,896
Portugal	25,497	1,373	1,611	1,301	808	1,062	1,084	1,439	1,054	781
Romania	48,136	6,506	6,206	4,515	3,305	4,078	6,431	6,753	5,240	4,563
Russia	433,427	43,156	54,838	55,370	33,513	41,959	60,344	59,720	41,593	45,092
Spain	18,443	1,390	1,875	1,588	1,102	1,453	2,002	2,387	1,810	1,970
Switzerland	11,768	1,339	1,786	1,493	862	1,193	1,465	1,199	885	936
United Kingdom	156,182	14,427	20,118	17,940	11,155	16,680	21,956	19,984	16,113	16,189
Yugoslavia	57,039	11,960	21,854	28,051	8,270	13,213	19,249	11,066	6,364	5,812
Other Europe	29,087	3,337	6,976	6,723	6,377	7,286	9,485	10,994	7,847	7,347

Asia	2,859,899	254,932	336,112	325,749	235,339	319,025	382,707	411,746	359,387	369,339
China	342,058	41,804	50,677	55,901	37,342	50,280	64,887	83,590	70,924	75,410
Hong Kong	116,894	7,181	10,282	7,938	5,015	5,421	5,004	4,514	4,450	4,389
India	352,528	38,938	65,673	66,644	47,032	65,507	79,139	58,072	55,371	59,728
Iran	76,899	6,481	8,003	7,684	4,696	5,898	7,306	9,829	8,098	9,920
Israel	41,340	3,871	4,892	4,907	3,686	5,206	6,963	6,667	4,999	6,682
Japan	66,582	7,688	10,424	9,106	6,702	8,655	9,929	9,107	7,213	7,510
Jordan	42,755	4,476	5,106	4,774	4,008	5,186	5,430	5,512	5,516	5,692
Korea	179,770	15,107	19,728	19,917	12,076	19,441	26,002	24,472	21,278	26,155
Philippines	534,338	40,465	50,644	48,493	43,133	54,651	57,654	71,133	68,792	52,391
Syria	22,906	2,255	3,542	3,350	2,046	2,549	3,350	3,080	2,550	3,310
Taiwan	132,647	9,457	12,457	9,932	7,168	9,314	9,389	8,545	9,053	9,237
Turkey	38,687	2,702	3,463	3,914	3,318	4,491	6,449	6,433	4,728	4,953
Vietnam	275,379	25,159	34,537	32,372	21,227	30,074	30,832	29,701	27,510	29,807
Other Asia	637,116	49,348	56,684	50,817	37,890	52,352	70,373	91,091	68,905	74,155
America	5,137,743	392,461	470,794	477,363	305,936	408,972	432,726	548,812	434,272	491,045
Canada and Newfoundland	194,788	21,289	29,991	27,142	16,447	22,439	29,930	23,913	20,324	22,366
Mexico	2,757,418	171,445	204,032	216,924	114,758	173,711	157,992	170,042	143,180	188,015
Caribbean	1,004,687	84,250	96,384	93,914	67,498	82,116	91,371	144,477	114,318	134,744
Cuba	159,037	17,897	25,832	27,435	8,685	15,385	20,651	44,248	25,441	48,057
Dominican Republic	359,818	17,373	21,139	22,386	26,112	30,063	27,365	37,997	27,875	31,801
Haiti	177,446	21,977	22,470	19,151	11,924	13,695	13,491	21,625	29,978	25,522
Jamaica	177,143	15,603	15,031	14,507	13,045	13,581	17,774	24,538	18,873	18,077
Other Caribbean	181,243	11,400	11,912	10,435	7,732	9,392	12,090	16,069	12,151	11,287
Central America	610,189	60,331	72,504	66,298	53,283	61,253	52,629	74,244	53,834	49,741
Belize	12,600	774	982	983	616	888	901	1,263	1,089	1,113
Costa Rica	17,054	1,390	1,863	1,686	1,322	1,811	2,479	3,459	2,722	2,287
El Salvador	273,017	22,301	30,876	30,472	27,854	29,297	20,891	31,258	20,009	18,937
Guatemala	126,043	9,861	13,399	15,870	14,195	18,655	16,466	23,674	17,198	15,791
Honduras	72,880	5,851	6,546	6,355	4,582	5,339	6,825	8,036	7,300	6,389

Region and country of last residence	1990 to 1999	2000	2001	2002	2003	2004	2005	2006	2007	2008
Nicaragua	80,446	18,258	16,908	9,171	3,503	3,842	3,196	4,035	3,587	3,486
Panama	28,149	1,896	1,930	1,761	1,211	1,421	1,869	2,519	1,929	1,738
Other Central America	—	—	—	—	—	—	—	—	—	—
South America	570,624	55,143	67,880	73,082	53,946	69,452	100,803	136,134	102,616	96,178
Argentina	30,065	2,472	3,426	3,791	3,193	4,672	6,945	7,239	5,375	5,170
Bolivia	18,111	1,744	1,804	1,660	1,365	1,719	2,164	4,000	2,326	2,350
Brazil	50,744	6,767	9,391	9,034	6,108	10,247	16,329	17,741	13,546	11,813
Chile	18,200	1,660	1,881	1,766	1,255	1,719	2,354	2,727	2,202	1,988
Colombia	137,985	14,125	16,234	18,409	14,400	18,055	24,705	42,017	32,055	29,349
Ecuador	81,358	7,624	9,654	10,524	7,022	8,366	11,528	17,624	12,011	11,541
Guyana	74,407	5,255	7,835	9,492	6,373	5,721	8,771	9,010	5,288	6,302
Paraguay	6,082	394	464	413	222	324	523	725	518	489
Peru	110,117	9,361	10,838	11,737	9,169	11,369	15,205	21,300	17,056	14,873
Suriname	2,285	281	254	223	175	170	287	341	193	225
Uruguay	6,062	396	516	499	470	750	1,110	1,639	1,340	1,380
Venezuela	35,180	5,052	5,576	5,529	4,190	6,335	10,870	11,758	10,696	10,689
Other South America	28	12	7	5	4	5	12	13	10	9
Other America	37	3	3	3	4	1	1	2	—	1
Africa	346,416	40,790	50,009	56,002	45,559	62,623	79,697	112,100	89,277	100,881
Egypt	44,604	4,323	5,333	6,215	3,928	6,590	10,296	13,163	10,178	10,728
Ethiopia	40,097	3,645	4,620	6,308	5,969	7,180	8,378	13,390	11,340	11,703
Liberia	13,587	1,225	1,477	1,467	1,081	1,540	1,846	3,736	3,771	3,478
Morocco	15,768	3,423	4,752	3,188	2,969	3,910	4,165	4,704	4,311	4,187
South Africa	21,964	2,814	4,046	3,685	2,088	3,335	4,425	3,173	2,842	2,638
Other Africa	210,396	25,360	29,781	35,139	29,524	40,068	50,587	73,934	56,835	68,147
Oceania	56,800	5,928	7,201	6,495	5,076	6,954	7,432	8,000	6,639	5,926
Australia	24,288	2,694	3,714	3,420	2,488	3,397	4,090	3,770	3,026	3,031
New Zealand	8,600	1,080	1,347	1,364	1,030	1,420	1,457	1,344	1,234	1,092
Other Oceania	23,912	2,154	2,140	1,711	1,558	2,137	1,885	2,886	2,379	1,803
Not Specified	25,928	14,971	17,894	16,688	9,086	24,646	39,299	16,315	42,081	18,789

— Represents zero or not available.

PRESIDENTS, VICE PRESIDENTS, AND SECRETARIES OF STATE

	President	Vice President	Secretary of State
1.	George Washington, Federalist 1789	John Adams, Federalist 1789	Thomas Jefferson 1789 Edmund Randolph 1794 Timothy Pickering 1795
2.	John Adams, Federalist 1797	Thomas Jefferson, Dem.-Rep. 1797	Timothy Pickering 1797 John Marshall 1800
3.	Thomas Jefferson, Dem.-Rep. 1801	Aaron Burr, Dem.-Rep. 1801 George Clinton, Dem.-Rep. 1805	James Madison 1801
4.	James Madison, Dem.-Rep. 1809	George Clinton, Dem.-Rep. 1809 Elbridge Gerry, Dem.-Rep. 1813	Robert Smith 1809 James Monroe 1811
5.	James Monroe, Dem.-Rep. 1817	Daniel D. Tompkins, Dem.-Rep. 1817	John Q. Adams 1817
6.	John Quincy Adams, Dem.-Rep. 1825	John C. Calhoun, Dem.-Rep. 1825	Henry Clay 1825
7.	Andrew Jackson, Democratic 1829	John C. Calhoun, Democratic 1829 Martin Van Buren, Democratic 1833	Martin Van Buren 1829 Edward Livingston 1831 Louis McLane 1833 John Forsyth 1834
8.	Martin Van Buren, Democratic 1837	Richard M. Johnson, Democratic 1837	John Forsyth 1837
9.	William H. Harrison, Whig 1841	John Tyler, Whig 1841	Daniel Webster 1841

President	Vice President	Secretary of State
10. John Tyler, Whig and Democratic 1841	None	Daniel Webster 1841 Hugh S. Legaré 1843 Abel P. Upshur 1843 John C. Calhoun 1844
11. James K. Polk, Democratic 1845	George M. Dallas, Democratic 1845	James Buchanan 1845
12. Zachary Taylor, Whig 1849	Millard Fillmore, Whig 1848	John M. Clayton 1849
13. Millard Fillmore, Whig 1850	None	Daniel Webster 1850 Edward Everett 1852
14. Franklin Pierce, Democratic 1853	William R. King, Democratic 1853	William L. Marcy 1853
15. James Buchanan, Democratic 1857	John C. Breckinridge, Democratic 1857	Lewis Cass 1857 Jeremiah S. Black 1860
16. Abraham Lincoln, Republican 1861	Hannibal Hamlin, Republican 1861 Andrew Johnson, Unionist 1865	William H. Seward 1861
17. Andrew Johnson, Unionist 1865	None	William H. Seward 1865
18. Ulysses S. Grant, Republican 1869	Schuyler Colfax, Republican 1869 Henry Wilson, Republican 1873	Elihu B. Washburne 1869 Hamilton Fish 1869
19. Rutherford B. Hayes, Republican 1877	William A. Wheeler, Republican 1877	William M. Evarts 1877

	President	Vice President	Secretary of State
20.	James A. Garfield, Republican 1881	Chester A. Arthur, Republican 1881	James G. Blaine 1881
21.	Chester A. Arthur, Republican 1881	None	Frederick T. Frelinghuysen 1881
22.	Grover Cleveland, Democratic 1885	Thomas A. Hendricks, Democratic 1885	Thomas F. Bayard 1885
23.	Benjamin Harrison, Republican 1889	Levi P. Morton, Republican 1889	James G. Blaine 1889 John W. Foster 1892
24.	Grover Cleveland, Democratic 1893	Adlai E. Stevenson, Democratic 1893	Walter Q. Gresham 1893 Richard Olney 1895
25.	William McKinley, Republican 1897	Garret A. Hobart, Republican 1897 Theodore Roosevelt, Republican 1901	John Sherman 1897 William R. Day 1898 John Hay 1898
26.	Theodore Roosevelt, Republican 1901	Charles Fairbanks, Republican 1905	John Hay 1901 Elihu Root 1905 Robert Bacon 1909
27.	William H. Taft, Republican 1909	James S. Sherman, Republican 1909	Philander C. Knox 1909
28.	Woodrow Wilson, Democratic 1913	Thomas R. Marshall, Democratic 1913	William J. Bryan 1913 Robert Lansing 1915 Bainbridge Colby 1920
29.	Warren G. Harding, Republican 1921	Calvin Coolidge, Republican 1921	Charles E. Hughes 1921
30.	Calvin Coolidge, Republican 1923	Charles G. Dawes, Republican 1925	Charles E. Hughes 1923 Frank B. Kellogg 1925

	President	Vice President	Secretary of State
31.	Herbert Hoover, Republican 1929	Charles Curtis, Republican 1929	Henry L. Stimson 1929
32.	Franklin D. Roosevelt, Democratic 1933	John Nance Garner, Democratic 1933 Henry A. Wallace, Democratic 1941 Harry S. Truman, Democratic 1945	Cordell Hull 1933 Edward R. Stettinius, Jr. 1944
33.	Harry S. Truman, Democratic 1945	Alben W. Barkley, Democratic 1949	Edward R. Stettinius, Jr. 1945 James F. Byrnes 1945 George C. Marshall 1947 Dean G. Acheson 1949
34.	Dwight D. Eisenhower, Republican 1953	Richard M. Nixon, Republican 1953	John F. Dulles 1953 Christian A. Herter 1959
35.	John F. Kennedy, Democratic 1961	Lyndon B. Johnson, Democratic 1961	Dean Rusk 1961
36.	Lyndon B. Johnson, Democratic 1963	Hubert H. Humphrey, Democratic 1965	Dean Rusk 1963
37.	Richard M. Nixon, Republican 1969	Spiro T. Agnew, Republican 1969 Gerald R. Ford, Republican 1973	William P. Rogers 1969 Henry Kissinger 1973
38.	Gerald R. Ford, Republican 1974	Nelson Rockefeller, Republican 1974	Henry Kissinger 1974
39.	Jimmy Carter, Democratic 1977	Walter Mondale, Democratic 1977	Cyrus Vance 1977 Edmund Muskie 1980

	President	Vice President	Secretary of State
40.	Ronald Reagan, Republican 1981	George H. W. Bush, Republican 1981	Alexander Haig 1981 George Schultz 1982
41.	George H. W. Bush, Republican 1989	J. Danforth Quayle, Republican 1989	James A. Baker 1989 Lawrence Eagleburger 1992
42.	William J. Clinton, Democratic 1993	Albert Gore, Jr., Democratic 1993	Warren Christopher 1993 Madeleine Albright 1997
43.	George W. Bush, Republican 2001	Richard B. Cheney, Republican 2001	Colin L. Powell 2001 Condoleezza Rice 2005
44.	Barack Obama, Democratic 2009	Joseph R. Biden, Democratic 2009	Hillary Rodham Clinton 2009

FURTHER READINGS

CHAPTER 1

A fascinating study of pre-Columbian migration is Brian M. Fagan's *The Great Journey: The Peopling of Ancient America*, rev. ed. (2004). Alice B. Kehoe's *North American Indians: A Comprehensive Account*, 2nd ed. (1992), provides an encyclopedic treatment of Native Americans. See also Alvin M. Josephy, Jr., ed., *America in 1492: The World of the Indian Peoples before the Arrival of Columbus* (1992), and Daniel K. Richter, *Facing East from Indian Country: A Native History of Early America* (2001).

The conflict between Native Americans and Europeans is treated well in James Axtell's *The Invasion Within: The Contest of Cultures in Colonial North America* (1986) and *Beyond 1492: Encounters in Colonial North America* (1992). Colin G. Galloway's *New Worlds for All: Indians, Europeans, and the Remaking of Early America* (1997) explores the ecological effects of European settlement.

The most comprehensive overviews of European exploration are two volumes by Samuel Eliot Morison: *The European Discovery of America: The Northern Voyages*, A.D. *500–1600* (1971) and *The Southern Voyages*, A.D. *1492–1616* (1974).

The voyages of Columbus are surveyed in William D. Phillips Jr. and Carla Rahn Phillips's *The Worlds of Christopher Columbus* (1992). For sweeping overviews of Spain's creation of a global empire, see Henry Kamen's *Empire: How Spain Became a World Power, 1492–1763* (2003) and Hugh Thomas's *Rivers of Gold: The Rise of the Spanish Empire, from Columbus to Magellan* (2004). David J. Weber examines Spanish colonization in *The Spanish Frontier in North America* (1992). For the French experience, see William J. Eccles's *France in America*, rev. ed. (1990). For an insightful comparison of Spanish and English modes of settlement, see J. H. Elliott, *Empires of the Atlantic World: Britain and Spain in America, 1492–1830* (2006).

Chapter 2

Two excellent surveys of early American history are Peter C. Hoffer's *The Brave New World: A History of Early America,* 2nd ed. (2006), and William R. Polk's *The Birth of America: From before Columbus to the Revolution* (2006).

Bernard Bailyn's *Voyagers to the West: A Passage in the Peopling of America on the Eve of the Revolution* (1986) provides a comprehensive view of migration to the New World. Jack P. Greene offers a brilliant synthesis of British colonization in *Pursuits of Happiness: The Social Development of Early Modern British Colonies and the Formation of American Culture* (1988). The best overview of the colonization of North America is Alan Taylor's *American Colonies: The Settling of North America* (2001). On the interactions among Indian, European, and African cultures, see Gary B. Nash's *Red, White, and Black: The Peoples of Early North America,* 5th ed. (2005). See Daniel K. Richter's *The Ordeal of the Longhouse: The Peoples of the Iroquois League in the Era of European Colonization* (1992) and Daniel P. Barr's *Unconquered: The Iroquois League at War in Colonial America* (2006) for a history of the Iroquois Confederacy.

Andrew Delbanco's *The Puritan Ordeal* (1989) is a powerful study of the tensions inherent in the Puritan outlook. For information regarding the Puritan settlement of New England, see Virginia DeJohn Anderson's *New England's Generation: The Great Migration and the Formation of Society and Culture in the Seventeenth Century* (1991). The best biography of John Winthrop is Francis J. Bremer's *John Winthrop: America's Forgotten Founding Father* (2003).

The pattern of settlement in the middle colonies is illuminated in Barry Levy's *Quakers and the American Family: British Settlement in the Delaware Valley* (1988). On the early history of New York, see Russell Shorto's *The Island at the Center of the World: The Epic Story of Dutch Manhattan and the Forgotten Colony That Shaped America* (2004). Settlement of the areas along the Atlantic in the South is traced in James Horn's *Adapting to a New World: English Society in the Seventeenth-Century Chesapeake* (1994). For a study of race and the settlement of South Carolina, see Peter H. Wood's *Black Majority: Negroes in Colonial South Carolina from 1670 through the Stono Rebellion* (1974). A brilliant book on relations between the Catawba Indians and their black and white neighbors is James H. Merrell's *The Indians' New World: Catawbas and Their Neighbors from European Contact through the Era of Removal* (1989). On the flourishing trade in captive Indians, see Alan Gallay's *The Indian Slave Trade: The Rise of the English Empire in the American South,*

1670–1717 (2002). On the Yamasee War, see Steven J. Oatis's *A Colonial Complex: South Carolina's Frontiers in the Era of the Yamasee War, 1680–1730* (2004).

CHAPTER 3

The diversity of colonial societies may be seen in David Hackett Fischer's *Albion's Seed: Four British Folkways in America* (1989). On the economic development of New England, see Christine Leigh Heyrman's *Commerce and Culture: The Maritime Communities of Colonial Massachusetts, 1690–1750* (1984) and Stephen Innes's *Creating the Commonwealth: The Economic Culture of Puritan New England* (1995). John Frederick Martin's *Profits in the Wilderness: Entrepreneurship and the Founding of New England Towns in the Seventeenth Century* (1991) indicates that economic concerns rather than spiritual motives were driving forces in many New England towns. For a fascinating account of the impact of livestock on colonial history, see Virginia DeJohn Anderson's *Creatures of Empire: How Domestic Animals Transformed Early America* (2004).

Paul Boyer and Stephen Nissenbaum's *Salem Possessed: The Social Origins of Witchcraft* (1974) connects the notorious witch trials to changes in community structure. Bernard Rosenthal challenges many myths concerning the Salem witch trials in *Salem Story: Reading the Witch Trials of 1692* (1993). Mary Beth Norton's *In the Devil's Snare: The Salem Witchcraft Crisis of 1692* (2002) emphasizes the role of Indian violence.

Discussions of women in the New England colonies can be found in Laurel Thatcher Ulrich's *Good Wives: Image and Reality in the Lives of Women in Northern New England, 1650–1750* (1980), Joy Day Buel and Richard Buel, Jr.'s *The Way of Duty: A Woman and Her Family in Revolutionary America* (1984), and Carol F. Karlsen's *The Devil in the Shape of a Woman: Witchcraft in Colonial New England* (1987). On women and religion, see Susan Juster's *Disorderly Women: Sexual Politics and Evangelicalism in Revolutionary New England* (1994). John Demos describes family life in *A Little Commonwealth: Family Life in Plymouth Colony*, new ed. (2000).

For an excellent overview of Indian relations with Europeans, see Colin G. Calloway's *New Worlds for All: Indians, Europeans, and the Remaking of Early America* (1997). On New England Indians, see Kathleen J. Bragdon's *Native People of Southern New England, 1500–1650* (1996). For analyses of Indian wars, see Alfred A. Cave's *The Pequot War* (1996) and Jill Lepore's *The Name of War: King Philip's War and the Origins of American Identity* (1998). The story of the Iroquois is told well in Daniel K. Richter's *The Ordeal of the Longhouse: The Peoples of the Iroquois League in the Era of European Colonization* (1992). Indians in the southern colonies are the focus of James Axtell's *The Indians' New South: Cultural Change in the Colonial Southeast* (1997).

For the social history of the southern colonies, see Allan Kulikoff's *Tobacco and Slaves: The Development of Southern Cultures in the Chesapeake, 1680–1800* (1986) and Kathleen M. Brown's *Good Wives, Nasty Wenches, and Anxious Patriarchs: Gender, Race, and Power in Colonial Virginia* (1996). Family life along the Chesapeake Bay is described in Gloria L. Main's *Tobacco Colony: Life in Early Maryland, 1650–1720* (1982) and Daniel Blake Smith's *Inside the Great House: Planter Family Life in Eighteenth-Century Chesapeake Society* (1980).

Edmund S. Morgan's *American Slavery, American Freedom: The Ordeal of Colonial Virginia* (1975) examines Virginia's social structure, environment, and labor patterns in a biracial context. On the interaction of the cultures of blacks and whites, see Mechal Sobel's *The World They Made Together: Black and White Values in Eighteenth-Century Virginia* (1987). African American viewpoints are presented in Timothy H. Breen and Stephen Innes's *"Myne Owne Ground": Race and Freedom on Virginia's Eastern Shore, 1640–1676*, new ed. (2004). David W. Galenson's *White Servitude in Colonial America: An Economic Analysis* (1981) looks at the indentured labor force.

Henry F. May's *The Enlightenment in America* (1976) and Donald H. Meyer's *The Democratic Enlightenment* (1976) examine intellectual trends in eighteenth-century America. Lawrence A. Cremin's *American Education: The Colonial Experience, 1607–1783* (1970) surveys educational developments.

On the Great Awakening, see Patricia U. Bonomi's *Under the Cope of Heaven: Religion, Society, and Politics in Colonial America*, updated ed. (2003), Timothy D. Hall's *Contested Boundaries: Itinerancy and the Reshaping of the Colonial American Religious World* (1994), and Frank Lambert's *Inventing the "Great Awakening"* (1999). For evangelism in the South, see Christine Leigh Heyrman's *Southern Cross: The Beginnings of the Bible Belt* (1997).

CHAPTER 4

The economics motivating colonial policies is covered in John J. McCusker and Russell R. Menard's *The Economy of British America, 1607–1789*, rev. ed. (1991). The problems of colonial customs administration are explored in Michael Kammen's *Empire and Interest: The American Colonies and the Politics of Mercantilism* (1970).

The Andros crisis and related topics are treated in Jack M. Sosin's *English America and the Revolution of 1688: Royal Administration and the Structure of Provincial Government* (1982). Stephen Saunders Webb's *The Governors-General: The English Army and the Definition of the Empire, 1569–1681* (1979) argues that the Crown was more concerned with military administration than with commercial regulation, and Webb's *1676: The End of American Independence* (1984) shows how the Indian wars undermined the autonomy of the colonial governments.

On the Jesuits, see Nicholas P. Cushner's *Why Have You Come Here? The Jesuits and the First Evangelization of Native America* (2006). The early Indian wars are treated in Jill Lepore's *The Name of War: King Philip's War and the Origins of American Identity* (1998) and in Francis Jennings's *The Invasion of America: Indians, Colonialism, and the Cant of Conquest* (1975). See also Richard Aquila's *The Iroquois Restoration: Iroquois Diplomacy on the Colonial Frontier, 1701–1754* (1983). Gregory Evans Dowd describes the unification efforts of Indians east of the Mississippi in *A Spirited Resistance: The North American Indian Struggle for Unity, 1745–1815* (1992). See also James H. Merrell's *Into the American Woods: Negotiators on the Pennsylvania Frontier* (1999).

A good introduction to the imperial phase of the colonial conflicts is Howard H. Peckham's *The Colonial Wars, 1689–1762* (1964). More analytical is Douglas Edward Leach's *Arms for Empire: A Military History of the British Colonies in North America, 1607–1763* (1973). Fred Anderson's *Crucible of War: The Seven Years' War and the Fate of Empire in British North America, 1754–1766* (2000) is the best history of the Seven Years' War. On the French colonies in North America, see Allan Greer's *The People of New France* (1997).

CHAPTER 5

For a narrative survey of the events leading to the Revolution, see Edward Countryman's *The American Revolution*, rev. ed. (2003). For Great Britain's perspective on the imperial conflict, see Ian R. Christie's *Crisis of Empire: Great Britain and the American Colonies, 1754–1783* (1966).

The intellectual foundations of revolt are traced in Bernard Bailyn's *The Ideological Origins of the American Revolution*, enlarged ed. (1992). To understand how these views were connected to organized protest, see Pauline Maier's *From Resistance to Revolution: Colonial Radicals and the Development of American Opposition to Britain, 1765–1776* (1972) and Jon Butler's *Becoming America: The Revolution before 1776* (2000).

Several books deal with specific events in the crisis. Oliver M. Dickerson's *The Navigation Acts and the American Revolution* (1951) stresses the change from trade regulation to taxation in 1764. Edmund S. Morgan and Helen M. Morgan's *The Stamp Act Crisis: Prologue to Revolution*, rev. ed. (1962), gives the colonial perspective on that crucial event. Also valuable are Hiller B. Zobel's *The Boston Massacre* (1970), Benjamin Woods Labaree's *The Boston Tea Party, 1773; Catalyst for Revolution* (1964), and David Ammerman's *In the Common Cause: American Response to the Coercive Acts of 1774* (1974). On the efforts of colonists to boycott the purchase of British goods, see T. H. Breen's *The Marketplace of Revolution: How Consumer Politics Shaped American Independence* (2004). An excellent overview of the political turmoil leading to war is John Ferling's *A Leap in the Dark: The Struggle to Create the American Republic* (2003). A fascinating account of the smallpox epidemic during the Revolutionary War is Elizabeth A. Fenn's *Pox Americana: The Great Smallpox Epidemic of 1775–1782* (2001).

Pauline Maier's *American Scripture: Making the Declaration of Independence* (1997) is the best analysis of the framing of that document. For accounts of how the imperial controversy affected individual colonies, see Edward Countryman's *A People in Revolution: The American Revolution and Political Society in New York, 1760–1790* (1981), Richard L. Bushman's *King and People in Provincial Massachusetts* (1985), James H. Hutson's *Pennsylvania Politics, 1746–1770: The Movement for Royal Government and Its Consequences* (1972), Rhys Isaac's *The Transformation of Virginia, 1740–1790* (1982), and A. Roger Ekirch's *"Poor Carolina": Politics and Society in Colonial North Carolina, 1729–1776* (1981).

Events west of the Appalachians are chronicled concisely by Jack M. Sosin in *The Revolutionary Frontier, 1763–1783* (1967). Military affairs in the early phases of the war are handled in John W. Shy's *Toward Lexington: The Role of the British Army in the Coming of the American Revolution* (1965) and in works described in Chapter 6.

CHAPTER 6

The Revolutionary War is the subject of Colin Bonwick's *The American Revolution*, 2nd ed. (2005), Gordon S. Wood's *The Radicalism of the American Revolution* (1991), and Jeremy Black's *War for America: The Fight for Independence, 1775–1783* (1991). John Ferling's *Setting the World Ablaze Washington, Adams, Jefferson, and the American Revolution* (2000) highlights the roles played by key leaders.

On the social history of the Revolutionary War, see John W. Shy's *A People Numerous and Armed: Reflections on the Military Struggle for American Independence*, rev. ed. (1990), Charles Royster's *A Revolutionary People at War: The Continental Army and American Character, 1775–1783* (1979), and E. Wayne Carp's *To Starve the Army at Pleasure: Continental Army Administration and American Political Culture, 1775–1783* (1984). Colin G. Calloway tells the neglected story of the Indian experiences in the Revolution in *The American Revolution in Indian Country: Crisis and Diversity in Native American Communities* (1995). The imperial, aristocratic, and racist aspects of the Revolution are detailed in Francis Jennings's *The Creation of America: Through Revolution to Empire* (2000).

Why some Americans remained loyal to the Crown is the subject of Robert M. Calhoon's *The Loyalists in Revolutionary America, 1760–1781* (1973) and Mary Beth Norton's *The British-Americans: The Loyalist Exiles in England, 1774–1789* (1972).

The definitive study of African Americans during the Revolutionary era remains Benjamin Quarles's *The Negro in the American Revolution* (1961). Mary Beth Norton's *Liberty's Daughters: The Revolutionary Experience of American Women, 1750–1800,* new ed. (1996), Linda K. Kerber's *Women of the Republic: Intellect and Ideology in Revolutionary America* (1980), and Carol Berkin's *Revolutionary Mothers: Women in the Struggle for America's Independence* (2005) document the role that women played in securing independence. Joy Day Buel and Richard Buel Jr.'s *The Way of Duty: A Woman and Her Family in Revolutionary America* (1984) shows the impact of the Revolution on one New England family.

The Standard introduction to the diplomacy of the Revolutionary era is Jonathan R. Dull's *A Diplomatic History of the American Revolution* (1985).

CHAPTER 7

A good overview of the Confederation period is Richard B. Morris's *The Forging of the Union, 1781–1789* (1987). Another useful analysis of this period is Richard Buel Jr.'s *Securing the Revolution: Ideology in American Politics, 1789–1815* (1972).

David P. Szatmary's *Shays's Rebellion: The Making of an Agrarian Insurrection* (1980) covers that fateful incident. For a fine account of cultural change during the period, see Joseph J. Ellis's *After the Revolution: Profiles of Early American Culture* (1979).

Excellent treatments of the post-Revolutionary era include Edmund S. Morgan's *Inventing the People: The Rise of Popular Sovereignty in England and America* (1988), Michael Kammen's *Sovereignty and Liberty: Constitutional Discourse in American Culture* (1988), and Joyce Appleby's *Inheriting the Revolution: The First Generation of Americans* (2000). On the political philosophies contributing to the drafting of the Constitution, see Ralph Lerner's *The Thinking Revolutionary: Principle and Practice in the New Republic* (1987). Woody Holton's *Unruly Americans and the Origins of the Constitution* (2007) emphasizes the role of taxes and monetary policies in the crafting of the Constitution. Among the better collections of essays on the Constitution are *Toward a More Perfect Union: Six Essays on the Constitution* (1988), edited by Neil L. York, and *The Framing and Ratification of the Constitution* (1987), edited by Leonard W. Levy and Dennis J. Mahoney.

Bruce Ackerman's *We the People,* vol. 1, *Foundations* (1991) examines Federalist political principles. For the Bill of Rights that emerged from the ratification struggles, see Robert A. Rutland's *The Birth of the Bill of Rights, 1776–1791* (1955).

CHAPTER 8

The best introduction to the early Federalists remains John C. Miller's *The Federalist Era, 1789–1801* (1960). Other works analyze the ideological debates among the nation's first leaders. Richard Buel Jr.'s *Securing the Revolution: Ideology in American Politics, 1789–1815* (1972), Joyce Appleby's *Capitalism and a New Social Order: The Republican Vision of the 1790s* (1984), Drew R. McCoy's *The Last of the Fathers: James Madison and the Republican Legacy* (1989), and Stanley Elkins and Eric McKitrick's *The Age of Federalism: The Early American Republic, 1788–1800* (1993) trace the persistence and transformation of ideas first fostered during the Revolutionary crisis. On the first ten constitutional amendments, see Leonard W. Levy's *Origins of the Bill of Rights* (1999).

The 1790s may also be understood through the views and behavior of national leaders. Joseph J. Ellis's *Founding Brothers: The Revolutionary Generation* (2000) is a superb group study. See also the following biographies: Richard Brookhiser's *Founding Father: Rediscovering George Washington* (1996) and *Alexander Hamilton, American* (1999) and Joseph J. Ellis's *Passionate Sage: The Character and Legacy of John Adams* (1993). For a female perspective, see Phyllis Lee Levin's *Abigail Adams: A Biography* (1987). The Republican viewpoint is the subject of Lance Banning's *The Jeffersonian Persuasion: Evolution of a Party Ideology* (1978).

Federalist foreign policy is explored in Jerald A. Comb's *The Jay Treaty: Political Battleground of the Founding Fathers* (1970) and William Stinchcombe's *The XYZ Affair* (1980). For specific domestic issues, see Thomas P. Slaughter's *The Whiskey Rebellion: Frontier Epilogue to the American Revolution* (1986) and Harry Ammon's *The Genet Mission* (1973). The treatment of Indians in the Old Northwest is explored in Richard H. Kohn's *Eagle and Sword: The Federalists and the Creation of the Military Establishment in America, 1783–1802* (1975). For the Alien and Sedition Acts, consult James Morton Smith's *Freedom's Fetters: The Alien and Sedition Laws and American Civil Liberties* (1956).

Several books focus on social issues of the post-Revolutionary period, including *Keepers of the Revolution: New Yorkers at Work in the Early Republic* (1992), edited by Paul A. Gilje and Howard B. Rock; Ronald Schultz's *The Republic of Labor: Philadelphia Artisans and the Politics of Class, 1720–1830* (1993); and Peter Way's *Common Labour: Workers and the Digging of North American Canals, 1780–1860* (1993).

The African American experience in the Revolutionary era is detailed in Mechal Sobel's *The World They Made Together: Black and White Values in Eighteenth-Century Virginia* (1987) and Gary B. Nash's *Forging Freedom: The Formation of Philadelphia's Black Community, 1720–1840* (1988).

CHAPTER 9

Marshall Smelser's *The Democratic Republic, 1801–1815* (1968) presents an overview of the Republican administrations. The standard biography of Jefferson is Joseph J. Ellis's *American Sphinx: The Character of Thomas Jefferson* (1996). On the life of Jefferson's friend and successor, see Drew R. McCoy's *The Last of the Fathers: James Madison and the Republican Legacy* (1989). Joyce Appleby's *Capitalism and a New Social Order: The Republican Vision of the 1790s* (1984) minimizes the impact of Republican ideology.

Linda K. Kerber's *Federalists in Dissent: Imagery and Ideology in Jeffersonian American* (1970) explores the Federalists while out of power. The concept of judicial review and the courts can be studied in Richard E. Ellis's *The Jeffersonian Crisis: Courts and Politics in the Young Republic* (1971). On John Marshall, see G. Edward White's *The Marshall Court and Cultural Change, 1815–1835* (1988) and James F. Simon's *What Kind of Nation: Thomas Jefferson, John Marshall, and the Epic Struggle to Create a United States* (2002). Milton Lomask's two volumes, *Aaron Burr: The Years from Princeton to Vice President, 1756–1805* (1979) and *The Conspiracy and the Years of Exile, 1805–1836* (1982) trace the career of that remarkable American.

For the Louisiana Purchase, consult Jon Kukla's *A Wilderness So Immense: The Louisiana Purchase and the Destiny of America* (2003). For a captivating account of the Lewis and Clark expedition, see Stephen Ambrose's *Undaunted Courage: Meriwether Lewis, Thomas Jefferson, and the Opening of the American West* (1996). Bernard W. Sheehan's *Seeds of Extinction: Jeffersonian Philanthropy and the American Indian* (1973) is more analytical in its treatment of the Jeffersonians' Indian policy and the opening of the West.

Burton Spivak's *Jefferson's English Crisis: Commerce, Embargo, and the Republican Revolution* (1979) discusses Anglo-American relations during Jefferson's administration; Clifford L. Egan's *Neither Peace Nor War: Franco-American Relations, 1803–1812* (1983) covers America's relations with France. An excellent revisionist treatment of the events that brought on war in 1812 is J. C. A. Stagg's *Mr. Madison's War: Politics, Diplomacy, and Warfare in the Early American Republic, 1783–1830* (1983). The war itself is the focus of Donald R. Hickey's *The War of 1812: A Forgotten Conflict* (1989). See also David Curtis Skaggs and Gerard T. Altoff's *A Signal Victory: The Lake Erie Campaign, 1812–1813* (1997).

CHAPTER 10

The standard overview of the Era of Good Feelings remains George Dangerfield's *The Awakening of American Nationalism, 1815–1828* (1965). A classic summary of the economic trends of the period is Douglass C. North's *The Economic Growth of the United States, 1790–1860* (1961). An excellent synthesis of the era is Charles Sellers's *The Market Revolution: Jacksonian America, 1815–1846* (1991).

On diplomatic relations during James Monroe's presidency, see William Earl Weeks's *John Quincy Adams and American Global Empire* (1992). For relations after 1812, see Ernest R. May's *The Making of the Monroe Doctrine* (1975).

Background on Andrew Jackson can be obtained from works cited in Chapter 11. The campaign that brought Jackson to the White House is analyzed in Robert Vincent Remini's *The Election of Andrew Jackson* (1963).

CHAPTER 11

An excellent survey of events covered in this chapter is Daniel Feller's *The Jacksonian Promise: America, 1815–1840* (1995). Even more comprehensive surveys of politics and culture during the Jacksonian era are Daniel Walker Howe's *What Hath God Wrought: The Transformation of America,*

1815–1848 (2007) and David S. Reynolds's *Waking Giant: America in the Age of Jackson* (2008). A more political focus can be found in Harry L. Watson's *Liberty and Power: The Politics of Jacksonian America* (1990).

A still-valuable standard introduction to the development of the political parties of the 1830s is Richard Patrick McCormick's *The Second American Party System: Party Formation in the Jacksonian Era* (1966). For an outstanding analysis of women in New York City during the Jacksonian period, see Christine Stansell's *City of Women: Sex and Class in New York, 1789–1860* (1986). In *Chants Democratic: New York City and the Rise of the American Working-Class, 1788–1850* (1984), Sean Wilentz analyzes the social basis of working-class politics. More recently, Wilentz has traced the democratization of politics in *The Rise of American Democracy: Jefferson to Lincoln,* abridged college ed. (2009).

The best biography of Jackson remains Robert Vincent Remini's three-volume work: *Andrew Jackson: The Course of American Empire, 1767–1821* (1977), *Andrew Jackson: The Course of American Freedom, 1822–1832* (1981), and *Andrew Jackson: The Course of American Democracy, 1833–1845* (1984). A more critical study of the seventh president is Andrew Burstein's *The Passions of Andrew Jackson* (2003). On Jackson's successor, consult John Niven's *Martin Van Buren: The Romantic Age of American Politics* (1983) and Ted Widmer's *Martin Van Buren* (2005). Studies of other major figures of the period include John Niven's *John C. Calhoun and the Price of Union: A Biography* (1988), Merrill D. Peterson's *The Great Triumvirate: Webster, Clay, and Calhoun* (1987), and Robert Vincent Remini's *Henry Clay: Statesman for the Union* (1991) and *Daniel Webster: The Man and His Time* (1997).

The political philosophies of Jackson's opponents are treated in Michael F. Holt's *The Rise and Fall of the American Whig Party: Jacksonian Politics and the Onset of the Civil War* (1999) and Harry L. Watson's *Andrew Jackson vs. Henry Clay: Democracy and Development in Antebellum America* (1998).

On the Eaton affair, see John F. Marszalek's *The Petticoat Affair: Manners, Mutiny, and Sex in Andrew Jackson's White House* (1998). Two studies of the impact of the bank controversy are William G. Shade's *Banks or No Banks: The Money Issue in Western Politics, 1832–1865* (1972) and James Roger Sharp's *The Jacksonians versus the Banks: Politics in the States after the Panic of 1837* (1970).

The outstanding book on the nullification issue remains William W. Freehling's *Prelude to Civil War: The Nullification Controversy in South Carolina, 1816–1836* (1965). John M. Belohlavek's *"Let the Eagle Soar!": The Foreign Policy of Andrew Jackson* (1985) is a thorough study of Jacksonian diplomacy. Ronald N. Satz's *American Indian Policy in the Jacksonian Era* (1974) surveys the controversial relocation policy.

Chapter 12

On economic development in the nation's early decades, see Stuart Bruchey's *Enterprise: The Dynamic Economy of a Free People* (1990). The classic study of transportation and economic growth is George Rogers Taylor's *The Transportation Revolution, 1815–1860* (1951). A fresh view is provided in Sarah H. Gordon's *Passage to Union: How the Railroads Transformed American Life, 1829–1929* (1996). On the Erie Canal, see Carol Sheriff's *The Artificial River: The Erie Canal and the Paradox of Progress, 1817–1862* (1996).

The impact of technology is traced in David J. Jeremy's *Transatlantic Industrial Revolution: The Diffusion of Textile Technologies between Britain and America, 1790–1830s* (1981). On the invention of the telegraph, see Kenneth Silverman's *Lightning Man: The Accursed Life of Samuel F. B. Morse* (2003). For the story of steamboats, see Andrea Sutcliffe's *Steam: The Untold Story of America's First Great Invention* (2004). The best treatment of public works, such as the Erie Canal in the development of nineteenth-century America, is John Lauritz Larson's *Internal Improvement: National Public Works and the Promise of Popular Government in the Early United States* (2001).

Paul E. Johnson's *A Shopkeeper's Millenium: Society and Revivals in Rochester, New York, 1815–1837* (1978) studies the role religion played in the emerging industrial order. The attitude of the worker during this time of transition is surveyed in Edward E. Pessen's *Most Uncommon Jacksonians: The Radical Leaders of the Early Labor Movement* (1967). Detailed case studies of working communities include Anthony F. C. Wallace's *Rockdale: The Growth of an American Village in the Early Industrial Revolution* (1978), Thomas Dublin's *Women at Work: The Transformation of Work and Community in Lowell, Massachusetts, 1826–1860* (1979), and Sean Wilentz's *Chants Democratic: New York and the Rise of the American Working Class, 1788–1850* (1984). Walter Licht's *Working for the Railroad: The Organization of Work in the Nineteenth Century* (1983) is rich in detail.

For a fine treatment of urbanization, see Charles N. Glaab and A. Theodore Brown's *A History of Urban America* (1967). On immigration, see *The Irish in America*, edited by Michael Coffey with text by Terry Golway (1997).

Chapter 13

Russel Blaine Nye's *Society and Culture in America, 1830–1860* (1974) provides a wide-ranging survey of the Romantic movement. On the reform impulse, consult Ronald G. Walter's *American Reformers, 1815–1860*, rev. ed.

(1997). Revivalist religion is treated in Nathan O. Hatch's *The Democratization of American Christianity* (1989), Christine Leigh Heyrman's *Southern Cross: The Beginnings of the Bible Belt* (1997), and Ellen Eslinger's *Citizens of Zion: The Social Origins of Camp Meeting Revivalism* (1999). On the Mormons, see Leonard Arrington's *Brigham Young: American Moses* (1985).

The best treatments of transcendentalist thought are Paul F. Boller's *American Transcendentalism, 1830–1860: An Intellectual Inquiry* (1974) and Philip F. Gura's *American Transcendentalism: A History* (2007). Several good works describe various aspects of the antebellum reform movement. For temperance, see W. J. Rorabaugh's *The Alcoholic Republic: An American Tradition* (1979) and Barbara Leslie Epstein's *The Politics of Domesticity: Women, Evangelism, and Temperance in Nineteenth-Century America* (1981). Stephen Nissenbaum's *Sex, Diet, and Debility in Jacksonian America: Sylvester Graham and Health Reform* (1980) looks at a pioneering reformer concerned with diet and lifestyle. On prison reform and other humanitarian projects, see David J. Rothman's *The Discovery of the Asylum: Social Order and Disorder in the New Republic*, rev. ed. (2002), and Thomas J. Brown's biography *Dorothea Dix: New England Reformer* (1998). Lawrence A. Cremin's *American Education: The National Experience, 1783–1876* (1980) traces early school reform.

On women during the antebellum period, see Nancy F. Cott's *The Bonds of Womanhood: "Woman's Sphere" in New England, 1780–1835*, rev. ed. (1997), and Ellen C. DuBois's *Feminism and Suffrage: The Emergence of an Independent Women's Movement in America, 1848–1869* (1978). Michael Fellman's *The Unbounded Frame: Freedom and Community in Nineteenth-Century American Utopianism* (1973) surveys the utopian movements.

CHAPTER 14

For background on Whig programs and ideas, see Michael F. Holt's *The Rise and Fall of the American Whig Party: Jacksonian Politics and the Onset of the Civil War* (1999). On John Tyler, see Edward P. Crapol's *John Tyler: The Accidental President* (2006). Several works help interpret the expansionist impulse. Frederick Merk's *Manifest Destiny and Mission in American History: A Reinterpretation* (1963) remains a classic. A more recent treatment of expansionist ideology is Thomas R. Hietala's *Manifest Design: Anxious Aggrandizement in Late Jacksonian America* (1985).

The best survey of western expansion is Richard White's *"It's Your Misfortune and None of My Own": A New History of the American West* (1991). Robert M. Utley's *A Life Wild and Perilous: Mountain Men and the Paths to the Pacific* (1997) tells the dramatic story of the rugged pathfinders who discovered corridors over the Rocky Mountains. The movement of settlers to the West is ably documented in John Mack Faragher's *Women and Men on the Overland Trail,* 2nd ed. (2001), and David Dary's *The Santa Fe Trail: Its History, Legends, and Lore* (2000). On the tragic Donner party, see Ethan Rarick's *Desperate Passage: The Donner Party's Perilous Journey West* (2008).

Gene M. Brack's *Mexico Views Manifest Destiny, 1821–1846: An Essay on the Origins of the Mexican War* (1975) takes Mexico's viewpoint on U.S. designs on the West. For the American perspective on Texas, see Joel H. Silbey's *Storm over Texas: The Annexation Controversy and the Road to Civil War* (2005). On the siege of the Alamo, see William C. Davis's *Three Roads to the Alamo: The Lives and Fortunes of David Crockett, James Bowie, and William Barret Travis* (1998). An excellent biography related to the emergence of Texas is Gregg Cantrell's *Stephen F. Austin: Empresario of Texas* (1999). On James K. Polk, see John H. Schroeder's *Mr. Polk's War: American Opposition and Dissent, 1846–1848* (1973). The best survey of the military conflict is John S. D. Eisenhower's *So Far from God: The U.S. War with Mexico, 1846–1848* (1989). The Mexican War as viewed from the perspective of the soldiers is ably described in Richard Bruce Winders's *Mr. Polk's Army: American Military Experience in the Mexican War* (1997). On the diplomatic aspects of Mexican-American relations, see David M. Pletcher's *The Diplomacy of Annexation: Texas, Oregon, and the Mexican War* (1973).

CHAPTER 15

Those interested in the problem of discerning myth and reality in the southern experience should consult William R. Taylor's *Cavalier and Yankee: The Old South and American National Character* (1961). Three recent efforts to understand the mind of the Old South and its defense of slavery are Eugene D. Genovese's *The Slaveholders' Dilemma: Freedom and Progress in Southern Conservative Thought, 1820–1860* (1992), Eric H. Walther's *The Fire-Eaters* (1992), and William W. Freehling's *The Road to Disunion: Secessionists Triumphant, 1854–1861* (2007).

Contrasting analyses of the plantation system are Eugene D. Genovese's *The World the Slaveholders Made: Two Essays in Interpretation,* with a new introduction (1988), and Gavin Wright's *The Political Economy of the Cotton South: Households, Markets, and Wealth in the Nineteenth Century* (1978). Stephanie McCurry's *Masters of Small Worlds: Yeoman Households, Gender Relations, and the Political Culture of the Antebellum South Carolina Low Country* (1995) greatly enriches our understanding of southern households, religion, and political culture.

Other essential works on southern culture and society include Bertram Wyatt-Brown's *Honor and Violence in the Old South* (1986), Elizabeth Fox-Genovese's *Within the Plantation Household: Black and White Women of the Old South* (1988), Catherine Clinton's *The Plantation Mistress: Woman's World in the Old South* (1982), Joan E. Cashin's *A Family Venture: Men and Women on the Southern Frontier* (1991), and Theodore Rosengarten's *Tombee: Portrait of a Cotton Planter* (1986).

A provocative discussion of the psychology of African American slavery can be found in Stanley M. Elkins's *Slavery: A Problem in American Institutional and Intellectual Life,* 3rd ed. (1976). John W. Blassingame's *The Slave Community: Plantation Life in the Antebellum South,* rev. and enlarged ed. (1979), Eugene D. Genovese's *Roll, Jordan, Roll: The World the Slaves Made* (1974), and Herbert G. Gutman's *The Black Family in Slavery and Freedom, 1750–1925* (1976) all stress the theme of a persisting and identifiable slave culture. On the question of slavery's profitability, see Robert William Fogel and Stanley L. Engerman's *Time on the Cross: The Economics of American Negro Slavery* (1974).

Other works on slavery include Lawrence W. Levine's *Black Culture and Black Consciousness: Afro-American Folk Thought from Slavery to Freedom* (1977); Albert J. Raboteau's *Slave Religion: The "Invisible Institution" in the Antebellum South* (1978); *We Are Your Sisters: Black Women in the Nineteenth Century,* edited by Dorothy Sterling (1984); Deborah Gray White's *Ar'n't I a Woman? Female Slaves in the Plantation South,* rev. ed. (1999); and Joel Williamson's *The Crucible of Race: Black-White Relations in the American South since Emancipation* (1984). Charles Joyner's *Down by the Riverside: A South Carolina Slave Community* (1984) offers a vivid reconstruction of one community.

Useful surveys of abolitionism include James Brewer Stewart's *Holy Warriors: The Abolitionists and American Slavery,* rev. ed. (1997), and Julie Roy Jeffrey's *The Great Silent Army of Abolitionism: Ordinary Women in the Antislavery Movement* (1998). On William Lloyd Garrison, see Henry Mayer's *All on Fire: William Lloyd Garrison and the Abolition of Slavery* (1998). For the pro-slavery argument as it developed in the South, see Larry E. Tise's *Proslavery: A History of the Defense of Slavery in America, 1701–1840* (1987) and James Oakes's *The Ruling Race: A History of American Slaveholders* (1982). The problems southerners had in justifying slavery are explored in Kenneth S. Greenberg's *Masters and Statesmen: The Political Culture of American Slavery* (1985).

CHAPTER 16

The best surveys of the forces and events leading to the Civil War include James M. McPherson's *Battle Cry of Freedom: The Civil War Era* (1988), Stephen B. Oates's *The Approaching Fury: Voices of the Storm, 1820–1861* (1997), Bruce Levine's *Half Slave and Half Free: The Roots of Civil War* (1992), and David M. Potter's *The Impending Crisis, 1848–1861* (1976). The most recent narrative of the political debate leading to secession is Michael A. Morrison's *Slavery and the American West: The Eclipse of Manifest Destiny and the Coming of the Civil War* (1997).

Mark J. Stegmaier's *Texas, New Mexico, and the Compromise of 1850: Boundary Dispute and Sectional Crisis* (1996) probes that crucial dispute, while Michael F. Holt's *The Political Crisis of the 1850s* (1978) traces the demise of the Whigs. Eric Foner, in *Free Soil, Free Labor, Free Men: The Ideology of the Republican Party before the Civil War* (1970), shows how events and ideas combined in the formation of a new political party. A more straightforward study of the rise of the Republicans is William E. Gienapp's *The Origins of the Republican Party, 1852–1856* (1987). The economic, social, and political crises of 1857 are examined in Kenneth M. Stampp's *America in 1857: A Nation on the Brink* (1990). On the Anthony Burns case, see Albert J. von Frank's *The Trials of Anthony Burns: Freedom and Slavery in Emerson's Boston* (1998). The *Dred Scott* case is ably assessed in Earl M. Maltz's *Dred Scott and the Politics of Slavery* (2007). For an assessment of the Revival of 1857–1858, see Kathryn Teresa Long, *The Revival of 1857–1858: Interpreting an American Religious Awakening* (1998).

Robert W. Johannsen's *Stephen A. Douglas* (1973) analyzes the issue of popular sovereignty. A more national perspective is provided in James A. Rawley's *Race and Politics: "Bleeding Kansas" and the Coming of the Civil War* (1969). On the role of John Brown in the sectional crisis, see Stephen B. Oates's *To Purge This Land with Blood: A Biography of John Brown* (1970) and David S. Reynolds's *John Brown, Abolitionist: The Man Who Killed Slavery, Sparked the Civil War, and Seeded Civil Rights* (2005). An excellent study of the South's journey to secession is William W. Freehling's *The Road to Disunion*, vol. 1, *Secessionists at Bay, 1776–1854* (1990), and *The Road to Disunion*, vol. 2, *Secessionists Triumphant, 1854–1861* (2007).

On the Buchanan presidency, see Jean H. Baker's *James Buchanan* (2004). On Lincoln's role in the coming crisis of war, see Don E. Fehrenbacher's *Prelude to Greatness: Lincoln in the 1850s* (1962). Harry V. Jaffa's *Crisis of the House Divided: An Interpretation of the Issues in the Lincoln-Douglas Debate*, 50th anniversary ed. (2009), details the debates, and Maury Klein's *Days of Defiance: Sumter, Secession, and the Coming of the Civil War* (1997) treats the

Fort Sumter controversy. An excellent collection of interpretive essays is *Why the Civil War Came* (1996), edited by Gabor S. Boritt.

CHAPTER 17

The best one-volume overview of the Civil War period is James M. McPherson's *Battle Cry of Freedom: The Civil War Era* (1988). A good introduction to the military events is Herman Hattaway's *Shades of Blue and Gray: An Introductory Military History of the Civil War* (1997). The outlook and experiences of the common soldier are explored in James M. McPherson's *For Cause and Comrades: Why Men Fought in the Civil War* (1997) and Earl J. Hess's *The Union Soldier in Battle: Enduring the Ordeal of Combat* (1997).

For emphasis on the South, turn first to Gary W. Gallagher's *The Confederate War* (1997). For a sparkling account of the birth of the Rebel nation, see William C. Davis's *"A Government of Our Own": The Making of the Confederacy* (1994). The same author provides a fine biography of the Confederate president in *Jefferson Davis: The Man and His Hour* (1991). On the best Confederate commander, see John M. Taylor's *Duty Faithfully Performed: Robert E. Lee and His Critics* (1999). On the key Union generals, see Lee Kennett's *Sherman: A Soldier's Life* (2001) and Josiah Bunting III's *Ulysses S. Grant* (2004).

Analytical scholarship on the military conflict includes Joseph L. Harsh's *Confederate Tide Rising: Robert E. Lee and the Making of Southern Strategy, 1861–1862* (1998), Steven E. Woodworth's *Jefferson Davis and His Generals: The Failure of Confederate Command in the West* (1990), and Paul D. Casdorph's *Lee and Jackson: Confederate Chieftains* (1992). Lonnie R. Speer's *Portals to Hell: Military Prisons of the Civil War* (1997) details the ghastly experience of prisoners of war.

The history of the North during the war is surveyed in Philip Shaw Paludan's *A People's Contest: The Union and Civil War, 1861–1865*, 2nd ed. (1996), and J. Matthew Gallman's *The North Fights the Civil War: The Home Front* (1994).

The central northern political figure, Abraham Lincoln, is the subject of many books. See Harry V. Jaffa's *A New Birth of Freedom: Abraham Lincoln and the Coming of the Civil War* (2000). On Lincoln's great speeches, see Ronald C. White Jr.'s *The Eloquent President: A Portrait of Lincoln through His Words* (2005). The election of 1864 is treated in John C. Waugh's *Reelecting Lincoln: The Battle for the 1864 Presidency* (1997). On Lincoln's assassination, see William Hanchett's *The Lincoln Murder Conspiracies* (1983).

Concerning specific military campaigns, see Larry J. Daniel's *Shiloh: The Battle That Changed the Civil War* (1997), Thomas Goodrich's *Black*

Flag: Guerrilla Warfare on the Western Border, 1861–1865 (1995), Stephen W. Sears's *To the Gates of Richmond: The Peninsula Campaign* (1992), James M. McPherson's *Crossroads of Freedom: Antietam* (2002), James Lee McDonough and James Pickett Jones's *"War So Terrible": Sherman and Atlanta* (1987), Robert Garth Scott's *Into the Wilderness with the Army of the Potomac*, rev. and enl. ed. (1992), Albert Castel's *Decision in the West: The Atlanta Campaign of 1864* (1992), and Ernest B. Furgurson's *Not War but Murder: Cold Harbor, 1864* (2000). On the final weeks of the war, see William C. Davis's *An Honorable Defeat: The Last Days of the Confederate Government* (2001).

The experience of the African American soldier is surveyed in Joseph T. Glatthaar's *Forged in Battle: The Civil War Alliance of Black Soldiers and White Officers* (1990) and Ira Berlin, Joseph P. Reidy, and Leslie S. Rowland's *Freedom's Soldiers: The Black Military Experience in the Civil War* (1998). For the African American woman's experience, see Jacqueline Jones's *Labor of Love, Labor of Sorrow: Black Women, Work and the Family, from Slavery to the Present* (1985).

Recent gender and ethnic studies include *Divided Houses: Gender and the Civil War*, edited by Catherine Clinton and Nina Silber (1992), Drew Gilpin Faust's *Mothers of Invention: Women of the Slaveholding South in the American Civil War* (1996), George C. Rable's *Civil Wars: Women and the Crisis of Southern Nationalism* (1989), and William L. Burton's *Melting Pot Soldiers: The Union's Ethnic Regiments*, 2nd ed. (1998).

CHAPTER 18

The most comprehensive treatment of Reconstruction is Eric Foner's *Reconstruction: America's Unfinished Revolution, 1863–1877* (1988). On Andrew Johnson, see Hans L. Trefousse's *Andrew Johnson: A Biography* (1989). An excellent brief biography of Grant is Josiah Bunting III's *Ulysses S. Grant* (2004).

Scholars have been sympathetic to the aims and motives of the Radical Republicans. See, for instance, Herman Belz's *Reconstructing the Union: Theory and Policy during the Civil War* (1969) and Richard Nelson Current's *Those Terrible Carpetbaggers: A Reinterpretation* (1988). The ideology of the Radicals is explored in Michael Les Benedict's *A Compromise of Principle: Congressional Republicans and Reconstruction, 1863–1869* (1974). On the black political leaders, see Phillip Dray's *Capitol Men: The Epic Story of Reconstruction through the Lives of the First Black Congressmen* (2008).

The intransigence of southern white attitudes is examined in Michael Perman's *Reunion without Compromise: The South and Reconstruction, 1865–1868* (1973) and Dan T. Carter's *When the War Was Over: The Failure of*

Self-Reconstruction in the South, 1865–1867 (1985). Allen W. Trelease's *White Terror: The Ku Klux Klan Conspiracy and Southern Reconstruction* (1971) covers the various organizations that practiced vigilante tactics. On the massacre of African Americans, see Charles Lane's *The Day Freedom Died: The Colfax Massacre, the Supreme Court, and the Betrayal of Reconstruction* (2008). The difficulties former slaves had in adjusting to the new labor system are documented in James L. Roark's *Masters without Slaves: Southern Planters in the Civil War and Reconstruction* (1977). Books on southern politics during Reconstruction include Michael Perman's *The Road to Redemption: Southern Politics, 1869–1879* (1984), Terry L. Seip's *The South Returns to Congress: Men, Economic Measures, and Intersectional Relationships, 1868–1879* (1983), and Mark W. Summers's *Railroads, Reconstruction, and the Gospel of Prosperity: Aid under the Radical Republicans, 1865–1877* (1984).

Numerous works study the freed blacks' experience in the South. Start with Leon F. Litwack's *Been in the Storm So Long: The Aftermath of Slavery* (1979). Joel Williamson's *After Slavery: The Negro in South Carolina during Reconstruction, 1861–1877* (1965) argues that South Carolina blacks took an active role in pursuing their political and economic rights. The Freedmen's Bureau is explored in William S. McFeely's *Yankee Stepfather: General O. O. Howard and the Freedmen* (1968). The situation of freed slave women is discussed in Jacqueline Jones's *Labor of Love, Labor of Sorrow: Black Women, Work and the Family, from Slavery to the Present* (1985).

The politics of corruption outside the South is depicted in William S. McFeely's *Grant: A Biography* (1981). The political maneuvers of the election of 1876 and the resultant crisis and compromise are explained in C. Vann Woodward's *Reunion and Reaction: The Compromise of 1877 and the End of Reconstruction* (1951) and in William Gillette's *Retreat from Reconstruction, 1869–1879* (1979). The role of religion in determining the fate of Reconstruction is the focus of Edward J. Blum's *Reforging the White Republic: Race, Religion, and American Nationalism, 1865–1898* (2005).

CREDITS

Part 1: p.1, The New York Public Library/Art Resource, NY; p. 3, Granger Collection.

Chapter 1: p. 5, Bettmann/Corbis; p. 9, Charles & Josette Lenars/Corbis; p. 11, Daniel S. Glover/University of Missouri Museum of Anthropology; p. 12, Bettmann/Corbis; p. 14, Paul Souders/Getty Images; p. 19, Bettmann/Corbis; p. 22, Bridgeman Art Library; p. 23, The Granger Collection; p. 24, The Granger Collection; p. 28, The Benson Latin American Collection, University of Texas; p. 29, Library of Congress; p. 32, Atlantide Phototravel/Corbis; p. 37, The Royal Library of Copenhagen; p. 39, Werner Forman/Art Resource, NY; p. 43, The Gallery Collection/Corbis; p. 46, Bettmann/Corbis; p. 48, Bettmann/Corbis.

Chapter 2: p. 52, The Granger Collection; p. 55, Summerfield Press/Corbis; p. 55, National Portrait Gallery, London; p. 58, Bridgeman Art Library; p. 61, The Granger Collection; p. 63, Bettmann/Corbis; p. 65, The Granger Collection; p. 70, The Granger Collection; p. 72, The Granger Collection; p. 76, The Granger Collection; p. 80, Library of Congress; p. 82, The Granger Collection; p. 88, The Mariners' Museum/Corbis; p. 89, South Carolina Library; p. 90, The Royal Library of Copenhagen; p. 93, Museum of the City of New York/Corbis; p. 95, Bettmann/Corbis; p. 96, Library of Congress; p. 99, Stapleton Collection/Corbis; p. 101, The Granger Collection.

Chapter 3: p. 108, The Granger Collection; p. 110, The Granger Collection; p. 112, Worcester Art Museum, Worcester, MA, Sarah C. Graver Fund; p. 112, Burstein Collection/Corbis; p. 116, Connecticut Historical Society Museum; p. 119, Granger Collection; p. 120, The Swem Library, the College of William & Mary; p. 122, Granger Collection; p. 126, Abby Aldrich Rockefeller Folk Art Center, Colonial Williamsburg; p. 128, Courtesy of the Maryland Historical Society; p. 130, North Wind Picture Archive; p. 131, Granger Collection; p. 133, The Granger Collection; p. 138, Photo courtesy Peabody Essex Museum; p. 140, Granger Collection; p. 146, Collection of the New-York Historical Society; p. 148, Library Company of Philadelphia; p. 151, Granger Collection; p. 152, Granger Collection; p. 155, National Portrait Gallery, London; p. 157, Bettmann/Corbis.

CHAPTER 4: **p. 162**, Granger Collection; **p. 165**, I. N. Phelps Stokes Collection Miriam and Ira D. Wallach Division of Art, Prints and Photographs, New York Public Library, Astor, Lenox and Tilden Foundations; **p. 166**, Granger Collection; **p. 169**, Granger Collection; **p. 172**, Snark/Art Resource, NY; **p. 173**, Three Lions/Getty Images; **p. 177**, Collection of the New-York Historical Society; **p. 180**, Library of Congress; **p. 183**, Library and Archives Canada.

CHAPTER 5: **p. 190**, Library of Congress; **p. 192**, Granger Collection; **p. 194**, Library of Congress; **p. 197**, Library of Congress; **p. 198**, Library of Congress; **p. 201**, Library of Congress; **p. 203**, Library of Congress; **p. 204**, I. N. Phelps Stokes Collection, Miriam and Ira D. Wallach Division of Art, Prints and Photographs, The New York Public Library, Astor, Lenox and Tilden Fundations; **p. 207**, Library of Congress; **p. 208**, Library of Congress; **p. 211**, Granger Collection; **p. 213**, Granger Collection; **p. 215**, Library of Congress; **p. 219**, American Antiquarian Society; **p. 220**, Library of Congress.

PART 2: **p. 227**, Giraudon/Art Resource; **p. 228**, Library of Congress.

CHAPTER 6: **p. 231**, Giraudon/Art Resource NY; **p. 234**, Library of Congress; **p. 236**, US Senate Collection; **p. 238**, Anne S. K. Brown Military Collection, Brown University Library; **p. 241**, Granger Collection; **p. 244**, The Granger Collection; **p.247**, The Granger Collection; **p. 252**, Library of Congress; **p. 253**, The Granger Collection; **p. 259**, Courtesy of the Maryland Historical Society 1960.108.3.11; **p. 261**, The Granger Collection; **p. 263**, The Granger Collection; **p. 264**, Library of Congress; **p. 265**, The Granger Collection.

CHAPTER 7: **p. 270**, Bettmann/Corbis; **p. 278**, Library Company of Philadelphia; **p. 280**, Historical Society of Pennsylvania; **p. 282**, The Granger Collection; **p. 284**, Library of Congress; **p. 285**, Library of Congress; **p. 288**, Library of Congress; **p. 291**, Independence National Historical Park; **p. 297**, Library of Congress.

CHAPTER 8: **p. 300**, Art Resource, NY; **p. 301**, Library of Congress; **p. 304**, The Granger Collection; **p. 305**, Library of Congress; **p. 308**, Independence National Historical Park; **p. 311**, Courtesy of the Maryland Historical Society; **p. 314**, Historical Society of Pennsylvania; **p. 316**, The Granger Collection; **p. 320**, Courtesy of the Burton Historical Collection; **p. 324**, The Granger Collection; **p. 327**, Art Resource, NY; **p. 328**, The Granger Collection; **p. 330**, Image copyright © The Metropolitan Museum of Art/Art Resource, NY; **p. 331**, National Portrait Gallery NPG.71.4; **p. 332**, The Granger Collection; **p. 335**, The Granger Collection; **p. 337**, Library of Congress.

CHAPTER 9: **p. 344**, Giraudon/Art Resource NY; **p. 347**, Library of Congress; **p. 348**, Miriam and Ira D. Wallach Division of Art, Prints and Photographs. New York Public Library; **p. 351**, Cincinnati Museum Center, Cincinnati Historical Society Library; **p. 354**, Copyright American Philosophical Society; **p. 355**, Copyright American Philosophical Society; **p. 357**, Library of Congress; **p. 359**, From the Collections of the New Jersey Historical Society, Newark, NJ; **p. 361**, Library of Congress; **p. 362**, Collection of the

New-York Historical Society; **p. 365,** Library of Congress; **p. 367,** Collection of the New-York Historical Society; **p. 372,** Library of Congress; **p. 375,** Collection of Davenport West, Jr.

PART 3: **p. 379,** Library of Congress; **p. 381,** Library of Congress.

CHAPTER 10: **p. 383,** Library of Congress; **p. 384,** Maryland Historical Society 1934.2.1; **p. 390,** The Granger Collection; **p. 392,** Library of Congress; **p. 393,** Library of Congress; **p. 397,** Henry Clay Memorial Foundation; **p. 399,** Bettmann/Corbis; **p. 400,** Image copyright © The Metropolitan Museum of Art/Art Resource, NY; **p. 402,** Gerard W. Gawalt and Janice E. Ruth, Manuscript Division, Library of Congress; **p. 405,** Library of Congress; **p. 406,** Corbis; **p. 408,** Library of Congress; **p. 409,** Collection of the New-York Historical Society.

CHAPTER 11: **p. 414,** Library of Congress; **p. 415,** Library of Congress; **p. 419,** Granger Collection; **p. 420,** Library of Congress; **p. 421,** National Portrait Gallery; **p. 423,** Library of Congress; **p. 425,** Library of Congress; **p. 429,** Western Historical Collections University of Oklahoma library; **p. 431,** Alamy; **p. 434,** Collection of the New-York Historical Society; **p. 435,** Saint Louis Art Museum, Gift of Bank of America; **p. 440,** Library of Congress; **p. 441,** Library of Congress; **p. 443,** Library of Congress.

CHAPTER 12: **p. 450,** Granger Collection; **p. 451,** Granger Collection; **p. 453,** Warder Collection; **p. 458,** Minnesota Historical Society; **p. 459,** Granger Collection; **p. 462,** Library of Congress; **p. 466,** New York State Historical Association; **p. 467,** American Textile History Museum, Lowell, MA; **p. 468,** Granger Collection; **p. 471,** Library of Congress; **p. 472,** Collection of the New-York Historical Society; **p. 473,** Board of Trustees, National Gallery of Art, Washington. 1980.62.9. (2794)/PA; **p. 476,** Library of Congress; **p. 477,** National Park Service, Ellis Island Collection; **p. 479,** American Antiquarian Society; **p. 481,** Library of Congress; **p. 483,** Library of Congress; **p. 485,** John W. Bennett Labor Collection, Special Collections and University Archives, W. E. B. Du Bois Library, University of Massachusetts Amherst; **p. 486,** Courtesy Pennsylvania Hospital Historic Collections, Philadelphia.

CHAPTER 13: **p. 492,** Bettmann/Corbis; **p. 495,** Alamy; **p. 498,** Library of Congress; **p. 501,** Corbis; **p. 502,** Alamy; **p. 504,** Wadsworth Atheneum of Art, Hartford, CT, bequest of Daniel Wadsworth; **p. 506,** Bettmann/Corbis; **p. 507,** Bettmann/Corbis; **p. 509,** Bettmann/Corbis; **p. 510,** American Antiquarian Society; **p. 511,** Library of Congress; **p. 512,** The Walters Art Museum, Baltimore; **p. 513,** Manuscript Department, University of Virginia; **p. 515,** Granger Collection; **p. 517,** Library of Congress; **p. 519,** New York Public Library; **p. 520,** Warder Collection; **p. 521,** Library of Congress.

CHAPTER 14: **p. 526,** Granger Collection; **p. 528,** Granger Collection; **p. 531,** Library of Congress; **p.533,** Library of Congress; **p. 534,** Image copyright © The Metropolitan Museum of Art/Art Resource, NY; **p. 536,** Courtesy of Bancroft Library; **p. 537,**

Library of Congress; **p. 540,** Kansas State Historical Society; **p. 541,** Richard Collier, Wyoming Dept. of State Parks and Cultural Resources; **p. 542,** Macduff Everton/Corbis; **p. 544,** Library of Congress; **p. 547,** National Archives; **p. 552,** Library of Congress; **p. 557,** Warder Collection.

PART 4: **p. 565,** Granger Collection; **p. 566** Library of Congress.

CHAPTER 15: **p. 569,** Bettmann/Corbis; **p. 571,** Library of Congress; **p. 574,** Prints and Photographs Division, Schomburg Center for Research, the New York Public Library; **p. 576,** Library of Congress; **p. 577,** Bettmann/Corbis; **p. 578,** Used with Permission of Documenting the American South, The University of North Carolina at Chapel Hill Libraries; **p. 581,** Library of Congress; **p. 582,** © Atwater Kent Museum of Philadelphia/Courtesy of Historical Society of Pennsylvania Collection, The Bridgeman Art Library; **p. 583,** The Charleston Museum; **p. 586,** 2006 Harvard University, Peabody Museum Photo 35-5-10/53044T1874; **p. 587,** National Archives; **p. 588,** Library of Congress; **p. 590,** Library of Congress; **p. 593,** Granger Collection; **p. 595,** Library of Congress; **p. 595,** Library of Congress; **p. 596,** Granger Collection; **p. 596,** Library of Congress; **p. 598,** Granger Collection.

CHAPTER 16: **p. 602,** Granger Collection; **p. 606,** Library of Congress; **p. 607,** The Long Island Museum of American Art, History & Carriages, Stony Brook NY, Gift of Mr. and Mrs. Ward Melville, 1955; **p. 608,** Granger Collection; **p. 610,** Library of Congress; **p. 613,** Granger Collection; **p. 616,** Library of Congress; **p. 617,** Granger Collection; **p. 619,** Library of Congress; **p. 620,** Granger Collection; **p. 625,** GLC5116.19 Map: The Border Ruffian Code in Kansas 1856, The Gilder Lehermen Collection, courtesy of the Gilder Lehrman Institute of American History. Not to be reproduced without written permission; **p. 626,** Library of Congress; **p. 627,** The New York Public Library; **p. 631,** Library of Congress; **p. 636,** Granger Collection; **p. 637,** Library of Congress; **p. 639,** Library of Congress; **p. 641,** Granger Collection; **p. 644,** Granger Collection.

CHAPTER 17: **p. 648,** Library of Congress; **p. 650,** Library of Congress; **p. 653,** Medford Historical Society Collection/Corbis; **p. 654,** Bettmann/Corbis; **p. 658,** Bettmann/Corbis; **p. 659,** Granger Collection; **p. 664,** Bettmann/Corbis; **p. 668,** Bettmann/Corbis; **p. 670,** Library of Congress; **p. 671,** Library of Congress; **p. 671,** Library of Congress; **p. 673,** Bettmann/Corbis; **p. 674,** Bettmann/Corbis; **p. 675,** Library of Congress; **p. 677,** Library of Congress; **p. 679,** Granger Collection; **p. 681,** Library of Congress; **p. 683,** National Archives; **p. 684,** Library of Congress; **p. 687,** Library of Congress; **p. 689,** Bettmann/Corbis; **p. 690,** Corbis; **p. 691,** Massachusetts Commandery Military Order of the Loyal Legion and the U.S. Army Military History Institute; **p. 693** Bettmann/Corbis; **p. 694,** Library of Congress; **p. 698,** Library of Congress.

CHAPTER 18: **p. 702,** Library of Congress; **p. 704,** Library of Congress; **p. 705,** Library of Congress; **p. 706,** Library of Congress; **p. 709,** Bettmann/Corbis; **p. 710,** Library of Congress; **p. 712,** Library of Congress; **p. 713,** Library of Congress; **p. 714,** Library of Congress; **p. 718,** National Archives; **p. 721,** Granger Collection; **p. 722,** Bettmann/ Corbis; **p. 723,** Library of Congress; **p. 727,** Library of Congress; **p. 728,** Library of Congress; **p. 731,** Library of Congress; **p. 733,** Library of Congress; **p. 736,** Library of Congress.

INDEX

Page numbers in *italics* refer to illustrations.

Abenakis, 80–81, *103*
abolitionism, Thoreau and, 507–8, *507*
abolition movement, 523, 566, 592–99
    African Americans in, 595–97
    African colonization proposed in,
        592–93
    free press and, 597
    Fugitive Slave Act and, 615–16, 623
    Polk on, 551
    radicalization of, 593–94
    reactions to, 597–98
    split in, 594–95
    women in, 520–21, 594–95, *595*
Acadia, *see* Nova Scotia
Acomas, 531
Act for the Impartial Administration of
    Justice (1774), 208
Act of Settlement (1701), 56–57
Act of Union (1707), 57
Act to Prevent Frauds and Abuses (1696),
    167
Adams, Abigail, 263, 266, 335
    on Shays's Rebellion, 282–83
Adams, John, 254, 266, 267, 285, *331*,
    344, 361
    Alien and Sedition Acts signed by, 335
    in Boston Massacre case, 202
    committee work of, 271
    and Declaration of Independence,
        219, 221
    description of, 330–31
    domestic discontent and, 334–36
    in election of 1789, 303

in election of 1796, 330–31
in election of 1800, 338–41, *340*
foreign policy under, 331–34
French conflict and, 331–33
and French Revolution, 318
Jefferson's split with, 334–35
lame-duck appointments of, 339, 348
on peace commission, 253, *253*, 304
political philosophy of, 331
Revolution and, 207, 253, 254, 263
as vice-president, 303, 304
on women's rights, 263
Adams, John Quincy, 270, 355, 373, 390,
    393–94, *406*, 417, 439, 550
    abolitionism and, 597–98
    as congressman, 426
    in election of 1824, 403–4,
        405–6, *405*
    in election of 1828, 408–11,
        410, 478
    Indian lands and, 432
    on Mexican War, 555
    Monroe Doctrine and, 401–3
    named secretary of state, 390
    Oregon Country issue and, 401
    presidency of, 406–8
    Transcontinental Treaty (Adams-Onís
        Treaty) and, 394, 401
    on Tyler, 528
Adams, Samuel, *201*
    and Boston Tea Party, 207
    in Committee of Correspondence, 206
    in ratification debate, 294

Adams, Samuel (*continued*)
  as revolutionary agitator, 201–2, *201*,
    203, 206
  warned by Paul Revere, 213
Adena-Hopewell culture, 9–11
Admiralty courts, vice-admiralty courts,
    167, 193, 196, 200, 203
Africa:
  agriculture in, 122
  European exploration of, 17, 18
  slaves in, 121
  slaves in return to, 592–93
African Americans, 109, 115–16, *144*,
    344–45
  in abolition movement, 595–97
  African roots of, 121–23, 589
  in agriculture, 720
  in antebellum southern society,
    120–27, *126*, 581–82
  black code restrictions on, 711–12, 714
  in Boston Massacre, 202
  citizenship of, 288, 714
  Civil War attacks on, 659
  as Civil War soldiers, 672–74, *673*,
    674, 720
  in Congress, 724
  constitutional rights lacked by,
    287–88, 306
  in early U.S., 302
  education of, 721, 726
  first, 64
  folklore of, 589
  free blacks, 345, 353, 582, *583*
  as indentured servants, 121
  Irish Americans' animosity
    toward, 478
  land policy and, 705–6, 723, 724
  marriage of, 125, 590, 711, 720
  minstrel shows and, 474–75, *476*
  mulattoes, 579, 582
  music and, 125, *126*, 590
  population of, 121, 123, 302
  in Reconstruction, 705–6, 711–12,
    720–24, *723*
  as Reconstruction politicians, 719,
    722–24, *723*
  religion of, 125, 497, 589–90, 720, 727
  as Revolutionary War soldiers, 217,
    258, 260–61, 345

Underground Railroad and, 596
  voting rights for, 397, 710, 711, 713,
    716, 719, 722, *722*, 725, 728, 732
  see also civil rights and liberties; race
    riots; slavery; slaves; slave trade;
    voting rights, for African Americans
African Methodist Episcopal (AME)
    Church, 497
agriculture, 277, 278
  in Africa, 122
  African Americans and, 720
  in Alabama, 415, 451, 574
  biological exchange in, 22
  in colonial period, 57, 59, 110–11, *110*,
    117–18, 131–32, 134–35, 142
  in early nineteenth century, 384,
    451–52, 457–58
  in early U.S., 280, 302
  in Georgia, 451–52, 573, 574
  in Illinois, 574
  of Indians, 7, 10, 13, 81, 110–11, 531
  in Kentucky, 328–29, 573
  in Louisiana, 574
  in Maryland, 573
  in Mississippi, 415, 574
  in Missouri, 573
  in New England, 131–32
  in North Carolina, 573, 574
  in Pennsylvania, *327*
  plantations and, 577–79, 583–84
  in pre-Columbian cultures, 7, 10, 13
  in South, 573–75, 577–79, 591
  in South Carolina, 573, 574, 575
  in South Carolina colony, 118
  steamboats' influence on, 457–58
  technology of, 451–52, 453–54
  in Texas, 574
  in Virginia, 573
  in Virginia colony, 59
  in West, 450, 452–54, 574
Alabama, 174, 353, 452
  agriculture in, 415, 451, 574
  Indian conflicts in, 369
  migration to, 591
  secession of, 642
  slave trade in, 583
  Union Loyalists in, 724
  War of 1812 in, 369
Alamance, Battle of (1771), 205

Alamo, 546–47
Alaska, 34
Albany Congress (1754), 179
alcohol, consumption of, 323, 472
    in colonial period, 147
    in Old Southwest, 592
    Puritans on, 136
    temperance and, 516–17
Alcott, Bronson, 505
Alden, John, 69
Alexander I, czar of Russia, 373, 409
Alexander VI, Pope, 20
Algeria, 333
Algiers, 351, 375
Algonquians, 13, 64, *80*, 81, *88*, 95, 172
Alien Act (1798), 335–36, 337–38
Alien Enemies Act (1798), 336
Allen, Ethan, 214
Allen, Richard, 497
Alliance, Treaty of (1778), 242–43, 318,
    333, 334
American and Foreign Anti-Slavery
    Society, 595
American Anti-Slavery Society, 593–94,
    595, 598
American Association for the
    Advancement of Science, 464
American Bible Society, 499
American Colonization Society, 592–93
American Crisis, The (Paine), 235
American Indians, *see* Indians, American
American (Know-Nothing) party,
    481–82, *481*, 624, 629
American Philosophical Society, 150
American Revolution, 212–54
    African-American soldiers in, 217,
        258, 260–61, 345
    American society in, 237–39
    backcountry in, 237, 243, 250
    Boston Tea Party and, 206–7
    British strategies in, 239–41, 243,
        248–50
    British surrender in, 252–53
    causes of, 221–23
    as civil war, 236
    and Committees of Correspondence,
        206
    coup attempt in, 272
    events leading to, 192–212

finance and supply of, 239, 244, 272
first battles of, 212–14
France and, 218, 228, 239, 242–43, 245,
    251, 253–54
frontier in, 245–47, *246*
Hessians in, 218, 235, 237
independence issue in, 219–23, 232,
    266
Indians in, 217, 241–42, 245, 246–47,
    246, 264–65, 276
Loyalists in, 216, 217, 236–37, 239, 241,
    242, 243, 245, 247, 248–50, 260, 261
mercenaries in, 218
militias in, 211–12, 214–16, 234–36,
    237–38, *238*, 242, 248–50, 260
nationalism in, 191, 266–67
naval warfare in, 251
Patriot forces in, 212–18, 237–38,
    242, 243–44
peace efforts in, 216, 243, 253–54, *253*
political revolution and, 254–58
slavery and, 217, 222, 237, 258, 259–62,
    320, 321
social revolution and, 258–66
South in, 248–53, *249*
Spain and, 218, 242, 243, 253, 254
spreading conflict in, 211–12
summary of, 231–32
support for, 228
and Treaty of Paris (1783), 254, 255
women in, 262–64
"American Scholar, The" (Emerson), 506
American Society for the Promotion of
    Temperance, 517
American Sunday School Union, 499
American System, 388–89, 404–6, 527
American Temperance Union, 517
American Unitarian Association, 494
American Woman's Home, The
    (C. Beecher), *519*
Americas:
    Columbus's exploration of, 16–21
    diversity in, 3
    early European visions of, 14–16
    European biological exchange with,
        21–25
    European exploration of, 2
    first migrations to, 2, *6*
    imperial rivalries in, 3

Americas (*continued*)
  name of, 21
  Norse discovery of, 15–16, *15*
  pre-Columbian, 7–14
  professional explorers of, 25–26
Amherst, Jeffrey, 182
Amish, 41
Amity and Commerce, Treaty of (1778),
    242
Anabaptists, 41
anaconda strategy, 656–57
Anasazis, 9, 11–12, *12*
Anderson, Robert, 644, 649–50
André, John, 251
Andros, Edmund, 165–66
Anglican Church (Church of England),
    42–43, 52, 55, 56, 69, 153, 158,
    494–95
  Andros's support of, 166
  education and, 159
  Puritan views of, 72, 75, 137
  in South, 128–29
  state support of, 265–66
  see also Episcopal Church
animals, domesticated, 7, 22, 27, 574
Annapolis Convention (1786), 283
Anne, queen of England, 57, 167
Anthony, Susan B., 520, *520*
Antietam (Sharpsburg), Battle of (1862),
    666–68, 672
Antifederalists:
  and Bill of Rights, 294
  in ratification debate, 292, 294
Anti-Masonic party, 435, 440, 445
antislavery movement, *see* abolition
    movement
Apaches, 13, 38, 531, 532
Apalachees, *102*
"Appeal of the Independent Democrats,"
    621
Appleby, Joyce, 344–45
Appomattox, Va., surrender at, 697–98
apprentices, 133, 346, 482
Arapahoes, 39, 531
Arbella, 72–73
archaeology, 5
architecture:
  Aztec, 29, 31
  Georgian ("colonial"), 127–28

Jefferson and, 316
  in New England, 130–31, *130*
  in pre-Columbian cultures, 11, 13, 29
Arizona, 531
  Gadsden Purchase and, 619
  in Spanish Empire, 532, 533
Arkansas, 538
  Civil War fighting in, 652
  cotton in, 451
  military government of, 707
  secession of, 650
Arkansas Territory, 396
Army, U.S., 333, 384, 385
  in Constitution, 287
  after War of 1812, 375
  see also specific wars
Arnold, Benedict, 214, 216, 242, 251
Articles of Capitulation, 94
Articles of Confederation (1781),
    228–29, 257–58, 270, 272, 278, 286
  calls for revision of, 283
  debt under, 271–72
  finance under, 271–72
  unanimity required under, 292
arts:
  performing, 473–75
  romanticism in, 503–8
  see also architecture; literature
Asbury, Francis, 266, 497
Ashburton, Lord, *528*, 529–30
Ashley Cooper, Lord Anthony, 86
Asia:
  exploration and, 18–19, 25
  trade with, 17
  see also specific countries
assembly, freedom of, 305
Astor, John Jacob, 488
astronomy, Mayan, 7
asylums, 517–18
Atkins, Josiah, 260
Atlanta, Ga., capture of, 682, 692, 693, *694*
Atlanta Confederacy, 639
Attucks, Crispus, 202
Auburn Penitentiary, 518
Austin, Stephen F., 545
Austria, 34
  in colonial wars, 181
  French Revolution and, 317
  in Napoleonic wars, 360

Ayala, Felipe Guamán Poma de, *37*
Aztecs, 8–9, *23*, 27, 28–31, *29*, 34

backcountry, 142, 143, 145, 204–5
  in American Revolution, 237, 243, 250
  education in, 153
  and lack of organized government,
    204–5
  ratification debate and, 295
  religion in, 154
  underrepresentation of, 258–59
  Whiskey Rebellion in, 323–24, *324*
  see also frontier
Bacon, Nathaniel, 65, *65*
Bacon's Rebellion, 65–67, *65*
Bagot, Charles, 391
Balboa, Vasco Nuñez de, 26, *35*
Baltimore, Benedict Calvert,
    fourth Lord, 166
Baltimore, Cecilius Calvert, second Lord,
    67–68, 85
Baltimore, George Calvert, first Lord,
    67–68
Baltimore, Md., 470, 471
  War of 1812 in, 371
Baltimore Carpenters' Society, 482
Baltimore Republican, 445
banking industry:
  1837 runs on, 439
  state-chartered banks and, 395
Bank of North America, 271–72
Bank of the United States (national
    bank), 311–13, *311*, 375, 395, 404,
    443, 528
  Andrew Jackson and, 432–39, *434*,
    446–47
  constitutionality of, 312, 385–86,
    432–35, *434*
  expiration of first charter of, 366
  Hamilton's recommendation for, 309,
    311–13
  Jefferson's acceptance of, 350
  McCulloch v. Maryland and, 399–400
  and Panic of 1819, 395
  removal of government deposits from,
    436–37
  second charter of, 385–86, 388, 389, 390
  and speculative binge (1834), 437
  Tyler on, 527

Baptists, 41, 129, 139, 143, 156, 158, 159,
    264, 495, 496, 571, 720
  in revivals, 497
  in split over slavery, 599, 623
  in Whig party, 440
Barbados, 86
Barbary pirates, 351, 375
  see also privateers
barley, 22, 142
"Barnburners," 605
Barton, Clara, 675, *675*
Bartram, John, 150
Bates, Edward, 649
Battle-Pieces (Melville), 510
Bayard, James, 373
beans, 7, 22, 81, 110
Beard, Charles A., 293
Beauregard, Pierre G. T., 650, 655
Beecher, Catharine, 518–19, *519*, 594
Beecher, Henry Ward, 726–27
Beecher, Lyman, 481, 494, 499–500
Bell, John, 641, 642, *643*
Bennington, Battle of (1777), 242
Benton, Thomas Hart, 369, 386, 422–23,
    426, 433, 544, 550, 556, 603–4
Bering Strait, 5
Berkeley, John, 97–98
Berkeley, William, 64, 65–66, 85, 128
Berlin Decree (1806), 360, 363
Bermuda, 61, 83, 84
Bernard, Sir Francis, 196
Bethune, Mary Jane McLeod, 721
Bhagavad Gita, 505
Bibb, Henry, 595
Bible, 81, 137, 496, 499, 571, 599, 676
Biddle, Nicholas, 395, 432–34,
    436–37, 439
Bienville, Jean Baptiste le Moyne, sieur
    de, 174
Bill of Rights, English (1689), 56, 167
Bill of Rights, U.S., *261*
  debate on, 304–6
  in ratification of Constitution,
    294, 295
  states subject to, 714–15
bills of attainder, 292
bills (declarations) of rights, state, 256
Bingham, George Caleb, *328*, *435*, *534*
biological exchange, 21–25

Birney, James G., 598
birthrates, 111–13
black codes, 711–12, 714
Blackfoot Indians, 531
Black Hawk, Sauk and Fox chief, 429
Black Hawk, Sioux chief, 543
Black Hawk War (1832), 429
blacks, see African Americans
Blackwell, Elizabeth, 488
Blaine, James G., 735–36
Bleeding Kansas, 624–26
blood sports, 473, *473*
Board of Customs Commissioners, 200
Board of Trade (Lords of Trade and
    Plantations), 164–65
  functions of, 167
Bohemians, 143
Boleyn, Anne, 43
bonds, 679
Bonnie Prince Charlie (Charles Edward
    Stuart), 143
Book of Common Prayer, 43
Book of Mormon, 500
Boone, Daniel, 247, 327–29, 455
  background of, 327–28
Boonesborough, Ky., 328
  Revolutionary War fighting at, 247
Booth, John Wilkes, 696, 708–9
Border Ruffian Code in Kansas
    (1856), *625*
Boston, Mass.:
  antislavery demonstrations in, 623
  Boston Tea Party, 206–7
  class stratification in, 145, 146
  in colonial period, 73, 145, 146,
    147, *165*
  customs officials in, 165, 200
  disciplined by Parliament (1774), 208
  Great Awakening in, 158
  Irish Americans in, 477
  in nineteenth century, 470, 471
  poverty in, 147
  redcoats quartered in, 202
  siege of (1775–1776), 216
  tax protests in, 206–7
  Unitarianism in, 493–94
Boston English High School, 514
Boston Manufacturing Company, 466
Boston Massacre, 202–3, *203*

Boston Port Act (1774), *207,* 208, 209
Boston State House, *169*
Boston Tea Party, 206–7
Boudinot, Elias, *429*
Bowie, Jim, 546
boxing, 473, *473*
boycotts, 209, 210
Braddock, Edward, 180
Bradford, William, 69, 75, 81
Brady, Mathew, *698*
Bragg, Braxton, 688
Brandywine Creek, Battle of (1777), 241
Brant, Joseph (Thayendanegea),
    247, *247*
Brazil, *24,* 94, 121
Breckinridge, John C., 640, 641, 642,
    643, 695
Breed's Hill, Battle of (1775), 214–16, *215*
Bridger, Jim, 540
British Empire, 34, 120, 121
  colonization in, 38, 47–49
  French Empire compared with, 80,
    104, 113, 162, 171, 176
  maps of, *184, 185*
  Spanish Empire compared with,
    33–34, 57, 104, 113, 162, 170–71
  trade in, 36
  see also American Revolution; colonial
    period; Great Britain
British military:
  American criticism of, 191
  and emancipation, 260–61
  quartering of, 195
  as standing army, 195, 202
  see also American Revolution;
    War of 1812
British navy, 251, 360–61
Brook Farm, 523
Brooks, Preston S., 627, *627*
Brown, Frederick, 626
Brown, John, 628, 637–39, *637,* 640–41
  death of, 638–39
  Harper's Ferry raided by, 637–39
  Kansas violence led by, 625–26
Brown, Watson, 638
Brown, William Wells, 595
Brownson, Orestes, 505
Brown University (College of Rhode
    Island), 159, 514–15

Bruce, Blanche K., *723*, 724
bubonic plague, 24
Buchanan, James, 549, 553, 638
    Dred Scott decision and, 632
    in election of 1856, 629–30
    and election of 1860, 639–40
    in Kansas crisis, 632–33
    Lecompton constitution supported by,
        633
    after Lincoln's election, 643–44
    and Panic of 1857, 633–34
    secession and, 643–44
Buddha, 505
Buena Vista, Battle of (1847), 558, 604
buffalo, 13, 39–40, 531, *531, 532*
Buffalo, N.Y., 471
Bull Run (Manassas), first Battle of
    (1861), 655–56, *656*
Bull Run (Manassas), second Battle of
    (1861), 665
Bunker Hill, Battle of (1775),
    214–16, *215*
Burgoyne, John, 214, 239–42, *241*
burial mounds, 10–11
Burke, Edmund, 168
burned-over district, 499–500
Burns, Anthony, 623
Burnside, Ambrose E., 669, 684
Burr, Aaron, 356–57, 358–59, *359*
    in election of 1796, 330
    in election of 1800, 338–39, *340*
    Hamilton's duel with, 357, 358, 581
Burr conspiracy, 358–59
Burton, Mary, 124–25
Butler, Andrew Pickens, 627
Butler, Benjamin F., *718*
Byrd, Lucy Parke, 114
Byrd, William, II, 114, 128

Cabeza de Vaca, Álvar Núñez, *35*, 36
cabinet, British, 168, 192
cabinet, U.S., 304, 315, 316
Cabot, John, 26
Cadore, Duke de, 363
Cajuns, 180
calendar, Mayan, 7
Calhoun, Floride, 419
Calhoun, John C., 337, 366, 388, 390,
    402, *421*, 442, 631

    Andrew Jackson's rift with, 424–26
    in Compromise of 1850, 610–12
    Eaton Affair and, 419–20
    on economic growth, 451
    in election of 1824, 403–4, 406
    on independent Treasury, 442
    Indian conflicts and, 393
    internal improvements and, 420–21
    on Mexican War, 602
    national bank issue and, 386, 436
    nullification issue and, 408, 421–28
    on slavery, 599
    and slavery on frontier, 603–4
    tariff issue and, 407–8
    Texas annexation and, 548
    Van Buren's rivalry with, 418–19
    vice-presidency resigned by, 427
California, 36, 402, 535–38
    annexation of, 544–45, 551,
        556–57
    and Compromise of 1850,
        611–12, 615
    gold rush in (1848), 463, 532,
        540, 542, 606–9
    Indians in, 532
    Mexican independence and,
        536–37, 545
    Mexican War and, 551, 556–57,
        560, 561
    missions in, 535–36, *536*
    Polk and, 551
    settlers in, 533, 538, 539, 541
    slavery and, 609, 611–12, 615
    in Spanish Empire, 38, 535
    statehood for, 545, 609, 610,
        611–12, 615
California News, 607
California Trail, 538, *539*
Callender, James, 335
Calvert, Leonard, 117
Calvin, John, 41–42, 137
Calvinism, Calvinists, 41–42, 43, 77, 137,
    143, 151, 154, 158, 493, 495, 496,
    499, 505
Camden, S.C., Revolutionary War
    fighting at, 248
Cameron, Simon, 649
campaigns, *see* elections and campaigns
Camp Winfield Scott, *664*

Canada, 44
  in American Revolution, 216–17, 241
  British acquisition of, 182, 183–87
  in colonial wars, 182, 186–87
  Indian conflicts and, 322–23, 364–65
  Maine border with, 443, 530
  migration to, 476, 477
  Quebec Act and, 208, 259
  and War of 1812, 364, 366–69
canals, 456–57, 458–59, 459, 463, 464,
    465, 487
Canning, George, 402
Cape Verde, 18, 21
capitalism, Hamilton and, 308, 315, 316
Captain Clark and His Men Shooting
    Bears, 357
Caribs, 20, 44
Carnegie, Andrew, 680
carpetbaggers, 724, 734
Carroll, John, 266
Carson, Christopher "Kit," 544
Carter, Landon, 222
Carteret, George, 97–98
Cartier, Jacques, 44
Cartwright, Peter, 497
Cass, Lewis, 532, 604, 605–6
Catawbas, 88, 90, 103
Catherine of Aragon, 42
Catholicism, Catholic Church, 69,
    125, 571
  in Canada, 208
  in Democratic party, 440
  in England, 46, 52, 56, 67–68
  first U.S. bishop in, 266
  in French colonies, 172, 173–74
  German Americans in, 479
  Indians and, 32–33, 32, 33, 36–37, 171,
    532, 535–36
  Irish Americans in, 478–79
  James II and, 166
  missionaries of, 33, 36–37, 172,
    173–74, 176, 532, 535–36
  prejudice against, 478, 479, 480–82,
    481
  Reformation attacks on, 40–43
  in Spanish Empire, 32–33, 32, 33,
    36–37, 171, 183, 532
Catlin, George, 531
cattle, 22, 27, 110–11, 118, 131, 574, 683

Cavaliers, 56
Cayugas, 103, 247
Celia (slave), 586–87
Cession, Treaty of, 352–53
Chamberlain, Joshua, 698
Champlain, Samuel de, 44, 171–72, 172
Chancellorsville, Battle of (1863), 684,
    686, 689
Chandler, Zachariah, 680
Channing, William Ellery, 494, 521
Charles I, king of England, 55, 55, 67,
    72, 117
  execution of, 56, 85
Charles II, king of England, 56, 65,
    85, 86, 91, 92, 162
  colonial administration under,
    65, 164
  death of, 165
  France policy of, 176
Charleston, S.C.:
  in Civil War, 695, 704
  in colonial period, 86, 143, 145, 146
  founding of, 86
  in Revolutionary War, 217, 248
  and secession of South, 642, 649–50
Charlestown peninsula, Revolution War
    fighting at, 213
Charles V, king of Spain, 34, 42
Charles VII, king of France, 17–18
Chase, Salmon P., 649, 676, 719
Chattanooga, Battle of (1863), 688
Chauncey, Charles, 158
checks and balances, 286
Cherokee Nation v. Georgia, 431
Cherokee Phoenix, 429
Cherokees, 88, 89, 90, 91, 102, 182, 246,
    247, 302, 325
  in Civil War, 661
  government of, 429, 430–31
  lands ceded by, 276
  post-Revolutionary War weakness of,
    276
  removal of, 428–32, 431
  Tecumseh and, 364
Chesapeake, U.S.S., 361
Chesnut, Mary Boykin, 578–79, 578
Cheves, Langdon, 395
Cheyennes, 39, 531, 542
Chibchas, 9

Chicago, Ill., growth of, 471
Chicago Tribune, 696
Chickamauga, Battle of (1863), 688
Chickasaws, 88, 91, *102,* 302, 325
  in Civil War, 661
  removal of, 428
  Tecumseh and, 364
child labor, 469, 484
Chile, 32
China, 91
  American plants in, 22
  Forty-niners from, 608–9
  Protestant missionaries to, 618
  trade with, 278, 438, 463, 618
Chinese Americans, 480
Chinooks, 532
Chippewas, 322
Choctaws, 91, *102,* 302, 325
  in Civil War, 661
  removal of, 428–29
  Tecumseh and, 364
cholera, 24
Church of England, *see* Anglican Church
Church of Jesus Christ of Latter-day
  Saints (Mormons), 500–503, *501,*
  502, 609
  westward journey of, 501–3, *503*
Cincinnati, Ohio, *351,* 471
"circuit riders", Methodist, 497
cities and towns:
  amenities in, 464
  in colonial period, 145–48
  early factories in, 466–69, *466*
  employment in, 146
  industrialization as impetus to, 415,
    470–71
  in nineteenth century, 470–71,
    474, 475
  poverty in, 147
  recreation in, 472–75
  rise of, 17–18
  transportation between, 147, 470–71
Citizen Genet, 318–19
citizenship and naturalization:
  of African Americans, 289, 714
  Constitutional Convention and, 289
  of Indians, 289
"Civil Disobedience" (Thoreau), 507–8
civil liberties, *see* civil rights and liberties

Civil Rights Act (1866), 714
civil rights and liberties:
  in Civil War, 680–82
  in colonial period, 170, 196, 254–56
civil service reform, 732
Civil War, English (1642–1649), 84–85,
  98, 163
Civil War, U.S., 520, 648–99
  African Americans attacked in, 659
  African-American soldiers in, 672–74,
    673, 674, 720
  aftermath of, 702–6
  anaconda strategy in, 656–57
  balance of force in, 653–55
  bond sales in, 679
  calls for peace in, 680–81, 695
  casualties in, 567, 663, 673, 683,
    698–99
  choosing sides in, 650–52
  civil liberties and, 680–82
  compromise attempted before, 645
  Confederate command structure in,
    664–65, 685–86, 688
  Congress in, 645, 651, 669, 670, 674,
    678–79, 703
  destruction of landscape in, 683–84
  diplomacy and, 659–60
  Eastern campaigns in, *686*
  economy in, 653–54, 678–80
  emancipation in, 669–74
  environment and, 683
  financing of, 678–79
  government during, 678–84
  human resources in, 654
  Indians in, 661
  Lincoln's appraisal of, 696–97
  Mexican War and generals of, 561
  military advantages in, 654
  naval warfare in, 657
  outbreak of fighting in, 650
  peninsular campaign in, 663–65, *666*
  presidential transition and, 644–45,
    648, 649
  recruitment and draft in, 657–59, *658,*
    659, 672
  religion and, 676–78, *677*
  and secession of South, 642–43,
    650–52, *651*
  slavery and, 696

Civil War, U.S. (*continued*)
   southern blockade in, 654, 657
   strategies in, 655–57, 689
   technology in, 699
   as total war, 689, 693–95, 698–99
   Union command changes in, 663, 665,
      668, 684, 687, 688
   Union finances in, 678–79
   West in, 660–63, *662*
   women in, 674–76, 677
   see also Confederate States of America;
      Reconstruction
Clark, George Rogers, 245–46
Clark, William, 354–55, *354, 355,*
      356, 357
   journals of, 354, *354,* 355, *355*
Clarke, James Freeman, 505
Clay, Henry, 366, 373, 390, *397,* 407,
      420, 488
   African colonization and, 592
   American System of, 388–89, 404–6
   in Compromise of 1850, 610–11, 613
   in duel, 581
   economic nationalism and, 439–40,
      444, 527, 551
   in election of 1824, 403, *404, 405,* 409
   in election of 1832, 436
   in election of 1840, 445
   in election of 1844, 548–50, *549*
   and election of 1848, 605
   Missouri Compromise and, 397–98
   national bank debate and, 386, 433–34,
      436, 437
   nullification and, 426–28
   tariff policy of, 437, 528
   Tyler administration and, 527–29
Clermont, 456
Cleveland, Ohio, 471
Clinton, De Witt, 458
Clinton, George:
   in election of 1804, 357
   in election of 1808, 363
   in ratification debate, 294
Clinton, Henry, 214, 216, 217, 243, 245,
      248
clipper ships, 462–63, *462*
Coast Guard, U.S., 308
Cobbett, William, 516
Coercive (Intolerable) Acts (1774), 208–9

Cohens v. Virginia, 398
Colbert, Jean Baptiste, 173
Cold Harbor, Battle of (1864), 689
Cole, Thomas, *504*
Colfax, Schuyler, 730
colleges and universities, 514–16
   land-grant, 678, 703
   religious movements and, 158–59, 494,
      495–96
   women's, 515–16
   see also education
Colombia, 32
colonial governments:
   assemblies' powers in, 73, 169–70,
      209–11
   charters in, 72, 85, 137, 139, 163, 165,
      166, 168
   in Connecticut, 165, 168
   covenant theory in, 137
   in Delaware, 168
   and Dominion of New England, 165–66
   in Dutch colonies, 92–94
   English administration and, 163–68
   in Georgia, 100–104, 163, 167
   governors' powers in, 168–69, 170
   in Maryland, 67–68, 166, 168, 169
   in Massachusetts, 72–75, 85, 165, 166,
      168, 169
   in New Jersey, 165, 167
   in New York, 165, 166
   in North Carolina, 167
   in Pennsylvania, 100, 166–67, 168
   in Plymouth, 69–71
   in Rhode Island, 85, 137, 165, 168
   self-government developed in, 168–70
   in South Carolina, 86–87, 167, 169
   in Virginia, 62, 63–66, 169
colonial period:
   agriculture in, 57, 59, 117–18, 131–32,
      134–35, 142
   alcoholic abuse in, 147
   architecture in, 127–28, 130–31, *130*
   assemblies' powers in, 169–70
   backcountry in, 142, 143, 145
   birth and death rates in, 111–13
   British folkways in, 109
   cities in, 145–48
   civil liberties in, 170, 196, 254–56
   class stratification in, 146

colonial wars in, 176–87
currency shortage in, 134–36
disease in, 61, 113
education in, 152–53
employment in, 146
Enlightenment in, 149–53
ethnic mix in, 142–45
European settlement in, 57–79, *58*
indentured servants in, 62, 64, 65, 109,
    119–20, *120*
Indian conflicts in, 64–66, 81–84, *82,*
    89–91, 96, 182, 191, 193
land policy in, 118–19, 142
mercantile system in, 163–64
newspapers in, 148
population growth in, 111–13
postal service in, 147–48
religion in, 136–38, 143, 153–59
science in, 149–51
sex ratios in, 113
slavery in, 86, 87, 118, 120–227,
    126, 135
social and political order in, 146–47
society and economy in, 117–45, 346
taverns in, 147, *148*
taxation in, 166, 170, 192–202
trade and commerce in, 57, 59, 65, 66,
    80, 87–91, 104, 118–19, 132–36, *135,*
    138, 163–64, 172, 191
transportation in, 147
triangular trade in, 135, *135*
ways of life in, 108–61
westward expansion and, 193,
    327–29
witchcraft in, 139–41
colonial wars, 176–87
    French and Indian War, *see* French and
        Indian War
    with Indians, 64–66, 81–84, *82,* 84,
        89–91, 96, 182, 191, 193
    King George's War, 176
    King William's War, 176
Colorado Territory, 538, 660
Columbia, S.C., fall of, 695, 704
Columbia University (King's College), 159
Columbus, Christopher, 2, 7, 16, *19*
    background of, 19
    voyages of, 19–21, *20*
Comanches, 39, 531, 532

Command of the Army Act (1867),
    716, 718
commerce, *see* economy; trade and
    commerce
Committee of Correspondence, 206, 209
Committee of Safety (Boston), 212
common law, 53
Common Sense (Paine), 218, *234*
Commonwealth v. Hunt, 483
communications, 463–65
Compromise of 1790, 310–11, 316
Compromise of 1850, 610–18, *610, 614*
Compromise of 1877, 735–39, *736*
Conciliatory Resolution (1775), 211
Concord, Battle of (1775), 212–14, *212*
Confederate States of America:
    command structure of, 664–65
    constitution of, 642
    devastation in, 703–5
    diplomacy of, 659–60
    finances of, 680
    formation of, 642–43, 650–52
    industry in, 654
    navy of, 660
    politics in, 682–83
    recruitment in, 659
    states' rights in, 682
    Union Loyalists in, 652, 715, 724
    Union soldiers from, 652
    see also Civil War, U.S.
Confederation Congress, 257, 270–83
    accomplishments of, 271
    Articles of Confederation revision
        endorsed by, 284
    and development of the West, 272–77
    diplomacy and, 278–79
    end of, 295–96
    land policies of, 272–77
    Loyalist property and, 279
    paper currency issued by, 280–81
    powers of, 257, 270–71
    trade and commerce regulated by, 257,
        277–78
    weaknesses of, 279–81, 283, 308
Confiscation Act (1862), 670
Congregationalists, 72, 78, 137, 153, 154,
    157, 158, 159, *265,* 494, 495
    Presbyterians' union with, 496
    in Whig party, 440

Congress, Confederate, 680
Congress, U.S.:
  abolition and, 597–98
  African Americans in, 724
  Barbary pirates and, 375
  in Civil War, 645, 651, 669, 670, 674,
    678–79, 703
  commerce regulated by, 400–401
  in Constitution, 286, 288, 289–92
  currency policy of, 734–35
  education promoted by, 514
  and election of 1876, 737
  emancipation and, 669, 670
  executive departments established by,
    303–4
  first meeting of, 303
  Grant's relations with, 729
  independent Treasury voted by,
    442–43
  Indian policy and, 428
  internal improvements and, 388,
    390, 463
  Johnson's conflict with, 713–14
  Johnson's impeachment and, 718–19
  land policy and, 326, 453, 528
  Mexican War and, 554
  Napoleonic Wars and, 363
  national bank issue in, 311, 312,
    385–86, 399–400, 434–35
  railroads and, 620
  in Reconstruction, 706, 707–8, 711–17,
    719, 732, 735
  slavery issue and, 603, 609, 631–32,
    633, 674
  and suspension of habeas corpus, 681
  tariff policy of, 426–28
  taxation power of, 287, 288
  Texas annexation and, 548
  trade policy of, 363, 392
  Tyler's conflicts with, 528
  and War of 1812, 363, 364, 366
  West Virginia admitted to
    Union by, 651
  see also House of Representatives, U.S.;
    Senate, U.S.
Connecticut:
  Constitution ratified by, 295
  at Hartford Convention, 374
  Revolutionary War troops from, 214

slave trade halted by, 259
  voting rights in, 411
Connecticut Anti-Slavery Society, 594
Connecticut colony, 204
  charter of, 85, 168
  European settlement of, 78
  government of, 165, 168
  Indian conflicts in, 81–84, 82
  in land disputes, 209
Connecticut (Great) Compromise, 287
conquistadores, 28
Conspiracy of 1741, 123–25
Constantinople, 15
Constellation, U.S.S., 333
Constitution, Confederate, 676
Constitution, U.S., 284–97, 300–301, 375
  Congress in, 286, 288, 289–92
  foreign policy in, 290
  habeas corpus in, 681
  implied powers and, 312–13,
    352–53, 399
  internal improvements and, 420–21
  judicial review principle and, 349
  Louisiana Purchase and, 352–53
  Mormons and, 501
  motivation of advocates of, 293
  national bank issue and, 312–13,
    385–86, 432–33, 434
  nullification issue and, 422
  presidency in, 289–92
  ratification of, 292–97, 296, 305
  Reconstruction and, 707–8, 710,
    713–14
  and separation of powers, 289–92
  slavery in, 287–88, 350–51
  state-compact theory of, 337, 424
  strict construction of, 353, 358, 359,
    404, 527
  treason in, 359
  see also Constitutional Convention
Constitution, U.S.S., 333
constitutional amendments, U.S.:
  Eighteenth, 292
  Fifteenth, 567, 719, 722, 739
  Fifth, 603, 631
  First, 306, 598
  Fourteenth, 567, 714–15, 716, 717, 739
  Ninth, 306
  Tenth, 292, 306, 312

Thirteenth, 288, 645, 674, 702, 711, 739
Twelfth, 357
Constitutional Convention (1787), 229,
  284–92, *284, 291*
  call for, 283
  delegates to, 284–86
  Madison at, 285–86, *285,* 290, 293
  political philosophy of, 286
  representation issue in, 287, 289–90
  separation of powers issue in, 289–92
  slavery issue in, 287–88, 289, 297
  trade and commerce issue in, 287
  women's rights ignored in, 288–89
Constitutional Union party, 641
constitutions:
  British, 53, 55
  state, 256, 258, 261, 266, 289, 715, 725
  see also Constitution, U.S.
Continental army, 237–38
  desertions from, 238, 244
  recruitment to, 238, 239
  supply problems of, 239, 244
  winter quarters of, 239, 241, 243–44, *244*
  see also American Revolution
Continental Association, 209–10
Continental Congress, First, 248
  call for, 209–11
  plan of union considered by, 209
Continental Congress, Second, 214, *220,*
  232, 239, 245
  extralegal nature of, 257
  governmental functions taken by, 217
  independence voted by, 219, *219,* 266
  and Indian rights, 264
  peace efforts and, 216, 243, 253, 254
  supply problems and, 245, 271–72
Continental Divide, *539*
"Continental System," 360
Contract Labor Act (1864), 678
contract rights, 398–99
contract theory of government,
  167, 221, 256
Convention of 1800, 334
Convention of 1818, 391–92, *391,* 534
Cooke, Jay, 679, 734
Copernicus, Nicolaus, 149
Copperheads, 681
Corbin, Margaret, 262
Corey, Giles, 141

corn (maize), 7, 11, 13, 22, 70, 81, 110,
  329, 574
Cornwallis, Lord, 217, 241, 248–53, *252*
Coronado, Francisco Vásquez de, *35, 36*
corporations, business:
  in Europe, 17, 54
  as "persons" in judicial reasoning, 715
  see also industry; *specific corporations*
Corps of Discovery, 354–55
Cortés, Hernán, 27–28, *28,* 31, *35*
cotton, 302, 345, 384, 394, 414–15,
  451–52, 570, 571, *572,* 573–74, *573*
  British trade in, 362, 421, 438, 566,
  574, 577
  in Civil War, 657, 704
  French trade in, 421, 438, 574
  in Panic of 1857, 634
  see also textile industry
cotton gin, *451,* 452
Council for New England, 79
Council of the Indies, 34
courts, *see* Admiralty courts, vice
  admiralty courts; legal system;
  Supreme Court, U.S.
covenant theory, 137
cowboys, *736*
Cowpens, Battle of (1781), 250
Crawford, William H., 390, 403–4, *405,*
  406, 441
Crédit Mobilier, 730
Creeks, 88, 90, 91, *102,* 277, 302,
  325, 393
  Andrew Jackson's campaign
  against, 369
  in Civil War, 661
  removal of, 428–29, 432
  Tecumseh and, 364
Creole incident (1841), 529
crime:
  in colonial period, 146–47
  immigration and, 119
Critique of Pure Reason (Kant), 504
Crittenden, John J., 645
Crockett, Davy, 546
Cromwell, Oliver, 56, 84–85, 163
Crown Point, Battle of (1775), 214
Crows, 543
cruel and unusual punishment, 56, 306
Cruikshank, Robert, *415*

Cuba, 26, 28, 183, 402
  Columbus in, 19
  Ostend Manifesto and, 618
Cudahy, Michael, 477
Cudahy Packing Company, 477
culture, U.S.:
  emergence of, 266–67
  in nineteenth century, 472–75
  see also arts; popular culture
Cumberland Gap, 328
Cumberland (National) Road, *387,* 388,
    390, 420–21, 456
Cumberland Road Bill, 390
currency:
  in American Revolution, 239, 272
  in Civil War, 679, *679*
  after Civil War, 729
  in colonial period, 134–36, 195
  Constitution and, 293
  in early U.S., 279, 280–81, 311–12
  gold, 734–35
  greenbacks and, 679, *679,* 729, 734–35
  national bank issue and, 432, 433, 437
  shortage of, 134–36, 279, 280–81
  in War of 1812, 385
Currency Act (1764), 194–95, 203
customs, 194, 308
Cutler, Manasseh, 276

Dakota Territory, 660
*Daniel Boone Escorting Soldiers through
    the Cumberland Gap* (Bingham), *328*
Danish colonists, 143
Dare, Elinor, 48
Dare, Virginia, 48
Dartmouth College, 159, 398–99
Dartmouth College v. Woodward, 398–99
Daughters of Liberty, 200, 210
Davenport, James, 157
Davis, Henry Winter, 707
Davis, Jefferson, 620, 676
  in Black Hawk War, 429
  capture of, 697
  Civil War strategy of, 657
  and Compromise of 1850, 610, 611
  as Confederate president, 642, 682–83
  in duel, 581
  enlistment efforts and, 658
  and first Battle of Bull Run, 655–56

Fort Sumter and, 650
  Lee's relationship with, 665
  in Mexican War, 558
  stubbornness of, 683, 695–96
Dawes, William, 212–13
Day, Henry, 485
Dearborn, Henry, 367–69
death rates, in colonial period, 111–13
debt:
  after American Revolution, 279,
    280–81, 319–21
  for Confederate cause, 711, 715
  and issuance of paper currency, 280–81
  Shays's Rebellion and, 281–82
  state, federal assumption of, 308–9,
    310, 314, 316
debt, national:
  Andrew Jackson on, 436
  under Articles of Confederation,
    271–72
  after Civil War, 728, 729
  in early U.S., 308–10, 314, 316, 326
  gold vs. greenbacks in repayment
    of, 729
  in Jefferson administration, 350
debtors, imprisonment of, 484
Decatur, Stephen, 351, 375
Declaration of American Rights
    (1774), 209
Declaration of Independence (1776),
    219–23, *219, 220,* 302, 492
  Independence Day and, 266
  sources of, 220–21
Declaration of Rights, Virginia (1776),
    220, 265, 285, 305
Declaration of Sentiments (1848), 520
Declaration of the Causes and Necessity
    of Taking Up Arms (1775), 216
Declaration of the Causes of Secession
    (South Carolina) (1860), 642
Declaration of the Rights and Grievances
    of the Colonies (1765), 198
Declaratory Act (1766), 199
Deere, John, 453
deficits, federal, *see* debt, national
deism, 149, 151, 154, 493
Delaware:
  Constitution ratified by, 295, *295*
  in early interstate cooperation, 283

secession rejected by, 651
voting rights in, 258, 411
Delaware, Thomas West, Lord, 59, 62
Delaware and Hudson Canal, 459
Delaware colony, 86, 100
European settlement of, 86, 109
government of, 168
Delawares, *103*, 142, 182, 193, 247
Democratic party, 317
"Barnburners" in, 605
in Civil War, 669, 680, 682
in election of 1832, 436
in election of 1836, 439–40
in election of 1840, 443–45, *444*
in election of 1844, 548–50
in election of 1848, 603–4
in election of 1852, 617
in election of 1856, 629–30
in election of 1860, 639–40
in election of 1864, 682
in election of 1868, 728
in election of 1874, 735
in election of 1876, 735–39
in formation of Republican party, 624
in formation of Whigs, 439
Free Soil party and, 605–6
independent Treasury and, 442–43
Irish Americans in, 440, 478
in Kansas-Nebraska crisis, 624
labor and, 484
origins of, 407
in Reconstruction South, 733–34
slavery issue in, 551, 624, 639–40
in South, 579
Democratic-Republicans, 407
see also Democratic party
Deseret, 502, 609
de Soto, Hernando, *35, 36*
Detroit, Mich., 471
Dial, 505
Dias, Bartholomeu, 18
Dickinson, Emily, 509, *509,* 676
Dickinson, John, 200–201, 216, 257
diphtheria, 24, 113
discovery and exploration, 14–38
of Africa, 17, 18
biological exchange from, 21–25
Dutch, *45*
English, *45,* 47–49

French, 44, *45,* 171–76
Norse, 15–16, *15*
Spanish, 19–21, *25,* 26, 33–38, *35*
technology in, 16–17
see also Columbus, Christopher
disease:
on Atlantic crossing, 476, *477*
in Civil War, 683
in colonial era, 61, 113
Indian susceptibility to, 14, 23–25, *23, 24,* 31, 32–33, 81, 88, 95, 96–97
Overland Trail and, 541
among poor southern whites, 580
in Southwest frontier, 591
distillation, 323
Distribution Act (1836), 437, 438
District of Columbia, *see* Washington, D.C.
divine right of kings, 55, 167
divorce, 262
Dix, Dorothea Lynde, 518, 675
Dominican Republic, 20
Dominion of New England, 165–66
Donner, George, 543–44
Donner party, 543–44
Doolittle, Amos, *213*
Douglas, Stephen A., 463, *620,* 629, 633, 634–37
and Compromise of 1850, 610, 614
death of, 680
in election of 1860, 639–40, 641–42, *643*
Kansas-Nebraska issue and, 620–24, *620*
Lecompton constitution and, 633, 635
Lincoln's debates with, 635–37, *636*
popular sovereignty supported by, 604
Douglass, Frederick, 590, 595–96, *596,* 697, *723*
draft:
in Civil War, 658–59, *658, 659*
in colonies, 84
Drake, Francis, 44
Dred Scott v. Sandford, 630–32, 634, 636, 640
drugs, from Americas, 23
Du Bois, W. E. B., *261*
duels, 581, *581*
"due-process clause," 715

Dunmore, John Murray, Lord, 260
Durand, John, *146*
Dutch Americans, 98, 142, 143, *144,*
    145, 153
Dutch East India Company, 91
Dutch Empire, 38–40, 84, 91–95
Dutch Reformed Church, 42, 142,
    153, 159
Dutch Republic, 44, 176
Dutch West India Company, 92, 94
Dwight, Timothy, 495
dysentery, 113

Eastern Woodlands Indians, 12–13
East India Company, 206
Eaton, John, 419–20
Eaton, Peggy, 419–20
Eaton Affair, 419–20, *419*
Economic Interpretation of the
    Constitution, An (Beard), 293
economy:
    agriculture and, 415–16
    American System and, 388–89
    in antebellum South, 575–76
    in Civil War, 653–54, 678–80
    in early nineteenth century, 374,
        383–88, 414–16, 436–37, 438–39,
        450–71
    in early U.S., 271–72, 279–81, 307–15
    Hamilton's views on, 307–15
    in Jacksonian era, 414–16, 436–37,
        438–39
    in laissez-faire policies, 446–47
    of North vs. South, 566
    and Panic of 1819, 394–95
    of South, 575–76
    transportation improvements and,
        455–63
    under Van Buren, 442–43
    after War of 1812, 374, 383–88
    of West, 526–27
    see also agriculture; banking industry;
        corporations, business; currency;
        debt; industry; manufactures; tariffs
        and duties; trade and commerce;
        specific panics and depressions
education:
    of African Americans, 721, 726
    in backcountry, 153

    in colonial period, 128, 152–53
    federal aid to, 274, 678, 703
    higher, 514–16
    in nineteenth century, 512–16,
        721, 726
    private, 514
    public, 484, 486, 513–14
    in Reconstruction, 721, 726
    religion and, 158–59, 514
    social reform and, 500, 512–16
    technical, 514–15
    township support of, 274
    women and, 487–88, 515–16, *515,* 519
    see also colleges and universities
Edwards, Jonathan, 154–58, 267, 495
Edward VI, king of England, 43
Eighteenth Amendment, 292
elections and campaigns:
    of 1789, 303
    of 1792, 317
    of 1796, 330–31
    of 1800, 229, 338–41, *340,* 348
    of 1804, 348, 357
    of 1808, *362,* 363
    of 1816, 389
    of 1820, 403
    of 1824, 403–6, 440, 441
    of 1828, 408–11, *409, 410,* 422, 441
    of 1832, 426, 433–34, 435–36
    of 1836, 439–40
    of 1840, 443–45, *443, 444,* 527, 598
    of 1844, 548–51, *549,* 598
    of 1848, 604–5
    of 1852, 617–18
    of 1854, 481
    of 1856, 628–30, *628*
    of 1858, 635–37
    of 1860, 566, 639–42, *641*
    of 1864, 682, 709
    of 1868, 719, 727–29
    of 1872, 732–33
    of 1874, 735
    of 1876, 735–39, *738*
    congressional mechanisms for, 289–90
    fraud and intimidation in, 732
    nomination process in, 403–4
    platforms introduced into, 435–36
    precinct-level organization in, 445–46
electoral college, in Constitution, 290–91

see also elections and campaigns
Electoral Commission, 737
electrical motors, 464
Eliot, John, 83
Elizabeth I, queen of England, 43, *43*, 44,
    46–47, 49, 52, 54, 55, 57, 69
emancipation, 669–74
  in Civil War, 669–74
  early proposals for, 592–93
  freedmen's plight after, 705–6, *705*
  in Revolutionary War, 260–61
  southern economy and, 704
Emancipation Proclamation (1863),
    668–69, *671*, 672, *712*
Embargo Act (1807), 361–63, 466
Emerson, Ralph Waldo, 380, 381, 505–7,
    506, 508, 510, 521
  on Brooks's attack on Sumner, 628
  on Fugitive Slave Act, 616
  on John Brown, 639
  lectures of, 506
  on Mexican War, 602
employment, *see* labor, employment
Empress of China, 278
enclosure movement, 54
encomenderos, 32, 37
encomiendas, 32, 33
Enforcement Acts (1870–1871), 732
engineering, 487
England:
  background on, 52–57
  Catholics in, 46, 52, 56, 67–68
  colonial administration under, 101–5,
      162, 163–68, 192–200, 202
  constitution of, 53, 55
  explorations by, 26, *45*, 47–49
  government of, *see* Parliament,
      British
  landownership in, 54
  liberties in, 53
  monarchy of, 54–57, 162
  nobles in, 53, 54
  population explosion in, 54
  privateers from, 44, 46, 86
  Reformation in, 42–43
  Scotland joined with, 57
  Spanish Armada defeated by, 46–47, *46*
  taxation in, 53, 55, 56, 193
  traders from, 36

after Wars of the Roses, 18
  see also Anglican Church; Great Britain
English Civil War (1642–1649), 84–85,
    98, 163
English language:
  African influence in, 125
  Dutch influence in, 94
Enlightenment, 149–53, 493, 503
environment:
  Civil War and, 683–84
  European attitude toward, 110–11
  Great Plains and, 541–42
  industrialization and, 469–70, *471*
  introduced species and, 110–11
  pollution and, 469
Episcopal Church, 265–66, 495
equality:
  American Revolution and,
      258–59, *259*
  Jacksonian era and, 416, 488
  racial, 636–37
"equal protection clause," 715
Era of Good Feelings, 390, 392
Erie Canal, 458–59, *459*
Eries, 96, *102*
Eriksson, Leif, 16
Erik the Red, 15–16
Erskine, David, 363
Essay Concerning Human Understanding
    (Locke), 150
Essex Junto, 356
Ethiopian Regiment, 260
Europe:
  American biological exchange with,
      21–25
  expansion of, 16–18
evangelism, evangelists, 153, 155,
    496–500
executive branch, 303–4
  see also presidency
exploration, *see* discovery and
    exploration
ex post facto laws, 292

factory system, 346
Fair Oaks (Seven Pines), Battle
    of (1862), 664
Fallen Timbers, Battle of (1794), 322
Fall River (Rhode Island) system, 469

families:
    in colonial period, 113
    and life on trail, 541
    slave, 590–91, *590*
    see also marriage
"family slavery," 123
farmers, *see* agriculture
Farragut, David, 657, 682
Federal Highways Act (1916), 388
Federalist, The (Hamilton, Madison and
        Jay), 293–94, 304
Federalists, 229, 283, 334, *335*, 390
    Alien and Sedition Acts of, 335–36
    and army authorization of 1798, 334
    and *Dartmouth College v. Woodward*,
        398–99
    decline of, 358
    in election of 1796, 330–31
    in election of 1800, 338–41
    in election of 1808, 363
    in election of 1816, 389
    in election of 1824, 403
    Essex Junto in, 356
    French Revolution and, 319
    Jay's Treaty and, 321
    land policy of, 326
    Louisiana Purchase as seen by, 353
    military spending of, 350
    Napoleonic wars and, 362, 363
    national bank and, 386
    officeholder conflicts and, 348
    in ratification debate, 292, 294
    Republican opposition to, 315–17
    Republicans' role reversal with,
        375, 385
    and War of 1812, 374, 375
Feke, Robert, *151*
Ferdinand II, king of Aragon, 18–19, 21
Ferguson, Patrick, 248–50
feudalism, 92
    English, 54
Fifteenth Amendment, 567, 719, *722*, 739
Fifth Amendment, 603, 631
Fillmore, Millard, *613*, 617, 619, *662*
    and Compromise of 1850, 613–15
    in election of 1856, 629
Finance Department, U.S., 271
Finney, Charles Grandison, 499–500, 522
Finnish settlers, 98, 142

firearms, right to bear, 305
"First, Second, and Last Scene of
        Mortality, The" (Punderson), *116*
First African Church, *721*
First Amendment, 306, 598
Fish, Hamilton, 729
fishing, 13
    in New England, *131*, 132, 134, 138,
        469–70
Fisk, Jim, 730
Fitzhugh, George, 599
Fletcher, John, 222
Fletcher v. Peck, 398
Florida, 38, 101, 277, 319, 358, 359
    acquisition of, 392–94
    after American Revolution, 254
    British colonies established in, 193
    Civil War in, 657
    in colonial wars, 183, 186
    in election of 1876, 737
    exploration of, 34–36
    Huguenots in, 36
    Louisiana Purchase and, 352–53
    Reconstruction in, 724, 734
    secession of, 642
    Seminoles in, 429, 432
    Spanish exploration and colonization
        of, 34–36, 89, 90, 532
    statehood for, 394
    and War of 1812, 364, 371
Floyd, John, 436
Flying Cloud, 463
folklore, African-American, 589
food:
    in colonial period, 131, 132
    of slaves, 584
    technology and, 464, 477
Foot, Samuel A., 422
Foot Resolution, 422–24
force bill (1833), 427, 436
Foreign Affairs Department, U.S., 271
forfeited-rights theory, 713
Fort Detroit, *320*
Fort Donelson, 661
Fort Duquesne (Pittsburgh, Pa.), 178,
        181, 186
Fort Henry, 661
Fort Jackson, Treaty of (1814), 369
Fort Laramie Treaty (1851), 543, *543*

Fort Le Boeuf, 178
Fort Louisbourg, attack on, 182
Fort McHenry, 371
Fort Necessity, 178
Fort Pickens, 644
Fort Pitt, 186
Fort Sacramento, *537*
Fort Stanwix, Battle of (1777), 242
Fort Stanwix, Treaty of (1784), 276
Fort Sumter, 644–45
    fall of (1861), 649–50, *650*
Fort Ticonderoga, Battle of (1775), 214
Fort Ticonderoga, Battle of (1777), 242
Fort Wagner, 673
Forty-niners (gold miners), 606–9, *608*
Foster, Stephen, 474
Fourteenth Amendment, 567, 714–15,
    716, 717, 739
Fox, George, 98
Foxes, *102*, 429
France, 134, 359
    American Revolution and, 218, 228,
      239, 242–43, 245, 251, 253–54, 309
    California and, 545
    Citizen Genet and, 318–19
    in colonial wars, 176–87, 190, 191
    explorations of, 44, *45*, 171–76
    after Hundred Years' War, 17–18
    late eighteenth-century conflict with,
      331–33, *332*, 335, *335*
    Louisiana purchased from, 352–53,
      396–97
    Monroe Doctrine and, 402
    in Napoleonic Wars, 360–64, *361*,
      401–2, 532
    navy of, 251
    privateers from, 44, 320
    Revolution in, 317–19
    Texas Republic recognized by, 548
    traders from, 36
    U.S. Civil War and, 659, 672
    U.S. trade with, 307, 360–64, *361*, 363,
      421, 438, 574
    see also French Empire
Franciscans, 33, 36, 38, 535–36
Franklin, Battle of (1864), 693
Franklin, Benjamin, 118, 120, 138–39,
    148, 150–51, *151*, 155, *180*, 187, 218,
    236, 336

    at Albany Congress, 179–80
    Boston Tea Party condemned by, 207
    on British in Philadelphia, 241
    on Constitution, 296–97
    at Constitutional Convention, 285
    and Declaration of Independence,
      219, 221
    as deist, 493
    Paxton Boys and, 205
    on peace commission, *235*, 253, 304
    Plan of Union of, 179–80
    on population growth, 111
    as postmaster-general, 217
Franklin, William, 236
Franklin, William Temple, *253*
Freake, Elizabeth, *112*
Freake, John, *112*
Freake, Mary, *112*
Fredericksburg, Battle of (1862),
    668–69, 684
free blacks, 592
Freedmen's Bureau, U.S., 706, *706*,
    713–14, 720
freedom of assembly, 305
freedom of petition, 256
freedom of speech, 256, 305, 336
freedom of the press, 336
    abolitionism and, 597
    in Bill of Rights, 305
    in colonial period, 148
Freeman, Elizabeth "Mum Bett," *261*
Freeport Doctrine, 636
Free Soil party, 605–6, *606*, 617, 624, 629
Free State Hotel, 625, *626*
Frémont, John Charles, 544, *544*, 629
    in election of 1856, 629
    Mexican War and, 556–58
French Americans, 143, *144*, 145, 336
    in Civil War, 658
French and Indian War (Seven Years'
    War) (1754–1763), 176–83,
    179, *183*
    American soldiers in, 191
    legacy of, 191–92
French Empire, 34, 84, 92, 121
    British Empire compared with, 80,
      104, 162, 171, 176
    colonization in, 36, 44
    fur trade in, 80, 92, 172, 176

French Empire (*continued*)
   in Indian conflicts, 89, 96–97, *172*
   Indian relations with, 80, 171–73, 176
   maps of, *175, 184, 185*
   missionaries in, 172, 173–74, 176
   religious restrictions in, 172
   trade in, 36, 172, 176
   see also France
French Revolution, 317–19
frontier, 526–27
   American Revolution and, 245–47
   in Civil War period, 660–63
   in colonial period, 143, 145
   in early nineteenth century, 450
   in early U.S., 322–23
   internal improvements and, 387–88
   in Jefferson administration, 350
   manifest destiny and, 380, 530, 550, 554
   mountain men and, 534
   Northwest Ordinance and, 274–77
   Overland Trail and, 539–42, *541*
   religious revivals on, 496–99
   slavery in, 603–6
   southern, 591–92
   statehood procedures for, 274
   transportation links to, 455–62
   and War of 1812, 364–66
   westward expansion and, 193, 259,
      272–77, 302, 326–29, 344–45, 350,
      352–53, 530–45
   Wilderness Road and, 327–29
   see also backcountry; West
Fugitive Slave Act (1850), 615–16
   protests against, 623
fugitive slave laws, 610, 612, 615–16, *616*,
   623, 629
Fuller, Margaret, 505
Fulton, Robert, 400, *400*, 456
Fundamental Constitutions
   of Carolina, 86
Fundamental Orders of Connecticut
   (1639), 78, 137
fur trade, 142, 471
   Dutch, 80, 92, 95–96
   French, 80, 92, 172, 176
   mountain men and, 533–34
   rendezvous system in, 533–34
Fur Traders Descending the Missouri, 1845
   (Bingham), *534*

Gadsden Purchase, 561, 619, 620, *621*
Gage, Thomas, 208, 212, 239
Gallatin, Albert, 348, 350, 366, 373
Gandhi, Mahatma K., 508
Garfield, James A., *513*, 730, 737, 738
Garfield, Lucretia Randolph, *513*
Garrison, William Lloyd, 288, 521, 555,
   593–95, *593*, 623
Gaspee, 205–6, 207
Gates, Horatio, 242, 248
Gates, Thomas, 59–62
General Assembly of Virginia, 63–64
General Court, Connecticut, 78
General Court, Massachusetts,
   73, 75, 77
Genet, Edmond-Charles-Édouard,
   318–19
Geneva Medical College, 488
gentry, in southern colonies,
   127–28, *128*
geography, Renaissance, 16
George I, king of England, 167
George II, king of England, 100, 167
   death of, 183
George III, king of England, 192,
   192, 248
   accession of, 183, 190
   on Boston Tea Party, 207
   on colonial rebellion, 210
   mercenaries recruited by, 218
   ministerial changes of, 198, 202
   Paine on, 218
   peace efforts and, 216, 243
Georgia, 345
   African-American soldiers outlawed
      by, 260
   agriculture in, 451–52, 573, 574
   Civil War fighting in, 657, 688,
      691–95, *694*
   Confederacy and states' rights
      in, 682
   Constitution ratified by, 295, *295*
   Indian conflicts in, 277, 369
   Indians removed from, 429–32, *431*
   land claims of, *273*, 276
   paper currency in, 281
   Reconstruction in, 719, 734
   secession of, 642
   slave trade in, 259

Union Loyalists in, 724
voting rights in, 258, 410
Georgia colony:
  backcountry of, 143, 145
  ethnic groups in, 101
  European settlement of, 100–104
  government of, 100–104, 163, 167
  Indians in, 89, 100
  slaves in, 123
German Americans, 98, 100, 101, 119,
  142–43, *144,* 145, 380, 475, 476,
  479–80, 488, 580
  in Civil War, 658
  in Democratic party, 440
  prejudice against, 480
German Reformed Church, 42
German states, Reformation in, 41
Germantown, Battle of (1777), 241
Gerry, Elbridge:
  at Constitutional Convention, 285, 289
  in ratification debate, 294
  XYZ affair and, 333
Gettysburg, Battle of (1863), 685–88, *687*
Gettysburg Address (1863), 688
Ghent, Treaty of (1814), 372–73, 374, 391
Gibbons, Thomas, 400–401
Gibbons v. Ogden, 400–401
Gilbert, Humphrey, 47
global warming, 7
Glorious Revolution, 56, 163, 166–67,
  176, 192, 195
Godwin, Abraham, *314*
gold:
  currency and, 734–35
  in Georgia, 431, *431*
  in mercantile system, 163–64
  national debt repayments in, 728, 729
  paper currency redeemable in,
    734–35
  Spanish Empire and, 20, 34, 36, 37, 38,
    170, 171
gold miners (Forty-niners), 606–9, *608*
gold rushes, 660
  California (1848), 463, 532, 540, 542,
    606–9
Gone With the Wind, 569
Good, Sarah, 140
Goodyear, Charles, 464
Gorges, Ferdinando, 79

Gosiutes, 532
Gould, Jay, 730
government:
  of Cherokees, 429, 430–31
  in Civil War, 678–84, 707–8
  contract theory of, 167, 221, 256
  of early U.S., 303–4
  English, 53, 56, 162, 167, 191–92,
    254, 255
  implied constitutional powers of, 399
  in Iroquois League, 95–97
  Locke on, 167
  new state constitutions and, 256
  post-Revolutionary War debates on,
    254–56
  in Reconstruction South, 707–8,
    715–17
  representative (republican) form of,
    254–56
  separation of powers in, 289–92
  transportation and, 463
Graduation Act (1854), 453
Grant, Ulysses S., 652, 661, 682, *689,*
  719, *728*
  background of, 561
  at Chattanooga, 688
  early cabinet appointments of, 729
  economic policy of, 729, 734–35
  in election of 1868, 727–29
  in election of 1872, 732–33
  Lee pursued by, 689–91
  Lee's surrender to, 698
  in post-Civil War army, 716, 718
  scandals under, 730–31
  at Shiloh, 661–63
  at Vicksburg, 684–85
Grasse, Admiral de, 252
Graves, Billy, 543
gravitation, 149
Gray, Thomas, 588
Great Awakening, 153–59, 493
Great Awakening, Second, 494–503
Great Britain:
  Burr conspiracy and, 358
  California and, 545
  Canadian border and, 391, 443
  colonial trade with, 118, 134–35, 191
  in colonial wars, 176–87, 190
  and Convention of 1818, 391–92

Great Britain (*continued*)
  cotton trade with, 362, 421, 438, 566,
    574, 577
  creation of, 54, 57
  early U.S. relations with, 279
  eighteenth-century politics of, 192
  French Revolution and, 318, 319
  Indian conflicts and, 302, *320,* 364, 365
  industry in, 465
  Jay's Treaty with, 319–21
  military of, 191, 195, 202
  Monroe Doctrine and, 402
  in Napoleonic wars, 318, 360–64,
    361, 363
  navy of, 251, 360–61
  Oregon Country and, 401, 534, 551,
    552–53
  rule of 1756 of, 320, 360
  slave trade and, 529
  Texas Republic relations with, 548
  U.S. Civil War and, 657, 659–60, 672
  U.S. trade with, 277, 279–80, 307,
    319–21, 332, 360–64, *361,* 363, 364,
    373, 391, 392, 394, 421, 438, 441, 574
  in War of 1812, 369–71
  see also American Revolution;
    British Empire; England;
    Parliament, British; War of 1812;
    specific colonies
Great (Connecticut) Compromise, 287
Great Migration of 1630s, 73
Great Plains:
  environment of, 541–42
  horses and, 38–40, 531
Great Revival, 497
Greeley, Horace, 732–33, *733*
Greenback (Independent National)
    party, 735
greenbacks, 679, *679,* 728, 734–35
Greene, Catharine, 452
Greene, Nathanael, 238, 452
  description of, 250
Greenland, 15
Green Mountain Boys, 214
Greenville, Treaty of (1795), *322,* 323,
    326
Grenville, George, 193–95, *194,* 198,
    198, 199
Grimké, Angelina, 594, *595*

Grimké, Sarah, 594, *595*
Griswald, Roger, *337*
Grundy, Felix, 366
Guadalupe Hidalgo, Treaty of (1848),
    502, 560
Guatemala, 31
guilds, 133, 482
Gullah, 589
Gutenberg, Johannes, 16

habeas corpus, 682, 683, 732
  Lincoln's suspension of, 651–52, 681
Habeas Corpus Act (1863), 681
haciendas, 33
Haiti (Saint Domingue), 20, 352
Hale, John P., 617
Half-Way Covenant (1662), 139
Halleck, Henry, 663, 665
Hamilton, Alexander, 229, 252, 272, 289,
    323, 334, 346
  Adams administration and, 333
  background of, 307
  Burr's duel with, 357, 358, 581
  Constitutional Convention and,
    283, 285, 290
  economic vision of, 307–15
  in election of 1796, 330
  and election of 1800, 338
  Federalist and, 293–94, 304
  French Revolution and, 318, 319
  Jefferson compared with, 315,
    316–17
  Jefferson's continuation of programs
    of, 350
  land policy of, 326
  national bank promoted by, 308, 309,
    311–13
  in ratification debate, 293–94
  as secretary of the Treasury, 303,
    307–15, *308*
  Washington's farewell and, 329
Hamilton, William, 245
Hammond, James H., 577
Hancock, John, 212–13, 222
Hanoverian succession, 192
Harper's Ferry, Va., 638, *653*
Harper's Weekly, 656, 703, *721*
Harris, Townsend, 619
Harris Convention (1858), 619

Harrison, William Henry, 364–65, 369
  in election of 1836, 440
  in election of 1840, *443*, 444–45, 527
Hartford, Treaty of (1638), 83
Hartford Convention (1814), 373–74, 423
Harvard Medical School, 488
Harvard University, 158–59
Hathorne, John, 141
Hawkins, John, 44
Hawthorne, Nathaniel, 462, 492, 505,
  508, 523
Hayes, Rutherford B., 736–39, *738*
Hayne, Robert Y., 423–24, 426, 575
Haynes, Lemuel, *265*
Hays, Mary Ludwig (Molly Pitcher),
  262, *263*
Hayward, James, 214
headright system, 118, 142
health and medicine:
  in Civil War, 675, *675*
  in colonial period, 112–13
  in Old Southwest, 591
  as profession, *486*, 487, 488
  of slaves, 583
  see also disease; drugs
heliocentrism, 149
hemp, 704
Henrico (Richmond), 62
Henrietta Maria, queen, 67
Henry, Joseph, 464
Henry, Patrick, 315
  Constitutional Convention avoided by,
    284, 294
  at Continental Congress, 211, *211*
  in ratification debate, 294, 295
  Virginia Resolves and, 197
Henry VII, king of England, 18, 26,
  46, 54
Henry VIII, king of England, 42–43
Herbert, Victor, 477–78
Hessians, 218, 235, 237
Hicks, Edward, *327*
Hidalgo y Costilla, Miguel, 533, *533*
highways and roads, 147, 387–88, 415,
  420–21, *456–57*
  in colonial period, 145, 147, 328
  federal funding for, 384, 387–88, 463
  to frontier regions, 145, 328, 455–56
  Maysville Road, 420

National (Cumberland) Road, *387*,
  388, 390, 420–21, 456
  state funding for, 437
  turnpike boom (1820s) and, 455
  Wilderness Road, 327–29, 455
Hill, Ambrose P., 665
Hill, D. H., 665
Hill, John, *459*
Hillsborough, earl of, 201
Hiroshige Utagawa, *619*
Hispanics:
  gold rush and, 608
  in Spanish America, 34, 532
Hispaniola, Columbus in, 20
Hobbs, Abigail, 141
Hoe, Richard, 511
Hoe rotary press, 511
Holmes, Oliver Wendell, Sr., 508
Holy Roman Empire, 34
Homestead Act (1862), 678, 703
Hood, John B., 691–93
Hooker, Joseph E., 684
  at Chancellorsville, 684, 689
Hooker, Thomas, 78
Hopewell culture, 10–11
Hopis, 11, 12, 531
horses, 110, 683
  Indians and, 38–40, 531
  Spanish introduction of, 27, 38–40
Horseshoe Bend, Battle of (1814), 369–70
House of Commons, British, 53, 73
  American Revolution and, 243, 253
House of Lords, British, 53, 73
House of Representatives, U.S.:
  in Constitution, 287, 289–90
  election of 1800 decided by, 339, *340*
  in election of 1824, 405
  Jay's Treaty opposed in, 321
  Johnson's impeachment in, 718, *718*
  violence in, 637
  see also Congress, U.S.
House of the Seven Gables, The
  (Hawthorne), 508
housing:
  in antebellum South, 579
  in colonial period, 130–31, *130*
  on frontier, 328
  of slaves, 583
  technological advances in, 464

Houston, Sam, 547, *547,* 581
    and Compromise of 1850, 611
    Kansas-Nebraska Act denounced by, 623
Howe, Elias, 464
Howe, Richard, Lord, 232
Howe, William, 214–16, 232–36, *233,*
    239, 241, 243
Hudson, Henry, 91–92
Hughson, John, 124
Huguenots, 36, 42, 86, 143, *144,* 172
Huitzilopochtli, 30
Hull, William, 367–68
human sacrifice, 30
Hundred Years' War (1338–1453), 17–18
Hungarian Americans, 658
Hunt, Harriet, 487–88
hunters and gatherers, 80–81
hunting, 13
Hurons, 96, *103,* 172
Hutchinson, Anne, 77–78, 79, 505
Hutchinson, Thomas, 196, 206, 208

Iberville, Pierre le Moyne, sieur d', 174
Idaho, 660
Ignatius of Loyola, 173
Illinois:
    agriculture in, 574
    German settlers in, 480
    Indian conflicts in, 429
    Mormons in, 501–2
    Revolutionary War fighting in, 245
immigration, 142–45, *144*
    Alien Act and, 336
    from British regions, 109
    of Chinese, 480
    Constitutional Convention and, 289
    of convicts, 119
    of Germans, 100, 101, 142–43, 145,
        479–80
    Great Migration and, 73
    of Highland Scots, 101, 143
    of Irish, 476–79
    nativism and, 480–82
    in nineteenth century, 475–82
    of Scandinavians, 98, 142, 480
    of Scotch-Irish, 22, 142, 143, 145
    of Swiss, 538
    see also specific ethnic groups and
        countries

impeachment, 290, 292
    of Andrew Johnson, 717–19, *718*
implied powers, 352–53, 399
impressment, 360–61, 373
Incas, 9, 27, 31, 34
income tax, 679
indentured servants, 62, 64, 65, 68, 109,
    116, 117, 119–20, *120*
    Africans as, 121
Independence Day, 266
Independents (religious group), 56
independent Treasury, 442–43, 551
Independent Treasury Act (1840),
    442–43, 528
India, 182, 438
    trade with, 391
Indiana, 323, 445
Indian conflicts:
    Andrew Jackson in, 369, 393–94,
        393, 546
    Black Hawk War, 429
    Canada and, 322–23, 364–65
    in colonial period, 64–66, 81–84,
        82, 89–91, 95–97, 141, 182, 184–86,
        191, 193
    in Connecticut colony, 81–84, *82,* 84
    in early U.S., 279, 302, 320–23
    French in, 89, 96–97, *172*
    in Georgia, 277
    Great Britain and, 302, *320,* 364
    in Illinois, 429
    in Revolutionary War, 264
    in South, 182
    Spain and, 277, 302, 325
    Tecumseh and, 364–66, *365,* 369
    Treaty of Paris (1763) and, 184–86
    in Virginia colony, 64–66
    and War of 1812, 364–66, 367–68
Indian Removal Act (1830), 428–29
Indians, American, 344–45
    agriculture of, 7, 10, 13, 81, 110–11, 531
    in American Revolution, 217, 241–42,
        245, 246–47, *246,* 276–77
    Americas settled by, 2, 5, *6*
    Andrew Jackson's policy toward, 428–31
    buffalo herds and, 13, 39–40, 531,
        531, 532
    Catholicism and, 32–33, *32, 33,*
        36–37, 171, *173,* 532, 535–36

Christian, 204
citizenship of, 289
in Civil War, 661
colonial trade with, 57, 80, 87–91,
    100, 173
Columbus's conflict with, 21
constitutional rights lacked by, 306
and diseases contracted from
    Europeans, 14, 23–25, *23, 24,* 26, 27,
    31, 32–33, 81, 88, 95
Dutch relations with, 92
in early U.S., 302
education and, 159
English vs. French relations with,
    80, 176
environment influenced by, 38–40,
    110–11
forced labor of, 2–3, 27, 37, *37*
in French and Indian War, 181
French relations with, 80, 171–73,
    173, 176
in fur trade, 80, 88, 97, 173, 534
gold rush and, 609
horses and, 38–40, *39,* 531
Kansas-Nebraska act and, 623
languages of, 23
Lewis and Clark expedition and, 354–55
massacres of, 21, 64, 81–84, 204–5, *204*
missionaries to, 33, 36–37, 83, 89, 172,
    173–74, 176, 535–36
named by Columbus, 19
in New England, 79–84, 141
in New York colony, 95–97, 142
nomadic, 13
Old Northwest land of, 274, 276–77
in Pennsylvania colony, 142
Plymouth colony and, 70
pre-Columbian civilizations of, 7–14,
    8, 9–12, 10
Quakers' relations with, 99–100
religious beliefs of, 33, 34, 37, *80,* 81
removal of, 428–31, *429, 430,* 452
reservation system and, 543
in Revolutionary War, 264–65
as slaves, 19, 83, 84, 88–91, 127, 264
technology of, 23, 38–40
tribal groups of, 12–14
Virginia colony and, 59, 61–63, 64–66
wagon trains and, 538–39, 540–41, 542

Western, 530–32
women, 13, 40
see also specific tribes
Indian Territory, 623
see also Oklahoma
indigo, 114, 248, 573
individualism, 380–81, 504, 505
Industrial Revolution, 465–71, 566
industry:
cities and, 470–71
in Civil War, 654
in early nineteenth century, 416,
    465–66, *470*
environment and, 469–70, *471*
family system in, 469
German Americans in, 479–80
Irish Americans in, 477
Lowell System in, 466–69
technological innovations and, 464–65
see also corporations, business;
    manufactures; *specific industries*
"In God We Trust" motto, 676
Institutes of the Christian Religion, The
    (Calvin), 42
Interior Department, U.S., 407, 561
internal improvements, 387–88, 389, 390,
    404, 405, 463
Andrew Jackson on, 420–21, *420*
Constitution and, 420–21
John Quincy Adams's promotion
    of, 407
Polk on, 551
Tyler on, 527
Whigs on, 440
Internal Revenue Act (1862), 679
Internal Revenue Service, 679
interposition, *see* nullification and
    interposition
Intolerable (Coercive) Acts (1774), 208–9
Ireland, 52, 54, 57
Irish Americans, 119, 143, 145, 380, 580
African Americans' animosity toward,
    478
in Democratic party, 440, 478
immigration by, 476–79, *477*
in labor force, 477
in nineteenth century, 476–79
prejudice against, 336, 478, 480, *481*
reasons for migration of, 476

iron industry, 575
Iroquoians, 13
Iroquois League, 92, 95–97, *103*, 142, *177*,
    246–47, 257, 264
  Albany Congress and, 179
  in American Revolution, 241–42
  in Colonial wars, 182
  French conflict with, 172, *172*
  post-Revolutionary War weakness
    of, 276
  Tuscaroras in, 90
Isabella I, queen of Castile, 18–19, 21
Islam, 115
Italian Americans, 143, 658

Jack (driver), *586*
Jackson, Andrew, 389, *393*, 403, *425*,
    438–39, 464
  assessment of presidency of, 445–47
  background of, 414, 417–18
  Calhoun's rift with, 424–26
  California annexation and, 544–45
  as commoner, 414, 417–18
  conflicting goals of, 418
  on debt, 436
  in duel, 581
  Eaton Affair and, 419–20, *419*
  in election of 1824, 404, *405*
  in election of 1828, 408–11, *408, 409,
    410,* 422, 441, 478
  in election of 1832, 436
  and election of 1844, 547
  in Florida campaign, 393–94
  government appointments of, 418
  Houston and, 547
  inauguration of, *415*, 418
  in Indian conflicts, 369, 393–94,
    393, 546
  Indian policy of, 428–31
  on Indians, 418
  internal improvements and,
    420–21, *420*
  Irish-American support of, 478
  land policy of, 437–38
  national bank issue and, 432–39, *434,*
    446–47
  nullification issue and, 424, 426–28,
    436, 439, 528
  Polk compared with, 550–51
  tariff issue and, 407–8, 426, 436
  ten-hour workday and, 484
  in War of 1812, 369, 371–72, *372,* 374
Jackson, "Drummer," *674*
Jackson, Rachel, 409, 420
Jackson, Thomas "Stonewall," 665
  background of, 561
  at Chancellorsville, 684
  death of, 684, *684*
  at first Bull Run, 655
  nickname given to, 655
  at second Bull Run, 665
Jamaica, 21
James I, king of England, 52, 54–55, *55,*
    57, 62, 69, 168
James II, king of England, 56, *166*
  accession of, 165
  colonization and, 93, 165
  France policy of, 176
  overthrow of, 166, 167, 192
Jamestown colony, 36, 38, 58–59, 61–63,
    66, 120, 127
Japan, trade with, 619, *619*
Jay, John, *304*
  background of, 304
  Federalist and, 293, 304
  on peace commission, 253, *253,* 304
  in ratification debate, 294
  treaty negotiated by, 319–21
Jayhawkers, 661
Jay's Treaty (1795), 319–21, *320,* 330, 332,
    334, 360
Jefferson, Thomas, 151–52, 228, 267, *316,*
    334–35, 346–48, *348, 362,* 384, 416,
    451, 599
  and Alien and Sedition Acts, 336–37
  background of, 316
  Barbary pirates and, 351
  Burr conspiracy and, 359
  on colonial protests, 209
  on Constitutional Convention, *291*
  debt issue and, 310
  Declaration of Independence drafted
    by, 219–20, *220,* 492
  as deist, 493
  domestic reforms of, 350–51
  as early Republican leader, 315–17
  economic policies of, 316–17, 350, 466
  education efforts of, 514

in election of 1796, 330
in election of 1800, 229, 338–41, *340*,
   346–47
in election of 1804, 348
exploration of West promoted by,
   353–54
French Revolution and, 317–18, 319
Hamilton compared with, 315, 316–17
inauguration of, 346–48
internal improvements and, 387–88
on Jackson, 417
land policy and, 274–77, 326
Louisiana Purchase and, 352–53
in *Marbury v. Madison*, 349–50
on Missouri Compromise, 398
Monroe Doctrine and, 402
Monroe's letter to, *402*
Napoleonic wars and, 360, 361, 362–63
national bank and, 312, 350
and religious freedom, 265–66, 306
second Washington term urged by, 317
as secretary of state, 303
on Shays's Rebellion, 282
as slaveholder, 261, 340
on territories, 274
on Whiskey Rebellion, 334
on women's rights, 263–64
Jeremiah, Thomas, 261
Jesuits, 33, 36, 172, 173–74, *173*
Jewish Americans, 87, 94–95, *95*, 101,
   143, *144*
Johnson, Andrew, 680, *710*, *714*, 727
   assassination plot against, 708
   congressional conflicts with, 713–14
   in election of 1864, 682, 709
   impeachment and trial of, 717–19, *718*
   Radical Republicans' conflict with,
      710, 715–16, 717–19
   Reconstruction plans of, 710–11,
      713–14
Johnson, Richard M., 366
Johnson, William, 582
Johnston, Albert Sidney, 661–63
Johnston, Joseph E., 655, 685–86, 689,
   695, 697
   at Seven Pines, 664
   Sherman's march countered by, 691
   surrender of, 698
Joint Committee on Reconstruction, 712

joint-stock companies, 54
Jolliet, Louis, 174, *175*
Jones, Jehu, 582
Jones, John Paul, 251
Jones, Mary, 676
*Journals of the Lewis and Clark
   Expedition,* 354, *354,* 355, *355*
journeymen, 133, 482
Judaism, 571
judicial review, 292, 398–99
Judiciary Act (1801), 339, 348
Julian, George W., 680, 712

Kaaterskill Falls (Cole), *504*
Kanagawa, Treaty of (1854), 619
Kansas, Civil War fighting in, 660–61
Kansas-Nebraska Act (1854), 619–28,
   620, 622, 629, 631
   proposed by Douglas, 619–24
   and violence in Kansas, 624
   and violence in Senate, 626–28
   Whig party destroyed over, 624
Kansas Territory, 36
   Lecompton constitution in, 632–33
   settlement of, 624–26
   slavery issue and, 620, 624–26,
      631–32
   statehood for, 625
   violence in (1856), 624–26
Kant, Immanuel, 504–5
Kearny, Stephen, 557
Kentucky, 247, 276, 279, 302, *322,* 455
   agriculture in, 328–29, 573
   Civil War fighting in, 661
   Indian lands ceded in, 276
   Indian removal and, 428
   secession debate in, 651–52
   settlement of, 327–29
   statehood for, 329
   tariff issue and, 407
   voting rights in, 410
Kentucky Resolutions (1798 and 1799),
   337, 423
Key, Francis Scott, 371
Kickapoos, *102*
King, Martin Luther, Jr., 508
King, Rufus, 357, 363, 389
King George's War (War of the Austrian
   Succession) (1744–1748), 176

King Philip's (Metacomet's) War
   (1675–1676), 83–84
King's College (Columbia
   University), 159
Kingsley, Bathsheba, 156
King's Mountain, Battle of (1780), 250
King William's War (War of the League
   of Augsburg) (1689–1697), 176
Kiowas, 39, 531, 543
KKK (Ku Klux Klan), 731–32, *731*
Klamaths, 532
Knight, Amelia, 541
Knights of the White Camellia, 731
Know-Nothing (American) party,
   481–82, *481*, 624, 629
Ku Klux Klan (KKK), 731–32, *731*
Ku Klux Klan Act (1871), 732

labor, employment:
   apprentice-journeyman system of,
      133, 346, 482
   in California missions, 535–36
   child, 469, 484
   in colonial cities, 146
   diversification of, 313, *314*
   in early nineteenth century, 346,
      467–69
   immigrant, 477
   organized, 482–85
   rise of professions, 485–88
   in southern colonies, 119–21, *120*
   of women, 116–17, 465, 467–69, *468*,
      521, 674–75
   working conditions of, 466–69
   see also indentured servants; slavery;
      slaves; working class
labor movement:
   in early nineteenth century, 482–85
   strikes and, 483, *183*, 484–85
   ten-hour workday and, 484
   see also working class; *specific unions*
Labrador (Markland), 392
Lady's Magazine, 264
Lafayette, Gilbert du Motier, Marquis
   of, 245
Lagunas, 531
Lakota Sioux, 543
Land Act (1796), 326
Land Act (1800), 326, 395

Land Act (1804), 327
land grants:
   for colleges, 678, 703
   for railroads, 463, 703
Land Ordinance (1785), 274
landownership:
   and confiscation of Loyalist estates,
      254, 259, 279, 398
   in England, 54
   European view of, 110–11
   in New England, 138
   in Virginia colony, 63–65
land policy, 528
   African Americans and, 705–6
   under Articles of Confederation,
      272–77
   in California, 537
   in colonial period, 118–19, 142
   Congress and, 326, 453, 528
   in early nineteenth century, 452–53
   in early U.S., 326–27
   Foot Resolution on, 422–24
   for freedmen, 705–6, 723, 724
   headright system and, 119, 142
   Homestead Act and, 703
   under Jackson, 437–38
   Morrill Land Grant Act and, 678, 703
   in New England, 129–30
   railroads and, 463
   Reconstruction and, 705–6, 723, 724
   in southern colonies, 118–19
   for surveys and sales, 118, 326–27,
      452–53
   in Texas, 545
   under Van Buren, 442
land speculators, 326, 395, 437
Lane Theological Seminary, 481
Lanphier, Jeremiah, 634
Larkin, Thomas O., 538, 554
La Salle, Robert Cavalier, sieur de,
   174, *175*
Las Casas, Bartolomé de, 33
Latin America:
   liberation of, 402
   see also specific countries
Latrobe, Benjamin, *259*
Laud, William, 55–57
Laurens, Henry, 222, *253*
Lawrence, 369

Lawrence, Kans.:
  Civil War destruction of, 661
  proslavery violence in (1856),
    625, *626*
law school, 487
Leaves of Grass (Whitman), 508, 510
Lecompton Constitution, 632–33
LeConte, Emma, 677
Lee, Ann (Mother Ann), 522
Lee, Charles, 245
Lee, Henry, 323
Lee, Richard Henry:
  at Continental Congress, 219, 257
  in ratification debate, 294
Lee, Robert E., 664–65, 695, *698*
  at Antietam, 666–68
  background of, 561
  at Chancellorsville, 684
  Confederate side chosen by, 652
  at Fredericksburg, 668–69
  at Gettysburg, 686–88
  Grant's pursuit of, 689–91
  at Harper's Ferry, 638
  surrender of, 698, 699
legal system:
  Admiralty courts in, 167, 193, 196,
    200, 203
  in colonial period, 167
  in Constitution, 291
  English, 53
  judicial nationalism in, 398–401
  judicial review in, 292, 398–99
  and Judiciary Act of 1801, 339
  as profession, 486–87
  testimony of blacks in, 711
  U.S., establishment of, 304
  see also Supreme Court, U.S.
Legal Tender Act (1862), 679
legislatures, in colonial period, 168
Leopard incident, 361
Lesser Antilles, 20
Letters from a Farmer in Pennsylvania
    (Dickinson), 200
Lewis, Meriwether, 354–55, *354, 355,*
    356, 357
  journals of, 354, *354, 355, 355*
Lexington, Battle of (1775), 212–14,
    212, 213
Liberator, 593

Liberia, 593
Liberty party, 550, 598
  Free Soil party and, 605
liberty trees, 196
Lienzo de Tlaxcala, *28*
Lincoln, Abraham:
  appraisal of Civil War by, 696–97
  assassination of, 708–9
  background of, 635
  and Battle of Petersburg, 691
  in Black Hawk War, 429
  border states held by, 651–52
  cabinet appointments of, 649, 716
  on Chattanooga, 688
  civil liberties curtailed by, 681–82
  Douglas's debates with, 635–37, *636*
  between election and inauguration,
    643–44, 648
  in election of 1860, 566, 640–42,
    641, 643
  in election of 1864, *681,* 682
  emancipation and, 669–74, *671*
  and first Battle of Bull Run, 655
  first inauguration of, 649
  funeral procession for, *709*
  Gettysburg Address of, 688
  on God's role in Civil War, 676–78
  McClellan's antagonism toward, 663,
    665, 668, *668*
  Mexican War opposed by, 555
  military strategy of, 656–57, 660–61,
    663, 688
  and outbreak of Civil War, 650
  Reconstruction plans of, 697, 707–8,
    710, 711
  secession and, 643–44
  second inauguration of, 696–97
  in senatorial election of 1858,
    635–37
  slavery issue and, 603, 635–37, 640,
    645, 649, 669–72, 696
  Union command structure and, 663,
    665, 668, 684, 688
  on use of African-American soldiers,
    673
  western fighting and, 660–61
  on Wilmot Proviso, 603
Lincoln, Benjamin, 248
Lincoln-Douglas debates, 635–37

literature:
  antislavery, 616–17
  in nineteenth century, 503
  romanticism in, 508–11
  transcendentalism and, 504–8
Livingston, Robert R., 219, 352, 400,
    400, 456
Locke, John, 86, 150, 167, 195, 221
Locofocos, 484
Logan, George, 333
Logan Act (1799), 333
Log Cabin, 445
"Log Cabin and Hard Cider"
    campaign, 445
Log College, 155
Longfellow, Henry Wadsworth, 508
Long Island, Battle of (1776), 234
"Long Parliament", English, 55
Longstreet, James A., 665, 724–25
Lords of Trade and Plantations (Board of
    Trade), 164–65, 167
lords proprietors, 86, 87
"Lost Colony" (Roanoke), 48–49
Louisiana, 396–97
  agriculture in, 574
  Civil War and, 672, 673
  cotton in, 451
  in election of 1876, 737
  Reconstruction in, 707, 722–23, 724,
    734, 738, 739
  secession of, 642
  slave trade in, 583
  statehood for, 353
Louisiana Purchase (1803), 352–55, 620
  boundaries of, 352, 391–92, *391*, 394
  exploration of, 353–55, *354, 355,
    356, 357*
  slavery in, 396, 397
Louisiana territory, 36, 180, 319, 396–97
  border of, 394
  Burr conspiracy and, 358–59
  French settlement of, 174–76
  Jefferson's purchase of, 352–53
  name of, 174
  northern border of, 391–92, *391*
  in Treaty of Paris (1763), 183, 186
  and War of 1812, 371–72
Louisville, 471
Louis XIV, king of France, 173, 176

Louis XVI, king of France, 318
Lovejoy, Elijah P., 597, *598*
Lowell, Francis Cabot, 466
Lowell, James Russell, 297, 508
Lowell System, 466–69
Loyalists (Tories), 206
  in American Revolution, 216, 217,
    236–37, 239, 241, 242, 243, 245, 247,
    248–50, 260, 261
  after American Revolution, 256
  confiscated estates of, 254, 259,
    279, 398
Luther, Martin, 41, 42
Lutheranism, 41, 143, 479
Lynch, Charles, 236
Lyon, Mary, 515
Lyon, Matthew, 336, *337*

McClellan, George B.:
  at Antietam, 666–68
  background of, 561
  in election of 1864, 682
  in formation of West Virginia, 651
  Lincoln's antagonism toward, 663, 665,
    668, *668*
  peninsular campaign of, 663–65, *666*
  at second Bull Run, 665
McCormick, Cyrus Hall, *453*, 454
McCulloch v. Maryland, 399–400, 432
Macdonough, Thomas, 370–71
McDowell, Irvin, 663, 664
  at first Bull Run, 655
machine tools, 487
McLane, Louis, 436
Macon, Nathaniel, 363
Madeira, 134
Madison, Dolley, 371
Madison, James, 151, 229, 301, 335,
    371, 375, 420
  African colonization and, 592
  Alien and Sedition Acts opposed by,
    336–37
  Bill of Rights and, 304–5
  at Constitutional Convention, 285–86,
    285, 290, 293
  debt issue and, 310
  as early Republican leader, 315, 316, 317
  in election of 1808, 363
  Federalist and, 293

government strengthening
  recommended by, 290, 384
on Indians, 428
internal improvements and, 388
land policy and, 326
in *Marbury v. Madison,* 349
Monroe Doctrine and, 402
Napoleonic Wars and, 363
national bank and, 312, 384, 385
in ratification debate, 294
as secretary of state, 348, 349
as slaveholder, 340
tariff policy and, 306–7
Virginia Plan, 286–87
and War of 1812, 363–64, 367, 373
Magellan, Ferdinand, 26
Magna Carta (1215), 53
Mahicans, *103*
Maine, 44
  Canadian border with, 443, 530
  in colonial period, 79, 80–81
  Indians in, 80–81
  statehood for, 397
  voting rights in, 411
  in War of 1812, 374
maize (corn), 7, 22, 70, 81, 110, 329, 574
malaria, 24, 113, 683
Mamout, Yarrow, *582*
Manassas (Bull Run), first Battle of
  (1861), 655–56, *656*
Manassas (Bull Run), second Battle of
  (1862), 665
Mandan Sioux, 354
manifest destiny, 380, 550, 554–55
  origin of term, 530
Manila, 183
Mann, Horace, 513
manufactures:
  cities and, 470–71
  in early nineteenth century, *384,*
    386–87, *407*–8, *465*–66
  in early U.S., 280, *280*, 306, 309,
    313–14
  Jefferson's embargo and, 384
  Lowell system and, 466–69
  of Shakers, 522
  in South, 575
  see also industry
manumission laws, 261–62

Marbury, William, 349–50
Marbury v. Madison, 349–50, 398, 631
Marine Corps, U.S., 217
Marion, Francis, 250
Markland (Labrador), 392
Marquette, Jacques, 174, *175*
marriage:
  African, 121
  of African Americans, 125, 590, 711, 720
  of clergy, 43
  in colonial period, 111–12, 113–14
  and cult of domesticity, 519
  divorce and, 262
  of indentured servants, 119
  interracial, 711
  in Oneida Community, 522
  of slaves, 125, 590
  women's rights and, 519
Marshall, John, 313, 347, *399,* 432
  African colonization and, 592
  Burr conspiracy and, 359
  Indian lands and, 431
  judicial nationalism of, 398–401
  in *Marbury v. Madison,* 349–50
  named as chief justice, 339
  XYZ affair and, 333
Martin, Luther, 294
Martin v. Hunter's Lessee, 398
Mary, queen of Scots, 46, 54
Mary I, queen of England, 43, 46, 165
Mary II, queen of England, 56, 166–67
Maryland:
  agriculture in, 573
  Civil War fighting in, 666–68, *667*
  Constitution ratified by, *295*
  free blacks in, 262
  Know-Nothing party in, 482
  land claims of, 257
  at navigation meeting of 1785, 283
  secession debate in, 651–52
  voting rights in, 411
  War of 1812 in, 371, 372
Maryland colony, 65, *67,* 68, 85
  charter of, 67–68
  European settlement of, 67–68
  government of, 67–68, 166, 168, 169
  Indians in, 186
  slavery in, *122,* 123, 126, *128*
  tobacco in, 117

Maryland Toleration Act (1649), 85
Mason, George, 220
  and Bill of Rights, 305
  at Constitutional Convention, 285,
    287–88, 289–90
  in ratification debate, 294
Mason, James M., 612, 660
Mason, John, 79
Masonic order, 435
Massachusetts:
  asylums in, 518
  Civil War troops from, 672–73, *691*
  constitution of, *261*
  Constitution ratified by, 295, *295, 297*
  education in, 512, 513, 514
  at Hartford Convention, 374
  Know-Nothing party in, 482
  Revolutionary War fighting in, 212–16
  Revolutionary War troops from,
    214–15, 260
  Shays's Rebellion in, 281–83
  slavery in, 260, 261, *261*
  taxation in, 281
  temperance in, 517
  voting rights in, 411
  and War of 1812, 374
Massachusetts Bay Company, 72
Massachusetts colony, 2–3, 84–85, 117
  in border disputes, 79
  charter of, 72–73, 85, 165, 168
  in colonial taxation disputes, 196,
    197–98, 201, 211
  in colonial wars, 177
  education in, 152–53
  European settlement of, 71–75, 109
  government of, 72–75, 85, 165, 166,
    168, 169
  governors' salary in, 206
  heresy repressed in, 139
  Plymouth combined with, 166
  religious freedom in, 139
  shipbuilding in, 132–34
  taxation in, 166
  trade and commerce in, 164–65
  see also Plymouth colony
Massachusetts Government Act (1774),
  208, 243
Massachusetts Indians, 81, *103*
mathematics, Mayan, 7

Mather, Cotton, 82, 115, 140, *140*
Mather, Increase, 136
Mayas, 7–8, *9*
Mayflower, 69
Mayflower Compact (1620), 69–71, 137
Mayhew, Jonathan, 158
Maysville Road Bill (1830), 420,
  421, 426
Meade, George, 689
  background of, 561
  at Gettysburg, 687–88
mechanics' lien laws, 484
media, *see* press
medicine, *see* health and medicine
"melting pot," 109
Melville, Herman, 508, 509–10, *511*, 523
Memphis, Tenn., race riot in (1866), 715
Mennonites, 41, 143
mentally ill, 518
mercantile system, 163–65, 307
Merrimack (Virginia), 657
Merrimack Mills and Boarding
  Houses, *467*
mestizos, 37, 532
Metacomet (Philip), Wampanoag chief,
  83–84
Metacomet's (King Philip's) War
  (1675–1676), 83–84
Methodists, 158, 265–66, 495, 571
  in revivals, 496–97, *498*
  split over slavery, 599, 623
Mexican Americans, 532
Mexican Revolution, 533
Mexican War (1845–1848), 553–61, *559*,
  603–4, 609
  California annexation and, 553–54,
    556–57
  casualties in, 560–61
  legacies of, 560–61
  opposition to, 554–55
  outbreak of, 553–54
  peace treaty in, 560
  Polk's intrigue with Santa Ana in, 558
  preparations for, 555–56
  slavery issue and, 507, 555
Mexico, 183, 502
  European diseases in, *23*, 24
  exploration of, 36
  Gadsden Purchase from, 619

as heart of Spanish Empire, 34
independence of, 170, 533, *533,*
    536, 545
pre-Columbian, 7–9
Texas independence from, 533,
    545–47
and U.S. efforts to annex California,
    544–45
U.S. trade with, 438, 538
Mexico City (Tenochtitlán), 9, 28–29, 31
    U.S. capture of, 558–60
Miamis, *102*
middle class:
    in antebellum South, 579
    performing arts and, 473–74
    reform movement and, 483
    in South, 579
    women's rights in, 518
Middle Colonies, 142–45
    ethnic mix in, 142–45
Middle Passage, 122
Milan Decree (1807), 360, 363
Milford, Conn., English settlers in, 79
military, U.S.:
    in Constitution, 287, 290
    in Jefferson administration, 350
    in Mexican War, 555
    see also specific branches and wars
Military Academy, U.S. (West Point), 514
Military Reconstruction Act (1867),
    716, 717
militias, 368, 369, 484
    in American Revolution, 211–12,
        214–16, 234–36, 237–38, *238,* 242,
        248–50, 260
    in War of 1812, 369, 371
Milwaukee, 471
mining:
    of coal, 575
    of gold, 608, *608*
    of silver, 660
Minnesota, 480
minstrel shows, 474–75, *476*
Minuit, Peter, 92
Minutemen, 213
missionaries:
    Catholic, 33, 36–37, 172, 173–74, 176,
        532, 535–36
    to China, 618

French, 172, 173–74, 176
to frontier, 496
Puritan, 83
Spanish, 33, 36–37, 89, 532, 535–36
Mississippi, 353, 452
    agriculture in, 415, 574
    Civil War fighting in, 685
    cotton in, 451
    migration to, 592
    Reconstruction in, 712, 719, 731, 733
    secession of, 642
    women's rights in, 521
Mississippian culture, 9, 11, *11*
Mississippi Rifle Club, 734
Mississippi River, 174
    in Civil War, 657, 685
    navigation rights to, 279,
        325–26, 352
    steamboats on, 456–58
    U.S. access to, 279, 325–26, 352
    in War of 1812, 370
Missouri:
    agriculture in, 573
    Civil War fighting in, 652, 661
    emancipation in, 673
    German settlers in, 480
    secession debate in, 651–52
    statehood for, 398
Missouri Compromise (1820), 395–98,
        396, 421, 604, 605, 612, 614, 620–21,
        623, 629, 630–32
Missouri Territory, 395–97
Mobile, Ala., capture of, 682
Mobile and Ohio Railroad, 463
Moby-Dick (Melville), 508, 510, *511*
"Model of Christian Charity, A"
    (Winthrop), 72
Mohawks, 92, 247, 264
Molasses Act (1733), 194
monarchy:
    English, 54–57, 162
    Locke on, 167
Monitor, 657
Monmouth Court House, Battle of
    (1778), 245
Monroe, James, 352, 389–91, *390,* 420
    African colonization and, 592
    as ambassador to France, 332
    in American Revolution, 235

Monroe, James (*continued*)
  description of, 390
  in election of 1816, 389
  in election of 1820, 390, 403
  Florida and, 393
  foreign policy under, 391–94,
    401–3, *402*
  Missouri Compromise and, 397–98
  and relations with Britain, 391–92
  as slaveholder, 340
  and War of 1812, 373
Monroe Doctrine, 401–3
Montana, 660
Montcalm, Louis Joseph de, 182
Montezuma II, Aztec Emperor, 31
Montgomery, Richard, 216–17
Montreal, 44
Moore's Creek Bridge, Battle
    of (1776), 217
Moravian Indians, 204–5
Moravians, 101, 143
Morgan, Daniel, 250
Morgan, J. Pierpont, 680
Mormons (Church of Jesus Christ of
    Latter-day Saints), 500–503, *501,
    502,* 609
  and Indians, 500, 503
  westward journey of, 501–3, *503*
Mormon Trail, *539*
Morocco, 351
  trade with, 278
Morrill Land Grant Act (1862), 678, 703
Morrill Tariff, 678, 703
Morris, Gouverneur, 285
Morris, Robert, 271–72, 309–10
Morristown, N.J., Washington's
    headquarters at (1776–1777), 239
Morse, Samuel F. B., 464, 465
Mother Ann (Ann Lee), 522
Mott, Lucretia, 520–21
Moultrie, William, 217
Mount, William Sydney, *607*
mountain men, 534, 544
Mount Vernon, *330*
movable type, 13
mulattoes, 582
Mulligan, James, 736
"Mulligan letters," 736
Murray, John, 494

Murray, Judith Sargent, 262–63
music, African-American, 125, *126,* 590
Muskogeans, 13

Napier press, 511
Napoléon I, Emperor of France, 318, 334,
    352–53, 360, 370, 373–74
Napoléon III, Emperor of France, 659
Narragansett Bay, 47
Narragansetts, 75–76, 81, 82, *82, 103*
Narrative of the Life of Frederick Douglass
    (Douglass), 596
Narváez, Pánfilo de, *35,* 36
Nash, Beverly, 722
Nashville, Battle of (1864), 693
Nast, Thomas, *712, 731*
national bank, *see* Bank of the United
    States
National Banking Act (1863), 678, 703
national conventions, 435–36
nationalism, American, 421–22, 439–40
  Clay's American System and, 388–89,
    404–6
  development of, 191, 266–67
  in diplomacy, 401–3
  economic, in early nineteenth
    century, 384, 389, 390, 439–40,
    444, 528, 551
  education and, 512
  of John Quincy Adams, 407
  judicial, 398–401
  Tyler and, 528
  after War of 1812, 366, 374–75, *375*
  of Webster, 424
national mint, 309
National-Republicans, 407, 433–34,
    436, 440
National (Cumberland) Road, *387,* 388,
    390, 420–21, 456
National Trades' Union, 484
National Typographical Union, 485, *485*
Native American Association, 481
Native Americans, *see* Indians, American
nativism, 480–82
naturalization, *see* citizenship and
    naturalization
Naturalization Act (1798), 336
Nausets, 81, *103*
Nauvoo, Ill., 501–2, *502*

Navajos, 11, 38, 531
Naval Academy, U.S. (Annapolis), 514
naval stores, 248
Navigation Act (1651), 163–64
Navigation Act (1660), 164
Navigation Act (1663), 164
Navigation Act (1817), 392
navigation acts, enforcement of, 164–65,
    167, 194
Navy, U.S., 251, 333, 350, 384, 385, 391
  in Civil War, 654–55, 657
  in Constitution, 287
  formation of, 217
  in War of 1812, 366–67, *367*, 369
  after War of 1812, 375
Navy Department, U.S., 333
Nebraska Territory, 533
  slavery issue and, 620, 623
"necessary and proper clause," 399
Netherlands, 34, 44, 47
  American Revolution and, 243, 309
  colonial trade with, 134
  colonization by, 91–94, 142
  Dutch Republic and, 44, 176
  empire of, 44, 84, 91–94
  in fur trade, 80, 92, 96
  privateers from, 44
  Puritans in, 69
  in rebellion against Spain, 44
  trade with, 277
Nevada:
  Indians in, 532
  statehood for, 660
New Amsterdam, 92, *93*
Newburgh Conspiracy, 272
New England:
  agriculture in, 131–32
  architecture in, 130–31, *130*
  colonial life in, 129–41
  in colonial wars, 191
  currency in, 194–95
  education in, 152–53
  European settlement of, 68–79, *71*
  fishing in, *131*, 132, 134, 138
  in French and Indian War, 191
  Great Awakening in, 153–59
  Hartford Convention and, 373–74
  Indians in, 79–84
  industry in, 132–34, *466*

Know-Nothing party in, 482
landownership in, 138
literature in (1800–1850), 505
Louisiana Purchase as seen in, 353
Mexican War as seen in, 555
post-Revolutionary War debt in, 310
religion in, 136–38, 139, 153–59; *see
    also* Puritans
secession considered by, 356, 374
sex ratios in, 113
shipbuilding in, 132–34
slaves in, 123
social distinctions in, 488–89
South compared with, 134
and Tariff of 1816, 386–87
temperance in, 516–17
trade and commerce in, 132–36, 138,
    302, 407–8, 466
transcendentalist movement in,
    504–8
in War of 1812, 370
New England, Dominion of, 165–66
New England Anti-Slavery Society, 593
New England Confederation, 84
New England Primer, The, 152
Newfoundland, *14,* 16, 35, 47, 134, 392
New France, 171–74, *173*
New Hampshire:
  in Constitutional Convention, 284
  Constitution ratified by, 295, *295*
  Dartmouth's charter altered by, 398–99
  at Hartford Convention, 374
  Revolutionary War troops from, 214
  voting rights in, 410, 411
New Hampshire colony, 79
  in land disputes, 204
New Harmony, 522–23
New Haven colony, 78
New Helvetia (Sutter's Fort), *537,* 538
New Jersey:
  constitution of, 264
  Constitution ratified by, 295, *295*
  Gibbons v. Ogden and, 400
  paper currency in, 281
  Revolutionary War fighting in, *233,*
    234–35, 239, 244, 245
  voting rights in, 264, 411
New Jersey, College of (Princeton
    University), 159

New Jersey colony, 86
  ethnic mix in, 142
  European settlement of, 97–98,
    97, 109
  government of, 165, 167
New Jersey Plan, 286–87
New Mexico, 36–38, 531, 533
  Gadsden Purchase and, 619
  Mexican War and, 557, 560
  Popé's rebellion in, 38
  slavery and, 609, 611, 613, 615
  in Spanish Empire, 36–38, 532
  statehood for, 609, 610, 613
New Netherland colony, 91, 94, 153
New Orleans, Battle of (1815), 371–72,
    372, 478
New Orleans, La., 174, 183, 186,
    457–58, 470
  in Civil War, 657
  mulattoes in, 582
  race riot in (1866), 715
  in War of 1812, 370, 371–72, 374
Newport, R.I., 143, 146
Newsom, Robert, 586
New Spain, 33
newspapers:
  in colonial period, 148
  proliferation of (1800–1850),
    511–12, 512
New Sweden, 92
Newton, Isaac, 149
New View of Society, A (Owen), 522
New York:
  canals in, 458–59
  Civil War troops from, 658
  at Constitutional Convention, 285
  Constitution ratified by, 295, 295
  and election of 1800, 339
  and election of 1844, 550
  Essex Junto and, 356–57
  in Gibbons v. Ogden, 400
  Indian lands ceded in, 276
  Jeffersonian Republicans in, 317
  Know-Nothing party in, 481–82
  land claims of, 257, 273
  Mormons in, 500–501
  paper currency in, 281
  prisons in, 518
  Revolutionary Loyalists in, 236–37

  Revolutionary War fighting in, 214,
    232–36, 233, 240, 242, 245, 247, 252
  slavery in, 261
  voting rights in, 411, 478
  in War of 1812, 368, 369
New York City, N.Y.:
  Civil War draft riots in, 659, 659
  in colonial period, 143, 145–46, 146
  ethnic mix in, 143
  Irish Americans in, 477
  in nineteenth century, 470–71, 472
  Panic of 1837 in, 442
  poverty in, 147
  slaves in, 123–25
  Tweed ring in, 736
New York colony, 86, 148
  in colonial taxation disputes, 198, 200
  Dutch origins of, 91–94, 142, 143, 153
  education in, 153
  ethnic mix in, 142, 143
  government of, 165, 166
  Indians in, 95–97, 142
  in land disputes, 204
  quartering of British in, 195
New York Herald, 733
New York Infirmary for Women and
    Children, 488
New York Mechanick Society, 314
New York militia, 368, 369
New York Tribune, 478, 625, 732
New York Weekly Journal, 148
Nez Perces, 532
Niña, 19
"Ninety-five Theses" (Luther), 41
Ninth Amendment, 306
Nisquallys, 532
nobles, English, 53, 54
Nonconformists, 69, 75
Norse explorers, 14, 15–16
North, Frederick, Lord, 202, 206–8, 207,
    211, 243, 253
North Carolina:
  agriculture in, 573, 574
  Confederacy and states' rights in, 682
  Constitution ratified by, 295, 297
  education in, 513
  free blacks in, 397
  Indian lands ceded in, 276
  Indians removed from, 276, 429–32

land claims of, 276
migration from, 591
newspapers in, 512
paper currency in, 281
Reconstruction in, 724, 734
Revolutionary Loyalists in, 237
Revolutionary War fighting in, 217, 247–51
Revolutionary War troops from, 250
secession of, 650
voting rights in, 258, 446
North Carolina colony:
backcountry of, 143, 205
colonization of, 48–49, *48*
European settlement of, 86, *87*
government of, 167
Indians in, 90
tar in, 118
North Star, 596
Northwest Ordinance (1787), 274–77, 605, 612
Norwegian settlers, 480
Notes on the State of Virginia (Jefferson), 261, 599
Nova Scotia, 44, 71, 171, 180
Noyes, John Humphrey, 522
nullification and interposition, 337–38, 421–28
Andrew Jackson and, 424, 426–28, 436, 439, 528
Calhoun and, 408, 421–28
South Carolina Ordinance and, 426
theory of, 337–38
Webster-Hayne debate on, 422–24
Nurse, Rebecca, *130*
nursing, 487–88

oats, 22, 131, 142
Oberlin College, 500, 515
Observations Concerning the Increase of Mankind (Franklin), 111
ocean transportation, 462–63
Ogden, Aaron, 400–401
Oglethorpe, James E., 100, 104
Ohio, 323
education in, 514
German settlers in, 480
Indian lands ceded in, 277
statehood for, 276, 350, 388, 514

Ohio Company, 178, 276
Ohio Life Insurance and Trust Company, 633
Ohio River, transportation on, 458
Ojibwas, 191
Oklahoma, 36
in Civil War, 661
see also Indian Territory
Old Northwest, 274–77, *275, 323*
slavery banned from, 276, 603, 605, 612
Old Southwest, 591–92
Olive Branch Petition (1775), 216
Oliver, John, 453
Omoo (Melville), 510
Oñate, Juan de, 37
Oneida Community, 522
Oneidas, *103*, 264
Onondagas, *103*
"On the Equality of the Sexes" (Murray), 262–63
Opechancanough, Powhatan chief, 64
opera houses, 473
opium, 438
Order of the Star Spangled Banner, 481
Ordinance of Secession (South Carolina) (1860), 642
Ordinance of Secession (Virginia) (1861), 650
Oregon Country, 392, 533–35, 561
and election of 1844, 550
Great Britain and, 401, 534, 551, 552–53, *553*
Polk and, 551, 552–53, *552*
Russia and, 401, 534
slavery issue and, 604
U.S.-British border in, 552–53, *552, 553*
U.S. settlement of, 538, 539, 541
Oregon (Overland) Trail, 534, 538, 539–42, *539, 540, 541*, 543
Oriskany, Battle of (1777), 242
Osborn, Sarah, 156, *157*
Osborne, Sarah, 140
Osceola, 429
Ostend Manifesto (1854), 618
O'Sullivan, John L., 530, 554, 560
O'Sullivan, T. H., *687*
Otis, James, 201, 210

Ottawas, 186, 322
Overland (Oregon) Trail, 539–42, *539,*
    540, 541, 543
Owen, Robert, 522–23
Oxbow Route, *539*

Paine, Thomas, 151
    in American Revolution, *234*
    background of, 218
painting, romanticism and, *504*
Paiutes, 532
Pakenham, Edward, 371–72
Palmer, Phoebe Worrall, 498
Palo Alto, Battle of (1846), 556
Panama, 26
Panic of 1819, 394–95, 407, 432, 452
Panic of 1837, 439, 441–42, *441,* 459, 463,
    484, 530, 534
Panic of 1857, 633–34
Panic of 1873, 734–35
Paragon, 400
Paris, Treaty of (1763), 183–87, 190, 221
Paris, Treaty of (1783), 254, *255,* 271,
    279, 304
Parker, John, 213
Parker, Theodore, 505, 523, 634
Parkman, Francis, 176
Parliament, British:
    American Revolution and, 243
    Charles I's conflict with, 55–56
    in colonial taxation disputes, 197–98,
        200, 203, 208, *208,* 219
    on Continental Congress, 210–11
    Continental Congress on, 210
    currency policies of, 194–95
    elections of, 202
    kings' conflict with, 55–56, 162, 168
    Restoration and, 56
    taxation and, 53
    trade regulated by, 163–64
    see also House of Commons, British;
        House of Lords, British
Parris, Samuel, 140
party system:
    cultural-ethnic identity and, 440, 478
    establishment of, 315
    Jefferson's role in, 348
    third parties and, 435–36, 481–82, 624
    Washington on, 329

patroonships, 92, 142
Paxton Boys, 204–5, *204*
Peabody, Elizabeth, 505
Peabody, Sophia, 505
Peale, Charles Willson, *236, 285, 316,*
    425, 582
Pea Ridge, Battle of (1862), 652
penal system, 517–18
Pendleton, George H. "Gentleman
    George," 728
Pendleton, William, 676
penitentiaries, 518
Penn, William, 98–99, 142–43,
    153, 167, 204
Pennsylvania:
    canals in, 459
    Civil War fighting in, 685–88
    Constitution ratified by, *295*
    in early interstate cooperation, 283
    Indian lands ceded in, 276
    paper currency in, 281
    Revolutionary War fighting in, 234,
        240, 241, 247
    slavery in, 259, 261
    voting rights in, 258–59, 410
    Whiskey Rebellion in, 323–24
Pennsylvania, University of (Philadelphia
    Academy), 150, 159
Pennsylvania Chronicle, 200
Pennsylvania colony, 87, 98–100,
    166–67
    backcountry of, 145
    discontent on frontier of, 204–5
    education in, 153
    ethnic groups in, 98–99,
        142–43, 145
    European settlement of, *97,*
        98–100, 109
    government of, 100, 168
    Indians in, 142, 186
    in land disputes, 204
    and protests against British, 200
    and Quakers, 98–100, 109
    religion in, 98–100, 142–43
Pennsylvania Dutch, 143
Pennsylvania Gazette, 150
Pennsylvania Journal, 197
"penny dailies," 511
Pequots, 81–83, *82, 103*

Pequot War (1637), 81–83
Perry, Matthew, 619, *619*
Perry, Oliver H., 369
Peru, 31, 171
pet banks, 437
Petersburg, Battle of (1864), 690
petition, freedom of, 256
Philadelphia, 351
Philadelphia, Battle of (1777), *240,* 241
Philadelphia, Pa., 470
  in colonial period, 143, 145
  Declaration of Independence written
    in, 219–20
  and First Continental Congress,
    209–11
  founding of, 99
  Irish Americans in, 477
  labor in, 484
  nativist clashes in (1844), 481
  Second Continental Congress and,
    214, 219–23
  as U.S. capitol, 311
Philadelphia Academy (University of
  Pennsylvania), 150, 159
Philadelphia-Lancaster Turnpike, 455
Philadelphia Navy Yard, 484
Philip (Metacomet), Wampanoag chief,
  83–84
Philip II, king of Spain, 46, 47
Philippines, 26, 183
Pickering, John, 349
Pickering, Thomas, 356
Pickering, Timothy, 333, 335
Pickett, George, 687
Pierce, Franklin, *610*
  in election of 1852, 617–18
  in election of 1856, 629
  foreign policy under, 618–19
  on Fugitive Slave Act, 623
  Kansas-Nebraska Act and, 622, 623
pigs, 22, 27, 110–11, 131, 574, 683
Pilgrims, 69
Pinchback, Pinckney B. S., 724
Pinckney, Charles, 114, 339
Pinckney, Charles Cotesworth,
  114, 332, 333
  in election of 1800, 338, *340*
  in election of 1804, 357
  in election of 1808, 363

Pinckney, Elizabeth Lucas "Eliza," 114–15
Pinckney, Thomas, 115, 332
  in election of 1796, 330
  and treaty with Britain, 325–26
Pinckney Treaty (1795), 325–26,
  325, 392
Pinta, 19
pirates, Barbary, 351, 375
  see also privateers
Pitcairn, John, 212, 213
Pitcher, Molly (Mary Ludwig Hays),
  262, *263*
Pitt, William, 181–83, 199
Pittsburgh, Pa. (Fort Duquesne), 178,
  181, 186, 471
Pizarro, Francisco, 31, *35*
Plains Indians, 12, 13, 38–40, *39,*
  530–32, 542
Plains of Mesa, Battle of the, *557*
Plan of Union (1801), 496
plantations, 345, 570, 577–79, 583–84
Plymouth colony, 36, 69–71, 75, 84,
  85, 110
  government of, 69–71
  Indian relations with, 70
  Massachusetts combined with, 166
  as Virginia Company division, 57, *60*
Pocahontas, 62–63, *63*
Poe, Edgar Allan, 509, *510*
Poles, 143
Polish Americans, 658
Politics in an Oyster House
  (Woodville), *512*
Polk, James K., 548–51
  Andrew Jackson compared with,
    550–51
  background of, 550–51
  in election of 1844, 548–51, *549*
  Mexican War and, 553–56, 557,
    560, 561
  reelection bid eschewed by, 604
  slavery issue and, 603, 604
pollution, 469
polygamy, 501, 522, 629
Ponce de León, Juan, 34–35, *35*
Pontiac, Ottawa chief, 186, 193
Poor Richard's Almanac (Franklin), 150
Popé, 38
Pope, John, 665

popular culture:
  in colonial period, 147, 472
  dueling and, 581
  in early nineteenth century, 472–75
  on the frontier, 329
  German immigrants and, *479*, 480
  Independence Day and, 266
  minstrel shows and, 474–75
  popular press and, 511–12
  slaves and, 125, *126*, 590
  southern planters and, 127–28
  and sports, 472–73, *473*
  taverns and, 147
  theater and, 473–74
  urban recreation and, 472–73
popular sovereignty, 604–5, 620, 631, 635
population:
  of cities, 470–71
  in colonial period, 111–13
  in early U.S., 301–3
  of Indians, 10, 12, 32–33
  Mayan, 8
  in nineteenth century, *454, 455*
  in South, *573*
  U.S., growth of, 414–15
Portugal:
  colonial trade with, 134
  exploration and discovery by, 18, *25, 26*
  in Napoleonic Wars, 362
  in slave trade, 127
Portuguese colonists, 143
Portuguese Empire, in Treaty
  of Tordesillas, 21
postal service, 147–48
  express, 464
Post Office Department, U.S., 217
potatoes, 22, 574, *574*
Pottawatomie Massacre (1856),
  625–26, 637
Potter, John "Bowie Knife," 637
poverty:
  alcoholism and, 516
  in antebellum South, 580
  in colonial period, 147
  education and, 513
  in post-Civil War South, 703–5
Powhatan, Chief, *58,* 59, 62–63
Powhatans, *103*
  colonists assisted by, 59

Pocahontas and, 62–63
  settler conflicts with, 64
predestination, 42
Preemption Act (1830), 453
Presbyterians, 42, 46, 55, 56, 143, 155,
  158, 159, 265, 494
  in Civil War, 599
  Congregationalists' union with, 496
  in revivals, 496, 497
  in Whig party, 440
Prescott, Samuel, 213
presidency:
  in Constitution, 289–92
  electors for, 290–91, 411
  executive privilege of, 321, 359
  nominations for, 403–4, 436
  powers of, 289, 290–92
  see also executive branch
presidios, 37
press:
  antislavery and, 593, 597
  colonial newspapers, 148
  freedom of, 148, 305, 336, 597
  popular, 511–12
Preston, Levi, 222–23
Price, Birch & Co., *587*
primogeniture, 54
Princeton, Battle of (1777), 235
Princeton University (College of
  New Jersey), 159
Principia (Newton), 149
printing technology, 16, 20, 511
prisons:
  debtors in, 484
  reform movements and, 517–18
privateers:
  American, 251
  Dutch, 44
  English, 44, 46
  French, 44, 320
proclamation line, 193
Proclamation of Amnesty (1865), 710
Proclamation of Amnesty and
  Reconstruction (1863), 707
professions, rise of, 485–88
progressivism, Theodore Roosevelt and,
  050–960
Prohibition movement, 292
Prohibitory Act (1775), 218, 243

property:
black ownership of, 712
voting rights and, 169–70, 258–59,
411, 478, 483
women's control of, 519, 521
prostitution, 117
Protestantism, 52, 579
anti-Catholicism and, 481
rationalism in, 493–94
in Reconstruction, 726–27
Reformation and, 40–43
see also specific denominations
Providence Plantations, 76–77
Prussia:
in colonial wars, 181
French Revolution and, 317
trade with, 278
Public Credit Act (1869), 729
public schools, 484
Pueblo-Hohokam culture, 9, 11
Pueblo Revolt, 38
Pueblos, 11, 34, 37, 531, 532
Puerto Rico, 26, 34–35, 402
Punderson, Prudence, *116*
Puritans, 85, 129, 136–37
Andros's conflict with, 166
Anglican Church as viewed by,
72, 75, 137
communitarian standards of,
137–38, 140
in Connecticut, 78, *82*
Cromwell and, 84, 163
dissension among, 75–77, *76*, 158
education and, 152–53
in England, 42, 43, 55
evolving doctrines of, 492–94
Great Awakening and, 158
Harvard founded by, 159
lifestyle of, 136
in Maine, 79
in Massachusetts, 68–69, 72, 73, 75, 77,
109, 117
missionaries of, 83
in New Hampshire, 79
Separatists, 43, 68–69, 72, 137
transcendentalism and, 505
in Virginia, 128
witchcraft and, 139–41
putting-out system, 466

quackery, 487
Quakers (Society of Friends), 41, *99*, 129,
139, 142, 143, 153, 204
educational efforts of, 153
and founding of Pennsylvania,
98–100, 109
transcendentalism and, 505
in Virginia, 128
Quantrill, William C., 661
Quarles, Benjamin, 672
Quartering Act (1765), 195, 199, 203
Quartering Act (1774), 208
quartering of military, 195, 203, 208, 305
Quebec, 44, 171, 174, 182, *183*
as British colony, 193
founding of, 171
Revolutionary War attack on, 216–17
Quebec, Battle of (1759), 182
Quebec Act (1774), 208, 259
Quechuas, *see* Incas
Queen's College (Rutgers University), 159

race riots:
in Memphis (1866), 715
in New Orleans (1866), 715
Radical Republicans:
assessment of, 725–26
in Civil War, 669, 680, 682
corruption charges against, 726
Johnson's relations with, 710, 713,
715–16, 717–19
presidential elections and, 404
in Reconstruction, 707–8, 710, 712–13,
725–26, 734
railroads, 463, 464, 465, 487, 606, 619
in Civil War, 654
in early nineteenth century, 421,
459–62, *460*, *461*, 463
economic benefits of, 462
Gadsden Purchase and, 619
Indian relocation and, 623
Kansas-Nebraska Act and, 620
land grants to, 463, 703
negative impact of, 462
in Panic of 1873, 734
steam power introduced to, 459
transcontinental, 619–20, 703
travel on, 462
Rainbow, 462

Raleigh, Walter, 47–48
ranchos, 537
Randolph, Edmund, 295, 303
Randolph, Edward, 164–65
Randolph, John, 358, 366, 408
"Real Whigs," 195
Reconstruction, 702–39, *725*
    African Americans in, 705–6, 711–12, 720–24, *723*
    black codes in, 711–12, 714
    carpetbaggers in, 724, 734
    Congress in, 706, 707–8, 711–17, 719, 732, 735
    "Conservative" parties in, 734
    conservative resurgence in, 733–34
    constitutional debates over, 707–8, 710, 713–14
    corruption and abuses in, 726
    education in, 721, 726
    end of, 738–39
    Johnson's plans for, 710–11, 713–14
    land policy in, 705–6, 723, 724
    Radical Republicans and, 707–8, 710, 712–13, 725–26, 734
    religion in, 726–27
    scalawags in, 724–25, 731, 734
    southern intransigence over, 711–12
    Supreme Court in, 717, 739
    white terror in, 731–32
Reconstruction Act, Second (1867), 717
Reconstruction Act, Third (1867), 717
Red Eagle, Creek chief, 369
Reed, Mary, 156
Reformation, 40–43
    in England, 42–43
reform movements, 484, 516–23
    antislavery, 592–97, 616–17
    for civil service, 732
    education, 512–16
    for prisons and asylums, 517–18
    Prohibition movement, 516–17
    utopian, 521–23
    for women's rights, 518–21, 596–97
    see also progressivism
Refunding Act (1870), 729
Regulators, 205, 217, 237
religion:
    abolitionists and, 616
    African, 122

African-American, 115, 125, 497, 589–90, 720, 727
American Indian, 33, 34, 37, *80*, 81
in backcountry, 154
and Civil War, 676–78, *677*
in colonial period, 136–38, 143, 153–59
deism and, 493
denominational splits in, 158
education and, 159–9, 514
Enlightenment and, 149–50
Franklin on, 151
freedom of, *see* religious freedom
on frontier, 496
fundamentalism and, 136
Great Awakening and, 153–59, 493
in Massachusetts, 139
in New England, 136–38, 153–59
rational, 492–94
in Reconstruction, 726–27
revival meetings and, 496–99, *498*
revivals in, *see* revivals, religious
Second Great Awakening and, 494–503
and slavery, 572
slavery justified through, 599
social reform in, 498, 499–500
in South, 128–29, 571–72
temperance and, 516
transcendentalism and, 505
Unitarianism and, 493–94
Universalism and, 494
utopian communities and, 521–22
witchcraft and, 139–41, *140*
women and, 115–16, 156–57, 158, 498, 572, 677
    see also specific religions and denominations
religious freedom, 41, 56, 94, 98–99, 143
    after American Revolution, 265–66
    in Bill of Rights, 305, 306
    French colonies and, 174
    in Maryland, 85
    in Massachusetts, 139
    in Pennsylvania, 99, 143
    Roger Williams and, 74–76, 77
    and separation of church and state, 74–76
    in South Carolina, 86–87
    voting rights and, 170, 411
rendezvous system, 533–34

"Report on Manufactures" (Hamilton), 309, 313, 316
"Reports on Public Credit" (Hamilton), 308–9
Representative Men (Emerson), 508
Republican party:
  in Civil War, 678
  in election of 1856, 629–30
  in election of 1860, 640–42
  in election of 1868, 727–29
  in election of 1872, 733
  in election of 1876, 735–39
  emergence of, 623–24
  KKK intimidation of, 731
  Liberal, 732, *733*
  Lincoln's early involvement with, 636
  in Reconstruction, 731
  scalawags in, 724, 731, 734
  slavery compromise sought by, 645
  see also Radical Republicans
Republicans, Jeffersonian, 229, 334–35, 390
  Adams criticized by, 331
  Alien and Sedition Acts and, 335–36
  and *Dartmouth College v. Woodward,* 398–99
  in election of 1796, 330
  in election of 1800, 338–41
  in election of 1816, 389
  in election of 1824, 404
  Federalists' role reversal with, 375
  formation of, 315–17
  French conflict and, 333, 335–36, *335*
  French Revolution and, 319
  Hartford Convention and, 374
  Jay's Treaty and, 321
  Jefferson's role with, 346–48
  land policy of, 326
  Louisiana Purchase and, 352–53
  national bank and, 350, 385
  officeholder conflicts and, 348
  split among, 358
  and War of 1812, 375
  Whiskey Rebellion and, 324
Republicans, Old, 358
Resaca de la Palma, Battle of (1846), 556
reservation (Indian) system, 543
Restoration, English, 56, 85–86

Revels, Hiram, *723*, 724
Revenue (Sugar) Act (1764), 194, 195, 196, 199, 203
Revenue Act (1767), 200
revenuers, 324
Revere, Paul, *203*, 280
  warning ride of, 212–13
Revival of 1857–1859, 634
revivals, religious:
  and "burned over" district, 499–500
  during Civil War, 676
  on the frontier, 496–99
  Great Awakening, 153–59, 493
  Mormons and, 500
  and Panic of 1857, 634
  Second Great Awakening, 494–503
  women in, 634
Revolutionary War, *see* American Revolution
Rhett, Robert Barnwell, 615
Rhode Island:
  Civil War troops from, 672
  Constitutional Convention avoided by, 284
  Constitution ratified by, *295, 297*
  at Hartford Convention, 374
  paper currency in, 281
  Revolutionary War troops from, *214, 260*
  slavery in, 259, 261
Rhode Island, College of (Brown University), 159, 514–15
Rhode Island colony, 87
  charter of, 85, 137, 168
  European settlement of, 75–78
  in events before American Revolution, 205
  government of, 85, 137, 165, 168
  as refuge, 143
Rhode Island (Fall River) system, 469
Ricard, Cyprien, 582
rice, 22, 117–18, 384, 573, 704
rich, the:
  in colonial period, 146, *146*
  in early nineteenth century, 488
  housing of, 464
  social origins of, 488
  in South, 127–28, 577–79
  wartime profits of, 680

Richmond, Va., *704*
  bread riot in (1863), 682
  capture of (1865), 697
  as Confederate capital, 655, 657
  first settlements in, 62
  as military goal of Union army, 655,
    657, 663–65, 690, 697
  Tredegar Iron Works in, 575, *576*
Richmond Enquirer, 627–28
riots:
  in Memphis (1866), 715
  in New Orleans (1866), 715
  in New York (1863), 659, *659*
  in Richmond (1863), 682
  see also race riots
Ripley, George, 505, 523
Rittenhouse, David, 150
river transportation:
  federal funding for, 384, 387–88
  to frontier regions, 456–59
  Gibbons v. Ogden, 400–401
  state funding for, 437
  steamboats on, 400–401, 456–58, *458*
roads, *see* highways and roads
Roanoke Island, 48–49, *48*
Rockefeller, John D., 680
Rockingham, Marquis of, 199
Rolfe, John, 62–63, 64
Rolfe, Rebecca (Pocahontas), 62–63, *63*
Rolfe, Thomas, 63
romanticism, 381, 503–8
  American literature and, 508–11
  in art and architecture, 503
  transcendentalism and, 504–8
rope, 133
Rosecrans, William S., 688
Rossiter, Thomas Pritchard, *291*
Rothman, David, 517
Roundheads, 56
Royal Proclamation of 1763, 193, 259
Ruffin, Edmund, 615
rule of 1756, 320, 360
Rump Parliament, 56
Rush, Benjamin, 267, 516
Rush, Richard, 391
Rush-Bagot Agreement (1817), 391
Russell, Jonathan, 373
Russia:
  California and, 535
  in colonial wars, 181

  in Napoleonic wars, 360
  Oregon Country and, 401, 534
  seal traders from, 36, 535
Rutgers University (Queen's College), 159
Rutledge, John, 287

Sacagawea, 354
St. Augustine, Fla., 36, 170
St. Leger, Barry, 241–42
St. Louis, Mo., 471
St. Mary's, Md., 110
Salem, Mass., 75, 123–25, *130, 138,*
    139–41, 140
Sampson, Deborah, 262
San Antonio, Tex., 170
Sandys, Edwin, 63
San Francisco, Calif., gold rush and, *607*
San Salvador, 19
Santa Anna, Antonio López de, 545–46,
    547, 558
Santa Barbara, Mission of, *536*
Santa Fe, N.Mex., 38, 170, 538
Santa Fe Trail, 538, *539*
Santa María, 19, 20
Santo Domingo, 26, 402
Saratoga, Battle of (1777), *240,* 241–42,
    241, 243
Sassacus, Pequot chief, 82
Sassamon, John, 83
Sauks, *102,* 429
Savannah, Battle of (1778), 248
Savannah, Ga., *101*
  fall of (1864), 693–94
  founding of, 100–101
scalawags, 724–25, 731, 734
Scandinavia, 15
  Reformation in, 41
Scandinavian Americans, 480
  in Civil War, 658
Scarlet Letter, The (Hawthorne), 508
Schumacher, Ferdinand, 480
Schurz, Carl, 711
Schwenkfeldians, 41
science:
  in colonial period, 149–51
  in early nineteenth century, 464
Scotch-Irish Americans, 22, 100, 109,
    142, 143, *144,* 145, 155, 328, 496, 580
Scotland, 42, 52, 54, 55
  English union with, 57

Scots, Highland, 101, 143
Scott, Dred, 630–32
Scott, Harriet Robinson, 630
Scott, Winfield, 366, 443
    in Civil War, 652, 656, 663
    in election of 1852, 617
    in Mexican War, 556, 559–60, 561
Scottish Americans, 98, 101, 142, 143,
        144, 145, 580
    in American Revolution, 217
    in Civil War, 658
search and seizure, unreasonable, 305
search warrants, 191
secession, considered by New England,
        356, 374
secession of South, 642–43, *651*
    Buchanan's response to, 644–45
    choosing sides in, 650–52
    efforts at compromise in, 645
    forfeited-rights theory and, 713
    Lincoln's response to, 644–45, 649,
        651–52
    movement for, 642–43
Second Great Awakening, 494–503
    burned-over district and, 499–500
    on frontier, 496–99
    Mormons and, 500–503
    New England colleges and, 495–96
    salvation and, 499
Sedition Act (1798), 335–36, 337–38, *337*
self-incrimination, 256, 305
"Self-Reliance" (Emerson), 506
Seminoles, 302, 392–93, *392*
    in Civil War, 661
    removal of, 428–29
Senate, U.S.:
    Compromise of 1850 in, 610–15
    in Constitution, 287, 289–90
    Convention of 1800 ratified by, 334
    Jay's Treaty approved by, 321
    Johnson's trial in, 719
    Louisiana Purchase approved by, 353
    violence on floor of (1856),
        626–28, *627*
    see also Congress, U.S.
Seneca Falls Convention (1848), 520
Senecas, *103*, 247
separation of church and state,
        75–77, 306
separation of powers, 256, 289–92

Separatists, 43, 69, 72, 137
serfdom, 54
servants, *see* indentured servants
Seven Pines (Fair Oaks), Battle
        of (1862), 664
Seven Years' War, *see* French and
        Indian War
Seward, William H., 672
    appointed secretary of state, 649
    assassination attempt on, 708
    and Compromise of 1850, 610, 612–13
    and election of 1856, 629
    in election of 1860, 640
sewer systems, 464
sewing machines, 464
sex ratios, 113
sexual relations:
    Puritans on, 136
    slavery and, 579
Seymour, Horatio, 719, 728
Shakers, 521–22, *521*
Shakespeare, William, 61
Sharpsburg (Antietam), Battle of (1862),
        666–68, 672
Shaw, Robert Gould, 672–73
Shawnees, 184, 193, 247, 322, 364–66,
        365, 445
Shays, Daniel, 281
Shays's Rebellion, 281–83, *282*
sheep, 22, 110, 131
Sheridan, Philip Henry, *690*
Sherman, John, 729
Sherman, Roger, 219, 285, 287
Sherman, William Tecumseh, 689, *693*
    Atlanta destroyed by, 682
    Johnston's surrender to, 698
    in march to sea, 691–95, *695*, 703–4
Shiloh, Battle of (1862), 661–63
shipbuilding, 118, 132–34, *133*
shoemakers' strike (1860), 484–85
Siberia, 5
Signing the Constitution (Rossiter), *291*
silver:
    in mercantile system, 163–64
    mining of, 660
    Spanish Empire and, 34, 37, 38, 170
Singer, Isaac Merritt, 464
"Sinners in the Hands of an Angry God"
        (Edwards), 156
Sioux, 39, 354, 429, 531, 543

"slash-and-burn" techniques, 110
Slater, Samuel, 465
slavery, 428, 519, 523, 561, 571, *571*
    American Revolution and, 222, 258,
        259–62, 345
    banned from Old Northwest,
        276, 605, 612
    California and, 609, 611–12, 615
    Civil War and, 669–72, 696
    in colonial period, 86, 118, 120–27,
        126, 135
    and Compromise of 1850, 610–18, *614*
    Congress and, 603, 609, 631–32,
        633, 674
    in Constitution, 287–88, 289, 350–51
    defense of, 598–99
    in District of Columbia, 443
    Dred Scott case and, 630–32, 634,
        636, 640
    economics of, 576
    and election of 1844, 548, 550
    emancipation and, 669–74, 704
    in Kansas-Nebraska crisis, 619–30
    Lincoln-Douglas debates on, 635–37
    Mexican War and, 554
    Missouri Compromise and, 395–98,
        396, 421, 604, 605, 612, 614, 620,
        629, 630–32
    New Mexico and, 609, 611, 615
    origins of, 120–21, 123
    and religion, 572
    religious justification of, 599
    southern defense of, 570, 598–99
    in territories, 603–10
    Texas annexation and, 547, 551–52
    Thirteenth Amendment and, 288, 674,
        702, 711, 739
    Tyler and, 527–28
    Wilmot Proviso and, 603
    see also abolition movement
Slavery is Dead? (Nast), *712*
slaves, 100, 108–9, 132, 145
    in Africa, 121
    African roots of, 33, 121–23, *126*
    in American Revolution, 209, 217, 237,
        320, 321
    after American Revolution, 277, 345
    black ownership of, 582
    childhood among, 590–91

    in colonial period, 115–16
    community of, 588–89
    as "contraband," 670, *670, 673*
    culture of, 120–27, *126*
    escaped, 392, *392,* 584, 596
    freed, 345, 582, *583*
    fugitive slave laws and, 610, 615–16,
        616, 623
    Indians as, 21, 83, 84, 88–91, 127
    in industry, 575–76
    infant mortality of, 583
    insurrections of, 122–25, 421, 587–88,
        593, 638, 639
    management of, 579
    manumission of, 261–62
    marriage of, 125, 590
    middle-class southerners and, 579
    in Old Southwest, 592
    plantations and, 578–79, 583–84
    population of, 578, *584, 585*
    religion and, 589–90
    sexual exploitation of, 579,
        586–87, 592
    as skilled workers, 126–27, 482
    in South, 120–27, 302, 583–91
    in southern mythology, 569–70, 573
    southern white culture and, 576–79
    in West, 452
    women, 584–86
slave trade, 3, 86, 87, 121, 122–23, *124,*
        135, *288,* 583, *587*
    Constitutional provisions on,
        287–88, 289
    in District of Columbia, 443, 615
    end of, 259, 350–51, 529, 583
    foreign outlawing of, 350–51,
        529, 583
    within U.S., 583, 584, 611, 615
Slavs, 127
Slidell, John, 554, 660
smallpox, *23,* 24–25, 81, 96–97, 113, 186,
        216–17, 239, 260
    inoculation for, 239
Smith, Emma, 501
Smith, Hyrum, 502
Smith, John, *58,* 59–61, 63
Smith, Joseph, Jr., 500–502
Smithson, James, 464
Smithsonian Institution, 464

smuggling, 193–94, 200, 205, 222, 277, 362, 364
Society of Friends, *see* Quakers
Sons of Liberty, 196, 201–2, *201*
Sons of Temperance, 517
South, 566–67, 569–99
   African-American culture in, 120–27, *126*, 581–82
   agricultural diversity in, 571, 574–75
   agriculture in, 117–18, 573–75, 576–79
   in American Revolution, 248–53, *249*
   Civil War devastation of, 693–95, 703–5
   in colonial period, 117–30
   cotton in, 451–52
   distinctiveness of, 570–76
   dueling in, 581
   economy of, 575–76
   education in, 152–53
   in French and Indian War, 182
   frontier of, 591–92
   gentry in, 127–28, *128*
   honor and violence in, 580–81
   immigrants in, 570
   Indian conflicts in, 182
   Irish Americans in, 477
   land policies in, 118–19
   literacy rates in, 512
   manufactures in, 575
   masculine culture in, 580–81, 592
   middle class in, 579
   Middle Colonies' trade with, 142
   and migration to Southwest, 590–91
   mythology of, 569–70, 573
   New England compared with, 134
   plantations in, 576–79, 583–84
   poor whites in, 580
   post-Civil War devastation in, 703–5
   religion in, 571–72
   secession of, 642–43, 650–52, *651*
   sex ratios in, 113
   slaves in, 120–27, 302, 340, 583–91
   society and economy in, 117–30
   soil exhaustion in, 575
   and Tariff of 1816, 386–87
   War of 1812 in, 369–70, *370*
   Whigs in, 440
   white society in, 576–81

   see also Civil War, U.S.; Confederate States of America; Reconstruction
South Carolina, 345
   African-American soldiers outlawed by, 260
   agriculture in, 573, 574, 575
   Civil War fighting in, 649–50, 657, 673, 694–95
   Constitution ratified by, *295*
   cotton in, 451, 452
   education in, 513
   in election of 1800, 339
   in election of 1876, 737
   government of, 86–87
   Indian lands ceded in, 276
   Indians in, 264
   land claims of, *273*
   migration from, 591
   nullification and, 408, 421–23, 424, 426–28
   paper currency in, 281
   post-Revolutionary War debt in, 310
   Reconstruction in, 719, 724, 734, 738, 739
   Revolutionary Loyalists in, 237
   Revolutionary War fighting in, 217, 247–51
   Revolutionary War troops from, 247–51
   secession of, 642, *644*
   slave trade in, 259, 351
   voting rights in, 411
South Carolina colony:
   agriculture in, 118
   backcountry of, 143, 205
   gentry of, 127–28
   government of, 86–87, 167, 169
   Huguenots in, 36
   Indians in, 87–91
   as refuge, 143
   Regulators in, 205
   settlement of, 86–87, *87*
   slaves in, 121, 123, 126, *126*
   trade and commerce in, 118
South Carolina Exposition and Protest (Calhoun), 408, 421–22, 423
South Carolina Ordinance, 426–27
South Carolina Red Shirts, 734
Southern Patriot, 267

Southwest, Old, 591–92
Spain, 352–53, 358, 392–94
American Revolution and, 218, 242, 243, 253, 254, 309
colonial trade with, 134
in colonial wars, 183, 186
decline of, 392
early U.S. relations with, 279, 318, 322
explorations by, 18–21, 25, 26, 33–38, 35, 36–37
Indian conflicts and, 277, 302, 325
Mexican independence from, 170, 533, 533, 536–37, 545
Mississippi River access and, 279
Monroe Doctrine and, 402
in Napoleonic wars, 360, 362, 402, 532
Oregon Country claim of, 401, 534
Pinckney Treaty with, 325–26
in slave trade, 127
and War of 1812, 365, 371
see also Spanish Empire
Spanish Americans, 143, 658
Spanish Armada, 46–47, 46
Spanish Empire, 26–38, 89, 91, 125
Aztecs defeated by, 9
British Empire compared with, 33–34, 57, 104, 162, 170–71
California as territory of, 38, 535
Catholicism and, 32–33, 32, 33, 36–37, 171, 183, 532
challenges to, 44–49
colonization in, 36–37
conquests of, 27–32
Cromwell's conflicts with, 85
decline of, 170–71, 392
decolonization of, 402
European diseases spread in, 23–25
Florida as territory of, 34, 36, 183, 352–53, 365, 393–94, 532
maps of, 175, 184, 185
Mexico as territory of, 34, 536–37
missionaries in, 36–37, 89, 333, 532, 535–36
privateers' attacks against, 44
in Treaty of Tordesillas, 21
Specie Circular, 437, 438
Specie Resumption Act (1875), 735
speculators:
in bonds, 309

in gold, 730
in land, 326, 395
speech, freedom of, 256, 305, 336
speedy trial, right to, 306
spoils system, patronage, 418
Spokanes, 532
sports, in nineteenth century, 472–73, 473
Spotsylvania Court House, Battle of (1864), 690
Squanto, 70
squatter sovereignty, 604
stagecoaches, 147
Stamp Act (1765), 195–99, 197, 222–23
colonial protests against, 195–99
repeal of, 198–99, 198
Stamp Act Congress (1765), 198, 200
Standish, Miles, 69
Stanton, Edwin M., 680, 716, 718
Stanton, Elizabeth Cady, 520–21, 520
Stark, John, 242
Star of the West, 644
"Star-Spangled Banner, The," 371
state and local power:
in Constitution, 286–87
and paper currency, 280–81
state-compact theory, 337
State Department, U.S., 303
states' rights, 350, 358, 404, 440, 527
Confederacy and, 682
at Constitutional Convention, 285, 291
Webster-Hayne debate on, 422–24
see also nullification and interposition
steamboats, 400–401, 400, 456–58, 458, 464, 465
Gibbons v. Ogden and, 400–401
steam engine, 465
Steinway, Heinrich, 480
Stephens, Alexander, 642, 682, 711
Steuben, Frederick Wilhelm Augustus Henry Ferdinand, baron von, 244–45
Stevens, John, 236
Stevens, Thaddeus, 680, 712, 713, 714, 718, 726, 728
Stewart, Alexander T., 477
Stiles, Isaac, 158
Stockton, Robert F., 557

Stono uprising (1739), 123
Stowe, Harriet Beecher, 569, 616–17, 727
Strauss, Levi, 480, 606
Stuart, Charles Edward (Bonnie Prince
    Charlie), 143
Stuart, Gilbert, *247*
Stuart, J. E. B., 665
    at Harper's Ferry, 638
Stuyvesant, Peter, 93, 94
suffrage, *see* voting rights
Sufis, 505
sugar, 73, 574, 704
Sugar (Revenue) Act (1764), 194, 195,
    196, 199, 203
Sullivan, John, 247
Sumner, Charles, 680, 712, *713,* 714, 715
    Brooks's attack on, 626–28, *627*
Sumter, Thomas, 250
Supreme Court, U.S.:
    appointments to, 304, 339
    in *Cherokee Nation v. Georgia,* 431
    civil rights decisions of, 739
    on Civil War, 650
    in Constitution, 291
    in *Dred Scott* case, 630–32
    establishment of, 304
    in *Gibbons v. Ogden,* 400–401
    implied powers broadened by, 313
    Indian lands and, 431
    judicial nationalism and, 398–401
    judicial review by, 398–99
    in *McCulloch v. Maryland,* 399–400
    in *Marbury v. Madison,* 349–50
    in Reconstruction, 717, 739
Surrender of Lord Cornwallis
    (Trumball), *252*
Susquehannocks, 204, *204*
Sutter, John A., 538
Sutter's Fort (New Helvetia), *537,* 538
Sweden, trade with, 277
Swedish Americans, 98, 142, *144,*
    145, 480
Swedish colonies, 92
Swiss Americans, 101, 143
Switzerland, Reformation in, 41–42

Tallmadge, James, Jr., 396
Tammany Hall, 484
Taney, Roger B., 436, 631, *631*

Taos Indians, 531
Tappan, Arthur, 593, 595
Tappan, Lewis, 593, 595
tar, 118
Tariff of 1816, 386–87, 394
Tariff of 1824, 407
Tariff of 1828 (Tariff of Abominations),
    408, 421–22, 426
Tariff of 1832, 426
Tariff of 1833, 437
Tariff of 1857, 633
tariffs and duties, 194, 257, 389, 404, 405,
    437, 528, 566
    Adams's view on, 407
    Andrew Jackson on, 407–8,
    426–28, 436
    in Civil War, 678, 703
    Constitution and, 421–22
    in early U.S., 280, *280,* 306–7, 313–14
    economic nationalism and, 375, 384,
    386, 389
    in Hamiltonian program, 307–8,
    313–14
    under Jefferson, 350
    under Polk, 551
    in South Carolina nullification crisis,
    421–23
    Tyler on, 527
    after War of 1812, 386–87, 389
    see also specific tariffs and duties
Tarleton, Banastre, 248, 250
taverns, 147, *148,* 472–73
taxation:
    under Articles of Confederation, 257,
    271
    British, 53, 55, 56, 193
    churches supported by, 265
    in Civil War, 678–79
    in colonial period, 166, 170,
    193–202, 265
    by Confederacy, 680
    congressional power of, 287, 288
    in Constitution, 287, 288
    in early U.S., 306–7, 309–10, 316
    Grenville's program of, 193–95
    in Hamiltonian program, 309–10
    income, 679
    in Massachusetts, 166, 281–82
    national bank and, 399–400

taxation (*continued*)
  representation and, 196–97, 201
  Townshend's program of, 200
  voting rights and, 258, 410–11
  on whiskey, 316, 323, 350
Taylor, Zachary:
  California statehood and, 609–10
  and Compromise of 1850, 611, 613
  death of, 613
  in election of 1848, 604–6
  in Mexican War, 554, 556, 557–58, 561
  New Mexico statehood and, 609, 613
tea, trade in, 463
Tea Act (1773), 206
teaching, 486, 487
technology:
  agricultural, 451–52, 453–54, 502
  in early nineteenth century, 346,
    464–65
  education and, 514–15
  exploration aided by, 16–17
  food and, 464, 477
  and growth of industry, 464–65
  of Indians, 23, 27
  of printing, 16, 511
  of Spanish vs. Indians, 27
  transportation and, 455, 462–63
Tecumseh, Shawnee chief, 364–66,
    365, 369
telegraph, 464, 465, 606, 660
temperance, 516–17, 517
  see also Prohibition movement
Tempest, The (Shakespeare), 61
tenancy, 54
ten-hour workday, 484
Tennent, William, 155, 156
Tennessee, 279, 455
  Civil War fighting in, 661–62, 688, 693
  emancipation in, 672, 674
  free blacks in, 397
  Indian conflicts in, 325
  Indian lands ceded in, 276
  Indian removal and, 276, 428
  military government of, 707
  in Reconstruction, 715, 716, 734
  secession of, 650
  statehood for, 329
  Union loyalists in, 715, 724
  voting rights in, 410–11

Tennessee militia, 369
Tennessee volunteers, 393
Tenochtitlán (Mexico City), 9, 28–29, 31
Tenskwatawa, 364
Tenth Amendment, 292, 306, 312
Tenure of Office Act (1867), 716, 718
Terror (1793–1794), 317
Texas, 36, 38, 394, 402, 532, 538,
    545–48, 609
  agriculture of, 574
  annexation of, 547–48, 551–52, 561
  border of, 611, 613, 615
  in Civil War, 661
  and Compromise of 1850, 611, 613, 615
  in election of 1844, 550
  German settlers in, 480
  independence of, from Mexico, 533,
    545–47
  Mexican War and, 553–54, 560, 561
  Reconstruction in, 719, 724
  secession of, 642
  slavery issue and, 545–46, 603, 611, 615
  U.S. settlers in, 545
Texas-New Mexico Act (1850), 615
Texas v. White, 717
textile industry, 384, 414–15, 465–70,
    467, 468, 566
  Lowell System in, 466–69
  mechanization of, 465–66
  water power and, 469–70
  see also cotton
Thames, Battle of the, 365, 369
Thanksgiving, 70
Thayendanegea (Joseph Brant), 247, 247
theater, 473–74
third parties:
  Anti-Masonic party, 435–36
  and emergence of Republican
    party, 624
  introduction of, 435–36
  Know-Nothing party, 481–82, 624
Thirteenth Amendment, 288, 645, 674,
    702, 711, 739
Thirty Years' War (1618–1648), 92
Thomas, George H., 688, 692–93
Thoreau, Henry David, 381, 505, 506–8,
    507, 510, 623
Tientsin, Treaty of (1858), 618
Tilden, Samuel J., 736–39, 738

timber industry, 110, 118, 132
Timucuas, *103*
Tippecanoe, Battle of (1811), 365, 445
Tituba (slave), 140
Tlaxcalans, 27–28, 31
tobacco, 23, 57, 73, *119*, 248, 277, 384, 573
  Civil War and, 704
  in early U.S., 302
  in Maryland colony, 68
  Rolfe's experiments with, 62–63
  soil depleted by, 118
  in Virginia colony, 62, 64, 117–18
Tocqueville, Alexis de, 494
Toleration Act (1689), 56, 167
Toltecs, 8
Tonnage Act (1789), 307
Toombs, Robert, 611
Tordesillas, Treaty of (1494), 21
Tories, *see* Loyalists (Tories)
Townshend, Charles, 199–200
Townshend Acts (1767):
  colonial protest against, 200
  modification and repeal of,
    202, 243
townships, 274
trade and commerce:
  agriculture and, 277, 278
  after American Revolution,
    277–78, *278*
  American Revolution and, 243, 277–78
  in California, 537–38
  with China, 278, 438, 463, 618
  in colonial period, 57, 59, 65, 66, 80,
    100, 104, 118–19, 132–36, *135*, 138,
    163–64, 173, 191, 193–202, 206–7
  in Confederation period, 277–78,
    279–81
  congressional power over, 257
  in Constitution, 287
  Continental Congress and, 210
  in cotton, 362, 421, 438, 452, 566, 574,
    575, 577, *577*
  in early U.S., 279–81
  with France, 307, 360–64, *361*, 363,
    421, 438, 574
  in French colonies, 36, 171–73, 176
  with Great Britain, 277, 279–80, 307,
    319–21, 332, *336*, 360–64, 373, 391,
    392, 394, 421, 438, 441, 574

with Indians, 57, 80, 100, 173
interstate, regulation of, 400–401
mercantile system in, 163–64, 307
with Mexico, 438, 538
Napoleonic Wars and, 360–64
in New England, 132–36, 138
in pre-Columbian cultures, 10, 12
in southern colonies, 118–19, *119*
in Spanish Empire, 36, 171
in Virginia colony, 59
with West Indies, 104, 132, 134–35,
    142, 191, 277, 320, 321, 360, 392
  see also fur trade; tariffs and duties;
    taxation; transportation
trade associations, 482–83
Trail of Tears, 429–32, *431*
Transcendental Club, 505
transcendentalism, 381, 504–8
transcontinental railroads, 678
Transcontinental Treaty (Adams-Onís
    Treaty) (1819), 394, 401
transportation, 450
  in colonial period, 147
  in early nineteenth century, 455–63,
    456–57
  government role in, 463
  highways and roads, 147, 328, 387–88,
    390, 415, 420–21, 455, *456–57*, 463
  internal improvements to, 387–88
  ocean, 462–63
  in post-Civil War era, 726
  railroads, 421, 459–62
  water, 283, 400–401, 462–63
  see also highways and roads; railroads
Travis, William B., 546
treason, 359
Treasury Department, U.S., 303, 679,
    729, 730
  Hamilton's program for, 314–15
  under Van Buren, 442–43
Treatise on Domestic Economy, A
    (Beecher), 518–19
Tredegar Iron Works, 575, *576*
Trent affair, 660
Trenton, Battle of (1776), 235
trial by jury, 53, 196, 256, 306
Trinidad, 21
Tripoli, 351
Trist, Nicholas P., 560

Trumbull, John, *252*
Truth, Sojourner, 596–97, *596*
Tryon, William, 205
Tubman, Harriet, 596
Tunis, 351
turkeys, 7, 22
Turner, Nat, 588, 589, 593
turnpikes, 455, 464
Tuscaroras, 90, *103*
Tuscarora War (1711–1713), 90
Tweed ring, 736
Twelfth Amendment, 357
Twice-Told Tales (Hawthorne), 508
Twining, David, *327*
Two Treatises on Government (Locke),
    167, 195
Tyler, John, 445, 527–30, 551–52, 645
Typee (Melville), 510
typhus, 24

Uncle Tom's Cabin (Stowe), 569–70,
    616–17, *617*, 727
Underground Railroad, 596
Unionists, 426
Union League, 719, 722, 731
Union Manufactories, *384*
Union Pacific Railroad, 730
Unitarians, 56, 493–94, 505
United States, U.S.S., 333
United States Sanitary Commission, 675
*Universal Asylum and Columbian
    Magazine*, 301
Universalists, 494
universities, *see* colleges and universities
Upanishads, 505
Ury, John, 125
Utah:
    and Compromise of 1850, 615
    Indians in, 531, 532
    Mormons in, 502–3, *503*
Utah Act (1850), 615
utopian communities, 521–23

Vallandigham, Clement L., 681–82
Valley Forge, winter quarters at
    (1777–1778), 241, 243–45, *244*
Van Buren, Martin, 406, 408, 440–45,
    440, *441*, 547
    background of, 441

Calhoun's rivalry with, 418
    Eaton Affair and, 420
    in election of 1832, 436
    in election of 1836, 440
    in election of 1840, *443*, 445
    in election of 1844, 548–50
    in election of 1848, 605, *606*, 617
    Great Britain post denied to, 425–26
    independent Treasury under, 442–43
    national bank issue and, 434
    ten-hour workday and, 484
van Honthorst, Gerrit, *55*
Van Rensselaer, Stephen, 367, 368
Vassar College, 515
Verdict of the People (Bingham), *435*
Vermont, 204
    constitution of, 261
    at Hartford Convention, 374
    Revolutionary War fighting in, 242
    Revolutionary War troops
        from, 214
    slavery in, 261
    statehood for, 329
    voting rights in, 410
Verrazano, Giovanni da, 44
Vesey, Denmark, 421, 587–88
Vespucci, Amerigo, 21
Vicksburg, Battle of (1863), 684–85,
    685, 688
vigilantes, 205, 207, 281–83, 323, 608
Vincennes, Ill., Revolutionary War
    fighting in, 245
Vindication of the Rights of Woman, A
    (Wollstonecraft), *264*
Virginia:
    agriculture in, 573
    Civil War fighting in, 655–56, 657,
        663–65, *667*, 669, 684, 689–91,
        691, *692*
    Constitution ratified by, 295, *295*
    and Declaration of Independence, 220
    emancipation in, 261–62, 599, 672
    land claims of, 257, *273*, 276, 302
    Loyalist property in, 398
    migration from, 591
    at navigation meeting of 1785, 283
    post-Revolutionary War debt in, 310
    Reconstruction in, 719, 724, 734
    religious freedom in, 265

Revolutionary War fighting in, 217, 247–48, 251–53
Revolutionary War troops from, 250
secession of, 650
slave trade in, 287–88
Virginia, University of, 316, 514
Virginia (Merrimack), 657
Virginia colony, *67*, 68, 69, 85, 143
  agriculture in, 59
  Anglican Church in, 128
  Bacon's Rebellion in, 65–67
  charter of, 57, 257
  in colonial taxation disputes, 201, 204
  Committees of Correspondence in, 206
  European settlement of, 58–67, *58, 60*, 109
  first permanent settlement in, 58–62
  gentry of, 128
  government of, 62, 63–66, 169
  Indians in, 59, 61–63, 64–66, 186
  John Smith's administration of, 59–61
  in land disputes, 209
  landownership in, 63–65
  Loyalists in, 217
  population of, 64, 111
  religion in, 62, 128
  Roanoke colony, 48–49, *48, 67*
  as royal colony, 64
  Sandys's reforms in, 63
  sex ratios in, 113
  slavery in, 120, 123, 126, 260
  Stamp Act and, 197
  "starving time" in, 61–62
  tobacco in, 62, 64, 117–18, *119*
Virginia Company, 58–59, *61*, 118
  origins of, 57, 58, *60*
Virginia Declaration of Rights (1776), 220, 265, 285, 305
Virginia Plan, 286–87, 291
Virginia Resolutions (1798), 337, 423
Virginia Resolves (1765), 197
Virginia Statue of Religious Freedom (1786), 265–66
Voltaire, 149
voter turnout, in election of 1840, 445
voting rights:
  for African Americans, 397, 710, 711, 713, 716, 719, 722, *722*, 725, 728, 732

property qualifications and, 169–70, 258–59, 411, 446, 478, 483
  religion and, 170
  residency requirements and, 575
  taxation and, 258, 410–11
  women and, 264, 519

Wade, Benjamin F., 680, 708, 710, 712
Wade-Davis Bill, 708
Wade-Davis Manifesto, 708
Walden (Thoreau), 507, 508
Wales, 52
Walker, Robert J., 632–33
Walker Tariff (1846), 551
Walloons, 143
Walpole, Horace, 199
Walpole, Robert, 168
Walton Road, 455
Wampanoags, 81, 83–84, *103*
wampum, *96*
Wanghsia, Treaty of (1844), 618
War Department, U.S., 271
War of 1812, 363–75, *367, 368, 375*, 384, 466, 574
  aftermath of, 374–75
  Baltimore attacked in, 371
  causes of, 364–66
  in Chesapeake, 371
  Hartford Convention and, 373–74
  Indian troubles in, 364–66
  militias in, 369, 371, 372
  naval warfare in, 366–67, *367*, 369
  New Orleans battle of, 371–72, *372*, 478
  northern front of, 366–69, *368, 370*
  peace treaty in, 372–73
  preparations for, 366–67
  southern front of, 369–70, *370*
  Washington, D.C. captured in, 371
War of Independence, *see* American Revolution
War of the Austrian Succession (King George's War) (1744–1748), 176
War of the League of Augsburg (War of the Palatinate) (King William's War), 176
War of the Spanish Succession (Queen Anne's War) (1701–1713), 176
Warren, Joseph, 215

Warren, Mercy Otis, 210–11
Warriors' Path, 328
wars, *see specific conflicts and wars*
Washington, D.C.:
    and Compromise of 1850, 611
    first inauguration in, 346–48
    as new capital, 347, *348*
    plan of 1792, *347*
    slaves in, 443, 597–98, 609, 610, 611,
        615, 670
    voting rights in, 716
    in War of 1812, 371
Washington, George, 115, 267, 282, 283,
        300, 307, 316, 332, 334, 335, *362, 463*
    Algerian conflict and, 333
    in American Revolution, 214, 222, 228,
        232–36, *233, 236,* 239, 244–45, *247,*
        248, 251–52, 260, 272
    appearance and background of, 214
    called from retirement, 334
    chosen as commander in chief, 214
    on Constitution, 297
    at Constitutional Convention, *284,*
        285, 286, *291*
    at Continental Congress, 209
    and Declaration of Independence, 221
    farewell address of, 329
    on foreign alliances, 329
    in French and Indian War, 178, 181
    French Revolution and, 318, 319
    Jay's Treaty and, 320–21
    on national bank issue, 312–13
    in presidential elections, 303, 317
    as slaveholder, 260
    Whiskey Rebellion and, *302,*
        323–24, *324*
Washington Federalist, 361
Washington Territory, 533
water, as commodity, 469–70, *171*
water transportation, 283, 400–401,
        462–63
    canals, 458–59, 464
    in early nineteenth century,
        456–59, *459*
Watervliet Arsenal, *654*
Watt, James, 465
Waud, Alfred R., *690*
Wayne, Anthony, 322
Webb, James Watson, *581*

Webster, Daniel, 399, 408, 440, 550
    African colonization and, 592
    in Compromise of 1850, 610–13
    in election of 1836, 440
    Hayne's debate with, 422–24
    on Jackson, 418
    national bank issue and, 386, 433–34
    on nullification issue, 422–24, *423*
    Texas annexation and, 551, 555
    in Tyler administration, 527, 528, 530
Webster-Ashburton Treaty (1842),
        528, 529, 530
Webster-Hayne debate, 422–24
Welsh Americans, 101, 142, 143,
        144, 580
Wesley, John, 495, *495*
West, 538–45
    agriculture in, 450, 452–54, 574
    in Civil War, 660–63, *662*
    gold rushes and mining in, 463, 532,
        540, 542, 606–9, 660
    North and South in conflict over, 566
    trails through, 538–45
    Whigs in, 440
    see also frontier
West, Benjamin, *253*
Western Indians, 12, 13
Western Reserve Eclectic Institute, *513*
West Indies, 26, 32–33, 73, *73,* 121,
        186, 191, 318
    French-U.S. conflict in, 333
    Napoleonic wars and, 360
    trade with, 104, 132, 134–35, 142, 191,
        277, 320, 321, 360, 392
Westos, *90*
West Virginia, formation of, 651
whaling, 132, *511*
wheat, 22, 142, 574
Whcatley, Phillis, 209, 222
Wheelwright, John, 79
Whig party:
    "Conscience" vs. "Cotton" members
        of, 605
    Constitutional Union party and, 641
    destruction of, 624
    economic policies of, 442–45, 528
    in election of 1840, 444–45, *444,* 528
    in election of 1844, 548–49
    in election of 1848, 604–5

in election of 1852, 617
in election of 1856, 629–30
in election of 1860, 641
formation of, 439–40
in formation of Republican party, 624
Free Soil party and, 605
on independent Treasury, 442–43
Mexican War and, 554, 561
scalawags and, 724–25
slavery issue in, 604, 624
Taylor supported by, 609
Whigs, British, 192, 222
whiskey, tax on, 316, 323, 350
Whiskey Rebellion, 323–24, *324*, 334
whiskey ring, 730
White, Hugh Lawson, 440
White, John, *22*, 48, *88*
Whitefield, George, 155–56, *155*
White League, *731*
"white republic," 727, *727*
Whitman, Walt, 508, 510–11, 521
Whitney, Eli, *451*, 452
Whittier, John Greenleaf, 508
Wilderness, Battle of the (1863),
    684, 689
Wilderness Road, 327–29, 455
Wilkinson, Eliza, 288–89
Wilkinson, James, 358
Willard, Emma, 515
William III, king of England,
    56, 166–67, 176
William and Mary, College of, 159
Williams, Roger, 75–77, 82
Wilmot, David, 603–4, 605
Wilmot Proviso, 603–4, 605, 615, 631
Wilson, Henry, *728*
Wilson, James, at Constitutional
    Convention, 285, 290
Winthrop, John, 72–75, *72*, 75, 78,
    113–14, 115
Winthrop, John, IV, 150
Winthrop, John, Jr., 150
Wirt, William, 436
Wisconsin:
    Civil War troops from, 658
    immigration to, 480
Wisconsin Territory, Indian conflicts
    in, 429
witchcraft, *130*, 139–41, *140*

Wolfe, James, 182
Wollstonecraft, Mary, *264*
women, 344
    in abolition movement, 520, 594–95
    African-American, 115–16
    American Indian, 13, 40
    American Revolution and, 262–64
    in Civil War, 674–76, 677
    in colonial period, 111–17
    Constitutional Convention and,
        288–89
    domestic role of, 116–17, 262–63,
        518–19, 578–79
    education and, 487–88, 515–16,
        515, 519
    employment of, 116–17, 465, 467–69,
        468, 521, 674–75
    legal status of, 114, 262–64, 519
    in Lowell System, 467–69
    marriage and child-bearing patterns
        of, 111–12, *112*, 262–64
    in mining frontier (California), 608
    in Old Southwest, 591–92
    on Oregon Trail, *540*, 541
    as professionals, 487–88
    Puritan, 115
    Quaker, 98, *99*, 115
    in Reconstruction, 704–5
    and religion, 115–16, 156–57, 158,
        572, 677
    in religious revivals, 498
    sexual exploitation of, 579,
        586–87, 592
    slave, 126, 579, 584–86, 592
    southern honor and, 581
    on southern plantations, 578–79
    theater and, 473
    witchcraft and, 141
women's rights, 518–21
    abolitionism and, 520–21, 594–95
    in Civil War, 674–75
    Sojourner Truth on, 596–97
    voting and, 264, 519, 521
Wood, Jethro, 453
Woodville, Richard Caton, *512*
Worcester v. Georgia, 431
workers:
    American Revolution and, 258
    see also labor, employment

working class:
  in early nineteenth century,
    467–69, *468*
  housing of, 464
  Irish Americans in, 477
  in Panic of 1837, 441–42
  religion of, 494
  at theater, 474
  see also labor, employment; labor
    movement
Workingmen's party, 483, 512
Wormley Conference (1877),
  737, 739
Worth, Jonathan, 739
Worthington, Amanda, 704–5

XYZ affair, *332*, 333

Yakimas, 532
Yale College, 159, 495
Yamasees, *102*
Yamasee War (1715), 90–91
Yancey, William Lowndes, 615, 640
yellow fever, 24
"ye old deluder Satan" Act (1647), 152–53
York, duke of, *see* James II, king of
    England
Yorktown, Battle of (1781), *249*,
    251–53, *252*
Young, Brigham, 502–3, *502*
Yumas, 532

Zenger, John Peter, 148
Zias, 531
Zunis, 11, 531